WILEY

IFRS

2006 Interpretation and Application of International Accounting and Financial Reporting Standards

**Subscriber
Update
Service**

BECOME A SUBSCRIBER!
Did you purchase this product from a bookstore?

If you did, it's important for you to become a subscriber. John Wiley & Sons, Inc. may publish, on a periodic basis, supplements and new editions to reflect the latest changes in the subject matter that you *need to know* in order stay competitive in this ever-changing industry. By contacting the Wiley office nearest you, you'll receive any current update at no additional charge. In addition, you'll receive future updates and revised or related volumes on a 30-day examination review.

If you purchased this product directly from John Wiley & Sons, Inc., we have already recorded your subscription for this update service.

To become a subscriber, please call **1-877-762-2974** or send your name, company name (if applicable), address, and the title of the product to:

mailing address: **Supplement Department
John Wiley & Sons, Inc.
One Wiley Drive
Somerset, NJ 08875**

e-mail: **subscriber@wiley.com**
fax: **1-732-302-2300**
online: **www.wiley.com**

For customers outside the United States, please contact the Wiley office nearest you:

Professional & Reference Division
John Wiley & Sons Canada, Ltd.
22 Worcester Road
Etobicoke, Ontario M9W 1L1
CANADA
(416) 236-4433
Phone: 1-800-567-4797
Fax: (416)236-4447
canada@jwiley.com

John Wiley & Sons Australia, Ltd.
33 Park Road
P.O. Box 1226
Milton, Queensland 4064
AUSTRALIA
Phone: 61-7-3859-9755
Fax: 61-7-3859-9715
Email: brisbane@johnwiley.com.au

John Wiley & Sons, Ltd.
The Atrium
Southern Gate, Chichester
West Sussex, PO19 8SQ
ENGLAND
Phone: (44) 1243 779777
Fax: (44) 1243 775878
Email: customer@wiley.co.uk

John Wiley & Sons (Asia) Pte. Ltd.
2 Clementi Loop #02-01
SINGAPORE 129809
Phone: 65-64632400
Fax: 65-64634604/5/6
Customer Service: 65-64604280
Email: enquiry@wiley.com.sg

WILEY

I F R S

2006

Interpretation and Application of International Accounting and Financial Reporting Standards

Barry J. Epstein
Abbas Ali Mirza

WILEY

JOHN WILEY & SONS, INC.

CONTENTS

PREFACE

IFRS: Interpretation and Application of International Financial Reporting Standards provides analytical explanations and copious illustrations of all current accounting principles promulgated by the IASB (and its predecessor, the IASC). The book integrates principles promulgated by the Board—international financial reporting standards (IFRS) and the earlier international accounting standards (IAS)—and by the Board's body for responding to more narrowly focused issues—the International Financial Reporting Interpretations Committee (IFRIC), which succeeded the Standing Interpretations Committee (SIC). These materials have been synthesized into a user-oriented topical format, eliminating the need for readers to first be knowledgeable about the names or numbers of the salient professional standards.

The focus of the book is the practitioner and the myriad practical problems faced in applying IFRS. Accordingly, the paramount goal has been to incorporate meaningful, real-world-type examples in guiding users in the application of IFRS to complex fact situations that must be dealt with in the actual practice of accounting. In addition to this emphasis, a major strength of the book is that it does explain the theory of IFRS in sufficient detail to serve as a valuable adjunct to, or substitute for, accounting textbooks. Not merely a reiteration of currently promulgated IFRS, it provides the user with the underlying conceptual basis for the rules, to enable the reasoning by analogy that is so necessary in dealing with a complex, fast-changing world of commercial arrangements and structures. It is based on the authors' belief that proper application of IFRS demands an understanding of the logical underpinnings of its technical requirements. This is perhaps more true of IFRS than of various national GAAP sets of standards, since IFRS is by design more "principles based" and hence less prescriptive, leaving practitioners with a proportionately greater challenge in actually applying the rules.

Each chapter of this book, or major section thereof, provides an overview discussion of the perspective and key issues associated with the topics covered; a listing of the professional pronouncements that guide practice; and a detailed discussion of the concepts and accompanying examples. A comprehensive checklist following the main text offers practical guidance to preparing financial statements in accordance with IFRS. Also included is a revised, detailed, tabular comparison between IFRS and US national GAAP, keyed to the chapters of this book. Also included is a set of three comprehensive financial statements that illustrate application of financial reporting standards to different types of enterprises. A feature added to the 2004 edition—copious examples of actual informative disclosures made by companies reporting under IFRS—has been expanded and are included in the relevant chapters of this book.

The authors' wish is that this book will serve practitioners, faculty, and students as a reliable reference tool, to facilitate their understanding of, and ability to apply, the complexities of the authoritative literature. Comments from readers, both as to errors and omissions and as to proposed improvements for future editions, should be addressed to Barry J. Epstein, c/o John Wiley & Sons, Inc., 155 N. 3rd Street, Suite 502, DeKalb, Illinois 60115, prior to May 15, 2006, for consideration for the 2007 edition.

Barry J. Epstein
Abbas Ali Mirza
November 2005

ABOUT THE AUTHORS

Barry J. Epstein, PhD, CPA, a partner in the firm Russell Novak & Company, has almost forty years' experience in the public accounting profession, as auditor, technical director/partner for several national and local firms, and as a consulting and testifying accounting and auditing expert on over seventy litigation matters to date. His current practice is concentrated on providing technical consultations to CPA firms and corporations on US GAAP and IFRS accounting and financial reporting matters; on US and international auditing standards; matters involving financial analysis; forensic accounting investigations; and on corporate governance matters. He regularly serves as an expert on litigation matters, including assignments for both the private sector and governmental agencies.

Dr. Epstein is a widely published authority on accounting and auditing. His current publications include *Wiley GAAP*, now in its 2nd edition, for which he is the lead coauthor. He has also appeared on over a dozen national radio and television programs discussing the crisis in corporate financial reporting and corporate governance, and has presented over a hundred educational programs to professional and corporate groups in the US and internationally. He previously chaired the Audit Committee of the AICPA's Board of Examiners, responsible for the Uniform CPA Examination, and has served on other professional panels at state and national levels.

Dr Epstein holds degrees from DePaul University (Chicago—BSC, accounting and finance, 1967) University of Chicago (MBA, economics and industrial relations, 1969), and University of Pittsburgh (PhD, information systems and finance, 1979).

Dr. Epstein wishes to acknowledge the contributions of coauthor Abbas Ali Mirza, particularly in the original conception of this book in 1996.

Abbas Ali Mirza, CPA, ACA, AICWA, has brought his expertise in auditing, finance, and taxation to a variety of positions with major international firms in the US, India, and the Middle East. He is currently a partner with Deloitte & Touche, based in the United Arab Emirates, where he is responsible for audit clients and is a member of the firm's regional Assurance and Advisory Committee, responsible for technical and learning support throughout the region. He is a frequent speaker and workshop leader at global conferences on international financial reporting, has coauthored regular newspaper columns and written features for the media in the Middle East and India, and has been widely quoted as a commentator on business issues.

Mr. Mirza is also a member of the Accounting Standards Committee of the Securities & Exchange Board of India, and is involved in professional and regulatory affairs in India and Dubai, UAE. He has spoken at several United Nations conferences on financial reporting and corporate governance matters, and is associated with a number of other professional initiatives germane to worldwide adoption of IFRS.

1 INTRODUCTION TO INTERNATIONAL FINANCIAL REPORTING STANDARDS

The year 2005 marked the start of a new era in global business, and the fulfillment of a thirty-year effort to create the financial reporting rules for a worldwide capital market. For during that year's financial reporting cycle, as many as 7,000 listed companies in the 25 European Union member states, plus many others in countries such as Russia, Australia, South Africa and New Zealand, were expected (in the EU, required) to produce annual financial statements in compliance with a single set of international rules—International Financial Reporting Standards (IFRS). Many others, while not publicly held and not currently required to comply with IFRS, will do so either immediately or over time, in order to conform to what is clearly becoming the new worldwide standard. Since there are about 15,000 SEC-registered companies in the USA that use US GAAP (plus countless nonpublicly held companies reporting under GAAP), the vast majority of the world's large businesses will now be reporting under one or the other of these two comprehensive systems of accounting and financial reporting rules.

Encouraging this process, the standard setters have agreed to try to converge their measurement and recognition rules, so that differences between these two sets of requirements are already disappearing. In fact, the chairman of the US standard setter has suggested that by 2010 there would be no major differences left, and the SEC has speculated that the remaining differences might become so trivial that the currently required reconciliations required in Form 20-F filings by foreign registrants might be dispensed with entirely well before the end of the decade. However, there are undoubtedly many obstacles left to overcome, particularly as national securities regulators learn to live with the idea of using rules developed outside their jurisdiction by an autonomous panel of experts.

Origins and Early History of the IASB

Financial reporting in the developed world evolved from two broad models, whose objectives were somewhat different. The earliest systematized form of accounting regulation developed in continental Europe, starting in France in 1673. Here a requirement for an annual fair value balance sheet was introduced by the government as a means of protecting the economy from bankruptcies. This form of accounting at the initiative of the state to control economic actors was copied by other states and later incorporated in the 1807 Napoleonic Commercial Code. This method of regulating the economy expanded rapidly throughout continental Europe, partly through Napoleon's efforts and partly through a willingness on the part of European regulators to borrow ideas from each other. This "code law" family of reporting practices was much developed by Germany after its 1870 unification, with the emphasis moving away from market values to historical cost and systematic depreciation. It was used later by governments as the basis of tax assessment when taxes on profits started to be introduced, mostly in the early twentieth century.

This model of accounting serves primarily as a means of moderating relationships between the individual company and the state. It serves for tax assessment, and to limit dividend payments, and it is also a means of protecting the running of the economy by sanctioning individual businesses that are not financially sound or were run imprudently. While the model has been adapted for stock market reporting and group (consolidated) structures, this is not its main focus.

The other model did not appear until the nineteenth century and arose as a consequence of the industrial revolution. Industrialization created the need for large concentrations of capital to undertake industrial projects (initially, canals and railways) and to spread risks between many investors. In this model the financial report provided a means of monitoring the activities of large businesses in order to inform their (nonmanagement) shareholders. Financial reporting for capital markets purposes developed initially in the UK, in a common-law environment where the state legislated as little as possible and left a large degree of interpretation to practice and for the sanction of the courts. This approach was rapidly adopted by the US as it, too, became industrialized. As the US developed the idea of groups of companies controlled from a single head office (towards the end of the nineteenth century), this philosophy of financial reporting started to become focused on consolidated accounts and the group, rather than the individual company. For different reasons neither the UK nor the US governments saw this reporting framework as appropriate for income tax purposes, and in this tradition, while the financial reports inform the assessment process, taxation retains a separate stream of law, which has had little influence on financial reporting.

The second model of financial reporting, generally regarded as the Anglo-Saxon financial reporting approach, can be characterized as focusing on the relationship between the business and the investor, and on the flow of information to the capital markets. Government still uses reporting as a means of regulating economic activity (e.g., the SEC's mission is to protect the investor and ensure that the securities markets run efficiently), but the financial report is aimed at the investor, not the government.

Neither of the two above-described approaches to financial reporting is particularly useful in an agricultural economy, or to one that consists entirely of microbusinesses, in the opinion of many observers. Nonetheless, as countries have developed economically (or as they were colonized) they have adopted variants of one or the other of these two models.

IFRS are an example of the second, capital market-oriented, systems of financial reporting rules. The original international standard setter, the International Accounting Standards Committee (IASC), was formed in 1973, during a period of considerable change in accounting regulation. In the US the Financial Accounting Standards Board (FASB) had just been created, in the UK the first national standard setter had recently been organized, the EU was working on the main plank of its own accounting harmonization plan (the Fourth Directive), and both the UN and the OECD were shortly to create their own accounting committees. The IASC was launched in the wake of the 1972 World Accounting Congress (a five-yearly get-together of the international profession) after an informal meeting between representatives of the British profession (Institute of Chartered Accountants in England and Wales—ICAEW) and the American profession (American Institute of Certified Public Accountants—AICPA).

A rapid set of negotiations resulted in the professional bodies of Canada, Australia, Mexico, Japan, France, Germany, the Netherlands, and New Zealand being invited to join with the US and UK to form the international body. Due to pressure (coupled with a financial subsidy) from the UK, the IASC was established in London, where its successor, the IASB, remains today.

The actual reasons for the IASC's creation are unclear. A need for a common language of business was felt, to deal with a growing volume of international business, but other, more political motives abounded also. For example, some believe that the major motivation was that the British wanted to create an international standard setter to trump the regional initiatives within the EU, which leaned heavily to the Code model of reporting, in contrast to what was the norm in the UK and almost all English-speaking nations.

In the first phase of its existence, the IASC had mixed fortunes. Once the International Federation of Accountants (IFAC) was formed in 1977 (at the next World Congress of Accountants), the IASC had to fight off attempts to become a part of IFAC. It managed to resist, coming to a compromise where IASC remained independent but all IFAC members were automatically members of IASC, and IFAC was able to nominate the membership of the standard-setting Board.

Both the UN and OECD were active in international rule making in the 1970s but the IASC successfully persuaded them that they should leave recognition and measurement rules to the IASC. However, having established itself as the unique international rule maker, IASC had great difficulty in persuading anyone to use its rules. Although member professional bodies were theoretically committed to pushing for the use of IFRS at the national level, in practice few national bodies were influential in standard setting in their respective countries, and others (including the US and UK) preferred their national standards to whatever IASC might propose. In Europe, IFRS were used by some reporting entities in Italy and Switzerland, and national standard setters in some countries such as Malaysia began to use IFRS as an input to their national rules, while not necessarily adopting them as written by the IASC or giving explicit recognition to the fact that IFRS were being adopted in part as national GAAP.

IASC entered a new phase in 1987, which led directly to its 2001 reorganization, when the then-Secretary General, David Cairns, encouraged by the US SEC, negotiated an agreement with the International Organization of Securities Commissions (IOSCO). IOSCO was looking for a common international "passport" with which companies could be accepted for a secondary listing in the jurisdiction of any IOSCO member. The concept was that, whatever the listing rules in a company's primary stock exc hange, there would be a common minimum package which all stock exchanges would accept from foreign companies seeking a secondary listing. IOSCO was prepared to use IFRS as the financial reporting basis for this passport, provided that the international standards could be brought up to the level IOSCO stipulated. For the first time, the IASC would have a clear client and a clear role for its standards.

Historically, a major criticism of IFRS was that it essentially endorsed all accounting methods then in wide usage, effectively becoming a "lowest common denominator" set of standards. The trend in national GAAP was to narrow the range of acceptable alternatives, although uniformity was not anticipated in the near term. The IOSCO agreement provoked frenetic activity to improve the existing standards by removing the many alternative treatments which were permitted under the standards. The IASC launched its comparability and improvements project to develop a "core set of standards" as demanded by IOSCO. These were complete by 1993, not without disagreements between members, but—to the great frustration of the IASC—were then not accepted by IOSCO. IASC leaders were unhappy, amongst other things, that IOSCO seemingly wanted to cherry-pick individual standards, rather than endorse the IASC's process and thus all the standards created thereby.

Ultimately, the collaboration was relaunched in 1995, with IASC under new leadership, and this began a further frenetic period where existing standards were again reviewed and revised, and new standards were created to fill perceived gaps. This time the set of standards included, amongst others, IAS 39, on recognition and measurement of financial instruments, which had been accepted, at the very last moment and with great difficulty, as a compromise, purportedly interim standard.

At the same time, the IASC had established a committee to contemplate its future structure. In part, this was the result of pressure exerted by the US SEC and the US private sector standard setter, the FASB, which were seemingly concerned that IFRS were not being developed by "due process." While there may have been other agendas by some of the parties (the FASB, for example, was opposed to IFRS at the time and hoped that US GAAP would instead be accepted by other nations), in fact the IFRS were in need of strengthening, particularly as to reducing the range of diverse but accepted alternatives for similar transactions and events.

If IASC was to be the standard setter endorsed by the world's stock exchange regulators, it would need a structure that reflected that level of responsibility. The historical Anglo-Saxon standard-setting model—where professional accountants set the rules for themselves—had largely been abandoned in the twenty-five years since the IASC was formed, and standards were mostly being set by dedicated and independent national boards such as the FASB, and not by profession-dominated bodies like the AICPA. The choice, as restructuring became inevitable, was between a large, representative approach—much like the existing IASC structure, but where national standard setters sent representatives—or a small, professional body of experienced standard setters which worked independently.

The end of this phase of the international standard setting, and the resolution of these issues, came about within a short period in 2000. In May, IOSCO members voted at their annual meeting to endorse IASC standards, albeit subject to a number of reservations (see discussion later in this chapter). This was a considerable step forward for the IASC, which was quickly surpassed by an announcement in June 2000 that the European Commission intended to adopt IFRS as the requirement for primary listings in all member states. This planned full endorsement by the EU eclipsed the less than enthusiastic IOSCO announcement, and since then the EU has appeared to be the more influential body as far as gaining acceptance for IFRS is concerned.

In July 2000, IASC members voted to abandon the old structure based on professional bodies and adopt a new structure: beginning in 2001, standards would be set by a professional board, financed by voluntary contributions raised by a new oversight body.

The New Structure

The formal structure put in place in 2000 has the IASC Foundation, a Delaware corporation, as its keystone. The Trustees of the IASC Foundation have both the responsibility to raise the $15 million a year needed to finance standard setting, and the responsibility of appointing members to the International Accounting Standards Board (IASB), the

International Financial Reporting Interpretations Committee (IFRIC) and the Standards Advisory Council (SAC).

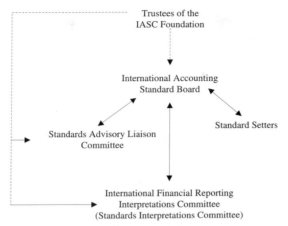

The Standards Advisory Council (SAC) meets with the IASB three times a year, generally for two days. The SAC consists of about 50 members, nominated in their personal (not organizational) capacity, but are usually supported by organizations that have an interest in international reporting. Members currently include analysts, corporate executives, auditors, standard setters, and stock exchange regulators. The members are supposed to serve as a channel for communication between the IASB and its wider group of constituents, to suggest topics for the IASB's agenda, and to discuss IASB proposals.

The International Financial Reporting Interpretations Committee (IFRIC) is a committee comprised mostly of technical partners in audit firms but also includes preparers and users. It succeeds the Standards Interpretations Committee (SIC), which had been created by the IASC. SIC/IFRIC's function is to answer technical queries from constituents about how to interpret IFRS—in effect, filling in the cracks between different rules. In recent times it has also proposed modifications to standards to the IASB, in response to perceived operational difficulties or need to improve consistency. IFRIC liaises with the US Emerging Issues Task Force and similar bodies liaison as standard setters, to try at preserve convergence at the level of interpretation. It is also establishing relations with stock exchange regulators, who may be involved in making decisions about the acceptability of accounting practices, which will have the effect of interpreting IFRS.

The liaison standard setters are national bodies from Australia, Canada, France, Germany, UK, USA, and Japan. Each of these bodies has a special relationship with a Board member, who normally maintains an office with the national standard setter and is responsible for liaison between the international body and the national body. This, together with the SAC, was the solution arrived at by the old IASC in an attempt to preserve some geographical representativeness. However, this has been somewhat overtaken by events: as far as the EU is concerned, its interaction with the IASB is through EFRAG (see below), which has no formal liaison member of the Board. The IASB Deputy Chairman has performed this function, but while France, Germany and the UK individually have liaison, EFRAG and the European Commission are, so far, outside this structure.

Furthermore, there are many national standard setters, particularly from developing countries, that have no seat on the SAC, and therefore have no direct link with the IASB, despite the fact that many of them seek to reflect IASB standards in their national standards.

At the October 2002 World Congress in Hong Kong, the IASB held an open meeting for national standard setters, which was met with enthusiasm. As a result, IASB began to provide time concurrent with formal liaison standard setters' meetings for any other interested standard setters to attend. While this practice is not enshrined in either the Constitution or the IASB's operating procedures, both are under review at the moment and changes may be in place for 2005.

Process of IFRS Standard Setting

The IASB has a formal due process which is set out in the *Preface to IFRS*, revised in 2001. As a minimum, a proposed standard should be exposed for comment, and these comments should be reviewed before issuance of a final standard, with debates open to the public. However, this formal process is rounded out in practice, with wider consultation taking place on an informal basis.

The IASB's agenda is determined in various ways. Suggestions are made by the Trustees, the SAC, liaison standard setters, the international audit firms and others. These are debated by the Board and tentative conclusions are discussed with the various consultative bodies. The IASB also has a joint agenda committee with the FASB. Long-range projects are first put on the research agenda, which means that preliminary work is being done on collecting information about the problem and potential solutions. Projects can also arrive on the current agenda outside that route.

The agenda has been dominated in the years since 2001 by the need to round out the legacy standards, so that there would be a full range of standards for European companies moving to IFRS in 2005, as well as to carry out urgent modifications in the name of convergence (acquisition accounting and goodwill) and improvements to existing standards. These needs have largely been met as of mid-2004.

Once a project reaches the current agenda, the formal process is that the staff (a group of about 20 technical staff permanently employed by the IASB) drafts papers which are then discussed by the Board in open meetings. Following that debate, the staff rewrites the paper, or writes a new paper which is debated at a subsequent meeting. In theory there is an internal process where the staff proposes solutions, and the Board either accepts or rejects them. In practice the process is more involved: sometimes (especially for projects like financial instruments) specific Board members are allocated a special responsibility for the project, and they discuss the problems regularly with the relevant staff, helping to build the papers that come to the Board. Equally, Board members may write or speak directly to the staff outside of the formal meeting process to indicate concerns about one thing or another.

The process usually involves: (1) discussion of a paper outlining the principal issues; (2) preparation of an Exposure Draft that incorporates the tentative decisions taken by the Board—during which process many of these are redebated, sometimes several times; (3) publication of the Exposure Draft; (4) analysis of comments received on the Exposure Draft; (5) debate and issue of the final standard, accompanied by application guidance and a document setting out the *Basis for Conclusions* (the reasons why the Board rejected some solutions and preferred others). Final ballots on the Exposure Draft and the final standard are carried out in secret, but otherwise the process is quite open, with outsiders able to consult project summaries on the IASB Web site and attend Board meetings if they wish. Of course, the informal exchanges between staff and Board on a day-to-day basis are not visible to the public, nor are the meetings where the Board takes strategic and administrative decisions.

The basic due process can be modified in different circumstances. If the project is controversial or particularly difficult, the Board may issue a discussion paper before proceeding to Exposure Draft stage. It reissued a discussion paper on stock options before proceeding to

IFRS 2, *Share-Based Payment.* It is also doing this with its reporting performance project and its project on standards for small and medium-sized enterprises. Such a discussion paper may just set out what the staff considers to be the issues, or it may do that as well as indicate the Board's preliminary views.

The Board may also hold some form of public consultation during the process. When revising IAS 39, *Financial Instruments: Recognition and Measurement* in 2003, it held round table discussions. Respondents to the Exposure Draft were invited to participate in small groups with Board members where they could put forward their views and engage in debate.

Apart from these formal consultative processes, the Board also carries out field trials of some standards (as it recently did on performance reporting and insurance), where volunteer preparers apply proposed new standards. The international audit firms receive Board papers as a result of their membership on IFRIC and are also invited to comment informally at various stages of standard development.

Constraints

The debate within the Board demonstrates the existence of certain pervasive constraints that will influence the decisions taken by the Board. A prime concern is *convergence.* In October 2002 the IASB signed an agreement with the FASB (the Norwalk Agreement) stating that the two boards would seek to remove differences and converge on high-quality standards. This agreement set in motion short-term adjustments and both standard setters have since issued Exposure Drafts changing their rules to converge with the other on certain issues. It also involves long-term development of joint projects (business combinations, performance reporting, revenue recognition, etc.).

This desire for convergence is driven by the perception that international investment is made more risky by the use of multiple reporting frameworks, and that the global market needs a single global reporting base—but also specifically by the knowledge that European companies wish to be listed in the US, and have to provide reconciliations of their equity and earnings to US GAAP when they do this (foreign companies registered with the SEC have to prepare the annual filing on Form 20-F which, if the entity does not prepare reports under US GAAP, requires a reconciliation between the entity's IFRS or national GAAP and US GAAP for earnings and equity. This reconciliation is costly to prepare and leads to companies publishing in effect two different operating results for the year, which is not always understood or appreciated by the market). If IFRS were substantially the same as US GAAP, the Form 20-F reconciliations hopefully would fade away (and the SEC has confirmed this is the likely outcome), so for European companies, convergence with US GAAP is an important issue.

A major concern for financial reporting is that of *consistency,* but this is a complex matter, since the Board has something of a hierarchy of consistency. As a paramount consideration, the Board would want a new standard to be consistent with its *Conceptual Framework* (discussed below). Thereafter, there may be a conflict between being consistent with US GAAP and being consistent with existing IAS/IFRS. However, there is little or no desire to maintain consistency with standards marked for extinction or major revision. For example, IASB believes that a number of extant standards are inconsistent with the *Framework* and need to be changed (e.g., IAS 20 on government grants), or are ineffective or obsolete (e.g., IAS 17 on leases), so there is little purpose in seeking to make a new standard consistent with them. Equally, since it aims to converge with US GAAP, it seems illogical to adopt a solution that is inconsistent with US GAAP, which will then have to be reconsidered as part of the convergence program.

Those members of the Board who have worked in North America are concerned that standards avoid creating abuse opportunities. Experience has sadly shown that there often will be attempts by preparers to engineer around accounting standards in order to be able to achieve the earnings or balance sheet amounts desired. This concern is sometimes manifested as a desire to avoid allowing exceptions. There is a justifiable perception that many standards become very complicated because they contain many exceptions to a simple basic rule.

IASB also manifests some concerns about the practicality of the solutions it mandates. While preparers might think that it is not sympathetic enough in this regard, it actually has limited the extent to which it requires restatements of previous years' reported results when the rules change, particularly in IFRS 1, *First-Time Adoption*. The *Framework* does include a cost/benefit constraint—that the costs of the financial reporting should not be greater than the benefits to be gained from the information—which is often mentioned in debate, although IASB considers that preparers are not the best ones to measure the benefits of disclosure.

There is also a procedural constraint that the Board has to manage, which is the relationship between the Exposure Draft and the final standard. IASB's due process requires that there should be nothing introduced in the final standard that was not exposed at the Exposure Draft stage, otherwise there would have to be reexposure of the material. This means that where there are several solutions possible, or a line can be drawn in several places, IASB may tend towards the most extreme position in the Exposure Draft, so as not to narrow its choices when redebating in the light of constituents' comments.

Conceptual Framework for Financial Reporting

The IASB inherited the IASC's *Framework for the Preparation and Presentation of Financial Statements* (the *Framework*). Like the other current conceptual frameworks among Anglo-Saxon standard setters, this derives from the US conceptual framework, or at least those parts of it completed in the 1970s. The *Framework* states that "the objective of financial statements is to provide information about the financial position, performance and changes in financial position of an enterprise that is useful to a wide range of users in making economic decisions." The information needs of investors are deemed to be of paramount concern, but if financial statements meet their needs, other users' needs would generally also be satisfied.

The *Framework* holds that users need to evaluate the ability of the enterprise to generate cash and the timing and certainty of its generation. The financial position is affected by the economic resources controlled by the entity, its financial structure, its liquidity and solvency, and its capacity to adapt to changes in the environment in which it operates.

The qualitative characteristics of financial statements are understandability, relevance, reliability and comparability. Reliability comprises representational faithfulness, substance over form, completeness, neutrality and prudence. It suggests that these are subject to a cost/benefit constraint, and that in practice there will often be a trade-off between characteristics. The *Framework* does not specifically include a "true and fair" requirement, but says that application of the specified qualitative characteristics should result in statements that present fairly or are true and fair (but note that IAS 1, *Presentation of Financial Statement,* does refer to the true and fair requirement).

Of great importance are the definitions of assets and liabilities. According to IASB, "an asset is a resource controlled by the enterprise as a result of past events and from which future economic benefits are expected to flow to the enterprise." A liability is a "present obligation of the enterprise arising from past events, the settlement of which is expected to result in an outflow from the enterprise of resources embodying future benefits." Equity is simply a residual arrived at by deducting the liabilities from assets. Neither asset nor liability are recognized in the financial statements unless they have a cost or value that can be measured reliably—which, as the *Framework* acknowledges, means that some assets and liabilities may remain unrecognized.

The asset and liability definitions have, in the past, not been central to financial reporting standards, many of which were instead guided by a "performance" view of the financial statements. For example, IAS 20 on government grants was suspended in 2004, in part because it allows government grants to be treated as a deferred credit and amortized to earnings, while a deferred credit does not meet the *Framework* definition of a liability. Similarly, IFRS 3 requires that where negative goodwill is identified in a business combination, this should be released to the income statement immediately—IAS 22 treated it as a deferred credit, which does not qualify as a liability.

Both FASB and IASB now intend to analyze solutions to reporting issues in terms of whether they cause any changes in assets or liabilities. The revenue recognition project which both are pursuing is an example of this. This project has tentatively embraced the view that where an entity receives an order and has a legally enforceable contract to supply goods or services, the entity has both an asset (the right to receive future revenue) and a liability (the obligation to fulfill the order) and it follows that, depending upon the measurement of the asset and the liability, some earnings could be recognized at that point. This would be a sharp departure from existing GAAP, under which executory contracts are almost never formally recognized, and never create earnings.

The IASB *Framework* is relatively silent on measurement issues. The three paragraphs that address this matter merely mention that several different measurement bases are available and that historical cost is the most common. Revaluation of tangible fixed assets is, for example, perfectly acceptable under IFRS for the moment. In practice IFRS have a mixed attribute model, based mainly in historical cost, but using value in use (the present value of expected future cash flows from the use of the asset within the entity) for impairment and fair value (market value) for some financial instruments, biological assets, business combinations and investment properties.

Hierarchy of Standards

The *Framework* is used by IASB members and staff in their debate, and they expect that those commenting on Exposure Drafts will articulate their arguments in terms of the *Framework*. However, the *Framework* is not intended normally to be used directly by preparers and auditors in determining their accounting methods. In its 2003 revision of IAS 8, IASB introduced a hierarchy of accounting rules that should be followed by preparers in seeking solutions to accounting problems. This hierarchy says that the most authoritative guidance is IFRS, and the preparer should seek guidance as follows:

1. IAS/IFRS and SIC/IFRIC Interpretations, when these specifically apply to a transaction or condition.
2. In the absence of such a directly applicable standard, judgement is to be used to develop and apply an accounting policy that is relevant to the economic decision-making needs of the users, and is reliable in that the financial statements: represent faithfully the financial position, financial performance and cash flows of the reporting entity; reflect the economic substance of transactions, events and conditions, rather than merely the legal forms thereof; are neutral; are prudent; and are complete in all material respects.
3. If this is not possible, the preparer should then look to recent pronouncements of other standard setters which use a similar conceptual framework to develop its stan-

dards, as well as other accounting literature and industry practices that do not conflict with higher level guidance.

4. Only if that also fails should the preparer look to the IASB *Framework* directly.

In effect, therefore, if IFRS do not cover a subject, the preparer should look to national GAAP, and the most obvious choice is US GAAP, partly because that is the most complete set of standards, and partly because in the global capital market, US GAAP is the alternative best understood (and use of US GAAP removes reconciliation items on the Form 20-F for foreign SEC registrants). In any event, given the professed intention of IFRS and US GAAP to converge, it would make little sense to seek guidance in any other set of standards, unless US GAAP were also silent on the matter needing clarification.

The IASB and the US

Although IASC and FASB were created almost contemporaneously, FASB largely ignored IASB until the 1990s. It was only at the beginning of the 1990s that FASB started to become interested in IASC. This was the period when IASC was starting to work with IOSCO, a body in which the SEC has always had a powerful voice. In effect, both the SEC and FASB were starting to look to the international, and IASC was also starting to take initiatives to encourage standard setters to meet together occasionally to debate technical issues of common interest.

IOSCO's efforts to create a single passport for secondary listings, and IASC's role as its standard setter, while intended to operate worldwide, would have the greatest significance for foreign issuers in terms of the US market. If the SEC were to accept IFRS in place of US GAAP, there would be no need for a Form 20-F reconciliation, and access to the US markets would be greatly facilitated. The SEC has therefore been a key actor in the later evolution of IASC. It encouraged IASC to build a relationship with IOSCO in 1987. It also observed that there were too many options under IAS. When IASC restarted its IOSCO work in 1995, the SEC issued a statement (April 1996) saying that, to be acceptable, IFRS must satisfy three criteria.

1. They must include a core set of standards that constituted a comprehensive basis of accounting;
2. The standards must be high quality, and enable investors to analyze performance meaningfully both across time periods and between companies; and
3. The standards must be rigorously interpreted and applied, otherwise comparability and transparency would not be achieved.

The plan with IOSCO involved IASC completion of its core set of standards, then handing these over to IOSCO, which in turn would ask its members to evaluate them, and finally IOSCO would issue its verdict. It was in this context the SEC issued a "concept release" in 2000, in which it asked for comments on the acceptability of the core set of standards, but crucially on whether there was a sufficient compliance and enforcement mechanism to ensure that standards were consistently and rigorously applied by preparers, that auditors would ensure this and stock exchange regulators would check compliance.

This latter element is something which is beyond the control of the IASC and IASB. The Standards Interpretations Committee was formed to help ensure uniform interpretation, and IFRIC has taken a number of initiatives to build liaison channels with stock exchange regulators and national interpretations bodies, but the rest is in the hands of the auditors, the audit oversight bodies, and the stock exchange oversight bodies. The SEC concepts release resulted in many comment letters, which can be viewed on the SEC Web site (www.sec.gov), but in the five years since its issue, the SEC has taken no definitive position.

The SEC's stance seems to be that it genuinely wants to see IFRS used by foreign registrants, but that it prefers convergence (so that no reconciliation is necessary) to acceptance without reconciliation of the IFRS as they were in 2000. The SEC in its public pronouncements regularly supports convergence. The SEC welcomed publicly the changes to US standards proposed by the FASB in December 2003, made to converge with IFRS.

Relations between FASB and IASB have grown ever warmer. The FASB joined the IASB for informal meetings in the early 1990s, and this led to the creation of the G4+1 group of Anglo-Saxon standard setters (US, UK, Canada, Australia and New Zealand, with the IASC as an observer) in which FASB was an active participant. IASB and FASB signed the Norwalk Agreement in October 2002, which set out a program of convergence, and their staffs now work together on a number of projects, including business combinations and revenue recognition. Video links are used to enable staff to observe and participate in board meetings. The two boards have a joint agenda committee whose aim is to harmonize the timing with which the boards discuss the same subjects. The boards are also committed to meeting twice a year in joint session.

However, this rosy picture of cooperation is not the full one. FASB works in a specific national legal framework, while IASB does not. Equally, both have what they term "inherited" GAAP (i.e., differences in approach that have a long history and are not easily removed). FASB also has a tradition of issuing very detailed, prescriptive ("rules-based") standards that give bright line audit guidance, which are intended to make compliance control easier and remove uncertainties. In the post-Enron world, after it became clear that such prescriptive rules had been abused, there was a flurry of interest in standards that supposedly express an objective and then explain how to reach it ("principles-based" standards), without attempting to prescribe responses to every conceivable fact pattern. However, as the SEC study into principles-based standards observed, use of principles alone, without detailed guidance, reduces comparability. The litigation environment in the US also makes companies and auditors reluctant to step into areas where judgments have to be taken in uncertain conditions.

The IASB and Europe

While France, Germany, the Netherlands and the UK were founding members of IASC and have remained heavily involved, the European Commission as such has generally had a difficult relationship with the international standard setter. It did not participate in any way until 1990, when it finally became an observer at Board meetings. It had had its own regional program of harmonization since the 1960s and in effect only officially abandoned this in 1995, when, in a policy paper, it recommended to member states that they seek to align their rules for consolidated financial statements on IAS. However, the Commission then went on to give IASB a great boost when it announced in June 2000 that it wanted to require all listed companies throughout the EU to use IFRS beginning in 2005 as part of its initiative to build a single European financial market. This intention was made concrete with the approval of the IFRS Regulation in June 2002 by the European Council of Ministers (the supreme EU decision-making authority).

The EU decision was all the more surprising in that, to be effective in legal terms, IFRS have to become enshrined in EU statute law, creating a situation where the EU is in effect rubber-stamping laws created by a small, self-appointed, private sector body. This is a delicate situation, which has proved within a very short time that it contains the seeds of unending disagreements: politicians are being asked in effect to endorse something over which they have no control, and are being lobbied by corporate interests who have failed to influence IASB directly to achieve their objectives. The EU endorsement of IFRS turns out to have the cost of exposing IASB to political pressures in the same way that FASB has at times been the focus of congressional manipulations in the US.

The EU created an elaborate machinery to mediate its relations with IASB. It preferred to work with another private sector body, created for the purpose, as the formal conduit for EU inputs to IASB. The European Financial Reporting Advisory Group (EFRAG) was formed in 2001 by a collection of European representative organizations (for details see www.efrag.org), including the European Accounting Federation (FEE) and European employer organization (UNICE). This in turn formed a small Technical Expert Group (TEG) which does the detailed work on IASB proposals. EFRAG consults widely within the EU, and particularly with national standard setters and the European Commission to canvass views on IASB proposals, and provides inputs to IASB. It responds formally to all discussion papers and Exposure Drafts.

At a second stage, when a final standard is issued, EFRAG is asked by the Commission to provide a report on the standard. This report should state whether the standard has the required qualities and is in conformity with the European company law directives. The European Commission then asks a new committee, the Accounting Regulation Committee (ARC), whether it wishes to endorse the standard. ARC consists of permanent representatives of the EU member state governments. It should normally only fail to endorse IFRS if it believes they are not in conformity with the overall framework of EU law; it should not take a strategic or policy view. However, the European Parliament also has the right to comment, if it wishes. If ARC fails to endorse a standard, the European Commission may still ask the Council of Ministers to override that decision.

Experience has shown that the system suffers from a number of problems. First, although EFRAG is intended to enhance EU inputs to IASB, it may in fact isolate people from IASB, or at least increase the costs of making representations. For example, when IASB revealed its intentions of issuing a standard on stock options, it received nearly a hundred comment letters from US companies (who report under US GAAP, not IFRS), but only one EFRAG, which represents about 90% of IASB's constituents. It is easy to feel in this context that EFRAG is seen at IASB as a single respondent, so people who have made the effort to work through EFRAG feel under-represented. In addition, EFRAG is bound to present a distillation of views, so it is already filtering respondents' views before they even reach IASB. The only recourse is for respondents to make representations not only to EFRAG but also directly to IASB.

However, resistance to the financial instruments standards, IAS 32 and IAS 39, has put the system under specific strain. These standards were already in existence when the European Commission announced its decision to adopt IFRS for European listed companies, and were exhaustively debated—but they have since become once more a political football. The first task of EFRAG and ARC was to endorse the existing standards of IASB. They did this—but excluded IAS 32 and 39 on the grounds that they were being extensively revised as part of IASB's then-ongoing *Improvements Project*.

During the exposure period of the improvements proposals—which exceptionally included round table meetings with constituents—the European Banking Federation, under particular pressure from French banks, lobbied IASB to modify the standard to permit macrohedging. The IASB agreed to do this, even though that meant the issuance of a new Exposure Draft and a further amendment to IAS 39 (which was finally issued in March 2004). The bankers did not like the terms of the amendment, and while it was still under discussion, they appealed to the French president and persuaded him to intervene. He wrote to the European Commission in July 2003, saying that the financial instruments standards were likely to make banks' figures volatile, would destabilize the European economy, and should not be approved. He also said that the Commission did not have a sufficient input to the standard setting process.

This manipulation of IAS 39 was further compounded when the European Central Bank complained in February 2004 that the "fair value option," introduced to IAS 39 as an improvement in final form in December 2003, could be used by banks to manipulate their prudential ratios, and asked IASB to limit the circumstances in which the option could be used. IASB agreed to do this, although again this meant issuing an Exposure Draft and a further amendment to IAS 39 which was not finalized until mid-2005. IASB, when it debated the issue, took a pragmatic line that no compromise of principle was involved, and that the principal bank regulator of the Board's largest constituent by far should be accommodated. The fact that the European Central Bank had not raised these issues at the original Exposure Draft stage was not discussed, nor was the legitimacy of a constituent deciding unilaterally it wanted to change a rule that had just been approved. The Accounting Standards Board of Japan lodged a formal protest and many other constituents have not been delighted.

The ARC has not yet approved IAS 32 and IAS 39, and may well not do so before 2005, given the European Central Bank amendment. Clearly the EU's involvement with IFRS is proving to be a mixed blessing for IASB, both exposing it to political pressures that are properly an issue for the Commission, not IASB, and putting its due process under stress. Some commentators consider that the EU might abandon IFRS, but this is not a realistic possibility, given that the EU has already tried and rejected the regional standard setting route. What is more probable is that we are enduring a period of adjustment, with both regulators and lobbyists uncertain as to how exactly the system works, testing its limits, but with some *modus vivendi* evolving over time. However, it is severe distraction for IASB that financial instruments, arguably the controversy of the 1990s, is still causing trouble, when it has on its agenda more radical ideas in the areas of revenue recognition, performance reporting and insurance contracts.

The Future Agenda for IFRS

IASB's future program has already been influenced by poor reception of its ideas in the area of reporting comprehensive income. Field tests of its proposals in 2003 have resulted in a proposal now to align this project more closely with that of FASB and split into two subprojects. The shorter-term objective will be to agree to a basic standard format with FASB, including some display of *other comprehensive income* (FASB) or *recognized income and expenditure* (IASB), which puts earnings together with valuation changes that presently flow directly to equity. An Exposure Draft is still possible in 2005. The longer-term objective will be to refine the definitions used within the income statement and report fair value and other subsequent measurement changes in a more systematic fashion. The longer-term project will probably be the subject of a discussion paper as its next step.

The FASB is also involved in a revenue recognition project. This project is trying to revisit revenue recognition through an analysis of assets and liabilities (mentioned above) instead of the existing approach which focuses on completed transactions and realized revenue. Such an approach has major implications for the timing of earnings recognition—it would potentially lead to recognition in stages throughout the transaction cycle. It is unlikely that this project will lead to short-term changes, given the fundamental nature of the issues involved.

Linked to these projects, which are revisions and extensions of the conceptual framework, is a joint project with the Canadian Accounting Standards Board on initial measurement and impairment, and a catch-up project with FASB on liabilities and equity.

IASB is continuing its revisions of its business combinations standards in coordination with FASB. Both Boards are nearing completion of Phase II of their projects. IASB has tentatively agreed that where there are minority interests, these should be included in group equity and that goodwill should be calculated for 100% of the shareholders, not for just the majority holding. It is still working on the definitions of contingent assets and liabilities acquired in a combination. IASB is also working on the criteria for consolidation (IAS 27) which it hopes to develop to deal more effectively with issues such as latent control and special-purpose entities. This may also turn into a joint project with FASB.

IASB is currently working on its own in the area of SME accounting (tailored standards for small and medium-sized entities), but this has now been taken up as well by the US standard setter and accounting profession. Broadly, the intention of this project (which was the subject of a Discussion Paper in 2004) is to produce a single accounting standard for SME which consists of simplified versions of the existing IFRS, analogous to what was done in the UK. IASB was initially reluctant to involve itself in this area, but was persuaded by a number of institutions, including the UN and the European Commission, that this was an urgent need. The crucial issue of what is an SME is couched in conceptual terms, as being an entity in which there is no public interest, but precise size terms are left to individual jurisdictions to determine. The definition excludes entities with listed equity or debt as well as those that which are economically significant.

The SME standard will likely be based on the "black letter paragraphs" of IFRS, with additional material as necessary. Where a preparer does not find the treatment needed, the entity should then refer to the substantive IFRS, although this does not then imply an obligation to comply with all the IFRS. The entity will be required to describe itself as reporting in accordance with the SME standard, and not as reporting in accordance with IFRS. The proposal is very similar to that of the UN's expert group, which provided a guideline to its member states on differential reporting and an abbreviated form of IFRS in 2001.

While IFRS 4, issued in March 2004, provides a first standard on accounting for insurance contracts, this is only an interim standard issued to meet the needs of 2005 adopters, and it permits the retention of many existing national practices. IASB is committed to a full standard, which it had hoped to have in place by 2007, although this now seems unlikely. The project should now enter full development. Analysis thus far, based on an asset and liability approach, would potentially allow recognition of some gain on the signing of a long-term contract. This will undoubtedly cause insurance regulators some concerns. IASB is also using fair value as a working measurement assumption, which has aroused opposition from insurers, many of whom have long used an approach which smoothed earnings over long periods and ignored the current market values of insurance assets and liabilities. They claim that fair value will introduce volatility, which is likely true: IASB members have observed that the volatility is in the marketplace, and that the insurers' accounts just do not reflect economic reality.

A project addressing IAS 30 disclosure requirements came to fruition in mid-2005 with the issuance of IFRS 7, covered in this book. It eliminates IAS 30 disclosures and merges them with those formerly in IAS 39, all of which are now incorporated into the new standard.

In mid-2005 IASB issued an Exposure Draft of an amendment to IAS 37. This evolved as part of the ongoing efforts to converge IFRS with US GAAP. In particular, it is responsive to the differences between IAS 37 (on provisions) and FAS 146, addressing certain disposal and exit activities and the costs properly accrued in connection with them. FAS 146 was promulgated, in part, to curtail the abuses commonly called providing "cookie jar reserves" during periods of corporate downsizing, when generous estimates were often made of future related costs, which in some instances served to absorb costs properly chargeable to future periods. In other cases, excess reserves (provisions) would later be released into income, thereby overstating operating results of the later periods. FAS 146 applies strict criteria so that reserves that do not meet the definition of liabilities cannot be recorded. The proposal also will hew more closely to US GAAP's approach to guarantees, which distinguish between the unconditional element—the promise to provide a service for some defined duration of time—and the conditional element, which is contingent on the future events, such as terminations, occurring.

If adopted, the amended IAS 37 would eliminate the terms contingent liability and contingent asset, and would restrict the meaning of constructive obligations so that these would be recognized as liabilities only if the reporting entity's actions result in other parties having a valid expectation on which they can reasonably rely that the entity will perform. Furthermore, the probability criterion would be deleted, so that only if a liability is not subject to reasonable measurement would it be justifiable to not record it. Certain changes are also made to IAS 19 by this draft (see discussion in Chapter 12).

IASB also intends to replace IAS 20, with an Exposure Draft presently promised for late 2005. (See discussion in Chapter 26.)

Other current IASB projects include: business combinations (application of purchase accounting method—Exposure Draft issued mid-2005); business combinations (accounting for noncontrolling interests—Exposure Draft issued mid-2005); conceptual framework (discussion paper due in mid-2006, in joint project with FASB); consolidation of special-purpose entities; emission rights (Exposure Draft to replace withdrawn IFRIC 3 expected mid-2006); insurance contracts (phase II); and performance reporting (new standard for presentation of information on the face of the financial statements).

Europe 2005 Update

The IASB's long effort to gain acceptance for IFRS began to bear fruit several years ago, when the EU abandoned a nascent quest to develop Euro-GAAP, and when IOSCO endorsed, with some qualifications, the "core set of standards" following major revisions to most of the then-extant IFRS. A significant impediment remains, however, as the US Securities and Exchange Commission still refuses to permit filings of financial statements prepared on the basis of IFRS without reconciliation of major items to US GAAP. However, the EU's decision to require IFRS-based filings will provide a further impetus to acceptance—as will the IASB-FASB agreement to work toward full convergence of the standards.

Beginning January 1, 2005, all European Union (EU) companies having securities listed on an EU exchange must prepare consolidated (group) accounts in conformity with IFRS. It is estimated that this requirement will affect approximately 7,000 companies, of which some 3,000 are in the United Kingdom. By 2004, some 200 to 300 EU companies had already begun to report on an IFRS basis. In all or almost all instances, comparative financial statements will be required, meaning that restatement of 2004 financials will also be necessary in the first year's (2005) presentations. However, by early 2005 the vast majority of companies affected by this requirement had not communicated the likely impacts of the change in basis of accounting to the stockholders, analysts or other constituents, and a surprisingly large fraction of analysts remained uneducated about IFRS.

In addition, it is likely that, within a reasonable period of time, all the EU states will *permit* IFRS in the consolidated accounts of nonlisted companies, although this permission, in some states, might not extend to certain types of companies such as small enterprises or charities. Moreover, most of the EU states will permit IFRS in the annual (i.e., not consolidated) accounts of all companies, again subject to some exceptions. In addition, some EU states have already begun to converge their national accounting rules with IFRS.

Privately held EU companies may also choose to utilize IFRS for many sound reasons (e.g., for comparability purposes), in anticipation of eventual convergence of national standards with IFRS, and at the specific request of stakeholders such as the entities' credit and investment constituencies.

The remaining impediment to full IFRS conformity among the affected EU companies pertains to the financial instruments standard, IAS 39, which has proved to be extraordinarily controversial, at least among some reporting entities, particularly financial institutions in some, but not all, European countries. Originally, as noted above, all IAS/IFRS standards were endorsed, *except* IAS 32 and IAS 39, as to which endorsement was postponed, nominally because of expected further amendments coming from IASB, but actually due to the philosophical or political dispute over use of fair value accounting for financial instruments and hedging provisions. The single most important of the concerns pertained to accounting for "core deposits" of banks, which drew objections from five of the six dissenting votes on the EFRAG (European Financial Reporting Advisory Group) Technical Expert Group (TEG). In fact, the dissents were a majority of the eleven-member TEG, but since it takes a two-thirds vote to refuse endorsement, the tepid support would be sufficient.

Notwithstanding that IASB had promised a "stable platform" of rules (i.e., no changes or new standards to be issued during the massive transition to IFRS in Europe, so that preparers could be spared the frustration of a moving target as they attempted to prepare, usually, January 1, 2004 restated balance sheets and 2004 and 2005 financial statements under IFRS), the controversy over IAS 39 resulted in a number of amendments being made in 2005, mostly in order to mollify EU member states. Thus, IAS 39 was (separately) amended to deal with macrohedging, cash flow hedges of forecast intragroup transactions, the "fair value option," and financial guarantee contracts. (These changes are all addressed in this book.)

Notwithstanding these efforts to satisfy EU member state concerns about specific aspects of IAS 39, the final EU approval was still qualified, with an additional "carve out" identified. Thus, there is the specter of semicompliance with IFRS, and independent auditors will have to grapple with this when financial statements prepared in accordance with Euro-IFRS are prepared for issuance in early 2006. At this point in time, the representation that financial statements are "in accordance with IFRS" can be invoked only when the reporting entity fully complies with IFRS, as the standards have been promulgated (and amended, when relevant), but without any deviations permitted in the EU legislation.

Impact of IFRS Adoption by EU Companies

The effect of the change to IFRS will vary from country to country and from company to company. National GAAP of many European countries were developed for tax and other regulatory purposes, so principles differ from state to state. The Web pages of many EU accounting firms currently highlight the complexity and potential confusion involved in transitioning to IFRS.

Complexity means cost. One survey of 1,000 European companies indicates that the average compliance cost across UK companies will be about £360,000. This figure rises to £446,000 for a top-500 company; £625,000 for companies with a market capitalization value between £1bn-£2bn; and over £1m for companies valued at more than £2bn.

Implementation, however, is not the only difficulty, and possibly not even the most significant one. Changes in principles can mean significant changes in profit and loss statements or balance sheets. In a 2002 survey of EU companies, two-thirds of respondents indicated that the adoption of IFRS would have a medium to high impact on their businesses.

One of the most important effects of the now-occurring change to IFRS will reverberate throughout companies' legal relationships. Obviously, companies must make appropriate disclosure to their stakeholders in order to properly explain the changes and their impact. Additionally, accountants and lawyers will also have to review the significantly expanded footnote disclosures required by IFRS in financial statements.

In addition to appropriate stakeholder disclosure, companies must re-examine legal relationships which are keyed to accounting reports. Changed accounting principles can undermine carefully crafted financial covenants in shareholder agreements, financing contracts and other transactional documents.

Drafters must examine the use of "material adverse change" triggers in the context of businesses whose earnings may be subject to accounting volatility. Debt, equity and lease financing arrangements may require restructuring due to unanticipated changes in reported results arising from the use of IFRS.

For example, IFRS may require a reclassification of certain financial instruments previously shown as equity on a company's balance sheet into their equity and debt components. Additionally, IFRS permits companies to adjust the carrying values of investment property (real estate) to fair market values with any gains being reflected in the income statement.

Executives may be concerned about compensation systems tied to earnings increases between measurement dates when earnings can be so volatile, or they may simply be concerned that compensation arrangements are keyed to results which are no longer realistic.

Few companies want to entertain dated or "frozen" GAAP for document purposes because of the costs involved in maintaining two separate systems of accounting. As a result, companies, their lawyers and accountants will have to re-examine agreements in light of the anticipated effect of IFRS on companies' financial statements.

APPENDIX A

CURRENT INTERNATIONAL FINANCIAL REPORTING STANDARDS (IAS/IFRS) AND INTERPRETATIONS (SIC/IFRIC)

(R) = Standard is revised or newly issued in 2004 or 2005

IAS 1	Presentation of Financial Statements (R)
IAS 2	Inventories
IAS 7	Cash Flow Statements
IAS 8	Accounting Policies, Changes in Accounting Estimates and Errors
IAS 10	Events After the Balance Sheet Date
IAS 11	Construction Contracts
IAS 12	Accounting for Taxes on Income
IAS 14	Reporting Financial Information by Segment
IAS 16	Property, Plant, and Equipment
IAS 17	Accounting for Leases
IAS 18	Revenue
IAS 19	Employee Benefits (R)
IAS 20	Accounting for Government Grants and Disclosure of Government Assistance
IAS 21	The Effects of Changes in Foreign Exchange Rates
IAS 23	Borrowing Costs
IAS 24	Related-Party Disclosures
IAS 26	Accounting and Reporting by Retirement Benefit Plans
IAS 27	Consolidated and Separate Financial Statements (R)
IAS 28	Accounting for Investments in Associates
IAS 29	Financial Reporting in Hyperinflationary Economies
IAS 30	Disclosures in the Financial Statements of Banks and Similar Financial Institutions (Superseded by IFRS 7 beginning in 2007)
IAS 31	Financial Reporting of Interests in Joint Ventures
IAS 32	Financial Instruments: Disclosures and Presentation (R)
IAS 33	Earnings Per Share
IAS 34	Interim Financial Reporting
IAS 36	Impairments of Assets (R)
IAS 37	Provisions, Contingent Liabilities, and Contingent Assets
IAS 38	Intangible Assets (R)
IAS 39	Financial Instruments: Recognition and Measurement (R)
IAS 40	Investment Property (R)
IAS 41	Agriculture
IFRS 1	First-Time Adoption of IFRS (R)

IFRS 2   Share-Based Payment (R)

IFRS 3   Business Combinations (R)

IFRS 4   Insurance Contracts (R)

IFRS 5   Noncurrent Assets Held for Sale and Discontinued Operations (R)

IFRS 6   Exploration for and Evaluation of Mineral Resources (R)

IFRS 7   Financial Instruments: Disclosures (R)

SIC 7   Introduction of the Euro (IAS 21)

SIC 10   Government Assistance—No Specific Relation to Operating Activities (IAS 20)

SIC 12   Consolidation—Special-Purpose Entities (IAS 27) (R)

SIC 13   Jointly Controlled Entities—Nonmonetary Contributions by Venturers (IAS 31)

SIC 15   Operating Leases—Incentives (IAS 17)

SIC 21   Income Taxes—Recovery of Revalued Nondepreciable Assets (IAS 12)

SIC 25   Income Taxes—Changes in the Tax Status of an Enterprise or Its Shareholders (IAS 12)

SIC 27   Evaluating the Substance of Transactions Involving the Legal Form of a Lease (IAS 1, IAS 17, and IAS 18)

SIC 29   Disclosure—Service Concession Arrangements (IAS 1)

SIC 31   Revenue—Barter Transactions Involving Advertising Services (IAS 18)

SIC 32   Intangible Assets—Web Site Costs (IAS 38)

IFRIC 1   Changes in Existing Decommissioning, Restoration and Similar Liabilities (IAS 1, IAS 8, IAS 16, IAS 23, IAS 36, IAS 37)

IFRIC 2   Members' Shares in Cooperative Entities and Similar Instruments (IAS 32, IAS 39) (R)

IFRIC 4   Determining Whether an Arrangement Contains a Lease (IAS 8, IAS 16, IAS 17, IAS 38) (R)

IFRIC 5   Rights to Interests Arising from Decommissioning, Restoration and Environmental Rehabilitation Funds (IAS 8, IAS 27, IAS 28, IAS 31, IAS 37, IAS 39, SIC 12) (R)

IFRIC 6   Liabilities Arising from Participating in a Specific Market—Waste Electrical and Electronic Equipment

APPENDIX B

CASE STUDY ILLUSTRATING POSSIBLE SUPPLEMENTAL TREATMENTS UNDER THE IOSCO RECOMMENDATIONS

The completion of a "core set of standards," as agreed by IOSCO, was a major achievement, and IASC quite naturally expected that, having performed on its side of the bargain, IOSCO would likewise deliver on its explicit and implicit commitments. After almost four years, IOSCO's technical committee gave a qualified endorsement in May 2000.

IOSCO's endorsement came with certain strings attached in the form of "supplemental treatments." As explained by IOSCO's Presidents' Committee resolution, these supplemental treatments are as follows:

- **Reconciliation**—Requiring reconciliation of certain items to show the effect of applying a different accounting method, in contrast with the method applied under IASC standards;
- **Disclosure**—Requiring additional disclosures, either in the presentation of the financial statements or in the footnotes; and
- **Interpretation**—Specifying use of a particular alternative provided in an IASC standard, or a particular interpretation in cases where the IASC standard is unclear or silent.

The resolution also establishes the notion of "waivers." It states that, as part of national or regional specific requirements, waivers of particular aspects of an IASC standard may be envisaged, without requiring that the effect of the accounting method used be reconciled to the effect of applying the IASC method. The clear intention is that the use of waivers will be restricted to exceptional circumstances, such as issues identified by a domestic regulator when a specific IASC standard is contrary to domestic or regional regulation.

While more recently the move to converge IFRS and US GAAP has taken center stage, the IOSCO supplemental treatments remain extant for securities regulators to impose as deemed relevant to national interests. The following case study suggests one such scenario.

Company X has presented its financial statements under International Financial Reporting Standards (IFRS) and is seeking listing on the national stock exchange of Country Y. The securities regulator of Country Y is a member of the IOSCO. It has recently decided to accept financial statements prepared under IFRS. However, supplemental treatments as envisaged by the IOSCO recommendations would need to be made for the purposes of listings on its national stock exchange.

A local practitioner who is also knowledgeable about IAS was consulted by Company X. The consultant pointed out the following items that would need to be adjusted before the financial statements could be presented to the stock exchange in Country Y:

1. Amortization of intangible assets over twenty-five years by the company as permitted by IAS 38;
2. Revaluation of building with disclosures strictly according to IAS 16;
3. Immediate expensing of borrowing costs relating to certain qualifying assets as permitted by IAS 23; and
4. Use of the "true and fair" override with respect to translation of monetary liabilities. Accounts payable denominated in a foreign currency were not translated at year-end rates because that would have resulted in the company recognizing income of $2 million. Strictly applying IAS 21, this translation gain would need to be booked to income. However, since the company was certain that when it would ultimately repay these amounts such a difference in the amount payable would not result, and thus, recognizing this huge sum as income would not be proper. It therefore invoked the "true and fair" override provisions of IAS 1 and did not recognize this income.

The following possible *supplemental adjustments* are required before Company X is allowed to list its shares on the national stock exchange of Country Y:

1. The GAAP in Country Y allows intangible assets to be amortized over five years. Since the company has amortized the intangible assets over twenty-five years, a *reconciliation* is required as envisaged by the IOSCO recommendations;

2. Disclosures made in Company X's financial statements under IAS 16 with respect to carrying amounts of a building based on cost would need to be supplemented by *addittonal disclosures* as envisioned in the IOSCO recommendations. For instance, additional disclosure with respect to significant balance sheet and income statement effect of revaluation would need to be provided;

3. Since the GAAP in Country Y only allows borrowing costs relating to qualifying assets to be capitalized, the financial statements prepared under IAS would need to be restated giving effect to this adjustment;

4. Because the GAAP in Country Y does not permit the "true and fair" override, the unrecognized income resulting from foreign currency translation gain would need to be booked in the income statement of Company X.

APPENDIX C

US GAAP RECONCILIATION AND RESTATEMENT—CASE STUDY

Hyderabad International Inc. prepares its financial statements in accordance with International Financial Reporting Standards (IFRS). The company wants to seek a listing on a US stock exchange. Therefore, it has approached an international financial reporting consultant, who specializes in both IFRS and US GAAP, to guide it in the reconciliation and restatement of its IFRS-based financial results to US GAAP. The approach taken by the consultant in restating the financial statements is very systematic and is based on the fundamental principles of double entry bookkeeping. In order to understand the logic behind the method employed by the consultant, one has to visualize the "opening" of the company's general ledger for the accounting period and debiting and crediting various accounts. The objective is to restate the IFRS-based financial results to financial statements prepared in accordance with US GAAP. The balance sheet and the income statement of Hyderabad International Inc. for the latest financial period are presented below.

Exhibit 1

Hyderabad International Inc.
Balance Sheet (under IFRS)
December 31, 2004

	(In DCU* Millions)	(In DCU Millions)
Current assets:		
Cash and bank	$ 500	
Accounts receivable	7,500	
Inventories	3,500	
Total current assets		$ 11,500
Current liabilities:		
Bank overdraft	(1,000)	
Accounts payable	(5,000)	
Accruals and provisions	(4,000)	
Total current liabilities		(10,000)
Net current assets		$ 1,500
Property, plant, and equipment	15,500	
Accumulated depreciation	(9,000)	
		6,500
Intangible assets	3,000	
Accumulated amortization	(1,000)	2,000
		10,000
Long-term loans		(3,000)
		7,000
Shareholders' equity:		
Equity capital	4,000	
Retained earnings	2,000	
Revaluation reserve	1,000	
Total shareholders' equity		$ 7,000

* *DCU are the Domestic Currency Units*

Exhibit 2

Hyderabad International Inc.
Income Statement (under IFRS)
For the Year Ended December 31, 2004

	(In DCU Millions)	*(In DCU Millions)*
Sales		$27,000
Less: Cost of sales		(15,000)
Gross profit		13,000
Distribution costs		5,000
Administrative expenses		1,500
Operating expenses:		
Depreciation	$1,000	
Amortization	1,000	
Staff costs	1,500	
Other operating expenses	1,500	5,000
Total distribution, admin. & operating expenses		$11,500
Income from operations		1,500
Interest expense		(700)
Interest income		200
Net income for the period		$ 1,000

Based on the differences noted between the two accounting frameworks, the IFRS/US GAAP consultant undertakes a restatement of the financial results. The following is a summary of some differences between IFRS and US GAAP identified by the consultant:

Revaluation of buildings. Under IAS 16, based on the "allowed alternative" treatment, property, plant, and equipment (PPE) can be revalued and carried from year to year at depreciated revalued amounts (instead of depreciated historical cost which is the prescribed treatment under the "benchmark treatment" of IAS 16). Although this treatment is followed in many countries including the UK, under US GAAP this practice would be regarded as a departure from GAAP. Consequently, when restating financial statements (initially prepared according to IFRS to financial statements prepared under US GAAP), the carrying amount of PPE that is revalued could be vastly different from the PPE carried at depreciated historical cost. Furthermore, depreciation charged to the Income Statement (when PPE is carried at revalued amounts) is comparatively higher. Thus, had the PPE been carried at depreciated historical cost (the way it is accounted for in the United States), the gross carrying amount of PPE would be lower by DCU 1,000 million compared to the IFRS-based figure. Also, for the year 2004, the depreciation charge would be lower by DCU 200 million compared to the IFRS-based depreciation expense.

The following journal entries are required in order to adjust the above:

Journal Entry 1

	Debit	*Credit*
Revaluation reserve	1,000	
Property, plant, & equipment		1,000
Accumulated depreciation	200	
Retained earnings		100
Depreciation		100

Research and development. During the current year, the company incurred research and development (R&D) expenditure. Part of this qualified as development expenditure under IAS 38. Such expenses amounting to DCU 1,000 million were, in accordance with IAS 38, treated as intangible assets. This is not the treatment prescribed by US GAAP that mandates that such expenses should be expensed when incurred and not allowed to be carried forward. Thus, on restating financial statements prepared in accordance with IFRS (to financial statements based on US GAAP), DCU 1,000 million would need to be reversed from intangible assets and charged to expenses (e.g., to "Other Operating Expenses"). The company amortized these capitalized "development costs" (treated as an intangible asset) over a period of five years using the straight-line method. For the year 2004, it charged an amortization expense of DCU 200 million to the income statement. This needs to be reversed.

The following journal entry illustrates the above adjustment:

Journal Entry 2

	Debit	Credit
Other operating expenses	1,000	
Intangible assets		1,000
Accumulated amortization	200	
Amortization		200

Expensed "in-process" R&D versus intangible asset or goodwill. During the previous financial year the company acquired a "dot.com" enterprise. Part of the acquisition price was attributed to in-process research and development (R&D). Under IAS 22, *acquired* in-process R&D is either a separately identifiable intangible asset or part of goodwill. (Note that for acquisitions after March 2004 the provisions of IFRS 3 apply, superseding IAS 22. However, regarding this matter, the prescribed treatements are essentially the same under both former and new standards.) However, under US GAAP, *acquired* in-process R&D is never recognized as an asset but is separated from goodwill and recognized as an expense in the year of acquisition. The company's accounting policy is to initially capitalize *acquired* in-process R&D as an intangible asset and later amortize it. Thus, the company capitalized in-process R&D of DCU 1,000 million on the acquisition of the dot.com enterprise in the previous financial year. It amortized this intangible asset over a period of five years using the straight-line method. Considering the treatment required under US GAAP (i.e., to expense *acquired* in-process R&D), the IFRS/US GAAP consultant (retained by the company) estimated that intangible assets were overstated (as of December 31, 2004) by DCU 600 million and that the net income for 2004 was understated by DCU 200 million. Further, the previous year's net income was overstated by DCU 800 million according to the consultant.

Based on the opinion of the consultant the following journal entry was recorded:

Journal Entry 3

	Debit	Credit
Retained earnings	1,000	
Intangible assets		1,000
Accumulated amortization	400	
Retained earnings		200
Amortization		200

Borrowing costs. Under IAS 23, borrowing costs relating to qualifying assets can either be expensed (under the benchmark treatment) or capitalized (under the allowed alternative treatment). In the United States, such borrowing costs are capitalized and added to the carrying amount of the related qualifying asset. During the current year, the construction of a qualifying asset (as defined in IAS 23) was completed. Interest expense on long-term borrowings utilized in the construction of the qualifying asset were expensed by the company in accordance with the benchmark treatment of IAS 23. The interest expense that was charged to the income statement in the previous financial period amounted to DCU 75 million and the interest expensed during the current year totaled DCU 25 million. The qualifying asset has a useful life of five years and is depreciated using the straight-line method.

The following adjusting entry is required in order to adjust the above treatment of borrowing costs under IFRS:

Journal Entry 4

	Debit	*Credit*
Property, plant, & equipment	100	
Retained earnings		75
Interest expense		25
Depreciation	20	
Accumulated depreciation		20

Foreign exchange differences—capitalization of losses from severe currency devaluation. At the end of the previous financial year the company imported machinery on deferred credit terms. The liability in foreign currency was carried forward to the current financial year. During the current financial year the currency of the country importing the machinery underwent severe devaluation. As a result, the company paid an extra sum of DCU 25 million over and above the contracted foreign currency liability relating to the imported machinery that was carried forward (as a foreign currency denominated payable) from the previous year. There was no practical means of hedging against this devaluation. Since this machinery was placed in service on the last day of the current financial year, no depreciation was charged on this asset.

Previously there had been an allowed alternative treatment in IAS 21, so that in rare circumstances, foreign exchange losses were allowed to be included in the carrying amount of a recently acquired asset. Such foreign exchange differences were to have resulted from "severe devaluation or depreciation of a currency against which there is no practical means of hedging and that affects liabilities which cannot be settled and which arise directly on the recent acquisition of an asset invoiced in a foreign currency." SIC 11 had clarified, among other issues, the meaning of the term "recent acquisition" used in IAS 21 and interpreted it as a period not exceeding twelve months.

Revised IAS 21 has eliminated this option, and recognition of the effects of exchange differences have to be included in current period earnings. The revisions to IAS 21 are effective in 2005. For purposes of this example, assume the differences arise before 2005 and that the now-eliminated option was elected by the reporting entity.

Under US GAAP, capitalization of foreign currency losses is not permitted. In other words, while restating financial statements in accordance with US GAAP, such foreign exchange differences would need to be charged to the income statement.

The consultant has suggested the following journal entry to take care of the above IFRS treatment:

Journal Entry 5

	Debit	*Credit*
Other operating expenses	25	
Property, plant, & equipment		25

Exhibit 3

Hyderabad International Inc.
Restated Balance Sheet (per US GAAP)
December 31, 2004 (in DCU Millions)

	Before restatement (per IFRS)	Debit	JE #	Credit	JE #	Restated (per US GAAP)
Assets						
Current assets:						
Cash and bank	$ 500					$ 500
Accounts receivable	7,500					7,500
Inventories	3,500					3,500
Total current assets	$11,500					$11,500
Property, plant, & equipment	$15,500	100	4	1,000	1	$14,575
				25	5	
Accumulated depreciation	(9,000)	200	1	20	4	(8,820)
	6,500					5,755
Intangible assets	3,000			1,000	2	1,000
				1,000	3	
		200	2			
Accumulated amortization	(1,000)	400	3			(400)
	2,000					600
Total	$20,000					$17,855
Liabilities & Equity						
Current liabilities:						
Bank overdraft	$ 1,000					$ 1,000
Accounts payable	5,000					5,000
Accruals and provisions	4,000					4,000
Total current liabilities	$10,000					$10,000
Long-term loans	$ 3,000					$ 3,000
Shareholders' equity:						
Equity capital	$ 4,000					$ 4,000
Retained earnings	2,000	1,000	3	100	1	
				200	3	
				75	4	
Decrease in net profit (1,000 − 480)		520				855
Revaluation reserve	1,000	1,000	1			0
	$ 7,000					$ 4,655
Total	$20,000					$17,855

Exhibit 4

Hyderabad International Inc.
Restated Income Sheet (per US GAAP)
Year Ended December 31, 2004 (in DCU Millions)

	Before restatement (per IFRS)	*Debit*	*JE #*	*Credit*	*JE #*	*Restated (per US GAAP)*
Sales	$27,000					$27,000
Less: Cost of sales	(15,000)					(15,000)
Gross profit	$13,000					$13,000
Distribution costs	5,000					5,000
Administrative expenses	1,500					1,500
Operating expenses:						
Depreciation	$ 1,000	20	4	100	1	$ 920
Amortization	1,000			200	2	
				200	3	600
Staff costs	1,500					1,500
		1,000	2			
Other operating expenses	1,500	25	5			2,525
	5,000					5,545
Total distribution, admin. and operating expenses	$11,500					$ 12,045
Income from operations	$ 1,500					955
Interest expense	(700)			25	4	(675)
Interest income	200					200
Net income for the period	$ 1,000					$ 480

Exhibit 5

Hyderabad International Inc.
Reconciliation of Net Profit Determined under International Accounting
Standards to Net Income in Accordance with US GAAP (in DCU millions)

Net Income determined under International Accounting Standards	(1,000)

Adjustments to conform to US GAAP

JE #		
1	Excess depreciation on revalued PPE reversed	(100)
2	Capitalized R&D expensed (plus reversal of amortization)	800
3	Adjustment relating to acquired in-process R&D	(200)
4	Expensed borrowing costs on qualifying assets capitalized	(25)
	(plus depreciation on capitalized borrowing costs adjusted)	20
5	Capitalized foreign currency losses (from severe devaluation) reversed	25
	Net income in accordance with US GAAP	(480)

APPENDIX D

USE OF PRESENT VALUE IN ACCOUNTING

Present value is a pervasive concept that has many applications in accounting. Currently, IFRS does not provide specific guidance to this subject matter, but in recognition of its importance, guidance drawn from US GAAP's Concepts Statement 7 (CON 7) is summarized on the following pages.

CON 7 provides a framework for using estimates of future cash flows as the basis for accounting measurements either at initial recognition or when assets are subsequently remeasured at fair value (fresh-start measurements). It also provides a framework for using the interest method of amortization. It provides the principles that govern measurement using present value, especially when the amount of future cash flows, their timing, or both are uncertain. However, it does not address recognition questions, such as which transactions and events should be valued using present value measures or when fresh-start measurements are appropriate.

Fair value is the objective for most measurements at initial recognition and for fresh-start measurements in subsequent periods. At initial recognition, the cash paid or received (historical cost or proceeds) is usually assumed to be fair value, absent evidence to the contrary. For fresh-start measurements, a price that is observed in the marketplace for an essentially similar asset or liability is fair value. If purchase prices and market prices are available, there is no need to use alternative measurement techniques to approximate fair value. However, if alternative measurement techniques must be used for initial recognition and for fresh-start measurements, those techniques should attempt to capture the elements that when taken together would comprise a market price if one existed. The objective is to estimate the price likely to exist in the marketplace if there were a marketplace—fair value.

CON 7 states that the only objective of using present value in accounting measurements is fair value. It is necessary to capture, to the extent possible, the economic differences in the marketplace between sets of estimated future cash flows. A present value measurement that fully captures those differences must include the following elements:

1. An estimate of the future cash flow, or in more complex cases, series of future cash flows at different times
2. Expectations about possible variations in the amount or timing of those cash flows
3. The time value of money, represented by the risk-free rate of interest
4. The risk premium—the price for bearing the uncertainty inherent in the asset or liability
5. Other factors, including illiquidity and market imperfections

How CON 7 measures differ from previously utilized present value techniques. Previously employed present value techniques typically used a single set of estimated cash flows and a single discount (interest) rate. In applying those techniques, adjustments for factors 2. through 5. described in the previous paragraph are incorporated in the selection of the discount rate. In the CON 7 approach, only the third factor listed (the time value of money) is included in the discount rate; the other factors cause adjustments in arriving at risk-adjusted expected cash flows. CON 7 introduces the probability-weighted, expected cash flow approach, which focuses on the range of possible estimated cash flows and estimates of their respective probabilities of occurrence.

Previous techniques used to compute present value used estimates of the cash flows most likely to occur. CON 7 refines and enhances the precision of this model by weighting different cash flow scenarios (regarding the amounts and timing of cash flows) by their estimated probabilities of occurrence and factoring these scenarios into the ultimate determination of fair value. The difference is that values are assigned to the cash flows other than the most likely one. To illustrate, a cash flow might be €100, €200, or €300 with probabilities of 10%, 50% and 40%, respectively. The most likely cash flow is the one with 50% probability, or €200. The expected cash flow is €230 (=€100 × .1) + (€200 × .5) + (€300 × .4).

The CON 7 method, unlike previous present value techniques, can also accommodate uncertainty in the timing of cash flows. For example, a cash flow of €10,000 may be received in one year, two years, or three years with probabilities of 15%, 60%, and 25%, respectively. Traditional present value techniques would compute the present value using the most likely timing of the payment—two years. The example below shows the computation of present value using the CON 7 method. Again, the expected present value of €9,030 differs from the traditional notion of a best estimate of €9,070 (the 60% probability) in this example.

Present value of €10,000 in one year discounted at 5%	€9,523	
Multiplied by 15% probability		€1,428
Present value of €10,000 in two years discounted at 5%	9,070	
Multiplied by 60% probability		5,442
Present value of €10,000 in three years discounted at 5%	8,638	
Multiplied by 25% probability		2,160
Probability weighted expected present value		€9,030

Measuring liabilities. The measurement of liabilities involves different problems from the measurement of assets; however, the underlying objective is the same. When using present value techniques to estimate the fair value of a liability, the objective is to estimate the value of the assets required currently to (1) settle the liability with the holder or (2) transfer the liability to an entity of comparable credit standing. To estimate the fair value of an entity's notes or bonds payable, accountants look to the price at which other entities are willing to hold the entity's liabilities as assets. For example, the proceeds of a loan are the price that a lender paid to hold the borrower's promise of future cash flows as an asset.

The most relevant measurement of an entity's liabilities should always reflect the credit standing of the entity. An entity with a good credit standing will receive more cash for its promise to pay than an entity with a poor credit standing. For example, if two entities both promise to pay €750 in three years with no stated interest payable in the interim, Entity A, with a good credit standing, might receive about €630 (a 6% interest rate). Entity B, with a poor credit standing, might receive about €533 (a 12% interest rate). Each entity initially records its respective liability at fair value, which is the amount of proceeds received—an amount that incorporates that entity's credit standing.

Present value techniques can also be used to value a guarantee of a liability. Assume that Entity B in the above example owes Entity C. If Entity A were to assume the debt, it would want to be compensated €630—the amount that it could get in the marketplace for its promise to pay €750 in three years. The difference between what Entity A would want to take the place of Entity B (€630) and the amount that Entity B receives (€533) is the value of the guarantee (€97).

Interest method of allocation. CON 7 describes the factors that suggest that an interest method of allocation should be used. It states that the interest method of allocation is more relevant than other methods of cost allocation when it is applied to assets and liabilities that exhibit one or more of the following characteristics:

1. The transaction is, in substance, a borrowing and lending transaction.
2. Period-to-period allocation of similar assets or liabilities employs an interest method.

3. A particular set of estimated future cash flows is closely associated with the asset or liability.
4. The measurement at initial recognition was based on present value.

Accounting for changes in expected cash flows. If the timing or amount of estimated cash flows changes and the asset or liability is not remeasured at a fresh-start measure, the interest method of allocation should be altered by a catch-up approach. That approach adjusts the carrying amount to the present value of the revised estimated future cash flows, discounted at the original effective interest rate.

Application of present value tables and formulas.

Present value of a single future amount. To take the present value of a single amount that will be paid in the future, apply the following formula; where *PV* is the present value of €1 paid in the future, *r* is the interest rate per period, and *n* is the number of periods between the current date and the future date when the amount will be realized.

$$PV = \frac{1}{(1+r)^n}$$

In many cases the results of this formula are summarized in a present value factor table.

(n) Periods	2%	3%	4%	5%	6%	7%	8%	9%	10%
1	0.9804	0.9709	0.9615	0.9524	0.9434	0.9346	0.9259	0.9174	0.9091
2	0.9612	0.9426	0.9246	0.9070	0.8900	0.8734	0.8573	0.8417	0.8265
3	0.9423	0.9151	0.8890	0.8638	0.8396	0.8163	0.7938	0.7722	0.7513
4	0.9239	0.8885	0.8548	0.8227	0.7921	0.7629	0.7350	0.7084	0.6830
5	0.9057	0.8626	0.8219	0.7835	0.7473	0.7130	0.6806	0.6499	0.6209

Example

Suppose one wishes to determine how much would need to be invested today to have €10,000 in five years if the sum invested would earn 8%. Looking across the row with n = 5 and finding the present value factor for the r = 8% column, the factor of 0.6806 would be identified. Multiplying €10,000 by 0.6806 results in €6,806, the amount that would need to be invested today to have €10,000 at the end of five years. Alternatively, using a calculator and applying the present value of a single sum formula, one could multiply €10,000 by $1/(1+.08)^5$, which would also give the same answer—€6,806.

Present value of a series of equal payments (an annuity). Many times in business situations a series of equal payments paid at equal time intervals is required. Examples of these include payments of semiannual bond interest and principal or lease payments. The present value of each of these payments could be added up to find the present value of this annuity, or alternatively a much simpler approach is available. The formula for calculating the present value of an annuity of €1 payments over *n* periodic payments, at a periodic interest rate of *r* is

$$PV\ Annuity = \left(1 - \frac{1}{(1+r)^n}\right)$$

The results of this formula are summarized in an annuity present value factor table.

(n) Periods	2%	3%	4%	5%	6%	7%	8%	9%	10%
1	0.9804	0.9709	0.9615	0.9524	0.9434	0.9346	0.9259	0.9174	0.9091
2	1.9416	1.9135	1.8861	1.8594	1.8334	1.8080	1.7833	1.7591	1.7355
3	2.8839	2.8286	2.7751	2.7233	2.6730	2.6243	2.5771	2.5313	2.4869
4	3.8077	3.7171	3.6299	3.5460	3.4651	3.3872	3.3121	3.2397	3.1699
5	4.7135	4.5797	4.4518	4.3295	4.2124	4.1002	3.9927	3.8897	3.7908

Example

Suppose four annual payments of €1,000 will be needed to satisfy an agreement with a supplier. What would be the amount of the liability today if the interest rate the supplier is charging is 6% per year? Using the table to get the present value factor, then n = 4 periods row, and the 6% column, gives you a factor of 3.4651. Multiply this by €1,000 and you get a liability of €3,465.10 that should be recorded. Using the formula would also give you the same answer with r = 6% and n = 4.

Caution must be exercised when payments are not to be made on an annual basis. If payments are on a semiannual basis n = 8, but *r* is now 3%. This is because *r* is the periodic interest rate, and the semiannual rate would not be 6%, but half of the 6% annual rate. Note that this is somewhat simplified, since due to the effect of compound interest 3% semiannually is slightly more than a 6% annual rate.

Example of the relevance of present values

A measurement based on the present value of estimated future cash flows provides more relevant information than a measurement based on the undiscounted sum of those cash flows. For example, consider the following four future cash flows, all of which have an undiscounted value of €100,000:

1. Asset A has a fixed contractual cash flow of €100,000 due tomorrow. The cash flow is certain of receipt.
2. Asset B has a fixed contractual cash flow of €100,000 due in twenty years. The cash flow is certain of receipt.
3. Asset C has a fixed contractual cash flow of €100,000 due in twenty years. The amount that ultimately will be received is uncertain. There is an 80% probability that the entire €100,000 will be received. There is a 20% probability that €80,000 will be received.
4. Asset D has an *expected* cash flow of €100,000 due in twenty years. The amount that ultimately will be received is uncertain. There is a 25% probability that €120,000 will be received. There is a 50% probability that €100,000 will be received. There is a 25% probability that €80,000 will be received.

Assuming a 5% risk-free rate of return, the present values of the assets are

1. Asset A has a present value of €99,986. The time value of money assigned to the one-day period is €14(€100,000 × .05/365 days).
2. Asset B has a present value of €37,689 [€100,000/$(1 + .05)^{20}$].
3. Asset C has a present value of €36,181 [(€100,000 × .8 + 80,000 × .2)/$(1 + .05)^{20}$].
4. Asset D has a present value of €37,689 [€120,000 × .25 + 100,000 × .5 + 80,000 × .25)/$(1 + .05)^{20}$].

Although each of these assets has the same undiscounted cash flows, few would argue that they are economically the same or that a rational investor would pay the same price for each. Investors require compensation for the time value of money. They also require a risk premium. That is, given a choice between Asset B with expected cash flows that are certain and Asset D with cash flows of the same expected amount that are uncertain, investors will place a higher value on Asset B, even though they have the same expected present value. CON 7 says that the risk premium should be subtracted from the expected cash flows before applying the discount rate. Thus, if the risk premium for Asset D was €500, the risk-adjusted present values would be €37,500 {[(€120,000 × .25 + 100,000 × .5 + 80,000 × .25) − 500]/$(1 + .05)^{20}$}.

Practical matters. Like any accounting measurement, the application of an expected cash flow approach is subject to a cost-benefit constraint. The cost of obtaining additional information must be weighed against the additional reliability that information will bring to the measurement. As a practical matter, an entity that uses present value measurements often has little or no information about some or all of the assumptions that investors would use in assessing the fair value of an asset or a liability. Instead, the entity must use the information that is available to it without undue cost and effort when it develops cash flow estimates. The entity's own assumptions about future cash flows can be used to estimate fair value using present value techniques, as long as there are no contrary data indicating that investors would use different assumptions. However, if contrary data exist, the entity must adjust its assumptions to incorporate that market information.

2 BALANCE SHEET

PERSPECTIVE AND ISSUES

As set forth by the IASB's *Framework for the Preparation and Presentation of Financial Statements ("Framework"),* the objective of financial reporting is to provide information regarding an entity's financial position, performance, and changes in financial position to a broad spectrum of users, to enable them to make rational and informed economic decisions. According to the *Framework,* the financial statements are meant to report on the "results of stewardship of the management, or the accountability of management for the resources entrusted to it."

IAS 1, *Presentation of Financial Statements,* which was substantially revised in 2003 and received a further amendment in 2005, refers to financial statements as "a structured financial representation of the financial position of and the transactions undertaken by an enterprise," and elaborates that the objective of general-purpose financial statements is to provide information about an enterprise's financial position, its performance, and its cash flows, which is then utilized by a wide spectrum of end users in making economic decisions. This information is communicated through a complete set of financial statements which, according to IAS 1, comprises the following components:

1. A balance sheet
2. An income statement
3. Another statement showing either

    a. All changes in equity, or
    b. Changes in equity other than those arising from capital transactions with owners and distributions to owners

4. A cash flow statement
5. Notes comprising a summary of significant accounting policies and other explanatory notes

The balance sheet is a statement of financial position that presents assets, liabilities, and shareholders' equity (net worth) at a given point in time. The balance sheet is sometimes described as a "stock" statement because it reflects the balances of the company's accounts at a moment in time, as opposed to the other basic financial statements, which are described as "flow" statements and all reflect summarized results of transactions over a period of time.

During the early era of financial reporting standard setting, throughout the nineteenth century and first half of twentieth century, the emphasis of legislation was almost entirely on the balance sheet, but by the mid-twentieth century shareholders were asking for more and more information about operating performance, leading to presentations of an increasingly complete income statement (or profit and loss account).

There is a continuing tension between the two financial statements, since—because of double entry bookkeeping conventions—they are linked together and cannot easily serve differing objectives. The stock markets look primarily at earnings expectations, which are largely based on historic performance, as measured by the income statement. If earnings measurement drives financial reporting, this means that, of necessity, the balance sheet carries the residuals of the earnings measurement process. For example, assets such as motor vehicles with service potential that is used up over several accounting periods will have their costs allocated to these periods through the depreciation process, with the balance sheet left to report a residual of that allocation process, which may or may not reflect the value of those assets on the balance sheet date. However, if reporting were truly balance sheet driven, the reporting entity would value the vehicles at each balance sheet date—for example by reference to their replacement costs in current condition—and the change in balance sheet values from one year to another would be reflected in the income statement.

By the 1960s many national GAAP standards were being promulgated to overtly favor the income statement over the balance sheet, but the pendulum began to swing back to a balance sheet-oriented strategy when standard setters—first, the FASB in the US; later others, including the International Accounting Standards Committee, predecessor of the current IASB—developed conceptual frameworks intended to serve as the fundamental theory of financial reporting. Undertaking that exercise had the result of causing accounting theory to revert to the original purpose—namely, to measure economic activity—and to implicitly adopt the definition of income as the change in wealth from period to period. With this in mind, measurement of that wealth, as captured in the balance sheet, became more central to new standards development efforts.

In practice, IFRS as currently written are a mixture of both approaches, depending on the transaction being recognized, measured, and reported. This mixed attribute approach is partially a legacy of earlier financial reporting rule making, but also reflects the practical difficulties of value measurement for many categories of assets and liabilities. For example, many financial instruments are remeasured at each balance sheet date, whereas property, plant, and equipment are normally held at original cost and are depreciated systematically over estimated useful lives, subject to further adjustment for impairment, as nescessary.

However, while existing requirements are not entirely consistent regarding financial statement primacy, both the IASB and the FASB, when developing new accounting standards, now are formally committed to a balance sheet approach. The *Framework* is expressed in terms of measuring assets and liabilities, and reportedly the two standard-setting bodies and their respective staffs analyze transactions affected by proposed standards from the perspective of whether they increase or diminish the assets and liabilities of the entity.

Overall, the IASB sees financial reporting as being based on the measuring of assets and liabilities, and has the overall goal of requiring reporting all changes to them (other than those which are a result of transactions with owners, such as the payment of dividends) in a statement of comprehensive income.

In 2003 the IASB pursued a project to create a new comprehensive statement of performance, to be called the *statement of comprehensive income*. Field visits suggested that the proposed statement was too far in advance of current practice to readily gain acceptance from preparers and users of financial reports, which caused the IASB to give further attention to a mode of presentation which would be more comprehensible to users and preparers. Some simplifications have since been agreed to, and other issues remain under discussion. In late 2004, IASB and FASB agreed to jointly conduct further consideration of these matters, effectively signaling a fresh start for this developing effort.

The focus on earnings in the capital markets does not mean that the balance sheet is irrelevant; clearly the financial structure of the company is an important aspect of the company's risk profile, which in turn is important to evaluating the potential return on an investment from the perspective of a current or potential stockholder. Lenders have an even greater interest in the entity's financial structure. This is why companies sometimes go to great lengths to keep some transactions off balance sheet, for example by using special-purpose entities and other complex financing structures. IAS 32 considers that any instrument that gives rise to a right to claim assets from an entity is a liability.

IAS 1 states that "each material class of similar items" should be presented separately in the financial statements. The standard expresses a preference for a presentation based on the current/noncurrent distinction, but allows a presentation by liquidity if that is more reliable and relevant. An asset or liability is current if it is part of the reporting entity's normal operating cycle (e.g., customer receivables) or if it will be realized or settled within twelve months. Only one of these conditions needs to be satisfied, so for example, inventory that stays on hand for two years should still be classified as current, while long-term liabilities should be reclassified as current for the final year before settlement. IAS 1 includes a sample balance sheet in its Application Guidance, but use of this format is optional.

Sources of IFRS
IAS 1, 8, 10, 24, 32, 36, 38, 39, 40, 41
IFRS 5, 6
Framework for the Preparation and Presentation of Financial Statements

DEFINITIONS OF TERMS

The IASB *Framework* describes the basic concepts by which financial statements are prepared. It does so by defining the objective of financial statements; identifying the qualitative characteristics that make information in financial statements useful; and defining the basic elements of financial statements and the concepts for recognizing and measuring them in financial statements.

The elements of financial statements are the broad classifications and groupings which convey the substantive financial effects of transactions and events on the reporting entity. To be included in the financial statements, an event or transaction must meet definitional, recognition, and measurement requirements, all of which are set forth in the *Framework*.

Elements of balance sheets.

Assets—Probable future economic benefits obtained or controlled by a particular entity as a result of past transactions or events.

The following three characteristics must be present for an item to qualify as an asset:

1. The asset must provide probable future economic benefit that enables it to provide future net cash inflows.
2. The entity is able to receive the benefit and restrict other entities' access to that benefit.
3. The event that provides the entity with the right to the benefit has occurred.

In addition, the asset must be capable of being measured reliably. The *Framework* says that reliable measurement means that the number must be free from material error and bias and can be depended upon by users to represent faithfully. In the Basis for Conclusions of IFRS 2, the IASB notes that the use of estimates is permitted, and that there may be a trade-off between the characteristics of being free from material error and having representational faithfulness.

Assets have features that help identify them in that they are exchangeable, legally enforceable, and have future economic benefit (service potential). It is that potential that eventually brings in cash to the entity and that underlies the concept of an asset.

Liabilities—*Probable future sacrifices of economic benefits arising from present obligations of a particular entity to transfer assets or provide services to other entities in the future as a result of past transactions or events.*

The following three characteristics must be present for an item to qualify as a liability:

1. A liability requires that the entity settle a present obligation by the probable future transfer of an asset on demand when a specified event occurs or at a particular date.
2. The obligation cannot be avoided.
3. The event that obligates the entity has occurred.

Liabilities are similarly recognized subject to the constraint that they can be measured reliably.

Liabilities usually result from transactions that enable entities to obtain resources. Other liabilities may arise from nonreciprocal transfers, such as the declaration of dividends to the owners of the entity or the pledge of assets to charitable organizations.

An entity may involuntarily incur a liability. A liability may be imposed on the entity by government or by the court system in the form of taxes, fines, or levies. A liability may arise from price changes or interest rate changes. Liabilities may be legally enforceable or they may be equitable obligations that arise from social, ethical, or moral requirements. Liabilities continue in existence until the entity is no longer responsible for discharging them.

The diagram that follows, which is taken from one of the statements produced from the conceptual framework project by the US standard setter, the FASB, identifies the three classes of events that affect an entity, and shows the relationship between assets and liabilities, on the one hand, and comprehensive income, on the other.

Equity—*The residual interest in the assets that remains after deducting its liabilities. In a business enterprise, the equity is the ownership interest.*

Equity arises from the ownership relation and is the basis for distributions of earnings to the owners. Distributions of enterprise assets to owners are voluntary. Equity is increased by owners' investments and comprehensive income and is reduced by distributions to owners. In practice, the distinction between equity and liabilities may be difficult to determine. Securities such as convertible debt and certain types of preferred stock may have characteristics of both equity (residual ownership interest) and liabilities (nondiscretionary future sacrifices). For both the IASB and the FASB, equity, aside from exchanges with owners, is a residual of the asset/liability recognition model.

All transactions and other events and circumstances that affect a business enterprise during a period

A. All changes in assets and liabilities not accompanied by changes in equity

1. Exchanges of assets for assets
2. Exchanges of liabilities for liabilities
3. Acquisitions of assets by incurring liabilities
4. Settlements of liabilities by transferring assets

B. All changes in assets or liabilities accompanied by changes in equity

1. Comprehensive income
   a. Revenues
   b. Gains
   c. Expenses
   d. Losses

2. All changes in equity from transfers between a business enterprise and its owners
   a. Investments by owners
   b. Distributions to owners

C. Changes within equity that do not affect assets or liabilities

CONCEPTS, RULES, AND EXAMPLES

General Concepts

Under IFRS, assets and liabilities are recorded at fair value at inception in financial statements, which for assets and liabilities arising from arm's-length transactions will be equal to negotiated prices. Subsequent measurement is usually under the historical cost principle, although in many cases subsequent changes in values are also recognized. All assets are now subject to impairment testing. IAS 36, *Impairment of Assets,* requires assets to be reduced in value if their carrying value exceeds the higher of fair value or value in use (expected future cash flows from the asset). IAS 39, *Financial Instruments: Recognition and Measurement,* IAS 40, *Investment Property,* and IAS 41, *Agriculture,* all include some element of subsequent measurement at fair value. Where assets are classified as held for sale, they are carried at the lower of their carrying amount or fair value less selling costs (IFRS 5).

Historical exchange prices, and the amortized cost amounts that are later presented, are sometimes cited as being useful because these amounts are objectively determined and capable of being verified independently. However, critics point out that, other than at transaction date, historical cost does not result in the presentation balance sheet numbers that are comparable between companies, so while they are reliable, they may not be relevant for decision-making purposes. This captures the fundamental conflict regarding accounting information: absolutely reliable or objective information may not be very relevant to current decision making.

Form of Balance Sheet

The titles commonly given to the primary financial statement that presents an entity's financial position include the balance sheet, the statement of financial position, and the statement of financial condition. (The statement of assets and liabilities, or some variant thereof, is also encountered, but usually connotes a presentation that is not consistent with IFRS or GAAP, such as a cash or tax basis of presentation.) The IASB routinely uses the term balance sheet, which is also used by the European Union in its accounting directives, and that title will be used throughout this book.

The three elements that are always to be displayed in the heading of a balance sheet are

1. The entity whose financial position is being presented
2. The title of the statement
3. The date of the statement

The entity's name should appear exactly as written in the legal document that created it (e.g., the certificate of incorporation, partnership agreement, etc.). The title should also clearly reflect the legal status of the enterprise as a corporation, partnership, sole proprietorship, or division of some other entity.

The balance sheet presents a "snapshot" of the resources and claims to resources at a moment in time. The last day of a month is normally used as the statement date (in jurisdictions where a choice is allowed) unless the entity uses a fiscal reporting period always ending on a particular day of the week, such as a Friday or Sunday (e.g., the last Friday in December, or the Sunday falling closest to December 31). In these cases, the balance sheet can appropriately be dated accordingly (i.e., December 26, October 1, etc.). In all cases, the implication is that the balance sheet captures the pertinent amounts as of the close of business on the date noted.

Balance sheets should generally be uniform in appearance from one period to the next, as indeed should all of the entity's financial statements. The form, terminology, captions, and pattern of combining insignificant items should be consistent. The goal is to enhance usefulness by maintaining a consistent manner of presentation unless there are good reasons to change these and the changes are duly reported.

Classification of Assets

Assets, liabilities, and stockholders' equity are separated in the balance sheet. IAS 1 says that companies should make a distinction between current and noncurrent assets and liabilities, except when a presentation based on liquidity provides information that is more reliable or relevant.

Current assets. An asset should be classified as a current asset when it satisfies any one of the following:

1. It is expected to be realized in, or is held for sale or consumption in, the normal course of the enterprise's operating cycle;
2. It is held primarily for trading purposes;
3. It is expected to be realized within twelve months of the balance sheet date;
4. It is cash or a cash equivalent asset that is not restricted in its use.

If a current asset category includes items that will have a life of more than twelve months, the amount that falls into the next financial year should be disclosed in the notes. All other assets should be classified as noncurrent assets, if a classified balance sheet is to be presented in the financial statements.

Thus, current assets include cash, cash equivalents and other assets that can be expected to be realized in cash, or sold or consumed during one normal operating cycle of the business. The operating cycle of an enterprise is the time between the acquisition of materials entering into a process and its realization in cash or an instrument that is readily convertible into cash. Inventories and trade receivables should still be classified as current assets in a classified balance sheet even if these assets are not expected to be realized within twelve months from the balance sheet date. However, marketable securities could only be classified as current assets if they are expected to be realized (sold, redeemed, or matured) within twelve months of the balance sheet date, even though most would deem marketable securities to be more liquid than inventories and possibly even than receivables. Management intention takes priority over liquidity potential. The following items would be classified as current assets:

1. **Inventories** are assets held, either for sale in the ordinary course of business or in the process of production for such sale, or in the form of materials or supplies to be consumed in the production process or in the rendering of services (IAS 2). The basis of valuation and the method of pricing, which is now limited to FIFO or weighted average cost, should be disclosed.

Inventories—at the lower of cost (FIFO) or net realizable value	$xxx

   In the case of a manufacturing concern, raw materials, work in process, and finished goods should be disclosed separately on the balance sheet or in the footnotes.

Inventories:		
Finished goods	$xxx	
Work in process	xxx	
Raw materials	xxx	$xxx

2. **Receivables** include accounts and notes receivable, receivables from affiliate companies, and officer and employee receivables. The term *accounts receivable*

represents amounts due from customers arising from transactions in the ordinary course of business. Allowances due to expected lack of collectibility and any amounts discounted or pledged should be stated clearly. The allowances may be based on a relationship to sales or based on direct analysis of the receivables. If material, the receivables should be analyzed into their component parts. The receivables section may be presented as follows:

Receivables:			
Customer accounts	$xxx		
Customer notes/commercial paper	xxx	$xxxx	
Less allowance for doubtful accounts		(xxx)	$xxxx
Due from associated companies			xxx
Due from officers and employees			xxx
Total			$xxxx

3. **Prepaid expenses** are assets created by the prepayment of cash or incurrence of a liability. They expire and become expenses with the passage of time, use, or events (e.g., prepaid rent, prepaid insurance, and deferred taxes). This item is frequently aggregated with others on the face of the balance sheet with details relegated to the notes, since it is rarely a material amount.

4. **Trading investments** are those that are acquired principally for the purpose of generating a profit from short-term fluctuations in price or dealer's margin. A financial asset should be classified as held-for-trading if it is part of a portfolio for which there is evidence of a recent actual pattern of short-term profit making. Trading assets include debt and equity securities and loans and receivables acquired by the enterprise with the intention of making a short-term profit. Derivative financial assets are always deemed held-for-trading unless they are designed as effective hedging instruments.

   As required by IAS 39, a financial asset held for trading should be measured at fair value, with changes in value reflected currently in earnings. There is a presumption that fair value can be reliably measured for financial assets that are held for trading.

5. **Cash** and cash equivalents include cash on hand, consisting of coins, currency, and undeposited checks; money orders and drafts; and deposits in banks. Anything accepted by a bank for deposit would be considered cash. Cash must be available for a demand withdrawal; thus, assets such as certificates of deposit would not be considered cash because of the time restrictions on withdrawal. Also, to be classified as a current asset, cash must be available for current use. According to IAS 1, cash that is restricted in use and whose restrictions will not expire within the operating cycle, or cash restricted for a noncurrent use, would not be included in current assets. According to IAS 7, cash equivalents include short-term, highly liquid investments that (1) are readily convertible to known amounts of cash, and (2) are so near their maturity (original maturities of three months or less) that they present negligible risk of changes in value because of changes in interest rates. Treasury bills, commercial paper, and money market funds are all examples of cash equivalents.

Noncurrent assets. IAS 1 uses the term "noncurrent" to include tangible, intangible, operating, and financial assets of a long-term nature. It does not prohibit the use of alternative descriptions, as long as the meaning is clear. The European Union uses the term *fixed assets* (which derives from nineteenth-century balance sheets, which drew a distinction between fixed and circulating assets). Noncurrent assets include held-to-maturity investments, investment property, property and equipment, intangible assets, assets held for sale, and miscellaneous other assets, as described in the following paragraphs.

Held-to-maturity investments are financial assets with fixed or determinable payments and fixed maturity that the enterprise has a positive intent and ability to hold to maturity (the term is from IAS 39, *Financial Instruments*). Examples of held-to-maturity investments are debt securities and mandatorily redeemable preferred shares. This category excludes loans and receivables originated by the enterprise, however, as under IAS 39 these represent a separate category of asset. Held-to-maturity investments are to be measured at amortized cost. (For a detailed discussion on financial instruments, refer to Chapters 5 and 10 of this book.)

Investment property. This denotes property being held to earn rentals, or for capital appreciation, or both, rather than for use in production or supply of goods or services, or for administrative purposes or for sale in the ordinary course of business. Investment property should be initially measured at cost. Subsequent to initial measurement an enterprise is required to elect either the fair value model or the cost model. (IAS 40 is the relevant standard: for a detailed discussion on investment property please refer to Chapter 10.)

Property, plant, and equipment. Tangible assets that are held by an enterprise for use in the production or supply of goods or services, or for rental to others, or for administrative purposes and which are expected to be used during more than one period. Included are such items as land, buildings, machinery and equipment, furniture and fixtures, motor vehicles and equipment. These should be disclosed, with the related accumulated depreciation, as follows:

Machinery and equipment	$xxx	
Less accumulated depreciation	(xxx)	$xxx
or		
Machinery and equipment (net of $xxx accumulated depreciation)		$xxx

Accumulated depreciation should be shown by major classes of depreciable assets. In addition to showing this amount on the balance sheet, the notes to the financial statements should contain balances of major classes of depreciable assets, by nature or function, at the balance sheet date, along with a general description of the method or methods used in computing depreciation with respect to major classes of depreciable assets (IAS 16).

Illustrative extract from published financial statements

Lectra SA
Notes to the Consolidated Balance Sheets
December 31, 2006

Note 3—Property, Plant, and Equipment

2005 *(in thousands of euros)*	*Land and buildings*	*Fixtures and fittings*	*Equipment and other*	*Total*
Gross value at January 1, 2005	9,796	8,110	20,691	38,597
Additions	42	282	1,409	1,733
Disposals	--	(41)	(858)	(899)
Translation adjustments	--	205	(1,223)	(1,428)
Gross value at December 31, 2005	9,838	8,146	20,019	38,003
Accumulated depreciation at December 31, 2005	(7,338)	(3,837)	(17,248)	(28,423)
Net value at December 31, 2005	2,500	4,309	2,771	9,580
2006 *(in thousands of euros)*				
Gross value at January 1, 2006	9,838	8,146	20,019	38,003
Additions	4	98	1,577	1,679
Disposals	--	(116)	(832)	(948)
Translation adjustments	--	(158)	(858)	(1,016)
Gross value at December 31, 2006	9,842	8,014	19,862	37,718
Accumulated depreciation at December 31, 2006	(7,419)	(4,186)	(17,428)	(29,033)
Net value at December 31, 2006	2,423	3,828	2,434	8,685

Change in depreciation

2005 *(in thousands of euros)*	*Land and buildings*	*Fixtures and fittings*	*Equipment and other*	*Total*
Accumulated depreciation at January 1, 2005	(7,263)	(3,321)	(17,031)	(27,615)
Additional depreciation	(75)	(498)	(1,488)	(2,061)
Disposal of assets	--	69	723	792
Translation adjustments	--	(87)	548	461
Accumulated depreciation at December 31, 2005	(7,338)	(3,837)	(17,248)	(28,423)
2006 *(in thousands of euros)*				
Accumulated depreciation at January 1, 2006	(7,338)	(3,837)	(17,248	(28,423)
Additional depreciation	(81)	(537)	(1,646)	(2,264)
Disposal of assets	--	74	778	852
Translation adjustments	--	114	688	852
Accumulated depreciation at December 31, 2006	(7,419)	(4,186)	(17,428)	(29,003)

Intangible assets. These are noncurrent assets of a business, without physical substance, the possession of which is expected to provide future benefits to the owner. Included in this category are the unidentifiable asset goodwill and the identifiable intangibles trademarks, patents, copyrights, and organizational costs.

IAS 38 stipulates that where an intangible is being amortized, it should be carried at cost net of accumulated amortization. Generally, the amortization of an intangible asset, or any impairment, is shown separately as a deduction from the asset cost, since that is a legal requirement in jurisdictions such as the European Union, but IAS 38 does not require this mode of presentation.

Illustrative extract from published financial statements

Lectra SA
Notes to the Consolidated Balance Sheets
December 31, 2006

Note 1—Intangible Assets

2005 *(in thousands of euros)*	*Management information software*	*Patents and trademarks*	*Other intangible assets*	*Total*
Gross value at January 1, 2005	8,555	1,703	5,232	15,490
External purchases	845	177	--	1,022
Internal development costs	381	--	--	381
Write-offs and disposals	--	--	(12)	(12)
Transfers	94	--	(94)	--
Translation adjustments	(38)	--	(12)	(50)
Gross value at December 31, 2005	9,837	1,880	5,114	16,831
Amortization at December 31, 2005	(6,913)	(1,523)	(4,422)	(12,858)
Net carrying value at December 31, 2006	2,924	357	692	3,973

2006 *(in thousands of euros)*	*Management information software*	*Patents and trademarks*	*Other intangible assets*	*Total*
Gross value at January 1, 2006	9,837	1,880	5,114	16,831
External purchases	1,061	137	42	1,240
Internal development costs	404	--	--	404
Write-offs and disposals	(17)	--	--	(17)
Transfers	(15)	--	15	--
Translation adjustments	(54)	--	(4)	(58)
Gross value at December 31, 2006	11,216	2,017	5,167	18,400
Amortization at December 31, 2006	(8,367)	(1,659)	(5,018)	(15,044)
Net carrying value at December 31, 2006	(2,849)	358	149	3,356

Changes in accumulated amortization

2005 *(in thousands of euros)*	*Management information software*	*Patents and trademarks*	*Other intangible assets*	*Total*
Amortization at January 1, 2005	(5,522)	(1,407)	(3,976)	(10,905)
Amortization charges	(1,490)	(116)	(446)	(2,052)
Disposals of assets	63	--	--	63
Translation adjustments	36	--	--	36
Amortization at December 31, 2005	(6,913)	(1,523)	(4,422)	(12,858)

2006 *(in thousands of euros)*				
Amortization at January 1, 2006	(6,913)	(1,523)	(4,422)	(12,858)
Amortization charges	(1,574)	(136)	(596)	(2,306)
Disposals of assets	97	--	--	97
Translation adjustments	23	--	--	23
Amortization at December 31, 2006	(8,367)	(1,659)	(5,018)	(15,044)

Assets held for sale. Where an entity has committed to a plan to sell an asset or group of assets, these should be reclassified as assets held for sale and should be measured at the lower of their carrying amount or their fair value less selling costs. (This requirement, set forth by IFRS 5, is discussed in Chapter 8).

Other assets. An all-inclusive heading for accounts that do not fit neatly into any of the other asset categories (e.g., long-term deferred expenses that will not be consumed within one operating cycle, and deferred tax assets).

Classification of Liabilities

The liabilities are normally displayed on the balance sheet in the order of payment due dates.

Current liabilities.   According to IAS 1, a liability should be classified as a current liability when

1.   It is expected to be settled in the normal course of business within the enterprise's operating cycle;
2.   It is due to be settled within twelve months of the balance sheet date;
3.   It is held primarily for the purpose of being traded; or
4.   The entity does not have an unconditional right to defer settlement beyond twelve months

All other liabilities should be classified as noncurrent liabilities. Obligations that are due on demand or are callable at any time by the lender are classified as current regardless of the present intent of the entity or of the lender concerning early demand for repayment. Current liabilities also include

1.   Obligations arising from the acquisition of goods and services entering into the entity's normal operating cycle (e.g., accounts payable, short-term notes payable, wages payable, taxes payable, and other miscellaneous payables).
2.   Collections of money in advance for the future delivery of goods or performance of services, such as rent received in advance and unearned subscription revenues.
3.   Other obligations maturing within the current operating cycle, such as the current maturity of bonds and long-term notes.

Certain liabilities, such as trade payables and accruals for operating costs, which form part of the working capital used in the normal operating cycle of the business, are to be classified as current liabilities even if they are due to be settled after more than twelve months from the balance sheet date.

Other current liabilities which are not settled as part of the operating cycle, but which are due for settlement within twelve months of the balance sheet date, such as dividends payable and the current portion of long-term debt, should also be classified as current liabilities. However, interest-bearing liabilities that provide the financing for working capital on a long-term basis and are not scheduled for settlement within twelve months should not be classified as current liabilities.

IAS 1 provides another exception to the general rule that a liability due to be repaid within twelve months of the balance sheet date should be classified as a current liability. If the original term was for a period longer than twelve months and the enterprise intended to refinance the obligation on a long-term basis prior to the balance sheet date, and that intention is supported by an agreement to refinance, or to reschedule payments, which is completed before the financial statements are approved, then the debt is to be reclassified as noncurrent as of the balance sheet date.

However, an entity would continue to classify as current liabilities its long-term financial liabilities when they are due to be settled within twelve months, if an agreement to refinance on a long-term basis was made after balance sheet date. Similarly if long-term debt becomes callable as a result of a breach of a loan covenant, and no agreement with the lender to provide a grace period of more than twelve months has been concluded by the balance sheet date, the debt must be classified as current. (This is different than under US GAAP, which permits a determination to be made as of the date of *issuance* of the financial statements, which may be months after the balance sheet date.)

The distinction between current and noncurrent liquid assets generally rests upon both the ability and the intent of the entity to realize or not to realize cash for the assets within the traditional one-year concept. Intent is not of similar significance with regard to the classification of liabilities, however, because the creditor has the legal right to demand satisfaction of a currently due obligation, and even an expression of intent not to exercise that right does not diminish the entity's burden should there be a change in the creditor's intention. Thus, whereas an entity can control its use of current assets, it is limited by its contractual obligations with regard to current liabilities, and accordingly, accounting for current liabilities (subject to the two exceptions noted above) is based on legal terms, not expressions of intent.

Noncurrent liabilities. Obligations that are not expected to be liquidated within the current operating cycle, including

1. Obligations arising as part of the long-term capital structure of the entity, such as the issuance of bonds, long-term notes, and lease obligations;
2. Obligations arising out of the normal course of operations, such as pension obligations, decommissioning provisions, and deferred taxes; and
3. Contingent obligations involving uncertainty as to possible expenses or losses. These are resolved by the occurrence or nonoccurrence of one or more future events that confirm the amount payable, the payee, and/or the date payable. Contingent obligations include such items as product warranties (see the section on provisions below).

For all long-term liabilities, the maturity date, nature of obligation, rate of interest, and description of any security pledged to support the agreement should be clearly shown. Also, in the case of bonds and long-term notes, any premium or discount should be reported separately as an addition to or subtraction from the par (or face) value of the bond or note. Long-term obligations which contain certain covenants that must be adhered to are classified as current liabilities if any of those covenants have been violated and the lender has the right to demand payment. Unless the lender expressly waives that right or the conditions causing the default are corrected, the obligation is current.

Offsetting assets and liabilities. In general, assets and liabilities may not be offset against each other. However, the reduction of accounts receivable by the allowance for doubtful accounts, or of property, plant, and equipment by the accumulated depreciation, are acts that reduce these assets by the appropriate valuation accounts and are not considered to be offsetting assets and liabilities.

Only where there is an actual right of setoff is the offsetting of assets and liabilities a proper presentation. This right of setoff exists only when all the following conditions are met:

1. Each of the two parties owes the other determinable amounts (although they may be in different currencies and bear different rates of interest).
2. The entity has the right to set off against the amount owed by the other party.
3. The entity intends to offset.
4. The right of setoff is legally enforceable.

In particular cases, laws of certain countries, including some bankruptcy laws, may impose restrictions or prohibitions against the right of setoff. Furthermore, when maturities differ, only the party with the nearest maturity can offset because the party with the longer maturity must settle in the manner determined by the earlier maturity party.

The question of setoff is sometimes significant for financial institutions which buy and sell financial instruments, often repackaging them as part of the process. IAS 39 provides detailed rules for determining when derecognition is appropriate and when assets and liabilities must be retained on balance sheet.

Classification of Stockholders' Equity

Stockholders' equity represents the interests of the stockholders in the net assets of a corporation. It shows the cumulative net results of past transactions and other events affecting the entity since its inception.

Share capital. This consists of the par or nominal value of preferred and common shares. The number of shares authorized, the number issued, and the number outstanding should be clearly shown. For preferred share capital, the preference features must also be stated, as the following example illustrates:

6% cumulative preference shares, $100 par value, callable at $115, 15,000 shares authorized, 10,000 shares issued and outstanding	$ 1,000,000
Common shares, $10 par value per share, 2,000,000 shares authorized, 1,500,000 shares issued and outstanding	$15,000,000

Preference share capital that is redeemable at the option of the holder may not be considered a part of equity—rather, it should be reported as a liability. IAS 32 makes it clear that substance prevails over form in the case of compound financial instruments; any instrument which includes a contractual obligation for the entity to deliver cash is considered to be a liability.

Retained earnings. This represents the accumulated earnings since the inception of the enterprise, less any earnings distributed to owners in the form of dividends. In some jurisdictions, notably in continental Europe, the law requires that a portion of retained earnings, equivalent to a small proportion of share capital, be set aside as a legal reserve. Historically, this was intended to limit dividend distributions by young or ailing businesses. This practice is expected to wane, and in any event is not congruent with financial reporting in accordance with IFRS and with the distinction made between equity and liabilities.

Also included in the equity section of the balance sheet is treasury stock representing issued shares that have been reacquired by the issuer, in jurisdictions where the purchase of the entity's own shares is permitted by law. These shares are generally stated at their cost of acquisition, as a reduction from shareholders' equity.

Finally, some elements of comprehensive income are included directly in equity (i.e., without first being included in results of operations), either as part of the analysis of equity or through a statement of recognized income and expenditure. These include net changes in the fair values of available-for-sale securities portfolios and unrealized gains or losses on translations of the financial statements of subsidiaries denominated in a foreign currency. These items of other comprehensive income will probably be incorporated in an expanded income statement in the future, if performance reporting projects currently being pursued by IASB and FASB come to fruition.

Minority interests should be shown separately from owners' equity of the parent company in group accounts (i.e., consolidated financial statements), but are included in the overall equity section.

Supplemental Disclosures

In addition to the recognition and measurement principles set forth under IFRS, there are also requirements for supplemental disclosures, generally shown as notes to the accounts. There is also a degree of fluidity between showing information "on the face of the accounts" (i.e., directly in the balance sheet or income statement) and in the notes: the main categories have to be preserved (see below), but the detail underlying the reported amounts may be shown in the notes. The two basic techniques are giving parenthetical explanations on the face of the accounts, and giving additional information in the notes.

Parenthetical explanations. Supplemental information is disclosed by means of parenthetical explanations following the appropriate balance sheet items. For example

Equity share capital ($10 par value, 200,000 shares authorized, 150,000 issued) $1,500,000

Parenthetical explanations have an advantage over both footnotes and supporting schedules, as they place the disclosure in the body of the statement, where their importance cannot be overlooked by users of the financial statements.

Footnotes. If the additional information cannot be disclosed in a relatively short and concise parenthetical explanation, a footnote should be used, with a cross-reference shown in the balance sheet. For example

Inventories (see Note 1) $2,550,000

The notes to the financial statements would then contain the following:

Note 1: Inventories are stated at the lower of cost or market. Cost is determined by the first-in, first-out method, and market is determined on the basis of estimated net realizable value. As of the balance sheet date, the market value of the inventory is $2,720,000.

To present adequate detail regarding certain balance sheet items, or move complex detail from the face of the accounts, a supporting schedule may be provided in the notes. Current receivables may be a single line item on the balance sheet, as follows:

Current receivables (see Note 2) $2,500,000

A separate schedule for current receivables would then be presented as follows:

Note 2
Current Receivables

Customers' accounts and notes	$2,000,000
Associated companies	300,000
Nonconsolidated affiliates	322,000
Other	18,000
	2,640,000
Less allowance for doubtful accounts	(140,000)
	$2,500,000

Valuation accounts are another form of schedule used to keep detail off the balance sheet. For example, accumulated depreciation reduces the book value for property, plant, and equipment, and a bond premium (discount) increases (decreases) the face value of a bond payable as shown in the following illustrations. The net amount is shown on the balance sheet, and the detail in the notes:

Property, plant, and equipment		
Equipment	$18,000,000	
Less accumulated depreciation	(1,625,000)	$16,375,000
Noncurrent liabilities		
Bonds payable	$20,000,000	
Less discount on bonds payable	(1,300,000)	$18,700,000
Bonds payable	$20,000,000	
Add premium on bonds payable	1,300,000	$21,300,000

Accounting policies. The policy note should begin with a clear statement on the nature of the comprehensive basis of accounting used. A reporting entity may only claim to follow IFRS if it complies with every single IFRS in force as of the reporting date. The European

Union made certain amendments to IFRS when endorsing them (carve-outs from IAS 32 and IAS 39), and those EU companies following these directives cannot claim to follow IFRS, and instead will have to acknowledge compliance with IFRS as endorsed by the EU.

IAS 1 requires financial statements to include clear and concise disclosure of all significant accounting policies that have been used in the preparation of those financial statements. Management must also indicate the judgments that it has made in the process of applying the accounting policies that have the most significant effect on the amounts recognized. The entity must also disclose the key assumptions about the future and any other sources of estimation uncertainty that have a significant risk of causing a material adjustment to later be made to the carrying amounts of assets and liabilities.

Financial statement users must be made aware of the accounting policies used by reporting entities, so that they can better understand the financial statements and make comparisons with the financial statements of others. The policy disclosures should identify and describe the accounting principles followed by the entity and methods of applying those principles that materially affect the determination of financial position, results of operations, or changes in cash flows.

IAS 1 requires that disclosure of these policies be an integral part of the financial statements. It recommends that these policies be disclosed in one location rather than being scattered throughout the footnotes. Though it makes it mandatory on enterprises to disclose all significant accounting policies, IAS 1 also recognizes that good disclosure cannot rectify an incorrect or inappropriate recognition or measurement decision.

IAS 8 (as discussed in Chapter 1) provides criteria for making accounting policy choices. Policies should be relevant to the needs of users and should be reliable (representationally faithful, reflecting economic substance, neutral, prudent, and complete).

Fairness exception under IAS 1. There is a subtle difference between US GAAP and what was required by many European countries regarding the use of an override to assure a fair presentation of the company's financial position and results of operations. While the US requires a fair presentation in accordance with GAAP, the European Fourth Directive requires that statements offer a *true and fair view* of the company's financial situation. If following the literal financial reporting requirements does not provide this result, then the entity should first consider the salutary effects of providing supplementary disclosures. However, if that is not seen as being sufficient to achieve a true and fair view, the entity may conclude that it must override (that is, ignore or contravene) the applicable accounting standard.

IAS 1 has a similar approach. It states the expectation that the use of IFRS will result, *in virtually all circumstances,* in financial statements that achieve a fair presentation. However, in extremely rare circumstances where the entity concludes that complying with a standard would be misleading, IAS 1 permits departure from the standards to achieve the greater good of fair presentation—provided, however, that the enterprise discloses the following:

1. That management has concluded that the financial statements fairly present the entity's financial position, results of operations, and cash flows;
2. That the entity has complied in all material respects with applicable IFRS except that it departed from a standard to achieve a fair presentation; and
3. The standard from which the entity has departed; the nature of the departure, including the accounting treatment which literal application of the standard would have required; the reason why that treatment would have been misleading in the circumstances; the alternative treatment which was in fact applied; and the financial impact of the departure on profit or loss, assets, liabilities, equity, and cash flows for each period presented.

The standard notes that deliberately departing from IFRS might not be permissible in some jurisdictions, in which case the entity should comply with the standard in question and disclose in the notes that it believes this to be misleading, and show the adjustments that would be necessary to avoid this distorted result.

It might be noted under US auditing standards there is a provision that an unqualified opinion may be rendered even when there has been a GAAP departure, if the auditor concludes that it provides a fairer presentation than would have resulted had GAAP been strictly adhered to (the so-called "Rule 203 exception," which may be eliminated under a new GAAP hierarchy standard currently proposed by FASB). Under IFRS, this logic is built into the accounting standards themselves, and thus is not dependent upon the level of service, if any, being rendered by an independent accountant, but rather makes it a management responsibility, including the need to disclose the logic and the financial statement impact.

Related-party disclosures. According to IAS 24, financial statements should include disclosure of material related-party transactions that are defined by the standard as "transfer of resources or obligations between related parties, regardless of whether a price is charged."

A *related party* is essentially any party that controls or can significantly influence the financial or operating decisions of the company to the extent that the company may be prevented from fully pursuing its own interests. Such groups would include associates, investees accounted for by the equity method, trusts for the benefit of employees, principal owners, key management personnel, and immediate family members of owners or management.

Disclosures should take place even if there is no accounting recognition made for such transactions (e.g., a service is performed without payment). Disclosures should generally not imply that such related-party transactions were on terms essentially equivalent to arm's-length dealings. Additionally, when one or more companies are under common control such that the financial statements might vary from those that would have been obtained if the companies were autonomous, the nature of the control relationship should be disclosed even if there are no transactions between the companies.

The disclosures generally should include

1. Nature of relationship
2. Description of transactions and effects of such transactions on the financial statements for each period for which an income statement is presented
3. Financial amounts of transactions for each period for which an income statement is presented and effects of any change in establishing the terms of such transactions different from that used in prior periods
4. Amounts due to and from such related parties as of the date of each balance sheet presented together with the terms and manner of settlement

Reporting comparative amounts for the preceding period. IAS 1 requires that financial statements should present corresponding figures for the preceding period. When the presentation or classification of items is changed, the comparative data must also be changed, unless it is impracticable to do so.

The related footnote disclosures must also be presented on a comparative basis, except for items of disclosure that would be not meaningful, or might even be confusing, if set forth in such a manner. Although there is no official guidance on this issue, certain details, such as schedules of debt maturities as of the year earlier balance sheet date, would seemingly be of little interest to users of the current statements and would be largely redundant with information provided for the more recent year-end. Accordingly, such details are often omitted from comparative financial statements. Most other disclosures, however, continue to be meaningful and should be presented for all years for which basic financial statements are displayed.

The IASB and FASB are proposing to converge their requirements for comparative data in due course, in the first phase of their joint project on reporting of entity performance.

To increase the usefulness of financial statements, many companies include in their annual reports five- or ten-year summaries of condensed financial information. This is not required by IFRS. These comparative statements allow investment analysts and other interested readers to perform comparative analysis of pertinent information. The presentation of comparative financial statements in annual reports enhances the usefulness of such reports and brings out more clearly the nature and trends of current changes affecting the enterprise. Such presentation emphasizes the fact that the statements for a series of periods are far more significant than those for a single period and that the accounts for one period are but an installment of what is essentially a continuous history.

Subsequent events. The balance sheet is dated as of the last day of the fiscal period, but a period of time will usually elapse before the financial statements are actually prepared and issued. During this period, significant events or transactions may have occurred that materially affect the company's financial position. These events and transactions are usually referred to as *subsequent events*. IAS 10 refers to these as "events after the balance sheet date." If not disclosed, significant events occurring between the balance sheet date and issue date could make the financial statements misleading to others not otherwise informed of such events.

There are two types of subsequent events described by IAS 10. The first type consists of events that provide additional evidence with respect to conditions that existed at the date of the balance sheet and which affect the estimates inherent in the process of preparing financial statements: these are called adjusting events. The second type consists of events that do not provide evidence with respect to conditions that existed at the date of the balance sheet, but arose subsequent to that date (and prior to the actual issuance of the financial statements): these are called nonadjusting events.

The principle is that the balance sheet should reflect as accurately as possible conditions that existed at balance sheet date, but not changes in conditions that occurred subsequently, even though they have the potential to influence investors' decisions. In the latter case disclosure is to be made.

Examples of post-balance-sheet date events

1. A loss on an uncollectible trade account receivable as a result of a customer's deteriorating financial condition leading to bankruptcy subsequent to the balance sheet date would usually (but not always) be indicative of conditions existing at the balance sheet date, thereby calling for adjustment of the financial statements before their issuance. On the other hand, a loss on an uncollectible trade account receivable resulting from a customer's major casualty, such as a fire or flood subsequent to the balance sheet date, would not be indicative of conditions existing at the balance sheet date, and adjustment of the financial statements would not be appropriate. However, if the amount is material, disclosure would be required.

2. A loss arising from the recognition after the balance sheet date that an asset such as plant and equipment had suffered a material decline in value arising out of reduced marketability for the product or service it can produce. Such a reduction would be considered an economic event in process at the balance sheet date and would require adjustment and recognition of the loss.

3. Nonadjusting events, which are those not existing at the balance sheet date, require disclosure but not adjustment. These could include

    a. Sale of a bond or share capital issue after the balance sheet date, even if planned before that date.

    b. Purchase of a business, if the transaction is consummated after year-end.

    c. Settlement of litigation when the event giving rise to the claim took place subsequent to the balance sheet date. The settlement is an economic event that would be accounted for in the period of occurrence. (However, if the event occurred before the balance sheet date, IAS 37 would require that the estimated amount of the contingency be accrued, in most instances, as discussed further in the next section of this chapter.)

d. Loss of plant or inventories as a result of fire or flood.

e. Losses on receivables resulting from conditions (such as a customer's major casualty) arising subsequent to the balance sheet date.

f. Gains or losses on certain marketable securities.

Contingent liabilities and assets. IAS 37 defines provisions, contingent assets, and contingent liabilities. Importantly, it differentiates provisions from contingent liabilities. Provisions are recognized as liabilities (if reliably estimatable), inasmuch as these are present obligations with probable outflows of resources embodying economic benefits needed to settle them. Contingent liabilities, on the other hand, are not recognized as liabilities under IFRS because they are either only *possible* obligations (i.e., not yet confirmed as being present obligations), or they are present obligations that do not meet the threshold for recognition (either because resource outflows are not *probable,* or because a sufficiently reliable estimate cannot be developed). Contingent liabilities are currently disclosed, although this treatment is likely to change.

Provisions are accrued by a charge against income if

1. The reporting entity has a present obligation as a result of past events;
2. It is probable that an outflow of the entity's resources will be required; and
3. A reliable estimate can be made of the amount.

If an estimate of the obligation cannot be made with a reasonable degree of certitude, accrual is not prescribed, but rather disclosure in the notes to the financial statements is needed.

For a provision to be made, the entity has to have incurred a constructive obligation. This may be an actual legal obligation, but it may also be only an obligation that arises as a result of an entity's stated polices. However, to preclude the use of reserves for manipulative purposes ("earnings management"), provisions for restructuring are subject to additional restrictions, and a provision may only be made once a detailed plan has been agreed and its implementation has commenced.

At the present date, the key recognition issue for contingent liabilities is the probability of a future cash outflow. The probability of this occurring is the threshold condition for recognition: a probable outflow triggers recording a provision, while an unlikely or improbable outflow creates only the need for a disclosure. In its ongoing business combinations project, the IASB (and also FASB) appears likely to conclude that a contingency is usually a combination of an *unconditional* right or obligation which is linked to a *conditional* right or obligation. The unconditional element is always to be recognized, although its value will be a function of the probability of the conditional element occurring. So if a company is being sued for €1m, and it considers that it has a 10% chance of losing, under the existing financial reporting rules, no provision would be made; if the new approach under consideration were to be adopted, this could be analyzed as an unconditional obligation to pay what the court decides, and this obligation would be measured as 10% of €1m. The probability of the loss then shifts from being a recognition criterion to being a measurement tool.

Other disclosures required by IAS 1. The reporting entity is required to provide details of any dividends proposed or declared before publication of the financial statements but not charged to equity. It should also indicate the amount of any cumulative preference dividends not recognized in the statement of changes in equity.

If not otherwise disclosed within the financial statements, these items should be reported in the footnotes.

1. The domicile and legal form of the entity, its country of incorporation, and the address of the registered office (or principal place of business, if different);
2. A description of the nature of the reporting entity's operations and its principal activities;
3. The name of the parent entity and the ultimate parent of the group; and
4. The number of employees either at the end of the period or an average during the period being reported upon.

These disclosures (which have been modeled on those set forth by the Fourth and Seventh EU Directives) are particularly of interest given the multinational character of many enterprises reporting in conformity with IFRS.

Balance Sheet Format

The format of a balance sheet is not specified in IFRS, although IAS 1 stipulates the following list of minimum categories to be displayed, to the extent relevant:

1. Property, plant, and equipment
2. Investment property
3. Intangible assets
4. Financial assets
5. Investments accounted for using the equity method
6. Biological assets
7. Inventories
8. Trade and other receivables
9. Cash and cash equivalents
10. Trade and other payables
11. Provisions
12. Financial liabilities
13. Liabilities for current tax
14. Deferred tax liabilities
15. Minority interest
16. Issued capital and reserves

In some countries, the legislation specifies the format of the financial statements—in particular the EU Fourth Directive mandates particular presentations—but in other jurisdictions entities have a free choice. The implementation guidance to IAS 1 gives an example of a balance sheet format in the European account format.

In general, the two types of formats are the report form and the account form. In the *report form* the balance sheet continues line by line from top to bottom as follows:

Assets	$xxx
Liabilities	$xxx
Stockholders' equity	xxx
Total liabilities and stockholders' equity	$xxx

In the *account form* the balance sheet appears in a balancing concept with assets on the left and liabilities and equity amounts on the right as follows:

Assets	$ xxx	Stockholders' equity	$ xxx
		Liabilities	xxx
Total assets	$ xxx	Total liabilities and stockholders' equity	$ xxx

The balance sheet format presented in Schedule 4 to the UK Companies Act of 1985, wherein a *net* asset total is presented (as a total of assets minus liabilities) as being equal to equity plus reserves, may be seen as a third variation, and is known as the UK GAAP format.

This is, in fact, a report format, as illustrated above, with merely a minor alteration made to explicitly reveal the equality between net assets and net worth.

The format of the balance sheet as illustrated by the appendix to IAS 1 is the following:

XYZ Limited
Consolidated Balance Sheet
December 31, 2004
(in thousands of currency units)

	2004	2004	2003	2003
Assets				
Noncurrent assets:	x		x	
Property, plant, and equipment	x		x	
Goodwill	x		x	
Other intangible assets	x		x	
Investments in associates	x		x	
Available-for-sale investments	x̲	xx	x̲	xx
Current assets:				
Inventories	x		x	
Trade and other receivables	x		x	
Other current assets	x		x	
Cash and cash equivalents	x̲	x̲x̲	x	x̲x̲
Total assets		x̲x̲		x̲x̲
Equity and Liabilities				
Capital and reserves				
Share capital (Note__)	x		x	
Other reserves (Note__)	x		x	
Retained earnings	x	xx	x̲	xx
Minority interest		xx		xx
Total equity		xx		x
Noncurrent liabilities:				
Long-term borrowings	x		x	
Deferred taxes	x		x	
Long-term provisions	x̲	x̲x̲	x̲	x̲x̲
Current liabilities:				
Trade and other payables	x		x	
Short-term borrowings	x		x	
Current portion of long-term borrowings	x		x	
Current tax payable	x		x	
Short-term provisions	x̲	x̲x̲	x̲	x̲x̲
Total equity and liabilities		x̲x̲		x̲x̲

Extract from Published Financial Statements

Barloworld
For the year ended September 30, 2004

	30 September	
R million	*2004*	*2003*
Assets		
Noncurrent assets	13,946	12,209
Property, plant, and equipment	7,728	6,672
Other noncurrent assets	1,096	699
Goodwill and intangible assets	2,674	1,580
Investment in associates and joint ventures	319	535
Finance lease receivables	1,631	2,267
Deferred taxation assets	498	456
Current assets	13,896	11,547
Inventories	5,134	5,010
Vehicle rental fleet	2,006	
Trade and other receivables	5,266	4,924
Taxation	47	66
Cash and cash equivalents	1,443	1,547
Total assets	27,842	23,756
Equity and liabilities		
Capital and reserves		
Share capital and premium	1,209	712
Other reserves	1,957	1,893
Retained income	7,988	7,087
Equity portion of convertible bond	--	36
Interest of shareholders of Barloworld Limited	11,154	9,728
Minority interest	721	708
Interest of all shareholders	11,875	10,436
Noncurrent liabilities	6,889	4,870
Interest-bearing	4,871	3,404
Deferred taxation liabilities	803	621
Noninterest-bearing	1,215	845
Current liabilities	9,078	8,450
Amounts due to bankers and short-term loans	2,839	2,559
Convertible bond	--	180
Taxation	468	461
Trade and other payables	5,272	4,746
Provisions	499	504
Total equity and liabilities	27,842	23,756

3 STATEMENTS OF INCOME, CHANGES IN EQUITY, AND RECOGNIZED INCOME AND EXPENSE

PERSPECTIVE AND ISSUES

In discussing the concept of performance, the IASB's *Framework* states that comprehensive income is the change in the entity's net assets over the course of the reporting period. Since mid-2004, the IASB and the FASB have been collaboratively pursuing projects on performance reporting, which has at least the potential to result in fundamental changes to the format and content of what currently is generally referred to as the income statement. One change that is deemed likely to be made is to require that the primary performance reporting financial statement include all changes in stockholders' equity that are now treated as being subject to exclusion from the income statement, apart from those resulting from investments by or distributions to owners. This joint effort has been bifurcated: the first component of the project is addressing narrow convergence issues such as the requirement under IFRS to present comparative financial statements (a requirement absent from US GAAP), while the second is to deal with larger issues, such as standards for presentation on the face of the required statement(s), the so-called "recycling" problem (how to report realized gains and losses when unrealized amounts were previously already reported in comprehensive income), and the use of totals and subtotals.

If indeed a combined statement of earnings and comprehensive income becomes mandatory, this will represent a triumph over the *all inclusive concept* of performance reporting. While this has been officially endorsed by world standard setters for many decades, in fact many standards promulgated over the years (e.g., IAS 39 requiring temporary changes in the fair value of investments other than trading securities are not included in current income) have deviated from adherence to this principle. While current sentiment appears to favor endorsement of a single statement, with net income being an intermediate caption in the financial statement, it remains possible that the ultimate consensus will favor a two-statement solution (much like the current situation).

Concepts of performance and measures of income have changed over the years, and current reporting still largely focuses on *realized* income and expense. However, unrealized gains and losses reflect real economic transactions and events, also, and are of great interest to decision makers. Under current IFRS, some of these unrealized gains and losses are *recognized*, while others are *unrecognized*. Both the financial reporting entities themselves and the financial analysts go to great lengths to identify within reported income those elements which are likely to be continuing into the future, since future period earnings and cash flows are main drivers of share prices.

IFRS rules for the presentation of income reflect a mixture of traditional realized income reporting, accompanied by fair value measures applied to unrealized gains and losses meeting certain criteria (e.g., financial instruments are accounted for differently from plant assets). For example, unrealized gains and losses arising from the translation of the foreign currency-denominated financial statements of foreign subsidiaries do not flow through the income statement. IAS 1 provides an option for grouping together all changes to equity deriving from performance, as opposed to exchanges with owners, in a separate *statement of changes in equity*. This corresponds more or less to the US GAAP concept of *other comprehensive income*.

The traditional income statement has been known by many titles. IFRS refer to this statement as the income statement, but in the EU Fourth Directive and in many Commonwealth countries it is referred to as the *profit and loss account*. In the United States other names, such as the statement of income, statement of earnings, or statement of operations, are sometimes used to denote the income statement. For convenience, this book uses the term income statement throughout, denoting the financial statement which reports all items entering into the determination of periodic earnings, but excluding items which are reported directly in stockholders' equity without passing through results of operations.

For many years, the income statement has been widely perceived by investors, creditors, management, and other interested parties as the single most important of an enterprise's basic financial statements. In fact, beginning in the mid-twentieth century, accounting theory development was largely driven by the desire to present a meaningful income statement, even to the extent that the balance sheet sometimes became the repository for balances of various accounts, such as deferred charges and credits, which could scarcely meet any reasonable definitions of assets or liabilities. This was done largely to serve the needs of investors, who are believed to use the past income of a business as the most important input to their predictions for entities' future earnings, which form the basis for their predictions of future share prices and dividends.

Creditors look to the income statement for insight into the borrower's ability to generate the future cash flows needed to pay interest and eventually to repay the principal amounts of the obligations. Even in the instance of secured debt, creditors do not look primarily to the balance sheet, inasmuch as seizure and liquidation of collateral is never the preferred outcome. Rather, generation of cash flows from operations—which is generally closely correlated to income—is seen as the primary source for debt service.

Management, then, must be concerned with the income statement by virtue of the importance placed on it by investors and creditors. In many large corporations, senior management receives substantial bonuses relating to either profit targets or share price performance. Consequently, managements sometimes devote considerable efforts in order to massage what appears in the income statement, in order to present the most encouraging view of the reporting entity's future prospects. This means that standard setters need to bear in mind the abuse possibilities of the rules they impose, and for that matter, the rules have been imposed in response to previous financial reporting abuses.

IFRS formerly allowed companies to segregate in their income statement any items not expected to recur, and to designate them as extraordinary gains or losses, but this led to predictable abuses. As one standard setter reportedly defined these items, "credits are ordinary items and debits are extraordinary items for some companies." In reaction, IASB eliminated the extraordinary item category entirely. On a related matter, recognition of provisions for restructuring is now somewhat restricted, in an attempt to prevent companies taking a larger-than-necessary charge against earnings in one period in order to retain greater flexibility (i.e., to absorb expenses or create earnings) in the next (often referred to as providing "cookie jar reserves").

The importance placed on income measurement has, as is well known, influenced behavior by some management personnel, who have sought to manipulate results to, say, meet Wall Street earnings estimates. The motivation for this improper behavior is readily understandable when one observes that recent markets have severely punished companies that missed earnings estimates by as little as a penny per share. One very popular vehicle for earnings management has centered on revenue recognition. Historically, certain revenue recognition situations, such as that involving prepaid service revenue, have lacked specific GAAP rules or have been highly subject to interpretation, opening the door to aggressive accounting by some entities. While in many businesses the revenue earning cycle is simple and straightforward and therefore difficult to manipulate, there are many other situations where it is a matter of interpretation as to when the revenue has actually been earned. For example, Xerox Corporation was fined by the SEC, and its auditors were sanctioned, for the manner in which the company allegedly distorted FAS 13 relative to recognition of lease income from long-term equipment rental contracts that were bundled with supplies and maintenance agreements.

The information provided by the income statement, relating to individual items of income and expense, as well as to the relationships between and among these items (such as the amounts reported as gross margin or profit before interest and taxes), facilitates financial analysis, especially that relating to the reporting entity's historical and possible future profitability. Even with the ascendancy of the balance sheet as the favored financial statement, financial statement users will always devote considerable attention to the income statement.

This chapter focuses on key income measurement issues and on matters of income statement presentation and disclosure. It also explains and illustrates the presentation of the *statement of changes in equity* and the *statement of recognized income and expense*.

Sources of IFRS
IAS 1, 8, 14, 16, 18, 21, 36, 37, 38, 39, 40
IFRS 1, 5
SIC 29
Framework for the Preparation and Presentation of Financial Statements

DEFINITIONS OF TERMS

Elements of Financial Statements

Comprehensive income. The change in equity of an entity during a period from transactions and other events and circumstances from nonowner sources. It includes all changes in net assets during a period, except those resulting from investments by owners and distributions to owners.

Expenses. Decreases in economic benefits during the accounting period in the form of outflows or depletions of assets or incurring liabilities that result in decreases in equity, other than those relating to distributions to equity participants. The term *expenses* is broad enough to include *losses* as well as normal categories of expenses; thus, IFRS differs from the corresponding US GAAP standard, which deems losses to be a separate and distinct element to be accounted for, denoting decreases in equity from peripheral or incidental transactions.

Income. Increases in economic benefits during the accounting period in the form of inflows or enhancements of assets that result in increases in equity, other than those relating to contributions from equity participants. The IASB's *Framework* clarifies that this definition of income encompasses both revenue and gains. As with expenses and losses, the corresponding US accounting standard holds that revenues and gains constitute two separate elements of financial reporting, with gains denoting increases in equity from peripheral or incidental transactions.

Statement of changes in equity. As prescribed by IAS 1, an enterprise should present, as a separate financial statement, a statement showing

1. The net profit or loss for the period;
2. Items of income (including gain) and expense (including loss) that are recognized in equity, as required by IAS 16, 21, 38, or 39, and the total of these items;
3. The cumulative effect of changes in accounting policy and the correction of errors (when the benchmark treatment, retrospective application and adjustment of beginning retained earnings, respectively, is elected under IAS 8);
4. Capital transactions and distributions with/to owners of the enterprise;
5. The balance of retained earnings (or accumulated loss) at the beginning of the period and at the balance sheet date, and the movements for the period; and
6. A reconciliation between the carrying amounts of each class of equity capital, share premium and each reserve at the beginning and the end of the period, separately disclosing each movement.

Statement of recognized income and expense. As an alternative to a statement of changes in equity (above), as prescribed by IAS 1, an enterprise may present, along with the traditional financial statements, a statement of recognized income and expense. This statement highlights items of income and expense that are not recognized in the income statement, and it reports all changes in equity, including net income, other than those resulting from investments by and distributions to owners (items 1-3 above). When an enterprise chooses to present the statement of recognized income and expense, it should, additionally, present in footnotes to the financial statements, items 4 to 6 shown under the discussion of the statement of changes in equity, above.

Other Terminology

Discontinued operations. IFRS 5 defines a "discontinued operation" as a component of an enterprise that has been disposed of, or is classified as held for sale, and

1. Represents a separate major line of business or geographical area of operations;
2. Is part of a single coordinated disposal plan;
3. Is a subsidiary acquired exclusively with a view to resale.

Component of an entity. In the context of discontinued operations, IFRS 5 defines a component of an entity as operations and cash flows that can be clearly distinguished, operationally and for financial reporting purposes, from the rest of the entity—a cash generating unit, or group of cash generating units.

Realization. The process of converting noncash resources and rights into money or, more precisely, the sale of an asset for cash or claims to cash.

Recognition. The process of formally recording or incorporating in the financial statements of an entity items that meet the definition of an element and satisfy the criteria for recognition.

Segment of a business. A distinguishable component of an enterprise which is engaged in providing products or services that are subject to risks and returns different from other "business segments" or "geographical segments." A segment may be in the form of a subsidiary, a division, a department, a joint venture, or other nonsubsidiary investee. Its assets, results of operations, and activities can be clearly distinguished (physically and operationally, and for financial reporting purposes) from the other assets, results of operations, and activities of the entity. Business segments are distinguishable components of an enterprise engaged in providing different products or services, or a different group of related products or services, primarily to customers outside an enterprise. Geographical segments are distinguishable components of an enterprise engaged in operations in different countries or group of countries within particular geographical areas as may be determined to be appropriate in an enterprise's particular circumstances.

CONCEPTS, RULES, AND EXAMPLES

Concepts of Income

Economists have generally employed a wealth maintenance concept of income. Under this concept (as specified by Hicks), income is the maximum amount that can be consumed during a period and still leave the enterprise with the same amount of wealth at the end of the period as existed at the beginning. Wealth is determined with reference to the current market values of the net productive assets at the beginning and end of the period. Therefore, the economists' definition of income would fully incorporate market value changes (both increases and decreases in wealth) in the determination of periodic income and this would correspond to measuring assets and liabilities at fair value, with the net of all the changes in net assets equating to comprehensive income.

Accountants, on the other hand, have traditionally defined income by reference to specific transactions that give rise to recognizable elements of revenue and expense during a reporting period. The events that produce reportable items of revenue and expense comprise a subset of economic events that determine economic income. Many changes in the market values of wealth components are deliberately excluded from the measurement of accounting income but are included in the measurement of economic income, although those exclusions have grown fewer as the use of fair values in financial reporting has been more widely embraced in recent years.

The discrepancy between the accounting and economic measures of income are the result of a preference on the part of accountants and financial statement users for information that is reliable, and also considerations of measurement of income for tax purposes in many jurisdictions. Since many fluctuations in the market values of assets are matters of conjecture, accountants have preferred to retain the historical cost/realization model, which generally postpones the recognition of value changes until there has been a completed transaction. While both accountants and economists understand that the earnings process occurs throughout the various stages of production, sales, and final delivery of the product, accountants have tended to stress the difficulty of measuring the precise rate at which this earnings process is taking place. That, coupled with a desire to not pay tax any earlier than necessary, has led accountants to conclude that income should be recognized only when it is fully realized.

Nonetheless, an application of the conceptual framework approach of recognizing assets and liabilities when they can be measured reliably enough is leading standard setters to experiment with the idea of recognizing transactions that are incomplete. This can be seen in IAS 39, where the changes in market value of some financial instruments are recognized, and in IAS 41, where the change in value of biological assets is recognized although not realized.

Recognition and Measurement

Recognition is signified by the inclusion of an item in the balance sheet or the income statement. Measurement is the determination of the amount at which the recognized item should be included. The IASB's *Framework* has identified the following recognition criteria, which remain in force:

1. **Item must meet the definition of an element.** To be recognized, an item must meet the definitions of either an asset or a liability (see Chapter 1). This may also involve recognition of income and expense; as discussed above, a gain in net assets would be income and a reduction of net assets would be an expense.

2. **Assessment of degree of uncertainty regarding future economic benefits.** The asset/liability definition says there must be a probable future inflow or outflow of future economic benefits. Recognition therefore involves consideration of the degree of uncertainty that the future economic benefits associated with an item will flow to or from the enterprise.

3. **Item's cost or value can be measured with reliability.** An item must possess a relevant attribute, such as cost or value, which can be quantified in monetary units with sufficient reliability. Measurability must be considered in terms of both relevance and reliability, the two primary qualitative characteristics of accounting information.

4. **Relevance.** An item is relevant if the information about it has the capacity to make a difference in investors', creditors', or other users' decisions. The relevance of information is affected by its nature and materiality.

5. **Reliability.** An item is reliable if the information about it is representationally faithful, free of material errors, and is neutral or free from bias. Further, to possess the quality of reliability, two more features should be present.

   a. The transactions and other events the information purports to represent should be accounted for and presented in accordance with their *substance* and economic reality and *not merely their legal form.*

   b. The preparers of financial statements, while dealing with and recognizing uncertainties, should exercise judgment or a degree of caution: in other words, *prudence.*

To be given accounting recognition, an asset, liability, or item of income or expense would have to meet the thresholds established by the above-mentioned five criteria.

Income. According to the IASB's *Framework*

Income is increases in economic benefits during the accounting period in the form of inflows or enhancements of assets or decreases of liabilities that result in increases in equity, other than those relating to contributions from equity participants. The definition of income encompasses both revenue and gains, and revenue arises in the course of ordinary activities of an enterprise and is referred to by different names, such as sales, fees, interest, dividends, royalties, and rent.

IAS 18 is the standard that deals with the accounting for revenue. It says that revenue is the gross inflow of economic benefits during the period (excluding transactions with owners).

The measurement basis is that revenue be measured at the fair value of the consideration received or receivable. *Fair value* is defined as

the amount for which an asset could be exchanged, or a liability settled, between knowledgeable, willing parties in an arm's-length transaction.

The historical cost measurement basis involves recognizing a completed marketplace transaction, in other words measuring at fair value at initial recognition. Revenue recognition is discussed in detail in Chapter 7.

Expenses. According to the IASB's *Framework*

Expenses are decreases in economic benefits during an accounting period in the form of outflows or depletions of assets or incurrences of liabilities, other than those relating to distributions to equity participants.

Expenses are expired costs, or items that were assets but are no longer assets because they have no future value. The matching principle requires that all expenses incurred in the generating of revenue be recognized in the same accounting period as the related revenues are recognized.

Costs such as materials and direct labor consumed in the manufacturing process are relatively easy to identify with the related revenue elements. These cost elements are included in inventory and expensed as cost of sales when the product is sold and revenue from the sale is recognized. This is associating cause and effect.

Some costs are more closely associated with specific accounting periods. In the absence of a cause and effect relationship, the asset's cost should be allocated to the benefitted accounting periods in a systematic and rational manner. This form of expense recognition involves assumptions about the expected length of benefit and the relationship between benefit and cost of each period. Depreciation of fixed assets, amortization of intangibles, and allocation of rent and insurance are examples of costs that would be recognized by the use of a systematic and rational method.

All other costs are normally expensed in the period in which they are incurred. This would include those costs for which no clear-cut future benefits can be identified, costs that were recorded as assets in prior periods but for which no remaining future benefits can be identified, and those other elements of administrative or general expense for which no rational allocation scheme can be devised. The general approach is first to attempt to match costs with the related revenues. Next, a method of systematic and rational allocation should be attempted. If neither of these measurement principles is beneficial, the cost should be immediately expensed.

Gains and losses. The *Framework* defines the term *expenses* broadly enough to include losses. IFRS include no definition of gains and losses that enables them to be separated from income and expense. Traditionally, gains and losses are thought by accountants to arise from purchases and sales outside the regular business trading of the company, such as on disposals of noncurrent assets that are no longer required. IAS 1 used to include an extraordinary category for display of items that were clearly distinct from ordinary activities. The IASB removed this category in its 2003 Improvements Project, concluding that these items arose from the normal business risks faced by an entity and that it is the nature or function of a transaction or other event, rather than its frequency, that should determine its presentation within the income statement.

According to the IASB's *Framework*

Gains (losses) represent increases (decreases) in economic benefits and as such are no different in nature from revenue (expenses). Hence they are not regarded as separate elements in IASB's Framework. *Characteristics of gains and losses include the following:*

1. *Result from peripheral transactions and circumstances that may be beyond entity's control*
2. *May be classified according to sources or as operating and nonoperating*

Statement of changes in equity and statement of recognized income and expense. IAS 1 offers preparers two principal mechanisms for reporting the changes in enterprise equity for a period. The first of these is a comprehensive statement of changes in equity. This statement should present

1. An enterprise's total recognized income and expense for the period, including those that are recognized directly in equity. Details must be given of each item of income, expense, gain, or loss that are required by other IFRS to be shown directly in equity, along with the total of these items, plus net profit or loss for the period. This will also include the cumulative effect of any changes in accounting policy and of correction of errors if retrospective adjustment is required, and
2. Other changes in the equity accounts, along with a reconciliation of beginning and ending balances in each of the components of equity (giving details by each class of equity capital) and balances of accumulated profit or loss (giving details of the movements for the period).

An example of the statement of changes in equity is presented in the following section of this chapter.

Under the second of the two permitted approaches, the enterprise would present a statement of recognized income and expenses for the period, which would only include the net effect of income, expense, gain or loss reported in the income statement for the period. That is, net income or loss, including if applicable the cumulative effect of changes in accounting policy and of the correction of any fundamental errors accounted for retrospectively, would be added to the other items of income, expense, gain or loss which are carried directly to equity, with the total of these being presented as the final amount in the statement of recognized income and expense. As revised in late 2004, IAS 19 permits companies to recognize all changes in actuarial gains and losses of defined benefit pension plans in the statement of recognized income and expense.

If the second approach is utilized, the changes in other capital accounts resulting from transactions with owners, as well as the changes in retained earnings (referred to in IAS 1 as accumulated profit or loss), must be presented elsewhere in the notes to the financial statements. An example of this second approach is also shown in the following section of this chapter.

IAS 1 explains that it is important to take into consideration all income, expenses, gains, and losses (including those not recognized in the income statement) in assessing the overall financial performance of an enterprise. Thus, the revised standard on presentation of financial statements has prescribed this new component of financial statements to capture those items of gains or losses that are not included in the determination of net income or loss for the period.

While the new standard refers to this as "a separate component of the financial statements," what is required is a new financial statement that (depending on which alternative version is adopted) may also require additional footnote materials.

Examples of the statements required by IAS 1—under both alternatives.

Example 1: If a statement of changes in equity is to be employed

XYZ Malta Inc.
Statement of Changes in Equity
For the Year Ended December 31, 2006
(in thousands of US dollars)

	Share capital	Share premium	Revaluation reserve	Currency translation	Accumulated profits	Total
Balance at Dec. 31, 2004	$1,000	$100	$200	$200	$100	$1,600
Changes in accounting policy	--	--	--	--	50	50
Opening balances, as restated	1,000	100	200	200	150	1,650
Currency translation difference	--	--	--	(50)	--	(50)
Surplus from revaluation of buildings	--	--	100	--	--	100
Net gains and losses not recognized in income statement	--	--	100	(50)	--	50
Net profit for the period	--	--	--	--	100	100
Issuance of share capital	100	10	--	--	--	110
Balance at Dec. 31, 2005	1,100	110	300	150	250	1,910
Currency translation difference	--	--	--	150	--	150
Deficit on revaluation of investments	--	--	--	--	(50)	(50)
Net gains and losses not recognized in income statement	--	--	--	150	(50)	100
Net profit for the period	--	--	--	--	200	200
Dividends	--	--	--	--	50	(50)
Balance at Dec. 31, 2006	$1,100	$110	$300	$300	$350	$2,160

Example 2: If a statement of recognized income and expense is to be presented (see note below)

ABC Barbados Co. Ltd.
Statement of Recognized Income and Expense
For the Year Ended December 31, 2006
(in thousands of US dollars)

	2006	2005
Surplus on revaluation of buildings	$ 500	$ --
Surplus (deficit) on revaluation of investments	1,000	(1,000)
Exchange differences on translation of the financial statements of a foreign subsidiary	2,000	(2,000)
Net income (expense) not recognized in the income statement	3,500	(3,000)
Net profit for the year	5,000	2,800
Total recognized income and expense	8,500	(200)
Effect of changes in accounting policy	$ --	$ 500

NOTE: If this approach is used, then a reconciliation of the opening and closing balances of share capital, reserves, and retained earnings (accumulated profits) as illustrated in the first example, above, should be presented in the footnotes to the financial statements.

Income Statement Classification and Presentation

Statement title. The legal name of the entity must be used to identify the financial statements and the title "Income Statement" (or "Profit and Loss Account") used to distinguish the statement from other information presented in the annual report.

Reporting period. The period covered by the income statement must clearly be identified, such as "year ended December 31, 2006," or "six months ended September 30, 2006." Income statements are normally presented annually (i.e., for a period of twelve months or a year). However, in some jurisdictions they may be required at quarterly or six-month intervals, and in exceptional circumstances (such as a newly acquired subsidiary harmonizing its account dates with those of its new parent), companies may need to prepare income statements for periods in excess of one year or for shorter periods as well. IAS 1 requires that when financial statements are presented for periods other than a year, the following additional disclosures should be made:

1. The reason for presenting the income statement (and other financial statements, such as the cash flow statement, statement of changes in equity, and notes) for a period other than one year; and
2. The fact that the comparative information presented (in the income statement, statement of changes in equity, cash flow statement, and notes) is not truly comparable.

Entities whose operations form a natural cycle may have a reporting period end on a specific day of the week (e.g., the last Friday of the month). Certain entities (typically retail enterprises) may prepare income statements for a fiscal period of fifty-two or fifty-three weeks instead of a year (thus, to always end on a day such as Sunday, on which no business is transacted, so that inventory may be taken). These entities should clearly state that the income statement has been presented, for instance, "for the fifty-two-week period ended March 28, 2006." IAS 1 states that it is deemed to be unlikely that the financial statements thus presented would be materially different from those that would be presented for one full year.

In order that the presentation and classification of items in the income statement be consistent from period to period, items of income and expenses should be uniform both with respect to appearance and categories from one time period through the next. If a decision is made to change classification schemes, the comparative prior period financials should be restated to conform and thus to maintain comparability between the two periods being presented together. Disclosure must be made of this reclassification, since the earlier period financial statements being presented currently will differ in appearance from those nominally same statements presented in the earlier year.

Major components of the income statement. IAS 1 stipulates that, at the minimum, the income statement must include line items that present the following items (if they are pertinent to the entity's operations for the period in question):

1. Revenue
2. Finance costs
3. Share of profits and losses of associates and joint ventures accounted for by the equity method
4. Tax expense
5. Discontinued operations
6. Profit or loss
7. Minority interest
8. Net profit attributable to equity holders in the parent

The foregoing items represent the barest minimum: the standard says that additional line items, headings, and subtotals should be presented on the face of the income statement when this is relevant to an understanding of the entity's financial performance. It should be carefully noted that this requirement cannot be dealt with by incorporating the items into the notes to the financial statements.

While the objectives of the line items are uniform across all reporting entities, the manner of presentation may differ. Specifically, IAS 1, (as also does the EU Fourth Directive), offers preparers two different ways of classifying operating and other expenses: by *nature* or by *function*. While entities are encouraged to apply one or the other of these on the face of the income statement, putting it in the notes is not prohibited.

The classification by nature identifies costs and expenses in terms of their character, such as salaries and wages, raw materials consumed, and depreciation of plant assets. On the other hand, the classification by function presents the expenses in terms of the purpose of the expenditure, such as for manufacturing, distribution, and administration. Note that finance costs must be so identified regardless of which classification is employed.

IFRS 5 governs the presentation and disclosures pertaining to discontinued operations. This is discussed later in this chapter.

IAS 1 furthermore stipulates that if a reporting entity discloses expenses by function, it must also provide information on the nature of the expenses, including depreciation and amortization and staff costs (salaries and wages). The standard does not provide detailed guidance on this requirement, but companies need only provide a note indicating the nature of the allocations made to comply with the requirement.

Finally, IAS 1 requires that dividends paid during the year, on a per share basis, be disclosed either on the face of the income statement, in the statement of changes in equity, or in the notes. Dividends declared but unpaid at year-end should also be disclosed.

While IAS does not require the inclusion of subsidiary schedules to support major captions in the income statement, it is commonly found that detailed schedules of line items are included in full sets of financial statements. These will be illustrated in the following section to provide a more expansive discussion of the meaning of certain major sections of the income statement.

Revenue. The term "ordinary activities," formerly found in IAS 1, was eliminated by the IASB's 2003 Improvements Project. However, companies typically show their regular trading operations first and then present any items to which they wish to direct analysts' attention.

1. **Sales or other operating revenues** are charges to customers for the goods and/or services provided to them during the period. This section of the income statement should include information about discounts, allowances, and returns, to determine net sales or net revenues.

2. **Cost of goods sold** is the cost of the inventory items sold during the period. In the case of a merchandising firm, net purchases (purchases less discounts, returns, and allowances plus freight-in) are added to beginning inventory to obtain the cost of goods available for sale. From the cost of goods available for sale amount, the ending inventory is deducted to compute cost of goods sold.

Example of schedule of cost of goods sold

ABC Merchandising Company
Schedule of Cost of Goods Sold
For the Year Ended December 31, 2006

Beginning inventory			$xxx
Add: Purchases		$xxx	
Freight-in		xxx	
Cost of purchases		xxx	
Less: Purchase discounts	$xx		
Purchase returns and allowances	xx	(xxx)	
Net purchases			xxx
Cost of goods available for sale			xxx
Less: Ending inventory			(xxx)
Cost of goods sold			$xxx

A manufacturing enterprise computes the cost of goods sold in a slightly different way. Cost of goods manufactured would be added to the beginning inventory to arrive at cost of goods available for sale. The ending inventory is then deducted from the cost of goods available for sale to determine the cost of goods sold. Cost of goods manufactured is computed by adding to raw (direct) materials on hand at the beginning of the period the raw materials purchases during the period and all other costs of production, such as labor and direct overhead, thereby yielding the cost of goods placed in production during the period. When adjusted for changes in work in process during the period and for raw materials on hand at the end of the period, this results in the calculation of goods produced.

Example of schedules of cost of goods manufactured and sold

XYZ Manufacturing Company
Schedule of Cost of Goods Manufactured
For the Year Ended December 31, 2006

Direct materials inventory, January 1	$xxx	
Purchases of materials (including freight-in and deducting purchase discounts)	xxx	
Total direct materials available	$xxx	
Direct materials inventory, December 31	(xxx)	
Direct materials used		$xxx
Direct labor		xxx
Factory overhead:		
Depreciation of factory equipment	$xxx	
Utilities	xxx	
Indirect factory labor	xxx	
Indirect materials	xxx	
Other overhead items	xxx	xxx
Manufacturing cost incurred in 2006		$xxx
Add: Work in process, January 1		xxx
Less: Work in process, December 31		(xxx)
Cost of goods manufactured		$xxx

XYZ Manufacturing Company
Schedule of Cost of Goods Sold
For the Year Ended December 31, 2006

Finished goods inventory, January 1	$xxx
Add: Cost of goods manufactured	xxx
Cost of goods available for sale	$xxx
Less: Finished goods inventory, December 31	(xxx)
Cost of goods sold	$xxx

3. **Operating expenses** are primary recurring costs associated with central operations, other than cost of goods sold, which are incurred to generate sales. Operating expenses are normally classified into the following two categories:

   a.   Distribution costs (or selling expenses)
   b.   General and administrative expenses

   Distribution costs are those expenses related directly to the company's efforts to generate sales (e.g., sales salaries, commissions, advertising, delivery expenses, depreciation of store furniture and equipment, and store supplies). General and administrative expenses are expenses related to the general administration of the company's operations (e.g., officers and office salaries, office supplies, depreciation of office furniture and fixtures, telephone, postage, accounting and legal services, and business licenses and fees).

4. **Other revenues and expenses** are incidental revenues and expenses not related to the central operations of the company (e.g., rental income from letting parts of premises not needed for company operations).

5. **Separate disclosure items** are items that are of such size, nature, or incidence that their disclosure becomes important in order to explain the performance of the enterprise for the period. Examples of items that, if material, would require such disclosure are as follows:

    a. Write-down of inventories to net realizable value, or of property, plant, and equipment to recoverable amounts, and subsequent reversals of such write-downs

    b. Costs of restructuring the activities of an enterprise and any subsequent reversals of such provisions

    c. Costs of litigation settlements

    d. Other reversals of provisions

6.   **Income tax expense.** The total of taxes payable and deferred taxation adjustments for the period covered by the income statement.

7.   **Discontinued operations.** With effect from January 1, 2005, IFRS 5, *Noncurrent Assets Held for Sale and Discontinued Operations* has superseded IAS 35, *Discontinuing Operations*. The new Standard was issued by the IASB as part of its convergence program with US GAAP, and harmonizes IFRS with those parts of the US standard, FAS 144, *Accounting for the Impairment or Disposal of Long-Lived Assets,* that deal with assets held for sale and discontinued operations.

       IFRS 5 creates a new "held for sale" category of asset into which should be put assets, or "disposal groups" of assets and liabilities that are to be sold. Such assets or groups of assets are to be valued at the lower of carrying value and fair value, less selling costs. Any resulting write-down appears, net of tax, as part of the caption "discontinued operations" in the income statement.

       The other component of this line is the posttax profit or loss of discontinued operations. A discontinued operation is defined as a component of an entity that either has been disposed of, or has been classified as held for sale. It must also

- Be a separate major line of business or geographical area of operations,
- Be a part of a single coordinated plan for disposal, or
- Is a subsidiary acquired exclusively with a view to resale.

The two elements of the single line of the income statement have to be analyzed in the notes, breaking out the related income tax expense between the two, as well as showing the components of revenue, expense, and pretax profit of the discontinued items.

       For the asset or disposal group to be classified as held for sale, and its related earnings to be classified as discontinued, IFRS 5 says that sale must be highly probable, the asset must be saleable in its current condition, and the sale price must be reasonable in relation to its fair value. The appropriate level of management in the group must be committed to a plan to sell the asset and an active program has been embarked upon. Sale should be expected within one year of classification and the standard sets out stringent conditions for any extension of this, which are based on elements outside of the control of the entity.

       Where an operation meets the criteria for classification as discontinued, but will be abandoned within one year rather than be sold, it should also be included in discontinued operations. Assets or disposal groups categorized as held for sale are not depreciated further.

Example of disclosure of discontinued operations under IFRS 5

Taj Mahal Enterprises
Statement of Income
For the Years Ended December 31, 2006 and 2005
(In UAE Dirhams)

	2006		2005	
Continuing Operations (Segments X & Y):				
Revenue	10,000		5,000	
Operating expenses	(7,000)		(3,500)	
Pretax profit from operating activities	3,000		1,500	
Interest expense	(300)		(200)	
Profit before tax	2,700		1,300	
Income tax expense	(540)		(260)	
Profit after taxes		2,160		1,040
Discontinuing operation (Segment Z):				
Discontinued operations (note)		(240)		80
Total enterprise:				
Profit (loss) attributable to shareholders		1920		1120

	2006		2005	
Note: Discontinued Operations				
Revenue	3,000		2,000	
Operating expenses	(1,800)		(1,400)	
Provision for end-of-service benefits	(900)		--	
Interest expense	(100)		(100)	
Pretax profit	200		500	
Income tax	(40)		(100)	
Discontinued earnings		160		400
Impairment loss	(500)		(400)	
Income tax	100		(80)	
Write-down of assets		(400)		(320)
Discontinued operations, net		(240)		(80)

Aggregating items. Aggregation of items should not serve to conceal significant information, as would the netting of revenues against expenses, or the combining of other elements that are individually of interest to readers, such as bad debts and depreciation. The categories "other" or "miscellaneous expense" should contain, at maximum, an immaterial total amount of aggregated, individually insignificant elements. Once this total approaches, for example, 10% of total expenses (or any other materiality threshold), some other aggregations, together with appropriate explanatory titles, should be selected.

Information is material if its omission or misstatement or nondisclosure could influence the economic decisions of users taken on the basis of the financial statements. Materiality depends on the size of the item judged in the particular circumstances of its omission (according to IASB's *Framework*). But it is often forgotten that materiality is also linked with understandability and the level of precision in which the financial statements are to be presented. For instance, the financial statements are often rendered more understandable by rounding information to the nearest thousand currency units (e.g., US dollars). This obviates the necessity of loading the financial statements with unnecessary detail. However, it should be borne in mind that the use of the level of precision that makes presentation possible in the nearest thousands of currency units is acceptable only as long as the threshold of materiality is not surpassed.

Offsetting items of revenue and expense. Materiality also plays a role in the matter of allowing or disallowing offsetting of the items of income and expense. IAS 1 addresses this issue and prescribes rules in this area. According to this standard, items of income and expense should be offset when, and only when

1. An international accounting standard requires or permits it. For example, IAS 30 (prior to being superseded by IFRS 7) permits banks and similar financial institutions to offset income and expense items relating to hedging; or
2. Gains, losses, and related expenses arising from the same or similar transactions and events are not material. Such amounts should be aggregated in such cases.

Usually, when more than one event occurs in a given reporting period, losses and gains on disposal of noncurrent assets are seen reported on a net basis, due to the fact that they are not material individually (compared to other items on the income statement). However, if they were material individually, they would need to be disclosed separately according to the requirements of IAS 1.

Views differ as to the treatment of disposal gains and losses arising from the routine replacement of noncurrent assets. Some experts believe that these should be separately disclosed as a disposal transaction, whereas others point out that if the depreciation schedule is estimated correctly, there should be no disposal gain or loss. Consequently, any difference between carrying value and disposal proceeds is akin to an adjustment to previous depreciation, and should logically flow through the income statement in the same caption where the depreciation was originally reported. Here again, the issue comes down to one of materiality: does it affect users' ability to make economic decisions?

IAS 1 further clarifies that when items of income or expense are offset, the enterprise should nevertheless consider, based on materiality, the need to disclose the gross amounts in the notes to the financial statements. This standard gives the following examples of transactions that are incidental to the main revenue-generating activities of an enterprise and whose results when presented by offsetting or reporting on a net basis, such as netting any gains with related expenses, reflect the substance of the transaction:

1. Gains or losses on the disposal of noncurrent assets, including investments and operating assets, are reported by deducting from the proceeds on disposal the carrying amounts of the asset and related selling expenses.
2. Expenditure related to a provision that is reimbursed under a contractual arrangement with a third party may be netted against the related reimbursement.

IASB Projects Affecting the Income Statement

Both the FASB and the IASB have set out to create standardized formats for the income statement in place of the current rules. These existing rules are generally thought to be unsatisfactory in that some transactions flow directly to equity while most others appear in the income statement first. Also, there is a perception that the conceptual frameworks under both sets of standards have not been rigorously applied, such that many extant standards deviate from the frameworks (and in many cases preceded the creation of the respective framework). The IASB made some progress with an initial effort to address performance reporting, the early recommendations of which involved reporting all elements of comprehensive income in a single financial statement. The IASB believes that there is an inherent inability to create a useful definition of a company's main business (e.g., as core operations, ordinary activities, etc.), and that the income statement should separate financial income and expense from all other income and expense, but that there be attempt to analyze the nonfinancial items into any core business element and the remaining "noise." The IASB field-tested the early proposals but then withdrew them in the face of opposition from constituents, recognizing that the proposals were too far in advance of business understanding of comprehensive income for acceptance of the need to abandon the traditional earnings statement format.

Subsequently, IASB has entered into a cooperative venture with FASB, to pursue a project entitled *Reporting Comprehensive Income*. This is divided into two segments, of which the first is expect to give rise to a public discussion document by the end of 2005. This is likely to recommend a single statement of comprehensive income that builds upon the existing income statement by incorporating the FASB's other comprehensive income or the IASB's recognized income and expense. The first segment of this project will also address the required primary financial statements, the number of years that should be presented for comparative purposes, and whether only the direct method should be permitted for the statement of cash flows.

The second segment of this project is expected to address issues such as recycling between net income and other comprehensive income, principles for disaggregating information and defining total and subtotals. Some commentators take the view that the Boards have in fact split the performance-reporting project into one segment that is achievable (and is mostly repackaging) and another segment for items on which they think it will be impossible to reach agreement.

4 CASH FLOW STATEMENT

PERSPECTIVE AND ISSUES

The IASC last revised IAS 7, *Cash Flow Statements*, in 1992, which became effective in 1994. IAS 7 had originally required that reporting entities prepare the statement of changes in financial position (commonly referred to as the funds flow statement), which was once a widely accepted method of presenting changes in financial position, as part of a complete set of financial statements. The cash flow statement is now universally accepted and required under most national GAAP as well as IFRS. While there are some variations in terms of presentation (most of which pertain to the section in which certain captions appear), the approach is highly similar across all current sets of standards.

The purpose of the statement of cash flows is to provide information about the operating cash receipts and cash payments of an entity during a period, as well as providing insight into its various investing and financing activities. It is a vitally important financial statement, because the ultimate concern of investors is the reporting entity's ability to generate cash flows which will support payments (typically but not necessarily in the form of dividends) to the shareholders. More specifically, the statement of cash flows should help investors and creditors assess

1. The ability to generate future positive cash flows
2. The ability to meet obligations and pay dividends
3. Reasons for differences between income and cash receipts and payments
4. Both cash and noncash aspects of entities' investing and financing transactions

Sources of IFRS
IAS 7

DEFINITIONS OF TERMS

Cash. Cash on hand and demand deposits with banks or other financial institutions.

Cash equivalents. Short-term highly liquid investments that are (1) readily convertible to known amounts of cash, and (2) so near their maturity (original maturity of three months or less) that they present negligible risk of changes in value because of changes in interest rates. Treasury bills, commercial paper, and money market funds are all examples of cash equivalents.

Direct method. A method that derives the net cash provided by or used in operating activities from major components of operating cash receipts and payments.

Financing activities. The transactions that cause changes in the size and composition of an enterprise's capital and borrowings.

Indirect (reconciliation) method. A method that derives the net cash provided by or used in operating activities by adjusting net income (loss) for the effects of transactions of a noncash nature, any deferrals or accruals of past or future operating cash receipts or payments, and items of income or expense associated with investing or financing activities.

Investing activities. The acquisition and disposal of long-term assets and other investments not included in cash equivalents.

Operating activities. The transactions not classified as financing or investing activities, generally involving producing and delivering goods or providing services.

CONCEPTS, RULES, AND EXAMPLES

Benefits of Cash Flow Statements

The concepts underlying the balance sheet and the income statement have long been established in financial reporting. They are, respectively, the stock measure or a snapshot at a point in time of an entity's resources and obligations, and a summary of the entity's economic transactions and performance over an interval of time. The third major financial statement, the cash flow statement, is a more recent innovation but has evolved substantially since introduced. What has ultimately developed into the cash flow statement began life as a flow statement that reconciled changes in enterprise resources over a period of time but in a fundamentally different manner than did the income statement.

Most of the basic progress on this financial statement occurred in the United States, where during the 1950s and early 1960s a variety of formats and concepts were experimented with. By the mid-1960s the most common reporting approach used in the United States was that of sources and applications (or uses) of funds, although such reporting did not become mandatory until 1971. Even then, *funds* could be defined by the reporting entity in at least four different ways, including as cash and as net working capital (current assets minus current liabilities).

One reason why the financial statement preparer community did not more quickly embrace a cash flow concept is that the accounting profession had long had a significant aversion to the cash basis measurement of enterprise operating performance. This was largely the result of its commitment to accrual basis accounting, which recognizes revenues when earned and expenses when incurred, and which views cash flow reporting as a back door approach to cash basis accounting. By focusing instead on funds, which most typically was defined as net working capital, items such as receivables and payables were included, thereby preserving the essential accrual basis characteristic of the flow measurement. On the other hand, this failed to give statement users meaningful insight into the entities' sources and uses of cash, which is germane to an evaluation of the reporting entity's liquidity and solvency.

By the 1970s there was widespread recognition of the myriad problems associated with funds flow reporting, including the required use of the "all financial resources" approach, under which all major noncash (and nonfund) transactions, such as exchanges of stock or debt for plant assets, were included in the funds flow statement. This ultimately led to a renewed call for cash flow reporting. Most significantly, the FASB's conceptual framework project of the late 1970s to mid-1980s identified usefulness in predicting future cash flows as a central purpose of the financial reporting process. This presaged the nearly universal move away from funds flows to cash flows as a third standard measurement to be incorporated in financial reports.

Cash flow statements thus became required in the late 1980s in the United States, with the United Kingdom following soon thereafter with an approach that largely mirrored the US standard, albeit with a somewhat refined classification scheme. The international accounting standard, which was adopted a year after that of the United Kingdom (both of these were revisions to earlier requirements that had mandated the use of funds flow statements), embraces the somewhat simpler US approach but offers greater flexibility, thus effectively incorporating the UK view without adding to the structural complexity of the cash flow statement itself.

Today, the clear consensus of national and international accounting standard setters is that the statement of cash flows is a necessary component of complete financial reporting. The perceived benefits of presenting the statement of cash flows in conjunction with the statement of financial position (balance sheet) and the statement of income (or operations) have been highlighted by IAS 7 to be as follows:

1. It provides an insight into the financial structure of the enterprise (including its liquidity and solvency) and its ability to affect the amounts and timing of cash flows in order to adapt to changing circumstances and opportunities.

The statement of cash flows discloses important information about the cash flows from operating, investing, and financing activities, information that is not available or as clearly discernible in either the balance sheet or the income statement. The additional disclosures which are either recommended by IAS 7 (such as those relating to undrawn borrowing facilities or cash flows that represent increases in operating capacity) or required to be disclosed by the standard (such as that about cash held by the enterprise but not available for use) provide a wealth of information for the informed user of financial statements. Taken together, the statement of cash flows coupled with these required or recommended disclosures provide the user with vastly more insight into the entity's performance and position, and its probable future results, than would the balance sheet and income statement alone.

2. It provides additional information to the users of financial statements for evaluating changes in assets, liabilities, and equity of an enterprise.

When comparative balance sheets are presented, users are given information about the enterprise's assets and liabilities at the end of each of the years. Were the statement of cash flows not presented as an integral part of the financial statements, it would be necessary for users of comparative financial statements either to speculate about how and why certain amounts reported on the balance sheet changed from one period to another, or to compute (at least for the latest year presented) approximations of these items for themselves. At best, however, such a do-it-yourself approach would derive the net changes (the increase or decrease) in the individual assets and liabilities and attribute these to normally related income statement accounts. (For example, the net change in accounts receivable from the beginning to the end of the year would be used to convert reported sales to cash-basis sales or cash collected from customers.)

While basic changes in the balance sheet can be used to infer cash flow implications, this is not universally the case. More complex combinations of events (such as the acquisition of another entity, along with its accounts receivables, which would be an increase in that asset which was not related to sales to customers by the reporting entity during the period) would not immediately be comprehensible and might lead to incorrect interpretations of the data unless an actual cash flow statement were presented.

3. It enhances the comparability of reporting of operating performance by different enterprises because it eliminates the effects of using different accounting treatments for the same transactions and events.

There was considerable debate even as early as the 1960s and 1970s over accounting standardization, which led to the emergence of cash flow accounting. The principal argument in support of cash flow accounting by its earliest proponents was that it avoids the arbitrary allocations inherent in accrual accounting. For example, cash flows provided by or used in operating activities are derived, under the indirect method, by adjusting net income (or loss) for items such as depreciation and amortization, which might have been computed by different entities using different accounting methods. Thus, accounting standardization will be achieved by converting the accrual-basis net income to cash-basis income, and the resultant figures will become comparable across enterprises.

4. It serves as an indicator of the amount, timing, and certainty of future cash flows. Furthermore, if an enterprise has a system in place to project its future cash flows, the statement of cash flows could be used as a touchstone to evaluate the accuracy of past projections of those future cash flows. This benefit is elucidated by the standard as follows:

    a. The statement of cash flows is useful in comparing past assessments of future cash flows against current year's cash flow information, and
    b. It is of value in appraising the relationship between profitability and net cash flows, and in assessing the impact of changing prices.

Exclusion of Noncash Transactions

The statement of cash flows, as its name implies, includes only actual inflows and outflows of cash and cash equivalents. Accordingly, it excludes all transactions that do not directly affect cash receipts and payments. However, IAS 7 does require that the effects of transactions not resulting in receipts or payments of cash be disclosed elsewhere in the financial statements. The reason for not including noncash transactions in the statement of cash flows and placing them elsewhere in the financial statements (e.g., the footnotes) is that it preserves the statement's primary focus on cash flows from operating, investing, and financing activities. It is thus important that the user of financial statements fully appreciate what this financial statement does—and does not—attempt to portray.

Components of Cash and Cash Equivalents

The statement of cash flows, under the various national and international standards, may or may not include transactions in cash equivalents as well as cash. Under US standards, for example, preparers may choose to define cash as "cash and cash equivalents," as long as the same definition is used in the balance sheet as in the cash flow statement (i.e., the cash flow statement must tie to a single caption on the balance sheet). IAS 7, on the other hand, rather clearly required that the changes in both cash and cash equivalents be explained by the cash flow statement.

Cash and cash equivalents include unrestricted cash (meaning cash actually on hand, or bank balances whose immediate use is determined by the management), other demand deposits, and short-term investments whose maturities at the date of acquisition by the enterprise were three months or less. Equity investments do not qualify as cash equivalents unless they fit the definition above of short-term maturities of three months or less, which would rarely, if ever, be true. Preference shares carrying mandatory redemption features, if acquired within three months of their predetermined redemption date, would meet the criteria above since they are, in substance, cash equivalents. These are very infrequently encountered circumstances, however.

Bank borrowings are normally considered as financing activities. However, in some countries, bank overdrafts play an integral part in the enterprise's cash management, and as such, overdrafts are to be included as a component of cash equivalents if the following conditions are met:

1. The bank overdraft is repayable on demand, and
2. The bank balance often fluctuates from positive to negative (overdraft).

Statutory (or reserve) deposits by banks (i.e., those held with the central bank for regulatory compliance purposes) are often included in the same balance sheet caption as cash. The financial statement treatment of these deposits is subject to some controversy in certain countries, which becomes fairly evident from scrutiny of published financial statements of banks, as these deposits are variously considered to be either a cash equivalent or an operating asset. If the latter, changes in amount would be presented in the operating activities section of the cash flow statement, and the item could not then be combined with cash in the balance sheet. Since the appendix to IAS 7, which illustrates the application of the standard to cash flow statements of financial institutions, does not include statutory deposits with the central bank as a cash equivalent, the authors have concluded that there is little logic to support the alternative presentation of this item as a cash equivalent. Given the fact that deposits with central banks are more or less permanent (and in fact would be more likely to increase over time than to be diminished, given a going concern assumption about the reporting financial institution) the presumption must be that these are not cash equivalents in normal practice.

Classifications in the Statement of Cash Flows

The statement of cash flows prepared in accordance with international accounting standards (and also in accordance with US GAAP) requires classification into these three categories:

1. *Investing activities* include the acquisition and disposition of property, plant and equipment and other long-term assets and debt and equity instruments of other enterprises that are not considered cash equivalents or held for dealing or trading purposes. Investing activities include cash advances and collections on loans made to other parties (other than advances and loans of a financial institution).
2. *Financing activities* include obtaining resources from and returning resources to the owners. Also included is obtaining resources through borrowings (short-term or long-term) and repayments of the amounts borrowed.
3. *Operating activities* include all transactions that are not investing and financing activities. In general, cash flows that relate to, or are the corollary of, items reported in the income statement are operating cash flows. Operating activities are principal revenue-producing activities of an enterprise and include delivering or producing goods for sale and providing services.

While both US GAAP and IFRS define these three components of cash flows, the international standards offer somewhat more flexibility in how certain types of cash flows are categorized. For example, under US GAAP, interest paid must be included in operating activities, but under the provisions of IAS 7 this may be consistently included in either operating or financing activities. (These and other discrepancies among the standards will be discussed further throughout this chapter.) This is a reflection of the fact that although interest expense is operating in the sense of being an item that is reported in the income statement, it also clearly relates to the entity's financing activities.

The following are examples of the statement of cash flows classification under the provisions of IAS 7:

	Operating	*Investing*	*Financing*
Cash inflows	• Receipts from sale of goods or services	• Principal collections from loans and sales of other entities' debt instruments	• Proceeds from issuing share capital
	• Sale of loans, debt, or equity instruments carried in trading portfolio	• Sale of equity instruments of other enterprises and from returns of investment in those instruments	• Proceeds from issuing debt (short-term or long-term)
	• Returns on loans (interest)	• Sale of plant and equipment	• Not-for-profits' donor-restricted cash that is limited to long-term purposes
	• Returns on equity securities (dividends)		
Cash outflows	• Payments to suppliers for goods and other services	• Loans made and acquisition of other entities' debt instruments	• Payment of dividends
	• Payments to or on behalf of employees	• Purchase of equity instruments* of other enterprises	• Repurchase of company's shares
	• Payments of taxes	• Purchase of plant and equipment	• Repayment of debt principal, including capital lease obligations
	• Payments of interest		
	• Purchase of loans, debt, or equity instruments carried in trading portfolio		

* *Unless held for trading purposes or considered to be cash equivalents.*

Noncash investing and financing activities should, according to IAS 7, be disclosed in the footnotes to financial statements ("elsewhere" is how the standard actually identifies this), but apparently are not intended to be included in the cash flow statement itself. This contrasts somewhat with the US standard, FAS 95, which encourages inclusion of this supplemental information on the face of the statement of cash flows, although this may, under that standard, be relegated to a footnote as well. Examples of significant noncash financing and investing activities might include

1. Acquiring an asset through a finance lease
2. Conversion of debt to equity
3. Exchange of noncash assets or liabilities for other noncash assets or liabilities
4. Issuance of stock to acquire assets

Basic example of a classified statement of cash flows

Liquid Corporation
Statement of Cash Flows
For the Year Ended December 31, 2006

Net cash flows from operating activities		$ xxx
Cash flows from investing activities:		
Purchase of property, plant, and equipment	$(xxx)	
Sale of equipment	xx	
Collection of notes receivable	xx	
Net cash **used** in investing activities		(xx)
Cash flows from financing activities:		
Proceeds from issuance of share capital	xxx	
Repayment of long-term debt	(xx)	
Reduction of notes payable	(xx)	
Net cash **provided** by financing activities		xx
Effect of exchange rate changes on cash		xx
Net increase in cash and cash equivalents		$ xxx
Cash and cash equivalents at beginning of year		xxx
Cash and cash equivalents at end of year		$xxxx

Footnote Disclosure of Noncash Investing and Financing Activities

Note 4: Supplemental Cash Flow Statement Information

Significant noncash investing and financing transactions:

Conversion of bonds into common stock	$ xxx
Property acquired under finance leases	xxx
	$ xxx

Reporting Cash Flows from Operating Activities

Direct vs. indirect methods. The operating activities section of the statement of cash flows can be presented under the direct or the indirect method. However, IFRS has expressed a preference for the direct method of presenting net cash from operating activities. In this regard the IASC was probably following in the well-worn path of the FASB in the United States, which similarly urged that the direct method of reporting be adhered to. For their part, most preparers of financial statements, like those in the US, have chosen overwhelmingly to ignore the recommendation of the IASC, preferring by a very large margin to use the indirect method in lieu of the recommended direct method.

The *direct method* shows the items that affected cash flow and the magnitude of those cash flows. Cash received from, and cash paid to, specific sources (such as customers and suppliers) are presented, as opposed to the indirect method's converting accrual-basis net income (loss) to cash flow information by means of a series of add-backs and deductions. Entities using the direct method are required by IAS 7 to report the following major classes of gross cash receipts and gross cash payments:

1. Cash collected from customers
2. Interest and dividends received[1]
3. Cash paid to employees and other suppliers

---

[1] *Alternatively, interest and dividends received may be classified as investing cash flows rather than as operating cash flows because they are returns on investments. In this important regard, the IFRS differs from the corresponding US rule, which does not permit this elective treatment, making the operating cash flow presentation mandatory.*

4. Interest paid[2]
5. Income taxes paid
6. Other operating cash receipts and payments

Given the availability of alternative modes of presentation of interest and dividends received, and of interest paid, it is particularly critical that the policy adopted be followed consistently. Since the face of the statement of cash flows will in almost all cases make it clear what approach has been elected, it is not usually necessary to spell this out in the accounting policy note to the financial statements, although this certainly can be done if it would be useful to do so.

An important advantage of the direct method is that it permits the user to better comprehend the relationships between the company's net income (loss) and its cash flows. For example, payments of expenses are shown as cash disbursements and are deducted from cash receipts. In this way the user is able to recognize the cash receipts and cash payments for the period. Formulas for conversion of various income statement amounts for the direct method presentation from the accrual basis to the cash basis are summarized below.

Accrual basis	*Additions*	*Deductions*	*Cash basis*
Net sales	+ Beginning AR	– Ending AR AR written off	= Cash received from customers
Cost of goods sold	+ Ending inventory Beginning AP	– Depreciation and amortization* Beginning inventory Ending AP	= Cash paid to suppliers
Operating expenses	+ Ending prepaid expenses Beginning accrued expenses	– Depreciation and amortization Beginning prepaid expenses Ending accrued expenses payable Bad debts expense	= Cash paid for operating expenses

* *Applies to a manufacturing entity only*

From the foregoing it can be appreciated that the amounts to be included in the operating section of the statement of cash flows, when the direct approach is utilized, are derived amounts that must be computed (although the computations are not onerous); they are not, generally, amounts that exist as account balances simply to be looked up and then placed in the statement. The extra effort needed to prepare the direct method operating cash flow data may be a contributing cause of why this method has been distinctly unpopular with preparers. (There is a further reason why the direct method proved to be unpopular with entities that report in conformity with US GAAP: FAS 95 requires that when the direct method is used, a supplementary schedule be prepared reconciling net income to net cash flows from operating activities, which effectively means that *both* the direct and indirect methods must be employed. This rule does not apply under international accounting standards, however.)

The *indirect method* (sometimes referred to as the reconciliation method) is the most widely used means of presentation of cash from operating activities, primarily because it is easier to prepare. It focuses on the differences between net operating results and cash flows. The indirect format begins with net income (or loss), which can be obtained directly from the income statement. Revenue and expense items not affecting cash are added or deducted to arrive at net cash provided by operating activities. For example, depreciation and amortization would be added back because these expenses reduce net income without affecting cash.

---

[2] *Alternatively, IAS 7 permits interest paid to be classified as a financing cash flow, because this is the cost of obtaining financing. As with the foregoing, the availability of alternative treatments differs from the US approach, which makes the operating cash flow presentation the only choice. It is not clear at this time how the alternative approaches under US GAAP and IFRS will be converged.*

The statement of cash flows prepared using the indirect method emphasizes changes in the components of most current asset and current liability accounts. Changes in inventory, accounts receivable, and other current accounts are used to determine the cash flow from operating activities. Although most of these adjustments are obvious (most preparers simply relate each current asset or current liability on the balance sheet to a single caption in the income statement), some changes require more careful analysis. For example, it is important to compute cash collected from sales by relating sales revenue to both the change in accounts receivable and the change in the related bad debt allowance account.

As another example of possible complexity in computing the cash from operating activities, the change in short-term borrowings resulting from the purchase of equipment would not be included, since it is not related to operating activities. Instead, these short-term borrowings would be classified as a financing activity. Other adjustments under the indirect method include changes in the account balances of deferred income taxes, minority interest, unrealized foreign currency gains or losses, and the income (loss) from investments under the equity method.

IAS 7 offers yet another alternative way of presenting the cash flows from operating activities. This could be referred to as the *modified indirect method*. Under this variant of the indirect method, the starting point is not net income but rather revenues and expenses as reported in the income statement. In essence, this approach is virtually the same as the regular indirect method, with two more details: revenues and expenses for the period. There is no equivalent rule under US GAAP.

The following summary, actually simply an expanded balance sheet equation, may facilitate understanding of the adjustments to net income necessary for converting accrual-basis net income to cash-basis net income when using the indirect method.

	Current assets*	–	Fixed assets	=	Current liabilities	+	Long-term liabilities	+	Income	Accrual income adjustment to convert to cash flow
1.	Increase			=					Increase	Decrease
2.	Decrease			=					Decrease	Increase
3.				=	Increase				Decrease	Increase
4.				=	Decrease				Increase	Decrease

*Other than cash and cash equivalents

For example, using row 1 in the above chart, a credit sale would increase accounts receivable and accrual-basis income but would not affect cash. Therefore, its effect must be removed from the accrual income to convert to cash income. The last column indicates that the increase in a current asset balance must be deducted from income to obtain cash flow.

Similarly, an increase in a current liability, row three, must be added to income to obtain cash flows (e.g., accrued wages are on the income statement as an expense, but they do not require cash; the increase in wages payable must be added back to remove this noncash flow expense from accrual-basis income).

Under the US GAAP, when the indirect method is employed, the amount of interest and income taxes paid must be included in the related disclosures (supplemental schedule). However, under international accounting standards, as illustrated by the appendix to IAS 7, instead of disclosing them in the supplemental schedules, they are shown as part of the operating activities under both the direct and indirect methods. (Examples presented later in the chapter illustrate this.)

The major drawback to the indirect method involves the user's difficulty in comprehending the information presented. This method does not show from where the cash was received or to where the cash was paid. Only adjustments to accrual-basis net income are shown. In some cases the adjustments can be confusing. For instance, the sale of equipment resulting in an accrual-basis loss would require that the loss be added to net income to arrive at net cash from operating activities. (The loss was deducted in the computation of net income, but because the sale will be shown as an investing activity, the loss must be added back to net income.)

Although the indirect method is more commonly used in practice, the IASC and the FASB both encouraged enterprises to use the direct method. As pointed out by IAS 7, a distinct advantage of the direct method is that it provides information that may be useful in estimating or projecting future cash flows, a benefit that is clearly not achieved when the indirect method is utilized instead. Both the direct and indirect methods are presented below.

Direct method

Cash flows from operating activities:		
Cash received from sale of goods	$xxx	
Cash dividends received*	xxx	
Cash provided by operating activities		$xxx
Cash paid to suppliers	(xxx)	
Cash paid for operating expenses	(xxx)	
Cash paid for income taxes**	(xxx)	
Cash disbursed for operating activities		$(xxx)
Net cash flows from operating activities		$xxx

  *   *Alternatively, could be classified as investing cash flow.*
 ** *Taxes paid are usually classified as operating activities. However, when it is practical to identify the tax cash flow with an individual transaction that gives rise to cash flows that are classified as investing or financing activities, then the tax cash flow is classified as an investing or financing activity as appropriate.*

Indirect method

Cash flows from operating activities:	
Net income before income taxes	$ xx
Adjustments for:	
Depreciation	xx
Unrealized loss on foreign exchange	xx
Interest expense	xx
Operating profit before working capital changes***	xx
Increase in accounts receivable	(xx)
Decrease in inventories	xx
Increase in accounts payable	xx
Cash generated from operations	xx
Interest paid	(xx)
Income taxes paid (see note**above)	(xx)
Net cash flows from operating activities	$xxx

Other Requirements

Gross vs. net basis. The emphasis in the statement of cash flows is on gross cash receipts and cash payments. For instance, reporting the net change in bonds payable would obscure the financing activities of the entity by not disclosing separately cash inflows from issuing bonds and cash outflows from retiring bonds.

IAS 7 specifies two exceptions where netting of cash flows is allowed. Items with quick turnovers, large amounts, and short maturities may be presented as net cash flows. Cash receipts and payments on behalf of customers when the cash flows reflect the activities of the customers rather than those of the enterprise may also be reported on a net rather than a gross basis.

Foreign currency cash flows. Foreign operations must prepare a separate statement of cash flows and translate the statement to the reporting currency using the exchange rate in effect at the time of the cash flow (a weighted-average exchange rate may be used if the result is substantially the same). This translated statement is then used in the preparation of the consolidated statement of cash flows. Noncash exchange gains and losses recognized on the income statement should be reported as a separate item when reconciling net income and operating activities. For a more detailed discussion about the exchange rate effects on the statement of cash flows, see Chapter 22.

Cash flow per share. There is presently no requirement either under the international accounting standards or under US GAAP to disclose such information in the financial statements of an enterprise, unlike the requirement to report earnings per share (EPS). In fact, cash flow per share is a somewhat disreputable concept, since it was sometimes touted in an earlier era as being indicative of an entity's "real" performance, when of course it is not a meaningful alternative to earnings per share because, for example, enterprises that are self-liquidating by selling productive assets can generate very positive total cash flows, and hence, cash flows per share, while decimating the potential for future earnings. Since, unlike a comprehensive cash flow statement, cash flow per share cannot reveal the components of cash flow (operating, investing, and financing), its usage could be misleading.

While cash flow per share is not well regarded, it should be noted that in recent years a growing number of entities have resorted to displaying a wide range of pro forma amounts, some of which roughly correspond to cash-based measures of operating performance. These non-GAAP/non-IFRS categories should be viewed with great caution, both because they convey the message that standard, GAAP- or IFRS-based measures of performance are somehow less meaningful, and also because there are no standard definitions of the non-GAAP/non-IFRS measures, opening the door to possible manipulation. This has, in the US, caused the securities regulatory body, the SEC, to mandate that all non-GAAP measures must be explicitly reconciled to the most similar GAAP measure. The international association of securities regulators, IOSCO, has offered a similar warning and recommendation for reconciliation.

Net Reporting by Financial Institutions

IAS 7 permits financial institutions to report cash flows arising from certain activities on a net basis. These activities, and the related conditions under which net reporting would be acceptable, are as follows:

1. Cash receipts and payments on behalf of customers when the cash flows reflect the activities of the customers rather than those of the bank, such as the acceptance and repayment of demand deposits
2. Cash flows relating to deposits with fixed maturity dates
3. Placements and withdrawals of deposits from other financial institutions
4. Cash advances and loans to banks customers and repayments thereon

Reporting Futures, Forward Contracts, Options, and Swaps

IAS 7 stipulates that cash payments for and cash receipts from futures contracts, forward contracts, option contracts, and swap contracts are normally classified as investing activities, except

1. When such contracts are held for dealing or trading purposes and thus represent operating activities
2. When the payments or receipts are considered by the enterprise as financing activities and are reported accordingly

Further, when a contract is accounted for as a hedge of an identifiable position, the cash flows of the contract are classified in the same manner as the cash flows of the position being hedged.

Reporting Extraordinary Items in the Cash Flow Statement

Under IFRS, prior to revisions to IAS 1 which became effective in 2005, cash flows associated with extraordinary items were to be disclosed separately as arising from operating, investing, or financing activities in the statement of cash flows, as appropriate. By way of contrast, US GAAP permits, but does not require, separate disclosure of cash flows related to extraordinary items. If an entity reporting under US GAAP chooses to make this disclosure, however, it is expected to do so consistently in all periods. Revised IAS 1 has eliminated the extraordinary categorization of gains or losses, so this no longer will impact the presentation of the cash flow statement under IFRS.

Reconciliation of Cash and Cash Equivalents

An enterprise should disclose the components of cash and cash equivalents and should present a reconciliation of the difference, if any, between the amounts reported in the statement of cash flows and equivalent items reported in the balance sheet. By contrast, under the US GAAP the definition must tie to a specific caption on the balance sheet. For example, if short-term investments are shown as a separate caption in the balance sheet, the definition of cash for the purposes of the statement of cash flows must include "cash" alone (and not also include short-term investments). On the other hand, if "cash and cash equivalents" is the adopted definition in the statement of cash flows, a single caption in the balance sheet must include both "cash" and "short-term investments."

Acquisitions and Disposals of Subsidiaries and Other Business Units

IAS 7 requires that the aggregate cash flows from acquisitions and from disposals of subsidiaries or other business units should be presented separately as part of the investing activities section of the statement of cash flows. The following disclosures have also been prescribed by IAS 7 in respect to both acquisitions and disposals:

1. The total consideration included
2. The portion thereof discharged by cash and cash equivalents
3. The amount of cash and cash equivalents in the subsidiary or business unit acquired or disposed
4. The amount of assets and liabilities (other than cash and cash equivalents) acquired or disposed, summarized by major category

Other Disclosures Required or Recommended by IAS 7

Certain additional information may be relevant to the users of financial statements in gaining an insight into the liquidity or solvency of an enterprise. With this objective in mind, IAS 7 sets forth other disclosures that are required or in some cases, recommended.

1. **Required disclosure**—Amount of significant cash and cash equivalent balances held by an enterprise that are not available for use by the group should be disclosed along with a commentary by management.
2. **Recommended disclosures**—The disclosures that are encouraged are the following:

    a. Amount of undrawn borrowing facilities, indicating restrictions on their use, if any

b. In case of investments in joint ventures, which are accounted for using proportionate consolidation, the aggregate amount of cash flows from operating, investing and financing activities that are attributable to the investment in the joint venture

c. Aggregate amount of cash flows that are attributable to the increase in operating capacity separately from those cash flows that are required to maintain operating capacity

d. Amount of cash flows segregated by reported industry and geographical segments

The disclosures above recommended by the IAS 7, although difficult to present, are unique since such disclosures are not required even under the US GAAP. They are useful in enabling the users of financial statements to understand the enterprise's financial position better.

Basic example of the preparation of the cash flow statement under IAS 7 using a worksheet approach

Using the following financial information for ABC (Eurasia) Ltd., preparation and presentation of the cash flow statement according to the requirements of IAS 7 are illustrated. (Note that all figures in this example are in thousands of US dollars.)

ABC (Eurasia) Ltd.
Balance Sheets
December 31, 2006 and 2005

	2006	2005
Assets		
Cash and cash equivalents	$ 3,000	$ 1,000
Debtors	5,000	2,500
Inventories	2,000	1,500
Preoperative expenses	1,000	1,500
Due from associates	19,000	19,000
Property, plant, and equipment cost	12,000	22,500
Accumulated depreciation	(5,000)	(6,000)
Property, plant, and equipment, net	7,000	16,500
Total assets	$37,000	$42,000
Liabilities		
Accounts payable	$ 5,000	$12,500
Income taxes payable	2,000	1,000
Deferred taxes payable	3,000	2,000
Total liabilities	10,000	15,500
Shareholders' equity		
Share capital	6,500	6,500
Retained earnings	20,500	20,000
Total shareholders' equity	27,000	26,500
Total liabilities and shareholders' equity	$37,000	$42,000

ABC (Eurasia) Ltd.
Statement of Income
For the Year Ended December 31, 2006

Sales	$ 30,000
Cost of sales	(10,000)
Gross operating income	20,000
Administrative and selling expenses	(2,000)
Interest expenses	(2,000)
Depreciation of property, plant and equipment	(2,000)
Amortization of intangible assets	(500)
Investment income	3,000
Net income before taxation	16,500
Taxes on income	(4,000)
Net income	$ 12,500

The following additional information is relevant to the preparation of the statement of cash flows:

1. Equipment with a net book value of $7,500 and original cost of $10,500 was sold for $7,500.
2. All sales made by the company are credit sales.
3. The company received cash dividends (from investments) amounting to $3,000, recorded as income in the income statement for the year ended December 31, 2006.
4. The company declared and paid dividends of $12,000 to its shareholders.
5. Interest expense for the year 2006 was $2,000, which was fully paid during the year. All administration and selling expenses incurred were paid during the year 2006.
6. Income tax expense for the year 2006 was provided at $4,000, out of which the company paid $2,000 during 2006 as an estimate.

A worksheet can be prepared to ease the development of the cash flow statement, as follows:

Cash Flow Worksheet

	2006	2005	*Change*	*Operating*	*Investing*	*Financing*	*Cash and equivalents*
Cash and equivalents	3,000	1,000	2,000				2,000
Receivables	5,000	2,500	2,500	(2,500)			
Inventories	2,000	1,500	500	(500)			
Preoperating expenses	1,000	1,500	(500)	500			
Due from associates	19,000	19,000	0				
Property, plant, and equipment	7,000	16,500	(9,500)	2,000	7,500		
Accounts payable	5,000	12,500	7,500	(7,500)			
Income taxes payable	2,000	1,000	1,000	1,000			
Deferred taxes payable	3,000	2,000	1,000	1,000			
Share capital	6,500	6,500	0				
Retained earnings	20,500	20,000	500	9,500	3,000	(12,000)	--
				3,500	10,500	(12,000)	2,000

XYZ (Eurasia) Ltd.
Statement of Cash Flows
For the Year Ended December 31, 2006
(Direct method)

Cash flows from operating activities

Cash receipts from customers	$ 27,500	
Cash paid to suppliers and employees	(20,000)	
Cash generated from operations	7,500	
Interest paid	(2,000)	
Income taxes paid	(2,000)	
Net cash flows from operating activities		$ 3,500

Cash flows from investing activities

Proceeds from the sale of equipment	7,500	
Dividends received	3,000	
Net cash flows from investing activities		10,500

Cash flows from financing activities

Dividends paid	(12,000)	
Net cash flows used in financing activities		(12,000)
Net increase in cash and cash equivalents		2,000
Cash and cash equivalents, beginning of year		1,000
Cash and cash equivalents, end of year		$ 3,000

Details of the computations of amounts shown in the statement of cash flows are as follows:

Cash received from customers during the year

Credit sales	30,000	
Plus: Accounts receivable, beginning of year	2,500	
Less: Accounts receivable, end of year	(5,000)	
Cash received from customers during the year		$27,500

Cash paid to suppliers and employees

Cost of sales	10,000	
Less: Inventory, beginning of year	(1,500)	
Plus: Inventory, end of year	2,000	
Plus: Accounts payable, beginning of year	12,500	
Less: Accounts payable, end of year	(5,000)	
Plus: Administrative and selling expenses paid	2,000	
Cash paid to suppliers and employees during the year		$20,000
Interest paid equals interest expense charged to the income statement (per additional information)		$ 2,000

Income taxes paid during the year

Tax expense during the year (comprising current and deferred portions)	4,000	
Plus: Beginning income taxes payable	1,000	
Plus: Beginning deferred taxes payable	2,000	
Less: Ending income taxes payable	(2,000)	
Less: Ending deferred taxes payable	(3,000)	
Cash paid toward income taxes		$ 2,000
Proceeds from sale of equipment (per additional information)		$ 7,500
Dividends received during 2006 (per additional information)		$ 3,000
Dividends paid during 2006 (per additional information)		$12,000

XYZ (Eurasia) Ltd.
Statement of Cash Flows
For the Year Ended December 31, 2006
(Indirect method)*

Cash flows from operating activities

Net income before taxation	$ 16,500	
Adjustments for:		
Depreciation of property, plant and equipment	2,000	
Amortization of preoperating expenses	500	
Investment income	(3,000)	
Interest expense	2,000	
Increase in accounts receivable	(2,500)	
Increase in inventories	(500)	
Decrease in accounts payable	(7,500)	
Cash generated from operations	7,500	
Interest paid	(2,000)	
Income taxes paid	(2,000)	
Net cash from operating activities		3,500

Cash flows from investing activities		
Proceeds from sale of equipment	7,500	
Dividends received	3,000	
Net cash from investing activities		10,500
Cash flows from financing activities		
Dividends paid	(12,000)	
Net cash used in financing activities		(12,000)
Net increase in cash and cash equivalents		2,000
Cash and cash equivalents, beginning of year		1,000
Cash and cash equivalents, end of year		$ 3,000

A Comprehensive Example of the Preparation of the Cash Flow Statement Using the T-Account Approach

Under a cash and cash equivalents basis, the changes in the cash account and any cash equivalent account is the bottom line figure of the statement of cash flows. Using the 2005 and 2006 balance sheets shown below, an increase of $17,000 can be computed. This is the difference between the totals for cash and treasury bills between 2005 and 2006 ($33,000 – $16,000).

When preparing the statement of cash flows using the direct method, gross cash inflows from revenues and gross cash outflows to suppliers and for expenses are presented in the operating activities section.

In preparing the reconciliation of net income to net cash flow from operating activities (indirect method), changes in all accounts other than cash and cash equivalents that are related to operations are additions to or deductions from net income to arrive at net cash provided by operating activities.

A T-account analysis may be helpful when preparing the statement of cash flows. A T-account is set up for each account, and beginning (2005) and ending (2006) balances are taken from the appropriate balance sheet. Additionally, a T-account for cash and cash equivalents from operating activities and a master or summary T-account of cash and cash equivalents should be used.

Example of preparing a statement of cash flows

The financial statements will be used to prepare the statement of cash flows.

Johnson Company
Balance Sheets
December 31, 2006 and 2005

	2006	*2005*
Assets		
Current assets:		
Cash	$ 29,000	$ 10,000
Treasury bills	4,000	6,000
Accounts receivable—net	9,000	11,000
Inventory	14,000	9,000
Prepaid expenses	10,000	13,000
Total current assets	$ 66,000	$ 49,000
Noncurrent assets:		
Investment in XYZ (35%)	16,000	14,000
Patent	5,000	6,000
Leased asset	5,000	--
Property, plant, and equipment	39,000	37,000
Less accumulated depreciation	(7,000)	(3,000)
Total assets	$124,000	$103,000

Liabilities
Current liabilities:

Accounts payable	$ 2,000	$ 12,000
Notes payable—current	9,000	--
Interest payable	3,000	2,000
Dividends payable	5,000	2,000
Income taxes payable	2,000	1,000
Lease obligation	700	--
Total current liabilities	21,700	17,000

Noncurrent liabilities:

Deferred tax liability	9,000	6,000
Bonds payable	10,000	25,000
Lease obligation	4,300	--
Total liabilities	$ 45,000	$ 48,000

Stockholders' equity

Common stock, $10 par value	$ 33,000	$ 26,000
Additional paid-in capital	16,000	3,000
Retained earnings	30,000	26,000
Total stockholders' equity	$ 79,000	$ 55,000
Total liabilities and stockholders' equity	$124,000	$103,000

Johnson Company
Statement of Earnings
For the Year Ended December 31, 2006

Sales	$100,000
Other income	8,000
	$108,000
Cost of goods sold, excluding depreciation	60,000
Selling, general, and administrative expenses	12,000
Depreciation	8,000
Amortization of patents	1,000
Interest expense	2,000
	$ 83,000
Income before taxes	$ 25,000
Income taxes (36%)	9,000
Net income	$ 16,000

Additional information (relating to 2006)

1. Equipment costing $6,000 with a book value of $2,000 was sold for $5,000.
2. The company received a $3,000 dividend from its investment in XYZ, accounted for under the equity method and recorded income from the investment of $5,000, which is included in other income.
3. The company issued 200 shares of common stock for $5,000.
4. The company signed a note payable for $9,000.
5. Equipment was purchased for $8,000.
6. The company converted $15,000 bonds payable into 500 shares of common stock. The book value method was used to record the transaction.
7. A dividend of $12,000 was declared.
8. Equipment was leased on December 31, 2006. The principal portion of the first payment due December 31, 2007, is $700.

	Summary of Cash and Cash Equivalent		
	Inflows	Outflows	
(d)	5,000	8,000	(g)
(h)	5,000	9,000	(i)
(n)	9,000		
(s)	15,000		
	34,000	17,000	
		17,000	Net increase in cash
	34,000	34,000	

	Cash and Cash Equivalents—Oper. Act.		
(a)	16,000		
(b)	8,000		
(c)	1,000	3,000	(d)
(e)	3,000	5,000	(f)
(f)	3,000		
(j)	2,000	5,000	(k)
(l)	3,000	10,000	(m)
(o)	1,000		
(p)	1,000		
	38,000	23,000	
		15,000	(s)
	38,000	38,000	

Accounts Receivable (Net)		
11,000		
	2,000	(j)
9,000		

Inventory		
9,000		
(k) 5,000		
14,000		

Prepaid Expenses		
13,000		
	3,000	(l)
10,000		

Investment in XYZ		
14,000		
(f) 5,000	3,000	(f)
16,000		

Patent		
6,000		
	1,000	(c)
5,000		

Leased Equipment		
(r) 5,000		
5,000		

Prop., Plant, & Equip.		
37,000		
	6,000	(d)
(g) 8,000		
39,000		

Accumulated Depr.		
	3,000	
	8,000	(b)
(d) 4,000		
	7,000	

Accounts Payable		
	12,000	
(m) 10,000		
	2,000	

Notes Payable		
	9,000	(n)
	9,000	

Interest Payable		
	2,000	
(o) 1,000	2,000	(o)
	3,000	

Dividends Payable		
	2,000	
(i) 9,000	12,000	(i)
	5,000	

Income Taxes Payable		
	1,000	
(p) 5,000	6,000	(p)
	2,000	

Deferred Tax Liability		
	6,000	
	3,000	(e)
	9,000	

Bonds Payable		
	25,000	
(q) 15,000		
	10,000	

Lease Obligation		
	5,000	(r)
	5,000	

Common Stock		
	26,000	
	2,000	(h)
	5,000	(q)
	33,000	

Addl. Paid-in Capital		
	3,000	
	3,000	(h)
	10,000	(q)
	16,000	

Retained Earnings		
	26,000	
	16,000	(a)
(i) 12,000		
	30,000	

Explanation of entries

a. Cash and Cash Equivalents—Operating Activities is debited for $16,000, and credited to Retained Earnings. This represents the net income figure.

b. Depreciation is not a cash flow; however, depreciation expense was deducted to arrive at net income. Therefore, Accumulated Depreciation is credited and Cash and Cash Equivalents—Operating Activities is debited.

c. Amortization of patents is another expense not requiring cash; therefore, Cash and Cash Equivalents—Operating Activities is debited and Patent is credited.

d. The sale of equipment (additional information, item 1.) resulted in a $3,000 gain. The gain is computed by comparing the book value of $2,000 with the sales price of $5,000. Cash proceeds of $5,000 are an inflow of cash. Since the gain was included in net income, it must be deducted from net income to determine cash provided by operating activities. This is necessary to avoid counting the $3,000 gain both in cash provided by operating activities and in investing activities. The following entry would have been made on the date of sale:

Cash	5,000	
Accumulated depreciation (6,000 – 2,000)	4,000	
Property, plant, and equipment		6,000
Gain on sale of equipment (5,000 – 2,000)		3,000

Adjust the T-accounts as follows: debit Summary of Cash and Cash Equivalents for $5,000, debit Accumulated Depreciation for $4,000, credit Property, Plant, and Equipment for $6,000, and credit Cash and Cash Equivalents—Operating Activities for $3,000.

e. The $3,000 increase in Deferred Income Taxes must be added to income from operations. Although the $3,000 was deducted as part of income tax expense in determining net income, it did not require an outflow of cash. Therefore, debit Cash and Cash Equivalents—Operating Activities and credit Deferred Taxes.

f. Item 2. under the additional information indicates that the investment in XYZ is accounted for under the equity method. The investment in XYZ had a net increase of $2,000 during the year after considering the receipt of a $3,000 dividend. Dividends received (an inflow of cash) would reduce the investment in XYZ, while the equity in the income of XYZ would increase the investment without affecting cash. In order for the T-account to balance, a debit of $5,000 must have been made, indicating earnings of that amount. The journal entries would have been

Cash (dividend received)	3,000	
Investment in XYZ		3,000
Investment in XYZ	5,000	
Equity in earnings of XYZ		5,000

The dividend received ($3,000) is an inflow of cash, while the equity earnings are not. Debit Investment in XYZ for $5,000, credit Cash and Cash Equivalents—Operating Activities for $5,000, debit Cash and Cash Equivalents—Operating Activities for $3,000, and credit Investment in XYZ for $3,000.

g. The Property, Plant, and Equipment account increased because of the purchase of $8,000 (additional information, item 5.). The purchase of assets is an outflow of cash. Debit Property, Plant, and Equipment for $8,000 and credit Summary of Cash and Cash Equivalents.

h. The company sold 200 shares of common stock during the year (additional information, item 3.). The entry for the sale of stock was

Cash	5,000	
Common stock (200 shares × $10)		2,000
Additional paid-in capital		3,000

This transaction resulted in an inflow of cash. Debit Summary of Cash and Cash Equivalents $5,000, credit Common Stock $2,000, and credit Additional Paid-in Capital $3,000.

i. Dividends of $12,000 were declared (additional information, item 7.). Only $9,000 was actually paid in cash resulting in an ending balance of $9,000 in the Dividends Payable account. Therefore, the following entries were made during the year:

Retained Earnings	12,000	
Dividends Payable		12,000
Dividends Payable	9,000	
Cash		9,000

These transactions result in an outflow of cash. Debit Retained Earnings $12,000 and credit Dividends Payable $12,000. Additionally, debit Dividends Payable $9,000 and credit Summary of Cash and Cash Equivalents $9,000 to indicate the cash dividends paid during the year.

j. Accounts Receivable (net) decreased by $2,000. This is added as an adjustment to net income in the computation of cash provided by operating activities. The decrease of $2,000 means that an additional $2,000 cash was collected on account above and beyond the sales reported in the income statement. Debit Cash and Cash Equivalents—Operating Activities and credit Accounts Receivable for $2,000.

k. Inventories increased by $5,000. This is subtracted as an adjustment to net income in the computation of cash provided by operating activities. Although $5,000 additional cash was spent to increase inventories, this expenditure is not reflected in accrual-basis cost of goods sold. Debit Inventory and credit Cash and Cash Equivalents—Operating Activities for $5,000.

l. Prepaid Expenses decreased by $3,000. This is added back to net income in the computation of cash provided by operating activities. The decrease means that no cash was spent when incurring the related expense. The cash was spent when the prepaid assets were purchased, not when they were expended on the income statement. Debit Cash and Cash Equivalents—Operating Activities and credit Prepaid Expenses for $3,000.

m. Accounts Payable decreased by $10,000. This is subtracted as an adjustment to net income. The decrease of $10,000 means that an additional $10,000 of purchases were paid for in cash; therefore, income was not affected but cash was decreased. Debit Accounts Payable and credit Cash and Cash Equivalents—Operating Activities for $10,000.

n. Notes Payable increased by $9,000 (additional information, item 4.). This is an inflow of cash and would be included in the financing activities. Debit Summary of Cash and Cash Equivalents and credit Notes Payable for $9,000.

o. Interest Payable increased by $1,000, but interest expense from the income statement was $2,000. Therefore, although $2,000 was expensed, only $1,000 cash was paid ($2,000 expense – $1,000 increase in interest payable). Debit Cash and Cash Equivalents—Operating Activities for $1,000, debit Interest Payable for $1,000, and credit Interest Payable for $2,000.

p. The following entry was made to record the incurrence of the tax liability:

Income tax expense	9,000	
Income taxes payable		6,000
Deferred tax liability		3,000

Therefore, $9,000 was deducted in arriving at net income. The $3,000 credit to Deferred Income Taxes was accounted for in entry (e) above. The $6,000 credit to Taxes Payable does not, however, indicate that $6,000 cash was paid for taxes. Since Taxes Payable increased $1,000, only $5,000 must have been paid and $1,000 remains unpaid. Debit Cash and Cash Equivalents—Operating Activities for $1,000, debit Income Taxes Payable for $5,000, and credit Income Taxes Payable for $6,000.

q. Item 6. under the additional information indicates that $15,000 of bonds payable were converted to common stock. This is a *noncash* financing activity and should be reported in a separate schedule. The following entry was made to record the transaction:

Bonds payable	15,000	
Common stock (500 shares × $10 par)		5,000
Additional paid-in capital		10,000

Adjust the T-accounts with a debit to Bonds Payable, $15,000; a credit to Common Stock, $5,000; and a credit to Additional Paid-in Capital, $10,000.

r.   Item 8. under the additional information indicates that leased equipment was acquired on the last day of 2005. This is also a noncash financing activity and should be reported in a separate schedule. The following entry was made to record the lease transaction:

Leased asset	5,000	
Lease obligation		5,000

s.   The cash and cash equivalents from operations ($15,000) is transferred to the Summary of Cash and Cash Equivalents.

Since all of the changes in the noncash accounts have been accounted for and the balance in the Summary of Cash and Cash Equivalents account of $17,000 is the amount of the year-to-year increase in cash and cash equivalents, the formal statement may now be prepared. The following classified SCF is prepared under the direct method and includes the reconciliation of net income to net cash provided by operating activities. The T-account, Cash and Cash Equivalents—Operating Activities, is used in the preparation of this reconciliation. The calculations for gross receipts and gross payments needed for the direct method are shown below.

Johnson Company
Statement of Cash Flows
For the Year Ended December 31, 2006

Cash flows from operating activities			
Cash received from customers	$102,000	(a)	
Dividends received	3,000		
Cash provided by operating activities			$105,000
Cash paid to suppliers	$ 75,000	(b)	
Cash paid for expenses	9,000	(c)	
Interest paid	1,000	(d)	
Taxes paid	5,000	(e)	
Cash paid for operating activities			(90,000)
Net cash provided by operating activities			$ 15,000
Cash flows from investing activities			
Sale of equipment	5,000		
Purchase of property, plant, and equipment	(8,000)		
Net cash used in investing activities			(3,000)
Cash flows from financing activities			
Sale of common stock	$ 5,000		
Increase in notes payable	9,000		
Dividends paid	(9,000)		
Net cash provided by financing activities			5,000
Net increase in cash and cash equivalents			$ 17,000
Cash and cash equivalents at beginning of year			16,000
Cash and cash equivalents at end of year			$ 33,000

Calculation of amounts for operating activities section of Johnson Co.'s statement of cash flows

(a)   Net sales + Beginning AR – Ending AR = Cash received from customers

       $100,000 + $11,000 – $9,000 = $102,000

(b)   Cost of goods sold + Beginning AP – Ending AP + Ending inventory – Beginning inventory = Cash paid to suppliers

       $60,000 + $12,000 – $2,000 + $14,000 – $9,000 = $75,000

(c)   Operating expenses + Ending prepaid expenses – Beginning prepaid expenses – Depreciation expense (and other noncash operating expenses) = Cash paid for operating expenses

       $12,000 + $10,000 – $13,000 = $9,000

(d)   Interest expense + Beginning interest payable – Ending interest payable = Interest paid

       $2,000 + $2,000 – $3,000 = $1,000

(e) Income taxes + Beginning income taxes payable – Ending income taxes payable + Beginning deferred income taxes – Ending deferred income taxes = Taxes paid

$$\$9,000 + \$1,000 - \$2,000 + \$6,000 - \$9,000 = \$5,000$$

Reconciliation of net income to net cash provided by operating activities

Net income	$16,000
Add (deduct) items not using (providing) cash:	
Depreciation	8,000
Amortization	1,000
Gain on sale of equipment	(3,000)
Increase in deferred taxes	3,000
Equity in XYZ	(2,000)
Decrease in accounts receivable	2,000
Increase in inventory	(5,000)
Decrease in prepaid expenses	3,000
Decrease in accounts payable	(10,000)
Increase in interest payable	1,000
Increase in income taxes payable	1,000
Net cash provided by operating activities	$15,000

(The reconciliation above is required by US GAAP when the direct method is used, but there is no equivalent requirement under IFRS. The reconciliation above illustrates the presentation of the operating section of the cash flow statement when the indirect method is used. The remaining sections [i.e., the investing and financing sections] of the statement of cash flows are common to both methods, hence have not been presented above.)

Schedule of noncash transactions (to be reported in the footnotes)

Conversion of bonds into common stock	$15,000
Acquisition of leased equipment	$ 5,000

Disclosure of accounting policy

For purposes of the statement of cash flows, the company considers all highly liquid debt instruments purchased with original maturities of three months or less to be cash equivalents.

Statement of Cash Flows for Consolidated Entities

A consolidated statement of cash flows must be presented when a complete set of consolidated financial statements is issued. The consolidated statement of cash flows would be the last statement to be prepared, as the information to prepare it will come from the other consolidated statements (consolidated balance sheet, income statement, and statement of retained earnings). The preparation of these other consolidated statements is discussed in Chapter 11.

The preparation of a consolidated statement of cash flows involves the same analysis and procedures as the statement for an individual entity, with a few additional items. The direct or indirect method of presentation may be used. When the indirect method is used, the additional noncash transactions relating to the business combination, such as the differential amortization, must also be reversed. Furthermore, all transfers to affiliates must be eliminated, as they do not represent a cash inflow or outflow of the consolidated entity.

All unrealized intercompany profits should have been eliminated in preparation of the other statements; thus, no additional entry of this sort should be required. Any income allocated to noncontrolling parties would need to be added back, as it would have been eliminated in computing consolidated net income but does not represent a true cash outflow. Finally, any dividend payments should be recorded as cash outflows in the financing activities section.

In preparing the operating activities section of the statement by the indirect method following a purchase business combination, the changes in assets and liabilities related to operations since acquisition should be derived by comparing the consolidated balance sheet as of the date of acquisition with the year-end consolidated balance sheet. These changes will be combined with those for the acquiring company up to the date of acquisition as adjustments to net income. The effects due to the acquisition of these assets and liabilities are reported under investing activities. Under the pooling-of-interests method the combination is treated as having occurred at the beginning of the year. Thus, the changes in assets and liabilities related to operations should be those derived by comparing the beginning-of-the-year balance sheet amounts on a consolidated basis with the end-of-the-year consolidated balance sheet amounts.

Example of cash flow reporting under IFRS

Nokia Group
Consolidated Cash Flow Statements
For the Years Ended December 31, 2004, 2003, and 2002

	Notes	*2004* *EURm*	*2003* *EURm*	*2002* *EURm*
Cash flow from operating activities:				
Net profit		3,207	3,592	3,381
Adjustments total	34	1,986	2,953	3,151
Net profit before change in net working capital		5,193	6,545	6,532
Change in net working capital	34	299	(194)	914
Cash generated from operations		5,492	6,351	7,446
Interest received		204	256	229
Interest paid		(26)	(33)	(94)
Other financial income and expenses, net received		41	118	67
Income taxes paid		(1,368)	(1,440)	(1,947)
Net cash from operating activities		4,343	5,252	5,701
Cash flow from investing activities:				
Acquisition of Group companies, net of acquired cash (2004: EUR 0 million, 2003: EUR 0 million, 2002: EUR 6 million)		--	(7)	(10)
Purchase of current available-for-sale investments, liquid assets		(10,318)	(11,695)	(7,392)
Purchase of noncurrent available-for-sale investments		(388)	(282)	(99)
Purchase of shares in associated companies		(109)	(61)	--
Additions to capitalized development costs		(101)	(218)	(418)
Long-term loans made to customers		--	(97)	(563)
Proceeds from repayment and sale of long-term loans receivable		368	315	314
Proceeds from (+)/payment of (-) other long-term receivables		2	(18)	(32)
Proceeds from (+)/payment of (-) short-term loans receivable		66	63	(85)
Capital expenditures		(548)	(432)	(432)
Proceeds from disposal of shares in Group companies, net of disposed cash		1	--	93
Proceeds from maturities and sale of current available-for-sale investments, liquid assets		9,737	8,793	4,390
Proceeds from sale of current available-for-sale investments		587	--	--
Proceeds from sale of noncurrent available-for-sale investments		346	381	162
Proceeds from sale of fixed assets		6	19	177
Dividends received		22	24	25
Net cash used in investing activities		(329)	(3,215)	(3,870)
Cash flow from financing activities:				
Proceeds from stock option exercises		--	23	163
Purchase of treasury shares		(2,640)	(1,355)	(17)
Capital investment by minority shareholders		--	--	26
Proceeds from long-term borrowings		1	8	100
Repayment of long-term borrowings		(3)	(56)	(98)
Repayment of short-term borrowings		(255)	(22)	(406)
Dividends paid		(1,413)	(1,378)	(1,348)
Net cash (used) in financing activities		(4,318)	(2,780)	(1,580)

	Notes	2004 EURm	2003 EURm	2002 EURm
Foreign exchange adjustment		(23)	(146)	(135)
Net increase (+)/decrease (–) in cash and cash equivalents		(327)	(889)	116
Cash and cash equivalents at beginning of period		2,784	3,673	3,557
Cash and cash equivalents at end of period		2,457	2,784	3,673
Cash and cash equivalents comprise of:				
Bank and cash		1,090	1,145	1,496
Current available-for sale investments, cash equivalents	16, 35	1,367	1,639	2,177
		2,457	2,784	3,673

See Notes to Consolidated Financial Statements.

The figures in the consolidated cash flow statement cannot be directly traced from the balance sheet without additional information as a result of acquisitions and disposals of subsidiaries and net foreign exchange differences arising on consolidation.

5 CASH, RECEIVABLES, AND FINANCIAL INSTRUMENTS

PERSPECTIVE AND ISSUES

Cash and receivables meet the definition of a financial instrument under IFRS. The accounting for financial instruments received a great deal of attention from the IASC—being the subject of its two most voluminous and controversial standards—and continued attention from the IASB is a certainty. The original intent, which was to address all matters of recognition, measurement, derecognition, presentation, and disclosure in a single comprehensive standard, proved to be unworkable (as was also the case under US GAAP), and thus matters have been dealt with piecemeal. The first standard, IAS 32, which became effective in 1996 and has most recently been revised effective 2005, addressed only matters of presentation and disclosure. The disclosure requirements set forth in IAS 32 have been removed from that standard, effective 2007, and are now incorporated into IFRS 7, which also includes financial institution disclosure requirements previously set forth by IAS 30. IFRS 7 is discussed in detail in this chapter.

The more intractable problems of recognition, measurement, and derecognition were dealt with by IAS 39, which became mandatory in 2001. IAS 39 has been amended several times in the past two years, largely as IASB struggled to gain EU acceptance for IFRS and a number of highly specific financial instruments-related concerns had to be resolved. IAS 39 was intended as only an interim standard, since it failed to comprehensively embrace fair value accounting for all financial assets and liabilities, which had been held out as the goal to which the IASC was committed at the time. Fair value accounting, particularly for liabilities, was and remains a controversial topic. Subsequent to IAS 39's promulgation, IASB has indicated that any decision to impose comprehensive fair value accounting for financial assets and liabilities is likely to be several years in the future, at best, and must be viewed as a longer-term objective.

IAS 39 established extensive new requirements for the recognition, derecognition, and measurement of financial assets and liabilities, and furthermore addressed, for the first time, special hedge accounting procedures to be applied under defined sets of circumstances. Hedging has become an increasingly common business risk management practice, but had previously created serious accounting anomalies not addressed by professional standards. Hedge accounting is designed to improve the matching of income statement recognition of related gains and losses, and is made necessary by the use of a "mixed attribute" accounting model, whereby some assets and liabilities are reported at (amortized) historical costs, and others are reported at fair values. Hedge accounting for financial assets and liabilities would be neither appropriate nor necessary, therefore, if all of these assets and liabilities were simply carried at fair value. While this has been stated as the ultimate goal of IFRS, it appears that it is at least several years away from becoming the rule, at the minimum.

Because of the complexity of IAS 39, a number of difficult implementation issues needed to be addressed, and in response the IASC constituted an IAS 39 Implementation Guidance Committee (IGC). Several hundred questions and answers were published by this committee, and a compendium of guidance was produced in connection with the 2003 revisions to IAS 39. More recently, however, much of the guidance formerly found in materials prepared by the IGC and also in certain of the Interpretations promulgated by SIC have been directly incorporated into revised IAS 32 and IAS 39 (revised 2004, effective 2005).

In this chapter, the overall requirements of IAS 32 and 39, and IFRS 7 will be set forth, while detailed application of IAS 39 is set forth in Chapter 10. In addition, this chapter will present detailed examples on a range of topics involving cash and receivables (e.g., the accounting for factored receivables) that are derived from the most widespread and venerable practices in these areas, even if not codified in the IAS.

Sources of IFRS
IAS 1, 32, 39   *IFRS* 7

DEFINITIONS OF TERMS

Accounts receivable. Amounts due from customers for goods or services provided in the normal course of business operations.

Aging the accounts. Procedure for the computation of the adjustment for uncollectible accounts receivable based on the length of time the end-of-period outstanding accounts have been unpaid.

Amortized cost of financial asset or financial liability. The amount at which the asset or liability was measured at original recognition, minus principal repayments, plus or minus the cumulative amortization of any premium or discount, and minus any write-down for impairment or uncollectibility.

Assignment. Formal procedure for collateralization of borrowings through the use of accounts receivable. It normally does not involve debtor notification.

Available-for-sale financial assets. Those nonderivative financial assets that are neither carried at fair value through current earnings nor held to maturity, and are not loans and receivables.

Carrying amount (value). For marketable equity securities, this is fair value (unless there is no available market value, in which case it is historical cost).

Cash. Coins and currency on hand and balances in checking accounts available for immediate withdrawal.

Cash equivalents. Short-term, highly liquid investments that are readily convertible to known amounts of cash. Examples include treasury bills, commercial paper, and money market funds.

Control. The power to obtain the future economic benefits that flow from an asset.

Credit risk. Possibility that a loss may occur from the failure of another party to perform according to the terms of a contract.

Current assets. Assets that are reasonably expected to be realized in cash or sold or consumed within a year or within the normal operating cycle of the entity.

Derecognize. Remove a financial asset or liability, or a portion thereof, from the entity's balance sheet.

Derivative. A financial instrument or other contract (1) whose value changes in response to changes in a specified interest rate, security price, commodity price, foreign exchange rate, index of prices or rates, a credit rating or credit index, or similar variable (which is known as the underlying), (2) that requires little or no initial net investment relative to other types of contracts that have a similar response to changes in market conditions, and (3) that is settled at a future date. Nonfinancial variables must be associated with an underlying that is not specific to a party to the contract.

Effective interest method. The means of computing amortization using the effective interest rate of a financial asset or liability. The effective interest rate is the rate that exactly discounts the expected stream of future cash payments through maturity or the next market-based repricing date to the current net carrying amount of the asset or liability. The computation includes all fees and points paid or received between parties to the contract.

Equity instrument. Any contract that evidences a residual interest in the assets of an entity after deducting all its liabilities.

Factoring. Outright sale of accounts receivable to a third-party financing entity. The sale may be with or without recourse.

Fair value. Amount for which an asset could be exchanged, or a liability settled, between knowledgeable willing parties in an arm's-length transaction.

Financial asset. Any asset that is

1. Cash
2. An equity instrument of another entity
3. A contractual right to receive cash or another financial asset from another entity
4. A contractual right to exchange financial instruments with another entity under conditions that are potentially favorable
5. A contract that will be settled in the reporting entity's own equity instruments and is a nonderivative for which the entity is or may be obligated to receive a variable number of its own equity instruments
6. A contract that will be settled in the reporting entity's own equity instruments and is a derivative that will or may be settled other than by an exchange of a fixed amount of cash or another financial asset for a fixed number of the entity's own equity instruments (which excludes instruments that are themselves contracts for the future receipt or delivery of the entity's equity instruments)

Financial asset or liability reported at fair value through current earnings. One which *either* is acquired or incurred for trading (i.e., is principally for the purpose of generating a profit from short-term fluctuations in price or dealer's margin, or which is part of identified commonly managed financial instruments and for which there is a pattern of short-term profit-taking by the entity, or which is a derivative unless designated for, and effective as, a hedging instrument) or upon initial recognition is designated for carrying at fair value through current earnings.

Financial instrument. Any contract that gives rise to both a financial asset of one entity and a financial liability or equity instrument of another entity.

Financial liability. Any liability that is

1. A contractual obligation to deliver cash or another financial asset to another entity
2. A contractual obligation to exchange financial instruments with another entity under conditions that are potentially unfavorable
3. A contract that will or may be settled in the entity's own equity instruments and is a nonderivative for which it is or may be obligated to deliver a variable number of its own equity instruments
4. A contract that will or may be settled in the entity's own equity instruments and is a derivative that will or may be settled other than by an exchange of a fixed amount of cash or another financial asset for a fixed number of the entity's own equity instruments (which excludes instruments that are themselves contracts for the future receipt or delivery of the entity's equity instruments)

Firm commitment. A binding agreement for the exchange of a specified quantity of resources at a specified price on a specified future date or dates.

Hedge effectiveness. The degree to which offsetting changes in fair values or cash flows attributable to the hedged risk are achieved by the hedging instrument.

Hedged item. An asset, liability, firm commitment, or forecasted future transaction that (1) exposes the entity to risk of changes in fair value or changes in future cash flows, and that (2) for hedge accounting purposes is designated as being hedged.

Hedging. Designating one or more hedging instruments such that the change in fair value is an offset, in whole or in part, to the change in the fair value or the cash flows of a hedged item.

Hedging instrument. For hedge accounting purposes, a designated derivative or (in limited instances) another financial asset or liability whose fair value or cash flows are expected to offset changes in the fair value or cash flows of a designated hedged item. Nonderivative financial assets or liabilities may be designated as hedging instruments for hedge accounting purposes only if they hedge the risk of changes in foreign currency exchange rates.

Held-to-maturity investments. Nonderivative financial assets with fixed or determinable payments and fixed maturities, that the entity has the positive intent and ability to hold to maturity, except for those designated upon initial recognition as carried at fair value, those available-for-sale, and loans and receivables.

Loans and receivables. Nonderivative financial assets with fixed or determinable payments that are not quoted in an active market, other than those that are to be sold immediately or in the short term, those designated upon initial recognition as carried at fair value, those designated as available-for-sale, and those for which the holder may not recover substantially all the initial investment other than due to credit deterioration.

Market risk. Possibility that future changes in market prices may make a financial instrument less valuable.

Market value. Amount obtainable from a sale, or payable on acquisition, of a financial instrument in an active market.

Marketable equity securities. Instruments representing actual ownership interest, or the rights to buy or sell such interests, that are actively traded or listed on a national securities exchange.

Monetary financial assets and financial liabilities. Financial assets and financial liabilities to be received or paid in fixed or determinable amounts of money.

Net realizable value. Amount of cash anticipated to be produced in the normal course of business from an asset, net of any direct costs of the conversion into cash.

Operating cycle. Average time between the acquisition of materials or services and the final cash realization from the sale of products or services.

Other than temporary decline. Downward movement in the value of a marketable equity security for which there are known causes. The decline indicates the remote likelihood of a price recovery.

Percentage-of-sales method. Procedure for computing the adjustment for uncollectible accounts receivable based on the historical relationship between bad debts and gross credit sales.

Pledging. Process of using an asset as collateral for borrowings. It generally refers to borrowings secured by accounts receivable.

Realized gain (loss). Difference between the cost or adjusted cost of a marketable security and the net selling price realized by the seller, which is to be included in the determination of net income in the period of the sale.

Recourse. Right of the transferee (factor) of accounts receivable to seek recovery for an uncollectible account from the transferor. It is often limited to specific conditions.

Repurchase agreement. An agreement to transfer a financial asset to another party in exchange for cash or other considerations, with a concurrent obligation to reacquire the asset at a future date for an amount equal to the cash or other consideration plus interest.

Risk of accounting loss. Includes (1) the possibility that a loss may occur from the failure of another party to perform according to the terms of a contract (credit risk), (2) the possibility that future changes in market prices may make a financial instrument less valuable (market risk), and (3) the risk of theft or physical loss.

Securitization. The process whereby financial assets are transformed into securities.

Short-term investments. Securities or other assets acquired with excess cash, having ready marketability and intended by management to be liquidated, if necessary, within the current operating cycle.

Temporary decline. Downward fluctuation in the value of a marketable equity security that has no known cause which suggests that the decline is of a permanent nature.

Transaction costs. Incremental costs directly attributable to the acquisition or disposal of a financial asset or liability.

CONCEPTS, RULES, AND EXAMPLES

Cash

The only actual guidance to the accounting for cash offered by IFRS is that found in IAS 1. Common practice is to define cash as including currency on hand, as well as current and other accounts maintained with banks. However, cash that is not available for immediate use is normally given separate disclosure to prevent misleading implications. IAS 1 (as revised effective 2005) generally requires that balance sheets be *classified* (i.e., that current and noncurrent assets and liabilities be grouped separately), unless presentation in the order of liquidity is deemed more reliable and relevant. If a classified balance sheet is presented, cash which is restricted and not available for use within one year of the balance sheet date should be included in noncurrent assets.

For a current asset classification to be warranted, it must furthermore be management's intention that the cash be available for current purposes. For example, cash in a demand deposit account, being held specifically for the retirement of long-term debts not maturing currently, should be excluded from current assets and shown as a noncurrent investment. This would apply only if management's intention was clear; otherwise it would not be necessary to segregate from the general cash account the funds that presumably will be needed for a scheduled debt retirement, as those funds could presumably be obtained from alternative sources, including new borrowings.

It has become more common for the caption "cash and cash equivalents" to appear in the balance sheet. This term includes other forms of near-cash items as well as demand deposits and liquid, short-term securities. To justify inclusion, however, cash equivalents must be available essentially upon demand (e.g., as investments which can be liquidated at once and with little risk of loss of principal).

In this regard, IAS 7 defines cash equivalents as short-term, highly liquid investments, readily convertible into known amounts of cash that are subject to an insignificant risk of changes in value. The reasonable, albeit arbitrary, limit of three months is placed on the maturity dates of any instruments acquired to be part of cash equivalents. (This is, not coincidentally, the same limit applied by the US standard on cash flow statements, FAS 95, promulgation of which preceded the revision of IAS 7 by several years.)

Compensating balances are cash amounts that are not immediately accessible by the owner. Pursuant to borrowing arrangements with lenders, an entity will often be required to maintain a minimum amount of cash on deposit (as a "compensating balance"). While stated to provide greater security for the loan, the actual purpose of this balance is to increase the yield on the loan to the lender. Since most organizations will need to maintain a certain working balance in their cash accounts simply to handle routine transactions and to cushion against unforeseen fluctuations in the demand for cash, borrowers often find compensating balance arrangements not objectionable and may well have sufficient liquidity to maintain these with little hardship being incurred. They may even be viewed as comprising "rotating" normal cash balances that are flowing into and out of the bank on a regular basis.

Notwithstanding how these are viewed by the debtor, however, the fact is that compensating balances are not available for unrestricted use, and penalties will result if they are withdrawn rather than being left intact, as called for under the arrangement. Therefore, the portion of an entity's cash account that is held as a compensating balance must be segregated and shown as a noncurrent asset if the related borrowings are noncurrent liabilities. If the borrowings are current liabilities, it is acceptable to show the compensating balance as a separately captioned current asset, but under no circumstances should these be included in the caption "cash."

In some jurisdictions, certain cash deposits held by banks, such as savings accounts or corporate time deposits, are subject to terms and conditions that might prevent immediate withdrawals. While not always exercised, these rights permit a delay in honoring withdrawal requests for a stated period of time, such as seven days or one month. These rules were instituted to discourage panic withdrawals and to give the depository institution adequate time to liquidate investments in an orderly fashion. Cash in savings accounts subject to a statutory notification requirement and cash in certificates of deposit maturing during the current operating cycle or within one year may be included as current assets, but as with compensating balances, should be separately captioned in the balance sheet to avoid the misleading implication that these funds are available immediately upon demand. Typically, such items will be included in the short-term investments caption, but these could be separately labeled as time deposits or restricted cash deposits.

Petty cash and other imprest cash accounts are usually presented in financial statements with other cash accounts. Due to materiality considerations, these need not be set forth in a separate caption unless so desired.

Receivables

Receivables include trade receivables, which are amounts due from customers for goods sold or services performed in the normal course of business, as well as such other categories of receivables as notes receivable, trade acceptances, third-party instruments, and amounts due from officers, stockholders, employees, or affiliated companies.

Notes receivable are formalized obligations evidenced by written promissory notes. The latter categories of receivables generally arise from cash advances but could develop from sales of merchandise or the provision of services. The basic nature of amounts due from trade customers is often different from that of balances receivable from related parties, such as employees or stockholders. Thus, the general practice is to insist that the various classes of receivables be identified separately either on the face of the balance sheet or in the notes. Revised IAS 1 does not explicitly require such presentation. Nonetheless, the authors believe that distinguishing among categories of receivables is an important financial reporting objective, however, and that the guidelines set forth in an earlier iteration of IAS 1 should continue to be observed.

IAS 39 addresses recognition and measurement of receivables. In addition, a number of international standards allude to the accounting for receivables. For example, IAS 18, *Reve-*

nue Recognition, addresses the timing of revenue recognition, which implicitly addresses the timing of recognition of the resulting receivables.

If the gross amount of receivables includes unearned interest or finance charges, these should be deducted in arriving at the net amount to be presented in the balance sheet. Deductions should be taken for amounts estimated to be uncollectible and also for the estimated returns, allowances, and other discounts to be taken by customers prior to or at the time of payment. In practice, the deductions that would be made for estimated returns, allowances, and trade discounts are usually deemed to be immaterial, and such adjustments are rarely made. However, if it is known that sales are often recorded for merchandise that is shipped on approval and available data suggests that a sizable proportion of such sales are returned by the customers, these estimated future returns must be accrued. Similarly, material amounts of anticipated discounts and allowances should be recorded in the period of sale.

The foregoing comments apply where revenues are recorded at the gross amount of the sale and subsequent sales discounts are recorded as debits (contra revenues). An alternative manner of recording revenue, which does away with any need to estimate future discounts, is to record the initial sale at the net amount; that is, at the amount that will be remitted if customers take advantage of the available discount terms. If customers pay the gross amount later (they fail to take the discounts), this additional revenue is recorded as income when it is remitted. The net method of recording sales, however, is rarely encountered in practice.

Bad Debts Expense

In theory, accruals should be made for anticipated sales returns, sales allowances, and discounts that pertain to sales already consummated as of the date of the financial statements. This is usually not done, however, because of materiality considerations. On the other hand, the recording of anticipated uncollectible amounts is almost always necessary, because these will be material to the presentation of the receivables on the balance sheet and also to the determination of periodic earnings. The direct write-off method, in which a receivable is charged off only when it is clear that it cannot be collected, is unsatisfactory since it results in a significant mismatching of revenues and expenses, and will also cause the balance sheet representation of receivables at amounts that exceed fair (i.e., realizable) value. Proper matching can be achieved only if bad debts expense is recorded in the same fiscal period as the revenues to which they are related. Since this expense cannot be known with certainty, an estimate must be made.

There are two popular estimation techniques. The percentage-of-sales method is principally oriented toward achieving the best possible matching of revenues and expenses. Aging the accounts is more oriented toward the presentation of the correct net realizable value of the trade receivables in the balance sheet. Both methods are acceptable and widely employed. However, with the ever-greater emphasis placed by accounting theory on the balance sheet, one might argue that the aging of receivables (or equivalent) would be the most appropriate method to employ.

Percentage-of-sales method of estimating bad debts. Historical data are analyzed to ascertain the relationship between credit sales and bad debts. The derived percentage is then applied to the current period's sales revenues to arrive at the appropriate debit to bad debts expense for the year. The offsetting credit is made to allowance for uncollectibles. When specific customer accounts are subsequently identified as uncollectible, they are written off against this allowance.

Example of percentage-of-sales method

Total credit sales for year:	€7,500,000
Bad debt ratio from prior years or other data source:	1.75% of sales
Computed year-end adjustment for bad debts expense:	€131,250
	(€7,500,000 × .0175)

The entry required is

Bad debts expense	131,250	
Allowance for uncollectibles		131,250

Note that the foregoing entry assumes that no bad debts expense has yet been recognized with respect to the year's credit sales. If some such expense has already been recognized, as a consequence of interim accruals, for example, the final adjusting entry would be suitably reduced.

Aging method of estimating bad debts. An analysis is prepared of the customer receivables at the balance sheet date. These accounts are categorized by the number of days or months they have remained outstanding. Based on the entity's past experience or on other available statistics, historical bad debts percentages are applied to each of these aggregate amounts, with larger percentages being applicable to the older accounts. The end result of this process is a computed total dollar amount that is the proper balance in the allowance for uncollectibles at the balance sheet date. As a result of the difference between the previous years' adjustments to the allowance for uncollectibles and the actual write-offs made to the account, there will usually be a balance in this account. Thus, the adjustment needed will be an amount other than that computed by the aging.

Example of the aging method

		Age of accounts		
	Under 30 days	*30-90 days*	*Over 90 days*	*Total*
Gross receivables	€1,100,000	€425,000	€360,000	
Bad debt percentage	0.5%	2.5%	15%	
Provision required	€5,500	€10,625	€54,000	€70,125

The credit balance required in the allowance account is €70,125. Assuming that a debit balance of €58,250 already exists in the allowance account (from charge-offs during the year), the necessary entry is

Bad debts expense	128,375	
Allowance for uncollectibles		128,375

Both of the estimation techniques should produce approximately the same result. This will be true especially over the course of a number of years. Nonetheless, it must be recognized that these adjustments are based on estimates and will never be totally accurate. When facts subsequently become available to indicate that the amount provided as an allowance for uncollectible accounts was incorrect, an adjustment classified as a change in estimate is made. According to IAS 8, adjustments of this nature are never considered to be accounting errors subject to subsequent correction or restatement. Only if an actual clerical or mechanical error occurred in the recording of allowance for uncollectibles would correction as an error be warranted.

Pledging, Assigning, and Factoring Receivables

An organization can alter the timing of cash flows resulting from sales to its customers by using its accounts receivable as collateral for borrowings or by selling the receivables outright. A wide variety of arrangements can be structured by the borrower and lender, but the most common are pledging, assignment, and factoring. The IFRS do not offer specific accounting guidance on these assorted types of arrangements, although the derecognition rules of IAS 39 generally apply to these as well as other financial instruments of the reporting entity.

Pledging of receivables. Pledging is an agreement whereby accounts receivable are used as collateral for loans. Generally, the lender has limited rights to inspect the borrower's records to achieve assurance that the receivables do exist. The customers whose accounts have been pledged are not aware of this event, and their payments are still remitted to the original obligee. The pledged accounts merely serve as security to the lender, giving comfort that sufficient assets exist that will generate cash flows adequate in amount and timing to repay the debt. However, the debt is paid by the borrower whether or not the pledged receivables are collected and whether or not the pattern of such collections matches the payments due on the debt.

The only accounting issue relating to pledging is that of adequate disclosure. The accounts receivable, which remain assets of the borrowing entity, continue to be shown as current assets in its financial statements but must be identified as having been pledged. This identification can be accomplished either parenthetically or by footnote disclosures. Similarly, the related debt should be identified as having been secured by the receivables.

Example of proper disclosure for pledged receivables

Current assets:
Accounts receivable, net of allowance for doubtful accounts of €600,000
  (€3,500,000 of which has been pledged as collateral for bank loans)   8,450,000

Current liabilities:
Bank loans payable (secured by pledged accounts receivable)   2,700,000

A more common practice is to include the disclosure in the notes to the financial statements.

Assignment of receivables. The assignment of accounts receivable is a more formalized transfer of the asset to the lending institution. The lender will make an investigation of the specific receivables that are being proposed for assignment and will approve those that are deemed to be worthy as collateral. Customers are not usually aware that their accounts have been assigned and they continue to forward their payments to the original obligee. In some cases, the assignment agreement requires that collection proceeds be delivered to the lender immediately. The borrower is, however, the primary obligor and is required to make timely payment on the debt whether or not the receivables are collected as anticipated. The borrowing is with recourse, and the general credit of the borrower is pledged to the payment of the debt.

Since the lender knows that not all the receivables will be collected on a timely basis by the borrower, only a fraction of the face value of the receivables will be advanced as a loan to the borrower. Typically, this amount ranges from 70 to 90%, depending on the credit history and collection experience of the borrower.

Assigned accounts receivable remain the assets of the borrower and continue to be presented in its financial statements, with appropriate disclosure of the assignment similar to that illustrated for pledging. Prepaid finance charges would be debited to a prepaid expense account and amortized to expense over the period to which the charges apply.

Factoring of receivables. This category of financing is the most significant in terms of accounting implications. Factoring traditionally has involved the outright sale of receivables to a financing institution known as a factor. These arrangements involved (1) notification to the customer to forward future payments to the factor, and (2) the transfer of receivables without recourse. The factor assumes the risk of an inability to collect. Thus, once a factoring arrangement was completed, the entity had no further involvement with the accounts except for a return of merchandise.

The classical variety of factoring provides two financial services to the business: (1) it permits the entity to obtain cash earlier, and (2) the risk of bad debts is transferred to the factor. The factor is compensated for each of the services. Interest is charged based on the anticipated length of time between the date the factoring is consummated and the expected collection date of the receivables sold, and a fee is charged based on the factor's anticipated bad debt losses.

Some companies continue to factor receivables as a means of transferring the risk of bad debts but leave the cash on deposit with the factor until the weighted-average due date of the receivables, thereby avoiding interest payments. This arrangement is still referred to as factoring, since the customer receivables have been sold. However, the borrowing entity does not receive cash but instead has created a new receivable, usually captioned "due from factor." In contrast to the original customer receivables, this receivable is essentially riskless and will be presented in the balance sheet without a deduction for estimated uncollectibles.

Merchandise returns will normally be the responsibility of the original vendor, who must then make the appropriate settlement with the factor. To protect against the possibility of merchandise returns that diminish the total of receivables to be collected, very often a factoring arrangement will not advance the full amount of the factored receivables (less any interest and factoring fee deductions). Rather, the factor will retain a certain fraction of the total proceeds relating to the portion of sales that are anticipated to be returned by customers. This sum is known as the factor's *holdback*. When merchandise is returned to the borrower, an entry is made offsetting the receivable from the factor. At the end of the return privilege period, any remaining holdback will become due and payable to the borrower.

Examples of journal entries to be made by the borrower in a factoring situation

1. Thirsty Corp. on July 1, 2005, enters into an agreement with Rich Company to sell a group of its receivables without recourse. A total face value of €200,000 accounts receivable (against which a 5% allowance had been recorded) is involved. The factor will charge 20% interest computed on the (weighted) average time to maturity of the receivables of 36 days plus a 3% fee. A 5% holdback will also be retained.
2. Thirsty's customers return for credit €4,800 of merchandise.
3. The customer return privilege period expires and the remaining holdback is paid to the transferor.

The entries required are as follows:

1. Cash	180,055	
Allowance for bad debts (€200,000 × .05)	10,000	
Interest expense (or prepaid) (€200,000 × .20 × 36/365)	3,945	
Factoring fee (€200,000 × .03)	6,000	
Factor's holdback receivable (€200,000 × .05)	10,000	
Bad debts expense		10,000
Accounts receivable		200,000

(Alternatively, the interest and factor's fee can be combined into a €9,945 charge to loss on sale of receivables.)

2. Sales returns and allowances	4,800	
Factor's holdback receivable		4,800

3. Cash	5,200	
Factor's holdback receivable		5,200

Transfers of Receivables with Recourse

In recent years, a newer variant on factoring has become popular. This variation has been called factoring with recourse, the terms of which suggest somewhat of a compromise between true factoring and the assignment of receivables. Accounting practice has varied considerably because of the hybrid nature of these transactions, and a strong argument can be made, in fact, that the factoring with recourse is nothing more than the assignment of receivables, and that the proper accounting (as discussed above) is to present this as a secured borrowing, not as a sale of the receivables. While "factoring with recourse" was previously held to qualify for derecognition by the transferor, this is now seen to be consistent with the derecognition rules of IAS 39, due to the nominal transferor's continuing involvement and retention of risk.

In the most recent amendments to IAS 32 and IAS 39, the IASB at first had signaled its intent to adopt a "continuing involvement model" for purposes of financial instrument derecognition rules, but ultimately decided to retain an approach largely consistent with the previous version of IAS 39, with some modification and clarification. Under revised IAS 39, although the transfer of the contractual right to receive cash flows is the paramount criterion for derecongnition of financial assets such as receivables, if not all the rewards and risks of ownership are disposed of then derecognition will not be permitted.

FINANCIAL INSTRUMENTS OTHER THAN CASH AND RECEIVABLES

Accounting for Financial Instruments: Evolution of the Current Standards

The quantity and variety of financial instruments have expanded dramatically over the recent decades. Accounting standard setters, including IASB, have lagged seriously behind "financial engineers," who have been creative in developing financial instruments which have been able to evade the presentation of the substance of these various arrangements. Compound nonderivative instruments (those having, for example, attributes of both debt and equity) and financial derivatives (e.g., options and futures) have presented the greatest challenges to standard setters. Derivative financial instruments in particular have been difficult to deal with, since traditional historical cost-based accounting does not provide satisfactory results, given the fact that many such instruments require little or no initial cash investment. Thus, under the historical cost model many if not most of these instruments would not be reported in a historical cost balance sheet notwithstanding the often very substantial risks being taken by the investor. For these and other reasons, the IASB signaled its desire to abandon historical costing for reporting financial instruments, in favor of a universal fair value approach. However, strong opposition to this change has made such a transition unlikely in the near term.

Standard setters have long since imposed modern financial reporting requirements for mundane instruments such as corporate stocks and bonds, although even in that realm compromises were made which preserve the "mixed (historical cost and fair value) attribute" characteristic of financial reporting standards. For example (as described in Chapter 10), marketable securities held as assets are reported in one of several different ways, depending upon management's intent. Meanwhile, accounting for financial liabilities (e.g., corporate debt obligations) remains tied to historical cost, in part due to opposition from debtors, particularly financial institutions, to the adoption of a fair value model.

Derivatives commonly employed in today's business environment include option contracts, interest rate caps, interest rate floors, fixed-rate loan commitments, note issuance facilities, letters of credit, forward contracts, forward interest rate agreements, interest rate collars, futures, swaps, mortgage-backed securities, interest-only obligations, principal-only obligations, indexed debt, and other optional characteristics which are directly incorporated within receivables and payables such as convertible bond conversion or call terms (embedded derivatives).

Derivative financial instruments are used most typically as a tool to assist in the management of some category of risk, such as possible unfavorable movements in stock prices, interest rate variations, currency fluctuations and commodity price volatility. To the extent derivatives are used for hedging activities, there has long been a consensus that, within the broad framework of an essentially historical cost-based system of accounting principles, there was a need for "special" accounting to reflect the effects of hedging. This is necessitated by the fact that many of the hedging assets and liabilities are normally reported under the historical cost model, while derivatives used to hedge changes in the value of these assets and liabilities must be reported at fair value, since historical costs are not meaningful.

While IAS 32 sets requirements for the classification by issuers of financial instruments as either liabilities or equity, and for offsetting of financial assets and liabilities, as well as for the disclosure of related information in the financial statements, IAS 39 tackled the somewhat more substantive questions of recognition, derecognition, measurement, and hedge accounting. Fair value reporting has been embraced, with a few important exceptions, for financial assets, while historical cost-based reporting has been largely preserved for financial liabilities. Special hedge accounting has been endorsed for those situations when a strict set of criteria are met, with the objectives of achieving good "matching" and of ensuring that all derivative financial instruments receive formal financial statement recognition, even if some value changes are excluded from current earnings.

While the application of fair value accounting to all financial instruments is still in the future, the IASB did make some changes to IAS 32 and IAS 39, some of which were to be implemented in 2005. These already enacted and further expected changes are discussed throughout the following sections of this chapter, and in Chapter 10, as they are pertinent. Detailed discussions of hedging and of derivative financial instruments are incorporated in Chapter 10.

Reporting and Disclosure of Financial Instruments under IAS 32

IAS 32's disclosure requirements have been removed from this standard and relocated to newly issued IFRS 7, which also incorporates requirements formerly found in IAS 30. IFRS 7 is discussed later in this chapter; however, since IFRS 7's mandatory adoption date is 2007, many entities will continue to meet the requirements established by IAS 32 for 2005 and 2006. Accordingly, these are detailed in the following paragraphs.

When first issued, IAS 32 was an important achievement for several reasons. It represented a commitment to a strict "substance over form" approach. The most signal accomplishment, perhaps, was the requirement that disparate elements of compound financial instruments be separately presented in the balance sheet.

Under IAS 32, financial assets and liabilities are defined as follows:

Financial asset: Any asset that is

1. Cash
2. An equity instrument of another entity
3. A contractual right to receive cash or another financial asset from another entity
4. A contractual right to exchange financial instruments with another entity under conditions that are potentially favorable
5. A contract that will be settled in the reporting entity's own equity instruments and is a nonderivative for which the entity is or may be obligated to receive a variable number of its own equity instruments

6. A contract that will be settled in the reporting entity's own equity instruments and is a derivative that will or may be settled other than by an exchange of a fixed amount of cash or another financial asset for a fixed number of the entity's own equity instruments (which excludes instruments that are themselves contracts for the future receipt or delivery of the entity's equity instruments).

Financial liability: Any liability that is

1. A contractual obligation to deliver cash or another financial asset to another entity
2. A contractual obligation to exchange financial instruments with another entity under conditions that are potentially unfavorable
3. A contract that will or may be settled in the entity's own equity instruments and is a nonderivative for which it is or may be obligated to deliver a variable number of its own equity instruments
4. A contract that will or may be settled in the entity's own equity instruments and is a derivative that will or may be settled other than by an exchange of a fixed amount of cash or another financial asset for a fixed number of the entity's own equity instruments (which excludes instruments that are themselves contracts for the future receipt or delivery of the entity's equity instruments).

According to the foregoing definition, financial instruments encompass a broad domain within the balance sheet. Included are both primary instruments, such as stocks and bonds, and derivative instruments, such as options, forwards, and swaps. Physical assets, such as inventories or plant assets, and such long-lived intangible assets as patents and goodwill, are excluded from the definition; although control of such assets may create opportunities to generate future cash inflows, it does not grant to the holder a present right to receive cash or other financial assets. Similarly, liabilities that are not contractual in nature, such as income taxes payable (which are statutory, but not contractual, obligations), are not financial instruments either.

Some contractual rights and obligations do not involve the transfer of financial assets. For example, a commitment to deliver commodities such as agricultural products or precious metals is not a financial instrument, although in practice these contracts are often used for hedging purposes by entities and are often settled in cash (technically, the contracts are closed out by entering into offsetting transactions before their mandatory settlement dates). The fact that the contracts call for delivery of physical product, unless canceled by a closing market transaction prior to the maturity date, prevents these from being included within the definition of financial instruments.

Presentation Issues Addressed by IAS 32

Distinguishing liabilities from equity. It sometimes happens that financial instruments of a given issuer may have attributes of both liabilities and equity. From a financial reporting perspective, the central issue is whether to account for these "compound" instruments in total as *either* liabilities or equity, *in toto*, or to disaggregate them into both liabilities and equity instruments. The notion of disaggregation has long been discussed—conceptually, of course, this should not have been difficult to resolve, since the time-honored accounting tradition of substance over form provided clear guidance on this matter—but it had not been effectively dealt with prior to IAS 32. The reluctance to resolve this derived from a variety of causes, including the concern that a strict doctrine of substance over form could trigger serious legal complications.

One example of the foregoing problem pertains to mandatorily redeemable preferred stock, which has historically been considered part of an entity's equity base despite having important characteristics of debt. Requiring that such quasi equity issuances be recategorized as debt might have resulted in many entities being deemed to be in violation of existing debt covenants and other contractual commitments. At a minimum, their balance sheets would imply a greater amount of leverage than previously, with possibly negative implications for lenders. Concerns such as this had previously caused the US standard setter, the FASB, to demur from adopting a strict "substance over form" approach in its financial instruments standards, despite having stated in its 1991 discussion memorandum that all debt-like instruments should be classified as debt, not equity. (Recently, however, the FASB adopted FAS 150, which does require debt-like instruments to be classified as liabilities.) The IASC, however, resolutely dealt with this matter, to its great credit.

Under the provisions of IAS 32, the issuer of a financial instrument must classify it, or its component parts, if a compound instrument (defined and discussed below), in accordance with the substance of the respective contractual arrangement. Thus it is quite clear that under IFRS, when the instrument gives rise to an obligation on the part of the issuer to deliver cash or another financial asset or to exchange financial instruments on potentially unfavorable terms, it is to be classified as a liability, not as equity. Mandatorily redeemable preferred stock and preferred stock issued with put options (options that can be exercised by the holder, potentially requiring the issuer to redeem the shares at agreed-upon prices) must, under this definition, be presented as liabilities.

The presentation of common stock subject to a buyout agreement with the entity's shareholders is less clear. Closely held entities frequently structure *buy-sell agreements* with each shareholder, which require that upon the occurrence of defined events, such as a shareholder's retirement or death, the entity will be required to redeem the former shareholder's ownership interest at a defined or determinable price, such as fair or book value. The practical effect of buy-sell agreements is that all but the final shareholder will eventually become creditors; the last to retire or die will be, by default, the residual owner of the business, since the entity will be unable to redeem that holder's shares unless a new investor enters the picture. IAS 32 does not address this type of situation explicitly, although circumstances of this sort are clearly alluded to by the standard, which notes that "if a financial instrument labeled as a share gives the holder an option to require redemption upon the occurrence of a future event that is highly likely to occur, classification as a financial liability on initial recognition reflects the substance of the instrument." Notwithstanding this guidance, entities can be expected to be quite reluctant to reclassify the majority of stockholders' equity as debt in cases such as that described above.

IAS 32 goes beyond the formal terms of a financial instrument in seeking to determine whether it might be a liability. Thus, for example, preferred stock which has mandatory redemption provisions, or which is "puttable" by the holder, is to be classified and accounted for as a liability upon its original issuance. In all instances, the substance of the instrument will guide the accounting for it.

Classification of compound instruments. Compound instruments are those which are sold or acquired jointly, but which provide the holder with more than a single economic interest in the issuing entity. For example, a bond sold with stock purchase warrants provides the holder with an unconditional promise to pay (the bond, which carries a rate of interest and a fixed maturity date) plus a right to acquire the issuer's shares (the warrant, which may be for common or preferred shares, at either a fixed price per share or a price based on some formula, such as a price that increases over time). In some cases, one or more of the component parts of the compound instrument may be financial derivatives, as a share purchase warrant would be. In other instances, each element might be a traditional, nonderivative instrument, as would be the case when a debenture is issued with common shares as a unit offering.

The accounting issue that is most obviously associated with compound instruments is how to allocate price or proceeds to the constituent elements. This becomes most important when the compound instrument consists of parts which are both liabilities and equity items. Proper classification of the elements is vital to accurate financial reporting, affecting potentially such matters as debt covenant compliance (if the debt to equity ratio, for example, is a covenant to be met by the debtor entity).

Under original IAS 32, the accounting issues were the same for the issuer and the holder of compound instruments. However, this is no longer the case, since revised IAS 32, effective 2005, made a significant change to the issuer's accounting for compound financial instruments. Previously, compound instruments (consisting of both liability and equity components) were to be analyzed into their constituent elements and accounted for accordingly. IAS 32, as issued, did not address recognition or measurement matters, and thus no single method of valuation for this purpose was prescribed. However, IAS 32 suggested two possible approaches: to allocate pro rata based on relative fair value, or to allocate to the more readily measured element full fair value and assign the residual to the other components. Depending on the facts and circumstances, this could have resulted in allocating fair value to the equity component, and assigning only a residual amount to the liability portion.

Under revised IAS 32, however, this has changed. Now, whether or not fair values are available for all components of the compound instrument, it is required that fair value be ascertained and then allocated to the liability components, with only the residual amount being assigned to equity. This position has been taken in order to be fully consistent with the definition of equity as instruments that evidence only a residual interest in the assets of an entity, after satisfying all of its liabilities. It therefore is no longer acceptable to assign a residual to the liability components, nor to allocate total proceeds proportionately to both liability and equity elements.

If the compound instruments include a derivative element (e.g., a put option), the value of those features, to the extent they are embedded in the compound financial instrument other than the equity component, is to be included in the liability component.

The sum of the carrying amounts assigned to the liability and equity components on initial recognition its always equal to the fair value that would be ascribed to the instrument as a whole. In other words, there can be no "day one" gains from issuing financial instruments.

Example of accounting by issuer of compound instrument

To illustrate the allocation of proceeds in a compound instrument situation, assume these facts.

1. 5,000 convertible bonds are sold by Needy Company on January 1, 2006. The bonds are due December 31, 2009.
2. Issuance price is par (€1,000 per bond); total issuance proceeds are €5,000,000.
3. Interest is due in arrears, semiannually, at a nominal rate of 5%.
4. Each (€1,000 face amount) bond is convertible into 150 shares of common stock of Needy Company.
5. At issuance date, similar, nonconvertible debt must yield 8%.

Required residual value method. Under the provisions of revised IAS 32, the issuer of compound financial instruments must assign full fair value to the portion which is to be classified as a liability, with only the residual value being allocated to the equity component. The computation for the above fact situation would be as follows:

1. Use the reference discount rate, 8%, to compute the market value of straight debt carrying a 5% yield:

PV of €5,000,000 due in 4 years, discounted at 8%	€3,653,451
PV of semiannual payments of €125,000 for 8 periods, discounted at 8%	841,593
Total	€4,495,044

2. Compute the amount allocable to the conversion feature

Total proceeds from issuance of compound instrument	€5,000,000
Value allocable to debt	4,495,044
Residual value allocable to equity component	€ 504,956

Thus, Needy Company received €4,495,044 in consideration of the actual debt being issued, plus a further €504,956 for the conversion feature, which is a call option on the underlying common stock of the issuer. The entry to record this would be

Cash	5,000,000	
Discount on bonds payable	504,956	
Bonds payable		5,000,000
Paid-in capital—bond conversion option		504,956

The bond discount would be amortized as additional interest over the term of the debt. See Chapter 13 for a complete discussion from the debtor's perspective.

Example of accounting by acquirer of compound instrument

From the perspective of the acquirer, compound financial instruments will often be seen as containing an embedded derivative—for example, a put option or a conversion feature of a debt instrument being held for an investment. This may be required to be valued and accounted for separately (which does not necessarily imply separate presentation in the financial statements, however). Per IAS 32, separate accounting is necessary if, and only if, the economic characteristics and risks of the embedded derivative are not closely related to the host; a separate instrument with the same terms would meet the definition of a derivative; and the combined instrument is not to be measured at fair value with changes included in current earnings (i.e., it is neither held for trading nor subject to the "fair value option" election).

In general, the embedded derivative is measured at fair value, with the host being assigned the residual of the purchase cost. When this cannot be measured, the embedded derivative should be assigned the differential between the hybrid instrument's cost and the fair value of the host portion, assuming this can be determined. If none of these can be determined, the embedded derivative is not separated, and the hybrid is to be carried at fair value in the trading portfolio.

To illustrate the allocation of purchase cost in a compound financial asset situation, assume these facts.

1. 500 convertible Needy Company bonds are acquired by Investor Corp. January 1, 2006. The bonds are due December 31, 2009.
2. The purchase price is par (€1,000 per bond); total cost is thus €500,000.
3. Interest is due in arrears, semiannually, at a nominal rate of 5%.
4. Each bond is convertible into 150 shares of common stock of the issuer.
5. At purchase date, similar, nonconvertible debt issued by borrowers having the same credit rating as Needy Company yield 8%.
6. At purchase date, Needy Company common shares are trading at €5, and dividends over the next 4 years are expected to be €.20 per share per year.
7. The relevant risk-free rate on 4-year obligations is 4%.
8. The historic variability of Needy Company's stock price can be indicated by a standard deviation of annual returns of 25%.

Per IAS 32, the fair value of the conversion feature should be determined, if possible, and assigned to that embedded derivative. In this example, the popular Black-Scholes model will be used (but other approaches are also acceptable).

1. Compute the standard deviation of proportionate changes in the fair value of the asset underlying the option multiplied by the square root of the time to expiration of the option

$$.25 \times \sqrt{4} = .25 \times 2 = .50$$

2. Compute the ratio of the fair value of the asset underlying the option to the present value of the option exercise price

    a. Since the expected dividend per share is €.20 per year, the present value of this stream over 4 years would (at the risk-free rate) be €.726.
    b. The shares are trading at €5.00.
    c. Therefore, the value of the underlying optioned asset, stripped of the stream of dividends that a holder of an unexercised option would obviously not receive, is

    €5.00 − .726 = €4.274 per share.

    d. The implicit exercise price is €1,000 ÷ 150 shares = €6.667 per share. This must be discounted at the risk-free rate, 4%, over 4 years, assuming that conversion takes place at the expiration of the conversion period, as follows:

    $$€6.667 \div 1.04^4 = 6.667 \div 1.170 = €5.699$$

    e. Therefore, the ratio of the underlying asset, €4.274, to the present value of the exercise price, €5.699, is .750.

3. Reference must now be made to a call option valuation table to assign a fair value to these two computed amounts (the standard deviation of proportionate changes in the fair value of the asset underlying the option multiplied by the square root of the time to expiration of the option, .50, and the ratio of the fair value of the asset underlying the option to the present value of the option exercise price, .750). For this example, assume that the table value is 13.44% (meaning that the fair value of the option is 13.44%) of the fair value of the underlying asset.

4. The valuation of the conversion option, then, is given as

    .1344 × €4.274 per share × 150 shares/bond × 500 bonds = €43,082

5. Since the fair value of the options (€43,082) has been determined, this is assigned to the conversion option. The difference between the cost of the hybrid investment, €500,000, and the amount allocated to the conversion feature, €43,082, or €456,918, should be attributed to the debt instrument.

6. The discount on the debt should be amortized, using the effective yield method, over the projected four-year holding period. The effective yield, taking into account the semi-annual interest payments to be received, will be about 7.54%.

If, for some reason, the value of the derivative (the conversion feature, in this case) could not be ascertained, the fair value of the debt portion would be computed, and the residual allocated to the derivative. This is illustrated as follows:

1. Use the reference discount rate, 8%, to compute the market value of straight debt carrying a 5% yield.

PV of €500,000 due in 4 years, discounted at 8%	€365,345
PV of semiannual payments of €12,500 for 8 periods, discounted at 8%	84,159
Total	€449,504

2. Compute the residual amount allocable to the conversion feature,

Total proceeds from issuance of compound instrument	€500,000
Value allocable to debt	449,504
Residual value allocable to embedded derivative	€ 50,496

Reporting interest, dividends, losses, and gains. IAS 32 establishes that income earned while holding financial instruments, and gains or losses from disposing of financial instruments should be reported in the income statement. Dividends paid on equity instruments issued should be charged directly to equity. (These will be reported in the statement of changes in equity.) The balance sheet classification of the instrument drives the income statement classification of the related interest or dividends. For example, if mandatorily redeemable preferred shares have been categorized as debt on the issuer's balance sheet, dividend payments on those shares must be reported in the income statement in the same manner as interest expense. Gains or losses on redemptions or refinancings of financial instruments classed as liabilities would be reported similarly in the income statement, while gains or losses on equity are credited or charged to equity directly.

Offsetting financial assets and liabilities. Under the provisions of IAS 32, offsetting financial assets and liabilities is permitted only when the entity *both* (1) has the legally enforceable right to set off the recognized amounts, and (2) intends to settle the asset and liability on a net basis, or to realize the asset and settle the liability simultaneously. Of great significance is the fact that offsetting does not give rise to gain or loss recognition, which distinguishes it from the derecognition of an instrument (which was not addressed by IAS 32, but was later dealt with by IAS 39).

Simultaneous settlement of a financial asset and a financial liability can be presumed only under defined circumstances. The most typical of such cases is when both instruments will be settled through a clearinghouse functioning for an organized exchange. Other situations may superficially appear to warrant the same accounting treatment but in fact do not give rise to legitimate offsetting. For example, if the entity will exchange checks with a single counterparty for the settlement of both instruments, it becomes exposed to credit risk for a time, however brief, when it has paid the other party for the amount of the obligation owed to it but has yet to receive the counterparty's funds to settle the amount it is owed by the counterparty. Offsetting would not be warranted in such a context.

The standard sets forth a number of other circumstances in which offsetting would *not* be justified. These include

1. When several different instruments are used to synthesize the features of another type of instrument (which typically would involve a number of different counterparties, thus violating a basic principle of offsetting).
2. When financial assets and financial liabilities arise from instruments having the same primary risk exposure (such as when both are forward contracts) but with different counterparties.
3. When financial assets are pledged as collateral for nonrecourse financial liabilities (as the intention is not typically to effect offsetting, but rather, to settle the obligation and gain release of the collateral).
4. When financial assets are set aside in a trust for the purpose of discharging a financial obligation but the assets have not been formally accepted by the creditor (as when a sinking fund is established, or when in-substance defeasance of debt is arranged).
5. When obligations incurred as a consequence of events giving rise to losses are expected to be recovered from a third party by virtue of an insurance claim (again, different counterparties means that the entity is exposed to credit risk, however slight).

Even the existence of a master netting agreement does not automatically justify the offsetting of financial assets and financial liabilities. Only if both the stipulated conditions (both the right to offset and the intention to do so) are met can this accounting treatment be employed.

Disclosure requirements under IAS 32. The disclosure requirements established by IAS 32 were later largely subsumed under those established by IAS 39. As revised in 2003, however, the disclosure requirements were again set forth in IAS 32. Most recently (mid-2005), all disclosure requirements have been removed from IAS 32 (which continues as the authoritative source of presentation requirements) and placed in new IFRS 7. Both IAS 32 and IFRS 7 disclosure requirements are discussed later in this chapter.

IAS 39: Financial Instruments—Recognition and Measurement

Evolution of the standard. Since the IASC's original efforts to develop a comprehensive standard on accounting and reporting for financial instruments failed to bear fruit and the program had to be bifurcated (leading to the issuance of IAS 32 in 1995), substantial attention has been directed to the development of a standard on recognition and measurement. The two major challenges were (1) to decide whether to impose uniform measurement and reporting standards on financial assets and financial liabilities and (2) to determine whether special hedge accounting would be necessary and acceptable. The IASC's experience was similar to that of national standard-setting bodies regarding both of these; strong opposition, coupled with some perceived practical difficulties, precluded the imposition of uniform asset and liability requirements, and special hedge accounting was therefore made a necessity.

The IASC's failure to develop, at that time, a comprehensive and uniform set of standards for all financial assets and liabilities must not be judged too harshly, since it mirrors the difficulties of the major national standard-setting bodies, none of which have been able to traverse this complex issue. In addition, the then-IASC's focus was necessarily on meeting the minimum threshold for completion of the "core set of standards" so that IOSCO consideration of endorsing the IAS for cross-border securities registrations could go forward. The IASB's attention will now turn to other matters, including the application of fair value accounting to all financial assets and liabilities, although this challenging task may take several more years to achieve.

The major changes wrought by IAS 39 were to greatly expand the use of fair values for measuring and reporting financial instruments and to address the important issue of financial derivatives, requiring that these be formally recognized and measured at fair value in most cases. IAS 39 is very similar to the corresponding US standard, FAS 133, although without the vast and detailed guidance offered by that standard, as is typical of US financial reporting rules. (While there is much debate over the relative virtues and limitations of "principles-based" and "rules-based" standards, most observers agree that financial instruments topics, which tend to be quite complex, benefit from the latter approach.)

Financial instrument recognition and measurement. The issuance of IAS 39 was the final and, some would argue, most important component of the IASC's "core set of standards" project, making possible the qualified endorsement of the international standards for use in cross-border securities registrations. Although ambitious and quite comprehensive, especially compared to other IFRS, IAS 39 was not a perfect document. Most of the complexities, however, are the result of continued endorsement of a "mixed attribute" (historical cost and fair value) model of financial reporting. If and when a pure fair value model of reporting financial instruments is adopted, the required accounting procedures will be substantially streamlined.

Both the US and international standard setters are clearly gravitating toward a pure fair value model for all financial instruments, perhaps with changes in value included in current period earnings in all cases. For various reasons, this solution has not been universally greeted with enthusiasm, and as a consequence both the US standard, FAS 133 (as amended), and the international standard, IAS 39, as most recently revised, have both endorsed continuation of mixed attribute models. This has necessitated the endorsement of accounting for hedging situations, which among other things requires that hedging be defined and that measures be established to evaluate the effectiveness of those hedges, in order to determine whether the special accounting is warranted in any given circumstance. A pure fair value reporting model for financial assets and liabilities would have obviated the need for these specially designed treatments.

Applicability. IAS 39 is applicable to all financial instruments *except* interests in subsidiaries, associates and joint ventures that are accounted for in accordance with IAS 27, 28, and 31, respectively; rights and obligations under operating leases, to which IAS 17 applies; most rights and obligations under insurance contracts; employers' assets and liabilities under employee benefit plans and employee equity compensation plans, to which IAS 19 applies; and equity instruments issued by the reporting entity.

IAS 39 as originally promulgated was not applicable to financial guarantee contracts, such as letters of credit, when these call for payments that would have to be made only if the primary debtor fails to perform; accounting for these types of arrangements was specified by IAS 37. However, amendments to IAS 39 and IFRS 4 made in 2005 have prescribed the accounting for guarantee contracts by the guarantor. It states that financial guarantees are initially to be measured at fair value, with subsequent measurement at the greater of the initial measurement and the best estimate as defined in IAS 37. The effect of this amendment was to bring the *recognition* decision under IAS 39, while leaving *measurement* guidance under IAS 37.

IAS 39 criteria apply where the guarantor will have to make payments when a defined change in credit rating, commodity prices, interest rates, security price, foreign exchange rate, an index of rates or prices, or other underlying indicator occurs. Also, if a guarantee arises from an event leading to the derecognition of a financial instrument, the guarantee must be recognized as set forth in this standard.

IAS 39 does not apply to contingent consideration arrangements pursuant to a business combination. Also, the standard does not apply to contracts that require payments dependent upon climatic, geological, or other physical factors or events, although if other types of derivatives are embedded therein, IAS 39 would set the requirements for recognition, measurement, disclosure, and derecognition.

IAS 39 must be applied to commodity-based contracts that give either party the right to settle by cash or some other financial instrument, with the exception of commodity contracts that were entered into and continue to meet the entity's expected purchase, sale, or usage requirements and were designated for that purpose at their inception. With regard to embedded derivatives, if their economic characteristics and risks are not closely related to the economic characteristics and risks of the host contract, and if a separate instrument with the same terms as the embedded derivative would meet the definition of a derivative, they are to be separated from the host contract and accounted for as a derivative in accordance with the standard.

Derecognition of financial assets. Revisions made to IAS 39 in 2004 have affected the derecognition accounting for financial assets. Derecognition of all or part of a financial instrument held as an asset may be warranted, depending on the facts and circumstances.

Derecognition of part of an instrument is justified only if one of the following conditions holds:

1. The part comprises specifically identified cash flows from a financial asset (or group of assets)—for example, an interest rate strip.
2. The part conprises a fully proportionate share of the cash flows from a financial asset (or group of assets)—for example, an arrangement whereby the counterparty obtains the rights to a 70% share of all cash flows of a debt instrument.

3. The part comprises a fully proportionate share of specifically identified cash flows from a financial asset (or group of assets)—for example, when an entity enters into an arrangement whereby the counterparty obtains the rights to a 70% share of interest cash flows from a financial asset.

Unless one of the foregoing conditions is met, the derecognition criteria are applied to the entire instrument.

Financial assets are to be derecognized only when (1) the contractual rights to the cash flows from the financial asset expire; or (2) the financial assets are transferred in a manner that qualifies for derecognition. A transfer of a financial asset occurs only if (1) the contractual rights to receive the cash flows of the financial asset are transferred or (2) the contractual rights to receive the cash flows of the financial asset are retained, but the entity assumes a contractual obligation to pay the cash flows to one or more recipients in an arrangement that meets the conditions set forth below.

When an entity (*transferor*) retains the contractual rights to receive the cash flows of a financial asset (referred to as the *original asset*), but assumes a contractual obligation to pay those cash flows to one or more entities (called the *eventual recipients*), the entity treats the transaction as a transfer of a financial asset only if all of the following three conditions are met:

1. The transferor has no obligation to pay amounts to the eventual recipients unless it collects equivalent amounts from the original asset.
2. The transferor is prohibited from selling or pledging the original asset except as security to the eventual recipients for the obligation to pay them cash flows.
3. The transferor has an obligation to remit any cash flows it collects on behalf of the eventual recipients without material delay; is not entitled to reinvest such cash flows, except for investments in cash or cash equivalents during the period from the collection date to the date of required remittance to the eventual recipients; and any interest earned thereon is paid to the eventual recipients.

When the reporting entity transfers a financial asset, as described in the foregoing paragraph, it is to evaluate the extent to which it retains the risks and rewards of ownership of the financial asset, which may involve consideration of control over the asset. In such a situation

1. If the reporting entity transfers substantially all the risks and rewards of ownership of the financial asset, it will derecognize the financial asset and recognize separately, as assets or liabilities, any rights and obligations created or retained in the transfer.
2. If it retains substantially all the risks and rewards of ownership of the financial asset, continued recognition of the financial asset is required.
3. If it neither transfers nor retains substantially all the risks and rewards of ownership of the financial asset, it must make a determination of whether it has retained control of the financial asset. In such case, (a) if it has not retained control, it is to derecognize the financial asset and recognize separately as assets or liabilities any rights and obligations created or retained in the transfer, but (b) if it has retained control, it will continue to recognize the financial asset to the extent of its continuing involvement in the financial asset.

The risks and rewards analysis, above, is effected by comparing the reporting entity's exposure, before and after the transfer, with the variability in the amounts and timing of the net cash flows of the transferred asset. Retention of substantially all the risks and rewards of ownership of a financial asset is indicated if the entity's exposure to the variability in the present value of the future net cash flows from the financial asset does not change significantly as a result of the transfer (e.g., because an asset has been sold subject to an agreement to buy it back at a fixed price or at the sale price plus a defined return to the counterparty).

On the other hand, transfer of substantially all the risks and rewards of an asset is indicated if the reporting entity's exposure to such variability is no longer significant in relation to the total variability in the present value of the future net cash flows associated with the financial asset (e.g., because the asset has been sold subject to an option to repurchase it at fair value, or a fully proportionate share of the cash flows from a larger financial asset has been sold in an arrangement, for example, a loan subparticipation, that meets the conditions set forth above).

It will often be clear that an asset transfer either did or did not involve the retention of substantially all risks and rewards of ownership. Thus, computations will commonly not be required to make this determination. However, in some instances it will be necessary to compute and compare the entity's exposure to the variability in the present value of the future net cash flows before and after the transfer. IAS 39 stipulates that the computation and comparison is to be made using an appropriate current market interest rate as the discount rate. All reasonably possible variability in net cash flows is to be considered, with greater weight being given to those outcomes that are more likely to occur.

Regarding control, IAS 39 has imposed a simple criterion. Retention of control by the reporting entity depends wholly on the transferee's ability to sell the asset. If the transferee has the practical ability to sell the asset in its entirety to an unrelated third party, and is able to exercise that ability unilaterally and without needing to impose additional restrictions on the transfer, the entity has not retained control. In all other cases, the entity has retained control.

Transfers that qualify for derecognition. IAS 39 addresses a number of circumstances that may arise in connection with a transfer of a financial instrument that is deemed to be accountable as asset derecognitions. These are discussed in the following paragraphs.

If the reporting entity retains the right to service the derecognized financial asset for a fee, it is to recognize either a servicing asset or a servicing liability for that servicing contract. If the servicing fee to be received will not compensate it adequately for performing the servicing, a servicing liability for the servicing obligation is to be recognized, measured at fair value. If the fee to be received is expected to be more than adequate compensation for the servicing, on the other hand, a servicing asset is to be recognized for the servicing right. The amount to be recognized as an asset is to be determined on the basis of an allocation of the carrying amount of the larger financial asset, discussed below.

If, because of the transfer, a financial asset is derecognized in its entirety but the transfer results in the entity obtaining a new financial asset or assuming a new financial liability, or incurring a servicing liability, the entity is to recognize the new financial asset, financial liability or servicing liability at fair value.

When a financial asset is derecognized in its entirety, the difference between the carrying amount and the sum of (1) the consideration received (including any new asset obtained less any new liability assumed) and (2) any cumulative gain or loss that had been recognized directly in equity is to be recognized in current earnings.

If the transferred asset is part of a larger financial asset (e.g., interest cash flows but not principal payments) and the portion that is transferred qualifies for derecognition in its entirety, the previous carrying amount of the larger financial asset must be allocated between the part that continues to be recognized and the part that is derecognized, based on the relative fair values of those parts on the date of the transfer. Any retained servicing asset is to be treated as a part that continues to be recognized for purposes of this fair value allocation process. The difference between the carrying amount allocated to the part derecognized and the sum of (1) the consideration received for the part derecognized (including any new asset obtained less any new liability assumed) and (2) any cumulative gain or loss allocated to it that had been recognized directly in equity is to be recognized currently in earnings. A cumulative gain or loss that was recognized directly in equity is to be allocated between the part that continues to be recognized and the part that is derecognized, based on their relative fair values.

When allocating the previous carrying amount of a larger financial asset between the part to remain recognized and that to be derecognized, the fair value of the former needs to be ascertained. If the reporting entity has a history of selling parts similar to the part that continues to be recognized, or if other market transactions exist for such parts, then recent prices of actual transactions would likely provide the best estimate of fair value. However, when there are no price quotes or recent market transactions to use as a reference, the best estimate of the fair value is the difference between the fair value of the larger financial asset as a whole and the consideration received from the transferee for the part that is derecognized.

Transfers that do not qualify for derecognition. If the reporting entity has retained substantially all the risks and rewards of ownership of the transferred asset, derecognition is not permitted. In effect, the transaction will be accounted for as a secured borrowing. Thus, the entity will continue to recognize the transferred asset in its entirety, and will also recognize a financial liability for the consideration received. In subsequent periods, the entity will recognize any income on the transferred asset and any expense incurred on the financial liability in the normal fashion.

If a transferred asset continues to be recognized, it and the corresponding liability may not be offset. Similarly, any income arising from the transferred asset and any expense incurred on the corresponding liability may not be offset.

If a transferor provides noncash collateral (e.g., debt or equity securities) to the transferee, the accounting for the collateral by the transferor and the transferee depends on whether the transferee has the right to sell or repledge the collateral and on whether the transferor has defaulted. If the transferee has the right by contract or custom to sell or repledge the collateral, then the transferor is to reclassify that asset in its balance sheet (e.g., as a loaned asset, pledged equity instrument or repurchase receivable), so that it is reported separately from other assets. If the transferee sells collateral pledged to it, the transferee must recognize the proceeds from the sale and a liability measured at fair value for its obligation to return the collateral.

If the transferor defaults under the terms of the contract and is no longer entitled to redeem the collateral, it will then derecognize the collateral, and the transferee is to recognize the collateral as its asset, initially measured at fair value or, if it has already sold the collateral, derecognize its obligation to return the collateral. Except for a default as just described, the transferor must continue to carry the collateral as its asset, and the transferee may not recognize the collateral as an asset.

Continuing involvement in transferred assets. If an entity neither transfers nor retains substantially all the risks and rewards of ownership of a transferred asset, but retains control of the transferred asset, it must continue to recognize the transferred asset to the extent of its continuing involvement. The extent of its continuing involvement in the transferred asset is gauged by the extent to which the entity is exposed to changes in the value of the transferred asset.

IAS 39 provides several examples that illustrate the concept of continuing involvement, indicating the amount to be reported as the asset by the transferor.

1. When the entity's continuing involvement takes the form of guaranteeing the transferred asset, the extent of the entity's continuing involvement is the lesser of (a) the amount of the asset and (b) the maximum amount of the consideration received that the entity could be required to repay (the *guarantee amount*).
2. When its continuing involvement takes the form of a written or purchased option (or both) on the transferred asset, the extent of the entity's continuing involvement is the amount of the transferred asset that the entity may repurchase. For a written put option on an asset measured at fair value, the extent of its continuing involvement is limited to the lower of the fair value of the transferred asset and the option exercise price.
3. When the entity's continuing involvement takes the form of a cash-settled option or similar provision on the transferred asset, the extent of continuing involvement is measured in the same way as that which results from noncash-settled options, above.

When an entity continues to recognize an asset to the extent of its continuing involvement, it also must recognize a corresponding liability. The transferred asset and the corresponding liability are measured on a basis that reflects the rights and obligations that the entity has retained. The liability is to be measured in such a way that the net carrying amount of the transferred asset and the corresponding liability is either (1) the amortized cost of the rights and obligations retained by the entity, if the transferred asset is measured at amortized cost; or (2) equal to the fair value of the rights and obligations retained by the entity when measured on a stand-alone basis, if the transferred asset is measured at fair value.

The reporting entity will continue to recognize any income arising on the transferred asset to the extent of its continuing involvement, and likewise will recognize any expense incurred on the corresponding liability. As regards the subsequent measurement of the transferred asset and the corresponding liability, recognized changes in fair values are to be accounted for consistently with each other and may not be offset.

When continuing involvement is limited to only a part of a financial asset (e.g., when an entity retains an option to repurchase only a part of the transferred asset), it should allocate the previous carrying amount of the asset between the part it continues to recognize and that which is no longer recognized on the basis of the relative fair values at the date of the transfer. The difference between (1) the carrying amount allocated to the part that is no longer recognized and (2) the sum of (a) the consideration received for the part no longer recognized and (b) any cumulative gain or loss allocated to it that had been recognized directly in equity is to be recognized in current period earnings. A cumulative gain or loss that had been recognized in equity is allocated between the parts recognized and no longer recognized on the basis of their relative fair values.

If the transferred asset is measured at amortized cost, the "fair value option" is not applicable to the corresponding liability.

Other asset transfer guidance applicable to special situations. In some cases, a reporting entity will transfer financial assets in a securitization transaction to a special-purpose entity (SPE) that it will be required to consolidate, and the SPE subsequently transfers a portion of those financial assets to third-party investors. The evaluation of whether a transfer of a portion of financial assets meets the derecognition criteria under IAS 39 generally will not differ if the transfer is directly to investors or through an SPE that first obtains the financial assets and then transfers a portion of those financial assets to third-party investors. If a transfer by a special-purpose entity to a third-party investor meets the conditions specified for derecognition in IAS 39, the transfer would be accounted for as a sale by the special-purpose entity and those derecognized assets or portions thereof would not be brought back on the balance sheet in the consolidated financial statements of the entity. (Note, however, that the entire subject of accounting for special-purpose entities is expected to be given renewed attention in the near future. Similar scrutiny by the US FASB has already resulted in the issuance of an important new standard, Interpretation 46[R].)

In other instances there may be dispositions with full recourse for transferee. If an entity sells receivables and provides a guarantee to the buyer to pay for any credit losses that may be incurred on the receivables as a result of the failure of the debtor to pay when due, while all other substantive benefits and risks (e.g., interest rate risk) of the receivables have been transferred to the buyer, the transaction qualifies as a transfer under IAS 39. In this scenario, the transferor has lost control over the receivables because the transferee has the ability to obtain the benefits of the transferred assets, and the risk retained by the transferor is limited to credit risk in the case of default. Under IAS 39, the guarantee is treated as a separate financial instrument to be recognized as a financial liability by the transferor.

Yet another situation involves a "right of first refusal." Derecognition is warranted if the transferor retains a right of first refusal that permits the transferor to purchase the transferred assets at their fair value at the date of reacquisition should the transferee decide to sell them. This is deemed appropriate since the reacquisition price is the fair value at the time of the reacquisition.

As noted earlier in this chapter, "factoring with recourse" is a popular form of receivables financing. Under the right of recourse, the transferor is obligated to compensate the transferee for the failure of the underlying debtors to pay when due. In addition, the recourse provision often entitles the transferee to sell the receivables back to the transferor at a fixed price in the event of unfavorable changes in interest rates or credit ratings of the underlying debtors. In many cases, such financing is promoted as being a sale of the customers' accounts, but applying a substance over form approach derecognition will not generally be warranted. Instead, this type of transaction should be accounted for as a collateralized borrowing by the transferor, since it does not qualify for derecognition. While the transferor has lost control, since the transferee has the ability to obtain the benefits of the transferred asset and is free to sell or pledge approximately the full fair value of the transferred asset, the transferor has effectively granted the transferee a *put option* on the transferred asset, since the transferee may sell the receivables back to the transferor in the event of both actual credit losses and changes in underlying credit ratings or interest rates. This is similar to other situations described in IAS 39, in which a transferor has not lost control and therefore a financial asset is not derecognized if the transferor retains substantially all the risks of ownership through an unconditional put option on the transferred assets held by the transferee.

As noted above, if an entity transfers a portion of a financial asset to others while retaining a part of the asset or assumes a related liability, the carrying amount of the financial asset should be allocated between the portion retained and the part sold or amount of liability retained, based on their relative fair values on the date of sale. The best evidence of the fair value of the retained interest in the bonds is obtained by reference to market quotations. Valuation models are generally used when market quotations do not exist. Gain or loss should be recognized based only on the proceeds for the portion sold.

If the fair value of the part of the asset retained cannot be measured reliably, then a "cost recovery" approach should be used to measure profit (that is, allocate all the cost to the portion sold). If a related liability is retained and cannot be valued, no gain should be recognized on the transfer, and the liability should be measured at the difference between the proceeds and the carrying amount of the part of the financial asset that was sold, with a loss recognized equal to the difference between the proceeds and the sum of the amount recognized for the liability and the previous carrying amount of the financial asset transferred.

Consider an example in which a portfolio of bonds is partially transferred to an unrelated party, with the balance retained by the reporting entity, with the yield to the transferee being different than that on the underlying bonds (e.g., because market rates had diverged from the coupon rates). There are two alternative methods for estimating the fair value of the retained interests in the bonds for purposes of allocating the basis in the bonds between the portion sold and the portion retained. The first method, deemed most suitable when there is no market evidence of the fair value of the bonds as a whole, requires making an estimate of the future cash flows of the underlying bonds based on their contractual payments, reduced by estimates of prepayments and credit losses. The cash flows are then discounted by an estimate of the appropriate risk-adjusted interest rate. This method produces a fair value of the retained interests in the bonds; the transferor would recognize a gain on sale computed by subtracting from the proceeds the amount allocated to the basis sold.

The other reasonable method is to obtain a market quotation on bonds that are similar to the bonds it acquired previously and are the subject of the current sale. This is prorated to the portion being sold, with a gain on sale being recognized as the difference between the prorated amount and the proceeds of the sale.

When the asset being partially transferred is one that has been originated by the transferor, some modifications in methodology might be necessary, due to a lack of an active market. However, reference to actual lending transactions of the transferor as a means of estimating the fair value of the retained beneficial interests in the loans might provide a more objective and reliable estimate of fair value than the discounted cash flow model described above, because it is based on actual market transactions. While the market interest rates may have changed between the origination dates of the loans and the subsequent sales date of a portion of the loans, the corresponding change in the value of the loans might be determined by reference to current market interest rates being charged by the transferor, or perhaps its competitors for similar loans (e.g., with similar remaining maturity, cash flow pattern, currency, credit risk, collateral, and interest basis). Alternatively, if there is no change in the credit risk of the borrowers subsequent to the origination of the loans, an estimate of the current market interest rate might be derived by using a benchmark interest rate of a higher quality than the loans, holding the credit spread constant, and adjusting for the change in the benchmark interest rate from the origination dates to the subsequent sales date.

A detailed example of accounting for partial transfers of financial assets is presented below.

Examples of allocation between asset sold and asset or liability retained

Assume that an investment in mortgage loans, carried at €14.5 million, is being sold, but the entity is retaining the "servicing rights" to these mortgages. Servicing rights entail making monthly collections of principal and interest and forwarding these to the holders of the mortgages; it also involves other activities such as taking legal action to compel payment by delinquent debtors, and so forth. For such efforts, the servicing party is compensated; in this example, the present value of future servicing income can be estimated at €1.2 million, while the mortgage portfolio, without servicing, is sold for €13.6 million. Since values of both components (the portion sold and the portion retained) can be reliably valued, gain or loss is determined by first allocating the carrying value pro rata to the two portions, as follows:

	Selling price or fair value	Percentage of total	Allocated amount
Mortgages without servicing rights	€13.6 M	91.89%	€13.32 M
Servicing rights	1.2	8.11	1.18
Total	€14.8 M	100.00%	€14.50 M

The sale of the portfolio, *sans* servicing rights, will result in a gain of €13.6 M – 13.32 M = €280,000. The servicing rights will be recorded as an asset in the amount €1.18 million.

Under other circumstances, transactions such as the foregoing will necessitate loss recognition. Assume the same facts as above, *except* that the selling price of the mortgage portfolio with servicing is only €13.1 million. In this case, the allocation of fair values and loss recognition will be as follows:

	Selling price or fair value	Percentage of total	Allocated amount
Mortgages without servicing rights	€13.1 M	91.61%	€13.28 M
Servicing rights	1.2	8.39	1.22
Total	€14.3 M	100.00%	€14.50 M

A loss on the sale of the mortgages amounting to €13.28 M – 13.1 M = €180,000 will be recognized. The servicing rights will be recorded as an asset in the amount €1.22 million.

Finally, consider a sale as above, but the obligation to continue servicing the portfolio, rather than representing an asset to the seller, is a liability, since the estimate of future costs to be incurred in carrying out these duties exceeds the future revenues to be derived therefrom. Assume this net liability has a present fair value of €1.1 million and that the selling price of the mortgages is €14.6 million. The allocation process and resulting gain or loss recognition is as follows:

	Selling price or fair value	Percentage of total	Allocated amount
Mortgages without servicing rights	€14.6 M	108.15%	€15.68 M
Servicing rights	(1.1)	(8.15)	(1.18)
Total	€14.8 M	100.00%	€14.50 M

A loss on the sale of the mortgages amounting to €15.68 M – 14.6 M = €1,080,000 will be recognized. The servicing rights will be recorded as a liability in the amount €1.1 million.

It should be added that, for the foregoing examples in which a net asset is retained, the servicing asset is deemed to be an intangible and accordingly will be accounted for under the provisions of IAS 38. Normally, this asset would be reported at amortized cost, unless impairment occurs which would necessitate a downward adjustment in carrying value. The net servicing liability would be considered similar to other liabilities and accounted for at its amortized amount.

Transfers of financial liabilities, with part of the obligation retained or with a new obligation created pursuant to the transfer, should be accounted for in a manner analogous to the foregoing examples. Using fair values and transaction prices, the carrying amount of the obligation should be allocated so that gain or loss can be computed and the liability retained or created can be appropriately recorded.

IAS 39 holds that a financial liability (or a part of a financial liability) should be removed from the balance sheet only when it is extinguished, that is, when the obligation specified in the contract is discharged, canceled, or expires, or when the primary responsibility for the liability (or a part thereof) is transferred to another party. Among other implications, this means that in-substance defeasance (which involves segregation of assets to be used for the future retirement of specific obligations of the entity) may no longer be given accounting recognition, since this does not entail actual discharge of the liability.

As described more fully in Chapter 10, revised IAS 39 has modified the criteria for derecognition of financial instruments. While previously there were several concepts which governed this determination, the revised standard (although retaining the primary concepts of *risks and rewards* and *control*) clarifies that the evaluation of the transfer of risks and rewards of ownership precedes the evaluation of the transfer of control for all derecognition determinations. New limitations are also placed on derecognition of parts of financial assets.

Under revised IAS 39, a determination must be made as to whether a financial asset has been *transferred;* derecognition can be effected only when there has been a transfer which meets the qualifications for derecognition accounting. Even if a transfer has occurred, if the reporting entity has retained substantially all such risks and rewards of ownership, it must continue to recognize the transferred asset.

Finally, when it is determined that when the entity has neither transferred nor retained substantially all the risks and rewards of ownership of the transferred asset, it must assess whether it has retained control over the transferred asset. When control has been retained, the transferred asset remains recognized by the transferor, to the extent of its continuing involvement in the transferred asset. On the other hand, if the transferor entity has not retained control, it derecognizes the transferred asset.

Initial recognition of financial assets at fair value. Initial recognition of financial assets is to be at fair value, increased by transaction costs only for those assets which are not to be carried at fair value with changes reflected currently through earnings. Similarly, issuance of financial liabilities is reflected at fair value less, for those not carried at fair value, transaction costs.

For financial instruments that are carried at amortized cost (held-to-maturity investments, originated loans, and most financial liabilities) the transaction costs are included in the calculation of amortized cost using the effective interest method. In effect, transaction costs are amortized through the income statement over the life of the instrument. This applies to loans and receivables and held-to-maturity investments, and also to investments in equity securities for which fair values cannot be determined by reference to quoted prices in active markets. It also applies to those derivatives which are linked to, and must be settled by delivery of, those unquoted equity instruments.

On the other hand, for financial instruments that are carried at fair value, such as available-for-sale investments and instruments held for trading, transaction costs are not included in the fair value measurement. In many instances, this will cause expense or loss recognition for the transaction costs at the date of acquisition.

For available-for-sale financial assets, if the financial asset has fixed or determinable payments and a fixed maturity (i.e., it is a debt investment), the transaction costs are amortized to net profit or loss using the effective interest method. If the financial asset does not have fixed or determinable payments and a fixed maturity (i.e., it is an equity investment), the transaction costs are recognized in income at the time of eventual sale.

Fair value option. An important change was made to IAS 39 as part of the *Improvements Project*. This has created the "fair value option" under which entities are granted permission to measure any financial asset or financial liability at fair value, with changes in fair value to be recognized in profit or loss. This is accomplished by designating the asset or liability, at initial recognition, as being accounted for at fair value with changes in fair value reflected currently in earnings. In presenting and disclosing information, the reporting entity may use an alternative caption for such instruments (e.g., "financial instruments at fair value [through net income]") instead of employing the term "trading." To prevent abuse, however, reclassification of financial instruments into (or out of) the new category during the holding period is prohibited. The purpose of the change was to simplify the application of IAS 39 (for example, for hybrid instruments and for entities with matched asset/liability positions) and to enable consistent measurement of financial assets and financial liabilities. This change obviated the need to provide the option to account for value changes in available-for-sale financial instruments through current earnings, so that feature of original IAS 39 has been eliminated.

Note that, because some European lenders objected to the fair value option, in order to implement IFRS-based reporting requirements in the EU in 2005 (when all publicly held companies must begin reporting consolidated financial statements in accordance with IFRS), a modification of the fair value option was imposed, which precludes using this for the reporting entity's own debt instruments. While this action by the EU authorities has not amended IFRS, per se, it will have some potential impact on comparability across entities, particularly those conforming with IFRS in their entirety, and those employing European-tailored IFRS.

When applying the fair value measure, the transaction costs which would have to be incurred if there were to be a sale of the asset are not recognized (i.e., fair value is **not** net of selling costs) and thus fair value for reporting purposes is without the impact of transaction costs on either acquisition or assumed disposition.

Example

Consider the following example of the acquisition of a financial asset. Assume an investment security is acquired as follows: 2,000 shares of Ravinia Corp. common stock, par value €5 per share, are purchased on the open market on October 15 for €76 per share, plus total commissions and fees of €1,775. The shares are held for trading and thus are recorded at [€76 × 2,000 =] €152,200, and the commissions and fees are expensed immediately. At December 31, the shares are quoted at €76 1/2, and a sale at that date would entail the payment of commissions and fees of €1,550. When the time comes to prepare the year-end balance sheet, this investment will be presented at [€76 1/2 × 2,000 shares =] €153,000. The potential cost of a sale, which would make the net realizable amount [€153,000 – 1,550 = € 151,450] lower than fair value, as defined by IAS 39, is to be ignored in all such remeasurements.

In rare instances, when the value of consideration given or received cannot be observed directly or indirectly by means of other market values, then IAS 39 directs that value be ascribed by means of computing the present value of all future cash payments or receipts, using the prevailing market rate of similar types of instruments as the discount rate.

Trade date vs. settlement date accounting. Normal securities trades clear or settle several days after the trade date. In practice, historically, some have recorded such transaction son the trade date, while others have waited until the settlement date to give formal recognition to the purchase or sale transaction. Under the provisions of IAS 39, as amended, an entity may elect to use either trade date accounting or settlement date accounting for purchases and sales of financial assets. However, it is required that the reporting entity apply the selected accounting policy in a consistent manner for both purchases and sales of financial assets that belong to the same balance sheet category (i.e., financial assets held for trading, those available for sale, those to be held to maturity, and loans and receivables originated by the entity and, optionally, loans which have been purchased and which are not quoted in an active market).

When trade date accounting is used, the asset is recognized at the trade date and all subsequent changes in value will be reflected as required under IAS 39. On the other hand, if settlement date accounting is used to record purchases, there would be a failure to recognize changes in value from trade to settlement date, before formally recording the asset. For that reason, IAS 39 requires that changes in the fair value of the underlying security during the interval from trade date to settlement date must be given accounting recognition, to the extent that changes in fair value would otherwise have been accounted for, consistent with the nature of the investment. Thus, for held-to-maturity investments, fair value changes between trade and settlement dates are not reported, since these investments are accounted for at amortized historical cost, not at fair values (unless a permanent impairment occurs, which is unlikely in the brief span from trade to settlement dates). In the case of trading securities, changes in fair value between the trade and settlement dates would be taken into income. For available-for-sale investments, the changes in fair value during the time interval from trade date to settlement date are reported in stockholders' equity.

Subsequent remeasurement issues. Before the issuance of IAS 39, the carrying values of financial instruments qualifying as investments were determined by a range of methods, varying by type of instrument, with many options available for the reporting entity to select from for any given category of investment asset. This situation was changed significantly by IAS 39, which requires that subsequent remeasurement of financial assets be at fair value excluding transaction costs, except for (1) loans and receivables, (2) held-to-maturity investments, and (3) any financial asset whose fair value cannot be reliably measured. Held-to-maturity investments and loans and receivables are to be reported at amortized cost; other financial assets which have indeterminate fair values but fixed maturities will be measured at amortized cost using the effective interest rate method, while those that do not have fixed maturities are to be measured at cost. In all cases, periodic review for possible impairment is needed, and if impairment exists, a loss is to be recognized in current period earnings. Derivative financial instruments that are assets must be valued at fair value.

One issue frequently raised pertains to how fair value should be gauged when the reporting entity owns a large enough fraction of the total class outstanding (or of the portion actively trading on a given day) such that a disposition would be expected to "move the market." The market could be affected in one of two ways: either the large block would fetch a premium price (in the nature of a "control premium" although the transferor's shares could not truly represent a controlling interest—if it did, the investment would have been accounted for under IAS 28 or 27, not under IAS 39), or it would cause a decline due to the imbalance of supply and demand. A published price quotation in an active market is the best estimate of fair value. This should be used, without adjustment for possible premiums or discounts that might result from the (hypothetical) sale of the entity's holdings.

Revised IAS 39 has provided additional guidance regarding the determination of fair values using valuation techniques. Specifically, it states that the goal is to establish what the transaction price would have been, on the measurement date, in an arm's-length exchange motivated by normal business considerations. Accordingly, any valuation technique employed must (1) incorporate all factors that market participants would consider in setting a price, and (2) be consistent with accepted economic methodologies for pricing financial instruments. The estimates and assumptions used must be consistent with available information about the estimates and assumptions that market participants would use in setting an actual price for the financial instrument.

The standard reiterates that the best estimates of fair value at initial recognition, for financial instruments that are not quoted in an active market, are the actual transaction prices. However, if fair values are evidenced by other observable market transactions, or are more usefully based on valuation techniques whose variables include only data from observable markets, those should be used instead.

Accounting for collateral held. Creditors sometimes require that debtors provide them with collateral as additional security for repayment obligations. It has often been suggested that, to enhance accountability, this collateral held be reported on the creditor's balance sheet (which would necessitate recognition of a liability for the return of the collateral, also) for as long as it is held. This approach has, in the past, been mandated under various financial reporting standards, but has been controversial for two reasons. First, it results in a "grossing up" of the creditor's balance sheet, since both the underlying receivable and the collateral would be shown as assets. Second, the collateral would appear on both creditor's and debtor's balance sheets simultaneously, since it would not qualify for derecognition by the debtor, which strikes many as inappropriate although not literally banned under GAAP or IFRS.

Revised IAS 32 provides new guidance on the accounting for collateral, as follows:

1. A reporting entity is required to disclose the carrying amount of financial assets pledged as collateral for liabilities, the carrying amount of financial assets pledged as collateral for contingent liabilities, and any material terms and conditions relating to assets pledged as collateral.
2. When an entity has accepted collateral that it is permitted to sell or repledge in the absence of default by the owner of the collateral, it is now required to disclose

   a. The fair value of the collateral accepted (both financial and nonfinancial assets);
   b. The fair value of any such collateral sold or repledged and whether the entity has an obligation to return it; and
   c. Any material terms and conditions associated with its use of this collateral.

Other issues. Financial assets that are hedged against exposure in changes in fair value must be accounted for at an adjusted carrying amount that reflects changes in fair value attributable to the risk designated as being hedged, with a derivative the hedging instrument likewise accounted for at fair value, as discussed later in this chapter. Financial instruments which have values less than zero are to be accounted for as financial liabilities; that is, at fair value if held for trading or if a derivative instrument, otherwise at amortized cost in most cases.

Changes in the value of held-to-maturity investments are generally not recognized. However, the use of the held-to-maturity classification is strictly limited to situations in which both intent and ability to hold are present, and past behavior is to be used to evaluate whether the expression of intent is indeed sincere. Intent to hold for an indefinite period would not be a basis for classification as held-to-maturity, nor would a willingness to dispose of the investment if certain changes in interest rates or market risks were to occur, or if improved yields on alternative investments or other factors were to develop.

If the issuer of the instrument that the entity holds as a financial asset has the right to settle it at an amount materially below amortized cost, the use of the held-to-maturity classification is not permitted. For instance, a normal call feature will not preclude held-to-maturity classification if the holder would recover substantially all of the carrying amount if the call feature is exercised by the issuer. If the entity holding the investment has a put option (giving it the right to demand early redemption, but not the obligation to do so), classification as held-to-maturity is not possible.

As a practical matter, the held-to-maturity category will be reserved to debt securities held as investments, since equity securities have indefinite life (thus rendering untestable the holder's representation of its intent to hold to maturity) or else have indeterminable returns to the holder (as with warrants and options). Notwithstanding the nature of the investment, use of the held-to-maturity classification is prohibited if the reporting entity has, during the current reporting year or two prior years, sold, transferred, or exercised the put option on a significant amount of held-to-maturity investments before maturity. However, IAS 39 provides certain exceptions to the foregoing rule: sales close to maturity or an exercised call date such that market rate changes would not affect the asset's fair value; a sale after substantially all of the original principal had been recovered; and sales due to isolated events beyond the entity's control, which are nonrecurring and which could not have been reasonably anticipated by it (e.g., a significant decline in the issuer's creditworthiness, changes in tax laws, or other changes in the legal or regulatory environment). To the extent that any of these conditions exist, sales from the held-to-maturity portfolio will not taint the remaining assets.

Reclassifications from and to held-to-maturity. Under the provisions of IAS 39, the determination that there is both intent and ability to hold financial assets to maturity must be made not merely at acquisition, but also at each subsequent balance sheet date. If at one of these later determination dates it is concluded that the criteria are no longer met, then the investment should be remeasured at fair value at that time. In such instance, the investment would be reclassified to the available-for-sale category, and accordingly the adjustment to fair value would be recognized directly in stockholders' equity. Reclassification from held-to-maturity has severe implications, however, since this would prevent the entity from so classifying other securities for the following two years (as discussed in Chapter 10).

Remeasurement of trading and available-for-sale financial assets. Changes in the value of trading securities are reported currently in earnings. IAS 39 defines derivative financial instruments as being, ipso facto, financial instruments held for trading, unless held for designated hedging purposes. Available-for-sale securities are also remeasured at fair value at each balance sheet date, but the changes in fair value must be reported in stockholders' equity. A formerly permitted optional treatment to show these changes in current income, is no longer permitted under revised IAS 39. However, under the fair value option, at acquisition any financial asset or liability may be designated for reporting of changes in fair value in current earnings, so effectively the elimination of the previous alternative accounting for available-for-sale securities is not an impediment.

Impairments of Available-for-Sale Investments

An impairment in value of equity securities classified as available-for-sale must be reflected in earnings. A financial asset is impaired if its carrying amount is greater than its estimated recoverable amount. Specifically, this is meant to be the result of other than the normal fluctuations in value characteristic of all investments, due to general movements in the underlying markets, etc. In the absence of an ability to demonstrate that a decline is neither significant nor prolonged, the conclusion must be that there is an impairment that must be recognized in income. Declines are measured at the individual security level, and thus, losses in one security's value cannot be offset by gains in another's value.

While temporary declines in value of available-for-sale investments are reported directly in stockholders' equity, impairment losses must be included in earnings. Similarly, reversals of impairment losses (if recovery can be objectively attributed to events occurring after the impairment recognition) should always be reported in earnings.

Under revised IAS 39, impairment losses on available-for-sale *equity* instruments cannot be reversed through profit or loss. That is, any increase in fair value subsequent to impairment must be recognized only by a direct credit to equity.

IAS 39 also provides new insights into the matter of how impairments that are inherent in a group of loans, receivables, or held-to-maturity investments, but cannot yet be identified with any individual financial asset in the groups, are to be evaluated, as follows:

- An asset that is individually identified as impaired should not be included in a group of assets that are collectively assessed for impairment.
- An asset that has been individually assessed for impairment and found not to be individually impaired should be included in a collective assessment of impairment. The occurrence of an event or a combination of events should not be a precondition for including an asset in a group of assets that are collectively evaluated for impairment.
- Assets should be grouped by similar credit risk characteristics that are indicative of the debtor's ability to pay all amounts due according to the contractual terms.
- Contractual cash flows and historical loss experience should provide the basis for estimating expected cash flow. Historical loss rates should be adjusted on the basis of relevant observable data that reflect current economic conditions.
- The methodology for measuring impairment should ensure that an impairment loss is not recognized immediately on initial recognition. Therefore, for the purposes of

measuring impairment in groups of assets, estimated cash flows (contractual principal and interest payments adjusted for estimated credit losses) should be discounted using an original effective interest rate that equates the present value of the originally estimated cash flows with the initial net carrying amount of those assets.

Accounting for Investments in Debt Securities

Under IAS 39 fair value is required for debt securities held for trading or available for sale, while amortized cost is prescribed for those in the held-to-maturity portfolio, as that is narrowly defined by the standard, as well as for those classified as loans and receivables, because these are not quoted in active markets. The held-to-maturity category is the most restrictive of the three; debt instruments can be so classified only if the reporting entity has the positive intent and the ability to hold the securities for that length of time. A mere intent to hold an investment for an indefinite period is not adequate to permit such a classification. On the other hand, a variety of isolated causes may necessitate transferring an investment in a debt security from the held-for-investment category without calling into question the investor's general intention to hold other similarly classified investments to maturity. Among these are declines in the creditworthiness of a particular investment's issuer or a change in tax law or regulatory rules. On the other hand, sales of investments which were classified as held-to-maturity for other reasons will call into question the entity's assertions, both in the past and in the future, about its intentions regarding these and other similarly categorized securities. For this reason, transfers from or sales of held-to-maturity securities will be very rare, indeed.

If it cannot be established that a particular debt security held as an investment will be held for trading or held to maturity, or that it qualifies as a loan or a receivable, it must be classed as available-for-sale. Whatever the original classification of the investment, however, transfers among the three portfolios will be made as intentions change.

Accounting for debt securities that are held for trading and those that are available for sale is based on fair value. For balance sheet purposes, increases or decreases in value are reflected by adjustments to the asset account; such adjustments are to be determined on an individual security basis. Changes in the values of debt securities in the trading portfolio are recognized in earnings immediately, while changes in the values of debt securities in the available-for-sale category are reported either in earnings or in stockholders' equity, based on the election made when IAS 39 was first adopted.

Transfers of Debt Securities among Portfolios

IAS 39 says very little regarding the reclassifications of investments. Nonetheless, from the basic principles espoused by the standard, it is clear that transfers of any given security between classifications should be accounted for at fair market value. IAS 39 states that transfers from the trading category should not take place, because classification as a trading security is based on the original intent in acquiring it. The standard, as most recently revised, also says that transfers to the trading category are prohibited.

If a debt security is being transferred from held-to-maturity to the available-for-sale portfolio, the unrealized gain or loss, not previously reflected in the investment account, must be added to the appropriate equity account at the date of transfer and reported in the statement of changes in equity at that time. If an impairment is being recognized, of course, this will be reported in earnings of the period.

Impairments in value of held-to-maturity investments. IAS 39 establishes a need for earnings recognition when impairment losses occur which affect investments included in the held-to-maturity portfolio. Evaluation of whether there is objective evidence of impairment is to be made at each balance sheet date; if this exists, the recoverable amount of the financial asset should be ascertained. Evidence of impairment could be provided by information about the financial difficulties of the issuer, an actual breach or default by the obligor, a debt restructuring by the issuer, a delisting of the issuer's securities or a high probability that this will occur in the near term, and similar developments. On the other hand, IAS 39 cautions that a change in status to not being publicly traded does not constitute evidence of a security's impairment, nor does a downward credit rating revision, taken alone, although in combination with other factors these could have significance.

For held-to-maturity securities, the standard provides that when it becomes probable that the holder will not be able to collect all amounts that are due contractually (including both interest and principal), an impairment loss is to be recognized. Similarly, when loans or receivables originated by the entity and not held for trading have such an impairment, a bad debt loss is to be recognized currently. In determining the amount of such loss, the carrying amount (amortized cost) is compared to its recoverable amount, defined as the present value of projected future cash flows, discounted using the instrument's original effective interest rate (**not** the current market interest rate). A write-down to this recoverable amount is indicated when impairment has been found to have occurred. Use of the current market rate of interest is prohibited because to use this rate would be to indirectly impose a fair value measure, which of course is contrary to the concept of accounting for held-to-maturity financial assets, loans and receivables originated by the entity, and purchased loans not quoted in an active market, at amortized historical cost.

When in a later period there is a reversal of the impairment recognized earlier with regard to held-to-maturity financial assets, loans, and receivables, this recovery should be appropriately reported in earnings. However, the reversal cannot result in carrying the asset at an amount in excess of that which it would have been reported at on that date, considering intervening periods' amortization if pertinent.

When the carrying value of a held-to-maturity financial asset is reduced due to findings of impairment, future interest income must be computed on the basis used to reduce the asset to its recoverable amount. That is, the *effective rate* or *yield* of the original investment (including the impact of any premium or discount amortization) will be used, not its contractual rate.

Having once been reduced in carrying value due to a finding of impairment, there often will be a heightened need to monitor further impairments in later periods. If such evidence is objectively determinable, yet another computation of recoverable amount (and possibly a further adjustment to the financial asset's carrying amount) will be required.

In the case of available-for-sale securities, adjustments due to changes in fair value would have been accumulated in stockholders' equity, so a later discovery that there has been a permanent impairment in value will necessitate accounting recognition. The appropriate amount of the accumulated fair value adjustment must be removed from equity and reported in earnings at the time objective evidence of impairment is determined to exist. The difference between acquisition cost and either current fair value (for equity-type instruments) or recoverable amount (for debt instruments) is the usual measure of impairment.

What may be considered the recoverable amount, as used in the context of available-for-sale financial assets, differs from that used to describe held-to-maturity assets. In the latter case, as noted above, projected future cash flows are to be discounted at the instrument's original effective rate, to avoid confounding the impairment measure by reference to current fair values, which would be inappropriate if applied to this class of investment. In the setting of available-for-sale instruments, however, fair value is both quite appropriate and required. Thus, if debt instruments are in the available-for-sale category and are being evaluated for impairment, future cash flows must be discounted at the *current market rate* of interest applicable to such instruments.

Remeasurement of financial liabilities. The remeasurement of financial liabilities is discussed and illustrated in Chapter 12.

Hedge Accounting

IAS 39 provides for special hedge accounting under defined circumstances. The standard defines three types of hedging relationships: fair value hedges, cash flow hedges, and hedges of net investment in a foreign entity. These are described in IAS 39 as follows:

- **Fair value hedges.** A hedge, using a derivative or other financial instrument, of the exposure to changes in the fair value of a recognized asset or liability, or an identified portion of such an asset or liability, that is attributable to a particular risk and will affect reported net income.
- **Cash flow hedges.** A hedge, using a derivative or other financial instrument, of the exposure to variability in cash flows that is attributable to a particular risk associated with a recognized asset or liability (such as all or a portion of future interest payments on variable-rate debt) or forecasted transaction (such as an anticipated purchase or sale) that will affect reported income or loss. Under revised IAS 39 (effective 2005), a hedge of an unrecognized firm commitment to buy an asset at a fixed price is now to be accounted for as a fair value hedge (previously this was to be treated as a cash flow hedge). However, a hedge of the foreign currency risk of a firm commitment can be treated as either a cash flow hedge or a fair value hedge.
- **Hedges of a net investment in a foreign entity** (as defined in IAS 21) using a derivative or other financial instrument.

The most contentious issue regarding hedging has been the decision to apply special hedge accounting to such transactions. If all financial instruments were marked to market (fair) values, there would be no need for special accounting except, perhaps, for hedges of unrecognized firm commitments and forecasted transactions. However, given that fair value accounting has yet to be fully accepted for financial instruments held as assets, and is even less widely accepted for financial instruments classed as liabilities, the topic of hedge accounting must be addressed. Under the provisions of IAS 39, a hedging relationship will qualify for special hedge accounting presentation if all of the following conditions are met:

1. At the inception of the hedge there is formal documentation of the hedging relationship and the entity's risk management objective and strategy for undertaking the hedge. That documentation should include identification of the hedging instrument, the related hedged item or transaction, the nature of the risk being hedged, and how the entity will assess the hedging instrument's effectiveness if offsetting the exposure to changes in the hedged item's fair value or the hedged transaction's cash flows that is attributable to the hedged risk.
2. The hedge is expected to be highly effective in achieving offsetting changes in fair value or cash flows attributable to the hedged risk, consistent with the originally documented risk management strategy for that particular hedging relationship.
3. For cash flow hedges, a forecasted transaction that is the subject of the hedge must be probable and present an exposure to price risk that could produce variation in cash flows that will affect reported income.
4. The effectiveness of the hedge can be reliably measured, that is, the fair value or cash flows of the hedged item and the fair value of the hedging instrument can be reliably measured.

5. The hedge was assessed and determined actually to have been effective throughout the financial reporting period.

Under IAS 39, a hedging relationship could be designated for a hedging instrument taken as a whole, or, in certain specified instances, for a component of a hedging instrument. Thus, an entity could designate the change in the intrinsic value of an option as the hedge, while the remaining component of the option (its time value) is excluded.

As noted, to qualify for hedge accounting, the effectiveness of a hedge would have to be subject to effectiveness testing. The method an entity adopts for this would depend on its risk management strategy, and this could vary for different types of hedges. If the principal terms of the hedging instrument and of the entire hedged asset or liability or hedged forecasted transaction are the same, the changes in fair value and cash flows attributable to the risk being hedged offset fully, both when the hedge is entered into and thereafter until completion. An interest rate swap is likely to be an effective hedge if the notional and principal amounts, term, repricing dates, dates of interest or principal receipts and payments, and basis for measuring interest rates are the same for the hedging instrument and the hedged item.

Also, to qualify for special hedge accounting under IAS 39's provisions, the hedge would have to relate to a specific identified and designated risk, and not merely to overall entity business risks, and must ultimately affect the entity's net profit or loss, not just its equity.

The standard provides that a hedge can be judged to be highly effective if, both at inception and throughout its life, the reporting entity can expect that changes in the fair value or cash flows (depending on the type of hedge) of the hedged item will be virtually fully offset by changes in the fair value or cash flows of the underlying or hedged item, and that actual results are within a range of 80% to 125% of full offset. While there is flexibility in terms of how an entity measures and monitors effectiveness (and this may even vary within an entity regarding different types of hedges), the fact that IAS 39 provides quantified upper and lower effectiveness thresholds underlines the importance of making such a determination. The documentation of the entity's hedging strategy must stipulate how this will be achieved, and hedging effectiveness must be assessed at least as often as financial reports are prepared.

Fair value hedges. With specific regard to fair value hedges, IAS 39 prescribes the following special hedge accounting:

1. The gain or loss from remeasuring the hedging instrument at fair value is to be recognized currently in net profit or loss; and
2. The gain or loss on the hedged item attributable to the hedged risk should adjust the carrying amount of the hedged item and be recognized currently in net profit or loss.

These requirements apply even if a hedged item is otherwise measured at fair value with changes in fair value recognized directly in equity. Hedge accounting must be discontinued, however, when the hedging instrument expires or is sold, terminated, or exercised, or when the hedge no longer meets the criteria for qualification for hedge accounting.

When there has been an adjustment made to the carrying amount of a hedged, interest-bearing instrument, it should be amortized to earnings, beginning no later than when it ceases to be adjusted for changes in fair value attributable to the risk being hedged.

Macrohedging. One of the long-standing debates regarding fair value hedging pertained to so-called "macrohedging." Historically, it was required that specific assets or liabilities be identified as the hedged items, but many financial managers have argued that actual fair value hedging is often conducted by acquiring a hedging position to protect against the effect of the value changes of the *net* asset or liability position maintained. This is known as "macrohedging" or hedging a portfolio of interest rate risks. Such an action, while sound from a management perspective, did not qualify for hedge accounting treatment under the original IAS 39.

In response to this perceived failure to address the accounting implications of common risk management strategies, IASB proposed, and subsequently adopted, an amendment to IAS 39 to permit hedge accounting for such macrohedge situations. As amended, IAS 39 permits the following rules to apply for purposes of accounting for a fair value hedge of a portfolio of interest rate risk:

1. The reporting entity identifies a portfolio of items whose interest rate risk it wishes to hedge. The portfolio may include both assets and liabilities, or could include only assets or only liabilities.

2. The reporting entity analyzes the portfolio into repricing time periods based on *expected*, rather than contractual, repricing dates.

3. The reporting entity then designates the hedged item as a percentage of the amount of assets (or liabilities) in each time period. All of the assets from which the hedged amount are drawn have to be items (a) whose fair value changes in response to the risk being hedged and (b) that could have qualified for fair value hedge accounting under the original IAS 39 had they been hedged individually. The time periods have to be sufficiently narrow to ensure that all assets (or liabilities) in a time period are homogeneous with respect to the hedged risk—that is, the fair value of each item moves proportionately to, and in the same direction as, changes in the hedged interest rate risk.

4. The reporting entity designates what interest rate risk it is hedging. This risk may be a portion of the interest rate risk in each of the items in the portfolio, such as a benchmark interest rate like LIBOR or US Prime.

5. The reporting entity designates a hedging instrument for each time period. The hedging instrument may be a portfolio of derivatives (for instance, interest rate swaps) containing offsetting risk positions.

6. The reporting entity measures the change in the fair value of the hedged item that is attributable to the hedged risk. The result is then recognized in profit or loss and in one of two separate line items in the balance sheet. The balance sheet line item depends upon whether the hedged item is an asset (in which case the change in fair value would be reported in a separate line item within assets) or is a liability (in which case the value change would be reported in a separate line item within liabilities). In either case this separate balance sheet line item is to be presented on the face of the balance sheet adjacent to the related hedged item—but it is not permissible to allocate it to individual assets or liabilities, or to separate classes of assets or liabilities (i.e., it is not acceptable to employ "basis adjustment").

7. The reporting entity measures the change in the fair value of the hedging instrument and recognized this as a gain or loss in profit or loss. It recognizes the fair value of the hedging instrument as an asset or liability in the balance sheet.

8. Ineffectiveness will be given as the difference in profit or loss between the amounts determined in steps 6 and 7.

A change in the amounts that are expected to be repaid or mature in a time period will result in ineffectiveness, measured as the difference between (a) the initial hedge ratio applied to the initially estimated amount in a time period and (b) that same ratio applied to the revised estimate of the amount.

Cash flow hedges. Gain or loss relating to the portion of a cash flow hedge that is determined to be effective is to be recognized directly in stockholders' equity, through the statement of changes in equity. The ineffective portion, if any, must be recognized currently in earnings.

Per IAS 39, the separate component of equity associated with the hedged item is to be adjusted to the lesser of two amounts: (1) the cumulative gain or loss on the hedging instrument needed to offset the cumulative change in expected future cash flows on the hedged item from inception of the hedge, less the portion associated with the ineffective component, or (2) the fair value of the cumulative change in expected future cash flows on the hedged item from inception of the hedge. Any remaining gain or loss (the ineffective portion) is either taken to earnings or equity as described above.

Revised IAS 39 requires that when a hedged forecast transaction occurs and results in the recognition of a *financial asset* or a *financial liability*, the gain or loss deferred in equity does not adjust the initial carrying amount of the asset or liability (thus, the formerly acceptable method of basis adjustment has been prohibited). This remains in equity and is recognized in profit or loss consistent with the recognition of gains and losses on the asset or liability. On the other hand, for hedges of forecast transactions that result in the recognition of a *nonfinancial asset* or a *nonfinancial liability*, the entity may elect whether to apply basis adjustment or retain the hedging gain or loss in equity and report it in profit or loss when the asset or liability affects profit or loss.

In the case of other cash flow hedges (i.e., those not resulting in recognition of assets or liabilities), amounts reflected in equity will be recognized in earnings in the period or periods when the hedged firm commitment or forecasted transaction also affects earnings.

Hedge accounting is to be discontinued when the hedging instrument is sold, expires, is terminated or exercised. If the gain or loss was accumulated in equity, it should remain there until such time as the forecasted transaction occurs, when it is added to the asset or liability recorded or is taken into earnings when the transaction impacts earnings. Hedge accounting is also discontinued prospectively when the hedge ceases meeting the criteria for qualification of hedge accounting. The accumulated gain or loss remains in equity until the committed or forecasted transaction occurs, whereupon it will be handled as discussed above.

Finally, if the forecasted or committed transaction is no longer expected to occur, hedge accounting is prospectively discontinued. In this case, the accumulated gain or loss included in equity must be immediately taken into earnings.

Hedges of a net investment in a foreign entity. Hedges of a net investment in a foreign entity are accounted for similarly to those of cash flows. To the extent it is determined to be effective, accumulated gains or losses are reflected in equity via the statement of changes in equity. The ineffective portion is reported in earnings.

In terms of financial reporting, the gain or loss on the effective portion of these hedges should be classified in the same manner as the foreign currency translation gain or loss. According to IAS 21, translation gains and losses are not reported in earnings but instead are reported directly in equity, with allocation being made to minority interest when the foreign entity is not wholly owned by the reporting entity. Likewise, any hedging gain or loss would be reported in equity. When the foreign entity is disposed of, the accumulated translation gain or loss would be reported in earnings, as would any related deferred hedging gain or loss.

When a hedge does not qualify for special hedge accounting (due to failure to properly document, ineffectiveness, etc.), any gains or losses are to be accounted for based on the nature of the hedging instrument. If a derivative financial instrument, the gains or losses must be reported in earnings.

Hedges of interest rate risk on a portfolio basis (also called macrohedging). Revised IAS 39 permits fair value hedge accounting to be used more readily for a portfolio hedge of interest rate risk than previously was the case. In particular, for such a hedge, it allows

1. The hedged item to be designated as an amount of a currency (e.g., an amount of dollars, euros, pounds, or rands) rather than as individual assets (or liabilities)
2. The gain or loss attributable to the hedged item to be presented either

   a. In a single separate line item within assets, for those repricing time periods for which the hedged item is an asset; or
   b. In a single separate line item within liabilities, for those repricing time periods for which the hedged item is a liability.

3. Prepayment risk to be incorporated by scheduling prepayable items into repricing time periods based on expected, rather than contractual, repricing dates. However, when the portion hedged is based on expected repricing dates, the effect that changes in the hedged interest rate have on those expected repricing dates are included when determining the change in the fair value of the hedged item. Consequently, if a portfolio that contains prepayable items is hedged with a non-prepayable derivative, ineffectiveness arises if the dates on which items in the hedged portfolio are expected to prepay are revised, or actual prepayment dates differ from those expected.

Assessing hedge effectiveness. Under the provisions of IAS 39, assuming other conditions are also met, hedge accounting may be applied as long as, and to the extent that, the hedge is effective. By effective, the standard is alluding to the degree to which offsetting changes in fair values or cash flows attributable to the hedged risk are achieved by the hedging instrument. A hedge is generally deemed effective if, at inception and throughout the period of the hedge, the ratio of changes in value of the underlying to changes in value of the hedging instrument are in a range of 80 to 125%.

Hedge effectiveness will be heavily impacted by the nature of the instruments used for hedging. For example, interest rate swaps will be almost completely effective if the notional and principal amounts match, and the terms, repricing dates, interest and principal payment dates, and basis for measurement are the same. On the other hand, if the hedged and hedging instruments are denominated in different currencies, effectiveness will not be 100% in most instances. Also, if the rate change is partially due to changes in perceived credit risk, there will be a lack of perfect correlation as well.

Hedges must be defined in terms of specific identified and designated risks. Overall (entity) risk cannot be the basis for hedging. Also, it must be possible to precisely measure the risk being hedged; thus, threat of expropriation (which may be an insurable risk) is not a risk that can be hedged, as that term is used in IAS 39. Similarly, investments accounted for by the equity method cannot be hedged, since that would be inconsistent with the equity method of accounting. In contrast, a net investment in a foreign subsidiary can be hedged, since this is a function of currency exchange rates alone.

If a hedge does not qualify for special hedge accounting because it is not effective, any gains or losses arising from changes in the fair value of a hedged item measured at fair value, subsequent to initial recognition, are reported as otherwise prescribed by IAS 39. That is, if an item is held for trading, changes in value are reported in earnings; if available for sale, the changes are reported in equity.

Disclosures Required under IAS 32

IAS 32 was effective in 1996 and established an expansive set of disclosure requirements. IAS 39, which became effective in 2001, carried forward these requirements with only minor changes and added further informational disclosure requirements. Both IAS 32 and IAS 39 were revised as part of the IASB's *Improvements Project* in 2003, and all disclosure requirements were relocated to IAS 32. Most recently (mid-2005) a new standard has been promulgated, IFRS 7, which set forth all financial instruments disclosure requirements, superseding (but not changing) the disclosure requirements previously found in both IAS 30 and IAS 32. Since IFRS 7 does not become mandatorily effective until 2007, the existing requirements under IAS 32 are given primary attention here. (Bank and other financial institution disclosure requirements, as set forth by IAS 30, are explained and copiously illustrated in Chapter 24.)

Primacy of risk considerations. The major objective of the disclosure requirements established by IAS 32 is to give financial statement users the ability to assess on- and off-balance-sheet risks, which prominently includes risks relating to future cash flows associated with the financial instruments. The standard presents the following typology of risk:

1. **Market risk,** which implies not merely the risk of loss but also the potential for gain, and which is in turn comprised of

    a. **Currency risk**—The risk that the value of an instrument will vary due to changes in currency exchange rates.

    b. **Fair value interest rate risk**—The risk that the value of the instrument will fluctuate due to changes in market interest rates.

    c. **Price risk**—A broader concept that subsumes interest rate risk, this is, the risk that prices will fluctuate due to factors specific to the financial instrument or due to factors that are generally affecting other securities trading in the same markets.

2. **Credit risk** is related to the failure of one party to perform as it is required to contractually.

3. **Liquidity risk** (also known as **funding risk**) is a function of the possible difficulty to be encountered in raising funds to meet commitments; it may result from an inability to sell a financial asset at its fair value.

4. **Cash flow interest rate risk** is the risk that the future cash flows associated with a monetary financial instrument will fluctuate in amount, as when a debt instrument carries a floating interest rate, potentially causing a change in cash flows while fair values will remain constant (absent a coincidentally occurring change in creditworthiness).

The standard does address the means by which interest rate and credit risk factors are to be addressed in the financial statements, while cash flow and liquidity risk are discussed in general terms only. These matters are elaborated upon in the following paragraphs.

Fair value interest rate risk in greater detail. Interest rate risk is the risk associated with holding fixed-rate instruments in a changing interest-rate environment. As market rates rise, the price of fixed-interest-rate instruments will decline, and vice versa. This relationship holds in all cases, irrespective of other specific factors, such as changes in perceived creditworthiness of the borrower. However, with certain complex instruments such as mortgage-backed bonds (a popular form of derivative instrument), where the behavior of the underlying debtors can be expected to be altered by changes in the interest rate environment (i.e., as market interest rates decline, prepayments by mortgagors increase in frequency, raising reinvestment rate risk to the bondholders and accordingly tempering the otherwise expected upward movement of the bond prices), the inverse relationship will become distorted.

IAS 32 requires that for each class of financial asset and financial liability, both those that are recognized (i.e., on-balance-sheet) and those that are not recognized (off-balance-sheet), the reporting entity should disclose information which will illuminate its exposure to interest rate risk. This includes disclosure of contractual repricing dates or maturity dates, whichever are earlier, as well as effective interest rates, if applicable.

These data provide the user of the financial statements with an ability to predict cash flows, since fixed-rate instruments will generate cash inflows (if assets) or outflows (if liabilities) at a given rate until the maturity date or the earlier repricing date, although other features, such as optional call dates or serial retirements, can complicate this further. The combination of information on contractual (or coupon) rates, maturity dates, and changing market conditions (not provided by the financial statements, but presumably available to anyone with access to the financial press) also provides insight into the price risk of the underlying debt instruments, while for debt having floating rates of interest, knowledge of market conditions provides insight into cash flow risk.

The standard also suggests, but does not require, that when **expected** repricings are to occur at dates that differ significantly from contractual dates, such information be provided as well. An example is when the entity is an investor in fixed-rate mortgage loans and when prepayments can be reliably estimated; as the funds thereby generated will need to be reinvested at then-current market rates, altering the patterns and amounts of future cash flows from what a simple reading of the balance sheet might otherwise suggest. Information based on management expectations should be clearly distinguished from that which is based on contractual provisions.

IAS 32 suggests that a meaningful way to present this information is to group financial assets and financial liabilities into categories as follows:

1. Those debt instruments that have fixed rates and thus expose the reporting entity to interest-rate (price) risk
2. Those debt instruments that have floating rates and thus expose the entity to cash flow risk
3. Those instruments, typically equity, which are not interest-rate sensitive

Effective interest rates, as used in this standard, means the internal rate of return, which is the discount rate that equates the present value of all future cash flows associated with the instrument with its current market price. Put another way, this is the measure of the time value of money as it relates to the financial instrument in question. Effective interest rates cannot be determined for derivative financial instruments such as swaps, forwards and options, although these are often affected by changes in interest rates, and the effective rate disclosures prescribed by IAS 32 do not apply in such cases. In any event, the risk characteristics of such instruments must be discussed in the footnote disclosures.

The nature of the reporting entity's business and the extent to which it holds financial assets or is obligated by financial liabilities will affect the manner in which such disclosures are presented, and no single method of making such disclosures will be suitable for every entity. The standard suggests that in many cases a tabular disclosure of amounts of financial instruments exposed to interest rate risk will be useful, with the instruments grouped according to repricing or maturity dates (e.g., within one year, from one to five years, and over five years from the balance sheet date). In other cases (for financial institutions, for example), finer distinctions of maturities might be warranted. Similar tabular presentations of data on floating-rate instruments (which create cash-flow risk rather than interest-rate [price] risk) should also be presented, when pertinent. When other risk factors are also present, such as credit risk (discussed in the following section), a series of tabular presentations, segregating instruments into risk classes and then categorizing each in terms of maturities and so on, may be necessary to convey the risk dimensions adequately to readers.

Sensitivity analysis has been alluded to in a number of accounting standards over the years. Since it has always been presented as an optional feature, it has rarely been employed in actual disclosures, despite having great potential for being useful to readers. In the context of financial instruments, sensitivity analysis would imply a discussion of the effect on portfolio value of a hypothetical change (e.g., a 1% change, plus or minus) in interest rates. There are at least two reasons why such information, unless accompanied by an adequate discussion of the particular characteristics of the financial instruments in question, might be misleading to financial statement readers.

First, because of the phenomenon known as convexity, the value change of each successive 1% change in interest rates is not a constant, but rather, a function of current market rates. For example, if the market rate at the balance sheet date is 8%, a move in rates to 9% might cause a €20,000 decline in value in a given bond portfolio, but a further 1% change in the market rate, from 9% to 10%, would not have a further €20,000 effect. Instead, the effect would be an amount greater or lesser depending on the coupon (contractual) rate of interest of the underlying financial instruments. A reader, however, would rarely appreciate this fact and would probably extrapolate the sensitivity data in a linear manner, which could be materially misleading in the absence of further narrative information.

Second, sensitivity data most often are presented in a manner that suggests that they apply symmetrically. Thus, in the foregoing example, the presumption is that a 1% market rate decline would boost the portfolio value by €20,000 and that a 1% rate increase would depress it by a similar amount. However, some instruments, most notably those with embedded options (mortgage-backed bonds, having prepayment options, are the most common example cited, although exotic derivatives can be far more difficult to analyze) will not exhibit symmetrical price behavior, and the asymmetries will become exaggerated as hypothetical market rates stray further from the current rates. As a practical matter, the only way to convey these subtleties in a meaningful fashion would be to incorporate extensive tables of information into the footnotes, which many users would find to be impossibly confusing.

For these and possibly other reasons, although recommended by IAS 32, it is not anticipated that sensitivity data will be provided widely in the near term. If provided, however, any assumptions and the methodologies employed should be explained adequately, along with any needed caveats concerning the validity of extrapolation over greater ranges of market rate changes and over time.

Credit risk in greater detail. IAS 32 also demands that for each class of financial asset, both recognized (i.e., on-balance-sheet) and unrecognized (off-balance-sheet), information be provided as to exposure to credit risk. Specifically, the maximum amount of credit risk exposure as of the balance sheet date, without considering possible recoveries from any collateral that may have been provided, should be stated and any significant concentrations of credit risk should be discussed.

Disclosure is required of the amount that best represents the maximum credit risk exposure at the balance sheet date. In many cases, this is simply the carrying value of such instruments; for example, accounts receivable net of any allowance for uncollectibles already provided would be the measure of credit risk associated with trade receivables. In other cases, the maximum loss would be an amount less than that which is revealed on the balance sheet, as when a legal right of offset exists but the financial asset was not presented on a net basis on the balance sheet because one of the required conditions set forth in IAS 32 (intention to settle on a net basis) was not met. In yet other circumstances, the maximum accounting loss that could be incurred would be greater, as when the asset is unrecognized in the balance sheet although otherwise disclosed in the footnotes as, for example, when the entity has guaranteed collection of receivables that have been sold to another party (often called factoring with recourse, discussed earlier).

There are a large number of potential combinations of factors that could affect maximum credit risk exposure, and in other than the most basic circumstances it is likely that extended narratives will be needed to convey the risks fully in the most meaningful way to users of the financial statements. For example, when an entity has financial assets owed from and financial liabilities owed to the same counter-party, with the right of offset but without having an intent to settle on a net basis, the maximum amount subject to credit risk may be lower than the carrying value of the asset. However, if past behavior suggests that the entity would probably respond to the debtor's difficulties by extending the maturity of the financial asset beyond the maturity of the related liability, it will voluntarily expose itself to greater risk since it will presumably settle its obligation and thus forfeit the opportunity to offset these related instruments.

When the maximum credit risk exposure associated with a particular financial asset or group of assets is the same as the amount presented on the face of the balance sheet, it is not necessary to reiterate this fact in the footnotes. The presumption is that there will be disclosures made for all material items for which this fact does not hold, however.

In addition to disclosure of maximum credit risk, IAS 32 requires disclosure of concentrations of credit risk when these are not otherwise apparent from the financial statements. Common examples of this involve trade accounts receivable that are due from debtors within one geographic region or operating within one industry segment, as when a large fraction of receivables are due from, say, housing construction contractors in the Netherlands, many of whom might find themselves in financial difficulty if economic conditions deteriorated in that narrowly defined market. In addition to geographic locale and industry, other factors to consider would include the creditworthiness of the debtors (e.g., if the reporting entity targets a market such as college students not having steady employment, or third-world governments) and the nature of the activities undertaken by the counterparties. The disclosures should provide a clear indication of the characteristics shared by the debtors.

Examples of disclosures of credit risk

Note 5: Interest Rate Swap Agreements

The differential to be paid or received is accrued as interest rates change and is recognized over the life of the agreements.

Note 8: Foreign Exchange Contracts

The corporation enters into foreign exchange contracts as a hedge against accounts payable denominated in foreign currencies. Market value gains and losses are recognized, and the resulting credit or debit offsets foreign exchange losses or gains on those payables.

Note 13: Financial Instruments with Off-Balance-Sheet Risk

In the normal course of business, the corporation enters into or is a party to various financial instruments and contractual obligations that, under certain conditions, could give rise to or involve elements of, market or credit risk in excess of that shown in the statement of financial condition. These financial instruments and contractual obligations include interest rate swaps, forward foreign exchange contracts, financial guarantees, and commitments to extend credit. The corporation monitors and limits its exposure to market risk through management policies designed to identify and reduce excess risk. The corporation limits its credit risk through monitoring of client credit exposure, reviews, and conservative estimates of allowances for bad debt and through the prudent use of collateral for large amounts of credit.

The corporation monitors collateral values on a daily basis and requires additional collateral when deemed necessary.

Note 6: Interest Rate Swaps and Forward Exchange Contracts

The corporation enters into a variety of interest rate swaps and forward foreign exchange contracts. The primary use of these financial instruments is to reduce interest rate fluctuations and to stabilize costs or to hedge foreign currency liabilities or assets. Interest rate swap transactions involve the exchange of floating-rate and fixed-rate interest payment of obligations without the exchange of underlying notional amounts. The company is exposed to credit risk in the unlikely event of nonperformance by the counterparty. The differential to be received or paid is accrued as interest rates change and is recognized over the life of the agreement. Forward foreign exchange contracts represent commitments to exchange currencies at a specified future date. Gains (losses) on these contracts serve primarily to stabilize costs. Foreign currency exposure for the corporation will result in the unlikely event that the other party fails to perform under the contract.

Note 3: Financial Guarantees

Financial guarantees are conditional commitments to guarantee performance to third parties. These guarantees are primarily issued to guarantee borrowing arrangements. The corporation's credit risk exposure on these guarantees is not material.

Note 8: Commitment to Extend Credit

Loan commitments are agreements to extend credit under agreed-upon terms. The corporation's commitment to extend credit assists customers to meet their liquidity needs. These commitments generally have fixed expiration or other termination clauses. The corporation anticipates that not all of these commitments will be utilized. The amount of unused commitment does not necessarily represent future funding requirements.

Note 9: Summary of Off-Balance-Sheet Financial Instruments

The off-balance-sheet financial instruments are summarized as follows (in thousands):

Financial instruments whose notional or contract amounts exceed the amount of credit risk:

	Contract or notional amount
Interest rate swap agreements	€8,765,400
Forward foreign exchange contracts	7,654,300

Financial instruments whose contract amount represents credit risk:

	Contract or notional amount
Financial guarantees	€6,543,200
Commitments to extend credit	5,432,100

Concentration of credit risk for certain entities. For certain corporations, industry or regional concentrations of credit risk may be disclosed adequately by a description of the business. Some examples of such disclosure language are

1. Credit risk for these off-balance-sheet financial instruments is concentrated in Asia and in the trucking industry.
2. All financial instruments entered into by the corporation relate to Japanese government, international, and domestic commercial airline customers.

Example of disclosure of concentration of credit risk

Note 5: Significant Group Concentrations of Credit Risk

The corporation grants credit to customers throughout Europe and the Middle East. As of December 31, 2005, the five areas where the corporation had the greatest amount of credit risk were as follows:

United Kingdom	€8,765,400
Germany	7,654,300
United Arab Emirates	6,543,200
Turkey	5,432,100
France	4,321,000

Disclosure of fair values. IAS 32 further requires that for each class of financial asset and financial liability, the reporting entity should disclose information about fair value. This requirement is not operative, however, in the case of financial assets or liabilities that are already to be carried at fair value, per IAS 39. An exception is provided when the fair value cannot be reliably determined for an investment in an equity instrument, or in a derivative related to such instrument. However, when an entity avails itself of this option, it must disclose that fact, coupled with a summary of pertinent characteristics of the instrument, such that readers can make their own assessments of fair value should they so choose. Proposed revisions to IAS 32 and IAS 39 would expand the information to be presented in those instances where fair value disclosures cannot be provided

Stockholders and others have every reason to expect that management understands the values of the assets it acquires for the business or of the obligations it incurs. Therefore, an admission in the financial statements to the effect that fair values could not be determined, if made more than infrequently, would appear either disingenuous or an admission of managerial malfeasance. For this reason, a good-faith attempt to determine the fair value data requested by IAS 32, coupled with disclosures that set forth whatever caveats are deemed necessary to make the information not misleading, is probably the best course to follow.

Beyond the basic concern of computing fair values, there is the further issue of what this information is intended to imply. This question arises most commonly in the context of financial obligations, which represent contractual commitments to repay fixed sums at fixed points in time, that are not subject to adjustment for market-driven changes in value.

For example, assume that an entity owes a bank loan carrying fixed 9.5% interest, with the principal due as a €300,000 balloon payment three years hence. If current rates are 7%, the fair value of this obligation is something greater than its face value (in fact, the computed present value of future cash flows, discounted at 7%, is €342,060, which will be the surrogate for fair value), yet the contractual obligation is unchanged at the original €300,000. What, then, is the purpose of communicating to financial statement users that the fair value is the higher, €342,060, amount?

The explanation of this disclosure is that the economic burden being borne by the entity is heavier than would have been the case had a floating market rate of interest been attached to the debt. The spread between the disclosed fair value, €342,060, and the face amount of the debt, €300,000, is the present value of the additional interest to be paid in the future under the fixed-rate agreement over the amount that would be payable at the current market rate. Thus, fair value disclosure does not measure future cash flows, per se, but rather is an indication of economic burden or benefit in the assumed absence of any restructuring or other alteration of the debt.

Fair value is the exchange price in a current transaction (other than in a forced or liquidation sale) between willing parties. If a quoted market price is available, it should be used, after adjustment for transaction costs that would normally be incurred in a real transaction of this type. If there is more than one market price, the one used should be the one from the most active market. The possible effects on market price from the sale of large holdings and/or from thinly traded issues should generally be disregarded for purposes of this determination, since it would tend to introduce too much subjectivity into this measurement process.

If quoted market prices are unavailable, management's best estimate of fair value can be used. A number of standardized techniques, which attempt to tie the prices of various financial instruments to those having readily determinable fair values, are widely employed for this purpose. Some bases from which an estimate may be made include

1. Matrix pricing models
2. Option pricing models
3. Financial instruments with similar characteristics adjusted for risks involved
4. Financial instruments with similar valuation techniques (i.e. present value) adjusted for risks involved

Fair value disclosures, by class of assets and liabilities, are to be presented in such a way that users can compare these amounts to corresponding carrying amounts.

Example

Note X: Financial Instruments Disclosures of Fair Value

The estimates of fair value of financial instruments are summarized as follows (in thousands):

Instruments for which carrying amounts approximate fair values:

	Carrying amount
Cash	€987.6
Cash equivalents	876.5
Trade receivables	765.4
Trade payables	(654.3)

Fair values approximate carrying values because of the short time until realization or liquidation.

Instruments for which fair values exceed carrying amounts:

	Carrying amount	*Fair value*
Short-term securities	€876.5	€987.6
Long-term investments	765.4	876.5

Estimated fair values are based on available quoted market prices, present value calculations, and option pricing models.

Instruments for which carrying amounts exceed fair values:

	Carrying amount	*Fair value*
Long-term debt	(€543.2)	(€432.1)

Estimated fair values are based on quoted market prices, present value calculations, and the prices of the same or similar instruments after considering risk, current interest rates, and remaining maturities.

Unrecognized financial instruments:

	Carrying amount	*Fair value*
Financial guarantees	(€6,543.2)	(€7,654.3)

Estimated fair values after considering risk, current interest rates and remaining maturities were based on the following:

1. **Credit commitments**—Value of the same or similar instruments after considering credit ratings of counterparties.
2. **Financial guarantees**—Cost to settle or terminate obligations with counterparties at reporting date.

Fair value not estimated:

	Carrying amount	Fair value
Long-term investment	€1,234.5	€--

Fair value could not be estimated without incurring excessive costs. Investment is carried at original cost and represents an 8% investment in the common stock of a privately held non-traded company that supplies the corporation. Management considers the risk of loss to be negligible.

Financial assets carried at amounts in excess of fair value. Prior to the implementation of IAS 39, there were certain circumstances in which an entity might have carried one or several financial assets at amounts that exceeded fair value, notwithstanding the general rule under accounting theory that such declines should be formally recognized in most instances. Normally, failure to recognize such declines would have been justified only when there is no objective evidence of impairment.

IAS 32 requires that when one or more financial assets are reported at amounts that exceed fair value, disclosure should be made of both carrying amount and fair value, either individually or grouped in an appropriate manner, and the reasons for not reducing the carrying value to fair value should be set forth, including the nature of the evidence that provides the basis for management's belief that the carrying value will be recovered. The purpose is to alert the financial statement readers to the risk that carrying amounts might later be reduced if a change in circumstances causes management to reassess the likelihood of recovery.

With the implementation of IAS 39, the issue of reporting investments or other financial assets at amounts in excess of fair value became virtually moot. Essentially, only held-to-maturity investments in debt instruments, loans and receivables originated by the entity, and purchased loans not quoted in an active market, might be presented at amounts in excess of fair value, for instance, when they carry a fixed interest rate that is lower than the prevailing market interest rates for similar instruments and there is no objective evidence of impairment.

Other disclosure requirements. IAS 32 encourages financial statement preparers to make other disclosures as warranted to enhance the readers' understanding of the financial statements and hence, of the operations of the entity being reported on. It suggests that these further disclosures could include such matters as

1. The total amount of change in the fair value of financial assets and financial liabilities that has been recognized in income for the period
2. The average aggregate carrying amount during the year being reported on of recognized financial assets and financial liabilities; the average aggregate principal, stated, notional, or similar amounts of unrecognized financial assets and financial liabilities; and the average aggregate fair value of all financial assets and financial liabilities, all of which information is particularly useful when the amounts on hand at the balance sheet dates are not representative of the levels of activity during the period

Revisions to IAS 32, effective in 2005, added the following disclosure requirements:

- The methods and significant assumptions applied in determining fair values of financial assets and financial liabilities separately for significant classes of financial assets and financial liabilities;
- The extent to which fair values of financial assets and financial liabilities are determined directly by reference to published price quotations in an active market or recent

market transactions on arm's-length terms or are estimated using a valuation technique;

- The extent to which fair values are determined in full or in part using a valuation technique based on assumptions that are not supported by observable market prices;
- If a fair value estimated using a valuation technique is sensitive to valuation assumptions that are not supported by observable market prices, a statement of this fact and the effect on the fair value of using a range of reasonably possible alternative assumptions; and
- The total amount of the change in fair value estimated using a valuation technique that was recognized in earnings in the reporting period.

Categorization of financial assets and liabilities. IAS 39 establishes four categories of financial assets and liabilities, as follows:

1. Held-for-trading;
2. Available-for-sale;
3. Held-to-maturity; and
4. Loans and receivables originated by the entity and not held for trading (optionally inclusive of purchased loans not quoted in an active market).

When relevant, the financial statements must disclose, per revised IAS 32, for each of these four categories of instruments, whether regular way purchases of securities are accounted for at trade date or settlement date.

Also to be disclosed are a description of the reporting entity's financial risk management objectives and policies, including its policy for each major type of forecasted transaction (for example, in the case of hedges of risks relating to future sales, that description should indicate the nature of the risks being hedged, approximately how many months or years of future sales have been hedged, and the approximate percentage of sales in those future months or years); whether gain or loss on financial assets and liabilities measured at fair value subsequent to initial recognition, other than those relating to hedges, has been recognized directly in equity, and if so, the cumulative amount recognized as of the balance sheet date; and, when fair value cannot be reliably measured for a group of financial assets or financial liabilities that would otherwise have to be carried at fair value, that fact should be disclosed together with a description of the financial instruments, their carrying amount, and an explanation of why fair value cannot be reliably measured.

For designated fair value hedges, cash flow hedges, and hedges of net investment in a foreign entity, there are to be separate descriptions of the hedges, the financial instruments designated as hedging instruments together with fair values at the balance sheet date, the nature of the risks being hedged, and for forecasted transactions, the periods in which the forecasted transactions are expected to occur, when they are expected to enter into the determination of net profit or loss (e.g., a forecasted acquisition of property may affect earnings over the asset's depreciable lifetime), plus a description of any forecasted transaction for which hedge accounting was previously employed but which is no longer expected to occur.

When there has been a gain or loss on derivative and nonderivative financial assets or liabilities designated as hedging instruments in cash flow hedges which has been recognized directly in equity, disclosure is to be made of the amount so recognized during the current reporting period, the amount removed from equity and included in earnings for the period, and the amount removed from equity and included in the initial measurement of acquisition cost or carrying amount of the asset or liability in a hedged forecasted transaction during the current period.

The financial statements must also disclose the following with regard to financial instruments: the amount of any gains or losses resulting from remeasuring available-for-sale instruments at fair value, included directly in equity in the current period, and the amount removed from equity and reported in current operating results; a description of any held-for-trading or available-for-sale financial assets for which fair value cannot be determined, together with (when possible) the range of possible fair values thereof; the carrying amount and gain or loss on sale of any financial assets whose fair value was not previously determinable; significant items of income, expense, gain and loss resulting from financial assets or liabilities, whether included in earnings or in equity, with separate (gross) reporting of interest income and interest expense, and with separate reporting of realized and unrealized gains and losses resulting from available-for-sale financial assets. It is not necessary to distinguish realized and unrealized gains and losses resulting from held-for-trading financial assets, however.

If there are impaired loans, the amount of interest accrued but not received in cash must be disclosed.

If the entity has participated in securitizations or repurchase agreements, these must be described, and the nature of any collateral and key assumptions made in computing retained or new interests are to be discussed. There must be disclosure of whether the financial assets have been derecognized.

Any reclassifications of financial assets from categories reported at fair value to those reported at amortized historical cost (either because now deemed held-to-maturity, or because fair values are no longer obtainable) are to be explained.

Finally, any impairments or reversals of impairments are to be disclosed, separately for each class (held-to-maturity, etc.) of investment.

Derivatives Related to the Entity's Own Shares

Regarding derivatives based on an entity's own shares, the revised IAS 32 has provided guidance as follows:

- A derivative that is indexed to the price of an entity's own shares and requires net cash or net share settlement, or that gives the counterparty a choice of net cash or net share settlement, is to be treated as a derivative asset or derivative liability (i.e., not as an equity instrument) and is to be accounted for as such under IAS 39.
- A derivative that is indexed to the price of an entity's own shares and gives the entity a right to require net cash or net share settlement instead of gross physical settlement is to be treated as a derivative asset or derivative liability (i.e., not as an equity instrument), unless the entity has an established history of settling such contracts through a gross exchange of a fixed number of the entity's own shares for a fixed amount of cash or other financial assets.
- Changes in the fair value of a derivative that is fully indexed to the price of an entity's own shares and that will result in the receipt or delivery of a fixed number of an entity's own shares in exchange for a fixed amount of cash or other financial assets are not recognized in the financial statements, since to do otherwise would be to allow changes in the value of the reporting entity's equity shares to be reflected in its earnings.
- When a derivative involves an obligation to pay cash in exchange for receiving an entity's own shares, there is a liability for the share redemption amount. The objective of this proposed amendment is to clarify the requirements affecting the classification of derivatives based on an entity's own shares to promote the consistent application of those requirements.

Disclosure Requirements under IFRS 7

As noted previously, IFRS 7 will supersede the disclosure requirements currently found in IAS 32, as well as the financial institution-specific requirements of IAS 30, which will be withdrawn. Presentation requirements set forth in IAS 32 will continue in effect under that standard. IFRS 7 may be adopted early, but will mandatorily become effective for years beginning in 2007.

IFRS was made necessary by the increasingly sophisticated (but opaque) methods that reporting entities have begun using to measure and manage their exposure to risks arising from financial instruments. At the same time, new risk management concepts and approaches have gained acceptance. IASB concluded that users of financial statements need information about the reporting entities' exposures to risks and how those risks are being managed.

Risk management information can influence the users' assessments of the financial position and performance of reporting entities, as well as of the amount, timing, and uncertainty of the respective entity's future cash flows. In short, greater transparency regarding those risks allows users to make more informed judgments about risk and return. This is entirely consistent with the fundamental objective of financial reporting and is consistent with the widely accepted efficient markets hypothesis.

With this as background, IASB determined that the disclosure requirements set forth in IAS 30 and IAS 32 needed to be revised and enhanced. A unified set of requirements has been imposed, eliminating the need for a separate standard dealing only with financial institutions.

IFRS 7 applies to all risks arising from all financial instruments, with limited exceptions. It furthermore applies to all entities, including those that have few financial instruments (e.g., an entity whose only financial instruments are accounts receivable and payable), as well as those that have many financial instruments (e.g., a financial institution, most assets and liabilities of which are financial instruments). Under IFRS 7, the extent of disclosure required depends on the extent of the entity's use of financial instruments and of its exposure to risk.

IFRS 7 requires disclosure of

1. The significance of financial instruments for an entity's financial position and performance (which incorporates many of the requirements previously set forth by IAS 32); and
2. Qualitative and quantitative information about exposure to risks arising from financial instruments, including specified minimum disclosures about credit risk, liquidity risk, and market risk. The *qualitative* disclosures describe managements' objectives, policies, and processes for managing those risks. The *quantitative* disclosures provide information about the extent to which the entity is exposed to risk, based on information provided internally to the entity's key management personnel. Together, these disclosures are expected to provide an overview of the reporting entity's use of financial instruments and the exposures to risks they create.

Exceptions to applicability. IFRS 7 identifies the following types of financial instruments to which the requirements do not apply:

1. Interests in subsidiaries, associates, and joint ventures accounted for in accordance with IAS 27, IAS 28, or IAS 31, respectively. However, given that in some cases those standards permit an entity to account for an interest in a subsidiary, associate, or joint venture using IAS 39, in those cases the reporting entities are to apply the disclosure requirements in those other standards as well as those in IFRS 7. Entities are also to apply IFRS 7 to all derivatives linked to interests in subsidiaries, associ-

ates, or joint ventures, unless the derivative meets the definition of an equity instrument per IAS 32.

2. Employers' rights and obligations arising from employee benefit plans, to which IAS 19 applies.
3. Contracts for contingent consideration in a business combination, per IFRS 3, in financial reporting by the acquirer.
4. Insurance contracts as defined in IFRS 4. However, IFRS 7 applies to derivatives that are embedded in insurance contracts if IAS 39 requires the entity to account for them separately.
5. Financial instruments, contracts, and obligations under share-based payment transactions to which IFRS 2 applies, except that IFRS 7 applies to certain contracts that are within the scope of IAS 39.

Applicability. IFRS 7 applies to both recognized and unrecognized financial instruments. *Recognized* financial instruments include financial assets and financial liabilities that are within the scope of IAS 39. *Unrecognized* financial instruments include some financial instruments that, although outside the scope of IAS 39, are within the scope of this IFRS (such as some loan commitments). The requirements also extend to contracts involving nonfinancial items if they are subject to IAS 39.

Classes of financial instruments and level of disclosure. Many of the IFRS 7 requirements pertain to grouped data. In such cases, the grouping into classes is to be effected in the manner that is appropriate to the nature of the information disclosed and that takes into account the characteristics of the financial instruments. Importantly, sufficient information must be provided so as to permit reconciliation to the line items presented in the balance sheet. Enough detail is required so that users are able to assess the significance of financial instruments to the reporting entity's financial position and results of operations.

IFRS 7 requires that carrying amounts of each of the following categories, as defined in IAS 39, is to be disclosed either on the face of the balance sheet or in the notes:

1. Financial assets at fair value through profit or loss, showing separately (a) those designated as such upon initial recognition via the "fair value option" and (b) those classified as held-for-trading in accordance with IAS 39;
2. Held-to-maturity investments;
3. Loans and receivables;
4. Available-for-sale financial assets;
5. Financial liabilities at fair value through profit or loss, showing separately, (a) those designated as such upon initial recognition via the "fair value option" and (b) those classified as held-for-trading in accordance with IAS 39; and
6. Financial liabilities carried at amortized cost.

Special disclosures apply to those financial assets and liabilities accounted for by the "fair value option." If the reporting entity designated a loan or receivable (or groups thereof) to be reported at fair value through profit or loss, it is required to disclose

1. The maximum exposure to *credit risk* of the loan or receivable (or group thereof) at the reporting date.
2. The amount by which any related credit derivatives or similar instruments mitigate that maximum exposure to credit risk.
3. The amount of change, both during the reporting period *and* cumulatively, in the fair value of the loan or receivable (or group thereof) that is attributable to *changes in the credit risk* of the financial asset determined either

 a. As the amount of change in its fair value that is not attributable to changes in market conditions that give rise to market risk; or

 b. Using an alternative method the entity believes more faithfully represents the amount of change in its fair value that is attributable to changes in the credit risk of the asset.

Changes in market conditions that give rise to market risk include changes in an observed (benchmark) interest rate, commodity price, foreign exchange rate, or index of prices or rates.

4. The amount of the change in the fair value of any related derivatives or similar instruments that has occurred during the period and cumulatively since the loan or receivable was designated.

If the reporting entity has designated a financial liability to be reported at fair value through profit or loss, it is to disclose

1. The amount of change, both during the period *and* cumulatively, in the fair value of the financial liability that is attributable to *changes in the credit risk* of that liability determined either

 a. As the amount of change in its fair value that is not attributable to changes in market conditions that give rise to market risk; or

 b. Using an alternative method the entity believes more faithfully represents the amount of change in its fair value that is attributable to changes in the credit risk of the liability.

Changes in market conditions that give rise to market risk include changes in a benchmark interest rate, the price of another entity's financial instrument, a commodity price, a foreign exchange rate, or an index of prices or rates. For contracts that include a unit-linking feature, changes in market conditions include changes in the performance of the related internal or external investment fund.

2. The difference between the financial liability's carrying amount and the amount the entity would be contractually required to pay at maturity to the holder of the obligation.

Reclassifications. If a financial asset has been reclassified to one that is measured: (1) at cost or amortized cost, rather than at fair value; or (2) at fair value, rather than at cost or amortized cost, the amount reclassified into and out of each category and the reason for that reclassification are to be disclosed.

Certain derecognition matters. If financial assets were transferred in such a way that part or all of those assets did not qualify for derecognition under IAS 39, the following disclosures are required for each class of such financial assets:

1. The nature of the assets;
2. The nature of the risks and rewards of ownership to which the entity remains exposed;
3. When the entity continues to recognize all of the assets, the carrying amounts of the assts and of the associated liabilities; and
4. When the entity continues to recognize the assets to the extent of its continuing involvement, the total carrying amount of the original assets, the amount of the assets that the entity continues to recognize, and the carrying amount of the associated liabilities.

Collateral. The reporting entity must disclose the carrying amount of financial assets it has pledged as collateral for liabilities or contingent liabilities, including amounts that have been reclassified in accordance with the provision of IAS 39 pertaining to rights to repledge; and the terms and conditions relating to its pledge.

Conversely, if the reporting entity holds collateral (of either financial or nonfinancial assets) and is permitted to sell or repledge the collateral in the absence of default by the owner of the collateral, it must now disclose the fair value of the collateral held and the fair value of any such collateral sold or repledged, and whether it has an obligation to return it; and the terms and conditions associated with its use of the collateral.

Allowances for bad debts or other credit losses. When financial assets are impaired by credit losses and the entity records the impairment in a separate account (whether associated with a specific asset or for the collective impairment of assets), rather than directly reducing the carrying amount of the asset, it is to disclose a reconciliation of changes in that account during the period, for each class of financial assets.

Certain compound instruments. If the reporting entity is the *issuer* of compound instruments, such as convertible debt, having multiple embedded derivatives having interdependent values (such as the conversion feature and a call feature, such that the issuer can effectively force conversion), these matters must be disclosed.

Defaults and breaches. If the reporting entity is the obligor under loans payable at the balance sheet date, it must disclose

1. The details of any defaults during the period, involving payment of principal or interest, or into a sinking fund, or of the redemption terms of those loans payable.
2. The carrying amount of the loans payable in default at the reporting date; and
3. Whether the default was remedied, or the terms of the loans payable were renegotiated, before the financial statements were authorized for issue.

Similar disclosures are required for any other breaches of loan agreement terms, if such breaches gave the lender the right to accelerate payment, unless these were remedied or terms were renegotiated before the reporting date.

Income statement and changes in equity disclosures. The reporting entity is to disclose the following items of income, expense, gains, or losses, either on the face of the financial statements or in the notes thereto:

1. Net gain or net losses on

    a. Financial assets or financial liabilities carried at fair value through profit or loss, showing separately those incurred on financial assets or financial liabilities designated as such upon initial recognition, and those on financial assets or financial liabilities that are classified as held-for-trading in accordance with IAS 39;

    b. Available-for-sale financial assets, showing separately the amount of gain or loss recognized directly in equity during the period and the amount removed from equity and recognized in profit or loss for the period;

    c. Held-to-maturity investments;

    d. Loans and receivables; and

    e. Financial liabilities carried at amortized cost;

2. Total interest income and total interest expense (calculated using the effective interest method) for financial assets or financial liabilities that are not carried at fair value through profit or loss;

3. Fee income and expense (other than amounts included in determining the effective interest rate) arising from

    a. Financial assets or financial liabilities that are not carried at fair value through profit or loss; and
    b. Trust and other fiduciary activities that result in the holding or investing of assets on behalf of individuals, trusts, retirement benefit plans, and other institutions

4. Interest income on impaired financial assets accrued in accordance with the provision of IAS 39 that stipulates that, once written down for impairment, interest income thereafter is to be recognized at the rate used to discount cash flows in order to compute impairment; and

5. The amount of any impairment loss for each class of financial asset.

Accounting policies disclosure. The reporting entity is to disclose the measurement basis (or bases) used in preparing the financial statements and the other accounting policies used that are relevant to an understanding of the financial statements.

Hedging disclosures. Hedge accounting is one of the more complex aspects of financial instruments accounting under IAS 39. IFRS 7 specifies that an entity engaged in hedging must disclose, separately for each type of hedge described in IAS 39 (i.e., fair value hedges, cash flow hedges, and hedges of net investments in foreign operations)

1. A description of each type of hedge;
2. A description of the financial instruments designated as hedging instruments and their fair values at the reporting date; and
3. The nature of the risks being hedged.

In the case of cash flow hedges, the reporting entity is to disclose

1. The periods when the cash flows are expected to occur and when they are expected to affect profit or loss;
2. A description of any forecasted transaction for which hedge accounting had previously been used, but which is no longer expected to occur;
3. The amount that was recognized in equity during the period;
4. The amount that was removed from equity and included in profit or loss for the period, showing the amount included in each line item in the income statement; and
5. The amount that was removed from equity during the period and included in the initial cost or other carrying amount of a nonfinancial asset or nonfinancial liability whose acquisition or incurrence was a hedged highly probable forecast transaction.

The reporting entity is to disclose separately

1. For fair value hedges, gains, or losses

    a. From the hedging instrument; and
    b. From the hedge item attributable to the hedged risk.

2. The ineffectiveness recognized in profit or loss that arises from cash flow hedges; and
3. The ineffectiveness recognized in profit or loss that arises from hedges of net investments in foreign operations.

Fair value disclosures. IFRS 7 requires that for each class of financial assets and financial liabilities, the reporting entity is to disclose the fair value of that class of assets and liabilities in a way that permits it to be compared with its carrying amount. Grouping by class is required, but offsetting assets and liabilities is generally not permitted (but will conform with balance sheet presentation). To be disclosed are

1. The methods and, if a valuation technique is used, the assumptions applied in determining fair values of each class of financial assets or financial liabilities (e.g., as to prepayment rates, rates of estimated credit losses, and interest rates or discount rates).
2. Whether fair values are determined, in whole or in part, directly by reference to published price quotations in an active market or are estimated using a valuation technique.
3. Whether the fair values recognized or disclosed in the financial statements are determined in whole or in part using a valuation technique based on assumptions that are *not* supported by prices from observable current market transactions in the same instrument (that is, without modification or repackaging) and *not* based on available observable market data. If fair values are recognized in the financial statements, and if changing one or more of those assumptions to reasonably possible alternative assumptions would change fair value significantly, then this fact must be stated, and the effect of those changes must be disclosed. Significance is to be assessed in light of the entity's profit or loss, and total assets or total liabilities, or, when changes in fair value are recognized in equity, total equity.
4. If 3. applies, the total amount of the change in fair value estimated using such a valuation technique that was recognized in profit or loss during the period.

In instances where the market for a financial instrument is not active, the reporting entity establishes the fair value using a valuation technique. The best evidence of fair value at initial recognition is the transaction price, so there could be a difference between the fair value at initial recognition and the amount that would be determined at that date using the valuation technique. In such a case, disclosure is required, by the class of financial instrument of

1. The entity's accounting policy for recognizing that difference in profit or loss to reflect a change in factors (including time) that market participants would consider in setting a price; and
2. The aggregate difference yet to be recognized in profit or loss at the beginning and end of the period and a reconciliation of changes in the balance of this difference.

Disclosures of fair value are not required in these circumstances.

1. When the carrying amount is a reasonable approximation of fair value, (e.g., for short-term trade receivables and payables);
2. For an investment in equity instruments that do not have a quoted market price in an active market, or derivatives linked to such equity instruments, that is measured at cost in accordance with IAS 39 because its fair value cannot be measured reliably; or
3. For an insurance contract containing a discretionary participation feature if the fair value of that feature cannot be measured reliably.

In instances identified in 2. and 3. immediately above, the reporting entity must disclose information to help users of the financial statements make their own judgments about the extent of possible differences between the carrying amount of those financial assets or financial liabilities and their fair value, including

1. The fact that fair value information has not been disclosed for these instruments because their fair value cannot be measured reliably;

2. A description of the financial instruments, their carrying amount, and an explanation of why fair value cannot be measured reliably;
3. Information about the market for the instruments;
4. Information about whether and how the entity intends to dispose of the financial instruments; and
5. If financial instruments whose fair value previously could not be reliably measured are derecognized, that fact, their carrying amount at the time of derecognition, and the amount of gain or loss recognized.

Disclosures about the nature and extent of risks flowing from financial instruments. Reporting entities are required to disclose various information that will enable the users to evaluate the nature and extent of risks the reporting entity is faced with as a consequence of financial instruments it is exposed to on the balance sheet date. Both qualitative and quantitative disclosures are required under IFRS 7, as described in the following paragraphs.

Qualitative disclosures. For each type of risk arising from financial instruments, the reporting entity is expected to disclose

1. The exposures to risk and how they arise;
2. Its objectives, policies and processes for managing the risk and the methods used to measure the risk; and
3. Any changes in 1. or 2. from the previous period.

Quantitative disclosures. For each type of risk arising from financial instruments, the entity must present

1. Summary quantitative data about its exposure to that risk at the reporting date. This is to be based on the information provided internally to key management personnel of the entity.
2. The disclosures required as set forth below (credit risk, et al.), to the extent not provided in 1., unless the risk is not material.
3. Concentrations of risk, if not apparent from 1. and 2.

If the quantitative data disclosed as of the balance sheet date are not representative of the reporting entity's exposure to risk during the period, it must provide further information that is representative.

Specific disclosures are mandated, concerning credit risk, liquidity risk, and market risk. These are set forth as follows in IFRS 7:

Credit risk disclosures. To be disclosed, by class of financial instrument, are

1. The amount that best represents the entity's maximum exposure to credit risk at the reporting date, before taking into account any collateral held or other credit enhancements;
2. In respect of the amount disclosed in a., a description of collateral held as security and other credit enhancements;
3. Information about the credit quality of financial assets that are *neither* past due *nor* impaired; and
4. The carrying amount of financial assets that would otherwise be past due or impaired whose terms have been renegotiated.

Regarding financial assets that are either past due or impaired, the entity must disclose, again by class of financial asset

1. An analysis of the age of financial assets that are past due as of the balance sheet date but which are not judged to be impaired;
2. An analysis of financial assets that are individually determined to be impaired as at the reporting date, including the factors that the entity considered in determining that they are impaired; and
3. For the amounts disclosed in 1. and 2., a description of collateral held by the entity as security and other credit enhancements and, unless impracticable, an estimate of their fair value.

Regarding any collateral and other credit enhancements obtained, if these meet recognition criteria in the relevant IFRS, the reporting entity is to disclose

1. The nature and carrying amount of the assets obtained; and
2. If the assets are not readily convertible into cash, its policies for disposing of such assets or for using them in its operations.

Liquidity risk. The entity is to disclose

1. A maturity analysis for financial liabilities that shows the remaining contractual maturities; and
2. A description of how the entity manages the liquidity risk inherent in a.

Market risk. A number of informative disclosures are mandated, as described in the following paragraphs.

Sensitivity analysis is generally required, as follows:

1. A sensitivity analysis for each type of market risk to which the entity is exposed at the reporting date, showing how profit or loss and equity would have been affected by changes in the relevant risk variable that were reasonably possible at that date;
2. The methods and assumptions used in preparing the sensitivity analysis; and
3. Changes from the previous period in the methods and assumptions used, and the reasons for such changes.

If the reporting entity prepares a sensitivity analysis, such as value-at-risk, that reflects interdependencies between risk variables (e.g., between interest rates and exchange rates and uses it to manage financial risks, it may use that sensitivity analysis in place of the analysis specified in the preceding paragraph. The entity would also have to disclose

1. An explanation of the method used in preparing such a sensitivity analysis, and of the main parameters and assumptions underlying the data provided; and
2. An explanation of the objective of the method used and of limitations that may result in the information not fully reflecting the fair value of the assets and liabilities involved.

Other market risk disclosures may also be necessary to fully inform financial statement users. When the sensitivity analyses are unrepresentative of a risk inherent in a financial instrument (e.g., because the year-end exposure does not reflect the actual exposure during the year), the entity is to disclose that fact, together with the reason it believes the sensitivity analyses are unrepresentative.

Examples of Financial Statement Disclosures

Barco Consolidated
Year ended December 31, 2004

Notes to the financial statements

Accounting principles

22. Derivative financial instruments

Derivative financial instruments are recognized initially at cost. Subsequent to initial recognition, derivative financial instruments are stated at fair value. The fair values of derivative interest contracts are estimated by discounting expected future cash flows using current market interest rates and yield curve over the remaining term of the instrument. The fair value of forward exchange contracts is their market price at the balance sheet date.

Derivative financial instruments that are either hedging instruments not designated or not qualified as hedges are carried at fair value with changes in value included in the income statement.

Where a derivative financial instrument is designated as a hedge of the variability in cash-flows of a recognized asset or liability, a firm commitment or a highly probable forecasted transaction, the effective part of any gain or loss on the derivative financial instrument is recognized directly in equity. Carryforward of unused tax credits and unused tax losses, to the extent that it is probable that taxable profit will be available against which the deductible temporary differences, carryforward of unused tax credit and tax losses can be utilized.

32. Derivative financial instruments

Derivative financial instruments are used to reduce the exposure to fluctuations in foreign exchange rates and interest rates. These instruments are subject to the risk of market rates changing subsequent to acquisition. These changes are generally offset by opposite effects on the item being hedged.

Foreign currency risk

Recognized assets and liabilities

Barco incurs foreign currency risk on recognized assets and liabilities when they are denominated in a currency other than the company's local currency. Such risks may be naturally covered when a receivable in a given currency is matched with a payable in the same currency.

Forward exchange contracts and option contracts are used to manage the currency risk arising from recognized receivables and payables, which are not naturally hedged. This is particularly the case for the US dollar, for which receivables are systematically higher than payables and for the Japanese yen, for which payables are systematically higher than receivables. No hedge accounting is applied to these contracts.

The balances on foreign currency receivables and payables are valued at the rates of exchange prevailing at the end of the accounting period. Derivative financial instruments that are used to reduce the exposure of these balances are rated in the balance sheet at fair value. Both changes in foreign currency balances and in fair value of derivative financial instruments are recognized in the income statement.

Forecasted transactions

In January 2004, Barco started to designate forward contracts to forecasted sales and costs. Hedge accounting is applied to these contracts. The portion of the gain or loss on the hedging instrument that will be determined as an effective hedge is recognized directly in equity.

Interest rate risk

Barco uses the following hedging instruments to manage its interest rate risk:

- Swap on outstanding loan
- An outstanding loan of USD 5,695 K (euro 4,181 K) with variable interest swapped into fixed 4.38%

- This hedging instrument is treated as cash-flow hedge, and gains or losses are recognized directly into equity

Cap/floor on loan agreements

Barco entered into the following loan agreements with variable interest rates, for which the variability is limited by a cap/floor:

- An outstanding loan of euro 14,250 K, with variable interest rate which is limited between 2% and 5%;
- An outstanding loan of USD 3,680 K (euro 2,702 K) with variable interest rate which is limited between 2.74% and 7%;
- An outstanding loan of USD 3,635 K (euro 2,669 K) with variable interest rate which is limited between 2.49% and 4.89%.

The cap/floor agreements do not meet the hedging requirements of IAS 39 and are therefore treated as financial instruments held for trading. They are valued at fair value and changes in fair value are recognized in the income statement.

Credit risk

Credit risk on accounts receivable. Credit evaluations are performed on all customers requiring credit over a certain amount. The credit risk is monitored on a continuous basis. In a number of cases collateral is being requested before a credit risk is accepted. Specific trade finance instruments such as letters of credit and bills of exchange are regularly used in order to minimize the credit risk.

Credit risk on liquid securities and short-term investments. A policy defining acceptable counterparties and the maximum risk per counterparty is in place. Short-term investments are done in marketable securities or in fixed-term deposits with reputable banks.

ADIDAS-SALOMON AG, GERMANY
Year ended December 31, 2004

Notes to the financial statements

23. Financial instruments

Management of foreign exchange risk. The Group is subject to currency exposure, primarily due to an imbalance of its global cash flows caused by the high share of product sourcing invoiced in US dollars, while sales other than in US dollars are invoiced mainly in European currencies, but also in Japanese yen, Canadian dollars, and other currencies. It is the Group's policy to hedge identified currency risks arising from forecasted transactions when it becomes exposed. In addition, the Group hedges balance sheet risks selectively.

Risk management is conducted by using natural hedges and arranging forward contracts, currency options and currency swaps. It is Group policy to have a high share of hedging instruments, such as currency options or option combinations, which provide protection and, at the same time, retain the potential to benefit from future favorable exchange rate developments in the financial markets. In 2004, the share of options hedging increased compared to 2003.

In 2004, the Group contracted currency options with premiums paid in a total amount of €22 million (2003: €17 million). Since currency options serve as cash flow hedges for future product transactions, the related premiums are recorded in income at the same time as the underlying transaction is recorded. The total amount of option premiums, which was charged to income in 2004, is €17 million (2003: €11 million). Paid option premiums (as part of the total capitalized fair value) in an amount of €25 million and €18 million were deferred as at December 31, 2004 and 2003, respectively.

The total net amount of US dollar purchases against other currencies was €1.7 billion and €1.6 billion in the years ending December 31, 2004 and 2003, respectively.

The notional amounts of all outstanding currency hedging instruments, which are mainly related to cash flow hedges, are summarized in the following table:

Notional Amounts of All Currency Hedging Instruments
(€ in millions)

	December 31 2004	December 31 2003
Forward contracts	871	1,104
Currency options	848	604
Total	1,719	1,708

The comparatively high amount of forward contracts is primarily due to currency swaps for liquidity management purposes and hedging transactions, in which the US dollar is not involved.

Out of the total amount of outstanding hedges, the following contracts relate to the coverage of the biggest single exposure, the US dollar.

Notional Amounts of US Dollar Hedging Instruments
(€ in millions)

	December 31 2004	December 31 2003
Forward contracts	326	234
Currency options	657	504
Total	983	738

The fair value of all outstanding currency hedging instruments is as follows:

Fair Value
(€ in millions)

	December 31 2004	December 31 2003
Forward contracts	(16)	6
Currency options	(10)	(16)
Total	(26)	(10)

Out of the negative fair value of €16 million of forward contracts, negative €18 million relate to hedging instruments falling under hedge accounting as per definition of IAS 39, split into a negative fair value of €19 million from cash flow hedges and a positive fair value of €1 million from net investment hedges (see further details below). The total fair value of outstanding currency options relates to cash flow hedges.

The fair value adjustments of outstanding cash flow hedges for forecasted sales will be reported in the income statement when the forecasted sales transaction is recorded, the wide majority being forecasted for 2005. One cash flow hedge, which related to an embedded derivative within a specific contract, was closed out in 2004 and the remaining fair value was reallocated from equity to the income statement. Other significant embedded derivatives did not exist at the balance sheet date.

In addition, Adidas-Salomon hedges part of its net investment in Salomon & Taylor Made Co., Ltd., Tokyo (Japan) with forward contracts. A related gain of €1 million in 2004 (2003: €1.5 million) is recognized in equity.

Management of interest rate risk. It has been the policy of the Group to concentrate its financing on short-term borrowings, but to protect against liquidity risks with longer-term financing agreements, and to protect against the risk of rising interest rates with interest rate caps, cross-currency interest rate swaps, and interest rate swaps. In view of the continuing decline of the borrowings, no additional caps were arranged in 2004. Additionally, maturing interest rate caps amounting to approximately €200 million were not renewed.

The interest rate hedges which were outstanding as at December 31, 2004 and 2003, respectively expire as detailed below.

Expiration Dates of Interest Rate Hedges
(€ in millions)

	December 31 2004	December 31 2003
Within 1 year	213	204
Between 1 and 3 years	553	721
Between 3 and 5 years	--	50
Over 5 years	96	102
Total	862	1,077

In contrast to 2003, the summary above also includes, in addition to the interest rate options, the notional amount of one long-term US dollar interest rate swap in an amount of €73 million (2003: €79 million) and one long-term cross-currency swap in an amount of €23 million (2003: €23 million).

The interest rate options had a negative fair value of €3.0 million and €2.6 million as at December 31, 2004 and 2003 respectively.

The interest rate swaps and cross-currency interest rate swaps had a negative fair value of €7.4 million as at December 31, 2004 and 2003 respectively.

Several of the instruments qualify as cash flow hedges pursuant to IAS 39. The related negative change in fair value of €0.2 million was debited in equity and will be expensed according to interest rate developments in parallel to the underlying hedged item. The negative change in the fair value of the remaining instruments of €0.2 million was recorded directly in the income statement, as incurred.

Credit risk. The Group's treasury arranges currency and interest rate hedges, and invests cash, with major banks of a high credit standing throughout the world, all being rated "A-" or higher in terms of Standard & Poor's long-term ratings (or a comparable rating from other rating agencies).

Generally, foreign Group companies are authorized to work with banks rated "BBB+" or higher. In exceptional cases, they are authorized to work with banks rated lower than "BBB+." To limit risk in these cases, restrictions such as limited amounts of cash deposits with these banks are stipulated.

6 INVENTORY

PERSPECTIVE AND ISSUES

The accounting for inventories is a major consideration for many entities because of its significance on both the income statement (cost of goods sold) and the balance sheet. Inventories are defined by IAS 2 as items that are

...held for sale in the ordinary course of business; in the process of production for such sale; or in the form of materials or supplies to be consumed in the production process or in the rendering of services.

The complexity of accounting for inventories arises from several factors.

1. The high volume of activity (or turnover) in the account
2. The various cost flow alternatives that are acceptable
3. The classification of inventories

There are two types of entities for which the accounting for inventories must be considered. The merchandising entity (generally, a retailer or wholesaler) has a single inventory account, usually entitled *merchandise inventory*. These are goods on hand that are purchased for resale. The other type of entity is the manufacturer, which generally has three types of inventory: (1) raw materials, (2) work in process, and (3) finished goods. *Raw materials inventory* represents the goods purchased that will act as inputs in the production process leading to the finished product. *Work in process* (WIP) consists of the goods entered into production but not yet completed. *Finished goods inventory* is the completed product that is on hand awaiting sale.

In the case of either type of entity the same basic questions need to be resolved.

1. At what point in time should the items be included in inventory (ownership)?

2. What costs incurred should be included in the valuation of inventories?
3. What cost flow assumption should be used?
4. At what value should inventories be reported (net realizable value)?

The standard that addresses these questions is IAS 2, which has been revised several times since it was first promulgated. IAS 2 discusses the definition, valuation, and classification of inventory. Over the years, the principal objective of the IASB in making amendments to this standard has been to reduce alternatives for the measurement of the carrying value of inventories. Most recently, LIFO costing has been eliminated as an acceptable pricing method.

The international accounting standards tend to be "principles-based" (as opposed to being "rules-based"), and for that reason practical application guidance contained in IAS 2 is not as comprehensive as it is under various national GAAP, such as that in the US. The materials in the body of this chapter essentially reflect the level of guidance provided under IAS 2. To supplement this material, the Appendix to this chapter contains additional guidance from other sources (specifically, from US GAAP), which provides a basis for comparing the treatment accorded to this subject in other jurisdictions.

Under the provisions of IAS 2, before its most recent revision, the first-in, first-out (FIFO) and weighted-average cost methods were defined as "benchmark treatments" with the last-in, first-out (LIFO) method cast as the "allowed alternative treatments." Since IFRS went to some length to avoid naming certain methods as being preferred or recommended (hence the term "benchmark," which was deemed to be somewhat more neutral, although the connotation was clearly that these were to be preferred), it is fair to say that all three methods were acceptable under IAS 2, prior to its recent revision. The IASB, as part of its recent Improvements Project, determined that the goals of achieving convergence among accounting standards and of promoting uniformity across entities reporting under IFRS would be served by eliminating the formerly "allowed alternative" of costing inventories by means of the last-in, first-out (LIFO) method. This has left the first-in, first-out (FIFO) and the weighted-average methods as the only two acceptable costing techniques under IFRS.

While convergence with US GAAP is now an announced goal of IFRS, banning use of the LIFO method will complicate the achievement of this objective. Notwithstanding that LIFO rarely corresponded to the physical movement of goods (although there were exceptions, such as when new receipts of goods were placed on top of, or in front of, older stock, and thus likely to be sold before older goods), LIFO has been popular in certain jurisdictions. For example, this method has long been acceptable in the US for tax purposes, and, given the decades-long experience of rising prices, LIFO resulted in lower reportable income and therefore in lower taxes. In the US, the tax laws demand that entities using LIFO for tax purposes also do so for general-purpose financial reporting. Accordingly, the US standard setter will find it difficult or impossible to converge to revised IAS 2, unless the tax laws are also changed, which is not currently being proposed.

An interpretation (SIC 1) by the erstwhile Standing Interpretations Committee (SIC) had stated that entities should use the same cost formula for all inventories having similar nature and use. It furthermore held that mere differences in geographic location would not justify the use of different cost formulas. Revised IAS 2 has incorporated these positions into the standard, and the SIC was thus withdrawn.

Sources of IFRS
IAS 2, 18, 34, 41

DEFINITIONS OF TERMS

Absorption (full) costing. Inclusion of all manufacturing costs (fixed and variable) in the cost of finished goods inventory.

By-products. Goods that result as an ancillary product from the production of a primary good; often having minor value when compared to the value of the principal product(s).

Consignments. Marketing method in which the consignor ships goods to the consignee, who acts as an agent for the consignor in selling the goods. The inventory remains the property of the consignor until sold by the consignee.

Direct (variable) costing. Inclusion of only variable manufacturing costs in the cost of ending finished goods inventory. While often used for management (internal) reporting, this method is not deemed acceptable for financial reporting purposes.

Finished goods. Completed but unsold products produced by a manufacturing firm.

First-in, first-out (FIFO). Cost flow assumption; the first goods purchased or produced are assumed to be the first goods sold.

Goods in transit. Goods being shipped from seller to buyer at year-end.

Gross profit method. Method used to estimate the amount of ending inventory based on the cost of goods available for sale, sales, and the gross profit percentage.

Inventory. Assets held for sale in the normal course of business, or which are in the process of production for such sale, or are in the form of materials or supplies to be consumed in the production process or in the rendering of services.

Joint products. Two or more products produced jointly, where neither is viewed as being more important; in some cases additional production steps are applied to one or more joint products after a split-off point.

Last-in, first-out (LIFO). Cost flow assumption; the last goods purchased are assumed to be the first goods sold.

Lower of cost and net realizable value. Inventories must be valued at lower of cost or realizable value.

Markdown. Decrease below original retail price. A markdown cancellation is an increase (not above original retail price) in retail price after a markdown.

Markup. Increase above original retail price. A markup cancellation is a decrease (not below original retail price) in retail price after a markup.

Net realizable value. Estimated selling price in the ordinary course of business less the estimated costs of completion and the estimated costs necessary to make the sale.

Periodic. Inventory system where quantities are determined only periodically by physical count.

Perpetual. Inventory system where up-to-date records of inventory quantities are kept.

Product financing arrangements. Arrangements whereby an entity buys inventory for another firm that agrees to purchase the inventory over a certain period at specified prices which include handling and financing costs; alternatively, an entity can buy inventory from another firm with the understanding that the seller will repurchase the goods at the original price plus defined storage and financing costs.

Raw materials. For a manufacturing firm, materials on hand awaiting entry into the production process.

Replacement cost. Cost to reproduce an inventory item by purchase or manufacture. In lower of cost or market computations, the term *market* means replacement cost, subject to the ceiling and floor limitations.

Retail method. Inventory costing method that uses a cost ratio to reduce ending inventory (valued at retail) to cost.

Specific identification. Inventory system where the seller identifies which specific items are sold and which remain in ending inventory.

Standard costs. Predetermined unit costs, which are acceptable for financial reporting purposes if adjusted periodically to reflect current conditions. While useful for management (internal) reporting under some conditions, this is not an acceptable costing method for financial statements presented in accordance with IFRS.

Weighted-average. Periodic inventory costing method where ending inventory and cost of goods sold are priced at the weighted-average cost of all items available for sale.

Work in process. For a manufacturing firm, the inventory of partially completed products.

CONCEPTS, RULES, AND EXAMPLES

Basic Concept of Inventory Costing

IFRS (IAS 2) established that the lower of cost and net realizable value should be the basis for the valuation of inventories. In contrast to IFRS dealing with property, plant, and equipment (IAS 36) or investment property (IAS 40), there is no option for revaluing inventories to current replacement cost or fair value, presumably due to the far shorter period of time over which such assets are held, thereby limiting the cumulative impact of inflation or other economic factors on reported amounts.

The cost of inventories of items that are ordinarily interchangeable, and goods or services produced and segregated for specific projects, are generally assigned carrying values by using the specific identification method. For most goods, however, specific identification is not a practical alternative. In cases where there are a large number of items of inventory and where the turnover is rapid, the extant standard prescribes two more useful methods of pricing inventories, namely the first-in, first-out (FIFO) method and the weighted-average method. A third alternative formerly endorsed by IFRS, the LIFO costing method, has now been designated as being unacceptable.

FIFO and weighted-average cost are now the only acceptable cost flow assumptions under IFRS. Either method can be used to assign cost of inventories, but once selected an entity must apply that cost flow assumption consistently (unless the change to the other method can be justified under the criteria set forth by IAS 8). Furthermore, an entity is constrained from applying different cost formulas to inventories having similar nature and use to the entity. On the other hand, for inventories having different natures or uses, different cost formulas may be justified. Mere difference in location, however, cannot be used to justify applying different costing methods to otherwise similar inventories.

Ownership of Goods

Inventory can only be an asset of the reporting entity if it is an economic resource of the entity at the balance sheet date. In general, an enterprise should record purchases and sales of inventory when legal title passes. Although strict adherence to this rule may not appear to be important in daily transactions, a proper inventory cutoff at the end of an accounting period is crucial for the correct determination of periodic results of operations. Thus, for accounting purposes, to obtain an accurate measurement of inventory quantity and corresponding monetary representation of inventory and cost of goods sold in the financial statements, it is necessary to determine when title has passed.

The most common error made in this regard is to assume that title is synonymous with possession of goods on hand. This may be incorrect in two ways: (1) the goods on hand may not be owned, and (2) goods that are not on hand may be owned. There are four matters that may cause confusion about proper ownership: (1) goods in transit, (2) consignment sales, (3) product financing arrangements, and (4) sales made with the buyer having generous or unusual right of return.

Goods in transit. At year-end, any *goods in transit* from seller to buyer may properly be includable in one, and only one, of those parties' inventories, based on the terms and conditions of the sale. Under traditional legal and accounting interpretation, goods are included in the inventory of the firm financially responsible for transportation costs. This responsibility may be indicated by shipping terms such as FOB, which is used in overland shipping contracts, and by FAS, CIF, C&F, and ex-ship, which are used in maritime contracts.

The term *FOB* stands for "free on board." If goods are shipped FOB destination, transportation costs are paid by the seller and title does not pass until the carrier delivers the goods to the buyer; thus these goods are part of the seller's inventory while in transit. If goods are shipped FOB shipping point, transportation costs are paid by the buyer and title passes when the carrier takes possession; thus these goods are part of the buyer's inventory while in transit. The terms *FOB destination* and *FOB shipping point* often indicate a specific location at which title to the goods is transferred, such as FOB Milan. This means that the seller retains title and risk of loss until the goods are delivered to a common carrier in Milan who will act as an agent for the buyer.

A seller who ships *FAS* (free alongside) must bear all expense and risk involved in delivering the goods to the dock next to (alongside) the vessel on which they are to be shipped. The buyer bears the cost of loading and of shipment; thus title passes when the carrier takes possession of the goods.

In a *CIF* (cost, insurance, and freight) contract the buyer agrees to pay in a lump sum the cost of the goods, insurance costs, and freight charges. In a C&F contract, the buyer promises to pay a lump sum that includes the cost of the goods and all freight charges. In either case, the seller must deliver the goods to the carrier and pay the costs of loading; thus both title and risk of loss pass to the buyer upon delivery of the goods to the carrier.

A seller who delivers goods *ex-ship* bears all expense and risk until the goods are unloaded, at which time both title and risk of loss pass to the buyer.

The foregoing is meant only to define normal terms and usage; actual contractual arrangements between a given buyer and a given seller can vary widely. The accounting treatment should in all cases strive to mirror the substance of the legal terms established between the parties.

Examples of accounting for goods in transit

The Vartan Gyroscope Company is located in Veracruz, Mexico, and obtains precision jeweled bearings from a supplier in Switzerland. The standard delivery terms are free alongside (FAS) a container ship in the harbor in Nice, France, so that Vartan takes legal title to the delivery once possession of the goods is taken by the carrier's dockside employees for the purpose of loading the goods on board the ship. When the supplier delivers goods with an invoiced value of $1,200,000 ($= Mexican pesos) to the wharf, it e-mails an advance shipping notice (ASN) and invoice to Vartan via an electronic data interchange (EDI) transaction, itemizing the contents of the delivery. Vartan's computer system receives the EDI transmission, notes the FAS terms in the supplier file, and therefore automatically logs it into the company computer system with the following entry:

Inventory	1,200,000	
Accounts payable		1,200,000

The goods are assigned an "In Transit" location code in Vartan's perpetual inventory system. When the precision jeweled bearings delivery eventually arrives at Vartan's receiving dock, the receiving staff records a change in inventory location code from "In Transit" to a code designating a physical location within the warehouse.

Vartan's secondary precision jeweled bearings supplier is located in Vancouver, British Columbia, and ships overland using free on board (FOB) Veracruz terms, so the supplier retains title until the shipment arrives at Vartan's location. This supplier also issues an advance shipping notice by EDI to inform Vartan of the estimated arrival date, but in this case Vartan's computer system notes the FOB Veracruz terms, and makes no entry to record the transaction until the goods arrive at Vartan's receiving dock.

Consignment sales. There are specifically defined situations where the party holding the goods is doing so as an agent for the true owner. In *consignments,* the consignor (seller) ships goods to the consignee (buyer), which acts as the agent of the consignor in trying to sell the goods. In some consignments, the consignee receives a commission; in other arrangements, the consignee "purchases" the goods simultaneously with the sale of the goods to the final customer. Goods out on consignment are properly included in the inventory of the consignor and excluded from the inventory of the consignee. Disclosure may be required of the consignee, however, since common financial analytical inferences, such as days' sales in inventory or inventory turnover, may appear distorted unless the financial statement users are informed. However, IFRS does not explicitly address this.

Example of a consignment arrangement

The Random Gadget Company ships a consignment of its wireless media control devices to a retail outlet of the Consumer Products Corporation. Random Gadget's cost of the consigned goods is €3,700, Random Gadget shifts the inventory cost into a separate inventory account to track the physical location of the goods. The entry follows:

Consignment out inventory	3,700	
Finished goods inventory		3,700

A third-party shipping company ships the cordless phone inventory from Random Gadget to Consumer Products. Upon receipt of an invoice for this €550 shipping expense, Random Gadget charges the cost to consignment inventory with the following entry:

Consignment out inventory	550	
Accounts payable		550

To record the cost of shipping goods from the factory to Consumer Products Corporation

Consumer Products sells half the consigned inventory during the month for €2,750 in credit card payments, and earns a 22% commission on these sales, totaling €605. According to the consignment arrangement, Random Gadget must also reimburse Consumer Products for the 2% credit card processing fee, which is €55 (€2,750 × 2%). The results of this sale are summarized as follows:

Sales price to Consumer Product's customer earned on behalf of Random Gadget		€2,750
Less: Amounts due to Consumer Product in accordance with arrangement		
22% sales commission		605
Reimbursement for credit card processing fee		55
		660
Due to Random Gadget		€2,090

Upon receipt of the monthly sales report from Consumer Products, Random Gadget records the following entries:

Accounts receivable	2,090	
Cost of goods sold	55	
Commission expense	605	
Sales		2,750

To record the sale made by Consumer Product acting as agent of Random Gadget, the commission earned by Consumer Product and the credit card fee reimbursement earned by Consumer Product in connection with the sale

| Cost of goods sold | 2,125 | |
| Consignment out inventory | | 2,125 |

To transfer the related inventory cost to cost of goods sold, including half the original inventory cost and half the cost of the shipment to Consumer Product [(€3,700 + €550= €4,250) × ½ =€2,125]

Product financing arrangements. A *product financing arrangement* is a transaction in which an entity sells and agrees to repurchase inventory with the repurchase price equal to the original sales price plus the carrying and financing costs. The purpose of this transaction is to allow the seller (sponsor) to arrange financing of its original purchase of the inventory. As such, this is an alternative to other common methods of financing, such as secured working capital loans, where the ownership does not change but the lender places a lien on the inventory, which may be seized for nonpayment of the debt. The substance of a product financing transaction is illustrated by the diagram below.

1. In the initial transaction the sponsor "sells" inventoriable items to the financing entity in return for the remittance of the sales price and at the same time agrees to repurchase the inventory at a specified price (usually the sales price plus carrying and financing costs) over a specified period of time.
2. The financing entity procures the funds remitted to the sponsor by borrowing from a bank (or other financial institution) using the newly purchased inventory as collateral.
3. The financing entity actually remits the funds to the sponsor and the sponsor presumably uses these funds to pay off the debt incurred as a result of the original purchase of the inventoriable debt.
4. The sponsor then repurchases the inventory for the specified price plus costs from the financing entity at a later time when the funds are available.

In a variant of this transaction, an entity can acquire goods from a manufacturer or dealer, with the contractual understanding that they will be resold to another entity at the same price plus handling, storage, and financing costs.

The purpose of either variation of product financing arrangement is to enable the sponsor to acquire or control inventory without incurring additional reportable debt. Transactions of this type are addressed fleetingly under IAS 18, which does note that a separate agreement to repurchase may negate the effect of a sale transaction. In effect, the substance of this type of transaction is that of a borrowing.

Under the pertinent US standard (FAS 49, *Accounting for Product Financing Arrangements*), such transactions are, in substance, no different from those where a sponsor obtains third-party financing to purchase its inventory. As a result, the FASB ruled that when an entity sells inventory with a related arrangement to repurchase it, proper accounting is to record a liability when the funds are received for the initial transfer of the inventory in the amount of the selling price. The sponsor is then to accrue carrying and financing costs in accordance with its normal accounting policies. These accruals are eliminated and the liability satisfied when the sponsor repurchases the inventory. The inventory is not to be taken off the balance sheet of the sponsor and a sale is not to be recorded. Thus, although legal title has passed to the financing entity, for purposes of measuring and valuing inventory, the inventory is considered to be owned by the sponsor. Although the other variation on this financing arrangement with a nominee entity acquiring the goods for the ultimate purchaser is not addressed in FAS 49, logic suggests that an analogous accounting treatment be prescribed.

Example of a product financing arrangement

The Mechanical Innovations Company has borrowed the maximum amount it has available under its short-term line of credit. Mechanical Innovations obtains additional financing by selling €280,000 of its product inventory to a third-party financing entity. The third party obtains a bank loan at 6% interest to pay for its purchase of the product inventory, while charging Mechanical Innovations 8% interest and €1,500 per month to store the product inventory at a public storage facility. As Mechanical Innovations obtains product orders, it purchases inventory back from the third party, which in turn authorizes the public warehouse to drop ship the orders directly to Mechanical Innovations' customers at a cost of €35 per order. Since this is a product financing arrangement, Mechanical Innovations cannot remove the product inventory from its accounting records or record revenue for sale of its inventory to the third party. Instead, the following entry records the initial financing arrangement:

Cash	280,000	
Short-term debt		280,000

After one month, Mechanical Innovations records accrued interest of €1,867 (€280,000 × 8% interest × 1/12 year) on the loan, as well as the monthly storage fee of €1,500, as shown in the following entry:

Interest expense	1,867	
Storage expense	1,500	
Accrued interest		1,867
Accounts payable		1,500

On the first day of the succeeding month, Mechanical Innovations receives a prepaid customer order for €3,800. The margin on the order is 40%, and therefore the related inventory cost is €2,280, Mechanical Innovations pays the third party €2,280 to buy back the required inventory as well as €35 to the public storage facility to ship the order to the customer, and records the following entries:

Short-term debt	2,280	
Cash		2,280
To repurchase inventory from the third-party financing entity		

Cash	3,800	
Sales		3,800
To record the sale to the customer		

Cost of goods sold	2,280	
Inventory		2,280
To record the cost of the sale to the customer		

Freight out	35	
Accounts payable		35
To record the cost of fulfilling the order		

Right to return purchases. A related inventory accounting issue that requires special consideration is the situation that exists when the buyer holds the right to return the merchandise acquired. This is not meant to address the normal sales terms found throughout commercial transactions (e.g., where the buyer can return goods, whether found to be defective or not, within a short time after delivery, such as five days). Rather, this connotes situations where the return privileges are well in excess of standard practice, so as to place doubt on the veracity of the purported sale transaction itself.

IAS 18 notes that when the buyer has the right to rescind the transaction under defined conditions and the seller cannot, with reasonable confidence, estimate the likelihood of this occurrence, the retention of significant risks of ownership makes this transaction not a sale. Again, US GAAP usefully elaborates on this situation (FAS 48, *Revenue Recognition When Right of Return Exits*), and may provide additional insight. Under both standards the sale is to be recorded if the future amount of the returns can reasonably be estimated. If the ability to make a reasonable estimate is precluded, the sale is not to be recorded until further returns are unlikely. Although legal title has passed to the buyer, the seller must continue to include the goods in its measurement and valuation of inventory.

In some situations, a "side agreement" may grant the nominal customer greatly expanded or even unlimited return privileges, when the formal sales documents (bill of sale, bill of lading, etc.) make no such reference. These situations would be highly suggestive of financial reporting irregularities, in an apparent attempt to overstate revenues in the current period (and risk reporting high levels of sales returns in the following period, if customers do indeed avail themselves of the generous terms). In such circumstances, these sales should in all likelihood not be recognized, and the goods nominally sold should be returned to the reporting entity's inventories.

Accounting for Inventories

Introduction. The major objectives of accounting for inventories are the matching of appropriate costs against revenues in order to arrive at the proper determination of periodic income, and the accurate representation of inventories on hand as assets of the reporting entity as of the balance sheet date. As it happens, these two goals are in conflict and, under any system of accounting in which the financial statements are fully articulated (i.e., where the balance sheet and income statement are linked together mechanically), it will be virtually impossible to achieve both fully.

The accounting for inventories is done under either a periodic or a perpetual system. In a *periodic inventory system,* the inventory quantity is determined periodically by a physical count. The quantity so determined is then priced in accordance with the cost method used. Cost of goods sold is computed by adding beginning inventory and net purchases (or cost of goods manufactured) and subtracting ending inventory.

Alternatively, a *perpetual inventory system* keeps a running total of the quantity (and possibly the cost) of inventory on hand by recording all sales and purchases as they occur. When inventory is purchased, the inventory account (rather than purchases) is debited. When inventory is sold, the cost of goods sold and reduction of inventory are recorded. Periodic physical counts are necessary only to verify the perpetual records and to satisfy the tax regulations (tax regulations require that a physical inventory be taken, at least annually).

Valuation of Inventories

According to IAS 2, the primary basis of accounting for inventories is cost. *Cost* is defined as the sum of all costs of purchase, costs of conversion, and other costs incurred in bringing the inventories to their present location and condition. This definition allows for significant interpretation of the costs to be included in inventory.

For raw materials and merchandise inventory that are purchased outright and not intended for further conversion, the identification of cost is relatively straightforward. The cost of these purchased inventories will include all expenditures incurred in bringing the goods to the point of sale and putting them in a salable condition. These costs include the purchase price, transportation costs, insurance, and handling costs. Trade discounts, rebates, and other such items are to be deducted in determining inventory costs; failure to do so would result in carrying inventory at amounts in excess of true historical costs.

The impact of interest costs as they relate to the valuation of inventoriable items (IAS 23) is discussed in Chapter 8. In general, even when the allowed alternative treatment prescribed by IAS 23 is employed, borrowing costs will not be capitalized in connection with inventory acquisitions, since the period required to ready the goods for sale will not be significant. However, where a lengthy production process is required to prepare the goods for sale, the provisions of IAS 23 would be applicable and a portion of borrowing costs would become part of the cost of inventory.

Conversion costs for manufactured goods should include all costs that are directly associated with the units produced, such as labor and overhead. The allocation of overhead costs, however, must be systematic and rational, and in the case of fixed overhead costs (i.e., those which do not vary directly with level of production) the allocation process should be based on normal production levels. In periods of unusually low levels of production, a portion of fixed overhead costs must accordingly be charged directly to operations, and not taken into inventory.

Costs other than material and conversion costs are inventoriable only to the extent they are necessary to bring the goods to their present condition and location. Examples might include certain design costs and other types of preproduction expenditures if intended to benefit specific classes of customers. On the other hand, all research costs and most development costs (per IAS 38, as discussed in Chapter 8) would typically *not* become part of inventory costs. Also generally excluded from inventory would be such costs as administrative and selling expenses, which must be treated as period costs; the cost of wasted materials, labor, or other production expenditures; and most storage costs. Included in overhead, and thus allocable to inventory, would be such categories as repairs, maintenance, utilities, rent, indirect labor, production supervisory wages, indirect materials and supplies, quality control and inspection, and the cost of small tools not capitalized.

Example of recording raw material or component parts cost

Accurate Laser-Guided Farm Implements, Inc. purchases lasers, a component that it uses in manufacturing its signature product. The company typically receives delivery of all its component parts and uses them in manufacturing its finished products during the fall and early winter, and then sells its stock of finished goods in the late winter and spring. The supplier invoice for a January delivery of lasers includes the following line items:

Lasers	€5,043
Shipping and handling	125
Shipping insurance	48
Sales tax	193
Total	€5,409

Since Accurate is using the lasers as components in a product that it resells, it will not pay the sales tax. However, both the shipping and handling charge and the shipping insurance are required for ongoing product acquisition, and so are included in the following entry to record receipt of the goods:

Inventory—components	5,216	
Accounts payable		5,216

To record purchase of lasers and related costs (€5,043 +€125 + €48)

On February 1, Accurate purchases a €5,000, two-month shipping insurance (known as "inland marine") policy that applies to all incoming supplier deliveries for the remainder of the winter production season, allowing it to refuse shipping insurance charges on individual deliveries. Since the policy insures all inbound components deliveries (not just lasers) it is too time-consuming to charge the cost of this policy to individual components deliveries using specific identification, the controller can estimate a flat charge per delivery based on the number of expected deliveries during the two-month term of the insurance policy as follows:

€5,000 insurance premium ÷ 200 expected deliveries during the policy term = €25 per delivery and then charge each delivery with €25 as follows:

Inventory—components	25	
Prepaid insurance		25

To allocate cost of inland marine coverage to inbound insured components shipments

In this case, however, the controller determined that shipments are expected to occur evenly during the two-month policy period and therefore will simply make a monthly standard journal entry as follows:

Inventory—components	2,500	
Prepaid insurance		2,500

To amortize premium on inland marine policy using the straight-line method

Note that the controller must be careful, under either scenario, to ensure that perpetual inventory records appropriately track unit costs of components to include the cost of shipping insurance. Failure to do so would result in an understatement of the cost of raw materials inventory on hand at the end of any accounting period.

Joint products and by-products. In some production processes, more than one product is produced simultaneously. Typically, if each product has significant value, they are referred to as *joint products*; if only one has substantial value, the others are known as *by-products*. Under IAS 2, when the costs of each jointly produced good cannot be clearly determined, a rational allocation among them is required. Generally, such allocation is made by reference to the relative values of the jointly produced goods, as measured by ultimate selling prices. Often, after a period of joint production the goods are split off, separately incurring additional costs before being completed and ready for sale. The allocation of joint costs should take into account the additional individual product costs yet to be incurred after the point at which joint production ceases.

By-products by definition are products that have limited value when measured with reference to the primary good being produced. IAS 2 suggests that by-products be valued at net realizable value, with the costs allocated to by-products thereby being deducted from the cost pool, being otherwise allocated to the sole or several principal products.

For example, products A and B have the same processes performed on them up to the split-off point. The total cost incurred to this point is €80,000. This cost can be assigned to products A and B using their relative sales value at the split-off point. If A could be sold for €60,000 and B for €40,000, the total sales value is €100,000. The cost would be assigned on the basis of each product's relative sales value. Thus, A would be assigned a cost of €48,000 (60,000/100,000 x 80,000) and B a cost of €32,000 (400,000/100,000 x 80,000).

If inventory is exchanged with another entity for similar goods, the earnings process is generally not culminated. Accordingly, the acquired items are recorded at the recorded, or book, value of the items given up.

In some jurisdictions, the categories of costs that are includable in inventory for tax purposes may differ from those that are permitted for financial reporting purposes under international accounting standards. To the extent that differential tax and financial reporting is possible (i.e., that there is no statutory requirement that the taxation rules constrain financial reporting) this situation will result in interperiod tax allocation. This is discussed more fully in Chapter 15.

Direct costing. The generally accepted method of allocating fixed overhead to both ending inventory and cost of goods sold is commonly known as *(full) absorption costing.* IAS 2 requires that absorption costing be employed. However, often for managerial decision-making purposes an alternative to absorption costing, known as *variable or direct costing,* is utilized. Direct costing requires classifying only direct materials, direct labor, and variable overhead related to production as inventory costs. All fixed costs are accounted for as period costs. The virtue of direct costing is that under this accounting strategy there will be a predictable, linear effect on marginal contribution from each unit of sales revenue, which can be useful in planning and controlling the business operation. However, such a costing method does not result in inventory that includes all costs of production, and therefore this is deemed not to be in accordance with IFRS on inventories (IAS 2). If an entity uses direct costing for internal budgeting or other purposes, adjustments must be made to develop alternative information for financial reporting purposes.

Differences in inventory costing between IFRS and tax requirements. In certain tax jurisdictions, there may be requirements to include or exclude certain overhead cost elements which are handled differently under IFRS for financial reporting purposes. For example, in the US the tax code requires elements of overhead to be allocated to inventory, while US GAAP (consistent with IFRS) demand that these be expensed currently as period costs. Since tax laws do not dictate GAAP or IFRS, the appropriate response to such a circumstance is to treat these as temporary differences, which will create the need for interperiod income tax allocation under IAS 12. Deferred tax accounting is fully discussed in Chapter 15.

METHODS OF INVENTORY COSTING UNDER IAS 2

Specific Identification

The theoretical basis for valuing inventories and cost of goods sold requires assigning the production and/or acquisition costs to the specific goods to which they relate. For example, the cost of ending inventory for an entity in its first year, during which it produced ten items (e.g., exclusive single family homes), might be the actual production cost of the first, sixth, and eighth unit produced if those are the actual units still on hand at the balance sheet date. The costs of the other homes would be included in that year's income statement as cost of goods sold. This method of inventory valuation is usually referred to as *specific identification.*

Specific identification is generally not a practical technique, as the product will generally lose its separate identity as it passes through the production and sales process. Exceptions to this would generally be limited to those situations where there are small inventory quantities, typically having high unit value and a low turnover rate. Under IAS 2, specific identification must be employed to cost inventories that are not ordinarily interchangeable, and goods and services produced and segregated for specific projects. For inventories meeting either of these criteria, the specific identification method is mandatory and alternative methods cannot be used.

Because of the limited applicability of specific identification, it is more likely to be the case that certain assumptions regarding the cost flows associated with inventory will need to be made. One of accounting's peculiarities is that these cost flows may or may not reflect the physical flow of inventory. Over the years, much attention has been given to both the flow of physical goods and the assumed flow of costs associated with those goods. In most jurisdictions, it has long been recognized that the flow of costs need not mirror the actual flow of the goods with which those costs are associated. For example, a key provision in an early US accounting standard stated that

> *...cost for inventory purposes shall be determined under any one of several assumptions as to the flow of cost factors; the major objective in selecting a method should be to choose the one which, under the circumstances, most clearly reflects periodic income.*

Under the current IFRS on inventories, revised IAS 2, there are two acceptable cost flow assumptions. These are: (1) first-in, first-out (FIFO) method and (2) the weighted-average method. There are variations of each of these cost flow assumptions that are sometimes used in practice, but if an entity presents its financial statements under IFRS it has to be careful not to apply a variant of these cost flow assumptions that would represent a deviation from the requirements of IAS 2. Furthermore, in certain jurisdictions, other costing methods, such as the last-in, first-out (LIFO) method and the base stock method, continue to be permitted. The LIFO method was an allowed alternative method of costing inventories under IAS 2 until its most recent revision, in 2003 (effective 2005), at which time it was banned. Certain important jurisdictions such as the US still allow the use of the LIFO method, and since use of LIFO for tax purposes necessitates use for financial reporting, the elimination of LIFO in the US is a controversial topic and may hinder full convergence with IFRS.

Given that LIFO is no longer permitted under IFRS, coverage of that costing method has been eliminated from this edition. Those needing guidance on LIFO costing methods should refer to the Appendix to Chapter 6 of the 2005 edition.

First-In, First-Out (FIFO)

The FIFO method of inventory valuation assumes that the first goods purchased will be the first goods to be used or sold, regardless of the actual physical flow. This method is thought to parallel most closely the physical flow of the units for most industries having moderate to rapid turnover of goods. The strength of this cost flow assumption lies in the inventory amount reported on the balance sheet. Because the earliest goods purchased are the first ones removed from the inventory account, the remaining balance is composed of items acquired closer to period end, at more recent costs. This yields results similar to those obtained under current cost accounting on the balance sheet, and helps in achieving the goal of reporting assets at amounts approximating current values.

However, the FIFO method does not necessarily reflect the most accurate or decision-relevant income figure when viewed from the perspective of underlying economic performance, as older historical costs are being matched against current revenues. Depending on the rate of inventory turnover and the speed with which general and specific prices are changing, this mismatching could potentially have a material distorting effect on reported income. At the extreme, if reported earnings are fully distributed to owners as dividends, the enterprise could be left without sufficient resources to replenish its inventory stocks due to the impact of changing prices. (This problem is not limited to inventory costing; depreciation based on old costs of plant assets also may understate the true economic cost of capital asset consumption, and serve to support dividend distributions that leave the entity unable to replace plant assets at current prices.)

The following example illustrates the basic principles involved in the application of FIFO:

	Units available	Units sold	Actual unit cost	Actual total cost
Beginning inventory	100	--	€2.10	€210
Sale	--	75	--	--
Purchase	150	--	2.80	420
Sale	--	100	--	--
Purchase	50	--	3.00	150
Total	300	175		$780

Given these data, the cost of goods sold and the ending inventory balance are determined as follows:

	Units	Unit cost	Total cost
Cost of goods sold	100	$2.10	€210
	75	2.80	210
	175		€420

	Units	*Unit cost*	*Total cost*
Ending inventory	50	3.00	$150
	75	2.80	210
	125		€360

Notice that the total of the units in cost of goods sold and ending inventory, as well as the sum of their total costs, is equal to the goods available for sale and their respective total costs.

The unique characteristic of the FIFO method is that it provides the same results under either the periodic or perpetual system. This will not be the case for any other costing method.

Weighted-Average Cost

The other acceptable method of inventory valuation under revised IAS 2 involves averaging and is commonly referred to as the weighted-average cost method. The cost of goods available for sale (beginning inventory and net purchases) is divided by the units available for sale to obtain a weighted-average unit cost. Ending inventory and cost of goods sold are then priced at this average cost. For example, assume the following data:

	Units available	*Units sold*	*Actual unit cost*	*Actual total cost*
Beginning inventory	100	--	€2.10	€210
Sale	--	75	--	--
Purchase	150	--	2.80	420
Sale	--	100	--	--
Purchase	50	--	3.00	150
Total	300	175		€780

The weighted-average cost is €780/300, or €2.60. Ending inventory is 125 units at €2.60, or €325; cost of goods sold is 175 units at €2.60, or €455.

When the weighted-average assumption is applied to a perpetual inventory system, the average cost is recomputed after each purchase. This process is referred to as a moving average. Sales are costed at the most recent average. This combination is called the moving average method and is applied below to the same data used in the weighted-average example above.

	Units on hand	*Purchases in euros*	*Sales in euros*	*Total cost*	*Inventory unit cost*
Beginning inventory	100	€ --	€ --	€210.00	€2.10
Sale (75 units @ $2.10)	25	--	157.50	52.50	2.10
Purchase (150 units, $420)	175	420.00	--	472.50	2.70
Sale (100 units @ $2.70)	75	--	270.00	202.50	2.70
Purchase (50 units, $150)	125	150.00	--	352.50	2.82

Cost of goods sold is 75 units at €2.10 and 100 units at €2.70, or a total of €427.50.

Net Realizable Value

As stated in IAS 2

Net realizable value is the estimated selling price in the ordinary course of business less the estimated costs of completion and the estimated costs necessary to make the sale.

The utility of an item of inventory is limited to the amount to be realized from its ultimate sale; where the item's recorded cost exceeds this amount, IFRS requires that a loss be recognized for the difference. The logic for this requirement is twofold: first, assets (in particular, current assets such as inventory) should not be reported at amounts that exceed net realizable value; and second, any decline in value in a period should be reported in that period's results of operations in order to achieve proper matching with current period's revenues. Were the inventory to be carried forward at an amount in excess of net realizable value, the loss would be recognized on the ultimate sale in a subsequent period. This would mean that a loss incurred in one period, when the value decline occurred, would have been deferred to a different period, which would clearly be inconsistent with several key accounting concepts, including conservatism.

Revised IAS 2 states that estimates of net realizable value should be applied on an item-by-item basis in most instances, although it makes an exception for those situations where there are groups of related products or similar items that can be properly valued in the aggregate. As a general principle, item-by-item comparisons of cost to net realizable value are required, lest unrealized "gains" on some items (i.e., where the net realizable values exceed historical costs) offset the unrealized losses on other items, thereby reducing the net loss to be recognized. Since recognition of unrealized gains in earnings is generally proscribed under GAAP, evaluation of inventory declines on a grouped basis would be an indirect or "backdoor" mechanism to recognize gains that should not be given such recognition. Accordingly, the basic requirement is to apply the net realizable value tests on an individual item basis.

Recoveries of previously recognized losses. IAS 2 stipulates that a new assessment of net realizable value should be made in each subsequent period; when the reason for a previous write-down no longer exists (i.e., when net realizable value has improved), it should be reversed. Since the write-down was taken into income, the reversal should also be reflected in earnings. As under prior rules, the amount to be restored to the carrying value will be limited to the amount of the previous impairment recognized. (Note that, under parallel requirements imposed by some national GAAP, such as that in the US, once inventory is written down to a lower amount of net realizable value, it cannot be restored to original cost even if conditions change in later reporting periods.)

Other Valuation Methods

There are instances in which an accountant must estimate the value of inventories. Whether for interim financial statements or as a check against perpetual records, the need for an inventory valuation without an actual physical count is required. Some of the methods used, which are discussed below, are the retail method and the gross profit method.

Retail method. IAS 2 notes that the retail method may be used by certain industry groups but does not provide details on how to employ this method, nor does it address the many variations of the technique. The conventional retail method is used by retailers as a method to estimate the cost of their ending inventory. The retailer can either take a physical inventory at retail prices or estimate ending retail inventory and then use the cost-to-retail ratio derived under this method to convert the ending inventory at retail to its estimated cost. This eliminates the process of going back to original invoices or other documents to determine the original cost for each inventoriable item. The retail method can be used under either of the two cost flow assumptions discussed earlier: FIFO or average cost. As with ordinary FIFO or average cost, the LCM rule can also be applied to the retail method when either one of these two cost assumptions is used.

The key to applying the retail method is determining the cost-to-retail ratio. The calculation of this number varies depending on the cost flow assumption selected. Essentially, the cost-to-retail ratio provides a relationship between the cost of goods available for sale and the retail price of these goods. This ratio is used to convert the ending retail inventory back to cost. Computation of the cost-to-retail ratio for each of the available methods is described below.

1. **FIFO cost**—The concept of FIFO indicates that the ending inventory is made up of the latest purchases; therefore, beginning inventory is excluded from computation of

the cost-to-retail ratio, and the computation becomes net purchases divided by their retail value adjusted for both net markups and net markdowns.

2. **FIFO (using a lower of cost or net realizable approach)**—The computation is basically the same as FIFO cost except that markdowns are excluded from the computation of the cost-to-retail ratio.

3. **Average cost**—Average cost assumes that ending inventory consists of all goods available for sale. Therefore, the cost-to-retail ratio is computed by dividing the cost of goods available for sale (Beginning inventory + Net purchases) by the retail value of these goods adjusted for both net markups and net markdowns.

4. **Average cost (using a lower of cost or net realizable approach)**—This is computed in the same manner as average cost except that markdowns are excluded for the calculation of the cost-to-retail ratio.

A simple example illustrates the computation of the cost-to-retail ratio under both the FIFO cost and average cost methods in a situation where no markups or markdowns exist.

	FIFO cost		*Average cost*	
	Cost	*Retail*	*Cost*	*Retail*
Beginning inventory	€100,000	€ 200,000	€100,000	€ 200,000
Net purchases	500,000	800,000	500,000	800,000
Total goods available for sale	€600,000	1,000,000	€600,000	1,000,000
Sales at retail		(800,000)		(800,000)
Ending inventory at retail		€ 200,000		€ 200,000

Cost-to-retail ratio	$\dfrac{500,000}{800,000}$ = 62.5%		$\dfrac{600,000}{1,000,000}$ = 60%	

Ending inventory at cost
200,000 x 0.625   € 125,000
200,000 x 0.60   € 120,000

Note that the only difference in the two examples is the numbers used to calculate the cost-to-retail ratio.

As shown above, the lower of cost or market aspect of the retail method is a result of the treatment of net markups and net markdowns. *Net markups* (defined as markups less markup cancellations) are net increases above the original retail price, which are generally caused by changes in supply and demand. *Net markdowns* (markdowns less markdown cancellations) are net decreases below the original retail price. An approximation of lower of cost or market is achieved by including net markups but excluding net markdowns from the cost-to-retail ratio.

To understand this approximation, assume that a toy is purchased for €6 and the retail price is set at €10. It is later marked down to €8. A cost-to-retail ratio including markdowns would be €6 divided by €8 or 75%, and ending inventory would be valued at €8 times 75%, or €6 (original cost). A cost-to-retail ratio excluding markdowns would be €6 divided by €10 or 60%, and ending inventory would be valued at €8 times 60%, or €4.80 (on a lower of cost or market basis). The write-down to €4.80 reflects the loss in utility that is evidenced by the reduced retail price.

The application of the lower of cost or market rule is illustrated for both the FIFO and average cost methods in the example below. Remember, if the markups and markdowns below had been included in the preceding example, *both* would have been included in the cost-to-retail ratio.

	FIFO cost (LCM)		Average cost (LCM)	
	Cost	*Retail*	*Cost*	*Retail*
Beginning inventory	€100,000	€ 200,000	€100,000	€ 200,000
Net purchases	500,000	800,000	500,000	800,000
Net markups	--	250,000	--	250,000
Total goods available for sale	€600,000	1,250,000	€600,000	1,250,000
Net markdowns		(50,000)		(50,000)
Sales at retail		(800,000)		(800,000)
Ending inventory at retail		€ 400,000		€ 400,000

Cost-to-retail ratio	$\frac{500,000}{1,050,000}$ =	47.6%	$\frac{600,000}{1,250,000}$ =	48%

Ending inventory at cost
400,000 x 0.476   € 190,400
400,000 x 0.48   € 192,000

Notice that under the FIFO (LCM) method all of the markups are considered attributable to the current period purchases. Although this is not necessarily accurate, it provides the most conservative estimate of the ending inventory.

There are a number of additional inventory topics and issues that affect the computation of the cost-to-retail ratio and, therefore, deserve some discussion. Purchase discounts and freight affect only the cost column in this computation. The sales figure that is subtracted from the adjusted cost of goods available for sale in the retail column must be gross sales after adjustment for sales returns. If sales are recorded at gross, deduct the gross sales figure. If sales are recorded at net, both the recorded sales and sales discount must be deducted to give the same effect as deducting gross sales (i.e., sales discounts are not included in the computation). Normal spoilage is generally allowed for in the firm's pricing policies, and for this reason it is deducted from the retail column after calculation of the cost-to-retail ratio. Abnormal spoilage, on the other hand, should be deducted from *both* the cost and retail columns *before* the cost-to-retail calculation, as it could distort the ratio. It is then generally reported as a loss separate from the cost of goods sold section. Abnormal spoilage is generally considered to arise from a major theft or casualty, while normal spoilage is usually due to shrinkage or breakage. These determinations and their treatments will vary depending on the firm's policies.

When applying the retail method, separate computations should be made for any departments that experience significantly higher or lower profit margins. Distortions arise in the retail method when a department sells goods with varying margins in a proportion different from that purchased, in which case the cost-to-retail percentage would not be representative of the mix of goods in ending inventory. Also, manipulations of income are possible by planning the timing of markups and markdowns.

The retail method is an acceptable method of valuing inventories for tax purposes in some, but not all, jurisdictions. The foregoing examples are not meant to imply that the method would be usable in any given jurisdiction; readers should ascertain whether or not it can be used.

Gross profit method. The gross profit method can be used to estimate ending inventory when a physical count is not possible or feasible. It can also be used to evaluate the reasonableness of a given inventory amount. The cost of goods available for sale is compared with the estimated cost of goods sold. For example, assume the following data:

Beginning inventory	€125,000
Net purchases	450,000
Sales	600,000
Estimated gross profit	32%

Ending inventory is then estimated as follows:

Beginning inventory	€125,000
Net purchases	450,000
Cost of goods available for sale	575,000
Cost of goods sold [€600,000 – (32% x €600,000)] or (68% x €600,000)	408,000
Estimated ending inventory	€167,000

The gross profit method, if used, should be limited to making interim reporting estimates, for analyses conducted by auditors, and for making estimates of inventory lost in fires or other catastrophes. The method is generally not acceptable for either tax or annual financial reporting purposes (and is not in conformity with IAS 2). Thus, its major purposes are for internal and interim reporting. For such purposes, however, it may prove to be extremely valuable.

Fair value as an inventory costing method. In general, inventories are to be carried at cost, although, as has been explained in the preceding sections of this chapter, cost may be ascertained by a variety of methods under IAS 2, and when recoverable amounts do not equal cost there is the further need to write down inventory to reflect such impairment. However, under defined circumstances, inventories may be carried at fair value, in excess of the actual cost of production or acquisition. Currently, IAS 41 provides that agricultural products that are carried in inventory are to be reported at fair value, subject to certain limitations.

Under the provisions of IAS 41, which became effective in 2003, all biological assets are to be measured at fair value less expected point-of-sale costs at each balance sheet date, unless fair value cannot be measured reliably. Agricultural produce is to be measured at fair value at the point of harvest less expected point-of-sale costs. Because harvested produce is a marketable commodity, there is no "measurable reliability" exception for produce.

Furthermore, the change in fair value of biological assets occurring during a reporting period is reported in net profit or loss, notwithstanding that these are "unrealized" as of the balance sheet date. IAS 41, however, does provide an exception to this fair value model for biological assets for situations where there is no active market at time of recognition in the financial statements, and no other reliable measurement method exists. In such instances, it provides that the cost model is to be applied to the specific biological asset for which such conditions hold, only. These biological assets should be measured at depreciated cost less any accumulated impairment losses.

More generally, the quoted market prices in active markets will represent the best measure of fair value of biological assets or agricultural produce. If an active market does not exist, IAS 41 provides guidance for choosing another measurement basis. Fair value measurement stops at the moment of harvest. IAS 2 applies after that date.

The details of IAS 41 are described in Chapter 24, Specialized Industries.

Other Cost Topics

Base stock. The base stock method assumes that a certain level of inventory investment is necessary for normal business activities and is therefore effectively a permanent asset of the business. The base stock inventory is carried at historical cost. Decreases in the base stock are considered temporary and are charged to cost of goods sold at replacement cost. Increases are carried at current year costs. The base stock approach is seldom encountered today in practice and it is not allowed for tax purposes in many jurisdictions. Although the original IAS 2 permitted the base stock method, it has been proscribed since an earlier revised version of IAS 2 became effective in 1995.

Standard costs. Standard costs are predetermined unit costs used by many manufacturing firms for planning and control purposes. Standard costs are often incorporated into the accounts, and materials, work in process, and finished goods inventories are all carried on this basis of accounting. The use of standard costs in financial reporting is acceptable if adjustments are made periodically to reflect current conditions and if its use approximates one of the recognized cost flow assumptions.

Inventories valued at net realizable value. In exceptional cases, inventories may be reported at net realizable value in accordance with well-established practices in certain industries. Such treatment is justified when cost is difficult to determine, quoted market prices are available, marketability is assured, and units are interchangeable. IAS 2 stipulates that producers' inventories of agricultural and forest products, agricultural produce after harvest, and minerals and mineral products, to the extent that they are measured at net realizable value in accordance with well-established practices, are to be valued in this manner. IAS 41 subsequently addressed this matter for biological assets only. When inventory is valued above cost, revenue is recognized before the point of sale; full disclosure in the financial statements would, of course, be required.

Inventories valued at fair value less costs to sell. In case of commodity broker-traders' inventories, IAS 2 stipulates that these inventories be valued at fair value less costs to sell. While allowing this exceptional treatment for inventories of commodity broker-traders, IAS 2 makes it mandatory that in such cases the fair value changes should be reported in profit and loss account for the period of change.

Disclosure Requirements

IAS 2 sets forth certain disclosure requirements relative to inventory accounting methods employed by the reporting entity. According to this standard, the following must be disclosed:

1. The accounting policies adopted in measuring inventories, including the costing methods (e.g., FIFO or weighted-average) employed
2. The total carrying amount of inventories and the carrying amount in classifications appropriate to the enterprise
3. The carrying amount of inventories carried at fair value less costs to sell
4. The amount of inventories recognized as expense during the period
5. The amount of any write-down of inventories recognized as an expense in the period.
6. The amount of any reversal of any previous write-down that is recognized in earnings for the period
7. The circumstances or events that led to the reversal of a write-down of inventories to net realizable value
8. The carrying amount of inventories pledged as security for liabilities

The type of information to be provided concerning inventories held in different classifications is somewhat flexible, but traditional classifications, such as raw materials, work in progress, finished goods, and supplies, should normally be employed. In the case of service providers, inventories (which are really akin to unbilled receivables) can be described as work in progress.

In addition to the foregoing, the financial statements should disclose either the cost of inventories recognized as an expense during the period (i.e., reported as cost of sales or included in other expense categories), or the operating costs, applicable to revenues, recognized as an expense during the period, categorized by their respective natures.

Costs of inventories recognized as expense includes, in addition to the costs inventoried previously and attaching to goods sold currently, the excess overhead costs charged to expense for the period because, under the standard, they could not be deferred to future periods.

Examples of Financial Statement Disclosures

Nokia Corporation
Period ending December 2004

Notes to the Consolidated Financial Statements

1. Accounting Principles

Inventories. Inventories are stated at the lower of cost or net realizable value. Cost is determined using standard cost, which approximates actual cost, on a first-in, first-out (FIFO) basis. Net realizable value is the amount that can be realized from the sale of the inventory in the normal course of business after allowing for the costs for realization. In addition to the cost of materials and direct labor, an appropriate proportion of production overheads are included in the inventory values. An allowance is recorded for excess inventory and obsolescence.

18. Inventories

	2004 EURm	2003 EURm
Raw material, supplies and other	326	346
Work in progress	477	435
Finished goods	502	388
Total	1,305	1,169

Barloworld Limited
Period ending September 30, 2004

Note 1. Principal Accounting Policies

1.17 Inventories

Inventories are stated at the lower of cost and net realizable value. Cost includes cost of purchase (including taxes, transport, and handling) net of trade discounts received, cost of conversion (including fixed and variable manufacturing overheads) and other costs incurred in bringing the inventories to their present location and condition. Where appropriate, cost is calculated on a specific identification basis. Otherwise the first-in, first-out method or, in certain subsidiaries, the weighted-average method is used. Net realizable value represents the estimated selling price less all estimated costs to completion and costs to be incurred in marketing, selling and distribution. When inventories are sold, the carrying amount is recognized as an expense in the period in which the related revenue is recognized. Any write-down of inventories to net realizable value, and all losses of inventories or reversals of previous write-downs or losses are recognized in income in the period the write-down, loss, or reversal occurs.

Note 9. Inventories

	Group 2004	Group 2003
Raw materials and components	395	425
Work in progress	297	277
Finished goods	2,329	2,079
Merchandise	1,394	1,506
Consumable stores	92	102
Buy-back commitments	618	615
Other inventories	9	6
	5,134	5,010
The value of inventories has been determined on the following basis:		
First-in first-out and specific identification	4,700	4,682

	Group	
	2004	*2003*
Weighted-average	434	328
	5,134	5,010
Inventory pledged as security for liabilities	6	42
The secured liabilities are included under trade and other payables (note 16)		
Inventory recognized as an expense during the year	24,787	23,232
Amount of write-down of inventory to net realizable value and losses of inventory	35	85
Amount of reversals of previous inventory write-downs	4	

Lectra S.A.
Period ending December 31, 2004

Accounting Policies

Inventories of raw materials are valued at the lower of purchase cost (based on weighted average cost, including related costs) and their net realizable value. Finished goods and work -in-progress are valued at the lower of standard industrial cost (adjusted at year-end on an actual cost basis) and their net realizable value. Cost price does not include interest expense. Allowance is made if net realizable value is less than the book value. Allowance for inventories of parts and consumables are calculated by comparing book value and probable realizable value after a specific analysis of the rotation and obsolescence of inventory items, taking into account the utilization of items for maintenance and after-sales activities and changes in the range of products marketed.

Note 6 Inventories	*€ in thousands*	
	2004	*2003*
Raw materials	15,221	14,734
Finished goods and work-in-progress [1]	17,357	12,581
Inventories, gross value	32,578	27,315
Raw materials	(4316)	(3,678)
Finished goods and work-in-progress [1]	(4,457)	(5,213)
Allowances	(8,773)	(8,891)
Raw materials	10,905	11,056
Finished goods and work-in-progress [1]	12,900	7,368
Inventories, net value	23,805	18,424

(1) Including demonstration and second-hand equipment.

€2,289,000 of inventory depreciated in full at January 1, 2004, was scrapped in the course of 2004, thereby diminishing the gross value of inventory and depreciation by the same amount.

APPENDIX

NET REALIZABLE VALUE UNDER US GAAP

In many jurisdictions, the term *lower of cost or market* is used, as contrasted to IAS 2's *lower of cost or net realizable value*. As a practical matter, this difference in terminology will have little or no impact, since *market* is usually defined operationally as being replacement cost or net realizable value. However, one important distinction is that *market* is usually defined as a conditional term that contemplates a range of values, based not only on the costs to complete and sell an item, but also, in some circumstances, on the expected or normal profit to be earned on the sale. Since IAS 2 provides only general guidance concerning the determination of net realizable value, it will be useful to look to other existing standards for insight into how these measures are to be developed in a practical situation.

Measuring the decline to net realizable value. The IAS 2 definition of net realizable value makes explicit reference only to "costs of completion and costs incurred in order to make the sale." However, as illustrated below, if expected or normal profit margins on sales of inventory items are not taken into account, excessive profits or losses might be recognized in future periods, due to an incomplete application of the net realizable value concept.

The application of these principles is illustrated in the following example. In this example, replacement cost will be used as the primary operational definition of inventory value when that amount is lower than carrying value determined by historical cost. Replacement cost is a valid measure of the future utility of the inventory item since increases or decreases in the purchase price generally foreshadow related increases or decreases in the selling price. Assume the following information for products A, B, C, D, and E:

Item	Cost	Replacement cost	Est. selling price	Cost to complete	Normal profit percentage
A	€2.00	€1.80	€ 2.50	€0.50	24%
B	4.00	1.60	4.00	0.80	24%
C	6.00	6.60	10.00	1.00	18%
D	5.00	4.75	6.00	2.00	20%
E	1.00	1.05	1.20	0.25	12.5%

Consider item A: The net realizable value defined in accordance with IAS 2 is €2.50 – 0.50 = €2.00 (estimated selling price less costs to complete and sell). As it happens, this is exactly equal to historical cost, suggesting that there would be no adjustment required. However, if no adjustment is recorded, the profit realized upon the sale next period will be €2.50 – 2.00 – 0.50 = €0, which would be an unnaturally low net margin given the historical experience of a 24% margin. To preserve the normal margin, which would amount to €0.60 (€2.50 x 24%), the inventory would have to be written down to €1.40 (€2.50 – 0.50 – 0.60). However, the actual cost to replace the item in inventory is known to be €1.80, which suggests that the normal margin of 24% cannot be replicated under current conditions.

The foregoing explains why some standards setters and accounting theoreticians (but it should be stressed, not the IASB) have concluded that inventory should be reported at the lower of cost or market, where *market* is defined as replacement cost subject to ceiling and floor values; where *ceiling* is defined as net realizable value (NRV), and *floor* as the NRV minus the normal profit margin. Using this approach (which is the standard in the United States), the amount of profit to be recognized in the period of later sale, absent other changes in the marketplace after the reporting date, will not be abnormally high or low.

To continue with this example, the data in the foregoing table are used to compute market values consistent with the definition set forth earlier. Note that the primary measure in all cases is replacement cost; if this falls between the ceiling and the floor, it becomes the measure of market, which is then compared to historical cost; the lower of cost or market is then used to actually value the inventory item. If the replacement cost exceeds the ceiling value (as for items D and E), the ceiling value becomes the market next to be compared to historical cost. On the other hand, if replacement cost is lower than the floor (as for items B and C), the floor is used as the market value to be compared next to the historical cost.

Determination of Net Realizable Value

Item	Cost	Replacement cost	NRV (ceiling)	NRV less profit (floor)	Market	LCM
A	€2.00	€1.80	€2.00	€1.40	€1.80	€1.80
B	4.00	1.60	3.20	2.24	2.24	2.24
C	6.00	6.60	9.00	7.20	7.20	6.00
D	5.00	4.75	4.00	2.80	4.00	4.00
E	1.00	1.05	0.95	0.80	0.95	0.95

Note that under a strict reading of IAS 2, NRV would be compared directly to historical cost; the other values in the above table would not be given any consideration. If a strict application of the net realizable value rule were insisted upon, in contrast, item A would be valued at €2.00 instead of €1.80, resulting in a zero profit upon sale; and item B would be valued at €3.20 instead of €2.24, also resulting in a zero profit upon ultimate disposition. In general, the impact of using net realizable value, rather than market, would be to preclude preservation of some (if not a normal amount of) profit upon later sale of the item.

7 REVENUE RECOGNITION, INCLUDING CONSTRUCTION CONTRACTS

REVENUE RECOGNITION
PERSPECTIVE AND ISSUES

The standard addressing revenue recognition principles in general terms is IAS 18. It prescribes the accounting treatment for revenue arising from certain types of transactions and events and, while useful, is not a comprehensive treatise on the peculiarities on all the diverse forms of revenue and of possible recognition strategies that could be encountered. The basic premise is that revenue should be measured at the fair value of the consideration that has been received when the product or service promised has been provided to the customer. Specific guidance applies to various categories of revenues.

Thus, in the normal sale of goods, revenue is presumed to have been realized when the significant risks and rewards have been transferred to the buyer, accompanied by the forfeiture of effective control by the seller, and the amount to be received can be reliably measured. For most routine transactions (e.g., by retail merchants), this occurs when the goods have been delivered to the customer.

Revenue recognition for service transactions, as set forth in revised IAS 18, requires that the percentage-of-completion method be used unless certain defined conditions are not met. Originally, reporting entities had a choice of methods—percentage-of-completion or completed contract. Current revenue recognition standards for services transactions closely parallel those for construction contracts under IAS 11, which is also covered in this chapter.

For interest, royalties and dividends, recognition is warranted when it is probable that economic benefits will flow to the entity. Specifically, interest is recognized on a time proportion basis, taking into account the effective yield on the asset. Royalties are recognized on an accrual basis, in accordance with the terms of the underlying agreement. Dividend income is recognized when the shareholder's right to receive payment has been established.

In recent years, particularly with the advent of Web-based "e-commerce" entities, there has been a large increase in the occurrence of barter transactions. The more controversial of the barter transactions involve the swapping of advertising services (e.g., whereby two or more e-commerce (or other) operations "swap" display advertising on the others' Web sites), particularly when these were valued by reference to arbitrary prices or were seldom equaled in cash transactions conducted at arm's-length (i.e., sales of advertising for cash). The interpretation SIC 31 established the requirement that, in order for revenue to be recognized in such advertising swap situations, an objective measure of the value of the services provided by the entity seeking to recognize revenue has to be available. In the absence of such reliable data, no revenue can be recognized.

IAS 18 also established certain disclosure requirements, including the revenue recognition accounting policies of the reporting entity.

While the existing general guidance on revenue recognition under IAS actually exceeds that which has thus far been provided under various national standards, it nonetheless is modest given the broad importance of the topic. IASB (and the US standard setter, FASB) has been pursuing a project intended to address revenue recognition, as well as the associated topics of distinguishing liabilities from equity. This project, still not near completion, is likely to have a major impact on financial reporting, since it promises to fundamentally change revenue recognition practices. This chapter contains a summary of this project as of mid-2005.

Sources of IFRS
IASB's *Framework for Preparation and Presentation of Financial Statements*
IAS 18, *SIC* 31

DEFINITIONS OF TERMS

Fair value. An amount for which an asset could be exchanged, or a liability settled, between knowledgeable, willing parties in an arm's-length transaction.

Ordinary activities. Those activities of an entity which it undertakes as part of its business and such related activities in which the entity engages in furtherance of, incidental to, or arising from those activities.

Revenue. Gross inflow of economic benefits resulting from an entity's ordinary activities is considered "revenue," provided those inflows result in increases in equity, other than increases relating to contributions from owners or equity participants. Revenue refers to the gross amount (of revenue) and excludes amounts collected on behalf of third parties.

CONCEPTS, RULES, AND EXAMPLES

Revenue. The IASB's *Framework* defines "income" to include both revenue and gains. IAS 18 deals only with revenue. Revenue is defined as income arising from the ordinary activities of an entity and may be referred to by a variety of names including sales, fees, interest, dividends and royalties. Revenue encompasses only the gross inflow of economic benefits received or receivable by the entity, on its own account. This implies that amounts collected on behalf of others—such as in the case of sales tax or value added tax, which also flow to the entity along with the revenue from sales—do not qualify as revenue. Thus, these other collections should not be included in an entity's reported revenue. Put another way, gross revenue from sales should be shown net of amounts collected on behalf of third parties.

Similarly, in an agency relationship the amounts collected on behalf of the principal is not regarded as revenue for the agent. Instead, the commission earned on such collections qualifies as revenue of the agent. For example, in the case of a travel agency, the collections from ticket sales do not qualify as revenue or income from its ordinary activities. Instead, it will be the commission on the tickets sold by the travel agency that will constitute that entity's gross revenue.

Scope of the standard. IAS 18 applies to the accounting for revenue arising from

- The sale of goods;
- The rendering of services; and
- The use of the entity's assets by others, yielding (for the entity) interest, dividends and royalties.

A sale of goods encompasses *both* goods produced by the entity for sale to others and goods purchased for resale by the entity. The rendering of services involves the performance by the entity of an agreed-upon task, based on a contract, over a contractually agreed period of time.

The use of the entity's assets by others gives rise to revenue for the entity in the form of

- **Interest,** which is a charge for the use of cash and cash equivalent or amounts due to the entity;
- **Royalties,** which are charges for the use of long-term assets of the entity such as patents or trademarks owned by the entity; and
- **Dividends,** which are distributions of profit to the holders of equity investments in the share capital of other entities.

The standard *does not* apply to revenue arising from

- Lease agreements that are covered by IAS 17;
- Dividends arising from investments in associates which are accounted for using the equity method, which are dealt with in IAS 28;
- Insurance contracts within the scope of IFRS 4;
- Changes in fair values of financial instruments, which is addressed by IAS 39;
- Natural increases in herds, agriculture and forest products, which is dealt with under IAS 41;
- The extraction of mineral ores, where an interim standard should be published before the end of 2004; and
- Changes in the value of other current assets.

Measurement of revenue. The quantum of revenue to be recognized is usually dependent upon the terms of the contract between the entity and the buyer of goods, the recipient of the services, or the users of the assets of the entity. Revenue should be measured at the fair value of the consideration received or receivable, net of any trade discounts and volume rebates allowed by the entity.

When the inflow of the consideration, which is usually in the form of cash or cash equivalents, is deferred, the fair value of the consideration will be an amount lower than the nominal amount of consideration. The difference between the fair value and the nominal value of the consideration, which represents the time value of money, is recognized as interest revenue.

When the entity offers interest-free extended credit to the buyer or accepts a promissory note from the buyer (as consideration) that bears either no interest or a below-market interest rate, such an arrangement would be construed as a financing transaction. In such a case the fair value of the consideration is ascertained by discounting the future inflows using an imputed rate of interest. The imputed rate of interest is either "the prevailing rate of interest for a similar instrument of an issuer with a similar credit rating, or a rate of interest that discounts the nominal amount of the instrument to the current cash sales price of the goods or services."

To illustrate this point, let us consider the following example:

> Hero International is a car dealership that is known to offer excellent packages for all new models of Japanese cars. Currently, it is advertising on the television that there is a special offer for all Year 2006 models of a certain make. The offer is valid for all purchases made on or before September 30, 2005. The special offer deal is either a cash payment in full of €20,000 or a zero down payment with extended credit terms of two years—24 monthly installments of €1,000 each. Thus, anyone opting for the extended credit terms would pay €24,000 in total.
>
> Since there is a difference of €4,000 between the cash price of €20,000 and the total amount payable if the car is paid for in 24 installments of €1,000 each, this arrangement is effectively a financing transaction (and of course a sale transaction as well). The cash price of €20,000 would be regarded as the amount of consideration attributable to the sale of the car. The difference between the cash price and the aggregate amount payable in monthly installments is interest revenue and is to be recognized over the period of two years on a time proportion basis (using the effective interest method).

Exchanges of similar and dissimilar goods and services. When goods or services are exchanged or swapped for *similar* goods or services, the earning process is not considered being complete. Thus the exchange is not regarded as a transaction that generates revenue. Such exchanges are common in certain commodity industries, such as oil or milk industries, where suppliers usually swap inventories in various locations in order to meet geographically diverse demand on a timely basis.

In contrast, when goods or services of a *dissimilar* nature are swapped, the earning process is considered to be complete, and thus the exchange is regarded as a transaction that generates revenue. The revenue thus generated is measured at the fair value of the goods or services received or receivable. If in this process cash or cash equivalents are also transferred, then the fair value should be adjusted by the amount of cash or cash equivalents (commonly referred to as "boot") transferred. In certain cases, the fair value of the goods or services received cannot be measured reliably. Under such circumstances, fair value of goods or services given up, adjusted by the amount of boot transferred, is the measure of revenue to be recognized. Barter arrangements are examples of such exchanges involving goods that are dissimilar in nature.

Identification of the transaction. While setting out clearly the criteria for the recognition of revenue under three categories—sale of goods, rendering of services and use of the entity's assets by others—the standard clarifies that these should be applied separately to each transaction. In other words, the recognition criteria should be applied to the separately identifiable components of a single transaction consistent with the principle of "substance over form."

For example, a washing machine is sold with an after-sale service warranty. The selling price includes a separately identifiable portion attributable to the after-sale service warranty. In such a case, the standard requires that the selling price of the washing machine should be apportioned between the two separately identifiable components and each one recognized according to an appropriate recognition criterion. Thus, the portion of the selling price attributable to the after-sales warranty should be deferred and recognized over the period during which the service is performed. The remaining selling price should be recognized immediately if the recognition criteria for revenue from sale of goods (explained below) are satisfied.

Similarly, the recognition criteria are to be applied to two or more separate transactions together when they are connected or linked in such a way that the commercial effect (or substance over form) cannot be understood without considering the series of transactions as a whole. For example, Company X sells a ship to Company Y and later enters into a separate contract with Company Y to repurchase the same ship from it. In this case the two transactions need to be considered together in order to ascertain whether or not revenue is to be recognized.

Revenue recognition criteria. According to the IASB's *Framework*, revenue is to be recognized when it is probable that future economic benefits will flow to the entity and reliable measurement of the quantum of revenue is possible. Based on these fundamental tenets of revenue recognition stated in the IASB's *Framework*, IAS 18 establishes criteria for recognition of revenue from three categories of transactions—the sale of goods, the rendering of services, and the use by others of the reporting entity's assets. In the case of the first two categories of transactions producing revenue, the standard prescribes certain additional criteria for recognition of revenue. In the case of revenue from the use by others of the entity's assets, the standard does not overtly prescribe additional criteria, but it does provide guidance on the bases to be adopted in revenue recognition from this source. This may, in a way, be construed as an additional criterion for revenue recognition from this source of revenue.

Revenue recognition from the sale of goods. Revenue from the sale of goods should be recognized if the *all* of the five conditions mentioned below are met.

- The reporting entity has transferred significant risks and rewards of ownership of the goods to the buyer;
- The entity does not retain *either* continuing managerial involvement (akin to that usually associated with ownership) *or* effective control over the goods sold;
- The quantum of revenue to be recognized can be measured reliably;
- The probability that economic benefits related to the transaction will flow to the entity exists; and
- The costs incurred or to be incurred in respect of the transaction can be measured reliably.

The determination of the point in time when a reporting entity is considered to have transferred the significant risks and rewards of ownership in goods to the buyer is critical to the recognition of revenue from the sale of goods. If upon examination of the circumstances of the transfer of risks and rewards of ownership by the entity it is determined that the entity could still be considered as having retained significant risks and rewards of ownership, the transaction could not be regarded as a sale.

Some examples of situations illustrated by the standard in which an entity may be considered to have retained significant risks and rewards of ownership, and thus revenue is not recognized, are set out below.

- A contract for the sale of an oil refinery stipulates that installation of the refinery is an integral and a significant part of the contract. Therefore, until the refinery is completely installed by the reporting entity that sold it, the sale would not be regarded as complete. In other words, until the completion of the installation, the entity that sold the refinery would still be regarded as the effective owner of the refinery even if the refinery has already been delivered to the buyer. Accordingly, revenue will not be recognized by the entity until it completes the installation of the refinery.
- Goods are sold on approval, whereby the buyer has negotiated a limited right of return. Since there is a possibility that the buyer may return the goods, revenue is not recognized until the shipment has been formally accepted by the buyer, or the goods have been delivered as per the terms of the contract, and the time stipulated in the contract for rejection has expired.
- In the case of "layaway sales," under terms of which the goods are delivered only when the buyer makes the final payment in a series of installments, revenue is not recognized until the last and final payment is received by the entity. Upon receipt of the final installment, the goods are delivered to the buyer and revenue is recognized. However, based upon experience, if it can reasonably be presumed that most such sales are consummated, revenue may be recognized when a significant deposit is received from the buyer and goods are on hand, identified and ready for delivery to the buyer.

If the reporting entity retains only an insignificant risk of ownership, the transaction is considered a sale and revenue is recognized. For example, a department store has a policy to offer refunds if a customer is not satisfied. Since the entity is only retaining an insignificant risk of ownership, revenue from sale of goods is recognized. However, since the enterprise's refund policy is publicly announced and thus would have created a valid expectation on the part of the customers that the store will honor its policy of refunds, a provision is also recognized for the best estimate of the costs of refunds, as explained in IAS 37.

Another important condition for recognition of revenue from the sale of goods is the existence of the probability that the economic benefits will flow to the entity. For example, for several years an entity has been exporting goods to a foreign country. In the current year, due to sudden restrictions by the foreign government on remittances of currency outside the country, collections from these sales were not made by the entity. As long as it is uncertain if these restrictions will be removed, revenue should not be recognized from these exports, since it may not be probable that economic benefits in the form of collections will flow to the entity. Once the restrictions are withdrawn and uncertainty is removed, revenue may be recognized.

Yet another important condition for recognition of revenue from the sale of goods relates to the reliability of measuring costs associated with the sale of goods. Thus, if expenses such as those relating to warranties or other postshipment costs cannot be measured reliably, then revenue from the sale of such goods should also not be recognized. This rule is based on the principle of matching of revenues and expenses.

Revenue recognition from the rendering of services. When the outcome of the transaction involving the rendering of services can be estimated reliably, revenue relating to that transaction should be recognized. The recognition of revenue should be with reference to the stage of completion of the transaction at the balance sheet date. The outcome of a transaction can be estimated reliably when each of the four conditions set out below are met.

- The amount of revenue can be measured reliably;
- The probability that the economic benefits related to this transaction will flow to the entity exists;
- The stage of completion of the transaction at the balance sheet date can be measured reliably; and
- The costs incurred for the transaction and the costs to complete the transaction can be measured reliably.

This manner of recognition of revenue, based on the stage of completion, is often referred to as the "percentage-of-completion" method. IAS 11 also mandates recognition of revenue on this basis. Revenue is recognized only when it is probable that the economic benefits related to the transaction will flow to the reporting entity. However, if there is uncertainty with regard to the collectability of an amount already included in revenue, the uncollectable amount should be recognized as an expense instead of adjusting it against the amount of revenue originally recognized.

In order to be able to make reliable estimates, an entity should agree with the other party to the following:

- Each other's enforceable rights with respect to the services provided;
- The consideration to be exchanged; and
- The manner and terms of settlement.

It is important that the entity has in place an effective internal financial budgeting and reporting system. This ensures that the entity can promptly review and revise the estimates of revenue as the service is being performed. It should be noted, however, that merely because there is a later need for revisions does not by itself make an estimate of the outcome of the transaction unreliable.

Progress payments and advances received from customers are emphatically *not* a measure of stage of completion. The stage of completion of a transaction may be determined in a number of ways. Depending on the nature of the transaction, the method used may include

- Surveys of work performed;
- Services performed to date as a percentage of total services to be performed; or
- The proportion that costs incurred to date bear to the estimated total costs of the transaction. (Only costs that reflect services performed or to be performed are included in costs incurred to date or in estimated total costs.)

In certain cases services are performed by an indeterminable number of acts over a specified period of time. Revenue in such a case should be recognized on a straight-line basis unless it is possible to estimate the stage of completion by some other method more reliably. Similarly when in a series of acts to be performed in rendering a service, a specific act is much more significant than other acts, the recognition is postponed until the significant act is performed.

During the early stages of the transaction it may not be possible to estimate the outcome of the transaction reliably. In all such cases, where the outcome of the transaction involving the rendering of services cannot be estimated reliably, revenue should be recognized only to the extent of the expenses recognized that are recoverable. However, in a later period when the uncertainty that precluded the reliable estimation of the outcome no longer exists, revenue is recognized as usual.

NOTE: The "percentage-of-completion" method is discussed in detail in the second part of this chapter. For numerical examples illustrating the method, please refer to the second part of this chapter relating to construction contracts.

Revenue recognition from interest, royalties, and dividends. Revenue arising from the use by others of the reporting entity's assets yielding interest, royalties and dividends should be recognized when both of the following two conditions are met:

1. It is probable that the economic benefits relating to the transaction will flow to the entity; and
2. The amount of the revenue can be measured reliably.

The bases prescribed for the recognition of the revenue are the following:

a. In the case of interest—the time proportion basis that takes into account the effective yield on the assets;
b. In the case of royalties—the accrual basis in accordance with the substance of the relevant agreement; and
c. In the case of dividends—when the shareholder's right to receive payment is established.

According to IAS 18, "the effective yield on an asset is the rate of interest used to discount the stream of future cash receipts expected over the life of the asset to equate to the initial carrying amount of asset." Interest revenue includes the effect of amortization of any discount, premium or other difference between the initial carrying amount of a debt security and its amount at maturity.

When unpaid interest has accrued before an interest-bearing investment is purchased by the entity, the subsequent receipt of interest is to be allocated between preacquisition and postacquisition periods. Only the portion of interest that accrued subsequent to the acquisition by the entity is recognized as income. The remaining portion of interest, which is attributable to the preacquisition period, is treated as a reduction of the cost of the investment, as explained by IAS 39. Similarly, dividends on equity securities declared from preacquisition profits are treated as reduction of the cost of investment. If it is difficult to make such an allocation except on an arbitrary basis, dividends are recognized as revenue unless they clearly represent a recovery of part of the cost of the equity securities.

Disclosures. A reporting entity should disclose the following:

- The accounting policies adopted for the recognition of revenue including the methods adopted to determine the stage of completion of transactions involving the rendering of services;
- The amount of each significant category of revenue recognized during the period including revenue arising from
  - The sale of goods;
  - The rendering of services; and
  - Interest, royalties, and dividends.
- The amounts revenue arising from exchanges of goods or services included in each significant category of revenue.

Accounting for barter transactions. The much-heralded era of e-commerce (i.e., commerce conducted via Internet, based on commercial Web sites directed at end consumers ["B-to-C" business] or at intermediate consumers, such as wholesalers and manufacturers

["B-to-B" business]), although past its over-touted boom period, is now an established feature of business life. It is likely that growing percentages of business will be conducted via electronic commerce.

The "dot-com bubble" was accompanied by another related trend, that of investors and others finding value in new "performance" measures such as gross sales volume and the number of "hits" registered on Web sites. Concurrently, the importance (for high technology and start-up entities in particular) of traditional measure of success, particularly profits, was often unjustifiably discounted. The confluence of these two structural changes provided an unfortunate opportunity to some entities to seek ways to inflate reported revenues, if not profits. It is commonplace for Web-based businesses to swap advertising with each other. With each entity "buying" advertising and "selling" advertising, a liberal interpretation of financial reporting standards could enable each of them to inflate reported revenues by attributing any value to the exchange. While corresponding expenses were also necessarily exaggerated and net earnings affected not at all (unless revenues and expenses were reported in different fiscal periods, which also occurred), with investors mesmerized by gross revenue, the impact was to encourage overvaluation of the entities' shares in the market.

As certain recently publicized financial reporting frauds have demonstrated, distortion of revenues via "swap" arrangements has hardly been constrained to the providing and acquiring of advertising (e.g., the "capacity swaps" of many US telecom and energy companies). However, the bartering of advertising services has been the first to receive the attention of the SIC, which issued SIC 31 to prescribe revenue recognition principles to be applied to these transactions.

This interpretation addresses how revenue from a barter transaction involving advertising services received or provided in a barter transaction should be reliably measured. The SIC agreed that the entity providing advertising should measure revenue from the barter transaction based on the fair value of the advertising services it has provided to its customer, and not on the value of that received. In fact, the SIC states categorically that the value of the services received cannot be used to reliably measure the revenue generated by the services provided.

Furthermore, SIC 31 holds that the fair value advertising services provided in a barter transaction can be reliably measured only by reference to nonbarter transactions that involve services similar to that in the barter transaction, when those transactions occur frequently, are expected to continue occurring after the barter transaction, represent a predominant source of revenue from advertising similar to the advertising in the barter transaction, involve cash and/or another form of consideration (e.g., marketable securities, nonmonetary assets, and other services) that has a reliably determinable fair value, and do not involve the same counterparty as in the barter transaction. All of these conditions must be satisfied in order to value the revenue to be recognized from the advertising barter transaction.

Clearly, based on the criteria mandated by SIC 31, the more common barter transactions, involving mere "swaps" of advertising among the members of the bartering group, henceforth cannot serve as a basis for revenue recognition by any of the parties thereto.

Accounting for multiple-element sales arrangements. The accounting for multiple-element revenue arrangements is not presently addressed under IAS, but the IASB's project on revenue recognition does deal with this increasingly common phenomenon. When entities offer customers multiple-element revenue arrangements, these provide for the delivery or performance of multiple products, services, or rights, which may take place at different times. The IASB has noted that the accounting for such arrangements has been one of the most contentious practice issues of revenue recognition. As part of its current project, it examined the application of an assets and liabilities approach to revenue recognition against the cases involving multiple-element revenue arrangements, and contrasted the impact of such an approach to the positions taken by the FASB's Emerging Issues Task Force's *Accounting for Revenue Arrangements with Multiple Deliverables* (EITF Issue 00-21, which was approved by the EITF in November 2002). The IASB noted that the EITF's approach was consistent with, but more extensive than, the revenue recognition criteria in IAS 18.

IASB compared an assets and liabilities approach with the EITF's approach, which instead focuses on when revenue is earned and whether delivering an element in an arrangement represents a separate earning process from delivery of other elements. It tentatively agreed that the case studies examined indicated that, in many cases, similar outcomes would in fact result from applying either approach. However, IASB noted that applying an assets and liabilities approach has certain advantages over the EITF's approach. First, it is not dependent on whether the delivered item is sold separately by any vendor or whether the customer could resell the deliverable. Second, the existence of rights of return does not have the potential to preclude the recognition of revenue for delivered items. Third, when a delivered asset in a multiple-element arrangement is inseparable from the undelivered items, an assets and liabilities approach avoids the need to recognize a "deferred debit" as an asset when the asset sacrificed is derecognized. Finally, the IASB approach measures the value of undelivered items by direct reference to a measurement attribute (e.g., fair value) rather than through an allocation process, which avoids assuming the same margin on each inseparable deliverable in a multiple-element arrangement. However, the IASB has issued no definitive literature.

IASB PROJECT: REVENUE RECOGNITION

The amount of accounting guidance offered by IAS 18 exceeded that which was heretofore provided under most, if not all, of the national GAAP standards but, even so, the direction given to practitioners has been modest when considered in light of the importance of the topic. Concerns over proper revenue recognition practices have long existed, and studies have shown that financial reporting irregularities that have come to light and required large restatements of previously issued reports have largely sprung from improper revenue recognition. Standard setters, including the IASB, have therefore concluded that more prescriptive guidance is needed, and are currently endeavoring to produce standards that will provide such.

The IASB started to work independently on the issues of revenue recognition and concepts of liabilities and equity. It subsequently, however, decided to work with the FASB as part of their joint convergence program. The FASB has two separate projects on these issues.

The revenue recognition project has explored various different approaches, but opinion seems to be coalescing on one grounded in recognition of assets and liabilities, and the extinguishment of the liabilities. The idea is that where an entity has a legally enforceable, noncancelable contract, it should start to recognize the assets and liabilities inherent in that contract. While this approach does not change the final net earnings on the completed contract, it opens up the issue of the timing of recognition, moving from the end of the transaction, where recognition has traditionally taken place, to the point where an executory contract exists, and then remeasuring as the transaction evolves towards completion.

A simple example would be where a customer sees a sofa in a furniture shop, and decides to buy it. However, he wants a different color from that available in the shop. He pays the retailer €1,000 for delivery of a similar sofa but of a different color, within one week. Assuming the contract is noncancelable, the retailer would have an asset of €1,000, plus an obligation to supply a sofa. If he could order the sofa from the manufacturer for €600 and have someone deliver it for €75, the liability is for €675, and the retailer has a surplus of €325. Arguably there is a risk that the manufacturer or delivery service will fail to perform, and the retailer might have to refund the money, but this is quantifiable in the same way as a product liability, which could be deducted from the surplus, and then released when the transaction is complete. Under this approach, the retailer can identify a "selling" profit that is distinct from the actual supplying of the item.

This approach is conceptually consistent with the *Framework,* and has the merit that it recognizes the principle that earning is a gradual process. For some businesses, the value of executory contracts is a significant indication of profits, but which is currently excluded from measurement, except in the area of financial instruments. Clearly, however, this approach depends upon being able to ascertain fair values for the different components of the earnings process. It relies upon the ability to identify the selling profit as a residual, and this often cannot be independently measured or observed, and thus there is the risk that it will be miscalculated.

A key issue is the identification of the liabilities at the different stages in the revenue-generating process, and this provides a conceptual link to the project on liabilities and equity. However, for that project the issue is where to draw the line between equity and liabilities, or indeed whether there are only two categories in the financing side of the balance sheet.

Neither standard setter is likely to move very rapidly on either of these conceptual issues since they involve major steps away from the traditional revenue recognition model. The more likely next phase will be publication of discussion documents, to start the process of persuading people to accept change.

Examples of Financial Statement Disclosures

Barco N.V.
For the Year ended December 31, 2004

Notes to the consolidated financial statements

Accounting principles

11. Revenue recognition

Revenue is recognized when it is probable that the economic benefits will flow to the group and the revenue can be reliably measured. For product sales, revenue is recognized when the significant risks and rewards of ownership of the goods have passed to the buyer. Sales are recognized when persuasive evidence of an arrangement exists, delivery has occurred, the fee is fixed and determinable, and collectibility is probable.

For contract revenue, the percentage of completion method is used, provided that the outcome of the contract can be assessed with reasonable certainty. For sales of services, revenue is recognized by reference to the stage of completion.

Novartis A.G.
For the year ended December 31, 2004

Revenue

Revenue is recognized when title and risk of loss for the products is transferred to the customer. Accruals for US Medicaid and similar rebates in the US and other countries, chargebacks, estimated returns, customer rebates and discounts are established concurrently with the recognition of revenue. Accordingly, sales are reported net of these allowances which, since they are estimated, may not fully reflect the final outcome.

The following briefly describes the nature of each accrual and how such accruals are estimated with specific reference to the US practices:

- The US Medicaid program, established under Title XIX of the Social Security Act, is a state administered program, using state and federal funds, to provide assistance to certain vulnerable and needy individuals and families. In 1990, the Medicaid Drug Rebate Program was established to reduce state and federal expenditures for prescription drugs. Under the rebate program, we have signed an agreement to provide a rebate on drugs paid for by a state. Provisions for estimating Medicaid Rebates are calculated using a combination of historical experience, product and population growth, anticipated price increases, the impact of contracting strategies and specific terms in the individual state agreements. These provisions are adjusted based upon the established refiling process with the individual states.

- We participate in prescription drug savings programs that offer savings to patients that are eligible Medicare participants. These savings vary based on a patient's current drug coverage and personal income levels.

- We have arrangements with certain parties establishing discounted prices for our products. A chargeback represents the difference between the invoice price to the wholesaler and the indirect customer's contract discount price. Provisions for estimating chargebacks are calculated using a combination of historical experience, product growth rates and the specific terms in each agreement.

- Where there is a historical experience of agreeing to customers returns, we record a reserve for estimated sales returns by applying historical experience of customer returns to the amounts invoiced and the amount of returned product to be destroyed versus product that can be placed back in inventory for resale.

- Our policy relating to supply of pharmaceuticals products is to maintain inventories on a consistent level from year to year based on the pattern of consumption. A process exists at Novartis Pharmaceuticals Corporation to monitor on a monthly basis inventory levels at wholesalers based on the gross sales volume, prescription volumes based on IMS data and information received from the key wholesalers. Bases on this information, the inventories on hand at wholesalers and other distribution channels in the US are less than one month at December 31, 2004. Similar processes exist in the Sandoz generics and the OTC businesses. We believe the third-party data sources of information are sufficiently reliable, however their accuracy cannot be verified.

- Customer rebates are offered to key managed care, group purchasing organizations and other direct and indirect customers to sustain and increase our product market share. These rebate programs provide that the customer receive a rebate after attaining certain performance parameters relating to product purchases, formulary status and/or preestablished market share milestones relative to competitors. Since rebates are contractually agreed upon, rebates are estimated based on the specific terms in each agreement, historical experience and product growth rates.

- Cash discounts are offered to customers to encourage prompt payment that is accrued at the time of invoicing.

- Shelf-stock adjustments are granted to customers based on the existing inventory of a customer following decreases in the invoice or contract price of the related product. Provisions for shelf-stock adjustments are determined at the time of the price decline or at the point of sale if a price decline is reasonably estimable and are based on estimated inventory levels.

- Historical data has been adjusted, where applicable, to give effect to subsequent events, including, primarily, the effect of increased turnover on such provisions.

The US market has the most complex arrangements in this area. The following tables show the extent of rebates made and payment experiences in the US in 2004 for our key subsidiaries affected, which are Novartis Pharmaceuticals Corporation, Sandoz Inc. and Novartis Consumer Health Inc. (OTC):

Notes to the consolidated financial statements

1.   Accounting policies

The Novartis Group ("Group" or "Novartis") consolidated financial statements are prepared in accordance with the historical cost convention except for the revaluation to market value of certain financial assets and liabilities and comply with the International Financial Reporting Standards (IFRS) formulated by the International Accounting Standards Board (IASB) and with International Accounting Standards (IAS) and interpretations formulated by its predecessor organization, the International Accounting Standards Committee (IASC), as well as with the following significant accounting policies.

Revenue and expense recognition. Revenue is recognized when title and risk of loss for the products is transferred to the customer.   Provisions for rebates and discounts granted to government agencies, wholesalers, managed care and other customers are recorded as a reduction of revenue at the time the related revenues are recorded or when the incentives are offered. They are calculated on the basis of historical experience and the specific terms in the individual agreements.   Cash discounts are offered to customers to encourage prompt payment.   They are recorded as a reduction of revenue at the time of invoicing. Shelf-stock adjustments are granted to customers based on the existing inventory of a customer following decreases in the invoice or contract price of the related product. Provisions for shelf-stock adjustments are determined at the time of the price decline or at the point of sale if a price decline is reasonably estimable and based on estimated inventory levels.   Where there is a historical experience of Novartis agreeing to customer returns, Novartis records a reserve for estimated sales returns by applying historical experience of customer returns to the amounts invoiced and the amount of returned products to be destroyed versus products that can be placed back in inventory for resale.

Expenses for research and service contracts in progress are recognized based on their percentage of completion.

CONSTRUCTION CONTRACT ACCOUNTING

PERSPECTIVE AND ISSUES

The principal concern of accounting for long-term construction contracts involves the timing of revenue (and thus profit) recognition.   It has been well accepted that, given the long-term nature of such projects, deferring revenue recognition until completion would often result in the presentation of periodic financial reports that fail to meaningfully convey the true level of activity of the reporting entity during the reporting period.   In extreme cases, in fact, there could be periods of no apparent activity, and others of exaggerated amounts, when in fact the entity was operating at a rather constant rate of production during all of the periods.   To avoid these distortions, the percentage of completion method was developed, which reports the revenues proportionally to the degree to which the projects are being completed, even absent full completion and, in many cases, even absent the right to collect for the work done to date.

The major challenges in using percentages of completion accounting are to accurately gauge the extent to which the projects are being finished, and to assess the ability of the entity to actually bill and collect for the work done.   Since many projects are priced at fixed amounts, or in some other fashion prevent the passing through to the customers the full amount of cost overruns, the computation of periodic profits must be sensitive not merely to the extent to which the project is nearing completion, but also to the terms of the underlying contractual arrangements.

IAS 11 is the salient IFRS addressing the accounting for construction contracts and other situations in which the percentage of completion method of revenue recognition would be appropriate.   This standard uses the recognition criteria established by the IASB's *Framework* as the basis for the guidance it offers on accounting for construction contracts.

The various complexities in applying IAS 11, including the estimation of revenues, costs, and progress toward completion, are set forth in the following discussion.

Sources of IFRS
IAS 10, 11, 23, 37

DEFINITIONS OF TERMS

Additional asset stipulation. A special provision in a construction contract which either gives the option to the customer to require construction of an additional asset or permits amendment to the construction contract so as to include an additional asset not envisioned by the original contract should be construed as a separate construction contract when

1. The additional asset differs significantly (in design, function, or technology) from the asset(s) covered by the original contract; or
2. The extra contract price fixed for the construction of the additional asset is negotiated without regard to the original contract price.

Back charges. Billings for work performed or costs incurred by one party that, in accordance with the agreement, should have been performed or incurred by the party billed.

Billings on long-term contracts. Accumulated billings sent to the purchaser at intervals as various milestones in the project are reached.

Change orders. Modifications of an original contract that effectively change the provisions of the contract without adding new provisions; synonymous with *variations*.

Claims. Amounts in excess of the agreed-on contract price that a contractor seeks to collect from a customer (or another party) for customer-caused delays, errors in specifications and designs, disputed variations in contract work, or other occurrences that are alleged to be the causes of unanticipated costs.

Combining (grouping) contracts. Grouping two or more contracts, whether with a single customer or with several customers, into a single profit center for accounting purposes, provided that

1. The group of contracts is negotiated as a single package;
2. The contracts combined are so closely interrelated that, in essence, they could be considered as a single contract negotiated with an overall profit margin; and
3. The contracts combined are either executed concurrently or in a sequence.

Construction contract. Contract specifically entered into for the construction of an asset or a combination of assets that are closely interrelated or interdependent in terms of their design, technology, and function or their end use or purpose.

Construction-in-progress (CIP). Inventory account used to accumulate the construction costs of the contract project. For the percentage-of-completion method, the CIP account also includes the gross profit earned to date.

Contract costs. Comprised of costs directly related to a specific contract, costs that are attributable to the contract activity in general and can be allocated to the contract, and other costs that are specifically chargeable to the customer under the terms of the contract.

Contract revenue. Comprised of initial amount of revenue stipulated by the contract plus any variations in contract work, claims, and incentive payments, provided that these extra amounts of revenue meet the recognition criteria set by the IASB's *Framework* (i.e., regarding the probability of future economic benefits flowing to the contractor and reliability of measurement).

Cost-plus contract. Construction contract in which the contractor is reimbursed for allowable costs plus either a percentage of these costs or a fixed fee.

Cost-to-cost method. Percentage-of-completion method used to determine the extent of progress toward completion on a contract. The ratio of costs incurred through the end of the current year divided by the total estimated costs of the project is used to recognize income.

Estimated cost to complete. Anticipated additional cost of materials, labor, subcontracting costs, and indirect costs (overhead) required to complete a project at a scheduled time.

Fixed-price contract. Construction contract wherein the contract revenue is fixed either in absolute terms or is fixed in terms of unit rate of output; in certain cases both fixed prices being subject to any cost escalation clauses, if allowed by the contract.

Incentive payments. Any additional amounts payable to the contractor if specified performance standards are either met or surpassed.

Percentage-of-completion method. Method of accounting that recognizes income on a contract as work progresses by matching contract revenue with contract costs incurred, based on the proportion of work completed. However, any expected loss, which is the excess of total incurred and expected contract costs over the total contract revenue, is recognized immediately, irrespective of the stage of completion of the contract.

Precontract costs. Costs that are related directly to a contract and are incurred in securing a contract (e.g., architectural designs, purchase of special equipment, engineering fees, and start-up costs). They are included as part of contract costs if they can be identified separately and measured reliably and it is probable that the contract will be obtained.

Profit center. Unit for the accumulation of revenues and cost for the measurement of income.

Segmenting contracts. Dividing a single contract, which covers the construction of a number of assets, into two or more profit centers for accounting purposes, provided that

1. Separate proposals were submitted for each of the assets that are the subject matter of the single contract
2. The construction of each asset was the subject of separate negotiation wherein both the contractor and the customer were in a position to either accept or reject part of the contract pertaining to a single asset (out of numerous assets contemplated by the contract)
3. The costs and revenues pertaining to each individual asset can be separately identified

Stage of completion. Proportion of the contract work completed, which may be determined using one of several methods that reliably measures it, including

1. Percentage-of-completion method
2. Surveys of work performed
3. Physical proportion of contract work completed

Subcontractor. Second-level contractor who enters into a contract with a prime contractor to perform a specific part or phase of a construction project.

Substantial completion. Point at which the major work on a contract is completed and only insignificant costs and potential risks remain.

Variation. Instruction by the customer for a change in the scope of the work envisioned by the construction contract.

CONCEPTS, RULES, AND EXAMPLES

Construction contract revenue may be recognized during construction rather than at the completion of the contract. This "as earned" approach to revenue recognition is justified because under most long-term construction contracts, both the buyer and the seller (contractor) obtain enforceable rights. The buyer has the legal right to require specific performance from the contractor and, in effect, has an ownership claim to the contractor's work in progress. The contractor, under most long-term contracts, has the right to require the buyer to make progress payments during the construction period. The substance of this business activity is that a continuous sale occurs as the work progresses.

IAS 11 recognizes the percentage-of-completion method as the only valid method of accounting for construction contracts. Under an earlier version of IAS 11, both the percentage-of-completion method and the completed-contract method were recognized as being acceptable alternative methods of accounting for long-term construction activities.

The thinking worldwide on this issue is equivocal and rather confusing. Many national GAAP recognize both methods as being appropriate, although they may not be viewed as equally acceptable under given circumstances. The United States, Canada, and Japan are usually noted as protagonists of both GAAP methods on this subject. There is another set of countries whose GAAP is in line with the current IAS on the subject. The national accounting standards of the United Kingdom, Australia, China, and New Zealand recognize only the percentage-of-completion method. Germany, on the other hand, seems to have taken the extreme viewpoint as a supporter of only the completed-contract method. Although it may seem that the world is completely divided on this matter, a closer look into this contentious issue offers a better insight into the diversity in approaches.

Although Germany seems to be alone in the contest of alternative methods of accounting for long-term contracts, its position is more explicable when it is recalled that this country has traditionally been known for its conservative approach and its emphasis on creditor protection and a close linkage between accounting recognition rules and the measurement of taxable income. Thus, it seems to have been guided primarily by the prudence concept in developing this accounting principle.

For countries that support both the methods, it is well known that some also express a clear preference for the percentage-of-completion method. US GAAP, for instance, exemplifies this position. It recommends the percentage-of-completion method as preferable when estimates are reasonably dependable and the following conditions exist:

1. Contracts executed by the parties normally include provisions that clearly specify the enforceable rights regarding goods or services to be provided and received by the parties, the consideration to be exchanged, and the manner and terms of settlement.
2. The buyer can be expected to satisfy its obligations under the contract.
3. The contractor can be expected to perform its contractual obligations.

The Accounting Standards Division of the AICPA believes that these two methods should not be used as acceptable alternatives for the same set of circumstances. US GAAP states that, in general, when estimates of costs to complete and extent of progress toward completion of long-term contracts are reasonably dependable, the percentage-of-completion method is preferable. When lack of dependable estimates or inherent hazards cause forecasts to be doubtful, the completed-contract method is preferable.

Percentage-of-Completion Method in Detail

A number of controversial issues are encountered when the percentage-of-completion method is used in practice. In the following paragraphs, the authors' address a number of these, offering proposed approaches to follow for those matters that have not been authoritatively resolved, or in many instances, even discussed by the international accounting standards.

IAS 11 defines the percentage-of-completion method as follows:

Under this method contract revenue is matched with the contract costs incurred in reaching the stage of completion, resulting in the reporting of revenue, expenses and profit which can be attributed to the proportion of work completed. ...Contract revenue is recognized as revenue in the income statement in the accounting periods in which the work is performed. Contract costs are usually recognized as an expense in the accounting periods in which the work to which they relate is performed. However, any expected excess of total revenue for the contract is recognized as an expense immediately.

Under the percentage-of-completion method, the construction-in-progress (CIP) account is used to accumulate costs and recognized income. When the CIP exceeds billings, the difference is reported as a current asset. If billings exceed CIP, the difference is reported as a current liability. Where more than one contract exists, the excess cost or liability should be determined on a project-by-project basis, with the accumulated costs and liabilities being stated separately on the balance sheet. Assets and liabilities should not be offset unless a right of offset exists. Thus, the net debit balances for certain contracts should not ordinarily be offset against net credit balances for other contracts. An exception may exist if the balances relate to contracts that meet the criteria for combining.

Under the percentage-of-completion method, income should not be based on advances (cash collections) or progress (interim) billings. Cash collections and interim billings are based on contract terms that do not necessarily measure contract performance.

Costs and estimated earnings in excess of billings should be classified as an asset. If billings exceed costs and estimated earnings, the difference should be classified as a liability.

Contract costs. Contract costs comprise costs that are identifiable with a specific contract, plus those that are attributable to contracting activity in general and can be allocated to the contract and those that are contractually chargeable to a customer. Generally, contract costs would include all direct costs, such as direct materials, direct labor, and direct expenses and any construction overhead that could specifically be allocated to specific contracts.

Direct costs or costs that are identifiable with a specific contract include

1. Costs of materials consumed in the specific construction contract
2. Wages and other labor costs for site labor and site supervisors
3. Depreciation charges of plant and equipment used in the contract
4. Lease rentals of hired plant and equipment specifically for the contract
5. Cost incurred in shifting of plant, equipment, and materials to and from the construction site
6. Cost of design and technical assistance directly identifiable with a specific contract
7. Estimated costs of any work undertaken under a warranty or guarantee
8. Claims from third parties

With regard to claims from third parties, these should be accrued if they rise to the level of "provisions" as defined by IAS 37. This requires that an obligation exist at the balance sheet date that is subject to reasonable measurement. However, if either of the above mentioned conditions is not met (and the possibility of the loss is not remote), this contingency will only be disclosed. Contingent losses are specifically required to be disclosed under IAS 11.

Contract costs may be reduced by incidental income if such income is not included in contract revenue. For instance, sale proceeds (net of any selling expenses) from the disposal of any surplus materials or from the sale of plant and equipment at the end of the contract may be credited or offset against these expenses. Drawing an analogy from this principle, it could be argued that if advances received from customers are invested by the contractor temporarily (instead of being allowed to lie idle in a current account), any interest earned on such investments could be treated as incidental income and used in reducing contract costs, which may or may not include borrowing costs (depending on how the contractor is financed, whether self-financed or leveraged). On the other hand, it may also be argued that instead of being subtracted from contract costs, such interest income should be added to contract revenue.

In the authors' opinion, the latter argument may be valid if the contract is structured in such a manner that the contractor receives lump-sum advances at the beginning of the contract (or for that matter, even during the term of the contract, such that the advances at any point in time exceed the amounts due the contractor from the customer). In these cases, such interest income should, in fact, be treated as contract revenue and not offset against contract costs. The reasoning underlying treating this differently from the earlier instance (where idle funds resulting from advances are invested temporarily) is that such advances were envisioned by the terms of the contract and as such were probably fully considered in the negotiation process that preceded fixing contract revenue. Thus, since negotiated as part of the total contract price, this belongs in contract revenues. (It should be borne in mind that the different treatments for interest income would in fact have a bearing on the determination of the percentage or stage of completion of a construction contract.)

Indirect costs or overhead expenses should be included in contract costs provided that they are attributable to the contracting activity in general and could be allocated to specific contracts. Such costs include construction overhead, cost of insurance, cost of design, and technical assistance that is not related directly to specific contracts. They should be allocated using methods that are systematic and rational and are applied in a consistent manner to costs having similar features or characteristics. The allocation should be based on the normal level of construction activity, not on theoretical maximum capacity.

Example of contract costs

A construction company incurs €700,000 in annual rental expense for the office space occupied by a group of engineers and architects and their support staff. The company utilizes this group to act as the quality assurance team that overlooks all contracts undertaken by the company. The company also incurs in the aggregate another €300,000 as the annual expenditure toward electricity, water, and maintenance of this office space occupied by the group. Since the group is responsible for quality assurance for all contracts on hand, its work, by nature, cannot be considered as being directed toward any specific contract but is in support of the entire contracting activity. Thus, the company should allocate the rent expense and the cost of utilities in accordance with a systematic and rational basis of allocation, which should be applied consistently to both types of expenditure (since they have similar characteristics).

Although the bases of allocation of this construction overhead could be many (such as the amounts of contract revenue, contract costs, and labor hours utilized in each contract) the basis of allocation that seems most rational is contract revenue. Further, since both expenses are similar in nature, allocating both the costs on the basis of the amount of contract revenue generated by each construction contract would also satisfy the consistency criteria.

Other examples of construction overhead or costs that should be allocated to contract costs are

1. Costs of preparing and processing payroll of employees engaged in construction activity
2. Borrowing costs that are capitalized under IAS 23 in conformity with the allowed alternative treatment (note that IASB's announced intent, as part of the Improvements Project, to eliminate the choice under IAS 23 of capitalizing borrowing costs that meet certain conditions, has since been dropped)

Certain costs are specifically excluded from allocation to the construction contract, as the standard considers them as not attributable to the construction activity. Such costs may include

1. General and administrative costs that are not contractually reimbursable
2. Costs incurred in marketing or selling
3. Research and development costs that are not contractually reimbursable
4. Depreciation of plant and equipment that is lying idle and not used in any particular contract

Types of contract costs. Contract costs can be broken down into two categories: costs incurred to date and estimated costs to complete. The *costs incurred to date* include precontract costs and costs incurred after contract acceptance. *Precontract costs* are costs incurred before a contract has been entered into, with the expectation that the contract will be accepted and these costs will thereby be recoverable through billings. The criteria for recognition of such costs are

1. They are capable of being identified separately.
2. They can be measured reliably.
3. It is probable that the contract will be obtained.

Precontract costs include costs of architectural designs, costs of learning a new process, cost of securing the contract, and any other costs that are expected to be recovered if the contract is accepted. Contract costs incurred after the acceptance of the contract are costs incurred toward the completion of the project and are also capitalized in the construction-in-progress (CIP) account. The contract does not have to be identified before the capitalization decision is made; it is only necessary that there be an expectation of the recovery of the costs. Once the contract has been accepted, the precontract costs become contract costs incurred to date. However, if the precontract costs are already recognized as an expense in the period in which they are incurred, they are not included in contract costs when the contract is obtained in a subsequent period.

Estimated costs to complete. These are the anticipated costs required to complete a project at a scheduled time. They would be comprised of the same elements as the original total estimated contract costs and would be based on prices expected to be in effect when the costs are incurred. The latest estimates should be used to determine the progress toward completion.

Although IAS 11 does not specifically provide instructions for estimating costs to complete, practical guidance can be gleaned from other international accounting standards, as follows: The first rule is that systematic and consistent procedures should be used. These procedures should be correlated with the cost accounting system and should be able to provide a comparison between actual and estimated costs. Additionally, the determination of estimated total contract costs should identify the significant cost elements.

A second important point is that the estimation of the costs to complete should include the same elements of costs included in accumulated costs. Additionally, the estimated costs should reflect any expected price increases. These expected price increases should not be blanket provisions for all contract costs, but rather, specific provisions for each type of cost. Expected increases in each of the cost elements such as wages, materials, and overhead items should be taken into consideration separately.

Finally, estimates of costs to complete should be reviewed periodically to reflect new information. Estimates of costs should be examined for price fluctuations and should also be reviewed for possible future problems, such as labor strikes or direct material delays.

Accounting for contract costs is similar to accounting for inventory. Costs necessary to ready the asset for sale would be recorded in the construction-in-progress account, as incurred. CIP would include both direct and indirect costs but would usually not include general and administrative expenses or selling expenses since they are not normally identifiable with a particular contract and should therefore be expensed.

Subcontractor costs. Since a contractor may not be able to do all facets of a construction project, a subcontractor may be engaged. The amount billed to the contractor for work done by the subcontractor should be included in contract costs. The amount billed is directly traceable to the project and would be included in the CIP account, similar to direct materials and direct labor.

Back charges. Contract costs may have to be adjusted for back charges. Back charges are billings for costs incurred that the contract stipulated should have been performed by another party. The parties involved often dispute these charges.

Example of a back charge situation

The contract states that the subcontractor was to raze the building and have the land ready for construction; however, the contractor/seller had to clear away debris in order to begin construction. The contractor wants to be reimbursed for the work; therefore, the contractor back charges the subcontractor for the cost of the debris removal.

The contractor should treat the back charge as a receivable from the subcontractor and should reduce contract costs by the amount recoverable. If the subcontractor disputes the back charge, the cost becomes a claim. Claims are an amount in excess of the agreed contract price or amounts not included in the original contract price that the contractor seeks to collect. Claims should be recorded as additional contract revenue only if the requirements set forth in IAS 11 are met.

The subcontractor should record the back charge as a payable and as additional contract costs if it is probable that the amount will be paid. If the amount or validity of the liability is disputed, the subcontractor would have to consider the probable outcome in order to determine the proper accounting treatment.

Fixed-Price and Cost-Plus Contracts

IAS 11 recognizes two types of construction contracts that are distinguished based on their pricing arrangements: (1) fixed-price contracts and (2) cost-plus contracts.

Fixed-price contracts are contracts for which the price is not usually subject to adjustment because of costs incurred by the contractor. The contractor agrees to a fixed contract price or a fixed rate per unit of output. These amounts are sometimes subject to escalation clauses.

There are two types of cost-plus contracts.

1. **Cost-without-fee contract**—Contractor is reimbursed for allowable or otherwise defined costs with no provision for a fee. However, a percentage is added that is based on the foregoing costs.

2. **Cost-plus-fixed-fee contract**—Contractor is reimbursed for costs plus a provision for a fee. The contract price on a cost-type contract is determined by the sum of the reimbursable expenditures and a fee. The fee is the profit margin (revenue less direct expenses) to be earned on the contract. All reimbursable expenditures should be included in the accumulated contract costs account.

There are a number of possible variations of contracts that are based on a cost-plus-fee arrangement. These could include cost-plus-fixed-fee, under which the fee is a fixed monetary amount; cost-plus-award, under which an incentive payment is provided to the contractor, typically based on the project's timely or on-budget completion; and cost-plus-a-percentage-fee, under which a variable bonus payment will be added to the contractor's ultimate payment based on stated criteria.

Some contracts may have features of both a fixed-price contract and a cost-plus contract. A cost-plus contract with an agreed maximum price is an example of such a contract.

Recognition of Contract Revenue and Expenses

Percentage-of-completion accounting cannot be employed if the quality of information will not support a reasonable level of accuracy in the financial reporting process. Generally, only when the outcome of a construction contract can be estimated reliably, should the contract revenue and contract costs be recognized by reference to the stage of completion at the balance sheet date.

Different criteria have been prescribed by the standard for assessing whether the outcome can be estimated reliably for a contract, depending on whether it is a fixed-price contract or a cost-plus contract. The following are the criteria in each case:

1. If it is a fixed-price contract

    NOTE: *All* conditions should be satisfied.

    a. It meets the recognition criteria set by the IASB's *Framework*; that is

        (1) Total contract revenue can be measured reliably.
        (2) It is probable that economic benefits flow to the entity.

    b. Both the contract cost to complete and the stage of completion can be measured reliably.

    c. Contract costs attributable to the contract can be identified properly and measured reliably so that comparison of actual contract costs with estimates can be done.

2. If it is a cost-plus contract

    NOTE: *All* conditions should be satisfied.

    a. It is probable that the economic benefits will flow to the entity.

    b. The contract costs attributable to the contract, whether or not reimbursable, can be identified and measured reliably.

When Outcome of a Contract Cannot Be Estimated Reliably

As stated above, unless the outcome of a contract can be estimated reliably, contract revenue and costs should not be recognized by reference to the stage of completion. IAS 11 establishes the following rules for revenue recognition in cases where the outcome of a contract cannot be estimated reliably:

1. Revenue should be recognized only to the extent of the contract costs incurred that are probable of being recoverable.
2. Contract costs should be recognized as an expense in the period in which they are incurred.

Any expected losses should, however, be recognized immediately.

It is not unusual that during the early stages of a contract, outcome cannot be estimated reliably. This would be particularly likely to be true if the contract represents a type of project with which the contractor has had limited experience in the past.

Contract Costs Not Recoverable Due to Uncertainties

Recoverability of contract costs may be considered doubtful in the case of contracts that have any of the following characteristics:

1. The contract is not fully enforceable.
2. Completion of the contract is dependent on the outcome of pending litigation or legislation.
3. The contract relates to properties that are likely to be expropriated or condemned.
4. The contract is with a customer who is unable to perform its obligations, perhaps because of financial difficulties.
5. The contractor is unable to complete the contract or otherwise meet its obligation under the terms of the contract, as when, for example, the contractor has been experiencing recurring losses and is unable to get financial support from creditors and bankers and may be ready to declare bankruptcy.

In all such cases, contract costs should be expensed immediately. Although the implication is unambiguous, the determination that one or more of the foregoing conditions holds will be subject to some imprecision. Thus, each such situation needs to be assessed carefully on a case-by-case basis.

If and when these uncertainties are resolved, revenue and expenses should again be recognized on the same basis as other construction-type contracts (i.e., by the percentage-of-completion method). However, it is not permitted to restore costs already expensed in prior periods, since the accounting was not in error, given the facts that existed at the time the earlier financial statements were prepared.

Revenue Measurement—Determining the Stage of Completion

The standard recognizes that the stage of completion of a contract may be determined in many ways and that an entity uses the method that measures reliably the work performed. The standard further stipulates that depending on the nature of the contract, one of the following methods may be chosen:

1. The proportion that contract costs incurred bears to estimated total contract cost (also referred to as the cost-to-cost method)
2. Survey of work performed method
3. Completion of a physical proportion of contract work (also called units-of-work-performed) method.

   NOTE: Progress payments and advances received from customers often do not reflect the work performed.

Each of these methods of measuring progress on a contract can be identified as being either an input or an output measure. The *input measures* attempt to identify progress in a contract in terms of the efforts devoted to it. The cost-to-cost method is an example of an input measure. Under the cost-to-cost method, the percentage of completion would be estimated by comparing total costs incurred to date to total costs expected for the entire job. *Output measures* are made in terms of results by attempting to identify progress toward completion by physical measures. The units-of-work-performed method is an example of an output measure. Under this method, an estimate of completion is made in terms of achievements to date. Output measures are usually not considered to be as reliable as input measures.

When the stage of completion is determined by reference to the contract costs incurred to date, the standard specifically refers to certain costs that are to be excluded from contract costs. Examples of such costs are

1. Contract costs that relate to future activity (e.g., construction materials supplied to the site but not yet consumed during construction)
2. Payments made in advance to subcontractors prior to performance of the work by the subcontractor

Example of the percentage-of-completion method

The percentage-of-completion method works under the principle that "recognized income (should) be that percentage of estimated total income...that incurred costs to date bear to estimated total costs." The cost-to-cost method has become one of the most popular measures used to determine the extent of progress toward completion.

Under the cost-to-cost method, the percentage of revenue to recognize can be determined by the following formula:

$$\frac{\text{Cost to date}}{\substack{\text{Cumulative costs incurred} \\ \text{+ Estimated costs} \\ \text{to complete}}} \times \substack{\text{Contract} \\ \text{price}} - \substack{\text{Revenue} \\ \text{previously} \\ \text{recognized}} = \substack{\text{Current} \\ \text{revenue} \\ \text{recognized}}$$

By slightly modifying this formula, current gross profit can also be determined.

$$\frac{\text{Cost to date}}{\substack{\text{Cumulative costs incurred} \\ \text{+ Estimated costs} \\ \text{to complete}}} \times \substack{\text{Expected} \\ \text{total gross} \\ \text{profit}} - \substack{\text{Gross profit} \\ \text{previously} \\ \text{recognized}} = \substack{\text{Current} \\ \text{gross} \\ \text{profit}}$$

Example of the percentage-of-completion (cost-to-cost) and completed-contract methods with profitable contract

Assume a €500,000 contract that requires 3 years to complete and incurs a total cost of €405,000. The following data pertain to the construction period:

	Year 1	Year 2	Year 3
Cumulative costs incurred to date	€150,000	€360,000	€405,000
Estimated costs yet to be incurred at year-end	300,000	40,000	--
Progress billings made during year	100,000	370,000	30,000
Collections of billings	75,000	300,000	125,000

Completed-Contract and Percentage-of-Completion Methods

	Year 1		Year 2		Year 3	
Construction in progress	150,000		210,000		45,000	
Cash, payables, etc.		150,000		210,000		45,000
Contract receivables	100,000		370,000		30,000	
Billings on contracts		100,000		370,000		30,000
Cash	75,000		300,000		125,000	
Contract receivables		75,000		300,000		125,000

Completed-Contract Method Only

Billings on contracts		500,000	
Cost of revenues earned		405,000	
Contracts revenues earned			500,000
Construction in progress			405,000

Percentage-of-Completion Method Only

	Year 1		Year 2		Year 3	
Construction in progress	16,667		73,333		5,000	
Cost of revenues earned	150,000		210,000		45,000	
Contract revenues earned		166,667		283,333		50,000
Billings on contracts			500,000		
Construction in progress						500,000

Income Statement Presentation

	Year 1	Year 2	Year 3	Total
Percentage-of-completion				
Contract revenues earned	€166,667*	€283,333**	€ 50,000***	€500,000
Cost of revenues earned	(150,000)	(210,000)	(45,000)	(405,000)
Gross profit	€ 16,667	€ 73,333	€ 5,000	€ 95,000
Completed-contract				
Contract revenues earned	--	--	€500,000	€500,000
Cost of contracts completed	--	--	(405,000)	(405,000)
Gross profit	--	--	€ 95,000	€ 95,000

$$* \quad \frac{€\,150,000}{450,000} \times 500,000 = €166,667$$

$$** \quad \frac{€\,360,000}{400,000} \times 500,000 - 166,667 = €283,333$$

$$*** \quad \frac{€405,000}{405,000} \times 500,000 - 166,667 - 283,333 = €50,000$$

Balance Sheet Presentation

	Year 1	Year 2	Year 3
Percentage-of-completion			
Current assets:			
Contract receivables		€25,000	€ 95,000	*
Costs and estimated earnings in excess of billings on uncompleted contracts			
Construction in progress	166,667**		
Less billings on long-term contracts	(100,000)	66,667	
Current liabilities:			
Billings in excess of costs and estimated earnings on uncompleted contracts, year 2 (€470,000*** – €450,000****)		20,000	
Completed-contract			
Current assets:			
Contract receivables		25,000	95,000	*
Costs in excess of billings on uncompleted contracts			
Construction in progress	150,000		
Less billings on long-term contracts	(100,000)	50,000	
Current liabilities:			
Billings in excess of costs on uncompleted contracts, year 2 (€470,000 – €360,000)		110,000	

* Since the contract was completed and title was transferred in year 3, there are no balance sheet amounts. However, if the project is complete but transfer of title has not taken place, there would be a balance sheet presentation at the end of the third year because the entry closing out the Construction-in-progress account and the Billings account would not have been made yet.

** €150,000 (Costs) + 16,667 (Gross profit)

*** €100,000 (Year 1 Billings) + 370,000 (Year 2 Billings)

**** €360,000 (Costs) + 16,667 (Gross profit) + 73,333 (Gross profit)

Recognition of Expected Contract Losses

When the current estimate of total contract cost exceeds the current estimate of total contract revenue, a provision for the entire loss on the entire contract should be made. Provisions for losses should be made in the period in which they become evident under either the percentage-of-completion method or the completed-contract method. In other words, when it is probable that total contract costs will exceed total contract revenue, the expected loss should be recognized as an expense immediately. The loss provision should be computed on the basis of the total estimated costs to complete the contract, which would include the contract costs incurred to date plus estimated costs (use the same elements as contract costs incurred) to complete. The provision should be shown separately as a current liability on the balance sheet.

In any year when a percentage-of-completion contract has an expected loss, the amount of the loss reported in that year can be computed as follows:

Reported loss = Total expected loss + All profit previously recognized

Example of the percentage-of-completion and completed-contract methods with loss contract

Using the previous information, if the costs yet to be incurred at the end of year 2 were €148,000, the total expected loss is €8,000 [= €500,000 – (360,000 + 148,000)], and the total loss reported in year 2 would be €24,667 (= €8,000 + 16,667). Under the completed-contract method, the loss recognized is simply the total expected loss, €8,000.

Journal entry at end of year 2	Percentage-of-Completion	Completed-contract
Loss on uncompleted long-term contract	24,667	8,000
Construction in progress (or estimated loss on uncompleted contact)	24,667	8,000

Profit or Loss Recognized on Contract
(Percentage-of-Completion Method)

	Year 1	Year 2	Year 3
Contract price	€500,000	€500,000	€500,000
Estimated total costs:			
Costs incurred to date	150,000	360,000	506,000*
Estimated cost yet to be incurred	300,000	148,000	--
Estimated total costs for the three-year period, actual for year 3	450,000	508,000	506,000
Estimated income (loss), actual for year 3	16,667	(8,000)	(6,000)
Less income (loss) previously recognized	--	16,667	(8,000)
Amount of estimated income (loss) recognized in the current period, actual for year 3	€ 16,667	€ (24,667)	€ 2,000

* *Assumed*

Profit or Loss Recognized on Contract
(Completed-Contract Method)

	Year 1	Year 2	Year 3
Contract price	€500,000	€500,000	€500,000
Estimated total costs:			
Costs incurred to date	150,000	360,000	506,000*
Estimated costs yet to be incurred	300,000	148,000	--
Estimated total costs for the three-year period, actual for year 3	50,000	(8,000)	(6,000)
Loss previously recognized	--	--	(8,000)
Amount of estimated income (loss) recognized in the current period, actual for year 3	€ --	€ (8,000)	€ 2,000

* *Assumed*

Upon completion of the project during year 3, it can be seen that the actual loss was only €6,000 (= €500,000 – 506,000); therefore, the estimated loss provision was overstated by €2,000. However, since this is a change of an estimate, the €2,000 difference must be handled prospectively; consequently, €2,000 of income should be recognized in year 3 (= €8,000 previously recognized – €6,000 actual loss).

Combining and Segmenting Contracts

The profit center for accounting purposes is usually a single contract, but under some circumstances the profit center may be a combination of two or more contracts, a segment of a contract, or a group of combined contracts. Conformity with explicit criteria set forth in IAS 11 is necessary to combine separate contracts, or segment a single contract; otherwise, each individual contract is presumed to be the profit center.

For accounting purposes, a group of contracts may be combined if they are so closely related that they are, in substance, parts of a single project with an overall profit margin. A group of contracts, whether with a single customer or with several customers, should be combined and treated as a single contract if the group of contracts

1. Are negotiated as a single package
2. Require such closely interrelated construction activities that they are, in effect, part of a single project with an overall profit margin
3. Are performed concurrently or in a continuous sequence

Segmenting a contract is a process of breaking up a larger unit into smaller units for accounting purposes. If the project is segmented, revenues can be assigned to the different elements or phases to achieve different rates of profitability based on the relative value of each element or phase to the estimated total contract revenue. According to IAS 11, a contract may cover a number of assets. The construction of each asset should be treated as a separate construction contract when

1. The contractor has submitted separate proposals on the separate components of the project
2. Each asset has been subject to separate negotiation and the contractor and customer had the right to accept or reject part of the proposal relating to a single asset
3. The cost and revenues of each asset can be separately identified

Contractual Stipulation for Additional Asset—Separate Contract

The contractual stipulation for an additional asset is a special provision in the international accounting standard. IAS 11 provides that a contract may stipulate the construction of an additional asset at the option of the customer, or the contract may be amended to include the construction of an additional asset. The construction of the additional asset should be treated as a separate construction contract if

1. The additional asset significantly differs (in design, technology or function) from the asset or assets covered by the original contract
2. The price for the additional asset is negotiated without regard to the original contract price

Changes in Estimate

Since the percentage-of-completion method uses current estimates of contract revenue and expenses, it is normal to encounter changes in estimates of contract revenue and costs frequently. Such changes in estimate of the contract's outcome are treated on a par with changes in accounting estimate as defined by IAS 8.

Disclosure Requirements under IAS 11

IAS 11 prescribes a number of disclosures; some of them are for all the contracts and others are only for contracts in progress at the balance sheet date. These are summarized below.

1. Disclosures relating to all contracts

   a. Aggregate amount of contract revenue recognized in the period
   b. Methods used in determination of contract revenue recognized in the period

2. Disclosures relating to contracts in progress

    a. Methods used in determination of stage of completion (of contracts in progress)
    b. Aggregate amount of costs incurred and recognized profits (net of recognized losses) to date
    c. Amounts of advances received (at balance sheet date)
    d. Amount of retentions (at balance sheet date)

Financial Statement Presentation Requirements under IAS 11

Gross amounts due from customers should be reported as an asset. This amount is the net of

1. Costs incurred plus recognized profits, less
2. The aggregate of recognized losses and progress billings.

This represents, in the case of contracts in progress, excess of contract costs incurred plus recognized profits, net of recognized losses, over progress billings.

Gross amounts due to customers should be reported as a liability. This amount is the net of

1. Costs incurred plus recognized profits, less
2. The aggregate of the recognized losses and progress billings.

This represents, in the case of contract work in progress, excess of progress billings over contract costs incurred plus recognized profits, net of recognized losses.

APPENDIX

ACCOUNTING UNDER SPECIAL SITUATIONS— GUIDANCE FROM US GAAP

A number of specialized situations that are fairly common in long-term construction contracting are not addressed by international accounting standards. To provide guidance on certain of these matters, the following interpretations are offered, analogized from existing practice under US GAAP.

Joint Ventures and Shared Contracts

Many contracts obtained by long-term construction companies are shared by more than one contractor. When the owner of the contract puts it up for bids, many contractors form syndicates or joint ventures to bid on and obtain a contract under which each contractor could not perform individually.

When this transpires, a separate set of books is maintained for the joint venture. If the percentages of interest for each venture are identical in more than one contract, the joint venture might keep its records almost like another construction company. Usually, the joint venture is for a single contract and ends on completion of that contract.

A joint venture is a form of a partnership, although a partnership for a limited purpose. An agreement of the parties and the terms of the contract successfully bid on will determine the nature of the accounting records. Income statements are usually cumulative statements showing all totals from the date of contract determination until the reporting date. Each venturer records its share of the amount from the venture's income statement less its previously recorded portion of the venture's income as a single line item similar to the equity method for investments. Similarly, balance sheets of the venture give rise to a single line asset balance of investment and advances in joint ventures. In most cases, footnote disclosure is similar to the equity method in displaying condensed financial statements of material joint ventures.

Under international standards (IAS 31), a venturer's interest in a joint venture may be accounted for by either the proportionate consolidation or the equity method of accounting. See Chapter 10 for a detailed discussion of joint venture accounting.

Accounting for Change Orders

Change orders are modifications of specifications or provisions of an original contract. Contract revenue and costs should be adjusted to reflect change orders that are approved by the contractor and customer. According to US GAAP, the accounting for the change order depends on the scope and price of the change. If the customer and contractor have agreed both the scope and price, contract revenue and cost should be adjusted to reflect the change order.

According to US GAAP, accounting for unpriced change orders depends on their characteristics and the circumstances in which they occur. Under the completed-contract method, costs attributable to unpriced change orders should be deferred as contract costs if it is probable that total contract costs, including costs attributable to the change orders, will be recovered from contract revenues. Recovery should be deemed probable if the future event or events are likely to occur.

According to US GAAP, the following guidelines should be followed when accounting for unpriced change orders under the percentage-of-completion method:

1. Costs attributable to unpriced change orders should be treated as costs of contract performance in the period in which the costs are incurred if it is not probable that the costs will be recovered through a change in the contract price.
2. If it is probable that the costs will be recovered through a change in the contract price, the costs should be deferred (excluded from the cost of contract performance) until the parties have agreed on the change in contract price, or alternatively, they should be treated as costs of contract performance in the period in which they are incurred, and contract revenue should be recognized to the extent of the costs incurred.
3. If an adjustment to the contract price will be made in an amount that will exceed the costs attributable to the change order, this may be given recognition under certain circumstances. Specifically, if the amount of the excess can be reliably estimated, and if realization is probable, then the original contract price should be so adjusted. However, since the substantiation of the amount of future revenue is difficult, revenue in excess of the costs attributable to unpriced change orders should only be recorded in circumstances in which realization is assured beyond a reasonable doubt, such as circumstances in which an entity's historical experience provides such assurance or in which an entity has received a bona fide pricing offer from a customer and records only the amount of the offer as revenue.

Accounting for Contract Options

According to US GAAP, an addition or option to an existing contract should be treated as a separate contract if any of the following circumstances exist:

1. The product or service to be provided differs significantly from the product or service provided under the original contract.
2. The price of the new product or service is negotiated without regard to the original contract and involves different economic judgments.
3. The products or services to be provided under the exercised option or amendment are similar to those under the original contract, but the contract price and anticipated contract cost relationship are significantly different.

If the addition or option does not meet the foregoing circumstances, the contracts should be combined. However, if the addition or option does not meet the criteria for combining, they should be treated as change orders.

Accounting for Claims

These represent amounts in excess of the agreed contract price that a contractor seeks to collect from customers for unanticipated additional costs. The recognition of additional contract revenue relating to claims is appropriate if it is probable that the claim will result in additional revenue and if the amount can be estimated reliably. US GAAP specifies that all of the following conditions must exist for the probable and estimable requirements to be satisfied:

1. The contract or other evidence provides a legal basis for the claim; or a legal opinion has been obtained, stating that under the circumstances there is a reasonable basis to support the claim.
2. Additional costs are caused by circumstances that were unforeseen at the contract date and are not the result of deficiencies in the contractor's performance.
3. Costs associated with the claim are identifiable or otherwise determinable and are reasonable in view of the work performed.

4.   The evidence supporting the claim is objective and verifiable, not based on management's "feel" for the situation or on unsupported representations.

When the foregoing requirements are met, revenue from a claim should be recorded only to the extent that contract costs relating to the claim have been incurred. When the foregoing requirements are not met, a contingent asset should be disclosed in accordance with US GAAP governing contingencies.

8 PROPERTY, PLANT, AND EQUIPMENT

PERSPECTIVE AND ISSUES

Long-lived tangible and intangible assets (which include plant, property, and equipment as well as development costs, various intellectual property intangibles, and goodwill) hold the promise of providing economic benefits to an enterprise for a period greater than that covered by the current year's financial statements. Accordingly, these assets must be capitalized rather than immediately expensed, and their costs must be allocated over the expected periods of benefit for the reporting entity. IFRS for long-lived assets address matters such as the determination of the amounts at which to initially record the acquisitions of such assets, the amounts at which to present these assets at subsequent reporting dates, and the appropriate method(s) by which to allocate the assets' costs to future periods. Under current IFRS, while historical cost is normally assumed to be the basis for financial reporting, it is also acceptable to periodically revalue long-lived assets if certain defined conditions are met.

Long-lived nonfinancial assets are primarily operational in character, (i.e., actively used in the business rather than being held as passive investments), and they may be classified into two basic types: tangible and intangible. *Tangible assets,* which are the subject of the present chapter, have physical substance and can be further categorized as follows:

1. Depreciable assets
2. Depletable assets
3. Other tangible assets

Intangible assets, on the other hand, have no physical substance. The value of an intangible asset is a function of the rights or privileges that its ownership conveys to the business entity. Intangible assets, which are explored at length in Chapter 9, can be further categorized as being either

1. Identifiable, or
2. Unidentifiable (i.e., goodwill).

Property (such as factory buildings) is often constructed by an enterprise over an extended period of time, and during this interval, when the property has yet to be placed in productive service, the enterprise may incur interest cost on funds borrowed to finance the construction. IAS 23 provides that such cost may be added to the carrying value of the asset under construction, in line with the US treatment, or may be expensed as incurred. European companies have historically generally expensed such costs as period costs as they are incurred, because this has been a more tax-efficient strategy. IAS 23 provides for either method, but once the reporting entity adopts the allowed alternative (capitalization) as its accounting policy, interest costs should be added to the carrying value of all qualifying assets.

Long-lived assets are sometimes acquired in nonmonetary transactions, either in exchanges of assets between the entity and another business organization, or else when assets are given as capital contributions by shareholders to the entity. IAS 16 requires such transactions to be measured at fair value, unless they lack commercial substance.

Increasingly, assets may be acquired or constructed with an attendant obligation to dismantle, remediate the environment, or otherwise clean up after the end of the assets' useful lives. Decommissioning costs now have to be estimated at initial recognition of the asset and recognized, in most instances, as additional asset cost and as a long-term liability, thus causing the costs to be spread over the useful lives of the assets via depreciation charges.

Measurement and presentation of long-lived assets subsequent to acquisition or construction involves both systematic allocation of cost to accounting periods, and possible special write-downs. Concerning cost allocation to periods of use, IFRS now require a "components approach" to depreciation. Thus, elements such as roofing and heating plant are to be separated from the cost paid for a building, and amortized over the lives appropriate for those (shorter-lived) assets.

It has long been held that an entity's balance sheet should never present assets at amounts in excess of some threshold level of economic utility; under different national GAAP standards, this was variously defined in terms of market value or an amount which could be recovered from future revenues to be derived from utilization of the asset. However, such rules were only infrequently formalized and less often enforced. For many years, there was no specific guidance within IFRS on how to account for any diminution in the value of long-lived assets that may have occurred during the reporting period. IAS 36, *Im-*

pairment of Assets, which was introduced in 1998, significantly altered the accounting landscape by providing thorough coverage of this subject. IAS 36 is equally applicable to tangible and intangible long-lived assets, and will be accordingly addressed in both this and the immediately succeeding chapters.

Sources of IFRS			
IFRS 5	*IAS* 16, 23, 36, 37	*IFRIC* 1	*SIC* 21

DEFINITIONS OF TERMS

Amortization. The general process of allocating the cost of a long-term asset over its useful life; the term is also used specifically to define the allocation process for intangible assets.

Boot. A term sometimes applied to monetary consideration given or received as a net settle-up in what is otherwise a nonmonetary asset exchange.

Carrying amount. The amount at which an asset is presented on the balance sheet, which is its cost (or other allowable basis, such as fair value), net of any accumulated depreciation and accumulated impairment losses thereon.

Cash generating unit. The smallest identifiable group of assets that generates cash inflows from continuing use, largely independent of the cash inflows associated with other assets or groups of assets; used for impairment testing purposes.

Commercial substance. The ability to change an entity's future cash flows; used in determining the accounting for certain nonmonetary exchanges.

Corporate assets. Assets, excluding goodwill, that contribute to future cash flows of the cash generating unit under review for impairment as well as other cash generating units of the entity.

Cost. Amount of cash or cash equivalent paid or the fair value of other consideration given to acquire or construct an asset.

Costs of disposal. The incremental costs directly associated with the disposal of an asset; these do not include financing costs or related income tax effects.

Decommissioning costs. The costs of dismantling an asset and restoring the land on which it was sited, and any other affected assets to their previous state.

Depreciable amount. Cost of an asset or the other amount that has been substituted for cost, less the residual value of the asset.

Depreciation. Systematic and rational allocation of the depreciable amount of an asset over its economic life.

Exchange. Reciprocal transfer between an enterprise and another entity that results in the acquisition of assets or services, or the satisfaction of liabilities, through a transfer of other assets, services, or other obligations.

Fair value. Amount that would be obtained for an asset in an arm's-length exchange transaction between knowledgeable, willing parties.

Fixed assets. Assets used in a productive capacity that have physical substance, are relatively long-lived, and provide future benefit that is readily measurable. Also referred to as property, plant, and equipment.

Impairment loss. The excess of the carrying amount of an asset over its recoverable amount.

Intangible assets. Nonmonetary assets, without physical substance, held for use in the production or supply of goods or services or for rental to others, or for administrative purposes, which are identifiable and are controlled by the enterprise as a result of past events, and from which future economic benefits are expected to flow.

Monetary assets. Assets whose amounts are fixed in terms of units of currency. Examples are cash, accounts receivable, and notes receivable.

Net selling price. The amount that could be realized from the sale of an asset by means of an arm's-length transaction, less costs of disposal.

Nonmonetary assets. Assets other than monetary assets. Examples are inventories; investments in common stock; and property, plant, and equipment.

Nonmonetary transactions. Exchanges and nonreciprocal transfers that involve little or no monetary assets or liabilities.

Nonreciprocal transfer. Transfer of assets or services in one direction, either from an enterprise to its owners or another entity, or from owners or another entity to the enterprise. An enterprise's reacquisition of its outstanding stock is a nonreciprocal transfer.

Property, plant, and equipment. Tangible assets with an expected useful life of more than one year, that are held for use in the process of producing goods or services for sale, that are held for rental to others, or that are held for administrative purposes; also referred to commonly as fixed assets.

Provision. A liability established to recognize a probable outflow of resources, whose timing or value is uncertain, where the reporting entity has a present obligation arising out of a past event.

Recoverable amount. The greater of an asset's net selling price or its value in use.

Residual value. Estimated amount expected to be obtained on ultimate disposition of the asset after its useful life has ended, net of estimated costs of disposal.

Similar productive assets. Productive assets that are of the same general type, that perform the same function, or that are employed in the same line of business.

Useful life. Period over which an asset will be employed in a productive capacity, as measured either by the time over which it is expected to be used, or the number of production units expected to be obtained from the asset by the enterprise.

CONCEPTS, RULES, AND EXAMPLES

Property, Plant, and Equipment

Property, plant, and equipment (also variously referred to as plant assets, fixed tangible assets, or PP&E) is the term most often used to denote tangible property to be used in a productive capacity that will benefit the enterprise for a period of greater than one year. This term is meant to distinguish these assets from intangibles, which are long-term, generally identifiable assets that do not have physical substance, or whose value is not fully indicated by their physical existence.

There are four concerns to be addressed in accounting for fixed assets.

1. The amount at which the assets should be recorded initially on acquisition;
2. How value changes subsequent to acquisition should be reflected in the accounts, including questions of both value increases and possible decreases due to impairments;
3. The rate at which the amount the assets are recorded should be allocated as an expense to future periods; and
4. The recording of the ultimate disposal of the assets.

Initial measurement. All costs required to bring an asset into working condition should be recorded as part of the cost of the asset. Examples of such costs include sales, value added, or other nonrefundable taxes or duties, finders' fees, freight costs, site preparation and other installation costs, and setup costs. Thus, any reasonable cost incurred prior to using the asset in actual production involved in bringing the asset to the buyer is capitalized. These costs are not to be expensed in the period in which they are incurred, as they are deemed to add value to the asset and indeed were necessary expenditures to obtain the asset, provided that this does not lead to recording the asset at an amount greater than fair value.

The costs required to bring acquired assets to the place where they are to be used includes such ancillary costs as testing and calibrating, where relevant. IAS 16 aims to draw a distinction between the costs of getting the asset to the state in which it is in a condition to be exploited (which are to be included in the asset's carrying value) and costs associated with the start-up operations, such as staff training, down time between completion of the asset and the start of its exploitation, losses incurred through running at below normal capacity etc., which are considered to be operating expenses. To be netted against such costs are any revenues received during the installation process. As an example, the standard cites the sales of samples produced during this procedure.

IAS 16, as revised in 2003, distinguishes the situation in the preceding paragraph from other situations where incidental operations unrelated to the asset may occur before or during the construction or development activities. For example, it notes that income may be earned through using a building site as a car parking lot until construction begins. Because incidental operations such as this are not necessary to bring the asset to the location and working condition necessary for it to be capable of operating in the manner intended by management, the income and related expenses of incidental operations are to be recognized in current earnings, and included in their respective classifications of income and expense in the income statement. These are not to be presented net, as in the earlier example of machine testing costs and sample sales revenues.

Administrative costs, as well as other types of overhead costs, are not normally allocated to fixed asset acquisitions, despite the fact that some such costs, such as the salaries of the personnel who evaluate assets for proposed acquisitions, are in fact incurred as part of the acquisition process. As a general principle, administrative costs are expensed in the period incurred, based on the perception that these costs are fixed and would not be avoided in the absence of asset acquisitions. On the other hand, truly incremental costs, such as a consulting fee or commission paid to an agent hired specifically to assist in the acquisition, may be treated as part of the initial amount to be recognized as the asset cost.

While interest costs incurred during the construction of certain assets may be added to the cost of the asset (see below), if an asset is purchased on deferred payment terms, the interest cost, whether made explicit or imputed, is *not* part of the cost of the asset. Accordingly, such costs must be expensed currently as interest charges. If the purchase price for the asset incorporates a deferred payment scheme, only the cash equivalent price should be capitalized as the initial carrying amount of the asset. If the cash equivalent price is not explicitly stated, the deferred payment amount should be reduced to present value by the application of an appropriate discount rate. This would normally be best approximated by use of the enterprise's incremental borrowing cost for debt having a maturity similar to the deferred payment term.

Decommissioning costs included in initial measurement. The elements of cost to be incorporated in the initial recognition of an asset are to include the estimated costs of its eventual dismantlement ("decommissioning costs"). That is, the cost of the asset is "grossed up" for these estimated terminal costs, with the offsetting credit being posted to a liability account. It is important to stress that recognition of a liability can only be effected when all the criteria set forth in IAS 37 for the recognition of provisions are met. These stipulate that a provision is to be recognized only when (1) the reporting entity has a *present* obligation, whether legal or constructive, as a result of a *past* event; (2) it is *probable* that an outflow of resources embodying economic benefits will be required to settle the obligation; and (3) a reliable estimate can be made of the amount of the obligation.

For example, assume that it were necessary to secure a government license in order to construct a particular asset, such as a power generating plant, and a condition of the license is that at the end of the expected life of the property the owner would dismantle it, remove any debris, and restore the land to its previous condition. These conditions would qualify as a present obligation resulting from a past event (the plant construction), which will probably result in a future outflow of resources. The cost of such future activities, while perhaps challenging to estimate due to the long time horizon involved and the possible intervening evolution of technology, can normally be accomplished with a requisite degree of accuracy. Per IAS 37, a best estimate is to be made of the future costs, which is then to be discounted to present value. This present value is to be recognized as an additional cost of acquiring the asset.

The cost of dismantlement and similar legal or constructive obligations do not extend to operating costs to be incurred in the future, since those would not qualify as "present obligations." The precise mechanism for making these computations is addressed in Chapter 12.

If estimated costs of dismantlement, removal, and restoration are included in the cost of the asset, the effect will be to allocate this cost over the life of the asset through the depreciation process. Each period the discounting of the provision should be "unwound," such that interest cost is accreted each period. If this is done, at the expected date on which the expenditure is to be incurred it will be appropriately stated. The increase in the carrying value of the provision should be reported as interest expense or a similar financing cost.

Examples of decommissioning or similar costs to be recognized at acquisition

Example 1—Leased premises. In accordance with the terms of a lease, the lessee is obligated to remove its specialized machinery from the leased premises prior to vacating those premises, or to compensate the lessor accordingly. The lease imposes a contractual obligation on the lessee to remove the asset at the end of the asset's useful life or upon vacating the premises, and therefore in this situation an asset (i.e., deferred cost) and liability should be recognized. If the lease is a capital lease, it is added to the asset cost; if an operating lease (less likely), a deferred charge would be reported.

Example 2—Owned premises. The same machinery described in Example 1 is installed in a factory that the entity owns. At the end of the useful life of the machinery, the entity will either incur costs to dismantle and remove the asset or will leave it idle in place. If the entity chooses to do nothing (i.e., not remove the equipment), this would adversely affect the fair value of the premises should the entity choose to sell the premises on an "as is" basis. Conceptually, to apply the matching principle in a manner consistent with Example 1, the cost of asset retirement should be recognized systematically and rationally over the productive life of the asset and not in the period of retirement. However, in this example, there is no *legal obligation* on the part of the owner of the factory and equipment to retire the asset and, thus, a cost would *not* be recognized at inception for this possible future loss of value.

Example 3—Promissory estoppel. Assume the same facts as in Example 2. In this case, however, the owner of the property sold to a third party an option to purchase the factory, exercisable at the end of five years. In offering the option to the third party, the owner verbally represented that the factory would be completely vacant at the end of the five-year option period and that all machinery, furniture, and fixtures would be removed from the premises. The property owner would reasonably expect that the purchaser of the option relied to the purchaser's detriment (as evidenced by the financial sacrifice of consideration made in exchange for the option) on the representation that the factory would be vacant. While the legal status of such a promise may vary depending on local custom and law, in general this is a constructive obligation and should be recognized as a decommissioning cost and related liability.

Example of timing of recognition of decommissioning cost

Teradactyl Corporation owns and operates a chemical company. At its premises, it maintains underground tanks used to store various types of chemicals. The tanks were installed when Teradactyl Corporation purchased its facilities seven years prior. On February 1, 2006, the legislature of the nation passed a law that requires removal of such tanks when they are no longer being used. Since the law imposes a legal obligation on Teradactyl Corporation, upon enactment recognition of a decommissioning obligation would be required.

Example of ongoing additions to the decommissioning obligation

Jermyn Manufacturing Corporation operates a factory. As part of its normal operations it stores production by-products and used cleaning solvents on-site in a reservoir specifically designed for that purpose. The reservoir and surrounding land, all owned by Jermyn, are contaminated with these chemicals. On February 1, 2006, the legislature of the nation enacted a law that requires cleanup and disposal of hazardous waste from existing production processes upon retirement of the facility. Upon the enactment of the law, immediate recognition would be required for the decommissioning obligation associated with the contamination that had already occurred. In addition, liabilities will continue to be recognized over the remaining life of the facility as additional contamination occurs.

Changes in decommissioning costs. IFRIC 1 addresses the accounting treatment to be followed where a provision for reinstatement and dismantling costs has been created when an asset was acquired. The Interpretation requires that where estimates of future costs are revised, these should be applied prospectively only, and there is no adjustment to past years' depreciation. IFRIC 1 is addressed in Chapter 13 of this book.

Initial recognition of self-constructed assets. Essentially the same principles that have been established for recognition of the cost of purchased assets also apply to self-constructed assets. All costs that must be incurred to complete the construction of the asset can be added to the amount to be recognized initially, subject only to the constraint that if these costs exceed the recoverable amount (as discussed fully later in this chapter), the excess must be expensed currently. This rule is necessary to avoid the "gold-plated hammer syndrome," whereby a misguided or unfortunate asset construction project incurs excessive costs that then find their way onto the balance sheet, consequently overstating the entity's current net worth and distorting future periods' earnings. Of course, internal (intracompany) profits cannot be allocated to construction costs. The standard specifies that "abnormal amounts" of wasted material, labor or other resources may not be added to the cost of the asset.

Self-constructed assets may include, in addition to the range of costs discussed earlier, the cost of borrowed funds used during the period of construction. Capitalization of borrowing costs, as set forth by IAS 23, is discussed in a later section of this chapter.

The other issue that arises most commonly in connection with self-constructed fixed assets relates to overhead allocations. While capitalization of all direct costs (labor, materials, and variable overhead) is clearly required and proper, a controversy exists regarding the treatment of fixed overhead. Two alternative views of how to treat fixed overhead are to either

1. Charge the asset with its fair, pro rata share of fixed overhead (i.e., use the same basis of allocation used for inventory); or
2. Charge the fixed asset account with only the identifiable incremental amount of fixed overhead.

While international standards do not address this concern, it may be instructive to consider the nonbinding guidance to be found in US GAAP. AICPA Accounting Research Monograph 1 has suggested that

> *. . . in the absence of compelling evidence to the contrary, overhead costs considered to have "discernible future benefits" for the purposes of determining the cost of inventory should be presumed to have "discernible future benefits" for the purpose of determining the cost of a self-constructed depreciable asset.*

The implication of this statement is that a logic similar to what was applied to determining which acquisition costs may be included in inventory might reasonably also be applied to the costing of fixed assets. Also, consistent with the standards applicable to inventories, if the costs of fixed assets exceed realizable values, any excess costs should be written off to expense and not deferred to future periods.

Exchanges of assets. IAS 16 discusses the accounting to be applied to those situations in which assets are exchanged for other similar or dissimilar assets, with or without the additional consideration of monetary assets. This topic is addressed later in this chapter, under the heading "Nonmonetary (Exchange) Transactions."

Costs incurred subsequent to purchase or self-construction. Costs that are incurred subsequent to the purchase or construction of the long-lived asset, such as those for repairs, maintenance, or betterments, may involve an adjustment to the carrying value, or may be expensed, depending on the precise facts and circumstances.

To be capitalized, costs must be associated with incremental benefits. Costs can be added to the carrying value of the related asset only when it is *probable* that future economic benefits beyond those originally anticipated for the asset will be received by the entity. For example, modifications to the asset made to extend its useful life (measured either in years or in units of potential production) or to increase its capacity (e.g., as measured by units of output per hour) would be capitalized. Similarly, if the expenditure results in an improved quality of output, or permits a reduction in other cost inputs (e.g., would result in labor savings), it is a candidate for capitalization. As with self-constructed assets, if the costs incurred exceed the defined threshold, they must be expensed currently. Where a modification involves changing part of the asset (e.g., substituting a more powerful power source), the cost of the part that is removed should be treated as a disposal.

For example, roofs of commercial buildings, linings of blast furnaces used for steel making, and engines of commercial aircraft all need to be replaced or overhauled before the related buildings, furnaces, or airframes themselves must be replaced. If componentized deprecation was properly employed, the roofs, linings, and engines were being depreciated over their respectively shorter useful lives, and when the replacements or overhauls are performed, on average, these will have been fully depreciated. To the extent that undepreciated costs of these components remain, they would have to be removed from the account (i.e., charged to expense in the period of replacement or overhaul) as the newly incurred replacement or overhaul costs are added to the asset accounts, in order to avoid having, for financial reporting purposes, "two roofs on one building."

It can usually be assumed that ordinary maintenance and repair expenditures will occur on a ratable basis over the life of the asset and should be charged to expense as incurred. Thus, if the purpose of the expenditure is either to maintain the productive capacity anticipated when the asset was acquired or constructed, or to restore it to that level, the costs are not subject to capitalization.

A partial exception is encountered if an asset is acquired in a condition that necessitates that certain expenditures be incurred in order to put it into the appropriate state for its intended use. For example, a deteriorated building may be purchased with the intention that it be restored and then utilized as a factory or office facility. In such cases, costs that otherwise would be categorized as ordinary maintenance items might be subject to capitalization, subject to the constraint that the asset not be presented at a value that exceeds its recoverable amount. Once the restoration is completed, further expenditures of similar type would be viewed as being ordinary repairs or maintenance, and thus expensed as incurred.

However, costs associated with required inspections (e.g., of aircraft) could be capitalized and depreciated. These costs would be amortized over the expected period of benefit (i.e., the estimated time to the next inspection). As with the cost of physical assets, removal of any undepreciated costs of previous inspections would be required. The capitalized inspection cost would have to be treated as a separate component of the asset.

The chart on the following page summarizes the treatment of expenditures subsequent to acquisition consistent with the foregoing discussion.

Depreciation of property, plant, and equipment. In accordance with one of the more important of the basic accounting conventions, the matching principle, the costs of fixed assets are allocated through depreciation to the periods that will have benefited from the use of the asset. Whatever method of depreciation is chosen, it must result in the systematic and rational allocation of the depreciable amount of the asset (initial cost less residual value) over the asset's expected useful life. The determination of the useful life must take a number of factors into consideration. These factors include technological change, normal deterioration, actual physical use, and legal or other limitations on the ability to use the property. The method of depreciation is based on whether the useful life is determined as a function of time or as a function of actual physical usage.

IAS 16 states that, although land normally has an unlimited useful life and is not to be depreciated, where the cost of the land includes estimated dismantlement or restoration costs, these are to be depreciated over the period of benefits obtained by incurring those costs. In some cases, the land itself may have a limited useful life, in which case it is to be depreciated in a manner that reflects the benefits to be derived from it.

Since, under the historical cost convention, depreciation accounting is intended as a strategy for cost allocation, it does not reflect changes in the market value of the asset being amortized (except in some cases where the impairment rules have been applied in that way—as discussed below). Thus, with the exception of land, which has infinite life, all tangible fixed assets must be depreciated, even if (as sometimes occurs, particularly in periods of general price inflation) their nominal or real values increase.

Furthermore, if the recorded amount of the asset is allocated over a period of time (as opposed to actual use), it should be the expected period of usefulness to the entity, not the physical life of the property itself that governs. Thus, such concerns as technological obsolescence, as well as normal wear and tear, must be addressed in the initial determination of the period over which to allocate the asset cost. The reporting entity's strategy for repairs and maintenance will also affect this computation, since the same physical asset might have a longer or shorter economic useful life in the hands of differing owners, depending on the care with which it is intended to be maintained.

Similarly, the same asset may have a longer or shorter economic life, depending on its intended use. A particular building, for example, may have a fifty-year expected life as a facility for storing goods or for use in light manufacturing, but as a showroom would have a shorter period of usefulness, due to the anticipated disinclination of customers to shop at enterprises housed in older premises. Again, it is not physical life, but useful economic life, that should govern.

Compound assets, such as buildings containing such disparate components as heating plant, roofs, and other structural elements, are most commonly recorded in several separate accounts, to facilitate the process of amortizing the different elements over varying periods. Thus, a heating plant may have an expected useful life of twenty years, the roof a life of fifteen years, and the basic structure itself a life of forty years. Maintaining separate ledger accounts eases the calculation of periodic depreciation in such situations, although for financial reporting purposes a greater degree of aggregation is usual.

Accounting for Costs Incurred Subsequent to Acquisition of Property, Plant, and Equipment

Type of expenditure	Characteristics	Expense when incurred	Capitalize — Charge to asset	Capitalize — Charge to accum. deprec.	Other
1. Additions	• Extensions, enlargements, or expansions made to an existing asset		x		
2. Repairs and maintenance					
a. Ordinary	• Recurring, relatively small expenditures 1. Maintain normal operating condition 2. **Do not** add materially to use value 3. **Do not** extend useful life	x x x			
b. Extraordinary (major)	• Not recurring, relatively large expenditures 1. Primarily increase the use value 2. Primarily extend the useful life		x	x	
3. Replacements and betterments	• Major component of asset is removed and replaced with the same type of component with comparable performance capabilities (replacement) or a different type of component having superior performance capabilities (betterment)				
a. Book value of old component is known	1. Primarily increase the use value 2. Primarily extend the useful life		x	x	• Remove old asset cost and accum. deprec. • Recognize any loss (or gain) on old asset • Charge asset for replacement component
b. Book value of old component is not known	• Provide greater efficiency in production or reduce production costs			x	
4. Reinstallations and rearrangements	1. Material costs incurred; benefits extend into future accounting periods 2. No measurable future benefit	x	x		

IAS 16 as revised in 2003 now requires a components approach for depreciation, where, as described above, each material component of a composite asset with different useful lives or different patterns of depreciation is accounted for separately for the purpose of depreciation and accounting for subsequent expenditure (including replacement and renewal). Thus, rather than recording a newly acquired, existing office building as a single asset, it is recorded as a building shell, a heating plant, a roof, and perhaps other discrete mechanical components, subject to a materiality threshold. Allocation of cost over useful lives, instead of being based on a weighted-average of the varying components' lives, is based on separate estimated lives for each component.

IAS 16 states that the depreciation method should reflect the pattern in which the asset's future economic benefits are expected to be consumed by the entity, and that appropriateness of the method should be reviewed at least annually in case there has been a change in the expected pattern. Beyond that, the standard leaves the choice of method to the entity, even though it does cite straight-line, diminishing balance and units of production methods.

Depreciation methods based on time.

1. Straight-line—Depreciation expense is incurred evenly over the life of the asset. The periodic charge for depreciation is given as

$$\frac{\text{Cost or amount substituted for cost, less residual value}}{\text{Estimated useful life of asset}}$$

2. Accelerated methods—Depreciation expense is higher in the early years of the asset's useful life and lower in the later years. IAS 16 only mentions one accelerated method, the diminishing balance method, but other methods have been employed in various national GAAP under earlier or contemporary accounting standards.

    a. Diminishing balance—the depreciation rate is applied to the net book value of the asset, resulting in a diminishing annual charge. There are various ways to compute the percentage to be applied. The formula below provides a mathematically correct allocation over useful life.

$$\text{Rate \%} = \left(1 - \sqrt[n]{\text{residual value/cost}}\right) \times 100$$

    where n is the expected useful life in years. However, companies generally use approximations or conventions influenced by tax practice, such as a multiple of the straight-line rate times the net carrying value at the beginning of the year.

$$\text{Straight-line rate} = \frac{1}{\text{Estimated useful life}}$$

    Example

    Double-declining balance depreciation (if salvage value is to be recognized, stop when book value = estimated salvage value)

    Depreciation = 2 x Straight-line rate x Book value at beginning of year

    Another method to accomplish a diminishing charge for depreciation is the sum-of-the-years' digits method, which is commonly employed in the United States and certain other venues.

    b. Sum-of-the-years' digits (SYD) depreciation =

    (Cost less salvage value) x Applicable fraction

$$\text{where applicable fraction} = \frac{\text{number of years of estimated life remaining as of the beginning of the year}}{\text{SYD}}$$

$$\text{and } SYD = \frac{n(n+1)}{2} \quad \text{and } n = \text{estimated useful life}$$

Example

An asset having a useful economic life of 5 years and no salvage value would have 5/15 (= 1/3) of its cost allocated to year 1, 4/15 to year 2, and so on.

In practice, unless there are tax reasons to employ accelerated methods, large companies tend to use straight-line depreciation. This has the merit that it is simple to apply, and where a company has a large pool of similar assets, some of which are replaced each year, the aggregate annual depreciation charge is likely to be the same, irrespective of the method chosen (consider a trucking company that has ten trucks, each costing $200,000, one of which is replaced each year: the aggregate annual depreciation charge will be $200,000 under any mathematically accurate depreciation method).

Partial-year depreciation. Although IAS 16 is silent on the matter, when an asset is either acquired or disposed of during the year, the full year depreciation calculation should be prorated between the accounting periods involved. This is necessary to achieve proper matching. However, if individual assets in a relatively homogeneous group are regularly acquired and disposed of, one of several conventions can be adopted, as follows:

1. Record a full year's depreciation in the year of acquisition and none in the year of disposal.
2. Record one-half year's depreciation in the year of acquisition and one-half year's depreciation in the year of disposal.

Example of partial-year depreciation

Assume the following:

Taj Mahal Milling Co., a calendar-year entity, acquired a machine on June 1, 2005, that cost €40,000 with an estimated useful life of four years and a €2,500 salvage value. The depreciation expense for each *full* year of the asset's life is calculated as follows:

	Straight-line		*Double-declining balance*					*Sum-of-years' digits*		
Year 1	€37,500* ÷ 4 = €9,375	50% x	€40,000	=	€20,000	4/10 x		€37,500*	=	€15,000
Year 2	€9,375	50% x	€20,000	=	€10,000	3/10 x		€37,500	=	€11,250
Year 3	€9,375	50% x	€10,000	=	€5,000	2/10 x		€37,500	=	€7,500
Year 4	€9,375	50% x	€5,000	=	€2,500	1/10 x		€37,500	=	€3,750

* *€40,000 – €2,500.*

Because the first full year of the asset's life does not coincide with the company's fiscal year, the amounts shown above must be prorated as follows:

	Straight-line	*Double-declining balance*					*Sum-of-years' digits*			
2005	7/12 x 9,375 = €5,469	7/12 x	€20,000	=	€11,667	7/12 x	€15,000	=	€ 8,750
2006	€9,375	5/12 x	€20,000	=	€ 8,333	5/12 x	€15,000	=	€ 6,250
		7/12 x	€10,000	=	€ 5,833	7/12 x	€11,250	=	€ 6,563
					€14,166				€12,813
2007	€9,375	5/12 x	€10,000	=	€ 4,167	5/12 x	€11,250	=	€ 4,687
		7/12 x	€ 5,000	=	€ 2,917	7/12 x	€ 7,500	=	€ 4,375
					€ 7,084				€ 9,062

2008		€9,375	5/12	x	€5,000	=	€2,083	5/12	x	€7,500	=	€3,125
			7/12	x	€2,500	=	€1,458	7/12	x	€3,750	=	€2,188
							€3,541					€5,313
2009	5/12 x 9,375 = €3,906		5/12	x	€2,500	=	€1,042	5/12	x	€3,750	=	€1,562

Depreciation method based on actual physical use—Units of production method. Depreciation may also be based on the number of units produced by the asset in a given year. IAS 16 identifies this as the units of production method, but it is also known as the sum of the units approach. It is best suited to those assets, such as machinery, that have an expected life that is most rationally defined in terms of productive output; in periods of reduced production (such as economic recession) the machinery is used less, thus extending the number of years it is likely to remain in service. This method has the merit that the annual depreciation expense fluctuates with the contribution made by the asset each year. Furthermore, if the depreciation finds its way into the cost of finished goods, the unit cost in periods of reduced production would be exaggerated and could even exceed net realizable value unless a units of production approach to depreciation were taken.

$$\text{Depreciation rate} = \frac{\text{Cost less residual value}}{\substack{\text{Estimated number of units to be produced} \\ \text{by the asset over its estimated useful life}}}$$

$$\substack{\text{Units of} \\ \text{production} \\ \text{depreciation}} = \text{Depreciation rate} \quad x \quad \substack{\text{Number of units} \\ \text{produced during} \\ \text{the period}}$$

Other depreciation methods. Although IAS 16 does not discuss other methods of depreciation (nor even all the variations noted in the foregoing paragraphs), at different times and in various jurisdictions other methods have been used. Some of these are summarized as follows:

1. **Retirement method**—Cost of asset is expensed in period in which it is retired.
2. **Replacement method**—Original cost is carried in accounts and cost of replacement is expensed in the period of replacement. (Neither the retirement nor replacement methods would be acceptable under IAS 16 because they do not reflect the pattern of consumption.)
3. **Group (or composite) method**—Averages the service lives of a number of assets using a weighted-average of the units and depreciates the group or composite as if it were a single unit. A group consists of similar assets, while a composite is made up of dissimilar assets.

$$\text{Depreciation rate} = \frac{\substack{\text{Sum of the straight-line} \\ \text{depreciation of individual assets}}}{\text{Total asset cost}}$$

Depreciation expense = Depreciation rate x Total group (composite) cost

A peculiarity of the composite approach is that gains and losses are not recognized on the disposal of an asset, but rather, are netted into accumulated depreciation. This is because it is a presumption of this method that although dispositions of individual assets may yield proceeds greater than or less than their respective book values, the ultimate gross proceeds from a group of assets will not differ materially from the aggregate book value thereof, and accordingly, recognition of those individual gains or losses should be deferred and effectively netted out.

4. **Revenue method**—The future cash flows expected to be derived from asset are estimated, and a percentage is calculated which reflects the cost of the asset as a

proportion of its expected revenue. When revenue is received, that percentage is applied to it as a depreciation charge. This is used, for example, for films, and could be considered to be a variant on the units of production method.

Residual value. Most depreciation methods discussed above require that depreciation is applied not to the full cost of the asset, but to the "depreciable amount": that is, the historical cost or amount substituted therefore (i.e., fair value) less the estimated residual value of the asset. As IAS 16 points out, residual value is often not material and in practice is frequently ignored, but it may impact upon some assets, particularly when the entity disposes of them early in their life (e.g., rental vehicles) or where the residual value is so high as to negate any requirement for depreciation (some hotel companies, for example, claim that they have to maintain their premises to such a high standard that their residual value under historical cost is higher than the original cost of the asset).

Under historical cost, residual value is defined as the expected worth of the asset, in present dollars (i.e., without any consideration of the impact of future inflation), at the end of its useful life. Residual value should, however, be measured net of any expected costs of disposal. In some cases, assets will have a negative residual value, as for example when the entity is likely to incur costs to dispose of the asset, or to return the property to an earlier condition, as in the case of certain operations, such as strip mines, that are subject to environmental protection or other laws. In such instances, periodic depreciation should total more than the asset's original cost, such that at the expected disposal date, an estimated liability has been accrued equal to the negative residual value. The residual value is, like all aspects of the depreciation method, subject to at least annual review.

If the revaluation method of measuring tangible fixed assets is chosen, residual value must be assessed anew at the date of each revaluation of the asset. This is accomplished by using data on realizable values for similar assets, ending their respective useful lives at the time of the revaluation, after having been used for purposes similar to the asset being valued. Again, no consideration can be paid to anticipated inflation, and expected future values are not to be discounted to present values to give recognition to the time value of money. As with historical cost based accounting for plant assets, if a negative residual value is anticipated, this should be effectively recognized over the useful life of the asset by charging extra depreciation, such that the estimated liability will have been accrued by the disposal date.

Useful lives. Useful life is affected by such things as the entity's practices regarding repairs and maintenance of its assets, as well as the pace of technological change and the market demand for goods produced and sold by the entity using the assets as productive inputs. If it is determined, when reviewing the depreciation method, that the estimated life is greater or less than previously believed, the change is handled as a change in accounting estimate, not as a correction of an accounting error. Accordingly, no restatement is to be made to previously reported depreciation; rather, the change is accounted for strictly on a prospective basis, being reflected in the period of change and subsequent periods.

Example of estimating the useful life

To illustrate this concept, consider an asset costing €100,000 and originally estimated to have a productive life of 10 years. The straight-line method is used, and there was no residual value anticipated. After 2 years, management revises its estimate of useful life to a total of 6 years. Since the net carrying value of the asset is €80,000 after 2 years (= €100,000 x 8/10), and the remaining expected life is 4 years (2 of the 6 revised total years having already elapsed), depreciation in years 3 through 6 will be €20,000 (= €80,000/4) each.

Tax methods. The methods of computing depreciation discussed in the foregoing sections relate only to financial reporting under IFRS. Tax laws in different nations of the world vary widely in terms of the acceptability of depreciation methods, and it is not possible for a general treatise such as this to address those in any detail. However, to the extent that depreciation allowable for income tax reporting purposes differs from that required or permitted for financial statement purposes, deferred income taxes would have to be computed. Interperiod income tax allocation is discussed more fully in Chapter 15.

Leasehold improvements. Leasehold improvements are improvements to property not owned by the party making these investments. For example, a lessee of office space may invest its funds to install partitions or to combine several suites by removing certain interior walls. Due to the nature of these physical changes to the property (done with the lessor's permission, of course), the lessee cannot remove or undo these changes and must abandon them upon termination of the lease, if the lessee does not remain in the facility.

There is no guidance under IFRS on how to account for leasehold improvements, per se. The recommendations made in the following paragraphs is derived from those under US GAAP but, in the authors' opinion, is straightforward and not subject to serious debate.

Leasehold improvements are often classified as intangibles because the reporting entity has only the (intangible) right to use the property, and does not own the physical property itself once it is attached to the leased property in a way that it cannot be removed or undone. On the other hand, leasehold improvements are not always perceived of as intangibles because they involve tangible physical enhancements made to property by or on behalf of the property's lessee. By law in many jurisdictions, when improvements are made to real property and those improvements are permanently affixed to the property, the title to those improvements automatically transfers to the owner of the property. The rationale behind this is that the improvements, when permanently affixed, are inseparable from the rest of the real estate. For purposes of the following discussion, whether leasehold improvements are depreciated or amortized is a mere semantic point, and does not alter the substance of this guidance. (The term amortization will be used here, however.)

A frequently encountered issue with respect to leasehold improvements relates to determination of the period over which they are to be amortized. Normally, the cost of long-lived assets is charged to expense over the estimated useful lives of the assets. However, the right to use a leasehold improvement expires when the related lease expires, irrespective of whether the improvement has any remaining useful life. Thus, the appropriate useful life for a leasehold improvement is the lesser of the useful life of the improvement or the term of the underlying lease.

Some leases contain a fixed, noncancelable term and additional renewal options. When considering the term of the lease for the purposes of amortizing leasehold improvements, normally only the initial fixed noncancelable term is included. There are exceptions to this general rule, however. If a renewal option is a bargain renewal option, which means that it is probable at the inception of the lease that it will be exercised and, therefore, the option period should be included in the lease term for purposes of determining the amortizable life of the leasehold improvements. Additionally, under the definition of the lease term there are other situations where it is probable that an option to renew for an additional period would be exercised. These situations include periods for which failure to renew the lease imposes a penalty on the lessee in such amount that a renewal appears, at the inception of the lease, to be reasonably assured. Other situations of this kind arise when an otherwise excludable renewal period precedes a provision for a bargain purchase of the leased asset or when, during periods covered by ordinary renewal options, the lessee has guaranteed the lessor's debt on the leased property.

Example

Mojo Corporation occupies a warehouse under a five-year operating lease commencing January 1, 2006, and expiring December 31, 2010. The lease contains three successive options to renew the lease for additional five-year periods. The options are not bargain renewals as they call for fixed rentals at the prevailing fair market rents that will be in effect at the time of exercise. When the initial calculation was made to determine whether the lease is an operating lease or a capital lease, only the initial noncancelable term of five years was included in the calculation. Consequently, for the purpose of determining the amortizable life of any leasehold improvements made by Mojo Corporation, only the initial five-year term is used. If Mojo Corporation decides, at the beginning of year four of the lease, to make a substantial amount of leasehold improvements to the leased property, it could be argued that it would now be probable that Mojo would exercise one or more of the renewal periods, since not doing so would impose the substantial financial penalty for abandoning expensive leasehold improvements. This would trigger accounting for the lease by treating the period or periods for which it is likely that the lessee will renew as a new agreement and require testing to determine whether the lease, prospectively, qualifies as a capital or operating lease.

Revaluation of Property, Plant, and Equipment

IAS 16 provides for two acceptable alternative approaches to accounting for long-lived tangible assets. The first of these is the historical cost method, under which acquisition or construction cost is used for initial recognition, subject to depreciation over the expected economic life and to possible write-down in the event of a permanent impairment in value. In many jurisdictions this is the only method allowed by statute, but a number of jurisdictions, particularly those with significant rates of inflation, do permit either full or selective revaluation and IAS 16 acknowledges this by also mandating what it calls the "revaluation model."

The logic of recognizing revaluations relates to both the balance sheet and the measure of periodic performance provided by the income statement. Due to the effects of inflation (which even if quite moderate when measured on an annual basis can compound dramatically during the lengthy period over which fixed assets remain in use) the balance sheet can become a virtually meaningless agglomeration of dissimilar costs.

Furthermore, if the depreciation charge to income is determined by reference to historical costs of assets acquired in much earlier periods, profits will be overstated, and will not reflect the cost of maintaining the entity's asset base. Under these circumstances, a nominally profitable enterprise might find that it has self-liquidated and is unable to continue in existence, at least not with the same level of productive capacity, without new debt or equity infusions. IAS 29, *Financial Reporting in Hyperinflationary Economies,* addresses adjustments to deprecation under conditions of hyperinflation. Use of the revaluation method is typically encountered in economies that from time to time suffer less significant inflation than that which necessitates application of the procedures specified by IAS 29.

Fair value. As the basis for the revaluation method, the standard stipulates that it is *fair value* (defined as the amount for which the asset could be exchanged between knowledgeable, willing parties in an arm's-length transaction) that is to be used in any such revaluations. Furthermore, the standard requires that, once an entity undertakes revaluations, they must continue to be made with sufficient regularity that the carrying amounts in any subsequent balance sheet are not materially at variance with then-current fair values. In other words, if the reporting entity adopts the revaluation method, it cannot report balance sheets that contain obsolete fair values, since that would not only obviate the purpose of the allowed treatment, but would actually make it impossible for the user to meaningfully interpret the financial statements.

IAS 16 suggests that fair value is usually determined by appraisers, using market-based evidence. Market values can also be used for machinery and equipment, but since such items often do not have readily determinable market values, particularly if intended for specialized applications, they may instead be valued at depreciated replacement cost. At the moment, the term fair value is employed by several IFRS without reference to any detailed guidance as to how it is applied. Such guidance may be forthcoming (e.g., the IASB's ongoing business combinations project is to address this very issue in the context of allocation of purchase cost to acquired assets. In the interim, it can be useful to refer to the 2004 FASB Exposure Draft on the measurement of fair value, which identifies three levels of fair value. It cited as the highest the observable market transactions for the same kind of asset; the second best being observable market transactions for similar assets; and the final being the use of valuation models having some market inputs, or some other basis. Under the FASB's proposal, when fair value would be used the entity would need to disclose which level of valuation had been employed, and if level three, what actual model was being employed.

Alternative concepts of current value. A number of different concepts have been proposed over the years to achieve accounting adjusted for inflation. Methods that address changes in specific prices, in contrast to those that attempt to adjust for general purchasing power changes, have measured reproduction cost, replacement cost, sound value, exit value, entry value, and net present value.

In brief, *reproduction cost* refers to the actual current cost of exactly reproducing the asset, essentially ignoring changes in technology in favor of a strict bricks-and-mortar concept. Since the same service potential could be obtained currently, in many cases, without a literal reproduction of the asset, this method fails to fully address the economic reality that accounting should ideally attempt to measure.

Replacement cost, in contrast, deals with the service potential of the asset, which is after all what truly represents value for its owner. An obvious example can be found in the realm of computers. While the cost to reproduce a particular mainframe machine exactly might be the same or somewhat lower today versus its original purchase price, the computing capacity of the machine might easily be replaced by one or a small group of microcomputers that could be obtained for a fraction of the cost of the larger machine. To gross up the balance sheet by reference to reproduction cost would be distorting, at the very least. Instead, the replacement cost of the service potential of the owned asset should be used to accomplish the revaluation contemplated by IAS 16.

Furthermore, even replacement cost, if reported on a gross basis, would be an exaggeration of the value implicit in the reporting entity's asset holdings, since the asset in question has already had some fraction of its service life expire. The concept of sound value addresses this concern. Sound value is the equivalent of the cost of replacement of the service potential of the asset, adjusted to reflect the relative loss in its utility due to the passage of time or the fraction of total productive capacity that has already been utilized.

Example of depreciated replacement cost (sound value) as a valuation approach

An asset acquired January 1, 2003, at a cost of €40,000 was expected to have a useful economic life of 10 years. On January 1, 2006, it is appraised as having a gross replacement cost of €50,000. The sound value, or depreciated replacement cost, would be 7/10 x €50,000, or €35,000. This compares with a book, or carrying, value of €28,000 at that same date. Mechanically, to accomplish a revaluation at January 1, 2006, the asset should be written up by €10,000 (i.e., from €40,000 to €50,000 gross cost) and the accumulated depreciation should be proportionally written up by €3,000 (from €12,000 to €15,000). Under IAS 16, the net amount of the revaluation adjustment, €7,000, would be credited to revaluation surplus, an additional equity account.

An alternative accounting procedure is also permitted by the standard, under which the accumulated depreciation at the date of the revaluation is written off against the gross carrying value of the asset. In the foregoing example, this would mean that the €12,000 of accumulated depreciation at January 1, 2006, immediately prior to the revaluation, would be credited to the gross asset amount, €40,000, thereby reducing it to €28,000. Then the asset account would be adjusted to reflect the valuation of €35,000 by increasing the asset account by €7,000 (€35,000 − €28,000), with the offset again in stockholders' equity. In terms of total assets reported in the balance sheet, this has exactly the same effect as the first method.

However, many users of financial statements, including credit grantors and prospective investors, pay heed to the ratio of net property and equipment as a fraction of the related gross amounts. This is done to assess the relative age of the enterprise's productive assets and, indirectly, to estimate the timing and amounts of cash needed for asset replacements. There is a significant diminution of information under the second method. Accordingly, the first approach described above, preserving the relationship between gross and net asset amounts after the revaluation, is recommended as being the preferable alternative if the goal is meaningful financial reporting.

Revaluation applied to all assets in the class. IAS 16 requires that if any assets are revalued, all other assets in those groupings or categories must also be revalued. This is necessary to prevent the presentation of a balance sheet that contains an unintelligible and possibly misleading mix of historical costs and current values, and to preclude selective revaluation designed to maximize reported net assets. Coupled with the requirement that revaluations take place with sufficient frequency to approximate fair values as of each balance sheet date, this preserves the integrity of the financial reporting process. In fact, given that a balance sheet prepared under the historical cost method will, in fact, contain noncomparable values for similar assets (due to assets having been acquired at varying times, at differing price levels), the revaluation approach has the possibility of providing more consistent financial reporting. Offsetting this potential improvement, at least somewhat, is the greater subjectivity inherent in the use of fair values, providing an example of the conceptual framework's trade-off between relevance and reliability.

Although IAS 16 requires revaluation of all assets in a given class, the standard recognizes that it may be more practical to accomplish this on a rolling, or cycle, basis. This could be done by revaluing one-third of the assets in a given asset category, such as machinery, in each year, so that as of any balance sheet date one-third of the group is valued at current fair value, another one-third is valued at amounts that are one year obsolete, and another one-third are valued at amounts that are two years obsolete. Unless values are changing rapidly, it is likely that the balance sheet would not be materially distorted, and therefore, this approach would in all likelihood be a reasonable means to facilitate the revaluation process.

Revaluation adjustments taken into income. In general, revaluation adjustments are to be shown directly in equity as revaluation surplus. If a revalued asset is subsequently found to be impaired, the impairment provision is first offset against the revaluation surplus, and only when that has been exhausted is it expensed. (Equally, if an asset carried at historical cost had been impaired, but was subsequently revalued above historical cost, because of some dramatic change in economic circumstances, the previous impairment provision would flow back through income, and only the increase above historical cost would go directly to equity.)

Under the provisions of IAS 16, the amount credited to revaluation surplus can either be amortized to retained earnings (but *not* through the income statement!) as the asset is being depreciated, or it can be held in the surplus account until such time as the asset is disposed of or retired from service. Any amortization is limited to an amount equal to the difference between historical cost amortization and that charged in the income statement, based on the revalued amount.

Deferred tax effects of revaluations. As described in detail in Chapter 15, the tax effects of temporary differences must be provided. Where plant assets are depreciated over longer lives for financial reporting purposes than for tax reporting purposes, a deferred tax liability will be created in the early years and then drawn down in later years. Generally speaking, the deferred tax provided will be measured by the expected future tax rate applied to the temporary difference at the time it reverses; unless future tax rate changes have already been enacted, the current rate structure is used as an unbiased estimator of those future effects.

In the case of revaluation of plant assets, it may be that taxing authorities will not permit the higher revalued amounts to be depreciated for purposes of computing tax liabilities. Instead, only the actual cost incurred can be used to offset tax obligations. On the other hand, since revaluations reflect a holding gain, this gain would be taxable if realized. Accordingly, a deferred tax liability is still required to be recognized, even though it does not relate to temporary differences arising from periodic depreciation charges.

SIC 21 confirms that measurement of the deferred tax effects relating to the revaluation of nondepreciable assets must be made with reference to the tax consequences that would follow from recovery of the carrying amount of that asset through an eventual sale. This is necessary because the asset will not be depreciated, and hence, no part of its carrying amount is considered to be recovered through use. As a practical matter this means that if there are differential capital gain and ordinary income tax rates, deferred taxes will be computed with reference to the former.

Impairment of Tangible Long-Lived Assets

Until the promulgation of IAS 36, there had been a wide range of practices dealing with impairment recognition and measurement. Many European jurisdictions had statutory obligations to compare the carrying value of assets with their market value, but these requirements were not necessarily applied rigorously. Some jurisdictions, typically those with a British company law tradition, had no requirement to reflect impairment unless it was permanent and long-term. The much more rigorous approach of IAS 36 reflects awareness by regulators that this has been a neglected area in financial reporting.

Principal requirements of IAS 36. In general, the standard requires that the entity tests for impairment when there is an indication that an asset might be impaired (but annually for intangible assets having an indefinite useful life). When carried out, the test is applied to the smallest group of assets for which the entity has identifiable cash flows, called a "cash generating unit." The carrying amount of the asset or assets in the cash generating unit (cash generating unit) is compared with the fair value and the present value of the cash flows expected to be generated by using the asset ("value in use"). If the higher of these future values is lower than the carrying amount, an impairment is recognized for the difference.

Identifying impairments. According to IAS 36, at each financial reporting date the reporting entity should determine whether there are conditions that would indicate that impairments may have occurred. Note that this is *not* a requirement that possible impairments be calculated for all assets at each balance sheet date, which would be a formidable undertaking for most enterprises. Rather, it is the existence of conditions that might be suggestive of a heightened risk of impairment that must be evaluated. However, if such indicators are present, then further analysis will be necessary.

The standard provides a set of indicators of potential impairment and suggests that these represent a minimum array of factors to be given consideration. Other more industry- or entity-specific gauges could be devised by the reporting enterprise.

At a minimum, the following external and internal signs of possible impairment are to be given consideration on an annual basis:

- Market value declines for specific assets or cash generating units, beyond the declines expected as a function of asset aging and use;
- Significant changes in the technological, market, economic, or legal environments in which the enterprise operates, or the specific market to which the asset is dedicated;
- Increases in the market interest rate or other market-oriented rate of return such that increases in the discount rate to be employed in determining value in use can be anticipated, with a resultant enhanced likelihood that impairments will emerge;
- Declines in the (publicly owned) entity's market capitalization suggest that the aggregate carrying value of assets exceeds the perceived value of the enterprise taken as a whole;
- There is specific evidence of obsolescence or of physical damage to an asset or group of assets;
- There have been significant internal changes to the organization or its operations, such as product discontinuation decisions or restructurings, so that the expected remaining useful life or utility of the asset has seemingly been reduced; and
- Internal reporting data suggest that the economic performance of the asset or group of assets is, or will become, worse than previously anticipated.

The mere fact that one or more of the foregoing indicators suggests that there might be cause for concern about possible asset impairment does not necessarily mean that formal impairment testing must proceed in every instance, although in the absence of a plausible explanation why the signals of possible impairment should not be further considered, the implication would be that some follow-up investigation is needed.

Computing recoverable amounts—General concepts. IAS 36 defines impairment as the excess of carrying value over recoverable amount, and defines recoverable amount as the greater of two alternative measures: net selling price and value in use. The objective is to recognize an impairment when the economic value of an asset (or cash generating unit comprised of a group of assets) is truly below its book (carrying) value. In theory, and for the most part in practice also, an entity making rational choices would sell an asset if its net selling price (fair value less costs of disposal) were greater than the asset's value in use, and would continue to employ the asset if value in use exceeded salvage value. Thus, the economic value of an asset is most meaningfully measured with reference to the greater of these two amounts, since the entity will either retain or dispose of the asset, consistent with what appears to be its highest and best use. Once recoverable amount has been determined, this is to be compared to carrying value; if recoverable amount is lower, the asset has been impaired, and this impairment must be given accounting recognition. It should be noted that value in use is an entity-specific value, in contrast to fair value, which is based on market price. Value in use is thus a much more subjective measurement than is fair value, since it takes account of factors available only to the individual business, which may be difficult to validate.

Determining net selling prices. The determination of the fair value less costs to sell (i.e., net selling price) and the value in use of the asset being evaluated will typically present some difficulties. For actively traded assets, fair value can be ascertained by reference to publicly available information (e.g., from price lists or dealer quotations), and costs of disposal will either be implicitly factored into those amounts (such as when a dealer quote includes pick-up, shipping, etc.) or else can be readily estimated. Most common productive tangible assets, such as machinery and equipment, will not easily be priced, however, since active markets for used items will either not exist or be relatively illiquid. It will often be necessary to reason by analogy (i.e., to draw inferences from recent transactions in similar assets), making adjustments for age, condition, productive capacity, and other variables. For example, a five-year-old machine having an output rate (for a given component) of 2,000 units per day, and an estimated useful life of eight years, might be valued at 30% (=3/8 × .8) of the cost of a new replacement machine having a capacity of 2,500 units per day. In many industries, trade publications and other data sources can provide a great deal of insight into the market value of key assets. As discussed above, the FASB expects to finalize guidance on measuring fair value and this may provide the model for the IASB's own efforts.

Computing value in use. The computation of value in use involves a two-step process: first, future cash flows must be estimated; and second, the present value of these cash flows must be calculated by application of an appropriate discount rate. These will be discussed in turn in the following paragraphs.

Projection of future cash flows must be based on reasonable assumptions. Exaggerated revenue growth rates, significant anticipated cost reductions, or unreasonable useful lives for plant assets must be avoided if meaningful results are to be obtained. In general, recent past experience is a fair guide to the near-term future, but a recent sudden growth spurt should not be extrapolated to more than the very near-term future. For example, if growth over the past five years averaged 5% but in the latest year equaled 15%, unless the recent rate of growth can be identified with factors that demonstrate it as being sustainable, a future growth rate of 5%, or slightly higher, would be more supportable.

Typically, extrapolation cannot be made to a greater number of future periods than the number of "base periods" upon which the projection is built. Thus, a five-year projection, to be sound, should be based on at least five years of actual historical performance data. Also, since no business can grow exponentially forever—even if, for example, a five-year historical analysis suggests a 20% annual (inflation adjusted) growth rate—beyond a horizon of a few years a moderation of that growth must be hypothesized. This is even more important for a single asset or small cash generating unit, since physical constraints and the ironclad law of diminishing marginal returns makes it virtually inevitable that a plateau will be reached, beyond which further growth will be tightly constrained. Basic economic laws suggest that, if exceptional returns are being reaped from the assets used to produce a product line, competitors will enter the market and limit future profitability.

IAS 36 stipulates that steady or declining growth rates must be utilized for periods beyond those covered by the most recent budgets and forecasts. It further states that, barring an ability to demonstrate why a higher rate is appropriate, the growth rate should not exceed the long-term growth rate of the industry in which the entity participates.

The guidance offered by IAS 36 suggests that only normal, recurring cash inflows and outflows from the continuing use of the asset being evaluated should be considered, to which would be added any estimated salvage value at the end of the asset's useful life. Noncash costs, such as depreciation of the asset, obviously must be excluded from this calculation, since, in the case of depreciation, this would in effect double count the very item being measured. Furthermore, projections should always exclude cash flows related to financing the asset—for example, interest and principal repayments on any debt incurred in acquiring the asset—since operating decisions (e.g., keeping or disposing of an asset) are to be evaluated separately from financing decisions (borrowing, leasing, buying with equity capital funds). Also, cash flow projections must relate to the asset in its existing state and in its current use, without regard to possible future enhancements. Income tax effects are also to be disregarded (i.e., the entire analysis should be on a pretax basis).

Cash generating units. Under IAS 36, when cash flows cannot be identified with individual assets, (as is frequently the case), these must be grouped in order to permit an assessment of future cash flows. The requirement is that this grouping be performed at the lowest level possible, which would be the smallest aggregation of assets for which discrete cash flows can be identified, and which are independent of other groups of assets. In practice, this unit may be a department, a product line, or a factory, for which the output of product and the input of raw materials, labor, and overhead can be identified.

Thus, while the precise contribution to overall cash flow made by, say, a given drill press or lathe may be impossible to surmise, the cash inflows and outflows of a department which produces and sells a discrete product line to an identified group of customers can be more readily determined. To comply with IFRS, the extent of aggregation must be the minimum necessary to develop cash flow information for impairment assessment, and no greater.

A too-high level of aggregation is prohibited for a very basic reason: doing so could permit some impairments to be concealed, by effectively offsetting impairment losses against productivity or profitability gains derived from the expected future use of other assets. Consider an entity which is, overall, quite profitable and which generates positive cash flow, although certain departments or product lines are significantly unprofitable and cash drains. If aggregation at the entity level were permitted, there would be no impairment to be recognized, which would thwart IAS 36's objectives. If impairment testing were done at the departmental or product line level, on the other hand—consistent with IAS 36 requirements—then some loss-producing assets would be written down for impairment, while the cash-generating assets would continue to be accounted for at amortized historical cost.

Put another way, excessive aggregation results (when there are both cash generating and cash using groups of operating assets, departments, or product lines) in the recognition of unrealized gains on some assets that nominally are being accounted for on the historical cost basis, which violates IFRS. These gains, while concealed and not reported as such, offset the impairment losses on assets (or groups of assets) whose value have suffered diminutions in value. IAS 36 does not permit this result to be obtained.

IAS 36 requires that cash generating units be defined consistently from period to period. In addition to being necessary for consistency in financial reporting from period to period, which is an important objective per se, it is also needed to preclude the opportunistic redefining of cash generating groups effected in order to minimize or eliminate impairment recognition.

Discount rate. The other measurement issue in computing value in use comes from identifying the appropriate discount rate to apply to projected future cash flows. The discount rate is comprised of subcomponents. The base component of the discount rate is the current market rate, which should be identical for all impairment testing at any given date. This must be adjusted for the risks specific to the asset, which thus adds the second component of discount rate.

In practice, this asset class risk adjustment can be built into the cash flows. Appendix A to the standard discusses what it describes as the *traditional approach* to present value calculation, where forecast cash flows are discounted using a rate that is adjusted for uncertainties. It also describes the *expected value* method, where the forecast cash flows are directly adjusted to reflect uncertainty and then discounted at the market rate. These are alternative approaches and care must be exercised to apply one or the other correctly. Most importantly, risk should not be adjusted for twice in computing the present value of future cash flows.

IAS 36 suggests that identifying the appropriate risk-adjusted cost of capital to employ as a discount rate can be accomplished by reference to the implicit rates in current market transactions (e.g., leasing transactions), or from the weighted-average cost of capital of publicly traded enterprises operating in the same industry grouping. Such statistics are available for certain industry segments in selected (but not all) markets. The entity's own recent transactions, typically involving leasing or borrowing to buy other long-lived assets, will be highly salient information in estimating the appropriate discount rate to use.

When risk-adjusted rates are not available, however, it will become necessary to develop a discount rate from surrogate data. The two steps to this procedure are (1) to identify the pure time value of money for the requisite time horizon over which the asset will be utilized: and (2) to add an appropriate risk premium to the pure interest factor, which is related to the variability of future cash flows. Regarding the first component, the life of the asset being tested for impairment will be critical; short-term obligations almost always carry a lower rate than intermediate or long-term ones, although there have been periods when "yield curve inversions" have been dramatic. As to the second element, projected future cash flows having greater variability (which is the technical definition of risk) will be associated with higher risk premiums.

Of these two discount rate components, the latter is likely to prove the more difficult to determine or estimate, in practice. IAS 36 provides a fairly extended discussion of the methodology to utilize, however, and this should be carefully considered before embarking on this procedure. It addresses such factors as country risk, currency risk, cash flow risk, and pricing risk.

The interest rate is considered to include an inflation risk component (i.e., to represent nominal rates, rather than real or inflation adjusted rates), and to calculate present value consistent with this fact the forecast cash flows should reflect the monetary amounts expected to be received in the future, rather than being adjusted to current price levels.

The interest rate to apply must reflect current market conditions as of the balance sheet date. This means that during periods when rates are changing rapidly the computed value in use of assets will also change, perhaps markedly, even if projected cash flows before discounting remain stable. This is not a computational artifact, however, but rather it reflects economic reality: as discount (interest) rates decline, holdings of productive assets become more economically valuable, holding all other considerations constant; and as rates rise, such holdings lose value because of the erosion of the value of their future cash flows. The accounting implication is that long-lived assets that were unimpaired one year earlier may fail an impairment test in the current period if rates have risen during the interim.

Corporate assets. Corporate assets, such as headquarters buildings and shared equipment, which do not themselves generate identifiable cash flows, need to be tested for impairment as are all other long-lived assets. However, these present a particular problem in practice due to the inability to identify cash flows deriving from the future use of these assets. A failure to test corporate assets for impairment would permit such assets to be carried at amounts that could, under some circumstances, be at variance with requirements under IFRS. It would also permit a reporting entity to deliberately evade the impairment testing requirements by opportunistically defining certain otherwise productive assets as being corporate assets.

To avoid such results, IAS 36 requires that corporate assets be allocated among or assigned to the cash generating unit or units with which they are most closely associated. For a large and diversified enterprise, this probably implies that corporate assets will be allocated among most or all of its cash generating units, perhaps in proportion to annual turnover (revenue). Since ultimately an enterprise must generate sufficient cash flows to recover its investment in all long-lived assets, whether assigned to operating divisions or to administrative groups, there are no circumstances in which corporate assets can be isolated and excluded from impairment testing.

Accounting for impairments. If the recoverable amount of the cash generating unit is lower than its carrying value, an impairment must be recognized. The mechanism for recording an impairment loss depends upon whether the entity is accounting for long-lived assets on the amortized historical cost or revaluation basis. Impairments computed for assets carried at historical cost will be recognized as charges against current period earnings, either included with depreciation for financial reporting, or identified separately in the income statement.

For assets grouped into cash generating units, it will not be possible to determine which specific assets have suffered impairment losses when the unit as a whole has been found to be impaired, and so IAS 36 prescribes a formulaic approach. If the cash generating unit in question has been allocated any goodwill, any impairment should be allocated fully to goodwill, until its carrying value has been reduced to zero. Any further impairment would be allocated proportionately to all the other assets in that cash generating unit.

The standard does not specify whether the impairment should be credited to the asset account or to the accumulated depreciation (contra asset) account. Of course, either approach has the same effect: net book value is reduced by the accumulated impairment recognized. European practice has generally been to add impairment provisions to the accumulated depreciation account. This is consistent with the view that reducing the asset account directly would be a contravention of the general prohibition on offsetting.

If the entity employs the revaluation method of accounting for long-lived assets, the impairment adjustment will be treated as the partial reversal of a previous upward revaluation. However, if the entire revaluation account is eliminated due to the recognition of an impairment, any excess impairment should be charged to expense (and thus be closed out to retained earnings). In other words, the revaluation account cannot contain a net debit balance.

Example of accounting for impairment

Xebob Corp. has one (of its many) departments that performs machining operations on parts that are sold to contractors. A group of machines have an aggregate book value at the latest balance sheet date (December 31, 2005) totaling €123,000. It has been determined that this group of machinery constitutes a cash generating unit for purposes of applying IAS 36.

Upon analysis, the following facts about future expected cash inflows and outflows become apparent, based on the diminishing productivity expected of the machinery as it ages, and the increasing costs that will be incurred to generate output from the machines:

Year	Revenues	Costs, **excluding** *depreciation*
2006	€ 75,000	€ 28,000
2007	80,000	42,000
2008	65,000	55,000
2009	20,000	15,000
Totals	€240,000	€140,000

The net selling price of the machinery in this cash generating unit is determined by reference to used machinery quotation sheets obtained from a prominent dealer. After deducting estimated disposition costs, the net selling price is calculated as €84,500.

Value in use is determined with reference to the above-noted expected cash inflows and outflows, discounted at a risk rate of 5%. This yields a present value of about €91,981, as shown below.

Year	Cash flows	PV factors	Net PV of cash flows
2006	€47,000	.95238	€44,761.91
2007	38,000	.90703	34,467.12
2008	10,000	.86384	8,638.38
2009	5,000	.82270	4,113.51
Total			€91,980.91

Since value in use exceeds net selling price, value in use is selected to represent the recoverable amount of this cash generating unit. This is lower than the carrying value of the group of assets, however, and thus an impairment must be recognized as of the end of 2005, in the amount of €123,000 − €91,981 = €31,019. This will be included in operating expenses (either depreciation or a separate caption in the income statement) for 2005.

Reversals of previously recognized impairments under historical cost method of accounting. IFRS provides for recognition of reversals of previously recognized impairments, unlike US GAAP. In order to recognize a recovery of a previously recognized impairment, a process similar to that which led to the original loss recognition must be followed. This begins with consideration, as of each balance sheet date, of whether there are indicators of possible impairment recoveries, utilizing external and internal sources of information. Data relied upon could include that pertaining to material market value increases; changes in the technological, market, economic or legal environment or the market in which the asset is employed; and the occurrence of a favorable change in interest rates or required rates of return on assets which would imply changes in the discount rate used to compute value in use. Also to be given consideration are data about any changes in the manner in which the asset is employed, as well as evidence that the economic performance of the asset has exceeded expectations and/or is expected to do so in the future.

If one or more of these indicators is present, it will be necessary to compute the recoverable amount of the asset in question or, if appropriate, of the cash generating unit containing that asset, in order to determine if the current recoverable amount exceeds the carrying amount of the asset, where it had been previously reduced for an impairment.

If that is the case, a recovery can be recognized under IAS 36. The amount of recovery to be recognized is limited, however, to the difference between the carrying value and the amount which would have been the current carrying value had the earlier impairment not been given recognition. Note that this means that restoration of the full amount at which the asset was carried at the time of the earlier impairment cannot be made, since time has elapsed between these two events and further depreciation of the asset would have been recognized in the interim.

Example of impairment recovery

To illustrate, assume an asset had a carrying value of €40,000 at December 31, 2005, based on its original cost of €50,000, less accumulated depreciation representing the one-fifth, or two years, of its projected useful life of ten years which already has elapsed. The carrying value of €40,000 is after depreciation for 2005 has been computed, but before impairment has been addressed. At that date, a determination was made that the asset's recoverable amount was only €32,000 (assume this was properly computed and that recognition of the impairment was warranted), so that an €8,000 adjustment must be made. For simplicity, assume this was added to accumulated depreciation, so that at December 31, 2005, the asset cost remains €50,000 and accumulated depreciation is stated as €18,000.

At December 31, 2006, before any adjustments are posted, the carrying value of this asset is €32,000. Depreciation for 2006 would be €4,000 (= €32,000 book value ÷ 8 years remaining life), which would leave a net book value, after current period depreciation, of €28,000. However, a determination is made that the asset's recoverable amount at this date is €37,000. Before making an adjustment to reverse some or all of the impairment loss previously recognized, the carrying value at December 31, 2006, as it would have existed had the impairment not been recognized in 2005 must be computed.

December 31, 2005 preimpairment carrying value	€40,000
2006 depreciation based on above	5,000
Indicated December 31, 2006 carrying value	€35,000

The December 31, 2006 carrying value would have been €40,000 – €5,000 = €35,000; this is the maximum carrying value which can be reflected on the December 31, 2006 balance sheet. Thus, the full recovery cannot be recognized; instead, the 2006 income statement will reflect (net) a *negative* depreciation charge of €35,000 – €32,000 = €3,000, which can be thought of (or recorded) as follows:

Actual December 31, 2005 carrying value	€32,000	
2006 depreciation based on above	4,000	(a)
Indicated December 31, 2006 carrying value	€28,000	
Indicated December 31, 2006 carrying value	€28,000	
Actual December 31, 2006 carrying value	35,000	
Recovery of previously recognized impairment	€ 7,000	(b)

Thus, the net effect on the 2006 income statement is (a) – (b) = €(3,000). The asset cannot be restored to its indicated recoverable amount at December 31, 2006, amounting to €37,000, as this exceeds the carrying amount that would have existed at this date had the impairment in 2005 never been recognized.

Where a cash generating unit including goodwill has been impaired, and the impairment has been allocated first to the goodwill and then pro rata to the other assets, *only* the amount allocated to nongoodwill assets can be reversed. The standard specifically prohibits the reversal of impairments to goodwill, on the basis that the goodwill could have been replaced by internally generated goodwill, which cannot be recognized under IFRS.

Reversals of previously recognized impairments under revaluation method of accounting. Reversals of impairments are accounted for differently if the reporting entity employed the revaluation method of accounting for long-lived assets. Under this approach, assets are periodically adjusted to reflect current fair values, with the write-up being recorded in the asset accounts and the corresponding credit reported directly in stockholders' equity, and not included in earnings. Impairments are viewed as being downward adjustments of fair value in this scenario, and accordingly are reported as reversals of previous revaluations, not reported in income unless the entire remaining, unamortized portion of the revaluation is eliminated as a consequence of the impairment. Any further impairment is reported in results of operations in such case.

When an asset (or cash generating group of assets) had first been revalued upward, then written down to reflect an impairment, and then later adjusted to convey a recovery of the impairment, the required procedure is to report the recovery as a reversal of the impairment, as with the historical cost method of accounting for long-lived assets. Since in most instances impairments will have been accounted for as reversals of upward revaluations, a still-later reversal of the impairment will be seen as yet another upward revaluation and accounted for as an addition to an equity account, not to be reported through earnings. In the event that an impairment will have eliminated the entire revaluation capital account, and an excess loss will have been reported in earnings, then a later recovery will be reported in earnings to the extent the earlier write-down had been so reported, with any balance taken directly to stockholders' equity.

Example of impairment recovery—revaluation method

To illustrate, assume an asset was acquired January 1, 2004, and it had a net carrying value of €45,000 at December 31, 2005, based on its original cost of €50,000, less accumulated depreciation representing the one-fifth, or two years, of its projected useful life of ten years, which has already elapsed, plus a revaluation write-up of €5,000, net. The increase in carrying value was recorded a year earlier, based on an appraisal showing the asset's then fair value was €56,250.

At December 31, 2006, an impairment is detected, and the recoverable amount at that date is determined to be €34,000. Had this not occurred, depreciation for 2006 would have been (€45,000 ÷ 8 years remaining life =) €5,625; book value after recording 2006 depreciation would have been (€45,000 − €5,625 =) €39,375. Thus the impairment loss recognized in 2006 is (€39,375 − €34,000 =) €5,375. Of this loss amount, €4,375 represents a reversal of the net amount of the previously recognized valuation increase remaining (i.e., undepreciated) at the end of 2006, as shown below.

Gross amount of revaluation at December 31, 2004	€6,250
Portion of the above allocable to accumulated depreciation	625
Net revaluation increase at December 31, 2004	5,625
Depreciation taken on appreciation for 2005	625
Net revaluation increase at December 31, 2005	5,000
Depreciation taken on appreciation for 2006	625
Net revaluation increase at December 31, 2006, before recognition of impairment	4,375
Impairment recognized as reversal of earlier revaluation	4,375
Net revaluation increase at December 31, 2006	€0

The remaining €1,000 impairment recognized at December 31, 2006, is reported as a current period expense, since it exceeds the available amount of revaluation surplus.

In 2007 there is a recovery of value that pertains to this asset; at December 31, 2007, it is valued at €36,500. This represents a €2,500 increase in carrying amount from the earlier year's balance, net of accumulated depreciation. The first €1,000 of this recovery in value is credited to income, since this is the amount of previously recognized impairment that was charged against earnings; the remaining €1,500 of recovery is accounted for as revaluation, and thus is to be credited to a stockholders' equity (revaluation surplus) account.

Deferred tax effects. Recognition of an impairment for financial reporting purposes will most likely not be accompanied by a deduction for current tax purposes. As a consequence of the nondeductibility of most impairment charges, the book value and tax basis of the impaired assets will diverge, with the difference thus created to gradually be eliminated over the remaining life of the asset, as depreciation for tax purposes varies from that which is recognized for financial reporting. Following the dictates of IAS 12, deferred taxes must be recognized for this new discrepancy. The accounting for deferred taxes is discussed in Chapter 14 and will not be addressed here.

Impairments that will be mitigated by recoveries or compensation from third parties. Impairments of tangible long-lived assets may result from natural or other damages, such as from floods or windstorms, and in some such instances there will be the possibility that payments from third parties (typically commercial insurers) will mitigate the gross loss incurred. The question in such circumstances is whether the gross impairment must be recognized, or whether it may be offset by the actual or estimated amount of the recovery to be received by the reporting entity.

IAS 16 holds that when property is damaged or lost, impairments and claims for reimbursements should be accounted for separately (i.e., not netted for financial reporting purposes). Impairments are to be accounted for per IAS 36 as discussed above; disposals (of damaged or otherwise impaired assets) should be accounted for consistent with guidance in IAS 16. Compensation from third parties, which are gain contingencies, should be recognized as income only when the funds become receivable. The cost of replacement items or of restored items is determined in accordance with IAS 16.

Disclosure requirements. For each class of long-lived asset, the amount of impairment losses recognized in earnings for each period being reported upon must be stated, with an indication of where in the income statement it has been included (i.e., as part of depreciation or with other charges). For each class of asset, the amount of any reversals of previously recognized impairment must also be stipulated, again with an identification of where in the income statement this has been included. If any impairment losses were recognized in stockholders' equity directly (i.e., as a reversal of a previously recognized upward revaluation), this must be disclosed. Finally, any reversals of impairment losses that were recognized in equity must be stated.

If the reporting entity applies IAS 14, the amounts of impairments and of reversals of impairments, recognized in income and in stockholders' equity during the year must also be stated. Note that the segment disclosures pertaining to impairments need not be categorized by asset class, and the income statement location of the charge or credit need not be stated (but will be understood from the disclosures relating to the primary financial statements themselves).

IAS 36 further provides that if an impairment loss for an individual asset or group of assets categorized as a cash generating unit is either recognized or reversed during the period, in an amount that is material to the financial statements taken as a whole, disclosures should be made of the following:

- The events or circumstances that caused the loss or recovery of loss;
- The amount of the impairment loss recognized or reversed;
- If for an individual asset, the nature of the asset and the reportable segment to which it belongs, using the primary format as defined under IAS 14;
- If for a cash generating unit, a description of that unit (e.g., defined as a product line, a plant, geographical area, etc.), the amount of impairment recognized or reversed by class of asset and by reportable segment based on the primary format, and, if the unit's composition has changed since the previous estimate of the unit's recoverable amount, a description of the reasons for such changes;
- Whether net selling price or value in use was employed to compute the recoverable amount;
- If recoverable amount is net selling price, the basis used to determine it (e.g., whether by reference to active market prices or otherwise); and
- If the recoverable amount is value in use, the discount rate(s) used in the current and prior period's estimate.

Furthermore, when impairments recognized or reversed in the current period are material in the aggregate, the reporting entity should provide a description of the main classes of assets affected by impairment losses or reversals of losses, as well as the main events and circumstances that caused recognition of losses or reversals. This information is not required to the extent that the disclosures above are given for individual assets or cash generating units.

Retirements and Other Disposals

In general, when an asset is no longer utilized by an entity it is removed from the balance sheet. In the case of long-lived tangible assets, both the asset and the related contra asset, accumulated depreciation, should be eliminated. The difference between the net carrying amount and any proceeds received will be given immediate recognition as a gain or loss arising from the disposition.

If the revaluation method of accounting has been employed, and the asset and the related accumulated depreciation account have been adjusted upward, if the asset is subsequently disposed of before it has been fully depreciated, the gain or loss computed will be identical to what would have been determined had the historical cost method of accounting been used. The reason is that, at any point in time, the net amount of the revaluation (i.e., the step-up in the asset less the unamortized balance in the step-up in accumulated depreciation) will be offset exactly by the remaining balance in the revaluation surplus account. Elimination of the asset, contra asset, and revaluation surplus accounts will balance precisely, and there will be no gain or loss on this aspect of the disposition transaction. The gain or loss will be determined exclusively by the discrepancy between the net book value, based on historical cost, and the proceeds from the disposition. Thus, the accounting outcome is identical under cost and revaluation methods.

Examples of accounting for asset disposal

On January 1, 2004, Zara Corp. acquired a machine at a cost of €12,000; it had an estimated life of six years, no residual value, and was expected to provide a level pattern of utility to the enterprise. Thus, straight-line depreciation in the amount of €2,000 was charged to operations. At the end of four years, the asset was sold for €5,000. Accounting was done on a historical cost basis. The entries to record depreciation and to report the ultimate disposal on January 1, 2008, are as follows:

1/1/04	Machinery	12,000	
	Cash, etc.		12,000
12/31/04	Depreciation expense	2,000	
	Accumulated depreciation		2,000
12/31/05	Depreciation expense	2,000	
	Accumulated depreciation		2,000
12/31/06	Depreciation expense	2,000	
	Accumulated depreciation		2,000
12/31/07	Depreciation expense	2,000	
	Accumulated depreciation		2,000
1/1/08	Cash	5,000	
	Accumulated depreciation	8,000	
	Machinery		12,000
	Gain on asset disposal		1,000

Now assume the same facts as above, but that the revaluation method is used. At the beginning of year four (2007) the asset is revalued at a gross replacement cost of €15,000. A year later it is sold for €5,000. The entries are as follows (note in particular that the gain on the sale is identical to that reported under the historical cost approach):

1/1/04	Machinery	12,000	
	Cash, etc.		12,000
12/31/04	Depreciation expense	2,000	
	Accumulated depreciation		2,000
12/31/05	Depreciation expense	2,000	
	Accumulated depreciation		2,000
12/31/06	Depreciation expense	2,000	
	Accumulated depreciation		2,000
1/1/07	Machinery	3,000	
	Accumulated depreciation		1,500
	Revaluation surplus		1,500
12/31/07	Depreciation expense	2,500	
	Accumulated depreciation		2,500
	Revaluation surplus	500	
	Retained earnings		500
1/1/08	Cash	5,000	
	Accumulated depreciation	10,000	
	Revaluation surplus	1,000	
	Machinery		15,000
	Gain on asset disposal		1,000

Accounting for Assets to Be Disposed Of

As part of its ongoing efforts to converge IFRS with US GAAP, IASB issued IFRS 5, *Noncurrent Assets Held for Sale and Discontinued Operations.* This has introduced new and substantially revised guidance for accounting for long-lived tangible (and other) assets that have been identified for disposal. IFRS 5 states that where management has decided to sell an asset, or group of assets, these should be classified in the balance sheet as "held-for-sale" and should be measured at the lower of carrying value or fair value less cost to sell. After reclassification, these assets will no longer be subject to systematic deprecation.

IFRS 5 states that assets and liabilities which are to be disposed of together in a single transaction are to be treated as a *disposal group.* The measurement basis for noncurrent assets classified as held-for-sale is to be applied to the group as a whole, and any resulting impairment loss will reduce the carrying amount of the noncurrent assets in the disposal group.

The reporting entity would classify a noncurrent asset (or disposal group) as held-for-sale if its carrying amount will be recovered principally through a sale transaction rather than through continuing use. The criteria are that

1. Management, of an appropriate seniority to approve the action, commits itself to a plan to sell;
2. The asset (or disposal group) is available for immediate sale in its present condition subject only to terms that are usual and customary for sales of such assets (or disposal groups);
3. An active program to locate a buyer and other actions required to complete the plan to sell the asset (or disposal group) are initiated;
4. The sale is *highly probable,* and is expected to qualify for recognition as a completed sale, within one year from the date of classification as held-for-sale (with limited exceptions, set out in Appendix B to the standard);
5. The asset (or disposal group) is being actively marketed for sale at a price that is reasonable in relation to its current fair value; and
6. Actions required to complete the plan indicate that it is unlikely that significant changes to the plan will be made or that the plan will be withdrawn.

Assets that are classified as being held for disposal are measured differently and presented separately from other noncurrent assets. IFRS 5 requires that noncurrent assets classified as held-for-sale be measured at the *lower* of carrying amount or fair value less costs to sell. If a newly acquired asset is intended for immediate disposal (e.g., when it has been acquired as part of a larger transaction, but is not needed in operations), it should initially be measured at fair value less cost to sell upon acquisition. If the sale is expected to occur more than a year after acquisition, the recorded amount would be the *present value* of the fair value less cost to sell.

The standard stipulates that, for assets not previously revalued (under IAS 16), any recorded decrease in carrying value (to fair value less cost to sell) would be an impairment loss taken as charge against income; subsequent changes in fair value would also be recognized, but not increases in excess of impairment losses previously recognized.

For an asset that is carried at a revalued amount (as permitted under IAS 16), revaluation under that standard will have to be effected immediately before it is reclassified as held-for-sale under this proposed standard, with any impairment loss recognized in the income statement. Subsequent increases or decreases in estimated costs to sell the asset will be recognized in the income statement. On the other hand, decreases in estimated fair value would be offset against revaluation surplus created under IAS 16, and subsequent increases in fair value would be recognized in full as a revaluation increase under IAS 16, identical to the accounting required before the asset was reclassified as held-for-sale.

A disposal group, as defined under IFRS 5, may include some assets which had been accounted for by the revaluation method. For such disposal groups subsequent increases in fair value are to be recognized, but only to the extent that the carrying values of the noncurrent assets in the group, after the increase has been allocated, do not exceed their respective fair value less costs to sell. The increase recognized would continue to be treated as a revaluation increase under IAS 16.

Finally, IFRS 5 states that noncurrent assets classified as held-for-sale are not to be depreciated. This is logical: the concept objective of depreciation accounting is to allocate asset cost to its useful economic life, and once an asset is denoted as being held for sale, this purpose is no longer meaningful. The constraints on classifying an asset as held-for-sale are, in part, intended to prevent entities from employing such reclassification as a means of avoiding depreciation. Even after classification as held for sale, however, interest and other costs associated with the asset are still recognized as expenses as required under IFRS.

If the asset held for sale is not later disposed of, it is to be reclassified to the operating asset category it is properly assignable to. The amount to be initially recognized upon such reclassification would be the lower of (1) the asset's carrying amount before the asset (or disposal group) was classified as held-for-sale, adjusted for any depreciation or amortization that would have been recognized during the interim had the asset (disposal group) not been classified as held-for-sale, and (2) the *recoverable amount* at the date of the subsequent decision not to sell. If the asset is part of a cash-generating unit (as defined under IAS 36), its recoverable amount will be defined as the carrying amount that would have been recognized after the allocation of any impairment loss incurred from that same cash-generating unit.

Under the foregoing circumstance, the reporting entity would include, as part of income from continuing operations in the period in which the criteria for classification as held-for-sale are no longer met, any required adjustment to the carrying amount of a noncurrent asset that ceases to be classified as held-for-sale. That adjustment would be presented in income from continuing operations. It is not an adjustment to prior period results of operations under any circumstances

If an individual asset or liability is removed from a disposal group classified as held-for-sale, the remaining assets and liabilities of the disposal group still to be sold will continue to be measured as a group only if the group meets the criteria for categorization as held-for-sale. In other circumstances, the remaining noncurrent assets of the group that individually meet the criteria to be classified as held-for-sale will need to be measured individually at the lower of their carrying amounts or fair values less costs to sell at that date.

Special industry situations. Accounting for tangible fixed assets in specialized industries such as mineral extraction or agriculture is dealt with in Chapter 24.

Disclosure Requirements: Tangible Long-Lived Assets

The disclosures required under IAS 16 for property, plant, and equipment, and under IAS 38 for intangibles, are similar. Furthermore, IAS 36 requires extensive disclosures when assets are impaired or when formerly recognized impairments are being reversed. The requirements that pertain to property, plant, and equipment are as follows:

For each class of tangible asset, disclosure is required of

1. The measurement basis used (amortized historical cost or revaluation approaches)
2. The depreciation method(s) used
3. Useful lives or depreciation rates used

4. The gross carrying amounts and accumulated depreciation at the beginning and at the end of the period
5. A reconciliation of the carrying amount from the beginning to the end of the period, showing additions, dispositions, acquisitions by means of business combinations, increases or decreases resulting from revaluations, reductions to recognize impairments, amounts written back to recognize recoveries of prior impairments, depreciation, the net effect of translation of foreign entities' financial statements, and any other material items. (An example of such a reconciliation is presented below.) This reconciliation need be provided for only the current period even if comparative financial statements are being presented.

In addition, the statements should also disclose the following facts:

1. Any restrictions on titles and any assets pledged as security for debt
2. The accounting policy regarding restoration costs for items of property, plant, and equipment
3. The expenditures made for property, plant, and equipment, including any construction in progress
4. The amount of outstanding commitments for property, plant, and equipment acquisitions

In addition, the statements should also disclose the following facts:

1. Whether, in determining recoverable amounts, future projected cash flows have been discounted to present values
2. Any restrictions on titles and any assets pledged as security for debt
3. The amount of outstanding commitments for property, plant, and equipment acquisitions

Example of reconciliation of asset carrying amounts

Date	Gross cost	Accumulated depreciation	Net book value
1/1/06	€4,500,000	€2,000,000	€2,500,000
Acquisitions	3,000,000		3,000,000
Disposals	(400,000)	(340,000)	(60,000)
Impairment		600,000	(600,000)
Depreciation		200,000	(200,000)
12/31/06	€7,100,000	€2,460,000	€4,640,000

Nonmonetary (Exchange) Transactions

Businesses sometimes engage in nonmonetary exchange transactions, where tangible or intangible assets are exchanged for other assets, without a cash transaction or with only a small amount of cash "settle up." These exchanges can involve productive assets such as machinery and equipment, which are not held for sale under normal circumstances, or inventory items, which are intended for sale to customers.

IAS 16 provides authoritative guidance to the accounting for nonmonetary exchanges of tangible assets. It requires that the cost of an item of property, plant, and equipment acquired in exchange for a similar asset is to be measured at *fair value*, provided that the transaction has commercial substance. The concept of a purely "book value" exchange, formerly employed, is now prohibited under most circumstances.

Commercial substance is a new notion under IFRS, and is defined as the event or transaction causing the cash flows of the entity to change. That is, if the expected cash flows after the exchange differ from what would have been expected without this occurring, the exchange has commercial substance and is to be accounted for at fair value. In assessing whether this has occurred, the entity has to consider if the amount, timing and uncertainty of the cash flows from the new asset are different from the one given up, or if the entity-specific portion of the company's operations will be different. If either of these is significant, then the transaction has commercial substance.

If the transaction does not have commercial substance, or the fair value of neither the asset received nor the asset given up can be measured reliably, then the asset acquired is valued at the carrying amount of the asset given up. Such situations are expected to be rare.

If there is a settle-up paid or received in cash or a cash equivalent, this is often referred to as *boot*.

Example of an exchange involving dissimilar assets and no boot

Assume the following:

1. Jamok, Inc. exchanges an automobile with a carrying value of €2,500 with Springsteen & Co. for a tooling machine with a fair market value of €3,200.
2. No boot is exchanged in the transaction.
3. The fair value of the automobile is not readily determinable.

In this case, Jamok, Inc. has recognized a gain of €700 (= €3,200 – €2,500) on the exchange, and the gain should be included in the determination of net income. The entry to record the transaction would be as follows:

Machine	3,200	
Automobile		2,500
Gain on exchange of automobile		700

Nonreciprocal transfers. In a nonreciprocal transfer, one party gives or receives property without the other party doing the opposite. Often these involve an entity and the owners of the entity. Examples of nonreciprocal transfers with owners include dividends-paid-in-kind, nonmonetary assets exchanged for common stock, split-ups, and spin-offs. An example of a nonreciprocal transaction with other than the owners is a donation of property either by or to the enterprise.

The accounting for most nonreciprocal transfers should be based on the fair market value of the asset given (or received, if the fair value of the nonmonetary asset is both objectively measurable and would be clearly recognizable under IFRS). However, nonmonetary assets distributed to owners of an enterprise in a spin-off or other form of reorganization or liquidation should be based on the recorded amount. Where no asset is given, the valuation of the transaction should be based on the fair value of the asset received.

Example of accounting for a nonreciprocal transfer

Assume the following:

1. Salaam donated property with a book value of €10,000 to a charity during the current year.
2. The property had a fair market value of €17,000 at the date of the transfer.

The transaction is to be valued at the fair market value of the property transferred, and any gain or loss on the transaction is to be recognized. Thus, Salaam should recognize a gain of €7,000 (= €17,000 – €10,000) in the determination of the current period's net income. The entry to record the transaction would be as follows:

Charitable donations	17,000	
Property		10,000
Gain on transfer of property		7,000

Capitalization of Borrowing Costs

Accounting literature says that the cost of an asset should include all the costs necessary to get the asset set up and functioning properly for its intended use in the place it is to be used. There has long been, however, a debate about whether borrowing costs should be included in the definition of all costs necessary, or whether instead such costs should be treated as purely a period expense. The concern is that two otherwise identical entities might report different asset costs simply due to decisions made regarding the financing of the enterprises, with the leveraged (debt issuing) entity having a higher reported asset cost. A corollary issue is whether an imputed cost of capital for equity financing should be treated as a cost to be capitalized, which would reduce or eliminate such a discrepancy in apparent asset costs.

The principal purposes to be accomplished by the capitalization of interest costs are as follows:

1. To obtain a more accurate original asset investment cost
2. To achieve a better matching of costs deferred to future periods with revenues of those future periods

In the US, the FASB took the position (in FAS 34) that borrowing costs, under defined conditions, are to be added to the cost of long-lived tangible assets (and inventory also, under very limited circumstances). However, the implicit cost of equity capital may not be similarly treated as an asset cost. This treatment, where defined criteria are met, is mandatory under US GAAP. IFRS has taken a different approach, offering the US GAAP rule as one alternative treatment, which is optional at the reporting entity's election.

Benchmark treatment under IFRS. IAS 23 defines so-called benchmark and allowed alternative treatments for certain financing costs incurred in connection with the acquisition or construction of long-lived assets. The benchmark treatment is to treat all financing costs as period expenses, recognized immediately in results of operations. Under this approach, these costs cannot be added to the carrying value of the assets.

Alternative treatment under IFRS. IAS 23 permits, but does not require, that interest actually incurred on borrowed funds used to finance the acquisition, construction, or production of a *qualifying asset* (defined below) can be added to the carrying value of the asset. The amount of interest so accounted for depends on whether funds were borrowed specifically for the project in question or whether a pool of borrowed funds was deployed for a variety of projects, some of which may be subject to the interest capitalization rules.

Qualifying assets are those that normally take an extended period of time to prepare for their intended uses. While IAS 23 does not give further insight into the limitations of this definition, many years' experience with FAS 34 provided certain insights that may prove germane to this matter. In general, interest capitalization has been applied to those asset acquisition and construction situations in which

1. Assets are being constructed for an entity's own use or for which deposit or progress payments are made
2. Assets are produced as discrete projects that are intended for lease or sale
3. Investments are being made that are accounted for by the equity method, where the investee is using funds to acquire qualifying assets for its principal operations which have not yet begun

Generally, inventories and land that are not undergoing preparation for intended use are not qualifying assets. When land is in the process of being developed, it is a qualifying asset. If land is being developed for lots, the capitalized interest cost is added to the cost of the land. The related borrowing costs are then matched against revenues when the lots are sold.

If, on the other hand, the land is being developed for a building, the capitalized interest cost should instead be added to the cost of the building. The interest cost is then matched against future revenues as the building is depreciated.

The capitalization of interest costs would probably *not* apply to the following situations:

1. The routine production of inventories in large quantities on a repetitive basis
2. For any asset acquisition or self-construction, when the effects of capitalization would not be material, compared to the effect of expensing interest
3. When qualifying assets are already in use or ready for use
4. When qualifying assets are not being used and are not awaiting activities to get them ready for use
5. When qualifying assets are not included in a consolidated balance sheet
6. When principal operations of an investee accounted for under the equity method have already begun
7. When regulated investees capitalize both the cost of debt and equity capital
8. When assets are acquired with grants and gifts restricted by the donor to the extent that funds are available from those grants and gifts

If funds are borrowed specifically for the purpose of obtaining a qualified asset, the interest costs incurred thereon should be deemed eligible for capitalization, net of any interest earned from the temporary investment of idle funds. It is likely that there will not be a perfect match between funds borrowed and funds actually applied to the asset production process, at any given time, although in some construction projects funds are drawn from the lender's credit facility only as vendors' invoices, and other costs, are actually paid. Only the interest incurred on the project should be included as a cost of the project, however.

In other situations, a variety of credit facilities may be used to generate a pool of funds, a portion of which is applied to the asset construction or acquisition program. In those instances, the amount of interest to be capitalized will be determined by applying an average borrowing cost to the amount of funds committed to the project. Interest cost could include the following:

1. Interest on debt having explicit interest rates
2. Interest related to finance leases
3. Amortization of any related discount or premium on borrowings, or of other ancillary borrowing costs such as commitment fees

The amount of interest to be capitalized is that portion that could have been avoided if the qualifying asset had not been acquired. Thus, the capitalized amount is the incremental amount of interest cost incurred by the entity to finance the acquired asset. A weighted-average of the rates of the borrowings of the entity should be used. The selection of borrowings to be used in the calculation of the weighted-average of rates requires judgment. In resolving this problem, particularly in the case of consolidated financial statements, the best criterion to use is the identification and determination of that portion of interest that could have been avoided if the qualifying assets had not been acquired.

The base (which should be used to multiply the weighted-average rate by) is the average amount of accumulated net capital expenditures incurred for qualifying assets during the relevant reporting period. Capitalized costs and expenditures are not synonymous terms. Theoretically, a capitalized cost financed by a trade payable for which no interest is recognized is not a capital expenditure to which the capitalization rate should be applied. Reasonable approximations of net capital expenditures are acceptable, however, and capitalized costs are generally used in place of capital expenditures unless there is a material difference.

If the average capitalized expenditures exceed the specific new borrowings for the time frame involved, the *excess* expenditures amount should be multiplied by the weighted-average of rates and not by the rate associated with the specific debt. This requirement more accurately reflects the interest cost that is actually incurred by the entity in bringing the long-lived asset to a properly functioning condition and location.

The interest being paid on the underlying debt may be either simple or subject to compounding. Simple interest is computed on the principal alone, whereas compound interest is computed on principal and on any accumulated interest that has not been paid. Compounding may be yearly, monthly, or daily. Most long-lived assets will be acquired with debt having interest compounded, and that feature should be considered when computing the amount of interest to be capitalized.

The total amount of interest actually incurred by the entity during the relevant time frame is the ceiling for the amount of interest cost capitalized. Thus, the amount capitalized cannot exceed the amount actually incurred during the period. On a consolidated financial reporting basis, this ceiling is defined as the sum of the parent's interest cost plus that incurred by its consolidated subsidiaries. If financial statements are issued separately, the interest cost capitalized should be limited to the amount that the separate entity has incurred, and that amount should include interest on intercompany borrowings, which of course would be eliminated in consolidated financial statements. The interest incurred is a gross amount and is not netted against interest earned except in rare cases.

IAS 23, while offering a choice between immediate expensing and capitalization of qualifying borrowing costs, did not indicate whether a given enterprise could use both procedures in accounting for different qualifying properties. SIC 2 responded to this previously unanswered question with a consensus that if interest capitalization is elected, it should be used for all qualifying assets and for all periods. It also states that if interest cost is capitalized, this fact must not result in the asset being reported at an amount in excess of recoverable amount. Any excess interest cost is thus an impairment, to be recognized immediately in expense.

Example of accounting for capitalized interest costs

Assume the following:

1. On January 1, 2005, Gemini Corp. contracted with Leo Company to construct a building for €20,000,000 on land that Gemini had purchased years earlier.
2. Gemini Corp. was to make five payments in 2005, with the last payment scheduled for the date of completion.
3. The building was completed December 31, 2005.
4. Gemini Corp. made the following payments during 2005:

January 1, 2005	€ 2,000,000
March 31, 2005	4,000,000
June 30, 2005	6,100,000
September 30, 2005	4,400,000
December 31, 2005	3,500,000
	€20,000,000

5. Gemini Corp. had the following debt outstanding at December 31, 2005:

   a. A 12%, 4-year note dated 1/1/05 with interest compounded quarterly. Both principal and interest due 12/31/08 (relates specifically to building project) €8,500,000

   b. A 10%, 10-year note dated 12/31/01 with simple interest and interest payable annually on December 31 €6,000,000

   c.   A 12%, 5-year note dated 12/31/03 with simple interest and interest payable annually on December 31   €7,000,000

The amount of interest to be capitalized during 2005 is computed as follows:

Average Accumulated Expenditures

Date	Expenditure	Capitalization period*	Average accumulated expenditures
1/1/05	€ 2,000,000	12/12	€2,000,000
3/31/05	4,000,000	9/12	3,000,000
6/30/05	6,100,000	6/12	3,050,000
9/30/05	4,400,000	3/12	1,100,000
12/31/05	3,500,000	0/12	--
	€20,000,000		€9,150,000

* *The number of months between the date when expenditures were made and the date on which interest capitalization stops (December 31, 2005).*

Potential Interest Cost to Be Capitalized

(€8,500,000	x	1.12551)*	− €8,500,000	=	€1,066,840
650,000	x	0.1108**		=	72,020
€9,150,000					€1,138,860

* *The principal, €8,500,000, is multiplied by the factor for the future amount of €1 for 4 periods at 3% to determine the amount of principal and interest due in 2005.*

** *Weighted-average interest rate*

	Principal	Interest
10%, 10-year note	€ 6,000,000	€ 600,000
12%, 5-year note	7,000,000	840,000
	€13,000,000	€1,440,000

$$\frac{\text{Total interest}}{\text{Total principal}} = \frac{€1,440,000}{€13,000,000} = 11.08\%$$

The actual interest is

12%, 4-year note [(€8,500,000 x 1.12551) − €8,500,000]	=	€1,066,840
10%, 10-year note (€6,000,000 x 10%)	=	600,000
12%, 5-year note (€7,000,000 x 12%)	=	840,000
Total interest		€2,506,840

The interest cost to be capitalized is the lesser of €1,138,860 (avoidable interest) or €2,506,840 (actual interest). The remaining €1,367,980 (= €2,506,840 − €1,138,860) must be expensed.

Determining the time period for interest capitalization. Three conditions must be met before the capitalization period should begin.

1. Expenditures for the asset are being incurred
2. Borrowing costs are being incurred
3. Activities that are necessary to prepare the asset for its intended use are in progress

As long as these conditions continue, interest costs can be capitalized.

Necessary activities are interpreted in a very broad manner. They start with the planning process and continue until the qualifying asset is substantially complete and ready to function as intended. These activities may include technical and administrative work prior to actual commencement of physical work, such as obtaining permits and approvals, and may continue after physical work has ceased. Brief, normal interruptions do not stop the capitalization of interest costs. However, if the entity intentionally suspends or delays the activities for some reason, interest costs should not be capitalized from the point of suspension or delay until substantial activities in regard to the asset resume.

If the asset is completed in a piecemeal fashion, the capitalization of interest costs stops for each part as it becomes ready to function as intended. An asset that must be entirely complete before the parts can be used as intended can continue to capitalize interest costs until the total asset becomes ready to function.

Suspension and cessation of capitalization. If there is an extended period during which there is no activity to prepare the asset for its intended use, capitalization of borrowing costs should be suspended. As a practical matter, unless the break in activity is significant, it is usually ignored. Also, if delays are normal and to be expected given the nature of the construction project (such as a suspension of building construction during the winter months), this would have been anticipated as a cost and would not warrant even a temporary cessation of borrowing cost capitalization.

Capitalization would cease when the project has been substantially completed. This would occur when the asset is ready for its intended use or for sale to a customer. The fact that routine minor administrative matters still need to be attended to would not mean that the project had not been completed, however. The measure should be *substantially* complete, in other words, not absolutely finished.

Costs in excess of recoverable amounts. If the capitalization of borrowing costs causes the carrying value of the asset to exceed its recoverable value (if property, plant, or equipment) or its net realizable value (if an item held for resale), it will be necessary to record an adjustment to write the asset carrying value down. In the case of plant, property, and equipment, a later write-up may occur due to use of the allowed alternative (i.e., revaluation) treatment, recognizing fair value increases, in which case, as described earlier, recovery of a previously recognized loss will be reported in earnings.

Consistency of application. IAS 23 did not address the question of whether an entity would be justified in capitalizing interest costs for some qualifying assets, while expensing currently interest incurred in the acquisition, construction, or production of other qualifying assets. SIC 2, which was subsequently incorporated into IAS 8, specified that an entity must apply its accounting policies consistently for all similar transactions, other events and conditions. The policy must be applied consistently to each category of assets.

Disclosure requirements. With respect to an entity's accounting for borrowing costs, the financial statements must disclose which policy (expensing or capitalization) is being utilized, as well as the actual borrowing costs capitalized during the period and the rate used to determine the amount of such costs eligible for capitalization. As noted, this rate will be the weighted-average of rates on all borrowings included in an allocation pool or the actual rate on specific debt identified with a given asset acquisition or construction project.

Examples of Financial Statement Disclosures

Novartis AG
For the Fiscal Year ending December 31, 2004

Notes to the consolidated financial statements

8.   Property, plant & equipment movements

(in USD millions)	Land	Buildings	Machinery	Plant under construction and other equipment	Totals 2004	2003
Cost, January 1	367	5,247	7,909	1,370	14,893	12,670
Consolidation changes	1	10	19	--	30	--
Reclassifications	4	404	583	(991)	--	(237)
Additions	13	94	250	912	1,269	1,329
Disposals	(5)	(102)	(308)	(58)	(473)	(284)
Translation effects	23	376	598	130	1,127	1,415
December 31	403	6,029	9,051	1,363	16,846	14,893

Accumulated depreciation

January 1	(1)	(2,544)	(4,751)		(7,296)	(6,349)
Consolidation changes			(1)		(1)	
Reclassifications						(334)
Depreciation charge		(186)	(594)		(780)	(737)
Depreciation on disposals		82	262		344	188
Impairment charge		(4)	(12)		(16)	(31)
Translation effects	(1)	(208)	(391)		(600)	(701)
December 31	(2)	(2,860)	(5,487)		(8,349)	(7,296)
Net book value— December 31	401	3,169	3,564	1,363	8,497	7,597
Commitments for purchases of property, plant, & equipment					325	209

Barco SA
For the Fiscal Year ending December 31, 2004

Notes to the consolidated financial statements

Property, plant, and equipment. Property, plant, and equipment are stated at cost less accumulated depreciation. Generally, depreciation is computed on a straight-line basis over the estimated useful life of the assets. The carrying amounts are reviewed at each balance sheet date to assess whether they are recorded in excess of their recoverable amounts, and where carrying values exceed this estimated recoverable amount, assets are written down to their recoverable amount.

Estimated useful life is

Buildings	20 years
Installations	10 years
Production machinery	5 years
Measurement equipment	4 years
Tools and models	3 years
Furniture	10 years
Office equipment	5 years
Computer equipment	3 years
Vehicles	5 years
Leasehold improvements	limited to outstanding period of lease asset
Demo material	1-3 years

Lectra SA
For the Year ending December 2004

Summary of significant accounting policies and scope of consolidation

Property, plant, and equipment are carried at cost less accumulated depreciation and impairment, if any. The book value of tangible assets is tested for impairment at the close of each fiscal year. When a tangible asset comprises significant components with different useful lives, the latter are analyzed separately. Consequently, costs incurred in replacing or renewing a component of a tangible asset are booked as a distinct asset and the asset replaced is eliminated. Subsequent expenditures relating to a tangible asset are capitalized if they increase the future economic benefits of the specific asset to which they are attached. All other costs are expensed directly at the time they are incurred. Depreciation is computed on the straight-line method over their estimated useful lives as follows:

Buildings	20-30 years
Fixtures and fittings	5-10 years
Outdoor installations	5-10 years
Technical installations, equipment and tools	4-5 years
Office equipment and computers	3-5 years
Office furniture	5-10 years

Fixed assets under finance leases are capitalized on the basis of the present value of future rental costs and depreciated over their estimated useful lives.

Notes to the consolidated financial statements

3. Property, plant & equipment

(in thousands of euros)	Land and buildings	Fixtures and fittings	Equipment and other	Total
Gross value at January 1, 2003	9,838	8,146	20,019	38,003
Additions	4	98	1,577	1,679
Disposals	--	(116)	(832)	(948)
Transfer	--	44	(44)	--
Translation adjustments	--	(158)	(858)	(1,016)
Gross value at December 31, 2003	9,842	8,014	19,862	37,718
Accumulated depreciation at December 31, 2003	(7,419)	(4,186)	(17,428)	(29,033)
Net value at December 31, 2003	2,423	3,828	2,434	8,685
Gross value at January 1, 2004	9,842	8,014	19,862	37,718
Additions	29	1,196	2,040	3,265
Disposals	--	(443)	(1,684)	(2,127)
Transfer	68	131	(199)	--
Changes in scope of consolidation	--	392	1,149	1,541
Translation adjustments	--	(56)	(262)	(318)
Gross value at December 31, 2004	9,939	9,234	20,906	40,079
Accumulated depreciation at December 31, 2004	(7,617)	(5,444)	(17,093)	(30,154)
Net value at December 31, 2004	2,322	3,790	3,813	9,925

Nestlé, S.A.
Period ending December 31, 2004

Property, plant, and equipment. Property, plant, and equipment are shown in the balance sheet at their historical cost. Depreciation is provided on the straight-line method so as to depreciate the initial cost over the estimated useful lives, which are as follows:

Buildings	25-50 years
Machinery and equipment	10-15 years
Tools, furniture, information technology, and sundry equipment	3-8 years
Vehicles	5 years

Financing costs incurred during the course of construction are expensed. Land is not depreciated. Premiums capitalized for leasehold land or buildings are amortized over the length of the lease. Depreciation of property, plant, and equipment is allocated to the appropriate headings of expenses by function in the income statement.

Notes to the consolidated financial statements

12. Property, plant & equipment movements

(in millions of CHF)	Land and buildings	Machinery and equipment	Tools, furniture, and other equipment	Vehicles	Totals 2004	2003
Gross value						
At January 1	11,990	22,916	6,296	776	41,778	40,797
Currency retranslation and inflation adjustments	(424)	(801)	(217)	19	(1,423)	(491)
Expenditures	591	1,828	738	140	3,295	3,337
Disposals	(306)	(1,023)	(697)	(112)	(2,038)	(2,010)
Modification of the scope of consolidation	(129)	(265)	(68)	(109)	(567)	145
At December 31	11,623	22,555	6,152	715	41,045	41,778

(in millions of CHF)	Land and buildings	Machinery and equipment	Tools, furniture, and other equipment	Vehicles	Totals 2004	2003
Accumulated depreciation and impairments						
At January 1	(4,810)	(14,594)	(4,456)	(479)	(24,339)	(23,772)
Currency retranslation and inflation adjustments	155	391	169	(17)	698	71
Depreciation	(358)	(1,315)	(748)	(85)	(2,506)	(2,408)
Impairments	(54)	(71)	(4)	(1)	(130)	(149)
Disposals	210	940	571	93	1,814	1,756
Modification of the scope of consolidation	83	253	54	90	470	162
At December 31	(4,774)	(14,396)	(4,414)	(409)	(23,993)	(24,339)
Net at December 31	6,849	8,159	1,738	306	17,052	17,439

At December 31, 2004, property, plant, and equipment include CHF 492 million (2003: CHF 409 million) of assets under construction. Net property, plant, and equipment held under finance leases at December 31, 2004, amount to CHF 358 million (2003: CHF 276 million). Net property, plant, and equipment of CHF 112 million (2003: CHF 112 million) are pledged as security for financial liabilities. Fire risks, reasonably estimated, are insured in accordance with domestic requirements.

9 INTANGIBLE ASSETS

PERSPECTIVE AND ISSUES

Long-lived assets are those that will provide economic benefits to an enterprise for a number of future periods. Accounting standards regarding long-lived assets involve determination of the appropriate cost at which to record the assets initially, the amount at which to present the assets at subsequent reporting dates, and the appropriate method(s) to be used to allocate the cost over the periods being benefited, if that is appropriate.

Long-lived nonfinancial assets may be classified into two basic types: tangible and intangible. Tangible assets have physical substance, while intangible assets either have no physical substance, or have a value that is not conveyed by what physical substance they do have. For example, the value of computer software is not reasonably measured by the cost of the diskettes or CDs on which these are contained.

The value of an intangible asset is a function of the rights or privileges that its ownership conveys to the business enterprise.

The accounting treatment of intangible assets is not yet in a fully settled and agreed mode. The nineteenth century model from which we draw many of our financial reporting practices was developed when productive capacity was defined by manufacturing plant and equipment. In the postindustrial, knowledge-based economy in which the more developed nations operate today there is a different perspective on what constitutes value for a business. Intellectual property, such as patents and trade names, may be more vital than manufacturing capacity to modern growth companies, typified by Dell Computers, which is a selling organization with a brand name, and whose manufacturing is done by subcontractors in low-cost nations.

The recognition and measurement of intangibles such as brand names is problematical because many brands are internally generated, over a number of years, and there is little or no historical cost to be recognized under IFRS or most national GAAP standards. Thus, the Dell brand does not appear on Dell's balance sheet, nor does the Nestlé brand appear on Nestlé's balance sheet. Concepts, designs, sales networks, brands, and processes are all important elements of what enables one company to succeed while another fails, but the theoretical support for representing them on the balance sheet is at an early stage of development. For that matter, few companies even attempt to monitor such values for internal management purposes, so it is hardly surprising that the external reporting is still evolving.

We can draw a distinction between internally generated intangibles which are difficult to measure and thus to recognize in the balance sheet, such as research and development assets and brands, and those that are purchased externally by an entity and therefore have a historical cost. While an intangible can certainly be bought individually, most intangibles arise from acquisitions of other companies, where a bundle of assets and liabilities are acquired.

In this area of activity, we can further distinguish between identifiable intangibles and unidentifiable ones.

Identifiable intangibles include patents, copyrights, brand names, customer lists, trade names, and other specific rights that typically can be conveyed by an owner without necessarily also transferring related physical assets. Goodwill, on the other hand, is a residual which incorporates all the intangibles that cannot be reliably measured separately, and is often analyzed as containing both these and benefits that the purchasing company expected to gain from the synergies or other efficiencies arising from a business combination and cannot normally be transferred to a new owner without also selling the other assets and/or the operations of the business.

Accounting for goodwill is addressed in IFRS 3, and will be considered in Chapter 11 in this book, in the context of business combinations. In this chapter we will address the recognition and measurement criteria for identifiable intangibles. This includes the criteria for separability and treatment of internally generated intangibles, such as research and development costs.

The subsequent measurement of intangibles depends upon whether they are considered to have indefinite economic value or a definable useful life. The standard on impairment of assets (IAS 36) pertains to both tangible and intangible long-lived assets. This chapter will consider the implications of this standard for the accounting for intangible, separately identifiable assets.

Sources of IFRS		
IFRS 3	*IAS* 36, 38	*SIC* 32

DEFINITIONS OF TERMS

Amortization. In general, the systematic allocation of the cost of a long-term asset over its useful economic life; the term is also used specifically to define the allocation process for intangible assets.

Carrying amount. The amount at which an asset is presented on the balance sheet, which is its cost (or other allowable basis), net of any accumulated depreciation and impairment losses.

Cash generating unit. The smallest identifiable group of assets that generates cash inflows from continuing use, largely independent of the cash inflows associated with other assets or groups of assets.

Corporate assets. Assets, excluding goodwill, that contribute to future cash flows of both the cash generating unit under review for impairment and other cash generating units.

Cost. Amount of cash or cash equivalent paid or the fair value of other consideration given to acquire or construct an asset.

Depreciable amount. Cost of an asset or the other amount that has been substituted for cost, less the residual value of the asset: the value to be allocated over years of use.

Depreciation. Systematic and rational allocation of the depreciable amount of an asset over its economic life.

Development. The application of research findings or other knowledge to a plan or design for the production of new or substantially improved materials, devices, products, processes, systems, or services prior to commencement of commercial production or use. This should be distinguished from *research*.

Fair value. Amount that would be obtained for an asset in an arm's-length exchange transaction between knowledgeable willing parties.

Goodwill. The excess of the cost of a business combination accounted for as an acquisition over the fair value of the net assets thereof, to be amortized over its useful economic life that, as a rebuttable presumption, is no greater than twenty years.

Impairment loss. The excess of the carrying amount of an asset over its recoverable amount.

Intangible assets. Nonfinancial assets without physical substance that are held for use in the production or supply of goods or services or for rental to others, or for administrative purposes, which are identifiable and are controlled by the enterprise as a result of past events, and from which future economic benefits are expected to flow.

Monetary assets. Assets whose amounts are fixed in terms of units of currency. Examples are cash, accounts receivable, and notes receivable.

Net selling price. The amount which could be realized from the sale of an asset by means of an arm's-length transaction, less costs of disposal.

Nonmonetary transactions. Exchanges and nonreciprocal transfers that involve little or no monetary assets or liabilities.

Nonreciprocal transfer. Transfer of assets or services in one direction, either from an enterprise to its owners or another entity, or from owners or another entity to the enterprise. An enterprise's reacquisition of its outstanding stock is a nonreciprocal transfer.

Recoverable amount. The greater of an asset's net selling price or its value in use.

Research. The original and planned investigation undertaken with the prospect of gaining new scientific or technical knowledge and understanding. This should be distinguished from *development*.

Residual value. Estimated amount expected to be obtained on ultimate disposition of the asset after its useful life has ended, net of estimated costs of disposal.

Useful life. Period over which an asset will be employed in a productive capacity, as measured either by the time over which it is expected to be used, or the number of production units expected to be obtained from the asset by the enterprise.

CONCEPTS, RULES, AND EXAMPLES

Background

Over the years, the role of intangible assets has grown ever more important for the operations and prosperity of many types of businesses, as the "knowledge-based" economy becomes more dominant. However, until recently, accounting standards have tended to give scant attention to, or ignore entirely, the appropriate means of reporting upon such assets. As a consequence, practice has not evolved beyond the traditional historical cost rules.

IFRS first addressed accounting for intangibles in a thorough way with IAS 38, which was promulgated in 1998 after a rather long and contentious gestation period that included the issuance of two Exposure Drafts. Research and development costs had earlier been addressed by IAS 9 (issued in 1978) and goodwill arising from a business combination was dealt with by IAS 22 (issued in 1983). IAS 38 is the first comprehensive standard on intangibles and it superseded IAS 9. It established recognition criteria, measurement bases, and disclosure requirements for intangible assets. The standard also stipulates that impairment testing for intangible assets (as specified by IAS 36) is to be undertaken on a regular basis. This is to ensure that only assets having *recoverable values* will be capitalized and carried forward to future periods as assets of the business.

IAS 38 was modified in 2004 to acknowledge that intangible assets could have indefinite useful lives. Originally it was intended that intangibles should have a maximum life of twenty years, but when IAS 38 was finally approved, it included a rebuttable presumption that an intangible would have a life of no more than twenty years. The most recent amendment to IAS 38 removed the rebuttable presumption, and brings IAS 38 into closer convergence with the corresponding US GAAP standard, FAS 142, including the provision of a list of intangibles that should normally be recognized.

The IASB and FASB have put on their long-term joint agendas a project on accounting for intangibles.

Scope of the standard. IAS 38 applies to all reporting entities. It prescribes the accounting treatment for intangible assets, including development costs, but does not address intangible assets covered by other IAS. For instance, deferred tax assets are covered under IAS 12; leases fall within the purview of IAS 17; goodwill arising on a business combination is dealt with by IFRS 3; assets arising from employee benefits are covered by IAS 19; and financial assets are defined by IAS 39 and covered by IAS 27, 28, 31, and 39. IAS 38 also does not apply to intangible assets arising in insurance companies from contracts with policyholders within the scope of IFRS 4, nor to exploration and evaluation assets in the extractive industries which will be subject to their own standard, nor to intangible assets classified as held-for-sale under IFRS 5.

Identifiable intangible assets include patents, copyrights, licenses, customer lists, brand names, import quotas, computer software, marketing rights, and specialized know-how. These items have in common the fact that there is little or no tangible substance to them, they have an economic life of greater than one year. In many but not all cases, the asset is separable; that is, it could be sold or otherwise disposed of without simultaneously disposing of or diminishing the value of other assets held.

Intangible assets are, by definition, assets that have no physical substance. However, there may be instances where intangibles also have some physical form. For example

- There may be tangible evidence of an asset's existence, such as a certificate indicating that a patent had been granted, but this does constitute the asset itself;
- Some intangible assets may be contained in or on a physical substance such as a compact disc (in the case of computer software); and
- Identifiable assets that result from research and development activities are intangible assets because the tangible prototype or model is secondary to the knowledge that is the primary outcome of those activities.

In the case of assets that have both tangible and intangible elements, there may be uncertainty about whether classification should be as tangible or intangible assets. For example, the IASB has deliberately not specified whether mineral exploration and evaluation assets should be considered as tangible or intangible. Judgment is therefore required in properly classifying such assets as either intangible or tangible assets. As a rule of thumb, the asset should be classified as an intangible asset or a tangible asset based on the relative or comparative dominance or significance of the tangible or the intangible components of the asset. For instance, computer software that is not an integral part of the related hardware equipment is treated as software (i.e., as an intangible asset). Conversely, certain computer software, such as the operating system, that is essential and an integral part of a computer, is treated as part of the hardware equipment (i.e., as property, plant, and equipment as opposed to an intangible asset).

Recognition Criteria

Identifiable intangible assets have much in common with tangible long-lived assets (property, plant, and equipment), and the accounting for them is accordingly very similar. Recognitions depends on whether the *Framework* definition of an asset is satisfied. The key criteria for determining whether intangible assets are to be recognized are

1. Whether the intangible asset can be separately identified from other aspects of the business enterprise;
2. Whether the use of the intangible asset is controlled by the enterprise as a result of its past actions and events;
3. Whether future economic benefits can be expected to flow to the enterprise; and
4. Whether the cost of the asset can be measured reliably.

Identifiability. IAS 38 says an intangible meets the identifiability requirement if

1. It is separable (i.e., is capable of being separated or divided from the entity and sold, transferred, licensed, rented or exchanged, either individually or together with a related contract, asset or liability); or
2. It arises from contractual or other legal rights, regardless of whether those rights are transferable or separable from the entity or form other rights and obligations.

IAS 38 offers a fairly comprehensive listing of possible separate classes of intangibles. These are

1. Brand names;
2. Mastheads and publishing titles;
3. Computer software;
4. Licenses and franchises;
5. Copyrights, patents and other industrial property rights, service and operating rights;
6. Recipes, formulae, models, designs and prototypes; and
7. Intangible assets under development

The nature of intangibles is such that, as discussed above, many are not recognized at the time that they come into being. The costs of creating many intangibles are typically expensed year by year, before it is clear that an asset has been created. The cost of internal intangible asset development cannot be capitalized retrospectively, and this means that such assets remain off-balance-sheet until and unless the entity is acquired by another entity. The acquiring entity has to allocate the acquisition price over the bundle of assets and liabilities acquired, irrespective of whether they were recognized in the acquired company's balance sheet, so the notion of identifiability is significant in enabling an allocation to be made.

IASB prefers that as many individual assets be recognized as possible in a business acquisition, because the residual amount of unallocated acquisition cost is treated as goodwill, which provides less transparency to investors and other financial statement users.

Control. The provisions of IAS 38 require that an enterprise should be in a position to control the use of any intangible asset that is to be reflected on the entity's balance sheet.

Control implies the power to both obtain future economic benefits from the asset as well as restrict others' access to those benefits. Normally enterprises register patents, copyrights, etc. to ensure control over these intangible assets.

A patent provides the registered owner (or licensee) the exclusive right to use the underlying product or process without any interference or infringement from others. In contrast with these, intangible assets arising from technical knowledge of staff, customer loyalty, long-term training benefits, etc., will have difficulty meeting this recognition criteria in spite of expected future economic benefits from them. This is due to the fact that the enterprise would find it impossible to fully control these resources or to prevent others from controlling them.

For instance, even if an enterprise expends considerable resources on training that will supposedly increase staff skills, the economic benefits from skilled staff cannot be controlled, since trained employees could leave their current employment and move on in their career to other employers. Hence, staff training expenditures, no matter how material in amount, do not so far qualify as an intangible asset.

Future economic benefits. Generally an asset is recognized only if it is *probable* that future economic benefits specifically associated therewith will flow to the reporting entity, and the cost of the asset can be *measured reliably*. Traditionally, the probability issue acts as an on-off switch. If the future cash flow is *more likely than not* to occur, the item is recognized, but if the cash flow is less likely to occur, nothing is recognized. However, under IFRS 3, where an intangible asset is acquired as part of a business combination, it is valued at fair value, and the fair value computation takes in the probability of the future cash flow. Under the fair value approach, however, the recorded amount is determined as the present value of the cash flow, adjusted for the likelihood of receiving it, as well as for the time value of money. Even with a low probability of cash flow ultimately occurring, fair value will have some positive measure, and an asset will be recognized.

The IASB acknowledged in the IFRS 3 Basis for Conclusions that there is a discrepancy between this standard and the *Framework*, but it took the view that this will most likely be resolved in due course by amending the *Framework*. In other words, there will be a more general movement to incorporating the concept of probability in the measurement of assets, instead of using likelihood as a recognition threshold criterion.

The future economic benefits envisaged by the standard may take the form of revenue from the sale of products or services, cost savings, or other benefits resulting from the use of the intangible asset by the enterprise. A good example of other benefits resulting from the use of the intangible asset is the use by an entity of a secret formula (which the enterprise has protected legally) that leads to reduced future production costs (as opposed to increased future revenue).

Measurement of Cost of Intangibles

The conditions under which the intangible asset has been acquired will determine the measurement of its cost.

The cost of an intangible asset acquired separately is determined in a manner largely analogous to that for tangible long-lived assets as described in Chapter 8. Thus, the cost comprises the purchase cost, including any taxes and import duties, less any trade discounts and rebates, plus any directly attributable expenditures incurred in preparing the asset for its intended use. Directly attributable expenditures would include fully loaded labor costs, thus including employee benefits arising directly from bringing the asset to its working condition. It would also include outside professional fees and other incremental costs.

As with tangible assets, capitalization of costs ceases at the point when the intangible asset is ready to be placed in service in the manner intended by management. Any costs incurred in using or redeploying intangible assets are accordingly to be excluded from the cost of those assets. Thus, any costs incurred while the asset is capable of being used in the manner intended by management, but while it has yet to be placed into service, would be expensed, not capitalized. Similarly, initial operating losses, such as those incurred while demand for the asset's productive outputs is being developed, cannot be capitalized. On the other hand, further expenditures made for the purpose of improving the asset's level of performance would qualify for capitalization. In all these particulars, guidance under IAS 38 mirrors that under IAS 16.

According to IAS 38, the cost of an intangible asset acquired as part of a business combination is its fair value as at the date of acquisition. If the intangible asset can be freely traded in an active market, then the quoted market price is the best measurement of cost. If the intangible asset has no active market, then cost is determined based on the amount that the enterprise would have paid for the asset in an arm's-length transaction at the date of acquisition. If the cost of an intangible asset acquired as part of a business combination cannot be measured reliably, then that asset is not separately recognized, but rather, is included in goodwill.

Intangibles acquired through an exchange of assets. In other situations, intangible assets may be acquired in exchange or partly in exchange for other dissimilar intangible or other assets. The same commercial substance rules apply under IAS 38 as under IAS 16. If the exchange will affect the future cash flows of the entity, then it has commercial substance, and the acquired asset is recognized at its fair value, and the asset given up is also measured at fair value. Any difference between carrying value of the asset(s) given up and those acquired will be given income statement recognition as a gain or loss. However, if there is no commercial substance to the exchange, or the fair values cannot be measured reliably, then the value used is that of the asset given up.

Internally generated goodwill is not recognized as an intangible asset because it fails to meet recognition criteria including

- Reliable measurement of cost,
- An identity separate from other resources, and
- Control by the reporting enterprise.

In practice, accountants are usually confronted with the desire to recognize internally generated goodwill based on the premise that at a certain point in time the market value of an enterprise exceeds the carrying value of its identifiable net assets. However, as IAS 38 categorically states, such differences cannot be considered to represent the cost of intangible assets *controlled by the enterprise,* and hence could not meet the criteria for recognition (i.e., capitalization) of such an asset on the books of the enterprise. Nonetheless, standard setters are concerned that when an entity tests a cash generating unit for impairment, internally generated goodwill cannot be separated from acquired goodwill, and that it forms a cushion against impairment of acquired goodwill.

Intangibles acquired at little or no cost by means of government grants. If the intangible is acquired free of charge or by payment of nominal consideration, as by means of a government grant (e.g., when the government grants the right to operate a radio station) or similar means, and assuming the historical cost treatment is being utilized to account for these assets, obviously there will be little or no amount reflected as an asset. If the asset is important to the reporting entity's operations, however, it must be adequately disclosed in the notes to the financial statements.

If the revaluation method of accounting for the asset is used, the fair value should be determined by reference to an active market. However, given the probable lack of an active market, since government grants are virtually never transferable, it is unlikely that this situation will be encountered. If an active market does not exist for this type of an intangible asset, the enterprise must recognize the asset at cost. Cost would include those that are directly attributable to preparing the asset for its intended use. Government grants are addressed in Chapter 26.

Internally Generated Intangibles other than Goodwill

In many instances, intangibles are generated internally by an entity, rather than being acquired via a business combination or some other purchase transaction. Because of the nature of intangibles, the measurement of the cost (i.e., the initial amounts at which these could be recognized as assets) is constrained by the fact that many of the costs have already been expensed by the time the entity is able to determine that an asset has indeed been created. For example, when launching a new magazine, an entity may have to run the magazine at a loss in its early years, expensing large promotional and other costs which all flow through the income statement, before such time as the magazine can be determined to have become established, and have branding that might be taken to represent an intangible asset. At the point the brand is determined to be an asset, all the costs of creating it have already been expensed, and no retrospective adjustment is allowed to create a recognized asset.

IAS 38 provides that internally generated intangible assets are to be capitalized and amortized over the projected period of economic utility, provided that certain criteria are met.

Expenditures pertaining to the creation of intangible assets are to be classified alternatively as being indicative of, or analogous to, either research activity or development activity. The former costs are entirely expensed as incurred; the latter are capitalized, if future economic benefits are reasonably likely to be received by the reporting entity. Per IAS 38,

1. Costs incurred in the *research* phase are expensed immediately; and
2. If costs incurred in the *development* phase meet the recognition criteria for an intangible asset, such costs should be capitalized. However, once costs have been expensed during the development phase, they cannot later be capitalized.

In practice, distinguishing research-like expenditures from development-like expenditures may not be easily accomplished. This would be especially true in the case of intangibles for which the measurement of economic benefits cannot be accomplished in anything approximating a direct manner. Assets such as brand names, mastheads, and customer lists can prove quite resistant to such direct observation of value (although in many industries there are rules of thumb, such as the notion that a customer list in the securities brokerage business is worth $1,500 per name, implying the amount of promotional costs a purchaser of a customer list could avoid incurring itself).

Thus, entities may incur certain expenditures in order to enhance brand names, such as engaging in image-advertising campaigns, but these costs will also have ancillary benefits, such as promoting specific products that are being sold currently, and possibly even enhancing employee morale and performance. While it may be argued that the expenditures create or add to an intangible asset, as a practical matter it would be difficult to determine what portion of the expenditures relate to which achievement, and to ascertain how much, if any, of the cost may be capitalized as part of brand names. Thus, it is considered to be unlikely that threshold criteria for recognition can be met in such a case. For this reason IAS 38 has specifically disallowed the capitalization of internally generated assets like brands, mastheads, publishing titles, customer lists, and items similar in substance to these.

Apart from the prohibited items, however, IAS 38 permits recognition of internally created intangible assets to the extent the expenditures can be analogized to the development phase of a research and development program. Thus, internally developed patents, copyrights, trademarks, franchises, and other assets will be recognized at the cost of creation, exclusive of costs which would be analogous to research, as further explained in the following paragraphs. The Basis for Conclusion to IAS 38 notes that "some view these requirements and guidance as being too restrictive and arbitrary" and that they reflect the standard setter's interpretation of the recognition criteria, but it agrees that they reflect the fact that it is difficult in practice to determine whether there is an internally generated asset separate from internally generated goodwill.

When an internally generated intangible asset meets the recognition criteria, the cost is determined using the same principles as for an acquired tangible asset. Thus, cost comprises all costs directly attributable to creating, producing, and preparing the asset for its intended use. IAS 38 closely mirrors IAS 16 with regard to elements of cost that may be considered as part of the asset, and the need to recognize the cash equivalent price when the acquisition transaction provides for deferred payment terms. As with self-constructed tangible assets, elements of profit must be eliminated from amounts capitalized, but incremental administrative and other overhead costs can be allocated to the intangible and included in the asset's cost. Initial operating losses, on the other hand, cannot be deferred by being added to the cost of the intangible, but rather must be expensed as incurred.

The standard takes this view based on the premise that an enterprise cannot demonstrate that the expenditure incurred in the research phase will generate probable future economic benefits, and consequently, that an intangible asset has been created (therefore, such expenditure should be expensed). Examples of research activities include: activities aimed at obtaining new knowledge; the search for, evaluation, and final selection of applications of research findings; and the search for and formulation of alternatives for new and improved systems, etc.

The standard recognizes that the development stage is further advanced towards ultimate commercial exploitation of the product or service being created than is the research stage. It acknowledges that an enterprise can possibly, in certain cases, identify an intangible asset and demonstrate that this asset will probably generate future economic benefits for the organization. Accordingly, IAS 38 allows recognition of an intangible asset during the development phase, provided the enterprise can demonstrate *all* of the following:

- Technical feasibility of completing the intangible asset so that it will be available for use or sale;
- Its intention to complete the intangible asset and either use it or sell it;
- Its ability to use or sell the intangible asset;
- The mechanism by which the intangible will generate probable future economic benefits;
- The availability of adequate technical, financial and other resources to complete the development and to use or sell the intangible asset; and
- The entity's ability to reliably measure the expenditure attributable to the intangible asset during its development.

Examples of development activities include: the design and testing of preproduction models; design of tools, jigs, molds, and dies; design of a pilot plant which is not otherwise commercially feasible; design and testing of a preferred alternative for new and improved systems, etc.

Recognition of internally generated computer software costs. The recognition of computer software costs poses several questions.

1. In the case of a company developing software programs for sale, should the costs incurred in developing the software be expensed, or should the costs be capitalized and amortized?
2. Is the treatment for developing software programs different if the program is to be used for in-house applications only?
3. In the case of purchased software, should the cost of the software be capitalized as a tangible asset or as an intangible asset, or should it be expensed fully and immediately?

In view of IAS 38's provisions the position can be clarified as follows:

1. In the case of a software-developing company, the costs incurred in the development of software programs are research and development costs. Accordingly, all expenses incurred in the research phase would be expensed. Thus, all expenses incurred until *technological feasibility* for the product has been established should be expensed. The enterprise would have to demonstrate technical feasibility and probability of its commercial success. Technological feasibility would be established if the enterprise has completed a detailed program design or working model. The enterprise should have completed the planning, designing, coding, and testing activities and established that the product can be successfully produced. Apart from being capable of production, the enterprise should demonstrate that it has the intention and ability to use or sell the program. Action taken to obtain control over the program in the form of copyrights or patents would support capitalization of these costs. At this stage the software program would be able to meet the criteria of identifiability, control, and future economic benefits, and can thus be capitalized and amortized as an intangible asset.
2. In the case of software internally developed for in-house use, for example, a computerized payroll program developed by the reporting enterprise itself, the accounting approach would be different. While the program developed may have some utility to the enterprise itself, it would be difficult to demonstrate how the program would generate future economic benefits to the enterprise. Also, in the absence of any legal rights to control the program or to prevent others from using it, the recognition criteria would not be met. Further, the cost proposed to be capitalized should be recoverable. In view of the impairment test prescribed by the standard, the carrying amount of the asset may not be recoverable and would accordingly have to be adjusted. Considering the above facts, such costs may need to be expensed.
3. In the case of purchased software, the treatment could differ and would need to be evaluated on a case-by-case basis. Software purchased for sale would be treated as inventory. However, software held for licensing or rental to others should be recognized as an intangible asset. On the other hand, cost of software purchased by an enterprise for its own use and which is integral to the hardware (because without that software the equipment cannot operate), would be treated as part of cost of the hardware and capitalized as property, plant, or equipment. Thus, the cost of an operating system purchased for an in-house computer, or cost of software purchased for computer-controlled machine tool, are treated as part of the related hardware.

   The costs of other software programs should be treated as intangible assets (as opposed to being capitalized along with the related hardware), as they are not an integral part of the hardware. For example, the cost of payroll or inventory software (purchased) may be treated as an intangible asset provided it meets the capitalization criteria under IAS 38. In practice, the conservative approach would be to expense such costs as they are incurred, since their ability to generate future economic benefits will always be questionable. If the costs are capitalized, useful lives should be conservatively estimated (i.e., kept brief) because of the well-known risk of technological obsolescence.

Example of software developed for internal use

The Hy-Tech Services Corporation employs researchers based in countries around the world. Employee time is the basis upon which charges to many customers are made. The geographically dispersed nature of its operations makes it extremely difficult for the payroll staff to collect time records, so the management team authorizes the design of an in-house, Web-based timekeeping system. The project team incurs the following costs:

Cost type	*Charged to expense*	*Capitalized*
Concept design	€2,500	
Evaluation of design alternatives	3,700	
Determination of required technology	8,100	
Final selection of alternatives	1,400	
Software design		€28,000
Software coding		42,000
Quality assurance testing		30,000
Data conversion costs	3,900	
Training	14,000	
Overhead allocation	6,900	
General and administrative costs	11,200	
Ongoing maintenance costs	6,000	
Totals	€57,700	€100,000

Thus, the total capitalized cost of this development project is €100,000. The estimated useful life of the timekeeping system is five years. As soon as all testing is completed, Hy-Tech's controller begins amortizing using a monthly charge of €1,666.67. The calculation follows:

€100,000 capitalized cost ÷ 60 months = €1,666.67 amortization charge

Once operational, management elects to construct another module for the system that issues an e-mail reminder for employees to complete their timesheets. This represents significant added functionality, so the design cost can be capitalized. The following costs are incurred:

Labor type	*Labor cost*	*Payroll taxes*	*Benefits*	*Total cost*
Software developers	€11,000	€842	€1,870	€13,712
Quality assurance testers	7,000	536	1,190	8,726
Totals	€18,000	€1,378	€3,060	€22,438

The full €22,438 amount of these costs can be capitalized. By the time this additional work is completed, the original system has been in operation for one year, thereby reducing the amortization period for the new module to four years. The calculation of the monthly straight-line amortization follows:

€22,438 capitalized cost ÷ 48 months = €467.46 amortization charge

The Hy-Tech management then authorizes the development of an additional module that allows employees to enter time data into the system from their cell phones using text messaging. Despite successfully passing through the concept design stage, the development team cannot resolve interface problems on a timely basis. Management elects to shut down the development project, requiring the charge of all €13,000 of programming and testing costs to expense in the current period.

After the system has been operating for two years, a Hy-Tech customer sees the timekeeping system in action and begs management to sell it as a stand-alone product. The customer becomes a distributor, and lands three sales in the first year. From these sales Hy-Tech receives revenues of €57,000, and incurs the following related expenses:

Expense type	*Amount*
Distributor commission (25%)	€14,250
Service costs	1,900
Installation costs	4,300
Total	€20,450

Thus, the net proceeds from the software sale is €36,550 (= €57,000 revenue less €20,450 related costs). Rather than recording these transactions as revenue and expense, the €36,550 net proceeds are offset against the remaining unamortized balance of the software asset with the following entry:

Revenue	57,000	
Fixed assets—software		36,550
Commission expense		14,250
Service expense		1,900
Installation expense		4,300

At this point, the remaining unamortized balance of the timekeeping system is €40,278, which is calculated as follows:

Original capitalized amount	€100,000
+ Additional software module	22,438
– 24 month's amortization on original capitalized amount	(40,000)
– 12 month's amortization on additional software module	(5,610)
– Net proceeds from software sales	(36,550)
Total unamortized balance	€40,278

Immediately thereafter, Hy-Tech's management receives a sales call from an application service provider who manages an Internet-based timekeeping system. The terms offered are so attractive that Hy-Tech abandons its in-house system at once and switches to the server system. As a result of this change, the company writes off the remaining unamortized balance of its timekeeping system with the following entry:

Accumulated depreciation	45,610	
Loss on asset disposal	40,278	
Fixed assets—software		85,888

Costs Not Satisfying the IAS 38 Recognition Criteria

The standard has specifically provided that expenditures incurred for nonfinancial intangible assets should be recognized as an expense unless

1. It relates to an intangible asset dealt with in another IAS;
2. The cost forms part of the cost of an intangible asset that meets the recognition criteria prescribed by IAS 38; or
3. It is acquired in a business combination and cannot be recognized as an identifiable intangible asset. In this case, this expenditure should form part of the amount attributable to goodwill as at the date of acquisition.

As a consequence of applying the above criteria, the following costs are expensed as they are incurred:

- Research costs;
- Preopening costs for a new facility or business, and plant start-up costs incurred during a period prior to full-scale production or operation, unless these costs are capitalized as part of the cost of an item of property, plant, and equipment;
- Organization costs such as legal and secretarial costs, which are typically incurred in establishing a legal entity;
- Training costs involved in operating a business or a product line;
- Advertising and related costs;

- Relocation, restructuring, and other costs involved in organizing a business or product line;
- Customer lists, brands, mastheads, and publishing titles that are internally generated.

In some countries enterprises have previously been allowed to defer and amortize setup costs and preoperating costs on the premise that benefits from them flow to the enterprise over future periods as well. IAS 38 does not condone this view.

The criteria for recognition of intangible assets as provided in IAS 38 are rather stringent, and many enterprises will find that expenditures either to acquire or to develop intangible assets will fail the test for capitalization. In such instances, all these costs must be expensed currently as incurred. Furthermore, once expensed, these costs cannot be resurrected and capitalized in a later period, even if the conditions for such treatment are later met. This is not meant, however, to preclude correction of an error made in an earlier period if the conditions for capitalization were met but interpreted incorrectly by the reporting entity at that time.

Subsequently Incurred Costs

Under the provisions of IAS 38, the capitalization of any subsequent costs incurred on intangible assets is difficult to justify. This is because the nature of an intangible asset is such that, in many cases, it is not possible to determine whether subsequent costs are likely to enhance the specific economic benefits that will flow to the enterprise from those assets. Thus, subsequent costs incurred on an intangible asset should be recognized as an expense when they are incurred unless

1. It is probable that those costs will enable the asset to generate specifically attributable future economic benefits in excess of its assessed standard of performance immediately prior to the incremental expenditure; and
2. Those costs can be measured reliably and attributed to the asset reliably.

Thus, if the above two criteria are both met, any subsequent expenditure on an intangible after its purchase or its completion should be capitalized along with its cost. The following example should help to illustrate this point better.

Example

An enterprise is developing a new product. Costs incurred by the R&D department in 2005 on the "research phase" amounted to €200,000. In 2006, technical and commercial feasibility of the product was established. Costs incurred in 2006 were €20,000 personnel costs and €15,000 legal fees to register the patent. In 2007, the enterprise incurred €30,000 to successfully defend a legal suit to protect the patent. The enterprise would account for these costs as follows:

- Research and development costs incurred in 2005, amounting to €200,000, should be expensed, as they do not meet the recognition criteria for intangible assets. The costs do not result in an identifiable asset capable of generating future economic benefits.
- Personnel and legal costs incurred in 2006, amounting to €35,000, would be capitalized as patents. The company has established technical and commercial feasibility of the product, as well as obtained control over the use of the asset. The standard specifically prohibits the reinstatement of costs previously recognized as an expense. Thus €200,000, recognized as an expense in the previous financial statements, cannot be reinstated and capitalized.
- Legal costs of €30,000 incurred in 2007 to defend the enterprise in a patent lawsuit should be expensed. Under US GAAP, legal fees and other costs incurred in successfully defending a patent lawsuit can be capitalized in the patents account, to the extent that value is evident, because such costs are incurred to establish the legal rights of the owner of the patent. However, in view of the stringent conditions imposed by IAS 38 concerning the

recognition of subsequent costs, only such subsequent costs should be capitalized which would enable the asset to generate future economic benefits *in excess of the originally assessed standards of performance*. This represents, in most instances, a very high, possibly insurmountable hurdle. Thus, legal costs incurred in connection with defending the patent, which could be considered as expenses incurred to maintain the asset at its originally assessed standard of performance, would not meet the recognition criteria under IAS 38.

- Alternatively, if the enterprise were to lose the patent lawsuit, then the useful life and the recoverable amount of the intangible asset would be in question. The enterprise would be required to provide for any impairment loss, and in all probability, even to fully write off the intangible asset. What is required must be determined by the facts of the specific situation.

Measurement subsequent to Initial Recognition

IAS 38 incorporates two alternative measurement bases: the cost model and the revaluation model. This is entirely comparable to what is prescribed under IAS 16 relative to tangible long-lived assets.

Cost model. After initial recognition, an intangible asset should be carried at its cost less any accumulated amortization and any accumulated impairment losses.

Revaluation model. As with tangible assets, the standard for intangibles permits revaluation subsequent to original acquisition, with the asset being written up to fair value. Inasmuch as most of the particulars of IAS 38 follow IAS 16 to the letter, and were described in detail in Chapter 8, these will not be repeated here. The unique features of IAS 38 are as follows:

1. If the intangibles were not initially recognized (i.e., they were expensed rather than capitalized) it would not be possible to later recognize them at fair value.
2. Deriving fair value by applying a present value concept to projected cash flows (a technique that can be used in the case of tangible assets under IAS 16) is deemed to be too unreliable in the realm of intangibles, primarily because it would tend to commingle the impact of identifiable assets and goodwill. Accordingly, fair value of an intangible asset should *only* be determined by reference to an active market in that type of intangible asset. Active markets providing meaningful data are not expected to exist for such unique assets as patents and trademarks, and thus it is presumed that revaluation will not be applied to these types of assets in the normal course of business. As a consequence, the standard effectively restricts revaluation of intangible assets to freely tradable intangible assets.

As with the rules pertaining to plant, property, and equipment under IAS 16, if some intangible assets in a given class are subjected to revaluation, all the assets in that class should be consistently accounted for unless fair value information is not or ceases to be available. Also in common with the requirements for tangible fixed assets, IAS 38 requires that revaluations be taken directly to equity through the use of a revaluation surplus account, except to the extent that previous impairments had been recognized by a charge against income.

Example of revaluation of intangible assets

A patent right is acquired July 1, 2005, for €250,000; while it has a legal life of 15 years, due to rapidly changing technology, management estimates a useful life of only five years. Straight-line amortization will be used. At January 1, 2006, management is uncertain that the process can actually be made economically feasible, and decides to write down the patent to an estimated market value of €75,000. Amortization will be taken over three years from that point. On January 1, 2008, having perfected the related production process, the asset is now appraised at a sound value of €300,000. Furthermore, the estimated useful life is now believed to be six more years. The entries to reflect these events are as follows:

7/1/05	Patent	250,000	
	Cash, etc.		250,000
12/31/05	Amortization expense	25,000	
	Patent		25,000
1/1/06	Loss from asset impairment	150,000	
	Patent		150,000
12/31/06	Amortization expense	25,000	
	Patent		25,000
12/31/07	Amortization expense	25,000	
	Patent		25,000
1/1/08	Patent	275,000	
	Gain on asset value recovery		100,000
	Revaluation surplus		175,000

Certain of the entries in the foregoing example will be explained further. The entry at year-end 2005 is to record amortization based on original cost, since there had been no revaluations through that time; only a half-year amortization is provided [(€250,000/5) x 1/2]. On January 1, 2006, the impairment is recorded by writing down the asset to the estimated value of €75,000, which necessitates a €150,000 charge to income (carrying value, €225,000, less fair value, €75,000).

In 2006 and 2007, amortization must be provided on the new lower value recorded at the beginning of 2006; furthermore, since the new estimated life was three years from January 2006, annual amortization will be €25,000.

As of January 1, 2008, the carrying value of the patent is €25,000; had the January 2006 revaluation not been made, the carrying value would have been €125,000 (€250,000 original cost, less two-and-one-half years amortization versus an original estimated life of five years). The new appraised value is €300,000, which will fully recover the earlier write-down and add even more asset value than the originally recognized cost. Under the guidance of IAS 38, the recovery of €100,000 that had been charged to expense should be taken into income; the excess will be credited to stockholders' equity.

Development costs pose a special problem in terms of the application of the revaluation method under IAS 38. In general, it will not be possible to obtain fair value data from active markets, as is required by IAS 38. Accordingly, the expectation is that the cost method will be almost universally applied for development costs.

Example of development cost capitalization

Assume that Creative, Incorporated incurs substantial research and development costs for the invention of new products, many of which are brought to market successfully. In particular, Creative has incurred costs during 2005 amounting to €750,000, relative to a new manufacturing process. Of these costs, €600,000 were incurred prior to December 1, 2005. As of December 31, the viability of the new process was still not known, although testing had been conducted on December 1. In fact, results were not conclusively known until February 15, 2006, after another €75,000 in costs were incurred post–January 1. Creative, Incorporated's financial statements for 2005 were issued February 10, 2006, and the full €750,000 in research and development costs were expensed, since it was not yet known whether a portion of these qualified as development costs under IAS 38. When it is learned that feasibility had, in fact, been shown as of December 1, Creative management asks to restore the €150,000 of post–December 1 costs as a development asset. Under IAS 38 this is prohibited. However, the 2006 costs (€75,000 thus far) would qualify for capitalization, in all likelihood, based on the facts known.

If, however, it is determined that fair value information derived from active markets is indeed available, and the enterprise desires to apply the revaluation method of accounting to development costs, then it will be necessary to perform revaluations on a regular basis, such that at any reporting date the carrying amounts are not materially different from the current fair values. From a mechanical perspective, the adjustment to fair value can be accomplished either by "grossing up" the cost and the accumulated amortization accounts proportionally, or by netting the accumulated amortization, prior to revaluation, against the asset account and then restating the asset to the net fair value as of the revaluation date. In either case, the net effect of the upward revaluation will be recorded in equity as revaluation surplus; the only exception would be when an upward revaluation is in effect a reversal of a previously recognized impairment which was reported as a charge against earnings or a revaluation decrease (reversal or a yet earlier upward adjustment) which was reflected in earnings.

The accounting for revaluations is illustrated as follows:

Example of accounting for revaluation of development cost

Assume Breakthrough, Inc. has accumulated development costs that meet the criteria for capitalization at December 31, 2005, amounting to €39,000. It is estimated that the useful life of this intangible asset will be six years; accordingly, amortization of €6,500 per year is anticipated. Breakthrough uses the allowed alternative method of accounting for its long-lived tangible and intangible assets. At December 31, 2007, it obtains market information regarding the then-current fair value of this intangible asset, which suggests a current fair value of these development costs is €40,000; the estimated useful life, however, has not changed. There are two ways to apply IAS 38: the asset and accumulated amortization can be "grossed up" to reflect the new fair value information, or the asset can be restated on a "net" basis. These are both illustrated below. For both illustrations, the book value (amortized cost) immediately prior to the revaluation is €39,000 – (2 x €6,500) = €26,000. The net upward revaluation is given by the difference between fair value and book value, or €40,000 – €26,000 = €14,000.

If the "gross up" method is used: Since the fair value after two years of the six-year useful life have already elapsed is found to be €40,000, the gross fair value must be 6/4 x €40,000 = €60,000. The entries to record this would be as follows:

Development cost (asset)	21,000	
Accumulated amortization—development cost		7,000
Revaluation surplus (stockholders' equity)		14,000

If the "netting" method is used: Under this variant, the accumulated amortization as of the date of the revaluation is eliminated against the asset account, which is then adjusted to reflect the net fair value.

Accumulated amortization—development cost	13,000	
Development cost (asset)		13,000
Development cost (asset)	14,000	
Revaluation surplus (stockholders' equity)		14,000

Amortization Period

IAS 38, as revised in 2004, requires the entity to determine whether an intangible has a finite or indefinite useful life. An indefinite future life means that there is no foreseeable limit on the period during which the asset is expected to generate future cash flows. The standard lists a number of factors to be taken into account:

1. The expected usage by the entity;
2. Typical product life cycles for the asset;
3. Technical, technological, commercial or other types of obsolescence;
4. The stability of the industry in which the asset operates;
5. Expected actions by competitors;
6. The level of maintenance expenditure required to obtain the future economic benefits, and the company's ability an intention to reach such a level;
7. The period of control over the asset and legal or similar limits on the use of the asset;

8. Whether the useful life of the asset is dependent on the useful life of other assets.

Assets having a finite useful life must be amortized over that useful life, and this may be done in any of the usual ways (pro rata over time, over units of production, etc.). If control over the future economic benefits from an intangible asset is achieved through legal rights for a finite period, then the useful life of the intangible asset should not exceed the period of legal rights, unless the legal rights are renewable and the renewal is a virtual certainty. Thus, as a practical matter, the shorter legal life will set the upper limit for an amortization period in most cases.

The amortization method used should reflect the pattern in which the economic benefits of the asset are consumed by the enterprise. Amortization should commence when the asset is available for use and the amortization charge for each period should be recognized as an expense unless it is included in the carrying amount of another asset (e.g., inventory). Intangible assets may be amortized by the same systematic and rational methods that are used to depreciate tangible fixed assets. Thus, IAS 38 would seemingly permit straight-line, diminishing balance, and units of production methods. If a method other than straight-line is used, it must accurately mirror the expiration of the asset's economic service potential.

IAS 38 offers several examples of how useful life of intangibles is to be assessed. These include the following types of assets:

Customer lists. Care is urged to ensure that amortization is only over the expected useful life of the acquired list, ignoring the extended life that may be created as the acquirer adds to the list by virtue of its own efforts and costs, after acquisition. In many instances the initial, purchased list will erode in value rather quickly, since contacts become obsolete as customers migrate to other vendors, leave business, and so forth. These assets must be constantly refreshed, and that will involve expenditures by the acquirer of the original list (and whether those costs justify capitalization and amortization is a separate issue). For example, the acquired list might have a useful economic life of only two years (i.e., without additional expenditures, the value will be fully consumed over that time horizon). Two years would be the amortization period, therefore.

Patents. While a patent has a legal life (depending on jurisdiction of issuance) of as long as several decades, realistically, due to evolving technology and end-product obsolescence or changing customer tastes and preferences, the useful economic life may be much less. IAS 38 offers an example of a patent having a 15-year remaining life and a firm offer to acquire by a third party in five years, at a fixed fraction of the original acquirer's purchase cost. In such a situation (which is probably unusual, however), amortization of the fraction not to be recovered in the subsequent sale, over a 5-year period, would be appropriate.

In other situations, it would be necessary to estimate the economic life of the patent and amortize the entire cost, in the absence of any firmly established residual value, over that period. It should be noted that there is increasing activity involving the monetizing of intellectual property values, including via the packaging of groups of patents and transferring them to special-purpose entities which then license them to third-party licensees. This shows promise of becoming an important way for patent holders to reap greater benefits from existing pools of patents held by them, but is in its infancy at this time and future success cannot be reliably predicted. Amortization of existing acquired patents or other intellectual property (intangible assets) should not be based on highly speculative values that might be obtained from such arrangements.

Additionally, whatever lives are assigned to patents for amortization purposes, these should regularly be reconsidered. As necessary, changes in useful lives should be implemented, which would be changes in estimate affecting current and future periods' amortization only, unless an accounting error had previously been made.

Copyrights. In many jurisdictions copyrights now have very lengthy terms, but for most materials so protected the actual useful lives will be very much shorter, sometimes only a year or two.

Renewable license rights. In many situations the entity may acquire license rights, such as broadcasting of radio or television signals, which technically expire after a fixed term but which are essentially renewable with little or no cost incurred as long as minimum performance criteria are met. If there is adequate evidence to demonstrate that this description is accurate and that the reporting entity has indeed been able, previously, to successfully accomplish this, then the intangible will be deemed to have an indefinite life and not be subjected to periodic amortization. However, this makes it more vital that impairment be regularly reviewed, since even if control of the rights remains with the reporting entity, changes in technology or consumer demand may serve to diminish the value of that asset. If impaired, a charge against earnings must be recognized, with the remaining unimpaired cost (if any) continuing to be recognized as an indefinite life intangible.

Similar actions would be warranted in the case of airline route authority. If readily renewable, without limitation, provided that minimal regulations are complied with (such as maintaining airport terminal space in a prescribed manner), the standard suggests that this be treated as an indefinite life intangible. Annual impairment testing would be required, as with all indefinite life intangibles (more often if there is any indication of impairment).

IAS 38 notes that a change in the governmental licensing regime may require a change in how these are accounted for. It cites an example of a change that ends perfunctory renewal and substitutes public auctions for the rights at each former renewal date. In such an instance, the reporting entity can no longer presume to have any right to continue after expiration of the current license, and must amortize its cost over the remaining term.

Residual Value

Tangible assets often have a positive residual value before considering the disposal costs because tangible assets can generally be sold, at least, for scrap, or possibly can be transferred to another user that has less need for or ability to afford new assets of that type. Intangibles, on the other hand, often have little or no residual worth. Accordingly, IAS 38 requires that a zero residual value be presumed unless an accurate measure of residual is possible. Thus, the residual value is presumed to be zero *unless*

- There is a commitment by a third party to purchase the asset at the end of its useful life; *or*
- There is an active market for that type of intangible asset, and residual value can be measured reliably by reference to that market and it is probable that such a market will exist at the end of the useful life.

IAS 38 specifies that the residual value of an intangible asset is the estimated net amount that the reporting entity currently expects to obtain from disposal of the asset at the end of its useful life, after deducting the estimated costs of disposal, if the asset were of the age and in the condition expected at the end of its estimated useful life. Changes in estimated selling prices or other variables that occur over the expected period of use of the asset are not to be included in the estimated residual value, since this would result in the recognition of projected future holding gains over the life of the asset (via reduced amortization that would be the consequence of a higher estimated residual value).

Residual value is to be assessed at each balance sheet date. Any change to the estimated residual, other than that resulting from impairment (accounted for under IAS 36) is to be accounted for prospectively, by varying future periodic amortization. Similarly, any change in amortization method (e.g., from accelerated to straight-line), based on an updated understanding of the pattern of future usage and economic benefits to be reaped therefrom, is dealt with as a change in estimate, again to be reflected only through changes in future periodic charges for amortization.

Periodic review of useful life assumptions and amortization methods employed. As for fixed assets accounted for in conformity with IAS 16, the standard on intangibles requires that the amortization period be reconsidered at the end of each reporting period, and that the method of amortization also be reviewed at similar intervals. There is the expectation that due to their nature intangibles are more likely to require revisions to one or both of these judgments. In either case, a change would be accounted for as a change in estimate, affecting current and future periods' reported earnings but not requiring restatement of previously reported periods.

Intangibles being accounted for as having an indefinite life must furthermore be reassessed periodically, as management plans and expectations almost inevitably vary over time. For example, a trademarked product, despite having wide consumer recognition and acceptance, can become irrelevant as tastes and preferences alter, and a limited horizon, perhaps a very short one, may emerge with little warning. Business history is littered with formerly valuable franchises that, for whatever reason—including management missteps—become valueless.

Impairment Losses

Where an asset is determined to have an indefinite useful life, the entity must conduct impairment tests annually, as well as whenever there is an indication that the intangible may be impaired. Furthermore, the presumption that the asset has an indefinite life must also be reviewed.

The impairment of intangible assets other than goodwill (such as patents, copyrights, trade names, customer lists, and franchise rights) should be considered in precisely the same way that long-lived tangible assets are dealt with. Carrying amounts must be compared to the greater of net selling price or value in use when there are indications that an impairment may have been suffered. Reversals of impairment losses under defined conditions are also recognized. The effects of impairment recognitions and reversals will be reflected in current period operating results, if the intangible assets in question are being accounted for in accordance with the cost method.

On the other hand, if the revaluation method of accounting for intangible assets is followed (use of which is possible only if strict criteria can be met), impairments will normally be charged to stockholders' equity to the extent that revaluation surplus exists, and only to the extent that the loss exceeds previously recognized valuation surplus will the impairment loss be reported as a charge against earnings. Recoveries are handled consistent with the method by which impairments were reported, in a manner entirely analogous to the explanation in Chapter 8 dealing with impairments of plant, property, and equipment.

Unlike other intangible assets that are individually identifiable, goodwill is amorphous and cannot exist, from a financial reporting perspective, apart from the tangible and identifiable intangible assets with which it was acquired and remains associated. Thus, a direct evaluation of the recoverable amount of goodwill is not actually feasible. Accordingly, IFRS requires that goodwill be combined with other assets which together define a cash generating unit, and that an evaluation of any potential impairment (if warranted by the facts and circumstances) be conducted on an aggregate basis. A more detailed consideration of goodwill is presented in Chapter 11.

Disposals of Intangible Assets

With regard to questions of accounting for the disposition of assets, the guidance of IAS 38 is consistent with that of IAS 16. Gain or loss recognition will be for the difference between carrying amount (net, if applicable, of any remaining revaluation surplus) and the net proceeds from the sale. The amendment to IAS 38 made in 2004 observes that a disposal of an intangible asset may be effected either by a sale of the asset or by entering into a finance lease. The determination of the date of disposal of the intangible asset is made by applying the criteria in IAS 18 for recognizing revenue from the sale of goods, or IAS 17 in the case of disposal by a sale and leaseback. As for other similar transactions, the consideration receivable on disposal of an intangible asset is to be recognized initially at fair value. If payment for such an intangible asset is deferred, the consideration received is recognized initially at the cash price equivalent, with any difference between the nominal amount of the consideration and the cash price equivalent to be recognized as interest revenue under IAS 18, using the effective yield method.

Web Site Development and Operating Costs

With the advent of the Internet and of "e-commerce," most businesses now have their own Web sites. Web sites have become integral to doing business and may be designed either for external or internal access. Those designed for external access are developed and maintained for the purposes of promotion and advertising of an entity's products and services to their potential consumers. On the other hand, those developed for internal access may be used for displaying company policies and storing customer details.

With substantial costs being incurred by many entities for Web site development and maintenance, the need for accounting guidance became evident. The 2001 interpretation, SIC 32, concluded that such costs represent an internally generated intangible asset that is subject to the requirements of IAS 38, and that such costs should be recognized if, and only if, an enterprise can satisfy the requirements set forth in IAS 38. Therefore, Web site costs have been likened to "development phase" (as opposed to "research phase") costs.

Thus the stringent qualifying conditions applicable to the development phase, such as "ability to generate future economic benefits," have to be met if such costs are to be recognized as an intangible asset. If an enterprise is not able to demonstrate how a Web site developed solely or primarily for promoting and advertising its own products and services will generate probable future economic benefits, all expenditure on developing such a Web site should be recognized as an expense when incurred.

Any internal expenditure on development and operation of the Web site should be accounted for in accordance with IAS 38. Comprehensive additional guidance is provided in the Appendix to SIC 32 and is summarized below.

1. Planning stage expenditures, such as undertaking feasibility studies, defining hardware and software specifications, evaluating alternative products and suppliers, and selecting preferences, should be expensed;
2. Application and infrastructure development costs pertaining to acquisition of tangible assets, such as purchasing and developing hardware, should be dealt with in accordance with IAS 16;
3. Other application and infrastructure development costs, such as obtaining a domain name, developing operating software, developing code for the application, installing developed applications on the Web server and stress testing, should be expensed when incurred unless the conditions prescribed by IAS 38 are met;

4. Graphical design development costs, such as designing the appearance of Web pages, should be expensed when incurred unless recognition criteria prescribed by IAS 38 are met;

5. Content development costs, such as expenses incurred for creating, purchasing, preparing, and uploading information onto the Web site, to the extent that these costs are incurred to advertise and promote an enterprise's own products or services, should be expensed immediately, consistent with how other advertising and related costs are to be accounted for under IFRS. Thus, these costs are not deferred, even until first displayed on the Web site, but are expensed when incurred;

6. Operating costs, such as updating graphics and revising content, adding new functions, registering Web site with search engines, backing up data, reviewing security access and analyzing usage of the Web site should be expensed when incurred, unless in rare circumstances these costs meet the criteria prescribed in IAS 38, in which case such expenditure is capitalized as a cost of the Web site; and

7. Other costs, such as selling and administrative overhead (excluding expenditure which can be directly attributed to preparation of Web site for use), initial operating losses and inefficiencies incurred before the Web site achieves planned , and training costs of employees to operate the Web site, should be expensed when incurred as required under IFRS.

Disclosure Requirements

The disclosure requirements set out in IAS 38 for intangible assets and those imposed by IAS 16 for property, plant, and equipment are very similar, and both demand extensive details to be disclosed in the financial statement footnotes. Another marked similarity is the exemption from disclosing "comparative information" with respect to the reconciliation of carrying amounts at the beginning and end of the period. While this may be misconstrued as a departure from the well-known principle of presenting all numerical information in comparative form, it is worth noting that it is in line with the provisions of IAS 1. IAS 1 categorically states that "(u)nless a Standard permits or requires otherwise, comparative information should be disclosed in respect of the previous period for all numerical information in the financial statements…." (Another standard that contains a similar exemption from disclosure of comparative reconciliation information is IAS 37—which is dealt with in Chapter 12.)

For each class of intangible assets (distinguishing between internally generated and other intangible assets), disclosure is required of

1. Whether the useful lives are indefinite or finite and if finite, the useful lives or amortization rates used;

2. The amortization method(s) used;

3. The gross carrying amount and accumulated amortization (including accumulated impairment losses) at both the beginning and end of the period;

4. A reconciliation of the carrying amount at the beginning and end of the period showing additions (analyzed between those acquired separately and those acquired in a business combination), assets classified as held for sale, retirements, disposals, acquisitions by means of business combinations, increases or decreases resulting from revaluations, reductions to recognize impairments, amounts written back to recognize recoveries of prior impairments, amortization during the period, the net effect of translation of foreign entities' financial statements, and any other material items; and

5. The line item of the income statement in which the amortization charge of intangible assets is included.

The standard explains the concept of "class of intangible assets" as a "grouping of assets of similar nature and use in an enterprise's operations." Examples of intangible assets that could be reported as separate classes (of intangible assets) are

1. Brand names;
2. Licenses and franchises;
3. Mastheads and publishing titles;
4. Computer software;
5. Copyrights, patents and other industrial property rights, service and operating right;
6. Recipes, formulae, models, designs and prototypes; and
7. Intangible assets under development.

The above list is only illustrative in nature. Intangible assets may be combined (or disaggregated) to report larger classes (or smaller classes) of intangible assets if this results in more relevant information for financial statement users.

In addition, the financial statements should also disclose the following:

1. For any asset assessed as having an indefinite useful life, the carrying amount of the asset and the reasons for considering that it has an indefinite life and the significant factors used to determine this;
2. The nature, carrying amount, and remaining amortization period of any individual intangible asset that is material to the financial statements of the enterprise as a whole;
3. For intangible assets acquired by way of a government grant and initially recognized at fair value, the fair value initially recognized, their carrying amount, and whether they are carried under the cost or revaluation method for subsequent measurement;
4. Any restrictions on title and any assets pledged as security for debt; and
5. The amount of outstanding commitments for the acquisition of intangible assets.

Where intangibles are carried using the revaluation model, the entity must disclose the effective date of the revaluation, the carrying amount of the assets, and what their carrying value would have been under the cost model, the amount of revaluation surplus applicable to the assets and the significant assumptions used in measuring fair value.

The financial statements should also disclose the aggregate amount of research and development expenditure recognized as an expense during the period. The entity is encouraged but not required to disclose any fully amortized assets still in use and any significant assets in use but not recognized because they did not meet the IAS 38 recognition criteria.

Examples of Financial Statement Disclosures

Novartis AG
For the Fiscal Year ending December 31, 2004

Notes to the consolidated financial statements

Intangible assets. Intangible assets are valued at cost and reviewed periodically for any diminution in value. Any resulting impairment loss is recorded in the income statement in Other Operating Income & Expense. In the case of business combinations, the excess of the purchase price over the fair value of net identifiable assets acquired is recorded as goodwill in the balance sheet. Goodwill, which is denominated in the local currency of the related acquisition, is amortized to income through Other Operating Income & Expense on a straight-line basis over the asset's useful life. The amortization period is determined at the time of the acquisition, based upon the particular circumstances, and ranges from 5 to 20 years. An exception is for goodwill on acquisitions after March 31, 2004, which is no longer amortized under IFRS 3 but instead is subject to annual impairment testing. Goodwill relating to acquisitions arising prior to January 1, 1995, has been fully written off against retained earnings.

Up to March 31, 2004, management determined the estimated useful life of goodwill arising from an acquisition based on its evaluation of the respective company at the time of the acquisition, considering factors such as existing market share, potential sales growth, and other factors inherent in the acquired company.

For all acquisitions after March 31, 2004, in accordance with IAS 38 (revised), In-Process Research & Development (IPR&D) is separately recorded as an intangible asset. It will start to be amortized when it results in a saleable product and is assessed at least annually for impairment.

Other acquired intangible assets are written off on a straight-line basis over the following periods:

Trademarks	10 to 15 years
Product and marketing rights	5 to 20 years
Software	3 years
Others	3 to 5 years

Trademarks are amortized on a straight-line basis over the estimated economic or legal life, whichever is shorter, while the practice of the Group has been to amortize product rights over estimated useful lives of 5 to 20 years. The useful lives assigned to acquired product rights are based on the maturity of the products and the estimated economic benefit that such product rights can provide. Marketing rights are amortized over their useful lives commencing in the year in which the rights first generate sales.

Long-lived property, plant & equipment and identifiable intangibles are reviewed for impairment whenever events or changes in circumstances indicate that the balance sheet carrying amount of the asset may not be recoverable. Goodwill is reviewed for impairment annually. When events or changes in circumstance indicate the value may not be fully recoverable, the Group estimates its value in use based on the future cash flows expected to result from the use of the asset and its eventual disposition. If the balance sheet carrying amount of the asset is more than the higher of its value in use to Novartis or its anticipated net selling price, an impairment loss for the difference is recognized. For purposes of assessing impairment, assets are grouped at the lowest level for which there are separately identifiable cash flows.

Considerable management judgment is necessary to estimate discounted future cash flows. Accordingly, actual outcomes could vary significantly from such estimates.

Research and Development. We are among the leaders in the pharmaceuticals industry in terms of research and development investment. In 2004, we invested approximately $3.5 billion in Pharmaceuticals Division research and development, which represents 18.8% of the Division's total net sales. Our Pharmaceuticals Division invested $3.1 billion and $2.4 billion on research and development in 2003 and 2002 respectively. There are currently more than 75 projects in clinical development. In 2005, as a result of these efforts, we expect to launch *Aclasata* and *Focalin XR*, as well as new indications or formulations for *Gleevec/Glivec*, *Diovan*, *Femara*, *Zelnorm/Zelmac*, and *Xolair*, in various markets worldwide.

We have long-term research commitments totaling $1.2 billion as of December 31, 2004, including $0.6 billion in milestone payments. We intend to fund these expenditures from internally developed resources.

The discovery and development of a new drug is a lengthy process, usually requiring 10 to 12 years from the initial research to bringing a drug to market, including 6 to 8 years from Phase I clinical trials to market. At each of these steps, there is a substantial risk that we will not achieve our goals. In such an event, we may be required to abandon a product in which we have made a substantial investment.

9.   Intangible asset movements

(in USD millions)	Goodwill	Research & Development	Product and marketing rights	Trademarks	Software	Other intangibles	Totals 2004	Totals 2003
Cost,								
January 1	2,097	--	3,578	441	122	615	6,853	6,144
Consolidation changes	--	139	158	104	--	90	491	24
Reclassifications*	6	--	1	(8)	1	--	--	(21)
Additions	535	--	15	4	16	148	718	521
Disposals	(20)	--	(29)	(5)	(10)	(49)	(113)	(316)
Translation effects	121	12	235	12	7	20	407	501
December 31	2,739	151	3,958	548	136	824	8,356	6,835
Accumulated amortization								
January 1	(620)	--	(981)	(153)	(96)	(295)	(2,145)	(1,749)
Reclassifications*	--	--	--	1	--	(1)	--	(2)
Amortization charge	(620)	--	(230)	(43)	(18)	(57)	(456)	(410)
Disposals	7	--	28	5	7	48	95	271
Impairment charge	75	--	(12)	--	--	--	(87)	(105)
Translation effects	44	=	(69)	(4)	(5)	(12)	(134)	(150)
December 31	840	=	(1,264)	(194)	(112)	(317)	(2,727)	(2,145)
Net book value—December 31	1,899	151	2,694	354	24	507	5,629	4,708

* *Reclassifications between various asset categories as a result of recording final acquisition balance sheets*

In 2004, impairment charges of $87 million were recorded, principally relating to the valuation of Sandoz activities in Germany due to the effects of competitive pressures on pricing.

In 2003 impairment charges of $105 million were recorded, principally relating to loss of market share which, in the near future was considered to be difficult to regain of the Sandoz activities in Germany; the divestment of Genetic Therapy Inc., US, a Pharmaceuticals Division research activity, to Cell Genesys Inc., US, and adjustments to CIBA Vision Business Unit intangibles related to the planned disposal of the refractive surgery activities.

Mittal Steel South Africa
Period ending December 2004

Intangible Assets

No value is attributed to internally developed trademarks, patents and similar rights and assets. Trademarks, concessions, patents and similar rights purchased by the company are capitalized. Intangible assets are amortized on a straight-line basis over their estimated useful lives.

Intangible assets acquired by the group are stated at cost less accumulated amortization and impairment losses. Amortization is charged to the income statement on a straight-line basis over the estimated useful lives of intangible assets, unless such lives are indefinite Subsequent expenditure on capitalized intangible assets is capitalized only when it increases the future benefits embodied in the specific asset to which it relates. All other expenditure is expensed as incurred.

13. Intangible assets

	Group	
	Year ended Dec. 31 2004 2003 Rm	Six months ended Dec. 31 2003 2002 Rm
Gross carrying amount		
At beginning of period	41	41
At end of period	<u>41</u>	<u>40</u>
Accumulated depreciation		
At beginning of period	9	8
Impairment charge included in depreciation charge	<u>2</u>	<u>1</u>
At end of period	<u>11</u>	<u>9</u>
Net carrying amount at end of period	30	32

F. Hoffman-La Roche Ltd.
Period ending December 2004

Intangible assets

Millions of CHF	Acquisition related	Patents, licenses, trademarks and other	2004 total	2003 total
Net book value				
At beginning of year	5,384	1,561	6,945	7,786
Igen acquisition	740	--	740	--
Disetronic acquisition	--	--	--	320
Disposal of Consumer Health (OTC) business	(234)	(6)	(240)	--
Additions	4	284	288	233
Disposals	--	(12)	(12)	(2)
Amortization charge	(728)	(298)	(1,026)	(1,013)
Impairment charge	(2)	(29)	(31)	(21)
Igen litigation	--	--	--	(117)
Currency translation effects	(258)	(66)	(324)	(241)
At end of year	4,906	1,434	6,340	6,945
At 31 December				
Cost	11,627	2,685	14,312	14,729
Accumulated amortization	(6,721)	(1,251)	(7,972)	(7,784)
Net book value	4,906	1,434	6,340	6,945

Of which	Remaining useful life	2004	2003
-Genentech acquisition	1-10 years	592	826
-Corange acquisition	3-13 years	2,345	2,705
-Chugai acquisition	8-16 years	680	781
-Disetronic acquisition	9 years	267	300
-Igen acquisition	12 years	634	--
-Kytril	4 years	755	988
-Others	Various	<u>1,067</u>	<u>1,345</u>
Total		<u>6,340</u>	<u>6,945</u>

The majority of the Group's intangible assets results from the acquisitions made by the Group. The patents, licenses, trademarks and other intangible assets are recorded at fair value in the acquisition accounting and are subsequently amortized over their useful lives. The Kytril intangible assets arise from the purchase by the Group of the global rights to Kytril (granisetron) from SmithKline Beecham in December 2000. The Group currently has no internally generated intangible assets from development as the criteria for the recognition as an asset are not met.

Lectra
Period ending December 31, 2004

Accounting policies

Intangible assets. Intangible assets are carried at their purchase cost less cumulative amortization and impairment, if any. Amortization is charged on a straight-line basis depending on the estimated useful life of the intangible asset. The book value of each intangible asset is tested for impairment at each closing date.

Management information software. Purchased management information software packages are amortized on a straight-line basis over three years, together with internal or external development costs incurred in their deployment. Costs incurred by the company in the development of software for its own use refer to direct development costs and to software configuration costs.

Patents and trademarks. Patents, trademarks and associated costs are amortized on a straight-line basis over three to ten years from the date of registration. The Group is not dependent on any patents or licenses that it does not own. In terms of intellectual property, no patents or other industrial property rights belonging to the Group are currently under license to third parties, other than its customers. The rights held by the Group, notably with regard to software specific to its business as a software developer and publisher, are used under license by its customers within the framework of sales activity.

Other intangible assets. Other intangible assets are amortized on a straight-line basis over two to five years.

Note 1. Intangible Assets

(In thousands of euros) **2003**	*Management information software*	*Patents and trademarks*	*Other intangible assets*	*Total*
Gross value at January 1, 2003	9,837	1,880	5,114	16,831
External purchases	1,061	137	42	1,240
Internal developments	404	--	--	404
Write-offs and disposals	(17)	--	--	(17)
Transfers	(15)	--	15	--
Translation adjustments	(54)	--	(4)	(58)
Gross value at December 31, 2003	11,216	2,017	5,167	18,400
Amortization at December 31, 2003	(8,367)	(1,659)	(5,018)	(15,044)
Net value at December 31, 2003	2,849	358	149	3,356
2004				
Gross value at January 1, 2004	11,216	2,017	5,167	18,400
External purchases	387	138	159	684
Internal developments	207	--	--	207
Write-offs and disposals	(39)	(3)	--	(42)
Transfers	(8)	--	8	--
Changes in scope of consolidation	183	204	--	387
Translation adjustments	(17)	--	(3)	(20)
Gross value at December 31, 2004	11,929	2,356	5,331	19,616
Amortization at December 31, 2004	(10,172)	(1,995)	(5,127)	(17,294)
Net value at December 31, 2004	1,757	361	204	2,322
Change in amoritzation **2004**				
Amortization at January 1, 2004	(8,367)	(1,659)	(5,018)	(15,044)
Amortization charges	(1,743)	(135)	(111)	(1,989)
Amortization write-backs	37	3	1	41
Changes in scope of consolidation	(119)	(204)	--	(323)
Translation adjustments	20	--	1	21
Amortization at December 31, 2004	(10,172)	(1,995)	(5,127)	(17,294)

Management information software. As part of an ongoing process of upgrading and reinforcing its information systems, in 2003 and 2004, the Group purchased licenses of new management information software together with additional licenses for software already in use in order to increase the number of users. Investments concerned license purchase costs together with the cost of developing and configuring the corresponding software.

Nokia
Period ending December 31, 2004

Note 1. Accounting principles

Other intangible assets. Expenditures on acquired patents, trademarks and licenses are capitalized and amortized using the straight-line method over their useful lives, but not exceeding 20 years. Where an indication of impairment exists, the carrying amount of any intangible asset is assessed and written down to its recoverable amount. Costs of software licenses associated with internal-use software are capitalized. These costs are included within other intangible assets and are amortized over a period not to exceed three years.

Note 10. Depreciation and amortization

Depreciation and amortization by asset category	*2004 EURm*	*2003 EURm*	*2002 EURm*
Intangible assets			
Capitalized development costs	244	327	233
Intangible rights	38	51	65
Goodwill	96	159	206
Other intangible assets	30	21	28
Property, plant, and equipment			
Buildings and constructions	32	34	37
Machinery and equipment	426	545	737
Other tangible assets	2	1	5
Total	868	1,138	1,311

Note 13. Intangible assets

	2004 EURm	*2003 EURm*
Capitalized development costs		
Acquisition cost Jan. 1	1,470	1,707
Additions	101	218
Impairment and write-offs	(115)	(455)
Accumulated amortization Dec. 31	(1,178)	(933)
Net carrying amount Dec. 31	278	537
Goodwill		
Acquisition cost Jan. 1	1,298	1,429
Additions	--	20
Impairment charges (Note 8)	--	(151)
Accumulated amortization Dec. 31	(1,208)	(1,112)
Net carrying amount Dec. 31	90	
		186
Other intangible assets		
Acquisition cost Jan. 1	554	524
Additions	86	87
Disposals	(7)	(44)
Translation differences	(4)	(13)
Accumulated amortization Dec. 31	(420)	(369)
Net carrying amount Dec. 31	209	185

The amount of capitalized development cost impairment and write-offs in 2004 includes a EUR 50 million impairment charge based on IFRS impairment review and EUR 65 million of other impairments (EUR 275 million and EUR 180 million in 2003, respectively).

	2004 EURm	2003 EURm
Machinery and equipment		
Acquisition cost Jan. 1	3,223	3,249
Additions	438	336
Disposals	(277)	(313)
Translation differences	(13)	(49)
Accumulated depreciation Dec. 31	(2,681)	(2,521)
Net carrying amount Dec. 31	690	702
Other tangible assets		
Acquisition cost Jan. 1	18	22
Additions	1	--
Disposals	--	(1)
Translation differences	2	(3)
Accumulated depreciation Dec. 31	(11)	(6)
Net carrying amount Dec. 31	10	12
Advance payments and fixed assets under construction		
Acquisition cost Jan. 1	53	60
Additions	25	44
Disposals	--	(10)
Transfers to:		
Other intangible assets	(1)	(4)
Buildings and constructions	(8)	--
Machinery and equipment	(30)	(35)
Translation differences	1	(2)
Net carrying amount Dec. 31	40	53
Total property, plant, and equipment	1,534	1,566

10 INTERESTS IN FINANCIAL INSTRUMENTS, ASSOCIATES, JOINT VENTURES, AND INVESTMENT PROPERTY

PERSPECTIVE AND ISSUES

Varying aspects of accounting for investments are addressed by several different IFRS. Previous improvements to these standards have eliminated most, but not all, options regarding how investments may be valued and presented in the financial statements. Fair value is now the predominant mode of investment valuation.

Under current standards, accounting for passive investments in financial instruments is generally at fair value, although an exception is made for held-to-maturity investments in debt instruments. Despite this general principle, the manner in which the changes in fair value are recognized in the financial statements still depends on management's intentions. Accounting for investments over which the investor has significant influence is generally by the equity method, although for the special case of joint ventures the proportional consolidation method is also permitted. Investments in real estate, other than as productive assets or goods held for sale in the ordinary course of business, are optionally accounted for at either fair value or historical cost.

Relevant standards include IAS 39, which provides guidance for passive investments in dept and equity instruments; IAS 28, governing the accounting for active investments in equity securities; IAS 31, dealing with joint ventures; and IAS 40, covering investments in real property other than as productive capacity or goods to be sold to customers. A number of SIC (interpretations) are also relevant to the discussion in the following pages.

Sources of IAS			
IAS 28, 31, 32, 39, 40	*IFRS* 7	*SIC* 13	*IFRIC* 5

DEFINITIONS OF TERMS

Associate. An entity over which an investor has significant influence but which is neither a subsidiary nor a joint venture of the investor company.

Available-for-sale financial assets. Those financial assets that are not held for trading or held to maturity, and are not loans and receivables originated by the entity.

Control. The power to obtain the future economic benefits that flow from an asset.

Cost method. A method of accounting for investment whereby the investment is recorded at cost; the income statement reflects income from the investment only to the extent that the investor receives distributions from the investee's accumulated net profits arising after the date of acquisition.

Current investment. An investment that is, by its nature, readily realizable and is intended to be held for not more than one year.

Derecognize. Remove a financial asset or liability, or a portion thereof, from the entity's balance sheet.

Derivative. A financial instrument (1) whose value changes in response to changes in a specified interest rate, security price, commodity price, foreign exchange rate, index of prices or rates, a credit rating or credit index, or similar variable (which is known as the "underlying"), (2) that requires no initial net investment or little initial net investment relative to other types of contracts that have a similar response to changes in market conditions, and (3) that is settled at a future date.

Differential. The difference between the carrying value of common stock investment and the book value of underlying net assets of the investee; this should be allocated between excess (or deficiency) of fair value over (or under) book value of net assets and goodwill (a negative goodwill) and amortized appropriately against earnings from investee.

Equity method. A method of accounting whereby the investment is initially recorded at cost and subsequently adjusted for the postacquisition change in the investor's share of net assets of the investee. The investor's income statement reflects the investor's share of the investee's results of operations.

Fair value. The amount for which an asset could be exchanged between a knowledgeable, willing buyer and seller in an arm's-length transaction.

Goodwill. The excess of the cost of the acquired entity over the sum of the amounts assigned to identifiable assets acquired net of any liabilities assumed.

Hedge effectiveness. The degree to which offsetting changes in fair values or cash flows attributable to the hedged risk are achieved by the hedging instrument.

Hedged item. An asset, liability, firm commitment, or forecasted future transaction that (1) exposes the entity to risk of changes in fair value or changes in future cash flows, and that (2) for hedge accounting purposes is designated as being hedged.

Hedging. Designating one or more hedging instruments such that the change in fair value is an offset, in whole or part, to the change in the fair value or the cash flows of a hedged item.

Hedging instrument. For hedge accounting purposes, a designated derivative or (in limited instances) another financial asset or liability whose fair value or cash flows are expected to offset changes in the fair value or cash flows of a designated hedged item. Nonderivative financial assets or liabilities may be designated as hedging instruments for hedge accounting purposes only if they hedge the risk of changes in foreign currency exchange rates.

Held-for-trading. A financial asset which is acquired principally for the purpose of generating a profit from short-term fluctuations in price or dealer's margin. Regardless of why acquired, a financial asset should be denoted as held-for-trading if there is a pattern of short-term profit taking by the entity. Derivative financial assets are always deemed held-for-trading unless designated and effective as hedging instruments.

Held-to-maturity investments. Financial assets with fixed or determinable payments and fixed maturities, that entity has positive intent and ability to hold to maturity, except for loans and receivables originated by the entity.

Investee. An entity that issued voting stock that is held by an investor.

Investee capital transaction. The purchase or sale by the investee of its own common shares, which alters the investor's ownership interest and is accounted for by the investor as if the investee were a consolidated subsidiary.

Investment. An asset held by an entity for purposes of accretion of wealth through distributions of interest, royalties, dividends, and rentals, or for capital appreciation or other benefits to be obtained.

Investment property. According to IAS 40, investment property is land or a building, or part of a building, or both, held by the owner or by the lessee under a finance lease, to earn rentals or for capital appreciation purposes or both, as opposed to being held as

- An owner-occupied property (i.e. for use in the production or supply of goods or services or for administrative purposes); or
- Property held for sale in the ordinary course of business.

Investor. A business entity that holds an investment in the voting stock of another entity.

Joint control. The contractually agreed-on joint sharing of control over the operations and/or assets of an economic activity.

Joint venture. A contractual arrangement whereby two or more parties undertake an economic activity subject to their joint control.

Long-term investment. An investment other than a current investment.

Market value. The amount obtainable from the sale of an investment in an active market.

Marketable. Assets for which there are active markets and from which market values, or other indicators that permit determination thereof, are available.

Owner-occupied property. Property held by the owner (i.e., the entity itself) or by a lessee under a finance lease for use in the production or supply of goods or services or for administrative purposes.

Significant influence. The power of the investor to participate in the financial and operating policy decisions of the investee; however, this is less than the ability to control those policies.

Subsidiary. An entity that is controlled by another entity (its parent).

Undistributed investee earnings. The investor's share of investee earnings in excess of dividends paid.

CONCEPTS, RULES, AND EXAMPLES

Accounting for Debt and Equity Investments

IAS 39 provides rules for the accounting for investments in debt and equity securities which differ markedly from preexisting requirements. It also addresses accounting for financial liabilities (see Chapter 12) and hedging using financial derivatives and other instruments, a subject which was introduced in Chapter 5 and which will be further explored later in the present chapter.

Under the provisions of IAS 39, the once important distinction between current and noncurrent investments is eliminated completely, even as IFRS now, for the first time (in revised IAS 1) requires presentation of classified balance sheets in most instances. Instead, the question of "management intent" is now of paramount concern, as manifested in the tripartite distinction of investments into (1) those held for trading, (2) those available for sale albeit not held for trading purposes, and (3) those intended to be held to maturity. The accounting for debt and equity securities held as investments is dependent upon which of these three categories they are placed in, as was described in detail in Chapter 5. In the following sections of this chapter, illustrations of the accounting for such investments will be presented.

For convenience, some of the key provisions of IAS 39 are repeated in the following discussion, but these are less extensive than the presentation in Chapter 5, which should be referred to by the reader.

Determining the cost of debt and equity investments. Debt and equity securities held as investment assets are recorded at cost, including transactions costs, as of the date when the investor entity becomes a party to the contractual provisions of the instrument. In general this date is readily determinable and unambiguous. For securities purchased "regular way" (when settlement date follows the trade date by several days), however, recognition may be on either the trade or the settlement date. Any change in fair value between these dates must be recognized (strictly speaking, regular-way trades involve a forward contract, which is a derivative financial instrument, but IAS 39 does not require that these be actually accounted for as derivatives).

Carrying amount for investments—general considerations. Debt and equity securities held as investments are to be accounted for at fair value, if held for trading or if otherwise available for sale. Transaction costs are excluded from the fair value determinations, and thus, unless there has been an increase in value since acquisition date, there will often be a loss recognized in the first holding period, due to the fact that when originally recorded, transaction costs were included.

In the case of investments held for trading purposes, changes in fair value from period to period are included in operating results. Given the explicit presumption that these securities will be disposed of in the near term, as market conditions may warrant, marking these to fair value through current earnings is entirely logical, and mandatory.

Changes in the value of investments classified as available-for-sale must now be recognized directly in equity, unless a decline in value is deemed to be an impairment. Under provisions of the original IAS 39, the changes in fair value could either be included in current operating results, or recognized directly in equity through the statement of changes in equity, although each reporting entity had been required to make a onetime election as to which of these alternatives it would conform to thereafter. However, revised IAS 39 (effective 2005) eliminated this option, so recognition through earnings is not permitted, although the new "fair value option" is available and accomplishes the same objective (see discussion below).

Debt securities to be held to maturity are maintained at amortized historical cost, unless objective evidence of impairment exists. Of course, this assumes that the conditions for classification as held to maturity as set forth by IAS 39 are met; namely, that management has demonstrated both the intent and the ability to hold the securities until the maturity date. The transaction costs included in the originally recorded basis are not eliminated, but are typically amortized as part of any premium or discount.

Fair value option. Amended IAS 39 permits an entity to designate any financial asset or financial liability, but only upon its initial recognition, as one to be measured at fair value, with changes in fair value recognized in current profit or loss. To preclude the obvious temptation to "cherry pick" which assets to treat this way from one period to the next, the reporting entity is prohibited from reclassifying financial instruments into or out of this category. Thus, the election is irrevocable upon initial recognition. Since it will not be known at the date of initial recognition whether the fair value of the instrument will increase or decrease in subsequent periods, manipulation of financial results cannot occur. The fair value option can be employed in connection with either available-for-sale or held-to-maturity investments.

Constraints on use of held-to-maturity classification. Under IAS 39, held-to-maturity investments are nonderivative financial assets having fixed or determinable payments and fixed maturity, that an entity has the positive intention and ability to hold to maturity other than those that

1. The entity designates as being carried at fair value though earnings at the time of initial recognition;
2. The entity designates as available for sale; or
3. Meet the definition of loans and receivables.

Importantly, an entity is not permitted to classify any financial assets as held to maturity if it has, during the current financial reporting year or during the two preceding financial reporting years, sold or reclassified more than insignificant amount of held-to-maturity investments before maturity other than sales or reclassifications that

1. Are so close to maturity or to the asset's call date (e.g., less than three months before maturity) that changes in the market rate of interest would not have a significant effect on the financial asset's fair value over that time interval;
2. Occur after the entity has collected substantially all of the financial asset's original principal through scheduled payments (e.g., from payments on serial bonds) or prepayments; or
3. Are attributable to an isolated event that is beyond the entity's control, is nonrecurring and could not have been reasonably anticipated by the entity.

In applying the foregoing rule, *more than insignificant* is evaluated in relation to the total amount of held-to-maturity investments.

It is clear that an entity cannot have a demonstrated ability to hold an investment to maturity if it is subject to a constraint that could frustrate its intention to hold the financial asset to maturity. One question that arises is whether a debt security that has been pledged as collateral or transferred to another party under a "repo" or securities lending transaction and continues to be recognized by the reporting entity, can still be classified as a held-to-maturity investment. Accordingly to the IGC, an entity's intent and ability to hold debt securities to maturity is not necessarily constrained if those securities have been pledged as collateral or are subject to a repurchase agreement or securities lending agreement. However, an entity does not have the positive intent and ability to hold the debt securities until maturity if it does not expect to be able to maintain or recover access to the securities. Thus, the specific facts and circumstances of the repo arrangement must be given careful consideration in concluding on the classification of the securities.

The strictures against early sales of securities that had been classified as held-to-maturity are quite severe. For example, if an investor sells a significant amount of financial assets classified as held-to-maturity, and does not thereafter classify any financial assets acquired subsequently as held-to-maturity, but maintains that it still intends to hold the remaining investments originally categorized as held-to-maturity to their respective maturities and accordingly does not reclassify them, the reporting entity will be deemed to be not in compliance with IAS 39. Thus, whenever a sale or transfer of more than an insignificant amount of financial assets classified as held-to-maturity results in the conditions in IAS 39 not being satisfied, no instruments should continue to be classified in that category. Any remaining held-to-maturity assets must be reclassified as available-for-sale. The reclassification is recorded in the reporting period in which the sales or transfers occurred and is accounted for as a change in classification as prescribed by the standard. Once this violation has occurred, at least two full years must pass before an entity can again classify financial assets as held-to-maturity.

Another question concerning continuing classification of investments as held-to-maturity relates to sales that are triggered by a change in the management of the investor entity. According to the IGC, such sales would definitely compromise the classification of other financial assets as held-to-maturity. A change in management is not identified under IAS 39 as an instance where sales or transfers from held-to-maturity do not compromise the classification as held-to-maturity. Sales that are made in response to such a change in management would, therefore, call into question the entity's intent to hold any of its investments to maturity.

The IGC cited an example similar to the following. A company held a portfolio of financial assets that was classified as held-to-maturity. In the current period, at the direction of the board of directors, the entire senior management team was replaced. The new management wishes to sell a portion of the held-to-maturity financial assets in order to carry out an expansion strategy designated and approved by the board, as part of its recovery strategy. Although the previous management team had been in place since the entity's inception and the company had never before undergone a major restructuring, the sale will nevertheless call into question this entity's intent to hold remaining held-to-maturity financial assets to maturity. If the sale goes forward, all held-to-maturity securities would have to be reclassified, and the entity will be precluded from using that classification for investments for another two years.

Another example of the stringency of the requirements for classifying securities as held-to-maturity is suggested by an IGC position on sales made to satisfy regulatory authorities. In some countries, regulators of banks or other industries may set capital requirements on an entity-specific basis based on an assessment of the risk in that particular entity. IAS 39 indicates that an entity that sells held-to-maturity investments in response to an unanticipated significant increase by the regulator of the industry's capital requirements may do so under that standard without necessarily raising a question about its intention to hold other investments to maturity. The IGC has ruled, however, that sales of held-to-maturity investments that are due to a significant increase in *entity-specific* capital requirements imposed by regulators will indeed "taint" the entity's intent to hold other financial assets as held-to-maturity. Thus, unless it can be demonstrated that the sales fulfill the condition in IAS 39 in that the sales were the result of an increase in capital requirements which was an isolated event that was beyond the entity's control and that is nonrecurring and could not have been reasonably anticipated by the entity.

Held-to-maturity investments can be disposed of before maturity under certain conditions. As noted above, an entity may not classify any financial asset as held-to-maturity unless it has both the positive intent and ability to hold it to maturity. To put teeth into this threshold criterion, IAS 39 stipulates that, if a sale of a held-to-maturity financial asset occurs, it calls into question the entity's intent to hold all other held-to-maturity financial assets to maturity. Exceptions are allowed for sales "close enough to maturity," and after collection of "substantially all" of the original principal.

Questions have arisen in practice on how these conditions be interpreted. The IGC has offered certain insights into the application of these exception criteria. As interpreted, these conditions relate to situations in which an entity can be expected to be indifferent whether to hold or sell a financial asset because movements in interest rates—occurring after substantially all of the original principal has been collected or when the instrument is close to maturity—will not have a significant impact on its fair value. In such situations, a sale would not affect reported net profit or loss and no price volatility would be expected during the remaining period to maturity.

More specifically, the condition "close enough to maturity" addresses the extent to which interest rate risk is substantially eliminated as a pricing factor. According to the IGC, if an entity sells a financial asset less than three months before its scheduled maturity, which would generally qualify for use of this exception. The impact on the fair value of the instrument for a difference between the stated interest rate and the market rate generally would be small for an instrument that matures in three months, in contrast to an instrument that matures in several years, for example.

The condition of having collected "substantially all" of the original principal provides guidance as to when a sale is for not more than an insignificant amount. Thus, if an entity sells a financial asset after it has collected 90% or more of the financial asset's original principal through scheduled payments or prepayments, the requirements of IAS 39 would probably not be deemed to have been violated. However, if the entity has collected only 10% of the original principal, then that condition clearly is not met. The 90% threshold is apparently not meant to be absolute, so some judgment is still needed to operationalize this exception.

In some cases a debt instrument will have a put option associated with it; this gives the holder (the investor) the right, but not the obligation, to require that the issuer redeem the debt, under defined conditions. The existence of the put option need not be an impediment to held-to-maturity classification. IAS 39 permits an entity to classify a puttable debt instrument as held-to-maturity, provided that the investor has the positive intent and ability to hold the investment until maturity and does not intend to exercise the put option. However, if an entity has sold, transferred, or exercised a put option on more than an insignificant amount of other held-to-maturity investments, the continued use of the held-to-maturity classification would be prohibited, subject to exceptions for certain sales (very close to maturity, after substantially all principal has been recovered, and due to certain isolated events). The IGC has stated that these same exceptions apply to transfers and exercises (rather than outright sales) of put options in similar circumstances. The IGC cautions, however, that classification of puttable debt as held-to-maturity requires great care, as it seems inconsistent with the likely intent when purchasing a puttable debt instrument. Given that the investor presumably would have paid extra for the put option, it would seem counter intuitive that the investor would be willing to represent that it does not intend to exercise that option.

In addition to debt securities being held to maturity, any financial asset that does not have a quoted market price in an active market, fair value of which cannot be reliably measured, will of necessity also be maintained at historical cost, unless there is evidence of impairment in value. Furthermore, loans or receivables which are originated by the reporting entity, and which are *not* held for trading purposes, are also to be maintained at historical cost, per IAS 39. Loans or receivables that are acquired from others, however, are accounted for in the same manner as other debt securities (i.e., they must be classified as held-for-trading, available-for-sale, or held-to-maturity, and accounted for accordingly).

Under IAS 39, held-to-maturity financial assets (i.e., debt instruments held for long-term investment) and originated loans are measured at amortized cost, using the effective interest method. This requires that any premium or discount be amortized not on the straight-line basis, but rather by the effective interest method, in order to achieve a constant yield on the amortized carrying value. One question that arises is how discount or premium arising in connection with the purchase of a variable-rate debt instrument should be amortized (i.e., whether it should be amortized to maturity or to the next repricing date.)

The IGC has ruled that this depends generally on whether, at the next repricing date, the fair value of the financial asset will be its par value. In theory, of course, a constantly repricing variable-rate instrument will sell at or very close to par value, since it offers a current yield fully reflective of market rates and the issuer's credit risk. Accordingly, the IGC notes that there are two potential reasons for the discount or premium: it either (1) could reflect the timing of interest payments—for instance, because interest payments are in arrears or have otherwise accrued since the most recent interest payment date or market rates of interest have changed since the debt instrument was most recently repriced to par—or (2) the market's required yield differs from the stated variable rate, for instance, because the credit spread required by the market for the specific instrument is higher or lower than the credit spread that is implicit in the variable rate.

Thus, a discount or premium that reflects interest that has accrued on the instrument since interest was last paid or changes in market rates of interest since the debt instrument was most recently repriced to par is to be amortized to the date that the accrued interest will be paid and the variable interest rate will be reset to the market rate. On the other hand, to the extent the discount or premium results from a change in the credit spread over the variable rate specified in the instrument, it is to be amortized over the remaining term to maturity of the instrument. In this case, the date the interest rate is next reset is not a market-based repricing date of the entire instrument, since the variable rate is not adjusted for changes in the credit spread for the specific issue.

Example

To illustrate, a twenty-year bond is issued at €10,000,000, which is the principal (i.e., par) amount. The debt requires quarterly interest payments equal to current three-month LIBOR plus 1% over the life of the instrument. The interest rate reflects the market-based required rate of return associated with the bond issue at issuance. Subsequent to issuance, the credit quality of the issuer deteriorates, resulting in a bond rating downgrade. Thereafter, the bond trades at a significant discount. Columbia Co. purchases the bond for €9,500,000 and classifies it as held-to-maturity. In this case, the discount of €500,000 is amortized to net profit or loss over the period to the maturity of the bond. The discount is not amortized to the next date interest rate payments are reset. At each reporting date, Columbia assesses the likelihood that it will not be able to collect all amounts due (principal and interest) according to the contractual terms of the instrument, to determine the need for recognizing an impairment loss as a charge against earnings.

With the foregoing principles in mind, a basic example of the accounting for investments is next presented.

Example of accounting for investments in equity securities

Assume that Raphael Corporation purchases the following equity securities for investment purposes during 2006:

Security description	Acquisition cost	Fair value at year-end
1,000 shares Belarus Steel common stock	€ 34,500	€ 37,000
2,000 shares Wimbledon pfd. "A" stock	125,000	109,500
1,000 shares Hillcrest common stock	74,250	88,750

Assume that, at the respective dates of acquisition, management of Raphael Corporation designated the Belarus Steel and Hillcrest common stock investments as being for trading purposes, while the Wimbledon preferred shares were designated as having been purchased for long term-investment purposes (and will thus be categorized as available-for-sale rather than trading). Accordingly, the entries to record the purchases were as follows:

Investment in equity securities—held-for-trading	108,750	
Cash		108,750
Investment in equity securities—available-for-sale	125,000	
Cash		125,000

At year-end, both portfolios are adjusted to fair value; the decline in Wimbledon preferred stock, series A, is judged to be a temporary market fluctuation because there is no objective evidence of impairment. The entries to adjust the investment accounts at December 31, 2006, are

Investment in equity securities—held-for-trading	17,000	
Gain on holding equity securities		17,000
Unrealized loss on securities—available-for-sale		
(an equity account)	15,500	
Investment in equity securities—available-for-sale		15,500

Thus, the change in value of the portfolio of trading securities is recognized in earnings, whereas the change in the value of the available-for-sale securities is reflected directly in stockholders' equity, after being reported in equity, via the statement of changes in equity.

Accounting for changes in value. Changes in the value of held-for-trading securities are reported in income currently. Changes in the value of available-for-sale securities are now required to be reflected directly in equity, unless the "fair value option" was elected and these investments were designated initially by the reporting entity. Changes in value of held-to-maturity securities, unless deemed to be impairments, are ignored. Impairments of held-to-maturity or available-for-sale securities are reflected in income currently. Values are normally determined with reference to market prices, but in some circumstances other approaches will need to be used, such as discounted cash flow analysis, using the discount rate apropos to the instrument's risk characteristics, term to maturity, and so forth.

When an investment in bonds is classified as available-for-sale, so that fair value changes are reported directly in equity until the investment is sold, the amortization of premium or discount on such an investment should nonetheless be reported in net profit or loss as part of interest income or expense. Amortization cannot be included as part of the change in fair value and included directly in equity. The IGC notes that, under other provisions of this standard, as well as under provisions of IAS 18 and IAS 32, these amounts are measured using the effective interest method, which means that the amortization of premium or discount is part of interest income or interest expense and, therefore, included in determining net profit or loss.

Accounting for changes in classification. There is a very limited ability to revise the classification of investments in financial instruments under IAS 39. This limitation is to avoid providing a vehicle by which to manipulate earnings by, for example, deciding period-by-period which value changes will be reflected in earnings and which will be reported directly in equity. The ability to reassign investments among classifications has been further limited under revised IAS 39.

Those investments which were at first denoted as held-for-trading can never be later defined as held-to-maturity or as available-for-sale, and those investments not originally classed as held-for-trading cannot later be so categorized, under revised IAS 39. This is directly a consequence of the desire to not permit changes in designation of investments in any way that would alter which value changes are being reported in current earnings. Likewise, securities investments not held for trading, but which have been designed under the "fair value option," and thus have their value changes reported in earnings, must be identified as such at acquisition, and this election cannot later be revoked.

Investments are also very unlikely to be reclassified to held-to-maturity after acquisition, since here, too, the original intent will be deemed to be of great importance. However, if, as a result of a change in intention or ability or in the rare circumstance that a reliable measure of fair value is no longer available or because the "two preceding financial years" constraint has passed, it becomes appropriate to carry a financial asset or financial liability at cost or amortized cost rather than at fair value, the fair value carrying amount of the financial asset or the financial liability on that date becomes its new cost or amortized cost, as applicable. If previously any gain or loss on that asset had been recognized directly in equity, then this is to be disposed of as follows:

1. If the asset has a fixed maturity, the gain or loss is to be amortized into earnings over the remaining term using the effective interest method. Any difference between the new amortized cost and the maturity amount is also to be amortized over the remaining term of the asset using the effective interest method, similar to the amortization of a premium or dismount. However, if subsequently the asset is determined to be impaired, any gain or loss that has been recognized directly in equity must be taken into income.

2. If the asset does not have a fixed maturity, the gain or loss shall remain in equity until the financial asset is sold or otherwise disposed of, at which point it is to be recognized in earnings. If it is subsequently determined to be impaired, any previous gain or loss that has been recognized directly in equity must be included in current earnings.

As noted earlier, investments classified as held-to-maturity may be mandatorily reclassified to available-for-sale if the entity, during the current year or the two prior years, has sold, transferred, or exercised a put option on more than an insignificant amount of similarly classified securities before maturity date. However, sales very close to the maturity dates (or exercised call dates) will not "taint" the classification of other held-to-maturity securities, nor will sales occurring after substantially all of the asset's principal has been collected (e.g., in the case of serial bonds or mortgage securities), or when made in response to isolated events beyond the entity's control (e.g., the debtor's impending financial collapse) when nonrecurring in nature and not subject to having been forecast by the entity.

If, as a result of a change in intention or ability, it is no longer appropriate to classify an investment as held-to-maturity, it must be reclassified as available-for-sale and remeasured at fair value, as of the date of transfer. Note that this may well be at an interim date, and fair value as of the next reporting date would not necessarily suffice to gauge the gain or loss to be recognized. The difference between the investment's carrying amount and fair value at the date of transfer is to be accounted for directly in equity.

Transfers out of the held-to-maturity category jeopardizes all other similar classifications. IAS 39 requires that a held-to-maturity investment must be reclassified (to either available-for-sale or trading) and remeasured at fair value if there is a change of intent or ability. The IGC has addressed the issue of whether such a reclassification might call into question the classification of other held-to-maturity investments. It finds that such reclassifications could well raise the specter of having to reclassify all similarly categorized investments. IAS 39's requirements concerning early sales of some held-to-maturity investments applies not only to sales, but also to transfers of such investments. The term "transfer" comprises any reclassification out of the held-to-maturity category. Thus, the transfer of more than an insignificant portion of held-to-maturity investments into the available-for-sale or trading category would not be consistent with an intent to hold other held-to-maturity investments to maturity.

Transfers between available-for-sale and trading investment categories. Under the provisions of revised IAS 39, investments held first for trading purposes cannot later be reclassified to available-for-sale; conversely, transfers to the trading portfolio are also now prohibited (whereas previously there were permitted but were expected to be infrequent, occurring only when there was evidence of trading behavior by the entity which strongly suggested that the investment in question will indeed be traded in the short term).

Accounting for Transfers between Portfolios

Transfers among portfolios, to the extent permitted, are to be made at fair value as of the date of transfer.

Example of accounting for transfers of debt securities

Marseilles Corporation purchases the following debt securities as investments in 2005:

Issue	Face value	Price paid*
DeLacroix Chemical 8% due 2010	€200,000	€190,000
Forsythe Pharmaceutical 9.90% due 2022	500,000	575,000
Luckystrike Mining 6% due 2007	100,000	65,000

* *Accrued interest is ignored in these amounts; the normal entries for interest accrual and receipt are assumed.*

Management has stated that Marseilles's objectives differed among the various investments. Thus, the DeLacroix bonds are considered to be suitable as a long-term investment, with the intention that they will be held until maturity. The Luckystrike bonds are a speculation; the significant discount from par value was seen as very attractive, despite the low coupon rate. Management believes the bonds were depressed because mining stocks and bonds have been out of favor, but believes the economic recovery will lead to a surge in market value, at which point the bonds will be sold for a quick profit. The Forsythe Pharmaceutical bonds are deemed a good investment, but with a maturity date sixteen years in the future, management is unable to commit to holding these to maturity.

Based on the foregoing, the appropriate accounting for the three investments in bonds would be as follows:

DeLacroix Chemical 8% due 2010

These should be accounted for as held-to-maturity; maintain at historical cost, with the discount (€10,000) to be amortized over term to maturity using the effective interest method.

Forsythe Pharmaceutical 9.90% due 2022

Account for these as available-for-sale, since neither the held-for-trading nor held-to-maturity criteria apply. These should be reported at fair value at each balance sheet date, with any unrealized gain or loss included in the equity account (consistent with the entity's normal accounting practice), unless an impairment occurs.

Luckystrike Mining 6% due 2007

As an admitted speculation, these should be accounted for as part of the trading portfolio, and also reported at fair value on the balance sheet. All adjustments to carrying value will be included in earnings each year, whether the fair value fluctuations are temporary or permanent in nature.

Transfers between portfolio categories are to be accounted for at fair value at the date of the transfer, as described above. However, only certain types of transfers are permitted under IAS 39, as the standard has been interpreted by the IGC. For example, transfers to or from the trading category are almost never permitted, since there is a strong presumption that trading securities are properly defined at the date of their acquisition. (In rare cases, securities available-for-sale will be recategorized as trading when other, very similar securities have in fact been actively traded by the reporting entity.)

To better understand the limited opportunity for reclassification of securities held as trading, available-for-sale or held-to maturity investments by the entity, and the accounting for such transfers as are permitted, consider the following events:

1.   Marseilles management decides in 2006, when the Forsythe bonds have a market (fair) value of €604,500, that the bonds will be disposed of in the short term, hopefully when the price hits €605,000. Under revised IAS 39, the decision to sell a financial asset does not make it a financial asset held for trading, and transfers into the trading portfolio are not allowed. Therefore, these bonds will continue to be held in the available-for-sale portfolio, and fair value changes will be taken directly to equity, unless this investment was denoted under the "fair value option" at acquisition date.

2. In 2006, Marseilles management also made a decision about its investment in DeLacroix Chemical bonds. These bonds, which were originally designated as held-to-maturity, were accounted for at amortized historical cost. Assume the amortization in 2005 was €2,000 (because the bonds were not held for a full year), so that the book value of the investment at year-end 2005 was €192,000. In 2006, at a time when the value of these bonds was €198,000, management concluded that it was no longer certain that they would be held to maturity. While the change in management's intention could be seen as providing support for a reclassification of this investment to the available-for-sale portfolio, to do so would raise a tainting concern which would jeopardize any classification of further investments as held-to-maturity.

According to IAS 39, investments in debt instruments may be categorized as held-to-maturity only when there is a positive intent to do so. The intent is absent when the reporting entity stands ready to sell that asset in response to changes in market conditions or the entity's liquidity needs, among other considerations. As described here, Marseilles management seemingly has reacted to either market conditions or its own liquidity needs in effectively retracting its commitment to hold the DeLacroix bonds to maturity. If reclassification were effected, there would be a virtually certain presumption that no other fixed maturity investment could thereafter be classified as held-to-maturity—there would be tainting which would preclude usage of that classification. This would apply even to other investments being held currently, where no intent to dispose before maturity had even been manifested. Thus (as interpreted by the IGC), the tainting issue must be taken extremely seriously.

It should also be understood that transfers into the held-to-maturity category would not be feasible, since essentially the characteristics of intent and ability as of the date of acquisition would not have been satisfied. Thus, the guidance under IAS 39 is substantially more rigid than the superficially identical set of criteria under US GAAP.

Accounting for impairments in value—general concerns. A financial asset will be deemed to have become impaired whenever the carrying amount exceeds the recoverable amount. This is to be assessed at each balance sheet date, making reference, for example, to any significant financial difficulties of the issuer, a contractual breach by the issuer, the probability of a bankruptcy or financial reorganization, or the disappearance of an active market for the issuer's securities (although the fact that an entity has "gone private" does not create the presumption of impairment).

In general, trading securities will be carried at fair value and any impairment will have been recognized as it was developing, with immediate recognition in the operating results of the investor. Available-for-sale securities will similarly have been adjusted to fair value, with any loss arising from impairment given recognition in earnings and, if such impairment had been given recognition, any previously accumulated unrealized fair value changes would have been eliminated from equity at that time. No reversal of the impairment loss is allowed, so that, if subsequent to impairment recognition there is an increase in the fair value of the available-for-sale investment, that increase is taken directly to equity, and not to current period earnings.

For securities being reported at amortized historical cost (those held to maturity, plus loans or receivables originated by the entity), the amount of the impairment to be recognized will be the difference between the carrying amount and the present value of expected future cash flows, discounted using the instrument's original discount rate. The current market discount rate is not to be used, since to do so would introduce an element of fair value accounting, which is not pertinent to such investments. Any write-down for impairment, which may be made directly or via an allowance account, must be reported in current operating results. If later events, such as a revision in the obligor's credit rating, result in a lessened measure of impairment, the previously recognized impairment may be partially or fully reversed, also through reported earnings.

Securities that are not carried at fair value because of the absence of fair value information are nonetheless subject to review for possible impairments. These are measured as the difference between carrying amount and the present value of expected future cash flows, discounted using the current market interest rate for similar instruments. Note that current rates, not the original effective rate, are the relevant reference, since these investments were being maintained at cost by default (i.e., due to the absence of reliable fair value data), not because they qualified for amortized historical cost due to being held to maturity. Accordingly, the application of fair value accounting, or a reasonable surrogate for it, is valid in such instances.

Once an asset is deemed impaired and written down to its estimated recoverable amount, future interest is accreted using the same discount rate used to compute the impaired value. Thus, for held-to-maturity investments, after being adjusted to recoverable amount, the interest accruals will continue to be consistent with the original effective rate. For securities not carried at fair value due to lack of sufficient information, however, future interest income, if any, will be accrued using the current rate employed to determine the recoverable amount to which the asset's carrying value was adjusted.

Market value decline is not necessarily evidence of impairment. To ascertain whether an investment has been impaired requires that its current (i.e., balance sheet date) fair value be assessed. IAS 39 provides guidance about how to determine fair values using valuation techniques. It states that the objective is to establish what a transaction price would have been on the measurement date in an arm's-length exchange motivated by normal business considerations. A valuation technique that would be acceptable for use would (1) incorporate all factors that market participants would consider in setting a price and (2) be consistent with accepted economic methodologies for pricing financial instruments. In applying valuation techniques, the reporting entity is to use estimates and assumptions that are consistent with available information about the estimates and assumptions that market participants would use in setting a price for the financial instrument.

Future impairment cannot be anticipated. A financial asset (or a group of assets) is impaired only if there is objective evidence of impairments as a result of one or more events that occurred after the initial recognition of the asset (which IAS 39 calls a "loss event") and that loss event (or events) has an impact on the estimated future cash flows of the financial asset (or group of assets) that can be reliably estimated. Losses that are anticipated to occur as a result of future events, no matter how likely this may be, cannot be given recognition. (This is consistent with guidance on provisions and contingencies under IAS 37.)

In practice, it may not be possible to identify a single, specific event that causes an impairment. Rather the combined effect of several events may be the cause. Revised IAS 39 does offer a useful tabulation of such factors, however. These include the following matters:

1. Significant financial difficulty of the issuer or obligor;
2. A default or delinquency in interest or principal payments, or other breach of contract by the borrower;
3. The lender, for economic or legal reasons relating to the borrower's financial difficulty, granting an otherwise unlikely concession to the borrower;
4. A growing likelihood that the borrower will enter bankruptcy or reorganize;
5. The elimination of an active market for the asset because of financial difficulties; or
6. Observable data about a measurable decrease in the estimated future cash flows from a *group* of financial assets since their initial recognition, although the decrease cannot yet be identified with the individual financial assets in the group, including:

(a) Adverse changes in the payment status of borrowers in the group (e.g., an increased number of late payments; increased frequency of credit card borrowers reaching their credit limits and are paying monthly minimums); or

(b) National or local economic indicators that correlate with defaults on the assets in the group (e.g., increased unemployment rate in the geographical area of the borrowers; decreased property prices (for mortgage assets); decreased commodity process (for loans to commodity producers); adverse changes in other industry conditions).

The fair value of an equity security that is classified as available-for-sale may fall below its cost, which is not necessarily evidence of impairment. When an entity reports fair value changes on available-for-sale financial assets in equity in accordance with IAS 39, it continues to do so until there is objective evidence of impairment, such as the circumstances identified in the standard. If objective evidence of impairment exists, any cumulative net loss that has been recognized directly in equity is removed and recognized in net profit or loss for the period.

Impairment testing for financial assets carried at amortized historical cost. IAS 39 requires that impairment be recognized for financial assets carried at amortized cost. That impairment may be measured and recognized individually or, for a group of similar financial assets, on a portfolio basis. As noted above, the amount of the loss is measured as the difference between the asset's carrying amount and the present value of estimated future cash flows discounted at the financial asset's original effective interest rate. Future credit losses that have not been incurred cannot be included in this computation (again, the concepts underlying IAS 37 must be observed). The original effective rate is not the nominal or contractual rate of the debt, but rather is the effective interest rate computed at the date of initial recognition of the investment. If an impairment is determined to exist, the carrying amount of the asset may either be reduced directly or via the use of an allowance (reserve) account. Any loss is to be recognized currently in earnings.

Where there is no ability to individually assess financial assets accounted for at amortized historical cost for impairment, IAS 39 directs that these assets be grouped and assessed on a portfolio basis. The grouped assets should have similar credit and other characteristics. Assets individually assessed and found to be impaired are excluded from such groupings.

A reversal of impairment is permitted when there is clear evidence that the reversal occurred subsequent to the initial impairment recognition and is the result of a discrete event, such as the improved credit rating of the debtor. This reversal is accounted for consistent with the impairment—that is, it is recognized in current period earnings. However, the amount of recovery is limited, so that the new carrying value of the asset is no greater than what its carrying value would have been had the impairment not occurred, adjusted for any amortization over the intervening period. For example, consider an asset that was carried at €8,000 and being accreted, at €500 per year, to a maturity value of €10,000 at the time it was found to be impaired and written down to €5,000. Two years later the credit-related problem was resolved and the fair value was assessed as €9,500. However, it can only be restored to a carrying value of €9,000, which is what would have been the carrying value had two further years' amortization (at €500 per year) been accreted.

If an asset has been individually assessed for impairment and was found not be individually impaired, according to IAS 39 it should be included in the collective assessment of impairment. According to the standard, this is to reflect that, in the light of the law of large numbers, impairment may be evident in a group of assets, but not yet meet the threshold for recognition when any individual asset in that group is assessed.

However, it is not permissible to avoid addressing impairment on an individual asset basis in order to use group assessment, in a deliberate effort to benefit from the implicit offsetting described above. If one asset in the group is impaired but the fair value of another asset in the group is above its amortized cost, nonrecognition of the impairment of the first asset is not permitted. If it is known that an individual financial asset carried at amortized cost is impaired, IAS 39 requires that the impairment of that asset be recognized. Measurement of impairment on a portfolio basis under IAS 39 is applicable *only* when there is indication of impairment in a group of similar assets, and impairment cannot be identified with an individual asset in that group.

In actually assessing impairment on a portfolio basis (a "collective assessment of impairment"), care should be taken to include only assets having similar credit risk characteristics, indicative of the debtors' ability to pay all amounts due according to the contractual terms. While contractual cash flows and historical loss experience will provide a basis for estimating *expected* cash flows, these historical data must be adjusted for relevant observable data reflecting current (balance sheet date) economic conditions.

IAS 39 further cautions that whatever methodology is used to measure impairment, it should ensure that an impairment loss is not recognized at the initial recognition of an asset. Put another way, the imputed interest rate on a newly acquired debt investment should be the rate that equates cost and the present value of future cash flows, and this rate is used consistently thereafter in valuing the asset as future cash flow expectations change. An impairment on "day one" thus cannot exist, and would indicate an error in methodology should it occur.

Assessment of loan impairment must take into consideration related interest rate swap. An originated loan with fixed interest rate payments is hedged against the exposure to interest rate risk by a "receive-variable pay-fixed" interest rate swap. The hedge relationship qualifies for fair value hedge accounting and is reported as a fair value hedge. Thus, the carrying amount of the loan includes an adjustment for fair value changes attributable to movements in interest rates. According to an interpretive finding by the IGC, an assessment of impairment in the loan should take into account the fair value adjustment for interest rate risk. Since the loan's original effective interest rate prior to the hedge is made irrelevant once the carrying amount of the loan is adjusted for any changes in its fair value attributable to interest rate movements, the original effective interest rate and amortized cost of the loan are adjusted to take into account recognized fair value changes. The adjusted effective interest rate is calculated using the adjusted carrying amount of the loan. An impairment loss on the hedged loan should therefore be calculated as the difference between its carrying amount after adjustment for fair value changes attributable to the risk being hedged and the expected future cash flows of the loan discounted at the adjusted effective interest rate.

Recognition of impairment of loans. Assume that, due to financial difficulties of Knapsack Co., one of its customers, the Galactic Bank, becomes concerned that Knapsack will not be able to make all principal and interest payments due on an originated loan when they become due. Galactic negotiates a restructuring of the loan, and it now expects that Knapsack will be able to meet its obligations under the restructured terms. Whether Galactic Bank will recognize an impairment loss—and in what magnitude—will depend, according to the IGC, on the specifics of the restructured terms. The IGC offers the following guidelines.

If, under the terms of the restructuring, Knapsack Co. will pay the full principal amount of the original loan five years after the original due date, but none of the interest due under the original terms, an impairment must be recognized, since the present value of the future principal and interest payments discounted at the loan's original effective interest rate (i.e., the recoverable amount) will be lower than the carrying amount of the loan.

If, on the other hand, Knapsack Co.'s restructuring agreement calls for it to pay the full principal amount of the original loan on the original due date, but none of the interest due under the original terms, the same result as the foregoing will again hold. The impairment will be measured as the difference between the former carrying amount and the present value of the future principal and interest payments discounted at the loan's original effective interest rate.

As yet another variation on the restructuring theme, if Knapsack will pay the full principal amount on the original due date with interest, only at a lower interest rate than the interest rate inherent in the original loan, again the same guidance is offered by the IGC, so that an impairment must be recognized.

This same outcome prevails if Knapsack agrees to pay the full principal amount five years after the original due date and all interest accrued during the original loan term, but no interest for the extended term. Since the present value of future cash flows is lower than the loan's carrying amount, impairment is to be recognized.

As a final option, the IGC offers the loan restructuring situation whereby Knapsack is to pay the full principal amount five years after the original due date and all interest, including interest for both the original term of the loan and the extended term. In this scenario, even though the amount and timing of payments has changed, Galactic Bank will nonetheless receive interest on interest, so that the present value of the future principal and interest payments discounted at the loan's original effective interest rate will equal the carrying amount of the loan. Therefore, there is no impairment loss.

Example of impairment of investments

Given the foregoing, assume now, with reference again to the Raphael Corporation example first presented earlier in this chapter, that in January 2007 new information comes to Raphael Corporation management regarding the viability of Wimbledon Corp. Based on this information, it is determined that the decline in Wimbledon preferred stock is probably not a temporary one, but rather is an impairment of the asset as that term is used in IAS 39. The standard prescribes that such a decline be reflected in earnings. The stock's fair value has remained at the amount last reported, €109,500, but this value is no longer viewed as being only a market fluctuation. Accordingly, the entry to recognize the fact of the investment's permanent impairment is as follows:

Impairment loss on holding equity securities	15,500	
Unrealized loss on securities—available-for-sale (an equity account)		15,500

Any later recovery in this value would be recognized in earnings if it can be objectively demonstrated that the recovery was based on subsequent developments. Otherwise, later market fluctuations will be reported in equity.

To illustrate this point, assume that in March 2008 new information comes to management's attention, which suggests that the decline in Wimbledon preferred had indeed been only a temporary decline; in fact, the value of Wimbledon now rises to €112,000. However, there is no evidence of any specific event occurring after the date of the impairment that is responsible for this recovery in value. Accordingly it would not be permitted under revised IAS 39 to reverse the impairment loss that had been included in earnings. The carrying value after the recognition of the impairment was €109,500, and the current period increase to €112,000 will have to be accounted for as an increase to be reflected in equity, rather than in earnings. The entry required to reflect this is

Investment in equity securities—available-for-sale	2,500	
Unrealized gain on securities—available-for-sale (an equity account)		2,500

If the recovery had been attributable to a reversal of the impairment, based on an event that occurred after the impairment, any increases in value above the original cost basis would not have been taken into earnings, since the investment is still considered to be available-for-sale, rather than a part of the trading portfolio. Increases in value up to the original cost basis would have been recognized in current earnings, had that condition been met (rather than the fact situation described here).

Structured notes as held-to-maturity investments. Among the more complex of what are commonly referred to as "engineered" financial products, which have become commonplace over the last decade, are "structured notes." Structured notes and related products are privately negotiated and not easily marketable once acquired. These instruments often appear to be straightforward debt investments, but in fact contain provisions which have the potential to greatly increase or decrease the return to the investor, based on (typically) the movement of some index related to currency exchange rates, interest rates, or, in some cases, stock price indices. The IGC has addressed the question of whether these assets can be considered as held-to-maturity investments. The IGC offers as an example a structured note tied to an equity price index, upon which the following illustration is based.

Example of structured debt instrument

Cartegena Co. purchases a five-year "equity-index-linked note" with an original issue price of €1,000,000 at a market price of €1,200,000 at the time of purchase. The note requires no interest payments prior to maturity. At maturity, the note requires payment of the original issue price of €1,000,000 plus a supplemental redemption amount that depends on whether a specified stock price index (e.g. the Dow Jones Industrial Average) exceeds a predetermined level at the maturity date. If the stock index does not exceed or is equal to the predetermined level, no supplemental redemption amount is paid. If the stock index exceeds the predetermined level, the supplemental redemption amount will equal 115% of the difference between the level of the stock index at maturity and the level of the stock index at original issuance of the note divided by the level of the stock index at original issuance.

Obviously, the investment is largely a gamble on an increase in the Dow Jones average over the five-year term, since Cartegena is paying a substantial premium and, as a worst case scenario, could lose its entire premium plus the opportunity cost of lost interest over the five years. Structured notes such as this are very difficult to dispose of on the secondary (i.e., resale) market, having been created (structured) to fit the unique needs or desires of the issuer and investor. Determining a fair value at any intermediate point in the five-year holding period would be difficult or impossible, absent arm's-length bids, particularly if the underlying index has yet to advance to a level at which a gain will be reaped by the investor.

In the present example, assume that Cartegena has the positive intent and ability to hold the note to maturity. According to guidance issued by the IGC, it can indeed classify this note as a held-to-maturity investment, because it has a fixed payment of €1,000,000 and a fixed maturity, and because Cartegena Co. has the positive intent and ability to hold it to maturity. However, the equity index feature is a call option not closely related to the debt host, and accordingly, it must be separated as an embedded derivative under IAS 39. The purchase price of €1,200,000 must be allocated between the host debt instrument and the embedded derivative. For instance, if the fair value of the embedded option at acquisition is €400,000, the host debt instrument is measured at €800,000 on initial recognition. In this case, the discount of €200,000 that is implicit in the host bond is amortized to net profit or loss over the term to maturity of the note using the effective interest method.

A similar situation arises if the investment is a bond with a fixed payment at maturity and a fixed maturity date, but with variable interest payments indexed to the price of a commodity or equity (commodity-indexed or equity-indexed bonds). If the entity has the positive intent and ability to hold the bond to maturity, it can be classified as held-to-maturity. However, as confirmed in an interpretation offered by the IGC, the commodity-indexed or equity-indexed interest payments result in an embedded derivative that is separated and accounted for as a derivative at fair value. The special exception in IAS 39, under which, if the two components cannot be reasonably separated the entire financial asset is classified as held for trading purposes, is found not to be applicable. According to the IGC, it should be straightforward to separate the host debt investment (the fixed payment at maturity) from the embedded derivative (the index-linked interest payments).

Accounting for sales of investments in financial instruments. In general, sales of investments are accounted for by eliminating the carrying value and recognizing a gain or loss for the difference between carrying amount and sales proceeds. Derecognition will occur only when the entity transfers control over the contractual rights which comprise the financial asset, or a portion thereof. IAS 39 sets forth certain conditions to define an actual transfer of control. Thus, for example, in most cases if the transferor has the right to reacquire the transferred asset, derecognition will not be warranted, unless the asset is readily obtainable in the market or reacquisition is to be at then-fair value. Arrangements which are essentially repurchase (repo) arrangements are similarly not sales and do not result in derecognition. In general, the transferee must obtain the benefits of the transferred asset in order to warrant derecognition by the transferor.

Revisions to IAS 39 (effective 2005) altered somewhat the criteria for derecognition of investments in financial instruments. A guiding principle has become the "continuing involvement approach," which prohibits derecognition to the extent to which the transferor has continuing involvement in an asset or a portion of an asset it has transferred.

Under the original IAS 39, and under the revised standard also, there are two main concepts—risks and rewards, and control—that govern derecognition decisions. However, as revised, IAS 39 clarifies that evaluation of the transfer of risks and rewards of ownership must in all instances precede the evaluation of the transfer of control. The reporting entity determines what asset is to be considered for derecognition, and a part of a larger financial asset can be considered for derecognition if, and only if, the part is one of

1. Specifically identified cash flows from a financial asset; or
2. A fully proportionate (pro rata) share of the cash flows from a financial asset; or
3. A fully proportionate (pro rata) share of specifically identified cash flows from a financial asset.

Unless one of the foregoing criteria are satisfied, derecognition of a portion of a financial asset is not permitted. In that case, the financial asset must be considered for derecognition in its entirety.

Revised IAS 39 establishes a key concept of *transfer*. As applied to a financial asset, derecognition may be reported when both (1) an entity has transferred a financial asset, *and* (2) the transfer qualifies for derecognition. It holds that a transfer has occurred if, and only if, the reporting entity either:

1. Retains the contractual rights to receive the cash flows of the financial asset, but also assumes a contractual obligation to pay those cash flows to one or more recipients in an arrangement that meets three specified conditions; or
2. Transfers the contractual rights to receive the cash flows of a financial asset.

Under revised IAS 39, if the reporting entity transfers a financial asset, it must assess whether if has transferred substantially all the risks and rewards of ownership of the transferred asset. If it instead has retained substantially all such risks and rewards, the transferred asset continues to be recognized by that entity. To the contrary, if it has transferred substantially all such risks and rewards, the reporting entity derecognizes the transferred asset.

If the transferor entity has neither transferred nor retained substantially all the risks and rewards of ownership of the transferred asset, it next assesses whether it has retained control over the transferred asset. Where the transferor entity has retained control, it will continue to recognize the transferred asset to the extent of its *continuing involvement* in the transferred asset. If it has not retained control, the entity derecognizes the transferred asset.

The transferor would be deemed to have a continuing involvement when: (1) it could, or could be required to, reacquire control of the transferred asset (e.g., it has a call option); or (2) compensation based on the performance of the transferred asset will be paid (e.g., a guarantee is given to the transferee).

Several earlier provisions in IAS 39 have been eliminated, consistent with the proposed move to a "continuing involvement approach" as a derecognition threshold. First, the idea that the transferor must not retain substantially all of the risk and returns of particular assets for any portion of those assets to qualify for derecognition has been dispensed with. And, second, the transferee "right to sell or repledge" condition for derecognition has been deleted.

In some instances, the asset will be sold as part of a compound transaction in which the transferor either retains part of the asset, obtains another financial instrument, or incurs a financial liability. If the fair values of all components of the transaction (asset retained, new asset acquired, etc.) are known, computing the gain or loss will be no problem. However, if one or more elements are not subject to an objective assessment, special requirement apply. In the unlikely event that the fair value of the component retained cannot be determined, it should be recorded at zero, thereby conservatively measuring the gain (or loss) on the transaction. Similarly, if a new financial asset is obtained and it cannot be objectively valued, it must be recorded at zero value.

On the other hand, if a financial liability is assumed (e.g., a guarantee) and it cannot be measured at fair value, then the initial carrying amount should be such (i.e., large enough) that no gain is recognized on the transaction. If necessitated by IAS 39's provisions, a loss should be recognized on the transaction. For example, if an asset carried at €4,000 is sold for €4,200 in cash, with the transferor assuming a guarantee obligation which cannot be valued (admittedly, such a situation is unlikely to occur in the context of a truly "arm's-length" transaction), no gain would be recognized and the financial liability would accordingly be initially recorded at €200. On the other hand, if the selling price were instead only €3,800, a loss of €200 would be immediately recognized, and the guarantee obligation would be given no value (but would be disclosed).

Presentation and Disclosure Issues

Income statement presentation. Under IAS 32 and IAS 39, significant items of income, expense, gain and loss deriving from financial assets and financial liabilities are to be given sufficient disclosure. (Note that disclosure requirements formerly set forth by IAS 39 were moved to IAS 32 in the revisions of these standards, effective 2005, and were subsequently moved from IAS 32 to IFRS 7, effective 2007.) This applies equally to those items included in the income statement, and those reflected directly in equity. Interest income and interest expense are to be disclosed on a "gross" basis (i.e., interest income is not to be netted against interest expense). Additional disclosure is required of interest accrued on impaired loans.

With regard to available-for-sale financial assets which have been adjusted to fair value, a distinction is to be maintained between the total gain or loss associated with derecognition (typically, from disposition) which is included in net income or loss for the period, and gains and losses which are value adjustments being made for the period. The most common terminology is to denote the former as realized and the latter as unrealized gains and losses.

Other disclosures required. In addition to the distinctions to be made in the income statement or the notes thereto, IAS 32 now also specifies a number of other mandatory disclosures. These include

- The methods and key assumptions used in determining fair values of financial assets and liabilities, separately by major class
- A statement as to whether reporting value changes in earnings or directly in equity was elected for available-for-sale securities
- A statement as to whether trade date or settlement date accounting is used for "regular way" trades, for each of the four categories of financial assets
- Disclosures pertaining to hedging, including describing the entity's risk management objectives and policies and policy for hedging each major type of forecasted transaction
- For designated fair value hedges, cash flow hedges, and hedges of net investments in a foreign entity (separately), descriptions of the hedges and of the hedging instruments used, and the fair values thereof, the nature of the risks being hedged, and for forecasted transactions that are expected to occur, when the forecasted transactions are expected to enter into the determination of net income as well as descriptions of hedges of forecasted transactions that are no longer anticipated
- For gains and losses on financial assets and liabilities designated as hedges that have been taken directly to equity, the amount so recognized in the current reporting period, the amount removed from equity and reported in earnings, and the amount removed from equity and added to the carrying value of an acquired asset or incurred liability during the reporting period
- The amounts of fair value adjustments pertaining to available-for-sale financial assets recognized in or removed from equity during the period
- The carrying amount and description of any trading or available-for-sale securities for which fair values could not be determined, with an explanation of why such assessments could not be made, including (where possible) ranges of likely fair values, as well as the amount of any gain or loss incurred on sales of assets for which previously fair values could not be determined
- For each securitization or repo agreement occurring during the period, and for remaining retained interests in earlier such transactions, the nature and extent of those transactions, including descriptions of collateral and quantitative information about key assumptions used in calculating fair values thereof, and a statement as to whether the financial assets had been derecognized
- Information about reclassifications of securities previously carried at fair value to the amortized cost basis
- The nature and amount of any impairment loss or reversals thereof, separately for each significant class of financial asset

Revised IAS 32 (effective 2005) clarified certain disclosure requirements for investments in financial assets. Disclosure was required of the extent to which fair values are estimated using a valuation technique, and the extent to which valuations using valuation techniques are based on assumptions that are not supported by observable market prices. Also required is information about the sensitivity of the estimated fair values to changes in those assumptions, based on a range of *reasonably possible* alternative assumptions that could be made. Note that the disclosure requirements under IAS 32 have been relocated to IFRS 7, effective 2007 (see discussion in Chapter 5).

Furthermore, the changes in fair values estimated using valuation techniques and recognized in profit or loss during the reporting period must be stated. Finally, revised IAS 32 requires disclosures about the nature and extent of transfers of financial assets that *do not* qualify for derecognition, along with an explanation of the risks inherent in any component that continues to be recognized after a transfer of financial assets that does not qualify for derecognition. (See also Chapter 5 and the Disclosure Checklist.)

Accounting for Hedging Activities

The topic of hedging is almost inextricably intertwined with the subject of financial derivatives, since most (but not all) hedging is accomplished using derivatives. Revised IAS 39 addresses both of these matters extensively, and the IGC has provided yet more instructional materials on these issues. In the following sections, a basic review of, first, derivative financial instruments, and second, hedging activities, will be presented.

Derivatives. As defined by IAS 39, a derivative is a financial instrument with all the following characteristics:

1. Its value changes in response to the change in a specified interest rate, security price, commodity price, foreign exchange rate, index of prices or rates, a credit rating or credit index, or similar variable (sometimes called the underlying);
2. It requires no initial net investment or little initial net investment relative to other types of contracts that have a similar response to changes in market conditions; and
3. It is settled at a future date.

Examples of financial instruments that meet the foregoing definition include the following, along with the underlying variable which affects the derivative's value.

Type of contract	*Main pricing—settlement variable (underlying variable)*
Interest rate swap	Interest rates
Currency swap (foreign exchange swap)	Currency rates
Commodity swap	Commodity prices
Equity swap (equity of another entity)	Equity prices
Credit swap	Credit rating, credit index, or credit price
Total return swap	Total fair value of the reference asset and interest rates
Purchased or written treasury bond option (call or put)	Interest rates
Purchased or written currency option (call or put)	Currency rates
Purchased or written commodity option (call or put)	Commodity prices
Purchased or written stock option (call or put)	Equity prices (equity of another entity)
Interest rate futures linked to government debt (treasury futures)	Interest rates
Currency futures	Currency rates
Commodity futures	Commodity prices
Interest rate forward linked to government debt (treasury forward)	Interest rates
Currency forward	Currency rates
Commodity forward	Commodity prices
Equity forward	Equity prices (equity of another entity)

The issue of what is meant by "little or no net investment" has been explored by the IGC. According to the IGC, professional judgment will be required in determining what constitutes little or no initial net investment, and is to be interpreted on a relative basis—the initial net investment is less than that needed to acquire a primary financial instrument with a similar response to changes in market conditions. This reflects the inherent leverage features typical of derivative agreements compared to the underlying instruments. If, for example, a "deep in the money" call option is purchased (that is, the option's value consists mostly of intrinsic value), a significant premium is paid. If the premium is equal or close to the amount required to invest in the underlying instrument, this would fail the "little initial net investment" criterion.

A margin account is not part of the initial net investment in a derivative instrument. Margin accounts are a form of collateral for the counterparty or clearinghouse and may take the form of cash, securities, or other specified assets, typically liquid ones. Margin accounts are separate assets that are to be accounted for separately. Accordingly, in determining whether an arrangement qualifies as a derivative, the margin deposit is not a factor in assessing whether the "little or no net investment" criterion has been met.

A financial instrument can qualify as a derivative even if the settlement amount does not vary proportionately. An example of this phenomenon was provided by the IGC.

Example of derivative transaction

Accurate Corp. enters into a contract that requires it to pay Aimless Co. €2 million if the stock of Reference Corp. rises by €5 per share or more during a six-month period. Conversely, Accurate Corp. will receive from Aimless Co. a payment of €2 million if the stock of Reference Corp. declines by €5 or more during that same six-month period. If price changes are within the ±€5 collar range, no payments will be made or received by the parties. This arrangement would qualify as a derivative instrument, the underlying being the price of Reference Corp. common stock. IAS 39 provides that "a derivative could require a fixed payment as a result of some future event that is unrelated to a notional amount."

In some instances what might first appear to be normal financial instruments are actually derivative transactions. The IGC offers the example of offsetting loans, which serve the same purpose and should be accounted for as an interest rate swap. The example is as follows:

Example of apparent loans that qualify as derivative transaction

Aguilar S.A. makes a five-year *fixed-rate* loan to Battapaglia Spa, while Battapaglia at the same time makes a five-year *variable-rate* loan for the same amount to Aguilar. There are no transfers of principal at inception of the two loans, since Aguilar and Battapaglia have a netting agreement. While superficially these appear to be two unconditional debt obligations, in fact this meets the definition of a derivative. Note that there is an underlying variable, no or little initial net investment, and future settlement, such that the contractual effect of the loans is the equivalent of an interest rate swap arrangement with no initial net investment. Nonderivative transactions are aggregated and treated as a derivative when the transactions result, in substance, in a derivative.

Indicators of this situation would include: (1) the transactions are entered into at the same time and in contemplation of one another, (2) they have the same counterparty, (3) they relate to the same risk, and (4) there is no apparent economic need or substantive business purpose for structuring the transactions separately that could not also have been accomplished in a single transaction. Note that even in the absence of a netting agreement, the foregoing arrangement would have been deemed to be a derivative.

Difficulty of identifying whether certain transactions involve derivatives. The definition of derivatives has already been addressed. While seemingly straightforward, the almost limitless and still expanding variety of "engineered" financial products often makes definitive categorization more difficult than this at first would appear to be. The IGC illustrates this with examples of two variants on interest rate swaps, both of which involve prepayments. The first of these, a prepaid interest rate swap (fixed-rate payment obligation prepaid at inception or subsequently) qualifies as a derivative; the second, a variable-rate payment obligation prepaid at inception or subsequently) would not be a derivative. The reasoning is set forth in the next paragraphs, which are adapted from the IGC guidance.

Example of interest rate swap to be accounted for as a derivative

First consider the "pay-fixed, receive-variable" interest rate swap that the party prepays at inception. Assume Agememnon Corp. enters into a €100 million notional amount five-year pay-fixed, receive-variable interest rate swap with Baltic Metals, Inc. The interest rate of the variable part of the swap resets on a quarterly basis to the three-month LIBOR. The interest rate of the fixed part of the swap is 10% per year. Agememnon Corp. prepays its fixed obligation under the swap of €50 million (= €100 million × 10% × 5 years) at inception, discounted using market interest rates, while retaining the right to receive interest payments on the €100 million reset quarterly based on three-month LIBOR over the life of the swap.

The initial net investment in the interest rate swap is significantly less than the notional amount on which the variable payments under the variable leg will be calculated. The contract requires little initial net investment relative to other types of contracts that have a similar response to changes in market conditions, such as a variable-rate bond. Therefore, the contract fulfills the "no or little initial net investment" provision of IAS 39. Even though Agememnon Corp. has no future performance obligation, the ultimate settlement of the contract is at a future date and the value of the contract changes in response to changes in the LIBOR index. Accordingly, the contract is considered to be a derivative contract. The IGC further notes that if the fixed-rate payment obligation is prepaid subsequent to initial recognition, which would be considered a termination of the old swap and an origination of a new instrument, which would have to be evaluated under IAS 39.

Now consider the opposite situation, a prepaid pay-variable, receive-fixed interest rate swap, which the IGC concludes is *not* a derivative. This result obtains because it provides a return on the prepaid (invested) amount comparable to the return on a debt instrument with fixed cash flows.

Example of interest rate swap *not* to be accounted for as a derivative

Assume that Synchronous Ltd. enters into a €100 million notional amount five-year "pay-variable, receive-fixed" interest rate swap with counterparty Cabot Corp. The variable leg of the swap resets on a quarterly basis to the three-month LIBOR. The fixed interest payments under the swap are calculated as 10% times the swap's notional amount, or €10 million per year. Synchronous Ltd. prepays its obligation under the variable leg of the swap at inception at current market rates, while retaining the right to receive fixed interest payments of 10% on €100 million per year.

The cash inflows under the contract are equivalent to those of a financial instrument with a fixed annuity stream, since Synchronous Ltd. knows it will receive €10 million per year over the life of the swap. Therefore, all else being equal, the initial investment in the contract should equal that of other financial instruments that consist of fixed annuities. Thus, the initial net investment in the pay-variable, receive-fixed interest rate swap is equal to the investment required in a non-derivative contract that has a similar response to changes in market conditions. For this reason, the instrument fails the "no or little net investment" criterion of IAS 39. Therefore, the contract is *not* to be accounted for as a derivative under IAS 39. By discharging the obligation to pay variable interest rate payments, Synchronous Ltd. effectively extends an annuity loan to Cabot Corp. In this situation, the instrument is accounted for as a loan originated by the entity unless Synchronous Ltd. has the intent to sell it immediately or in the short term.

In yet other instances arrangements that technically meet the definition of derivatives are not to be accounted for as such.

Example of derivative not to be settled for cash

Assume National Wire Products Corp. enters into a fixed-price forward contract to purchase two million kilograms of copper. The contract permits National Wire to take physical delivery of the copper at the end of twelve months or to pay or receive a net settlement in cash, based on the change in fair value of copper. While such a contract meets the definition of a derivative, it is not necessarily accounted for as a derivative. The contract is a derivative instrument because there is no initial net investment, the contract is based on the price of an underlying, copper, and it is to be settled at a future date. However, if National Wire intends to settle the contract by taking delivery and has no history of settling in cash, the contract is not accounted for as a derivative under IAS 39. Instead, it is accounted for as an executory contract for the purchase of inventory.

Just as some seemingly derivative transactions may be accounted for as not involving a derivative instrument, the opposite situation can also occur, where some seemingly nonderivative transactions would be accounted for as being derivatives.

Example of nonfinancial derivative to be settled for cash

Argyle Corp. enters into a forward contract to purchase a commodity or other nonfinancial asset that contractually is to be settled by taking delivery. Argyle has an established pattern of settling such contracts prior to delivery by contracting with a third party. Argyle settles any market value difference for the contract price directly with the third party. This pattern of settlement prohibits Argyle Corp. from qualifying for the exemption based on normal delivery; the contract is accounted for as a derivative. IAS 39 applies to a contract to purchase a nonfinancial asset if the contract meets the definition of a derivative and the contract does not qualify for the exemption for delivery in the normal course of business. In this case, Argyle does not expect to take delivery. Under the standard, a pattern of entering into offsetting contracts that effectively accomplishes settlement on a net basis does not qualify for the exemption on the grounds of delivery in the normal course of business.

Forward contracts. Forward contracts to purchase fixed-rate debt instruments (such as mortgages) at fixed prices are to be accounted for as derivatives. They meet the definition of a derivative because there is no or little initial net investment, there is an underlying variable (interest rates), and they will be settled in the future. However, such transactions are to be accounted for as a regular way transaction, if regular way delivery is required. "Regular way" delivery is defined by IAS 39 to include contracts for purchases or sales of financial instruments that require delivery in the time frame generally established by regulation or convention in the marketplace concerned. Regular way contracts are explicitly defined as *not* being derivatives.

Swaps. Interest rate (and currency) swaps have become widely used financial arrangements. Swaps are to be accounted for as derivatives whether an interest rate swap settles gross or net. Regardless of how the arrangement is to be settled, the three key defining characteristics are present in all interest rate swaps—namely, that value changes are in response to changes in an underlying variable (interest rates or an index of rates), that there is little or no initial net investment, and that settlements will occur at future dates. Thus, swaps are always derivatives.

Derivatives that are not based on financial instruments. Not all derivatives involve financial instruments. Consider Corboy Co., which owns an office building and enters into a put option, with a term of five years, with an investor that permits it to put the building to the investor for €15 million. The current value of the building is €17.5 million. The option, if exercised, may be settled through physical delivery or net cash, at Corboy's option. Corboy's accounting depends on Corboy's intent and past practice for settlement. Although the contract meets the definition of a derivative, Corboy does not account for it as a derivative if it intends to settle the contract by delivering the building if it exercises its option, and there is no past practice of settling net.

The investor, however, cannot conclude that the option was entered into to meet the investor's expected purchase, sale, or usage requirements because the investor does not have the ability to require delivery. Therefore, the investor has to account for the contract as a derivative. Regardless of past practices, the investor's intention does not affect whether settlement is by delivery or in cash. The investor has written an option, and a written option in which the holder has the choice of physical delivery or net cash settlement can never satisfy the normal delivery requirement for the exemption from IAS 39 for the investor. However, if the contract required physical delivery and the reporting entity had no past practice of settling net in cash, the contract would not be accounted for as a derivative.

Embedded derivatives. In certain cases, IAS 39 requires that an embedded derivative be separated from a host contract. The embedded derivative must then be accounted for separately as a derivative, at fair value. That does not, however, require separating them in the balance sheet; IAS 39 does not address the presentation in the balance sheet of embedded derivatives. However, IAS 32 requires separate disclosure of financial assets carried at cost and financial assets carried at fair value, although this could be in the notes rather than on the face of the balance sheet.

The concept of embedded derivatives embraces such elements as conversion features, such as are found in convertible debts. For example, an investment in a bond (a financial asset) may be convertible into shares of the issuing entity or another entity at any time prior to the bond's maturity, at the option of the holder. The existence of the conversion feature in such a situation generally precludes classification as a held-to-maturity investment because that would be inconsistent with paying for the conversion feature—the right to convert into equity shares before maturity.

An investment in a convertible bond can be classified as an available-for-sale financial asset provided it is not purchased for trading purposes. The equity conversion option is an embedded derivative. If the bond is classified as available-for-sale with fair value changes recognized directly in equity until the bond is sold, the equity conversion option (the embedded derivative) is generally separated. The amount paid for the bond is split between the debt security without the conversion option and the equity conversion option itself. Changes in the fair value of the equity conversion option are recognized in the income statement unless the option is part of a cash flow hedging relationship. If the convertible bond is carried at fair value with changes in fair value reported in net profit or loss, separating the embedded derivative from the host bond is not permitted.

When an evaluation made using the criteria in IAS 39 leads to a conclusion that the embedded derivative must be separately accounted for, the initial carrying amounts of a host and the embedded derivative must be determined. Since the embedded derivative must be recorded at fair value with changes in fair value reported in net profit or loss, the initial carrying amount assigned to the host contract on separation is determined as the difference between the cost (i.e., the fair value of the consideration given) for the hybrid (combined) instrument and the fair value of the embedded derivative.

IAS 32, as revised and effective 2005, requires that in separating the liability and equity components contained in a compound financial instrument, the issuer must first allocate fair value to the liability component, leaving only the residual (the difference between aggregate fair value and that allocated to liabilities) to be assigned to the equity component. However, IAS 32 is not applicable to the separation of a derivative from a hybrid instrument under IAS 39. It would be inappropriate to allocate the basis in the hybrid instrument under IAS 39 to the derivative and nonderivative components based on their relative fair values, since that might result in an immediate gain or loss being recognized in net profit or loss on the subsequent measurement of the derivative at fair value.

Example of separate contracts that cannot be deemed an embedded derivative

Erewohn AG acquires a five-year floating-rate debt instrument issued by Spacemaker Co. At the same time, it enters into a five-year "pay-variable, receive-fixed" interest rate swap with the St. Helena Bank. Erewohn argues that the combination of the debt instrument and swap is a "synthetic fixed-rate instrument" and accordingly classifies the instrument as a held-to-maturity investment, since it has the positive intent and ability to hold it to maturity. Erewohn contends that separate accounting for the swap is inappropriate, since IAS 39 requires an embedded derivative to be classified together with its host instrument if the derivative is linked to an interest rate that can change the amount of interest that would otherwise be paid or received on the host debt contract.

The company's analysis is not correct. Embedded derivative instruments are terms and conditions that are included in nonderivative host contracts. It is generally inappropriate to treat two or more separate financial instruments as a single combined instrument (synthetic instrument accounting) for the purposes of applying IAS 39. Each of the financial instruments has its own terms and conditions and each may be transferred or settled separately. Therefore, the debt instrument and the swap are classified separately.

Hedging Accounting under IAS 39

When there is a hedging relationship between a hedging instrument and another item (the underlying), and certain conditions are met, then special "hedging accounting" will be applied. The purpose is to relate the value changes in the hedging instrument and the underlying so that these affect earnings in the same period. Hedging instruments are often financial derivatives, such as options or futures, but this is not a necessary condition. Hedging may be engaged in to protect against changes in fair values, changes in expected cash flows, or changes in the value of an investment in a foreign operation, such as a subsidiary, due to currency rate movements. There is no requirement that entities engage in hedging, but the principles of good management will often dictate that this be done.

For a simplistic example of the need for, and means of, hedging, consider an entity that holds US Treasury bonds as an investment. The bonds have a maturity some ten years in the future, but the entity actually intends to dispose of these in the intermediate term, for example, within four years to partially finance a plant expansion currently being planned. Obviously, an unexpected increase in general interest rates during the projected four-year holding period would be an unwelcome development, since it would cause a decline in the market value of the bonds and could accordingly result in an unanticipated loss of principal. One means of guarding against this would be to purchase a put option on these bonds, permitting the entity to sell them at an agreed-upon price, which would be most valuable should there be a price decline. If interest rates do indeed rise, the increasing value of the "put" will (if properly structured) offset the declining value of the bonds themselves, thus providing an effective fair value hedge. (Other hedging strategies are also available, including selling short Treasury bond futures, and the entity of course could have reduced or eliminated the need to hedge entirely by having invested in Treasury bonds having a maturity more closely matched to its anticipated cash need.)

Special hedge accounting is necessitated by the fact that fair value changes in not all financial instruments are reported in current earnings. Thus, if the entity in the foregoing example holding the Treasuries has elected to report changes in available-for-sale investments (which would include the Treasury bonds in this instance) directly in equity, but the changes in the hedging instrument's fair value were to be reported in current operations, there would be a fundamental mismatching which would distort the real hedging relationship that had been established. To avoid this result, the entity may elect to apply special hedge accounting as prescribed by IAS 39, as was discussed in some detail in Chapter 5. It should be noted, though, that hedge accounting is optional. An entity that carries out hedging activities for risk management purposes may well decide not to apply hedge accounting for some hedging transactions if it wishes to reduce the cost and burden of complying with the hedge accounting requirements in IAS 39.

Accounting for gains and losses from fair value hedges. The accounting for qualifying gains and losses on fair value hedges is as follows:

1. On the hedging instrument, they are recognized in earnings.
2. On the hedged item, they are recognized in earnings even if the gains or losses would normally have been recognized directly in equity if not hedged.

The foregoing rule applies even in the case of investments (classified as available-for-sale) for which unrealized gains and losses are being accumulated directly in equity, if that method was appropriately elected by the reporting entity, as permitted by IAS 39. In all instances, to the extent that there are differences between the amounts of gain or loss on hedging and hedged items, these will be due either to amounts excluded from assessment effectiveness, or to hedge ineffectiveness; in either event, these are recognized currently in earnings.

As an example, consider an available-for-sale security, the carrying amount of which is adjusted by the amount of gain or loss resulting from the hedged risk, a fair value hedge. It is assumed that the entire investment was hedged, but it is also possible to hedge merely a portion of the investment. The facts are as follows:

Hedged item:	Available-for-sale security
Hedging instrument:	Put option
Underlying:	Price of the security
Notional amount:	100 shares of the security

Example 1

On July 1, 2004, Gardiner Company purchased 100 shares of Dizzy Co. common stock at a cost of €15 per share and classified it as an available-for-sale security. On October 1, Gardiner Company purchased an at-the-money put on Dizzy with an exercise price of €25 and an expiration date of April 2007. This put purchase locks in a profit of €650, as long as the price is equal to €25 or lower, but allows continued profitability if the price of the Dizzy stock goes above €25. (In other words, the put cost a premium of €350, which if deducted from the locked-in gain [= €2,500 market value less €1,500 cost] leaves a net gain of €650 to be realized.)

The premium paid for an at-the-money option (i.e., where the exercise price is current market value of the underlying) is the price paid for the right to have the entire remaining option period in which to exercise the option. In the present example, Gardiner Company specifies that only the intrinsic value of the option is to be used to measure effectiveness. Thus, the time value decreases of the put will be charged against the income of the period, and not offset against the change in value of the underlying, hedged item. Gardiner Company then documents the hedge's strategy, objectives, hedging relationships, and method of measuring effectiveness. The following table shows the fair value of the hedged item and the hedging instrument.

	Case One			
	10/1/06	*12/31/06*	*3/31/07*	*4/17/07*
Hedged item:				
Dizzy share price	€ 25	€ 22	€ 20	€ 20
Number of shares	100	100	100	100
Total value of shares	€2,500	€2,200	€2,000	€2,000
Hedging instrument:				
Put option (100 shares)				
Intrinsic value	€ 0	€ 300	€ 500	€ 500
Time value	350	215	53	0
Total	€ 350	€ 515	€ 553	€ 500
Intrinsic value				
Gain (loss) on put from last				
measurement date	€ 0	€ 300	€ 200	€ 0

Entries to record the foregoing changes in value, ignoring tax effects and transaction costs, are as follows:

7/1/06	Purchase:	Available-for-sale securities	1,500	
		Cash		1,500
9/30/06	End of quarter:	Valuation allowance—available-for-sale securities	1,000	
		Shareholders' equity		1,000
10/1/06	Put purchase:	Put option	350	
		Cash		350
12/31/06	End of year:	Put option	300	
		Hedge gain/loss (intrinsic value gain)		300
		Gain/loss	135	
		Put option (time value loss)		135
		Hedge gain/loss	300	
		Available-for-sale securities (market value loss)		300
3/31/07	End of quarter:	Put option	200	
		Hedge gain/loss (intrinsic value changes)		200
		Gain/loss	162	
		Put option (time value loss)		162
		Hedge gain/loss	200	
		Available-for-sale securities (market value loss)		200
4/17/07	Put expires:	Put option	0	
		Hedge gain/loss (intrinsic value changes)		0
		Gain/loss	53	
		Put option (time value changes)		53
		Hedge gain/loss	0	
		Available-for-sale securities (market value changes)		0

An option is said to be "in-the-money" if the exercise price is above the market value (for a put option) or below the market value (for a call option). At or before expiration, an in-the-money put should be sold or exercised (to let it simply expire would be to effectively discard a valuable asset). It should be stressed that this applies to so-called "American options," which may be exercised at any time prior to expiration; so-called "European options" can only be exercised at the expiration date. Assuming that the put option is sold immediately before its expiration date, the entry would be

4/17/07	Put sold:	Cash	500	
		Put option		500

On the other hand, if the put is exercised (i.e., the underlying security is delivered to the counterparty, which is obligated to pay €25 per share for the stock), the entry would be

4/17/07	Cash	2,500	
	Shareholders' equity	1,000	
	Valuation allowance—available-for-sale securities		1,000
	Available-for-sale securities		1,000
	Put option		500
	Gain on sale of securities		1,000

The cumulative effect on retained earnings of the hedge and sale is a net gain of €650 (= €1,000 – €350).

Example 2

To further illustrate fair value hedge accounting, the facts in the preceding example will now be slightly modified. Now, the share price increases after the put option is purchased, thus making the put worthless, since the shares could be sold for a more advantageous price on the open market.

Case Two

	10/1/06	12/31/06	3/31/07	4/17/07
Hedged item:				
Dizzy share price	€ 25	€ 28	€ 30	€ 31
Number of shares	100	100	100	100
Total value of shares	€2,500	€2,800	€3,000	€3,100
Hedging instrument:				
Put option (100 shares)				
Intrinsic value	€ 0	€ 0	€ 0	€ 0
Time value	350	100	25	0
Total	€ 350	€ 100	€ 25	€ 0
Intrinsic value				
Gain (loss) on put from last measurement date	€ 0	€ 0	€ 0	€ 0

Entries to record the foregoing changes in value, ignoring tax effects and transaction costs, are as follows:

Date		Account	Debit	Credit
7/1/06	Purchase:	Available-for-sale securities	1,500	
		Cash		1,500
9/30/06	End of quarter:	Valuation allowance—available-for-sale security	1,000	
		Shareholders' equity		1,000
10/1/06	Put purchase:	Put option	350	
		Cash		350
12/31/06	End of year:	Put option	0	
		Hedge gain/loss (intrinsic value gain)		0
		Hedge gain/loss	250	
		Put option (time value loss)		250
		Available-for-sale security	300	
		Shareholders' equity		300
3/31/07	End of quarter:	Put option	0	
		Hedge gain/loss (intrinsic value change)		0
		Hedge gain/loss	75	
		Put option (time value loss)		75
		Available-for-sale securities	200	
		Shareholders' equity		200
4/17/07	Put expires:	Put option	0	
		Hedge gain/loss (intrinsic value change)		0
		Hedge gain/loss	25	
		Put option (time value change)		25
		Available-for-sale securities	100	
		Shareholders' equity		100

The put expired unexercised and Gardiner Company must decide whether to sell the security. If it continues to hold, normal IAS 39 accounting would apply. In this example, since it was hypothesized that Gardiner had elected to record the effects of value changes (apart from those which were hedging related) directly in shareholders' equity, it would continue to apply this accounting after the expiration of the put option. Assuming, however, that the security is instead sold, the entry would be

Date	Account	Debit	Credit
4/17/07	Cash	3,100	
	Shareholders' equity	1,600	
	Available-for-sale securities		1,500
	Valuation allowance—available-for-sale securities		1,600
	Gain on sale of securities		1,600

Accounting for gains and losses from cash flow hedges. Cash flow hedges generally involve forecasted transactions or events. The intention is to defer the recognition of gains or losses arising from the hedging activity itself until the forecasted transaction takes place, and then to have the formerly deferred gain or loss affect earnings when the forecasted transaction affects earnings. While overwhelmingly it will be derivative financial instruments that are used to hedge cash flows relating to forecasted transactions, IAS 39 contemplates the use of non-derivatives for this purpose as well in the case of hedges of foreign currency risk. Forecasted transactions may include future cash flows arising from presently existing, recognized assets or liabilities—for example, future interest rate payments to be made on debt carrying floating interest rates are subject to cash flow hedging.

The accounting for qualifying gains and losses on cash flow hedges is as follows:

1. On the hedging instrument, the portion of the gain or loss that is determined to be an effective hedge will be recognized directly in equity.

2. Also on the hedging instrument, the ineffective portion should be reported in earnings, if the instrument is a derivative; otherwise, it should be reported in a manner consistent with the accounting for other financial assets or liabilities as set forth in IAS 39. Thus, if an available-for-sale security has been used as the hedging instrument in a particular cash flow hedging situation, and the entity has elected to report value changes in equity, then any ineffective portion of the hedge should continue to be recorded in equity.

According to IAS 39, the separate component of equity associated with the hedged item should be adjusted to the lesser (in absolute terms) of either the cumulative gain or loss on the hedging instrument necessary to offset the cumulative change in expected future cash flows on the hedged item from hedge inception, excluding the ineffective portion, or the fair value of the cumulative change in expected future cash flows on the hedged item from inception of the hedge. Furthermore, any remaining gain or loss on the hedging instrument (i.e., the ineffective portion) must be recognized currently in earnings or directly in equity, as dictated by the nature of the instrument and entity's accounting policy (for available-for-sale instruments, where there is a choice of reporting directly in equity or in earnings). If the entity's policy regarding the hedge is to exclude a portion from the measure of hedge effectiveness (e.g., time value of options in the preceding example in this section of Chapter 10), then any related gain or loss must be incorporated into either earnings or equity based on the nature of the item and the elected policy.

Example of "plain vanilla" interest rate swap

On July 1, 2006, Abbott Corp. borrows €5 million with a fixed maturity (no prepayment option) of June 30, 2010, carrying interest at the US prime interest rate + 1/2%. Interest payments are due semiannually; the entire principal is due at maturity. At the same date, Abbott Corp. enters into a "plain-vanilla-type" swap arrangement, calling for fixed payments at 8% and the receipt of prime + 1/2%, on a notional amount of €5 million. At that date prime is 7.5%, and there is no premium due on the swap arrangement since the fixed and variable payments are equal. (Note that swaps are privately negotiated and, accordingly, a wide range of terms will be encountered in practice; this is simply intended as an example, albeit a very typical one.)

The foregoing swap qualifies as a cash flow hedge under IAS 39. Given the nature of this swap, it is reasonable to assume no ineffectiveness, but in real world situations this must be carefully evaluated with reference to the specific circumstances of each case; IAS 39 does not provide a short-cut method (which contrasts with the corresponding US GAAP standard). IAS 39 defines effectiveness in terms of results: if at inception and throughout the life of the hedge, the entity can expect an almost complete offset of cash flow variations, and in fact (retrospectively) actual results are within a range of 80 to 125%, the hedge will be judged highly effective.

In the present example, assume that in fact the hedge proves to be highly effective. Also, assume that the prime rate over the four-year term of the loan, as of each interest payment date, is as follows, along with the fair value of the remaining term of the interest swap at those dates:

Date	Prime rate (%)	Fair value of swap*
December 31, 2006	6.5	€(150,051)
June 30, 2007	6.0	(196,580)
December 31, 2007	6.5	(111,296)
June 30, 2008	7.0	(45,374)
December 31, 2008	7.5	0
June 30, 2009	8.0	23,576
December 31, 2009	8.5	24,038
June 30, 2010	8.0	0

* *Fair values are determined as the present values of future cash flows resulting from expected interest rate differentials, based on current prime rate, discounted at 8%.*

Regarding the fair values presented in the foregoing table, it should be assumed that the market (fair) values of the swap contract are precisely equal to the present value, at each valuation date (assumed to be the interest payment dates), of the differential future cash flows resulting from utilization of the swap. Future variable interest rates (prime + 1/2%) are assumed to be the same as the existing rates at each valuation date (i.e., the yield curve is flat and there is no basis for any expectation of rate changes, and therefore, the best estimate at any given moment is that the current rate will persist over time). The discount rate, 8%, is assumed to be constant over time.

Thus, for example, the fair value of the swap at December 31, 2006, would be the present value of an annuity of seven payments (the number of remaining semiannual interest payments due) of €25,000 each (pay 8%, receive 7%, based on then-existing prime rate of 6.5%) to be made to the swap counterparty, discounted at an annual rate of 8%. (Consistent with the convention for quoting interest rates as bond-equivalent yields, 4% is used for the semiannual discounting, rather than the rate that would compound to 8% annually.) The present value of a stream of seven €25,000 payments to the swap counterparty amounts to €150,051 at December 31, 2006, which is the swap liability to be reported by Abbott Corp. at that date. The offset is a debit to equity, since the hedge is continually judged to be 100% effective in this case.

The semiannual accounting entries will be as follows:

December 31, 2006

Interest expense	175,000	
Accrued interest (or cash)		175,000

To accrue or pay interest on the debt at the variable rate of prime + 1/2% (7.0%)

Interest expense	25,000	
Accrued interest (or cash)		25,000

To record net settle-up on swap arrangement [8.0 – 7.0%]

Shareholders' equity	150,051	
Obligation under swap contract		150,051

To record the fair value of the swap contract as of this date (a net liability because fixed rate payable is below expected variable rate based on current prime rate)

June 30, 2007

Interest expense	162,500	
Accrued interest (or cash)		162,500

To accrue or pay interest on the debt at the variable rate of prime + 1/2% (6.5%)

Interest expense	37,500	
Accrued interest (or cash)		37,500

To record net settle-up on swap arrangement [8.0 – 6.5%]

Shareholders' equity	46,529	
Obligation under swap contract		46,529

To record the fair value of the swap contract as of this date (increase in obligation because of further decline in prime rate)

December 31, 2007

Interest expense	175,000	
Accrued interest (or cash)		175,000

To accrue or pay interest on the debt at the variable rate of prime + 1/2% (7.0%)

Interest expense	25,000	
Accrued interest (or cash)		25,000

To record net settle-up on swap arrangement [8.0 – 7.0%]

Obligation under swap contract	85,284	
Shareholders' equity		85,284

To record the fair value of the swap contract as of this date (decrease in obligation due to increase in prime rate)

June 30, 2008

Interest expense	187,500	
Accrued interest (or cash)		187,500

To accrue or pay interest on the debt at the variable rate of prime + 1/2% (7.5%)

Interest expense	12,500	
Accrued interest (or cash)		12,500

To record net settle-up on swap arrangement [8.0 – 7.5%]

Obligation under swap contract	65,922	
Shareholders' equity		65,922

To record the fair value of the swap contract as of this date (further increase in prime rate reduces fair value of derivative)

December 31, 2008

Interest expense	200,000	
Accrued interest (or cash)		200,000

To accrue or pay interest on the debt at the variable rate of prime + 1/2% (8.0%)

Interest expense	0	
Accrued interest (or cash)		0

To record net settle-up on swap arrangement [8.0 – 8.0%]

Obligation under swap contract	45,374	
Shareholders' equity		45,374

To record the fair value of the swap contract as of this date (further increase in prime rate eliminates fair value of the derivative)

June 30, 2009

Interest expense	212,500	
Accrued interest (or cash)		212,500

To accrue or pay interest on the debt at the variable rate of prime + 1/2% (8.5%)

Accrued interest (or cash)	12,500	
Interest expense		12,500

To record net settle-up on swap arrangement [8.0 – 8.5%]

Receivable under swap contract	23,576	
Shareholders' equity		23,576

To record the fair value of the swap contract as of this date (increase in prime rate creates net asset position for derivative)

December 31, 2009

Interest expense	225,000	
Accrued interest (or cash)		225,000

To accrue or pay interest on the debt at the variable rate of prime + 1/2% (9.0%)

Accrued interest (or cash)	25,000	
Interest expense		25,000

To record net settle-up on swap arrangement [8.0 – 9.0%]

Receivable under swap contract	462	
Shareholders' equity		462

To record the fair value of the swap contract as of this date (increase in asset value due to further rise in prime rate)

June 30, 2010

Interest expense	212,500	
Accrued interest (or cash)		212,500

To accrue or pay interest on the debt at the variable rate of prime + 1/2% (8.5%)

Accrued interest (or cash)	12,500	
Interest expense		12,500

To record net settle-up on swap arrangement [8.0 – 8.5%]

Shareholders' equity	24,038	
Receivable under swap contract		24,038

To record the fair value of the swap contract as of this date (value declines to zero as expiration date approaches)

Example of option on an interest rate swap

The facts of this example are a further variation on the previous one (the "plain vanilla" swap). Abbott Corp. anticipates, as of June 30, 2006, that as of June 30, 2008, it will become a borrower of €5 million with a fixed maturity four years hence (i.e., at June 30, 2012). Based on its current credit rating, it will be able to borrow at the US prime interest rate + 1/2%. As of June 30, 2006, it is able to purchase a "swaption" (an option on an interest rate swap, calling for fixed pay at 8% and variable receipt at prime + 1/2%, on a notional amount of €5 million, for a term of four years) for a single payment of €25,000. The option will expire in two years. At June 30, 2006, the prime is 7.5%.

NOTE: The interest rate behavior in this example differs somewhat from the prior example, to better illustrate the "one-sidedness" of options, versus the obligation under a plain vanilla swap arrangement or of other nonoption contracts, such as futures and forwards.

It will be assumed that the time value of the swaption expires ratably over the two years.

This swaption qualifies as a cash flow hedge under IAS 39. However, while the change in fair value of the contract is an effective hedge of the cash flow variability of the prospective debt issuance, the premium paid is a reflection of the time value of money and would not be an effective part of the hedge. Accordingly, it is to be expensed as incurred, rather than being deferred.

The table below gives the prime rate at semiannual intervals including the two-year period prior to the debt issuance, plus the four years during which the debt (and the swap, if the option is exercised) will be outstanding, as well as the fair value of the swaption (and later, the swap itself) at these points in time.

Date	*Prime rate (%)*	*Fair value of swaption/swap*[*]
December 31, 2006	7.5	€ 0
June 30, 2007	8.0	77,925
December 31, 2007	6.5	0
June 30, 2008	7.0	(84,159)
December 31, 2008	7.5	0
June 30, 2009	8.0	65,527
December 31, 2009	8.5	111,296
June 30, 2010	8.0	45,374
December 31, 2010	8.0	34,689
June 30, 2011	7.5	0
December 31, 2011	7.5	0
June 30, 2012	7.0	0

[*] *Fair value is determined as the present value of future expected interest rate differentials, based on current prime rate, discounted at 8%. An "out-of-the-money" swaption is valued at zero, since the option does not have to be exercised. Since the option is exercised on June 30, 2008, the value at that date is recorded, although negative.*

The value of the swaption contract is only recorded (unless and until exercised, of course, at which point it becomes a contractually binding swap) if it is positive, since if "out-of-the-money," the holder would forego exercise in most instances and thus there is no liability by the holder to be reported. This illustrates the asymmetrical nature of options, where the most that can be lost by the option holder is the premium paid, since exercise by the holder is never required, unlike the case with futures and forwards, in which both parties are obligated to perform.

The present example is an illustration of counterintuitive (but not really illogical) behavior by the holder of an out-of-the-money option. Despite having a negative value, the option holder determines that exercise is advisable, presumably because it expects that over the term of the debt unfavorable movements in interest rates will occur.

At June 30, 2008, the swaption is an asset, since the reference variable rate (prime + 1/2%) is greater than the fixed swap rate, and thus the expectation is that the option will be exercised at expiration. This would (if present rates hold steady, which is the naïve assumption) result in a series of eight semiannual payments from the swap counterparty in the amount of €12,500. Discounting this at a nominal 8%, the present value as of the debt origination date (to be June 30, 2008) would be €84,159, which, when further discounted to June 30, 2007, yields a fair value of €77,925.

Note that the following period (at December 31, 2007) prime drops to such an extent that the value of the swaption evaporates entirely. Actually, the value becomes negative, which will not be reported since the holder is under no obligation to exercise the option under unfavorable conditions; the carrying value is therefore eliminated as of that date.

At the expiration of the swaption contract, the holder does (for this example) exercise, notwithstanding a negative fair value, and from that point forward the fair value of the swap will be reported, whether positive (an asset) or negative (a liability). Once exercised, the swap represents a series of forward contracts, the fair value of which must be fully recognized under IAS 39. (Note that, in the real world, the holder would have likely had another choice: to let the unfavorable swaption expire unexercised, but to negotiate a new interest rate swap, presumably at more favorable terms given that prime is only 7% at that date; for example, a swap of 7.5% fixed versus prime + 1/2% would likely be available at little or no cost.)

As noted above, assume that, at the option expiration date, despite the fact that prime + 1/2% is below the fixed pay rate on the swap, the management is convinced that rates will climb over the four-year term of the loan, and thus it does exercise the swaption at that date. Given this, the accounting journal entries over the entire six years are as follows:

June 30, 2006

Swaption contract	25,000	
Cash		25,000
To record purchase premium on swaption contract		

December 31, 2006

Gain/loss on hedging arrangement	6,250	
Swaption contract		6,250
To record change in time value of swaption contract—charge premium to income since this represents payment for time value of money, which expires ratably over two-year term		

June 30, 2007

Swaption contract	77,925	
Shareholders' equity		77,925
To record the fair value of the swaption contract as of this date		
Gain/loss on hedging arrangement	6,250	
Swaption contract		6,250
To record change in time value of swaption contract—charge premium to income since this represents payment for time value of money, which expires ratably over two-year term		

December 31, 2007

Shareholders' equity	77,925	
Swaption contract		77,925
To record the change in fair value of the swaption contract as of this date; since contract is out-of-the-money, it is not written down below zero (i.e., a net liability is not reported)		

| Gain/loss on hedging arrangement | 6,250 | |
| Swaption contract | | 6,250 |

To record change in time value of swaption contract—charge premium to income since this represents payment for time value of money, which expires ratably over two-year term

June 30, 2008

| Shareholders' equity | 84,159 | |
| Swaption contract | | 84,159 |

To record the fair value of the swaption contract as of this date—a net liability is reported since swap option was exercised

| Gain/loss on hedging arrangement | 6,250 | |
| Swaption contract | | 6,250 |

To record change in time value of swaption contract—charge premium to income since this represents payment for time value of money, which expires ratably over two-year term

December 31, 2008

| Interest expense | 200,000 | |
| Accrued interest (or cash) | | 200,000 |

To accrue or pay interest on the debt at the variable rate of prime + 1/2% (8.0%)

| Interest expense | 0 | |
| Accrued interest (or cash) | | 0 |

To record net settle-up on swap arrangement [8.0 – 8.0%]

| Swap contract | 84,159 | |
| Shareholders' equity | | 84,159 |

To record the change in the fair value of the swap contract as of this date

June 30, 2009

| Interest expense | 212,500 | |
| Accrued interest (or cash) | | 212,500 |

To accrue or pay interest on the debt at the variable rate of prime + 1/2% (8.5%)

| Accrued interest (or cash) | 12,500 | |
| Interest expense | | 12,500 |

To record net settle-up on swap arrangement [8.0 – 8.5%]

| Swap contract | 65,527 | |
| Shareholders' equity | | 65,527 |

To record the fair value of the swap contract as of this date

December 31, 2009

| Interest expense | 225,000 | |
| Accrued interest (or cash) | | 225,000 |

To accrue or pay interest on the debt at the variable rate of prime + 1/2% (9.0%)

| Accrued interest (or cash) | 25,000 | |
| Interest expense | | 25,000 |

To record net settle-up on swap arrangement [8.0 – 9.0%]

| Swap contract | 45,769 | |
| Shareholders' equity | | 45,769 |

To record the fair value of the swap contract as of this date

June 30, 2010

| Interest expense | 212,500 | |
| Accrued interest (or cash) | | 212,500 |

To accrue or pay interest on the debt at the variable rate of prime + 1/2% (8.5%)

| Accrued interest (cash) | 12,500 | |
| Interest expense | | 12,500 |

To record net settle-up on swap arrangement [8.0 – 8.5%]

| Shareholders' equity | 65,922 | |
| Swap contract | | 65,922 |

To record the change in the fair value of the swap contract as of this date (declining prime rate causes swap to lose value)

December 31, 2010

Interest expense	212,500	
Accrued interest (or cash)		212,000

To accrue or pay interest on the debt at the variable rate of prime + 1/2% (8.5%)

Accrued interest (or cash)	12,500	
Interest expense		12,500

To record net settle-up on swap arrangement [8.0 – 8.5%]

Shareholders' equity	10,685	
Swap contract		10,685

To record the fair value of the swap contract as of this date (decline is due to passage of time, as the prime rate expectations have not changed from the earlier period)

June 30, 2011

Interest expense	200,000	
Accrued interest (or cash)		200,000

To accrue or pay interest on the debt at the variable rate of prime + 1/2% (8.0%)

Accrued interest (or cash)	0	
Interest expense		0

To record net settle-up on swap arrangement [8.0 – 8.5%]

Shareholders' equity	34,689	
Swap contract		34,689

To record the fair value of the swap contract as of this date

December 31, 2011

Interest expense	200,000	
Accrued interest (or cash)		200,000

To accrue or pay interest on the debt at the variable rate of prime + 1/2% (8.0%)

Accrued interest (or cash)	0	
Interest expense		0

To record net settle-up on swap arrangement [8.0 – 8.0%]

Swap contract	0	
Shareholders' equity		0

No change to the fair value of the swap contract as of this date

June 30, 2012

Interest expense	187,500	
Accrued interest (or cash)		187,500

To accrue or pay interest on the debt at the variable rate of prime + 1/2% (7.5%)

Interest expense	12,500	
Accrued interest (or cash)		12,500

To record net settle-up on swap arrangement [8.0 – 7.5%]

Shareholders' equity	0	
Swap contract		0

No change to the fair value of the swap contract, which expires as of this date

Example of using options to hedge a future purchase of inventory

Friendly Chemicals Corp. uses petroleum as a feedstock from which it produces a range of chemicals for sale to producers of synthetic fabrics and other consumer goods. It is concerned about the rising price of oil and decides to hedge a major purchase it plans to make in mid-2007 Oil futures and options are traded on the New York Mercantile Exchange and in other markets; Friendly decides to use options rather than futures because it is only interested in protecting itself from a price increase; if prices decline, it wishes to reap that benefit rather than suffer the loss which would result from holding a futures contract in a declining market environment.

At December 31, 2006, Friendly projects a need for 10 million barrels of crude oil of a defined grade to be purchased by mid-2007; this will suffice for production through mid-2008. The current world price for this grade of crude is €14.50 per barrel, but prices have been rising recently. Management desires to limit its crude oil costs to no higher than €15.75 per barrel, and accordingly purchases, at a cost of €2 million, an option to purchase up to 10 million barrels at a cost of €15.55 per barrel, at any time through December 2007. When the option premium is added to this €15.55 per barrel cost, it would make the total cost €15.75 per barrel if the full 10 million barrels are acquired.

Management has studied the behavior of option prices and has concluded that changes in option prices that relate to time value are not correlated to price changes and hence are ineffective in hedging price changes. On the other hand, changes in option prices that pertain to pricing changes (intrinsic value changes) are highly effective as hedging vehicles. The table below reports the value of these options, analyzed in terms of time value and intrinsic value, over the period from December 2006 through December 2007.

| Date | Price of oil/barrel | Fair value of option relating to | |
		Time value*	Intrinsic value
December 31, 2006	€14.50	€2,000,000	€ 0
January 31, 2007	14.90	1,900,000	0
February 28, 2007	15.30	1,800,000	0
March 31, 2007	15.80	1,700,000	2,500,000
April 30, 2007	16.00	1,600,000	4,500,000
May 31, 2007	15.85	1,500,000	3,000,000
June 30, 2007**	16.00	700,000	2,250,000
July 31, 2007	15.60	650,000	250,000
August 31, 2007	15.50	600,000	0
September 30, 2007	15.75	550,000	1,000,000
October 31, 2007	15.80	500,000	1,250,000
November 30, 2007	15.85	450,000	1,500,000
December 31, 2007***	15.90	400,000	1,750,000

* This example does not address how the time value of options would be computed in practice.
** Options for five million barrels exercised; remainder held until end of December, then sold.
*** Values cited are immediately prior to sale of remaining options.

At the end of June 2007, Friendly Chemicals exercises options for five million barrels, paying €15.55 per barrel for oil that is then selling on world markets for €16.00 each. It holds the remaining options until December, when it sells these for an aggregate price of €2.1 million, a slight discount to the nominal fair value at that date.

The inventory acquired in mid-2007 is processed and included in goods available for sale. Sales of these goods, in terms of the five million barrels of crude oil which were consumed in their production, are as follows:

Date	Equivalent barrels sold in month	Equivalent barrels on hand at month end
June 30, 2007	300,000	4,700,000
July 31, 2007	250,000	4,450,000
August 31, 2007	400,000	4,050,000
September 30, 2007	350,000	3,700,000
October 31, 2007	550,000	3,150,000
November 30, 2007	500,000	2,650,000
December 31, 2007	650,000	2,000,000

Based on the foregoing facts, the journal entries prepared on a **monthly** basis (for illustrative purposes) for the period December 2006 through December 2007 are as follows:

December 31, 2006

Option contract	2,000,000	
Cash		2,000,000

To record purchase premium on option contract for up to 10 million barrels of oil at price of €15.55 per barrel

January 31, 2007

Gain/loss on hedging transaction	100,000	
Option contract		100,000

To record change in time value of option contract—charge premium to income since this represents payment for time value of money, which expires ratably over two-year term and does not qualify for hedge accounting treatment

Option contract	0	
Shareholders' equity		0

To reflect change in intrinsic value of option contracts (no value at this date)

February 28, 2007

Gain/loss on hedging transaction	100,000	
Option contract		100,000

To record change in time value of option contract—charge premium to income since this represents payment for time value of money, which expires ratably over two-year term and does not qualify for hedge accounting treatment

Option contract	0	
Shareholders' equity		0

To reflect change in intrinsic value of option contracts (no value at this date)

March 31, 2007

Gain/loss on hedging transaction	100,000	
Option contract		100,000

To record change in time value of option contract—charge premium to income since this represents payment for time value of money, which expires ratably over two-year term and does not qualify for hedge accounting treatment

Option contract	2,500,000	
Shareholders' equity		2,500,000

To reflect change in intrinsic value of option contracts

April 30, 2007

Gain/loss on hedging transaction	100,000	
Option contract		100,000

To record change in time value of option contract—charge premium to income since this represents payment for time value of money, which expires ratably over two-year term and does not qualify for hedge accounting treatment

Option contract	2,000,000	
Shareholders' equity		2,000,000

To reflect change in intrinsic value of option contracts (further increase in value)

May 31, 2007

Gain/loss on hedging transaction	100,000	
Option contract		100,000

To record change in time value of option contract—charge premium to income since this represents payment for time value of money, which expires ratably over two-year term and does not qualify for hedge accounting treatment

Shareholders' equity	1,500,000	
Option contract		1,500,000

To reflect change in intrinsic value of option contracts (decline in value)

June 30, 2007

Gain/loss on hedging transaction	800,000	
Option contract		800,000

To record change in time value of option contract—charge premium to income since this represents payment for time value of money, which expires ratably over two-year term and does not qualify for hedge accounting treatment; since one-half the options were exercised in June, the remaining unexpensed time value of that portion is also entirely written off at this time

| Option contracts | 1,500,000 | |
| Shareholders' equity | | 1,500,000 |

To reflect change in intrinsic value of option contracts (further increase in value) **before** *accounting for exercise of options on five million barrels*

June 30 value of options before exercise	4,500,000
Allocation to oil purchased at €15.55	2,250,000
Remaining option valuation adjustment	2,250,000

The allocation to exercised options will be used to adjust the carrying value of the inventory, and ultimately will be transferred to cost of goods sold as a contra cost, as the five million barrels are sold, at the rate of 45¢ per equivalent barrel.

| Inventory | 77,750,000 | |
| Cash | | 77,750,000 |

To record purchase of five million barrels of oil at option price of €15.55/barrel

| Inventory | 2,250,000 | |
| Option contract | | 2,250,000 |

To increase the recorded value of the inventory to include the fair value of options given up in acquiring the oil (taken together, the cash purchase price and the fair value of options surrendered add to €16 per barrel, the world market price at date of purchase)

| Shareholders' equity | 2,250,000 | |
| Inventory | | 2,250,000 |

To remove deferred gain from equity and include in initial measurement of inventory

| Cost of goods sold | 4,935,000 | |
| Inventory | | 4,935,000 |

To record cost of goods sold

July 31, 2007

| Gain/loss on hedging transaction | 50,000 | |
| Option contract | | 50,000 |

To record change in time value of option contract—charge premium to income since this represents payment for time value of money, which expires ratably over two-year term, and does not qualify for hedge accounting treatment

| Shareholders' equity | 2,000,000 | |
| Option contract | | 2,000,000 |

To reflect change in intrinsic value of remaining option contracts (decline in value)

| Cost of goods sold | 3,887,500 | |
| Inventory | | 3,887,500 |

To record cost of goods sold

August 31, 2007

| Loss on hedging transaction | 50,000 | |
| Option contract | | 50,000 |

To record change in time value of option contract—charge premium to income since this represents payment for time value of money, which expires ratably over two-year term, and does not qualify for hedge accounting treatment

| Shareholders' equity | 250,000 | |
| Option contract | | 250,000 |

To reflect change in intrinsic value of remaining option contracts (decline in value)

| Cost of goods sold | 6,220,000 | |
| Inventory | | 6,220,000 |

To record cost of goods sold

September 30, 2007

| Gain/loss on hedging transaction | 50,000 | |
| Option contract | | 50,000 |

To record change in time value of option contract—charge premium to income since this represents payment for time value of money, which expires ratably over two-year term, and does not qualify for hedge accounting treatment

Option contract	1,000,000	
Shareholders' equity		1,000,000

To reflect change in intrinsic value of remaining option contracts (increase in value)

Cost of goods sold	5,442,500	
Inventory		5,442,500

To record cost of goods sold

October 31, 2007

Gain/loss on hedging transaction	50,000	
Option contract		50,000

To record change in time value of option contract—charge premium to income since this represents payment for time value of money, which expires ratably over two-year term, and does not qualify for hedge accounting treatment

Option contract	250,000	
Shareholders' equity		250,000

To reflect change in intrinsic value of remaining option contracts (further increase in value)

Cost of goods sold	8,552,500	
Inventory		8,552,500

To record cost of goods sold

November 30, 2007

Gain/loss on hedging transaction	50,000	
Option contract		50,000

To record change in time value of option contract—charge premium to income since this represents payment for time value of money, which expires ratably over two-year term, and does not qualify for hedge accounting treatment

Option contract	250,000	
Shareholders' equity		250,000

To reflect change in intrinsic value of remaining option contracts (further increase in value)

Cost of goods sold	7,775,000	
Inventory		7,775,000

To record cost of goods sold

December 31, 2007

Gain/loss on hedging transaction	50,000	
Option contract		50,000

To record change in time value of option contract—charge premium to income since this represents payment for time value of money, which expires ratably over two-year term, and does not qualify for hedge accounting treatment

Option contract	250,000	
Shareholders' equity		250,000

To reflect change in intrinsic value of remaining option contracts (further increase in value) before sale of options

Cost of goods sold	10,107,500	
Inventory		10,107,500

To record cost of goods sold

Cash	2,100,000	
Loss on sale of options	50,000	
Option contract		2,150,000

Shareholders' equity	1,750,000	
Gain on sale of options		1,750,000

To record sale of remaining option contracts; the cash price was €50,000 lower than carrying value of asset sold (options having unexpired time value of €400,000 plus intrinsic value of €1,750,000), but transfer of shareholders' equity to income recognizes formerly deferred gain; since no further inventory purchases are planned in connection with this hedging activity, the unrealized gain is taken into income

Hedging on a "net" basis and "macrohedging." The IGC has addressed the issue of whether a reporting entity can group financial assets together with financial liabilities for the purpose of determining the net cash flow exposure to be hedged for hedge accounting purposes. It ruled that while an entity's hedging strategy and risk management practices may assess cash flow risk on a net basis, IAS 39 does not permit designating a net cash flow exposure as a hedged item for hedge accounting purposes. IAS 39 provides an example of how a bank might assess its risk on a net basis (with similar assets and liabilities grouped together) and then qualify for hedge accounting by hedging on a gross basis.

In 2004 IASB amended IAS 39 to permit "macrohedging" (more formally, hedging a portfolio hedge of interest rate risk). This permits an entity to apply *fair value* hedging (but not cash flow hedging) to a grouping of assets and/or liabilities, which essentially means that the net exposure can be hedged, without a need to separately put hedge positions on for each of the individual assets and/or liabilities. (See discussion in Chapter 5.)

Partial term hedging. IAS 39 indicates that a hedging relationship may not be designated for only a portion of the time period in which a hedging instrument is outstanding. On the other hand, it is permitted to designate a derivative as hedging only a portion of the time period to maturity of a hedged item. For example, if Aquarian Corp. acquires a 10% fixed-rate government bond with a remaining term to maturity of ten years, and classifies the bond as available-for-sale, it may hedge itself against fair value exposure on the bond associated with the present value of the interest rate payments until year five by acquiring a five-year "pay-fixed, receive-floating" swap. The swap may be designated as hedging the fair value exposure of the interest rate payments on the government bond until year five and the change in value of the principal payment due at maturity to the extent affected by changes in the yield curve relating to the five years of the swap.

Interest rate risk managed on a net basis should be designated as hedge of gross exposure. If an entity manages its exposure to interest rate risk on a net basis, a number of complex financial reporting issues must be addressed, regarding the ability to use hedge accounting. The IGC has offered substantial guidance on a number of matters, the more generally applicable of which are summarized in the following paragraphs.

The IGC has concluded that a derivative that is used to manage interest rate risk on a net basis be designated as a hedging instrument in a fair value hedge or a cash flow hedge of a gross exposure under IAS 39. An entity may designate the derivative used in interest rate risk management activities either as a fair value hedge of assets or liabilities or as a cash flow hedge of forecasted transactions, such as the anticipated reinvestment of cash inflows, the anticipated refinancing or rollover of a financial liability, and the cash flow consequences of the resetting of interest rates for an asset or a liability.

The IGC also notes that firm commitments to purchase or sell assets at fixed prices create fair value exposures, but are accounted for as cash flow hedges. (Note, however, the IASB has proposed to reverse the former rule, such that hedges of firm commitments will henceforth be accounted for as fair value hedges.) In economic terms, it does not matter whether the derivative instrument is considered a fair value hedge or a cash flow hedge. Under either perspective of the exposure, the derivative has the same economic effect of reducing the net exposure. For example, a receive-fixed, pay-variable interest rate swap can be considered to be a cash flow hedge of a variable-rate asset or a fair value hedge of a fixed-rate liability. Under either perspective, the fair value or cash flows of the interest rate swap offsets the exposure to interest rate changes. However, accounting consequences differ depending on whether the derivative is designated as a fair value hedge or a cash flow hedge, as discussed below.

Consider the following illustration. Among its financial resources and obligations, a bank has the following assets and liabilities having maturities of two years:

	Variable interest	*Fixed interest*
Assets	60,000	100,000
Liabilities	(100,000)	(60,000)
Net	(40,000)	40,000

The bank enters into a two-year interest rate swap with a notional principal of €40,000 to receive a variable interest rate and pay a fixed interest rate, in order to hedge the net exposure of the two-year maturity financial assets and liabilities. According to the IGC, this may be designated either as a fair value hedge of €40,000 of the fixed-rate assets or as a cash flow hedge of €40,000 of the variable-rate liabilities. It cannot be designated as a hedge of the net exposure, however.

Determining whether a derivative that is used to manage interest rate risk on a net basis should be designated as a hedging instrument in a fair value hedge or a cash flow hedge of a gross exposure is based on a number of critical considerations. These include the assessment of hedge effectiveness in the presence of prepayment risk, and the ability of the information systems to attribute fair value or cash flow changes of hedging instruments to fair value or cash flow changes, respectively, of hedged items. For accounting purposes, the designation of the derivative as hedging a fair value exposure or a cash flow exposure is important because both the qualification requirements for hedge accounting and the recognition of hedging gains and losses differ for each of these categories. The IGC has observed that it will often be easier to demonstrate high effectiveness for a cash flow hedge than for a fair value hedge.

Another important issue involves the effects of prepayments on the fair value of an instrument and the timing of its cash flows, as well as the impacts on the effectiveness test for fair value hedges and the probability test for cash flow hedges, respectively. Effectiveness is often more difficult to achieve for fair value hedges than for cash flow hedges when the instrument being hedged is subject to prepayment risk. For a fair value hedge to qualify for hedge accounting, the changes in the fair value of the derivative hedging instrument must be expected to be highly effective in offsetting the changes in the fair value of the hedged item. This test may be difficult to meet if, for example, the derivative hedging instrument is a forward contract having a fixed term, and the financial assets being hedged are subject to prepayment by the borrower.

Also, it may be difficult to conclude that, for a portfolio of fixed-rate assets that are subject to prepayment, the changes in the fair value for each individual item in the group will be expected to be approximately proportional to the overall changes in fair value attributable to the hedged risk of the group. Even if the risk being hedged is a benchmark interest rate, to be able to conclude that fair value changes will be proportional for each item in the portfolio, it may be necessary to disaggregate the asset portfolio into categories based on term, coupon, credit, type of loan, and other characteristics.

In economic terms, a forward derivative instrument could be used to hedge assets that are subject to prepayment, but it would be effective only for small movements in interest rates. A reasonable estimate of prepayments can be made for a given interest rate environment and the derivative position can be adjusted as the interest rate environment changes. However, for accounting purposes, the expectation of effectiveness has to be based on existing fair value exposures and the potential for interest rate movements, without consideration of future adjustments to those positions. The fair value exposure attributable to prepayment risk can generally be hedged with options.

For a cash flow hedge to qualify for hedge accounting, the forecasted cash flows, including the reinvestment of cash inflows or the refinancing of cash outflows, must be highly probable, and the hedge expected to be highly effective in achieving offsetting changes in the cash flows of the hedged item and hedging instrument. Prepayments affect the timing of cash flows and, therefore, the probability of occurrence of the forecasted transaction. If the hedge is established for risk management purposes on a net basis, an entity may have sufficient levels of highly probable cash flows on a gross basis to support the designation for accounting purposes of forecasted transactions associated with a portion of the gross cash flows as the hedged item. In this case, the portion of the gross cash flows designated as being hedged may be chosen to be equal to the amount of net cash flows being hedged for risk management purposes.

The IAS 39 Implementation Guidance Committee has also emphasized that there are important systems considerations relating to the use of hedge accounting. It notes that the accounting differs for fair value hedges and cash flow hedges. It is usually easier to use existing information systems to manage and track cash flow hedges than it is for fair value hedges.

Under fair value hedge accounting, the assets or liabilities that are designated as being hedged are remeasured for those changes in fair values during the hedge period that are attributable to the risk being hedged. Such changes adjust the carrying amount of the hedged items and, for interest-sensitive assets and liabilities, may result in an adjustment of the effective yield of the hedged item. As a consequence of fair value hedging activities, the changes in fair value have to be allocated to the hedged assets or liabilities being hedged in order to be able to recompute their effective yield, determine the subsequent amortization of the fair value adjustment to net profit or loss, and determine the amount that should be recognized in net profit or loss when assets are sold or liabilities extinguished. To comply with the requirements for fair value hedge accounting, it generally will be necessary to establish a system to track the changes in the fair value attributable to the hedged risk, associate those changes with individual hedged items, recompute the effective yield of the hedged items, and amortize the changes to net profit or loss over the life of the respective hedged item.

Under cash flow hedge accounting, the cash flows relating to the forecasted transactions that are designated as being hedged reflect changes in interest rates. The adjustment for changes in the fair value of a hedging derivative instrument is initially recognized in equity. To comply with the requirements for cash flow hedge accounting, it is necessary to determine when the adjustments to equity from changes in the fair value of a hedging instrument should be recognized in net profit or loss. For cash flow hedges, it is not necessary to create a separate system to make this determination. The system used to determine the extent of the net exposure provides the basis for scheduling out the changes in the cash flows of the derivative and the recognition of such changes in net profit or loss. The timing of the recognition in earnings can be predetermined when the hedge is associated with the exposure to changes in cash flows.

The forecasted transactions that are being hedged can be associated with a specific principal amount in specific future periods, composed of variable-rate assets and cash inflows being reinvested or variable-rate liabilities and cash outflows being refinanced, each of which create a cash flow exposure to changes in interest rates. The specific principal amounts in specific future periods are equal to the notional amount of the derivative hedging instruments and are hedged only for the period that corresponds to the repricing or maturity of the derivative hedging instruments so that the cash flow changes resulting from changes in interest rate are matched with the derivative hedging instrument. IAS 39 specifies that the amounts recognized in equity should be included in net profit or loss in the same period or periods during which the hedged item affects net profit or loss.

If a hedging relationship is designated as a cash flow hedge relating to changes in cash flows resulting from interest rate changes, the documentation required by IAS 39 would include information about the hedging relationship; the entity's risk management objective and strategy for undertaking the hedge; the type of hedge; the hedged item; the hedged risk; the hedging instrument; and the method of assessing effectiveness.

Information about the hedging relationship would include the maturity schedule of cash flows used for risk management purposes, to determine exposures to cash flow mismatches on a net basis would provide part of the documentation of the hedging relationship. The entity's risk management objective and strategy for undertaking the hedge would be addressed in terms of the entity's overall risk management objective and strategy for hedging exposures to interest rate risk would provide part of the documentation of the hedging objective and strategy. The fact that the hedge is a cash flow hedge would also be noted.

The hedged item will be documented as a group of forecasted transactions (interest cash flows) that are expected to occur with a high degree of probability in specified future periods, for instance, scheduled on a monthly basis. The hedged item may include interest cash flows resulting from the reinvestment of cash inflows, including the resetting of interest rates on assets, or from the refinancing of cash outflows, including the resetting of interest rates on liabilities and rollovers of financial liabilities. The forecasted transactions meet the probability test if there are sufficient levels of highly probable cash flows in the specified future periods to encompass the amounts designated as being hedged on a gross basis.

The risk designated as being hedged is documented as a portion of the overall exposure to changes in a specified market interest rate, often the risk-free interest rate or an interbank offered rate, common to all items in the group. To help ensure that the hedge effectiveness test is met at inception of the hedge and subsequently, the designated hedged portion of the interest rate risk could be documented as being based off the same yield curve as the derivative hedging instrument.

Each derivative hedging instrument is documented as a hedge of specified amounts in specified future time periods corresponding with the forecasted transactions occurring in the specified future periods designated as being hedged.

The method of assessing effectiveness is documented by comparing the changes in the cash flows of the derivatives allocated to the applicable periods in which they are designated as a hedge to the changes in the cash flows of the forecasted transactions being hedged. Measurement of the cash flow changes is based on the applicable yield curves of the derivatives and hedged items.

When a hedging relationship is designated as a cash flow hedge, the entity might satisfy the requirement for an expectation of high effectiveness in achieving offsetting changes by preparing an analysis demonstrating high historical and expected future correlation between the interest rate risk designated as being hedged and the interest rate risk of the hedging instrument. Existing documentation of the hedge ratio used in establishing the derivative contracts may also serve to demonstrate an expectation of effectiveness.

If the hedging relationship is designated as a cash flow hedge, an entity may demonstrate a high probability of the forecasted transactions occurring by preparing a cash flow maturity schedule showing that there exist sufficient aggregate gross levels of expected cash flows, including the effects of the resetting of interest rates for assets or liabilities, to establish that the forecasted transactions that are designated as being hedged are highly probable of occurring. Such a schedule should be supported by management's stated intent and past practice of reinvesting cash inflows and refinancing cash outflows.

For instance, an entity may forecast aggregate gross cash inflows of €10,000 and aggregate gross cash outflows of €9,000 in a particular time period in the near future. In this case, it may wish to designate the forecasted reinvestment of gross cash inflows of €1,000 as the hedged item in the future time period. If more than €1,000 of the forecasted cash inflows are contractually specified and have low credit risk, the entity has very strong evidence to support an assertion that gross cash inflows of €1,000 are highly probable of occurring and support the designation of the forecasted reinvestment of those cash flows as being hedged for a particular portion of the reinvestment period. A high probability of the forecasted transactions occurring may also be demonstrated under other circumstances.

If the hedging relationship is designated as a cash flow hedge, an entity will assess and measure effectiveness under IAS 39, at a minimum, at the time an entity prepares its annual or interim financial reports. However, an entity may wish to measure it more frequently on a specified periodic basis, at the end of each month or other applicable reporting period. It is also measured whenever derivative positions designated as hedging instruments are changed or hedges are terminated to ensure that the recognition in net profit or loss of the changes in the fair value amounts on assets and liabilities and the recognition of changes in the fair value of derivative instruments designated as cash flow hedges are appropriate.

Changes in the cash flows of the derivative are computed and allocated to the applicable periods in which the derivative is designated as a hedge and are compared with computations of changes in the cash flows of the forecasted transactions. Computations are based on yield curves applicable to the hedged items and the derivative hedging instruments and applicable interest rates for the specified periods being hedged. The schedule used to determine effectiveness could be maintained and used as the basis for determining the period in which the hedging gains and losses recognized initially in equity are reclassified out of equity and recognized in net profit or loss.

If the hedging relationship is designated as a cash flow hedge, an entity will account for the hedge as follows: (1) the portion of gains and losses on hedging derivatives determined to result from effective hedges is recognized in equity whenever effectiveness is measured and (2) the ineffective portion of gains and losses resulting from hedging derivatives is recognized in net profit or loss.

The amounts recognized in equity should be included in net profit or loss in the same period or periods during which the hedged item affects net profit or loss. Accordingly, when the forecasted transactions occur, the amounts previously recognized in equity are recognized in net profit or loss. For instance, if an interest rate swap is designated as a hedging instrument of a series of forecasted cash flows, the changes in the cash flows of the swap are recognized in net profit or loss in the periods when the forecasted cash flows and the cash flows of the swap offset each other.

If the hedging relationship is designated as a cash flow hedge, the treatment of any net cumulative gains and losses recognized in equity if the hedging instrument is terminated prematurely, the hedge accounting criteria are no longer met, or the hedged forecasted transactions are no longer expected to take place, will be as described in the following. If the hedging instrument is terminated prematurely or the hedge no longer meets the criteria for qualification for hedge accounting (for instance, the forecasted transactions are no longer highly probable), the net cumulative gain or loss reported in equity remains in equity until the forecasted transaction occurs. If the hedged forecasted transactions are no longer expected to occur, the net cumulative gain or loss is reported in net profit or loss for the period.

IAS 39 states that a hedging relationship may not be designated for only a portion of the time period in which a hedging instrument is outstanding. If the hedging relationship is designated as a cash flow hedge, and the hedge subsequently fails the test for being highly effective, IAS 39 does not preclude redesignating the hedging instrument. The standard indicates that a derivative instrument may not be designated as a hedging instrument for only a portion of its remaining period to maturity but does not refer to the derivative instrument's original period to maturity. If there is a hedge effectiveness failure, the ineffective portion of the gain or loss on the derivative instrument is recognized immediately in net profit or loss and hedge accounting based on the previous designation of the hedge relationship cannot be continued. In this case, the derivative instrument may be redesignated prospectively as a hedging instrument in a new hedging relationship, provided this hedging relationship satisfies the necessary conditions. The derivative instrument must be redesignated as a hedge for the entire time period it remains outstanding.

For cash flow hedges, IAS 39 states that "if the hedged firm commitment or forecasted transaction results in the recognition of an asset or liability, then at the time the asset or liability is recognized the associated gains or losses that were recognized directly in equity, should enter into the initial measurement of the carrying amount of the asset or liability" (basis adjustment). If a derivative is used to manage a net exposure to interest rate risk and the derivative is designated as a cash flow hedge of forecasted interest cash flows or portions thereof on a gross basis, there will be no basis adjustment when the forecasted cash flow occurs. There is no basis adjustment because the hedged forecasted transactions do not result in the recognition of assets or liabilities and the effect of interest rate changes that are designated as being hedged is recognized in net profit or loss in the period in which the forecasted transactions occur. Although the types of hedges described herein would not result in basis adjustment if instead the derivative is designated as a hedge of a forecasted purchase of a financial asset or issuance of a liability, the derivative gain or loss would be an adjustment to the basis of the asset or liability upon the occurrence of the transaction.

IAS 39 permits a portion of a cash flow exposure to be designated as a hedged item. While IAS 39 does not specifically address a hedge of a portion of a cash flow exposure for a forecasted transaction, it specifies that a financial asset or liability may be a hedged item with respect to the risks associated with only a portion of its cash flows or fair value, if effectiveness can be measured. The ability to hedge a portion of a cash flow exposure resulting from the resetting of interest rates for assets and liabilities suggests that a portion of a cash flow exposure resulting from the forecasted reinvestment of cash inflows or the refinancing or rollover of financial liabilities can also be hedged. The basis for qualification as a hedged item of a portion of an exposure is the ability to measure effectiveness.

Furthermore, IAS 39 specifies that a nonfinancial asset or liability can be hedged only in its entirety or for foreign currency risk but not for a portion of other risks because of the difficulty of isolating and measuring the risks attributable to a specific risk. Accordingly, assuming effectiveness can be measured, a portion of a cash flow exposure of forecasted transactions associated with, for example, the resetting of interest rates for a variable-rate asset or liability can be designated as a hedged item.

Since forecasted transactions will have different terms when they occur, including credit exposures, maturities, and option features, there may be an issue over how an entity can satisfy the tests in IAS 39 requiring that the hedged group have similar risk characteristics. According to the IGC, the standard provides for hedging a group of assets, liabilities, firm commitments, or forecasted transactions with similar risk characteristics. IAS 39 provides additional guidance and specifies that portfolio hedging is permitted if two conditions are met, namely: the individual items in the portfolio share the same risk for which they are designated and the change in the fair value attributable to the hedged risk for each individual item in the group will be expected to be approximately proportional to the overall change in fair value.

When an entity associates a derivative hedging instrument with a gross exposure, the hedged item typically is a group of forecasted transactions. For hedges of cash flow exposures relating to a group of forecasted transactions, the overall exposure of the forecasted transactions and the assets or liabilities that are repricing may have very different risks. The exposure from forecasted transactions may differ based on the terms that are expected as they relate to credit exposures, maturities, option, and other features. Although the overall risk exposures may be different for the individual items in the group, a specific risk inherent in each of the items in the group can be designated as being hedged.

The items in the portfolio do not necessarily have to have the same overall exposure to risk, providing they share the same risk for which they are designated as being hedged. A common risk typically shared by a portfolio of financial instruments is exposure to changes in the risk-free interest rate or to changes in a specified rate that has a credit exposure equal to the highest credit-rated instrument in the portfolio (that is, the instrument with the lowest credit risk). If the instruments that are grouped into a portfolio have different credit exposures, they may be hedged as a group for a portion of the exposure. The risk they have in common that is designated as being hedged is the exposure to interest rate changes from the highest credit-rated instrument in the portfolio. This ensures that the change in fair value attributable to the hedged risk for each individual item in the group is expected to be approximately proportional to the overall change in fair value attributable to the hedged risk of the group. It is likely there will be some ineffectiveness if the hedging instrument has a credit quality that is inferior to the credit quality of the highest credit-rated instrument being hedged, since a hedging relationship is designated for a hedging instrument in its entirety.

For example, if a portfolio of assets consists of assets rated A, BB, and B, and the current market interest rates for these assets are LIBOR+ 20 basis points, LIBOR+ 40 basis points, and LIBOR+ 60 basis points, respectively, an entity may use a swap that pays fixed interest rate and for which variable interest payments are made based on LIBOR to hedge the exposure to variable interest rates. If LIBOR is designated as the risk being hedged, credit spreads above LIBOR on the hedged items are excluded from the designated hedge relationship and the assessment of hedge effectiveness.

Equity Method of Accounting for Investments

The preceding discussion addressed investments in which the investor has essentially a passive position, due to holding only a small minority ownership interest (or, in the case of debt, no actual ownership interest at all). In such situations, the investor is unable to control or materially influence decisions to be made by management of the investee. The use of fair value accounting has been deemed most appropriate in such circumstances.

In other situations an investor will have active control over the decisions taken by the management of the investee, or have joint control over those decisions, to be made in conjunction with its coinvestors. A third logical possibility is that the investor will have something less than control (or joint control), but will clearly also not be a mere passive investor. This last named circumstance is that where there is significant influence over an investee.

The notion of applying what is now known as equity-method accounting to investment situations where the investor is able to exercise significant influence developed in the early 1950s, as an application of the "substance over form" philosophy of financial reporting. It was not actually made mandatory, however, until the late 1960s, in the US. Because the actual determination of the existence of significant influence was anticipated to be difficult, a somewhat arbitrary, refutable presumption of such influence was set at a 20% voting interest in the investee. This became the de facto standard for all later accounting requirements seeking to emulate the pioneering one set forth under US GAAP.

The necessity of applying a method of accounting such as the equity method, when significant influence over the investee is held by the investor, can easily be understood when one considers how readily manipulation of the investor's financial position and results of operations could be achieved in its absence. If an investee has substantial income, but the investor, employing the cost method of accounting for the investment, uses its influence to defer the investee's declaration of dividends, the result would be that the investor would not be reporting its share of the investee's economic operating results, even though it had been in a position to cause a distribution of dividends, had it chosen to do so. This might be motivated, for example, by a desire to put aside future earnings to compensate for an expected, or feared, decline in the investor's own operations.

Conversely, the investor could effect or encourage a dividend distribution even in the absence of earnings by the investee. This could be motivated by a need for reportable earnings, perhaps to offset disappointing performance in the investor's own operations. In either case, the opportunity to manipulate reported results of operations would be of great concern.

More importantly, however, the use of the cost method would simply not reflect the economic reality of the investor's interest in an entity whose operations were indicative, in part at least, of the reporting entity's (i.e., the investor's) management decisions and operational skills. Thus, the clearly demonstrable need to reflect substance, rather than mere form, made the development of the equity method highly desirable.

The pure equity method is not the only possible means of accomplishing the goal of reporting the economic performance of the investor. Other suggested solutions include the expanded equity method and proportionate consolidation. IASB and the various national standard-setting bodies have directed differing levels of attention to these alternatives over the years; the simple equity method has received the most universal support.

The equity method permits an entity (the investor) controlling a certain share of the voting interest in another entity (the investee) to incorporate its pro rata share of the investee's operating results into its earnings. However, rather than include its share of each component of the investee's revenues, expenses, assets and liabilities into its financial statements, the investor will only include its share of the investee's net income as a separate line item in its income. Similarly, only a single line in the investor's balance is presented, but this reflects, to a degree, the investor's share in each of the investee's assets and liabilities. For this reason, the equity method has been referred to as "one-line consolidation."

It is important to recognize that the bottom-line impact on the investor's financial statements is identical whether the equity method or full consolidation is employed; only the amount of detail presented within the statements will differ. An understanding of this principle will be useful as the need to identify the "goodwill" component of the cost of the investment is explained, below.

Expanded equity method. Less commonly presented than the pure equity method of accounting are the expanded equity method and the proportionate consolidation method. These alternative approaches effectively are successive points along a continuum ranging from a pure historical cost basis to full consolidation. In contrast to the one-line consolidation approach of the simple equity method, the expanded equity method is an attempt to provide more meaningful detail about the various assets and liabilities, and revenues and expenses, in which the investor has an economic interest. Thus, if using the expanded equity method, the investor's interest in the investee's aggregate current assets would be presented, as a single number, in the current asset section of the investor's balance sheet. Similarly, the investor's share of the investee's noncurrent assets, current liabilities, and noncurrent liabilities would be captioned separately in the corresponding section of the investor's balance sheet.

On the income statement, using this expanded equity method, the investor's share of significant items of revenue, expense, gains, and losses would be set forth separately. This would not extend to every item of the income statement, but would highlight the major ones. Greater or lesser degrees of detail would be possible, depending on the investor's preferences, since there are no definitive standards governing this method.

A major advantage of this method of reporting an investor's interest in the investee is that the investor's financial statements will provide a more meaningful insight into the true economic scope of its operations, including indications of the gross volume of business being transacted. Furthermore, financial position will not be distorted by, for example, effectively merging the investee's current assets with the investor's noncurrent assets, which would be the result of placing equity in investee in the noncurrent asset section, as is required under common practice. As the amount of detail expands, the expanded equity method edges into proportionate consolidation, however.

The expanded equity method has not been endorsed, as such, although the equity method as defined by US GAAP (in APB Opinion 18) does incorporate elements of this approach. Specifically, APB 18 mandates one-line consolidation for the balance sheet, but requires that certain components of the investee's income statement (such as extraordinary items) retain their character when incorporated into the investor's income statement. Thus APB 18's requirements do go beyond a strict application of the equity method.

Proportionate consolidation. This is a more fully developed variant of the expanded equity method, whereby the investor's share of each element of the investee's balance sheet and income statement is reported in the investor's statements. Although there is nonauthoritative GAAP in the United States supporting this method of accounting for investments in joint ventures, and under IFRS (as discussed later in the chapter) this method is prescribed optionally for joint ventures, it has not been widely advocated for investments in which the investor does not exercise, at a minimum, joint control. Nonetheless, from a conceptual perspective, it does have appeal since it would convey the full scope of economic activities over which the reporting entity could be said to have either direct control or indirect yet significant impact.

Equity method as prescribed by IAS 28. The equity method is generally not available to be used as a substitute for consolidation. Consolidation is required when a majority voting interest is held by the reporting entity (the parent) in another entity (the subsidiary). The equity method is intended for use where the reporting entity (the investor) has significant influence over the operations of the other entity (the investee), but lacks control.

In general, significant influence is inferred when the investor owns between 20% and 50% of the investee's voting common stock. However, the 20% threshold stipulated in IAS 28 is not an absolute one. Specific circumstances may suggest that significant influence exists even though the investor's level of ownership is under 20%, in which case the equity method should be applied. In other instances, significant influence may be absent despite a level of ownership above 20%. Therefore, the existence of significant influence in the 20% to 50% ownership range should be treated as a refutable presumption. This 20% lower threshold is identical to that prescribed under US GAAP.

In considering whether significant influence exists, IAS 28 identifies the following factors as evidence that such influence is present: (1) investor representation on the board of directors or its equivalent, (2) participation in policy-making processes, (3) material transactions between the investor and investee, (4) interchange of managerial personnel, and (5) provision of essential technical information. There may be other factors present that suggest a lack of significant influence, such as organized opposition by the other shareholders, majority ownership by a small group of shareholders not inclusive of the investor, and inability to achieve representation on the board or to obtain information on the operations of the investee. Whether sufficient contrary evidence exists to negate the presumption of significant influence is a matter of judgment and requires a careful evaluation of all pertinent facts and circumstances, over an extended period of time in some cases.

When equity method is required. IAS 28 stipulates that the equity method should be employed by the investor for all investments in associates, unless the investment is acquired and held exclusively with a view to its disposal within twelve months from acquisition, or if it is in reorganization or in bankruptcy, or operates under severe long-term restrictions that would preclude making distributions to investors. In the latter cases, the use of the equity method of accounting would not be deemed appropriate; rather, the investment would be carried at its historical cost.

The IASB's Improvements Project made a number of changes to IAS 28 (effective 2005), among which is an exclusion from IAS 28's requirements for investments in associates held by venture capital organizations, mutual funds, unit trusts, and similar entities that are measured at fair value in accordance with IAS 39, when such measurement is well-established practice in those industries. When those investments are measured at fair value, changes in fair value are included in profit or loss in the period of the change.

When considering whether the investor has significant influence—and thus must apply the equity method of accounting—a number of factors must be taken into consideration. For example, beyond the mere 20% threshold of ownership, relevant indicia of significant influence would often include these factors.

1. Representation on the board of directors or equivalent governing body of the investee;
2. Participation in policy-making processes;
3. Material transactions between the investor and the investee;
4. Interchange of managerial personnel; or
5. Provision of essential technical information.

Another complicating factor in ascertaining whether the reporting entity has significant influence over the investee is that the investor may own securities such as share warrants, share call options, or other debt or equity instruments that are convertible into common shares, or other similar instruments that have the potential, if exercised or converted, to give the entity additional voting power or reduce another party's relative power over the financial and operating policies of another entity (i.e., potential voting rights). The existence and effect of potential voting rights that are currently exercisable or currently convertible, Iing potential voting rights held by other entities, must be considered when assessing whether an entity has the power to have significant influence in the financial and operating policy decisions of the investee. This issue is discussed in greater detail later in this chapter.

The standard does distinguish between the accounting for investments in associates in consolidated financials and that in separate financials of the investor. As amended by IAS 39, IAS 28 provides that in the separate financials of the investor the investment in the associate may be carried at either cost, by the equity method, or as an available-for-sale financial asset consistent with IAS 39's provisions, if the investor also prepares consolidated financial statements. If the investor does not issue consolidated financial statements, the choices are expanded to include, if warranted by the facts, treating the investment as a trading security as well.

In practice, many parent-only financial statements apply equity method accounting to subsidiaries and significant influence investees alike. This probably does provide the most meaningful reporting, avoiding detailed inclusion of any assets, liabilities, revenues, or expenses other than the parent company's own in its financial statements, while not distorting the bottom line measure of economic performance.

Complications in applying equity method accounting. Complexities in the use of the equity method arise in two areas. First, the cost of the investment to the investor might not be equal to the fair value of the investor's share of investee net assets; this is analogous to the existence of goodwill in a purchase business combination. Or the fair value of the investor's share of the investee's net assets may not be equal to the book value thereof; this situation is analogous to the purchase cost allocation problem in consolidations. Since the ultimate income statement result from the use of equity method accounting must generally be the same as full consolidation, an adjustment must be made for each of these differentials.

The second major complexity relates to interperiod income tax allocation. The equity method causes the investor to reflect current earnings based on the investee's operating results; however, for income tax purposes the investor reports only dividends received and gains or losses on disposal of the investment. Thus, temporary differences result, and IAS 12 provides guidance as to the appropriate method of computing the deferred tax effects of these differences.

In the absence of these complicating factors, use of the equity method by the investor is straightforward: The original cost of the investment is increased by the investor's share of the investee's earnings and is decreased by its share of investee losses and by dividends received. The basic procedure is illustrated below.

Example of a simple case ignoring deferred taxes

Assume the following information:

On January 2, 2006, Regency Corporation (the investor) acquired 40% of Elixir Company's (the investee) voting common stock on the open market for €100,000. Unless demonstrated otherwise, it is assumed that Regency Corporation can exercise significant influence over Elixir Company's operating and financing policies. On January 2, Elixir's stockholders' equity is comprised of the following accounts:

Common stock, par €1, 100,000 shares authorized,	
50,000 shares issued and outstanding	€ 50,000
Additional paid-in capital	150,000
Retained earnings	50,000
Total stockholders' equity	€250,000

Note that the cost of Elixir Company common stock was equal to 40% of the book value of Elixir's net assets. Assume also that there is no difference between the book value and the fair value of Elixir Company's assets and liabilities. Accordingly, the balance in the investment account in Regency's records represents exactly 40% of Elixir's stockholders' equity (net assets). Assume further that Elixir Company reported a 2006 net income of €30,000 and paid cash dividends of €10,000. Its stockholders' equity at year-end would be as follows:

Common stock, par €1, 100,000 shares authorized,	
50,000 shares issued and outstanding	€ 50,000
Additional paid-in capital	150,000
Retained earnings	70,000
Total stockholders' equity	€270,000

Regency Corporation would record its share of the increase in Elixir Company's net assets during 2006 as follows:

Investment in Elixir Company	12,000	
Equity in Elixir income (€30,000 × 40%)		12,000
Cash	4,000	
Investment in Elixir Company (€10,000 × 40%)		4,000

When Regency's balance sheet is prepared at December 31, 2006, the balance reported in the investment account would be €108,000 (= €100,000 + €12,000 – €4,000). This amount represents 40% of the book value of Elixir's net assets at the end of the year (40% × €270,000). Note also that the equity in Elixir income is reported as one amount on Regency's income statement under the caption "Other income and expense."

IAS 12 established the requirement that deferred income taxes be provided for the tax effects of timing differences. Under this standard, discussed in detail in Chapter 15, the liability method must be employed, under which the provision of a net deferred tax asset or liability is adjusted at each balance sheet date to reflect the current expectations regarding the amount that ultimately is to be received or paid.

In order to compute the deferred tax effects of income recognized by an investor employing the equity method of accounting for its investment, it must make an assumption regarding the means by which undistributed earnings of its investee will be realized. Earnings can generally be realized either through subsequent receipt of dividends, or by disposition of the investment at a gain, which presumably would reflect the investee's undistributed earnings as of that date. In many jurisdictions, these alternative modes of income realization will have differing tax implications. For example, in many jurisdictions the assumption of future dividends would result in taxes at the investor's marginal tax rate on ordinary income (net of any dividends received deduction or exclusion permitted by the local taxing authorities). If the sale of the investment is expected to be the route by which earnings are realized, this would commonly result in a capital gain, which in some jurisdictions is taxed at a different rate, or not taxed at all.

Example of a simple case including deferred taxes

Assume the same information as in the example above. In addition, assume that Regency Corporation has a combined (federal, state, and local) marginal tax rate of 34% on ordinary income and that it anticipates realization of Elixir Company earnings through future dividend receipts. In Regency's tax jurisdiction, there is an 80% deduction for dividends received from nonsubsidiary investees, meaning that only 20% of the income is subject to ordinary tax. Regency Corporation's entries at year-end 2006 will be as follows:

1.	Investment in Elixir Company	12,000	
	Equity in Elixir income		12,000
2.	Income tax expense	816	
	Deferred taxes		816

(Taxable portion of investee earnings to be received in the future as dividends times marginal tax rate: €12,000 × 20% × 34% = €816)

3.	Cash	4,000	
	Investment in Elixir Company		4,000
4.	Deferred taxes	272	
	Taxes payable—current		272

[Fraction of investee earnings currently taxed (€4,000/12,000) × 816 = €272]

Under the liability method of interperiod income tax allocation, as required by IAS 12, the tax provision should be based on the projected tax effect of the temporary difference reversal, and this may be subsequently adjusted for a variety of reasons, including alterations in tax rates and revision to management expectations (see Chapter 15 for a complete discussion).

Furthermore, when the taxable income (from dividends or the sale of the investment) is ultimately realized, the actual incidence of tax may still differ from the amount of deferred tax provided, as adjusted. This may occur because, assuming graduated rates and other complexities apply, the actual tax effect is a function of the entity's other current items of income and expense in the year of realization. Also, notwithstanding good-faith expectations, the realization of the investee's earnings may come in a manner other than anticipated (e.g., a sudden decision to sell rather than hold the investment could precipitate capital gains when future dividend income was planned for).

To illustrate this last point, assume that in 2007, before any further earnings or dividends are reported by the investee, the investor sells the entire investment for €115,000. The tax impact is

Selling price	€115,000
Less cost	100,000
Gain	€ 15,000
Capital gain rate (marginal corporate rate)	× 34%
Tax liability	€ 5,100

The entries to record the sale, the tax thereon, and the amortization of deferred taxes provided previously on the undistributed 2005 earnings are as follows:

1.	Cash		115,000	
	Investment in Elixir Company			108,000
	Gain on sale of investment			7,000
2.	Income tax expense		4,556	
	Deferred tax liability		544	
	Taxes payable—current			5,100

In the above, income tax expense of €4,556 is the sum of two factors: (1) the capital gains rate of 34% applied to the actual book gain realized (€115,000 selling price less €108,000 carrying value), for a tax of €2,380, and (2) the difference between the capital gains tax rate (34%) and the effective rate on dividend income (20% × 34% = 6.8%) on the undistributed 2006 earnings of Elixir Company previously recognized as ordinary income by Regency Corporation [€8,000 × (34% – 6.8%) = €2,176].

Note that if the realization through a sale of the investment had been anticipated at the time the 2006 balance sheet was being prepared, the deferred tax liability account would have been adjusted (possibly to the entire €5,100 amount of the ultimate obligation), with the offsetting entry applied to 2006 ordinary tax expense. The example above explicitly assumes that sale of the investment was not anticipated prior to 2007.

Accounting for a differential between cost and book value. The simple examples presented thus far avoided the major complexity of equity method accounting, the allocation of the differential between the cost to the investor and the investor's share in the net equity (net assets at book value) of the investee. Since the net impact of equity method accounting must equal that of full consolidation accounting, this differential must be analyzed into the following components and accounted for accordingly:

1. The difference between the book and fair values of the investee's net assets at the date the investment is made.
2. The remaining difference between the fair value of the net assets and the cost of the investment, that is generally attributable to goodwill.

According to IAS 28, any difference between the cost of the investment and the investor's share of the fair values of the net identifiable assets of the associate should be identified and accounted for in accordance with IFRS 3 (as detailed in Chapter 11). Thus, the differential should be allocated to specific asset categories, and these differences will then be amortized to the income from investee account as appropriate, for example, over the economic lives of fixed assets whose fair values exceeded book values. The difference between fair value and cost will be treated like goodwill and, in accordance with the provisions of IFRS 3 not subject to amortization, but rather will be reviewed for impairment on a regular basis, with write-downs taken for any impairment identified, to be included in earnings of the investor in the period of impairment.

Example of a complex case ignoring deferred taxes

Assume again that Regency Corporation acquired 40% of Elixir Company's shares on January 2, 2006, but that the price paid was €140,000. Elixir Company's assets and liabilities at that date had the following book and fair values:

	Book value	Fair value
Cash	€ 10,000	€ 10,000
Accounts receivable (net)	40,000	40,000
Inventories (FIFO cost)	80,000	90,000
Land	50,000	40,000
Plant and equipment (net of accumulated depreciation)	140,000	220,000
Total assets	€320,000	€400,000
Liabilities	(70,000)	(70,000)
Net assets (stockholders' equity)	€250,000	€330,000

The first order of business is the calculation of the differential, as follows:

Regency's cost for 40% of Elixir's common stock	€140,000
Book value of 40% of Elixir's net assets (€250,000 × 40%)	(100,000)
Total differential	€ 40,000

Next, the €40,000 is allocated to those individual assets and liabilities for which fair value differs from book value. In the example, the differential is allocated to inventories, land, and plant and equipment, as follows:

Item	Book value	Fair value	Difference debit (credit)	40% of difference debit (credit)
Inventories	€ 80,000	€ 90,000	€ 10,000	€ 4,000
Land	50,000	40,000	(10,000)	(4,000)
Plant and equipment	140,000	220,000	80,000	32,000
Differential allocated				€32,000

The difference between the allocated differential of €32,000 and the total differential of €40,000 is essentially identical to goodwill of €8,000. As shown by the following computation, goodwill represents the excess of the cost of the investment over the fair value of the net assets acquired.

Regency's cost for 40% of Elixir's common stock	€140,000
40% of Elixir's net assets (€330,000 × 40%)	(132,000)
Excess of cost over fair value (goodwill)	€ 8,000

At this point it is important to note that the allocation of the differential is not recorded formally by either Regency Corporation or Elixir Company. Furthermore, Regency does not remove the differential from the investment account and allocate it to the respective assets, since the use of the equity method (one-line consolidation) does not involve the recording of individual assets and liabilities. Regency leaves the differential of €40,000 in the investment account, as part of the balance of €140,000 at January 2, 2006. Accordingly, information pertaining to the allocation of the differential is maintained by the investor, but this information is outside the formal accounting system, which is comprised of journal entries and account balances.

After the differential has been allocated, the amortization pattern is developed. To develop the pattern in this example, assume that Elixir's plant and equipment have 10 years of useful life remaining and that Elixir depreciates its fixed assets on a straight-line basis. Under the provisions of IFRS 3, Regency may not amortize the unallocated differential, which is akin to goodwill, but must consider its possible impairment whenever preparing financial statements to conform with IFRS. Regency would prepare the following amortization schedule:

Item	Differential debit (credit)	Useful life	Amortization 2006	2007	2008
Inventories (FIFO)	€ 4,000	Sold in 2006	€4,000	€ --	€ --
Land	(4,000)	Indefinite	--	--	--
Plant and equipment (net)	32,000	10 years	3,200	3,200	3,200
Goodwill	8,000	N/A	--	--	--
Totals	€40,000		€7,200	€3,200	€3,200

Note that the entire differential allocated to inventories is amortized in 2006 because the cost flow assumption used by Elixir is FIFO. If Elixir had been using weighted-average costing instead of FIFO, amortization might have been computed on a different basis. Prior to the 2003 revision to IAS 2, LIFO costing was also permitted and this would have had an even more dramatically different impact on the pattern of eliminating the differential. However, now LIFO has been banned and this will simplify addressing the differential between cost of the investment and fair value of the underlying net identifiable assets. Note also that the differential allocated to Elixir's land is not amortized, because land is not a depreciable asset. Goodwill likewise is no longer subject to amortization.

The amortization of the differential, to the extent required under IFRS, is recorded formally in the accounting system of Regency Corporation. Recording the amortization adjusts the equity in Elixir's income that Regency recorded based on Elixir's income statement. Elixir's income must be adjusted because it is based on Elixir's book values, not on the cost that Regency incurred to acquire Elixir. Regency would make the following entries in 2006, assuming that Elixir reported net income of €30,000 and paid cash dividends of €10,000:

1.	Investment in Elixir	12,000	
	Equity in Elixir income (€30,000 × 40%)		12,000
2.	Equity in Elixir income (amortization of differential)	7,200	
	Investment in Elixir		7,200
3.	Cash	4,000	
	Investment in Elixir (€10,000 × 40%)		4,000

The balance in the investment account on Regency's records at the end of 2006 is €140,800 [= €140,000 + €12,000 – (€7,200 + €4,000)], and Elixir's stockholders' equity, as shown previously, is €270,000. The investment account balance of €140,000 is not equal to 40% of €270,000. However, this difference can easily be explained, as follows:

Balance in investment account at December 31, 2006		€140,800
40% of Elixir's net assets at December 31, 2006		108,000
Difference at December 31, 2006		€ 32,800
Differential at January 2, 2006	€40,000	
Differential amortized during 2006	(7,200)	
Unamortized differential at December 31, 2006		€ 32,800

As the years go by, the balance in the investment account will come closer and closer to representing 40% of the book value of Elixir's net assets. After twenty years, the remaining difference between these two amounts would be attributed to the original differential allocated to land (a €4,000 credit) and the amount analogous to goodwill (€8,000), unless written off due to impairment. This €4,000 difference would remain until Elixir sold the property.

To illustrate how the sale of land would affect equity method procedures, assume that Elixir sold the land in the year 2026 for €80,000. Since Elixir's cost for the land was €50,000, it would report a gain of €30,000, of which €12,000 (= €30,000 × 40%) would be recorded by Regency, when it records its 40% share of Elixir's reported net income, ignoring income taxes. However, from Regency's viewpoint, the gain on sale of land should have been €40,000 (€80,000 – €40,000) because the cost of the land from Regency's perspective was €40,000 at January 2, 2006. Therefore, besides the €12,000 share of the gain recorded above, Regency should record an additional €4,000 gain [(= €40,000 – €30,000) × 40%] by debiting the investment account and crediting the equity in Elixir income account. This €4,000 debit to the investment account will negate the €4,000 differential allocated to land on January 2, 2006, since the original differential was a credit (the fair value of the land was €10,000 less than its book value).

Example of a complex case including deferred taxes

The impact of interperiod income tax allocation in the foregoing example is similar to that demonstrated earlier in the simplified example. However, a complication arises with regard to the portion of the differential allocated to goodwill, since in some jurisdictions amounts representing goodwill are not amortizable for tax purposes and, therefore, will be a permanent (not a timing) difference that does not give rise to deferred taxes. The other components of the differential in this example are all generally defined as being timing differences.

The entries recorded by Regency Corporation in 2006 would be

1.	Investment in Elixir	12,000	
	Equity in Elixir income		12,000
2.	Income tax expense	816	
	Deferred tax liability (€12,000 × 20% × 34%)		816
3.	Cash	4,000	
	Investment in Elixir		4,000
4.	Deferred tax liability	272	
	Taxes payable—current (€4,000/€12,000 × €816)		272
5.	Equity in Elixir income	7,200	
	Investment in Elixir		7,200
6.	Deferred tax liability	490	
	Income tax expense (€7,200 × 20% × 34%)		490

Reporting disparate elements of the investee's income statement. As suggested earlier in this section, the expanded equity method would require that the major captions in the investee's income statement maintain their character when reported, pro rata, by the investor. IAS 28 does not mandate use of the expanded equity method, although it notes in its disclosure requirements that the investor's share of extraordinary and prior period items should be noted. Although the standard is silent on separate reporting on the face of the financial statements themselves, the authors are of the opinion that, to the extent that certain items would be a material part of the investor's income statement and thus have the potential to mislead users of those financial statements, it would be prudent and fully consistent with the spirit of IAS 28 to report these separately. For example, if corrected prior period financial statements are reported by the investee to address accounting errors made in the originally released financial statements, the investor's share of those corrections, if material, might be identified separately (or via footnote explanation) rather than simply be included in the equity in the investee company earnings.

One solution, of course, is to include the investor's share of these items with similar items in the investor's financial statements. That is, the expanded equity method concept should be applied, judiciously, to the investor's income statement. This would not extend, however, to separate reporting of any items of operating income or expense (gross sales, salaries, depreciation, etc.).

Example of accounting for separately reportable items

Assume that a correction of an accounting error is reported in an investee's income statement as reissued in the current period (e.g., as a comparative financial statement), and this item is considered material from the investor's viewpoint.

Investee's income statement:

Net income as originally reported	€ 80,000
Correction of accounting error – failure to record depreciation	(18,000)
Net income as corrected	€ 62,000

If an investor owned 30% of the voting common stock of this investee, the investor would make the following journal entries:

1.	Investment in investee company	24,000	
	Equity in investee income before correction of accounting error		24,000
	(€80,000 × 30%)		
2.	Equity in investee correction of accounting error	5,400	
	Investment in investee company		5,400
	(€18,000 × 30%)		

The equity in the investee's correction of an accounting error should be reported separately in the appropriate section on the investor's income statement.

Intercompany transactions between investor and investee. Transactions between the investor and the investee may require that the investor make certain adjustments when it records its share of the investee earnings. According to the realization concept, profits can be recognized by an entity only when realized through a sale to outside (unrelated) parties in arm's-length transactions (sales and purchases) between the investor and investee. Similar problems can arise when sales of fixed assets between the parties occur. In all cases, there is no need for any adjustment when the transfers are made at book value (i.e., without either party recognizing a profit or loss in its separate accounting records).

In preparing consolidated financial statements, all intercompany (parent-subsidiary) transactions are eliminated. However, when the equity method is used to account for investments, only the *profit component* of intercompany (investor-investee) transactions is eliminated. This is because the equity method does not result in the combining of all income statement accounts (such as sales and cost of sales) and therefore will not cause the financial statements to contain redundancies. In contrast, consolidated statements would include redundancies if the gross amounts of all intercompany transactions were not eliminated.

IAS 28 as originally issued was not explicit regarding the percentage of unrealized profits on investor-investee transactions to be eliminated. Logical arguments can be made to eliminate 100% of intercompany profits not realized through a subsequent transaction with unrelated third parties, that would replicate the approach used when preparing consolidated financial statements. However, good arguments can also be presented for the elimination of only the percentage held by the investor. Now-superseded interpretation SIC 3 held that when applying the equity method, unrealized profits should be eliminated for both "upstream" and "downstream" transactions (i.e., sales from investee to investor, and from investor to investee) to the extent of the investor's interest in the investee. Revised IAS 28 has incorporated the guidance formerly found in SIC 3 into the text of the revised standard itself.

Elimination of the investor's interest in the investee, rather than the entire unrealized profit on the transaction, is based on the logic that in an investor-investee situation, the investor does not have control (as would be the case with a subsidiary), and thus the nonowned percentage of profit is effectively realized through an arm's-length transaction. This is essentially the same logic as is set forth in IAS 31, dealing with joint venture accounting. For joint ventures, IAS 31 prescribes proportionate consolidation, which implies likewise that profits on intercompany transactions be eliminated only to the extent of the investor's interest in the venture. However, notwithstanding the use of proportionate elimination of intercompany profits, to the extent that losses are indicative of impairment in the value of the investment, this rule would not apply.

For purposes of determining the percentage interest in unrealized profit or loss to be eliminated, a group's interest in an associate is the aggregate of the holdings in that associate by the parent and its subsidiaries (excluding any interests held by minority interests of subsidiaries). Any holdings of the group's other associates (i.e., equity method investees) or joint ventures are ignored for the purpose of applying the equity method. When an associate has subsidiaries, associates, or joint ventures, the profits or losses and net assets taken into account in applying the equity method are those recognized in the associate's consolidated financial statements (including the associate's share of the profits or losses and net assets of its associates and joint ventures), after any adjustments necessary to give effect to the investor's accounting policies.

Example of accounting for intercompany transactions

Continue with the same information from the previous example and also assume that Elixir Company sold inventory to Regency Corporation in 2007 for €2,000 above Elixir's cost. Thirty percent of this inventory remains unsold by Regency at the end of 2007. Elixir's net income for 2007, including the gross profit on the inventory sold to Regency, is €20,000; Elixir's income tax rate is 34%. Regency should make the following journal entries for 2007 (ignoring deferred taxes):

1.	Investment in Elixir	8,000	
	Equity in Elixir income (€20,000 × 40%)		8,000
2.	Equity in Elixir income (amortization of differential)	3,600	
	Investment in Elixir		3,600
3.	Equity in Elixir income	158	
	Investment in Elixir (€2,000 × 30% × 66% × 40%)		158

The amount in the last entry needs further elaboration. Since 30% of the inventory remains unsold, only €600 of the intercompany profit is unrealized at year-end. This profit, net of income taxes, is €396. Regency's share of this profit (€158) is included in the first (€8,000) entry recorded. Accordingly, the third entry is needed to adjust or correct the equity in the reported net income of the investee.

Eliminating entries for intercompany profits in fixed assets are similar to those in the examples above. However, intercompany profit is realized only as the assets are depreciated by the purchasing entity. In other words, if an investor buys or sells fixed assets from or to an investee at a price above book value, the gain would only be realized piecemeal over the asset's remaining depreciable life. Accordingly, in the year of sale the pro rata share (based on the investor's percentage ownership interest in the investee, regardless of whether the sale is upstream or downstream) of the unrealized portion of the intercompany profit would have to be eliminated. In each subsequent year during the asset's life, the pro rata share of the gain realized in the period would be added to income from the investee.

Example of eliminating intercompany profit on fixed assets

Assume that Radnor Co., that owns 25% of Empanada Co., sold to Empanada a fixed asset having a five-year remaining life, at a gain of €100,000. Radnor Co. expects to remain in the 34% marginal tax bracket. The sale occurred at the end of 2005; Empanada Co. will use straight-line depreciation to amortize the asset over the years 2006 through 2010.

The entries related to the foregoing are

2005:

1.	Gain on sale of fixed asset	25,000	
	Deferred gain		25,000
	To defer the unrealized portion of the gain		
2.	Deferred tax benefit	8,500	
	Income tax expense		8,500
	Tax effect of gain deferral		

Alternatively, the 2005 events could have been reported by this single entry.

Equity in Empanada income	16,500	
Investment in Empanada Co.		16,500

2006 through 2010 (each year):

1.	Deferred gain	5,000	
	Gain on sale of fixed assets		5,000
	To amortize deferred gain		
2.	Income tax expense	1,700	
	Deferred tax benefit		1,700
	Tax effect of gain realization		

The alternative treatment would be

Investment in Empanada Co.	3,300	
Equity in Empanada income		3,300

In the example above, the tax currently paid by Radnor Co. (34% × €25,000 taxable gain on the transaction) is recorded as a deferred tax benefit in 2005 since taxes will not be due on the book gain recognized in the years 2006 through 2010. Under provisions of IAS 12, deferred tax benefits should be recorded to reflect the tax effects of all deductible timing differences. Unless Radnor Co. could demonstrate that future taxable amounts arising from existing temporary differences exist, this deferred tax benefit might be offset by an equivalent valuation allowance in Radnor Co.'s balance sheet at year-end 2005, because of the doubt that it will ever be realized. Thus, the deferred tax benefit might not be recognizable, net of the valuation allowance, for financial reporting purposes unless other temporary differences not specified in the example provided future taxable amounts to offset the net deductible effect of the deferred gain.

NOTE: *The deferred tax impact of an item of income for book purposes in excess of tax is the same as a deduction for tax purposes in excess of book.*

This is discussed more fully in Chapter 15.

Accounting for a partial sale or additional purchase of the equity investment. This section covers the accounting issues that arise when the investor either sells some or all of its equity or acquires additional equity in the investee. The consequence of these actions could involve discontinuation of the equity method of accounting, or resumption of the use of that method.

Example of accounting for a discontinuance of the equity method

Assume that Plato Corp. owns 10,000 shares (30%) of Xenia Co. common stock for which it paid €250,000 ten years ago. On July 1, 2006, Plato sells 5,000 Xenia shares for €375,000. The balance in the Investment in Xenia Co. account at January 1, 2006, was €600,000. Assume that all the original differential between cost and book value has been amortized. To calculate the gain (loss) on this sale of 5,000 shares, it is necessary first to adjust the investment account so that it is current as of the date of sale. Assuming that the investee had net income of €100,000 for the six months ended June 30, 2006, the investor should record the following entries:

1.	Investment in Xenia Co.	30,000	
	Equity in Xenia income (€100,000 × 30%)		30,000
2.	Income tax expense	2,040	
	Deferred tax liability (€30,000 × 20% × 34%)		2,040

The gain on sale can now be computed, as follows:

Proceeds on sale of 5,000 shares	€375,000
Book value of the 5,000 shares (€630,000 × 50%)	315,000
Gain from sale of Xenia common	€ 60,000

Two entries will be needed to reflect the sale: one to record the proceeds, the reduction in the investment account, and the gain (or loss); the other to record the tax effects thereof. Recall that the investor must have computed the deferred tax effect of the undistributed earnings of the investee that it had recorded each year, on the basis that those earnings either would eventually be paid as dividends or would be realized as capital gains. When those dividends are ultimately received or when the investment is disposed of, the deferred tax liability recorded previously must be amortized.

To illustrate, assume that the investor in this example, Plato Corp., provided deferred taxes at an effective rate for dividends (considering the assumed 80% exclusion of intercorporate dividends) of 6.8%. The realized capital gain will be taxed at an assumed 34%. For tax purposes, this gain is computed as (€375,000 − €125,000 =) €250,000, giving a tax effect of €85,000. For accounting purposes, the deferred taxes already provided are 6.8% × (€315,000 − €125,000), or €12,920. Accordingly, an additional tax expense of €72,080 is incurred on the sale, due to the fact that an additional gain was realized for book purposes (€375,000 − €315,000 = €60,000; tax at 34% = €20,400) *and* that the tax previously provided for at dividend income rates was lower than the real capital gains rate [€190,000 × (34% − 6.8%) = €51,680 extra tax due]. The entries are as follows:

1.	Cash	375,000	
	Investment in Xenia Co.		315,000
	Gain on sale of Xenia Co. stock		60,000
2.	Deferred tax liability	12,920	
	Income tax expense	72,080	
	Taxes payable—current		85,000

The gains (losses) from sales of investee stock are reported on the investor's income statement in the other income and expense section, assuming that a multistep income statement is presented.

According to IAS 28, an investor should discontinue use of the equity method when (1) it ceases to have significant influence in an associate while retaining some or all of its investment, or (2) the use of the equity method is no longer deemed to be appropriate because the associate is operating under severe and long-lasting restrictions that will limit its ability to transfer funds to the investor entity. When the equity method of accounting is discontinued due to a loss of significant influence, the carrying amount of the investment at the date that it ceases to be an associate shall be regarded as its cost on initial measurement as a financial asset under IAS 39.

In the foregoing example, the sale of stock reduced the percentage of the investee owned by the investor to 15%. In a situation such as this, discontinuation of the equity method is generally prescribed, although it is not inconceivable that significant influence can still be demonstrated at that ownership level, which would require continued application of equity method accounting.

The balance in the investment account on the date the equity method is suspended (€315,000 in the example) continues as an asset, but it then becomes subject to the IAS 39 requirement that it be accounted for at fair value. Passive equity investments are classified as either held-for-trading or available-for-sale; in this fact situation, categorization as available-for-sale is most likely. Under IAS 39, changes in fair value of available-for-sale investments are reported either in earnings or directly in equity, depending on the election made by the reporting entity upon first adoption. For purposes of this example, assume election of reporting changes in the fair value of available-for-sale investments will be shown in equity.

The change in ownership precipitates a change in accounting principle from equity method to fair value. This change does not require computation of a cumulative effect or any retroactive disclosures in the investor's financial statements. In periods subsequent to this change, the investor records cash dividends received from the investment as dividend revenue. Any dividends received in excess of the investor's share of post-disposal-date earnings of the investee (which are unlikely) should be credited to the investment account rather than to income, as they would represent a return of capital, rather than income.

An entity may hold an investment in another entity's common stock that is below the level that would create a presumption of significant influence, which it later increases so that the threshold for application of the equity method is exceeded. The guidance of IAS 28 would suggest that when the equity method is first applied, the difference between the carrying value of the investment and the fair value of the underlying net identifiable assets must be computed (as described earlier in the chapter). Even though IAS 39's fair value provisions were being applied, there will likely be a difference between the fair value of the passive investment (gauged by market prices for publicly-traded securities) and the fair value of the investee's underlying net assets (which are driven by the ability to generate cash flows, etc.). Thus, when the equity method accounting threshold is first exceeded for a formerly passively held investment, determination of the "goodwill-like" component of the investment will typically be necessary.

Example of accounting for a return to the equity method of accounting

Continuing the same example, Xenia Co. reported earnings for the second half of 2006 and all of 2007, respectively, of €150,000 and €350,000; Xenia paid dividends of €100,000 and €150,000 in December of those years. During the period from July 2006 through December 2007, Plato Corp. accounted for its investment in Xenia Co. as an investment in marketable securities, at fair value, with changes in carrying value being reflected directly in equity. At December 31, 2006, the fair value of Plato's holding of Xenia's stock is assessed at €335,000; at December 31, 2007, the fair value is €365,000.

In January 2008, the Plato Corp. purchased 10,000 Xenia shares in the open market for €700,000, thereby increasing its ownership share to 45% and necessitating a return to equity method accounting. The fair value of Plato's interest in the underlying identifiable net assets of Xenia at this date is €1,000,000. The relevant entries are as follows:

1.	Cash	15,000	
	Income from Xenia dividends		15,000
	To report dividends paid in 2006		
2.	Investment in Xenia Corp.	20,000	
	Unrealized gain on available-for-sale investment		20,000
	To reflect increased value of investment		
3.	Income tax expense	1,020	
	Unrealized gain on available-for-sale investment	6,800	
	Taxes payable—current		1,020
	Taxes payable—deferred		6,800
	To record taxes on dividends at current effective tax rate [€15,000 x .068] and deferred taxes on value increase [€20,000 x .34] in 2006		
4.	Cash	22,500	
	Income from Xenia dividends		22,500
	To report dividends paid in 2007		
5.	Investment in Xenia Corp.	30,000	
	Unrealized gain on available-for-sale investment		30,000
	To reflect increased value of investment		
6.	Income tax expense	1,530	
	Unrealized gain on available-for-sale investment	10,200	
	Taxes payable—current		1,530
	Taxes payable—deferred		10,200
	To record taxes on dividends at current effective tax rate [€22,500 x .068] and deferred taxes on value increase [€30,000 x .34] in 2006		
7.	Investment in Xenia Co.	700,000	
	Cash		700,000
	To record additional investment in Xenia		
8.	Unrealized gain on available-for-sale investment	33,000	
	Income from investment		33,000
	See explanation for this entry below		

The explanation for the last entry above is as follows. IAS 28 does not suggest that a return to the previously discontinued equity method would result in a restatement of the investment account and the additional equity and retained earnings accounts to "catch up" to what the balances would have been had that not taken place. Accordingly, the authors believe that the new cost basis of the investment at the time the equity method is reestablished should be the adjusted carrying amount immediately prior thereto. In the present example, the carrying amount was as follows:

Balance 6/30/06	€ 315,000
Adjust to fair value 12/06	20,000
Adjust to fair value 12/07	30,000
Balance, 12/07	€ 365,000
Additional investment, 1/08	700,000
Carrying value, 1/08	€1,065,000

The difference between the new cost basis, €1,065,000, and Plato's equity in Xenia's net identifiable assets, (€1,065,000 – €1,000,000 =) €65,000, would be treated similar to goodwill. Since goodwill is no longer subject to amortization, this must be assessed for impairment each year, as described in IFRS 3.

It would not be appropriate to carry forward the amount reflected in the additional equity account, €33,000, since the investment is no longer to be accounted for under IAS 39. Accordingly, in the authors' opinion, this should be reported as current period earnings, analogous to how the disposition of any other available-for-sale investment would be accounted for (where the unrealized gain or loss had been reported in equity, not in earnings during the holding period). The income will have been realized by adoption or readoption of the equity method. Note that the €33,000 balance is the net of the cumulative €50,000 upward revaluation recognized in 2006 and 2007 and the €17,000 tax provision, at capital gain rates (assumed in this example to be 34%), which was expected to pertain to the ultimate realization of this value increase. If, at the time the equity method is resumed, the effective tax rate is expected to differ from that used to compute deferred taxes earlier (e.g., due to the effect of the significant influence over the investee's dividend decisions), then there would be a need for an adjustment to the deferred tax provision.

To illustrate the latter point, assume that Plato now expects to realize all its income from Xenia in the form of dividends, to be taxed at an effective rate of 6.8%. The entry to adjust the deferred tax liability would be

Taxes payable—deferred	13,600	
Tax expense		13,600
To record adjustment to deferred taxes		

Note that the offset to the deferred tax adjustment is to current period (i.e., 2008) tax expense, under the rules of IAS 12, as described more fully in Chapter 15.

The foregoing illustration adjusts the additional equity account to earnings, since the resumption of equity method accounting is seen as an economic event of that period, similar to an outright sale of the investment. However, IAS 28 is silent on this matter and an argument could perhaps be made that this adjustment should be made to retained earnings directly, in effect as an adjustment to prior periods' earnings. This is the accounting prescribed under US GAAP.

Investor accounting for investee capital transactions. Investor accounting for investee capital transactions that affect the worth of the investor's investment is not addressed by IAS 28. However, given that ultimately the effect of using equity method accounting is intended to mirror full consolidation, it is logical that investee transactions of a capital nature, which affect the investor's share of the investee's stockholders' equity, should be accounted for as if the investee were a consolidated subsidiary. These transactions principally include situations where the investee purchases treasury stock from, or sells unissued shares or shares held in the treasury to, outside shareholders (i.e., owners other than the reporting entity). (Note that, if the investor participates in these transactions on a pro rata basis, its percentage ownership will not change and no special accounting would be necessary.) Similar results will be obtained when holders of outstanding options or convertible securities acquire additional investee common shares via exercise or conversion.

When the investee engages in one of the foregoing capital transactions, the investor's ownership percentage will be altered. This gives rise to a gain or loss, depending on whether the price paid (for treasury shares acquired) or received (for shares issued) is greater or lesser than the per share carrying value of the investor's interest in the investee. However, since no gain or loss can be recognized on capital transactions, these purchases or sales will be reflected in paid-in capital and/or retained earnings directly, without being reported through the investor's income statement. This method is consistent with the treatment that would be accorded to a consolidated subsidiary's capital transactions.

Example of accounting for an investee capital transaction

Assume that Roger Corp. purchases, on 1/2/06, 25% (2,000 shares) of Energetic Corp.'s outstanding shares for €80,000. The cost is equal to both the book and fair values of Roger's interest in Energetic's underlying net assets (i.e., there is no differential to be accounted for as goodwill). One week later, Energetic Corp. acquires 1,000 shares of its stock from other shareholders, in a treasury stock transaction, for €50,000. Since the price paid (€50/share) exceeded Roger Corp.'s per share carrying value of its interest, (€80,000 ÷ 2,000 shares =) €40, Roger Corp. has in fact suffered economic harm by virtue of this transaction. Also, Roger's percentage ownership of Energetic Corp. has increased, because the number of shares held by third parties, and total shares outstanding, have been reduced.

Roger Corp.'s new interest in Energetic's net assets is

$$\frac{2,000 \text{ shares held by Roger Corp.}}{7,000 \text{ shares outstanding in total}} \text{ x } \text{Energetic Corp. net assets}$$

$$= .2857 \times (€320,000 - €50,000) = €77,143$$

The interest held by Roger Corp. has thus been diminished by €80,000 – €77,143 = €2,857. Therefore, Roger Corp. should make the following entry:

Paid-in capital (or retained earnings)	2,857	
Investment in Energetic Corp.		2,857

Roger Corp. should charge the loss against paid-in capital only if paid-in capital from past transactions of a similar nature exists; otherwise, the debit must be made to retained earnings. Had the transaction given rise to a gain, it would have been credited to paid-in capital only (never to retained earnings) following the accounting principle that transactions in one's own shares cannot produce reportable earnings.

Note that the amount of the charge to paid-in capital (or retained earnings) in the entry above can be verified as follows: Roger Corp.'s share of the posttransaction net equity (2/7) times the excess price paid to outside interests (€50 – €40 = €10) times the number of shares purchased = 2/7 × €10 × 1,000 = €2,857.

Other than temporary impairment in value of equity method investments. IAS 28 provides that if there is a decline in value of an investment accounted for by the equity method which is determined to be "other than temporary" in nature, the carrying value of the investment should be adjusted downward. This criterion must be applied on an individual investment basis.

Other requirements of IAS 28. The standard requires that there be disclosure of the percentage of ownership that is held by the investor in each investment and, if it differs, the percentage of voting rights that are controlled. The method of accounting that is being applied to each significant investment should also be identified.

In addition, there may have been certain assumptions or adjustments made in developing information so that the equity method was applied. For example, the investee may have used different accounting principles than the investor, for which the investor made allowances in determining its share of the investee's operating results. The reported results of an investee that formerly used LIFO inventory accounting, for instance, may have been adjusted by the investor to conform to its FIFO costing method. Also, the investee's fiscal year may have differed from the investor's, and the investor may have converted this to its fiscal year by adding and subtracting stub period data. Revised IAS 28, effective 2005, states that a fiscal year-end difference of no more than three months will be permissible if unadjusted investee financial statements are to be employed. In any such case, if the impact is material, the fact of having made these adjustments should be disclosed, although it would be unusual to report the actual amount of such adjustments to users of the investor's financial statements.

If an associate has outstanding cumulative preferred stock, held by interests other than the investor, the investor should compute its equity interest in the investee's earnings after deducting dividends due to the preferred shareholders, whether or not declared. If material, this should be explained in the investor's financial statements.

When, due to the investor's recognition of recurring investee losses, the carrying value of the equity method investment has been reduced to zero, normally the investor will not recognize any share of further investee losses. If an investor ceases recognition of its share of losses of an investee, disclosure must be made in the notes to the financial statements of the unrecognized share of losses, both incurred during the current reporting period and cumulatively to date. The reason for the disclosure of cumulative unrecognized losses is that this is a measure of the amount of future investee earnings that will have to be realized before any further income will be reported in earnings by the investor.

There are certain exceptions to this rule. If the investor has incurred obligations or made payments on behalf of the associate to satisfy obligations of the associate that the investor has guaranteed or to which it is otherwise committed, whether funded or not, it should record further losses up to the amount of the guarantee or other commitment.

There are many common situations in which this occurs. For example, in the case of some closely held companies the investor negotiates banking facilities (both funded and unfunded) on the basis of the financial strength of the entire controlled group, not solely on the basis of the financial condition of the investee utilizing the borrowed funds. Where the investor has participated in the lending arrangements, even if its commitment is only moral, rather than contractual, it should be assumed that it will suffer losses beyond the nominal limit of its actual investment in the investee's shares, should that be necessary. For purposes of determining the total amount of losses which can be reflected in the investor's earnings, the interest in an associate is the carrying amount of the investment under the equity method plus items that, in substance, form part of the investor's investment in equity of the associate. Thus, for example, an item for which settlement is neither planned nor likely to occur in the foreseeable future is, in substance, an extension to or deduction from the entity's investment in equity. These additional investment items may include preferred shares and long-term receivables or loans; they would not include trade receivables or trade payables.

Impact of Potential Voting Interests on Application of Equity Method Accounting for Investments in Associates

Historically, actual voting interests in equity method investees has been the criterion used to determine (1) if equity method accounting for investees is to be employed; and (2) what percentage to apply in determining the allocation of the equity method investee's earnings to be included in the earnings of the equity method investor. However, the SIC has now addressed the situation in which the equity method investor has, in addition to its actual voting shareholder interest, a further potential voting interest in the investee.

The potential interest may exist in the form of options, warrants, convertible shares, or a contractual arrangement to acquire additional shares, including shares that it may have sold to another shareholder in the investee or to another party, with a right or contractual arrangement to reacquire the shares transferred.

As to whether the potential shares should be considered in reaching a decision as to whether significant influence is present, and thus whether reporting entity is to be regarded as the equity method investor and should therefore apply equity method accounting. Revised IAS 28 holds that this is indeed a factor to weigh (a position first taken by the now-withdrawn SIC 33). It has concluded that the existence and effect of potential voting rights that are presently exercisable or presently convertible should be considered, in addition to the other factors set forth in IAS 28, when assessing whether an entity significantly influences another entity. All potential voting rights should be considered, including potential voting rights held by other entities (which would counter the impact of the reporting entity's potential voting interest).

For example, an entity holding a 15% voting interest in another entity, but having options, not counterbalanced by options held by another party, to acquire another 15% voting interest, would thus effectively have a 30% current and potential voting interest, making use of the equity method of accounting for the investment required, under the provisions of revised IAS 28.

Regarding whether the potential share interest should be considered when determining what fraction of the investee's income should be allocated to the investor, the general answer is no. The proportion allocated to an investor that accounts for its investment using the equity method under IAS 28 should be determined based solely on present ownership interests.

However, the entity may, in substance, have a present ownership interest when it sells and simultaneously agrees to repurchase some of the voting shares it had held in the investee, but does not lose control of access to economic benefits associated with an ownership interest. In this circumstance, the proportion allocated should be determined taking into account the eventual exercise of potential voting rights and other derivatives that, in substance, presently give access to the economic benefits associated with an ownership interest. Note that the right to reacquire shares alone is not enough to have those shares included for purposes of determining the percentage of the investee's income to be reported by the investor. Rather, the investor must have ongoing access to the economic benefits of ownership of those shares.

Revised IAS 28 provides that losses recognized under the equity method in excess of the investor's common stock ownership will be applied to the other components of the investor's interest in an associate in the order of their seniority (i.e., in order of priority in liquidation). The investor will apply the requirements of IAS 39 to determine whether any additional impairment loss is recognized with respect to the other component of the investor's interest.

Once the investor's interest has been reduced to zero by its absorption of investee losses, any additional losses are provided for, and a liability is recognized, only to the extent that the investor has incurred obligations or made payments on behalf of the associate. If the associate subsequently reports profits, the investor would resume recognizing its share of those profits only after its share of the profits equals the share of net losses not recognized.

Apart from the foregoing considerations of investee loss recognition, the investor must assess possible impairment of value of the investment as required under IAS 36. This requires that the "value in use" of the investment be ascertained. In making such a determination, the investor must estimate

1. Its share of the present value of the estimated future cash flows expected to be generated by the investee as a whole, including the cash flows from the operations of the investee and the proceeds on the ultimate disposal of the investment; or
2. The present value of the estimated future cash flows expected to arise from dividends to be received from the investment and from its ultimate disposal.

Under appropriate assumptions (given a perfectly functioning capital market), both methods give the same result. Any resulting impairment loss for the investment is allocated in accordance with IAS 36. Accordingly, it would first be allocated to that component of the investment carrying value that reflects any underlying, remaining goodwill, as described earlier in this chapter.

Disclosure Requirements

IAS 28, as most recently revised (effective 2005), provides for extensive disclosures. These include

1. The fair value of investments in associates for which there are published price quotations;
2. Summarized financial information of associates, including the aggregated amounts of assets, liabilities, revenues, and profit or loss;
3. The reasons why the presumption that an investor does not have significant influence is overcome if the investor holds, directly or indirectly through subsidiaries, less than 20% of the voting or potential voting power of the investee but concludes that it has significant influence;
4. The reasons why the presumption that an investor has significant influence is overcome if the investor holds, directly or indirectly through subsidiaries, 20% or more of the voting or potential voting power of the investee but concludes that is does not have significant influence;
5. The reporting date of the financial statements of an associate when such financial statements are used in applying the equity method and are as of a reporting date or for a period that is different from that of the investor, and the reasons for using a different reporting date or different period;
6. The nature and extent of any restrictions on the ability of associates to transfer funds to the investor in the form of cash dividends, repayment of loans or advances (i.e., borrowing arrangements, regulatory restraint, etc.);
7. The unrecognized share of net losses of an associate, both for the period and cumulatively, if an investor has discontinued recognition of its share of losses of an associate.

Investments in associates accounted for using the equity method must be classified as long-term assets and disclosed as a separate item in the balance sheet. The investor's share of the after-tax profit or loss of such associates investments should be disclosed as a separate item in the income statement. The investor's share of any discontinuing operations of such associates also should be separately disclosed. Furthermore, the investor's share of changes in the associate's equity recognized directly in equity by the investor is to be disclosed in the statement of changes in equity required by IAS 1.

To comply with the requirements of IAS 37, the investor must disclose

1. Its share of the contingent liabilities of an associate for which it is also contingently liable; and
2. Those contingent liabilities that arise because the investor is severally liable for all liabilities of the associate.

Accounting for Investments in Joint Ventures

IFRS address accounting for interests in joint ventures as a topic separate from accounting for other investments. Joint ventures share many characteristics with investments that are accounted for by the equity method: The investor clearly has significant influence over the investee but does not have absolute control, and hence full consolidation is typically unwarranted. According to the provisions of IAS 31, two different methods of accounting are possible, although not as true alternatives for the same fact situations: the proportional consolidation method and the equity method.

Joint ventures can take many forms and structures. Joint ventures may be created as partnerships, as corporations, or as unincorporated associations. The standard identifies three distinct types, referred to as jointly controlled operations, jointly controlled assets, and jointly controlled entities. Notwithstanding the formal structure, all joint ventures are characterized by certain features: having two or more venturers that are bound by a contractual arrangement, and by the fact that the contractual agreement establishes joint control of the entity.

The contractual provision(s) establishing joint control most clearly differentiates joint ventures from other investment scenarios in which the investor has significant influence over the investee. In fact, in the absence of such a contractual provision, joint venture accounting would not be appropriate, even in a situation in which two parties each have 50% ownership interests in an investee. The actual existence of such a contractual provision can be evidenced in a number of ways, although most typically it is in writing and often addresses such matters as the nature, term of existence, and reporting obligations of the joint venture; the governing mechanisms for the venture; the capital contributions by the respective venturers; and the intended division of output, income, expenses, or net results of the venture.

The contractual arrangement also establishes joint control over the venture. The thrust of such a provision is to ensure that no venturer can control the venture unilaterally. Certain decision areas will be stipulated as requiring consent by all the venturers, while other decision areas may be defined as needing the consent of only a majority of the venturers. There is no specific set of decisions that must fall into either grouping, however.

Typically, one venturer will be designated as the manager or operator of the venture. This does not imply the absolute power to govern; however, if such power exists, the venture would be a subsidiary, subject to the requirements of IAS 27 and not accounted for properly under IAS 31. IAS 31 (as amended by the IASB's Improvements Project in late 2003) does not apply to interests in jointly controlled entities held by venture capital organizations, mutual funds, unit trusts, and similar entities that are measured at fair value in accordance with IAS 39, when such measurement is well established practice in those industries. When such investments are measured at fair value, changes in fair value are included in profit or loss in the period of the change.

Specific accounting guidance is dependent on whether the entity represents jointly controlled operations, jointly controlled assets, or a jointly controlled entity.

Jointly controlled operations. The first of three types of joint ventures, this is characterized by the assigned use of certain assets or other resources, in contrast to an establishment of a new entity, be it a corporation or partnership. Thus, from a formal or legal perspective, this variety of joint venture may not have an existence separate from its sponsors; from an economic point of view, however, the joint venture can still be said to exist, which means that it may exist as an accounting entity. Typically, this form of operation will utilize assets owned by the venture partners, often including plant and equipment as well as inventories, and the partners will sometimes incur debt on behalf of the operation. Actual operations may be conducted on an integrated basis with the partners' own, separate operations, with certain employees, for example, devoting a part of their efforts to the jointly controlled operation. The European consortium Airbus may be a prototype of this type of entity.

IAS 31 is concerned not with the accounting by the entity conducting the jointly controlled operations, but by the venturers having an interest in the entity. Each venturer should recognize in its separate financial statements all assets of the venture that it controls, all liabilities that it incurs, all expenses that it incurs, and its share of any revenues produced by the venture. Often, since the assets are already owned by the venturers, they would be included in their respective financial statements in any event; similarly, any debt incurred will be reported by the partner even absent this special rule. Perhaps the only real challenge, from a measurement and disclosure perspective, would be the revenues attributable to each venture's efforts, which will be determined by reference to the joint venture agreement and other documents.

Note that joint control may be precluded when an investee is in legal reorganization or in bankruptcy, or operates under severe long-term restrictions on its ability to transfer funds to the venturer; in such cases, application of IAS 31 would not be appropriate.

Jointly controlled assets. In certain industries, such as oil and gas exploration and transmission and mineral extraction, jointly controlled assets are frequently employed. For example, oil pipelines may be controlled jointly by a number of oil producers, each of which uses the facilities and shares in its costs of operation. Certain informal real estate partnerships may also function in this fashion.

IAS 31 stipulates that in the case of jointly controlled assets, each venturer must report in its own financial statements its share of all jointly controlled assets, appropriately classified according to their natures. It must also report any liabilities that it has incurred on behalf of these jointly controlled assets, as well as its share of any jointly incurred liabilities. Each venturer will report any income earned from the use its share of the jointly controlled assets, along with the pro rata expenses and any other expenses it has incurred directly.

Jointly controlled entities. The major type of joint venture is the jointly controlled entity, which is really a form of partnership (although it may well be structured legally as a corporation) in which each partner has a form of control, rather than only significant influence. The classic example is an equal partnership of two partners; obviously, neither has a majority and either can block any important action, so the two partners must effectively agree on each key decision. Although this may be the model for a jointly controlled entity, it may in practice have more than two venturers and, depending on the partnership or shareholders' agreement, even minority owners may have joint control. For example, a partnership whose partners have 30%, 30%, 30%, and 10% interests, respectively, may have entered into a contractual agreement that stipulates that investment or financing actions may be taken only if there is unanimity among the partners.

Jointly controlled entities control the assets of the joint venture and may incur liabilities and expenses on its behalf. As a legal entity, it may enter into contracts and borrow funds, among other activities. In general, each venturer will share the net results in proportion to its ownership interest. As an entity with a distinct and separate legal and economic identity, the jointly controlled entity will normally produce its own financial statements and other tax and legal reports.

IAS 31 provides alternative accounting treatments that may be applied by the venture partners to reflect the operations and financial position of the venture. The objective is to report economic substance, rather than mere form, but there is not universal agreement on how this may best be achieved.

The benchmark treatment under the standard is the use of proportionate consolidation, which requires that the venture partner reflect its share of all assets, liabilities, revenues, and expenses on its financial statements as if these were incurred or held directly. In fact, this technique is very effective at conveying the true scope of an entity's operations, when those operations include interests in one or more jointly controlled entities. In this regard, IFRS are more advanced than US, UK, or other national standards, which at best permit proportionate consolidation but do not mandate this accounting treatment.

If the venturer employs the proportionate consolidation method, it will have a choice between two presentation formats that are equally acceptable. First, the venture partner may include its share of the assets, liabilities, revenues, and expenses of the jointly controlled entity with similar items under its sole control. Thus, under this method, its share of the venture's receivables would be added to its own accounts receivable and presented as a single total on its balance sheet. Alternatively, the items that are undivided interests in the venture's assets, and so on, may be shown on separate lines of the venture's financial statements, although still placed within the correct grouping. For example, the venture's receivables might be shown immediately below the partner's individually owned accounts receivable. In either case, the same category totals (aggregate current assets, etc.) will be presented; the only distinction is whether the venture-owned items are given separate recognition. Even if presented on a combined basis, however, the appropriate detail can still be shown in the financial statement footnotes, and indeed to achieve a fair presentation, this might be needed.

The proportionate consolidation method should be discontinued when the partner no longer has the ability to control the entity jointly. This may occur when the interest is held for disposal within twelve months from acquisition date, or when external restrictions are placed on the ability to exercise control. In some cases a partner will waive its right to control the entity, possibly in exchange for other economic advantages, such as a larger interest in the operating results. In such instances, IAS 39 should be used to guide the accounting for the investment.

Under the provisions of IAS 31, a second accounting method, the equity method, is also considered to be acceptable. The equity method in this context is as described in IAS 28 and as explained in the preceding section. As with the proportionate consolidation method, use of the equity method must be discontinued when the venturer no longer has joint control or significant influence over the jointly controlled entity. In such a case, IAS 39 would be the relevant accounting requirement.

Accounting for jointly controlled entities as passive investments. Although the expectation is that investments in jointly controlled entities will be accounted for by the proportionate consolidation or equity method (the benchmark and allowed alternative treatments, respectively), in certain circumstances the venturer should account for its interest following the guidelines of IAS 39, that is, as a passive investment. This would be the prescription when the investment has been acquired and is being held with a view toward disposition within twelve months of the acquisition, or when the investee is operating under severe long-term restrictions that severely impair its ability to transfer funds to its venturer owners.

If the investment is seen as being strictly temporary, effectively it is being held for trading purposes in the same manner as a temporary investment in marketable securities would be. In such a situation it would not be logical to apply either the proportionate consolidation or equity method, since it would not be the venture's share of the operating results of the venture that provided value to the venturer, but rather, the change in fair value.

Similarly, if the venture were operating under such severe restrictions, expected to persist beyond a short time horizon, that transfers of funds from the jointly controlled entity to its venture parents were precluded, it would be misleading and conceptually invalid to treat the venture's operating results as bearing directly on the venture parents' earnings results. In such a case, an inability to transfer funds would mean that the venture partners would be unable to obtain any benefit, in the short run at least, from their investment in the jointly controlled entity.

As amended by IAS 39, IAS 31 provides that in the separate financial statements of an investor that issues consolidated financial statements as well, the cost method may alternatively be employed to present the investment in the joint venture.

Change from joint control to full control status. If one of the venturers' interest in the jointly controlled entity is increased, whether by an acquisition of some or all of another of the venturers' interest, or by action of a contractual provision of the venture agreement (resulting from a failure to perform by another venturer, etc.), the proportionate consolidation method of accounting ceases to be appropriate and full consolidation will become necessary. Guidance on preparation of consolidated financial statements is provided by IAS 27 and is discussed fully in Chapter 11.

Accounting for Transactions between Venture Partner and Jointly Controlled Entity

Transfers at a gain to the transferor. A general, underlying principle of financial reporting is that earnings are to be realized only by engaging in transactions with outside parties. Thus, gains cannot be recognized by transferring assets (be they productive assets or goods held for sale in the normal course of the business) to a subsidiary, affiliate, or joint venture, to the extent this really would represent a transaction by an entity with itself. Were this not the rule, entities would establish a range of related entities to sell goods to, thereby permitting the reporting of profits well before any sale to real, unrelated customers ever took place. The potential for abuse of the financial reporting process in such a scenario is too obvious to need elaboration.

IAS 31 stipulates that when a venturer sells or transfers assets to a jointly controlled entity, it may recognize profit only to the extent that the venture is owned by the other venture partners, and then only to the extent that the risks and rewards of ownership have indeed been transferred to the jointly controlled entity. The logic is that a portion of the profit has in fact been realized, to the extent that the purchase was agreed on by unrelated parties that jointly control the entity making the acquisition. For example, if venturers A, B, and C jointly control venture D (each having a 1/3 interest), and A sells equipment having a book value of €40,000 to the venture for €100,000, only 2/3 of the apparent gain of €60,000, or €40,000, may be realized. In its balance sheet immediately after this transaction, A would report its share of the asset reflected in the balance sheet of D, 1/3 × €100,000 = €33,333, minus the unrealized gain of €20,000, for a net of €13,333. This is identical to A's remaining 1/3 interest in the pretransaction basis of the asset (1/3 × €40,000 = €13,333). Thus, there is no step up in the carrying value of the proportionate share of the asset reflected in the transferor's balance sheet.

If the asset is subject to depreciation, the deferred gain on the transfer (1/3 × €60,000 = €20,000) would be amortized in proportion to the depreciation reflected by the venture, such that the depreciated balance of the asset reported by A is the same as would have been reported had the transfer not taken place. For example, assume that the asset has a useful economic life of five years after the date of transfer to D. The deferred gain (€20,000) would be amortized to income at a rate of €4,000 per year. At the end of the first post-transfer year, D would report a net carrying value of €100,000 – €20,000 = €80,000; A's proportionate interest is 1/3 × €80,000 = €26,667. The unamortized balance of the deferred gain is €20,000 – €4,000 = €16,000. Thus the net reported amount of A's share of the jointly controlled entity's asset is €26,667 – €16,000 = €10,667. This amount is precisely what A would have reported the remaining share of its asset at on this date: 1/3 × (€40,000 – €8,000) = €10,667.

Of course, A has also reported a gain of €40,000 as of the date of the transfer of its asset to joint venture D, but this represents the gain that has been realized by the sale of 2/3 of the asset to unrelated parties B and C, the covertures in D. In short, two-thirds of the asset has been sold at a gain, while one-third has been retained and is continuing to be used and depreciated over its remaining economic life and is reported on the cost basis in A's financial statements.

The matters described above have been further emphasized by the Standing Interpretation Committee's interpretation, SIC 13, which holds that gains or losses will result from contributions of nonmonetary assets to a jointly controlled entity *only* when significant risks and rewards of ownership have been transferred, and the gain or loss can be reliably measured. However, no gain or loss would be recognized when the asset is contributed in exchange for an equity interest in the jointly controlled entity when the asset is similar to assets contributed by the other venturers. Any unrealized gain or loss should be netted against the related assets, and not presented as deferred gain or loss in the venture's consolidated financial statements.

Transfers of assets at a loss. The foregoing illustration was predicated on a transfer to the jointly controlled entity at a nominal gain to the transferor, of which a portion was realized for financial reporting purposes. The situation when a transfer is at an amount below the transferor's carrying value is not analogous; rather, such a transfer is deemed to be confirmation of a permanent decline in value, which must be recognized by the transferor immediately rather than being deferred. This reflects the conservative bias in accounting: Unrealized losses are often recognized, while unrealized gains are deferred.

Assume that venturer C (a 1/3 owner of D, as described above) transfers an asset it had been carrying at €150,000 to jointly controlled entity D at a price of €120,000. If the decline is deemed to be other than temporary in nature (that presumptively it is, since C would not normally have been willing to engage in this transaction if the decline were expected to be reversed in the near term), C must recognize the full €30,000 at the time of the transfer. Subsequently, C will pick up its 1/3 interest in the asset held by D (1/3 × €120,000 = €40,000) as its own asset in its balance sheet, before considering any depreciation, and so on.

Accounting for Assets Purchased from a Jointly Controlled Entity

Transfers at a gain to the transferor. A similar situation arises when a venture partner acquires an asset from a jointly controlled entity: The venturer cannot reflect the gain recognized by the joint venture, to the extent that this represents its share in the results of the venture's operations. For example, again assuming that A, B, and C jointly own D, an asset having a book value of €200,000 is transferred by D to B for a price of €275,000. Since B has a 1/3 interest in D, it would (unless an adjustment were made to its accounting) report €25,000 of D's gain as its own, which would violate the realization concept under GAAP.

To avoid this result, B will record the asset at its cost, €275,000, less the deferred gain, €25,000, for a net carrying value of €250,000, which represents the transferor's basis, €200,000, plus the increase in value realized by unrelated parties (A and C) in the amount of €50,000.

As the asset is depreciated, the deferred gain will be amortized apace. For example, assume that the useful life of the asset in B's hands is ten years. At the end of the first year, the carrying value of the asset is €275,000 – €27,500 = €247,500; the unamortized balance of the deferred gain is €25,000 – €2,500 = €22,500. Thus the net carrying value, after offsetting the remaining deferred gain, will be €247,500 – €22,500 = €225,000. This corresponds to the remaining life of the asset (9/10 of its estimated life) times its original net carrying amount, €250,000. The amortization of the deferred gain should be credited to depreciation expense to offset the depreciation charged on the nominal acquisition price and thereby to reduce it to a cost basis as required by GAAP.

Transfers at a loss to the transferor. If the asset was acquired by B at a loss to D, on the other hand, and the decline was deemed to be indicative of an other than temporary diminution in value, B should recognize its share of this decline. This contrasts with the gain scenario discussed immediately above, and as such is entirely consistent with the accounting treatment for transfers from the venture partner to the jointly controlled venture.

For example, if D sells an asset carried at €50,000 to B for €44,000, and the reason for this discount is an other than temporary decline in the value of said asset, the venture, D, records a loss of €6,000 and each venture partner will in turn recognize a €2,000 loss. B would report the asset at its acquisition cost of €44,000 and will also report its share of the loss, €2,000. This loss will not be deferred and will not be added to the carrying value of the asset in B's hands (as would have been the case if B treated only the €4,000 loss realized by unrelated parties A and C as being recognizable).

Disclosure Requirements

A venture partner is required to disclose in the notes to the financial statements its ownership interests in all significant joint ventures, including its ownership percentage and other relevant data. If the venturer uses proportionate consolidation and merges its share of the assets, liabilities, revenues, and expenses of the jointly controlled entity with its own assets, liabilities, revenues, and expenses, or if the venturer uses the equity method, the notes should disclose the amounts of the current and long-term assets, current and long-term liabilities, revenues, and expenses related to its interests in jointly controlled ventures.

Furthermore, the joint venture partner should disclose any contingencies that the venturer has incurred in relation to its interests in any joint ventures, noting any share of contingencies jointly incurred with other joint venturers. In addition, the venturer's share of any contingencies of the joint venture (as distinct from contingencies incurred in connection with its investment in the venture) for which it may be contingently liable must be reported. Finally, those contingencies that arise because the venturer is contingently liable for the liabilities of the other partners in the jointly controlled entity must be set forth. These disclosures are a logical application of the rules set forth in IAS 37, which is discussed in Chapter 12 of this book.

A venture partner should also disclose in the notes to her/his financial statements information about any commitments s/he has outstanding in respect to interests s/he has in joint ventures. These include any capital commitments s/he has and her/his share of any joint commitments s/he may have incurred with other venture partners, as well as her/his share of the capital commitments of the joint ventures themselves, if any.

Accounting for Investment Property

Investment property. An investment in land or a building, part of a building, or both, if held by the owner (or a lessee under a finance lease) with the intention of earning rentals or for capital appreciation or both, is defined by IAS 40 as an investment property. An investment property is capable of generating cash flows independently of other assets held by the entity. Investment property is sometimes referred to as being "passive" investments, to distinguish it from actively managed property such as plant assets, the use of which is integrated with the rest of the entity's operations. This characteristic is what distinguishes investment property from owner-occupied property, which is property held by the entity or a lessee under a finance lease, for use in its business (i.e., for use in production or supply of goods or services or for administrative purposes).

Revised IAS 40, effective in 2005, for the first time permits property interests held in the form of operating leases to be classified and accounted for as investment property. This may be done if

1. The other elements of the definition of investment property (see below) are met;
2. The operating lease is accounted for as if it were a finance lease in accordance with IAS 17 (that is, it is capitalized); and
3. The lessee uses the fair value model set out in IAS 40 for the asset recognized.

This classification option—to report the lessee's property interest as investment property—is available on a property-by-property basis. On the other hand, IAS 40 requires that all investment property should be consistently accounted for, employing either the fair value or cost model. Given these requirements, it is held that once the investment alternative is selected for one leased property, all property classified as investment property must be accounted for consistently, on the fair value basis.

The best way to understand what investment property constitutes is to look at examples of investments that are considered by the standard as investment properties, and contrast these with those investments that do not qualify for this categorization.

According to the standard, examples of investment property are

- Land held for long-term capital appreciation as opposed to short-term purposes like land held for sale in the ordinary course of business;
- Land held for an undetermined future use;
- Building owned by the reporting entity (or held by the reporting entity under a finance lease) and leased out under one or more operating leases; and
- Vacant building held by an entity to be leased out under one or more operating leases.

According to IAS 40, investment property does *not* include

- Property employed in the business, (i.e., held for use in production or supply of goods or services or for administrative purposes, the accounting for which is governed by IAS 16);
- Property being constructed or developed on behalf of others, the accounting of which is outlined in IAS 11;
- Property held for sale in the ordinary course of the business, the accounting for which is specified by IAS 2; and
- Property under construction or being developed for future use as investment property. IAS 16 is applied to such property until the construction or development is completed, at which time, IAS 40 governs. However, existing investment property that is being redeveloped for continued future use would qualify as investment property.

Apportioning property between investment property and owner-occupied property. In many cases it will be clear what constitutes investment property as opposed to owner-occupied property, but in other instances making this distinction might be less obvious. Certain properties are not held entirely for rental purposes or for capital appreciation purposes. For example, portions of these properties might be used by the entity for manufacturing or for administrative purposes. If these portions, earmarked for different purposes, could be sold separately, then the entity is required to account for them separately. However, if the portions cannot be sold separately, the property would be deemed as investment property if an insignificant portion is held by the entity for business use.

When ancillary services are provided by the entity and these ancillary services are a relatively insignificant component of the arrangement, as when the owner of a residential building provides maintenance and security services to the tenants, the entity treats such an investment as investment property. On the other hand, if the service provided is a comparatively significant component of the arrangement, then the investment would be considered as an owner-occupied property.

For instance, an entity that owns and operates a motel and also provides services to the guests of the motel would be unable to argue that it is an investment property as that term is used by IAS 40. Rather, such an investment would be classified as an owner-occupied property. Judgment is therefore required in determining whether a property qualifies as investment property. It is so important a factor that if an entity develops criteria for determining when to classify a property as an investment property, it is required by this standard to disclose these criteria in the context of difficult or controversial classifications.

Property leased to a subsidiary or a parent company. Property leased to a subsidiary or its parent company is considered an investment property from the perspective of the entity. However, for the purposes of consolidated financial statements, from the perspective of the group as a whole, it will not qualify as an investment property, since it is an owner-occupied property when viewed from the parent company level.

Recognition and measurement. Investment property will be recognized when it becomes probable that the entity will enjoy the future economic benefits which are attributable to it, and when the cost or fair value can be reliably measured. In general, this will occur when the property is first acquired or constructed by the reporting entity. In only unusual circumstances would it be concluded that the owner's likelihood of receipt of the economic benefits would be less than probable, necessitating deferral of initial recognition of the asset.

Initial measurement will be at cost, which is equivalent to fair value, assuming that the acquisition was the result of an arm's-length exchange transaction. Included in the purchase cost will be such directly attributable expenditure as legal fees and property transfer taxes, if incurred in the transaction. If the asset is self-constructed, cost will include not only direct expenditures on product or services consumed, but also overhead charges which can be allocated on a reasonable and consistent basis, in the same manner as these are allocated to inventories under the guidelines of IAS 2. To the extent that the acquisition cost includes an interest charge, if the payment is deferred, the amount to be recognized as an investment asset should not include the interest charges. Furthermore, start-up costs (unless they are essential in bringing the property to its working condition), initial operating losses (incurred prior to the investment property achieving planned level of occupancy) or abnormal waste (in construction or development) do not constitute part of the capitalized cost of an investment property. If an investment property is acquired in exchange for equity instruments of the reporting entity, the cost of the investment property is the fair value of the equity instruments issued, although the fair value of the investment property received is used to measure its cost if it is more clearly evident than the fair value of the equity instruments issued.

Subsequent expenditures. In some instances there may be further expenditure incurred on the investment property after the date of initial recognition. Consistent with similar situations arising in connection with plant, property and equipment (dealt with under IAS 16), if it can be demonstrated that the subsequent expenditure will enhance the generation of future economic benefits to the entity, then those costs may be added to the carrying value of the investment property. That is, the cost can be capitalized only when it is probable that it increases the future economic benefits, in excess of its standard of performance assessed immediately before the expenditure was made. By implication, all other subsequent expenditure should be expensed in the periods they are incurred.

Sometimes, the appropriate accounting treatment for subsequent expenditure would depend upon the circumstances that were considered in the initial measurement and recognition of the investment property. For example, if a property (e.g., an office building) is acquired for investment purposes in a condition that makes it incumbent upon the entity to perform significant renovations thereafter, then such renovation costs (which would constitute subsequent expenditures) will be added to the carrying value of the investment property when incurred later.

Fair value model vs. historical cost. Analogous to the financial reporting of plant and equipment under IAS 16, IAS 40 provides that investment property may be reported at either fair value or at depreciated (historical) cost less accumulated impairment. The cost model is the benchmark treatment prescribed by IAS 16 for plant assets. The fair value approach under IAS 40 more closely resembles that used for financial instruments than it does the allowed alternative (revaluation) method for plant assets, however. Also, under IAS 40 if the cost method is used, fair value information must nonetheless be disclosed.

Fair value. When investment property is carried at fair value, at each subsequent financial reporting date the carrying amount must be adjusted to the then-current fair value, with the adjustment being reported in the net profit or loss for the period in which it arises. The inclusion of the value adjustments in earnings—in contrast to the revaluation approach under IAS 16, whereby adjustments are generally reported in equity—is a reflection of the different roles played by plant assets and by other investment property. The former are used, or consumed, in the operation of the business, which is often centered upon the production of goods and services for sale to customers. The latter are held for possible appreciation in value, and hence those value changes are highly germane to the assessment of periodic operating performance. With this distinction in mind, the decision was made to not only permit fair value reporting, but to require value changes to be included in earnings.

IAS 40 represents the first time that fair value accounting is being embraced as an accounting model for nonfinancial assets. This has been a matter of great controversy, and to address the many concerns voiced during the exposure draft stage, the IASC added more guidance on the subject to the final standard. This standard is quite comprehensive, and it includes some very insightful and practical hints on applying the standard.

Fair value is defined by the standard as the most probable price reasonably obtainable in the marketplace at the balance sheet date. Fair value would not be appropriately measured with reference to either a past or a future date. Further, the definition envisions "knowledgeable, willing parties" as being the arbiters of fair value. This presupposes that both the buyer and seller are willing to enter into the transaction, and that they each have reasonable knowledge about the nature and characteristics of the investment property, its potential uses, and the state of the market as of the valuation date. Put another way, fair value presumes that neither the buyer nor the seller is acting under coercion; and fair value is not a price that is based on a "distress sale."

The standard goes into great detail to explain the concept of a "willing buyer" (i.e., one who is motivated but not compelled to buy) and a "willing seller" (i.e., one who is neither overeager nor a forced seller). For instance, in explaining the concept of a "willing seller," the standard clarifies that the motivation to sell at market terms for the best price obtainable in the open market is derived "after proper marketing." This expression has been explained very eloquently by the standard to mean that in order to be considered as "after proper marketing," the investment property would need to be "exposed to the market" in the most appropriate manner to effect its disposal at the best price obtainable. The length of exposure time, according to the standard, must be "sufficient" to allow the investment property to be brought to the attention of an "adequate number" of potential purchasers.

As if there were not enough unknowns in the equation, the standard further qualifies this by stating that the "exposure period" is assumed to occur "prior to the balance sheet date." With respect to the length of the exposure period, the standard opines that "it may vary with market conditions." Some may find this an example of "overkill" which confuses, rather than clarifies the standard and impedes attempts to apply it. However, given that this is the maiden attempt by the IASC to mandate fair value accounting for nonfinancial assets, it may in hindsight be warranted.

The standard *encourages* an entity to determine the fair value based on a valuation by an independent valuer who holds a recognized and relevant professional qualification and who has had recent experience in the location and category of the investment property being valued. While terms such as "relevant" are not defined, IAS 40 does offer a significant amount of practical guidance on issues relating to the determination of fair values. These practical hints will likely greatly facilitate the correct application of the principles enshrined in the standard. They are summarized as follows:

- Factors that could distort the value, such as the incorporation of particularly favorable or unfavorable financing terms, the inclusion of sale and leaseback arrangements, or any other concession by either buyer or seller, are not to be given any consideration in the valuation process;
- On the other hand, the actual conditions in the marketplace at the valuation date, even if these represent somewhat atypical climatic factors, will govern the valuation process. For example, if the economy is in the midst of a recession and rental properties' prices are depressed, no attempt should be made to normalize fair value, since that would add a subjective element and depart from the concept of fair value as of the balance sheet date;
- Fair values should be determined without any deduction for transaction costs that the entity may incur on the sale or other disposal of the investment property;
- Fair value should reflect the actual state of the market and circumstances as of the balance sheet date, not as of either a past or a future date;
- In the absence of current prices on an active market, an entity should use information from a variety of sources, including: current prices on an active market of dissimilar properties with suitable adjustments for the differences, recent prices on less active markets, with necessary adjustments, and discounted cash flow projections based on reliable estimates of future cash flows using an appropriate discount rate;
- Fair value differs from "value in use" as defined in IAS 36. Whereas fair value is reflective of market knowledge and estimates of participants in the market in general, value in use reflects the entity's knowledge and estimates that are entity-specific and are thus not applicable to entities in general. In other words, value in use is an estimate at the entity level or at a "microlevel," while fair value is a "macrolevel" concept that is reflective of the perceptions of the market participants in general;
- Entities are alerted to the possibility of double counting in determining the fair value of certain types of investment property. For instance, when an office building is leased on a furnished basis, the fair value of office furniture and fixtures is generally included in the fair value of the investment property (in this case the office building). The IASC's apparent rationale is that the rental income relates to the furnished office building; when fair values of furniture and fixtures are included along with the fair value of the investment property, the entity does not recognize them as separate assets; and
- Lastly, the fair value of investment property should neither reflect the future capital expenditure (that would improve or enhance the property), nor the related future benefits from this future expenditure.

Inability to measure fair value reliably. There is a rebuttable presumption that, if an entity acquires or constructs property that will qualify as investment property under this standard, it will be able to assess fair value reliably on an ongoing basis. In rare circumstances, however, when an entity acquires for the first time an investment property (or when an existing property first qualifies to be classified as investment property following the completion of development or construction, or when there has been change of use), there may be clear evidence that the fair value of the investment property cannot reliably be determined, on a continuous basis.

Under such exceptional circumstances, the standard stipulates that the entity should measure that investment property using the benchmark treatment in IAS 16 until the disposal of the investment property. According to IAS 40, the residual value of such investment property measured under the benchmark treatment in IAS 16 should be presumed to be zero. The standard further states that under the exceptional circumstances explained above, in the case of an entity that uses the fair value model, the entity should measure the other investment properties held by it at fair values. In other words, notwithstanding the fact that one of the investment properties, due to exceptional circumstances, is being carried under the benchmark (cost) treatment in IAS 16, an entity that uses the fair value model should continue carrying the other investment properties at fair values. While this results in a mixed measure of the aggregate investment property, it underlines the perceived importance of the fair value method.

Transfers to or from investment property. Transfers to or from investment property should be made only when there is demonstrated "change in use" as contemplated by the standard. A change in use takes place when there is a transfer

- From investment property to owner-occupied property, when owner-occupation commences;
- From investment property to inventories, on commencement of development with a view to sale;
- From an owner-occupied property to investment property, when owner-occupation ends;
- Of inventories to investment property, when an operating lease to a third party commences; or
- Of property in the course of development or construction to investment property, at end of the construction or development.

In the case of an entity that employs the cost model, transfers between investment property, owner-occupied property and inventories do not change the carrying amount of the property transferred and thus do not change the cost of that property for measurement or disclosure purposes. When the investment property is carried under the fair value model, vastly different results follow as far as recognition and measurement is concerned. These are explained below.

1. **Transfers from (or to) investment property to (or from) plant and equipment (in the case of investment property carried under the fair value model).** In some instances, property that at first is appropriately classified as investment property under IAS 40 may later become plant, property, and equipment as defined under IAS 16. For example, a building is obtained and leased to unrelated parties, but at a later date the entity expands its own operations to the extent that it now chooses to utilize the building formerly held as a passive investment for its own purposes, such as for the corporate executive offices. The amount reflected in the accounting records as the fair value of the property as of the date of change in status would become the cost basis for subsequent accounting purposes. Previously recognized changes in value, if any, would not be reversed.

    Similarly, if property first classified as owner-occupied property and treated as plant and equipment under the benchmark treatment of IAS 16 is later redeployed as investment property, it is to be measured at fair value at the date of the change in its usage. If the value is lower than the carrying amount (i.e., if there is a previously unrecognized decline in its fair value) then this will be reflected in earnings in the period of redeployment as an investment property. On the other hand, if there has been an unrecognized increase in value, the accounting will depend on whether this is a reversal of a previously recognized value impairment. If the increase is a reversal of a decline in value, the increase should be recognized currently in earnings; the amount so reported, however, should not exceed the amount needed to restore the carrying amount to what it would have been, net of depreciation, had the earlier impairment loss not occurred.

If, on the other hand, there was no previously recognized impairment which the current value increase is effectively reversing (or, to the extent that the current increase exceeds the earlier decline), then the increase should be reported directly in equity, by means of the statement of changes in equity. If the investment property is later disposed of, any resultant gain or loss computation should *not* include the effect of the amount reported directly in equity.

2. **Transfers from inventory to investment property (in the case of investment property carried under the fair value model).** It may also happen that property originally classified as inventory, originally held for sale in the normal course of the business, is later redeployed as investment property. When reclassified, the initial carrying amount should be fair value as of that date. Any gain or loss resulting from this reclassification would be reported in current period's earnings. IAS 40 does not contemplate reclassification from investment property to inventory, however. When the entity determines that property held as investment property is to be disposed of, that property should be retained as investment property until actually sold. It should not be derecognized (eliminated from the balance sheet) or transferred to an inventory classification.

3. **Transfer on completion of construction or development of self-constructed investment property (to be carried at fair value).** On completion of construction or development of self-constructed investment property that will be carried at fair value, any difference between the fair value of the property at that date and its previous carrying amount should be recognized in the net income or loss for the period.

Disposal and retirement of investment property. An investment property should be derecognized (i.e., eliminated from the balance sheet of the entity) on disposal or when it is permanently withdrawn from use and no future economic benefits are expected from its disposal. The word "disposal" has been used in the standard to mean not only a sale but also the entering into of a finance lease by the entity. Any gains or losses on disposal or retirement of an investment property should be determined as the difference between the net disposal proceeds and the carrying amount of the asset and should be recognized in the net income or loss for the period.

Disclosure requirements. It is anticipated that in certain cases investment property will be property that is owned by the reporting entity and leased to others under operating-type lease arrangements. The disclosure requirements set forth in IAS 17 (and discussed in Chapter 14) continue unaltered by IAS 40. In addition, IAS 40 stipulates a number of new disclosure requirements set out below.

1. **Disclosures applicable to all investment properties**

   - When classification is difficult, an entity that holds an investment property will need to disclose the criteria used to distinguish investment property from owner-occupied property and from property held for sale in the ordinary course of business.
   - The methods and any significant assumptions that were used in ascertaining the fair values of the investment properties are to be disclosed as well. Such disclosure also includes a statement about whether the determination of fair value was supported by market evidence or relied heavily on other factors (which the entity

needs to disclose as well) due to the nature of the property and the absence of comparable market data.

- If investment property has been revalued by an independent appraiser, having recognized and relevant qualifications, and who has recent experience with properties having similar characteristics of location and type, the extent to which the fair value of investment property (either used in case the fair value model is used or disclosed in case the cost model is used) is based on valuation by such an independent valuer. If there is no such valuation, that fact should be disclosed as well.
- The following should be disclosed in the income statement:

  - The amount of rental income derived from investment property;
  - Direct operating expenses (including repairs and maintenance) arising from investment property that generated rental income; and
  - Direct operating expenses (including repairs and maintenance) arising from investment property that did not generate rental income.
  - The existence and the amount of any restrictions which may potentially affect the realizability of investment property or the remittance of income and proceeds from disposal to be received; and
  - Material contractual obligations to purchase or build investment property or for repairs, maintenance or improvements thereto.

2. **Disclosures applicable to investment property measured using the fair value model**

   - In addition to the disclosures outlined above, the standard requires that an entity that uses the fair value model should also present a reconciliation of the carrying amounts of the investment property, from the beginning to the end of the reporting period. The reconciliation will separately identify additions resulting from acquisitions, those resulting from business combinations, and those deriving from capitalized expenditures subsequent to the property's initial recognition. It will also identify disposals, gains or losses from fair value adjustments, the net exchange differences, if any, arising from the translation of the financial statements of a foreign entity, transfers to and from inventories and owner-occupied properties, and any other movements. (Comparative reconciliation data for prior periods need not be presented).
   - Under exceptional circumstances, due to lack of reliable fair value, when an entity measures investment property using the benchmark treatment under IAS 16, the above reconciliation should disclose amounts separately for that investment property from amounts relating to other investment property. In addition, an entity should also disclose

     - A description of such a property,
     - An explanation of why fair value cannot be reliably measured,
     - If possible, the range of estimates within which fair value is highly likely to lie, and
     - On disposal of such an investment property, the fact that the entity has disposed of investment property not carried at fair value along with its carrying amount at the time of disposal and the amount of gain or loss recognized.

3. **Disclosures applicable to investment property measured using the cost model**

   - In addition to the disclosure requirements outlined in 1. above, the standard requires that an entity that applies the cost model should also disclose: the depreciation methods used, the useful lives or the depreciation rates used, and the gross carrying amount and the accumulated depreciation (aggregated with accumulated impairment losses) at the beginning and end of the period. It should also disclose a reconciliation of the carrying amount of investment property at the beginning and the end of the period showing the following details: additions resulting from acquisitions, those resulting from business combinations, and those deriving from capitalized expenditures subsequent to the property's initial recognition. It should also disclose disposals, depreciation, impairment losses recognized and reversed, the net exchange differences, if any, arising from the translation of the financial statements of a foreign entity, transfers to and from inventories and owner-occupied properties, and any other movements. (Comparative reconciliation data for prior periods need not be presented.)

- The fair value of investment property carried under the cost model should also be disclosed. In exceptional cases, when the fair value of the investment property cannot be reliably estimated, the entity should instead disclose

  - A description of such property,
  - An explanation of why fair value cannot be reliably measured, and
  - If possible, the range of estimates within which fair value is highly likely to lie.

Transitional Provisions

Fair value model. Under the fair value model, an entity should report the effect of adopting this standard on its effective date (or earlier) as an adjustment to the opening balance of retained earnings for the period in which the standard is first adopted. In addition

- If the entity has previously disclosed publicly (in financial statements or otherwise) the fair value of its investment property in earlier periods (determined on a basis that satisfies the definition of fair value given in the standard), the entity is encouraged, but not required, to

  - Adjust the opening balance of retained earnings for the earliest period presented for which such fair value was disclosed publicly; and
  - Restate comparative information for those periods.

- If the entity has not previously disclosed publicly the information described in 1., the entity should not restate comparative information and should disclose that fact.

Cost model. IAS 8 applies to any change in accounting policies that occurs when an entity first adopts this standard and chooses to use the cost model. The effect of the change in accounting policies includes the reclassification of any amount held in revaluation surplus for investment property.

Rights to Interests Arising from Decommissioning, Restoration, and Environmental Rehabilitation Funds

As discussed in Chapter 8, when an obligation exists for decommissioning or otherwise removing or remediating damages caused by a long-lived asset at the end of its useful economic life, this must be accounted for as a cost of the asset, depreciated or amortized over its useful life. The corresponding obligation, recorded at inception at the present value of the amount estimated to be incurred at the termination date, is accreted for time value of money (i.e., interest) and, subject to the usual uncertainties of the estimation process, will equal the amount due at that point.

The required accounting is independent of whether or not funds are set aside to pay for the expected decommissioning or other costs. However, in some cases, funds are provided by the entity over the course of the asset's use so that there will be little or no risk that the entity would be unable to meet its terminal obligation. In some cases, providing a sinking fund is simply a matter of prudent financial management, but in other instances payments into a fund, not under the control of the reporting entity, may be mandated by law or regulation. IFRIC 5, which is effective in 2006, addresses the accounting for the entities' interests in such funds.

The purpose of various decommissioning, restoration and environmental rehabilitation funds ("decommissioning funds") is to segregate assets to fund some or all of the costs of decommissioning, or in undertaking environmental rehabilitation. The funds typically have one of the following structures:

1. They are established by a single contributor to fund its own decommissioning obligations, whether for a particular site, or for a number of geographically dispersed sites.
2. They are established with multiple contributors, to fund their individual or joint decommissioning obligations, and the contributors will be entitled to reimbursement for decommissioning expenses to the extent of their contributions plus any actual earnings on those contributions less pro rata costs of administering the fund. Contributors may be contingently obligated to make additional contributions, as in the event of the bankruptcy of another contributor.
3. They are established with multiple contributors to fund their individual or joint decommissioning obligations when the required level of contributions is based on the current activity of a contributor and the benefit obtained by that contributor is based on its past activity. In such cases there is a potential mismatch in the amount of contributions made by a contributor (based on current activity) and the value realizable from the fund (based on past activity).

The guidance in IFRIC 5 was intended to apply to those situations where

1. The fund is separately administered by independent trustees.
2. The entities make contributions to the fund, which are invested in a range of assets that may include both debt and equity investments, and are available to help pay these entities' decommissioning costs. The fund trustees determine how contributions are invested, within the constraints set by the fund's governing documents and any applicable legislation or other regulations.
3. The contributing entities retain the obligation to pay their decommissioning costs. However, they are able to obtain reimbursement of decommissioning costs from the fund up to the lower of the decommissioning costs incurred and the contributor's share of assets of the fund.
4. The contributing entities may have restricted access or no access to any surplus of assets of the fund over those used to meet eligible decommissioning costs.

IFRIC 5 directs the accounting for the fund contributions in the financial statements of the contributing entities, if both of the following features are present:

1. The assets are administered separately (either by being held in a separate legal entity or as segregated assets within *another* entity); *and*
2. The contributing entity's right to access the assets is restricted.

If there is a residual interest in the fund, that goes beyond a right to reimbursement (e.g., a contractual right to distributions once all decommissioning has been completed, or on winding up the fund), this may be an equity instrument within the scope of IAS 39. Accordingly, accounting for such an interest is not within the scope of IFRIC 5.

Consistent with underlying principles of IFRS, offsetting is not permitted. Therefore, the entity making contributions to a fund must recognize its obligation to pay decommissioning costs as a liability, and separately recognize its interest in the fund, unless the entity has been relieved of its obligation and would not be liable to pay decommissioning costs even if the fund fails to pay.

The reporting entity is to determine whether it has control, joint control or significant influence over the fund by reference to IAS 27, IAS 28, IAS 31 and SIC12. If one of these conditions exists, the entity is required to account for its interest in the fund in accordance with the applicable standard (i.e., equity method accounting might be necessary, etc.).

In most cases, significant influence or control will not be in the hands of the contributing entity. IFRIC 5 status that, when the entity does not have control, joint control, or significant influence over the fund, it is to recognize the right to receive reimbursement from the fund as a reimbursement in accordance with IAS 37. This is to be measured at the lesser of

1. The amount of the decommissioning obligation recognized; and
2. The contributor's share of the fair value of the net assets of the fund attributable to contributors.

Any changes in the carrying value of the right to receive reimbursement, other than contributions to and payments from the fund, are to be recognized in profit or loss in the period in which these changes occur.

In some instances the entity making contributions to a fund has an obligation to make additional contributions in the future. For example, in a multicontributor fund, entities might be contingently liable for further contributions if other fund participants declare bankruptcy, or if the value of the investment assets held by the fund decreases to an extent that they are insufficient to fulfill the fund's reimbursement obligations. IFRIC 5 states that such an obligation is a contingent liability within the scope of IAS 37. Accordingly, the entity would need to recognize a liability only if it is deemed *probable* that additional contributions will have to be made.

Disclosures required. The reporting entity that makes contributions to such a fund is required to disclose the nature of its interest in a fund and any restrictions on access to the assets in the fund. When there is an obligation to make potential additional contributions that is not recognized as a liability (i.e., it was not deemed probable of occurrence), the reporting entity is required to make the disclosures required by IAS 37.

If the contributor accounts for its interest in the fund as set forth above, it must also make the disclosures required under IAS 37.

APPENDIX

Schematic Summarizing Treatment of Investment Property
(*Source: IAS 40, Appendix A*)

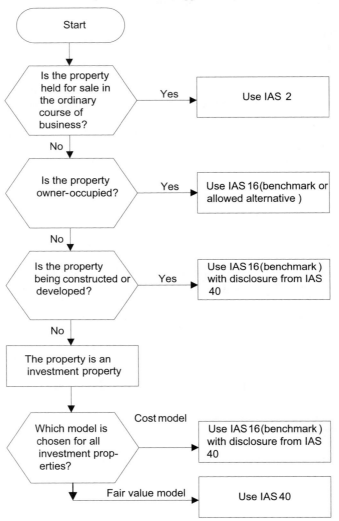

Examples of Financial Statement Disclosures

Barco
For the year ended December 31, 2004

Accounting principles

Investments in associated companies

Investments in associated companies over which the Company has significant influence (typically those that are 20-50% owned) are accounted for under the equity method of accounting and are carried in the balance sheet at the lower of the equity method amount and the recoverable amount, and the pro rata share of income (loss) of associated companies is included in income.

Joint ventures

The Company's interest in the jointly controlled entity is accounted for by proportionate consolidation, which involves recognizing a proportionate share of the joint venture's assets, liabilities, income and expenses with similar items in the consolidated financial statements on a line-by-line basis.

Barloworld limited
For the year ended September 30, 2004

I. Joint ventures

Notes to the annual financial statements

Note 1.15. Interests in joint ventures

A joint venture is a contractual arrangement whereby the group and other parties undertake an economic activity which is subject to joint control. The group's interests in joint ventures are accounted for using the equity method. Where a group enterprise transacts with a jointly controlled entity, unrealized profits and losses are eliminated to the extent of the group's interest in the relevant entity.

Note 7. Investment in associates and joint ventures

	Group		Group	
	2004 Rm	*2003 Rm*	*2004 Rm*	*2003 Rm*
Investment in associates and joint ventures[*]				
Investment in associates	83	416		
Interest in joint ventures	236	119		
	319	535		
	Associates		*Joint ventures*	
Cost of investment excluding goodwill	588	281	103	107
Share of retained earnings	161	131	22	12
Beginning of year	131	80	12	15
Increase for the year	53	58	17	17
Normal and exceptional profit for the year[**]	64	81	43	33
Dividends received	(11)	(23)	(26)	(16)
Other movements	(23)	(7)	(7)	(20)
Avis associate now a subsidiary	(653)			
Carrying value excluding amounts owing	96	412	125	119
Loans and advances (to)/from associates and joint ventures	(13)	4	111	
Carrying value including amounts owing	83	416	236	119
Carrying value by category				
Listed associates—shares at carrying value		323		
Unlisted associates and joint ventures—				
shares at carrying value	96	89	125	119
	96	412	125	119
Valuation of shares				
Market value—listed associate companies		595		
Directors' valuation of unlisted associate companies and	193	189	237	204
joint ventures	193	784	237	204

	Group		Group	
	2004 Rm	2003 Rm	2004 Rm	2003 Rm
	Associates		Joint ventures	
Aggregate of associate companies and joint ventures' net assets, revenue, and profit (100%)				
Property, plant, and equipment and other noncurrent assets	270	3,140	63	74
Current assets	311	2,302	702	314
Long-term liabilities	91	591	167	99
Current liabilities	150	155	403	151
Revenue	835	1,584	3,362	2,083
Profit after tax	77	135	85	71

* *Refer notes 36 and 37 for a detailed list of associate and joint venture companies.*
** *Refer note 3 for a breakdown by business segment of equity accounted income.*

Note 37. Significant joint ventures

		Percentage held by investors	
		2004	2003
Investor company/ joint venture	*Principle products or activities*		
Barloworld Equipment Company			
Barloworld Optron Technologies (Pty) Limited	GPS technology on earthmoving equipment	50.0	
The Used Equipment Co (Pty) Limited	Traders in used Caterpillar equipment	50.0	
Barloworld Motor (Pty) Limited			
NMI Durban South Motors (Pty) Limited	Motor retailer	50.0	50.0
Auric Auto (Pty) Limited	Motor retailer	49.0	
Pretoria Portland Cement Company Limited			
Slagment (Pty) Limited	Slag-based products	33.3	33.3
Barloworld Holdings Plc			
Finaltair Barloworld SA	Energy generation	50	50

II. Associates

Note 1.18. Investments in associates

An associate is an enterprise over which the group is in a position to exercise significant influence, through participation in the financial and operating policy decisions of the investee. The results and assets and liabilities of associates are incorporated in these financial statements using the equity method of accounting. The carrying amount of such investments is reduced to recognize any decline, other than a temporary decline, in the value of individual investments. On acquisition of the investment in an associate, any difference (whether positive or negative) between the cost of acquisition and the group's share of the fair values of the net identifiable assets of the associate is included in the carrying value of the associate but accounted for as goodwill as per note 1.11 above. Where a group enterprise transacts with an associate of the group, unrealized profits and losses are eliminated to the extent of the group's interest in the relevant associate.

Note 38. Related party transactions

Various transactions are entered into by the company and its subsidiaries during the year with related parties. Unless specifically disclosed these transactions occurred under terms that are no less favorable than entered into with third parties. Intragroup transactions are eliminated on consolidation. The following is a summary of transactions with related parties during the year and balances due at year-end:

R millions	Joint control of significant influence holders in the group	Associates of the group	Joint ventures in which the group is a venturer
Group			
2004			
Goods and services sold to			
Old Mutual Life Assurance Company SA Limited	25		
The Used Equipment Co (Pty) Limited			103
Avis Southern Africa Limited prior to acquisition of 100% of the company		61	
Herberts—Plascon (Pty) Limited		64	
Mine Support Products (Pty) Limited		49	
International Paints (Pty) Limited		24	
Amanzi Lime Services (Pty) Limited		21	
Select Trucks LLC		21	
Other sales to related parties		52	25
	25	292	128
Goods and services purchased from			
Avis Southern Africa Limited prior to acquisition of 100% of the company		56	
Select Trucks LLC		58	
Other purchases from related parties		48	4
		162	4
Other transaction			
Interest paid to Old Mutual Life Assurance Company SA Limited on short-term borrowings	25		
Management fees received from associates		13	
	25	13	
Amounts due from/(to) related parties as at end of year*			
The Used Equipment Co (Pty) Limited (payment terms 60 days)			110
Old Mutual Life Assurance Company SA Limited—short-term borrowings	(2)		
Loans and other trade related amounts due from related parties		44	3
	(2)	44	113
Group			
2003			
Goods and services sold to			
Avis Southern Africa Limited		119	
Herberts—Plascon (Pty) Limited		70	
Select Trucks LLC		56	
Sizwe Paints (Pty) Limited		52	
Mine Support Products (Pty) Limited		52	
Amanzi Lime Services (Pty) Limited		29	
Other sales to related parties		28	3
		406	3
Goods and services purchased from			
Avis Southern Africa		42	
Select Trucks LLC		89	
Longridge (Pty) Limited		67	
NMI Durban South Motors (Pty) Limited			4
		198	4
Other transactions			
Interest paid to Old Mutual Life Assurance Company SA Limited on short-term borrowings	68		
Management fees received from associates		15	
	68	15	

R millions	Joint control of significant influence holders in the group	Associates of the group	Joint ventures in which the group is a venturer
Old Mutual Life Assurance Company SA Limited—short-term borrowings	(81)		
Loans and other trade-related amounts due from related parties		37	
	(81)	37	

Note 36. Investment in associate companies

Investor company/associate	Principal products or activities	Issued share capital R000	Percentage held by investors 2004	2003
Barloworld Australia (Pty) Limited				
Chemcorp Australia (Pty) Limited 1	Paint colorant manufacturer	200		50
Mercedes-Benz of Melbourne (Pty) Limited 1	Motor retailer	9,380	49	49
Barloworld Coatings (Pty) Limited				
Herberts–Plascon (Pty) Limited	Automotive coatings	21	49	49
International Paints (Pty) Limited	Industrial coatings	20	49	49
Longridge (Pty) Limited	Paint colorant manufacturer	1		50
Sizwe Paints (Pty) Limited	Decorative paint distributor		30	30
Valspar (SA) (Pty) Limited	Can coatings manufacturer	17	20	20
Barloworld Equipment Company				
Surcotec (Pty) Limited	Metal spraying and general engineering			40
Umndeni Circon (Pty) Limited	Generator set manufacturing	1	33	33
Barloworld Holdings Plc				
Barzem Enterprises (Pty) Limited 4	Caterpillar dealer	48	35	35
Select Trucks LLC 2	Used truck dealer			50
Barloworld Investments (Pty) Limited				
Avis Southern Africa Limited	Car rental	171,282		35
Barloworld Australia (Pty) Limited				
Investment Facility Company 383 (Pty) Limited t/a Sizwe Car Rental	Short-term car rental	231,500	49	
Midlands Car Hire Limited t/a Avis Rent-A-Car Zambia [6]	Short-term car rental	100	45	
Barloworld Robor (Pty) Limited				
Bonskia Investment (Pty) Limited	Steel and metal traders			49
Mine Support Products (Pty) Limited	Pit props	1	50	50
Stewarts & Lloyds Trading (Wadeville) (Pty) Limited	Steel and metal traders		40	65
Pretoria Portland Cement Company Limited				
Amanzi Lime Serves (Pty) Limited	Lime services	4		50
Kgale Quarries [5]	Aggregate manufacture	378		50
Shaleje Service Trust	Administration service		38	38

All companies are incorporated in (or operate principally in) the Republic of South Africa except where otherwise indicated.

[1] *Australia*

[2] *United States of America*

[3] *Spain*

[4] *Zimbabwe*

[5] *Botswana*

[6] *Zambia*

Novartis Group
Period Ending December 31, 2004

Investment in Associated Companies

Novartis has investments in associated companies (defined generally as investments of between 20% and 50% of a company's voting shares) that are accounted for by using the equity method. Due to the various estimates that have been made in applying the equity method, the amounts recorded in the consolidated financial statements in respect of Roche Holding AG and Chiron Corporation may require adjustments in the following year after more financial and other information becomes publicly available.

Note 10. Investment in Associated Companies

Novartis has the following significant investments in associated companies, which are accounted for by using the equity method:

	Balance sheet value		Pretax income statement effect	
	2004	*2003*	*2004*	*2003*
	USD millions	*USD millions*	*USD millions*	*USD millions*
Roche Holding AG, Switzerland	6,234	5,662	97	(354)
Chiron Corporation, USA	1,143	1,118	33	134
Others	73	68	12	20
Total	7,450	6,848	142	(200)

The accounting standards of the Group's associated are adjusted to IFRS in cases where IFRS is not already used.

Due to the various estimates that have been made in applying the equity method accounting treatment for Roche Holding AG ("Roche") and Chiron Corporation ("Chiron"), adjustments may be necessary in succeeding years as more financial and other information becomes publicly available.

Roche Holding AG: The Group's holding in Roche voting shares was 33.3% at December 31, 2004 and 2003. This investment represents 6.3% of the total outstanding voting and nonvoting equity instruments. In order to apply the equity method of accounting, independent appraisers have been used to estimate the fair value of Roche so as to determine the Novartis share of property, plant & equipment and intangible assets and the amount of the residual goodwill at the time of acquisition. The purchase price allocations were made on publicly available information at the time of acquisition of the shares.

The purchase price allocation is as follows:

	USD millions
Identified intangible assets	4,161
Other net assets	104
Residual goodwill	2,971
Total purchase price	7,236
Net income effect—2004	27
Other accumulated equity adjustments	(1,029)
December 31, 2004 balance sheet value	6,234

The identified intangible assets principally relate to the value of currently marketed products and are being amortized on a straight-line basis over their estimated average useful life of 20 years. The residual goodwill is also being amortized on a straight-line basis over 20 years.

The income statement effects from applying Novartis accounting policies to the Roche figures for 2004 and 2003 are as follows:

	2004 USD millions	*2003 USD millions*
Depreciation and amortization of fair value adjustments to:		
Property, plant & equipment and intangible assets	(166)	(143)
Goodwill	(136	127
Prior year adjustment	30	(269)
Novartis share of estimated Roche current year consolidate pretax income	369	185

	2004 USD millions	2003 USD millions
Pretax income statement effect	97	(354)
Deferred tax	(70)	(44)
Net income effect	27	(398)

The market value of the Novartis interest in Roche at December 31, 2004 was USD 7.1 billion (Reuters symbol: RO.S.).

Chiron Corporation: The Group's holding in the common stock of Chiron was 42.5% and 42.3% at December 31, 2004 and 2003, respectively. The recording of the results of the strategic interest in Chiron is based on the estimated Chiron equity at December 31 of each year. The amounts for Chiron incorporated into the Novartis consolidated financial statements take into account the effects stemming from differences in accounting policies between Novartis and Chiron (primarily Novartis' amortization over 10 years of in-process research and development arising on Chiron's acquisitions which are written off by Chiron in the year of acquisition).

The income statement effects from applying Novartis accounting policies to the Chiron figures for 2004 and 2003 figures are as follows:

	2004 USD millions	2003 USD millions
Amortization of goodwill	(18)	(20)
Prior year adjustment	4	4
Novartis share of estimated Chiron current year consolidated pretax income	47	150
Pre-tax income statement effect	33	134
Deferred tax	(1)	(37)
Net income effect	32	97

The market value of the Novartis interest in Chiron at December 31, 2004, was USD 2.6 billion (NASDAQ symbol: CHIR).

Nokia
For the year ended December 31, 2004

Notes to the consolidated financial statements

Note 15. Investments in associated companies

	2004 EURm	2003 EURm
Net carrying amount Jan. 1	76	49
Additions	150	59
Share of results	(26)	(18)
Translation differences	1	(2)
Other movements	(1)	(12)
Net carrying amount Dec. 31	200	76

In 2004, Nokia increased its ownership in Symbian from 32.2% to 47.9% by acquiring part of the shares of Symbian owned by Psion for EUR 102 million (GBP 70 million). EUR 68 million (GBP 47 million) of the total acquisition cost was paid in cash and the remaining purchase price is considered as contingent consideration to be paid in 2005 and 2006. Nokia also participated in a rights issue to raise EUR 73 million (GBP 50 million) additional funding to Symbian. The issue was pro rata to existing shareholders. In 2003, Nokia increased its ownership in Symbian from 19.0% to 32.2% by acquiring part of the shares of Symbian owned by Motorola representing 13.2% of all the shares in Symbian, for EUR 57 million (GBP 39.6 million) in cash. Shareholdings in associated companies are comprised of investments in unlisted companies in all periods presented.

Note 33. Associated companies

	2004 EURm	2003 EURm	2002 EURm
Share of results of associated companies	(26)	(18)	(19)
Dividend income	2	3	1
Share of shareholders' equity of associated companies	37	18	30
Liabilities to associated companies	3	3	7

Note 36. Principal Nokia Group companies at December 31, 2004

	Parent holding %	*Group majority %*
US Nokia Inc.	–	100.00
DE Nokia GmbH	100.00	100.00
GB Nokia UK Limited	–	100.00
KR Nokia TMC Limited	100.00	100.00
CN Nokia Capitel Telecommunications Ltd	–	52.90
NL Nokia Finance International B.V.	100.00	100.00
HU Nokia Kornarom Kft	100.00	100.00
BR Nokia do Brazil Technologia Ltda	99.99	100.00
IT Nokia Italia Spa	100.00	100.00
IN Nokia India Ltd	100.00	100.00
CN Dongguan Nokia Mobile Phones Company Ltd	–	70.00
CN Beijing Nokia Hang Xing		
Telecommunications Systems Co. Ltd	–	69.00

Shares in listed companies

Group holding more than 5%	*Group holding %*	*Group voting %*
Nectrom Holding S.A.	79.33	86.21

Under a binding sale agreement signed on December 31, 2004, Nokia will sell its entire holding in Nextrom Holding S.A. and the remaining loan agreement to Knill Group. The transaction is expected to be completed during the first quarter of 2005. The negative impact of EUR 12 million from the divestiture was recognized in other operating expenses in 2004.

	Group holding %	*Group voting %*
Associated companies		
Symbian Limited	47.90	47.90

A complete list of subsisidaries and associated companies is included in Nokia's Statutory Accounts.

(In million of CHF)	*2003*	*2002*
Balance sheet		
Long-term assets	235	269
Current assets	173	145
Noncurrent liabilities	(88)	(89)
Current liabilities	(187)	(181)
Net assets	133	144

Mittal Steel South Africa Limited
Period ending December 2004

Accounting Policies

Investments in joint ventures

A joint venture is an entity jointly controlled by the group and one or more other venturers in terms of a contractual arrangement. It may involve a corporation, partnership or other entity in which the group has an interest. Investments in joint ventures are accounted for in the group financial statements using the equity method for the period during which the group has the ability to exercise significant influence or joint control. Equity accounted income represents the group's proportionate share of profits of these entities and the share of taxation thereon. The group's share of retained earnings net of any dividends received are transferred to a nondistributable reserve. All unrealized profits and losses are eliminated. Where necessary, accounting policies are changed to ensure consistency with group policies.

The group's interest in joint ventures is carried in the balance sheet at an amount that reflects the group's share of the net assets. Goodwill on the acquisition of joint ventures is treated in accordance with the group's accounting policy for goodwill. Carrying amounts of investments in joint ventures are reduced to their recoverable amount where this is lower than their carrying amount.

Where the group's share of losses of a joint venture exceeds the carrying amount of the joint venture, the joint venture is carried at zero. Additional losses are only recognized to the extent that the group has incurred obligations in respect of a joint venture.

Annexure 1: Investments in joint ventures

	Number of shares held	Percentage holding		Group carrying amount		Company carrying amount		Year-end other than Dec. 31
		As of Dec. 31 2004 %	As of Dec. 31 2004 %	As of Dec.31 2004 Rm	As of Dec.31 2004 Rm	As of Dec.31 2004 Rm	As of Dec.31 2004 Rm	
Joint venture								
Unlisted shares								
Consolidated Wire Industries Limited	1,999,999	50	50	55	50	14	14	
Ensimbini Terminals (Pty) Limited	1,000	50	50	14	13	10	10	30 June
Morsteel International Holdings BV	35,001	50	50	521	355			
Microsteel (Pty) Limited	2,000	50	50					30 June
Pietersburg Iron Company (Pty) Limited	4,000	50		6		6		
Total investment				596	418	30	24	
Directors' valuation of unlisted shares in joint ventures				759	479	30	24	

Where the above entities' financial year-ends are not connected with that of the company, financial information has been obtained from management accounts.

The group's effective share of income statement, balance sheet and cash flow items in respect of joint ventures is as follows:

	As at Dec. 31, 2004 Rm	As at Dec. 31, 2003 Rm
Balance sheets		
Noncurrent assets	292	152
Current assets	1,192	834
Total assets	1,484	986
Shareholders' equity	596	428
Noncurrent liabilities		
Interest-bearing borrowings	214	114
Current liabilities		
Interest-bearing borrowings	166	66
Other	508	378
Total equity and liabilities	1,484	986

	Year ended Dec. 31, 2004 Rm	Six months ended Dec. 31, 2003 Rm
Income Statements		
Revenue	9,789	3,293
Operating expenses	(9,480)	(3,205)
Net operating profit	309	88
Net financing costs	(1)	(3)
Income from investments		3
Income from equity accounted investments	39	
Profit before taxation	347	88
Taxation		
Normal	(89)	(21)

	Year ended Dec. 31, 2004 Rm	Six months ended Dec. 31, 2003 Rm
Income Statements		
Net profit attributable to ordinary shareholders	258	67
Cash flow statements		
Net cash flows from operating activities	(185)	115
Net cash flows from investing activities	(15)	(4)
Net cash flows from financing activities	124	14
Foreign currency translations	(8)	9
Net increase/(decrease) in cash and cash equivalents	(84)	134

11 BUSINESS COMBINATIONS AND CONSOLIDATED FINANCIAL STATEMENTS

PERSPECTIVE AND ISSUES

Accounting for business combinations has undergone a thorough overhaul in recent years, first in the US, later by the IASB, and by standard setters in other jurisdictions as well. IFRS 3, introduced in 2004, like FAS 141, the US GAAP standard, ends the use of pooling of interests accounting, and treats goodwill arising from an acquisition as an intangible asset with an indefinite life, not subject to periodic amortization. The standard also requires that, where there is a minority interest, the assets and liabilities in a subsidiary are now to be valued at full fair value, including the minority interest's portion.

IASB is currently pursuing a project (recently renamed *Control [Including Special Purpose Entities]*) to address both the basis (policy) on which a parent entity should consolidate its investments in subsidiaries, and the actual procedures for consolidation. It is intended that this will provide more rigorous guidance on the concept of control, which is the basis for consolidation under IAS 27. Among other matters to be resolved is that of special-purpose entities (SPE), which are utilized for "off the books" financings, leasing activities, and other purposes. Under US GAAP, these have been redefined as "variable interest entities" and stricter, if much more complex, criteria have been established, with the objective of forcing adherence to the "substance over form" strategy of consolidating SPEs when they are, effectively, economically integrated with the reporting entity. (Note: SIC 12 currently sets forth the IFRS requirements in this area.)

When a combination is accounted for as an acquisition, as now is virtually always the case, the assets acquired and liabilities assumed are recorded at their respective fair values, using purchase accounting. If the fair value of the net assets acquired equal an amount other than the total acquisition price, the excess (or less commonly, the deficiency) is generally referred to as goodwill (a deficiency is commonly, if confusingly, called negative goodwill). Goodwill of this kind can arise only in the context of a business combination. While fair values of many assets and liabilities can readily be determined (and in an arm's-length transaction should be known to the parties) certain recognition and measurement problems do inevitably arise. Among these are the value of contingent consideration promised to former owners of the acquired entity, and the determination as to whether certain expenses that arise by virtue of the transaction, such as those pertaining to elimination of duplicate facilities, should be treated as part of the transaction or as an element of postacquisition accounting.

At an operational level, acquired entities are either maintained as operating subsidiaries or their assets and liabilities are absorbed into the acquirer's existing business. The financial reporting of the surviving entity or the consolidated financial reporting of the parent company will be identical in either case, but in the latter the subsidiary's own (separate company) financial statements preserve its historical cost carrying values, so there will be a need to maintain "memo" records so that asset and liability step-ups or step-downs (to reflect fair values as of the acquisition date, further adjusted for amortization and other occurrences thereafter until the financial statement date) can be made in preparing consolidated financial statements. Where the assets and liabilities are transferred to the acquirer, the records for the acquiring unit will reflect the new carrying values of assets and liabilities as at the date of acquisition.

Major accounting issues affecting business combinations and the preparation of consolidated or combined financial statements are as follows:

1. The proper recognition and measurement of the assets and liabilities of the combining entities,
2. The elimination of intercompany balances and transactions in the preparation of consolidated financial statements.

This chapter also discusses the accounting applicable to special problem areas, such as reverse acquisitions, and emerging practices having complex accounting implications, such as special-purpose entities.

Sources of IFRS		
IFRS 3	*IAS* 27, 36, 37, 38	*SIC* 12

DEFINITIONS OF TERMS

Accounting consolidation. The process of combining the financial statements of a parent company and one or more legally separate and distinct subsidiaries.

Acquisition. A business combination in which one entity (the acquirer) obtains control over the net assets and operations of another (the acquiree) in exchange for the transfer of assets, incurrence of liability, or issuance of equity.

Business combination. The bringing together of separate enterprises into one economic entity as a result of one enterprise obtaining control over the net assets and operations of another.

Combination. Any transaction whereby one enterprise obtains control over the assets and properties of another enterprise, regardless of the resulting form of the enterprise emerging from the combination transaction.

Combined financial statements. Financial statements presenting the financial position and/or results of operations of legally separate entities, related by common ownership, as if they were a single entity.

Consolidated financial statements. The financial statements of a group presented as those of a single economic entity.

Control. The ability to direct the strategic financing and operating policies of an entity so as to access benefits flowing from the entity and increase, maintain, or protect the amount of those benefits.

Cost method. A method of accounting whereby the investment is recognized at cost. The investor recognizes income from the investment only to the extent that the investor receives distributions from accumulated net profits of the investee arising after the date of acquisition.

Date of acquisition. The date on which control of the net assets and operations of the acquiree is effectively transferred to the acquirer (i.e., the date of exchange effecting the acquisition).

Fair value. The amount for which an asset could be exchanged or a liability settled between knowledgeable, willing parties in an arm's-length transaction.

Goodwill. The excess of the cost of a business acquisition accounted for as an acquisition (i.e., by the purchase method) over the fair value of the acquirer's share of net assets obtained.

Group. A parent and all its subsidiaries.

Minority interest. That portion of the profit or loss and of net assets of a subsidiary attributable to equity interests that are not owned, directly or indirectly through subsidiaries, by the parent.

Negative goodwill. This amount represents the net excess of fair value of the net assets of a business acquisition accounted for as a purchase over the cost of the acquisition, in transactions referred to as "bargain purchases."

Parent. An entity that has one or more subsidiaries.

Purchase method. An accounting method used for a business combination that recognizes that one combining entity was acquired by another. It establishes a new basis of accountability for the acquiree. The purchase method is to be used for all acquisitions other than those among affiliated entities.

Purchased preacquisition earnings. An account used to report the earnings of a subsidiary attributable to percentage ownership acquired at the interim date in the current reporting period.

Subsidiary. An entity, including an unincorporated entity such as a partnership, that is controlled by another entity (known as the parent).

Unrealized intercompany profit. The excess of the transaction price over the carrying value of an item (usually inventory or long-lived assets) transferred from (or to) a parent to (or from) the subsidiary, or among subsidiaries, and not sold to an outside entity as of the balance sheet date. For purposes of consolidated financial statements, recognition must be deferred until subsequent realization through a transaction with an unrelated party.

CONCEPTS, RULES, AND EXAMPLES

Introduction to Business Combinations

All business combinations are now, for accounting purposes under IFRS, considered to be acquisitions, whereby one entity (the parent) takes management control of another entity, or of its assets and liabilities. This is independent of the legal form of the business combination. Thus, two entities may consolidate to create a new, third enterprise. Alternatively, one entity may purchase, for cash or for stock, the stock of another enterprise, which may or may not be followed by a formal merging of the acquired entity into the acquirer. In yet other cases, one entity may simply purchase the assets of another, with or without assuming the debts of that enterprise. One enterprise may enter into an agreement for another to manage its assets and liabilities.

Uniting of Interests

The use of pooling-of-interests (or unitings of interests) accounting had been widespread for about fifty years, particularly in the US. Under this method of accounting for business combinations, the premerger book values of each combining entity's assets and liabilities would simply be added together, with no remeasurement to fair value. While there was a logical foundation for pooling of interests accounting (it originally had evolved to address certain combinations, typically of entities of approximately the same size and of similar operations, in which identification of an acquirer was made difficult by the fact that all or most of the ownership interests of the combining entities remained as owners of the combined entity), over time, the criteria had eroded and there were abuses. Under pooling accounting the real cost of an acquisition was concealed and future earnings were (usually) enhanced, since there were no adjustments of carrying values of depreciable assets to fair values, which would create higher future depreciation charges.

US GAAP eliminated pooling accounting outright (effective mid-2001) and the IASB followed suit, under IFRS 3, from early 2004. With the exceptions of selected types of combinations, such as those involving existing affiliated entities, where there are conceptually sound reasons to not permit fair value adjustments at the time of what may not be arm's-length acquisition transactions, all business combinations must now be treated as acquisitions of one entity by another, with the acquiree's assets and liabilities being recorded at fair values.

Acquisition Accounting

In most business combinations, one enterprise gains control over another, and the identity of the acquirer can readily be determined. Under IFRS, it is necessary to identify the acquirer in virtually all business combinations, since pooling accounting has, from early 2004, been eliminated as an acceptable method of accounting for such transactions. Generally, the combining enterprise that obtains more than one-half of the voting rights of the other combining enterprises is the acquirer. In exceptional cases, the party that is the acquirer does not obtain over one-half of the voting rights; but the identity of the acquirer will be the party that obtains power

1. Over more than one half of the voting rights of the other enterprise by virtue of agreement with the other investors (e.g., voting trust arrangements or other contractual provisions)

2. To govern the financial and operating policies of the other enterprise, under a statute or agreement

3. To appoint and remove the majority of the board of directors or equivalent governing body of the other enterprise

4. To cast the majority of votes at meetings of the board of directors or equivalent body

Other indicators of which party was the acquirer in any given business combination are as follows (these are suggestive only, not conclusive):

1. The fair value of one entity is significantly greater than that of the other combining enterprises; in such a case, the larger entity would be deemed the acquirer.

2. The combination is effected by an exchange of voting stock for cash; the entity paying the cash would be deemed to be the acquirer.

3. Management of one enterprise is able to dominate selection of management of the combined entity; the dominant entity would be deemed to be the acquirer.

The major accounting issue in business acquisitions pertains to the allocation of the purchase price to the individual assets obtained and liabilities assumed. In this regard, IFRS 3, as discussed in its *Basis for Conclusions*, takes the position that what is being recognized is the assets and liabilities that existed within the acquiree at acquisition date, and their measurement is based on their value to the acquiree, not on their subsequent use. Any assets or liabilities that flow from the combination, as opposed to those existing at the moment of combination, are not recognized within the allocation of the purchase price. This is an important distinction, if a subtle one, and represents a change of position from former standard IAS 22, which allowed certain restructuring provisions to be recognized within the combination calculation.

In general, restructuring provisions arising from business combinations will no longer be recognized as liabilities affecting the purchase price allocation process, since this would not meet the criteria under IAS 37. Previously, planned efforts to "rationalize" operations following a business combination (a common objective when the acquiree's operations were in the same business segments as the acquirer's) were often used to justify the provision of reserves at the acquisition date. These reserves (i.e., accrued liabilities) were sometimes used to defray future operating costs unrelated to the intended restructuring—and this often became a vehicle for the accomplishment of improper earnings manipulations.

It is clear that possible future costs to be incurred for intended restructurings do not give rise to a recognizable liability at the acquisition date, consistent with the IFRS definition of liabilities (per the IASB *Framework*, probable future sacrifices of economic benefits arising from present obligations of a particular entity to transfer assets or provide services to other entities in the future as a result of past transactions or events). Accordingly, if and when these costs are later actually incurred, they are to be charged to expense at such later date.

Furthermore, most restructuring costs that are associated with combinations are truly contingent on the consummation of the acquisition or merger transaction. If the transaction fails to close, for whatever reason, the restructuring process will not proceed. At the transaction date, it therefore cannot be stated that the obligation exists. On the other hand, if the acquirer or the acquiree had independently announced a restructuring program prior to the transaction, it is possible that the accrual would meet the criteria of IAS 37 for the recognition of provisions. Similarly, if an earlier contractual arrangement had been made with, say, officers or directors of the acquiree, which promised certain termination benefits if the entity were to be acquired, then a liability would be recognized during the purchase price allocation process, since this contractual arrangement would be a contingency arising from past events and confirmed by the future event (the acquisition).

As has traditionally been the case, if the fair value of net assets (i.e., identifiable tangible and intangible assets acquired less all liabilities assumed) is less than the aggregate purchase cost, the excess will be deemed to represent goodwill. Goodwill is considered to be an unidentifiable intangible asset with an indefinite life, and thus not subject to periodic amortization. It is, of course, subject to impairment testing, as set forth by IAS 36. If the fair value of net assets acquired is greater than the cost (so-called bargain purchase transactions), this difference will be negative goodwill, and is immediately taken into income. These matters are dealt with in detail later in this chapter.

When less than 100% of the shares of the acquired entity is owned by the acquirer, a complication arises in the preparation of consolidated statements, and a minority interest (discussed below) must be determined and presented. The acquired assets and liabilities are still fully included in the parent's consolidated financial statements, and are valued at fair value, which has implications for the presentation of minority interest.

The other major distinguishing characteristic of the purchase accounting method is that none of the equity accounts of the acquired entity (including its retained earnings) will be carried forward to appear on consolidated financial statements. In other words, ownership interests of the acquired entity's shareholders are eliminated against the parent's investment for the purposes of consolidated financial statements.

Reverse acquisitions. IFRS 3 acknowledges the possibility of reverse acquisitions, where the acquirer becomes a subsidiary of the acquired company. These are characterized by an entity issuing shares in exchange for shares in its target acquiree, such that control passes to the acquiree due to the number of additional shares issued by the acquirer. In such cases, notwithstanding the nominal or legal identification of the acquirer and acquiree, for accounting purposes, the enterprise whose shareholders now control the combined entity is the acquirer.

Accounting for acquisitions. The purchase method is to be used to report acquisitions; the transaction is to be recorded in a manner similar to that applied to other purchases of assets. That is, the purchase price must be allocated among the various assets that are obtained, net of any liabilities assumed in the transaction, commensurate with the fair values of those assets. In the unlikely event that the price equals the fair value of the net assets, the allocation process will be straightforward, with each asset being recorded at fair value. If the price exceeds the fair value of the net identifiable assets, the difference is treated as goodwill, as discussed below, since the individual identifiable assets cannot be recorded at amounts greater than their respective fair values. Similarly, if the fair values of the net identifiable assets acquired exceeds the price paid, negative goodwill exists, the accounting for which is also discussed later in this chapter.

The acquisition should be recognized as of the date it is effected, since this form of business combination is a discrete transaction occurring at a point in time, caused by a change in ownership and resulting in changes in the bases of accountability. IFRS 3 specifies that the acquisition date is that when control of the net assets and operations of the acquired entity is effectively transferred to the acquirer. The results of operations of the acquiree are included in the consolidated statements only from the date of the transaction. Financial statements for earlier periods are not restated to reflect the combination (although pro forma results for earlier periods can, of course, be presented for purposes of supplementary analysis).

Acquisitions should be accounted for at the cost paid or incurred. Cost is the amount of cash paid or the fair value of other consideration given to the shareholders of the acquired entity. It also includes transaction costs such as legal and accounting fees, investment banking charges, and so on. Depending on the terms of the acquisition agreement, it may include certain contingent consideration as well (discussed below).

Individual assets and liabilities should be recognized separately at the date acquired, if it is both probable that any associated economic benefits will flow to the enterprise, and a reliable measure of cost or fair value to the acquirer is available. Acquired intangible assets are presumed for these purposes always to have probable future benefits. In the case of most acquisitions, these conditions will readily be met, since in an arm's-length transaction the parties normally will have knowledge of the price paid and the acquirer would not have consummated the purchase unless all the attendant benefits would flow to it in subsequent periods.

Determining purchase price. In some acquisitions, a package consisting of different forms of consideration may be given. As is often stipulated in accounting rules, the primary measure should be the fair value of any assets given up in the transaction; these may include, in addition to cash, promissory notes, shares, and even operating assets of the acquirer. Except when actual cash is exchanged, fair values may differ from book values. Thus, promissory notes may carry a rate of interest other than a market rate, in which case a premium or discount will be ascribed to the obligation. (For example, if a €10 million, 5% interest-bearing two-year note is exchanged as consideration in a business acquisition, in an environment where the buyer would normally pay 8% on borrowed funds, the actual purchase price will be computed as being somewhat lower than the nominal €10 million.)

Similarly, the acquirer's common stock will virtually always have a market value different from par or stated amounts. If there is an active market for the shares, reference should be made to the price quoted: IFRS 3 holds that this provides the best evidence of fair value, and must be used "except in rare circumstances." If the market price on any given day can be demonstrated not to be a reliable indicator, other evidence or methods should be considered.

For example, the prices over a period of days before and after the announcement of the terms of the acquisition transaction should be reviewed. If the stock is thinly traded, or not traded at all, or if shares in a listed company are offered with restrictions (not salable for a fixed period of time, etc.), it would be necessary to ascertain a reasonable value, possibly in consultation with investment bankers or other experts. In extreme cases, the fair value of the proportionate interest in the acquired entity's net assets, or the fair value of the fraction of the acquirer's net assets represented by the shares issued would be used as a measure, whichever is more objectively determinable. If dissenting minority shareholders of the acquiree are paid in cash, the price paid may also serve as a reliable indicator of the value of the transaction. Of course, the parties to the transaction, being at arm's length, should also be able to place an objective value on the stock being exchanged, inasmuch as they had negotiated for this price.

If the acquirer exchanges certain of its assets, either operating assets that had been subject to depreciation, or investment securities or other investments assets, such as idle land, for the stock of the acquired entity, a more complicated assessment of fair value will have to be made. Book or carrying value—even if the assets had been adjusted to fair value under the revaluation method permitted by IAS 16—should not be taken as being fair value for purposes of accounting for the business combination, unless corroborated by other evidence.

If the acquisition is to be paid for on a deferred basis, the cost to be reflected will be the present value of the future payments, discounted at the acquiring entity's normal borrowing cost, given the terms of the arrangement, provided that the future payments are probable and can be measured reliably. If it cannot be measured at the date of acquisition, it must be adjusted subsequently. However, where an additional payment is made to the seller as a result of guarantees given by the acquirer as to the value of assets given up (e.g., the market value of the acquirer's shares), the adjustment is not made to the cost of the acquisition, but to the value of the consideration initially given to the seller.

Step acquisitions. In many instances, control over another entity is not achieved in a single transaction, but rather, after a series of transactions. For example, one enterprise may acquire a 25% interest in another entity, followed by another 20% some time later, and then followed by another 10% at yet a later date. The last step gives the acquirer a 55% interest and, thus, control. The accounting issue is to determine at what point in time the business combination took place and how to measure the cost of the acquisition.

IFRS 3 stipulates that the cost of the acquisition is measured with reference to the cost and fair value data as of that exchange transaction. In the foregoing example, therefore, it would be necessary to look to the consideration given for each of the three separate purchases of stock. If one or more of these transaction were noncash, these would have to be valued as described earlier in this section. To the extent that the value of the consideration given differed from the fair value of the underlying net assets, measured at the date of the respective exchange, goodwill or negative goodwill would have to be computed and accounted for as stipulated under IFRS. Conceivably, some of these purchases could be made at premiums over fair value and others could be consummated at discounts from fair values.

In the example above, the first acquisition results in a 25% holding in the investee, which is over the threshold where significant influence is assumed to be exerted by the investor. Thus, the equity method should be employed beginning at the time of the first exchange and continuing through the second exchange (when a 45% ownership interest is achieved). Application of the equity method is explained in Chapter 10; one important aspect, however, is that the difference between cost and the fair value of the underlying interest in the net assets of the investee is to be treated as goodwill or negative goodwill and accounted for consistent with the provisions of IFRS 3. Accordingly, the amount implicitly representing goodwill or negative goodwill needs to be computed as discussed in this chapter. The amount of goodwill (or negative goodwill) at the date of the first exchange transaction should not be merged into the next step transaction computation of goodwill. In other words, each step in the transaction sequence should be accounted for as a separate acquisition.

When control is achieved, the fair value of the subsidiary's net assets will be represented by a blending of fair values computed at different points in time. Since fair values are measured as each step in the acquisition process occurs, and once made are not later adjusted due to a further acquisition of ownership interest, a mixture of values inevitably occurs. Unlike business acquisitions effected in a single transaction, the ultimate resulting balance sheet will not reflect the fair values of the acquiree's assets and liabilities as of the date control is achieved.

In the foregoing example, the fair value of net assets is determined 25% by the first purchase transaction, another 20% by the second transaction, and the final 10% by the third transaction, at the time control is achieved. Since values will vary and will be dependent upon the dates of the respective transactions, it is possible that both goodwill and negative goodwill might be present, simultaneously. (As explained elsewhere in this chapter, control is normally signified by majority ownership, although it can be triggered by holding potential shares, such as options, even when actual ownership of outstanding shares fails to reach majority level.)

Recording the Assets Acquired and Liabilities Assumed

The assets acquired and liabilities assumed in the business combination should be recorded at fair values. If the acquirer obtained a 100% interest in the acquired entity, this process is straightforward. As mentioned above, if the cost exceeds the fair value of the net assets acquired, the excess is deemed to be goodwill, and capitalized as an intangible asset, subject to amortization.

Determining fair values. Accounting for acquisitions requires a determination of the fair value for each of the acquired company's identifiable tangible and intangible assets and for each of its liabilities at the date of combination (except for assets which are to be resold and which are to be accounted for at fair value less costs to sell under IFRS 5). IFRS 3 gives some illustrative examples as to how to treat certain assets, particularly intangibles, but provides no general guidance on determining fair value. The Phase II revisions to IFRS 3, promised by IASB, are expected to provide more detailed guidance on this topic.

The list below is drawn from Appendix B of IFRS 3.

1. **Financial instruments traded in an active market**—Current market values.

2. **Financial instruments not traded in an active market**—Estimated fair values, determined on a basis consistent with relevant price-earnings ratios, dividend yields, and expected growth rates of comparable securities of entities having similar characteristics.

3. **Receivables**—Present values of amounts to be received determined by using current interest rates, less allowances for uncollectible accounts.

4. **Inventories**

   a. Finished goods and merchandise inventories—Estimated selling prices less the sum of the costs of disposal and a reasonable profit.

   b. Work in process inventories—Estimated selling prices of finished goods less the sum of the costs of completion, costs of disposal, and a reasonable profit.

   c. Raw material inventories—Current replacement costs.

5. **Plant and equipment**—At market value as determined by appraisal; in the absence of market values, use depreciated replacement cost. Land and building are to be valued at market value.

6. **Identifiable intangible assets** (such as patents and licenses)—Fair values determined primarily with reference to active markets as per IAS 38; in the absence of market data, use the best available information, with discounted cash flows being useful only when information about cash flows which are directly attributable to the asset, and which are largely independent of cash flows from other assets, can be developed.

7. **Net employee benefit assets or obligations for defined benefit plans**—The actuarial present value of promised benefits, net of the fair value of related assets. (Note that an asset can be recognized only to the extent that it would be available to the enterprise as refunds or reductions in future contributions.)

8. **Tax assets and liabilities**—The amount of tax benefit arising from tax losses or the taxes payable in respect to net earnings or loss. The amount to be recorded is net of the tax effect of restating other identifiable assets and liabilities at fair values.

9. **Liabilities** (such as notes and accounts payable, long-term debt, warranties, claims payable)—Present value of amounts to be paid determined at appropriate current interest rates; discounting is not required for short-term liabilities where the effect is immaterial.

10. **Onerous contract obligations and other identifiable liabilities**—At the present value of the amounts to be disbursed.

11. **Contingent liabilities**—The amount that a third party would charge to assume those liabilities. The amount must reflect expectations about cash flows rather than

the single most likely outcome. (Note that the subsequent measurement should fall under IAS 37 and in many cases would call for derecognition. IFRS 3 provides an exception for such contingent liabilities, in that subsequent measurement is to be at the higher of the amount recognized under IFRS 3 or the amount mandated by IAS 37.)

Identifiable in-process research and development acquired in business combination. Often, in business combinations, part of the consideration paid is in recognition of ongoing product development efforts by the acquiree. IFRS requires immediate expensing of research costs incurred, but capitalization and amortization of development expenditures. In a slight departure from this general principle, purchased in-process research and development (IPR&D) acquired as part of a business combination should generally be recorded as an intangible asset. This asset is separate and distinct from goodwill. Thus costs ineligible for recognition when incurred by the acquiree may need to be recognized when acquired in a business purchase transaction.

To qualify for capitalization, in-process research and development must meet all the following criteria: it must be separately identifiable, be a resource that is controlled, be a probable source of future economic benefits, and have a reliably measurable fair value. IPR&D is separately identifiable if it arises from contractual or other legal rights. If the IPR&D is not contractual or separable, it would form part of the amount attributable to goodwill.

Subsequent expenditure on IPR&D acquired in a business combination, if recognized as an asset separate from goodwill, would be accounted for in accordance with the requirements in IAS 38. If the subsequent expenditure is properly characterized as research, the expenditure would be recognized as an expense when it is incurred, but if in the nature of development, the expenditure would be capitalized, assuming that the entity can satisfy all of the criteria for deferral in IAS 38.

Subsequent adjustment to assets acquired and liabilities assumed. IFRS 3 states that the amounts initially recognized may be subsequently changed only if an error occurred (or where the agreement has contingent aspects). In such a case, in compliance with IAS 8, the adjustment is made retrospectively to the financial statements so that, as revised, they appear as if the error had never happened. Where there is a change in estimate, on the other hand, this is to be accounted for prospectively, and the adjustment will flow through income for the current and, if appropriate, future periods. The only exception to this rule is in the case of an adjustment to deferred taxes. Where a deferred tax asset did not qualify for recognition originally, but is subsequently realized, the benefit is treated as income but an adjustment is also made to the originally recorded goodwill, also through income.

SIC 22 has provided clarification regarding how the adjustment to the pertinent asset or liability account(s) should be computed. SIC 22 states that such adjustments should be calculated as if the newly assigned values had been used from the date of the acquisition. Thus, in the case of a depreciating asset such as a patent, the adjustment should take into account the amount of depreciation or amortization that would have been recognized subsequent to the date of acquisition, had the asset been fully recognized as of that date. This is necessary to avoid having later periods charged with more annual depreciation than would have been the case had the lack of ability to properly allocate costs at the date of the acquisition not occurred as it did.

SIC 22 also states that adjustments to amounts included in the income statement, such as depreciation or amortization of goodwill, are included in the corresponding category of income or expense presented on the face of the income statement. That is, these adjustments cannot be segregated from the normal categorization that would have been appropriate, and, for example, shown as some type of nonoperating or nonrecurring transaction.

Finally, SIC 22 requires disclosure of the amount of an adjustment recognized in the income statement of the current period that relates to comparative and prior periods. For example, if the adjustment increases depreciation expense in the current period by €15,000, and €10,000 of the increase results from the recalculation of the effects of the adjustment to identifiable assets over the comparative year, that fact would be disclosed. This is necessary to avoid misleading implications from being drawn from the comparative amounts being presented.

However, IFRS 3 also addresses the situation where fair values can only be assigned provisionally in the initial accounting, because of some lack of information. Such provisional values can be used for a maximum of twelve months from the date of acquisition. If it is necessary to prepare a balance sheet before the end of the twelve-month period, the provisional values should be used. When provisional values are used, the subsequent adjustments are carried out retrospectively, from the date of acquisition.

Allocation of Cost of Acquisition When the Acquirer Obtains Less Than 100% of the Acquiree's Voting Interest

When an acquirer obtains a majority interest, but not 100% ownership, in another entity, the process of recording the transaction is potentially more complicated. The portion of the acquired operation not owned by the acquirer, but claimed (in an economic sense) by outside interests, is referred to as **minority interest**. Not all standard setters agree whether, in a situation in which goodwill or negative goodwill will be reported, to value it with reference only to the price paid by the new (majority) owner, or whether to gross up the balance sheet for the minority's share as well. Former standard IAS 22 had permitted both approaches, but IFRS 3 specifies that identifiable assets and liabilities are valued entirely at fair value, and the minority interest is correspondingly adjusted to reflect the relevant proportion of the net assets.

Under IFRS 3 all identifiable (i.e., excluding goodwill) assets and liabilities are recognized at their respective fair values, including those corresponding to the minority's ownership interest. This means that there is a step-up in recorded amounts to reflect the valuation being placed on the enterprise indirectly by the new majority owner.

Under this approach, the minority interest shown in a consolidated balance sheet will be the minority ownership percentage times the net assets of the subsidiary as reported in the parent's consolidated balance sheet. Goodwill will be reported, as under the benchmark treatment, to reflect only the excess paid by the majority owner in excess of the fair value of the net identifiable assets acquired.

This approach uses the purchase price for the majority interest as an indicator of the value of the entire acquired entity. The strength of this approach is that the acquired entity's assets and liabilities are valued on a consistent basis, presumably using the most recent, objectively determined valuation data, derived from the arm's-length purchase transaction.

Goodwill and Negative Goodwill

Goodwill. Goodwill represents the excess purchase price paid in a business acquisition over the fair value of the identifiable net assets obtained. Presumably, when an acquiring enterprise pays this premium price, it sees value that transcends the worth of the tangible assets and the identifiable intangibles, or else the deal would not have been consummated on such terms. Goodwill arising from acquisitions must be recognized as an asset.

The balance in the goodwill account should be reviewed at each balance sheet date to determine whether the asset has suffered any impairment. If goodwill is no longer deemed probable of being fully recovered through the profitable operations of the acquired business, it should be partially written down or fully written off. Any write-off of goodwill must be charged to expense. Once written down, goodwill cannot later be restored as an asset, again reflecting the concern that the independent measurement of goodwill is not possible and that acquired goodwill may, postacquisition, be replaced by internally generated goodwill, which is not to be recognized.

It should be noted that goodwill is recorded, in the case of acquisitions of less than 100%, only to reflect the price paid, by the new parent company, in excess of the fair values of the net identifiable assets of the subsidiary. That is, under current IFRS no goodwill is imputed to the minority interests based on the price paid by the majority (although this may change when the IASB completes Phase II of its review of business combinations). Thus, while the net identifiable assets attributable to the minority are written up to the values implied by the majority's purchase decision, goodwill will not be imputed for the minority share.

Example of purchase transaction—goodwill

Oman Heating Corp. acquired all of the common stock of Euro Boiler Manufacturing Co. on January 2, 2005, at a cost of €32 million, consisting of €15 million in cash and the balance represented by a long-term note to former Euro stockholders. As of January 2, 2005, immediately prior to the transaction, Euro's balance sheet is as follows, with both book and fair values indicated (€000 omitted):

	Book value	Fair value		Book value	Fair value
Cash	€ 1,000	€ 1,000	Current liabilities	€26,200	€26,200
Accounts receivable, net	12,200	12,000	Long-term debt	46,000	41,500
Inventory	8,500	9,750	Guarantee of debt	--	75
Other current assets	500	500			
Property, plant, and equipment, net	38,500	52,400			
Customers list	--	1,400			
Patents	2,400	3,900			
			Stockholders'		
In-process research and development	--	8,600	equity (deficit)	(9,100)	21,775
Totals	€63,100	€89,550		€63,100	€89,550

The fair value of inventory exceeded the corresponding book value because Euro Boiler had been using LIFO for many years to cost its inventory, prior to revised IAS 2's banning this method, and actual replacement cost was therefore somewhat higher than carrying value at the date of the acquisition. The long-term debt's fair value was slightly lower than carrying value (cost) because the debt carries a fixed interest rate and the market rates have risen since the debt was incurred. Consequently, Euro Boiler benefits economically by having future debt service requirements which are less onerous than they would be if it were to borrow at current rates. Conversely, of course, the fair value of the lender's note receivable has declined since it now represents a loan payable at less than market rates. Finally, the fair values of Euro Boiler's receivables have also declined from their carrying amount, due to both the higher market rates of interest and to the greater risk of uncollectibility because of the change in ownership. The higher interest rates impact the valuation in two ways: (1) when computing the discounted present value of the amounts to be received, the higher interest rate reduces the computed present value, and (2) the higher interest rates may serve as an incentive for customers to delay payments to Euro rather than borrow the money to repay the receivables, with that delay resulting in cash flows being received later than anticipated thus causing the present value to decline.

Euro Boiler's customer list has been appraised at €1.4 million and is a major reason for the company's acquisition by Oman Heating. Having been internally developed over many years, the customer list is not recorded as an asset by Euro, however. The patents have been amortized down to €2.4 million in Euro Boiler's accounting records, consistent with IFRS, but an appraisal finds that on a fair value basis the value is somewhat higher.

Similarly, property, plant, and equipment has been depreciated down to a book value of €38.5 million, but has been appraised at a sound value (that is, replacement cost new adjusted for the fraction of the useful life already elapsed) of €52.4 million.

A key asset being acquired by Oman Heating, is the in-process research and development (IPR&D), which pertains to activities undertaken over a period of several years aimed at making significant process and product improvements which would enhance Euro Boiler's market position and will be captured by the new combined operations. It has been determined that duplicating the benefits of this ongoing R&D work would cost Oman Heating €8.6 million. The strong motivation to make this acquisition, and to pay a substantial premium over book value, is based on Euro Boiler's customer list and its IPR&D. Euro Boiler has previously expensed all R&D costs incurred, as required under IFRS, since it conservatively believed that these costs were in the nature of research, rather than development.

Euro Boiler had guaranteed a €1.5 million bank debt of a former affiliated entity, but this was an "off the books" event since guarantees issued between corporations under common control were commonly deemed exempt from recognition. The actual contingent obligation has been appraised as having a fair value (considering both the amount and likelihood of having to honor the commitment) of €75,000.

Thus, although Euro Boiler's balance sheet reflects a stockholders' deficit (including the par value of common stock issued and outstanding, additional paid-in capital, and accumulated deficit) of €9.1 million, the value of the acquisition, including the IPR&D, is much higher. The preliminary computation of goodwill is as follows:

Purchase price		€32,000,000
Net working capital	€(2,950,000)	
Property, plant, and equipment	52,400,000	
Customer list	1,400,000	
Patents	3,900,000	
In-process research and development	8,600,000	
Guarantee of indebtedness of others	(75,000)	
Long-term debt	(41,500,000)	21,775,000
Goodwill (excess of cost over fair value)		€10,225,000

Under IFRS (IFRS 3), the fair value allocated to the in-process research and development must be expensed unless it is separately identifiable, is a resource that is controlled, is a probable source of future economic benefits, and has a reliably measurable fair value. Oman Heating determines that €1,800,000 of the cost of IPR&D meets all these criteria and supports capitalization. All other assets and liabilities are recorded by Oman Heating at the allocated fair values, with the excess cost being assigned to goodwill. The entry to record the purchase (for preparation of consolidated financial statements, for example) is as follows:

Cash	1,000,000	
Accounts receivable, net	12,000,000	
Inventory	9,750,000	
Other current assets	500,000	
Property, plant, and equipment	52,400,000	
Customer list	1,400,000	
Patents	3,900,000	
Goodwill	10,225,000	
Research and development expense	6,800,000	
Development costs capitalized	1,800,000	
Current liabilities		26,200,000
Guarantee of indebtedness of others		75,000
Long-term debt		41,500,000
Notes payable to former stockholders		17,000,000
Cash		15,000,000

Note that, while the foregoing example is for a stock acquisition, an asset and liability acquisition would be accounted for in the exact same manner. Also, since the debt is recorded at fair value, which will often differ from face (maturity) value, the differential (premium or discount) must be amortized using the effective yield method from acquisition date to the maturity date of the debt, and thus there will be differences between actual payments of interest and the amounts recognized in the income statements as interest expense. Finally, note that property, plant, and equipment is recorded "net"—that is, the allocated fair value becomes the "cost" of these assets; accumulated depreciation previously recorded in the accounting records of the acquired entity does not carry forward to the postacquisition financial statements of the consolidated entity.

Impairment of goodwill. Assume that an entity acquires another enterprise in a transaction accounted for as a purchase, and that after allocation of the purchase price to all identifiable assets and liabilities an unallocated excess cost of €500,000 remains. Also assume that, for purposes of impairment, it is determined that the acquired business comprises seven discrete cash generating units. The goodwill recorded on the acquisition must be allocated to some or all of those seven cash generating units. If it is the case that the goodwill is associated with only some of the seven cash generating units, the goodwill recognized in the balance sheet should be allocated to only those assets or groups of assets.

IAS 36 requires that the recoverable amount of each *cash generating unit* is calculated and compared with the carrying value of the assets, including goodwill, allocated to that unit. If the recoverable amount is less than the carrying value, an impairment write-down must be made.

An impairment loss is first absorbed by goodwill, and only when goodwill has been eliminated entirely is any further impairment loss credited to other assets in the group (on a pro rata basis, unless it is possible to measure the recoverable amounts of the individual assets). This is perhaps somewhat arbitrary, but it is also logical, since the excess earnings power represented by goodwill must be deemed to have been lost if the recoverable amount of the cash generating unit is less than its carrying amount. It is also a conservative approach, and will diminish or eliminate the display of that often misunderstood and always suspiciously viewed asset, goodwill, before the carrying values of identifiable intangible and tangible assets are adjusted.

Reversal of previously recognized impairment of goodwill. In general under IFRS, reversal of an impairment identified with a cash generating unit is permitted. However, due to the special character of this asset, IAS 36 has imposed a requirement that reversals may not be recognized for previous write-downs in goodwill. Thus, a later recovery in value of the cash generating unit will be allocated only to the nongoodwill assets. (The adjustments to those assets cannot be for amounts greater than would be needed to restore them to the carrying amounts at which they would be currently stated had the earlier impairment not been recognized—i.e., at the former carrying values less the depreciation that would have been recorded during the intervening period.)

Negative goodwill. In certain purchase business combinations, the purchase price is less than the fair value of the net assets acquired. These are often identified as being "bargain purchase" transactions. This difference has traditionally been referred to as "negative goodwill." IFRS 3 suggests that, since arm's-length business acquisition transactions will usually favor neither party, the likelihood of the acquirer obtaining a bargain is considered remote. According to this standard, apparent instances of bargain purchases giving rise to negative goodwill are more often the result of measurement error (i.e., where the fair values assigned to assets and liabilities were incorrect to some extent) or of a failure to recognize a contingent or actual liability (such as for employee severance payments). However, negative goodwill can also derive from the risk of future losses, recognized by both parties and incorporated into the transaction price. (One such example was the case of the sale by BMW of its Rover car division to a consortium for £1. It did indeed suffer subsequent losses and eventually failed.)

IFRS 3 requires that, before negative goodwill is recognized, the allocation of fair values is to be revisited, and that all liabilities—including contingencies—be reviewed. After this is completed, if indeed the fair values of identifiable assets acquired net of all liabilities assumed exceeds the total cost of the transaction, then negative goodwill will be acknowledged. The accounting treatment of negative goodwill has passed through a number of evolutionary stages beginning with the original IAS 22, which was later twice revised with major changes to the prescribed accounting treatment of negative goodwill.

Under current IFRS 3, negative goodwill is taken immediately into income. Essentially, this is regarded, for financial reporting purposes, as a gain realized upon the acquisition transaction, and accounted for accordingly.

Example of purchase transaction—negative goodwill

Hoegedorn Corp. acquires, on March 4, 2005, all the capital stock of Gemutlicheit Co. for €800,000 in cash. A formerly successful enterprise, Gemutlicheit had recently suffered from declining sales and demands for repayment of its outstanding bank debt, which were threatening its continued existence. Hoegedorn management perceived an opportunity to make a favorable purchase of a company operating in a related line of business, and accordingly made this modest offer, which was accepted by the stockholders of Gemutlicheit, the acquiree. Gemutlicheit's balance sheet at the date of acquisition is as follows, with both book and fair values indicated (€000 omitted):

	Book value	Fair value		Book value	Fair value
Cash	€ 800	€ 800	Current liabilities	€ 2,875	€ 2,875
Accounts receivable, net	3,600	3,400	Long-term debt	11,155	11,155
Inventory	1,850	1,800			
Property, plant, and equipment	6,800	7,200	Stockholders'		
Net operating loss carryforwards	--	2,400	equity (deficit)	(980)	1,570
Totals	€13,050	€15,600		€13,050	€15,600

Gemutlicheit had provided a valuation allowance for the deferred income tax asset attributable to the net operating loss carryforward tax benefit, since recurring and increasing losses made it more likely than not that these benefits would not be realized, consistent with IFRS (IAS 12). Hoegedorn Corp., which is highly profitable, is in the same line of business, and intends to continue Gemutlicheit's operation, expects to be able to realize these benefits, and therefore will have no valuation allowance against this asset.

Thus, although Gemutlicheit's balance sheet reflects a stockholders' deficit (including outstanding common stock, additional paid-in capital and accumulated deficit) of €980,000, the value of the acquisition is much higher, and furthermore the acquirer is able to negotiate a bargain purchase. The preliminary computation of negative goodwill is as follows:

Net working capital	€ 3,125,000	
Property, plant, and equipment	7,200,000	
Net operating loss carryforward	2,400,000	
Long-term debt	(11,155,000)	1,570,000
Purchase price		800,000
Negative goodwill (excess of fair value over cost)		€ 770,000

IFRS 3 requires that negative goodwill be taken into earnings immediately, after first verifying that all acquired or assumed liabilities, including contingencies, have been fully accounted for, and that assets acquired were not overstated. In the present example, these matters were reviewed and the amounts shown above were fully supported.

The entry to record the purchase is therefore as follows:

Cash	800,000	
Accounts receivable, net	3,400,000	
Inventory	1,800,000	
Property, plant, and equipment	7,200,000	
Deferred income tax asset	2,400,000	
Current liabilities		2,875,000
Long-term debt		11,155,000
Cash		800,000
Gain on bargain purchase transaction		770,000

Contingent Consideration

In many business combinations, the purchase price is not completely fixed at the time of the exchange, but is instead dependent on the outcome of future events. There are two major types of future events that might commonly be used to modify the purchase price: the performance of the acquired entity (acquiree), and the market value of the consideration given for the acquisition.

The most frequently encountered contingency involves the postacquisition performance of the purchased entity or operations. The contractual agreement dealing with this is often referred to as an "earn out" provision. It typically calls for additional payments to be made to the former owners of the acquiree if defined revenue or earnings thresholds are met or exceeded. These may extend for several years after the acquisition date, and may define varying thresholds for different years. For example, if the acquiree, during its final pretransaction year, generated revenues of €4 million, there might be additional sums due if the acquired operations produced €4.5 million or greater revenues in year one after the acquisition, €5 million or greater in year two, and €6 million in year three.

If the contingent consideration is deemed likely to become payable, and furthermore can be measured reliably at the date of the acquisition, an estimate should be included in the cost of the acquisition. This is a change from past practice, and is at variance with current US GAAP requirements, but is a logical change, since a contingent liability that is probable and measurable is to be accrued currently.

If all or some of the accrued contingent consideration is not later earned and paid, an adjustment has to be made to the cost of the acquisition. Since the inclusion of the contingent payment most likely resulted in initial or increased recognition of goodwill, the revision for nonpayment will normally cause an adjustment to be made to goodwill.

If, at the transaction date, the contingent consideration is either deemed not probable, or cannot be reliably estimated, no estimate is made at that date. However, if in the future a payment does become probable, and can be reliably estimated, an adjustment should be made to recognize this additional acquisition cost at that time. As noted previously, this probably will result in the initial or increased recognition of goodwill.

Whether accrued at the transaction date or not, the ultimate payment of contingent consideration may exceed what was recorded. Any additional cost should be assigned to assets acquired, which is generally going to be goodwill.

The less often observed type of postacquisition adjustment that can occur is where the acquirer has guaranteed the value of the consideration given. For example, if €3 million of shares were issued to effect the purchase, the acquiring entity might warrant that the market price would not fall below, say, €2.8 million over a defined time horizon, generally no longer than one or two years. If the value of the consideration given declines below this threshold level, and the acquirer is obliged to make a further payment of shares, this is not accounted for as an additional cost of the business combination. Rather, the newly increased number of shares issued is adjusted against the value of the equity originally issued, not against the purchase price of the acquiree. Thus, the acquirer's capital accounts would be adjusted, typically by increasing the aggregate par or stated value of shares issued (since more shares will now be given), and decreasing additional paid-in capital.

Disclosure requirements. IFRS 3 has added a sizable number of new disclosures to existing requirements. The principle stated is that users should be able to evaluate the nature and financial effect of any combinations that were carried out during the period or after the balance sheet date. The detailed requirements include disclosure of

1. The number of equity instruments issued or issuable as purchase consideration and the fair value of those instruments.
2. The amounts recognized as at the date of acquisition for each class of the acquiree's assets and liabilities.
3. The carrying amount of each class of the acquiree's assets and liabilities immediately before the business combination.
4. The amount of any excess of the fair value of the acquiree's identifiable net assets over the cost of acquisition (i.e., the negative goodwill), and the line item in the income statement in which the excess is recognized.
5. A description of the factors that contributed to a cost of acquisition that results in the recognition of goodwill, or a description of the nature of any excess of the fair value of the acquiree's identifiable net assets over the cost of acquisition.
6. The amount of the acquiree's profit or loss included in the profit or loss of the reporting entity for the period.
7. In aggregate, the information required to be disclosed for each business combination for those business combinations that are individually immaterial.
8. The revenue and the profit or loss of the combined entity for the reporting period as though the date of acquisition for all of the business combinations during the reporting period had been the beginning of the reporting period, unless that disclosure would require undue cost and effort.
9. In periods following a business combination, any gain or loss related to the assets acquired or liabilities assumed that is of such size, nature, or incidence that disclosure is relevant to an understanding of the combined entity's financial performance.
10. The reconciliation of the carrying amount of goodwill should be amended to require net exchange differences arising on the translation of the financial statements of a foreign entity also to be shown separately.

Transitional arrangements. IFRS 3 applies to all combinations consummated after March 31, 2004. For previous combinations, the standard is to be applied prospectively. Where an entity already has goodwill, amortization ceases and instead impairment testing will be required instead. This would apply also to goodwill implicit in an investment accounted for by the equity method.

Any negative goodwill existing at the time IFRS 3 was first adopted was to be credited directly to retained earnings. This would apply also to negative goodwill implicit in an investment accounted for by the equity method.

An intangible asset acquired in a business combination before IFRS 3 was first adopted, that does not meet the recognition criteria in the revised IAS 38, is to be reclassified as goodwill. The revisions to IAS 38 apply to intangible assets recognized at the time the standards are adopted. Any resulting change in estimated useful life (including a change from a finite life to an indefinite life) should be accounted for prospectively as a change in estimate.

Proposed Amendments to IFRS 3

IFRS 3 as originally issued included a scope exception for mutual entities and entities under common control (e.g., brother-sister companies, owned completely or substantially by the same owners). The IASB decided subsequently that this was unnecessary and issued a proposed amendment withdrawing the scope exceptions in 2004, which was not adopted as a final standard. The substance of that draft has now been adopted in a more substantive proposal, described below.

IFRS 3 was the first phase of a two-part IASB project dealing with accounting for business combinations. It was promised at the time IFRS 3 was promulgated that another standard would be forthcoming, addressing a number of consolidated financial reporting issues and allied topics. This second phase was expected to deal with specific accounting procedures arising in purchase accounting and with special business combination issues, such as joint venturing and combinations of entities already under common control.

In mid-2005, IASB issued the Exposure Draft of this substantive amendment to IFRS 3. This will, if adopted, require an acquirer to recognize an acquired business at its full fair value at the acquisition date, rather than at its cost. It also will require that the acquirer measure and recognize individual assets acquired and liabilities assumed at their fair values at the acquisition date, with limited exceptions. The major implication is that even in business combinations in which the acquirer obtains control of a business by acquiring less than 100% of the equity interests in the acquiree, or in step acquisitions, full fair value of assets and liabilities, including goodwill, will be reported after the transaction (or final step) has occurred. The draft presents IASB's conclusions that

- Recognition should be given to the minority interest's share of goodwill (i.e., the price paid for the majority interest should be extrapolated to an implied value for the entire acquiree, including the minority share, resulting in a "step up" in the amount of reported minority interest for goodwill).
- Acquisition cost is to be measured at fair value, as the sum of (1) the assets transferred by the acquirer, liabilities incurred by the acquirer, and equity interests issued by the acquirer, including contingent consideration, and (2) any noncontrolling equity investment in the acquiree owned by the acquirer immediately before the acquisition date. This differs from current IFRS 3 in that the fair value of all contingent consideration will be included in the purchase price, compared to current practice which recognizes only that contingent consideration which meets IAS 37 criteria.
- The acquirer should be required to assess whether any portion of the transaction price paid, and any asset acquired or liabilities assumed or incurred, are not part of the exchange for the acquiree. For example, transaction costs would be excluded from the cost to be allocated to acquired assets, in a change from current practice. Only the consideration transferred or the assets acquired or liabilities assumed or incurred that are part of the exchange for the acquiree will be accounted for as part of the business combination accounting.
- The acquirer will be required to measure and recognize the acquisition-date fair value of the assets acquired and liabilities assumed as part of the business combination, with limited exceptions, which will be
  - Goodwill, which will be measured and recognized as the excess of the fair value of the acquiree, as a whole, over the net amount of the recognized identifiable assets acquired and liabilities assumed. Thus, if the acquirer owns less than 100% of the equity interests in the acquiree at the acquisition date, goodwill attributable to the

noncontrolling interest will be recognized, contrary to current practice under existing IFRS 3.

- Noncurrent assets (or disposal group) classified as held-for-sale, deferred tax assets or liabilities, and assets or liabilities related to the acquiree's employee benefit plans will be measured in accordance with other IFRS (IFRS 5, IAS 12, and IAS 19, respectively).
- Acquiree operating leases, where no asset or related liability will be recognized if the lease terms reflect market conditions.

- The acquirer will recognize, separately from goodwill, an acquiree's intangible assets that meet the definition of an intangible asset set forth in IAS 38 and which are identifiable (i.e., if they arise from contractual-legal rights or are separable).
- In a business combination where the acquisition-date fair value of the acquirer's interest in the acquiree exceeds the fair value of the consideration transferred for that interest (the "bargain purchase" situation), the acquirer will be required to account for that excess by reducing goodwill until the goodwill related to that business combination is reduced to zero and then by recognizing any remaining excess in profit or loss.
- The acquirer will be required to recognize any adjustments made during the measurement period to the provisional values of the assets acquired and liabilities assumed as if the accounting for the business combination had been completed at the acquisition date. This will necessitate adjusting comparative information for prior periods presented in financial statements.
- Increase or decreases in the parent's ownership interest after a business combination should be accounted for as equity transactions, not as acquisition transactions.

The proposed standard will provide extended guidance on the accounting for combinations of mutual entities, those achieved by contract alone (providing control without ownership, for example), step acquisitions, those transferring less than 100% ownership, and bargain purchases.

Regarding mergers of mutually owned entities, the proposed standard would mandate that an amount equal to the fair value of the acquiree would be recognized as a direct addition to capital or equity, not to retained earnings.

As to situations where an acquirer (1) obtains control of an acquiree by contract, (2) transfers no consideration for control of the acquiree for the net assets of the acquiree, and (3) obtains no equity interest in the acquiree, either on the acquisition date or previously, the fair value of the acquiree would be attributed to the noncontrolling interests of the acquiree (that is, the equity holders of the acquiree) in the consolidated financial statements of the acquirer.

The new standard would also greatly expand disclosures required in all business combinations. According to the Exposure Draft, one set of disclosures would be designed to enable users of the financial statements to evaluate the nature and financial effect of business combinations that occur both (1) during the reporting period; and (2) after the balance sheet date but before the financial statements are authorized for issue. These would include, for those combinations that occur during the reporting period

- Name and description of the acquiree.
- Acquisition date.
- Percentage of voting equity instruments acquired.
- Primary reasons for the combination, including a description of the factors that contributed to the recognition of goodwill.
- Acquisition-date fair value of the acquiree and basis for measuring that value.

- Acquisition-date fair value of the consideration transferred, including the fair value of each major class of consideration, such as
  - Cash
  - Other tangible or intangible assets, including a business or subsidiary of the acquirer
  - Contingent consideration
  - Debt instruments
  - Equity or member interests of the acquirer, including the number of instruments or interests issued or issuable, and the method of determining the fair value of those instruments or interests
    - Acquirer's previously acquired noncontrolling equity investment in the acquiree in a business combination achieved in stages.
- Amounts recognized as of the acquisition date for each major class of assets acquired and liabilities assumed in the form of a condensed balance sheet.
- Maximum potential amount of future payments (undiscounted) the acquirer could be required to make under the terms of the acquisition agreement; if there is no limitation on the maximum future payments, that would be disclosed.
- For a "bargain purchase" business combination, the amount of any gain recognized, the line item in the income statement where the gain is recognized, and a description of the reasons why the acquirer was able to achieve a gain.
- For a business combination achieved in stages, the amount of any gain or loss recognized, and the line item in the income statement where that gain or loss is recognized.
- For a business combination in which the acquirer and acquiree have a preexisting relationship
  - The nature of the preexisting relationship
  - The measurement of the settlement amount of the preexisting relationship, if any, and the valuation method used to determine the settlement amount.
  - The amount of any settlement gain or loss recognized and the line item in the income statement where that gain or loss is recognized.
- Amount of costs incurred in connection with the business combination, the amount recognized as an expense, and the line item or items in the income statement where those expenses are recognized.

The acquirer will also be required to disclose the information set forth above in the aggregate for individually immaterial business combinations that are material collectively. If a material business combination is completed after the balance sheet date but before the financial statements are authorized for issue, these disclosures will also be made, unless disclosure of any of the information is impracticable—but if impracticable, that fact and the reasons will have to be disclosed.

An acquirer will furthermore be required to disclose the following information for each material business combination that occurs during the reporting period, or in the aggregate for individually immaterial business combinations that are material collectively and occur during the reporting period:

1. Amounts of revenue and profit or loss of the acquiree since the acquisition date that are included in the consolidated income statement for the reporting period.
2. The revenue and operating results of the combined entity for the current reporting period as though the acquisition date for all business combinations that occurred during the year had been as of the beginning of the annual reporting period.

If disclosure of any of this information is impracticable, that fact and the reasons would have to be disclosed.

The acquirer will also be required to disclose information that enables users of the financial statements to evaluate the financial effects of adjustments recognized in the current reporting period relating to business combinations that were effected in the current or previous reporting periods. This information would include, for each material business combination or in the aggregate for individually immaterial business combinations that are material collectively

1. If the amounts recognized in the financial statements for the business combination have been determined only provisionally

   a. The reasons why the initial accounting for the business combination is not complete.
   b. The assets acquired or the liabilities assumed for which the measurement period is still open.
   c. The nature and amount of any measurement period adjustments recognized during the reporting period.

2. A reconciliation of the beginning and ending balances of liabilities for contingent consideration and contingencies that are required to be remeasured to fair value after initial recognition, showing separately the changes in fair value during the reporting period and amounts paid or otherwise settled in accordance with IAS 37 and IAS 39.

3. A description of the discrete event or circumstance that occurred after the acquisition date that resulted in deferred tax assets acquired as part of the business combination being recognized as income within twelve months after the acquisition date.

4. The amount and an explanation of any gain or loss recognized in the current reporting period that *both*

   a. Relates to the identifiable assets acquired or liabilities assumed in a business combination that was effected in the current or previous reporting period, and
   b. Is of such a size, nature or incidence that disclosure is relevant to understanding the combined entity's financial statements.

The acquirer will additionally be required to disclose information that enables users of its financial statements to evaluate changes in the carrying amount of goodwill during the reporting period. To meet this objective, if the total amount of goodwill is significant in relation to the fair value of the acquiree, the acquirer will have to disclose for each material business combination that occurs during the reporting period, the total amount of goodwill and the amount that is expected to be deductible for tax purposes.

The acquiree will also disclose the information in the preceding paragraph (1) in aggregate for individually immaterial business combinations that are material collectively (2) if a material business combination is completed after the balance sheet date but before the financial statements are authorized for issue unless such disclosure is impracticable, in which case that fact and the reasons therefor must be disclosed.

The acquirer will have to disclose a reconciliation of the carrying amount of goodwill at the beginning and end of the reporting period, showing separately

1. The gross amount and accumulated impairment losses at the beginning of the reporting period.

2. The additional goodwill recognized during the reporting period, except goodwill included in a disposal group than, on acquisition, meets the criteria to be classified as held-for-sale in accordance with IFRS 5.
3. Adjustments resulting from the subsequent recognition of deferred tax assets during the reporting period.
4. Goodwill included in a disposal group classified as held-for-sale in accordance with IFRS 5 and goodwill derecognized during the reporting period without having previously been included in a disposal group classified as held-for-sale.
5. Impairment losses recognized during the reporting period in accordance with IAS 36.
6. The net exchange differences arising during the reporting period in accordance with IAS 21.
7. Any other changes in the carrying amount during the reporting period.
8. The gross amount and accumulated impairment losses at the end of the reporting period.

Finally, the proposed standard stipulates that if the specific disclosures required by this and other IFRS do not meet the objectives set out above, the acquirer will be expected to disclose any additional information necessary to meet those objectives.

The proposed standard, which will amend IFRS 3, is anticipated to become effective in 2007.

Consolidated Financial Statements

Requirements for consolidated financial statements. IAS 27, as most recently revised, prescribes the requirements for the presentation of consolidated financial statements. A parent entity must present consolidated financial statements in order to comply with IFRS, unless *all* of the following conditions apply:

1. It is a wholly owned subsidiary, or if the owners of the minority interests, including those not otherwise entitled to vote, unanimously agree that the parent need not present consolidated financial statements;
2. Its securities are not publicly traded;
3. It is not in the process of issuing securities in public securities markets; and
4. The immediate or ultimate parent publishes consolidated financial statements that comply with IFRS.

Under the provisions of revised IAS 27, when the conditions above are all satisfied and as a consequence the parent chooses not to present consolidated financial statements, but to instead present separate financial statements, then all investments in subsidiaries, jointly controlled entities and associates that are consolidated, proportionally consolidated or accounted for under the equity method in consolidated financial statements prepared in accordance with the requirements of IAS 27 or in financial statements prepared in accordance with the requirements of IAS 31 or IAS 28, must be accounted for either at cost, or as available-for-sale financial assets in accordance with IAS 39. The same method must be applied for each category of investments. In other words, if consolidated financial reporting is foregone, then equity method accounting or proportional consolidation is also precluded.

Revised IAS 27 stipulates that under the cost method, an investor recognizes its investment in the investee at cost. Income is recognized only to the extent that the investor receives distributions from the accumulated net profits of the investee arising after the date of acquisition by the investor. Distributions received in excess of such profits are to be regarded as recoveries of the investment, and are to be accounted for as a reduction of the cost of the investment (i.e., as a return of capital).

Furthermore, investments in subsidiaries, jointly controlled entities and associates that are accounted for in accordance with IAS 39 in the consolidated financial statements are to be accounted for in the same way in the investor's separate financial statements and in the financial statements of a parent that need not present consolidated financial statements.

IAS 27 holds that users of the financial statements of a parent entity, joint venturer, or investor in an associate are usually concerned with and need to be informed about the financial position, results of operations, and changes in financial position of the group as a whole. This need is served by consolidated financial statements or financial statements in which the associate is accounted for under the equity method that present financial information about the group as a single economic entity without regard for the legal boundaries of the separate legal entities.

The "substance over form" imperative, which is not always heeded in financial reporting, is normally given great weight in these reporting matters. On the other hand, separate financial statements present financial information about the entity's position viewed as an investor. The implication is that, even when permissible under IFRS, separate financial reporting is not viewed as being more useful than consolidated reporting. For this reason, the following disclosures have to be made in the investor's separate financial statements and in the financial statements of a parent that need not present consolidated financial statements:

1. The reasons why separate financial statements are being presented;
2. The name of the immediate or ultimate parent and a reference to the consolidated financial statements and/or the financial statements in which associates and jointly controlled entities are accounted for under the equity method or proportionate consolidation method in accordance with IAS 28 and IAS 31, respectively; and
3. A description of the method used to account for investments in subsidiaries, associates and jointly controlled entities.

In addition to the foregoing elective option to not present consolidated financial statements, IAS 27 essentially continues its predecessor's prohibition of consolidation when there is an absence of control over a subsidiary. Consolidated financial statements are to consolidate a parent and all of its subsidiaries, foreign and domestic, when those entities are controlled by the parent. For making this determination, control is presumed to exist when the parent owns, directly or indirectly through subsidiaries, more than one-half of the voting power of an entity—unless, in exceptional circumstances, it can be clearly demonstrated that this ownership does not connote control. Control also exists when the parent owns one-half or less of the voting power of an entity when there is

1. Power over more than one-half of the voting rights by virtue of an agreement with other investors (e.g., a voting trust);
2. Power to govern the financial and operating policies of the entity under a statute or an agreement;
3. Power to appoint or remove the majority of the members of the board of directors or equivalent governing body and control of the entity is by that board or body; or
4. Power to cast the majority of votes at meetings of the board of directors or equivalent governing body and control of the entity is by that board or body.

Control may furthermore be precluded when an investee is in legal reorganization or in bankruptcy or operates under severe long-term restrictions on its ability to transfer funds to the investor. Thus, under unusual circumstances, a majority owned subsidiary would be excluded from consolidation.

Additionally (under the terms of IFRS 5), a subsidiary must be excluded from consolidation when control is intended to be temporary because the subsidiary is acquired and held exclusively with a view to subsequent disposal within twelve months from acquisition. Investments in such subsidiaries should be treated as a disposal group, and accounted for at fair value less costs to sell, with any later changes in fair value included in profit or loss of the period of the change. Categorization as a disposal group is dependent upon the subsidiary being available for sale in its present condition, as well as there being both a management commitment to sell and a high probability of disposal actually taking place within twelve months from the date of acquisition.

The exceptions to consolidation are strictly limited and cannot be generalized from the situations described above. Thus, a subsidiary cannot be excluded from consolidation simply because the investor is a venture capital organization, mutual fund, unit trust, or similar entity. Also, a subsidiary cannot be excluded from consolidation because its business activities are dissimilar from those of the other entities within the group. It is presumed that more relevant information is provided by consolidating such subsidiaries and disclosing additional information in the consolidated financial statements about the different business activities of subsidiaries. The disclosure model of IAS 14 for segment information may be relevant to such an exercise in the case of nonhomogeneous consolidated subsidiaries.

Impact of Potential Voting Interests on Consolidation

Historically, actual voting interests in subsidiaries has been the criterion used to determine

1. If consolidated financial statements are to be presented; and
2. What percentage to apply in determining the allocation of a subsidiary's income, included in consolidated earnings, between the parent and the minority interests.

However, as revised, IAS 27 also addresses the situation where the parent entity has, in addition to its actual voting shareholder interest, a further potential voting interest in the subsidiary. (This was first addressed by SIC 33, which was withdrawn when IAS 27 was revised.)

A potential interest may exist due to the existence of options, warrants, convertible shares, or a contractual agreement to acquire additional shares, including shares that the investor or parent entity may have sold to another shareholder in the subsidiary or to another party, with a right or contractual arrangement to reacquire the shares transferred at a later date.

As to whether the potential shares should be considered in reaching a decision as to whether control is present, and thus whether the reporting entity is to be regarded as the parent company and should therefore prepare consolidated financial statements, IAS 27 holds that this is indeed a factor to weigh. It concluded that the existence and effect of potential voting rights that are *presently* exercisable or *presently* convertible should be considered, in addition to the other factors set forth in IAS 27, when assessing whether an enterprise controls another enterprise. All potential voting rights should be considered, including any potential voting rights held by other enterprises, which would mitigate or even eliminate the impact of the reporting entity's potential voting interest.

For example, an entity holding 40% voting rights in another entity, but having options to acquire another 15% voting interest, the effect of which is not offset by options held by another party, would effectively have a 55% current and potential voting interest, making consolidation required under IAS 27.

On the other hand, concerning whether the potential share interest should be taken into account when determining what fraction of the subsidiary's income should be allocated to the parent, the general answer is no. IAS 27 states that the proportion allocated to the parent and to minority interests, respectively, when preparing consolidated financial statements should be determined solely on present ownership interests. That is, potential ownership may necessitate consolidated financial reporting, but income or loss allocation is still to be based on actual, not potential, ownership percentages.

However, the enterprise may, in substance, have a present ownership interest when it sells and simultaneously agrees to repurchase some of the voting shares it had held in the subsidiary. In such a situation, it does not lose control of access to economic benefits associated with an ownership interest. In this circumstance, the proportion allocated should be determined by taking into account the eventual exercise of potential voting rights and other derivatives that, in substance, give present access to the economic benefits associated with an ownership interest. Note that the right to reacquire shares alone is not enough to have those shares included for purposes of determining the percentage of the subsidiary's income to be reported by the parent. Rather, the parent must have ongoing access to the economic benefits of ownership of those shares.

Intercompany transactions and balances. In preparing consolidated financial statements, any transactions among members of the group must be eliminated. For example, a parent may sell merchandise to its subsidiary, at cost or with a profit margin added, before the subsidiary ultimately sells the merchandise to unrelated parties in arm's-length transactions. Furthermore, any balances due to or from members of the consolidated group at the date of the balance sheet must also be eliminated. The reason for this requirement: to avoid grossing up the financial statements for transactions or balances that do not represent economic events with outside parties. Were this rule not in effect, a consolidated group could create the appearance of being a much larger enterprise than it is in reality, merely by engaging in multiple transactions with itself.

If assets have been transferred among the entities in the controlled group at amounts in excess of the transferor's cost, and they have not yet been further transferred to outside parties (e.g., inventories) or not yet consumed (e.g., plant assets subject to depreciation) by the date of the balance sheet, the amount of profit not yet realized through an arm's-length transaction must be eliminated.

Different fiscal periods of parent and subsidiary. A practical consideration in preparing consolidated financial statements is to have information on all constituent entities current as of the parent's year-end. If the subsidiaries have different fiscal years, they may prepare updated information as of the parent's year-end, to be used for preparing consolidated statements. Failing this, IAS 27 permits combining information as of different dates, as long as this discrepancy does not exceed three months. Of course, if this option is elected, the process of eliminating intercompany transactions and balances may become a bit more complicated, since reciprocal accounts (e.g., sales and cost of sales) will be out of balance for any events occurring after the earlier fiscal year-end but before the later one.

Uniformity of accounting policies. There is a presumption that all the members of the consolidated group should use the same accounting principles to account for similar events and transactions. However, in many cases this will not occur, as, for example, when a subsidiary is acquired that uses FIFO costing for its inventories while the parent has long employed the LIFO method. (Note that LIFO is no longer permitted under provisions of revised IAS 2. The average cost method is still permitted as an alternative to FIFO.) IAS 27 does not demand that one or the other entity change its method of accounting; rather, it merely requires that there be adequate disclosure of the accounting principles employed.

If a subsidiary was acquired during the period, the results of the operations of the subsidiary should be included in consolidated financial statements only for the period it was owned. Since this may cause comparability with earlier periods presented to be impaired, there must be adequate disclosure in the accompanying footnotes to make it possible to interpret the information properly. The posttax profits or losses of operations that have been sold or classified as held for sale during the period should be disclosed separately on the face of the income statement as discontinued operations.

Consolidated Statements in Subsequent Periods with Minority Interests

When a company acquires some, but not all, of the voting stock of another entity, the shares held by third parties represent a *minority interest* in the acquired company. Under IFRS, if a parent company owns more than half of another entity (or controls that entity in some other way, as discussed above), the two should be consolidated for financial statement purposes (unless to do so would mislead the statement users because control is temporary or the businesses are heterogeneous, etc.). The minority interest in the assets and earnings of the consolidated entity must also be accounted for.

When consolidated statements are prepared, the full amount of assets and liabilities (in the balance sheet) and income and expenses (in the income statement) of the subsidiary are generally presented. Accordingly, a contra must be shown for the portion of these items that does not belong to the parent company. In the balance sheet this contra is normally a credit item shown between total liabilities and stockholders' equity, representing the minority interest in consolidated net assets equal to the minority's percentage ownership in the net assets of the subsidiary entity. Although less likely, a debit balance in minority interest could result when the subsidiary has a deficit in its stockholders' equity and when there is reason to believe that the minority owners will make additional capital contributions to erase that deficit. This situation sometimes occurs where the entities are closely held and the minority owners are related parties having other business relationships with the parent company and/or its stockholders. In other circumstances, a debit in minority interest would be charged against parent company retained earnings under the concept that the loss will be borne by that company.

IAS 27 as revised stipulates that minority interest be presented in the consolidated balance sheet as a separate component of, but within, stockholders' equity. Previously, IAS 27 permitted minority interest to be shown in a separate caption positioned between liabilities and equity. However, IASB determined that it did not meet the definition of a liability and should be included within equity.

In the income statement, the minority interest in the income (or loss) of a consolidated subsidiary is shown as a deduction from (or addition to) the consolidated net income account. As above, if the minority interest in the net assets of the subsidiary has already been reduced to zero, and if a net debit minority interest will not be recorded (the usual case), the minority's interest in any further losses should not be recorded. (However, this must be explained in the footnotes.) Furthermore, if past minority losses have not been recorded, the minority's interest in current profits will not be recognized until the aggregate of such profits equals the aggregate unrecognized losses. This closely parallels the rule for equity method accounting recognition of profits and losses.

IAS 27 states that income attributable to minority interest be separately presented in the statement of earnings or operations. Generally, this is accomplished by presenting net income before minority interest, followed by the allocation to the minority, and then followed by net income.

Example of consolidation process involving a minority interest

Assume the following:

Alto Company and Bass Company
Balance Sheets at January 1, 2006
(before combination)

	Alto Company	*Bass Company*
Assets		
Cash	€ 30,900	€ 37,400
Accounts receivable (net)	34,200	9,100
Inventories	22,900	16,100
Equipment	200,000	50,000
Less accumulated depreciation	(21,000)	(10,000)
Patents	--	10,000
Total assets	€267,000	€112,600
Liabilities and stockholders' equity		
Accounts payable	€ 4,000	€ 6,600
Bonds payable, 10%	100,000	--
Common stock, €10 par	100,000	50,000
Additional paid-in capital	15,000	15,000
Retained earnings	48,000	41,000
Total liabilities and stockholders' equity	€267,000	€112,600

Note that in the foregoing, the net assets of Bass Company may be computed by one of two methods.

Method 1: Subtract the book value of the liability from the book values of the assets.

$$€112,600 – €6,600 = €106,000$$

Method 2: Add the book value of the components of Bass Company's stockholders' equity.

$$€50,000 + €15,000 + €41,000 = €106,000$$

Alto requires 90% of the shares of Bass. At the date of the combination, the fair value of all (i.e., 100% of) the assets and liabilities were determined by appraisal, as follows:

Bass Company Item	*Book value (BV)*	*Fair market value (FMV)*	*Difference between BV and FMV*
Cash	€ 37,400	€ 37,400	€ --
Accounts receivable (net)	9,100	9,100	--
Inventories	16,100	17,100	1,000
Equipment (net)	40,000	48,000	8,000
Patents	10,000	13,000	3,000
Accounts payable	(6,600)	(6,600)	--
Totals	€106,000	€118,000	€12,000

The equipment has a book value of €40,000 (€50,000 less 20% depreciation of €10,000). An appraisal concluded that the equipment's replacement cost was €60,000 less 20% accumulated depreciation of €12,000, resulting in a net fair value of €48,000.

When a minority interest exists, as in this example, the concept employed is to record all the assets and liabilities at their fair values as of the date of the acquisition, including the portion represented by the minority interest's ownership share. There will be no mixture of costs for the net identifiable assets acquired in the business combination on the consolidated balance sheet; all items will be presented at fair values as of the acquisition date. Goodwill, however, will be presented only to the extent that the acquirer paid more than the fair values of the net identifiable assets; there will not be any goodwill attributable to the minority interest.

In the present example, Bass's identifiable (i.e., before goodwill) net assets will be reported in the Alto consolidated balance sheet at €118,000. These amounts are computed as follows:

Bass Company net assets, at FMV	€118,000	
90% thereof (majority interest)		€106,200
Bass Company net assets, at FMV	118,000	
10% thereof (minority interest)		11,800
Total identifiable net assets		€118,000

Assume that on January 1, 2006, Alto acquired 90% of Bass in exchange for 5,400 shares of €10 par common stock having a market value of €120,600.

Working papers for the consolidated balance sheet as of the date of the transaction will be as shown below.

Alto Company and Bass Company Consolidated Working Papers
For Date of Combination—1/1/06

Purchase accounting
90% interest

	Alto Company	Bass Company	Adjustments and eliminations Debit	Credit	Minority interest	Consolidated balances
Balance sheet, 1/1/06						
Cash	€ 30,900	€ 37,400				€ 68,300
Accounts receivable	34,200	9,100				43,300
Inventories	22,900	16,100	€ 1,000b			40,000
Equipment	200,000	50,000	10,000b			260,000
Accumulated depreciation	(21,000)	(10,000)		€ 2,000b		(33,000)
Investment in stock of						
Bass Company	120,600			120,600a		
Difference between fair and						
book value			12,000a	12,000b		
Excess of cost over fair						
value (goodwill)			14,400a			14,400
Patents		10,000	3,000b			13,000
Total assets	€387,600	€112,600				€406,000
Accounts payable	€ 4,000	€ 6,600				€ 10,600
Bonds payable	100,000					100,000
Capital stock	154,000	50,000	45,000a		€ 5,000	154,000
Additional paid-in capital	81,600	15,000	13,500a		1,500	81,600
Retained earnings	48,000	41,000	36,900a		4,100	48,000
Share of revaluation				1,200a	1,200	
Minority interest					€11,800	11,800 MI
Total liabilities and equity	€387,600	€112,600	€135,800	€135,800		€406,000

Based on the foregoing, the consolidated balance sheet as of the date of acquisition will be as follows:

Alto Company and Bass Company
Consolidated Balance Sheet at January 1, 2006
(immediately after combination)

Assets

Cash	€ 68,300
Accounts receivable, net	43,300
Inventories	40,000
Equipment	260,000
Less accumulated depreciation	(33,000)
Goodwill	14,400
Patents	13,000
Total assets	€406,000

Liabilities and stockholders' equity

Accounts payable	€ 10,600
Bonds payable, 10%	100,000
Total liabilities	110,600
Common stock, €10 par	154,000
Additional paid-in capital	81,600
Retained earnings	48,000
Equity holders of parent	283,600
Minority interest	11,800
Total equity	295,400
Total liabilities and equity	€406,000

1. Investment on Alto Company's books

    The entry to record the 90% purchase-acquisition on Alto Company's books was

Investment in stock of Bass Company	120,600	
Capital stock		54,000
Additional paid-in capital		66,600

    To record the issuance of 5,400 shares of €10 par stock to acquire a 90% interest in Bass Company

    Although common stock is used for the consideration in our example, Alto Company could have used debentures, cash, or any other form of consideration acceptable to Bass Company's stockholders to make the purchase combination.

2. Difference between investment cost and fair value

    The difference between the investment cost and the parent company's equity in the net assets of the subsidiary at fair value is computed as follows:

Investment cost			€120,600
Computation of goodwill			
Book value of Bass Company at acquisition date			
Capital stock		€ 50,000	
Additional paid-in capital		15,000	
Retained earnings		41,000	
		€106,000	
Majority share (% stock ownership)		x 90%	
Acquired share of book value	(a)	95,400	
Allocation of step up to fair value of net assets			
Fair value of net assets		€118,000	
Book value of net assets		106,000	
Excess fair value over book value (step up)		12,000	
Majority share (% stock ownership)		x 90%	
Majority share of step up	(b)	10,800	
Majority's share of net assets at fair value (b) – (a)		€106,200	€106,200
Goodwill to be recognized			€ 14,400

Adjustment of asset values		
Inventory	1,000	
Equipment	10,000	
Patents	3,000	
Accumulated depreciation		2,000
Difference between fair value and book value		12,000

3. Elimination entries on preceding workpaper (a)

    The basic reciprocal accounts are the investment in subsidiary account on the parent's books and the subsidiary's stockholder equity accounts. Only the parent's share of the subsidiary's accounts may be eliminated as reciprocal accounts. The remaining 10% portion is allocated to the minority interest. The entries below include documentation showing the company source for the information. The workpaper entry to eliminate the basic reciprocal accounts is as follows:

Capital stock—Bass Co.	45,000	
Additional paid-in capital—Bass Co.	13,500	
Retained earnings—Bass Co.	36,900*	
Minority interest in revaluation		1,200
Difference between fair and book value	12,000	
Goodwill	14,400	
Investment in stock of Bass Co.—Alto Co.		120,600

    * *€41,000 x 90% = €36,900*

    Note that only 90% of Bass Company's stockholders' equity accounts are eliminated.

    The minority interest column is the 10% interest of Bass Company's net assets owned by outside third parties. Minority interest must be disclosed because 100% of the book values of Bass Company are included in the consolidated statements, although Alto Company controls only 90% of the net assets.

The example does not include any other intercompany accounts as of the date of combination. If any existed, they would be eliminated to present the consolidated entity fairly. Several examples of other reciprocal accounts will be shown later for the preparation of consolidated financial statements subsequent to the date of acquisition.

Consolidation process in periods subsequent to acquisition. Given the foregoing, the following additional information is available in the first year after the acquisition (2006):

1. Alto Company uses the partial equity method to record changes in the value of the investment account. The partial equity method means that the parent reports its share of earnings, and so on, of the subsidiary on its books using the equity method, but any differential between acquisition cost and underlying fair value of net assets, and so on, is not addressed on an ongoing basis; rather, these matters await the typical year-end accounting adjustment process.

2. During 2006, Alto Company sold merchandise to Bass Company that originally cost Alto Company €15,000, and the sale was made for €20,000. On December 31, 2006, Bass Company's inventory included merchandise purchased from Alto Company at a cost to Bass Company of €12,000.

3. Also during 2006, Alto Company acquired €18,000 of merchandise from Bass Company. Bass Company uses a normal markup of 25% above its cost. Alto Company's ending inventory includes €10,000 of the merchandise acquired from Bass Company.

4. Bass Company reduced its intercompany account payable to Alto Company to a balance of €4,000 as of December 31, 2006, by making a payment of €1,000 on December 30. This €1,000 payment was still in transit on December 31, 2006.

5. On January 2, 2006, Bass Company acquired equipment from Alto Company for €7,000. The equipment was originally purchased by Alto Company for €5,000 and had a book value of €4,000 at the date of sale to Bass Company. The equipment had an estimated remaining life of four years as of January 2, 2006.

6. On December 31, 2006, Bass Company purchased for €44,000, 50% of the outstanding bonds issued by Alto Company. The bonds mature on December 31, 2009, and were originally issued at par. The bonds pay interest annually on December 31 of each year, and the interest was paid to the prior investor immediately before Bass Company's purchase of the bonds.

The worksheet for the preparation of consolidated financial statements as of December 31, 2006, is presented on the following pages, on the assumption that purchase accounting is used for the business combination.

The investment account balance at the statement date should be reconciled to ensure that the parent company made the proper entries under the method of accounting used to account for the investment. Any adjustments (e.g., depreciation) made with respect to the step-up to fair values will be recognized only in the worksheets.

An analysis of the investment account at December 31, 2006, is as presented below.

	Investment in Stock of Bass Company		
Original cost	120,600		
% of Bass Co.'s income			% of Bass Co.'s dividends
(€9,400 x 90%)	8,460	3,600	declared (€4,000 x 90%)
Balance, 12/31/06	125,460		

Any errors will require correcting entries before the consolidation process is continued. Correcting entries will be posted to the books of the appropriate company; eliminating entries are not posted to either company's books.

The difference between the investment cost and the book value of the net assets acquired was determined and allocated in the preparation of the date of combination consolidated statements presented earlier. The same computations are used in preparing financial statements for as long as the investment is owned.

The following adjusting and eliminating entries will be required to prepare consolidated financials as of December 31, 2006. Note that a consolidated income statement is required, and therefore, the nominal (i.e., income and expense) accounts are still open. The number or letter in parentheses to the left of the entry corresponds to the key used on the worksheets presented after the following discussion.

Step 1—Complete the transaction for any intercompany items in transit at the end of the year.

(a)	Cash	1,000	
	Accounts receivable		1,000

This adjusting entry will now properly present the financial positions of both companies, and the consolidation process may be continued.

Step 2—Prepare the eliminating entries.

(a)	Sales	38,000	
	Cost of goods sold		38,000

Total intercompany sales of €38,000 include €20,000 in a downstream transaction from Alto Company to Bass Company and €18,000 in an upstream transaction from Bass Company to Alto Company.

(b)	Cost of goods sold	5,000	
	Inventory		5,000

The ending inventories are overstated because of the unrealized profit from the intercompany sales. The debit to cost of goods sold is required because a decrease in ending inventory will increase cost of goods sold to be deducted on the income statement. Supporting computations for the entry are as follows:

	In ending inventory of	
	Alto Company	*Bass Company*
Intercompany sales not resold, at selling price	€10,000	€12,000
Cost basis of remaining intercompany merchandise		
From Bass to Alto (÷ 125%)	(8,000)	
From Alto to Bass (÷ 133 1/3%)	_____	(9,000)
Unrealized profit	€ 2,000	€ 3,000

NOTE: When preparing consolidated working papers for 2007 (the next fiscal period), an additional eliminating entry will be required if the goods in 2006's ending inventory are sold to outsiders during 2007. The additional entry will recognize the profit for 2007 that was eliminated as unrealized in 2006. This entry is necessary since the entry at the end of 2006 was made only on the worksheet. The 2007 entry will be as follows:

	Retained earnings—Bass Co., 1/1/07	*2,000*	
	Retained earnings—Alto Co., 1/1/07	*3,000*	
	Cost of goods sold, 2007		*5,000*

(c)	Accounts payable	4,000	
	Accounts receivable		4,000

This entry eliminates the remaining intercompany receivable/payable owed by Bass Company to Alto Company. This eliminating entry is necessary to avoid overstating the consolidated entity's balance sheet. The receivable/payable is not extinguished, and Bass Company must still transfer €4,000 to Alto Company in the future.

(d)	Gain on sale of equipment	3,000	
	Equipment		2,000
	Accumulated depreciation		250
	Depreciation expense		750

This entry eliminates the gain on the intercompany sale of the equipment, eliminates the overstatement of equipment, and removes the excess depreciation taken on the gain. Supporting computations for the entry are as follows:

	Cost	At date of intercompany sale accum. depr.	2006 depr. ex.	End of period accum. depr.
Original basis				
(to seller, Alto Co.)	€5,000	(€1,000)	€ 1,000	(€2,000)
New basis				
(to buyer, Bass Co.)	7,000	--	1,750	(1,750)
Difference	(€2,000)		(€ 750)	€ 250

If the intercompany sale had not occurred, Alto Company would have depreciated the remaining book value of €4,000 over the estimated remaining life of four years. However, since Bass Company's acquisition price (€7,000) was more than Alto Company's basis in the asset (€4,000), the depreciation recorded on the books of Bass Company will include part of the intercompany unrealized profit. The equipment must be reflected on the consolidated statements at the original cost to the consolidated entity. Therefore, the write-up of €2,000 in the equipment, the excess depreciation of €750, and the gain of €3,000 must be eliminated. The ending balance of accumulated depreciation must be shown at what it would have been if the intercompany equipment transaction had not occurred. In future periods, a retained earnings account will be used instead of the gain account; however, the other concepts will be extended to include the additional periods.

(e)	Bonds payable	50,000	
	Investment in bonds of Alto Company		44,000
	Gain on extinguishment of debt		6,000

This entry eliminates the book value of Alto Company's debt against the bond investment account of Bass Company. On a consolidated entity basis, this transaction must be shown as a retirement of debt, even though Alto Company has the outstanding intercompany debt to Bass Company. Any gains or losses on debt extinguishment will be reported in the income statement. In future periods Bass Company will amortize the discount, thereby bringing the investment account up to par value. In future periods the retained earnings account will be used in the eliminating entry instead of the gain account, as the gain is closed out with other nominal accounts.

(f)	Equity in subsidiary's income—Alto Co.	8,460	
	Dividends declared—Bass Co.		3,600
	Investment in stock of Alto Co.		4,860

This elimination entry adjusts the investment account back to its balance at the beginning of the period and also eliminates the subsidiary income account.

(g)	Capital stock—Bass Co.	45,000	
	Additional paid-in capital— Bass Co.	13,500	
	Retained earnings—Bass Co.	36,900	
	Minority interest in revaluation		1,200
	Difference between fair and book value	12,000	
	Goodwill	14,400	
	Investment in stock of Bass Company—Alto Co.		120,600

This entry eliminates 90% of Bass Company's stockholders' equity at the beginning of the year, 1/1/06. Note that the changes during the year were eliminated in entry (f).

(h)	Adjustment of asset values		
	Inventory	1,000	
	Equipment	10,000	
	Patents	3,000	
	Accumulated depreciation		2,000
	Difference between fair value and book value		12,000

This entry allocates the differential (excess of fair value over the book values of the assets acquired). Note that this entry is the same as the allocation entry made to prepare consolidated financial statements for January 1, 2006, the date of acquisition.

(i)

Cost of goods sold		1,000	
Depreciation expense		2,000	
Other operating expenses—patent amortization		300	
Inventory			1,000
Accumulated depreciation			2,000
Patents			300

The elimination entry amortizes the revaluations to fair market value made in entry (h). The inventory has been sold and therefore becomes part of cost of goods sold. The remaining revaluations will be amortized as follows:

	Revaluation	*Amortization period*	*Annual amortization*
Equipment (net)	€8,000	4 years	€2,000
Patents	3,000	10 years	300

The amortizations will continue to be made on future worksheets. For example, at the end of the next year (2007), the amortization entry (i) would be as follows:

Differential	3,300	
Depreciation expense	2,000	
Other operating expenses—patent amortization	300	
Inventory		1,000
Accumulated depreciation		4,000
Patents		600

The initial debit of €3,300 to differential is an aggregation of the prior period's charges to income statement accounts (€1,000 + €2,000 + €300). During subsequent years, some accountants prefer reducing the allocated amounts in entry (h) for prior period's charges. In this case the amortization entry in future periods would reflect just that period's amortizations.

In adjusting for the minority interest in the consolidated entity's equity and earnings, the following guidelines should be observed:

1. Only the parent's share of the subsidiary's shareholders' equity is eliminated in the basic eliminating entry. The minority interest's share is presented separately.
2. The entire amount of intercompany reciprocal items is eliminated. For example, all receivables/payables and sales/cost of sales with a 90% subsidiary are eliminated.
3. For intercompany transactions in inventory and fixed assets, the possible effect on minority interest depends on whether the original transaction affected the subsidiary's income statement. Minority interest is adjusted only if the subsidiary is the selling entity. In this case, the minority interest is adjusted for its percentage ownership of the common stock of the subsidiary. The minority interest is not adjusted for unrealized profits on downstream sales. The effects of downstream transactions are confined solely to the parent's (i.e., controlling) ownership interests.

The minority interest's share of the subsidiary's income is shown as a deduction on the consolidated income statement since 100% of the sub's revenues and expenses are combined, even though the parent company owns less than a 100% interest. For our example, the minority interest deduction on the income statement is computed as follows:

Bass Company's reported income	€9,400
Less unrealized profit on an upstream inventory sale	(2,000)
Bass Company's income for consolidated financial purposes	€7,400
Minority interest share	x 10%
Minority interest on income statement	€ 740

The minority interest's share of the net assets of Bass Company is shown on the consolidated balance sheet between liabilities and controlling interest's equity. The computation for the minority interest shown in the balance sheet for our example is as follows:

Bass Company's capital stock, 12/31/06	€50,000	
Minority interest share	x 10%	€ 5,000
Bass Company's additional paid-in capital, 12/31/06	€15,000	
Minority interest share	x 10%	1,500
Bass Company's retained earnings, 1/1/06	€41,000	
Minority interest share	x 10%	4,100
Bass Company's 2006 income for consolidated purposes	€ 7,400	
Minority interest share	x 10%	740
Bass Company's dividends during 2006	€ 4,000	
Minority interest share	x 10%	(400)
Total minority interest, 12/31/06		€10,940

Alto Company and Bass Company Consolidated Working Papers
Year Ended December 31, 2006

Purchase accounting
90% owned subsidiary
Subsequent year, partial equity method

	Alto Company	Bass Company	Adjustments and eliminations Debit	Adjustments and eliminations Credit	Minority interest	Consolidated balances
Income statements for year ended 12/31/06						
Sales	€750,000	€420,000	€ 38,000a			€1,132,000
Cost of sales	581,000	266,000	5,000b 1,000i	€ 38,000a		815,000
Gross margin	169,000	154,000				317,000
Depreciation and interest expense	28,400	16,200	2,000i	750d		45,850
Other operating expenses	117,000	128,400	300i			245,700
Net income from operations	23,600	9,400				25,450
Gain on sale of equipment	3,000		3,000d			
Gain on bonds				6,000e		6,000
Equity in subsidiary's income	8,460		8,460f			
Minority income (€7,400 x .10)					€ 740	(740)
Net income	€ 35,060	€ 9,400	€ 57,760	€ 44,750	€ 740	€ 30,710
Statement of retained earnings for year ended 12/31/06						
1/1/06 retained earnings						
Alto Company	€ 48,000					€ 48,000
Bass Company		€ 41,000	€ 36,900g		€ 4,100	
Add net income (from above)	35,060	9,400	57,760	€ 44,750	740	30,710
Total	83,060	50,400			4,840	78,710
Deduct dividends	15,000	4,000		3,600f	400	15,000
Balance, 12/31/06	€ 68,060	€ 46,400	€ 94,660	€ 48,350	€ 4,440	€ 63,710
Balance sheet						
Cash	€ 45,300	€ 6,400	€ 1,000l			€ 52,700
Accounts receivable (net)	43,700	12,100		€ 1,000l 4,000c		50,800
Inventories	38,300	20,750	1,000h	5,000b 1,000i		54,050
Equipment	195,000	57,000	10,000h	2,000d		260,000
Accumulated depreciation	(35,200)	(18,900)		250d 2,000h 2,000i		(58,350)

	Alto Company	Bass Company	Adjustments and eliminations Debit	Adjustments and eliminations Credit	Minority interest	Consolidated balances
Investment in stock of Bass				4,860[f]		
Company	125,460			120,600[g]		
Differential			2,000[g]	2,000[h]		
Goodwill			14,400[g]			14,400
Investment in bonds of Alto						
Company		44,000		44,000[e]		
Patents		9,000	3,000[h]	300[i]		11,700
	€412,560	€130,350				€ 385,300
Accounts payable	€ 8,900	€ 18,950	4,000[c]			€ 23,850
Bonds payable	100,000		50,000[e]			50,000
Capital stock	154,000	50,000	45,000[g]		€ 5,000	154,000
Additional paid-in capital	81,600	15,000	13,500[g]		1,500	81,600
Retained earnings (from above)	68,060	46,400	94,660	48,350	4,440	63,710
Minority share of revaluation				1,200	1,200	
Minority interest					€10,940	12,140
	€412,560	€130,350	€238,560	€238,560		€385,300

The remainder of the consolidation process consists of the following worksheet techniques:

1. Take all income items across horizontally, and foot the adjustments, minority interest, and consolidated columns down to the net income line.
2. Take the amounts on the net income line (on income statement) in the adjustments, minority interest, and consolidated balances columns down to retained earnings items across the consolidated balances column. Foot and crossfoot the retained earnings statement.
3. Take the amounts of ending retained earnings in each of the four columns down to the ending retained earnings line in the balance sheet. Foot the minority interest column and place its total in the consolidated balances column. Take all the balance sheet items across to consolidated balances column.

Other Accounting Issues Arising in Business Combinations

Depending on the tax jurisdiction, an acquirer may or may not succeed to the available tax loss carryforward benefits of an acquired entity. IFRS requires that a liability approach be used in accounting for the tax effects of temporary differences, which includes the tax effects of tax loss carryforwards. If an acquirer is permitted to use the predecessor's tax benefits, the amount to be reflected in its balance sheet will be measured in accordance with IAS 12, which is the amount of the benefits expected to be realized. As expectations change over time, this amount will be amended, with any such adjustments being taken into tax expense of the period in which expectations change. If the acquirer can only utilize the benefits to offset taxes on earnings of the operations acquired (i.e., it cannot shelter other sources of earnings), it will be necessary to project profitable operations to support recording this benefit as an asset.

Subsequent identification of, or changes in value of, assets and liabilities acquired. IFRS 3 stipulates that individual assets and liabilities should be recognized in an acquisition to the extent that there are probable future economic benefits that will flow to the acquirer and a reliable measure is available of the fair value. In some cases, due to one or both of these criteria not being met at the date of the transaction, some assets or liabilities may not be recognized (which would normally have the ramification that goodwill would be larger). The standard stipulates that where the acquirer knows that there are possible assets and liabilities which cannot be recognized certainly at acquisition date, it may assign provisional values for a maximum of twelve months from the date of acquisition. In these circumstances adjustments may be made to the acquisition transaction, and these should be done as at the acquisition date. Deferred tax assets that did not meet the criteria for recognition at the time of acquisition but are subsequently realized should trigger a change in goodwill. The only other adjustment possible is the correction of an error. Changes in estimates flow through the income statement in the period where they are recognized.

The reason for this requirement is to avoid having changes made to goodwill or negative goodwill over an unlimited time horizon.

Changes in majority interest. IFRS 3 does not directly address step acquisitions. The currently outstanding (mid-2005) Exposure Draft of an amendment to IFRS 3 proposes to require that the acquisition of a tranche of shares that conveys control should cause the acquiror to revise the previous share purchases to fair value. The project does not specifically deal with the acquisition of further shares once a majority has been obtained. The parent's ownership interest can change as a result of purchases or sales of the subsidiary's common shares by the parent or as a consequence of capital transactions of the subsidiary. The latter circumstance is generally handled precisely as demonstrated in the equity method discussion in Chapter 10. If the parent's relative book value interest in the subsidiary has changed, gains or losses are treated as incurred in an entity's own treasury stock transactions. Gains are credited to paid-in capital; losses are charged to any paid-in capital or to retained earnings created previously.

When the parent's share of ownership increases through a purchase of additional stock, simply debit investment and credit cash for the cost. A problem occurs with consolidated income statements when the change in ownership takes place in midperiod. Consolidated statements should be prepared based on the ending ownership level. The authors' suggested approach is illustrated in the following example.

Example of a consolidation with a change in the majority interest

Assume that Alto Company increased its ownership of Bass Company from 90% to 95% on October 1, 2006. The investment was acquired at book value of €5,452.50 and is determined as follows:

Capital stock at 10/1/06		€50,000
Additional paid-in capital, 10/1/06		15,000
Retained earnings at 10/1/06		
Balance, 1/1/06	€41,000	
Net income for 9 months (€9,400 x .75)	7,050*	
Preacquisition dividends	(4,000)	44,050
		€ 109,050
		x 5%
Book value acquired		€5,452.50

* *Assumes income was earned ratably throughout the year.*

The consolidated net income should reflect a net of

90%	x	€9,400	x	12/12	=		€8,460.00
5%	x	€9,400	x	3/12	=		117.50
95%							€8,577.50

The interim stock purchase will result in a new account being shown on the consolidated income statement. The account is *purchased preacquisition earnings*, which represents the percentage of the subsidiary's income earned, in this case, on the 5% stock interest from January 1, 2006, to October 1, 2006. The basic eliminating entries would be based on the 95% ownership as follows:

Equity in subsidiary's income—Alto Co.	8,577.50	
Dividends declared—Bass Co.		3,600.00
Investment in stock of Bass Co.		4,977.50

Capital stock—Bass Co.	47,500.00
Additional paid-in capital—Bass Co.	14,250.00
Retained earnings—Bass Co.	38,750.00**
Purchased preacquisition earnings	352.50***
Differential	25,200.00
Investment in stock of Bass Co.—Alto Co.	126,052.50

** 95% x €41,000 beginning 2006 balance	€38,950
Less preacquisition dividend of 5% x €4,000	(200)
Retained earnings available, as adjusted	€38,750
*** 5% x €9,400 x 9/12 = €352.50	

Purchased preacquisition earnings is shown as a deduction, along with minority interest, to arrive at consolidated net income. Purchased preacquisition earnings are used only with interim acquisition under the purchase accounting method; all poolings are assumed to take place at the beginning of the period regardless of when, during the period, the acquisition was actually made.

Combined Financial Statements

When a group of entities is under common ownership, control, or management, it is often useful to present combined (or combining, showing the separate as well as the combined entities) financial statements. In this situation, the economic substance of the nominally independent entities' operations may be more important to statement users than is the legal form of those enterprises. When consolidated statements are not presented, combined statements may be used to show the financial position, or operating results, of a group of companies that are each subsidiaries of a common parent.

IFRS 3 as originally issued excludes such combinations from its scope, but an amendment was issued in draft form in May 2004 and superseded by a much more expansive proposed amendment in mid-2005, as described above, which would bring mutual entities within the scope of IFRS 3. The draft would call for any combination to be accounted for in the same way as a commercial acquisition, and on the basis that one of the entities was an acquirer. Where there is no consideration, as in a combination by contract, the fair value of the assets and liabilities of the acquiree would be attributed to the "minority" interest (actually the acquiree's unrelated shareholders). Where two mutuals combine, the aggregate of the fair value of the acquiree's net assets and of any assets given, liabilities assumed or equity issued by the acquirer would be added to the acquiror's paid-in capital.

Combinations of Entities under Common Control

IFRS 3 explicitly does **not** apply to entities under common control (e.g., brother-sister corporations). A question arises, however, when a parent (Company P) transfers ownership in one of its subsidiaries (Company B) to another of its subsidiaries (Company A) in exchange for additional shares of Company A. In such an instance, A's carrying value for the investment in B should be P's basis, not B's book value. Furthermore, if A subsequently retires the interests of minority owners of B, the transaction should be accounted for as a purchase, whether it is effected through a stock issuance by A or by a cash payment to the selling shareholders.

Furthermore, when a purchase transaction is closely followed by a sale of the parent's subsidiary to the newly acquired (target) entity, these two transactions should be viewed as a single transaction. Accordingly, the parent should recognize gain or loss on the sale of its subsidiary to the target company, to the extent of minority interest in the target entity. As a result, there will be a new basis (step-up) not only for the target company's assets and liabilities, but also for the subsidiary company's net assets. Basis is stepped up to the extent of minority participation in the target entity to which the subsidiary company was transferred.

Accounting for Special-Purpose Entities

An issue related to the accounting for entities under common control arises when one enterprise has been created solely or largely for the purpose of accommodating the other's need for financing or for engaging in certain strictly limited transactions with or on behalf of the sponsoring entity. Common objectives are to effect a lease, conduct research and development activities, or to securitize financial assets. These special-purpose entities, (SPE) or special-purpose vehicles (SPV) have received a good deal of attention in recent years, largely as a consequence of several notable financial frauds, which utilized SPE to conceal large amounts of the reporting entity's debt and/or to create the appearance of revenues and/or earnings which did not actually exist.

SPE have often been used to escape the requirements of lease capitalization or other financial reporting requirements that the sponsoring enterprise wishes to evade. While there are often legitimate (i.e., those not driven by financial reporting) reasons for the use of special-purpose entities (SPE), at least a side effect, if not the main one, is that the sponsoring entity's apparent financial strength (e.g., leverage) will be distorted.

In many instances an adroitly structured SPE will not be owned, or majority owned, by the true sponsor. Were ownership the only criterion for determining whether entities need to be consolidated for financial reporting purposes, this factor could result in a "form over substance" decision to not consolidate the SPE with its sponsor. However, under the provisions of SIC 12, ownership is not the critical element in determining the need for consolidation; rather, a "beneficial interest" test is used to determine whether the SPE should be consolidated. Beneficial interest can take various forms, including ownership of debt instruments, or even a lessee relationship.

SIC 12 states that consolidation of an SPE should be effected if the substance of its relationship with another entity indicates that it is effectively controlled by the other entity. Control can derive from the nature of the predetermined activities of the SPE (what the interpretation refers to as being on "autopilot"), and emphatically can exist even when the sponsor has less than a majority interest in the SPE. SIC 12 specifically notes that the following conditions would suggest that the sponsor controls the SPE:

1. The activities of the SPE are conducted so as to provide the sponsor with the benefits thereof;
2. The sponsor in substance has decision-making powers to obtain most of the benefits of the SPE, or else an autopilot mechanism has been established such that the decision-making powers have been delegated;
3. The sponsor has the right to obtain the majority of the benefits of the SPE and consequently is exposed to risks inherent in the SPE activities; or
4. The sponsor retains the majority of the residual or ownership risks of the SPE or its assets, in order to obtain the benefits of the SPE activities.

SIC 12 is particularly concerned that autopilot arrangements may have been put into place specifically to obfuscate the determination of control. It cautions that although difficult to assess in some situations, control is to be attributed to the enterprise having the principal beneficial interest. The entity which arranged the autopilot mechanism would generally have had, and continue to have, control, and thus the need for consolidation with the sponsor for financial reporting purposes would accordingly be indicated. SIC 12 offers a number of examples of conditions which would be strongly indicative of control and thus of a need to consolidate the SPE financial statements with those of its sponsor.

Common SPE situations involve entities set up to effect a lease, a securitization of financial assets, or to conduct research and development activities. The concept of control used in IAS 27 requires having the ability to direct or dominate decision making accompanied by the objective of obtaining benefits from the SPE's activities. Thus, determining whether a given SPE should be consolidated by the sponsor or beneficiary reporting entity remains a matter of judgment under IFRS. Note that under US GAAP (FIN 46[R]), which replaced the concept of SPE with a similar but more complex concept of variable interest entities (VIE), consolidation questions are resolved by mechanical, but complex, analyses.

Some entities will separately evaluate the matter of asset derecognition, as when assets are transferred to an SPE. In certain circumstances, a transfer of assets may result in those assets being derecognized and the transfer will be accounted for as a sale, with gain or loss recognition being warranted. Even if the transfer qualifies as a sale, however, the provisions of IAS 27 and SIC 12 may necessitate that the enterprise consolidate the SPE, thus reversing or obviating sale recognition and elimination of any gain or loss. SIC 12 does not address the circumstances where sale treatment would apply for the reporting entity or when the consequences of such a sale would have to be eliminated upon consolidation.

SIC 12 was modified by IFRIC in late 2004 to clarify the scope exclusion for postemployment benefit plans and extend this to other long-term employee benefit plans.

Accounting for Leveraged Buyouts

Possibly one of the most complex accounting issues has been the appropriate accounting for leveraged buyouts (LBO). At the center of this issue is the question of whether a new basis of accountability is created by the LBO transaction. If so, a step-up in the reported value of assets and/or liabilities is warranted. If not, the carryforward bases of the predecessor entity should continue to be reported in the company's financial statements.

IFRS do not address this issue directly. However, guidance can be gleaned from the decisions made by the standard setters in the United States, which have dealt with this question. Although this guidance is neither definitive or binding on preparers of IFRS-based financial reports, it is instructive.

Under relevant US GAAP, partial or complete new basis accounting is appropriate only when the LBO transaction is characterized by a change in control of voting interest. A series of mechanical tests were developed by which this change in interest is to be measured. Three groups of interests were identified: the shareholders in the newly created company, management, and the shareholders in the old company (who may or may not also have an interest in the new company). Depending on the relative interests of these groups in the old entity (referred to as OLDCO) and in the new enterprise (NEWCO), there will be either (1) a finding that the transaction was a purchase (new basis accounting applies) or (2) that it was a recapitalization or a restructuring (carryforward basis accounting applies).

Among the tests decreed to determine proper accounting for any given LBO transaction is the *monetary test*. This test requires that at least 80% of the net consideration paid to acquire OLDCO interests must be monetary. In this context, monetary means cash, debt, and the fair value of any equity securities given by NEWCO to selling shareholders of OLDCO. Loan proceeds provided by OLDCO to assist in the acquisition of NEWCO shares by NEWCO shareholders are excluded from this definition. If the portion of the purchase that is effected through monetary consideration is less than 80%, but other criteria are satisfied, there will be a step-up. This step-up will be limited to the percentage of the transaction represented by monetary consideration.

US GAAP guidance also presents an extensive series of examples illustrating the circumstances that would and would not meet the purchase accounting criteria to be employed in LBO. These examples should be consulted as needed when addressing an actual LBO transaction accounting issue. It is not known whether IFRS will eventually address this type of acquisition transaction.

Spin-Offs

Occasionally, an entity disposes of a wholly or partially owned subsidiary or of an investee by transferring it unilaterally to the entity's shareholders. The proper accounting for such a transaction, generally known as a spin-off, depends on the percentage of the company that is owned.

If the ownership percentage is relatively minor, 25% for example, the transfer to stockholders would be viewed as a *dividend in kind* and would be accounted for at the fair value of the property (i.e., shares in the investee) transferred.

However, when the entity whose shares are distributed is majority or wholly owned, the effect is not merely to transfer a passive investment, but to remove the operations from the former parent and to vest them with the parent's shareholders. This transaction is a true spin-off transaction, not merely a property dividend. Although international accounting standards have not addressed this matter, as a point of reference, US GAAP requires that spin-offs and similar nonreciprocal transfers to owners be accounted for at the recorded book values of the assets and liabilities transferred.

If the operations (or subsidiary) being spun off are distributed during a fiscal period, it may be necessary to estimate the results of operations for the elapsed period prior to spin-off to ascertain the net book value as of the date of the transfer. Stated another way, the operating results of the subsidiary to be disposed of should be included in the reported results of the parent through the actual date of the spin-off.

In most instances, the subsidiary being spun off will have a positive net book value. This net worth represents the cost of the nonreciprocal transfer to the owners, and like a dividend, will be reflected as a charge against the parent's retained earnings at the date of spin-off. In other situations, the operations (or subsidiary) will have a net deficit (negative net book value). Since it is unacceptable to recognize a credit to the parent's retained earnings for other than a culmination of an earnings process, the spin-off should be recorded as a credit to the parent's paid-in capital. In effect, the stockholders (the recipients of the spun-off subsidiary) have made a capital contribution to the parent company by accepting the operations having a negative book value. As with other capital transactions, this would **not** be presented in the income statement, only in the statement of changes in stockholders' equity (and in the statement of cash flows).

Non-Sub Subsidiaries

An issue that has sometimes been of concern to accountants is the use of what have been called *non-sub subsidiaries*. This situation arises when an entity plays a major role in the creation and financing of what is often a start-up or experimental operation but does not take an equity position at the outset. For example, the parent might finance the entity by means of convertible debt or debt with warrants for the later purchase of common shares. The original equity partner in such arrangements most often will be the creative or managerial talent that generally exchanges its talents for a stock interest. If the operation prospers, the parent will exercise its rights to a majority voting stock position; if it fails, the parent presumably avoids reflecting the losses in its statements.

Although this strategy may seem to avoid the requirements of equity accounting or consolidation, the economic substance clearly suggests that the operating results of the subsidiary should be reflected in the financial statements of the real parent, even absent stock ownership. In theory the control criteria of IAS 27 should apply, and where the "parent" entity's interest includes convertible debt, there may well be latent control.

Disclosure Requirements

Consolidated financial statements. IAS 27 has its own disclosure requirements in addition to those set out in IFRS 3 (discussed earlier in the chapter).

If any subsidiary is not included in the consolidated financial statements, the reasons must be set forth. If an entity over which the parent does not have majority voting control is included in the consolidated financial statements, the reasons for this must also be explained.

The financial statements must disclose if the reporting date for a subsidiary is different from that of the parent, and if so, why this is the case. If there are any significant restrictions on the subsidiary's ability to transfer funds to the parent, this must be explained.

If a subsidiary was acquired or disposed of during the period, the effect of the event on the consolidated financial statements should be discussed. If parent-only financial statements are being presented (which is permitted, but not as a substitute for consolidated financial reporting), the method of accounting for interests in subsidiaries should be stated.

Example of Financial Statement Disclosures

Adidas-Salomon AG, Germany
Year ended December 31, 2004

2.   **Summary of significant accounting policies**

The consolidated financial statements are prepared in accordance with the consolidation, accounting, and valuation principles described below.

Principles of consolidation. The consolidated financial statements include the accounts of Adidas-Salomon AG and its significant direct and indirect subsidiaries, which are prepared in accordance with uniform accounting principles.

A company is a subsidiary if Adidas-Salomon AG directly or indirectly controls the financial and operating policies of the respective enterprise.

The number of consolidated companies evolved as follows for the years ending December 31, 2004 and 2003, respectively.

Number of consolidated companies

	2004	*2003*
January 1	111	106
Newly founded/consolidated companies	1	6
Divestments/exclusion from consolidation	(6)	--
Merged companies	(1)	(1)
Purchased companies	2	--
December 31	107	111

Three subsidiaries have not been included in the consolidated financial statements in 2004 (2003: four subsidiaries), since they have no or little active business and are insignificant to the Group's financial position, results of operations, and cash flows. The shares in these companies are accounted at cost.

A schedule of the shareholdings of Adidas-Salomon AG is shown in Attachment I to these notes. A collective listing of these shareholdings in accordance with §313 section 4 of the German Commercial Code will be filed with the Commercial Register at the Local Court in Fürth (Bavaria).

Consolidation of equity is made in compliance with the book value method by offsetting the initial investments in subsidiaries against the relevant equity portion at fair value held by the parent company as at acquisition date.

All significant intercompany transactions and balances, and any unrealized gains and losses arising from intercompany transactions are eliminated in preparing the consolidated financial statements.

20. Minority interests

Minority interests are attributable to eight and eleven subsidiaries as at December 31, 2004, and 2003, respectively.

These subsidiaries were mainly set up together with former independent distributors and licensees for the Adidas brand. Salomon & Taylor Made Co., Ltd., Tokyo (Japan) is a public company, which was listed on the Tokyo Stock Exchange from 1995 until 2004.

Minority interests evolved as follows in the years ending December 31, 2004 and 2003, respectively:

Minority Interests
(€in thousands)

	2004	*2003*
Minority interests as at January 1	56,579	55,513
Currency translation differences	1,196	(5,195)
Net gain (loss) on cash flow hedges, net of tax	22	(108)
Acquisition of minority interests	(30,181)	--
Exclusion from consolidation	880	--
Share in net profit	9,221	11,391
Dividends to third parties	(7,107)	(5,022)
Minority interests as at December 31	28,850	56,579

Novartis Group
Period Ending December 31, 2004

1. Accounting policies

Principles of consolidation. The annual closing date of the individual financial statements is December 31. The financial statements of consolidated companies operating in high-inflation countries are adjusted to eliminate the impact of high inflation. The purchase method of accounting is used for acquired businesses. Companies acquired or disposed of during the year are included in the consolidated financial statements from the date of acquisition or up to the date of disposal. The Group was formed on December 20, 1996, when all assets and liabilities of Sandoz AG and Ciba-Geigy AG were transferred by universal succession to Novartis AG. The uniting of interests method was used to account for this transaction. If it were undertaken today, the merger would require a different accounting treatment. Intercompany income and expenses, including unrealized gross profits from internal Novartis transactions and intercompany receivables and payables have been eliminated.

2. Changes in the scope of consolidation

Acquisitions prior to March 31, 2004, were accounted for in accordance with IAS 22. Acquisitions since April 1, 2004, are accounted for in accordance with IFRS 3 and goodwill is no longer amortized but instead is assessed annually for impairment. The following significant changes in the scope of consolidation were made during 2004 and 2003.

Acquisitions 2004

Sandoz. On June 30, Novartis acquired 100% of the shares of the Danish generics company Durascan A/S from AstraZeneca. Goodwill of USD 23 million has been recorded on this transaction. On August 13, Novartis completed the acquisition of 100% of the shares of Sabex Inc., a Canadian generic manufacturer with a leading position in generic injectables, for USD 565 million in cash. Based on a preliminary estimate, goodwill of SD 329 million has been recorded on this transaction. A total of USD 61 million of sales and USD 10 million of operating loss were recorded since the closure of these two transactions in 2004. The operating loss is mainly due to one-off costs related to purchase accounting and integration costs.

Medical nutrition. On February 13, Novartis completed the acquisition of Mead Johnson's global adult medical nutrition business for USD 385 million in cash. These activities are included in the consolidated financial statements from that date with USD 220 million of sales and a USD 31 million operating loss being recorded in 2004. Goodwill of USD 183 million has been recorded on this transaction which is being amortized on a straight-line basis over twenty years.

Acquisitions 2003

Pharmaceuticals. On May 8, 2003, an additional 51% of the share capital of Idenix Pharmaceuticals Inc., Cambridge, Massachusetts was acquired for an initial payment of USD 255 million in cash to its existing shareholders. As part of the acquisition, Novartis agreed to pay additional amounts to the shareholders of Idenix Pharmaceuticals Inc. based on the achievement of clinical and regulatory milestones, marketing approvals and sales targets. The total additional value of these milestone payments is up to USD 357 million. Novartis cannot estimate when or if these additional milestone payments will be made. This company is included in the consolidated financial statements from May 2003. Since net liabilities were also assumed, total goodwill amounted to USD 297 million on this transaction which is being amortized over fifteen years.

Corporate. In 2003 the Group increased its investment in Roche Holding AG to 33.3% by acquiring further voting shares for USD 120 million. The Group's holding represents approximately 6.3% of Roche Holding AG's total shares and equity instruments.

23. Acquisitions and divestments of businesses

1. Cash flow arising from major acquisitions and divestments.

The following is a summary of the cash flow impact of the major divestments and acquisitions of businesses.

	2004 acquisition USD millions	2004 investments USD millions	2003 acquisitions USD millions
Property, plant, & equipment	(29)	3	(1)
Currently marketed products including trademarks	(262)		(24)
In-process research and development	(139)		
Other intellectual property	(90)		
Financial assets	(5)		
Inventories	(69)	4	(1)
Trade accounts receivable and other current assets	(20)		(1)
Marketable securities, cash, and short-term deposits	(6)		
Long-term and short-term debt to third parties	8	(2)	
Bank borrowing	86		
Trade accounts payable and other liabilities including deferred taxes	109	(3)	36
Net identifiable assets acquired/divested	(417)	2	9
Acquired liquidity	6	—	18
Subtotal	(411)	2	27
Refinancing of acquired debt	(86)		
Goodwill	(535)		(303)
Divestment loss		(1)	
Translation effects	—	—	4
Net cash flow	(1,032)	1	(272)

Note 2 provides further information regarding changes in the consolidation scope. All acquisitions were for cash.

2.   Assets and liabilities arising from the 2004 acquisitions.

	Fair value USD millions	Revaluation due to purchase accounting USD millions	Acquiree's carrying amount USD millions
Property, plant, & equipment	29	2	27
Currently marketed products including trademarks	262	137	125
In-process research and development	139	138	1
Other intellectual property	90	90	
Financial assets	5		5
Inventories	69	18	51
Trade accounts receivable and other current assets	20	1	19
Marketable securities, cash, and short-term deposits	6		6
Long-term and short-term debt to third parties	(8)		(8)
Bank borrowing	(86)		(86)
Trade accounts payable and other liabilities including deferred taxes	(109)	(74)	(35)
Net identifiable assets acquired	417	312	105
Less acquired liquidity	(6)		
Refinancing of acquired debt	86		
Goodwill	535		
Total cash flow from acquisition of businesses	1,032		

Professional fees and related expenses incurred for the acquisitions amount to USD 12 million.

Nestle Group
Period Ending December 31, 2004

in millions of CHF	2004	2003
Fair value of net assets acquired		
Property, plant, & equipment	72	395
Financial assets	21	(18)
Intangible assets	154	11
Minority interests	(9)	18
Purchase of minority interests in existing participations	41	8
Net working capital	(12)	100
Financial liabilities	(24)	(507)
Employee benefits, deferred taxes and provisions	(73)	(38)
Liquid assets	8	30
	178	(1)
Goodwill	476	4,726
Total acquisition cost	654	4,725
Less:		
Cash and cash equivalents acquired	(8)	(30)
Consideration payable	(13)	(3,041)
Payment of consideration payable on prior years acquisition	--	296
Cash outflow on acquisitions	633	1,950

The Group's sales and net profit are not significantly impacted by acquisitions for which the agreement date is on or after March 31, 2004, even if the acquisition date for all these acquisitions had been January 1, 2004.

12 CURRENT LIABILITIES, PROVISIONS, CONTINGENCIES, AND EVENTS AFTER THE BALANCE SHEET DATE

PERSPECTIVE AND ISSUES

Accounting for all of a reporting entity's liabilities is clearly necessary in order to accurately convey its financial position to investors, creditors and other stakeholders. Different kinds of liabilities have differing implications: *short-term trade payables* indicate a near-term outflow, while *long-term debt* covers a wide range of periods, and *provisions* have yet other significance to those performing financial analysis. At the same time, a company with a long operating cycle will have operating liabilities that stretch for more than a year ahead, and some long-term debt may call for repayment within one year, so the distinction is not so clear, and balance sheet presentation is an issue. Transparency of disclosure will also be a consideration, beyond mere questions of current or noncurrent classification.

Historically, it has long been recognized that prudence would normally necessitate the recognition of even uncertain liabilities, while uncertain assets were not to be recognized. IAS 37, the key standard on provisions, addresses the boundaries of recognition. In general, IASB is also evolving to a new position on contingent liabilities, where the assessed probability of occurrence will be built into the measurement of liabilities, thereby changing the boundaries of accounting recognition for liabilities.

The recognition and measurement of provisions can have a major impact on the way in which the financial position of an entity is viewed. IAS 37 addresses so-called "onerous contract" provisions, which require a company to take into current earnings the entire cost of fulfilling contracts that continue into the future under defined conditions. This can be a very sensitive issue for a company experiencing trading difficulties.

Another sensitive issue is the accounting for decommissioning or similar asset retirement costs, which increasingly are becoming a burden for companies engaged in mineral extraction and manufacturing, but also potentially for those engaged in agriculture and other industry segments. Where historically it was assumed that these costs were future events to be recognized in later periods, it is now clear that these are costs of asset ownership and operation that need to be reflected over the productive lives of the assets, and that the estimated costs are to be recognized as a formal obligation of the reporting entity.

The reporting entity's financial position may also be affected by events, both favorable and unfavorable, which occur between the balance sheet date and the date when the financial statements are authorized for issue. Under IAS 10, such post-balance-sheet date events require either formal recognition or only disclosure, depending on the character and timing of the event in question, which are referred to as "adjusting" and "nonadjusting," respectively.

In practice, there may be some ambiguity as to when the financial statements are actually "authorized for issuance." For this reason, the revised standard recognizes that the process involved in authorizing the financial statements for issue will vary and may be dependent upon the reporting entity's management structure, statutory requirements, and the procedures prescribed for the preparing and finalizing of the financial statements. Thus, IAS 10 illustrates in detail the principles governing the determination of the financial statements' authorization date, which date is required to be disclosed.

Sources of IFRS	
IAS 1, 10, 37, 39	*IFRIC* 1, 6

DEFINITIONS OF TERMS

Adjusting events after the balance sheet date. Those post-balance-sheet events that provide evidence of conditions that existed at the balance sheet date and require that the financial statements be adjusted.

Authorization date. The date when the financial statements would be considered legally authorized for issue.

Constructive obligation. An obligation resulting from an enterprise's actions such that the enterprise

- By an established pattern of past practice, published policies or a sufficiently specific current statement, has indicated to third parties that it will accept certain responsibilities; and
- As a result, has created a valid expectation in the minds of third parties that it will discharge those responsibilities.

Contingent asset. A possible asset that arises from past events and whose existence will be confirmed only by the occurrence or nonoccurrence of one or more uncertain future events not wholly within the control of the reporting enterprise.

Contingent liability. An obligation that is either

- A possible obligation arising from past events, the outcome of which will be confirmed only on the occurrence or nonoccurrence of one or more uncertain future events which are not wholly within the control of the reporting enterprise; or

- A present obligation arising from past events which is not recognized either because it is not probable that an outflow of resources will be required to settle an obligation, or where the amount of the obligation cannot be measured with sufficient reliability.

Current liabilities. Enterprise obligations whose liquidation is reasonably expected to require the use of existing resources properly classified as current assets or the creation of other current liabilities. Obligations that are due on demand or will be due on demand within one year or the operating cycle, if longer, are current liabilities.

Estimated liability. An obligation that is known to exist, although the obligee may not be known, and the amount and timing of payment is subject to uncertainty. Now referred to as provisions.

Events after the balance sheet date. Events that occur after an enterprise's accounting year-end (also referred to as the balance sheet date) and the date they are authorized for issue that would necessitate either adjusting the financial statements or disclosure. The concept is comprehensive enough to cover both favorable and unfavorable post-balance-sheet date events.

Guarantee. A commitment to honor an obligation of another party in the event certain defined conditions are not met.

Indirect guarantee of indebtedness of others. A guarantee under an agreement that obligates one enterprise to transfer funds to a second enterprise upon the occurrence of specified events under conditions whereby (1) the funds are legally available to the creditors of the second enterprise, and (2) those creditors may enforce the second enterprise's claims against the first enterprise.

Legal obligation. An obligation that derives from the explicit or implicit terms of a contract, or from legislation or other operation of law.

Liability. A present obligation of the reporting enterprise arising from past events, the settlement of which is expected to result in an outflow from the enterprise of resources embodying economic benefits.

Nonadjusting events after the balance sheet date. Those post-balance-sheet events that are indicative of conditions that arose after the balance sheet date and which thus would not necessitate adjusting financial statements. Instead, if significant, these would require disclosure.

Obligating event. An event that creates a legal or constructive obligation that results in an enterprise having no realistic alternative but to settle that obligation.

Onerous contract. A contract in which the unavoidable costs of meeting the obligations under the contract exceed the economic benefits expected to be received therefrom.

Operating cycle. The average length of time necessary for an enterprise to convert inventory to receivables to cash.

Possible loss. A contingent loss based on the occurrence of a future event or events whose likelihood of occurring is more than remote but less than likely.

Probable loss. A contingent loss based on the occurrence of a future event or events that are likely to occur.

Provision. Liabilities having uncertain timing or amount.

Remote loss. A contingent loss based on the occurrence of a future event or events whose likelihood of occurring is slight.

Restructuring. A program that is planned and controlled by management and which materially changes either the scope of business undertaken by the enterprise or the manner in which it is conducted.

CONCEPTS, RULES, AND EXAMPLES

Current Liabilities

Classification of balance sheets. IAS 1 requires that the reporting entity must present current and noncurrent assets, and current and noncurrent liabilities, as separate classifications on the face of its balance sheet, except when a liquidity presentation provides more relevant and reliable information. In those exceptional instances, all assets and liabilities are to be presented broadly in order of liquidity. Whether classified or employing the order of liquidity approach, for any asset or liability reported as a discrete line item that combines amounts expected to be recovered or settled within no more than twelve months after the balance sheet date and more than twelve months after the balance sheet date, the reporting entity must disclose the amount expected to be recovered or settled after more than twelve months.

IAS 1 also makes explicit reference to the requirements imposed by IAS 32 concerning financial assets and liabilities. Since such common balance sheet items as trade and other receivables and payables are within the definition of financial instruments, information about maturity dates is already required under IFRS. While most trade payables and accrued liabilities will be due within thirty to ninety days, and thus are understood by all financial statement readers to be current, this requirement would necessitate additional disclosure, either on the face of the balance sheet or in the footnotes thereto, when this assumption is not warranted.

The other purpose of presenting a classified balance sheet is to highlight those assets and obligations that are "continuously circulating" in the phraseology of IAS 1. That is, the goal is to identify specifically resources and commitments that are consumed or settled in the normal course of the operating cycle. In some types of businesses, such as certain construction enterprises, the normal operating cycle may exceed one year. Thus, some assets or liabilities might fail to be incorporated into a definition based on the first goal of reporting, providing insight into liquidity, but be included in one that meets the second goal.

As a compromise, if a classified balance sheet is indeed being presented, the convention for financial reporting purposes is to consider assets and liabilities current if they will be realized and liquidated within one year or one operating cycle, whichever is longer. Since this may vary in practice from one reporting entity to another, however, it is important for users to read the accounting policies set forth in notes to the financial statements. The classification criterion should be set forth there, particularly if it is other than the rule most commonly employed: one-year threshold.

Nature of current liabilities. Current liabilities are generally perceived to be those that are due within a brief time span. The convention has long been to use one year from the balance sheet date as the threshold for categorization as current, subject to the operating cycle issue for liabilities linked to operations. Examples of liabilities which are not expected to be settled in the normal course of the operating cycle but which, if due within twelve months would be deemed current, are current portions of long-term debt and bank overdrafts, dividends declared and payable, and various nontrade payables.

Current liabilities would almost always include not only obligations that are due on demand (typically including bank lines of credit, other demand notes payable, and certain overdue obligations for which forbearance has been granted on a day-to-day basis), but also the currently scheduled payments on longer-term obligations, such as installment notes. Also included in this group would be trade credit and accrued expenses, and deferred revenues and advances from customers for which services are to be provided or product delivered within one year. If certain conditions are met (described below), short-term obligations that are intended to be refinanced may be excluded from current liabilities.

Like all liabilities, current liabilities may be known with certainty as to amount, due date, and payee, as is most commonly the case. However, one or more of these elements may be unknown or subject to estimation. Consistent with basic principles of accrual accounting, however, the lack of specific information on, say, the amount owed, will not serve to justify a failure to record and report on such obligations. The former commonly used term "estimated liabilities" has been superseded per IAS 37 by the term "provisions." Provisions and contingent liabilities are discussed in detail later in this chapter.

Offsetting current assets against related current liabilities. IAS 1 states that current liabilities are not to be reduced by the deduction of a current asset (or vice versa) unless required or permitted by another IAS. In practice, there are few circumstances that would meet this requirement; certain financial institution transactions are the most commonly encountered exceptions. As an almost universal rule, therefore, assets and liabilities must be shown "broad," even where the same counterparties are present (e.g., amounts due from and amounts owed to another entity).

Types of liabilities. Current obligations can be divided into those where

1. Both the amount and the payee are known;
2. The payee is known but the amount may have to be estimated;
3. The payee is unknown and the amount may have to be estimated; and
4. The liability has been incurred due to a loss contingency.

These types of liabilities are discussed in the following sections.

Amount and Payee Known

Accounts payable arise primarily from the acquisition of materials and supplies to be used in the production of goods or in conjunction with providing services. Payables that arise from transactions with suppliers in the normal course of business, which customarily are due in no more than one year, may be stated at their face amount rather than at the present value of the required future cash flows.

Notes payable are more formalized obligations that may arise from the acquisition of materials and supplies used in operations or from the use of short-term credit to purchase capital assets. Although international accounting standards do not explicitly address the matter, it is widely agreed that monetary obligations, other than those due currently, should be presented at the present value of the amount owed, thus giving explicit recognition to the time value of money. However, most would agree that this exercise would not be needed to present current obligations fairly. (Of course, if the obligations are interest-bearing at a reasonable rate determined at inception, this is not an issue.)

Dividends payable become a liability of the enterprise when a dividend has been declared. However, jurisdictions vary as to how this is interpreted. Under most continental European company law, only the shareholders in general meeting can declare a dividend, and so the function of the directors is to propose a dividend, which itself does not give rise to a liability. In other jurisdictions, the decision of the board of directors would trigger recognition of a liability. Since declared dividends are usually paid within a short period of time after the declaration date, they are classified as current liabilities, should a balance sheet be prepared in between the two events.

Unearned revenues or advances result from customer prepayments for either performance of services or delivery of product. They may be required by the selling enterprise as a condition of the sale or may be made by the buyer as a means of guaranteeing that the seller will perform the desired service or deliver the product. Unearned revenues and advances should be classified as current liabilities at the balance sheet date if the services are to be performed or the products are to be delivered within one year or the operating cycle, whichever is longer.

Returnable deposits may be received to cover possible future damage to property. Many utility companies require security deposits. A deposit may be required for the use of a reusable container. Refundable deposits are classified as current liabilities if the firm expects to refund them during the current operating cycle or within one year, whichever is longer.

Accrued liabilities have their origin in the end-of-period adjustment process required by accrual accounting. They represent economic obligations, even when the legal or contractual commitment to pay has not yet been triggered, and as such must be given recognition if the matching concept is to be adhered to. Commonly accrued liabilities include wages and salaries payable, interest payable, rent payable, and taxes payable.

Agency liabilities result from the legal obligation of the enterprise to act as the collection agent for employee or customer taxes owed to various federal, state, or local government units. Examples of agency liabilities include value-added tax, sales taxes, income taxes withheld from employee paychecks, and employee social security contributions, where mandated by law. In addition to agency liabilities, an employer may have a current obligation for unemployment taxes. Payroll taxes typically are not legal liabilities until the associated payroll is actually paid, but in keeping with the concept of accrual accounting, if the payroll has been accrued, the associated payroll taxes should be as well.

Obligations that are, by their terms, due on demand or will become due on demand within one year (or operating cycle, if longer) from the balance sheet date, even if liquidation is not expected to occur within that period, must be classified as current liabilities. Current IAS are not explicit as to how long-term obligations having features such as subjective acceleration provisions, or acceleration based on covenant violations which are deemed likely to occur over the following year, should be accounted for.

However, when the reporting entity breaches an undertaking or covenant under a long-term loan agreement, thereby causing the liability to become due and payable on demand, it must be classified as current at the balance sheet date, even if the lender has agreed, after the balance sheet date and before the authorization of the financial statements for issue, not to demand payment as a consequence of the breach (i.e., to give forbearance to the borrower).

On the other hand, if the lender has granted forbearance before the balance sheet date (extending for at least one year from the balance sheet date), then noncurrent classification would be warranted. Similarly, if the lender has agreed by the balance sheet date to provide a grace period within which the entity can rectify a breach of an undertaking or covenant under a long-term loan agreement and during that time the lender cannot demand immediate repayment, the liability is to be classified as noncurrent if it is due for settlement, without that breach of an undertaking or covenant, at least twelve months after the balance sheet date *and either:*

1. The entity rectifies the breach within the period of grace; *or*
2. When the financial statements are authorized for issue, the grace period is incomplete and it is probable that the breach will indeed be rectified.

Failure to rectify the breach confirms that current classification of the liability was warranted, and the financial statements would be adjusted to conform to that fact.

Short-term obligations expected to be refinanced. Long-term financial liabilities within twelve months of maturity are current liabilities. In some cases, the reporting entity has plans or intentions to refinance the debt ("roll it over") and thus does not expect its maturity to cause it to employ its working capital. Under provisions of IAS 1, this debt must be shown as current when due to be settled within twelve months of the balance sheet date, notwithstanding that its original term was for a period of more than twelve months; and that an agreement to refinance, or to reschedule payments, on a long-term basis is completed after the balance sheet date and before the financial statements are authorized for issuance. Note that this rule contrasts with the equivalent provision under US GAAP, which does permit (if certain additional conditions are met) noncurrent presentation. The two Boards are unlikely to try to converge in the short term.

However, if the reporting entity has the ability, unilaterally, to refinance or "roll over" the debt for at least twelve months after the balance sheet date, under the terms of an existing loan facility, it is classified an noncurrent, even if it is otherwise due to be repaid within twelve months of the balance sheet date, if a "rollover" is the entity's intent. This differs from the situation in which refinancing or "rolling over" the obligation is not at the discretion of the entity (as when there is no agreement to refinance), in which case the potential to refinance (which is no more than the borrower's hope in such instance) is not considered and the obligation is classified as current.

Example of short-term obligations to be refinanced

The Marrakech Warehousing Company has obtained a €3,500,000 bridge loan to assist it in completing a new warehouse. All construction is completed by the balance sheet date, after which Marrakech has the following three choices for refinancing the bridge loan:

- Enter into a 30-year fixed-rate mortgage for €3,400,000 at 7% interest, leaving Marrakech with a €100,000 obligation to fulfill from short-term funds. Under this scenario, Marrakech reports as current debt the €100,000, as well as the €50,000 portion of the mortgage due within one year, with the remainder of the mortgage itemized as long-term debt. The presentation follows:

  Current liabilities
Short-term notes	100,000
Current portion of long-term debt	50,000

  Noncurrent liabilities
7% mortgage note due in 2036	3,350,000

- Pay off the bridge loan with Marrakech's existing variable rate line of credit (LOC), which expires in two years. The maximum amount of the LOC is 80% of Marrakech's accounts receivable. Over the two-year remaining term of the LOC, the lowest level of qualifying accounts receivable is expected to be €2,700,000. Thus only €2,700,000 of the debt can be classified as long-term, while €800,000 is classified as a short-term obligation. The presentation follows:

  Current liabilities
Short-term note—variable rate line of credit	800,000

  Noncurrent liabilities
Variable rate line of credit due in 2008	2,700,000

- Obtain a loan bearing interest at 10% from Marrakech's owner, with a balloon payment due in five years. Under the terms of this arrangement, the owner can withdraw up to €1,500,000 of funding at any time, even though €3,500,000 is currently available to Marrakech. Under this approach, €1,500,000 is callable, and therefore must be classified as a short-term obligation. The remainder is classified as long-term debt. The presentation follows:

Current liabilities	
Short-term note—majority stockholder	1,500,000
Noncurrent liabilities	
10% balloon note payable to majority stock-holder, due in 2011	2,000,000

Long-term debt subject to demand for repayment. What may be thought of as the polar opposite of short-term debt to be refinanced long-term is the situation where the entity is obligated under a long-term (noncurrent) debt arrangement where the lender has either the right to demand immediate or significantly accelerated repayment, or such acceleration rights vest with the lender upon the occurrence of certain events. For example, long-term (and even many short-term) debt agreements typically contain covenants, which effectively are negative or affirmative restrictions on the borrower as to undertaking further borrowings, paying dividends, maintaining specified levels of working capital, and so forth. If a covenant is breached by the borrower, the lender will typically have the right to call the debt immediately, or to otherwise accelerate repayment.

In other cases, the lender will have certain rights under a "subjective acceleration clause" inserted into the loan agreement, giving it the right to demand repayment if it perceives that its risk position has deteriorated as a result of changes in the borrower's business operations, liquidity, or other sometimes vaguely defined factors. Obviously, this gives the lender great power and subjects the borrower to the real possibility that the nominally long-term debt will, in fact, be short-term.

IAS 1 addresses the matter of breach of loan covenants, but does not address the less common phenomenon of subjective acceleration clauses in loan agreements. As to the former, it provides that continued classification of the debt as noncurrent, when one or more of the stipulated default circumstances has occurred, is contingent upon meeting two conditions: First, the lender has agreed, prior to approval of the financial statements, not to demand payment as a consequence of the breach (giving what is known as a debt compliance waiver); and second, that it is considered not probable that further breaches will occur within twelve months of the balance sheet date. If one or both of these cannot be met, the debt must be reclassified to current status if a classified balance sheet is, as is generally required under IAS 1, to be presented.

Logic suggests that the existence of subjective acceleration clauses convert nominally long-term debt into currently payable debt. US GAAP, in fact, formally recognizes this reality, requiring current presentation whenever such clauses are present. The authors therefore suggest that in the presence of these or similar provisions, it would be misleading to categorize debt as noncurrent, regardless of the actual maturity date, since continued forbearance by the lender would be required, and this cannot be controlled by the obligor. Such debt should be shown as current, with sufficient disclosure to inform the reader that the debt could effectively be "rolled over" until the nominal maturity date, at the sole discretion of the lender.

Payee Known but Amount May Need to Be Estimated

Provisions. Under IAS 37, *Provisions, Contingent Liabilities, and Contingent Assets*, those liabilities for which amount or timing of expenditure is uncertain are deemed to be provisions.

IAS 37 provides a comprehensive definition of the term "provision." It mandates, in a clear-cut manner, that a provision should be recognized *only* if

• The enterprise has a present obligation (legal or constructive) as a result of a past event;

- It is probable that an outflow of resources embodying economic benefits will be required to settle the obligation; and
- A reliable estimate can be made of the amount of the obligation.

Thus, a whole range of vaguely defined reserves found in financial statements in days past are clearly not permitted under IFRS. This includes the oft-manipulated restructuring reserves commonly found created during the business combination process when purchase accounting was used (which is, subsequent to March 2004, the only acceptable method of accounting for such transactions). Now, unless there is a *present obligation* as of the purchase combination date, such reserves cannot be established—in most instances, any future restructuring costs will be recognized after the merger event and charged against the successor entity's earnings.

Many other previously employed reserves are likewise barred by the strict conditions set forth by IAS 37. However, the mere need to estimate the amount to be reflected in the provision is not evidence of a failure to qualify for recognition. If an actual obligation exists, despite one or more factors making the amount less than precisely known, recognition is required.

IAS 37 offers in-depth guidance on the topic of provisions. Each of the key words in the definition of the term "provision" is explained in detail by the standard. Explanations and clarifications offered by the standard are summarized below.

- **Present obligation.** The standard opines that in almost all cases it will be clear when a present obligation exists. The notion of an obligation in the standard includes not only a legal obligation (e.g., deriving from a contract or legislation) but also a constructive obligation. It explains that a constructive obligation exists when the entity from an established pattern of past practice or stated policy has created a valid expectation that it will accept certain responsibilities.
- **Past event.** There must be some past event which has triggered the present obligation—for example, an accidental oil spillage. An accounting provision cannot be created in anticipation of a future event. The entity must also have no realistic alternative to settling the obligation caused by the event.
- **Probable outflow of resources embodying economic benefits.** For a provision to qualify for recognition it is essential that it is not only a present obligation of the reporting entity, but also it should be probable that an outflow of resources embodying benefits used to settle the obligation will in fact result. For the purposes of this standard, probable is defined as "more likely than not." A footnote to the standard states that this interpretation of the term "probable" does not necessarily apply to other IAS. The use of terms such as probable, significant, or impracticable creates problems of interpretation, both within a given set of standards (e.g., IFRS) and across different sets. The IASB and FASB are intending to converge on their interpretation and use of such terms in order to reduce the level of confusion.
- **Reliable estimate of the obligation.** The standard recognizes that using estimates is common in the preparation of financial statements and suggest that by using a range of possible outcomes, an enterprise will usually be able to make an estimate of the obligation that is sufficiently reliable to use in recognizing a provision. Where no reliable estimate can be made, though, no liability is recognized.

Other salient features of provisions explained by the standard include the following:

1. For all estimated liabilities that are included within the definition of provisions, the amount to be recorded and presented on the balance sheet should be the *best estimate*, at the balance sheet date, of the amount of expenditure that will be required to

settle the obligation. This is often referred to as the "expected value" of the obligation, which may be operationally defined as the amount the entity would pay, currently, to either settle the actual obligation or provide consideration to a third party to assume it (e.g., as a single occurrence insurance premium). For estimated liabilities comprised of large numbers of relatively small, similar items, weighting by probability of occurrence can be used to compute the aggregate expected value; this is often used to compute accrued warranty reserves, for example. For those estimated liabilities consisting of only a few (or a single) discrete obligations, the most likely outcome may be used to measure the liability when there is a range of outcomes having roughly similar probabilities; but if possible outcomes include amounts much greater (and lesser) than the most likely, it may be necessary to accrue a larger amount if there is a significant chance that the larger obligation will have to be settled, even if that is not the most likely outcome as such.

The concept of "expected value" can be best explained through a numeric illustration.

> Good Samaritan Inc. manufactures and sells pinball machines under warranty. Customers are entitled to refunds if they return defective machines with valid proof of purchase. Good Samaritan Inc. estimates that if all machines sold and still in warranty had major defects, total replacement costs would equal €1,000,000; if all those machines suffered from minor defects, the total repair costs would be €500,000. Good Samaritan's past experience, however, suggests that only 10% of the machines sold will have major defects, and that another 30% will have minor defects. Based on this information, the expected value of the product warranty costs to be accrued at year-end would be computed as follows:
>
> Expected value of the cost of refunds:
>
> | | | | |
> |---|---|---|---|
> | Resulting from major defects: | €1,000,000 × 0.10 | = | €100,000 |
> | Resulting from minor defects: | € 500,000 × 0.30 | = | 150,000 |
> | No defects: | €   0 × 0.60 | = | -- |
> | | Total | = | €250,000 |

2. The "risks and uncertainties" surrounding events and circumstances should be taken into account in arriving at the best estimate of a provision. However, as pointedly noted by the standard, uncertainty should not be used to justify the creation of excessive provisions or a deliberate overstatement of liabilities.

3. The standard also addresses the use of present values or discounting (i.e., recording the estimated liability at present value, after taking into account the time value of money). While the entire subject of present value measurement in accounting has been widely debated, in practice there is a notable lack of consistency (with some standards requiring it, others prohibiting it, and many others remaining silent on the issue). IAS 37 has stood firm on the subject of present value measurement, despite some opposition voiced in response to the Exposure Draft and an ongoing plea for more guidance on how this is to be determined. The standard requires the use of discounting when the effect would be material, but it can be ignored if immaterial in effect. Thus, provisions estimated to be due farther into the future will have more need to be discounted than those due currently. As a practical matter, all but trivial provisions should be discounted unless the timing is unknown (which makes discounting a computational impossibility).

IAS 37 clarifies that the discount rate applied should be consistent with the estimation of cash flows (i.e., if cash flows are projected in nominal terms). That is, if the estimated amount expected to be paid out reflects whatever price inflation is anticipated to occur between the balance sheet date and the date of ultimate settlement of the estimated obligation, then a nominal discount rate should be used. If future cash outflows are projected in real terms, net of any price inflation, then a real interest rate should be applied. In either case, past experience must be used to ascertain likely timing of future cash flows, since discounting cannot otherwise be performed.

4. Future events that may affect the amount required to settle an obligation should be reflected in the provision amount where there is sufficient objective evidence that such future events will in fact occur. For example, if an enterprise believes that the cost of cleaning up a plant site at the end of its useful life will be reduced by future changes in technology, the amount recognized as a provision for cleanup costs should reflect a reasonable estimate of cost reduction resulting from any anticipated technological changes. In many instances making such estimates will not be possible, however.

5. IFRIC 1 mandates that changes in decommissioning provisions should be recognized prospectively (i.e., by amending future depreciation charges).

6. Gains from expected disposals of assets should not be taken into account in arriving at the amount of the provision (even if the expected disposal is closely linked to the event giving rise to the provision).

7. Reimbursements by other parties should be taken into account when computing the provision, only if it is virtually certain that the reimbursement will be received. The reimbursement should be treated as a separate asset on the balance sheet, not netted against the estimated liability. However, in the income statement, the provision may be presented net of the amount recognized as a reimbursement. In the authors' observation, recognition of such contingent assets would be very rare in practice due to the long time horizons and concerns about the viability of the parties promising to make reimbursement payments over the long term. A government-backed fund, on the other hand, could probably be deemed reliable.

8. Changes in provisions should be considered at each balance sheet date, and provisions should be adjusted to reflect the current best estimate. If upon review it appears that it is no longer probable that an outflow of resources embodying economics will be required to settle the obligation, then the provision should be reversed through current period results of operations.

9. Use of provision is to be restricted to the purpose for which it was recognized originally. A reserve for plant dismantlement, for example, cannot be used to absorb environmental pollution claims or warranty payments. If an expenditure is set against a provision that was originally recognized for another purpose, that would camouflage the impact of the two different events, distorting income performance and possibly constituting financial reporting fraud.

10. Provisions for future operating losses should not be recognized. This is explicitly proscribed by the standard, since future operating losses do not meet the definition of a liability at the balance sheet date (as defined in the standard) and the general recognition criteria set forth in the standard.

11. Present obligations under *onerous contracts* should be recognized and measured as a provision. The standard introduces the concept of onerous contracts, which it defines as contracts under which the unavoidable costs of satisfying the obligations exceed the economic benefits expected. Executory contracts that are not onerous do not fall within the purview of this standard. In other words, the expected negative implications of such contracts (executory contracts which are not onerous) cannot be recognized as a provision.

The standard mandates that unavoidable costs under a contract represent the "least net costs of exiting from the contract." Such unavoidable costs should be measured at the *lower* of

- The cost of fulfilling the contract; **or**
- Any compensation or penalties arising from failure to fulfill the contract.

12. Provisions for restructuring costs are recognized only when the general recognition criteria for provisions are met. A constructive obligation to restructure arises only when an enterprise has a *detailed formal plan* for the restructuring which identifies at least: the business or the part of the business concerned, principal locations affected, approximate number of employees that would need to be compensated for termination resulting from the restructuring (along with their function and location), expenditure that would be required to carry out the restructuring, and information as to when the plan is to be implemented.

Furthermore, the recognition criteria also require that the enterprise should have raised a valid expectation among those affected by the restructuring that it will, in fact, carry out the restructuring by starting to implement that plan or announcing its main features to those affected by it. Thus, until both the conditions mentioned above are satisfied, a restructuring provision cannot be made based upon the concept of constructive obligation. In practice, given the strict criteria of IAS 37, restructuring costs are more likely to become recognizable when actually incurred in a subsequent period.

Only *direct* expenditures arising from restructuring should be provided for. Such direct expenditures should be both necessarily incurred for the restructuring *and* not associated with the ongoing activities of the enterprises. Thus, a provision for restructuring would not include costs like: cost of retraining or relocating the enterprise's current staff members or costs of marketing or investments in new systems and distribution networks (such expenditures are in fact categorically disallowed by the standard, as they are considered to be expenses relating to the future conduct of the business of the enterprise, and thus are not liabilities relating to the restructuring program). Also, identifiable future operating losses up to the date of an actual restructuring are not to be included in the provision for a restructuring (unless they relate to an onerous contract). Furthermore, in keeping with the general measurement principles relating to provisions outlined in the standard, the specific guidance in IAS 37 relating to restructuring prohibits taking into account any gains on expected disposal of assets in measuring a restructuring provision, even if the sale of the assets is envisaged as part of the restructuring.

A management decision or a board resolution to restructure taken before the balance sheet date does not automatically give rise to a constructive obligation at the balance sheet date unless the enterprise has, before the balance sheet date: either started to implement the restructuring plan, or announced the main features of the restructuring plan to those affected by it in a sufficiently specific manner such that a valid expectation is raised in them (i.e., that the entity will in fact carry out the restructuring and that benefits will be paid to them).

Examples of events that may fall within the definition of restructuring are

- A fundamental reorganization of an enterprise that has a material effect on the nature and focus of the enterprise's operations;
- Drastic changes in the management structure—for example, making all functional units autonomous;

- Removing the business to a more strategic location or place by relocating the headquarters from one country or region to another; and
- The sale or termination of a line of business (if certain other conditions are satisfied, such that a restructuring could be considered a discontinued operation under IFRS 5).

13. Disclosures mandated by the standard for provisions are the following:

- For each class of provision, the carrying amount at the beginning and the end of the period, additional provisions made during the period, amounts used during the period, unused amounts reversed during the period, and the increase during the period in the discounted amount arising from the passage of time and the effect of change in discount rate (comparative information is not required).
- For each class of provision, a brief description of the nature of the obligation and the expected timing of any resulting outflows of economic benefits, an indication of the uncertainties regarding the amount or timing of those outflows (including, where necessary in order to provide adequate information, disclosure of major assumptions made concerning future events), and the amount of any expected reimbursement, stating the amount of the asset that has been recognized for that expected reimbursement.
- In extremely rare circumstances, if the above disclosures as envisaged by the standard are expected to seriously prejudice the position of the enterprise in a dispute with third parties on the subject matter of the provision, then the standard takes a lenient view and allows the reporting entity to disclose the general nature of the dispute together with the fact that, and reason why, the information has not been disclosed. This is to satisfy the concerns of those who believe that mere disclosure of certain provisions will encourage potential claimants to assert themselves, thus becoming a "self-fulfilling prophecy."

For the purposes of making the above disclosures, it may be essential to group or aggregate provisions. The standard also offers guidance on how to determine which provisions may be aggregated to form a class. As per the standard, in determining which provisions may be aggregated to report as a class, the nature of the items should be sufficiently similar for them to be aggregated together and reported as a class. For example, while it may be appropriate to aggregate into a single class all provisions relating to warranties of different products, it may not be appropriate to group and present, as a single class, amounts relating to normal warranties and amounts that are subject to legal proceedings.

Example footnote illustrating disclosures required under IAS 37 with respect to provisions

Provisions

At December 31, 2005, provisions consist of the following (all amounts in euros):

	Opening balance	Additions	Provision utilized	Unutilized provision reversed	Closing balance
Provision for environmental costs	1,000,000	900,000	(800,000)	(100,000)	1,000,000
Provision for staff bonus	2,000,000	1,000,000	(900,000)	--	2,100,000
Provision for restructuring costs	1,000,000	500,000	(100,000)	(200,000)	1,200,000
Provision for decommissioning costs	5,000,000	500,000	(2,000,000)	--	3,500,000
	9,000,000	2,900,000	(3,800,000)	(300,000)	7,800,000

Provision for environmental costs. Statutory decontamination costs relating to old chemical manufacturing sites are determined based on periodic assessments undertaken by environmental specialists employed by the company and verified by independent experts.

Provision for staff bonus. Provisions for staff bonus represents contractual amounts due to the company's middle management, based on one month's basic salary, as per current employment contracts.

Provision for restructuring costs. Restructuring provisions arise from a fundamental reorganization of the company's operations and management structure.

Provision for decommissioning costs. Provision is made for estimated decommissioning costs relating to oilfields operated by the company based on engineering estimates and independent experts' reports.

The following paragraphs provide examples of provisions that would need to be recognized, based on the rules laid down by the standard. It also discusses common provisions and the accounting treatment that is often applied to these particular items.

Dry-docking costs. In some countries it is required by law, for the purposes of obtaining a certificate of seaworthiness, that ships must periodically (e.g., every three to five years) undergo extensive repairs and incur maintenance costs that are customarily referred to as "dry-docking costs." Depending on the type of vessel and its remaining useful life, such costs could be significant in amount. Before IAS 37 came into effect, some argued that dry-docking costs should be periodically accrued (in anticipation) and amortized over a period of time such that the amount is spread over the period commencing from the date of accrual to the date of payment. Using this approach, if every three years a vessel has to be dry-docked at a cost of €5 million, then such costs could be recognized as a provision at the beginning of each triennial period and amortized over the following three years.

Under the requirements set forth by IAS 37, provisions for future dry-docking expenditures cannot be accrued, since these future costs are not contractual in nature and can be avoided (e.g., by disposing of the vessel prior to its next overhaul). In general, such costs are to be expensed when incurred. However, consistent with IAS 16, if a separate component of the asset cost was recognized at inception (e.g., at acquisition of the vessel) and depreciated over its (shorter) useful life, then the cost associated with the subsequent dry-docking can likewise be capitalized as a separate asset component and depreciated over the interval until the next expected dry-docking. While the presumption is that this asset component would be included in the property and equipment accounts, in practice, some enterprises record major inspection or overhaul costs as a deferred charge (a noncurrent prepaid expense account) and amortize them over the expected period of benefit, which has the same impact on total assets and periodic results of operations.

Unlawful environmental damage. Cleanup costs and penalties resulting from unlawful environmental damage (e.g., an oil spill by a tanker ship which contaminates the water near the sea port) would need to be provided for in those countries which have laws requiring cleanup, since it would lead to an outflow of resources embodying economic benefits in settlement regardless of the future actions of the enterprise.

In case the enterprise which has caused the environmental damage operates in a country that has not yet enacted legislation requiring cleanup, in some cases a provision may still be required based on the principle of constructive obligation (as opposed to a legal obligation). This may be possible if the enterprise has a widely publicized environmental policy in which it undertakes to clean up all contamination that it causes and the enterprise has a clean track record of honoring its published environmental policy. The reason a provision would be needed under the second situation is that the recognition criteria have been met—that is, there is a present obligation resulting from a past obligating event (the oil spill) and the conduct of the enterprise has created a valid expectation on the part of those affected by it that the enterprise will clean up the contamination (a constructive obligation) and the outflow of resources embodying economic benefits is probable.

The issue of determining what constitutes an "obligating event" under IAS 37 has recently been addressed, in a highly particularized setting, by IFRIC 6, *Liabilities Arising from Participating in a Specific Market—Waste Electrical and Electronic Equipment.* This was in response to a European Union Directive on Waste Electrical and Electronic Equipment (WE&EE), which regulates the collection, treatment, recovery and environmentally sound disposal of waste equipment. Such items contain toxic metals and other materials and have become a concern in recent years, due to the large quantities (e.g., obsolete computers) of goods being dumped by household and business consumers.

The EU Directive deals only with private household WE&EE sold before August 13, 2005 ("historical household equipment"). Assuming enactment of legislation by member states, it is to be mandated that the cost of waste management for this historical household equipment will be borne by the producers of that type of equipment, with levies being assessed on them in proportion to their market shares. This will be done with reference to those manufacturers that are in the market during a period to be specified in the applicable legislation of each EU member state (the "measurement period").

The accounting issue is simply this: what is the obligating event that creates the liabilities for these producers of the defined historical household equipment, which of course all has already been sold by the producers in months and years gone by. IFRIC 6 concludes that it is participation in the market during the measurement period that will be the obligating event, rather than the earlier event (manufacture of the equipment) or a later event (incurrence of costs in the performance of waste management activities). Accordingly, initial recognition of the liability will occur when the measurement period occurs.

While IFRIC 6 was promulgated in response to a specific, and unusual, situation, it does well illustrate how significant making such determinations (the obligating event, in this instance) can be with regard to presentation in the financial statements.

Provision for restructuring costs. An enterprise which publicly announces, before the balance sheet date, its plans to shut down a division in accordance with a board decision and a detailed formal plan, would need to recognize a provision for the best estimate of the costs of closing down the division. In such a case the recognition criteria are met as follows: a present obligation has resulted from a past obligating event (public announcement of the decision to the public at large) which gives rise to a constructive obligation from that date, since it creates a valid expectation that the division will be shut down and an outflow of resources embodying economic benefits in settlement is probable.

On the other hand, if the enterprise had not publicly announced its plans to shut down the division before the balance sheet date, or did not start implementing its plan before the balance sheet date, no provision would need to be made since the board decision alone would not give rise to a constructive obligation at the balance sheet date (since no valid expectation has in fact been raised in those affected by the restructuring that the enterprise will start to implement that plan). When a reporting entity commences implementation of a restructuring plan, or announces its main features to those affected, only after the balance sheet date, disclosure is required by the provisions of IAS 10. Applying the materiality logic common in financial reporting, such disclosure would only be mandatory if the restructuring is material and if nondisclosure could reasonably be expected to influence the economic decisions made by users on the basis of the financial statements.

Onerous contract. An enterprise relocates its offices to a more prestigious office complex because the old office building that it was occupying (and has been there for the last twenty years), does not suit the new corporate image it wants to project. However, the lease of the old office premises cannot be canceled at the present time since it continues for the next five years. This is a case of an onerous contract wherein the unavoidable costs of meeting the obligations under the contract exceed the economic benefits under it. A provision is thus required to be made for the best estimate of unavoidable lease payments.

Decommissioning costs. An oil company installed an oil refinery on leased land. The installation was completed before the balance sheet date. Upon expiration of the lease contract, seven years hence, the refinery will have to be relocated to another strategic location that would ensure uninterrupted supply of crude oil. These estimated relocation or decommissioning costs would need to be recognized at the balance sheet date. Accordingly, a provision should be recognized for the present value of the estimated decommissioning costs to take place after seven years.

In 2004, the IASB's committee dealing with implementation issues (IFRIC) issued a final interpretation, *Changes in Decommissioning, Restoration and Similar Liabilities,* which provides further guidance on this topic. Specifically, this interpretation specifies how the following matters would be accounted for:

1. Changes in the estimated outflows of resources embodying economic benefits (e.g., cash flows) required to settle the obligation;
2. Changes in current market assessments of the discount rate as defined in IAS 37 (i.e., including changes in both the time value of money and the risks specific to the liability); and
3. Increases that reflect the passage of time (also referred to as the unwinding of the discount, or as accretion of the estimated liability amount).

The interpretation holds that, regarding changes in either the estimated future cash flows or in the assessed discount rate, these would be added to (or deducted from) the related asset to the extent the change relates to the portion of the asset that will be depreciated in future periods. These charges or credits will thereafter be reflected in periodic results of operations over future periods. Thus, no prior period adjustments will be permitted in respect to such changes in estimates, consistent with IAS 8.

Regarding accretion of the discount over the asset's useful life, so that the liability for decommissioning costs reaches full value at the date of decommissioning, the interpretation holds that this must be included in current income, presumably as a finance charge. Importantly, the interpretation states that this cannot be capitalized as part of the asset cost.

Example of adjustment for changes in discount rate

To illustrate the accounting for this change, assume an oil refinery was recorded inclusive of an estimated removal cost, at present value, of €2,333,000. Now assume that, after two years have elapsed, the relevant discount rate is assessed at 6%. There have been no changes in the estimated ultimate removal costs, which are still expected to total €4,000,000. The accreted recorded liability value at this date is €2,722,000, but given the new discount rate, it needs to be adjusted to €2,989,000, for an increase of €267,000 as of the beginning of the third year. The provision account must be credited by this amount, as shown in the journal entry below.

The asset account and accumulated depreciation must also be adjusted for this change in discount rate. Under the proposed requirement, this would be done by recomputing the amount that would have been capitalized, using the initial discount rate for the first two years, followed by the new discount rate over the remaining five years (note that the new rate is not imposed on the period already elapsed, because the rate originally used was correct during those earlier periods). If the €4,000,000 future value were discounted for five years at 6% and two years at 8%, the adjusted initial present value would have been €2,563,000, instead of the €2,333,000 actually recorded. To adjust for this, the asset must be increased by (€2,563,000 – €2,333,000 =) €230,000.

Had the revised present value of the removal costs been capitalized, €732,286 (= €2,563,000 × 2/7) would have been depreciated to date, instead of the €666,571 (= €2,333,000 × 2/7) that was in fact recorded, for a net difference in accumulated depreciation of €65,715. This amount must be credited to the contra asset account.

Asset	230,000	
Expense	102,715	
Accumulated depreciation		65,715
Decommissioning liability		267,000

The remaining part of the entry above, a debit to expense totaling €102,715, is the net effect of the increase in the net book value of the asset (€230,000 – €65,715 =) €164,285, offset by the increased provision, €267,000, which is an expense of the period.

Taxes payable include federal or national, state or provincial, and local income taxes. Due to frequent changes in the tax laws, the amount of income taxes payable may have to be estimated. That portion deemed currently payable must be classified as a current liability. The remaining amount is classified as a long-term liability. Although estimated future taxes are broadly includable under the category "provisions," specific rules in IAS 12 prohibit discounting these amounts to present values.

Property taxes payable represent the unpaid portion of an entity's obligation to a state or other taxing authority that arises from ownership of real property. Often these taxes are levied in arrears, based on periodic reassessments of value and on governmental budgetary needs. Accordingly, the most acceptable method of accounting for property taxes is a monthly accrual of property tax expense during the fiscal period of the taxing authority for which the taxes are levied. The fiscal period of the taxing authority is the fiscal period that includes the assessment or lien date.

A liability for property taxes payable arises when the fiscal year of the taxing authority and the fiscal year of the entity do not coincide or when the assessment or lien date and the actual payment date do not fall within the same fiscal year. For example, XYZ Corporation is a calendar-year corporation that owns real estate in a state that operates on a June 30 fiscal year. In this state, property taxes are assessed and become a lien against property on July 1, although they are not payable until April 1 and August 1 of the next calendar year. XYZ Corporation would accrue an expense and a liability on a monthly basis beginning on July 1. At year-end (December 31), the firm would have an expense for six months' property tax on their income statement and a current liability for the same amount.

Bonus payments may require estimation since the amount of the bonus payment may be affected by the amount of income taxes currently payable.

Compensated absences refer to paid vacation, paid holidays, and paid sick leave. IAS 19 addresses this issue and requires that an employer should accrue a liability for employees' compensation of future absences if the employees' right to receive compensation for future absences is attributable to employee services already rendered, the right vests or accumulates, ultimate payment of the compensation is probable, and the amount of the payment can be reasonably estimated.

If an employer is required to compensate an employee for unused vacation, holidays, or sick days, even if employment is terminated, the employee's right to this compensation is said to vest. Accrual of a liability for nonvesting rights depends on whether the unused rights expire at the end of the year in which earned or accumulated and are carried forward to succeeding years. If the rights expire, a liability for future absences should not be accrued at year-end because the benefits to be paid in subsequent years would not be attributable to employee services rendered in prior years. If unused rights accumulate and increase the benefits otherwise available in subsequent years, a liability should be accrued at year-end to the extent that it is probable that employees will be paid in subsequent years for the increased benefits attributable to the accumulated rights, and the amount can reasonably be estimated.

Pay for employee leaves of absence that represent time off for past services should be considered compensation subject to accrual. Pay for employee leaves of absence that will provide future benefits and that are not attributable to past services rendered would not be subject to accrual. Although in theory such accruals should be based on expected future rates of pay, as a practical matter these are often computed on current pay rates that may not materially differ and have the advantage of being known. Also, if the payments are to be made some time in the future, discounting of the accrual amounts would seemingly be appropriate, but again this may not often be done for practical considerations.

Similar arguments can be made to support the accrual of an obligation for post-employment benefits other than pensions if employees' rights accumulate or vest, payment is probable, and the amount can be reasonably estimated. If these benefits do not vest or accumulate, these would be deemed to be contingent liabilities. Contingent liabilities are discussed in IAS 37 and are considered later in this chapter.

Short sale obligations. When an individual or enterprise sells securities that are not owned, this is referred to as a "short sale," and is usually accomplished by means of securities borrowed from a brokerage firm. In such cases, the borrowed securities are not recorded as an asset by the borrower. The IASC's IAS 39 Implementation Guidance Committee has noted that a short seller accounts for the obligation to deliver securities that it has sold as a "liability held for trading." Therefore, if an enterprise sells an unrecorded financial asset that is subject to a securities borrowing agreement, the enterprise recognizes the proceeds from the sale as an asset, and the obligation to return the asset as a liability held for trading. Liabilities held for trading, just like held for trading securities that are assets of the entity, must be measured at fair value. Changes in fair value will be reflected currently in earnings.

Payee Unknown and the Amount May Have to Be Estimated

The following are further examples of estimated liabilities, which also will fall within the definition of provisions under IAS 37. Accordingly, discounting should be applied to projected future cash flows to determine the amounts to be reported on the balance sheet if the effect of discounting is material, and if timing can be estimated with sufficient accuracy to accomplish this process.

Premiums are usually offered by an enterprise to increase product sales. They may require the purchaser to return a specified number of box tops, wrappers, or other proofs of purchase. They may or may not require the payment of a cash amount. If the premium offer terminates at the end of the current period but has not been accounted for completely if it extends into the next accounting period, a current liability for the estimated number of redemptions expected in the future period will have to be recorded. If the premium offer extends for more than one accounting period, the estimated liability must be divided into a current portion and a long-term portion.

Product warranties providing for repair or replacement of defective products may be sold separately or may be included in the sale price of the product. If the warranty extends into the next accounting period, a current liability for the estimated amount of warranty expense anticipated for the next period must be recorded. If the warranty spans more than the next period, the estimated liability must be partitioned into a current and long-term portion.

Example of product warranty expense accrual

The River Rocks Corporation manufactures clothes washers. It sells €900,000 of washing machines during its most recent month of operations. Based on its historical warranty claims experience, it reserves an estimated warranty expense of 2% of revenues with the following entry:

Warranty expense	18,000	
Reserve for warranty claims		18,000

During the following month, River Rocks incurs €10,000 of actual labor and €4,500 of actual materials expenses to repair warranty claims, which it charges to the warranty claims reserve with the following entry:

Reserve for warranty claims	14,500	
Labor expense		10,000
Materials expense		4,500

River Rocks also sells three-year extended warranties on its washing machines that begin once the initial one-year manufacturer's warranty is completed. During one month, it sells €54,000 of extended warranties, which it records with the following entry:

Cash	54,000	
Unearned warranty revenue		54,000

This liability remains unaltered for one year from the purchase date, during the period of normal warranty coverage, after which the extended warranty servicing period begins. River Rocks recognizes the warranty revenue on a straight-line basis over the 36 months of the warranty period, using the following entry each month:

Unearned warranty revenue	1,500	
Warranty revenue		1,500

Other customer incentives are usually offered by an enterprise to increase product sales. They may require the customers to accumulate "points" earned in proportion to products or services purchased or consumed. A common example is airline frequent flyer mileage programs, which reward loyal passengers with free trips following a threshold amount of paid travel, usually gauged by mileage traveled. Over time, airlines accumulate experience which lets them accurately predict what fraction of earned miles will eventually be redeemed for "free" travel. A provision must be made for the cost of such travel, if and when redemption occurs.

Example of an accrued sales incentive cost

Central European Airlines, a specialty airline offering flights to Central Europe's wine producing regions, offers frequent flier miles to its passengers. Anyone remitting 15,000 mileage points earns a free flight on Central European, which costs the airline €120 per flight granted, or approximately €0.008 per mileage point remitted. In April, the airline granted 23,000,000 mileage points, having a total value of €184,000 (=23,000,000 miles flown × €0.008). Central European's history of mileage claims remitted over the past three years suggests that 40% of all mileage points are eventually remitted. Thus, Central European records the following liability in April, based on recognition of 40% of the total value of points granted:

Passenger transportation expense	73,600	
Unremitted mileage points liability		73,600

Also in April, 8,475,000 mileage points are remitted by Central European passengers for free flights. The implicit cost of these remittances is as follows:

Mileage points remitted		8,475,000
Cost per mileage point	×	€ 0.008
Total liability reduction	=	€ 67,800

Central European records the liability with the following entry:

Unremitted mileage points liability	67,800	
Passenger transportation expense		67,800

The actual cost of transportation of passengers paid or accrued by Central European at the time the flights occur is thus reduced by the amount accrued at the time the points currently being redeemed were awarded.

A year later, Central European finds that the mileage points remittance rate has risen from 40% to 42%. At this time, there are 163,000,000 mileage points outstanding. Central European records a liability for the incremental increase of 2% in the remittance level with the following entry:

Passenger transportation expense	26,080	
Unremitted mileage points liability		26,080

The entry is based on the following calculation:

Mileage points outstanding		163,000,00
Net increase in remittance percentage	×	2%
Cost per mileage point	×	€ 0.008
Total liability	=	€26,080

Central European receives an offer to sell 20,000,000 mileage points to the Wine Tourist branded credit card, which in turn sells the points to its cardholders in exchange for purchases made with its credit card. The sale price is €0.005 per mile sold, resulting in the following entry:

Cash	100,000	
Revenue		100,000

Central European must also record the related cost of this transaction. Based on its estimated 42% mileage points remittance rate and €0.008 cost per mileage point, Central European arrives at the following estimated cost of this transaction:

Mileage points sold		20,000,000
Mileage remittance percentage	×	42%
Cost per mileage point	×	€ 0.008
Total estimated cost	=	€67,200

Central European records the following entry to record the expense associated with the mileage points sale:

Passenger transportation expense	67,200	
Unremitted mileage points liability		67,200

Contingent Liabilities

The term contingent liability is used differently under IFRS than under US GAAP. IAS 37 defines a contingent liability as an obligation that is either

- A *possible* obligation arising from past events, the outcome of which will be confirmed only on the occurrence or nonoccurrence of one or more uncertain future events which are not wholly within the control of the reporting enterprise; *or*
- A *present* obligation arising from past events, which is not recognized either because it is not probable that an outflow of resources will be required to settle an obligation or the amount of the obligation cannot be measured with sufficient reliability.

Under IAS, the reporting entity is not to give formal recognition to a contingent liability. Instead, it should disclose in the notes to the financial statements the following information:

1. An estimate of its financial effect;
2. An indication of the uncertainties relating to the amount or timing of any outflow; and
3. The possibility of any reimbursement.

Disclosure of this information may be foregone if the possibility of any outflow in settlement is remote, or if the information cannot be obtained without undue cost or effort.

Contingent liabilities may develop in a way not initially anticipated. Thus, it is imperative that they be reassessed continually to determine whether an outflow of resources embodying economic benefits has become probable. If the outflow of future economic benefits becomes probable, then a provision is required to be recognized in the financial statements of the period in which the change in such a probability occurs (except in extremely rare cases, when no reliable estimate can be made of the amount needed to be recognized as a provision).

Contingent liabilities must be distinguished from estimated liabilities, although both involve uncertainties that will be resolved by future events. However, an estimate exists because of uncertainty about the amount of an event requiring an acknowledged accounting recognition. The event is known and the effect is known, but the amount itself is uncertain. For example, depreciation is an estimate, but not a contingency, because the actual fact of physical depreciation is acknowledged, although the amount is obtained by an assumed accounting method.

In a contingency, whether there will be an impairment of an asset or the occurrence of a liability is the uncertainty that will be resolved in the future. The amount is also usually uncertain, although that is not an essential characteristic defining the contingency. Collectibility of receivables is a contingency because both the amount of loss and the identification of which customer will not pay as promised in the future is unknown. Similar logic would hold for obligations related to product warranties. Both the amount and the customer are currently unknown.

Assessing the likelihood of contingent events. It is tempting to express quantitatively the likelihood of the occurrence of contingent events (e.g., an 80% probability), but this exaggerates the degree of precision possible in the estimation process. For this reason, accounting standards have not been written to require quantification of the likelihood of contingent outcomes. Rather, qualitative descriptions, ranging along the continuum from remote to probable, have historically been prescribed.

IAS 37 sets the threshold for accrual at "more likely than not," which most experts have defined as being very slightly over a 50% likelihood. Thus, if there is even a hint that the obligation is more likely to exist than to not exist, it will need to be formally recognized if an amount can be reasonably estimated for it. The impact will be both to make it much less ambiguous when a contingency should be recorded, and to force recognition of far more of these obligations at earlier dates than they are being given recognition at present. (Note that under longstanding US GAAP, only "probable" contingent losses are accrued, although less likely outcomes, called "reasonably possible" contingencies, must be given disclosure in the financial statement footnotes.)

When a loss is probable and no estimate is possible, these facts should be disclosed in the current period. The accrual of the loss should be made in the period in which the amount of the loss can be estimated. This accrual of a loss in future periods is a change in estimate. It is **not** a prior period adjustment.

Disappearance of contingent liabilities and assets. In the context of Phase II of its Business Combinations project, the IASB has extensively redebated the accounting for contingent items. It has concluded that a contingent liability consists of both a certain obligation and an uncertain obligation. For example, a premium or reward to be claimed by buyers of a sufficient quantity of the entity's goods involves a certain liability, the obligation to pay the premium when claimed correctly, and an uncertain obligation, which is a function of how many people are likely to claim it. The certain obligation meets the *Framework* definition of a liability, while the uncertain obligation provides an input into the measurement of this liability. If this approach is incorporated into the expected amendment to IFRS 3, the probability of the obligation coming to fruition will no longer be the trigger for recognition; it will become instead the basis of measurement. In the case of the premiums owed to customers, the entity should work out the expected value of the future cash flows by combining the probabilities, and this would determine the value of the liability. In the future, therefore, contingent assets and contingent liabilities will no longer exist: the same events will trigger an actual asset or liability, and the level of uncertainty will be factored into the carrying value.

Remote contingent losses. With the exception of certain remote contingencies for which disclosures have traditionally been given, contingent losses that are deemed remote in terms of likelihood of occurrence are not accrued or disclosed in the financial statements. For example, every business risks loss by fire, explosion, government expropriation, or guarantees made in the ordinary course of business. These are all contingencies because of the uncertainty surrounding whether the future event confirming the loss will or will not take place. The risk of asset expropriation exists, but this has become less common an occurrence in recent decades and, in any event, would be limited to less developed or politically unstable nations. Unless there is specific information about the expectation of such occurrences, which would thus raise the item to the possible category in any event, thereby making it subject to disclosure, these are not normally discussed in the financial statements.

Litigation. The most difficult area of contingencies accounting involves litigation. In some developed nations there is a great deal of commercial and other litigation, some of which exposes reporting entities to risks of incurring very material losses. Accountants must generally rely on attorneys' assessments concerning the likelihood of such events. Unless the attorney indicates that the risk of loss is remote or slight, or that the impact of any loss that does occur would be immaterial to the company, the accountant will require that the entity add explanatory material to the financial statements regarding the contingency. In cases where judgments have been entered against the entity, or where the attorney gives a range of expected losses or other amounts, certain accruals of loss contingencies for at least the minimum point of the range must be made. Similarly, if the reporting entity has made an offer in settlement of unresolved litigation, that offer would normally be deemed the lower end of the range of possible loss and, thus, subject for accrual. In most cases, however, an estimate of the contingency is unknown and the contingency is reflected only in footnotes.

Example of illustrative footnotes—contingent liabilities

1. A former plant manager of the establishment has filed a claim related to injuries sustained by him during an accident in the factory. The former employee is claiming approximately €3.5 million as damages for permanent disability, alleging that the establishment had violated a safety regulation. At December 31, 2005, no provision has been made for this claim, as management intends to vigorously defend these allegations and believes the payment of any penalty is not probable.

2. Based on allegations made by a competitor, the company is currently the subject of a government investigation relating to antitrust matters. If the company is ultimately accused of violations of the country's antitrust laws, fines could be assessed. Penalties would include sharing of previously earned profits with a competitor on all contracts entered into from inception. The competitor has indicated to the governmental agency investigating the company that the company has made excessive profits ranging from €50 million to €75 million by resorting to restrictive trade practices that are prohibited by the law of the country. No provision for any penalties or other damages has been made at year-end since the company's legal counsel is confident that these allegations will not be sustained in a court of law.

Financial Guarantee Contracts

Guarantees are commonly encountered in the commercial world; these can range from guarantees of bank loans made as accommodations to business associates to negotiated arrangements made to facilitate sales of the entity's goods or services. Guarantees had not been comprehensively addressed by IFRS prior to a recent (mid-2005) amendment to IAS 39 and IFRS 4 to explicitly deal with certain financial guarantee contracts. In contrast, under

US GAAP (FAS 5, in particular) there had long been a tradition of, at minimum, disclosure of guarantees, and in many circumstances the accrual of the anticipated loss to be suffered by the guarantor. Most recently, US GAAP saw the promulgation of a detailed standard, FIN 45, which established a new regime for measuring, recording, and reporting all guarantees.

IFRS has been revised to provide guidance on the accounting for all financial guarantees—those which are in effect insurance, the accounting for which is therefore to be guided by the provisions of IFRS 4, and those which are not akin to insurance, and which are to be accounted for consistent with IAS 39, which has been amended appropriately. For purposes of applying the new guidance, a financial guarantee contract is defined as a contract that requires the issuer to make specified payments to reimburse the holder for a loss it incurs because a specified debtor fails to make payment when due. These are generally to be accounted for under provisions of amended IAS 39, as follows:

- Financial guarantee contracts are initially recognized at fair value. For those financial guarantee contracts issued in stand-alone arm's-length transactions to unrelated parties, fair value at inception will be equal to the consideration received, unless there is evidence to the contrary.
- In subsequent periods, the guarantee is to be reported at the higher of (1) the amount determined in accordance with IAS 37, or (2) the amount initially recognized less, if appropriate, the cumulative amortization (to income) that was recognized in accordance with IAS 18.

If certain criteria are met, the issuer (guarantor) may elect to use the fair value option set forth in IAS 39. That is, the guarantee may be designated as simply being carried at fair value, with all changes being reported currently in earnings. (See Chapter 5 for discussion of the *fair value option*, as most recently revised.)

The original proposal, released in 2004, was to have dealt with a class of arrangement that required the guarantor to make payments in response to adverse changes in the debtor's credit rating, even if no event of default occurred. However, in the amendments to IAS 39 and IFRS 4 that were adopted, these are excluded from the definition of financial guarantees. Rather, these credit derivatives (as they are often known) are to be accounted for at fair value under IAS 39. These are derivative financial instruments, not insurance. The accounting for such derivatives is not affected by the amendments.

The amended language of IAS 39 observes that financial guarantee contracts can have various legal forms (e.g., a guarantee, some types of letter of credit, a credit default contract, or an insurance contract), but that the proper accounting treatment does not depend on legal form.

The basic requirement of these amendments is that financial guarantee contracts, as defined, are to be accounted for under IAS 39, not under IFRS 4. However, there is an important exception: if the guarantor/issuer had previously asserted explicitly that it regarded those as insurance contracts, and had accounted for them consistent with such a declaration, then it is permitted to make a onetime election (on a contract-by-contract basis) as to whether the contracts will be accounted for as insurance or as financial instruments. This is an irrevocable election.

Apart from this special optional treatment, all financial guarantees are to be accounted for as set forth above. Free-standing guarantees (e.g., when a party other than the merchandise vendor guarantees the customer's borrowings made to effect the transaction), if arm's length, will typically be priced at fair value. For instance, if a €10,000 loan is drawn down so that the borrower can acquire machinery from a dealer, and a third party agrees to guarantee this debt to the bank for a onetime premium of €250, for a loan term of four years, that amount probably represents the fair value of the loan guarantee, which should be recorded accordingly. If it qualifies under IAS 18 for recognition as revenue on a straight-line basis, it would be amortized to income at the rate of €62.50 per year.

Assume that, subsequently, the machinery purchaser's creditworthiness is impaired by a severe downturn in its industry segment performance, so that, by the end of the second year, the fair value of this guarantee (which has two more years to run) is €200. That could be measured, among other ways, by the onetime premium that would be charged to transfer this risk to another arm's-length guarantor. Since the carrying value of the liability is €125 after two years' amortization has occurred, the *higher* of the amount determined under IAS 37 or the carrying value, €200 must be reported on the balance sheet as the guarantee obligation. An expense of (€200 – €125 =) €75 must be recognized in the current (second) year as the cost of the additional risk borne by the reporting entity (but note that €62.50 in fee income is also being recognized in that year). The new book value, €200, will be amortized over the remaining two years ratably, assuming of course no default occurs.

Note that IAS 37 stipulates that the "best estimate" of the amount to be reported as a provision is the amount that would rationally be offered to eliminate the obligation. In general, this should comport with the notion of "fair value." Both imply a pobability-weighted assessment, which may be made explicitly or implicitly depending upon the circumstances. Both also imply a present value equivalent of future resource outflows, assuming that the timing of such outflows could be estimated.

When the guarantor is not "arm's-length," determining the fair value of the guarantee at inception may be more difficult, since there is no "onetime premium" being paid to secure this arrangement. Typically, the guarantee is a sales inducement (e.g., when the machinery dealer finds it must guarantee the buyer's bank loan in order to consummate the sale), and thus is effectively a discount on the price otherwise obtainable for the merchandise (or services). The full expense would be recognized at the date of the transaction since this expense was incurred in order to generate the sale; thus it is best "matched" against revenue recognized in the current reporting period. The guarantee liability is accounted for as set forth above (adjusted to the higher of fair value or amortized original value, if amortization is proper under IAS 18).

Example of estimating the fair value of a guarantee

Paso Robles Company guarantees a €1,000,000 debt of Sauganash Company for the next three years in conjunction with selling equipment to Sauganash. Paso Robles evaluates its risk of payment as follows:

(1) There is no possibility that Paso Robles will pay to honor the guarantee during year 1 (or, equivalently, there is zero risk of default by Sauganash in year 1).

(2) There is a 15% chance that Paso Robles will pay during year 2 (i.e., that there will be a partial or complete default by Sauganash that year). If it has to pay, there is a 30% chance that it will have to pay €500,000 and a 70% chance that it will have to pay only €250,000.

(3) There is a 20% chance that Paso Robles will pay during year 3. If it has to pay, there is a 25% chance that it will have to pay €600,000 and a 75% chance that it will have to pay €300,000.

The expected cash outflows from the guarantor are computed as follows:

Year 1   100% chance of paying €0 = €0

Year 2   85% chance of paying €0 and a 15% chance of paying (.30 × €500,000 + .70 × €250,000) = (€325,000 × 15%) = €48,750

Year 3   80% chance of paying €0 and a 20% chance of paying (.25 × €600,000 + .75 × €300,000) = (€375,000 × 20%) = €75,000

The present value of the expected cash flows is computed as the sum of the years' probability-weighted cash flows, here assuming an appropriate discount rate of 8%.

Year 1	€	0	×	$1/1.08$	=	€ 0
Year 2	€48.750		×	$1/(1.08)^2$	=	41,795
Year 3	€75,000		×	$1/(1.08)^3$	=	59,537
	Fair value of the guarantee					€101,332

Based on the foregoing, a liability of €101,332 should be recognized at inception. This would effectively reduce the net selling price of the equipment sold to Sauganash by a like amount, thereby reducing the profit to be reported on the sale transaction. Assume that the equipment cost was €650,000; the entry recording the sale (assume specific identification is used for inventory costing) and the guarantee is as follows:

Cash	1,000,000	
Cost of goods sold	650,000	
Sales expense—guarantee of customer debt	101,332	
Revenue		1,000,000
Guarantee liability		101,332
Inventory		650,000

The profit reported in the current period would be €1,000,000 – €650,000 – €101,332 = €248,668. The guarantee liability would be amortized to income over the term of the three-year loan; if no default occurs, the dealer recovers the full sales expense it incurred by offering the discount.

Contingent Assets

Per IAS 37, a contingent asset is a possible asset that arises from past events and whose existence will be confirmed only by the occurrence or nonoccurrence of one or more uncertain future events that are not wholly within the control of the reporting enterprise.

Contingent assets usually arise from unplanned or unexpected events that give rise to the possibility of an inflow of economic benefits to the enterprise. An example of a contingent asset is a claim against an insurance company that the enterprise is pursuing legally.

Contingent assets should not be recognized; instead, they should be disclosed if the inflow of the economic benefits is probable. As with contingent liabilities, contingent assets need to be continually assessed to ensure that developments are properly reflected in the financial statements. For instance, if it becomes virtually certain that the inflow of economic benefits will arise, the asset and the related income should be recognized in the financial statements of the period in which the change occurs. If, however, the inflow of economic benefits has become probable (instead of virtually certain), then it should be disclosed as a contingent asset.

Example of illustrative footnotes—gain contingency/contingent asset

1. During the current year, a trial court found that a major multinational company had infringed on certain patents and trademarks owned by the company. The court awarded €100 million in damages for these alleged violations by the defendant. In accordance with the court order, the defendant will also be required to pay interest on the award amount and legal costs as well. Should the defendant appeal to an appellate court, the verdict of the trial court could be reduced or the amount of the damages could be reduced. Therefore, at December 31, 2005, the company has not recognized the award amount in the accompanying financial statements since it is not virtually certain of the verdict of the appellate court.

2. In June 2005, the company settled its longtime copyright infringement and trade secrets lawsuit with a competitor. Under the terms of the settlement, the competitor paid the company €2.5 million, which was received in full and final settlement in October 2005, and the parties have dismissed all remaining litigation. For the year ended Decem-

ber 31, 2005, the company recognized the amount received in settlement as "other income," which is included in the accompanying financial statements.

The IASB's ongoing project dealing with business combinations (described in Chapter 11) would revise the definition of contingent asset to converge with the US GAAP definition. If adopted, this would define a contingent asset as "a present right that arises from past events that may result in future cash inflow (or other economic benefits) based on the occurrence or nonoccurrence of one or more uncertain future events not wholly within the control of the enterprise." As discussed under contingent liabilities, in the future it is likely that the category contingent assets would disappear, to be replaced by a measurement which factors in uncertainty.

Disclosures Prescribed by IAS 37 for Contingent Liabilities and Contingent Assets

For the moment, an enterprise should disclose, for each class of contingent liability at the balance sheet date, a brief description of the nature of the contingent liability and, where practicable, an estimate of its financial effect measured in the same manner as provisions, an indication of the uncertainties relating to the amount or timing of any outflow, and the possibility of any reimbursement.

In aggregating contingent liabilities to form a class, it is essential to consider whether the nature of the items is sufficiently similar to each other such that they could be presented as a single class.

In the case of contingent assets where an inflow of economic benefits is probable, an enterprise should disclose a brief description of the nature of the contingent assets at the balance sheet date and, where practicable, an estimate of their financial effect, measured using the same principles as provisions.

Where any of the above information is not disclosed because it is not practical to do so, that fact should be disclosed. In extremely rare circumstances, if the above disclosures as envisaged by the standard are expected to seriously prejudice the position of the enterprise in a dispute with third parties on the subject matter of the contingencies, then the standard takes a lenient view and allows the enterprise to disclose the general nature of the dispute, together with the fact that, and reason why, the information has not been disclosed.

Reporting Events Occurring After the Balance Sheet Date

The issue addressed by IAS 10 is to what extent anything that happens during the post-year-end period when the financial statements are being prepared should be reflected in those financial statements. The standard distinguishes between events that provide information about the state of the entity at balance sheet date, and those that concern the next financial period. A secondary issue is the cutoff point beyond which the financial statements are considered to be finalized.

Authorization date. The determination of the authorization date (i.e., the date when the financial statements could be considered legally authorized for issuance, generally by action of the board of directors of the reporting entity) is critical to the concept of events after the balance sheet date. It serves as the cutoff point after the balance sheet date, up to which the post-balance-sheet events are to be examined in order to ascertain whether such events qualify for the treatment prescribed by IAS 10. This standard explains the concept through the use of illustrations.

The general principles that need to be considered in determining the authorization date of the financial statements are set out below.

- When an entity is required to submit its financial statements to its shareholders for approval after they have already been issued, the authorization date in this case would mean the date of original issuance and not the date when these are approved by the shareholders; and

- When an enterprise is required to issue its financial statements to a supervisory board made up wholly of nonexecutives, authorization date would mean the date on which management authorizes them for issue to the supervisory board.

Consider the following examples:

1. The preparation of the financial statements of Xanadu Corp. for the accounting period ended December 31, 2005, was completed by the management on February 15, 2006. The draft financial statements were considered at the meeting of the board of directors held on February 18, 2006, on which date the Board approved them and authorized them for issuance. The annual general meeting (AGM) was held on March 28, 2006, after allowing for printing and the requisite notice period mandated by the corporate statute. At the AGM the shareholders approved the financial statements. The approved financial statements were filed by the corporation with the Company Law Board (the statutory body of the country that regulates corporations) on April 6, 2006.

    Given these facts, the date of authorization of the financial statements of Xanadu Corp. for the year ended December 31, 2005, is February 18, 2006, the date when the board approved them and authorized them for issue (and not the date they were approved in the AGM by the shareholders). Thus, all post-balance-sheet events between December 31, 2005, and February 18, 2006, need to be considered by Xanadu Corp. for the purposes of evaluating whether or not they are to be accounted or reported under IAS 10.

2. Suppose in the above cited case the management of Xanadu Corp. was required to issue the financial statements to a supervisory board (consisting solely of nonexecutives including representatives of a trade union). The management of Xanadu Corp. had issued the draft financial statements to the supervisory board on February 16, 2006. The supervisory board approved them on February 17, 2006, and the shareholders approved them in the AGM held on March 28, 2006. The approved financial statements were filed with the Company Law Board on April 6, 2006.

    In this case the date of authorization of financial statements would be February 16, 2006, the date the draft financial statements were issued to the supervisory board. Thus, all post-balance-sheet events between December 31, 2005, and February 16, 2006, need to be considered by Xanadu Corp. for the purposes of evaluating whether or not they are to be accounted or reported under IAS 10.

Adjusting and nonadjusting events (after the balance sheet date). Two kinds of events after the balance sheet date are distinguished by the standard. These are, respectively, "adjusting events after the balance sheet date" and "nonadjusting events after the balance sheet date." Adjusting events are those post-balance-sheet events that provide evidence of conditions that actually existed at the balance sheet date, albeit they were not known at the time. Financial statements should be adjusted to reflect adjusting events after the balance sheet date.

Examples of *adjusting events*, given by the standard, are the following:

1. Resolution after the balance sheet date of a court case that confirms a present obligation requiring either an adjustment to an existing provision or recognition of a provision instead of mere disclosure of a contingent liability;

2. Receipt of information after the balance sheet date indicating that an asset was impaired or that a previous impairment loss needs to be adjusted. For instance, the bankruptcy of a customer subsequent to the balance sheet date usually confirms the existence of loss at the balance sheet date, and the disposal of inventories after the balance sheet date provides evidence (not always conclusive, however) about their net realizable value at the balance sheet date;

3. The determination after the balance sheet date of the cost of assets purchased, or the proceeds from assets disposed of, before the balance sheet date;

4. The determination subsequent to the balance sheet date of the amount of profit sharing or bonus payments, where there was a present legal or constructive obligation at the balance sheet date to make the payments as a result of events before that date; and

5. The discovery of frauds or errors, after the balance sheet date, that show that the financial statements were incorrect at year-end before the adjustment.

Commonly encountered situations of adjusting events are illustrated below.

- During the year 2005 Taj Corp. was sued by a competitor for €10 million for infringement of a trademark. Based on the advice of the company's legal counsel, Taj accrued the sum of €5 million as a provision in its financial statements for the year ended December 31, 2005. Subsequent to the balance sheet date, on February 15, 2006, the Supreme Court decided in favor of the party alleging infringement of the trademark and ordered the defendant to pay the aggrieved party a sum of €7 million. The financial statements were prepared by the company's management on January 31, 2006, and approved by the Board on February 20, 2006. Taj Corp. should adjust the provision by €2 million to reflect the award decreed by the Supreme Court (assumed to be the final appellate authority on the matter in this example) to be paid by Taj Corp. to its competitor. Had the judgment of the Supreme Court been delivered on February 25, 2006, or later, this post-balance-sheet event would have occurred after the cutoff point (i.e., the date the financial statements were authorized for original issuance). If so, adjustment of financial statements would not have been required.

- Penn Corp. carries its inventory at the lower of cost and net realizable value. At December 31, 2005, the cost of inventory, determined under the first-in, first-out (FIFO) method, as reported in its financial statements for the year then ended, was €5 million. Due to severe recession and other negative economic trends in the market, the inventory could not be sold during the entire month of January 2006. On February 10, 2006, Penn Corp. entered into an agreement to sell the entire inventory to a competitor for €4 million. Presuming the financial statements were authorized for issuance on February 15, 2006, the company should recognize a write-down of €1 million in the financial statements for the year ended December 31, 2005.

In contrast with the foregoing, nonadjusting events are those post-balance-sheet events that are indicative of conditions that arose after the balance sheet date. Financial statements should not be adjusted to reflect nonadjusting events after the balance sheet date. An example of a nonadjusting event is a decline in the market value of investments between the balance sheet date and the date when the financial statements are authorized for issue. Since the fall in the market value of investments after the balance sheet date is not indicative of their market value at the balance sheet date (instead it reflects circumstances that arose subsequent to the balance sheet date) the fall in market value need not, and should not, be recognized in the financial statements at the balance sheet date.

Not all nonadjusting events are significant enough to require disclosure, however. The revised standard gives examples of nonadjusting events that would impair the ability of the users of financial statements to make proper evaluations or decisions if not disclosed. Where nonadjusting events after the balance sheet date are of such significance, disclosure should be made for each such significant category of nonadjusting event, of the nature of the event and an estimate of its financial effect or a statement that such an estimate cannot be made. Examples given by the standard of such significant nonadjusting post-balance-sheet events are the following:

1. A major business combination or disposing of a major subsidiary;
2. Announcing a plan to discontinue an operation;

3. Major purchases and disposals of assets or expropriation of major assets by government;
4. The destruction of a major production plant by fire;
5. Announcing or commencing the implementation of a major restructuring;
6. Abnormally large changes in asset prices or foreign exchange rates;
7. Significant changes in tax rates and enacted tax laws;
8. Entering into significant commitments or contingent liabilities; and
9. Major litigation arising from events occurring after the balance sheet date.

Dividends proposed or declared after the balance sheet date. Dividends on equity shares proposed or declared after the balance sheet date should not be recognized as a liability at the balance sheet date. Such declaration is a nonadjusting subsequent event, in other words. While at one time IFRS did permit accrual of post-balance-sheet date dividend declarations, this has not been permissible for some time. Furthermore, the revisions made to IAS 10 as part of the IASB's Improvements Project in late 2003 (effective 2005) also eliminated the formerly permitted display of post-balance-sheet date dividends as a separate component of equity. Footnote disclosure is, on the other hand, required unless immaterial.

Going concern considerations. Deterioration in an entity's financial position after the balance sheet date could cast substantial doubts about an enterprise's ability to continue as a going concern. IAS 10 requires that an enterprise should not prepare its financial statements on a going concern basis if management determines after the balance sheet date either that it intends to liquidate the enterprise or cease trading, or that it has no realistic alternative but to do so. IAS 10 notes that disclosures prescribed by IAS 1 under such circumstances should also be complied with.

Disclosure requirements. The following disclosures are mandated by IAS 10:

1. The date when the financial statements were authorized for issue and who gave that authorization. If the enterprise's owners have the power to amend the financial statements after issuance, this fact should be disclosed;
2. If information is received after the balance sheet date about conditions that existed at the balance sheet date, disclosures that relate to those conditions should be updated in the light of the new information; and
3. Where nonadjusting events after the balance sheet date are of such significance that nondisclosure would affect the ability of the users of financial statements to make proper evaluations and decisions, disclosure should be made for each such significant category of nonadjusting event, of the nature of the event and an estimate of its financial effect or a statement that such an estimate cannot be made.

Accounting for Financial Liabilities and IAS 39

IAS 39 established new requirements for accounting for financial liabilities that are held for trading and those that are derivatives. These have to be accounted for at fair value and are addressed in detail in Chapters 5, 10, and 13. However, other financial liabilities continue to be reported at amortized historical cost. The Joint Working Group of standard setters, which in the 1990s discussed a possible successor to IAS 39, suggested the notion of employing fair value to account for all financial assets and liabilities. Some standard setters, both internationally and in the US, are enthusiastic for the extension of the use of fair value, because they believe it provides more comparable and representationally faithful information. However, a move towards the use of full fair value is undoubtedly many years away.

Initial measurement of financial liabilities. IAS 39 stipulates that all financial liabilities are to be initially measured at cost, which (assuming they are each incurred in an arm's-length transaction) is also fair value. Any related transaction costs are included in this initial measurement. In rare instances when the fair value of the consideration received is not reliably determinable, resort is to be made to a computation of the present value of all future cash flows related to the liability. In such a case, the discount rate to apply would be the prevailing rate on similar instruments issued by a party having a similar credit rating.

Remeasurement of financial liabilities. IAS 39 provides that, subsequent to initial recognition, an enterprise should measure all financial liabilities, other than liabilities held for trading purposes and derivative contracts that are liabilities, at amortized cost. Where the initial recorded amount is not the contractual maturity value of the liability (e.g., as when transaction costs are added to the issuance price, or when there was a premium or discount upon issuance) periodic amortization should be recorded, using the constant effective yield method.

In its 2003 revisions, the IASB introduced what is known as the "fair value option," which allowed entities to designate any liability as being held at fair value, with changes in fair value flowing through the income statement. However, this widening of the standard, intended to provide flexibility, has been strenuously opposed by banking regulators and by some EU authorities, and in response (to gain support for the EU mandate that all publicly held entities begin reporting consolidated financial statements prepared in accordance with IFRS in 2005) the IASB issued an amendment which constrains its use in respect of liabilities.

Examples of Financial Statement Disclosures

Novartis AG
For the Fiscal Year ending December 31, 2004

Notes to the consolidated financial statements

28. Commitments and contingencies.

Spin-off of Novartis Agribusiness. All remaining significant matters in connection with the 1999 Master Agreement between Novartis AG and AstraZeneca Plc for the spin-off and merger of their respective agrochemical businesses into Syngenta AG have been completed during 2003.

Chiron Corporation. In connection with its original investment in January 1996 in Chiron

- Novartis has agreed to purchase up to $500 million of new Chiron equity at fair value, at Chiron's request. To date, Chiron has made no such request.
- Novartis has agreed to guarantee up to $703 million of Chiron debt. Utilization of the guarantee in excess of $403 million reduces the equity put amount mentioned above. Novartis' obligation under the guarantee is only effective if Chiron defaults on the debt.
- Chiron has granted to Novartis an option to purchase newly issued shares of equity securities directly from Chiron at fair market value. Novartis may exercise this option at any time subject to certain conditions, including a limitation on Novartis' aggregate ownership not to exceed 55% of Chiron's then outstanding common stock.

The outstanding equity put and guarantee expire no later than 2011.

Leasing commitments. Commitments arising from fixed-term operational leases in effect at December 31 are as follows:

	2004
	($ millions)
2005	233
2006	181
2007	123
2008	80
2009	63
Thereafter	246
Total	926
Expense of current year	287

Research and development commitments. The Group has entered into long-term research agreements with various institutions, including potential milestone payments. As of December 31, 2004, they are as follows:

	Unconditional Commitments 2004	*Potential milestone payments 2004*	*Total 2004*
	($ millions)	*($ millions)*	*($ millions)*
2005	285	91	376
2006	169	70	239
2007	76	88	164
2008	75	67	142
2009	38	133	171
Thereafter	22	133	155
Total	665	582	1,247

Other commitments The Novartis Group entered into various purchase commitments for services and materials as well as for equipment as part of the ordinary business. These commitments are not in excess of current market prices in all material respects and reflect on normal business operations.

Contingencies. Group companies have to observe the laws, government orders, and regulations of the country in which they operate. A number of them are currently involved in administrative proceedings arising out of the normal conduct of their business. In the opinion of Group management, however, the outcome of these actions will not materially affect the Group's financial position, result of operations, or cash flow.

The material components of the Group's potential environmental liability consist of a risk assessment based on investigation of the various sites identified by the Group as at risk for environmental exposure. The Group's future remediation expenses are affected by a number of uncertainties. These uncertainties include, but are not limited to, the method and extent of remediation, the percentage of material attributable to the Group at the remediation sites relative to that attributable to other parties, and the financial capabilities of the other potentially responsible parties.

The Group is also subject to certain legal and product liability claims. Whilst provisions have been made for probable losses that management deems to be reasonable or appropriate there are uncertainties connected with these estimates. Note 19 contains more extensive discussion of these matters.

The Group does not expect the resolution of such uncertainties to have a material effect on the consolidated financial statements.

Clariant Group
Consolidated Financial Statements
Period Ending December 2004

14. Movements in provisions for long-term liabilities

CHF mn	*Provisions for pension plans and other post-employment benefits*	*Environ-mental provisions*	*Long-term personnel provisions*	*Other long-term provisions*	*Total provisions for long-term liabilities 2004*	*Total provisions for long-term liabilities 2003*
At January 1	498	218	125	52	893	882
Additions	49	17	21	19	106	200
Amounts used	(48)	(16)	(25)	(31)	(120)	(165)
Unused amounts reversed	(14)	(9)	(2)	(4)	(29)	(48)
Changes due to the passage of time and changes in discount rates	7	1	2	0	10	12
Translation effects	(13)	(7)	(5)	2	(23)	10
At December 31	479	204	116	38	837	893
Debts falling due						
Between 1 and 3 years	43	28	29	8	108	117
Between 3 and 5 years	56	9	59	6	130	165
Over 5 years	380	167	28	24	599	611
At December 31	479	204	116	38	837	893

Provisions for pension plans and other postemployment benefits. Provisions for pension plans relate to defined benefit plans, defined contribution plans, and postemployment medical plans in which many of the Group's subsidiaries participate. Major defined benefit plans are maintained in Switzerland, the USA, Germany, Japan, and the UK. Postemployment medical plans are maintained in the USA, Canada, and France. Most subsidiaries also have defined contribution plans. See Note 13 of the Consolidated Financial Statements for further information on the Group's employee benefit plans.

Environmental provisions. Provisions for environmental liabilities are made when there is a legal or constructive obligation for the Group, which will result in an outflow of economic resources. It is difficult to estimate the action required by Clariant in the future to correct the effects on the environment of prior disposal or release of chemical substances by Clariant or other parties, and the associated costs, pursuant to environmental laws and regulations. The material components of the environmental provisions consist of the cost to fully clean and refurbish contaminated sites and to treat and contain contamination at sites where the environmental exposure is less severe. The Group's future remediation expenses are affected by a number of uncertainties which include, but are not limited to, the method and extent of remediation and the percentage of material attributable to Clariant at the remediation sites relative to that attributable to other parties. The environmental provisions reported in the balance sheet concern a number of different obligations, mainly in Switzerland, the USA, Germany, the UK, Brazil and Italy.

Provisions are made for remedial work where there is an obligation to remedy environmental damage, as well as for containment work where required by environmental regulations. All provisions relate to environmental liabilities arising in connection with activities that occurred prior to the date when Clariant took control of the relevant site.

Long-term personnel provisions. Long-term personnel provisions include long-term compensated absences such as sabbatical leave, jubilee or other long-service benefits, long-term disability benefits, profit sharing and bonuses payable twelve months or more after the end of the period in which they are earned.

Other long-term provisions. Other long-term provisions include provisions for obligations relating to tax and legal cases in various countries where settlement is expected after twelve months or more.

17. Movements in provisions for short-term liabilities

CHF mn	Restructuring provisions	Short-term personnel provisions	Other short-term provisions	Total provisions for short-term liabilities 2004	Total provisions for short-term liabilities 2003
At January 1	45	129	189	363	460
Additions and reclassifications	56	119	137	312	317
Amounts used	(40)	(119)	(125)	(284)	(376)
Unused amounts reversed	(1)	(13)	(19)	(33)	(43)
Translation effects	0	(2)	9	7	5
At December 31	60	114	191	365	363

Restructuring provisions. Restructuring provisions are established where there is a legal or constructive obligation for the Group that will result in the outflow of economic resources and which is expected to occur within the next twelve months. The term restructuring refers to activities that have as a consequence, staff redundancies and the shut-down of production lines or entire sites. However, expenses for termination benefits which are borne by the pension and termination plans are included in pension plan liabilities (see Note 13).

Short-term personnel provisions. Liabilities from personnel costs include holiday entitlements, compensated absences such as annual leave, profit sharing and bonuses payable within twelve months, and nonmonetary benefits such as medical care, housing, and cars for current employees payable within twelve months, for which no invoice has been received.

Other short-term provisions. Other short-term provisions are recorded for liabilities (comprising tax, legal and other items in various countries) falling due within the next twelve months, for which no invoice has been received at the reporting date and/or for which the amount can only be reliably estimated.

29. Commitments and contingencies

Leasing commitments. Commitments arising from fixed-term operational leases mainly from Infraserv companies at December 31 are as follows:

CHF mn	2004	2003
2004		90
2005	75	75
2006	57	55
2007	46	47
2008	40	46
2009	32	--
Thereafter	39	67
Total	289	380
Guarantees in favor of third parties	31	76

Expenses for operating leases were CHF 95 million in 2004 and CHF 99 million in 2003.

Contingencies. Clariant operates in countries where political, economic, social, legal and regulatory developments can have an impact on the operational activities. The effects of such risks on the Company's results, which arise during the normal course of business, are not foreseeable and are therefore not included in the accompanying financial statements.

In the ordinary course of business, Clariant is involved in lawsuits, claims, investigations and proceedings, including product liability, intellectual property, commercial, environmental and health and safety matters. Although the outcome of any legal proceedings cannot be predicted with certainty, management is of the opinion that there are no such matters pending which would be likely to have any material adverse effect in relation to its business, financial position, or results of operations.

Purchase commitments. In the regular course of business, Clariant enters into relationships with suppliers whereby the Group commits itself to purchase certain minimum quantities of materials in order to benefit from better pricing conditions. At present, purchase commitments on such contracts amount to about CHF 85 million.

Environmental risk. Clariant is exposed to environmental liabilities and risks relating to its past operations, principally in respect of remediation costs. Provisions for nonrecurring remediation costs are made when there is a legal or constructive obligation and the cost can be reliably estimated. It is difficult to estimate the action required by Clariant in the future to correct the effects on the environment of prior disposal or release of chemical substances by Clariant or other parties, and the associated costs, pursuant to environmental laws and regulations. The material components of the environmental provisions consist of costs to fully clean and refurbish contaminated sites and to treat and contain contamination at sites where the environmental exposure is less severe. The Group's future remediation expenses are affected by a number of uncertainties which include, but are not limited to, the method and extent of remediation and the percentage of material attributable to Clariant at the remediation sites relative to that attributable to other parties. The Group permanently monitors the various sites identified at risk for environmental exposure. Clariant believes that its provisions are adequate based upon currently available information, however given the inherent difficulties in estimating liabilities in this area, there is no guarantee that additional costs will not be incurred.

30. Exchange rates of principal currencies

Rates used to translate the consolidated balance sheets (closing rate)

	December 31, 2004	*December 31, 2003*
1 USD	1.13	1.24
1 GBP	2.18	2.20
100 JPY	1.10	1.16
1 EUR	1.54	1.56

Average sales-weighted rates used to translate the consolidated income statements and consolidated statements of cash flow

	2004	*2003*
1 USD	1.25	1.35
1 GBP	2.28	2.20
100 JPY	1.15	1.16
1 EUR	1.54	1.52

Nestlé Group
Period Ending December 2004

Contingent assets and liabilities

Contingent assets and liabilities arise from conditions or situations, the outcome of which depends on future events. They are disclosed in the notes to the accounts.

The Group is exposed to contingent liabilities amounting to about CHF 690 million (2003: CHF 470 million) representing various potential litigations (CHF 550 million) and other items (CHF 140 million).

Contingent assets for litigation claims in favor of the Group amount to about CHF 170 million (2003: CHF 170 million).

Provisions. Provisions recognize contingencies which may arise and which have been prudently provided. A provision for uninsured risks is constituted to cover risks not insured with third parties, such as consequential loss. Provision for Swiss taxes is made on the basis of the Company's taxable capital, reserves, and profit for the year. A general provision is maintained to cover possible foreign taxes liabilities.

Contingencies. At December 31, 2004 and 2003, the total of guarantees for credit facilities granted to Group companies and Commercial Paper Programs, together with the buy-back agreements relating to notes issued, amounted to CHF 12.275 million and CHF 15.038 million, respectively.

HVB Group
Period Ending December 2004

77. Contingent liabilities and other commitments

€ millions	2004	2003
Contingent liabilities*	31,334	33,060
Rediscounted bills of exchange	19	23
Guarantees and indemnities	31,315	33,037
Loan guarantees	7,432	9,409
Guarantees and indemnity agreements	20,989	21,231
Documentary credits	2,894	2,397
Other commitments	55,742	58,422
Commitments arising from sale option to resell transactions	787	771
Irrevocable credit commitments	46,865	51,575
Book credits	40,050	45,228
Guarantees	3,765	44,253
Mortgage and municipal loans	2,818	1,741
Bills of exchange	232	353
Delivery obligations from securities lending transactions	5,706	4,001
Other commitments	2,384	2,075
Total	87,076	91,482

* *Contingent liabilities are offset by contingent assets to the same amount*

Neither contingent liabilities nor other commitments contain any significant items. Commitments under guarantee and indemnity agreements, as well as irrevocable credit commitments to nonconsolidated companies, amounted to €361 million (2003: €352 million) and €85 million (2003: €56 million), respectively.

The largest single item under other commitments is placement and transfer obligations totaling €507 million (2003: €487 million). Other commitments arising particularly from rental, leasing, and maintenance agreements, and from rental of office space and use of technical equipment amount to €473 million (2003: €490 million). The contracts run for standard market periods, and no charges have been put off to future years.

The Bank has declared its willingness to offset any losses incurred by hotel operating companies in which it holds an indirect majority stake, by means of income subsidies.

As part of real estate financing and development operations, the Bank has assumed rental obligations or issued rent guarantees on a case-by-case basis to make fund constructions more marketable—in particular for the lease funds and (closed) KG real estate funds offered by its H.F.S. Hypo-Fondsbeteiligungen fur Sachwerte GmbH subsidiary. Identifiable risks arising from such guarantees have been included. The Bank has provided performance guarantees for the holders of shares in bond/money market funds offered by some of its capital investment companies.

Other financial commitments arising from longer-term rental and leasing agreements exist at the nonconsolidated HVB Immobilien AG and the latter's nonconsolidated subsidiaries.

Commitments for uncalled payments on shares not fully paid up amounted to €418 million at year-end 2004 (2003: €463 million), and similar liabilities for shares in cooperatives totaled €1 million (2003: €1 million). Under Section 24 of the German Private Limited Companies Act, the Bank was also liable for such calls in respect of two private limited companies for an aggregate of €16 million (2003: €16 million).

Lectra
Period Ending December 31, 2004

Notes to the consolidated financial statements

Postclosing Events

New Acquisition

On December 22, 2004, Lectra announced the acquisition of Humantec. This company, founded in 1993 and based in Germany, is today a significant player in its markets. It ranks alongside Lectra among the world's top three automated leather cutting equipment vendors. It is well-established in Europe and North America, and has recently expanded its business in Asia. Humantec reported consolidated revenues of approximately €9.2 million in 2004 and a net income of around €0.6 million. The transaction comprises the acquisition of 100% of Humantec Industriesysteme GmbH and its sister company in the United States, Humantec Systems, Inc. for a consideration of €2.9 million in cash and 330,000 Lectra shares. This consideration will be paid at the time of closing, scheduled to take place before March 31, 2005, the Lectra shares being drawn from treasury shares currently held by the company. Humantec will be consolidated in Lectra's financial statements in 2005. Based on currently available information, the transaction is expected to give rise to goodwill of approximately €5 million.

Dividend. Subject to the approval of shareholders at their meeting scheduled for April 29, 2005, the company plans to declare a dividend of €0.13 per share in respect of fiscal year 2004 (the *avoir fiscal* or tax credit has been abolished with effect from January 1, 2005), an increase of €0.01 (+8%) relative to the previous year.

HVB Group
For the year ended December 31, 2004

Events after December 31, 2004

In January 2005, we announced that the workout portfolios of the entire German real estate finance business of the parent bank would be transferred to the new Real Estate Restructuring segment together with the remaining portfolios of the Real Estate Workout segment. This will involve a volume of h15.4 billion. Starting with the first quarter of 2005, we will report separately on this new segment in our segment reports in the interim report. There were no further events after December 31, 2004, worth reporting.

Lectra S.A.
Fort the year ended December 31, 2004

I. Provisions:

Provision for risks and charges

All known risks at balance sheet date are reviewed in detail and an allowance is made if an obligation exists. At the time of the effective payment, the provision is deducted from the corresponding expenses.

Provisions for warranties. A provision for warranties covers, on the basis of historical data, costs from warranties granted by the Group to its customers at the time of sale of CAD/CAM equipment, for replacement of parts, travel of technicians, and labor. This provision is recorded at the time the sale is booked by the company.

Provisions for future benefits (including provisions for retirement indemnities). The Group is subject to a variety of deferred employee benefits plans, depending on the subsidiary concerned. These comprise

- *Defined contributions plans:* These refer to benefits payable subsequent to the period of employment. Under these plans, for certain employee categories, the Group pays defined contributions to an outside insurance company or pension fund. For the Group, defined contributions plans concern retirement plans exclusively. Defined contributions plans do not create future liabilities for the Group and hence do not require the setting up of provisions.

- *Defined benefits plans:* These refer to benefits payable subsequent to the period of employment that guarantees contractual additional income for certain employee categories (in some cases these plans are governed by specific industrywide agreements). For the Group, the plans cover lump-sum termination payments solely as required by legislation or as defined by the relevant industrywide agreement. The guaranteed additional income represents a future liability. This liability is calculated by estimating employees' future accumulated benefits in return for services performed during the current and previous fiscal years.

    The resulting provision reflects the discounted value of this liability calculated as required by IAS 19. Actuarial assumptions notably include a rate of salary increase, a discount rate (based on an average annual bond yield) and a turnover rate, in accordance with local regulations where appropriate, based on observed historical data. The Group has opted to record actuarial differences in full in the statement of income. The total charge represented by all of the foregoing is recognized in staff costs in the statement of income.

Notes to the consolidated balance sheets

12. Provisions for risks and charges

(in thousands of euros)	Provisions for litigations	Provisions for warranty	Provisions for deferred employee benefits	Other provisions for risks and charges	Total
Provisions for risks and charges at January 1	34	544	2,482	375	3,435
Allowances	12	512	347	319	1,190
Used amounts reversed	(3)	(636)	(375)	(102)	(1,116)
Unused amounts reversed	--	(10)	(166)	(73)	(249)
Changes in scope of consolidation	2,250	434	960	1,054	4,698
Translation adjustments	(1)	--	(10)	(3)	(14)
Provisions for risks and charges at December 31	2,292	844	3,238	1,570	7,944

Provisions for deferred benefits consist entirely of lump-sum payments payable upon retirement or, in certain countries and depending on local legislation, upon resignation or dismissal. These provisions concern France, Italy and Japan.

The increase in "Provisions for Risks and Charges" in the balance sheet at December 31, 2004, stems mainly from changes in scope of consolidation.

In addition to a provision for warranty and a provision for deferred benefits, the opening balance sheet of Investronica at April 1, 2004, includes a provision for restructuring and a provision for litigation, both related to the acquisition.

13 FINANCIAL INSTRUMENTS—
LONG-TERM DEBT

PERSPECTIVE AND ISSUES

Long-term debt represents future sacrifices of economic benefits to be repaid over a period of more than one year or, if longer, over more than one operating cycle. Long-term debt includes such familiar obligations as bonds payable, notes payable, lease obligations, pension and deferred compensation plan obligations, deferred income taxes, and unearned revenue. The accounting for bonds and long-term notes is covered in this chapter. Since at present, IFRS explicitly address only a few of these topics, the accounting recommendations herein are those of the authors, based on practices in many nations. Most of these are commonsense suggestions not likely to prove controversial.

The proper valuation basis for long-term debt is the present value of future payments using the market rate of interest, either that stated or implied in the transaction, at the date the debt was incurred. An exception to the use of the market rate of interest stated or implied in the transaction in valuing long-term notes occurs when it is necessary to use an imputed interest rate, if the debt is either noninterest-bearing or bears a clearly nonmarket rate of interest.

Changes were made in 2003 to IAS 32 and IAS 39 which pertain to a number of matters addressed in this chapter, including the classification of instruments with contingent settlement provisions, and the method to be employed in allocating proceeds from the issuance of compound financial instruments. The "fair value option" permitted entities to designate any financial asset or financial liability, at acquisition or issuance, respectively, to be accounted for at fair value, with changes in fair value being included in current period earnings. The objective was to provide the entities making this election the opportunity to eliminate the otherwise tedious computations associated with hedge accounting (such as determining hedge effectiveness each period). However, this proved to be controversial and became an issue in the process of gaining EU endorsement of IFRS, necessary to facilitate the 2005 mandate to publicly held companies for reporting on the basis of IFRS.

Sources of IFRS

IAS 32, 39   *IFRIC* 1

DEFINITIONS OF TERMS

Amortization. The process of allocating an amount to expense over the periods benefited.

Bond. A written agreement whereby a borrower agrees to pay a sum of money at a designated future date plus periodic interest payments at the stated rate.

Bond issue costs. Costs related to issuing a bond (i.e., legal, accounting, underwriting fees, and printing and registration costs).

Bonds outstanding method. The method of accounting for serial bonds that assumes the discount or premium applicable to each bond of the issue is the same dollar amount per bond per year.

Book value approach. The method of recording the stock issued from a bond conversion at the carrying value of the bonds converted.

Callable bond. A bond in that the issuer reserves the right to call and retire the bond prior to its maturity.

Carrying value. The face amount of a debt issue increased or decreased by the applicable unamortized premium or discount plus unamortized issue costs.

Collateral. Asset(s) pledged to settle the obligation to repay a loan, if not repaid.

Contingent settlement provisions. A requirement in a financial instrument that could result in the payment of cash, depending upon the occurrence or nonoccurrence of an event, or on the outcome of uncertain circumstances that are beyond the control of the obligor.

Convertible debt. Debt that may be converted into common stock at the holder's option after specific criteria are met.

Covenant. A clause in a debt (or preferred stock) contract written for the protection of the lender (or preferred stock investor) that outlines the rights and actions of the parties involved when certain conditions occur (e.g., when the debtor's current ratio declines below a specified level).

Debenture. Long-term debt not secured by collateral.

Defeasance. Extinguishment of debt by creating a trust to service it.

Discount. Created when a debt instrument sells for less than face value and occurs because the stated rate on the instrument is less than the market rate at the date of issue.

Effective interest method. The method of amortizing the discount or premium to interest expense so as to result in a constant rate of interest when applied to the amount of debt, net of any unamortized premium or discount, outstanding at the beginning of any given period.

Effective rate. See market rate.

Face value. The stated or principal amount due on the maturity date.

Imputation. The process of interest rate approximation that is accomplished by examining the circumstances under which the note was issued.

Long-term debt. Probable future sacrifices of economic benefits arising from present obligations that are not currently payable within one year or one operating cycle of the business, whichever is longer.

Market rate. The current rate of interest available for obligations issued under the same terms and conditions.

Market value approach. The method of recording the stock issued from a bond conversion at the current market price of the bonds converted or the stock issued.

Maturity date. The date on which the face value (principal) of the bond or note becomes due.

Maturity value. See face value.

Premium. Created when a debt instrument sells for more than its face value and occurs because the stated rate on the instrument is greater than the market rate at the time of issue.

Principal. See face value.

Secured debt. Debt that has collateral to satisfy the obligation (i.e., a mortgage on specific property), if not otherwise repaid.

Serial bond. Debt whose face value matures in installments.

Stated rate. The interest rate written on the face of the debt instrument.

Straight-line method. The method of amortizing the premium or discount to interest expense such that there is an even allocation of interest expense over the life of the debt, causing the effective rate to vary from one period to the next.

Take-or-pay contract. A contract in which a purchaser of goods agrees to pay specified fixed or minimum amounts periodically in return for products, even if delivery is not taken. It results from a project financing arrangement where the project produces the products.

Throughput agreement. An agreement similar to a take-or-pay contract except that a service is provided by the project under the financing arrangement.

Troubled debt restructuring. Occurs when the creditor, for economic or legal reasons related to the debtor's financial difficulties, grants a concession to the debtor (deferment or reduction of interest or principal) that it would not otherwise consider.

Unconditional purchase obligation. An obligation to transfer a fixed or minimum amount of funds in the future or to transfer goods or services at fixed or minimum prices.

Yield. See market rate.

CONCEPTS, RULES, AND EXAMPLES

Notes and Bonds

Long-term debt generally takes one of two forms: notes or bonds. *Notes* generally represent debt issued to a single investor without intending for the debt to be broken up among many investors. Their maturity, usually lasting one to seven years, tends to be shorter than that of a bond. *Bonds* also result from a single agreement. However, a bond is intended to be broken up into various subunits, typically $1,000 (or equivalent) each, which can be issued to a variety of investors.

Notes and bonds share common characteristics: a written agreement stating the amount of the principal, the interest rate, when the interest and principal are to be paid, and the restrictive covenants, if any, that must be met. The interest rate is affected by many factors including the cost of money, the business risk factors, and the inflationary expectations associated with the business.

Nominal vs. effective rates. The stated rate on a note or bond often differs from the market rate at the time of issuance. When this occurs, the present value of the interest and principal payments will differ from the maturity, or face value. If the market rate exceeds the stated rate, the cash proceeds will be less than the face value of the debt because the present value of the total interest and principal payments discounted back to the present yields an amount that is less than the face value. Because an investor is rarely willing to pay more than the present value, the bonds must be issued at a discount. The discount is the difference between the issuance price (present value) and the face, or stated, value of the bonds. This discount is then amortized over the life of the bonds to increase the recognized interest expense so that the total amount of the expense represents the actual bond yield.

When the stated rate exceeds the market rate, the bond will sell for more than its face value (at a premium) to bring the effective rate to the market rate and will decrease the total interest expense. When the market and stated rates are equivalent at the time of issuance, no discount or premium exists and the instrument will sell at its face value. Changes in the market rate subsequent to issuance are irrelevant in determining the discount or premium or the amount of periodic amortization.

Notes are a common form of exchange in business transactions for cash, property, goods, and services. Most notes carry a stated rate of interest, but it is not uncommon for noninterest-bearing notes or notes bearing an unrealistic rate of interest to be exchanged. Notes such as these, which are long-term in nature, do not reflect the economic substance of the transaction since the face value of the note does not represent the present value of the consideration involved. Not recording the note at its present value will misstate the cost of the asset or services to the buyer, as well as the selling price and profit to the seller. In subsequent periods, both the interest expense and revenue will be misstated.

In general, the transaction price (cash, or the fair value of any noncash consideration) will define the fair value of a financial instrument, including liabilities, at initial recognition. For most liabilities, this will be equivalent to the present value of all associated contractual cash flows, discounted at the relevant interest rate. However, when part of the consideration is other than the instrument, fair value may be estimated using a valuation technique (e.g., option pricing models). When a long-term loan is received which bears no interest or a nonmarket rate of interest, the present value must be computed with reference to contractual cash flows and current market rates. Any extra amount given is reflected in current earnings unless some other asset has been obtained.

Accordingly, it is suggested that all commitments to pay (and receive) money at a determinable future date be subjected to present value calculations and, if necessary, interest imputation, with the exceptions of the following:

1. Normal accounts payable due within one year
2. Amounts to be applied to purchase price of goods or services or that provide security to an agreement (e.g., advances, progress payments, security deposits, and retainages)
3. Obligations payable at some indeterminable future date (warranties)
4. Lending and depositor savings activities of financial institutions whose primary business is lending money
5. Transactions where interest rates are affected by prescriptions of a governmental agency (e.g., revenue bonds, tax exempt obligations, etc.)

Notes issued solely for cash. When a note is issued solely for cash, its present value is assumed to be equal to the cash proceeds. The interest rate is that rate which equates the cash proceeds to the amounts to be paid in the future (i.e., *no* interest rate is to be imputed). For example, a €1,000 note due in three years that sells for €889 has an implicit rate of 4% (€1,000 × .889, where .889 is the present value factor of a lump sum at 4% for three years). This rate is to be used when amortizing the discount.

Notes issued for cash and a right or privilege. Often when a note bearing an unrealistic rate of interest is issued in exchange for cash, an additional right or privilege is granted, such as the issuer agreeing to sell merchandise to the purchaser at a reduced rate. The difference between the present value of the receivable and the cash loaned should logically be regarded as an addition to the cost of the products purchased for the purchaser/lender and as unearned revenue to the issuer. This treatment stems from the desire to match revenue and expense in the proper periods and to differentiate between those factors that affect income from operations and income or expense from nonoperating sources. In the situation above, the discount (difference between the cash loaned and the present value of the note) will be amortized to interest revenue or expense, while the unearned revenue or contractual right is amortized to sales and inventory, respectively. The discount affects income from nonoperational sources, while the unearned revenue or contractual right affects the gross profit computation. This differentiation is necessary because the amortization rates used differ for the two amounts.

Example of accounting for a note issued for both cash and a contractual right

1. Miller borrows €10,000 via a noninterest-bearing 3-year note from Krueger.
2. Miller agrees to sell €50,000 of merchandise to Krueger at less than the ordinary retail price for the duration of the note.
3. The fair rate of interest on a note such as this is 10%.

As set forth in the discussion above, the difference between the present value of the note and the face value of the loan is to be regarded as part of the cost of the products purchased under the agreement. The present value factor for an amount due in 3 years at 10% is .75132. Therefore, the present value of the note is €7,513 (=€10,000 × .75132). The €2,487 (= €10,000 – €7,513) difference between the face value and the present value is to be recorded as a discount on the note payable and as unearned revenue on the future purchases. The following entries would be made to record the transaction:

Miller				*Krueger*		
Cash	10,000			Note receivable	10,000	
Discount on note payable	2,487			Contract right with supplier	2,487	
Note payable		10,000		Cash		10,000
Unearned revenue		2,487		Discount on note receivable		2,487

The discount on note payable (and note receivable) should be amortized using the effective interest (constant yield) method, while the unearned revenue account and contract right with supplier account are amortized on a pro rata basis as the right to purchase merchandise is used up. Thus, if Krueger purchased €20,000 of merchandise from Miller in the first year, the following entries would be necessary:

Miller				*Krueger*		
Unearned revenue	995[*]			Inventory (or cost of sales)	995	
Sales		995		Contract right with supplier		995
Interest expense	751			Discount on note receivable	751	
Discount on note payable		751[**]		Interest revenue		751

[*] *€2,487 × (20,000/50,000)*
[**] *€7,513 × 10%*

The amortization of unearned revenue and contract right with supplier accounts will fluctuate with the amount of purchases made. If there is a balance remaining in the account at the end of the loan term, it is amortized to the appropriate account in that final year.

Noncash transactions. When a note is issued for consideration such as property, goods, or services, and the transaction is entered into at arm's length, the stated interest rate is presumed to be fair unless (1) no interest rate is stated, (2) the stated rate is unreasonable, or (3) the face value of the debt is materially different from the consideration involved or the current market value of the note at the date of the transaction. As discussed above, it is recommended that when the rate on the note is not considered fair, the note is to be recorded at the fair market value of the property, goods, or services received or at an amount that reasonably approximates the market value of the note, whichever is the more clearly determinable. When this amount differs from the face value of the note, the difference is to be recorded as a discount or premium and amortized to interest expense.

Example of accounting for a note exchanged for property

1. Alpha sells Beta a machine that has a fair market value of €7,510.
2. Alpha receives a 3-year noninterest-bearing note having a face value of €10,000.

In this situation, the fair market value of the consideration is readily determinable and thus represents the amount at which the note is to be recorded. The following entry is necessary:

Machine	7,510	
Discount on notes payable	2,490	
Notes payable		10,000

The discount will be amortized to interest expense over the 3-year period using the interest rate implied in the transaction.

If the fair market value of the consideration or note is not determinable, the present value of the note must be determined using an *imputed* interest rate. This rate will then be used to establish the present value of the note by discounting all future payments on the note at this rate. General guidelines for imputing the interest rate include the prevailing rates of similar instruments from creditors with similar credit ratings and the rate the debtor could obtain for similar financing from other sources. Other determining factors include any collateral or restrictive covenants involved, the current and expected prime rate, and other terms pertaining to the instrument. The objective is to approximate the rate of interest that would have resulted if an independent borrower and lender had negotiated a similar transaction under comparable terms and conditions. This determination is as of the issuance date, and any subsequent changes in interest rates would be irrelevant.

Bonds represent a promise to pay a sum of money at a designated maturity date plus periodic interest payments at a stated rate. Bonds are used primarily to borrow funds from the general public or institutional investors when a contract for a single amount (a note) is too large for one lender to supply. Dividing up the amount needed into €1,000 or €10,000 units makes it easier to sell the bonds.

In most situations, a bond is issued at a price other than its face value. The amount of the cash exchanged is equal to the total of the present value of the interest and principal payments. The difference between the cash proceeds and the face value is recorded as a premium if the cash proceeds are greater or a discount if they are less. The journal entry to record a bond issued at a premium follows:

Cash	(proceeds)
Premium on bonds payable	(difference)
Bonds payable	(face value)

The premium will be recognized over the life of the bond issue. If issued at a discount, "Discount on bonds payable" would be debited for the difference. As the premium is amortized, it will reduce interest expense on the books of the issuer (a discount will increase interest expense). The premium (discount) would be added to (deducted from) the related liability when a balance sheet is prepared.

The *effective interest method* is the prescribed method of accounting for a discount or premium arising from a note or bond, although some other method may be used (e.g., straight-line) if the results are not materially different. Under the effective interest method, the discount or premium is to be amortized over the life of the debt so as to produce a constant rate of interest when applied to the amount outstanding at the beginning of any given period. Therefore, interest expense is equal to the market rate of interest at the time of issuance multiplied by this beginning figure. The difference between the interest expense and the cash paid represents the amortization of the discount or premium. The effective rate is a required disclosure under IAS 32.

As with other aspects of financial reporting requirements, if alternative methods do not result in material disparities versus the prescribed approaches to measurement, they may also be used. Thus, where use of the straight-line amortization method does not result in a material distortion as compared to the effective interest method, it would also be acceptable, although not endorsed under IFRS. Interest expense under the *straight-line method* is equal to the cash interest paid plus the amortized portion of the discount or minus the amortized portion of the premium. The amortized portion is equal to the total amount of the discount or premium divided by the life of the debt from issuance in months multiplied by the number of months the debt has been outstanding that year.

Example of applying the effective interest method

1. A three-year, 12%, €10,000 bond is issued at 1/1/05, with interest payments semiannually.
2. The market rate is 10%.

The amortization table would appear as follows:

Date	Credit cash	Debit int. exp.	Debit prem.	Unam. prem. bal.	Carrying Value
1/1/05				€507.61	€10,507.61(a)
7/1/05	€ 600.00(b)	€ 525.38(c)	€ 74.62(d)	432.99(e)	10,432.99(f)
1/1/06	600.00	521.65	78.35	354.64	10,354.64
7/1/06	600.00	517.73	82.27	272.37	10,272.37
1/1/07	600.00	513.62	86.38	185.99	10,185.99
7/1/07	600.00	509.30	90.70	95.29	10,095.29
1/1/08	600.00	504.71(g)	95.29	--	€10,000.00
	€3,600.00	€3,092.39	€507.61		

(a)*PV of principal and interest payments*
€10,000(.74622)   =   € 7,462.20
€ 600(5.07569)   =   3,045.41
€10,507.61

(b) €10,000.00 × .06

(c)€10,507.61 × .05
(d €600.00 – €525.38
(e)€507.61 – €74.62
(f)€10,507.61 – €74.62
(or €10,000 + €432.99)
(g)*Rounding error = €.05*

When the interest date does not coincide with the year-end, an adjusting entry must be made. The proportional share of interest payable should be recognized along with the amortization of the discount or premium. Within the amortization period, the discount or premium can be amortized using the straight-line method, as a practical matter, or can be computed more precisely as described above.

If the bonds are issued between interest dates, discount or premium amortization must be computed for the period between the sale date and the next interest date. This is accomplished by "straight-lining" the period's amount calculated using the usual method of amortization. In addition, the purchaser prepays the seller the amount of interest that has accrued since the last interest date. This interest is recorded as a payable by the seller. At the next interest date, the buyer then receives the full amount of interest regardless of how long the bond has been held. This procedure results in interest being paid equivalent to the time the bond has been outstanding.

Various costs may be incurred in connection with issuing bonds. Examples include legal, accounting, and underwriting fees; commissions; and engraving, printing, and registration costs. These costs should be deducted from the initial carrying amount of the bonds and amortized using the effective interest method; generally the amount involved is insignificant enough that use of the simpler straight-line method would not result in a material difference. These costs do not provide any future economic benefit and therefore should not be considered an asset. Since these costs reduce the amount of cash proceeds, they in effect increase the effective interest rate and probably should be accounted for the same as an unamortized discount. Short-term debt obligations that are expected to be refinanced on a long-term basis, and that accordingly are classified as long-term debt according to IAS 1, are discussed in Chapter 12.

The diagram below illustrates the recommended accounting treatments for monetary assets (and liabilities).

ACCOUNTING FOR MONETARY ASSETS AND LIABILITIES

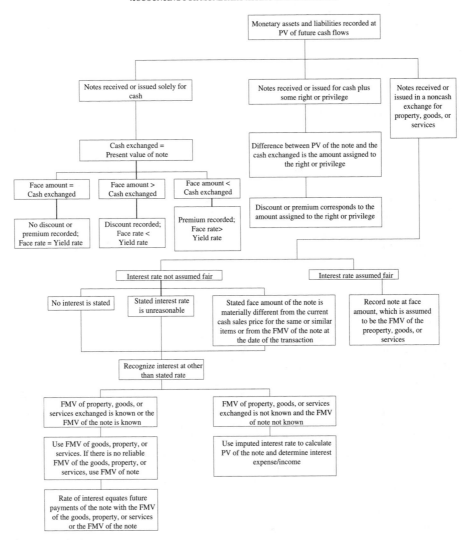

Extinguishment of Debt

According to IAS 39, removing a financial liability (or part of a financial liability) from the reporting entity's balance sheet is warranted only when the obligation is *extinguished*.

This will be deemed to have occurred when the obligation specified in the contract is discharged or canceled or expires.

In some instances, the debt issuer exchanges newly issued debt carrying different terms (as to maturities, interest rates, etc.) for outstanding debt. Under IAS 39, under such circumstances the original debt will be deemed extinguished, and a new liability will be deemed to have been incurred. Likewise, substantial modifications to the terms of existing financial liabilities, or to a part of that debt, whether this is attributable to financial exigencies or not, are now to be accounted for as extinguishments.

If there is a difference between the book value (i.e., carrying amount) of a financial liability extinguished or transferred (or relevant portion thereof) and the consideration paid to accomplish this, including the fair value of noncash assets transferred or liabilities assumed, this gain or loss will be recognized in current earnings.

When only a part of an existing liability is repurchased, the carrying value is allocated pro rata between the part extinguished and the part that remains outstanding. This allocation is to be based upon relative fair values. Gain on loss is recognized as the difference between the carrying value allocated to the portion extinguished and the consideration paid to accomplish this extinguishment, using the same approach as described above.

Substantial modification of the terms of existing debt. When an existing borrower and lender of debt exchange instruments with substantially different terms, this represents an extinguishment of the old debt and results in derecognition of that debt and recognition of a new debt instrument. IAS 39 defines "substantial modification of the terms" of an existing debt instrument and the standard requires that those modifications should be accounted for as extinguishments, provided that the discounted present value of cash flows under the terms of the new debt differs by at least 10% from the discounted present value of the remaining cash flows of the original debt instrument.

In computing the discounted present values for determining whether the 10% limit has been exceeded, the effective interest rate of the (old) debt being modified or exchanged is to be used. If the difference in present values is at least 10% the transaction is to be accounted for as an extinguishment of the old debt. In such case, the new, modified debt is initially recognized at fair value. On the other hand, a difference of less than 10%, is to be amortized over the remaining term of the debt instrument. In this instance, the debt is not to be remeasured at fair value and any costs or fees incurred adjust the carrying value of the debt and will be amortized by the effective interest method.

If an exchange of debt instruments, or if a modification of terms is accounted for under IAS 39 as an extinguishment, costs or fees incurred are to be recognized as part of the gain or loss incurred in the extinguishment. In nonextinguishement instances, any costs or fees incurred in the transaction are to be accounted for as adjustments to the carrying amount of the liability, to be amortized over the remaining term of the modified loan.

Under IAS 39, the reasons for the debt modification or exchange are irrelevant to the determination of the accounting to be applied. In this regard, IFRS contrasts with US GAAP, which historically had applied different accounting to those debt modifications which were identified as "troubled debt restructurings."

Example of accounting for debt exchange or restructuring with gain recognition

Assume that Debtor Corp. owes Friendly Bank €90,000 on a 5% interest-bearing non-amortizing note payable in five years, plus accrued and unpaid interest, due immediately, of €4,500. Friendly Bank agrees to a restructuring to assist Debtor Corp., which is suffering losses and is threatening to declare bankruptcy. The interest rate is reduced to 4%, the principal is reduced to €72,500, and the accrued interest is forgiven outright. Future payments will be on normal terms.

Whether there is recognition of a gain on the restructuring depends on the 10% threshold. The relevant discount rate to be used to compare the present values of the old and the new debt obligations is 5%. The present value of the old debt is simply the principal amount, €90,000, plus the interest due at present, €4,500, for a total of €94,500.

The present value of the replacement debt is the discounted present value of the reduced principal and the reduced future interest payments; the forgiven interest does not affect this. The new principal, €72,500, discounted at 5%, equals €56,806. The stream of future interest payments (€72,500 × .04 = €2,900 annually in arrears), discounted at 5%, equals €12,555. The total present value, therefore, is €69,361, which is about 27% below the present value of the old debt obligation. Thus, the 10% threshold is exceeded, and a gain will be recognized at the date of the restructuring.

However, given Debtor's current condition, the market rate of interest for its debt would actually be 12%, and since the new obligation must be recorded at fair value, this must be computed. The present value of the reduced principal, €72,500, discounted at 12%, has a present value of €41,138. The stream of future interest payments (€72,500 × .04 = €2,900 annually, in arrears), discounted at 12%, has a present value of €10,454. The total obligation thus has a fair value of €51,592.

The entry to record this event would be

Debt obligation (old) payable	90,000	
Interest payable	4,500	
Discount on debt obligation (new)	20,908	
Debt obligation (new) payable		72,500
Gain on debt restructuring		42,908

Note that the new debt obligation is recorded at a net of €51,592, not at the face value of €72,500. The difference, €20,908, is a discount to be amortized to interest expense over the next five years, in order to reflect the actual market rate of 12%, rather than the nominal 4% being charged. Amortization should be accomplished on the effective yield method.

Example of accounting for debt exchange or restructuring with gain deferral

Assume now that Hopeless Corp. owes Callous Bank €90,000 on a 5% interest-bearing non-amortizing note payable in five years, plus accrued and unpaid interest, due immediately, of €4,500. Callous Bank agrees to a restructuring to assist Hopeless Corp., which is also suffering losses and is threatening to declare bankruptcy. However, Callous is only willing to reduce the principal amount from €90,000 to €85,000, and reduce interest to 4.5% from 5%. It is not willing to forego the currently owed €4,500 interest payment, and furthermore requires that the loan maturity be shortened to three years, from five, in order to limit its risk. Hopeless agrees to the new terms.

In order to comply with IAS 39, the present value of the new debt must be compared to the present value of the old, existing obligation. As in the preceding example, the present value of the old debt is simply the principal amount, €90,000, plus the interest due at present, €4,500, for a total of €94,500.

The present value of the replacement debt is the discounted present value of the reduced principal and the reduced future interest payments, plus the interest using a 5% discount factor (= .86384 for the new three-year term), has a present value of €73,426. The stream of future interest payments (€85,000 × .045 = €3,825 annually in arrears), discounted at 5% (= 2.7231 annuity factor), has a present value of €10,416. The total present value, therefore, is (€73,426 + €10,416 + €4,500 =) €88,342, which is about 7% below the present value of the old debt obligation. Accordingly, since the 10% threshold is not exceeded, the difference of (€94,500 − €88,342 =) €6,158 is not recognized as a gain at the date of the restructuring, but rather is deferred and amortized over the new three-year term of the restructured loan.

The entry to record this event would be

Debt obligation (old) payable	90,000	
Discount on debt obligation (new)	1,158	
Debt obligation (new) payable		85,000
Deferred gain on debt restructuring		6,158

Note that the new debt obligation is recorded at a net of €83,842, not at the face value of €85,000. The difference of €1,158 represents a discount to be amortized to interest expense over the subsequent three years; this will result in an interest expense at the actual market rate of 5%, rather than at the nominal 4.5% rate. Amortization should be computed on the effective yield method, although if the discrepancy is not material the straight-line method may be employed. The deferred gain, €6,158, will be amortized over the three-year revised term. While the discount amortization will be added to interest expense. IAS 39 is silent as to how the amortization of the deferred gain should be handled. However, by reference to how a gain in excess of the 10% threshold (and thus been subject to immediate recognition) would have been reported, it is thought likely that this amortization should be included in "other income," and should not be offset against interest expense.

Presentation of the gain or loss from debt restructurings is not explicitly dealt with under IFRS. However, since IAS 8 has been revised, as part of the IASB's Improvements Project, to eliminate the income statement presentation of extraordinary items, there is no difficulty in making the appropriate decision. Gain or loss on debt extinguishments should, in the authors' opinion, be displayed as items of "other" income or expense in the income statement.

Defeasance of debt. Defeasance refers to the practice of effectively eliminating an obligation by pledging assets to the satisfaction thereof. For a period, it was in vogue to eliminate the balance sheet display of the liabilities "satisfied" and the assets pledged for that purpose, notwithstanding that the issuer remained legally obligated for the debt's satisfaction (For example, if the assets pledged prove to be insufficient to the task, the obligor must fulfill the obligation). This technique, *in-substance defeasance,* enjoyed some popularity which was largely due to the accounting treatment that had been permitted under earlier standards, particularly under US GAAP. By permitting the obligor to remove both the segregated assets and the debt from its balance sheet, a more positive financial leverage situation was implied, even though reported net worth would be unaffected.

This financial reporting practice was subsequently prohibited under US GAAP. More recently, in-substance defeasance was considered by IAS 39 and was rejected as an appropriate financial reporting option. According to this standard, payments to a third party (including a trust) do not relieve the debt or of its primary obligation to the creditor of record, in the absence of legal release. Accordingly, in-substance defeasance cannot be accounted for as elimination of debt and of the segregated assets.

Computing the gain or loss on debt extinguishments. The difference between the net carrying value and the acquisition price is to be recorded as a gain or loss. If the acquisition price is greater than the carrying value, a loss is incurred and must be accounted for. A gain is generated if the acquisition price is less than the carrying value. These gains or losses are to be recognized in the period in which the retirement takes place. These should be reported as "other" income or expense, because this is the same income statement category where interest expense is normally reported. It would not be appropriate, however, to include any gain or loss in the interest pool from which capitalized interest is computed under IAS 23 (discussed in Chapter 8).

The unamortized premium or discount and issue costs should be amortized to the acquisition date and recorded prior to determination of the gain or loss. If the extinguishment of debt does not occur on the interest date, the interest payable accruing between the last interest date and the acquisition date must also be recorded.

Example of accounting for the extinguishment of debt

1. A 10%, ten-year, €200,000 bond is dated and issued on 1/1/06 at €98, with the interest payable semiannually.
2. Associated bond issue costs of €14,000 are incurred.

3. Four years later, on 1/1/10, the entire bond issue is repurchased at €102 per €100 face value and is retired.
4. The straight-line method of amortization is used since the result is not materially different from that when the effective interest method is used.

The gain or loss on the repurchase is computed as follows:

Reacquisition price [(102/100) × €200,000]	€204,000	
Net carrying amount:		
Face value	€200,000	
Unamortized discount [2% × €200,000 × (6/10)]	(2,400)	
Unamortized issue costs [€14,000 × (6/10)]	(8,400)	189,200
Loss on bond repurchase		€ 14,800

Convertible Debt

Bonds are frequently issued with the right to convert them into common stock of the company at the holder's option when certain terms and conditions are met (i.e., a target market price is reached). Convertible debt is used for two reasons. First, when a specific amount of funds is needed, convertible debt often allows fewer shares to be issued (assuming that conversion ultimately occurs) than if the funds were raised by directly issuing the shares. Thus, less dilution is suffered by the other shareholders. Second, the conversion feature allows debt to be issued at a lower interest rate and with fewer restrictive covenants than if the debt were issued without it. That is because the bondholders are receiving the benefit of the conversion feature in lieu of higher current interest returns.

This dual nature of debt and equity, however, creates a question as to whether the equity element should receive separate recognition. Support for separate treatment is based on the assumption that this equity element has economic value. Since the convertible feature tends to lower the rate of interest, it can easily be argued that a portion of the proceeds should be allocated to this equity feature. On the other hand, a case can be made that the debt and equity elements are inseparable, and thus that the instrument is either all debt or all equity. IFRS had not previously addressed this matter directly, although the focus of the IASB *Framework* on "true and fair presentation" could be said to support the notion that the proceeds of a convertible debt offering be allocated between debt and equity accounts. The promulgation of IAS 32 resulted in the defining of convertible bonds (among other instruments) as being compound financial instruments, the component parts of which must be classified according to their separate characteristics.

Features of convertible debt. Revised IAS 32 addresses the accounting for compound financial instruments from the perspective of issuers. Convertible debt probably accounts for most of the compound instruments that will be of concern to those responsible for financial reporting. IAS 32 requires the issuer of such a financial instrument to present the liability component and the equity component separately on the balance sheet. Allocation of proceeds between liability and equity proceeds as follows:

1. Upon initial recognition, the fair value of the liability component of compound (convertible) debt instruments is computed as the present value of the contractual stream of future cash flows, discounted at the rate of interest applied at inception by the market to instruments of comparable credit status and providing substantially the same cash flows, on the same terms, but absent the conversion option. For example, if a 5% interest-bearing convertible bond would have commanded an 8% yield if issued without the conversion feature, the contractual cash flows are to be discounted at 8% in order to calculate the fair value of the unconditional debt component of the compound instrument.

2. The equity portion of the compound instrument is actually an embedded option to convert the liability into equity of the issuer. The fair value of the option is determined by time value and by the intrinsic value, if there is any. This option has value on initial recognition even when it is out of the money.

The issuance proceeds from convertible debt should be assigned to the components as described below.

Features of convertible debt typically include (1) a conversion price 15% to 20% greater than the market value of the stock when the debt is issued; (2) conversion features (price and number of shares) that protect against dilution from stock dividends, splits, and so on; and (3) a callable feature at the issuer's option that is usually exercised once the conversion price is reached (thus forcing conversion or redemption).

Convertible debt also has its disadvantages. If the stock price increases significantly after the debt is issued, the issuer would have been better off simply by issuing the stock. Additionally, if the price of the stock does not reach the conversion price, the debt will never be converted (a condition known as overhanging debt).

Accounting for Compound Instruments

For purposes of accounting decisions, the most important compound instruments are those which incorporate some elements of liability and other elements of equity instruments. Convertible bonds, and bonds with detachable stock purchase warrants, are the most common such instruments. In some cases, one or more of the component parts of the compound instrument may be financial derivatives, as a share purchase warrant would be. In other instances, each element might be a traditional, nonderivative instrument, as would be the case when a debenture is issued with common shares as a unit offering.

The accounting issue that is most obviously associated with compound instruments is how to allocate the proceeds among the constituent elements. When the compound instrument consists of parts which are both liabilities and equity items, proper classification of the elements is vital to accurate financial reporting, affecting potentially such matters as debt covenant compliance (if the debt to equity ratio, for example, is a covenant to be met by the debtor entity.)

Revised IAS 32, effective 2005, has made a significant change to the *issuer's* accounting for compound financial instruments. Previously, under original IAS 32, compound instruments were to be analyzed into their constituent elements and accounted for by either allocating the proceeds pro rata based on relative fair values, or allocating to the more readily measured element full fair value and assigning only the residual to the other components. Depending on the facts and circumstances, this could have resulted in allocating fair value to the equity component, and assigning only a residual amount to the liability portion.

Under revised IAS 32, however, it is required that whether or not fair values are available for all components of the compound instrument, full fair value be allocated to the liability components, with only the residual being assigned to equity. This position has been taken in order to be fully consistent with the definition of equity instruments. Equity evidences the residual interest in the assets of an entity after deducting all of its liabilities. To be consistent, liabilities must be stated at their full amounts, which in this instance is developed from the allocated proceeds upon issuance, at fair value, as subsequently adjusted for amortization of any associated discount or premium. To have assigned a lower amount to the debt would thus understate the interest of creditors in the entity's assets, and overstate the interest of the shareholders, in violation of IFRS.

It will no longer be acceptable to assign a residual to the liability components after first assigning a "fair value" measure to the equity. It will also be unacceptable to allocate total proceeds proportionately to both liability and equity elements.

If the compound instruments include a derivative element (e.g., a put option), the value of those features, to the extent they are embedded in the compound financial instrument other than the equity component, is to be included in the liability component.

The sum of the carrying amounts assigned to the liability and equity components on initial recognition is always equal to the fair value that would be ascribed to the instrument as a whole. In other words, there can be no "day one" gains from issuing financial instruments.

Residual allocation method. As noted, the only acceptable method of allocating proceeds from the issuance of convertible debt is to assign to the equity component (e.g., the conversion feature) the residual amount, after first assigning the full fair value of the debt, minus the conversion feature, to the liability component. To illustrate this approach, consider the following fact situation.

Example of the residual allocation method

Istanbul Corp. sells convertible bonds having aggregate par (face) value of €25 million to the public at a price of €98 on January 2, 2006. The bonds are due December 31, 2013, but can be called at €102 anytime after January 2, 2009. The bonds carry a coupon of 6% and are convertible into Istanbul Corp. common stock at an exchange ratio of twenty-five shares per bond (each bond having a face value of €1,000). Taking the discount on the offering price into account, the bonds were priced to yield about 6.3% to maturity.

The company's investment bankers have advised it that without the conversion feature, Istanbul's bonds would have had to carry an interest yield of 8% to have been sold in the current market environment. Thus, the market price of a pure bond with a 6% coupon at January 2, 2006, would have been about €883.48 (the present value of a stream of semiannual interest payments of €30 per bond, plus a terminal value of €1,000, discounted at a 4% semiannual rate).

This suggests that of the €980 being paid for each bond, €883.48 is being paid for the pure debt obligation, and another €96.52 is being offered for the conversion feature. Given this analysis, the entry to record the original issuance of the €25 million in debt securities on January 2, 2006, would be as follows:

Cash	24,500,000	
Discount on bonds payable	2,913,000	
Bonds payable		25,000,000
Paid-in capital—conversion feature		2,413,000

The discount should be amortized to interest expense, ideally by the effective yield method (constant return on increasing base) over the eight years to the maturity date. For purposes of this example, however, straight-line amortization (€2,913,000 ÷ 16 periods = €182,000 per semiannual period) will be used. Thus, the entry to record the June 30, 2005 interest payment would be as follows:

Interest expense	932,000	
Discount on bonds payable		182,000
Cash		750,000

The paid-in capital account arising from the foregoing transaction would form a permanent part of the capital of Istanbul Corp. If the bonds are later converted, this would be transferred to the common stock accounts, effectively forming part of the price paid for the shares ultimately issued. If the bondholders *decline* to convert and the bonds are eventually paid off at maturity, the paid-in capital from the conversion feature will form a type of "donated capital" to the entity, since the bondholders effectively will have forfeited this capital that they had contributed to the company.

If the bonds are not converted, the discount on the bonds payable will continue to be amortized until maturity. However, if they are converted, the remaining unamortized balance in this account, along with the face value of the bonds, will constitute the "price" being paid for the stock to be issued.

To illustrate this, assume the following:

On July 1, 2009, all the bonds are tendered for conversion to common stock of Istanbul Corp. The remaining book value of the bonds will be converted into common stock, which does not carry any par or stated value. The first step is to compute the book value of the debt.

Bonds payable		€25,000,000
Discount on bonds payable		
Original discount	€2,913,000	
Less amortization to date (4.4 yrs.)	(1,638,000)	1,275,000
Net book value of obligation		€23,725,000

The entry to record the conversion, given the foregoing information, is as follows:

Bonds payable	25,000,000	
Paid-in capital—conversion feature	2,413,000	
Discount on bonds payable		1,275,000
Common stock, no par value		26,138,000

Note that in the foregoing entry, the effective price recorded for the shares being issued is the book value of the remaining debt, adjusted by the price previously recorded to reflect the sale of the conversion feature. In the present instance, given the book value at the conversion date (a function of when the conversion privilege was exercised), and given the conversion ratio of twenty-five shares per bond, an effective price of €41.82 per share is being paid for the stock to be issued. This is determined without any reference to the market value at the date of the conversion. Presumably, the market price is higher, as it is unlikely that the bondholders would surrender an asset earning 6%, with a fixed maturity date, for another asset having a lower value and having an uncertain future worth (although if the dividend yield were somewhat higher than the equivalent bond interest, an unlikely event, this might happen).

Induced Conversion of Debt

A special situation may occur in that the conversion privileges of convertible debt are modified after issuance of the debt. These modifications may take the form of reduced conversion prices or additional consideration paid to the convertible debt holder. The debtor offers these modifications or "sweeteners" to induce prompt conversion of the outstanding debt. This is in addition to the normal strategy of calling the convertible debt to induce the holders to convert, assuming the underlying economic values make this attractive (debtors often do this when only a small fraction of the originally issued convertible debt remains outstanding). The issuance of these "sweeteners" should be accounted for as a reduction in the proceeds of the stock offering, thereby reducing paid-in capital from the transaction.

A previously acceptable alternative accounting treatment, recording the sweetener payments as an expense in the period of conversion, is no longer deemed appropriate given the proceeds allocation scheme mandated by revised IAS 32. That latter approach derived from a recognition that if it had been part of the original arrangement, a change in the exchange ratio or other adjustment would have affected the allocation of the original proceeds between debt and equity, and the discount or premium originally recognized would have been different in amount, and hence periodic amortization would have differed as well.

Debt Issued with Stock Warrants

Warrants are certificates enabling the holder to purchase a stated number of shares of stock at a certain price within a certain period. They are often issued with bonds to enhance the marketability of the bonds and to lower the bond's interest rate.

Detachable warrants are similar to other features, such as the conversion feature discussed earlier, which under IAS 32 make the debt a compound financial instrument and which necessitates that there be an allocation of the original proceeds among the constituent elements. Since warrants, which will often be traded in the market, are easier to value than are conversion features, prior to the most recent revision to IAS 32 it was logical to employ pro rata allocation based on relative market values. However, since revised IAS 32 requires allocation of only residual value to the equity element of compound instruments consisting of both liability and equity components, that approach is no longer acceptable.

Accounting for Collateral Given by Debtor to Creditor

In some instances, the borrower (debtor) will provide the lender (creditor) with valuable assets, most typically highly liquid assets such as marketable securities, to further secure the lending relationship and to provide the creditor with added protection. Under the provisions of IAS 39, the borrower is required to disclose the carrying amount of financial assets pledged as collateral for liabilities, as well as any significant terms and conditions relating to pledged assets. If the debtor delivers collateral to the creditor and the creditor is permitted to sell or repledge the collateral without constraints, then the debtor should disclose the collateral separately from other assets not used as collateral.

In other instances, the collateral is in the form of a security interest or mortgage deed. In those instances disclosure is still required, but the creditor is not able to take actions such as repledging or selling the collateral, as would be possible if actual assets such as negotiable instruments had been delivered.

Instruments Having Contingent Settlement Provisions

Some financial instruments are issued which have contingent settlement provisions—that is, which may or may not require the issuer/obligor to utilize its resources in subsequent settlement. For example, a note can be issued that will be payable either in cash or in the issuer's stock, depending on whether certain contingent events, such as the stock price exceeding a defined target over a defined number of days immediately preceding the maturity date of the note, are met or not. This situation differs from convertible debt, which is exchangeable into stock of the borrower, at the holder's option.

Revised IAS 32 incorporates the conclusion previously set forth in SIC 5, *Classification of Financial Instruments—Contingent Settlement Provisions*, that a financial instrument is a financial liability when the manner of settlement depends on the occurrence or nonoccurrence of uncertain future events or on the outcome of uncertain circumstances that are beyond the control of *both* the issuer and the holder. Contingent settlement provisions are ignored when they apply only in the event of liquidation of the issuer or are not genuine.

Examples of such contingent conditions would be changes in a stock market index, the consumer price index, a reference interest rate or taxation requirements, or the issuer's future revenues, net income or debt to equity ratio. The issuer cannot impact these factors and thus cannot unilaterally avoid settlement as a liability, delivering cash or other assets to resolve the obligation.

Under revised IAS 32, certain exceptions to the foregoing rule have been established. These exist when

1. The part of the contingent settlement provision that could require settlement in cash or another financial asset (or otherwise in such a way that it would be a financial liability) is not genuine; or

2. The issuer can be required to settle the obligation in cash or another financial asset (or otherwise to settle it in such a way that it would be a financial liability) only in the event of liquidation of the issuer.

By "not genuine," IAS 32 means that there is no reasonable expectation that settlement in cash or other asset will be triggered. Thus, a contract that requires settlement in cash or a variable number of the entity's own shares only on the occurrence of an event that is extremely rare, highly abnormal and very unlikely to occur is an equity instrument. Similarly, settlement in a fixed number of the entity's own shares may be contractually precluded in circumstances that are outside the control of the entity, but if these circumstances have no genuine possibility of occurring, classification as an equity instrument is appropriate.

If the settlement option is only triggered upon liquidation, this possibility is ignored in classifying the instrument, since the going concern assumption, underlying IFRS-basis financial reporting, presumes ongoing existence rather than liquidation.

In other instances the instrument includes a "put" option (i.e., an option that gives the holder the right, but not the obligation, to cause the issuer to redeem it at a fixed or determinable price). Notwithstanding certain prominent features suggesting an equity ownership, under the provisions of the revised IAS 32, any such instruments would have to be classified as liabilities. Again, this is because the issuer does not retain an unconditional right to avoid settlement using cash or other resources of the entity.

It also happens that entities will enter into contractual obligations of a fixed amount or of an amount that fluctuates in part or in full in response to changes in a variable other than the market price of the entity's own equity instruments, but which the entity must or can settle by delivery of its own equity instruments, the number of which depends on the amount of the obligation. Under revised IAS 32, such an obligation must be reported as a financial liability of the entity, unless the terms are such that this is deemed "not genuine." The reasoning is that if the number of an entity's own shares or other own equity instruments required to settle an obligation varies with changes in their fair value so that the total fair value of the entity's own equity instruments to be delivered always equals the amount of the contractual obligation, then the counterparty does not hold a true residual interest in the entity. Furthermore, settlement in shares could require the issuing entity to deliver more or fewer of its own equity instruments than would be the case at the date of entering into the contractual arrangement. This leads the IASB to conclude that such an obligation is a financial liability of the entity even though the entity must or can settle it by delivering its own equity instruments.

Changes in Noncurrent Estimated Liabilities

Increasingly, due to environmental and other concerns, entities are obligated to dismantle, remove and restore items of property, plant, and equipment during or at the end of the useful lives of the assets. The cost of such dismantlement or remediation is, per IAS 16, deemed to be a part of the cost of the assets and will be expensed via depreciation over the periods of use of these assets. IAS 37 contains requirements on how to measure decommissioning, restoration and similar liabilities, which will generally be presented in the balance sheet as noncurrent liabilities. IFRIC 1 provides guidance on how to account for the effect of changes in the measurement of existing decommissioning, restoration and similar liabilities.

Changes in these estimated liabilities may occur for two principal reasons. First, there likely may be one or more revisions to the estimated outflows of resources embodying economic benefits. Given the long-term nature of these obligations, and the constantly changing factors, such as technology, which will impact these costs, it would indeed be peculiar if such estimates did not change over time. For example, the estimated costs of decommissioning a nuclear-powered electric generating plant may vary significantly both in timing and amount as the plan is being used and as remediation technology advances. Timing is important because the *present value* of projected future cash outflows is used to measure this obligation; as the horizon lengthens or shortens, this will have a material effect on the amount of the liability to be reported.

Second, there may be revisions to the current market-based discount rate. As the discount rate rises, the present value of future cash outflows declines; as rates decline, present value of future costs increases.

IFRIC 1 applies to changes in the measurement of any existing decommissioning, restoration or similar liability that is *both* (1) recognized as part of the cost of an item of property, plant, and equipment in accordance with IAS 16; and (2) recognized as a liability in accordance with IAS 37. If the changes result from changes in the estimated timing or amount of the outflow of resources embodying economic benefits required to settle the obligation, or a change in the discount rate, this change is to be accounted for as explained in the following paragraphs.

Under provisions of IAS 16, plant assets can be carried either at depreciated cost or at revalued amounts. If the related asset is measured using the cost model, then changes in the liability are to be added to (if estimated cost increases), or deducted from (if estimated cost decreases), the cost of the related asset in the current period, subject to the reasonable condition, however, that the amount deducted from the cost of the asset cannot exceed the asset's carrying amount. In other words, the carrying value of the long-lived assets cannot "go negative." If the indicated decrease in the estimated liability in the current period, due to a reduction in the remediation or dismantlement obligation, were to exceed the carrying amount of the asset, the excess is to be recognized immediately in results of operations.

If the adjustment to the estimated liability results in an addition to the cost of an asset, it must be determined whether the new, higher carrying amount of the asset is deemed to be fully recoverable. If there is indication of a possible inability to recover this carrying value, then the reporting entity is required to test the asset for impairment by estimating its recoverable amount, and to account for the impairment loss, if any, in accordance with IAS 36. (See Chapter 8 for a full discussion.)

On the other hand, if the related asset is measured using the permitted revaluation model, then any changes in the liability will modify the revaluation surplus or deficit previously recognized in connection with that asset. Accordingly, a decrease in the liability will be credited directly to revaluation surplus in the equity section of the balance sheet, with the exception that it is to be recognized in current period results of operations to the extent that it reverses a revaluation deficit on the asset that was previously recognized in profit or loss. Similarly, an increase in the liability is to be recognized in results of operations, subject to the requirement that it be debited directly to revaluation surplus to the extent of any credit balance existing in the revaluation surplus arising from that asset.

In the event that a decrease in the liability (due to a reduction in estimated remediation or dismantlement costs, measured at present value) exceeds the carrying amount that would have been recognized had the asset been carried under the cost model, this excess must be recognized immediately in operating results.

The objectives of the revaluation model, where used, have to be borne in mind when estimated dismantlement or other costs are revised. A change in this liability is an indication that the asset may have to be revalued in order to ensure that the carrying amount does not differ materially from that which would be determined using fair value at the balance sheet date. Any such revaluation must be taken into account in determining the amounts to be taken to results of operations and to equity. If a revaluation is indeed necessary, IFRIC 1 stipulates that all the assets of that class are to be revalued.

IAS 1 requires disclosure on the face of the statement of changes in equity of each item of income or expense that is recognized directly in equity. In complying with this requirement, the change in the revaluation surplus arising from a change in the liability is to be separately identified and disclosed as to its source.

Under IFRS, the adjusted depreciable amount of the asset is depreciated over its respective useful life. Thus, once the related asset has reached the end of its useful economic life, all subsequent changes in the liability are to be recognized in results of current operations as they occur. This rule applies to both assets accounted for under the cost model and those reported in accordance with the revaluation model.

As time advances, of course, the present value of the obligation for dismantlement and similar costs, holding other factors constant, will increase. This periodic "unwinding of the discount" is to be recognized in current results of operations according to its character, which is a finance cost. The permitted capitalization of interest cost under IAS 23 is not relevant to this situation (it is intended to address construction period finance costs which are deemed part of the original cost of plant assets, only).

Examples of Financial Statement Disclosures

Adidas-Salomon AG, Germany
Year ended December 31, 2003

15. Borrowings and credit lines

In response to the decline in net borrowings by €352 million to €594 million in 2004 from €946 million in 2003, the Group has terminated its €300 million Belgian Commercial Paper Program and its multinational ABS Program. Additionally, the €750 million German Commercial Paper Program was not utilized in 2004.

With settlement on October 8, 2003, Adidas-Salomon issued a €400 million convertible bond through its wholly owned Dutch subsidiary, Adidas-Salomon International Finance B.V., guaranteed by Adidas-Salomon AG. The bond was issued in tranches of €50,000 each with a maturity up to fifteen years. The bond is, at the option of the respective holder, subject to certain conditions, convertible from and including November 18, 2003, up to and including September 20, 2018, into ordinary no-par-value bearer shares of Adidas-Salomon AG at the conversion price of €102.00 which was fixed upon issue. The coupon of the bond is 2.5% and is payable annually in arrears on October 8 of each year, commencing on October 8, 2004. The bond is convertible into approximately four million no-par-value shares.

The convertible bond is not callable by the issuer until October 2009 and callable thereafter, subject to a 130% trigger between October 2009 and October 2012 and subject to a 115% trigger between October 2012 and 2015, unconditionally thereafter. Investors have the right to put the bond in October 2009, October 2012, and October 2015.

The fair values of the liability component and the equity conversion component were determined on the issuance of the bond. The fair value of the liability component, included in long-term borrowings, was calculated using a market interest rate of approximately 5.3% for an equivalent straight bond. The residual amount of €116.6 million (less transaction costs of €2.3 million related thereto), representing the value of the equity conversion component, is included in shareholders' equity in capital reserve.

In subsequent periods, the liability component continues to be presented on the amortized cost basis, until conversion or maturity of the bond. The equity conversion component is determined on the issuance of the bond and will not change in subsequent periods.

In December 2004, Adidas-Salomon AG as guarantor of the bonds irrevocably waived its right towards all current and future bondholders to elect the cash payment (in lieu of the delivery of all or part of the shares) upon exercise of the conversion right through a bondholder pursuant to §9(1) and (2) of the Terms and Conditions of the Bonds.

The Adidas-Salomon stock traded above 110% (€12.20) of the conversion price of €102 on more than 20 trading days within the last 30 trading days in the fourth quarter of 2004. Consequently, bondholders have the right to convert their convertible bonds into equity, beginning January 1, 2005.

Gross borrowing declined in 2004 by €176 million (2003; €349 million).

Borrowings are denominated in a variety of currencies in which the Group conducts its business. The largest portions of effective gross borrowings (before liquidity swaps for cash management purposes) as at December 31, 2004, are denominated in euros (59%; 2003: 64%) and US dollars (31%; 2003: 26%).

Month-end weighted-average interest rates on borrowings in all currencies ranged from 3.0% to 3.8% and from 2.5% to 3.2% for the years ended December 31, 2004 and 2003, respectively.

As at December 31, 2004, the Group had cash credit lines and other longer-term financing arrangements totaling €3 billion (2003: €3.4 billion); thereof unused credit lines accounting for €2.0 billion (2003: €2.4 billion). In addition, the Group had separate lines for the issuance of letters of credit in an amount of approximately €0.3 billion (2003: €0.4 billion). The continuing decline reflects a shift in payment practices with product suppliers in the Far East, from letters of credit to settlements in open account.

The Group's outstanding financings are unsecured.

The private placement and convertible bond documentations each contain a negative-pledge clause and a minimum equity covenant. As at December 31, 2004, actual shareholders' equity was well above the amount of the minimum equity covenant.

Borrowings as at December 31, 2004

€ in millions

	Up to 1 year	Between 1 and 3 years	Between 3 and 5 years	After 5 years	Total
Bank borrowings	168	4	0	0	172
Commercial paper	0	0	0	0	0
Asset-backed securities	0	0	0	0	0
Private placements	18	141	239	194	592
Convertible bond	--	--	285	--	285
Total	184	145	524	194	1,049

Borrowings as at December 31, 2003

€ in millions

	Up to 1 year	Between 1 and 3 years	Between 3 and 5 years	After 5 years	Total
Bank borrowings	0	0	124	0	124
Commercial paper	0	0	29	0	29
Asset-backed securities	0	0	109	0	109
Private placements	0	0	450	234	684
Convertible bond	--	--	--	279	279
Total	0	0	712	513	1,225

In comparison to former years, when all borrowings with short-term maturities, which were back by long-term arrangements, were reported as long-term borrowings, the Group now reports short-term borrowings.

The borrowings relating to the outstanding convertible bond changed in value and classification, reflecting the accruing interest on the debt component in accordance with IFRS requirements and the first possibility to redeem the bond in 2009.

Information regarding the Group's protection against interest rate risks is also included in these notes (see note 23).

Novartis AG, Switzerland
For the Year ended December 31, 2004

18. Long-term financial debts

	2004	2003
	($ millions)	
Straight bonds	3,185	2,972
Liabilities to banks and other financial institutions [1]	114	142
Finance lease obligations	117	122
Total (including current portion of long-term debt)	3,416	3,236
Less current portion of long-term debt	(680)	(45)
Total long-term debts	2,736	3,191

	2004	2003
Straight bonds		
US dollar 6.625% Euro Medium Term Note 1995/2005 of Novartis Corporation, Florham Park, New Jersey, USA	300	300
US dollar 6.625% Euro Medium Term Note 1995/2005 of Novartis Corporation, Florham Park, New Jersey, USA	250	250
US dollar 9.0% bonds 2006 of Gerber Products Company, Fremont, Michigan, USA	35	35
EUR 900 million 4.0% bond 2001/2006 of Novartis Securities Investment Ltd., Hamilton, Bermuda [2]	1,228	1,127
EUR 1 billion 3.75% bond 2002/2007 of Novartis Securities Investment Ltd., Hamilton, Bermuda	1,372	1,260
Total straight bonds	3,185	2,972

[1] *Average interest rate 3.4% (2003: 3.4%)*
[2] *Swapped into Swiss francs in 2002.*

	2004	2003
	($ millions)	
Breakdown by maturity:		
2004		45
2005	680	677
2006	1,288	1,178
2007	1,388	1,274
2008	20	23
2009	16	39
Thereafter	24	--
Total	3,236	2,840

	2004	2003
	($ millions)	
Breakdown by currency:		
USD	707	719
EUR	1,474	1,382
CHF	1,228	1,127
Others	7	8
Total	3,416	3,236

Fair value comparison

	2004		2003	
	Balance sheet	Fair values	Balance sheet	Fair values
	($ millions)			
Straight bonds	3,185	3,272	2,972	3,057
Others	231	231	264	264
Total	3,416	3,503	3,236	3,321

Collateralized long-term debts and pledged assets

	2004	2003
	($ millions)	
Total amount of collateralized long-term financial debts	20	50
Total net book value of property, plant, and equipment pledged as collateral for long-term financial debts	88	101

The percentage of fixed-rate debt to total financial debt was 47% and 51% at December 31, 2004 and 2003, respectively.

The financial debts, including short-term financial debts, contain only general default covenants. The Group is in compliance with these covenants.

Barloworld Limited
For the Year ended September 30, 2004

Note 14. Noncurrent liabilities

	Group		Company	
Rm	2004	2003	2004	2003
Total SA rand and foreign currency borrowings (note 32.3)	6,190	4,154	1,550	
Less: Current portion redeemable and repayable within one year (note 15)	(1,319)	(750)		
Interest bearing	4,871	3,404	1,550	
Liability portion of convertible bond [1]				
Convertible bond		216		
Equity portion		(36)		
Less: Current portion transferred to short-term loans (note 15)		(180)		
Noninterest-bearing liabilities	1,215	845	46	
Postretirement benefit provisions	151	130		
Other provisions	352	124	46	
Noncurrent provisions (note 17)	503	254	46	
Bills and leases discounted with recourse and repurchase obligations	413	444		
Fair value of derivatives	34			
Retirement benefit obligation (note 30)	69	13		
Other creditors	196	134		
Deferred tax liabilities (note 13)	803	621		
Total noncurrent liabilities	6,889	4,870	1,596	

[1] *US $75 million was raised in 1994 through Barloworld International Investments Plc by way of a 10-year convertible bond issue guaranteed by Barloworld Limited. The bonds carried a coupon rate of 7% and were convertible into Barloworld Limited ordinary shares at a conversion price per share of R35.20 at a fixed exchange rate of R4.055 per US dollar. The bonds were convertible at the option of the holder between May 1995 and September 2004. The company, under certain circumstances, had a call option to convert the bonds into ordinary shares at any time from September 20, 1999, to maturity date. During the current year bonds to the value of $10.4 million (2003: nil) were repurchased with the remainder converted through the issue of 1, 431, 918 Barloworld shares.*

| | Liabilities secured | | Net book value of assets encumbered | |
	2004	2003	2004	2003
Included above are secured liabilities as follows:				
Secured liabilities				
Secured loans				
South African rands	48		59	
Foreign currencies	1,684	924	1,867	909
Liabilities under capitalized finance leases (note 28)				
South African rands	530	452	491	661
Foreign currencies	935	898	818	789
Total secured liabilities	3,197	2,274	3,235	2,359
Assets encumbered are made up as follows:				
Property, plant, and equipment (note 4)			1,062	1,203
Finance lease receivables (note 8)			1,926	909
Investments (note 5)			247	247
			3,235	2,359

14 LEASES

PERSPECTIVE AND ISSUES

Leasing has long been a popular financing option for the acquisition of business property. During the past few decades, however, the business of leasing has experienced staggering growth. The tremendous popularity of leasing is quite understandable, as it offers great flexibility, often coupled with a range of economic advantages over ownership. Thus, with leasing, a lessee (borrower) is typically able to obtain 100% financing, whereas under a traditional credit purchase arrangement the buyer would generally have to make an initial equity investment. In many jurisdictions, a leasing arrangement offers tax benefits compared to the purchase option. The lessee is protected to an extent from the risk of obsolescence, although the lease terms will vary based on the risk of obsolescence. For the lessor, there will be a regular stream of lease payments, which include interest that often will be at rates above commercial lending rates, and, at the end of the lease term, usually some residual value.

The accounting for lease transactions involves a number of complexities, which derive partly from the range of alternative structures that are available to the parties. For example, in many cases leases can be configured to allow manipulation of the tax benefits, with other features such as lease term and implied interest rate adjusted to achieve the intended overall economics of the arrangement. Leases can be used to transfer ownership of the leased asset, and they can be used to transfer some or all of the risks of ownership. In any event, the financial reporting objective is to have the economic substance of the transaction dictate the accounting treatment.

The accounting for lease transactions is one of the best examples of the application of the principle of substance over form, as set forth in the IASB's *Framework*. If the transaction effectively transfers ownership to the lessee, the substance of the transaction is that of a sale, and this should be recognized as such even though the transaction takes the contractual form of a lease.

Modest changes were made to IAS 17 as part of the Improvements Project undertaken by IASB beginning in 2002. These latest changes serve to clarify the classification of leases jointly including land and buildings, and also to reduce available alternatives for accounting for initial direct costs in the financial statements of lessors. An earlier revision eliminated alternatives formerly available for the recognition of finance income by lessors, which may now only be based on net book investment (i.e., carrying value). IFRIC Interpretation 4 addresses how to determine whether specific arrangements contain a lease agreement.

The guidance on lease accounting under IFRS is not as fully elaborated as is that provided under certain national GAAP. The IASB has indicated that it intends to thoroughly review the existing rules with the possible result that IAS 17 will either be revised or superseded by a new standard, possibly with the result that all leases be accounted for as property rights and liabilities by lessees, thus improving comparability across entities. It is not a current IASB agenda topic, however.

While almost any type of arrangement that satisfies the definition of a lease is covered by this standard, the following specialized types of lease agreements are excluded:

1. Lease agreements to explore for or use natural resources, such as oil, gas, timber, metals, and other mineral rights
2. Licensing agreements for such items as motion picture films, video recordings, plays, manuscripts, patents, and copyrights

The accounting for rights to explore and develop natural resources has yet to be formally addressed by IAS; IFRS 6, which deals with exploration and evaluation assets arising in the mineral exploration process, offers no accounting guidance for leases. Licensing agreements are addressed by IAS 38, which is discussed in Chapter 9.

Sources of IFRS		
IAS 17, 24, 36, 38	*SIC* 15, 27	*IFRIC* 4

DEFINITIONS OF TERMS

Bargain purchase option (BPO). A provision in the lease agreement allowing the lessee the option of purchasing the leased property for an amount that is sufficiently lower than the fair value of the property at the date the option becomes exercisable. Exercise of the option must appear reasonably assured at the inception of the lease.

Contingent rentals. Those lease rentals that are not fixed in amount but are based on a factor other than simply the passage of time; for example, based on percentage of sales, price indices, market rates of interest, or use of the leased asset.

Economic life of leased property. IAS 17 (revised) defines economic life of a leased asset as either the period over which the asset is expected to be economically usable by one or more users or the number of production or similar units expected to be obtained from the leased asset by one or more users. (This was the definition of useful life under the original IAS 17.)

Executory costs. Those costs such as insurance, maintenance, and taxes incurred for leased property, whether paid by the lessor or lessee. If paid by the lessee, the lessee's obligation to pay such costs are excluded from the minimum lease payments.

Fair value of leased property (FMV). The amount for which an asset could be exchanged between a knowledgeable, willing buyer and a knowledgeable, willing seller in an arm's-length transaction. When the lessor is a manufacturer or dealer, the fair value of the property at the inception of the lease will ordinarily be its normal selling price net of volume or trade discounts. When the lessor is not a manufacturer or dealer, the fair value of the property at the inception of the lease will ordinarily be its cost to the lessor unless a significant amount of time has lapsed between the acquisition of the property by the lessor and the inception of the lease, in which case fair value should be determined in light of market conditions prevailing at the inception of the lease. Thus, fair value may be greater or less than the cost or carrying amount of the property.

Finance lease. A lease that transfers substantially all the risks and rewards associated with the ownership of an asset. The risks related to ownership of an asset include the possibilities of losses from idle capacity or technological obsolescence and of variations in return due to changing economic conditions; rewards incidental to ownership of an asset include expectation of profitable operations over the asset's economic life and expectation of gain from appreciation in value or the ultimate realization of the residual value. Title may or may not eventually be transferred to the lessee.

Gross investment in the lease. The sum total of (1) the minimum lease payments under a finance lease (from the standpoint of the lessor), plus (2) any unguaranteed residual value accruing to the lessor.

Inception of the lease. The date of the written lease agreement or, if earlier, the date of a commitment by the parties to the principal provisions of the lease.

Initial direct costs. Initial direct costs, such as commissions and legal fees, incurred by lessors in negotiating and arranging a lease. These generally include (1) costs to originate a lease incurred in transactions with independent third parties that (a) result directly from and are essential to acquire that lease and (b) would not have been incurred had that leasing transaction not occurred; and (2) certain costs directly related to specified activities performed by the lessor for that lease, such as evaluating the prospective lessee's financial condition; evaluating and recording guarantees, collateral, and other security arrangements; negotiating lease terms; preparing and processing lease documents; and closing the transaction.

Lease. An agreement whereby a lessor conveys to the lessee, in return for payment or series of payments, the right to use an asset (property, plant, equipment, or land) for an agreed-upon period of time. Other arrangements essentially similar to leases, such as hire-purchase contracts, bare-boat charters, and so on, are considered leases for purposes of the standard.

Lease term. The initial noncancelable period for which the lessee has contracted to lease the asset together with any further periods for which the lessee has the option to extend the lease of the asset, with or without further payment, which option it is reasonably certain (at the inception of the lease) that the lessee will exercise.

Lessee's incremental borrowing rate. The interest rate that the lessee would have to pay on a similar lease, or, if that is not determinable, the rate that at the inception of the lease the lessee would have incurred to borrow over a similar term (i.e., a loan term equal to the lease term), and with a similar security, the funds necessary to purchase the leased asset.

Minimum lease payments (MLP).

1. *From the standpoint of the lessee.* The payments over the lease term that the lessee is or can be required to make in connection with the leased property. The lessee's obligation to pay executory costs (e.g., insurance, maintenance, or taxes) and contingent rents are excluded from minimum lease payments. If the lease contains a bargain purchase option, the minimum rental payments over the lease term plus the payment called for in the bargain purchase option are included in minimum lease payments.

   If no such provision regarding a bargain purchase option is included in the lease contract, the minimum lease payments include the following:

   a. The minimum rental payments called for by the lease over the lease contract over the term of the lease (excluding any executory costs), plus
   b. Any guarantee of residual value, at the expiration of the lease term, to be paid by the lessee or a party related to the lessee.

2. *From the standpoint of the lessor.* The payments described above plus any guarantee of the residual value of the leased asset by a third party unrelated to either the lessee or lessor (provided that the third party is financially capable of discharging the guaranteed obligation).

Net investment in the lease. The difference between the lessor's gross investment in the lease and the unearned finance income.

Noncancelable lease. A lease that is cancelable only

1. On occurrence of some remote contingency
2. With the concurrence (permission) of the lessor
3. If the lessee enters into a new lease for the same or an equivalent asset with the same lessor
4. On payment by the lessee of an additional amount such that at inception, continuation of the lease appears reasonably assured

Nonrecourse (debt) financing. Lending or borrowing activities in which the creditor does not have general recourse to the debtor but rather has recourse only to the property used for collateral in the transaction or other specific property.

Operating lease. A lease that does not meet the criteria prescribed for a finance lease.

Penalty. Any requirement that is imposed or can be imposed on the lessee by the lease agreement or by factors outside the lease agreement to pay cash, incur or assume a liability, perform services, surrender or transfer an asset or rights to an asset, or otherwise forego an economic benefit or suffer an economic detriment.

Rate implicit in the lease. The discount rate that at the inception of the lease, when applied to the minimum lease payments, and the unguaranteed residual value accruing to the benefit of the lessor, causes the aggregate present value to be equal to the fair value of the leased property to the lessor, net of any grants and tax credits receivable by the lessor.

Related parties in leasing transactions. Entities that are in a relationship where one party has the ability to control the other party or exercise significant influence over the operating and financial policies of the related party. Examples include the following:

1. A parent company and its subsidiaries
2. An owner company and its joint ventures and partnerships
3. An investor and its investees

Significant influence may be exercised in several ways, usually by representation on the board of directors but also by participation in the policy-making process, material intercompany transactions, interchange of managerial personnel, or dependence on technical information. The ability to exercise significant influence must be present before the parties can be considered related.

Renewal or extension of a lease. The continuation of a lease agreement beyond the original lease term, including a new lease where the lessee continues to use the same property.

Residual value of leased property. The fair value, estimated at the inception of the lease, that the enterprise expects to obtain from the leased property at the end of the lease term.

Sale and leaseback accounting. A method of accounting for a sale-leaseback transaction in which the seller-lessee records the sale, removes all property and related liabilities from its balance sheet, recognizes gain or loss from the sale, and classifies the leaseback in accordance with this section.

Unearned finance income. The excess of the lessor's gross investment in the lease over its present value.

Unguaranteed residual value. Part of the residual value of the leased asset (estimated at the inception of the lease) the realization of which by the lessor is not assured or is guaranteed by a party related to the lessor.

Useful life. The estimated remaining period over which the economic benefits embodied by the asset are expected to be consumed, without being limited to the lease term. (The former definition of this term, as employed in the original standard IAS 17, has now been assigned to the term **economic life**.)

CONCEPTS, RULES, AND EXAMPLES

Classification of Leases—Lessee

For accounting and reporting purposes the lessee has two alternatives in classifying a lease.

1. Operating
2. Finance

Finance leases (known as *capital* leases under the corresponding US GAAP, because such leased property is treated as owned, and accordingly, capitalized on the balance sheet) are those that essentially are alternative means of financing the acquisition of property or of substantially all the service potential represented by the property. Due to the relative paucity of guidance on lease accounting under IFRS there will be many issues on which informal direction will be taken from US GAAP. Accordingly, the terms *finance* and *capital* will be treated as synonymous in this chapter.

The proper classification of a lease is determined by the circumstances surrounding the leasing transaction. According to IAS 17, whether a lease is a finance lease or not will have to be judged based on the *substance* of the transaction, rather than on its mere *form*. If substantially all of the benefits and risks of ownership have been transferred to the lessee, the lease should be classified as a finance lease; such a lease is normally noncancelable and the lessor is assured (subject to normal credit risk) of recovery of the capital invested plus a reasonable return on its investment. IAS 17 stipulates that substantially all of the risks or benefits of ownership are deemed to have been transferred if *any one* of the following four criteria has been met:

1. The lease transfers ownership to the lessee by the end of the lease term.

2. The lease contains a bargain purchase option (an option to purchase the leased asset at a price that is expected to be substantially lower than the fair value at the date the option becomes exercisable) and it is reasonably certain that the option will be exercisable.

3. The lease term is for the major part of the economic life of the leased asset; title may or may not eventually pass to the lessee.

4. The present value (PV), at the inception of the lease, of the minimum lease payments is at least equal to substantially all of the fair value of the leased asset, net of grants and tax credits to the lessor at that time; title may or may not eventually pass to the lessee.

5. The leased assets are of a specialized nature such that only the lessee can use them without major modifications being made.

Further indicators which suggest that a lease might be properly considered to be a finance lease are

6. If the lessee can cancel the lease, the lessor's losses associated with the cancellation will be borne by the lessee.

7. Gains or losses resulting from the fluctuations in the fair value of the residual accrue to the lessee.

8. The lessee has the ability to continue the lease for a supplemental term at a rent that is substantially lower than market rent (a bargain renewal option).

Thus, under IAS 17, an evaluation of all eight of the foregoing criteria would be required to properly assess whether there is sufficient evidence to conclude that a given arrangement should be accounted for as a finance lease. Of the eight criteria set forth in the standard, the first five are essentially determinative in nature; that is, meeting any one of these would normally result in concluding that a given arrangement is in fact a finance lease. The final three criteria, however, are more suggestive in nature, and the standard states that these "could" lead to classification as a finance lease.

The interest rate used to compute the present value should be the lessee's *incremental borrowing rate* unless it is practicable to determine the rate *implicit* in the lease, in which case the implicit rate should be used. It is interesting to note that under US GAAP, in order to use the rate implicit in the lease to discount the minimum lease payments, this rate must be lower than the lessee's incremental borrowing rate. Logically, of course, if the lessee's incremental borrowing rate were lower than a rate offered implicitly in a lease, and the prospective lessee was aware of this fact, it would be more attractive to borrow and purchase, so the limitation under the US rule may be somewhat superfluous. IAS 17 does not set this as a condition, however.

In general, if a lease agreement meets one of the eight criteria set forth above, it is likely to be classified as a finance lease in the financial statements of the lessee. Prior to the most recent revisions to IAS 17, leases involving both land and buildings could only be considered finance leases if title were expected to transfer at the end of the lease term. However, the *Improvements Project* resulted in an amendment that revised IAS 17 regarding this issue. Separate analyses of the land and building components of the lease are now required, and capital treatment of the building lease component is not dependent on, or require, the land portion of the lease being capitalized. If title to the land is not expected to transfer to the lessee (i.e., there is no automatic title transfer at lease termination, and also no bargain purchase option), that component will be treated as an operating lease, which does not limit the accounting for the building component to also being operating. (This conforms to the corresponding rule under US GAAP.)

The language used in the third and fourth criteria, as set forth above, makes them rather subjective and somewhat difficult to apply in practice. Thus, given the same set of facts, it is possible for two enterprises to reach different conclusions regarding the classification of a given lease. The IAS 17 approach differs from that adopted by the corresponding US standard, FAS 13, in that more subjective criteria are established under IFRS.

The purpose of the third criterion is to define leases covering essentially all of the asset's useful life as being financing arrangements. Under the US standard, a threshold of 75% of the useful life has been specified for classifying a lease as a finance lease, which thus creates a "bright line" test that can be applied mechanically. The corresponding language under IAS 17 stipulates that capitalization results when the lease covers a "major part of the economic life" of the asset. Reasonable persons obviously can debate whether "major part" implies a proportion lower than 75% (say, as little as 51%), or implies a higher proportion (such as 90%).

The purpose of the fourth criterion is to define what are essentially arrangements to fully compensate the lessor for the entire value of the leased property as financing arrangements. Thus, a threshold of "the present value of minimum lease payments equaling at least 90% of leased asset fair value" is set under the US standard, while the corresponding language, "substantially all of the fair value of the leased asset," is employed under IFRS. Again, there is room for debate over whether "substantially all" implies a threshold lower than 90% or (less likely) even higher.

IAS 17 addresses the issue of change in lease classification resulting from alterations in lease terms, stating that if the parties agree to alter the terms of the lease, other than by renewing the lease, in a manner that would have resulted in a different classification of the lease, had the changed terms been in effect at inception of the lease, then the revised lease agreement is to be considered a new lease agreement.

Leases Involving Land and Buildings

IAS 17, as most recently revised in 2003, addresses leases involving both land and buildings; in general, the accounting treatment of such leases is the same as for simple leases of other assets. As revised, the standard requires that leases for land and buildings be analyzed into their component parts, with each element separately accounted for, unless title to both elements is expected to pass to the lessee by the end of the lease term. It continues the operating lease treatment requirement for the land portion of the lease, unless title is expected to pass to the lessee by the end of the lease term, in which case finance lease treatment is warranted. The buildings element is to be classified as a finance or operating lease in accordance with IAS 17's provisions.

Under revised IAS 17, the minimum lease payments at the inception of a lease of land and buildings (including any up-front payments) are to be allocated between the land and the buildings elements in proportion to their relative fair values at the inception of the lease. In those circumstances where the lease payments cannot be allocated reliably between these two elements, the entire lease is to be classified as a finance lease, unless it is clear that both elements are operating leases.

Furthermore, the amendment to IAS 17 has specified that for a lease of land an buildings in which the value of the land element at the inception of the lease is immaterial, the land and buildings may be treated as a single unit for the purpose of lease classification, in which case the criteria set forth in IAS 17 will govern the classification as a finance or operating lease. If this is done, the economic life of the buildings is regarded as the economic life of the entire leased asset.

Additional guidance, drawn from US GAAP, and an example of accounting for a combined land and building lease, are presented in Appendix A.

Classification of Leases—Lessor

The lessor has the following alternatives in classifying a lease:

1. Operating lease
2. Finance lease

    a. Plain or regular finance lease, hereinafter referred to as direct financing lease, which is the term used by US GAAP

    b. Finance lease by manufacturers or dealers, hereinafter referred to as sales-type lease, the term used by US GAAP

    c. Leveraged lease, wherein financing is through a third-party creditor instead of the lessor

Consistent accounting by lessee and lessor. Since the events or transactions that take place between the lessor and the lessee are based on an agreement (the lease) that is common to both the parties, it is normally appropriate that the lease be classified in a consistent manner by both parties. Thus, if any one of the eight criteria specified above for classification of a finance lease by the lessee is met, the lease should also be classified as a finance lease by the lessor. If the lease qualifies as a finance lease from the standpoint of the lessor, it would be classified either as a sales-type lease, a direct financing lease, or a leveraged lease, depending on the conditions present at the inception of the lease. Of course, neither party to the lease can control whether the other applies proper accounting to the transaction.

Notwithstanding this general observation, IAS 17 alludes to an exception to this general rule when it speaks about the "differing circumstances" sometimes leading to the same lease being classified differently by the lessor and lessee, as when the lessor benefits by having a third-party residual value guarantee in place. The standard does not elaborate, unfortunately, but once again it is possible to be informed by reference to US GAAP, which clearly sets forth the circumstances or factors which, if not satisfied from the standpoint of the lessor, would lead to different classifications by the lessor and the lessee. FAS 13 stipulates that the following two conditions both need to be satisfied in addition to meeting any one of the criteria established for capitalization determination by the lessee, before a lease could be classified as a finance (capital) lease from the standpoint of a lessor:

1. Collectibility of the minimum lease payments is reasonably predictable.
2. No important uncertainties surround the amount of nonreimbursable costs yet to be incurred by the lessor under the lease.

Under US GAAP, therefore, if a lease transaction does not meet the criteria for classification as a sales-type lease, a direct financing lease, or a leveraged lease as specified above (by satisfying both of the above noted extra criteria), it is to be classified in the financial statements of the lessor as an operating lease. If the lessee has accounted for the lease as a capital lease, the asset being leased may appear on the balance sheets of both lessee and lessor. This is an anomaly, but not a serious problem, since rarely will those using or relying on the financial statements of one party (lessor or lessee) also be relying on the financial statements of the other party.

Although guidance under IAS 17 does not establish additional conditions that must be fulfilled for the lessor to treat a lease as a financing transaction, as the US standard does, use of the "differing circumstances" language opens up the possibility that in any given situation, additional subjective considerations could be defined. This remains a matter for each enterprise to address on an individual basis, however.

Distinction among Sales-Type, Direct Financing, and Leveraged Leases

A lease is classified as a sales-type lease when the criteria set forth above have been met and the lease transaction is structured such that the lessor (generally a manufacturer or dealer) recognizes a profit or loss on the transaction in addition to interest revenue. For this to occur, the fair value of the property, or if lower, the sum of the present values of the minimum lease payments and the estimated unguaranteed residual value, must differ from the cost (or carrying value, if different). The essential substance of this transaction is that of a sale, thus its name. Common examples of sales-type leases: (1) when an automobile dealership opts to lease a car to its customers in lieu of making an actual sale, and (2) the re-lease of equipment coming off an expiring lease.

A direct financing lease differs from a sales-type lease in that the lessor does not realize a profit or loss on the transaction other than the interest revenue to be earned over the lease term. In a direct financing lease, the fair value of the property at the inception of the lease is equal to the cost (or carrying value, if the property is not new). This type of lease transaction most often involves entities regularly engaged in financing operations. The lessor (usually a bank or other financial institution) purchases the asset and then leases the asset to the lessee. This transaction merely replaces the conventional lending transaction where the borrower uses the borrowed funds to purchase the asset.

There are many economic reasons why a lease transaction may be considered. These include

1. The lessee (borrower) is generally able to obtain 100% financing.
2. There may be tax benefits for the lessee (such as the ability to expense the asset over its lease term, instead of a longer depreciable life).
3. The lessor receives the equivalent of interest as well as an asset with some remaining value at the end of the lease term (unless title transfers as a condition of the lease).
4. The lessee is protected from risk of obsolescence (although presumably this risk protection is priced into the lease terms).

In summary, it may help to visualize the following chart when considering the classification of a lease:

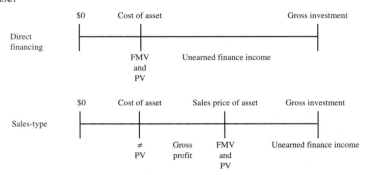

One specialized form of a direct financing lease is a *leveraged lease*. This type is mentioned separately both here and in the following section on how to account for leases because it is to receive a different accounting treatment by a lessor. A leveraged lease meets all the definitional criteria of a direct financing lease, but differs because it involves at least three parties: a lessee, a long-term creditor, and a lessor (commonly referred to as the equity participant). Other characteristics of a leveraged lease are as follows:

1. The financing provided by the long-term creditor must be without recourse as to the general credit of the lessor, although the creditor may hold recourse with respect to the leased property. The amount of the financing must provide the lessor with substantial leverage in the transaction.
2. The lessor's net investment declines during the early years and rises during the later years of the lease term before its elimination.

Accounting for Leases—Lessee

As discussed in the preceding section, there are two classifications under IAS 17 that apply to a lease transaction in the financial statements of the lessee. They are as follows:

1. Operating
2. Finance

Operating leases. The accounting treatment accorded an operating lease is relatively simple; rental expense should be charged to income as the payments are made or become payable. IAS 17 stipulates that rental expense be "recognized on a systematic basis that is representative of the time pattern of the user's benefits, even if the payments are not on that basis." In many cases, the lease payments are being made on a straight-line basis (i.e., equal payments per period over the lease term), and recognition of rental expense would normally also be on a straight-line basis.

However, even if the lease agreement calls for an alternative payment schedule or a scheduled rent increase over the lease term, the lease expense should still be recognized on a straight-line basis unless another systematic and rational basis is a better representation of actual physical use of the leased property. In such instances it will be necessary to create either a prepaid asset or a liability, depending on the structure of the payment schedule. In SIC 15, it has been held that all incentives relating to a new or renewed operating lease are to be considered in determining the total cost of the lease, to be recognized on a straight-line basis over the term of the lease. Thus, for example, a rent holiday for six months, offered as part of a five-year lease commitment, would not result in the reporting of only six months' rent expense during the first full year. Rather, four and one-half years' rent would be allocated over the full five-year term, such that monthly expense would equal 90% (=54 months' payments/60-month term) of the stated monthly rental payments that begin after the holiday ends. This accounting method would apply to both lessor and lessee.

The accounting would differ if rental increases were directly tied to expanded space utilization, however, but not if related merely to the extent that the property were being used. For example, if the lease agreement provides for a scheduled increase(s) in contemplation of the lessee's increased (i.e., more intensive) physical use of the leased property (e.g., more sustained usage of machinery after an initial set-up period), the total amount of rental payments, including the scheduled increase(s), should be charged to expense over the lease term on a straight-line basis; the increased rent should not impact the accounting. On the other hand, if the scheduled increase(s) is due to additional leased property (e.g., expanding to adjacent space after two years), recognition should be proportional to the amount of leased property, with the increased rents recognized over the years that the lessee has control over the use of the additional leased property. (These suggestions, and many other recommendations made in this chapter, are based on guidance from US GAAP, since the IAS does not address these detailed implementation matters at the present time.) Scheduled increases could envision more than one of these events occurring, making the accounting more complex.

Notice that in the case of an operating lease there is no balance sheet recognition of the leased asset because the substance of the lease is merely that of a rental. There is no reason to expect that the lessee will derive any future economic benefit from the leased asset beyond the lease term. There may, however, be a deferred charge or credit on the balance sheet if the payment schedule under terms of the lease does not correspond with the expense recognition, as suggested in the preceding paragraph.

Finance leases. Assuming that the lease agreement satisfies one of the eight criteria set forth above (while recognizing that the last three of the eight are not absolutely determinative, but are instead merely suggestive or persuasive), it must be accounted for as a finance lease.

According to IAS 17, the lessee is to record a finance lease as an asset and an obligation (liability) at an amount equal to the lesser of (1) the fair value of the leased property at the inception of the lease, net of grants and tax credits receivable by the lessors, or (2) the present value of the minimum lease payments.

For purposes of this computation, the minimum lease payments are considered to be the payments that the lessee is obligated to make or can be required to make, excluding contingent rent and executory costs such as insurance, maintenance, and taxes. The minimum lease payments generally include the minimum rental payments, and any guarantee of the residual value made by the lessee or a party related to the lessee. If the lease includes a bargain purchase option (BPO), the amount required to be paid under the BPO is included in the minimum lease payments. The present value shall be computed using the incremental borrowing rate of the lessee unless it is practicable for the lessee to determine the implicit rate computed by the lessor, in which case it is to be employed, whether higher or lower than the incremental borrowing rate.

(Under US GAAP, an important exception is made when the FMV of the leased asset is lower than the PV of the minimum lease payments, which exception has not yet been considered under IAS 17. In such a case an implicit rate is computed through a series of trial-and-error calculations. This rule is entirely logical, since it is well established in GAAP that assets are not to be recorded at amounts greater than fair value or net realizable value at acquisition. This exception has been illustrated in a numerical case study that follows in Appendix A.)

The lease term to be used in the present value computation is the fixed, noncancelable term of the lease, plus any further terms for which the lessee has the option to continue to lease the asset, with or without further payment, provided that it is reasonably certain, as of the beginning of the lease, that lessee will exercise such a renewal option.

Depreciation of leased assets. The depreciation of the leased asset will depend on which criterion resulted in the lease being qualified as a finance lease. If the lease transaction met the criteria as either transferring ownership or containing a bargain purchase option, the asset arising from the transaction is to be depreciated over the estimated useful life of the leased property, which will, after all, be used by the lessee (most likely) after the lease term expires. If the transaction qualifies as a finance lease because it met either the criterion of encompassing the major part of the asset's economic life, or because the present value of the minimum lease payments represented substantially all of the fair value of the underlying asset, then it must be depreciated over the shorter of the lease term or the useful life of the leased property. The conceptual rationale for this differentiated treatment arises because of the substance of the transaction. Under the first two criteria, the asset actually becomes the property of the lessee at the end of the lease term (or on exercise of the BPO). In the latter situations, title to the property remains with the lessor.

Thus, the leased asset is to be depreciated (amortized) over the shorter of the lease term or its useful life if title does not transfer to the lessee, but when it is reasonably certain that the lessee will obtain ownership by the end of the lease term, the leased asset is to be depreciated over the asset's useful life. The manner in which depreciation is computed should be consistent with the lessee's normal depreciation policy for other depreciable assets owned by the lessee, recognizing depreciation on the basis set out in IAS 16. Therefore, the accounting treatment and method used to depreciate (amortize) the leased asset is very similar to that used for an owned asset. The leased asset should not be depreciated (amortized) below the estimated residual value.

In some instances when the property is to revert back to the lessor, there may be a guaranteed residual value. This is the value at lease termination that the lessee guarantees to the lessor. If the fair value of the asset at the end of the lease term is greater than or equal to the guaranteed residual amount, the lessee incurs no additional obligation. On the other hand, if the fair value of the leased asset is less than the guaranteed residual value, the lessee must make up the difference, usually with a cash payment. The guaranteed residual value is often used as a device to reduce the periodic payments by substituting the lump-sum amount at the end of the term that results from the guarantee. In any event the depreciation (amortization) must still be based on the estimated residual value. This results in a rational and systematic allocation of the expense through the periods and avoids having to recognize a disproportionately large expense (or loss) in the last period as a result of the guarantee.

The annual (periodic) rent payments made during the lease term are to be apportioned between the reduction in the obligation and the finance charge (interest expense) in a manner such that the finance charge (interest expense) represents a constant periodic rate of interest on the remaining balance of the lease obligation. This is commonly referred to as the *effective rate* interest method. However, it is to be noted that IAS 17 also recognizes that an approximation of this pattern can be made, as an alternative. The effective rate method, which is used in many other applications, such as mortgage amortization, is almost universally understood, and therefore should be applied in virtually all cases.

At the inception of the lease the asset and the liability relating to the future rental obligation are reported in the balance sheet of the lessee at the same amounts. However, since the depreciation charge for use of the leased asset and the finance expense during the lease term differ due to different policies being used to recognize them, as explained above, it is likely that the asset and related liability balances would not be equal in amount after inception of the lease.

The following examples illustrate the treatment described in the foregoing paragraphs:

Example of accounting for a finance lease—asset returned to lessor at termination

Assume the following:

1. The lease is initiated on 1/1/06 for equipment with an expected useful life of three years. The equipment reverts back to the lessor on expiration of the lease agreement.
2. The FMV of the equipment is €135,000.
3. Three payments are due to the lessor in the amount of €50,000 per year beginning 12/31/06. An additional sum of €1,000 is to be paid annually by the lessee for insurance.
4. Lessee guarantees a €10,000 residual value on 12/31/08 to the lessor.
5. Irrespective of the €10,000 residual value guarantee, the leased asset is expected to have only a €1,000 salvage value on 12/31/08.
6. The lessee's incremental borrowing rate is 10% (lessor's implicit rate is unknown).
7. The present value of the lease obligation is as follows:

PV of guaranteed residual value	=	€10,000 × 0.7513*	= € 7,513
PV of annual payments	=	€50,000 × 2.4869**	= 124,345
			€131,858

* *The present value of an amount of €1 due in three periods at 10% is 0.7513.*
** *The present value of an ordinary annuity of €1 for three periods at 10% is 2.4869.*

The first step in accounting for any lease transaction is to classify the lease. In this case, the lease term is for three years, which is equal to 100% of the expected useful life of the asset. Notice that the test of fair value versus present value is also fulfilled, as the PV of the minimum lease payments (€131,858) could easily be considered as being equal to substantially all the FMV (€135,000), being equal to 97.7% of the FMV. Thus, this lease should be accounted for as a finance lease.

In assumption 7 above the present value of the lease obligation is computed. Note that the executory costs (insurance) are not included in the minimum lease payments and that the incremental borrowing rate of the lessee was used to determine the present value. This rate was used because the implicit rate was not determinable.

NOTE: *To have used the implicit rate it would have to have been known to the lessee.*

The entry necessary to record the lease on 1/1/06 is

| Leased equipment | 131,858 | |
| Lease obligation | | 131,858 |

Note that the lease is recorded at the present value of the minimum lease payments, which in this case is less than the fair value. If the present value of the minimum lease payments had exceeded the fair value, the lease would be recorded at fair value, as defined under IAS 36, dealing with impairment of long-lived assets.

The next step is to determine the proper allocation between interest and a reduction in the lease obligation for each lease payment. This is done using the effective interest method as illustrated below.

Year	*Cash payment*	*Interest expense*	*Reduction in lease obligation*	*Balance of lease obligation*
Inception of lease				€131,858
1	€50,000	€13,186	€36,814	95,044
2	50,000	9,504	40,496	54,548
3	50,000	5,452	44,548	10,000

The interest is calculated at 10% (the incremental borrowing rate) of the balance of the lease obligation for each period, and the remainder of the €50,000 payment is allocated to a reduction in the lease obligation. The lessee is also required to pay €1,000 for insurance on an annual basis. The entries necessary to record all payments relative to the lease for each of the three years are shown below.

	12/31/06		*12/31/07*		*12/31/08*	
Insurance expense	1,000		1,000		1,000	
Interest expense	13,186		9,504		5,452	
Lease obligation	36,814		40,496		44,548	
Cash		51,000		51,000		51,000

The leased equipment recorded as an asset must also be amortized (depreciated). The balance of this account is €131,858; however, as with any other asset, it cannot be depreciated below the estimated residual value of €1,000 (note that it is depreciated down to the actual estimated residual value, *not* the guaranteed residual value). In this case, the straight-line depreciation method is applied over a period of three years. This three-year period represents the lease term, *not* the life of the asset, because the asset reverts back to the lessor at the end of the lease term. Therefore, the following entry will be made at the end of each year:

| Depreciation expense | 43,619 | |
| Accumulated depreciation | | 43,619 [(€131,858 − €1,000) ÷ 3] |

Finally, on 12/31/08 we must recognize the fact that ownership of the property has reverted back to the owner (lessor). The lessee made a guarantee that the residual value would be €10,000 on 12/31/08; as a result, the lessee must make up the difference between the guaranteed residual value and the actual residual value with a cash payment to the lessor. The following entry illustrates the removal of the leased asset and obligation from the books of the lessee:

Lease obligation	10,000	
Accumulated depreciation	130,858	
Cash		9,000
Leased equipment		131,858

The foregoing example illustrated a situation where the asset was to be returned to the lessor. Another situation exists (where there is a bargain purchase option or automatic transfer of title) where the asset is expected to remain with the lessee. Recall that, under IAS 17, leased assets are amortized over their useful life when title transfers or a bargain purchase option exists. In such a circumstance, the lease liability will not be amortized completely as of the termination date, in many cases. At the end of the lease, the balance of the lease obligation should equal the guaranteed residual value, the bargain purchase option price, or a termination penalty.

Example of accounting for a finance lease—asset ownership transferred to lessee *and* fair market value of leased asset lower than present value of minimum lease payments

Assume the following:

1. A three-year lease is initiated on 1/1/06 for equipment with an expected useful life of five years.
2. Three annual lease payments of €52,000 are required beginning on 1/1/06 (note that the payment at the beginning of the year changes the PV computation). The lessor pays €2,000 per year for insurance on the equipment.
3. The lessee can exercise a bargain purchase option on 12/31/08 for €10,000. The expected residual value at 12/31/09 is €1,000.
4. The lessee's incremental borrowing rate is 10% (lessor's implicit rate is unknown).
5. The fair market value of the property leased is €140,000.

Once again, the classification of the lease must take place prior to the accounting for it. This lease is classified as a finance lease because it contains a bargain purchase option (BPO). Note that in this case, the PV versus FMV test is also clearly fulfilled.

The PV of the lease obligation is computed as follows:

PV of bargain purchase option	=	€10,000	×	0.7513*	=	€	7,513
PV of annual payments	=	(€52,000 − €2,000)	×	2.7355**	=		136,755
							€144,288

   * *The present value of an amount of €1 due in three periods at 10% is 0.7513.*
  ** *The present value of an annuity due of €1 for three periods at 10% is 2.7355.*

Notice that in the example above, the present value of the lease obligation is greater than the fair value of the asset. Also notice that since the lessor pays €2,000 a year for insurance, this payment is treated as executory costs and hence excluded from calculation of the present value of annual payments. In conclusion, since the PV is greater than the fair value, the lease obligation (as well as the leased asset) must be recorded at the fair value of the asset leased (being the lower of the two). The entry on 1/1/05 is as follows:

Leased equipment	140,000	
Obligation under finance lease		140,000

According to IAS 17, the apportionment between interest and principal is to be such that interest recognized reflects the use of a constant periodic rate of interest applied to the remaining balance of the obligation. As noted above, a special rule applies under US GAAP (which are illustrated here) when the present value of the minimum lease payments exceeds the fair value of the leased asset (i.e., when the asset is impaired) at lease inception. When the PV exceeds the fair value of the leased asset, a new, effective rate must be computed through a series of trial-and-error calculations. (Note, however, that an impairment after the inception date would be recognized as expense in the period of the impairment, following the procedures set forth in IAS 36, and this would not affect the recorded amount of the lease obligation (i.e., the liability) and thus would not alter the initially determined interest rate. In this example, the interest rate was determined to be 13.265%. The amortization of the lease takes place as follows:

Year	Cash payment	Interest expense	Reduction in lease obligation	Balance of lease obligation
Inception of lease				€140,000
1/1/06	€50,000	€ --	€50,000	90,000
1/1/07	50,000	11,939	38,061	51,939
1/1/08	50,000	6,890	43,110	8,829
12/31/09	10,000	1,171	8,829	--

The following entries are required in years 2005 through 2007 to recognize the payment and depreciation (amortization).

		2006		2007		2008	
1/1	Operating expense	2,000		2,000		2,000	
	Obligation under finance lease	50,000		38,061		43,110	
	Accrued interest payable			11,939		6,890	
	Cash		52,000		52,000		52,000
12/31	Interest expense	11,939		6,890		1,171	
	Accrued interest payable		11,939		6,890		
	Obligation under finance lease						1,171
12/31	Depreciation expense	27,800		27,800		27,800	
	Accumulated depreciation (€139,000, five years)		27,800		27,800		27,800
12/31	Obligation under finance lease					10,000	
	Cash						10,000

Impairment of leased asset. IAS 17 did not originally address the issue of how impairments of leased assets are to be assessed or, if determined to have occurred, how they would need to be accounted for. Subsequently, IAS 17 was revised to note that the provisions of IAS 36 should be applied to leased assets in the same manner as they would be applied to owned assets. Impairments to the leased asset (occurring after the inception of the lease) are recognized by charges to expense in the current reporting period. IAS 36 is discussed more fully in Chapter 8.

Accounting for Leases—Lessor

As illustrated above, there are four classifications of leases with which a lessor must be concerned.

1. Operating
2. Sales-type
3. Direct financing
4. Leveraged

Operating leases. As is the case for the lessee, the operating lease requires a less complex accounting treatment than does a finance lease. The payments received by the lessor are to be recorded as rent income in the period in which the payment is received or becomes receivable. As with the lessee, if the rentals vary from a straight-line basis, or if the lease agreement contains a scheduled rent increase over the lease term, the revenue is nonehteless to be recognized on a straight-line basis unless an alternative basis of systematic and rational allocation is more representative of the time pattern of earning process contained in the lease.

Additionally, if the lease agreement provides for a scheduled increase(s) in contemplation of the lessee's increased (i.e., more intensive) physical use of the leased property, the total amount of rental payments, including the scheduled increase(s), is allocated to revenue over the lease term on a straight-line basis. However, if the scheduled increase(s) is due to additional leased property (e.g., larger space, more machines), recognition should be proportional to the leased property, with the increased rents recognized over the years that the lessee has control over use of the additional leased property.

The lessor must report the leased property on the balance sheet under the caption "Investment in leased property." This account should be displayed with or near the property, plant, and equipment owned by the lessor, and depreciation should be determined in the same manner as for the rest of the lessor's owned property, plant, and equipment. IAS 17 stipulates that "when a significant portion of the lessor's business comprises operating leases, the lessor should disclose the amount of assets by each major class of asset together with the related accumulated depreciation at each balance sheet date." Further, "assets held for operating are usually included as property, plant, and equipment in the balance sheet."

Previously, lessors under operating leases were given the choice of either amortizing initial direct costs over the term of the lease or expensing such costs immediately. Under amended IAS 17, however, this choice was eliminated, and now all initial direct costs incurred must be added to the carrying amount of the leased asset and recognized as an expense over the lease term on the same basis as the lease income. Initial direct costs are incurred by lessors in negotiating and arranging an operating lease, and may include commissions, legal fees, and those internal costs that are actually incremental (i.e., would not exist if the lease were not being negotiated) and directly attributable to negotiating and arranging the lease.

Although there is no guidance on this matter under IFRS, logically any incentives granted by the lessor to the lessee are to be treated as reductions of rent and recognized on a straight-line basis over the term of the lease. This is also the position taken under US GAAP.

Depreciation of leased assets should be on a basis consistent with the lessor's normal depreciation policy for similar assets, and the depreciation expense should be computed on the basis set out in IAS 16.

Finance leases. The accounting by the lessor for finance leases depends on which variant of finance lease is at issue. In sales-type leases, an initial profit, analogous to that earned by a manufacturer or dealer, is recognized, whereas a direct financing lease does not give rise to an initial recognition of profit.

Sales-type leases. In the accounting for a sales-type lease, it is necessary for the lessor to determine the following amounts:

1. Gross investment
2. Fair value of the leased asset
3. Cost

From these amounts, the remainder of the computations necessary to record and account for the lease transaction can be made. The first objective is to determine the numbers necessary to complete the following entry:

Lease receivable	xx	
Cost of goods sold	xx	
Sales		xx
Inventory		xx
Unearned finance income		xx

The gross investment (lease receivable) of the lessor is equal to the sum of the minimum lease payments (excluding contingent rent and executory costs) from the standpoint of the lessor, plus the nonguaranteed residual value accruing to the lessor. The difference between the gross investment and the present value of the two components of gross investment (i.e., minimum lease payments and nonguaranteed residual value) is recorded as "unearned finance income" (also referred to as "unearned interest revenue"). The present value is to be computed using the lease term and implicit interest rate (both of which were discussed earlier).

IAS 17 stipulates that the resulting unearned finance income is to be amortized and recognized into income using the effective rate (or yield) interest method, which will result in a constant periodic rate of return on the "lessor's net investment" (which is computed as the "lessor's gross investment" less the "unearned finance income"). A choice of amortization approaches was offered under the original standard, but the selection of options has since been eliminated, so that the constant effective rate on book (carrying) value is now the only acceptable method of income recognition.

Consideration of "prudence" is called for by IAS 17 in recognizing finance income, which is in any event an underlying, qualitative characteristic or attribute of financial statements prepared under the IAS. The IASB's *Framework* makes it incumbent on financial statement preparers to exercise prudence. In other words, it requires caution in the exercise of judgment. IAS 17 clarifies this in the context of spreading income on a systematic basis, by giving the example of recognition of uncertainties relative to collectibility of lease rentals or to fluctuation of interest rates in the future. For instance, the uncertainties surrounding collectibility of lease rentals usually increase with the lease term (i.e., the longer the lease term, the greater are the risks involved), and thus in keeping with the principle of prudence, modification of the pattern of income recognition may be required to compensate.

For example, a lessor may decide to delay the recognition of finance income into the later years in the case of leases with terms spread over twenty years and above, as opposed to short-term leases with terms of three to five years, since predicting with certainty long-term collectibility, which depends on a number of factors such as the future financial position of the lessee, is a very difficult task. Effectively, more of the earlier collections might be seen as returns on investment, rather than income, until longer-term viability has been demonstrated.

Recall that the fair value of the leased property is by definition equal to the normal selling price of the asset adjusted by any residual amount retained (including any unguaranteed residual value, investment credit, etc.). According to IAS 17, the selling price to be used for a sales-type lease is equal to the fair value of the leased asset, or if lower, the sum of the present values of the MLP and the estimated unguaranteed residual value accruing to the lessor, discounted at a commercial rate of interest. In other words, the normal selling price less the present value of the unguaranteed residual value is equal to the present value of the MLP. (Note that this relationship is sometimes used while computing the MLP when the normal selling price and the residual value are known; this is illustrated in a case study that follows.)

Under IAS 17, initial direct costs incurred in connection with a sales-type lease (i.e., where the lessor is a manufacturer or dealer) must be expensed as incurred. This is a reasonable requirement, since these costs offset some of the profit recognized at inception, as do other selling expenses. Thus, the costs recognized at the inception of such lease arrangements would include the carrying value of the equipment or other items being leased, as well as incidental costs of negotiating and executing the lease. The profit recognized at inception would be the gross profit on the sale of the leased asset, less all operating costs, including the initial direct costs of creating the lease arrangement.

The estimated unguaranteed residual values used in computing the lessor's gross investment in a lease should be reviewed regularly. In case of a permanent reduction (impairment) in the estimated unguaranteed residual value, the income allocation over the lease term is revised and any reduction with respect to amounts already accrued is recognized immediately.

To attract customers, manufacturer or dealer lessors sometimes quote artificially low rates of interest. This has a direct impact on the recognition of initial profit, which is an integral part of the transaction and is inversely proportional to the finance income to be generated by it. Thus, if finance income is artificially low, this results in recognition of excessive profit from the transaction at the time of the sale. Under such circumstances, the standard requires that the profit recognized at inception, analogous to a cash sale of the leased asset, be restricted to that which would have resulted had a commercial rate of interest been used in the deal. Thus, the substance, not the form, of the transaction should be reflected in the financial statements. (The present value of the scheduled lease payments, discounted at the appropriate commercial rate, must be computed to derive the effective selling price of the leased asset under these circumstances. See Appendix D to Chapter 1 for a discussion of present value calculations.)

The difference between the selling price and the amount computed as the cost of goods sold is the gross profit recognized by the lessor on the inception of the lease (sale). Manufacturer or dealer lessors often give an option to their customers of either leasing the asset (with financing provided by them) or buying the asset outright. Thus, a finance lease by a manufacturer or dealer lessor, also referred to as a sales-type lease, generates two types of revenue for the lessor.

1. The gross profit (or loss) on the sale, which is equivalent to the profit (or loss) that would have resulted from an outright sale at normal selling prices, adjusted if necessary for a noncommercial rate of interest.
2. The finance income or interest earned on the lease receivable to be spread over the lease term based on a pattern reflecting a constant periodic rate of return on either the lessor's net investment outstanding or the net cash investment outstanding in respect of the finance lease.

The application of these points is illustrated in the example below.

Example of accounting for a sales-type lease

XYZ Inc. is a manufacturer of specialized equipment. Many of its customers do not have the necessary funds or financing available for outright purchase. Because of this, XYZ offers a leasing alternative. The data relative to a typical lease are as follows:

1. The noncancelable fixed portion of the lease term is five years. The lessor has the option to renew the lease for an additional three years at the same rental. The estimated useful life of the asset is ten years. Lessee guarantees a residual value of €40,000 at the end of five years, but the guarantee lapses if the full three renewal periods are exercised.
2. The lessor is to receive equal annual payments over the term of the lease. The leased property reverts back to the lessor on termination of the lease.
3. The lease is initiated on 1/1/06. Payments are due on 12/31 for the duration of the lease term.
4. The cost of the equipment to XYZ Inc. is €100,000. The lessor incurs cost associated with the inception of the lease in the amount of €2,500.
5. The selling price of the equipment for an outright purchase is €150,000.
6. The equipment is expected to have a residual value of €15,000 at the end of five years and €10,000 at the end of eight years.
7. The lessor desires a return of 12% (the implicit rate).

The first step is to calculate the annual payment due to the lessor. Recall that the present value (PV) of the minimum lease payments is equal to the selling price adjusted for the present value of the residual amount. The present value is to be computed using the implicit interest rate and the lease term. In this case, the implicit rate is given as 12% and the lease term is 8 years (the fixed noncancelable portion plus the renewal period, since the lessee guarantee terms make renewal virtually inevitable). Thus, the structure of the computation would be as follows:

Normal selling price – PV of residual value = PV of minimum lease payment

Or, in this case,

€150,000	–	(0.40388* × €10,000)	=	4.96764** × Minimum lease payment
€145,961.20	÷	4.96764	=	Minimum lease payment
		€29,382.40	=	Minimum lease payment

* *0.40388 is the present value of an amount of €1 due in eight periods at a 12% interest rate.*
** *4.96764 is the present value of an annuity of €1 for eight periods at a 12% interest rate.*

Prior to examining the accounting implications of a lease, we must determine the lease classification. In this example, the lease term is eight years (discussed above) while the estimated useful life of the asset is 10 years; thus this lease qualifies as something other than an operating lease. (Note that it also meets the FMV versus PV criterion because the PV of the minimum lease payments of €145,961.20, which is 97% of the FMV [€150,000], could be considered to be equal to substantially all of the fair value of the leased asset.) Now it must be determined if this is a sales-type, direct financing, or leveraged lease. To do this, examine the FMV or selling price of the asset and compare it to the cost. Because the two are not equal, we can determine this to be a sales-type lease.

Next, obtain the figures necessary to record the entry on the books of the lessor. The gross investment is the total minimum lease payments plus the unguaranteed residual value, or

$$(€29,382.40 \times 8) + €10,000 = €245,059.20$$

The cost of goods sold is the historical cost of the inventory (€100,000) plus any initial direct costs (€2,500) less the PV of the unguaranteed residual value (€10,000 × 0.40388). Thus, the cost of goods sold amount is €98,461.20 (€100,000 + €2,500 – €4,038.80). Note that the initial direct costs will require a credit entry to some account, usually accounts payable or cash. The inventory account is credited for the carrying value of the asset, in this case €100,000.

The adjusted selling price is equal to the PV of the minimum payments, or €145,961.20. Finally, the unearned finance income is equal to the gross investment (i.e., lease receivable) less the present value of the components making up the gross investment (the minimum lease payment of €29,382.40 and the unguaranteed residual of €10,000). The present value of these items is €150,000 [(€29,382.40 × 4.96764) + (€10,000 × 0.40388)]. Therefore, the entry necessary to record the lease is

Lease receivable	245,059.20	
Cost of goods sold	98,461.20	
Inventory		100,000.00
Sales		145,961.20
Unearned finance income		95,059.20
Accounts payable (initial direct costs)		2,500.00

The next step in accounting for a sales-type lease is to determine proper handling of the payment. Both principal and interest are included in each payment. According to IAS 17, interest is recognized on a basis such that a constant periodic rate of return is earned over the term of the lease. This will require setting up an amortization schedule as illustrated below.

Date or year ended	Cash payment	Interest	Reduction in principal	Balance of net investment
1/1/06				€150,000.00
12/31/06	€ 29,382.40	€18,000.00	€ 11,382.40	138,617.00
12/31/07	29,382.40	16,634.11	12,748.29	125,869.31
12/31/08	29,382.40	15,104.32	14,278.08	111,591.23
12/31/09	29,382.40	13,390.95	15,991.45	95,599.78
12/31/10	29,382.40	11,471.97	17,910.43	77,689.35
12/31/11	29,382.40	9,322.72	20,059.68	57,629.67
12/31/12	29,382.40	6,915.56	22,466.84	35,162.83
12/31/13	29,382.40	4,219.57	25,162.83	10,000.00
	€235,059.20	€95,059.20	€140,000.00	

A few of the columns need to be elaborated on. First, the net investment is the gross investment (lease receivable) less the unearned finance income. Notice that at the end of the lease term, the net investment is equal to the estimated residual value. Also note that the total interest earned over the lease term is equal to the unearned interest (unearned finance income) at the beginning of the lease term.

The entries below illustrate the proper treatment to record the receipt of the lease payment and the amortization of the unearned finance income in the year ended 12/31/06.

Cash	29,382.40	
Lease receivable		29,382.40
Unearned finance income	18,000.00	
Interest revenue		18,000.00

Notice that there is no explicit entry to recognize the principal reduction. This is done automatically when the net investment is reduced by decreasing the lease receivable (gross investment) by €29,382.40 and the unearned finance income account by only €18,000. The €18,000 is 12% (implicit rate) of the net investment. These entries are to be made over the life of the lease.

At the end of the lease term, 12/31/13, the asset is returned to the lessor and the following entry is required:

Asset	10,000	
Leased receivable		10,000

If the estimated residual value has changed during the lease term, the accounting computations would have also changed to reflect this.

Direct financing leases. The accounting for a direct financing lease exhibits many similarities to that for a sales-type lease. Of particular importance is that the terminology used is much the same; however, the treatment accorded these items varies greatly. Again, it is best to preface the discussion by determining the objectives in the accounting for a direct financing lease. Once the lease has been classified, it must be recorded. To do this, the following amounts must be determined:

1. Gross investment
2. Cost
3. Residual value

As noted, a direct financing lease generally involves a leasing company or other financial institution and results in only interest revenue being earned by the lessor. This is because the FMV (selling price) and the cost are equal, and therefore no dealer profit is recognized on the actual lease transaction. Note how this is different from a sales-type lease, which involves both a profit on the transaction and interest revenue over the lease term. The reason for this difference is derived from the conceptual nature underlying the purpose of the lease transaction. In a sales-type lease, the manufacturer (distributor, dealer, etc.) is seeking an alternative means to finance the sale of his product, whereas a direct financing lease is a result of the consumer's need to finance an equipment purchase. Because the consumer is unable to obtain conventional financing, he or she turns to a leasing company that will purchase the desired asset and then lease it to the consumer. Here the profit on the transaction remains with the manufacturer while the interest revenue is earned by the leasing company.

Like a sales-type lease, the first objective is to determine the amounts necessary to complete the following entry:

Lease receivable	xxx	
Asset		xxx
Unearned finance income		xxx

The gross investment is still defined as the minimum amount of lease payments (from the standpoint of a lessor) exclusive of any executory costs, plus the unguaranteed residual value. The difference between the gross investment as determined above and the cost (carrying value) of the asset is to be recorded as the unearned finance income because there is no manufacturer's/dealer's profit earned on the transaction. The following entry would be made to record initial direct costs:

Initial direct costs	xx	
Cash		xx

Under IAS 17, the net investment in the lease is defined as the gross investment less the unearned income plus the unamortized initial direct costs related to the lease. Initial direct costs are incremental costs that are directly attributable to negotiating and arranging a lease, except for such costs incurred by manufacturer or dealer lessors. Originally, initial direct costs could optionally either be amortized over the lease term, or charged to expense immediately. Revisions made to IAS 17 effective beginning 2005, have eliminated the choice of how a lessor accounts for initial direct costs incurred in negotiating a lease, and it is now a requirement that costs that are incremental and directly attributable to the lease are to be capitalized and allocated over the lease term.

Employing initial direct cost capitalization, the unearned lease (i.e., interest) income and the initial direct costs will be amortized to income over the lease term so that a constant periodic rate is earned either on the lessor's net investment outstanding or on the net cash investment outstanding in the finance lease (i.e., the balance of the cash outflows and inflows in respect of the lease, excluding any executory costs that are chargeable to the lessee). Thus, the effect of the initial direct costs is to reduce the implicit interest rate or, yield, to the lessor over the life of the lease.

An example follows that illustrates the preceding principles.

Example of accounting for a direct financing lease

Emirates Refining needs new equipment to expand its manufacturing operation; however, it does not have sufficient capital to purchase the asset at this time. Because of this, Emirates Refining has employed Consolidated Leasing to purchase the asset. In turn, Emirates will lease the asset from Consolidated. The following information applies to the terms of the lease:

1. A three-year lease is initiated on 1/1/06 for equipment costing €131,858, with an expected useful life of five years. FMV at 1/1/06 of equipment is €131,858.
2. Three annual payments are due to the lessor beginning 12/31/06. The property reverts back to the lessor on termination of the lease.
3. The unguaranteed residual value at the end of year three is estimated to be €10,000.
4. The annual payments are calculated to give the lessor a 10% return (the implicit rate).
5. The lease payments and unguaranteed residual value have a PV equal to €131,858 (FMV of asset) at the stipulated discount rate.
6. The annual payment to the lessor is computed as follows:

PV of residual value	=	€10,000 × .7513* = €7,513
PV of lease payments	=	Selling price – PV of residual value
	=	€131,858 – €7,513 = €124,345
Annual payment	=	€124,345 ÷ 2.4869** = €50,000

   * *.7513 is the PV of an amount due in three periods at 10%.*
   ** *2.4869 is the PV of an ordinary annuity of €1 per period for three periods, at 10% interest.*

7. Initial direct costs of €7,500 are incurred by ABC in the lease transaction.

As with any lease transaction, the first step must be to classify the lease appropriately. In this case, the PV of the lease payments (€124,345) is equal to 94% of the FMV (€131,858), thus could be considered as equal to substantially all of the FMV of the leased asset. Next, the unearned interest and the net investment in lease are to be determined.

Gross investment in lease [(3 × €50,000) + €10,000]	€160,000
Cost of leased property	131,858
Unearned finance income	€_28,142

The unamortized initial direct costs are to be added to the gross investment in the lease, and the unearned finance income is to be deducted to arrive at the net investment in the lease. The net investment in the lease for this example is determined as follows:

Gross investment in lease	€160,000
Add:	
Unamortized initial direct costs	7,500
Less:	
Unearned finance income	28,142
Net investment in lease	€139,358

The net investment in the lease (Gross investment – Unearned finance income) has been increased by the amount of initial direct costs. Therefore, the implicit rate is no longer 10%, and the implicit rate must be recomputed, which is the result of performing an internal rate of return calculation. The lease payments are to be €50,000 per annum and a residual value of €10,000 is available at the end of the lease term. In return for these payments (inflows), the lessor is giving up equipment (an outflow) and incurring initial direct costs (also an outflow), with a net investment of €139,358 (€131,858 + €7,500). The way to obtain the new implicit rate is through a trial-and-error calculation as set up below (or employ a calculator or computer routine that does this iterative computation automatically).

$$\frac{50,000}{(1+i)} \; 1 + \; \frac{50,000}{(1+i)} \; 2 + \; \frac{50,000}{(1+i)} \; 3 + \; \frac{10,000}{(1+i)} \; 3 = \$139,358$$

Where: i = implicit rate of interest

In this case, the implicit rate is equal to 7.008%. Thus, the amortization table would be set up as follows:

	(a)	(b)	(c)	(d)	(e)	(f)
				Reduction in	Reduction in	
		Reduction in	PV x Implicit	initial direct	PVI net in-	PVI net investment
	Lease	unearned	rate	costs	vestment	in lease
	payments	Interest	(7.008%)	(b-c)	(a-b + d)	$(f)_{(n+1)} = (f)_n - (e)$
At inception						€139,358
2006	€ 50,000	€13,186 (1)	€ 9,766	€3,420	€ 40,234	99,124
2007	50,000	9,504 (2)	6,947	2,557	43,053	56,071
2008	50,000	5,455 (3)	3,929	1,526	46,071	10,000
	€150,000	€28,145*	€20,642	€7,503	€129,358	

*Rounded

(b.1) €131,858 × 10% = €13,186
(b.2) [€131,858 – (€50,000 – 13,186)] × 10% = €9,504
(b.3) [€95,044 – (€50,000 – 9,504)] × 10% = €5,455

Here the interest is computed as 7.008% of the net investment. Note again that the net investment at the end of the lease term is equal to the estimated residual value.
    The entry made initially to record the lease is as follows:

Lease receivable** [(€50,000 × 3) + €10,000]	160,000	
Asset acquired for leasing		131,858
Unearned lease revenue		28,142

When the payment (or obligation to pay) of the initial direct costs occurs, the following entry must be made:

Initial direct costs	7,500	
Cash		7,500

Using the schedule above, the following entries would be made during each of the indicated years:

	2006		2007		2008	
Cash	50,000		50,000		50,000	
Lease receivable**		50,000		50,000		50,000
Unearned finance income	13,186		9,504		5,455	
Initial direct costs		3,420		2,557		1,526
Interest income		9,766		6,947		3,929

Finally, when the asset is returned to the lessor at the end of the lease term, it must be recorded on the books. The necessary entry is as follows:

Used asset	10,000	
Lease receivable**		10,000

**Also commonly referred to as the "gross investment in lease."*

Leveraged leases. Leveraged leases are discussed in detail in Appendix B of this chapter because of the complexity involved in the accounting treatment based on guidance available under US GAAP, where this topic has been given extensive coverage. Under IFRS, this concept has been defined, but with only a very brief outline of the treatment to be accorded to this kind of lease. A leveraged lease is defined in IAS 17 as a finance lease which is structured such that there are at least three parties involved: the lessee, the lessor, and one or more long-term creditors who provide part of the acquisition finance for the leased asset, usually without any general recourse to the lessor. Succinctly, this type of a lease is given the following unique accounting treatment:

1. The lessor records his or her investment in the lease net of the nonrecourse debt and the related finance costs to the third-party creditor(s).
2. The recognition of the finance income is based on the lessor's net cash investment outstanding in respect of the lease.

Sale-Leaseback Transactions

Sale-leaseback describes a transaction where the owner of property (the seller-lessee) sells the property and then immediately leases all or part of it back from the new owner (the buyer-lessor). These transactions may occur when the seller-lessee is experiencing cash flow or financing problems or because there are tax advantages in such an arrangement in the lessee's tax jurisdiction. The important consideration in this type of transaction is recognition of two separate and distinct economic transactions. However, it is important to note that there is not a physical transfer of property. First, there is a sale of property, and second, there is a lease agreement for the same property in which the original seller is the lessee and the original buyer is the lessor. This is illustrated as follows:

A sale-leaseback transaction is usually structured such that the sales price of the asset is greater than or equal to the current market value. The higher sales price has the concomitant effect of a higher periodic rental payment over the lease term than would otherwise have been negotiated. The transaction is usually attractive because of the tax benefits associated with it, and because it provides financing to the lessee. The seller-lessee benefits from the higher price because of the increased gain on the sale of the property and the deductibility of the lease payments, which are usually larger than the depreciation that was previously being taken. The buyer-lessor benefits from both the higher rental payments and the larger depreciable basis.

Under IAS 17, the accounting treatment depends on whether the leaseback results in a finance lease or an operating lease. If it results in a finance lease, any excess of sale proceeds over previous carrying value may not be recognized immediately as income in the financial statements of the seller-lessee. Rather, it is to be deferred and amortized over the lease term.

Accounting for a sale-leaseback that involves the creation of an operating lease depends on whether the sale portion of the compound transaction was on arm's-length terms. If the leaseback results in an operating lease, and it is evident that the transaction is established at fair value, then any profit or loss should be recognized immediately. On the other hand, if the sale price is *not* established at fair value, then

a.   If sale price is below fair value, any profit or loss should be recognized immediately, except that when a loss is to be compensated by below fair market future rentals, the loss should be deferred and amortized in proportion to the rental payments over the period the asset is expected to be used.

b.   If the sale price is above fair value, the excess over fair value should be deferred and amortized over the period for which the asset is expected to be used.

IAS 17 stipulates that, in case of operating leasebacks, if at the date of the sale and leaseback transaction the fair value is less than the carrying amount of the leased asset, the difference between the fair value and the carrying amount should immediately be recognized. In other words, impairment is recognized first, before the actual sale-leaseback transaction is given recognition. This logically follows from the fact that impairments are essentially catch-up depreciation charges, belated recognition that the consumption of the utility of the assets had not been correctly recognized in earlier periods.

However, in case the sale and leaseback result in a finance lease, no such adjustment is considered necessary unless there has been an impairment in value, in which case the carrying value should be reduced to the recoverable amount in accordance with the provisions of IAS 36.

The guidance under IFRS pertaining to sale-leaseback transactions is limited, and many variations in terms and conditions are found in actual practice. To provide further insight, albeit not with the suggestion that this constitutes IFRS, selected guidance found under US GAAP is offered in Appendix A to this chapter.

Other leasing guidance. SIC 27 addresses arrangements between an enterprise and an investor that involve the legal form of a lease. SIC 27 establishes that the accounting for such arrangements is in all instances to reflect the substance of the relationship. All aspects of the arrangement are to be evaluated to determine its substance, with particular emphasis on those that have an economic effect. To assist in doing this, SIC 27 identifies certain indicators that may demonstrate that an arrangement might not involve a lease under IAS 17. For example, a series of linked transactions that in substance do not transfer control over the asset, and which keep the right to receive the benefits of ownership with the transferor, would not be a lease. Also, transactions arranged for specific objectives, such as the transfer of tax attributes, would generally not be accounted for as leases.

SIC 27 deals most specifically with those arrangements that have characteristics of leases coupled with corollary subleases, whereby the lessor is the sublessee and the lessee is the sublessor, which may also involve a purchase option. The financing party (the lessee-sublessor) is often guaranteed a certain economic return on such transactions, further revealing that the substance might in fact be that of a secured borrowing rather than a series of lease arrangements. Since nominal lease and sublease payments will net to zero, the exchange of funds is often limited to the fee given by the property owner to the party providing financing; tax advantages are often the principal objective of these transactions. Accounting questions arising from the transactions include recognition of fees received by the financing party; the presentation of separate investment and sublease payment obligation accounts as an asset and a liability, respectively; and the accounting for resulting obligations.

SIC 27 imposes a substance over form solution to this problem. Accordingly, when an arrangement is found to not meet the definition of a lease, a separate investment account and a lease payment obligation would not meet the definitions of an asset and a liability, and should not be recognized by the entity. It presents certain indicators which imply that a given arrangement is not a lease (e.g., when the right to use the property for a given term is not in fact transferred to the nominal lessee) and that lease accounting cannot be applied.

The interpretation provides that the fee paid to the financing provider should be recognized in accordance with IAS 18. Fees received in advance would generally be deferred and recognized over the lease term when future performance is required in order to retain the fee, when limitations are placed on the use of the underlying asset, or when the nonremote likelihood of early termination would necessitate some fee repayment.

Finally, SIC 27 identifies certain factors that would suggest that other obligations of an arrangement, including any guarantees provided and obligations incurred upon early termination, should be accounted for under either IAS 37 (contingent liabilities) or IAS 39 (financial obligations), depending on the terms.

IFRIC 4 describes arrangements, comprising transactions or series of related transactions, that do not take the legal form of a lease, but which convey rights to use assets in return for series of payments. Examples of such arrangements include

- Outsourcing arrangements (e.g., the outsourcing of the data processing functions of an entity).
- Various arrangements in the telecommunications industry, in which suppliers of network capacity enter into contracts to provide other entities with rights to capacity.
- "Take-or-pay" and similar contracts, in which purchasers must make specified payments regardless of whether they take delivery of the contracted products or services (these often are styled as capacity contracts, giving one party exclusive rights to the counterparty's output).

IFRIC 4 provides guidance for determining whether such arrangements are, or contain, leases that should be accounted for in accordance with IAS 17. (It does not address how such arrangements, if determined to be leases, should be classified). In some of these arrangements, the underlying asset that is the subject of the lease is a portion of a larger asset. IFRIC 4 does not address how to ascertain if the portion of a larger asset is itself the underlying asset for the purposes of applying IAS 17. However, arrangements in which the underlying asset would represent a unit of account under either IAS 16 or IAS 38 are within the scope of this interpretation. Leases which would be excluded from IAS 17 (as noted earlier in this chapter) are not subject to the provisions of IFRIC 4.

Determining whether an arrangement is, or contains, a lease is required to be based on the substance of the arrangement. It requires an assessment of whether

1. Fulfillment of the arrangement is dependent on the use of a specific asset or assets; *and*
2. The arrangement conveys a right to use the asset.

An arrangement is not the subject of a lease if its fulfillment is not dependent on the use of the specified asset. Thus, if terms call for delivery of a specified quantity of goods or services, and the entity has the right and ability to provide those goods or services using other assets not specified in the arrangement, it is not subject to this interpretation. On the other hand, a warranty obligation that permits or requires the substitution of the same or similar assets when the specified asset is not operating properly, or a contractual provision (whether or not contingent) permitting or requiring the supplier to substitute other assets for any reason on or after a specified date, do not preclude lease treatment before the date of substitution.

IFRIC 4 states that an asset has been *implicitly specified* if, for example, the supplier owns or leases only one asset with which to fulfill the obligation, and it is not economically feasible to perform its obligation through the use of alternative assets.

An arrangement conveys the right to use the asset if the arrangement conveys to the purchaser (putatively, the lessee) the right to control the use of the underlying asset. This occurs if

1. The purchaser has the ability or right to operate the asset (or direct others to operate the asset) in a manner it determines while obtaining or controlling more than an insignificant amount of the output or other value of the asset;
2. The purchaser has the ability or right to control physical access to the underlying asset while obtaining or controlling more than an insignificant amount of the output or other utility of the asset; or
3. Fact and circumstances suggest that it is remote that one or more parties other than the purchaser will take more than an insignificant amount of the output of the asset, or other value that will be produced or generated by the asset during the term of the arrangement, and the price that the purchaser will pay for the output is neither contractually fixed per unit of output nor equal to the current market price per unit of output as of the time of delivery of the output.

According to IFRIC 4, the assessment of whether an arrangement contains a lease is to be made at the inception of the arrangement. This is defined as the earlier of the date of the arrangement or the date the parties commit to the principal terms of the arrangement, on the basis of all of the facts and circumstances. Once determined, a reassessment is permitted only if

1. There is a change in the contractual terms, unless the change only renews or extends the arrangement;
2. A renewal option is exercised or an extension is agreed to by the parties, unless the term of the renewal or extension had initially been included in the lease term in accordance with IAS 17 (a renewal or extension of the arrangement that does not include modification of any of the terms in the original arrangement before the end of the term of the original arrangement is to be evaluated only with respect to the renewal or extension period);
3. There is a change in the determination of whether fulfillment is dependent on a specified asset; or
4. There is a substantial change to the asset, (e.g., a substantial physical change to property, plant, or equipment).

Any reassessment of an arrangement is to be based on the facts and circumstances as of the date of reassessment, including the remaining term of the arrangement. Changes in estimate (e.g., as to the expected output to be delivered) may not be used to trigger a reassessment. If the reassessment concludes that the arrangement contains (or does not contain) a lease, lease accounting is to be applied (or cease to be applied) from when the change in circumstances giving rise to the reassessment occurs (if other than exercise of a renewal or extension), or the inception of the renewal or extension period.

If an arrangement is determined to contain a lease, both parties are to apply the requirements of IAS 17 to the lease element of the arrangement. Accordingly, the lease must be classified as a finance lease or an operating lease. Other elements of the arrangement, not within the scope of that standard, are to be accounted for as required by relevant IFRS. For the purpose of applying IAS 17, payments and other consideration required must be separated, at inception or upon a reassessment of the arrangement, into that being made for the lease and that applicable to the other elements, on the basis of relative fair values. Minimum lease payments (per IAS 17) include only payments for the lease itself.

In some instances it will be necessary to make assumptions and estimates in order to separate the payments for the lease from payments for the other elements. IFRIC 4 suggests that a purchaser might estimate the lease payment portion by reference to a lease for a comparable asset that contains no other elements, or might estimate the payments for the other elements by reference to comparable agreements, deriving the payments for the other component by deduction. However, if a purchaser concludes that it is impracticable to separate the payments reliably, the procedure to be followed depends on whether the lease is operating or finance in nature.

If a finance lease, the purchaser/lessee is to recognize an asset and a liability at an amount equal to the fair value of the underlying asset that was identified as being the subject of the lease. As payments are later made, the liability will be reduced and an imputed finance charge on the liability will be recognized using the purchaser's incremental borrowing rate of interest (as described earlier in this chapter).

If an operating lease, the purchaser/lessee is to treat all payments as lease payments for the purposes of complying with the disclosure requirements of IAS 17, but (1) disclose those payments separately from minimum lease payments of other arrangements that do not include payments for nonlease elements, and (2) state that the disclosed payments also include payments for nonlease elements in the arrangement.

IFRIC 4 is effective for years beginning in 2006, but earlier application is permitted, with appropriate disclosure.

DISCLOSURE REQUIREMENTS UNDER IAS 17

Lessee Disclosures

1. **Finance Leases**

    IAS 17 mandates the following disclosures for lessees under finance leases, in addition to disclosures required under IAS 32 for all financial instruments:

    a. For each class of asset, the net carrying amount at balance sheet date
    b. A reconciliation between the total of minimum lease payments at the balance sheet date, and their present value. In addition, an enterprise should disclose the total of the minimum lease payments at the balance sheet date, their present value, for each of the following periods:

    (1) Due in one year or less
    (2) Due in more than one but no more than five years
    (3) Due in more than five years

    c. Contingent rents included in profit or loss for the period
    d. The total of minimum sublease payments to be received in the future under noncancelable subleases as of the balance sheet date
    e. A general description of the lessee's significant leasing arrangements including, but not necessarily limited to the following:

    (1) The basis for determining contingent rentals

(2) The existence and terms of renewal or purchase options and escalation clauses

(3) Restrictions imposed by lease arrangements such as on dividends or assumptions of further debt or further leasing

2. **Operating Leases**

   IAS 17 sets forth in greater detail the disclosure requirements that will be applicable to lessees under operating leases. While some of these were suggested under original IAS 17 or are implicitly needed to provide adequate disclosure, the revised standard offers preparers more explicit guidance.

   Lessees should, in addition to the requirements of IAS 32, make the following disclosures for operating leases:

   a. Total of the future minimum lease payments under noncancelable operating leases for each of the following periods:

      (1) Due in one year or less
      (2) Due in more than one year but no more than five years
      (3) Due in more than five years

   b. The total of future minimum sublease payments expected to be received under noncancellable subleases at the balance sheet date

   c. Lease and sublease payments included in profit or loss for the period, with separate amounts of minimum lease payments, contingent rents, and sublease payments

   d. A general description of the lessee's significant leasing arrangements including, but not necessarily limited to the following:

      (1) The basis for determining contingent rentals
      (2) The existence and terms of renewal or purchase options escalation clauses
      (3) Restrictions imposed by lease arrangements such as on dividends or assumption of further debt or on further leasing

Lessor Disclosures

1. **Finance Leases**

   IAS 17 requires enhanced disclosures compared to the original standard. Lessors under finance leases are required to disclose, in addition to disclosures under IAS 32, the following:

   a. A reconciliation between the total gross investment in the lease at the balance sheet date, and the present value of minimum lease payments receivable as of the balance sheet date, categorized into

      (1) Those due in one year or less
      (2) Those due in more than one year but not more than five years
      (3) Those due beyond five years

   b. Unearned finance income
   c. The accumulated allowance for uncollectible minimum lease payments receivable
   d. Total contingent rentals included in income
   e. A general description of the lessor's significant leasing arrangements

2. **Operating Leases**

For lessors under operating leases, IAS 17 has prescribed the following expanded disclosures:

a. For each class of asset, the gross carrying amount, the accumulated depreciation and accumulated impairment losses at the balance sheet date

   (1) Depreciation recognized in income for the period
   (2) Impairment losses recognized in income for the period
   (3) Impairment losses reversed in income for the period

b. Depreciation recognized on assets held for operating lease use during the period
c. The future minimum lease payments under noncancellable operating leases, in the aggregate and classified into

   (1) Those due in no more than one year
   (2) Those due in more than one but not more than five years
   (3) Those due in more than five years

d. Total contingent rentals included in income for the period
e. A general description of leasing arrangements to which it is a party

Examples of Financial Statement Disclosures

Mittal Steel South Africa Limited
For the year ended December 31, 2004

1. Accounting policies

Leased assets. Leases involving plant and equipment whereby the lessor provides finance to the group with the asset as security and where the group assumes substantially all the benefits and risks of ownership are classified as finance leases. Assets acquired in terms of finance leases are capitalized at the lower of fair value and the present value of the minimum lease payments at inception of the lease and depreciated over the useful life of the asset. The capital element of future obligations under the leases is included as a liability in the balance sheet. Each lease payment is allocated between the liability and finance charges so as to achieve a constant rate on the finance balance outstanding. The interest element of the finance charge is charged against income over the lease period, using the effective interest rate method.

For a sale and leaseback transaction that results in a finance lease, any excess of sales proceeds over the carrying amount is deferred and recognized on a straight-line basis over the period of the lease.

Leases of assets to the group under which all the risks and benefits of ownership are effectively retained by the lessor, are classified as operating leases. Payments made under operating leases are charged against income on a straight-line basis over the period of the lease.

12. Property, plant and equipment

	Group		Company	
		Six		Six
	Year	months	Year	months
	ended	ended	ended	ended
The net carrying amount of machinery, plant, and equipment	Dec. 31	Dec. 31	Dec. 31	Dec. 31
includes assets held under finance leases	2004 Rm	2003 Rm	2004 Rm	2003 Rm
Gross carrying amount				
At beginning of period	571	571	571	571
At end of period	571	571	571	571
Accumulated depreciation and impairment losses				
At beginning of period	299	285	299	285
Depreciation charges	27	14	27	14
At end of period	326	299	326	299
Net carrying amount at end of period	245	272	245	272

The replacement value of assets for insurance purposes amount to R72 billion (December 2003: R55 billion). A register of land is available for inspection at the registered office of the company.

21. Interest bearing borrowings

	Group		Company	
		Six		Six
	Year	months	Year	months
	ended	ended	ended	ended
	Dec. 31	Dec. 31	Dec. 31	Dec. 31
	2004 Rm	2003 Rm	2004 Rm	2003 Rm
Interest-bearing borrowings				
Noncurrent borrowings	81	92		
Short-term borrowings		978		978
Current portion of noncurrent borrowings	10	10		
Total short-term borrowings	10	988		978
Total interest-bearing borrowings	91	1080		978

Short-term borrowings comprise an unsecured call facility which bears interest at call borrowing rates

A finance lease liability at an effective interest rate of 8.42% (December 2003: 8.57%) has not been included in the above interest-bearing borrowings. It has been set off against an interest-bearing loan to the lessee (a subsidiary of Mittal Steel South Africa) as provided for in the lease agreement as follows:

Gross finance lease liability			143	273
Loan to lessor set off against finance lease liability			143	273
Minimum lease payments				
Less than 1 year			143	152
More than 1 year and less than 5 years				142
Total			143	294
Less: future finance charges				21
Present value of lease liabilities			143	273
Representing lease liabilities				
Current			143	131
Noncurrent (more than 1 year and less than 5 years)				142
Total			143	273

HVB Group
Period ending December 2004

Lease operations. Under IAS 17, lease operations are divided into finance leases and operating leases. Unlike an operating lease, a finance lease is a lease that transfers substantially all the risks and rewards incident to ownership of an asset. Title may or may not eventually be transferred.

HVB Group as lessor. Under finance leases, the lessor recognizes in the balance sheet a receivable at an amount equal to the net investment in the lease and not the leased asset. Interest and similar income is recognized on the basis of a constant, periodic rate of return relating to the net investment outstanding. The term "net investment" is defined in detail in Note 48. HVB Group leases both movable property and real estate as a lessor under finance leases.

In contrast, assets held under operating leases are recognized as, and valued using the same principles as, property, plant, and equipment. Revenue under these arrangements is recognized on a straight-line basis over the lease term. HVB Group leases both movable property and real estate as a lessor under operating leases. Operating leases with HVB Group as lessor are comparatively insignificant.

HVB Group as lessee. Under a finance lease, the asset is recognized as property, plant, and equipment, and the obligation as a liability. Each asset is stated at the lower of the following two values: either the fair value of the leased asset at the inception of the lease, or the present value of the minimum lease payments. In calculating the present value of the minimum lease payments, the interest rate implicit in the lease is applied.

The lease payments are broken down into two components: the finance charge (treated as interest expense) and the redemption payment (which reduces the amount of the outstanding liability). Lease payments relating to operating leases are treated as rental expense and recognized in general administrative expenses. Contracts in which the Bank acts as lessee are comparatively insignificant.

Nokia Group
Period ending December 2004

Accounting policies

Leases. The Group has entered into various operating leases, the payments under which are treated as rentals and charged to the profit and loss account on a straight-line basis over the lease terms.

31. Leasing contracts.

The Group leases office, manufacturing, and warehouse space under various noncancellable operating leases. Certain contracts contain renewal options for various periods of time.

The future costs for noncancelable leasing contracts are as follows:

Leasing payments, EURm	Operating leases
2005	175
2006	137
2007	94
2008	78
2009	70
Thereafter	57
Total	611

Rental expense amounted to EUR 236 million in 2004 (EUR 285 million in 2003, and EUR 384 million in 2002).

32. Related-party transactions

The Group recorded net rental expense of EUR 2 million in 2004 (EUR 2 million in 2003 and EUR 2 million in 2002) pertaining to a sale-leaseback transaction with Nokia Pension Foundation involving certain buildings and a lease of the underlying land.

F. Hoffmann-LaRoche
Period ending December 2004

Leases. Leases of property, plant, and equipment where the Group has substantially all of the risks and rewards of ownership are classified as finance leases. Finance leases are capitalized at the start of the lease at fair value, or the present value of the minimum lease payments, if lower. The rental obligation, net of finance charges, is included in debt. Assets acquired under finance leases are depreciated in accordance with the Group's above policy on property, plant, and equipment. The interest element of the finance cost is charged against income over the lease term on the effective interest rate method.

Leases where substantially all of the risks and rewards of ownership are not transferred to the Group are classified as operating leases. Payments made under operating leases are charged against income on a straight-line basis over the period of the lease.

Finance leases. As at December 31, 2004, the capitalized cost of machinery and equipment under finance leases amounts to 867 million Swiss francs (2003: 1,036 million Swiss francs) and the net book value of these assets amounts to 640 million Swiss francs (2003: 846 million Swiss francs).

Finance leases: present value of future minimum lease payments
in millions of CHF

	2004	*2003*
Within one year	19	32
Between one and five years	510	569
More than five years	172	289
Total present value of minimum lease payments	701	890

Group companies are party to a number of finance leases, the most significant of which are those entered into by Genentech in respect of its manufacturing facility in Vacaville, California, and certain buildings on its South San Francisco site. Upon lease expiry Genentech may either purchase the property at a predetermined amount, sell the property to a third party or renew the lease. If the property is sold to a third party at an amount lower than the amount financed by the lessor, Genentech has agreed a residual value guarantee to pay the lessor up to an agreed percentage of the amount financed by the lessor. Genentech is also required to maintain financial covenants in the form of certain predefined financial ratios and is limited to the amount of debt it can assume. The carrying value of these lease obligations is 577 million US dollars (653 million Swiss francs).

Genentech lease
in millions of US dollars

	Approximate initial fair value of property	*Lease expiry*	*Maximum residual value guarantee*
Vacaville	425	November 2006	372
South San Francisco	160	June 2007	136
Total	585		508

Operating leases. Total operating lease rental expense was 245 million Swiss francs (2003: 219 million Swiss francs)

Operating leases: future minimum payments under noncancelable leases
in millions of CHF

	2004	*2003*
Within one year	103	114
Between one and five years	163	177
Thereafter	63	15
Total minimum annual payments	329	306

Group companies are party to a number of operating leases, mainly for plant and machinery, including motor vehicles, and for certain short-term property rentals. The arrangements do not impose any significant restrictions on the Group.

APPENDIX A

SPECIAL SITUATIONS NOT ADDRESSED BY IAS 17 BUT WHICH HAVE BEEN INTERPRETED UNDER US GAAP

In the following section, a number of interesting and common problem areas that have not been addressed by IFRS are briefly considered. The guidance found in US GAAP is referenced, as this is likely to represent the most comprehensive source of insight into these matters. However, it should be understood that this constitutes only possible approaches to selected fact situations, and is not authoritative guidance.

Sale-Leaseback Transactions

The accounting treatment from the seller-lessee's perspective will depend on the degree of rights to use retained by the seller-lessee. The degree of rights to use retained may be categorized as follows:

1. Substantially all
2. Minor
3. More than minor but less than substantially all

The guideline for the determination substantially all is based on the classification criteria presented for the lease transaction. For example, a test based on the 90% recovery criterion seems appropriate. That is, if the present value of fair rental payments is equal to 90% or more of the fair value of the sold asset, the seller-lessee is presumed to have retained substantially all the rights to use the sold property. The test for retaining minor rights would be to substitute 10% or less for 90% or more in the preceding sentence.

If substantially all the rights to use the property are retained by the seller-lessee and the agreement meets at least one of the criteria for capital lease treatment, the seller-lessee should account for the leaseback as a capital lease, and any profit on the sale should be deferred and either amortized over the life of the property or treated as a reduction of depreciation expense. If the leaseback is classified as an operating lease, it should be accounted for as one, and any profit or loss on the sale should be deferred and amortized over the lease term. Any loss on the sale would also be deferred unless the loss were perceived to be a real economic loss, in which case the loss would be recognized immediately and not deferred.

If only a minor portion of the rights to use are retained by the seller-lessee, the sale and the leaseback should be accounted for separately. However, if the rental payments appear unreasonable based on the existing market conditions at the inception of the lease, the profit or loss should be adjusted so that the rentals are at a reasonable amount. The amount created by the adjustment should be deferred and amortized over the life of the property if a capital lease is involved or over the lease term if an operating lease is involved.

If the seller-lessee retains more than a minor portion but less than substantially all the rights to use the property, any excess profit on the sale should be recognized on the date of the sale. For purposes of this paragraph, excess profit is derived as follows:

1. If the leaseback is classified as an operating lease, the excess profit is the profit that exceeds the present value of the minimum lease payments over the lease term. The seller-lessee should use its incremental borrowing rate to compute the present value of the minimum lease payments. If the implicit rate of interest in the lease is known, it should be used to compute the present value of the minimum lease payments.
2. If the leaseback is classified as a capital (i.e., finance) lease, the excess profit is the amount greater than the recorded amount of the leased asset.

When the fair value of the property at the time of the leaseback is less than its undepreciated cost, the seller-lessee should immediately recognize a loss for the difference. In the example below, the sales price is less than the book value of the property. However, there is no economic loss because the FMV is greater than the book value.

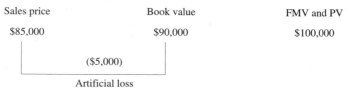

Sales price	Book value	FMV and PV
$85,000	$90,000	$100,000

($5,000)

Artificial loss

The artificial loss must be deferred and amortized as an addition to depreciation.

The following diagram summarizes the accounting for sale-leaseback transactions.

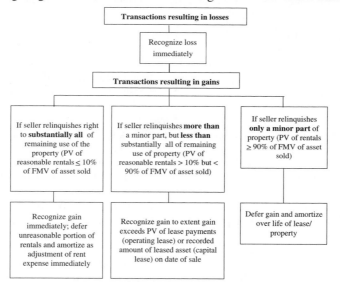

In the foregoing circumstances, when the leased asset is land only, any amortization should be on a straight-line basis over the lease term, regardless of whether the lease is classified as a capital or an operating lease.

Executory costs are not to be included in the calculation of profit to be deferred in a sale-leaseback transaction. The buyer-lessor should account for the transaction as a purchase and a direct financing lease if the agreement meets the criteria of **either** a direct financing lease **or** a sales-type lease. Otherwise, the agreement should be accounted for as a purchase and an operating lease.

Sale-leaseback involving real estate. Under US GAAP, three requirements are necessary for a sale-leaseback involving real estate (including real estate with equipment) to qualify for sale-leaseback accounting treatment. Those sale-leaseback transactions not meeting the three requirements should be accounted for as a deposit or as a financing. The three requirements are

1. The lease must be a normal leaseback.
2. Payment terms and provisions must adequately demonstrate the buyer-lessor's initial and continuing investment in the property.

3. Payment terms and provisions must transfer all the risks and rewards of ownership as demonstrated by a lack of continuing involvement by the seller-lessee.

A normal leaseback involves active use of the leased property in the seller-lessee's trade or business during the lease term.

The buyer-lessor's initial investment is adequate if it demonstrates the buyer-lessor's commitment to pay for the property and indicates a reasonable likelihood that the seller-lessee will collect any receivable related to the leased property. The buyer-lessor's continuing investment is adequate if the buyer is contractually obligated to pay an annual amount at least equal to the level of annual payment needed to pay that debt and interest over no more than (1) twenty years for land and (2) the customary term of a first mortgage loan for other real estate.

Any continuing involvement by the seller-lessee other than normal leaseback disqualifies the lease from sale-leaseback accounting treatment. Some examples of continuing involvement other than normal leaseback include

1. The seller-lessee has an obligation or option (excluding the right of first refusal) to repurchase the property.
2. The seller-lessee (or party related to the seller-lessee) guarantees the buyer-lessor's investment or debt related to that investment or a return on that investment.
3. The seller-lessee is required to reimburse the buyer-lessor for a decline in the fair value of the property below estimated residual value at the end of the lease term based on other than excess wear and tear.
4. The seller-lessee remains liable for an existing debt related to the property.
5. The seller-lessee's rental payments are contingent on some predetermined level of future operations of the buyer-lessor.
6. The seller-lessee provides collateral on behalf of the buyer-lessor other than the property directly involved in the sale-leaseback.
7. The seller-lessee provides nonrecourse financing to the buyer-lessor for any portion of the sales proceeds or provides recourse financing in which the only recourse is the leased asset.
8. The seller-lessee enters into a sale-leaseback involving property improvements or integral equipment without leasing the underlying land to the buyer-lessor.
9. The buyer-lessor is obligated to share any portion of the appreciation of the property with the seller-lessee.
10. Any other provision or circumstance that allows the seller-lessee to participate in any future profits of the buyer-lessor or appreciation of the leased property.

Example of accounting for a sale-leaseback transaction

To illustrate the accounting treatment in a sale-leaseback transaction, suppose that Lessee Corporation sells equipment that has a book value of €80,000 and a fair value of €100,000 to Lessor Corporation, and then immediately leases it back under the following conditions:

1. The sale date is January 1, 2006, and the equipment has a fair value of €100,000 on that date and an estimated useful life of 15 years.
2. The lease term is 15 years, noncancelable, and requires equal rental payments of €13,109 at the beginning of each year.
3. Lessee Corp. has the option annually to renew the lease at the same rental payments on expiration of the original lease.
4. Lessee Corp. has the obligation to pay all executory costs.
5. The annual rental payments provide the lessor with a 12% return on investment.
6. The incremental borrowing rate of Lessee Corp. is 12%.
7. Lessee Corp. depreciates similar equipment on a straight-line basis.

Lessee Corp. should classify the agreement as a capital lease since the lease term exceeds 75% (which is deemed to be a major part) of the estimated economic life of the equipment, and because the present value of the lease payments is greater than 90% (deemed to be substantially all) of the fair value of the equipment. Assuming that collectibility of the lease payments is reasonably predictable and that no important uncertainties exist concerning the amount of nonreimbursable costs yet to be incurred by the lessor, Lessor Corp. should classify the transaction as a direct financing lease because the present value of the minimum lease payments is equal to the fair market value of €100,000 (€13,109 × 7.62817).

Lessee Corp. and Lessor Corp. would normally make the following journal entries during the first year:

Upon Sale of Equipment on January 1, 2006

Lessee Corp.			*Lessor Corp.*		
Cash	100,000		Equipment	100,000	
Equipment*		80,000	Cash		100,000
Unearned profit on					
sale-leaseback		20,000			
Leased equipment	100,000		Lease receivable		
Lease obligations		100,000	(€13,109 × 15)	196,635	
			Equipment		100,000
			Unearned interest		96,635

*Assumes new equipment

To Record First Payment on January 1, 2006

Lessee Corp.			*Lessor Corp.*		
Lease obligations	13,109		Cash	13,109	
Cash		13,109	Lease receivable		13,109

To Record Incurrence and Payment of Executory Costs

Lessee Corp.			*Lessor Corp.*	
Insurance, taxes, etc.	xxx		(No entry)	
Cash (accounts payable)		xxx		

To Record Depreciation Expense on the Equipment, December 31, 2006

Lessee Corp.			*Lessor Corp.*	
Depreciation expense	6,667		(No entry)	
Accum. depr.— capital				
leases (€100,000 ÷ 15)		6,667		

To Amortize Profit on Sale-Leaseback by Lessee Corp., December 31, 2006

Lessee Corp.			*Lessor Corp.*	
Unearned profit on sale-			(No entry)	
leaseback	1,333			
Depr. expense				
(€20,000 ÷ 15)		1,333		

To Record Interest for December 31, 2006

Lessee Corp.			*Lessor Corp.*		
Interest expense	10,427		Unearned interest in-		
Accrued interest			come	10,427	
payable		10,427	Interest income		10,427

Partial Lease Amortization Schedule

Date	Cash payment	Interest expense	Reduction of obligation	Lease obligation
Inception of lease				€100,000
1/1/05	€13,109	€ --	€13,109	86,891
1/1/06	13,109	10,427	2,682	84,209

Leases Involving Real Estate—Guidance under US GAAP

While required practice regarding lease accounting is rather clearly set forth under IAS 17, as is typical under IFRS this is presented in rather general terms. US GAAP, by contrast, offers a great deal of very specific guidance on this topic. It is instructive to at least consider the US GAAP rules for lease accounting, which may provide some further insight and, in some circumstances, offer operational guidance to those attempting to apply IAS 17 to particular fact situations. Under US GAAP (which consists of many discrete standards and a large volume of interpretive literature), leases involving real estate are categorized into four groups:

1. Leases involving land only
2. Leases involving land and building(s)
3. Leases involving real estate and equipment
4. Leases involving only part of a building

Leases Involving Land Only

Lessee accounting. If the lease agreement transfers ownership or contains a bargain purchase option, the lessee should account for the lease as a capital lease and record an asset and related liability in an amount equal to the present value of the minimum lease payments. If the lease agreement does not transfer ownership or contain a bargain purchase option, the lessee should account for the lease as an operating lease.

Lessor accounting. If the lease gives rise to dealer's profit (or loss) and transfers ownership (i.e., title), the standards require that the lease shall be classified as a sales-type lease and accounted for under the provisions of the US standard dealing with sales of real estate, in the same manner as would a seller of the same property. If the lease transfers ownership, both the collectibility and the no material uncertainties criteria are met, but if it does not give rise to dealer's profit (or loss), the lease should be accounted for as a direct financing or leveraged lease, as appropriate. If the lease contains a bargain purchase option and both the collectibility and no material uncertainties criteria are met, the lease should be accounted for as a direct financing, leveraged, or operating lease as appropriate. If the lease does not meet the collectibility and/or no material uncertainties criteria, the lease should be accounted for as an operating lease.

Leases Involving Land and Building

Lessee accounting. Under US GAAP, if the agreement transfers title or contains a bargain purchase option, the lessee should account for the agreement by separating the land and building components and capitalize each separately. The land and building elements should be allocated on the basis of their relative fair market values measured at the inception of the lease. The land and building components are accounted for separately because the lessee is expected to own the real estate by the end of the lease term. The building should be depreciated over its estimated useful life without regard to the lease term.

When the lease agreement neither transfers title nor contains a bargain purchase option, the fair value of the land must be determined in relation to the fair value of the aggregate properties included in the lease agreement. If the fair value of the land is less than 25% of the fair value of the leased properties in aggregate, the land is considered immaterial. Conversely, if the fair value of the land is 25% or greater of the fair value of the leased properties in aggregate, the land is considered material.

When the land component of the lease agreement is considered immaterial (FMV land < 25% total FMV), the lease should be accounted for as a single lease unit. The lessee should capitalize the lease if one of the following occurs:

1. The term of the lease is 75% or more of the economic useful life of the real estate
2. The present value of the minimum lease payments equals 90% or more of the fair market value of the leased real estate less any lessor tax credits

If neither of the two criteria above is met, the lessee should account for the lease agreement as a single operating lease.

When the land component of the lease agreement is considered material (FMV land ≥ 25% total FMV), the land and building components should be separated. By applying the lessee's incremental borrowing rate to the fair market value of the land, the annual minimum lease payment attributed to land is computed. The remaining payments are attributed to the building. The division of minimum lease payments between land and building is essential for both the lessee and lessor. The lease involving the land should **always** be accounted for as an operating lease. Under US GAAP, the lease involving the building(s) must meet either the 75% (of useful life) or 90% (of fair value) test to be treated as a capital lease. If neither of the two criteria is met, the building(s) will also be accounted for as an operating lease.

Lessor accounting. The lessor's accounting depends on whether the lease transfers ownership, contains a bargain purchase option, or does neither of the two. If the lease transfers ownership and gives rise to dealer's profit (or loss), US GAAP requires that the lessor classify the lease as a sales-type lease and account for the lease as a single unit under the provisions of FAS 66 in the same manner as a seller of the same property. If the lease transfers ownership, meets both the collectibility and no important uncertainties criteria, but does not give rise to dealer's profit (or loss), the lease should be accounted for as a direct financing or leveraged lease as appropriate.

If the lease contains a bargain purchase option and gives rise to dealer's profit (or loss), the lease should be classified as an operating lease. If the lease contains a bargain purchase option, meets both the collectibility and no material uncertainties criteria, but does not give rise to dealer's profit (or loss), the lease should be accounted for as a direct financing lease or a leveraged lease, as appropriate.

If the lease agreement neither transfers ownership nor contains a bargain purchase option, the lessor should follow the same rules as the lessee in accounting for real estate leases involving land and building(s).

However, the collectibility and the no material uncertainties criteria must be met before the lessor can account for the agreement as a direct financing lease, and in no such case may the lease be classified as a sales-type lease (i.e., ownership must be transferred).

The treatment of a lease involving both land and building can be illustrated in the following examples.

Example of accounting for land and building lease containing transfer of title

Assume the following:

1. The lessee enters into a ten-year noncancelable lease for a parcel of land and a building for use in its operations. The building has an estimated useful life of 12 years.
2. The FMV of the land is €75,000, while the FMV of the building is €310,000.
3. A payment of €50,000 is due to the lessor at the beginning of each of the 10 years of the lease.
4. The lessee's incremental borrowing rate is 10%. (Lessor's implicit rate is unknown.)
5. Ownership will transfer to the lessee at the end of the lease.

The present value of the minimum lease payments is €337,951 (€50,000 × 6.75902*). The portion of the present value of the minimum lease payments that should be capitalized for each of the two components of the lease is computed as follows:

FMV of land			€ 75,000		
FMV of building			310,000		
Total FMV of leased property			€385,000		
Portion of PV allocated to land	€337,951	×	$\dfrac{75,000}{385,000}$	=	€ 65,835
Portion of PV allocated to building	€337,951	×	$\dfrac{310,000}{385,000}$	=	272,116
Total PV to be capitalized					€337,951

The entry made to record the lease initially is as follows:

Leased land	65,835	
Leased building	272,116	
Lease obligation		337,951

*6.75902 is the PV of an annuity due for ten periods at 10%.

Subsequently, the obligation will be decreased in accordance with the effective interest method. The leased building will be amortized over its expected useful life.

Example of accounting for land and building lease without transfer of title or bargain purchase option

Assume the same facts as in the previous example except that title does not transfer at the end of the lease.

The lease is still a capital lease because the lease term is more than 75% of the useful life. Since the FMV of the land is less than 25% of the leased properties in aggregate, (€75,000/€385,000 = 19%), the land component is considered immaterial and the lease will be accounted for as a single lease. The entry to record the lease is as follows:

Leased property	337,951	
Lease obligation		337,951

Assume the same facts as in the previous example except that the FMV of the land is €110,000 and the FMV of the building is €275,000. Once again, title does not transfer.

Because the FMV of the land exceeds 25% of the leased properties in aggregate (€110,000/€385,000 = 28%), the land component is considered material and the lease would be separated into two components. The annual minimum lease payment attributed to the land is computed as follows:

$$\frac{\text{FMV of land}}{\text{PV factor}} \quad \frac{€100,000}{6.75902^*} = €16,275$$

The remaining portion of the annual payment is attributed to the building.

Annual payment	€ 50,000
Less amount attributed to land	(16,275)
Annual payment attributed to building	€33,725

The present value of the minimum annual lease payments attributed to the building is then computed as follows:

Minimum annual lease payment attributed to building	€ 33,725
PV factor	× 6.75902*
PV of minimum annual lease payments attributed to building	€227,948

The entry to record the capital portion of the lease is as follows:

Leased building	227,948	
Lease obligation		227,948

*6.75902 is the PV of an annuity due for ten periods at 10%.

There would be no computation of the present value of the minimum annual lease payment attributed to the land since the land component of the lease will be treated as an operating lease. For this reason, each year, €16,275 of the €50,000 lease payment will be recorded as land rental expense. The remainder of the annual payment (€33,725) will be applied against the lease obligation using the effective interest method.

Leases involving real estate and equipment. When real estate leases also involve equipment or machinery, the equipment component should be separated and accounted for as a separate lease agreement by both lessees and lessors. According to US GAAP, "the portion of the minimum lease payments applicable to the equipment element of the lease shall be estimated by whatever means are appropriate in the circumstances." The lessee and lessor should apply the capitalization requirements to the equipment lease independently of accounting for the real estate lease(s). The real estate leases should be handled as discussed in the preceding two sections. In a sale-leaseback transaction involving real estate with equipment, the equipment and land are not separated.

Leases involving only part of a building. It is common to find lease agreements that involve only part of a building, as, for example, when a floor of an office building is leased or when a store in a shopping mall is leased. A difficulty that arises in this situation is that the cost and/or fair market value of the leased portion of the whole may not be determinable objectively.

For the lessee, if the fair value of the leased property is objectively determinable, the lessee should follow the rules and account for the lease as described in "leases involving land and building." If the fair value of the leased property cannot be determined objectively but the agreement satisfies the 75% test, the estimated economic life of the building in which the leased premises are located should be used. If this test is not met, the lessee should account for the agreement as an operating lease.

From the lessor's position, both the cost and fair value of the leased property must be objectively determinable before the procedures described under "leases involving land and building" will apply. If either the cost or the fair value cannot be determined objectively, the lessor should account for the agreement as an operating lease.

Termination of a Lease

The lessor shall remove the remaining net investment from his or her books and record the leased equipment as an asset at the lower of its original cost, present fair value, or current carrying value. The net adjustment is reflected in the income of the current period.

The lessee is also affected by the terminated agreement because he or she has been relieved of the obligation. If the lease is a capital lease, the lessee should remove both the obligation and the asset from his or her accounts and charge any adjustment to the current period income. If accounted for as an operating lease, no accounting adjustment is required.

Renewal or Extension of an Existing Lease

The renewal or extension of an existing lease agreement affects the accounting of both the lessee and the lessor. US GAAP specifies two basic situations in this regard: (1) the renewal occurs and makes a residual guarantee or penalty provision inoperative or (2) the renewal agreement does not do the foregoing and the renewal is to be treated as a new agreement. The accounting treatment prescribed under the latter situation for a lessee is as follows:

1. If the renewal or extension is classified as a capital lease, the (present) current balances of the asset and related obligation should be adjusted by an amount equal to the difference between the present value of the future minimum lease payments un-

der the revised agreement and the (present) current balance of the obligation. The present value of the minimum lease payments under the revised agreement should be computed using the interest rate that was in effect at the inception of the original lease.

2. If the renewal or extension is classified as an operating lease, the current balances in the asset and liability accounts are removed from the books and a gain (loss) recognized for the difference. The new lease agreement resulting from a renewal or extension is accounted for in the same manner as other operating leases.

Under the same circumstances, US GAAP prescribes the following treatment to be followed by the lessor:

1. If the renewal or extension is classified as a direct financing lease, then the existing balances of the lease receivable and the estimated residual value accounts should be adjusted for the changes resulting from the revised agreement.

    NOTE: Remember that an upward adjustment of the estimated residual value is not allowed.

    The net adjustment should be charged or credited to an unearned income account.

2. If the renewal or extension is classified as an operating lease, the remaining net investment under the existing sales-type lease or direct financing lease is removed from the books and the leased asset recorded as an asset at the lower of its original cost, present fair value, or current carrying amount. The difference between the net investment and the amount recorded for the leased asset is charged to income of the period. The renewal or extension is then accounted for as for any other operating lease.

3. If the renewal or extension is classified as a sales-type lease *and* it occurs at or near the end of the existing lease term, the renewal or extension should be accounted for as a sales-type lease.

    NOTE: A renewal or extension that occurs in the last few months of an existing lease is considered to have occurred at or near the end of the existing lease term.

If the renewal or extension causes the guarantee or penalty provision to be inoperative, the lessee adjusts the current balance of the leased asset and the lease obligation to the present value of the future minimum lease payments (according to the relevant standard, "by an amount equal to the difference between the PV of future minimum lease payments under the revised agreement and the present balance of the obligation"). The PV of the future minimum lease payments is computed using the implicit rate used in the original lease agreement.

Given the same circumstances, the lessor adjusts the existing balance of the lease receivable and estimated residual value accounts to reflect the changes of the revised agreement (remember, no upward adjustments to the residual value). The net adjustment is charged (or credited) to unearned income.

Leases between Related Parties

Leases between related parties are classified and accounted for as though the parties are unrelated, except in cases where it is clear that the terms and conditions of the agreement have been influenced significantly by the fact of the relationship. When this is the case, the classification and/or accounting is modified to reflect the true economic substance of the transaction rather than the legal form.

If a subsidiary's principal business activity is leasing property to its parent or other affiliated companies, consolidated financial statements are presented. The US GAAP standard on related parties requires that the nature and extent of leasing activities between related parties be disclosed.

TREATMENT OF SELECTED ITEMS IN ACCOUNTING FOR LEASES UNDER US GAAP

	Lessor		Lessee	
	Operating	Direct financing and sales-type	Operating	capital
Initial direct costs	Capitalize and amortize over lease term in proportion to rent revenue recognized (normally SL basis)	Direct financing: Record in separate account; Add to net investment in lease; Compute new effective rate that equates gross amt. of min. lease payments and unguar. residual value with net invest. Amortize so as to produce constant rate of return over lease term. Sales-type: Expense in period incurred	N/A	N/A
Investment tax credit retained by lessor	N/A	Reduces FMV of leased asset for 90% test	N/A	Reduces FMV of leased asset for 90% test
Bargain purchase option	N/A	Include in: Minimum lease payments 90% test	N/A	Include in: Minimum lease payments 90% test
Guaranteed residual value	N/A	Include in: Minimum lease payments 90% test Sales-type: Include PV in sales revenues	N/A	Include in: Minimum lease payments 90% test
Unguaranteed residual value	N/A	Include In: "Gross Investment in Lease" Not included in: 90% test Sales-type: Exclude from sales revenue Deduct PV from cost of sales	N/A	Include in: Minimum lease payments 90% test
Contingent rentals	Revenue in period earned	Not part of minimum lease payments; revenue in period earned	Expense in period incurred	Not part of minimum lease payments; expense in period incurred
Amortization period	Amortize down to estimated residual value over estimated economic life of asset	N/A	N/A	Amortize down to estimated residual value over lease term or estimated economic life[c]
Revenue (expense)[a]	Rent revenue (normally SL basis) Amortization (depreciation expense)	Direct financing: Interest revenue on net investment in lease (gross investment less unearned interest income) Sales-type: Dealer profit in period of sale (sales revenue less cost of leased asset) Interest revenue on net investment in lease	Rent expense (normally SL basis)[b]	Interest expense and depreciation expense

[a] Elements of revenue (expense) listed for the items above are not repeated here (e.g., treatment of initial direct costs).

[b] If payments are not on a SL basis, recognize rent expense on a SL basis unless another systematic and rational method is more representative of use benefit obtained from the property, in which case, the other method should be used.

[c] If lease has automatic passage of title or bargain purchase option, use estimated economic life; otherwise, use the lease term.

Accounting for Leases in a Business Combination

A business combination, in and of itself, has no effect on the classification of a lease. However, if, in connection with a business combination, the lease agreement is modified to change the original classification of the lease, it should be considered a new agreement and reclassified according to the revised provisions.

In most cases, a business combination that is accounted for by the pooling-of-interest method or by the purchase method will not affect the previous classification of a lease unless the provisions have been modified as indicated in the preceding paragraph.

The acquiring company should apply the following procedures to account for a leveraged lease in a business combination accounted for by the purchase method:

1. The classification of leveraged lease should be kept.
2. The net investment in the leveraged lease should be given a fair market value (present value, net of tax) based on the remaining future cash flows. Also, the estimated tax effects of the cash flows should be given recognition.
3. The net investment should be broken down into three components: net rentals receivable, estimated residual value, and unearned income.
4. Thereafter, the leveraged lease should be accounted for as described above in the section on leveraged leases.

Sale or Assignment to Third Parties—Nonrecourse Financing

The sale or assignment of a lease or of property subject to a lease that was originally accounted for as a sales-type lease or a direct financing lease will not affect the original accounting treatment of the lease. Any profit or loss on the sale or assignment should be recognized at the time of transaction except under the following two circumstances:

1. When the sale or assignment is between related parties, apply the provisions presented above under "Leases between Related Parties."
2. When the sale or assignment is with recourse, it should be accounted for using the provisions of the US GAAP standard on sale of receivables with recourse.

The sale of property subject to an operating lease should not be treated as a sale if the seller (or any related party to the seller) retains substantial risks of ownership in the leased property. A seller may retain substantial risks of ownership by various arrangements. For example, if the lessee defaults on the lease agreement or if the lease terminates, the seller may arrange to do one of the following:

1. Acquire the property or the lease
2. Substitute an existing lease
3. Secure a replacement lessee or a buyer for the property under a remarketing agreement

A seller will not retain substantial risks of ownership by arrangements where one of the following occurs:

1. A remarketing agreement includes a reasonable fee to be paid to the seller
2. The seller is not required to give priority to the releasing or disposition of the property owned by the third party over similar property owned by the seller

When the sale of property subject to an operating lease is not accounted for as a sale because the substantial risk factor is present, it should be accounted for as a borrowing. The proceeds from the sale should be recorded as an obligation on the seller's books. Rental payments made by the lessee under the operating lease should be recorded as revenue by the seller even if the payments are paid to the third-party purchaser. The seller shall account for each rental payment by allocating a portion to interest expense (to be imputed in accordance with the provisions of APB 21), and the remainder will reduce the existing obligation. Other normal accounting procedures for operating leases should be applied except that the depreciation term for the leased asset is limited to the amortization period of the obligation.

The sale or assignment of lease payments under an operating lease by the lessor should be accounted for as a borrowing as described above.

Nonrecourse financing is a common occurrence in the leasing industry whereby the stream of lease payments on a lease is discounted on a nonrecourse basis at a financial institution with the lease payments collateralizing the debt. The proceeds are then used to finance future leasing transactions. Even though the discounting is on a nonrecourse basis, US GAAP prohibits the offsetting of the debt against the related lease receivable unless a legal right of offset exists or the lease qualified as a leveraged lease at its inception.

Money-Over-Money Lease Transactions

In cases where a lessor obtains nonrecourse financing in excess of the leased asset's cost, a technical bulletin states that the borrowing and leasing are separate transactions and should not be offset against each other unless a right of offset exists. Only dealer profit in sales-type leases may be recognized at the beginning of the lease term.

Acquisition of Interest in Residual Value

Recently, there has been an increase in the acquisition of interests in residual values of leased assets by companies whose primary business is other than leasing or financing. This generally occurs through the outright purchase of the right to own the leased asset or the right to receive the proceeds from the sale of a leased asset at the end of its lease term.

In instances such as these, the rights should be recorded by the purchaser at the fair value of the assets surrendered. Recognition of increases in the value of the interest in the residual (i.e., residual value accretion) to the end of the lease term are prohibited. However, a nontemporary write-down of the residual value interest should be recognized as a loss. This guidance also applies to lessors who sell the related minimum lease payments but retain the interest in the residual value. Guaranteed residual values also have no effect on this guidance.

Accounting for a Sublease

A sublease is used to describe the situation where the original lessee re-leases the leased property to a third party (the sublessee), and the original lessee acts as a sublessor. Normally, the nature of a sublease agreement does not affect the original lease agreement, and the original lessee/sublessor retains primary liability.

The original lease remains in effect, and the original lessor continues to account for the lease as before. The original lessee/sublessor accounts for the lease as follows:

1. If the original lease agreement transfers ownership or contains a bargain purchase option and if the new lease meets any one of the four criteria specified in US GAAP (i.e., transfers ownership, BPO, the 75% test, or the 90% test) and both the collectibility and uncertainties criteria, the sublessor should classify the new lease as a sales-type or direct financing lease; otherwise, as an operating lease. In either situation, the original lessee/sublessor should continue accounting for the original lease obligation as before.

2. If the original lease agreement does not transfer ownership or contain a bargain purchase option, but it still qualified as a capital lease, the original lessee/sublessor

should (with one exception) apply the usual criteria set by US GAAP in classifying the new agreement as a capital or operating lease. If the new lease qualifies for capital treatment, the original lessee/sublessor should account for it as a direct financing lease, with the unamortized balance of the asset under the original lease being treated as the cost of the leased property. The one exception arises when the circumstances surrounding the sublease suggest that the sublease agreement was an important part of a predetermined plan in which the original lessee played only an intermediate role between the original lessor and the sublessee. In this situation, the sublease should be classified by the 75% and 90% criteria as well as collectibility and uncertainties criteria. In applying the 90% criterion, the fair value for the leased property will be the fair value to the original lessor at the inception of the original lease. Under all circumstances, the original lessee should continue accounting for the original lease obligation as before. If the new lease agreement (sublease) does not meet the capitalization requirements imposed for subleases, the new lease should be accounted for as an operating lease.

3. If the original lease is an operating lease, the original lessee/sublessor should account for the new lease as an operating lease and account for the original operating lease as before.

APPENDIX B

LEVERAGED LEASES UNDER US GAAP

One of the most complex accounting subjects regarding leases is the accounting for a leveraged lease. Once again, as with both sales-type and direct financing, the classification of the lease by the lessor has no effect on the accounting treatment accorded the lease by the lessee. The lessee simply treats it as any other lease and thus is interested only in whether the lease qualifies as an operating or a capital lease. The lessor's accounting problem is substantially more complex than that of the lessee.

Leveraged leases are not directly addressed under IFRS. However, such three-party leasing transactions may be encountered occasionally. This guidance under US GAAP is therefore offered to fill a void in IFRS literature.

To qualify as a leveraged lease, a lease agreement must meet the following requirements, and the lessor must account for the investment tax credit (when in effect) in the manner described below.

NOTE: Failure to do so will result in the lease being classified as a direct financing lease.

1. The lease must meet the definition of a direct financing lease. (The 90% of FMV criterion does not apply.)[1]
2. The lease must involve at least three parties.
   a. An owner-lessor (equity participant)
   b. A lessee
   c. A long-term creditor (debt participant)
3. The financing provided by the creditor is nonrecourse as to the general credit of the lessor and is sufficient to provide the lessor with substantial leverage.
4. The lessor's net investment (defined below) decreases in the early years and increases in the later years until it is eliminated.

The last characteristic (item 4) poses the accounting problem.

The leveraged lease arose as a result of an effort to maximize the tax benefits associated with a lease transaction. To accomplish this, it was necessary to involve a third party to the lease transaction (in addition to the lessor and lessee), a long-term creditor. The following diagram illustrates the existing relationships in a leveraged lease agreement:

The leveraged lease arrangement*

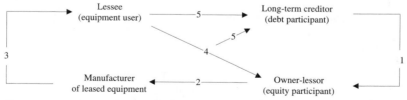

* *Adapted from "A Straightforward Approach to Leveraged Leasing" by Pierce R. Smith, **The Journal of Commercial Bank Lending**, July 1973, pp. 40-47.*

---

[1] *A direct financing lease must have its cost or carrying value equal to the fair value of the asset at the inception of the lease. Thus, even if the amounts are not significantly different, leveraged lease accounting should not be used.*

1. The owner-lessor secures long-term financing from the creditor, generally in excess of 50% of the purchase price. US GAAP indicates that the lessor must be provided with sufficient leverage in the transaction; thus the 50%.
2. The owner then uses this financing along with his or her own funds to purchase the asset from the manufacturer.
3. The manufacturer delivers the asset to the lessee.
4. The lessee remits the periodic rent to the lessor.
5. The debt is guaranteed by either using the equipment as collateral, the assignment of the lease payments, or both, depending on the demands established by the creditor.

The FASB concluded that the entire lease agreement be accounted for as a single transaction and not a direct financing lease plus a debt transaction. The feeling was that the latter did not readily convey the net investment in the lease to the user of the financial statements. Thus, the lessor is to record the investment as a net amount. The gross investment is calculated as a combination of the following amounts:

1. The rentals receivable from the lessee, net of the principal and interest payments due to the long-term creditor
2. A receivable for the amount of the investment tax credit (ITC) to be realized on the transaction (repealed in the United States but may yet exist in other jurisdictions)
3. The estimated residual value of the leased asset
4. The unearned and deferred income, consisting of

    a. The estimated pretax lease income (or loss), after deducting initial direct costs, remaining to be allocated to income
    b. The ITC remaining to be allocated to income over the remaining term of the lease

The first three amounts described above are readily obtainable; however, the last amount, the unearned and deferred income, requires additional computations. To derive this amount, it is necessary to create a cash flow (income) analysis by year for the entire lease term. As described in item 4 above, the unearned and deferred income consists of the pretax lease income (Gross lease rentals – Depreciation – Loan interest) and the unamortized investment tax credit. The total of these two amounts for all the periods in the lease term represents the unearned and deferred income at the inception of the lease.

The amount computed as the gross investment in the lease (foregoing paragraphs) less the deferred taxes relative to the difference between pretax lease income and taxable lease income is the net investment for purposes of computing the net income for the period. To compute the periodic net income, another schedule must be completed that uses the cash flows derived in the first schedule and allocates them between income and a reduction in the net investment.

The amount of income is first determined by applying a rate to the net investment. The rate to be used is the rate that will allocate the entire amount of cash flow (income) when applied in the years in which the net investment is positive. In other words, the rate is derived in much the same way as the implicit rate (trial and error), except that only the years in which there is a positive net investment are considered. Thus, income is recognized only in the years in which there is a positive net investment.

The income recognized is divided among the following three elements:

1. Pretax accounting income
2. Amortization of investment tax credit
3. The tax effect of the pretax accounting income

The first two are allocated in proportionate amounts from the unearned and deferred income included in calculation of the net investment. In other words, the unearned and deferred income consists of pretax lease accounting income and any investment tax credit. Each of these is recognized during the period in the proportion that the current period's allocated income is to the total income (cash flow). The last item, the tax effect, is recognized in the tax expense for the year. The tax effect of any difference between pretax lease accounting income and taxable lease income is charged (or credited) to deferred taxes.

When tax rates change, all components of a leveraged lease must be recalculated from the inception of the lease, using the revised after-tax cash flows arising from the revised tax rates.

If, in any case, the projected cash receipts (income) are less than the initial investment, the deficiency is to be recognized as a loss at the inception of the lease. Similarly, if at any time during the lease period the aforementioned method of recognizing income would result in a future period loss, the loss shall be recognized immediately.

This situation may arise as a result of the circumstances surrounding the lease changing. Therefore, any estimated residual value and other important assumptions must be reviewed on a periodic basis (at least annually). Any change is to be incorporated into the income computations; however, there is to be no upward revision of the estimated residual value.

The following example illustrates the application of these principles to a leveraged lease.

Example of simplified leveraged lease

Assume the following:

1. A lessor acquires an asset for €100,000 with an estimated useful life of 3 years in exchange for a €25,000 down payment and a €75,000 3-year note with equal payments due on 12/31 each year. The interest rate is 18%.
2. The asset has no residual value.
3. The PV of an ordinary annuity of €1 for three years at 18% is 2.17427.
4. The asset is leased for 3 years with annual payments due to the lessor on 12/31 in the amount of €45,000.
5. The lessor uses the ACRS method of depreciation for tax purposes and elects to reduce the ITC rate to 4%, as opposed to reducing the depreciable basis.
6. Assume a constant tax rate throughout the life of the lease of 40%.

Chart 1 analyzes the cash flows generated by the leveraged leasing activities. Chart 2 allocates the cash flows between the investment in leveraged leased assets and income from leveraged leasing activities. The allocation requires finding that rate of return which, when applied to the investment balance at the beginning of each year that the investment amount is positive, will allocate the net cash flow fully to net income over the term of the lease. This rate can be found only by a computer program or by an iterative trial-and-error process. The example that follows has a positive investment value in each of the three years, and thus the allocation takes place in each time period. Leveraged leases usually have periods where the investment account turns negative and is below zero.

Allocating principal and interest on the loan payments is as follows:

€75,000 ÷ 2.17427 = €34,494

Year	Payment	Interest 18%	Principal	Balance
Inception of lease	€ --	€ --	€ --	€75,000
1	34,494	13,500	20,994	54,006
2	34,494	9,721	24,773	29,233
3	34,494	5,261	29,233	--

Chart 1

	A	B	C	D	E	F	G	H	I
					Income tax payable (rcvbl.)	Loan principal		Cash flow (A+G-C	Cumulative cash
	Rent	Depr.	Interest on loan	Taxable income (A-B-C)	Dx40%	payments	ITC	-E-F)	flow
Initial	€ --	€ --	€ --	€ --	€ --	€ --	€ --	€(25,000)	€(25,000)
Year 1	45,000	25,000	13,500	6,500	2,600	20,994	4,000	11,906	(13,094)
Year 2	45,000	38,000	9,721	(2,721)	(1,088)	24,773	--	11,594	(1,500)
Year 3	45,000	37,000	5,261	2,739	1,096	29,233	--	9,410	7,910
Total	€135,000	€100,000	€28,482	€ 6,518	€ 2,608	€75,000	€4,000	€ 7,910	

The chart below allocates the cash flows determined above between the net investment in the lease and income. Recall that the income is then allocated between pretax accounting income and the amortization of the investment for credit. The income tax expense for the period is a result of applying the tax rate to the current periodic pretax accounting income.

The amount to be allocated in total in each period is the net cash flow determined in column H above. The investment at the beginning of year 1 is the initial down payment of €25,000. This investment is then reduced on an annual basis by the amount of the cash flow not allocated to income.

Chart 2

	1	2	3	4	5	6	7
		Cash Flow Assumption				Income Analysis	
	Investment beginning of year	Cash flow	Allocated to investment	Allocated to income	Pretax income	Income tax expense	Investment tax credit
Year 1	€25,000	€11,906	€ 7,964	€ 3,942	€3,248	€ 1,300	1,994
Year 2	17,036	11,594	8,908	2,686	2,213	885	1,358
Year 3	8,128	9,410	8,128	1,282	1,057	423	648
		€32,910	€25,000	€7,910	€6,518	€$2,608	€4,000

Rate of return = 15.77%

1. Column 2 is the net cash flow after the initial investment, and columns 3 and 4 are the allocation based on the 15.77% rate of return. The total of column 4 is the same as the total of column H in Chart 1.

2. Column 5 allocates column D in Chart 1 based on the allocations in column 4. Column 6 allocates column E in Chart 1, and column 7 allocates column G in Chart 1 in the same basis.

The journal entries below illustrate the proper recording and accounting for the leveraged lease transaction. The initial entry represents the cash down payment, investment tax credit receivable, the unearned and deferred revenue, and the net cash to be received over the term of the lease.

The remaining journal entries recognize the annual transactions that include the net receipt of cash and the amortization of income.

	Year 1		Year 2		Year 3	
Rents receivable [Chart 1 (A-C-F)]	31,518					
Investment tax credit receivable	4,000					
Cash		25,000				
Unearned and deferred income		10,518				
[Initial investment, Chart 2 (5+7) totals]						
Cash	10,506		10,506		10,506	
Rent receivable		10,506		10,506		10,506

	Year 1	*Year 2*	*Year 3*
[Net for all cash transactions, Chart 1 (A-C-F) line by line for each year]			
Income tax receivable (cash)	4,000		
Investment tax credit receivable		4,000	
Unearned and deferred income	5,242	3,571	1,705
Income from leveraged leases		5,242	3,571	1,705
[Amortization of unearned income, Chart 2 (5+7) line by line for each year]			

The following schedules illustrate the computation of deferred income tax amount. The annual amount is a result of the temporary difference created due to the difference in the timing of the recognition of income for book and tax purposes. The income for tax purposes can be found in column D in Chart 1, while the income for book purposes is found in column 5 of Chart 2. The actual amount of deferred tax is the difference between the tax computed with the temporary difference and the tax computed without the temporary difference. These amounts are represented by the income tax payable or receivable as shown in column E of Chart 1 and the income tax expense as shown in column 6 of Chart 2. A check of this figure is provided by multiplying the difference between book and tax income by the annual rate.

Year 1

Income tax payable	€ 2,600	
Income tax expense	(1,300)	
Deferred income tax (Dr)		€1,300
Taxable income	€ 6,500	
Pretax accounting income	(3,248)	
Difference	€ 3,252	
€3,252 × 40% = €1,300		

Year 2

Income tax receivable	€ 1,088	
Income tax expense	885	
Deferred income tax (Cr)		€1,973
Taxable loss	€ 2,721	
Pretax accounting income	2,213	
Difference	€ 4,934	
€4,934 × 40% = €1,973		

Year 3

Income tax payable	€ 1,096	
Income tax expense	(423)	
Deferred income tax (Dr)		€ 673
Taxable income	€ 2,739	
Pretax accounting income	(1,057)	
Difference	€ 1,682	
€1,682 × 40% = €673		

15 INCOME TAXES

PERSPECTIVE AND ISSUES

Accounting for income taxes is complicated by the fact that, in most jurisdictions, the amounts of revenues and expenses recognized in a given period for taxation purposes will not correspond to what is reported under GAAP (whether the various national GAAP or IFRS). The matching principle (still relevant, although no longer a central concept affecting financial reporting) implies that for financial reporting purposes the amount presented as current period tax expense should relate appropriately to the amount of pretax accounting income being reported. That expense would rarely if ever equal the current period's tax payment obligation. The upshot is that deferred income tax assets and/or liabilities must be recognized, being measured, approximately, as the difference between the amounts currently owed and the amounts recognizable for financial reporting purposes.

Under the provisions of IAS 12, which was substantially revised as effective in 1998 (with further limited revisions made in 2000), the *liability method* of computing interperiod income tax allocation is required. This method is oriented toward the balance sheet and has as its highest objective the accurate, appropriate measurement of assets and liabilities—specifically, toward the appropriate representation of deferred tax benefits and obligations as assets and liabilities meeting the definitions set forth by the IASB's *Framework*. In order to achieve this, at each balance sheet date the amounts in the deferred tax asset and/or liability accounts are to be assessed, with the necessary adjustment(s) made to achieve the correct balance(s) to be reported in the tax provisions for the period.

Under revised IAS 12, deferred tax assets and liabilities are to be presented at the amounts which are expected to flow to or from the reporting entity when the benefits are ultimately realized or the obligations are settled. IAS 12 makes no significant distinction between operation losses and other types of deductible temporary differences, and requires that both be given recognition, when realization is deemed to be probable. Discounting of these amounts to present values is not permitted, as the standard setters continue to debate the role of discounting in the presentation of assets and liabilities on the balance sheet.

Both deferred tax assets and liabilities are measured by reference to expected tax rates, which in general are defined as being the enacted, effective rates as of the balance sheet date. IAS 12 also has altered the criteria to be used for the recognition of the tax effects of temporary differences arising from ownership interests in investees and subsidiaries, and for the accounting related to goodwill and negative goodwill arising from business acquisitions. Presentation of deferred tax assets or liabilities as current assets or liabilities is prohibited. Extensive disclosures have been mandated by IAS 12, as set forth in this chapter.

Sources of IFRS
IAS 12   *SIC* 21, 25

DEFINITIONS OF TERMS

Accounting profit. Net profit or loss for the reporting period before deducting income tax expense.

Current tax expense (benefit). The amount of income taxes payable (recoverable) in respect of the taxable profit (tax loss) for a period.

Deductible temporary differences. Temporary differences that result in amounts that are deductible in determining future taxable profit when the carrying amount of the asset or liability is recovered or settled.

Deferred tax asset. The amounts of income taxes recoverable in future periods in respect of deductible temporary differences, carryforwards of unused tax losses, and carryforwards of unused tax credits.

Deferred tax expense (benefit). The change during a reporting period in the deferred tax liabilities and deferred tax assets of an entity.

Deferred tax liability. The amounts of income taxes payable in future periods in respect of taxable temporary differences.

Gains and losses included in nonowner movements in equity but excluded from net income. Certain items which, under IFRS, are events occurring currently but which are reported directly in equity, such as changes in market values of available-for-sale portfolios of marketable equity securities.

Interperiod tax allocation. The process of apportioning income tax expense among reporting periods without regard to the timing of the actual cash payments for taxes. The objective is to reflect fully the tax consequences of all economic events reported in current or prior financial statements and, in particular, to report the expected tax effects of the reversals of temporary differences existing at the reporting date.

Operating loss carryback or carryforward. The excess of tax deductions over taxable income. To the extent that this results in a carryforward (to be offset against future periods' taxable income under local laws), the tax effect thereof is included in the entity's deferred tax asset, unless this is not expected to be realized.

Permanent differences. Differences between accounting profit and taxable profit as a result of the treatment accorded certain transactions by the income tax regulations which differs from the accounting treatment. Permanent differences will not reverse in subsequent periods, and accordingly, do not create a need for deferred tax recognition.

Tax basis. The amount attributable (explicitly or implicitly) to an asset or liability by the taxation authorities in determining taxable profit.

Tax credits. Reductions in the tax liability as a result of certain expenditures accorded special treatment under the tax regulations.

Tax expense. The aggregate of current tax expense and deferred tax expense for a reporting period.

Taxable profit (loss). The profit (loss) for a taxable period, determined in accordance with the rules established by the pertinent taxing authorities, which determine income taxes payable (recoverable).

Taxable temporary differences. Temporary differences that result in taxable amounts in determining taxable profit of future periods when the carrying amount of the asset or liability is recovered or settled.

Temporary differences. The differences between tax and financial reporting bases of assets and liabilities that will result in taxable or deductible amounts in future periods. Temporary differences include "timing differences" as previously defined under IFRS as well as certain other differences, such as those arising from business combinations. There are some temporary differences that cannot be associated with particular assets or liabilities, but nonetheless do result from events that received financial statement recognition, and will have tax effects in future periods.

Unrecognized tax benefits. Deferred tax benefits that have not been recognized because they are not deemed probable of being realized.

CONCEPTS, RULES, AND EXAMPLES

Basic Concepts of Interperiod Income Tax Allocation

Over the years, various theories have been advanced regarding the appropriate reporting of income tax expense when there are differences in the timing of recognition of revenue and expense for tax and financial reporting purposes. The most popular of these were the deferral method and the liability method. (A third approach, the "net of tax" method, for a time received a moderate amount of academic support but was far less widely employed [or understood] by practitioners; its only actual widespread use was as a valuation technique to record assets and liabilities acquired in purchase business combinations.)

The deferral method, which was widely employed from the 1960s until about 1990, was soundly based on the matching principle and was never misrepresented as being designed to produce an accurate balance sheet. However, in practice the deferral method suffered from great complexity and sometimes also resulted in material distortions of the balance sheet. This was considered an acceptable, if regrettable, side effect, particularly during the late 1960s and 1970s, a period when more attention was directed at income measurement than at meaningfulness of corporate balance sheets.

Following the adoption of the IASC's *Framework*, which now serves as the conceptual underpinning for accounting standards promulgated by IASB, it was inevitable that substantial changes in accounting for income taxes would be made. That follows because the deferred charges and credits resulting from the application of the deferral method (as had been permitted by the original IAS 12) were generally not true assets or liabilities, as defined by the *Framework*. Accordingly, it became indefensible to continue to place these items on the balance sheet. The liability method (explained below), which completely avouids this problem, became the method of choice.

A separate but also important debate had long existed regarding which items of timing differences for which deferred tax effects were to be presented. At one extreme were proponents of no allocation, who favored reporting only the amount of taxes currently payable as income tax expense in the financial statements. Occupying the middle ground were advocates of partial allocation, who accepted the need to provide deferred taxes, but only for those timing differences whose ultimate reversal could be reasonably predicted. At the other extreme were those favoring comprehensive allocation, which holds that deferred tax effects are to be reported for all timing differences, even if ultimate reversal is far in the future or cannot be predicted at all. Reported net income would often vary markedly depending on which of these approaches were employed.

This debate was effectively resolved in 1979 when an earlier revision of IAS 12 decreed the need for comprehensive allocation, albeit with exceptions for a few items for which the tax effects were deemed not likely to reverse within three years. That version of IAS 12 did permit the utilization of either the deferral or the liability method, which are of course based on diametrically opposed theories. Partially for that reason, the standard was viewed as being flawed, as it, in common with many early IFRS, attempted to find the virtue in each of the major approaches used by various national GAAP at that time.

IASC's goal was to ultimately narrow the range of alternatives that would be deemed acceptable in accounting for given economic events, and it has accomplished that with regard to income tax accounting. The current version of IAS 12 clearly demands that the liability method be employed, using comprehensive allocation, with no alternative methodologies being permitted.

Measurement of Tax Expense

Current tax expense. Income tax expense will be comprised of two components: current tax expense and deferred tax expense. Either of these can be a benefit (i.e., a credit amount in the income statement), rather than an expense (a debit), depending on whether there is taxable profit or loss for the period. For convenience, the term "tax expense" will be used to denote either an expense or a benefit. Current tax expense is easily understood as the tax effect of the entity's reported taxable income or loss for the period, as determined by relevant rules of the various taxing authorities to which it is subject. Deferred tax expense, in general terms, arises as the tax effect of timing differences occurring during the reporting period.

Using the liability method, the reporting entity's current period total income tax expense cannot be computed directly (except when there are no temporary differences). Rather, it must be calculated as the sum of the two components: current tax expense and deferred tax expense. This total will not, in general, equal the amount that would be derived by applying the current tax rate to pretax accounting profit. The reason is that deferred tax expense is defined as the change in the deferred tax asset and liability accounts occurring in the current period, and this change may encompass more than the mere effect of the current tax rate times the net temporary differences arising or being reversed in the present reporting period.

IAS 12 has mandated a purely balance sheet oriented approach, much like that imposed under current US GAAP. Thus, it results in the inclusion in current period deferred tax expense the effects of changing tax rates on as-yet-unreversed temporary differences which originated in prior periods. In other words, current period tax expense may include not merely the tax effects of currently reported revenue and expense items, but also certain tax effects of items reported previously.

Although the primary objective of income tax accounting is no longer the proper matching of current period revenue and expenses, the matching principle remains important in financial reporting theory. Therefore, the tax effects of items excluded from the income statement are also excluded from the income statement. This is referred to as *intraperiod* tax allocation, and is to be distinguished from the *interperiod* allocation that is the major subject of IAS 12 and of this chapter.

An Overview of the Liability Method

The liability method is balance sheet oriented. The primary goal of the liability method is to present the estimated actual taxes to be payable in current and future periods as the income tax liability on the balance sheet. (This equally applies in the case of current and future tax refunds.) To accomplish this goal it is necessary to consider the effect of certain enacted future changes in the tax rates when computing the current period's tax provision. The computation of the amount of deferred taxes is based on the rate expected to be in effect when the temporary differences reverse. The annual computation is considered a tentative estimate of the liability (or asset) that is subject to change as the statutory tax rate changes or as the taxpayer moves into other tax rate brackets.

The IASB's *Framework* defines liabilities as obligations resulting from past transactions and involving "giving up resources embodying economic benefits in order to satisfy the claim of [another] party." Assets are defined as "the potential to contribute, directly or indirectly, to the flow of cash . . . to the enterprise." The fact that the deferred debits and credits generated through the use of the formerly-permitted deferral method did not meet the definitions of assets and liabilities prescribed by the *Framework* was one of the primary reasons for the IASC's mid-1990s reconsideration of IAS 12, which culminated in the issuance of the 1996 revision to IAS 12.

Application of the liability method is, in concept at least, relatively simple when compared to the deferral method. Unlike the deferral method, there is no need to maintain a historical record of the timing of origination of the various unreversed differences, since the effective rates at which the various components were established is not relevant. As the liability method is strictly a balance sheet approach, the primary concern is to state the obligation for taxes payable (or tax benefits receivable) as accurately as possible, based on expected tax impact of future reversals. This is accomplished by multiplying the aggregate unreversed temporary differences, including those originating in the current period, by the tax rate(s) expected to be in effect in the future to determine the expected future liability (or benefit). This expected liability (or benefit) is the amount presented on the balance sheet at the end of the period. The difference between this amount and the amount on the books at the beginning of the period, to greatly simplify the actual process, is the deferred tax expense or benefit to be reported in operating results for the current reporting period.

An example of application of the liability method of deferred income tax accounting follows.

Simplified example of interperiod allocation using the liability method

Ghiza International has no permanent differences in either years 2005 or 2006. The company has only two temporary differences, depreciation and prepaid rent. No consideration is given to the nature of the deferred tax account (i.e., current or long-term) as it is not considered necessary for purposes of this example. Ghiza has a credit balance in its deferred tax account at the beginning of 2005 in the amount of €180,000. This balance consists of €228,000 (€475,000 depreciation temporary difference x 48% tax rate) of deferred taxable amounts and €48,000 (€100,000 prepaid rent temporary difference x 48% tax rate) of deferred deductible amounts.

For purposes of this example, it is assumed that there was a constant effective 48% tax rate in all periods prior to 2005. The pretax accounting income and the temporary differences originating and reversing in 2005 and 2006 are as follows:

Ghiza International

		2005		2006	
Pretax accounting income			€800,000		€1,200,000
Timing differences:					
Depreciation:	originating	€(180,000)		€(160,000)	
	reversing	60,000	(120,000)	100,000	(60,000)
Prepaid rental income:	originating	75,000		80,000	
	reversing	(25,000)	50,000	(40,000)	40,000
Taxable income			€730,000		€1,180,000

The tax rates for years 2005 and 2006 are 46% and 38%, respectively. These rates are assumed to be independent of one another, and the 2006 change in the rate was not known until it took place in 2006.

Computation of tax provision—2005:

Balance of deferred tax account, 1/1/05		
Depreciation (€475,000 x 48%)		€228,000
Prepaid rental income (€100,000 x 48%)		(48,000)
		€180,000
Aggregate temporary differences, 12/31/05		
Depreciation (€475,000 + €120,000)	€595,000	
Prepaid rental income (€100,000 + €50,000)	(150,000)	
	€445,000	
Expected future rate (2005 rate)	x 46%	
Balance required in the deferred tax account, 12/31/05		204,700
Required addition to the deferred tax account		€ 24,700
Income taxes currently payable (€730,000 x 46%)		335,800
Total tax provision		€360,500

Computation of tax provision—2006:

Balance of deferred tax account, 1/1/06		
Depreciation (€595,000 x 46%)		€273,700
Prepaid rental income (€150,000 x 46%)		(69,000)
		€204,700
Aggregate timing differences, 12/31/06		
Depreciation (€595,000 + €60,000)	€655,000	
Prepaid rental income (€150,000 + €40,000)	(190,000)	
	€465,000	
Expected future rate (2006 rate)	x 38%	
Balance required in the deferred tax account, 12/31/06		176,700
Required reduction in the deferred tax account		€ (28,000)
Income taxes currently payable (€1,180,000 x 38%)		448,400
Total tax provision		€420,400

Liability Method Explained in Detail

While conceptually the liability method is straightforward, in practice there are a number of complexities that need to be addressed. In the following discussion, these measurement and reporting issues will be discussed in greater detail.

1. Nature of temporary differences

2. Treatment of operating loss carryforwards
3. Measurement of deferred tax assets and liabilities
4. Valuation allowance for deferred tax assets that are not assured of realization
5. Effect of tax law changes on previously recorded deferred tax assets and liabilities
6. Effect of tax status changes on previously incurred deferred tax assets and liabilities
7. Tax effects of business combinations
8. Intercorporate income tax allocation
9. Exceptions to the general rules of IAS 12

Detailed examples of deferred income tax accounting under IAS 12 are presented throughout the following discussion of these issues.

Nature of Temporary Differences

The preponderance of the typical reporting entity's revenue and expense transactions are treated identically for tax and financial reporting purposes. Some transactions and events, however, will have different tax and accounting implications. In many of these cases, the difference relates to the period in which the income or expense will be recognized. Under earlier iterations of IAS 12, the latter differences were referred to as *timing differences* and were said to originate in one period and to reverse in a later period. Common timing differences included those relating to depreciation methods, deferred compensation plans, percentage-of-completion accounting for long-term construction contracts, and cash versus accrual accounting methods.

The latest revisions to IAS 12 introduced the concept of *temporary differences*, which is a somewhat more comprehensive concept than that of timing differences. Temporary differences include all the categories of items defined under the earlier concept, and add a number of additional items, as well. Temporary differences are thus defined to include *all* differences between the tax and financial reporting bases of assets and liabilities, if those differences will result in taxable or deductible amounts in future years.

Examples of temporary differences that were also deemed to be timing differences under the original IAS 12 are the following:

1. **Revenue recognized for financial reporting purposes before being recognized for tax purposes.** Examples include revenue accounted for by the installment method for tax purposes, but reflected in income currently; certain construction-related revenue recognized on a completed-contract method for tax purposes, but on a percentage-of-completion basis for financial reporting; earnings from investees recognized by the equity method for accounting purposes but taxed only when later distributed as dividends to the investor. These are taxable temporary differences, which give rise to deferred tax liabilities.

2. **Revenue recognized for tax purposes prior to recognition in the financial statements.** These include certain types of revenue received in advance, such as prepaid rental income and service contract revenue. Referred to as deductible temporary differences, these items give rise to deferred tax assets.

3. **Expenses that are deductible for tax purposes prior to recognition in the financial statements.** This results when accelerated depreciation methods or shorter useful lives are used for tax purposes, while straight-line depreciation or longer useful economic lives are used for financial reporting; and when there are certain preoperating costs and certain capitalized interest costs that are deductible currently for tax purposes. These items are taxable temporary differences and give rise to deferred tax liabilities.

4. **Expenses that are reported in the financial statements prior to becoming deductible for tax purposes.** Certain estimated expenses, such as warranty costs, as well as such contingent losses as accruals of litigation expenses, are not tax deductible until the obligation becomes fixed. These are deductible temporary differences, and accordingly give rise to deferred tax assets.

In addition to these familiar and well-understood timing differences, temporary differences include a number of other categories that also involve differences between the tax and financial reporting bases of assets or liabilities. These are

1. **Reductions in tax deductible asset bases arising in connection with tax credits.** Under tax provisions in certain jurisdictions, credits are available for certain qualifying investments in plant assets. In some cases, taxpayers are permitted a choice of either full accelerated depreciation coupled with a reduced investment tax credit, or a full investment tax credit coupled with reduced depreciation allowances. If the taxpayer chose the latter option, the asset basis is reduced for tax depreciation, but would still be fully depreciable for financial reporting purposes. Accordingly, this election would be accounted for as a taxable timing difference, and give rise to a deferred tax liability.

2. **Increases in the tax bases of assets resulting from the indexing of asset costs for the effects of inflation.** Occasionally, proposed and sometimes enacted by taxing jurisdictions, such a tax law provision allows taxpaying entities to finance the replacement of depreciable assets through depreciation based on current costs, as computed by the application of indices to the historical costs of the assets being remeasured. This reevaluation of asset costs gives rise to deductible temporary differences that would be associated with deferred tax benefits.

3. **Certain business combinations accounted for by the acquisition method.** Under certain circumstances, the costs assignable to assets or liabilities acquired in purchase business combinations will differ from their tax bases. The usual scenario under which this arises is when the acquirer must continue to report the predecessor's tax bases for tax purposes, although the price paid was more or less than book value. Such differences may be either taxable or deductible and, accordingly, may give rise to deferred tax liabilities or assets. These differences were treated as timing differences under the original IAS 12, and will now be recognized as temporary differences by revised IAS 12.

4. **Assets which are revalued for financial reporting purposes although the tax bases are not affected.** This is analogous to the matter discussed in the preceding paragraph. Under certain IFRS (such as IAS 16 and IAS 40), assets may be upwardly adjusted to current fair values although for tax purposes these adjustments are ignored until and unless the assets are disposed of. The discrepancies between the adjusted book carrying values and the tax bases are temporary differences under IAS 12, and deferred taxes are to be provided on these variations. This is required even if there is no intention to dispose of the assets in question, or if, under the salient tax laws, exchanges for other similar assets (or reinvestment of proceeds of sales in similar assets) would effect a postponement of the tax obligation.

There are other items that would not have been deemed timing differences under the original IAS 12, but which are temporary differences under revised IAS 12. These include the following:

1. **Assets and liabilities acquired in transactions that are not business combinations which are not deductible or taxable in determining taxable profit.** In some tax jurisdictions, the cost of certain assets are never deductible in computing taxable profit. Depending on jurisdiction, buildings, intangibles, or other assets may not be subject to depreciation or amortization. Thus, the asset in question has a differing accounting basis than tax basis, and this defines a temporary difference under revised IAS 12. Similarly, certain liabilities may not be recognized for tax purposes. While IAS 12 agrees that these represent temporary differences and that, under the principles of interperiod tax allocation using the liability method, this should result in the recognition of deferred tax liabilities or assets, the decision was made to not permit this. The reason given is that the new result would be to "gross up" the recorded amount of the asset or liability to offset the recorded deferred tax liability or benefit, and this would make the financial statements "less transparent." It could also be argued that when an asset has, as one of its attributes, nondeductibility for tax purposes, the price paid for this asset would have been affected accordingly, so that any such "gross-up" would cause the asset to be reported at an amount in excess of fair value.

2. **Assets and liabilities acquired in business combinations.** When assets and liabilities are valued at fair value, as required under IFRS 3, but the tax basis is not adjusted (i.e., there is a carryforward basis for tax purposes), there will be differences between the tax and financial reporting bases of these assets and liabilities, which will constitute temporary differences. Deferred tax benefits and obligations need to be recognized for these differences.

3. **Goodwill that cannot be amortized (deducted) for tax purposes.** Prior to IFRS 3, goodwill was subject to amortization for financial reporting purposes but in some tax jurisdictions this could not be deducted, so there was a question regarding the deferred tax effects to be recognized. Goodwill or negative goodwill were residual amounts, and any attempt to compute the deferred tax effects thereof would have resulted in "grossing up" the financial statement balance of that very account (goodwill or negative goodwill, as the case may be). Although such a presentation could have been rationalized, it would have been of dubious usefulness to the users of the financial statements. For this reason, IAS 12 held that no deferred taxes were to be provided on the difference between the tax and book bases of nondeductible goodwill or nontaxable negative goodwill. Under IFRS 3, goodwill is no longer amortized, and negative goodwill is included in income upon consummating a business acquisition that is deemed a bargain purchase. There is less likely to be any issue of tax/book differences under the current requirements.

Measurement of Deferred Tax Assets and Liabilities

The procedure to compute the gross deferred tax provision (i.e., before addressing whether the deferred tax asset is probable of being realized and therefore should be recognized) is as follows:

1. Identify (i.e., take an inventory of) all temporary differences existing as of the reporting date.
2. Segregate the temporary differences into those that are taxable and those that are deductible. This step is necessary because under IAS 12 only those deferred tax benefits which are probable of being realized are recognized, whereas all deferred obligations are given full recognition.

3. Accumulate information about the *deductible* temporary differences, particularly the net operating loss and credit carryforwards that have expiration dates or other types of limitations.

4. Measure the tax effect of aggregate *taxable* temporary differences by applying the appropriate expected tax rates (federal plus any state, local, and foreign rates that are applicable under the circumstances).

5. Similarly, measure the tax effects of *deductible* temporary differences, including net operating loss carryforwards.

It should be emphasized that separate computations should be made for each tax jurisdiction, since in assessing the propriety of recording the tax effects of deductible temporary differences it is necessary to consider the entity's ability to absorb deferred tax benefits against tax liabilities. Inasmuch as benefits receivable from one tax jurisdiction will not reduce taxes payable to another jurisdiction, separate calculations will be needed. Also, for purposes of balance sheet presentation (discussed below in detail), the offsetting of deferred tax assets and liabilities is permissible only within jurisdictions, since there would never be a legal right to offset obligations due to and from different taxing authorities. Similarly, separate computations should be made for each taxpaying component of the business. Thus, if a parent company and its subsidiaries are consolidated for financial reporting purposes but file separate tax returns, the reporting entity comprises a number of components, and the tax benefits of any one will be unavailable to reduce the tax obligations of the others.

The principles set forth above are illustrated by the following examples.

Basic example of the computation of deferred tax liability and asset

Assume that Noori Company has pretax financial income of €250,000 in 2006, a total of €28,000 of taxable temporary differences, and a total of €8,000 of deductible temporary differences. Noori has no operating loss or tax credit carryforwards. The tax rate is a flat (i.e., not graduated) 40%. Also assume that there were no deferred tax liabilities or assets in prior years.

Taxable income is computed as follows:

Pretax financial income	€250,000
Taxable temporary differences	(28,000)
Deductible temporary differences	8,000
Taxable income	€230,000

The journal entry to record required amounts is

Current income tax expense	92,000	
Deferred tax asset	3,200	
Income tax expense—deferred	8,000	
Deferred tax liability		11,200
Income taxes currently payable		92,000

Current income tax expense and income taxes currently payable are each computed as taxable income times the current rate (€230,000 x 40%). The deferred tax asset of €3,200 represents 40% of deductible temporary differences of €8,000. The deferred tax liability of €11,200 is calculated as 40% of taxable temporary differences of €28,000. The deferred tax expense of €8,000 is the *net* of the deferred tax liability of €11,200 and the deferred tax asset of €3,200.

In 2007, Noori Company has pretax financial income of €450,000, aggregate taxable and deductible temporary differences are €75,000 and €36,000, respectively, and the tax rate remains a flat 40%. Taxable income is €411,000, computed as pretax financial income of €450,000 minus taxable differences of €75,000 plus deductible differences of €36,000. Current income tax expense and income taxes currently payable each are €164,400 (€411,000 x 40%).

Deferred amounts are calculated as follows:

	Deferred tax liability	Deferred tax asset	Income tax expense—deferred
Required balance at 12/31/07			
€75,000 x 40%	€30,000		--
€36,000 x 40%		€14,400	--
Balances at 12/31/06	11,200	3,200	--
Adjustment required	€18,800	€11,200	€7,600

The journal entry to record the deferred amounts is

Deferred tax asset	11,200	
Income tax expense—deferred	7,600	
Deferred tax liability		18,800

Because the *increase* in the liability in 2007 is larger (by €7,600) than the increase in the asset for that year, the result is a deferred tax *expense* for 2007.

Considerations for Recognition of Deferred Tax Assets

Although the case for presentation in the financial statements of any amount computed for deferred tax liabilities is clear, it can be argued that deferred tax assets should be included in the balance sheet only if they are, in fact, very likely to be realized in future periods. Since realization will almost certainly be dependent on the future profitability of the reporting entity, it may become necessary to ascertain the likelihood that the enterprise will be profitable. Absent convincing evidence of that, the concepts of conservatism and realization would suggest that the asset be treated as a contingent gain, and not accorded recognition until and unless ultimately realized.

Under IAS 12, deferred tax assets resulting from temporary differences and from tax loss carryforwards are to be given recognition only if realization is deemed to be *probable*. To operationalize this concept, the standard sets forth several criteria, which variously apply to deferred tax assets arising from temporary differences and from tax loss carryforwards. The standard establishes that

1. It is *probable* that future taxable profit will be available against which a deferred tax asset arising from a deductible temporary difference can be utilized when there are sufficient taxable temporary differences relating to the same taxation authority which will reverse either

   a. In the same period as the reversal of the deductible temporary difference, or
   b. In periods into which the deferred tax asset can be carried back or forward; or

2. If there are insufficient taxable temporary differences relating to the same taxation authority, it is probable that the enterprise will have taxable profits in the same period as the reversal of the deductible temporary difference or in periods to which the deferred tax can be carried back or forward, or there are tax planning opportunities available to the enterprise that will create taxable profit in appropriate periods.

Thus, there necessarily will be an element of judgment in making an assessment about how probable the realization of the deferred tax asset is, for those circumstances in which there is not an existing balance of deferred tax liability equal to or greater than the amount of the deferred tax asset. If it cannot be concluded that realization is probable, the deferred tax asset is not given recognition.

As a practical matter, there are a number of positive and negative factors which may be evaluated in reaching a conclusion as to amount of the deferred tax asset to be recognized. Positive factors (those suggesting that the full amount of the deferred tax asset associated with the gross temporary difference should be recorded) might include

1. Evidence of sufficient future taxable income, exclusive of reversing temporary differences and carryforwards, to realize the benefit of the deferred tax asset
2. Evidence of sufficient future taxable income arising from the reversals of existing taxable temporary differences (deferred tax liabilities) to realize the benefit of the tax asset
3. Evidence of sufficient taxable income in prior year(s) available for realization of an operating loss carryback under existing statutory limitations
4. Evidence of the existence of prudent, feasible tax planning strategies under management control which, if implemented, would permit the realization of the tax asset. These are discussed in greater detail below.
5. An excess of appreciated asset values over their tax bases, in an amount sufficient to realize the deferred tax asset. This can be thought of as a subset of the tax strategies idea, since a sale or sale/leaseback of appreciated property is once rather obvious tax planning strategy to salvage a deferred tax benefit which might otherwise expire unused.
6. A strong earnings history exclusive of the loss that created the deferred tax asset. This would, under many circumstances, suggest that future profitability is likely and therefore that realization of deferred tax assets is probable.

Although the foregoing may suggest that the reporting entity will be able to realize the benefits of the deductible temporary differences outstanding as of the balance sheet date, certain negative factors should also be considered in determining whether realization of the full amount of the deferred tax benefit is probable under the circumstances. These factors could include

1. A cumulative recent history of accounting losses. Depending on extent and length of time over which losses were experienced, this could reduce the assessment of likelihood of realization below the important "probable" threshold.
2. A history of operating losses or of tax operating loss or credit carryforwards that have expired unused
3. Losses that are anticipated in the near future years, despite a history of profitable operations

Thus, the process of determining how much of the computed gross deferred tax benefit should be recognized involves the weighing of both positive and negative factors to determine whether, based on the preponderance of available evidence, it is probable that the deferred tax asset will be realized. IAS 12 notes that a history of unused tax losses should be considered "strong evidence" that future taxable profits might prove elusive. In such cases, it would be expected that primary reliance would be placed on the existence of taxable temporary differences which, upon reversal, would provide taxable income to absorb the deferred tax benefits that are candidates for recognition in the financial statements. Absent those taxable temporary differences, recognition would be much more difficult.

Example

To illustrate this computation in a more specific fact situation, assume the following facts:

1. Malpasa Corporation reports on a calendar year and adopted revised IAS 12 in 2004.
2. As of the December 31, 2005 balance sheet, Malpasa has taxable temporary differences of €85,000 relating to depreciation, deductible temporary differences of €12,000 relating to deferred compensation arrangements, a net operating loss carryforward (which arose in 2003) of €40,000, and a capital loss carryover of €10,000. Note that capital losses can only be offset against capital gains (not ordinary income), but may be carried forward until used.

3. Malpasa's expected tax rate for future years is 40% for ordinary income, and 25% for net long-term capital gains.

The first steps are to compute the required balances of the deferred tax asset and liability accounts, without consideration of whether the tax asset would be probable of realization. The computations would proceed as follows:

Deferred tax liability

Taxable temporary difference (depreciation)	€85,000
Effective tax rate	× 40%
Required balance	€34,000

Deferred tax asset

Deductible temporary differences	€12,000
Deferred compensation	40,000
Net operating loss	€52,000
Effective tax rate	× 40%
Required balance (a)	€20,800
Capital loss	€10,000
Effective tax rate	× 25%
Required balance (b)	€2,500

Total deferred tax asset

Ordinary (a)	€20,800
Capital (b)	2,500
Total required balance	€23,300

The next step would be to consider whether realization of the deferred tax asset is probable. Malpasa management must evaluate both positive and negative evidence to determine this matter. Assume now that management identifies the following factors which may be relevant:

1. Before the net operating loss deduction, Malpasa reported taxable income of €5,000 in 2005. Management believes that taxable income in future years, apart from NOL deductions, should continue at about the same level experienced in 2005.
2. The taxable temporary differences are not expected to reverse in the foreseeable future.
3. The capital loss arose in connection with a transaction of a type that is unlikely to recur. The company does not generally engage in activities that have the potential to result in capital gains or losses.
4. Management estimates that certain productive assets have a fair value exceeding their respective tax bases by about €30,000. The entire gain, if realized for tax purposes, would be a recapture of depreciation previously taken. Since the current plans call for a substantial upgrading of the company's plant assets, management feels that it could easily accelerate those actions to realize taxable gains, should it be desirable to do so for tax planning purposes.

Based on the foregoing information, Malpasa Corporation management concludes that a €2,500 adjustment to deferred tax assets is required. The reasoning is as follows:

1. There will be some taxable operating income generated in future years (€5,000 annually, based on the earnings experienced in 2005), which will absorb a modest portion of the reversal of the deductible temporary difference (€12,000) and net operating loss carryforwad (€40,000) existing at year-end 2005.
2. More important, the feasible tax planning strategy of accelerating the taxable gain relating to appreciated assets (€30,000) would certainly be sufficient, in conjunction with operating income over several years, to permit Malpasa to realize the tax benefits of the deductible temporary difference and NOL carryover.
3. However, since capital loss carryovers are only usable to offset future capital gains and Malpasa management is unable to project future realization of capital gains, the associated tax benefit accrued (€2,500) will probably not be realized, and thus cannot be recognized.

Based on this analysis, deferred tax benefits in the amount of €20,800 should be recognized.

The criterion prescribed by IAS 12 is significantly different than that which is employed under the corresponding US GAAP standard, FAS 109. In conformity with that standard, all deferred tax assets are first recorded, after which a valuation allowance or reserve is established to offset that portion which is not deemed "more likely than not" to be realizable. The net effect will be generally similar under either approach, but the consensus opinion is that the US GAAP realization threshold, "more likely than not," represents a somewhat lower boundary than does IAS 12's "probable." While the former is acknowledged to imply a probability of just slightly over 50%, the latter is thought to connote a likelihood in the range of at least 75-80%, or possibly higher. Worded yet another way, it would seemingly be more difficult to support the existence of a valid deferred tax asset under IFRS than under US GAAP rules as they now exist.

Future temporary differences as a source for taxable profit to offset deductible differences. In some instances, an entity may have deferred tax assets that will be realizable when future tax deductions are taken, but it cannot be concluded that there will be sufficient taxable profits to absorb these future deductions. However, the enterprise can reasonably predict that if it continues as a going concern, it will generate other temporary differences such that taxable (if not book) profits will be created. It has indeed been argued that the going concern assumption underlying much of accounting theory is sufficient rationale for the recognition of deferred tax assets in such circumstances.

However, IAS 12 makes it clear that this is not valid reasoning. The new taxable temporary differences anticipated for future periods will themselves reverse in even later periods; these cannot do "double duty" by also being projected to be available to absorb currently existing deductible temporary differences. Thus, in evaluating whether realization of currently outstanding deferred tax benefits is probable, it is appropriate to consider the currently outstanding taxable temporary differences, but not taxable temporary differences which are projected to be created in later periods.

Tax planning opportunities that will help realize deferred tax assets. When an entity has deductible temporary differences and taxable temporary differences pertaining to the same tax jurisdiction, there is a presumption that realization of the relevant deferred tax assets is probable, since the relevant deferred tax liabilities should be available to offset these. However, before concluding that this is valid, it will be necessary to consider further the *timing* of the two sets of reversals. If the deductible temporary differences will reverse, say, in the very near term, and the taxable differences will not reverse for many years, it is a matter for concern that the tax benefits created by the former occurrence may expire unused prior to the latter event occurring. Thus, when the existence of deferred tax obligations serves as the logical basis for the recognition of deferred tax assets, it is also necessary to consider whether, under pertinent tax regulations, the benefit carryforward period is sufficient to assure that the benefit will not be lost to the reporting enterprise.

For example, if the deductible temporary difference is projected to reverse in two years but the taxable temporary difference is not anticipated to occur for another ten years, and the tax jurisdiction in question offers only a five-year tax loss carryforward, then (absent other facts suggesting that the tax benefit is probable of realization) the deferred tax benefit could not be given recognition under IAS 12.

However, the entity might have certain tax planning opportunities available to it, such that the pattern of taxable profits could be altered to make the deferred tax benefit, which might otherwise be lost, probable of realization. For example, again depending on the rules of the salient tax jurisdiction, an election might be made to tax interest income on an accrual rather than a cash received basis, which might accelerate income recognition such that it would be available to offset or absorb the deductible temporary differences. Also, claimed tax deductions might be deferred to later periods, similarly boosting taxable profits in the short term.

More subtly, a reporting entity may have certain assets, such as buildings, which have appreciated in value. It is entirely feasible, in many situations, for an enterprise to take certain steps, such as selling the building to realize the taxable gain thereon and then either leasing back the premises or acquiring another suitable building, to salvage the tax deduction that would otherwise be lost to it due to the expiration of a loss carryforward period. If such a strategy is deemed to be reasonably available, even if the entity does not expect to have to implement it (for example, because it expects other taxable temporary differences to be originated in the interim), it may be used to justify recognition of the deferred tax benefits.

Consider the following example of how an available tax planning strategy might be used to support recognition of a deferred tax asset that otherwise might have to go unrecognized.

Example of the impact of a qualifying tax strategy

Assume that Kirloski Company has a €180,000 operating loss carryforward as of 12/31/06, scheduled to expire at the end of the following year. Taxable temporary differences of €240,000 exist that are expected to reverse in approximately equal amounts of €80,000 in 2007, 2008, and 2009. Kirloski Company estimates that taxable income for 2007 (exclusive of the reversal of existing temporary differences and the operating loss carryforward) will be €20,000. Kirloski Company expects to implement a qualifying tax planning strategy that will accelerate the total of €240,000 of taxable temporary differences to 2007. Expenses to implement the strategy are estimated to approximate €30,000. The applicable expected tax rate is 40%.

In the absence of the tax planning strategy, €100,000 of the operating loss carryforward could be realized in 2007 based on estimated taxable income of €20,000 plus €80,000 of the reversal of taxable temporary differences. Thus, €80,000 would expire unused at the end of 2007 and the net amount of the deferred tax asset at 12/31/07 would be recognized at €40,000, computed as €72,000 (= €180,000 x 40%) minus the valuation allowance of €32,000 (€80,000 x 40%).

However, by implementing the tax planning strategy, the deferred tax asset is calculated as follows:

Taxable income for 2007:	
Expected amount without reversal of taxable temporary differences	€ 20,000
Reversal of taxable temporary differences due to tax planning strategy, net of costs	210,000
	230,000
Operating loss to be carried forward	(180,000)
Operating loss expiring unused at 12/31/07	€ 0

The deferred tax asset to be recorded at 12/31/06 is €54,000. This is computed as follows:

Full benefit of tax loss carryforward €180,000 x 40% =		€72,000
Less:	Net-of-tax effect of anticipated expenses related to implementation of the strategy €30,000 – (€30,000 x 40%) =	18,000
Net		€54,000

Kirloski Company will also recognize a deferred tax liability of €96,000 at the end of 2006 (40% of the taxable temporary differences of €240,000).

Subsequently revised expectations that a deferred tax benefit is realizable. It may happen that, in a given reporting period, a deferred tax asset is deemed not probable of being realized and accordingly is not recognized, but in a later reporting period the judgment is made that the amount is in fact realizable. If this change in expectation occurs, the deferred tax asset previously not recognized will now be recorded. This does not constitute a prior period adjustment because no accounting error occurred. Rather, this is a change in estimate and is to be included in current earnings. Thus, the tax provision in the period when the estimate is revised will be affected.

Similarly, if a deferred tax benefit provision is made in a given reporting period, but later events suggest that the amount is, in whole or in part, not probable of being realized, the provision should be partially or completely reversed. Again, this adjustment will be included in the tax provision in the period in which the estimate is altered, since it is a change in an accounting estimate. Under either scenario the footnotes to the financial statements will need to provide sufficient information for the users to make meaningful interpretations, since the amount reported as tax expense will seemingly bear an unusual relationship to the reported pretax accounting profit for the period.

If the deferred tax provision in a given period is misstated due to a clerical error, such as miscalculation of the effective expected tax rate, this would constitute an accounting error, and this must be accounted for according to IAS 8's provisions; as revised, this standard requires restatement of prior period financial statements and does not permit adjusting opening retained earnings for the effect of the error. Errors are thus distinguished from changes in accounting estimate, as the latter are accounted for prospectively, without restatement of prior period financial statements. Correction of accounting errors is discussed in Chapter 21.

Example: determining the extent to which the deferred tax asset is realizable.

Assume that Zacharias Corporation has a deductible temporary difference of €60,000 at December 31, 2006. The applicable tax rate is a flat 40%. Based on available evidence, management of Zacharias Corporation concludes that it is probable that all sources will not result in future taxable income sufficient to realize more than €15,000 (i.e., 25%) of the deductible temporary difference. Also, assume that there were no deferred tax assets in previous years and that prior years' taxable income was inconsequential.

At 12/31/06 Zacharias Corporation records a deferred tax asset in the amount of €6,000 (= €60,000 x 25% x 40%). The journal entry at 12/31/06 is

Deferred tax asset	6,000	
Income tax benefit—deferred		6,000

The deferred income tax benefit of €6,000 represents the tax effect of that portion of the deferred tax asset (25%) that is probable of being realized. For 2007 assume that Zacharias Corporation's results are

Pretax financial loss	€(32,000)
Reversing deductible differences from 2006	(10,000)
Loss carryforward for tax purposes	€(42,000)

The total of the loss carryforward (€42,000, as computed above) plus the amount of deductible temporary differences from 2006 not reversing in 2007 (€50,000) equals €92,000. Before considering how much of the benefit is probable of being realized, a deferred tax asset of €36,800 (= €92,000 x 40%) is computed at the end of 2007. However, the management of Zacharias Corporation has to consider what portion of this deferred tax asset is probable of being realized. It concludes that it is probable that €25,000 of the tax loss carryforward will *not* be realized. Thus, the net tax loss carryforward that is *probable* of being realized is €92,000 – €25,000 = €67,000, which yields a tax benefit of €26,800 (= €67,000 x 40%).

Since the balance in the deferred tax asset account had been €6,000, the adjustment needed is now as follows. The journal entry at 12/31/07 is

Deferred tax asset	20,800	
Income tax benefit—deferred		20,800

Effect of Tax Law Changes on Previously Recorded Deferred Tax Assets and Liabilities

The balance sheet oriented measurement approach of IAS 12 necessitates the reevaluation of the deferred tax asset and liability balances at each year-end. Although IAS 12 does not directly address the question of changes to tax rates or other provisions of the tax law (e.g., deductibility of items) which may be enacted that will affect the realization of future deferred tax assets or liabilities, the effect of these changes should be reflected in the year-end deferred tax accounts in the period the changes are enacted. The offsetting adjustments should be made through the current period tax provision.

When revised tax rates are enacted, they may affect not only the unreversed effects of items which were originally reported in the continuing operations section of the income statement, but also the unreversed effects of items first presented as extraordinary items or in other income statement captions. Although it might be conceptually superior to report the effects of tax law changes on such unreversed temporary differences in these same income statement captions, as a practical matter the complexities of identifying the diverse treatments of these originating transactions or events would make such an approach unworkable. Accordingly, remeasurements of the effects of tax law changes should generally be reported in the tax provision associated with continuing operations.

Example of the computation of a deferred tax asset with a change in rates

Assume that the Fanuzzi Company has €80,000 of deductible temporary differences at the end of 2005, which are expected to result in tax deductions of approximately €40,000 each on tax returns for 2006-2008. Enacted tax rates are 50% for the years 2001-2005, and 40% for 2006 and thereafter.

The deferred tax asset is computed at 12/31/05 under each of the following independent assumptions:

1. If Fanuzzi Company expects to offset the deductible temporary differences against taxable income in the years 2006-2008, the deferred tax asset is €32,000 (€80,000 x 40%).
2. If Fanuzzi Company expects to realize a tax benefit for the deductible temporary differences by loss carryback refund, the deferred tax asset is €40,000 (= €80,000 x 50%).

Assume that Fanuzzi Company expects to realize a tax asset of €32,000 at the end of 2005. Also assume that taxes payable in each of the years 2001-2004 were €8,000 (or 50% of taxable income). Realization of €24,000 of the €32,000 deferred tax asset is assured through carryback refunds even if no taxable income is earned in the years 2006-2007. Whether some or all of the remaining €8,000 will be recognized depends on Fanuzzi Company's assessment of the levels of future taxable earnings (i.e., whether the probable threshold is exceeded).

The foregoing estimate of the certain tax benefit, based on a loss carryback to periods of higher tax rates than are statutorily in effect for future periods, should be utilized only when future losses (for tax purposes) are expected. This restriction applies since the benefit thus recognized exceeds benefits that would be available in future periods, when tax rates will be lower.

Changes in tax law may affect rates, and may also affect the taxability or deductibility of income or expense items. While the latter type of change occurs infrequently, the impact is similar to the more common tax rate changes.

Example of effect of change in tax law

Leipzig Corporation has, at December 31, 2005, gross receivables of €12,000,000 and an allowance for bad debts in the amount of €600,000. Also assume that expected future taxes will be at a 40% rate. Effective January 1, 2006, the tax law is revised to eliminate deductions for accrued bad debts, with existing allowances required to be taken into income ratably over three years (a three-year spread). A balance sheet of Leipzig Corporation prepared on January 1, 2006, would report a deferred tax benefit in the amount of €240,000 (i.e., €600,000 × 40%, which is the tax effect of future deductions to be taken when specific receivables are written off and bad debts are incurred for tax purposes); a current tax liability of €80,000 (one-third of the tax obligation); and a noncurrent tax liability of €160,000 (two-thirds of the tax obligation). Under the requirements of IAS 12, the deferred tax benefit must be entirely reported as noncurrent in classified balance sheets, inasmuch as no deferred tax benefits or obligations can be shown as current.

Reporting the Effect of Tax Status Changes

Changes in the tax status of the reporting entity should be reported in a manner that is entirely analogous to the reporting of enacted tax law changes. When the tax status change becomes effective, the consequent adjustments to deferred tax assets and liabilities are reported in current tax expense as part of the tax provision relating to continuing operations.

The most commonly encountered changes in status are those attendant to an election, where permitted, to be taxed as a partnership or other flow-through enterprise. (This means that the corporation will not be treated as a taxable entity but rather as an enterprise that "flows through" its taxable income to the owners on a current basis. This favorable tax treatment is available to encourage small businesses, and often will be limited to entities having sales revenue under a particular threshold level, or to entities having no more than a maximum number of shareholders.) Enterprises subject to such optional tax treatment may also request that a previous election be terminated. When a previously taxable corporation becomes a nontaxed corporation, the stockholders become personally liable for taxes on the company's earnings, whether the earnings are distributed to them or not (similar to the relationship among a partnership and its partners).

As issued, IAS 12 did not explicitly address the matter of reporting the effects of a change in tax status, although (as discussed in earlier editions of this book) the appropriate treatment was quite obvious given the underlying concepts of that standard. This ambiguity was subsequently resolved by the issuance of SIC 25, which stipulates that in most cases the current and deferred tax consequences of the change in tax status should be included in net profit or loss for the period in which the change in status occurs. The tax effects of a change in status are included in results of operations because a change in a reporting entity's tax status (or that of its shareholders) does not give rise to increases or decreases in the pretax amounts recognized directly in equity.

The exception to the foregoing general rule arises in connection with those tax consequences which relate to transactions and events that result, in the same or a different period, in a direct credit or charge to the recognized amount of equity. For example, an event that is recognized directly in equity is a change in the carrying amount of property, plant, or equipment revalued under IAS 16. Those tax consequences that relate to change in the recognized amount of equity, in the same or a different period (not included in net profit or loss) should be charged or credited directly to equity.

The most common situation giving rise to a change in tax status would be the election by a corporation, in those jurisdictions where it is permitted to do so, to be taxed as a partnership, trust, or other flow-through entity. If a corporation having a net deferred tax liability elects nontaxed status, the deferred taxes will be eliminated through a credit to current period earnings. That is because what had been an obligation of the corporation has been eliminated (by being accepted directly by the shareholders, typically); a debt thus removed constitutes earnings for the formerly obligated party.

Similarly, if a previously nontaxed corporation becomes a taxable entity, the effect is to assume a net tax benefit or obligation for unreversed temporary differences existing at the date the change becomes effective. Accordingly, the financial statements for the period of such a change will report the effects of the event in the current tax provision. If the entity had at that date many taxable temporary differences as yet unreversed, it would report a large tax expense in that period. Conversely, if it had a large quantity of unreversed deductible temporary differences, a substantial deferred tax benefit (if probable of realization) would need to be recorded, with a concomitant credit to the current period's tax provision in the income statement. Whether eliminating an existing deferred tax balance or recording an initial deferred tax asset or liability, the income tax footnote to the financial statements will need to fully explain the nature of the events that transpired.

In some jurisdictions, nontaxed corporation elections are automatically effective when filed. In such a case, if a reporting entity makes an election before the end of the current fiscal year, it is logical that the effects be reported in current year income to become effective at the start of the following period. For example, an election filed in December 2005 would be reported in the 2005 financial statements to become effective at the beginning of the company's next fiscal year, January 1, 2006. No deferred tax assets or liabilities would appear on the December 31, 2005 balance sheet, and the tax provision for the year then ended would include the effects of any reversals that had previously been recorded. Practice varies, however, and in some instances the effect of the elimination of the deferred tax assets and liabilities would be reported in the year the election actually becomes effective.

Reporting the Effect of Accounting Changes Made for Tax Purposes

Occasionally, an entity will initiate or be required to adopt changes in accounting that affect income tax reporting, but that will not impact on financial reporting. For example, in certain jurisdictions at varying times, the following changes have been mandated: use of the direct write-off method of bad debt recognition instead of providing an allowance for bad debts, while continuing to use the reserve method as required by GAAP for financial reporting; the "full costing" method of computing inventory valuations for tax purposes (adding some items that are administrative costs to overhead), while continuing to expense currently those costs not inventoriable under GAAP; and use of accelerated capital recovery (depreciation) methods for tax reporting while continuing to use normal methods for financial reporting. Often, these changes really involve two distinct temporary differences. The first of these is the onetime, catch-up adjustment which either immediately or over a prescribed time period affects the tax basis of the asset or liability in question (net receivables or inventory, in the examples above), and which then reverses as these assets or liabilities are later realized or settled and are eliminated from the balance sheet. The second change is the ongoing differential in the amount of newly acquired assets or incurred liabilities being recognized for tax and accounting purposes; these differences also eventually reverse. This second type of change is the normal temporary difference which has already been discussed. It is the first change that differs from those previously discussed earlier in the chapter.

Implications of Changes in Tax Rates and Status Made in Interim Periods

Tax rate changes may occur during an interim reporting period, either because a tax law change mandated a mid-year effective date, or because tax law changes were effective at year-end but the reporting entity has adopted a fiscal year-end other than the natural year (December 31). The IFRS on interim reporting, IAS 34 (addressed in detail in Chapter 19), has essentially embraced a mixed view on interim reporting—with many aspects conforming to a "discrete" approach (each interim period standing on its own) but others, including accounting for income taxes, conforming to the "integral" manner of reporting. Whatever the philosophical strengths and weaknesses of the discrete and integral approaches in general, the integral approach was clearly warranted in the matter of accounting for income taxes.

The fact that income taxes are assessed annually is the primary reason for concluding that taxes are to be accrued based on an entity's estimated average annual effective tax rate for the full fiscal year. If rate changes have been enacted to take effect later in the fiscal year, the expected effective rate should take into account the rate changes as well as the anticipated pattern of earnings to be experienced over the course of the year. Thus, the rate to be applied to interim period earnings (or losses, as discussed further below) will take into account the expected level of earnings for the entire forthcoming year, as well as the effect of enacted (or substantially enacted) changes in the tax rates to become operative later in the fiscal year. In other words, and as expressed by IAS 34, the estimated average annual rate would "reflect a blend of the progressive tax rate structure expected to be applicable to the full year's earnings enacted or substantially enacted changes in the income tax rates scheduled to take effect later in the financial year."

While the principle espoused by IAS 34 is both clear and logical, a number of practical issues can arise. The standard does address in detail the various computational aspects of an effective interim period tax rate, some of which are summarized in the following paragraphs.

Many modern business entities operate in numerous nations or states and therefore are subject to a multiplicity of taxing jurisdictions. In some instances the amount of income subject to tax will vary from one jurisdiction to the next, since the tax laws in different jurisdictions will include and exclude disparate items of income or expense from the tax base. For example, interest earned on government-issued bonds may be exempted from tax by the jurisdiction which issued them, but be defined as fully taxable by other tax jurisdictions the entity is subject to. To the extent feasible, the appropriate estimated average annual effective tax rate should be separately ascertained for each taxing jurisdiction and applied individually to the interim period pretax income of each jurisdiction, so that the most accurate estimate of income taxes can be developed at each interim reporting date. In general, an overall estimated effective tax rate will not be as satisfactory for this purpose as would a more carefully constructed set of estimated rates, since the pattern of taxable and deductible items will fluctuate from one period to the next.

Similarly, if the tax law prescribes different income tax rates for different categories of income, then to the extent practicable, a separate effective tax rate should be applied to each category of interim period pretax income. IAS 34, while mandating such detailed rules of computing and applying tax rates across jurisdiction or across categories of income, nonetheless recognized that such a degree of precision may not be achievable in all cases. Thus, IAS 34 allows usage of a weighted-average of rates across jurisdictions or across categories of income provided it is a reasonable approximation of the effect of using more specific rates.

In computing an expected effective tax rate given for a tax jurisdiction, all relevant features of the tax regulations should be taken into account. Jurisdictions may provide for tax credits based on new investment in plant and machinery, relocation of facilities to backward or underdeveloped areas, research and development expenditures, levels of export sales, and so forth, and the expected credits against the tax for the full year should be given consideration in the determination of an expected effective tax rate. Thus, the tax effect of new investment in plant and machinery, when the local taxing body offers an investment credit for qualifying investment in tangible productive assets, will be reflected in those interim periods of the fiscal year in which the new investment occurs (assuming it can be forecast to occur later in a given fiscal year), and not merely in the period in which the new investment occurs. This is consistent with the underlying concept that taxes are strictly an annual phenomenon, but it is at variance with the purely discrete view of interim financial reporting.

IAS 34 notes that, although tax credits and similar modifying elements are to be taken into account in developing the expected effective tax rate to apply to interim earnings, tax benefits which will relate to onetime events are to be reflected from the interim period when those events take place. This is perhaps most likely to be encountered in the context of capital gains taxes incurred in connection with occasional dispositions of investments and other capital assets; since it is not feasible to project the timing of such transactions over the course of a year, the tax effects should be recognized only as the underlying events actually do transpire.

While in most cases tax credits are to be handled as suggested in the foregoing paragraphs, in some jurisdictions tax credits, particularly those which relate to export revenue or capital expenditures, are in effect government grants. Accounting for government grants is set forth in IAS 20; in brief, grants are recognized in income over the period necessary to properly match them to the costs which the grants are intended to offset or defray. Thus, compliance with both IAS 20 and IAS 34 would require that tax credits be carefully analyzed to identify those which are in substance grants, and that credits be accounted for consistent with their true natures.

When an interim period loss gives rise to a tax loss carryback, it should be fully reflected in that interim period. Similarly, if a loss in an interim period produces a tax loss carryforward, it should be recognized immediately, but only if the criteria set forth in IAS 12 are met. Specifically, it must be deemed probable that the benefits will be realizable before the loss benefits can be given formal recognition in the financial statements. In the case of interim period losses, it may be necessary to assess not only whether the enterprise will be profitable enough in future fiscal years to utilize the tax benefits associated with the loss, but furthermore, whether interim periods later in the same year will provide earnings of sufficient magnitude to absorb the losses of the current period.

IAS 12 provides that changes in expectations regarding the realizability of benefits related to net operating loss carryforwards should be reflected currently in tax expense. Similarly, if a net operating loss carryforward benefit is not deemed probable of being realized until the interim (or annual) period when it in fact becomes realized, the tax effect will be included in tax expense of that period. Appropriate explanatory material must be included in the notes to the financial statements, even on an interim basis, to provide users with an understanding of the unusual relationship reported between pretax accounting income and the provision for income taxes.

Income Tax Consequences of Dividends Paid

Historically, some taxing jurisdictions have levied income tax rates on corporate earnings at differential rates, depending on whether the earnings are retained by the entity or are distributed to shareholders. Typically, the rationale for this disparate treatment is that it motivates business entities to make distributions to shareholders, which is deemed a socially worthwhile goal by some (although it doesn't really alter wealth accumulation unless distortions are introduced by fiscal policy). A secondary reason for such rules is that this partially ameliorates the impact of the double taxation of corporate profits (which are typically first taxed at the corporate level, then taxed again as distributed to shareholders as taxable dividends). IAS 12 specifically abstained from addressing the issue of how to account for this phenomenon, but this was subsequently dealt with by a 2001 amendment.

Under the provisions of IAS 12, tax effects are to be provided for current taxable earnings without making any assumptions about future dividend declarations. In other words, the tax provision is to be computed using the tax rate applicable to undistributed earnings, even if the enterprise has a long history of making earnings distributions subsequent to year-end, which when made will generate tax savings. If dividends are later declared, the tax effect of this event will be accounted for in the period in which the proposed dividend is paid or becomes accruable as a liability by the enterprise, if earlier. Since there is typically no legal requirement to declare distributions to shareholders, this approach is clearly appropriate because to recognize tax benefits associated with dividend payments before declaration would be to anticipate income (in the form of tax benefits) before it is earned.

The standard holds that the tax effect of the dividend declaration (or payment) is to be included in the current period's tax provision, not as an adjustment to the earlier period's earnings, taken through the retained earnings account. This is true even when it is clear that the dividend is a distribution being made out of the earlier period's profits. The logic of this requirement is that the tax benefits are more closely linked to events reported in the income statement (i.e., the past or current transactions producing net income) than they are to the dividend distribution. In other words, it is the transactions and events resulting in earnings and not the act of distributing some of these earnings to shareholders that is of the greatest pertinence to financial statement users.

If dividends are declared before the end of the year, but are payable after year-end, the dividends become a legal liability of the reporting entity and taxes should be computed at the appropriate rate on the amount thus declared. If the dividend is declared after year-end but before the financial statements are issued, under IAS 10 a liability cannot be recognized on the balance sheet at year-end, and thus the tax effect related thereto also cannot be given recognition. Disclosure would be made, however, of this post-year-end event.

To illustrate the foregoing, consider the following example:

> Amir Corporation operates in a jurisdiction where income taxes are payable at a higher rate on undistributed profits than on distributed earnings. For the year 2006, the company's taxable income is €150,000. Amir also has net taxable temporary differences amounting to €50,000 for the year, thus creating the need for a deferred tax provision. The tax rate on distributed profits is 25%, and the rate on undistributed profits is 40%; the difference is refundable if profits are later distributed. As of the balance sheet date no liability for dividends proposed or declared has been reflected on the balance sheet. On March 31, 2007, however, the company distributes dividends of €50,000.

> The tax consequences of dividends on undistributed profits, current and deferred taxes for the year 2006, and the recovery of 2006 income taxes when dividends are subsequently declared would be as follows:

> 1. Amir Corporation recognizes a current tax liability and a current tax expense for 2006 of €150,000 x 40% = €160,000;
> 2. No asset is recognized for the amount that will be (potentially) recoverable when dividends are distributed;
> 3. Deferred tax liability and deferred tax expense for 2006 would be €50,000 x 40% = €20,000, and
> 4. In the following year (2007) when the company recognizes dividends of €50,000, the company will also recognize the recovery of income taxes of €50,000 x (40% – 25%) = €7,500 as a current tax asset and a reduction of the current income tax expense.

The only exception to the foregoing accounting for tax effects of dividends that are subject to differential tax rates arises in the situation of a dividend-paying corporation which is required to withhold taxes on the distribution and remit these to the taxing authorities. In general, withholding tax is offset against the amounts distributed to shareholders, and is later forwarded to the taxing bodies rather than to the shareholders, so that the total amount of the dividend declaration is not altered. However, if the corporation pays the tax in addition to the full amount of the dividend payments to shareholders, some might view this as a tax falling on the corporation and, accordingly, add this to the tax provision reported on the income statement. IAS 12, however, makes it clear that such an amount, if paid or payable to the taxing authorities, is to be charged to equity as part of the dividend declaration if it does not affect income taxes payable or recoverable by the enterprise in the same or a different period.

Finally, IAS 12 provides that disclosure will be required of the potential income tax consequences of dividends. The reporting enterprise should disclose the amounts of the potential income tax consequences which are practically determinable, and whether there are any potential income tax consequences not practically determinable.

Accounting for Income Taxes in Business Combinations

One of the more complex aspects of interperiod income tax accounting occurs when business combinations are consummated and are treated as acquisitions as now defined by IFRS 3, which superseded former IAS 22 in 2004. The principal complexity relates to the recognition, at the date of the purchase, of the deferred tax effects of the differences between the tax and financial reporting bases of assets and liabilities acquired. Further difficulties arise in connection with the recognition of goodwill and negative goodwill. If the reporting entity expects that the ultimate tax allocation will differ from the initial one (such as when disallowance by the tax authorities of an allocation made to identifiable intangibles is anticipated by the taxpayer), yet another complex accounting matter must be dealt with.

Under the provisions of IAS 12, the tax effects of any differences in tax and financial reporting bases are to be reflected, from the date of the purchase, as deferred tax assets and liabilities. The same rules that apply to the recognition of deferred tax assets and liabilities arising under other circumstances (i.e., the origination of temporary differences by the reporting entity) are equally applicable to such instances, *except* for the initial recognition of an asset or liability in a transaction other than a business combination when, at the time of the transaction, neither accounting profit nor taxable profit is affected. Accordingly, if deferred tax assets are not deemed to be probable of ultimate realization, they are not recognized in any of these circumstances.

Depending on the tax jurisdictions in which they occur, and how the transactions are structured, acquisitions may be either taxable or nontaxable in nature. In a taxable acquisition, the total purchase price paid will be allocated to assets and liabilities for both tax and financial reporting purposes, although under some circumstances the specifics of these allocations may differ, and to the extent the allocation is made to nondeductible goodwill there will be differences in future periods' taxable and accounting profit. In a nontaxable acquisition, the predecessor entity's tax bases for the various assets and liabilities will be carried forward, while for financial reporting purposes the purchase price will be allocated to the assets and liabilities acquired. Thus, in most cases, there may be significant differences between the tax and financial reporting bases. For this reason, both taxable and nontaxable acquisitions can involve the application of deferred income tax accounting.

Accounting for Purchase Business Combinations at Acquisition Date

IAS 12 requires that the tax effects of the tax-book basis differences of all assets and liabilities generally be presented as deferred tax assets and liabilities as of the acquisition date. In general, this grossing-up of the balance sheet is a straightforward matter.

Example of temporary differences in business acquisition

An example, in the context of the business acquisition of Windlass Corp., follows:

1. The income tax rate is a flat 40%.
2. The acquisition of a business is effected at a cost of €500,000.
3. The fair values of assets acquired total €750,000.
4. The carryforward tax bases of assets acquired total €600,000.
5. The fair and carryforward tax bases of the liabilities assumed in the purchase are €250,000.
6. The difference between the tax and fair values of the assets acquired, €150,000, consists of taxable temporary differences of €200,000 and deductible temporary differences of €50,000.
7. There is no doubt as to the realizability of the deductible temporary differences in this case.

Based on the foregoing facts, allocation of the purchase price is as follows:

Gross purchase price	€ 500,000
Allocation to identifiable assets and (liabilities):	
Assets other than goodwill and deferred tax benefits	750,000
Deferred tax benefits	20,000
Liabilities, other than deferred tax obligations	(250,000)
Deferred tax obligations	(80,000)
Net of the above allocations	440,000
Allocation to goodwill	€ 60,000

Goodwill and negative goodwill. Goodwill arises when part of the price paid in a business combination accounted for as a purchase cannot be allocated to identifiable assets; what was formerly known as negative goodwill results from bargain purchases. Accounting for goodwill and for negative goodwill has been substantially altered by IFRS 3. Goodwill is no longer subject to periodic amortization, but must be regularly tested for impairment and, if impaired, written down to fair value, with the adjustment being reflected in current period earnings. Negative goodwill (more properly, the excess of fair value over cost), which is much less commonly encountered, is now reported in current period earnings, rather than being deferred and amortized as under prior IFRS.

Goodwill may be tax deductible, depending on tax jurisdiction, or may be nondeductible. If it is deductible, the mandated amortization period will cause the carrying value for tax purposes over time to differ from that reflected in the financial statements prepared in conformity with IFRS. Since under IFRS goodwill is no longer to be amortized over its expected economic life, a temporary difference will develop, with the book carrying value being greater than the tax carrying amount, absent any impairment recognition for financial reporting purposes. If impairment charges are taken, however, book carrying value may be lower than the corresponding tax basis.

The situation with negative goodwill is as follows: if the fair value of net assets acquired exceeds the cost of the acquisition, it is first incumbent upon the acquirer to reassess values assigned. However, in the (likely) case that this does not lead to the elimination of what appeared to be negative goodwill, that amount is to be reported currently in income. This will likely result in a difference between tax and book carrying value for the negative goodwill (depending on local tax rules, of course), and this also is a timing difference to be considered in computing deferred taxes for the entity.

If goodwill or negative goodwill is not deductible or taxable, respectively, in a given tax jurisdiction (that is, it is a permanent difference), in theory its tax basis is zero, and thus there is a difference between tax and financial reporting bases, to which one would logically expect deferred taxes would be attributed. However, given the residual nature of goodwill or negative goodwill, recognition of deferred taxes would in turn create yet more goodwill, and thus more deferred tax, etc. There would be little purpose achieved by loading up the balance sheet with more goodwill and related deferred tax in such circumstances, and the computation itself would be quite challenging. Accordingly, IAS 12 prohibits grossing up goodwill in such a fashion. Similarly, no deferred tax benefit will be computed and presented in connection with the financial reporting recognition of negative goodwill.

The accounting for a taxable purchase business combination is essentially similar to that for a nontaxable one. However, unlike the previous example, in which there were numerous assets with different tax and financial reporting bases, there are likely to be only a few differences in the case of taxable purchases. In jurisdictions in which goodwill is not deductible, attempts are often made for tax purposes to allocate excess purchase cost to tangible assets as well as to other intangibles, such as covenants not to compete. (Such attempts may or not survive review by the tax authorities, of course.) In jurisdictions where goodwill is deductible, presumably this is not a motivation, although because goodwill is often viewed as a suspect asset, entities will still be more comfortable if purchase cost can be attributed to "real" assets, even when goodwill can be amortized for tax purposes.

IAS 12 does not permit recognition of deferred tax effects associated with goodwill. It is true that some book-tax temporary differences in goodwill would, if any other asset or liability were at issue, give rise to deferred tax assets or liabilities. For example, in some tax jurisdictions goodwill is not only not subject to period expensing (via amortization), but also the goodwill cannot be considered part of the tax basis in the subsidiary, so that when the parent ultimately sells the acquired entity, including its goodwill, the gain or loss on the transaction has to be adjusted so that goodwill is not deducted at that time. In other words, the tax basis of the goodwill is zero at acquisition and throughout the holding period of the business acquired. This differs from the book basis (under IFRS 3, goodwill is not subject to amortization, so absent any impairment the original amount allocated to goodwill remains intact until disposed of), which is the normal definition of a temporary difference. Nonetheless, no deferred tax can be associated with this.

This requirement applies equally to any subsequent change in the carrying value of goodwill, which is deemed to relate to the original acquisition of the goodwill. For example, if the book goodwill is later written down in value due to an assessed impairment, this does not generate deferred tax recognition.

A similar situation arises if assets other than goodwill are acquired and are not subject to depreciation for tax purposes (unusual, but not an impossible situation, given the wide disparity of local income tax laws). For example, if an asset is acquired and depreciated for book (financial reporting) purposes, and has an expected residual value of zero, but neither depreciation nor capital gains or losses are recognized for tax purposes, the tax basis of the asset is zero. The book-tax difference is in effect a permanent difference, and no deferred tax effects can be recognized under provisions of IAS 12.

Accounting for Purchase Business Combinations After the Acquisition

Under the provisions of the revised IAS 12, net deferred tax benefits are not to be carried forward as assets unless the deferred tax assets are deemed *probable* of being realized. The assessment of this probability was discussed earlier in the chapter.

In an example (Windlass) given above, it was specified that all deductible temporary differences were fully realizable, and therefore the deferred tax benefits associated with those temporary differences were recorded as of the acquisition date. In other situations there may be substantial doubt concerning realizability; that is, it may not be probable that the benefits will be realized. Accordingly, under IAS 12, the deferred tax asset would not be recognized at the date of the business acquisition. If so, the allocation of the purchase price would have to reflect that fact, and more of the purchase cost would be allocated to goodwill than would otherwise be the case.

If, at a later date, it is determined that some or all of the deferred tax asset that was not recognized at the date of the acquisition is, in fact, probable of being ultimately realized, the effect of that reevaluation will be reflected in tax expense (benefit) in the period during which the reevaluation is made. Furthermore, the portion of the extra goodwill recognized at the time of the business acquisition must be written off to expense.

Example of revising estimate of tax benefit realizability in business combination

To illustrate this last concept, assume that a business acquisition occurs on January 1, 2005, and that deferred tax assets of €100,000 are *not* recognized at that time, due to an assessment that realization is not probable. The unrecognized tax benefit is implicitly allocated to goodwill during the purchase price assignment process. On January 1, 2007, the likelihood of ultimately realizing the tax benefit is reassessed as being probable, with realization projected for later years. The entries at that date are as follows:

Deferred tax benefit	100,000	
Goodwill		100,000

In some situations, the amount of deferred tax benefits will, upon reassessment, exceed the balance in the goodwill account, or there may have been no goodwill recognized in connection with the business acquisition at all. IAS 12 stipulates that this reassessment cannot result in a recognition of negative goodwill. The implication is that, while negative goodwill could have been first recognized at the time of a business acquisition which involved recognition of deferred assets (and, under IFRS 3, reported immediately in earnings), it will not be possible to later recognize deferred tax benefits under such circumstances.

A related issue arises when the acquirer had unrecognized deferred tax benefits unrelated to the impending business combination. The asset was unrecognized because it was not probable that this benefit could be realized by that entity. As a result of the acquisition, however, this previously unrecognized asset becomes probable of realization, for example, because under relevant tax laws the earnings of the acquired entity will provide the acquirer with an opportunity to utilize its deductible temporary differences. According to IAS 12, the acquirer's deferred tax asset will now be given recognition, with the consequence that goodwill otherwise to be recorded in the transaction will be reduced, or negative goodwill will be increased or first given recognition (if negative goodwill is created, of course, this will be recognized immediately in income under IFRS 3).

Tax Allocation for Business Investments

As noted in Chapter 10, there are two basic methods of accounting for passive or minority investments in the common stock of other corporations: (1) the cost method and (2) the equity method. The *cost method* requires that the investing corporation (investor) record the investment at its purchase price, and no additional entry is made to the account over the life of the asset (this does not include any valuation contra accounts). The cost method is used in instances where the investor is not considered to have significant influence over the investee. The ownership threshold generally used is 20% of ownership. This figure is not considered an absolute, but it will be used to identify the break between application of the cost and equity methods. Under the cost method, ordinary income is recognized as dividends are declared by the investee, and capital gains (losses) are recognized on disposal of the investment. For tax purposes, no provision is made during the holding period for the allocable undistributed earnings of the investee. Deferred tax computation is not necessary when using the cost method because there is no temporary difference.

The *equity method* is generally used whenever an investor owns more than 20% of an investee or has significant influence over its operations. The equity method calls for recording the investment at cost and then increasing this carrying amount by the allocable portion of the investee's earnings. The allocable portion of the investee's earnings is then included in the pretax accounting income of the investor. Dividend payments are no longer included in pretax accounting income but are considered to be a reduction in the carrying amount of the investment. However, for tax purposes, dividends are the only revenue realized. As a result, the investor needs to recognize deferred income tax expense on the undistributed earnings of the associate that will be taxed in the future.

IAS 28 distinguishes between an associate and a subsidiary and prescribes different accounting treatments for each. An associate is considered to be a corporation whose stock is owned by an investor which holds more than 20% but no greater than 50% of the outstanding stock. An association situation occurs when the investor has significant influence but not control over the corporation in which it has invested. A subsidiary, on the other hand, exists when one enterprise exerts control over another, which is presumed when it holds more than 50% of the stock of the other entity.

In an important exception to the general rule that deferred taxes must be recognized for all book-tax basis differences, IAS 12 provides that when the parent, investor, or joint venturer can prevent the taxable event from occurring, deferred taxes are not recognized. Specifically, under IAS 12, two conditions must *both* be satisfied to justify *not* reflecting deferred taxes in connection with the earnings of a subsidiary (a control situation), branches and associates (significant influence), and joint ventures. These are (1) that the parent, investor or venturer is able to control the timing of the reversal of the temporary difference and (2) it is probable that the difference will not reverse in the foreseeable future. Unless *both* conditions are met, the tax effects of these temporary differences must be given recognition.

When a parent company that has the ability to control the dividend and other policies of its subsidiary determines that dividends will not be declared, and thus that the undistributed profit of the subsidiary will not be taxed at the parent company level, no deferred tax liability is to be recognized. If this intention is later altered, the tax effect of this change in estimate would be reflected in the current period's tax provision.

On the other hand, an investor, even one having significant influence, cannot absolutely determine the associate's dividend policy. Accordingly, it has to be presumed that earnings will eventually be distributed and that these will create taxable income at the investor company level. Therefore, deferred tax liability must be provided for the reporting entity's share of all undistributed earnings of its associates for which it is accounting by the equity method, unless there is a binding agreement for the earnings of the investee to not be distributed within the foreseeable future.

In the case of joint ventures there are a wide range of possible relationships between the venturers, and in some cases the reporting entity has the ability to control the payment of dividends. As in the foregoing, if the reporting entity has the ability to exercise this level of control and it is probable that distributions will not be made within the foreseeable future, no deferred tax liability will be reported.

In all these various circumstances, it will be necessary to assess whether distributions within the foreseeable future are probable. The standard does not define "foreseeable future" and thus this will remain a matter of subjective judgment. The criteria of IAS 12, while subjective, are less ambiguous than under the original standard, which permitted nonrecognition of deferred tax liability when it was "reasonable to assume that (the associates's) profits will not be distributed."

Example of tax allocation for investee and subsidiary income

To illustrate the application of these concepts, assume that Parent Company owns 30% of the outstanding common stock of Investee Company and 70% of the outstanding common stock of Subsidiary Company. Additional data for the year 2006 are as follows:

	Investee Company	*Subsidiary Company*
Net income	€50,000	€100,000
Dividends paid	20,000	60,000

How the foregoing data are used to recognize the tax effects of the stated events is discussed below.

Income tax effects from investee company. The 2006 accounting profit of Parent Company will include equity in its associate's income equal to €15,000 (= €50,000 x 30%). Parent's taxable income, however, will include dividend income of €6,000 (= €20,000 x 30%), and, under applicable tax law, a credit of 80% of the €6,000, or €4,800, will also be allowed for the dividends received. This 80% dividends received deduction is a permanent difference between accounting and taxable profits.

The amount of the deferred tax credit in 2006 depends on the expectations of Parent Company as to the manner in which the €9,000 of undistributed income will be received. In many tax jurisdictions, the effective tax rate will differ based on method of realization; dividend income may be taxed at a different rate than capital gains (achieved on the sale of an investment in an associate, for example). If the expectation of receipt is via dividends, the temporary difference is 20% of €9,000, or €1,800, and the deferred tax credit for this originating temporary difference in 2006 is the current tax rate times €1,800. However, if the expectation is that receipt will be through future sale of the investment, the gain on which would be fully taxed, the temporary difference is €9,000 and the deferred tax credit is the current capital gains rate times the €9,000.

The entries below illustrate these alternatives. A tax rate of 34% is used for both ordinary income and for capital gains. Note that the amounts in the entries below relate only to Investee Company's incremental impact on Parent Company's tax accounts.

	Expectations for undistributed income	
	Dividends	*Capital gains*
Income tax expense	1,020	2,208
Deferred tax liability	612[b]	1,800[c]
Income taxes payable	408[a]	408[a]

[a]*Computation of income taxes payable:*

Dividend income—30% x (€20,000)	*€6,000*
Less 80% dividends received deduction	*(4,800)*
Amount included in Parent's taxable income	*€1,200*
Tax liability—34% x (€1,200)	*€ 408*

[b]*Computation of deferred tax liability (dividend assumption):*
Originating temporary difference:

Parent's share of undistributed income—30% x (€30,000)	*€9,000*
Less 80% dividends received deduction	*(7,200)*
Originating temporary difference	*€1,800*
Deferred tax liability—34% x (€1,800)	*€ 612*

[c]*Computation of deferred tax liability (capital gain assumption):*

Originating temporary difference: Parent's share of undistrib-	
uted income—30% x (€30,000)	*€9,000*
Deferred tax liability—20% x (€9,000)	*€1,800*

Income tax effects from subsidiary company. The accounting profit of Parent Company will also include equity in Subsidiary income of €70,000 (= 70% x €100,000). This €70,000 will be included in pretax consolidated income if Parent and Subsidiary issue consolidated financial statements. Depending on the rules of the particular tax jurisdiction, it may be that for tax purposes, Parent and Subsidiary will not file a consolidated tax return (e.g., because the prescribed minimum level of control, that is, 80%, is not present). In the present example, assume that it will not be possible to file consolidated tax returns. Consequently, the taxable income of Parent will include dividend income of €42,000 (= 70% x €60,000). Assume further that there will be an 80% dividends received deduction, which will amount to €33,600. The originating temporary difference results from Parent's equity (€28,000) in Subsidiary's undistributed earnings of €40,000.

The amount of the deferred tax credit in 2006 depends on the expectations of Parent Company as to the manner in which this €28,000 of undistributed income will be received. The same expectations can exist as discussed previously, for Parent's equity in Investee's undistributed earnings (i.e., through future dividend distributions or capital gains).

The entries below illustrate these alternatives. A marginal tax rate of 34% is assumed. The amounts in the entries below relate only to Subsidiary Company's incremental impact on Parent Company's tax accounts.

	Expectations for undistributed income	
	Dividends	*Capital gains*
Income tax expense	4,760	12,376
Deferred tax liability	1,904[b]	9,520[c]
Income taxes payable	2,856[a]	2,856[a]

[a]*Computation of income taxes payable:*

Dividend income—70% x (€60,000)	€42,000
Less 80% dividends received deduction	(33,600)
Amount included in Parent's taxable income	€ 8,400
Tax liability—34% x (€5,600)	€ 2,856

[b]*Computation of deferred tax liability (dividend assumption):*
Originating temporary difference:

Parent's share of undistributed income—70% x (€40,000)	€28,000
Less 80% dividends received deduction	(22,400)
Originating temporary difference	€ 5,600
Deferred tax liability—34% x (€5,600)	€ 1,904

[c]*Computation of deferred tax liability (capital gain assumption):*
Originating temporary difference: Parent's share of undistrib-

uted income—70% x (€40,000)	€28,000
Deferred tax liability—34% x (€28,000)	€ 9,520

If a parent company owns a large enough percentage of the voting stock of a subsidiary and the parent, so that it may consolidate the subsidiary for both financial and tax reports, no temporary differences exist between pretax consolidated income and taxable income. Under the rules in some jurisdictions, it may be possible to submit separate tax returns even if consolidated returns could alternatively be filed; in such circumstances, there may be a tax rule that grants a 100% dividends received deduction, to avoid incurring double taxation. If, in the circumstances noted above, consolidated financial statements are prepared but a consolidated tax return is not, it would be the case that a dividends received deduction of 100% would be allowed. Accordingly, the temporary difference between pretax consolidated income and taxable income is zero if the parent assumes that the undistributed income will be realized in dividends.

Tax Effects of Compound Financial Instruments

IAS 32 established the important notion that when financial instruments are compound, the separately identifiable components are to be accounted for according to their distinct natures. For example, when an entity issues convertible debt instruments, those instruments have characteristics of both debt and equity securities, and accordingly, the issuance proceeds should be allocated among those components. (Originally the allocation was to be proportional to fair values of the components, but as amended, IAS 32 requires that the full fair value of the liability component be recognized, with only the residual allocated to equity, consistent with the concept that equity is only the residual interest in an entity.) A problem arises when the taxing authorities do not agree that a portion of the proceeds should be allocated to a secondary instrument. For example, when convertible bonds are sold, for tax reporting purposes the entire proceeds are considered to be the basis of the debt instrument in most jurisdictions, with no basis being allocated to the conversion feature. Accordingly this will create a temporary difference between the interest expense to be recognized for financial reporting purposes and interest to be recognized for income tax purposes, because of the amortization of discount or premium, and in turn this will create deferred tax implications.

Example of tax effects of compound financial instrument at issuance

Consider the following scenario. Tamara Corp. issues 6% convertible bonds with a face value of €3,000,000, due in ten years, with the bonds being convertible into Tamara common stock at the holders' option. Proceeds of the offering amount to €3,200,000, for an effective yield of approximately 5.13% at a time when "straight" debt with similar risks and time to maturity is yielding just under 6.95% in the market. Since the fair value of the debt component is thus €2.8 million out of the actual proceeds of €3.2 million, the convertibility feature is seemingly worth €400,000 in the financial marketplace. Under revised IAS 32, the full fair value of the liability component must be allocated to it, with only the residual value being attributed to equity.

The entry to record the issuance of the bonds follows:

Cash	3,200,000	
Unamortized debt discount	200,000	
Debt payable		3,000,000
Equity—paid-in capital account		400,000

Unamortized debt discount will be amortized as additional interest cost over the life of the bonds (ten years, in this example) for financial reporting purposes, but for tax purposes the deductible interest cost will be limited, typically, to the actual interest paid. In this example, the "originating" phase of the temporary difference will be when the compound security is first sold; the "reversing" of this temporary difference will occur as the debt discount is amortized, until the net carrying value of the debt equals the face value.

Example of tax effects of compound financial instrument in subsequent periods

To illustrate, continue the preceding example and assume that the tax rate is 30%, and for simplicity, also assume that the debt discount will be amortized on a straight-line basis over the ten-year term (€200,000 ÷ 10 = €20,000 per year), although in theory amortization using the "effective yield" method is preferred. The tax effect of the total debt discount is €200,000 × 30% = €60,000. Annual interest expense is €20,000 + (€3,000,000 × 6%) = €200,000. The entries to establish deferred tax liability accounting at inception, and to reflect interest accrual and reversal of the deferred tax account are as follows:

At inception (in addition to the entry shown above)

Equity—paid-in capital account	60,000	
Deferred tax payable		60,000

Each year thereafter

Interest expense	200,000	
Interest payable		180,000
Unamortized debt discount		20,000
Deferred tax payable	6,000	
Tax expense—deferred		6,000

Note that the offset to deferred tax liability at inception is a charge to equity, in effect reducing the credit to paid-in capital for the equity portion of the compound financial instrument to a net of tax basis, since allocating a portion of the proceeds to the equity component caused the creation of a nondeductible deferred charge, debt discount. When the deferred charge is later amortized, however, the reversing of the temporary difference leads to a reduction in tax expense to better "match" the higher interest expense reported in the financial statements than on the tax return.

Accounting for Income Taxes: Intraperiod Tax Allocation

While IAS 12 is concerned predominantly with the requirements of *interperiod* income tax allocation (deferred tax accounting), it also addresses the questions of *intraperiod* tax allocation. Intraperiod tax allocation relates to the matching in the income (or other financial) statement of various categories of comprehensive income or expense (continuing operations, corrections of errors, etc.) with the tax effects of those items. The general principle is that tax effects should follow the items to which they relate. The computation of the tax effects of these items is, however, complicated by the fact that many, if not most, jurisdictions feature progressive tax rates. For that reason, a question arises as to whether overall "blended" rates should be apportioned across all the disparate elements (ordinary income, corrections of errors, etc.), or whether the marginal tax effects of items other than ordinary income should be reported instead.

IAS 12 does not answer this question, or even address it. It might, however, be instructive to consider the two approaches, since this will affect the presentation of the income statement and, in the case of fundamental errors, the statement of retained earnings as well.

The blended rate approach would calculate the average, or effective, rate applicable to all an entity's taxable earnings for a given year (including the deferred tax effects of items that will be deductible or taxable in later periods, but that are being reported in the current year's financial statements). This effective rate is then used to compute income taxes on each of the individually reportable components. For example, if an entity has an effective blended rate of 46% in a given year, after considering the various tax brackets and any available credits against the gross amount of the tax computed, this rate is used to calculate the taxes on ordinary income, extraordinary income, the results of discontinued operations, the correction of fundamental errors, and the effects of changes in accounting principles, if any.

The alternative to the blended rate approach is what can be called the marginal tax effect approach. Using this computational technique, a series of "with-and-without" calculations will be made to identify the marginal, or incremental, effects of items other than those arising from ordinary, continuing operations. This is essentially the approach dictated under US GAAP (FAS 109 and its predecessor standards) and is the primary approach employed under UK GAAP as well. Since the prescription of this with-and-without method is detailed most extensively in current US GAAP, that explanation is referred to extensively in the following discussion.

Prior to the promulgation of current US GAAP, the with-and-without technique was applied under prior US standards in a step-by-step fashion proceeding down the face of the income statement. For example, an entity having continuing operations, discontinued operations, and extraordinary items would calculate tax expense as follows:

1. Tax would be computed for the aggregate results and for continuing operations. The difference between the two amounts would be allocated to the total of discontinued operations and extraordinary items.
2. Tax expense would be computed on discontinued operations. The residual amount (i.e., the difference between tax on the discontinued operations and the tax on the total of discontinued operations and extraordinary items) would then be allocated to extraordinary items.

Thus, the amount of tax expense allocated to any given classification in the statement of income (and the other financial statements, if relevant) was partially a function of the location in which the item was traditionally presented in the income and retained earnings statements.

Under current US GAAP, total income tax expense or benefit for the period is allocated among continuing operations, discontinued operations, extraordinary items, and stockholders' equity. The standard creates a few anomalies since, as defined in current US GAAP, the tax provisions on income from continuing operations include not only taxes on the income earned from continuing operations, as expected, but also a number of other tax effects including the following:

1. The impact of changes in tax laws and rates, which includes the effects of such changes on items that were previously reflected directly in stockholders' equity
2. The impact of changes in tax status
3. Changes in estimates about whether the tax benefits of deductible temporary differences or net operating loss or credit carryforwards are probable of realization.

> *NOTE: Under current US GAAP the actual criterion is "more likely than not," which differs from IAS's "probable" criterion.*

Under current US GAAP, stockholders' equity is charged or credited with the initial tax effects of items that are reported directly in stockholders' equity, including that related to corrections of the effects of accounting errors of previous periods, which under the international standards are known as fundamental errors. The effects of tax rate or other tax law changes on items for which the tax effects were originally reported directly in stockholders' equity are reported in continuing operations if they occur in any period after the original event. This approach was adopted by current US GAAP because of the presumed difficulty of identifying the original reporting location of items that are affected possibly years later by changing rates; the expedient solution was to require all such effects to be reported in the tax provision allocated to continuing operations.

Example of intraperiod allocation using a "with-and-without" approach

Assume that there were €50,000 in deductible temporary differences at 12/31/05; these remain unchanged during the current year, 2006.

Income from continuing operations	€400,000
Loss from discontinued operations	(120,000)
Gain on involuntary conversion	60,000
Correction of accounting error:	
understatement of depreciation in 2005	(20,000)
Tax credits	5,000

- Tax rates are: 15% on first €100,000 of taxable income; 20% on next €100,000; 25% on next €100,000; 30% thereafter.
- Effective (average) future tax rates were expected to be 20% at December 31, 2005, but are expected to be 28% at December 31, 2006.
- Retained earnings at December 31, 2005, totaled €650,000.

Intraperiod tax allocation proceeds as follows:

Step 1 — Tax on total taxable income of €320,000 (= €400,000 − €120,000 + €60,000 − €20,000) is €61,000 (that is, €66,000 based on rate structure, less tax credit of €5,000).

Step 2 — Tax on income from continuing operations, which includes the gain on the involuntary conversion (which can no longer be deemed extraordinary, since that classification has been eliminated by revised IAS 8) of €460,000 is €103,000, net of the tax credit.

Step 3 — The difference, €42,000, is allocated pro rata to discontinued operations, and the correction of the error in prior year depreciation, which for this example is deemed not practical to account for by restating the earlier year (in practice, this would not be readily accepted). Note the effect of these intraperiod allocations are both at 30%, the marginal rate.

Step 4 — Adjustment of the deferred tax asset, amounting to a €4,000 increase due to an effective tax rate estimate change [= €50,000 x (.28 − .20)] is allocated to continuing operations, regardless of the actual source of the temporary difference.

A summary combined income and retained earnings statement is presented below.

Income from continuing operations,		
before income taxes		€460,000
Income taxes on income from continuing operations:		
Current	€108,000	
Deferred	(4,000)	
Tax credits	(5,000)	99,000
Income from continuing operations, net		361,000
Loss from discontinued operations,		
net of tax benefit of €36,000		(84,000)
Net income		277,000

Retained earnings, January 1, 2006	650,000
Correction of accounting error, net of tax effects (€6,000)	(14,000)
Retained earnings, December 31, 2006	€913,000

Applicability to international accounting standards. Since IAS 12 is silent on the method to be used to compute the tax effects of individual captions in the statement of income and the statement of retained earnings (or changes in stockholders' equity), in the authors' opinion financial statement preparers have the option of using essentially a with-and-without or blended rate approach. Both can be rationalized from either practical or theoretical perspectives. The blended rate method would clearly be easier to apply, since only one set of computations using progressive tax rates would be needed. The blended rate method also avoids the implication that items other than income from continuing operations represented the "last units of currency" earned, since the rates applicable to those items would not be the highest marginal rates. On the other hand, the with-and-without method averts the situation where the blended rate applied to income from continuing operations is subject to wide variation due simply to the occasional existence of extraordinary and other unusual items.

On balance, and given the lack of a prescribed methodology in IAS 12, the authors slightly favor the blended rate approach. Whichever methodology is employed, however, it is vital that the notes to the financial statements clearly describe how the computation was made and disclose the tax effects of the various components presented. IAS 12 does, however, permit the tax effects of all extraordinary items to be presented in one amount, if computation of each extraordinary item is not readily accomplished.

Balance Sheet Classification of Deferred Taxes

Somewhat surprisingly, IAS 12 stated that should the reporting entity classify its balance sheet (into current and noncurrent assets and liabilities), deferred tax assets and liabilities should never be included in the current category. (Subsequent to the most recent revision to IAS 12, revised IAS 1 was promulgated, which essentially requires presentation of a classified balance sheet unless a liquidation ordering is deemed more meaningful; the prohibition against current classification of deferred taxes remains.) While not articulated in the standard, presumably the anticipated difficulties of assessing the amount and pattern of temporary difference reversals led to this decision. Arguably, the extent of any required scheduling would have been rather limited, since the only concern would have been to assess whether the expected reversals would occur before or after the one-year demarcation line between current and noncurrent. However, having established this clear prohibition, IAS 12 is undeniably easier to apply.

Deferred tax assets pertaining to certain tax jurisdictions may be fully or partially recognizable under IFRS rules, while those pertaining to others may not be recognized at all, based on the circumstances. Applying IAS 12's "probable" criterion to the expected timing and availability of taxable temporary differences and other items entering into the computation of taxable profit in each jurisdiction is necessary to make these determinations.

The offsetting of tax assets and liabilities is never allowed in the balance sheet, except to the extent that they pertain to taxes levied by, and refund due from, the same taxing authority. Amounts due to or from independent taxing bodies would not be subject to offsetting, inasmuch as amounts due to one agency cannot be withheld because refunds are due from others. In practice, offsetting is almost never applied even when the same authority is the counterparty, since due dates of amounts owed may not coincide with expected refund dates.

Finally, when entities included in consolidated financial statements are taxed separately, a tax asset recognized by one member of the group should not be offset against a liability recognized by another member of the same group, unless a legal right of offset exists, which would be rare. For example, in some jurisdictions the tax loss carryforward of an acquired affiliate entity cannot be used to reduce taxable profit of another member of the group, even if consolidated tax returns are being prepared. In such a case, the deferred tax asset recognized in connection with the tax loss carryforward cannot be offset against a deferred tax liability of another member of the consolidated group. Further, in evaluating whether realization of the tax asset is probable, the existence of the tax liability could not be considered.

Financial Statement Disclosures

Revised IAS 12 mandated a number of disclosures, including some which had not been required under earlier practice. The purpose of these disclosures is to provide the user with an understanding of the relationship between pretax accounting profit and the related tax effects, as well as to aid in predicting future cash inflows or outflows related to tax effects of assets and liabilities already reflected in the balance sheet. The more recently imposed disclosures were intended to provide greater insight into the relationship between deferred tax assets and liabilities recognized, the related tax expense or benefit recognized in earnings, and the underlying natures of the related temporary differences resulting in those items. There is also enhanced disclosure for discontinued operations under IAS 12. Finally, when deferred tax assets are given recognition under defined conditions, there will be disclosure of the nature of the evidence supporting recognition. The specific disclosures are presented in greater detail in the following paragraphs.

Balance sheet disclosures. A reporting entity is required to disclose the amount of a deferred tax asset and the nature of evidence supporting its recognition, when

1. Utilization of the deferred tax asset is dependent on future taxable profits in excess of the profits arising from the reversal of the existing taxable temporary differences; *and*
2. The enterprise has suffered a loss in the same tax jurisdiction to which the deferred tax assets relate in either the current or preceding period.

Income statement disclosures. IAS 12 places primary emphasis on disclosure of the components of income tax expense or benefit. The following information must be disclosed about the components of tax expense for each year for which an income statement is presented.

The components of tax expense or benefit, which may include some or all of the following:

1. Current tax expense or benefit
2. Any adjustments recognized in the current period for taxes of prior periods
3. The amount of deferred tax expense or benefit relating to the origination and reversal of temporary differences
4. The amount of deferred tax expense or benefit relating to changes in tax rates or the imposition of new taxes
5. The amount of the tax benefit arising from a previously unrecognized tax loss, tax credit, or temporary difference of a prior period that is used to reduce current period tax expense
6. The amount of the tax benefit from a previously unrecognized tax loss, tax credit, or temporary difference of a prior period that is used to reduce deferred tax expense
7. Deferred tax expense arising from the write-down of a deferred tax asset because it is no longer deemed probable of realization

In addition to the foregoing, IAS 12 also requires that disclosures be made of the following items which are to be separately stated:

1. The aggregate current and deferred tax relating to items that are charged or credited to equity
2. The relationship between tax expense or benefit and accounting profit or loss either (or both) as

   a. A numerical reconciliation between tax expense or benefit and the product of accounting profit or loss times the applicable tax rate(s), with disclosure of how the rate(s) was determined; or
   b. A numerical reconciliation between the average effective tax rate and applicable rate, also with disclosure of how the applicable rate was determined

3. An explanation of changes in the applicable rate vs. the prior reporting period
4. The amount and date of expiration of unrecognized tax assets relating to deductible temporary differences, tax losses and tax credits
5. The aggregate amount of any temporary differences relating to investments in subsidiaries, branches, and associates and interests in joint ventures for which deferred liabilities have not been recognized
6. For each type of temporary difference, including unused tax losses and credits, disclosure of

   a. The amount of the deferred tax assets and liabilities included in each balance sheet presented; and
   b. The amount of deferred income or expense recognized in the income statement, if not otherwise apparent from changes in the balance sheets

7. Disclosure of the tax expense or benefit related to discontinued operations

Finally, disclosure must be made of the amount of deferred tax asset and the evidence supporting its presentation in the balance sheet, when both these conditions exist: utilization is dependent upon future profitability beyond that assured by the future reversal of taxable temporary differences, *and* the entity has suffered a loss in either the current period or the preceding period in the jurisdiction to which the deferred tax asset relates.

Examples of informative disclosures about income tax expense

The disclosure requirements imposed by IAS 12 are extensive and in some instances complicated. The following examples have been adapted from the standard itself, with some modifications.

Note: Income tax expense

Major components of the provisions for income taxes are as follows:

	2005	2006
Current tax expense	€75,500	€82,450
Deferred tax expense (benefit), relating to the origination and reversal of temporary differences	12,300	(16,275)
Effect on previously provided deferred tax assets and liabilities resulting from increase in statutory tax rates	--	7,600
Total tax provision for the period	€87,800	€73,775

The aggregate current and deferred income tax expense (benefit) which was charged (credited) to stockholders' equity for the periods

	2005	2006
Current tax, related to correction of error	€(5,200)	€ --
Deferred tax, related to revaluation of investments	--	45,000
Total	€(5,200)	€45,000

The relationship between tax expense and accounting profit is explained by the following reconciliations:

NOTE: Only one required.

	2005	2004
Accounting profit	€167,907	€132,398
Tax at statutory rate (43% in 2005; 49% in 2006)	€ 72,200	€ 64,875
Tax effect of expenses which are not deductible:		
Charitable contributions	600	1,300
Civil fines imposed on the entity	15,000	
Effect on previously provided deferred tax assets and liabilities		
resulting from increase in statutory rates	--	7,600
Total tax provision for the period	€ 87,800	€ 73,775
Statutory tax rate	43.0	49.0
Tax effect of expenses which are not deductible:		
Charitable contributions	0.4	1.0
Civil fines imposed on the entity	8.9	--
Effect on previously provided deferred tax assets and liabilities		
resulting from increase in statutory rates	--	5.7
Total tax provision for the period	52.3	55.7

In 2006, the federal government imposed a 14% surcharge on the income tax, which has affected 2006 current tax expense as well as the recorded amounts of deferred tax assets and liabilities, since when these benefits are ultimately received or settled, the new higher tax rates will be applicable.

Deferred tax assets and liabilities included in the accompanying balance sheets as of December 31, 2005 and 2006 are as follows, as classified by categories of temporary differences:

	2005	2006
Accelerated depreciation for tax purposes	€26,890	€22,300
Liabilities for postretirement health care that are deductible only when paid	(15,675)	(19,420)
Product development costs deducted from taxable profits in prior years	2,500	--
Revaluation of fixed assets, net of accumulated depreciation	--	2,160
Deferred tax liability, net	€13,715	€ 5,040

Examples of Financial Statement Disclosures

Hong Kong Land Holdings Ltd
For the period ending December 31, 2004

Notes to the financial statements

1. Deferred tax

Deferred tax is provided, using the liability method, in respect of all temporary differences between the tax bases of assets and liabilities and their carrying values. Provision for deferred tax is made on the revaluation of certain noncurrent assets and, in relation to acquisitions, on the difference between the fair values of the net assets acquired and their tax base.

Provision for withholding tax, which could arise on the remittance of retained earnings relating to subsidiaries, is only made where there is a current intention to remit such earnings. Deferred tax assets relating to carryforward of unused tax losses are recognized to the extent that it is probable that future taxable profit will be available against which the unused tax losses can be utilized.

Critical accounting estimates and judgments

iii) Income taxes

The Group is subject to income taxes in numerous jurisdictions. Significant judgment is required in determining the worldwide provision for income taxes. There are many transactions and calculations for which the ultimate tax determination is uncertain during the ordinary course of business. The Group recognizes liabilities for anticipated tax audit issues based on estimates of whether additional taxes will be due. Where the final tax outcome of these matters is different from the amounts that were initially recorded, such differences will impact the income tax and deferred tax provisions in the period in which such determination is made.

6. Tax

	2004 US $m	2003 US $m
Current tax	(18.1)	(15.1)
Deferred tax		
Revaluation surpluses of investment properties	(288.9)	(76.4)
Other temporary differences	(7.3)	(1.3)
	(296.2)	75.1
	314.3	60.0

11. Deferred tax assets

Deferred tax assets of US $5.1 million (2003: US $7.4 million) arising from unused tax losses of US $27.5 million (2003: US $41.3 million) have not been recognized.

17. Deferred tax liabilities

	2004 US $m	2003 US $m
Accelerated capital allowances	20.2	16.7
Revaluation surpluses of investment properties	860.9	572.5
Other temporary differences	4.1	4.1
	885.2	593.3

Clariant
Period ending December 2004

Taxes

CHF mn	2004	2003
Current income taxes	(139)	(221)
Deferred income taxes	(1)	(110)
	(140)	(111)

The main elements contributing to the difference between the Group's overall expected tax expense/rate and effective tax expense/rate are:

	2004		2003	
	CHF mn	%	CHF mn	%
Income before taxes and minority interests	297		284	
Expected tax expense/rate	(96)	32.3	(92)	32.4
Effect of taxes on items not tax-deductible	(46)	15.5	(34)	12.0
Effect of utilization and changes in recognition of tax losses and tax credits	15	(5.1)	38	(13.4)
Effect of tax losses and tax credits of current year not recognized	(4)	1.3	(116)	40.8
Effect of adjustments to current taxes due to prior periods	(7)	2.4	2	(0.7)
Effect of tax exempt income	14	(4.7)	82	(28.9)
Effect of other items	(16)	5.4	9	(3.2)
Effective tax expense/rate	(140)	47.1	(111)	39.0

CHF mn	12/31/2004	12/31/2003
Deferred tax liabilities on		
Tangible and intangible assets	318	279
Prepaid pensions, other accruals and provisions	55	105
Total deferred tax liabilities	373	384
Deferred tax assets on		
Tangible and intangible assets	63	33
Employee benefit liabilities	83	61
Other accruals and provisions	88	172
Total deferred tax assets	279	291

Tax losses on which no deferred tax was calculated are as follows:

CHF mn	12/31/2004	12/31/2003
Expiry by		
2004	–	14
2005	34	22
2006	32	16
2007	31	105
2008	930	1,303
After 2008	1,289	1,165
Total	2,316	2,625

CHF mn	12/31/2004	12/31/2003
Unrecognized tax credits	3	4

The tax credits expires between 2005 and 2010.

F. Hoffman-LaRoche
Period ending December 2004

Taxation

Income taxes include all taxes based upon the taxable profits of the Group, including withholding taxes payable on the distribution of retained earnings within the Group. Other taxes not based on income, such as property and capital taxes, are included within other operating expenses or financial income according to their nature.

Liabilities for income taxes, mainly withholding taxes, which could arise on the remittance of retained earnings, principally relating to subsidiaries, are only recognized where there is a probable intention to remit such earnings.

Deferred income tax assets and liabilities are recognized on temporary differences between the tax bases of assets and liabilities and their carrying amounts in the financial statements. Deferred income tax assets relating to the carryforward of unused tax losses are recognized to the extent that it is probable that future taxable profit will be available against which the unused tax losses can be utilized.

Current and deferred income tax assets and liabilities are offset when the income taxes are levied by the same taxation authority and when there is a legally enforceable right to offset them. Deferred income taxes are determined based on the currently enacted tax rates applicable in each tax jurisdiction where the Group operates.

Income tax expenses in millions of CHF

	2004	2003
Current income taxes	2,167	1,794
Adjustments recognized for current tax of prior periods	25	39
Deferred income taxes	153	(388)
Total charge for income taxes	2,345	1,445

Since the Group operates across the world, it is subject to income taxes in many different tax jurisdictions. The Group calculates its average expected tax rate as a weighted-average of the tax-rates in the tax jurisdictions in which the Group operates. Within the Group's average expected tax rate, the increasing significance of Genentech and Chugai causes an increase in the rate which has been offset by ongoing improvement of the Group's structures.

The Group's effective tax rate can be reconciled to the Group's average expected tax rate as follows:

	2004	2003
Group's average expected tax rate	24.14%	24.3%
Tax effect of		
Unrecognized tax losses	1.5%	0.1%
Nontaxable income/nondeductible expenses	0.3%	0.1%
Impairment of financial assets	0.0%	1.2%
Other differences	2.1%	0.5%
Continuing businesses before exceptional items effective tax rate	25.0%	25.8%

	2004			2003		
	Profit before tax	*Income taxes*	*Tax rate*	*Profit before tax*	*Income taxes*	*Tax rate*
Continuing businesses before exceptional items effective tax rate	6,568	(1,645)	25.0%	5,119	(1,319)	25.8%
Amortization of goodwill	(572)	--		(489)	--	
Major legal cases	--	--		216	(87)	
Changes in Group organization	(199)	33		--	--	
Exceptional income from bond conversion and redemption	908	(290)		--	--	
Continuing businesses effective tax rate	6,705	(1,902)	28.4%	4,846	(1,406)	29.0%
Discontinuing businesses	277	(75)		430	(80)	
Changes in Group organization in discontinuing businesses	2,503	(368)		(395)	41	
Group's effective tax rate	9,485	(2,345)	24.7%	4,881	(1,445)	29.6%

Income tax assets (liabilities) *in millions of CHF*

	2004	2003
Current income taxes		
Current income tax assets	159	238
Current income tax liabilities	(947)	(714)
Net current income tax assets (liability)	(788)	(476)
Deferred income taxes		
Deferred income tax assets	1,047	900
Deferred income tax liabilities	(3,564)	(3,133)
Net deferred income tax asset (liability)	(2,517)	(2,233)

Deferred income tax assets are recognized for tax loss carryforwards only to the extent that realization of the related tax benefit is probable. The Group has unrecognized tax losses, including valuation allowances, of 172 million Swiss francs (2003: 594 million Swiss francs), of which 88 million Swiss francs expires within four years and 40 million Swiss francs expire within six years. The remaining 44 million Swiss francs of losses expire after fifteen years or more. Deferred income tax liabilities have not been established for the withholding tax and other taxes that would be payable on the unremitted earnings of certain foreign subsidiaries, as such amounts are currently regarded as permanently reinvested. These unremitted earnings totaled 27.6 billion Swiss francs at December 31, 2004 (2003: 22.8 billion Swiss francs).

The deferred income tax assets and liabilities and the deferred income tax charges (credits) are attributable to the following items:

Deferred income taxes: movements in recognized assets (liabilities)
in millions of CHF

2004	*Property, plant and equipment, and intangible assets*	*Restructuring provisions*	*Other temporary differences*	*Total*
Net deferred income tax asset (liability) at beginning of year	(3,597)	125	1,239	(2,233)
(Charged) credited to the income statement	390	(22)	(521)	(153)
(Charged) credited to equity	--	--	(19)	(19)
Acquisition of Igen	(259)	--	93	(166)
Disposal of Consumer Health (OTC) business	4	--	(2)	2
Currency translation effects and other	403	(79)	(278)	52
Net deferred income tax asset (liability) at end of year	(3,059)	30	512	(2,517)

2003	Property, plant and equipment, and intangible assets	Restructuring provisions	Other temporary differences	Total
Net deferred income tax asset (liability) at beginning of year	(3,343)	135	441	(2,767)
(Charged) credited to the income statement	(322)	(18)	728	388
(Charged) credited to equity	--	--	1	1
Disetronic	(80)	--	(3)	(83)
Disposal of Vitamins and Fine Chemicals business	7,223	(3)	109	329
Currency translation effects and other	(75)	11	(37)	(101)
Net deferred income tax asset (liability) at end of year	(3,597)	125	1,239	(2,233)

Mittal Steel South Africa Limited
Period ending December 2004

Income Taxation

Income tax on the profit or loss for the year comprises current and deferred tax. Income tax is recognized in the income statement except to the extent that it relates to items recognized directly in equity, in which case it is recognized in equity.

Current taxation comprises tax payable calculated on the basis of the expected taxable income for the year, using tax rates expected at the balance sheet date, and any adjustments of the tax payable for the previous year.

Additional income taxes that arise from the distribution of dividends are recognized at the same time as the liability to pay the related dividend.

Deferred Taxation

Deferred taxation is provided using the balance sheet liability method on all temporary differences between the carrying amounts for financial reporting purposes and the amounts used for taxation purposes, except differences relating to goodwill not deductible for taxation purposes and the initial recognition of assets or liabilities which affect neither accounting nor taxable profit or loss.

A deferred tax asset is recognized to the extent that it is probable that future taxable profits will be available against which the associated unused tax losses and deductible temporary differences can be utilized.

Deferred taxation is calculated using taxation rates that have been enacted at balance sheet date. The effect on deferred taxation of any changes in taxation rates is charged to the income statement, except to the extent that it relates to items previously charged or credited directly to equity.

Taxation

Charge to income

	Group		Company	
	Year ended Dec.31 2004 Rm	Six months ended Dec.31 2003 Rm	Year ended Dec.31 2004 Rm	Six months ended Dec.31 2003 Rm
South African normal taxation				
Current: Current period (excluding Controlled Foreign Companies)	(1,589)	(141)	(1,559)	(135)
Prior year (excluding Controlled Foreign Companies)	(6)			
Controlled foreign companies	(6)	(5)	(6)	(5)
	(1,601)	(146)	(1,565)	(140)
Deferred: Current year	(583)	(68)	(162)	(65)
Prior year	(3)	7	(3)	7
	(586)	(61)	(165)	(58)
Share of associates and joint ventures taxation	(89)	(21)	--	--
Secondary tax on companies	(209)	(51)	(207)	(51)
	(2,485)	(279)	(1,937)	(249)

Reconciliation of taxation rates

	%	%	%	%
Taxation as a percentage of profit before taxation	32.7	37.4	26.1	36.2
Taxation effect of				
Current taxation prior year	(0.1)			
Deferred taxation prior year		0.9		1.0
Share of associates and joint ventures taxation	0.2	0.7		
Exempt income		1.1		0.3
Disallowable expenditure	(0.7)	(2.1)	(0.7)	(2.2)
Dividends received				3.2
Secondary tax on companies	(2.8)	(6.8)	(2.8)	(7.4)
Proportional net income of controlled foreign entities – taxable in RSA			(0.1)	(0.6)
Impairment		(0.4)	7.7	
Fixed assets and finance leases	(0.2)	(1.1)	(0.2)	(0.7)
Other	(0.1)	0.3		0.2
Standard tax rate	30.0	30.0	30.0	30.0

APPENDIX

ACCOUNTING FOR INCOME TAXES IN INTERIM PERIODS

Interim Reporting

IAS 34, *Interim Financial Reporting*, established new requirements for interim reporting, while not making the reporting of interim results mandatory. While the DSOP preceding this standard's promulgation essentially endorsed a discrete approach (applying measurement principles to each interim period on a stand-alone basis), the final standard represents a judicious mix of integral and discrete viewpoints. As noted in the main body of this chapter, IAS 34 adopts an integral viewpoint with regard to income tax expense, as indeed was necessitated by the fact that taxing authorities almost universally apply their requirements to a full year, taken as a whole, with no attempt at interim measurement of results of operations.

In this appendix, supplementary guidance is offered, largely based on US GAAP, to assist in applying the principles of income tax accounting set forth in IAS 12 to interim periods when the enterprise elects (or is required by local law) to report on such as basis. This guidance should be understood as being illustrative rather than authoritative. Care should be taken in particular regarding areas of financial reporting which are guided by recently issued or revised international accounting standards (such as that for discontinuing operations).

The general consensus is that the appropriate perspective for interim period reporting is to view the interim period as an integral part of the year rather than as a discrete period. For purposes of computing income tax provisions, this objective is usually achieved by projecting income for the full annual period, computing the tax thereon, and applying the effective rate to the interim period income or loss, with quarterly (or monthly) revisions to the expected annual results and the tax effects thereof, as necessary.

Notwithstanding this general principle, however, there are certain complexities that arise only in the context of interim financial reporting. Included in this group of issues are (1) recognizing the tax benefits of losses based on expected earnings of later interim or annual periods, (2) reporting the benefits of net operating loss carryforwards in interim periods, and (3) reporting the effects of tax law changes in interim periods. Other matters requiring interpretation include the classification of deferred taxes on interim balance sheets and the allocation of interim period tax provisions between current and deferred expense.

Basic example of interim period accounting for income taxes

Andorra Woolens, Inc. estimates that accounting profit for the full fiscal year ending June 30, 2006, will be €400,000. The company expects the annual premium on an officer's life insurance policy to be €12,000, and dividend income (from a less than 20% ownership interest) is expected to be €100,000. Under pertinent tax rules, premiums paid on officer's life insurance is not an expense. Furthermore, there is a dividends received deduction of 70% for intercorporate investments of under 20%. Deferred organization costs are being amortized for financial reporting purposes (having been assessed as having limited life), but cannot be deducted for tax purposes in the company's jurisdiction. Organization cost amortization is €30,000 per year.

The company recognized income of €75,000 in the first quarter of the year. The deferred tax liability arises solely in connection with depreciation temporary differences; these differences totaled €150,000 at the beginning of the year and are projected to equal €280,000 at year-end. The effective rate expected to apply to the reversal at both year beginning and year-end is 34%. The change in the taxable temporary difference during the current interim period is €30,000.

Andorra Woolens must first calculate its estimated effective income tax rate for the year. This rate is computed using all the tax planning alternatives available to the company (e.g., tax credits, foreign rates, capital gains rates, etc.).

Estimated pretax accounting income		€ 400,000
Permanent differences:		
Add: Nondeductible officer's life insurance premium	€12,000	
Nondeductible amortization of organization costs	30,000	42,000
		442,000
Less: Dividends received deduction (€100,000 x 70%)		(70,000)
Estimated book taxable income		372,000
Less: Change in taxable temporary difference		(130,000)
Estimated taxable income for the year		€ 242,000
Tax on estimated taxable income (see below)		€ 70,530
Effective tax rate for **current** tax provision		
[€70,530/(€400,000 – €130,000)]		26.1%

Tax rate schedule			Taxable	
At least	*Not more than*	*Rate*	*income*	*Tax*
€ --	€50,000	15%	€ 50,000	€ 7,500
50,000	75,000	25%	25,000	6,250
75,000	--	34%	167,000	56,780
				€70,530

The deferred tax provision for the interim period should be based on the actual change in the temporary difference (depreciation, in this example) during the interim period. In this case the depreciation temporary difference grew by €30,000 during the period, and the expected tax rate that will apply to the reversal, in future years, is the marginal rate of 34%. Accordingly, the tax provision for the period is as follows:

Ordinary income for the interim period	€75,000
Less: Change in temporary difference	30,000
Net ordinary income	45,000
Applicable tax rate	26.1%
Current tax provision	€11,755
Tax effect of temporary difference (€30,000 x 34%)	10,200
Total provision	€21,955

Therefore, the entry necessary to record the income tax expense at the end of the first quarter is as follows:

Income tax expense	21,955	
Income taxes payable—current		11,755
Deferred tax liability		10,200

The financial statement presentation would remain the same as has been illustrated in prior examples.

In the second quarter, Andorra Woolens, Inc. revises its estimate of income for the full fiscal year. It now anticipates only €210,000 of book income, including only €75,000 of dividend income, because of dramatic changes in the national economy. Other permanent differences are still expected to total €42,000.

Estimated pretax accounting income		€ 210,000
Permanent differences:		
Add: Nondeductible officer's life insurance premium	€12,000	
Nondeductible amortization of organization costs	30,000	42,000
		252,000
Less: Dividends received deduction (€75,000 x 70%)		(52,500)
Estimated book taxable income		199,500
Less: Change in taxable temporary difference		(130,000)
Estimated taxable income for the year		€ 69,500
Tax on estimated taxable income (see below)		€ 12,375
Effective tax rate for *current* tax provision		
[€12,375/(€210,000 – €130,000)]		15.5%

Tax rate schedule			Taxable	
At least	*Not more than*	*Rate*	*income*	*Tax*
€ --	€50,000	15%	€ 50,000	€ 7,500
50,000	75,000	25%	19,500	4,875
				€12,375

The actual earnings for the second quarter were €22,000, and the change in the temporary difference was only €10,000. The tax provision for the second quarter is computed as follows:

Ordinary income for the half year	€97,000
Less: Change in temporary difference	40,000
Net ordinary income	57,000
Applicable tax rate	15.5%
Current tax provision	€ 8,835
Tax effect of temporary difference (€40,000 x 34%)	13,600
Total provision	€22,435

Under the general principle that changes in estimate are reported prospectively, the results of prior quarters are not restated for changes in the estimated effective annual tax rate. Given the provision for current and deferred income taxes that was made in the first interim period, shown above, the following entry is required to record the income taxes as of the end of the second quarter:

Income tax expense	480	
Income taxes payable—current	2,920	
Deferred tax liability		3,400

The foregoing illustrates the basic problems encountered in applying the promulgated US GAAP to interim reporting. In the following paragraphs, we discuss some items requiring modifications to the approach described above.

Net Operating Losses in Interim Periods

The tax effects of operating losses are treated no differently than any other temporary differences; if probable of being realized, the tax effects are reflected as deferred tax benefits in the period the loss is incurred. If not deemed probable, no tax effects are recognized; if the estimation of realizability changes in a later period, the deferred tax benefit is then recorded, with the offset being included in current period tax expense. However, given the desire to treat interim periods as integral parts of the annual period of which they are a component, the accounting treatment of net operating losses raises a number of issues. These include (1) calculation of the expected annual tax rate for purposes of interim period income tax provisions and (2) recognition of an asset for the tax effects of a loss carryforward.

Carryforward from prior years. Loss carryforward benefits from prior years first given recognition (i.e., by recordation of a deferred tax benefit when none had been recognized in the period the loss was incurred) in interim periods are included in the ordinary tax provision. Common practice is to compute the expected annual effective tax rate on ordinary income at each interim reporting date, and use this rate to provide income taxes on ordinary income on a cumulative basis at each interim date. The tax effects of extraordinary items, discontinued operations, and other nonoperating categories were excluded from this computation; those tax effects are typically separately determined on a with-and-without basis, as explained later in this appendix.

Recognition of a previously unrecognized tax benefit should be included as a credit in the tax provision of the interim period when there is a reevaluation of the likelihood of future tax benefits being realized. Similarly, a reduction of the deferred tax benefit resulting from a revised judgment that the benefits are not probable of being realized would cause a catch-up adjustment to be included in the current interim period's ordinary tax provision. In either situation, the effect is *not* prorated to future interim periods by means of the effective tax rate estimate. To illustrate, consider the following example.

Example of carryforward from prior years

Dacca Corporation has a previously unrecognized €50,000 net operating loss carryforward; a flat 40% tax rate for current and future periods is assumed. Income for the full year (before NOL) is projected to be €80,000; in the first quarter a pretax loss of €10,000 will be reported.

Projected annual income	€80,000
x Tax rate	40%
Projected tax liability	€32,000

Accordingly, in the income statement for the first fiscal quarter, the pretax operating loss of €10,000 will give rise to a tax *benefit* of €10,000 x 40% = €4,000.

In addition, a tax benefit of €20,000 (€50,000 loss carryforward x 40%) is given recognition and is included in the current interim period tax provision relating to continuing operations. Thus, total tax benefit for the first fiscal quarter will be €24,000 (= €4,000 + €20,000).

If Dacca's second quarter results in a pretax operating income of €30,000, and the expectation for the full year remains unchanged (i.e., operating income of €80,000), the second quarter tax provision is €12,000 (€30,000 x 40%).

The tax provision for the fiscal first half-year will be a benefit of €12,000, as follows:

Cumulative pretax income through second quarter	
(€30,000 – €10,000)	€ 20,000
x Effective rate	40%
Tax provision before recognition of NOL carryforward benefit	€ 8,000
Benefit of NOL carryforward first recognized in first quarter	(20,000)
Total tax provision (benefit)	€(12,000)

The foregoing example assumes that during the first quarter, Dacca's judgment changed as to the full realizability of the previously unrecognized benefit of the €50,000 loss carryforward. Were this *not* the case, however, the benefit would have been recognized only as actual tax liabilities were incurred (through current period earnings) in amounts to offset the NOL benefit.

To illustrate the latter situation, assume the same facts about earnings for the first two quarters, and assume now that Dacca's judgment about realizability of prior period NOL does not change. Tax provisions for the first quarter and first half are as follows:

	First quarter	*First half-year*
Pretax income (loss)	€(10,000)	€20,000
x Effective rate	40%	40%
Tax provision before recognition of NOL carryforward benefit	€ (4,000)	€ 8,000
Benefit of NOL carryforward recognized	0	(8,000)
Tax provision (benefit)	€ (4,000)	€ 0

Notice that recognition of a tax benefit of €4,000 in the first quarter is based on the expectation of at least a breakeven full year's results. That is, the benefit of the first quarter's loss was deemed probable of realization. Otherwise, no tax benefit would have been reported in the first quarter.

Estimated loss for the year. When the full year is expected to be profitable, it will be irrelevant that one or more interim periods results in a loss, and the expected effective rate for the full year should be used to record interim period tax benefits, as illustrated above. However, when the full year is expected to produce a loss, computation of the expected annual tax benefit rate must logically take into account the extent to which a deferred tax asset will be recordable at year-end. For the first set of examples, below, assume that the realization of tax benefits related to operating loss carryforwards are not entirely probable. That is, only a portion of the benefits will be recognized.

For each of the following examples we assume that the L'avventura Corporation is anticipating a loss for the fiscal year of €150,000. A deferred tax liability of €30,000 is currently recorded on the company's books; all of the credits will reverse in the fifteen-year carryforward period permitted by applicable tax law. Assume that future taxes will be at a 40% rate.

Example 1

Assume that the company can carry back the entire €150,000 to the preceding three years. The tax potentially refundable by the carryback would (remember, this is only an estimate until year-end) amount to €48,000 (an assumed amount). The effective rate is then 32% (€48,000/€150,000).

| | Ordinary income (loss) | | | Tax (benefit) expense | | |
| | | | | | Less | |
Reporting period	Reporting period	Year-to-date		Year-to-date	previously provided	Reporting period
1st qtr.	€ (50,000)	€ (50,000)		€(16,000)	€ --	€(16,000)
2nd qtr.	20,000	(30,000)		(9,600)	(16,000)	6,400
3rd qtr.	(70,000)	(100,000)		(32,000)	(9,600)	(22,400)
4th qtr.	(50,000)	(150,000)		(48,000)	(32,000)	(16,000)
Fiscal year	€(150,000)					€(48,000)

Note that both the income tax expense (2nd quarter) and benefit are computed using the estimated annual effective rate. This rate is applied to the year-to-date numbers just as in the previous examples, with any adjustment being made and realized in the current reporting period. This treatment is appropriate because the accrual of tax benefits in the first, third, and fourth quarters is consistent with the effective rate estimated at the beginning of the year; in contrast to those circumstances in which a change in estimate is made in a quarter relating to the realizability of tax benefits not provided previously (or provided for only partially).

Example 2

In this case assume that L'avventura Corporation can carry back only €50,000 of the loss and that the remainder must be carried forward. Realization of income to offset the loss is not deemed to be probable. The estimated carryback of €50,000 would generate a tax refund of €12,000 (again assumed). The company is assumed to be in the 40% tax bracket (a flat rate is used to simplify the example). The benefit of the operating loss carryforward is recognized only to the extent that it is deemed to be probable of realization. In this example, management has concluded that only one-fourth of the gross benefit will be realized in future years. Accordingly, only €10,000 of estimated tax benefit related to the carryforward of the projected loss is recordable. Considered in conjunction with the carryback of €12,000, the company will obtain a €22,000 tax benefit relating to the projected current year loss, for an effective tax benefit rate of 14.7%. The calculation of the estimated annual effective rate is as follows:

Expected net loss			€150,000
Tax benefit from carryback		€12,000	
Benefit of carryforward (€100,000 x 40%)	€40,000		
Portion not deemed to be probable of realization	(30,000)	10,000	
Total recognized benefit			€ 22,000
Estimated annual effective rate (€22,000 ÷ €150,000)			14.7%

	Ordinary income (loss)			Tax (benefit) expense		
				Year-to-date		
Reporting period	Reporting period	Year-to-date			Less previously provided	Reporting period
			Computed	Limited to		
1st qtr.	€ 10,000	€ 10,000	€ 1,470	€ --	€ --	€ 1,470
2nd qtr.	(80,000)	(70,000)	(11,733)	--	1,470	(10,263)
3rd qtr.	(100,000)	(170,000)	(14,667)	(22,000)	(10,263)	(4,404)
4th qtr.	20,000	(150,000)	(22,000)	--	(22,000)	--
Fiscal year	€(150,000)					€(22,000)

In the foregoing, the tax expense (benefit) is computed by multiplying the year-to-date income or loss by the estimated annual effective rate, and then subtracting the amount of tax liability or benefit provided in prior interim periods. It makes no difference if the current period indicates an income or a loss, assuming of course that the full-year estimated results are not being revised. However, if the cumulative loss for the interim periods to date exceeds the projected loss for the full year on which the effective tax benefit rate had been based, no further tax benefits can be recorded, as illustrated above in the provision for the third quarter.

Operating loss occurring during an interim period. An instance may occur in which the company expects net income for the year and incurs a net loss during one of the reporting periods. In this situation, the estimated annual effective rate, which was calculated based on the expected net income figure, is applied to the year-to-date income or loss to arrive at a total year-to-date tax provision. The amount previously provided is subtracted from the year-to-date figure to arrive at the provision for the current reporting period. If the current period operations resulted in a loss, the tax provision for the period will reflect a tax benefit.

Tax Provision Applicable to Discontinuing Operations Occurring in Interim Periods

Discontinuing operations are to be shown net of the related tax effects. The interim treatment accorded discontinuing operations does not differ from the fiscal year-end reporting required by GAAP. However, common practice is not to include these items in computation of the estimated annual tax rate. These items are generally recognized in the interim period in which they occur; that is, they are not annualized. Recognition of the tax effects of a loss due to any of the aforementioned situations would be made if the benefits are expected to be realized during the year or if they will be recognizable as a deferred tax asset at year-end under the provisions of IAS 12.

If a situation arises where realization is not probable in the period of occurrence but becomes assured in a subsequent period in the same fiscal year, the previously unrecognized tax benefit should be reported in income until it reduces the tax provision to zero, with any excess reported in other categories of income (e.g., discontinuing operations) that provided a means of realization for the tax benefit.

If the decision to dispose of operations occurs in any interim period other than the first period, the income (loss) applicable to the discontinuing segment has already been used in computing the estimated annual effective tax rate. Therefore, a recomputation of the total tax is not required. However, the total tax is to be divided into two components.

1. That tax applicable to income (loss) before discontinuing operations
2. That tax applicable to the income (loss) from the discontinuing segment

This division is accomplished as follows: A revised estimated annual effective rate is calculated for the income (loss) before discontinuing operations. This recomputation is then applied to the income (loss) from the preceding periods. The total tax applicable to the discontinuing segment is then composed of the difference between the total tax originally computed and the tax recomputed on remaining income before discontinuing operations.

Example

Realtime Corporation anticipates net income of €150,000 during the fiscal year. The net permanent differences for the year will be €10,000. The company also anticipates tax credits of €10,000 during the fiscal year. For purposes of this example, we assume a flat statutory rate of 50%. The estimated annual effective rate is then calculated as follows:

Estimated pretax income	€150,000
Net permanent differences	(10,000)
Taxable income	140,000
Statutory rate	50%
Tax	70,000
Anticipated credits	(10,000)
Total estimated tax	€ 60,000
Estimated effective rate (€60,000 ÷ €150,000)	40%

The first two quarters of operations were as follows:

	Income (loss)			Tax provision		
Reporting period	*Reporting period*	*Year-to-date*		*Year-to-date*	*Less previously provided*	*Reporting period*
1st qtr.	€30,000	€30,000		€12,000	€ --	€12,000
2nd qtr.	25,000	55,000		22,000	12,000	10,000

In the third quarter, Realtime made the decision to dispose of Division X. During the third quarter, the company earned a total of €60,000. The company expects the disposal to result in a onetime charge to income of €50,000 and estimates that losses subsequent to the disposal will be €25,000. The company estimates revised income in the fourth quarter to be €35,000. The two components of pretax accounting income (discontinuing operations and revised income before discontinuing operations) are shown below.

		Division X	
Reporting period	*Revised income before discontinuing operations*	*Loss from operations*	*Provision for loss on disposal*
1st qtr.	€ 40,000	€(10,000)	€ --
2nd qtr.	40,000	(15,000)	--
3rd qtr.	80,000	(20,000)	(75,000)
4th qtr.	35,000	--	--
Fiscal year	€195,000	€(45,000)	€(75,000)

Realtime must now recompute the estimated annual tax rate. Assume that all the permanent differences are related to the revised continuing operations. However, €3,300 of the tax credits were applicable to machinery used in Division X. Because of the discontinuance of operations, the credit on this machinery would not be allowed. Any recapture of prior period credits must be used as a reduction in the tax benefit from either operations or the loss on disposal. Assume that the company must recapture €2,000 of investment tax credit which is related to Division X.

The recomputed estimated annual rate for continuing operations is as follows:

Estimated (revised) ordinary income	€195,000
Less net permanent differences	(10,000)
	€185,000
Tax at statutory rate of 50%	€ 92,500
Less anticipated credits from continuing operations	(6,700)
Tax provision	€ 85,800
Estimated annual effective tax rate (€85,800 ÷ €195,000)	44%

The next step is then to apply the revised rate to the quarterly income from continuing operations as illustrated below.

	Income before discontinuing operations		Estimated annual effective	Tax provision		
Reporting period	*Reporting period*	*Year-to-date*	*rate*	*Year-to-date*	*Less previously provided*	*Reporting period*
1st qtr.	€ 40,000	€ 40,000	44%	€17,600	€ --	€17,600
2nd qtr.	40,000	80,000	44%	35,200	17,600	17,600
3rd qtr.	80,000	160,000	44%	70,400	35,200	35,200
4th qtr.	35,000	195,000	44%	85,800	70,400	15,400
Fiscal year	€195,000					€85,800

The tax benefit applicable to the operating loss from discontinuing operations and the loss from the disposal must now be calculated. The first two quarters are calculated on a differential basis as shown below.

	Tax applicable to ordinary income		Tax (benefit) expense
Reporting period	Previously reported	Recomputed (above)	applicable to Division X
1st qtr.	€ 12,000	€17,600	€ (5,600)
2nd qtr.	10,000	17,600	(7,600)
			€(13,200)

The only calculation remaining applies to the third quarter tax benefit pertaining to the operating loss and the loss on disposal of the discontinuing segment. The calculation of this amount is made based on the revised estimate of annual ordinary income, both including and excluding the effects of the Division X losses. This is shown below.

	Loss from operations of Division X	Provision for loss on Disposal
Estimated annual income from continuing operations	€195,000	€195,000
Net permanent differences	(10,000)	(10,000)
Loss from Division X operations	(45,000)	--
Provision for loss on disposal of Division X	--	(75,000)
Total	€140,000	€110,000
Tax at the statutory rate of 50%	€ 70,000	€ 55,000
Anticipated credits (from continuing operations)	(6,700)	(6,700)
Recapture of previously recognized tax credits as a result of disposal	--	2,000
Taxes after effect of Division X losses	63,300	50,300
Taxes computed on estimated income before the effect of Division X losses	85,800	85,800
Tax benefit applicable to Division X	(22,500)	(35,500)
Amounts recognized in quarters one and two (€5,600 + €7,600)	(13,200)	--
Tax benefit to be recognized in the third quarter	€ (9,300)	€ (35,500)

The quarterly tax provisions can be summarized as follows:

Reporting period	Pretax income (loss)			Tax (benefit) applicable to		
	Continuing operations	Operations of Division X	Provision for loss on disposal	Continuing operations	Operations of Division X	Provision for loss on disposal
1st qtr.	€ 40,000	€(10,000)	€ --	€17,600	€ (5,600)	€ --
2nd qtr.	40,000	(15,000)	--	17,600	(7,600)	--
3rd qtr.	80,000	(20,000)	(75,000)	35,200	(9,300)	(35,500)
4th qtr.	35,000	--	--	15,400	--	--
Fiscal year	€195,000	€(45,000)	€(75,000)	€85,800	€(22,500)	€(35,500)

The following income statement shows the proper financial statement presentation of these unusual and infrequent items. The notes to the statement indicate which items are to be included in the calculation of the annual estimated rate.

Income Statement

Net sales*		€xxxx
Other income*		xxx
		xxxx
Costs and expenses		
Cost of sales*	€xxxx	
Selling, general, and administrative expenses*	xxx	
Interest expense*	xx	
Other deductions*	xx	
Unusual items	xxx	
Infrequently occurring items	xxx	xxxx
Income (loss) from continuing operations before income taxes and other items listed below		xxxx
Provision for income taxes (benefit)**		xxx
Income (loss) from continuing operations before items listed below		xxxx
Discontinuing operations:		
Income (loss) from operations of discontinuing Division X (less applicable income taxes of €xxxx)	xxxx	
Income (loss) on disposal of Division X, including provision of €xxxx for operating losses during phaseout period (less applicable taxes of €xxxx)	xxxx	xxxx
Income (loss) before cumulative effect of a change in accounting principle		xxxx
Cumulative effect on prior years of a change in accounting principle (less applicable income taxes of €xxxx***)		xxxx
Net income (loss)		€xxxx

* *Components of ordinary income (loss).*

** *Consists of total income taxes (benefit) applicable to ordinary income (loss), unusual items, and infrequent items.*

*** *This amount is shown net of income taxes. Although the income taxes are generally disclosed (as illustrated), this is not required.*

16 EMPLOYEE BENEFITS

PERSPECTIVE AND ISSUES

The prescribed rules for the accounting for employee benefits under IFRS have evolved markedly over two decades. The current standard, IAS 19, was last subjected to a major revision in 1998, with further limited amendments made in 2000, 2002, and 2004. IAS 19 provides broad guidance, applicable to all employee benefits, not merely to pension plans. The approach set forth by IAS 19 is largely consistent with that of major national accounting standard setters. Compared to pre-1998 iterations of IAS 19, the range of acceptable alternative accounting treatments has been narrowed substantially, as has also occurred with other IFRS, and this reduction in the number of allowable alternative methods will likely continue as the process of "convergence" moves forward.

The objective of employee benefit accounting is primarily the appropriate determination of periodic cost. Under current IAS 19, only one basic method, the "projected unit credit" variation on the *accrued benefit valuation* method, is permitted for the periodic determination of this cost. IAS 19 endorses a smoothing methodology, and thus creates a "corridor" approach to recognition of actuarial gains and losses. It requires annual valuations, whereas the earlier mandate had been for triennial valuations. It also addresses past service cost recognition and other matters that had not been given any attention in earlier standards. Revised IAS 19 is more precise in defining the extent to which components of pension cost are to be disclosed in the financial statements, and it reduces the latitude formerly given to financial statement preparers regarding amortizing certain cost elements, such as that associated with plan amendments.

IAS 19 identifies and provides accounting direction for five categories of employee benefits: short-term benefits such as wages, bonuses, and emoluments such as medical care; postemployment benefits such as pensions and other postretirement benefits; other long-term benefits such as sabbatical leave; termination benefits; and equity compensation arrangements. Meaningful IFRS guidance is provided on each of these, whereas the earlier standards focused only on pensions. Nonetheless, the most explicit and detailed of these instructions are for defined benefit pension and other postretirement benefits plans, with less detailed instructions given on the other types of employee benefits; this is understandable given the extreme complexity of both the plans and the accounting therefor. Another major category of employee benefit program, stock-based compensation arrangements, have now been fully dealt with by a recent standard, IFRS 2, which is addressed in detail in Chapter 17.

Pension plans generally exist in two basic varieties; defined contribution and defined benefit. The accounting for the latter is, by far, the more difficult. Given the central role that accounting estimates play in the accounting for defined benefit plans, some diversity in financial reporting will be unavoidable, and full disclosure of key assumptions and methods is the best means of preventing misunderstandings by financial statement users. Defined benefit plan accounting in particular remains a controversial subject because of the heavy impact that various management assumptions have on expense determination, and also because IAS 19 embraces the concept of expense smoothing to a much greater extent than do other accounting standards. Many believe any smoothing strategy to be inappropriate, and a number of financial reporting frauds have been uncovered in recent years that used improper smoothing as a central component of the fraudulent scheme. It remains possible that future revisions to IAS 19 and its corresponding standards under US and other national GAAP may reduce or eliminate the extent to which periodic defined benefit pension cost determinations rely on such techniques.

Because of the long-term nature of employee benefit plans, IAS 19 provides for delayed recognition of certain cost components, such as those resulting from changes in actuarial estimates Thus, certain changes are not recognized immediately but instead are recognized over subsequent years in a gradual and systematic way. Estimates and averages may be used as long as material differences are not created as a result. Explicit assumptions and estimates of future events should be made for each specified variable included in pension costs.

IAS 19 also establishes requirements for disclosures to be made by employers when defined contribution or defined benefit pension plans are settled, curtailed, or terminated. Some previously deferred amounts are required to be recognized immediately under such circumstances.

IAS 19 defines all postemployment benefits other than pensions as defined benefit plans and, thus, all the accounting complications of defined benefit pension plans are mirrored here. These difficulties may be exacerbated, in the case of postretirement health care plans, by the need to project the future escalation in health care costs over a rather lengthy time horizon, which is a famously difficult exercise to undertake.

IAS 19 was amended in mid-2002 to prohibit the recognition of gains or losses that arise solely from past service cost and actuarial losses or gains, respectively, when a surplus in the plan exists. This amendment to IAS 19 addressed what some viewed as a counterintuitive result produced by the interaction of two aspects of the standard; namely, the option to defer the gains and losses in the pension fund and the limit on the amount that can be recognized as an asset (the "asset ceiling"). The effect of the amendment, which is viewed as an interim solution only, is to prevent such counterintuitive loss or gain recognition. The asset ceiling requirement was left unchanged.

While accounting for employee benefits by the various national standards and IFRS has been in the process of converging for many years, a number of important differences remain. IASB concluded that the differences between IAS 19 and the national standards would best be addressed in a broad-scope convergence project. This is an ongoing effort, with resolution tied to certain other IASB projects, including one that is attempting to address how comprehensive income should be reported. The major issues being addressed are discussed later in this chapter.

In June 2002, IASB began a limited convergence project on postemployment benefits. It resulted in the promulgation of an amendment dealing with the recognition of actuarial gain and losses, and in proposals (not acted upon) on the treatment of group defined benefit plans in the individual or separate financial statements of entities within a consolidated group, and additional disclosures.

Sources of IFRS
IAS 19

DEFINITIONS OF TERMS

Accrued benefit obligation. Actuarial present value of benefits (whether vested or non-vested) attributed by the pension benefit formula to employee service rendered before a specified date and based on employee service and compensation (if applicable) prior to that date.

Accrued benefit valuation methods. Actuarial valuation methods that reflect retirement benefits based on service rendered by employees to the date of the valuation. Assumptions about projected salary levels to the date of retirement must be incorporated, but service to be rendered after the balance sheet date is not considered in the calculation of pension cost or of the related obligation.

Accrued pension cost. Cumulative net pension cost accrued in excess of the employer's contributions.

Accrued postretirement benefit obligation. The actuarial present value of benefits attributed to employee service rendered as of a particular date. Prior to an employee's full eligibility date, the accrued postretirement benefit obligation as of a particular date for an employee is the portion of the expected postretirement benefit obligation attributed to that employee's service rendered to that date. On and after the full eligibility date, the accrued and expected postretirement benefit obligations for an employee are the same.

Actuarial present value. Value, as of a specified date, of an amount or series of amounts payable or receivable thereafter, with each amount adjusted to reflect (1) the time value of money (through discounts for interest) and (2) the probability of payment (by means of decrements for events such as death, disability, withdrawal, or retirement) between the date specified and the expected date of payment.

Actuarial valuation. The process used by actuaries to estimate the present value of benefits to be paid under a retirement plan and the present values of plan assets and sometimes also of future contributions.

Amortization. Usually refers to the process of reducing a recognized liability systematically by recognizing revenues or reducing a recognized asset systematically by recognizing expenses or costs. In pension accounting, amortization is also used to refer to the systematic recognition in net pension cost over several periods of previously unrecognized amounts, including unrecognized prior service cost and unrecognized actuarial gain or loss.

Asset ceiling. The maximum amount of defined benefit asset that can be recognized is the lower of (1) the surplus or deficit in the benefit plan plus (minus) any unrecognized losses (gains) or (2) the total of (a) any cumulative unrecognized net actuarial losses and past service cost, and (b) the present value of any economic benefits available in the form of refunds from the plan or reductions in future contributions to the plan, determined using the discount rate that reflects market yields at the balance sheet date on high-quality corporate bonds or, if necessary, on government bonds.

Attribution. Process of assigning pension benefits or cost to periods of employee service.

Career-average-pay formula (career-average-pay plan). Benefit formula that bases benefits on the employee's compensation over the entire period of service with the employer. A career-average-pay plan is a plan with such a formula.

Contributory plan. Pension plan under which employees contribute part of the cost. In some contributory plans, employees wishing to be covered must contribute; in other contributory plans, employee contributions result in increased benefits.

Current service cost. The cost to the employer under a retirement benefit plan for the services rendered by employees during the period, exclusive of cost elements identified as past service cost, experience adjustments, and the effects of changes in actuarial assumptions.

Curtailment. Event that significantly reduces the expected years of future service of present employees or eliminates, for a significant number of employees, the accrual of defined benefits for some or all of their future services. Curtailments include (1) termination of employee's services earlier than expected, which may or may not involve closing a facility or discontinuing a segment of a business, and (2) termination or suspension of a plan so that employees do not earn additional defined benefits for future services. In the latter situation, future service may be counted toward vesting of benefits accumulated based on past services.

Defined benefit pension plan. Any postemployment benefit plan other than a defined contribution plan. These are generally retirement benefit plans under which amounts to be paid as retirement benefits are determinable, usually by reference to employees' earnings and/or years of service. The fund (and/or employer) is obligated either legally or constructively to pay the full amount of promised benefits whether or not sufficient assets are held in the fund.

Defined contribution pension plan. Benefit plans under which amounts to be paid as retirement benefits are determined by the contributions to a fund together with accumulated investment earnings thereon; the plan has no obligation to pay further sums if the amounts available cannot pay all benefits relating to employee services in the current and prior periods.

Employee benefits. All forms of consideration to employees in exchange for services rendered.

Equity compensation benefits. Benefits under which employees are entitled to receive employer's equity financial instruments, or which compensate employees based on the future value of such instruments.

Equity compensation plans. Formal or informal arrangements to provide equity compensation benefits.

Expected long-term rate of return on plan assets. Assumption as to the rate of return on plan assets reflecting the average rate of earnings expected on the funds invested, or to be invested, to provide for the benefits included in the projected benefit obligation.

Expected postretirement benefit obligation. The actuarial present value as of a particular date of the benefits expected to be paid to or for an employee, the employee's beneficiaries, and any covered dependents pursuant to the terms of the postretirement benefit plan.

Expected return on plan assets. Amount calculated as a basis for determining the extent of delayed recognition of the effects of changes in the fair value of assets. The expected return on plan assets is determined based on the expected long-term rate of return on plan assets and the market related value of plan assets.

Experience adjustments. Adjustments to benefit costs arising from the differences between the previous actuarial assumptions as to future events and what actually occurred.

Fair value. Amount that an asset could be exchanged for between willing, knowledgeable parties in an arm's-length transaction.

Final-pay plan. A defined benefit plan that promises benefits based on the employee's remuneration at or near the date of retirement. It may be the compensation of the final year, or of a specified number of years near the end of the employee's service period.

Flat-benefit formula (flat-benefit plan). Benefit formula that bases benefits on a fixed amount per year of service, such as $20 of monthly retirement income for each year of credited service. A flat-benefit plan is a plan with such a formula.

Fund. Used as a verb, to pay over to a funding agency (as to fund future pension benefits or to fund pension cost). Used as a noun, assets accumulated in the hands of a funding agency for the purpose of meeting pension benefits when they become due.

Funding. The irrevocable transfer of assets to an entity separate from the employer's entity, to meet future obligations for the payment of retirement benefits.

Gain or loss. Change in the value of either the projected benefit obligation or the plan assets resulting from experience different from that assumed or from a change in an actuarial assumption.

Interest cost component (of net periodic pension cost). Increase in the present value of the accrued benefit obligation due to the passage of time.

Measurement date. Date as of which plan assets and obligations are measured.

Mortality rate. Proportion of the number of deaths in a specified group to the number living at the beginning of the period in which the deaths occur. Actuaries use mortality tables, which show death rates for each age, in estimating the amount of pension benefits that will become payable.

Net periodic pension cost. Amount recognized in an employer's financial statements as the cost of a pension plan for a period. Components of net periodic pension cost are service cost, interest cost (which is implicitly presented as part of service cost), actual return on plan assets, gain or loss, amortization of unrecognized prior service cost, and amortization of the unrecognized net obligation or asset existing at the date of initial application of IAS 19.

Other long-term employee benefits. Benefits other than postemployment, termination and stock equity compensation benefits, which do not fall due wholly within one year of the end of the period in which service was rendered.

Past service cost. The actuarially determined cost arising on the introduction of a retirement benefit plan, on the making of improvements to such a plan, or on the completion of minimum service requirements for eligibility in such a plan, all of which give employees credit for benefits for service prior to the occurrence of one or more of these events.

Pay-as-you-go. A method of recognizing the cost of retirement benefits only at the time that cash payments are made to employees on or after retirement.

Plan amendment. Change in terms of an existing plan or the initiation of a new plan. A plan amendment may increase benefits, including those attributed to years of service already rendered.

Plan assets. The assets held by a long-term employee benefit fund, and qualifying insurance policies. Regarding assets held by a fund, these are assets (other than nontransferable financial instruments issued by the reporting entity) that both

1. Are held by a fund that is legally separate from the reporting entity and exists solely to pay or fund employee benefits, and
2. Are available to be used only to pay or fund employee benefits, are not available to the reporting entity's own creditors (even in the event of bankruptcy), and cannot be returned to the reporting entity unless either

   a. The remaining assets of the fund are sufficient to meet all related employee benefit obligations of the plan or the entity, or
   b. The assets are returned to the reporting entity to reimburse it for employee benefits already paid by it.

Regarding the qualifying insurance policy, this must be issued by a nonrelated party if the proceeds of the policy both

1. Can be used only to pay or fund employee benefits under a defined benefit plan, and
2. Are not available to the reporting entity's own creditors (even in the event of bankruptcy) and cannot be returned to the reporting entity unless either

   a. The proceeds represent surplus assets that are not needed for the policy to meet all related employee benefit obligations, or
   b. The proceeds are returned to the reporting entity to reimburse it for employee benefits already paid by it.

Postretirement benefits. All forms of benefits, other than retirement income, provided by an employer to retirees. Those benefits may be defined in terms of specified benefits, such as health care, tuition assistance, or legal services, that are provided to retirees as the need for those benefits arises, or they may be defined in terms of monetary amounts that become payable on the occurrence of a specified event, such as life insurance benefits.

Prepaid pension cost. Cumulative employer contributions in excess of accrued net pension cost.

Prior service cost. Cost of retroactive benefits granted in a plan amendment.

Projected benefit obligation. The actuarial present value as of a date of all benefits attributed by the pension benefit formula to employee service rendered prior to that date. The projected benefit obligation is measured using assumptions as to future compensation levels if the pension benefit formula is based on those future compensation levels (pay-related, final-pay, final-average-pay, or career-average-pay plans).

Projected benefit valuation methods. Actuarial valuation methods that reflect retirement benefits based on service both rendered and to be rendered by employees, as of the date of the valuation. Contrasted with accumulated benefit valuation methods, projected benefit valuation methods will result in a more level assignment of costs to the periods of employee service, although this will not necessarily be a straight-line allocation. Assumptions about projected salary levels must be incorporated. This was the allowed alternative method under the prior version of IAS 19, but is prohibited under the current standard.

Retirement benefit plans. Formal or informal arrangements whereby employers provide benefits for employees on or after termination of service, when such benefits can be determined or estimated in advance of retirement from the provisions of a document or from the employers' practices.

Retroactive benefits. Benefits granted in a plan amendment (or initiation) that are attributed by the pension benefit formula to employee services rendered in periods prior to the amendment. The cost of the retroactive benefits is referred to as prior service cost.

Return on plan assets. Interest, dividends and other revenues derived from plan assets, together with realized and unrealized gains or losses on the assets, less administrative costs including taxes payable by the plan.

Service. Employment taken into consideration under a pension plan. Years of employment before the inception of a plan constitute an employee's past service; years thereafter are classified in relation to the particular actuarial valuation being made or discussed. Years of employment (including past service) prior to the date of a particular valuation constitute prior service.

Settlement. Transaction that (1) is an irrevocable action, (2) relieves the employer (or the plan) of primary responsibility for a pension benefit obligation, and (3) eliminates significant risks related to the obligation and the assets used to effect the settlement. Examples include making lump-sum cash payments to plan participants in exchange for their rights to receive specified pension benefits and purchasing nonparticipating annuity contracts to cover vested benefits.

Short-term employee benefits. Benefits other than termination and equity compensation benefits which are due within one year after the end of the period in which the employees rendered the related service.

Terminal funding. A method of recognizing the projected cost of retirement benefits only at the time an employee retires.

Termination benefits. Employee benefits payable as a result of the entity's termination of employment before normal retirement or the employee's acceptance of early retirement inducements.

Unrecognized prior service cost. Portion of prior service cost that has not been recognized as a part of net periodic pension cost.

Vested benefits. Those benefits that, under the conditions of a retirement benefit plan, are not conditional on continued employment.

CONCEPTS, RULES, AND EXAMPLES

Importance of Pension and Other Benefit Plan Accounting

For a variety of cultural, economic, and political reasons, the existence of private pension plans has increased tremendously over the past forty years, and these arrangements are the most common and desired of the assorted "fringe benefits" offered by employers in many nations. Under the laws of some nations, employers may be required to have such programs in place for their permanent employees. For many entities, pension costs have become a very material component of the total compensation paid to employees. Unlike for wages and other fringe benefits, the timing of the payment of cash to either the plan's administrators or to the plan beneficiaries can vary substantially from the underlying economic event (that is, the plans are not always fully funded on a current basis). This creates the possibility of misleading financial statement representation of the true costs of conducting business, unless a valid accrual method is employed. For this reason, and also because of the complexity of these arrangements and the impact they have on the welfare of the workers, accounting for the cost of pension plans and similar schemes (postretirement benefits other than pensions, etc.) has received a great deal of attention from national and international standards setters.

Basic Objectives of Accounting for Pension and Other Benefit Plan Costs

Need for pension accounting rules. The principal objectives of pension accounting are to measure the compensation cost associated with employees' benefits and to recognize that cost over the employees' respective service periods. The relevant standard, IAS 19, is concerned only with the accounting aspects of pensions (and other benefit plans). The funding of pension benefits is considered to be financial management and legal concerns, and accordingly, is not addressed by this pronouncement.

When an entity provides benefits, the amounts of which can be estimated in advance, to its retired employees and their beneficiaries, the arrangement is deemed to be a pension plan. The typical plan is written, and the amounts of future benefits can be determined by reference to the plan documents. However, the plan and its provisions can also be implied from unwritten but established past practices. The accounting for most types of retirement plans is suggested by, if not heavily detailed in, IAS 19. Plans may be unfunded, insured, trust fund, defined contribution and defined benefit plans, and deferred compensation contracts, if equivalent. Independent (i.e., not employer sponsored) deferred profit sharing plans and pension payments which are made to selected employees on a case-by-case basis are not considered pension plans.

The establishment of a pension plan represents a long-term financial commitment to employees. Although some entities manage their own plans, this commitment usually takes the form of contributions that are made to an independent trustee or, in some countries, to a governmental agency. These contributions are used by the trustee to acquire plan assets of various kinds, although the available types of investments may be restricted by governmental regulations in certain jurisdictions. Plan assets are used to generate a financial return, which typically consists of earned interest and/or appreciation in asset values.

The earnings from the plan assets (and occasionally, the proceeds from their liquidation) provide the trustee with cash to pay the benefits to which the employees become entitled at the date of their retirements. These benefits in turn are defined by the terms of the pension plan, which is known as the plan's benefit formula. In the case of defined benefit plans, the benefit formula incorporates many factors, including the employee's current and future compensation, service longevity, age, and so on. The benefit formula is the best indictor of the plan's obligations at any point in time. It is used as the basis for determining the pension cost to be recognized each fiscal year.

Income statement vs. balance sheet objectives. As the accounting requirements for pensions and other forms of postemployment benefits have evolved over the years, the primary objective has been to assign the periodic costs of such plans properly to the periods in which the related benefits are received by the employers incurring these costs. These benefits are obviously received when the workers are productively working at their jobs, not during the later years when they are enjoying their retirements. Matching expected future costs to currently occurring revenues is the central challenge of pension accounting.

For this reason, accounting long ago recognized that the "pay-as-you-go" method of expense recognition, under which expense recognition would be deferred until the benefit payments to retirees were actually made, would cause an unacceptable mismatching of costs and benefits and a significant distortion of the income statement. The probable result of this mismatching would be the overstating of earlier years' results of operations and understating those of later years when large retirement payments are being made. As pensions and other fringe benefits expanded over the past generation to become a material and ever-increasing fraction of workers' compensation, this problem could no longer be ignored by accounting standards setters.

The reason that pay-as-you-go accounting had not been eliminated long ago is that many pension plans and similar employee benefit plan arrangements are rather complex, and the accounting necessary to report on them properly is also difficult and was slow in evolving. Most significantly, in the case of defined benefit plans, actual costs may not be known for many years, even decades, since a variety of future events (employee turnover, performance of investments, salary increases, etc.) will affect the ultimate burden on the employer. Accordingly, the measurement of expense on a current basis demands that many complicated estimates be made, some involving actuarial computations, and accountants have often been reluctant to anchor the financial statements to estimates that are potentially very imprecise. Only when the distortions of pay-as-you-go accounting became unacceptably great, due to the growing occurrence and magnitude of these benefit plans, were professional standards revised to prohibit continued use of that mode of accounting.

As pensions became an almost universal fixture of the employment landscape (in some nations, private pensions are mandated by law; in other countries, participation in government-sponsored plans is required), the failure to require such accounting became an impediment to meaningful financial reporting. Notwithstanding the limitations of actuarial and other estimates, financial statements incorporating the accrual of pension costs are vastly more accurate and useful than those based on a pay-as-you-go approach.

Evolution of IFRS on pension costs. About thirty years ago, major accounting standard-setting bodies began urging that pension costs be accrued properly in financial statements. At first, a wide range of actuarial methods were permitted, each of which could produce more meaningful results than the pay-as-you-go method, but over time the range of options permitted has been narrowed in major jurisdictions.

As presently constituted, pension accounting rules have tended to focus overwhelmingly on the income statement. That is, the dominant objective has been to match income and expense properly on a current basis, so that the periodic measurement of operating performance is within the bounds of material accuracy.

The meaningful presentation of the balance sheet has been somewhat less of a priority, however. Thus, even when an employer has retained full responsibility for the ultimate payment of pension benefits (as with defined benefit plans), the employer's statement of financial position has usually not set forth the assets and obligations of the pension scheme. This has been due partly to the fact that various "smoothing" approaches have been made to expense measurement, making the balance sheet (given the rigors of double entry bookkeeping) a repository for the resulting deferred charges and credits, inevitably making an accurate depiction from the balance sheet side less meaningful. Furthermore, accountants and other have been genuinely ambivalent about the validity of presenting information about the assets and obligations of the pension plan on the face of the employer's balance sheet, believing that the pension plan constitutes a separate economic and reporting entity even when the ultimate legal (or at least, moral) obligation belongs to the employer.

IAS 19 is a substantial advance over its predecessor standards and is very similar in approach to the corresponding US GAAP standards (FAS 87, 88, and 106). In fact, it offers broader coverage than the US standards, touching on compensated absences and stock compensation arrangements (which are the subjects of more extensive coverage in separate US GAAP standards, however), and on various short-term arrangements as well. IAS 19 broke with the past IFRS practice of permitting a range of methodologies resulting in potentially quite different financial statement results. Finally, IAS 19 greatly expanded the disclosures required by employers having defined benefit plans, again largely mimicking the US requirements.

By mandating one specific actuarial costing method, IAS 19 effectively required employers sponsoring defined benefit plans to engage in annual actuarial valuations, which has increased the cost of compliance for those having such plans. Overall, the effect of IAS 19 has been to significantly increase the comparability of financial statements of entities with a wide range of employee benefit plans and thus, from a standard-setting perspective, must be deemed a success.

Basic Principles of IAS 19

Applicability: pension plans. IAS 19 is applicable to both defined contribution and defined benefit pension plans. The accounting for *defined contribution* plans is normally straightforward, with the objective of matching the cost of the program with the periods in which the employees earn their benefits. Since contributions are formula-driven (e.g., as a percentage of wages paid), typically the payments to the plan will be made currently; if they do not occur by the balance sheet date, an accrual will be recognized for any unpaid current contribution liability. Once made or accrued, the employer has no further obligation for the value of the assets held by the plan or for the sufficiency of fund assets for payment of the benefits, absent any violation of the terms of the agreement by the employer. Employees thus suffer or benefit from the performance of the assets in which the contributions made on their behalf were invested; often the employees themselves are charged with responsibility for selecting those investments.

IAS 19 requires that disclosure be made of the amount of expense recognized in connection with a defined contribution pension plan. If not explicitly identified in the statement of income, this should therefore be disclosed in the notes to the financial statements.

Compared to defined contribution plans, the accounting for *defined benefit* plans is vastly more complex, because the employer (sponsor) is responsible not merely for the current contribution to be made to the plan on behalf of participants, but additionally for the sufficiency of the assets in the plan for the ultimate payments of benefits promised to the participants. Thus the current contribution is at best a partial satisfaction of its obligation, and the amount of actual cost incurred is not measured by this alone. The measurement of pension cost under a defined benefit plan necessarily involves the expertise of actuaries—persons who are qualified to estimate the numbers of employees who will survive (both as employees, in the case of vesting requirements which some of them may not yet have met; and as living persons who will be present to receive the promised retirement benefits), the salary levels at which they will retire (if these are incorporated into the benefit formula, as is commonly the case), their expected life expectancy (since benefits are typically payable for life), and other factors which will influence the amount of resources needed to satisfy the employer's promises. Actuarial determinations cannot be made by accountants, who lack the training and credentials, but the results of actuaries' efforts will be critical to the ability to properly account for defined benefit plan costs. Accounting for defined benefit plans is described at length in the following pages.

Applicability: other employee benefit plans. IAS 19 explicitly applies to not merely pension plans (which were dealt with by earlier iterations of this standard as well, although in rather less detail), but also four other categories of employee and postemployment benefits. These are

1. *Short-term employee benefits,* which include normal wages and salaries as well as compensated absences, profit sharing and bonuses, and such nonmonetary fringe benefits as health insurance, housing subsidies, and employer-provided automobiles, to the extent these are granted to current (not retired) employees.
2. *Other long-term employee benefits,* such as long-term (sabbatical) leave, long-term disability benefits and, if payable after twelve months beyond the end of the reporting period, profit sharing and bonus arrangements and deferred compensation.
3. *Termination benefits,* which are payments to be made upon termination of employment under defined circumstances, generally when employees are induced to leave employment before normal retirement age.

4. *Equity compensation benefits,* which are stock option plans, phantom stock plans, and similar compensation schemes which reward employees based upon the performance of the companies' share prices.

Each of the foregoing categories of employee benefits will be explained later in this chapter.

IAS 19 also addresses postemployment benefits *other than pensions,* such as retiree medical plan coverage, as part of its requirements for pension plans, since these are essentially similar in nature. These are also discussed further later in this chapter.

IAS 19 considers all plans other than those explicitly structured as defined contribution plans to be defined benefit plans, with the accounting and reporting complexities that this implies. Unless the employer's obligation is strictly limited to the amount of contribution currently due, typically driven by a formula based on entity performance or by employee wages or salaries, the obligations to the employees (and the amount of recognizable expense) will have to be estimated in accordance with actuarial principles.

Cost recognition distinguished from funding practices. Although it is arguably a sound management practice to fund retirement benefit plans on a current basis, in some jurisdictions the requirement to do this is either limited or absent entirely. Furthermore, in some jurisdictions the currently available tax deduction for contributions to pension plans may be limited, reducing the incentive to make such contributions until such time as the funds are actually needed for making payouts to retirees. Since the objective of periodic financial reporting is to match costs and revenues properly on a current basis, the pattern of funding is obviously not always going to be a useful guide to proper accounting for pension costs.

"Pay-as-you-go," accrued benefit, and projected benefit methods of accounting for postretirement benefits. Before the establishment of strict accounting and financial reporting rules, it was not uncommon to account for pensions and other similar costs on the "pay-as-you-go" basis. Briefly, this methodology recognized current period expense equal to only the amounts of benefits actually paid out to retirees and other beneficiaries in the reporting period. In support of this approach, the argument was usually made (1) it was very difficult, or expensive, to accurately measure (i.e., on an actuarial basis) the real cost of such plans and (2) the effect on periodic earnings would not be much different in any event. However, pay-as-you-go obviously violates the concept of accrual basis accounting, and the presumption that periodic expense is not materially distorted is often not supported in fact. This method of accounting for pensions and other postretirement programs has accordingly been barred since the first version of IAS 19 was promulgated in 1983.

While adherence to the accrual concept precluded pay-as-you-go accounting for the cost of employee benefit plans, for plans other than those which qualify as defined contribution arrangements there remained a range of acceptable, accrual-basis-consistent methods. Earlier versions of IAS 19 granted wide discretion in selection of costing methods, for which it was rightly criticized. The various techniques all fall within two general groupings which are known as the *accrued benefit* and *projected benefit* methods. While IAS 19 has now ended the acceptability of the projected benefit methods, an understanding of the two approaches will be helpful to gaining a fuller comprehension of the intricacies of the financial reporting of pension plan related costs in the financial statements of the sponsoring entity.

The *accrued (or accumulated) benefit methods* are based on services provided by employees through the date of valuation (i.e., the balance sheet date), without considering future services to be rendered by them. Periodic pension cost is a function of services that are provided in the current period. Since the obligation for future pension payments is computed as the discounted present value of the amounts to be paid in later years, accrued benefit methods will calculate increasing charges (even if wage levels are constant) as employees approach retirement, since the present values of future payments will increase as the time to retirement shortens. Periodic charges also increase, in most actual instances, because attrition rates (employees who leave, thereby forfeiting their rights to retirement payments) decline over time, inasmuch as older employees show less inclination to change employment. While wages will typically increase over time as employees age, both as a result of compensation increases due to seniority and performance improvements, and also as a result (if the past is any guide) of ongoing wage inflation, this should not be the cause of increasing pension costs as time to retirement grows shorter, since even accrued benefit valuation methods must be based on assumptions about future salary progression.

Notwithstanding that over time these assumptions and expectations cannot be precisely accurate, the presumption should be that "estimation errors" will be randomly distributed, and that over the long run, good-faith estimates of salary progression and the resultant effects on periodic pension costs will be reasonably accurate. Consequently, periodic pension costs should not drift upward as employees age because of wage increases.

The *projected benefit valuation method*, on the other hand, uses actuarial estimation techniques that consider the services already rendered as well as those to be rendered by the employees. The goal is to allocate the entire retirement cost smoothly over each employee's respective working life. The pension obligation at any point in time is computed as the present value of the aggregate future payments earned to the balance sheet date. As with accrued benefit valuation methods, future salary progression must be taken into account in determining periodic pension costs over the working lives of employees. The difference, however, is that future costs are spread more evenly over the full period of employment (although this does not imply that straight-line allocation would be an absolute requirement) as compared to the accrued benefit valuation methods, and in particular, pension-related costs will not show the constantly increasing pattern exhibited by the alternative approach simply due to the shortening time horizon as retirement dates draw near.

Proponents of both accrued and projected benefit valuation approaches cite the matching concept for theoretical support. In fact, for major employers having a workforce comprised of individuals of all ages, which typically replace older retiring workers with younger ones, pension costs will be similar under either methodology on an aggregate basis. While pension costs relative to older workers will be higher and costs relating to younger workers will be lower, if the accrued benefit valuation method is used versus what would be reflected if the projected benefit valuation method were used, with a stable mix of ages of workers, total periodic pension cost will not significantly vary. For smaller employers, or those with a workforce skewed toward younger or older workers, the periodic pattern of pension costs will diverge under these two methods, holding all other considerations constant.

Example of accrued and projected benefit methods

To understand the essential difference between accrued benefit and projected benefit methods, consider a simple case of a single employee hired today with no expectation of future salary increases, and promised a total retirement benefit of €10,000 if he retires after at least 10 years' service, or €14,000 if after 20 years' service. Ignoring present valuing (which does have to be taken into account in the actual accounting for employee benefit costs, however), the accrued benefit method would allocate 1/10 of the €10,000 = €1,000 in promised benefits to each of the first 10 years of service, and then 1/10 of the €4,000 increment = €400 to each of the next 10 years, since accrued benefit methods would not assume the employee would continue employment beyond the tenth year until after that threshold is surpassed. Projected benefit methods, on the other hand, would assign 1/20 of the €14,000 = €700 to each of the first 20 years' employment, being based on service rendered and to be rendered until expected retirement. This all presumes the employee is expected to work at least 20 years (based on experience, the employee's age, etc.).

In actual practice, with multiple employees, statistical estimates are used such that full accrual of benefits is normally not made for all employees, given that a certain fraction will opt out before becoming vested, etc.

The foregoing discussion was introduced merely to provide a background about the alternative methods which, conceptually, could be proposed to address the measurement of periodic pension (and similar) costs, and also to report on the alternatives which had been authorized for use previously under IFRS. Under revised IAS 19, promulgated in 1998 and modified in several respects in more recent years, only the accrued benefit valuation method may be utilized. This will reflect retirement benefits based on service already rendered by employees to the date of the valuation. Assumptions about projected salary levels to the date of retirement must be incorporated, but service to be rendered after the balance sheet date is not. The following discussion will detail this method.

Net Periodic Pension Cost

General discussion. Absent specific information to the contrary, it is assumed that a company will continue to provide retirement benefits well into the future. The accounting for the plan's costs should be reflected in the financial statements and these amounts should not be discretionary. All pension costs—with the exception noted below—should be charged against income. No amounts should be charged directly to retained earnings. The principal focus of IAS 19 is on the allocation of cost to the periods being benefited, which are the periods in which the covered employees provide service to the reporting entity.

In a limited amendment to IAS 19 enacted in 2004, entities now have the option to fully recognize actuarial gains and losses in the period in which they occur, outside of operating results, in a statement of recognized income and expense. This eliminates these gains and losses from income determination but includes them in a "middle step" statement, and not directly as charges or credits to retained earnings.

Periodic measurement of cost for defined contribution plans. Under the terms of a defined contribution plan (in some cases referred to as a "money purchase" plan), the employer will be obligated for fixed or determinable contributions in each period, often computed as a percentage of the wage and salary base paid to the covered employees during the period. For one example, contributions might be set at 4% of each employee's wages and salaries, up to €50,000 wages per annum. Generally, the contributions must actually be made by a specific date, such as ninety days after the end of the reporting entity's fiscal year, consistent with local law. The expense must be accrued for accounting purposes in the year the cost is incurred, whether the contribution is made currently or not.

IAS 19 requires that contributions payable to a defined contribution plan be accrued currently, even if not paid by year-end. If the amount is due over a period extending more than one year from the balance sheet date, the long-term portion should be discounted at the rate applicable to long-term corporate bonds, if that information is known, or applicable to government bonds in the alternative.

Employers may choose to make further discretionary contributions to benefit plans in certain periods. For example, if the entity enjoys a particularly profitable year, the board of directors may vote to grant another 2% of wages as a bonus contribution to the employees' benefit plan. The extent to which this is done will depend, among other factors, on the tax laws of the relevant jurisdiction. Normally, an entity making such a discretionary contribution does not do so simply to reward past performance by its workers. Rather, it does so in the belief that the gesture will cause its employees to be motivated to be more productive and loyal in the forthcoming years. IAS 19 addresses profit sharing and bonus plans as a subset of its requirements concerning short-term compensation arrangements; it stipulates that such a payment should be recognized only when paid or when the entity has a legal or constructive obligation to make it, and when the payment can be reliably estimated. There appears to be no basis for deferring recognition of the expense after that point, however, even though longer-term benefits to the entity might be hoped for.

Past service costs arise when a plan is amended retroactively, so that additional contributions are made with respect to services rendered in past years. For example, if a plan formerly required contributions of 5% of salaries and is amended retroactively (which is not the norm) to provide for contributions of 6%, an extra 1% of each employee's aggregate salary for all prior years will be transferred to the employee's pension account. When plans are amended in this fashion, it is generally management's belief that it will provide an incentive for greater efforts in the future. IAS 19 does not explicitly address retroactive amendments to defined contribution plans, but by analogizing from the requirements concerning similar amendments to defined benefit plans, it is clear that, if fully vested immediately (as would almost inevitably be the case), these would have to be expensed currently.

Terminations of defined contribution plans generally provide no difficulties from an accounting perspective, since costs have been recognized currently in most instances. However, if certain costs, such as those associated with past services and with discretionary bonus contributions made in past years, have not yet been fully amortized, the remaining unrecognized portions of those costs must be expensed in the period when it becomes probable that the plan is to be terminated. This should be the period when the decision to terminate is made, which on occasion may precede the actual termination of the plan.

Periodic measurement of cost for defined benefit plans. Defined benefit plans present a far greater challenge to accountants than do defined contribution plans, since the amount of expense to be recognized currently will need to be determined on an actuarial basis. Under current IFRS, only the accrued benefit valuation method may be used to measure defined benefit plan pension cost. Furthermore, only a single variant of the accrued benefit method—the "projected unit credit" method—is permitted. A number of alternative approaches, which also fell under the general umbrella of the accrued benefit method are no longer accepted under IFRS. Accordingly, only the projected unit credit method will be discussed in the following presentation.

Net periodic pension cost will consist of the sum of the following six components:

1. Current (pure) service cost
2. Interest cost for the current period on the accrued benefit obligation
3. The expected return on plan assets
4. Actuarial gains and losses, to the extent recognized
5. Past service costs, to the extent recognized
6. The effects of any curtailments or settlements

Disclosures required by IAS 19 effectively require that these cost components be displayed in the notes to the financial statements.

It is important to stress that current service cost, the core cost element of all defined benefit plans, must be determined by a qualified actuary. While the other items to be computed and presented are also developed by actuaries in most cases, they can be verified or even calculated directly by others, including the entity's internal or external accountants. The current service cost, however, is not an immediately apparent computation, as it relies upon a detailed census of employees (age, expected remaining working life, etc.) and the employer's experience (turnover, etc.), and is an intricate and elaborate computational exercise in many cases. Current service cost can only be developed by this careful, employee-by-employee analysis, and this is best left to those with the expertise to complete it.

Current service cost. Current service cost must be determined by an actuarial valuation and will be affected by assumptions such as expected turnover of staff, average retirement age, the plan's vesting schedule, and life expectancy after retirement. The probable progression of wages over the employees' remaining working lives will also have to be taken into consideration if retirement benefits will be affected by levels of compensation in later years, as will be true in the case of career average and final pay plans, among others.

It is worth stressing this last point: when pension arrangements call for benefits to be based on the employees' ultimate salary levels, experience will show that those benefits will increase, and any computation based on current salary levels will surely understate the actual economic commitment to the future retirees. Accordingly, IFRS requires that, for such plans, future salary progression must be considered in determining current period pension costs. This is why the services of a consulting actuary are vital; it is not something to be assigned to accountants. While future salary progression (where appropriate to the plan's benefit formula) must be incorporated (via estimated wage increase rates), current pension cost is a function of the services provided by the employee in the reporting period, emphatically not including services to be provided in later periods.

Under IAS 19, service cost is based on the present value of the defined benefit obligation, and is attributed to periods of service without regard to conditional requirements under the plan calling for further service. Thus, vesting is not taken into account in the sense that there is no justification for nonaccrual prior to vesting. However, in the actuarial determination of pension cost, the statistical probability of employees leaving employment prior to vesting must be taken into account, lest an overaccrual of costs be made.

Example of service cost attribution

To explain the concept of service cost, assume a single employee is promised a pension of €1,000 per year for each year worked before retirement, for life, upon retirement at age sixty or thereafter. Further assume that this is the worker's first year on the job, and he is 30 years of age. The consulting actuary determines that if the worker, in fact, retires at age 60, he will have a life expectancy of 15 years, and at the present value of the required benefits (€1,000/yr × 15 years = €15,000) discounted at the long-term corporate bond rate, 8%, equals €8,560. In other words, based on the work performed thus far (one year's worth), this employee has earned the right to a lump-sum settlement of €8,560 at age 60. Since this is 30 years into the future, this amount must be reduced to present value, which at 8% is a mere €851, which is the pension cost to be recognized currently.

In year two, this worker earns the right to yet another annuity stream of €1,000 per year upon retirement, which again has a present value of €8,560 at the projected retirement age of 60. However, since age 60 is now only 29 years hence, the present value of that promised benefit at the end of the current (second) year is €919, which represents the service cost in year two. This pattern will continue: As the employee ages, the current cost of pension benefits grows apace with, for example, the cost in the final working year being €8,560, before considering interest on the previously accumulated obligation—which would, however, add another €18,388 of expense, for a total cost for this one employee in his final working year of €26,948. It should be noted, however, that in "real-life" situations for employee groups in the aggregate, this may not hold, since new younger employees will be added as older employees die or retire, which will tend to smooth out the annual cost of the plan.

Interest on the accrued benefit obligation. As noted, since the actuarial determination of current period cost is the present value of the future pension benefits to be paid to retirees by virtue of their service in the current period, the longer the time until the expected retirement date, the lower will be the service cost recognized. However, over time this accrued cost must be further increased, until at the employees' respective retirement dates the full amounts of the promised payments have been accreted. In this regard, the accrued pension liability is much like a sinking fund that grows from contributions plus the earnings thereon.

Consider the example of service cost presented in the preceding section. The €851 obligation recorded in the first year of that example will have grown to €919 by the end of the second year. This €68 increase in the obligation for future benefits due to the passage of time is reported as a component of pension cost, denoted as interest cost.

While service cost and interest are often the major components of expense recognized in connection with defined benefit plans, there are other important elements of benefit cost to be accounted for. IAS 19 identifies the expected return on plan assets, actuarial gains and losses, past service costs, and the effects of any curtailments or settlements as categories to be explicitly addressed in the disclosure of the details of annual pension cost for defined benefit plans. These will be discussed in the following sections, in turn.

The expected return on plan assets. IAS 19 has adopted the approach of the corresponding US standard in accepting the notion that since pension plan assets are intended as long-term investments, the random and perhaps sizable fluctuations from period to period should not be allowed to excessively distort the operating results reported by the sponsoring entity. This standard identifies the expected return rather than the actual return on plan assets as the salient component of pension cost, with the difference between actual and expected return being an *actuarial gain or loss* to be dealt with as described below (deferred to future periods or, if significant, partially recognized in the current period). Expected return for a given period is determined at the start of that period, and is based on long-term rates of return for assets to be held over the term of the related pension obligation. Expected return is to incorporate anticipated dividends, interest, and changes in fair value, and is furthermore to be reduced in respect of expected plan administration costs.

For example, assume that at the start of 2006 the plan administrator expects, over the long term, and based on historical performance of plan assets, that the plan's assets will receive annual interest and dividends of 6%, net of any taxes due by the fund itself, and will enjoy a market value gain of another 2.5%. It is also noted that plan administration costs will average .75% of plan assets, measured by fair value. With this data, an expected rate of return for 2006 would be computed as 6.00% + 2.50% − .75% = 7.75%. This rate would be used to calculate the return on assets, which would be used to offset service cost and other benefit plan cost components for the year 2006.

The difference between this assumed rate of return, 7.75% in this example, and the actual return enjoyed by the plan's assets would be added to or subtracted from the cumulative actuarial gains and losses. In theory, over the long run, if the expected returns are accurately estimated, these gains and losses will largely offset, inasmuch as they are the result of random, short-term fluctuations in market returns and of demographic and other changes in the group covered by the plan (such as unusual turnover, mortality, or changes in salaries). Since these are expected to largely offset, and given the very long time horizon over which pension benefit plan performance is to be judged, the notion of deferring and thus smoothing recognition of these net gains or losses was appealing, although certainly subject to criticism since actual economic results will not be reported as they occur.

Prior to a 2000 amendment to IAS 19, assets were properly considered to be plan assets only if *all* of the following three conditions were met:

1.   The pension or other benefit plan is an entity which is legally separate from the sponsoring employer or entity;
2.   The assets of the plan are only to be used to settle employee benefit obligations, are not available to the sponsoring entity's creditors, and either cannot be returned to

the sponsor at all or can be returned only to the extent that assets remaining in the fund are sufficient to meet the plan's obligations; and

3. The sponsor will have no legal or constructive obligation to directly pay the employee benefit obligations, assuming that the fund contains sufficient assets to satisfy those obligations.

The aforementioned amendment modified IAS 19's definition of plan assets to explicitly include certain insurance policies, and to eliminate the condition relating to sufficiency of assets in the funds. It also slightly amended and reworded the balance of the former definition. The new definition includes assets held by a long-term employee benefit fund, and qualifying insurance policies. Regarding assets held by a fund, these are assets (other than nontransferable financial instruments issued by the reporting entity) that both

1. Are held by a fund that is legally separate from the reporting entity and exist solely to pay or fund employee benefits, and
2. Are available to be used only to pay or fund employee benefits, are not available to the reporting entity's own creditors (even in the event of bankruptcy), and cannot be returned to the reporting entity unless either

    a. The remaining assets of the fund are sufficient to meet all related employee benefit obligations of the plan or the entity, or
    b. The assets are returned to the reporting entity to reimburse it for employee benefits already paid by it.

Regarding the qualifying insurance policy, this must be issued by a nonrelated party if the proceeds of the policy both

1. Can be used only to pay or fund employee benefits under a defined benefit plan, and
2. Are not available to the reporting entity's own creditors (even in the event of bankruptcy), and cannot be returned to the reporting entity unless either

    a. The proceeds represent surplus assets that are not needed for the policy to meet all related employee benefit obligations, or
    b. The proceeds are returned to the reporting entity to reimburse it for employee benefits already paid by it.

It should be stressed that the definition of plan assets is significant for several reasons: plan assets are excluded from the sponsoring employer's balance sheet and will also serve as the basis for determining the actual and expected rates of return, which impact on the periodic determination of pension cost. By adopting a somewhat more expansive definition of plan assets, the amended IAS 19 affected the future computation of pension costs.

The IAS 19 amendment adopted in 2000 also added certain new requirements which relate to recognition and measurement of the right of reimbursement of all or part of the expenditure to settle a defined benefit obligation. It established that only when it is virtually certain that another party will reimburse some or all of the expenditure required to settle a defined benefit obligation, the sponsoring entity would recognize its right to reimbursement as a separate asset, which would be measured at fair value. In all other respects, however, the asset (amount due from the pension plan) is to be treated in the same way as plan assets. In the income statement, defined benefit plan expense may be presented net of the reimbursement receivable recognized.

In some situations, a plan sponsor would be able to look to another entity to pay some or all of the cost to settle a defined benefit obligation, but the assets held by that other party were not deemed to be plan assets as defined in IAS 19 (prior to the revision in 2000). For example, when an insurance policy would match postemployment benefits, the assets of the insurer were not included in plan assets because the insurer was not established solely to pay or fund employee benefits. In such cases, the sponsor recognized its right to reimbursement as a separate asset, rather than as a deduction in determining the defined benefit liability (i.e., no right of offset was deemed to exist in such instances); in all other respects (e.g., the use of the corridor), the sponsoring entity would treat that asset in the same way as plan assets. In particular, the defined benefit liability recognized under IAS 19 had been increased (reduced) to the extent that net cumulative actuarial gains (losses) on the defined benefit obligation and on the related reimbursement remain unrecognized under this standard, as explained earlier in this chapter. A brief description of the link between the reimbursement and the related obligation would be required.

If the right to reimbursement arises under an insurance policy that exactly matches the amount and timing of some or all of the benefits payable under a defined benefit plan, the fair value of the reimbursement was formerly deemed to be present value of the related obligation (subject to any reduction required if the reimbursement was not recoverable in full).

As amended, however, qualifying insurance policies are now to be included in plan assets, arguably because those plans have similar economic effects to funds whose assets qualify as plan assets under the revised definition.

Actuarial gains and losses, to the extent recognized. Changes in the amount of the actuarially determined pension obligation and differences in the actual versus the expected yield on plan assets, as well as demographic changes (e.g., composition of the workforce, changes in life expectancy, etc.) contribute to actuarial (or "experience") gains and losses. While immediate recognition of these gains or losses could clearly be justified conceptually (because these are real and have already occurred), there are both theoretical arguments opposed to such immediate recognition (the distortive effects on the measure of current operating performance resulting from very long-term investments, much of which will reverse of their own accord over time), as well as great opposition by financial statement preparers and users. For this reason, IAS 19 does not require such immediate recognition, unless the fluctuations are so great that deferral is not deemed to be wise. It essentially acceded to the US approach and defined a 10% "corridor" as representing the range of variation deemed to be "normal." While the use of a 10% threshold is arbitrary, it does carry an aura of acceptability, since it had been employed for over a decade previously under US GAAP.

Thus, if the unrecognized actuarial gain or loss is no more than 10% of the larger of the present value of the defined benefit obligation or the fair value of plan assets, measured at the beginning of the reporting period, no recognition in the current period will be necessary (i.e., there will be continued deferral of the accumulated net actuarial gain or loss). On the other hand, if the accumulated net actuarial gain or loss exceeds this 10% corridor, the magnitude creates greater doubt that future losses or gains will offset these, and for that reason some recognition will be necessary.

It is suggested by IAS 19 that this excess be amortized over the expected remaining working lives of the then-active employee participants, but the standard actually permits any reasonable method of amortization as long as (1) recognition is at no slower a pace than would result from amortization over the working lives of participants, and (2) that the same method is used for both net gains and net losses. It is also acceptable to fully recognize all actuarial gains or losses immediately, without regard to the 10% corridor.

The corridor and the amount of any excess beyond this corridor must be computed anew each year, based on the present value of defined benefits and the fair value of plan assets, each determined as of the beginning of the year. Thus, there may have been an unrecognized actuarial gain of €450,000 at the end of year one, which exceeds the 10% corridor boundary by €210,000, and is therefore to be amortized over the average twenty-one-year remaining working life of the plan participants, indicating a €10,000 reduction in pension cost in year two. If, at the end of year two, market losses or other actuarial losses reduce the accumulated actuarial gain below the threshold implied by the 10% corridor. Accordingly, in year three there will be no further amortization of the net actuarial gain. This determination, therefore, must be made at the beginning of each period. Depending on the amount of unrecognized actuarial gain or loss at the end of year three, there may or may not be amortization in year four, and so on.

Past service costs, to the extent recognized. Past service costs refer to increases in the amount of a defined benefit liability that results from the initial adoption of a plan, or from a change or amendment to an existing plan which increases the benefits promised to the participants with respect to previous service rendered. Less commonly, a plan amendment could reduce the benefits for past services, if local laws permit this. Employers will amend plans for a variety of reasons, including competitive factors in the employment marketplace, but often it is done with the hope and expectation that it will engender goodwill among the workers and thus increase future productivity. For this reason, it is sometimes the case that these added benefits will not vest immediately, but rather must be earned over some defined time period.

IAS 19 requires immediate recognition of past service cost as an expense when the added benefits vest immediately. However, when these are not immediately vested, recognition is to be on a straight-line basis over the period until vesting occurs. For example, if at January 1, 2006, the sponsoring entity grants an added €4,000 per employee in future benefits, and given the number of employees expected to receive these benefits this computes to a present value of €455,000, but vesting will not be until January 1, 2011, then a past service cost of €455,000 ÷ 5 years = €91,000 per year will be recognized. (To this amount interest must be added, as with service cost as described above.)

The effects of any curtailments or settlements. Periodic defined benefit plan expense is also affected by any curtailments or settlements which have been incurred. The standard defines a curtailment as arising in connection with isolated events such as plant closings, discontinuations of operations, or termination or suspension of a benefit plan. Often, corporate restructurings will be accompanied by curtailments in benefit plans. Recognition can be given to the effect of a curtailment when the sponsor is demonstrably committed to make a material reduction in the number of covered employees, or it amends the terms of the plan such that a material element of future service by existing employees will no longer be covered or will receive reduced benefits. The curtailment must actually occur for it to be given recognition.

Settlements occur when the entity enters into a transaction which effectively transfers the obligation to another entity, such as an insurance company, so that the sponsor has no legal or constructive obligation to fund any benefit shortfall. Merely acquiring insurance which is intended to cover the benefit payments does not constitute a settlement, since a funding mechanism does not relieve the underlying obligation.

Under the current standard's predecessor, curtailment and settlement gains were recognized when the event occurred, but losses were to be recognized when probable of occurrence. Revised IAS 19 concluded that being *probable* was not sufficient under IFRS to warrant expense or loss recognition in the context of pension plan curtailments or settlements. Thus, both gains and losses are to be recognized when the event occurs.

The effect of a curtailment or settlement is measured with reference to the change in present value of the defined benefits, any change in fair value of related assets (normally there is none), and any related actuarial gains or losses and past service cost which had not yet been recognized. The net amount of these elements will be charged or credited to pension expense in the period the curtailment or settlement actually occurs.

Example of a settlement

Assume that a company's pension plan, at the current date, reports obligations amounting to €1,150 in vested future benefits and another €400 in nonvested benefits. It settles the €1,150 vested benefit portion of its projected benefit obligation by using plan assets to purchase a non-participating annuity contract at a cost of €1,150. After this settlement, nonvested benefits and the effects of projected future compensation levels remain in the plan. In accordance with IAS 19, a pro rata amount of the unrecognized net actuarial loss on assets and unrecognized past service cost are recognized due to settlement. Because the projected benefit obligation is reduced from €1,550 to €400, for a decrease of 74%, the pro rata amount used for recognition purposes is 74%. These changes are noted in the following table:

	Before settlement	*Effect of settlement*	*After settlement*
Assets and obligations			
Vested benefit obligation	€(1,150)	€1,150	€ 0
Nonvested benefits	(400)		(400)
Pension benefit obligation before salary increases projection	(1,550)	1,150	(400)
Effects of projected future salary increases	(456)		(456)
Pension benefit obligation	(2,006)	1,150	(856)
Plan assets at fair value	1,159	(1,150)	369
Items not yet recognized in earnings			
Funded status	(487)		(487)
Unrecognized net actuarial loss on assets	174	(129)	45
Unrecognized prior service cost	293	(217)	76
Unamortized net asset at IAS 19 adoption	(3)	0	(3)
Prepaid (accrued) benefit cost	€ (23)	€ (346)	€(369)

The entry used by the company to record this transaction does not include the purchase of the annuity contract, since the pension plan acquires the contract with existing funds. The recognition of the pro rata amount of the unrecognized net actuarial loss on assets and unrecognized prior service cost is recorded with the following entry:

Loss from settlement of pension obligation	346	
Accrued/prepaid pension cost		346

Example of a curtailment

Use information from the previous example, assume that the company shuts down one of its factories, which terminates the employment of a number of its staff. The terminated employees have nonvested benefits of €120 and a projected benefit obligation of €261. As a result of this curtailment of the plan, 19% of the pension benefit obligation has been eliminated (€381 obligation reduction resulting from the curtailment, divided by the beginning €2,006 pension benefit obligation). Accordingly, 19% of the unrecognized past service cost will also be recognized. The analysis follows:

	Before curtailment	*Effect of curtailment*	*After curtailment*
Assets and obligations			
Vested benefit obligation	€(1,150)	€ 0	€(1,150)
Nonvested benefits	(400)	120	(280)
Pension benefit obligation before salary increases projection	(1,550)	120	(1,430)
Effects of projected future salary increases	(456)	261	(195)
Pension benefit obligation	(2,006)	381	(1,625)
Plan assets at fair value	1,159		1,159
Items not yet recognized in earnings			
Funded status	(487)	381	(106)
Unrecognized net actuarial loss on assets	174	(33)	141
Unrecognized prior service cost	293	(56)	237
Unamortized net asset at IAS 19 adoption	(3)	0	(3)
Prepaid (accrued) benefit cost	€ (23)	€ 292	€ 269

The company records the recognition of the pro rata amount of the unrecognized prior service cost and unamortized net actuarial loss, which is offset against the net gain of €381 resulting from the reduction in the pension benefit obligation.

Accrued/prepaid pension cost	292	
Gain from curtailment of pension obligation		292

Transition adjustment. The final element of periodic pension cost under IAS 19 related to the effect of first adopting the accounting standard, which was mandatory for years beginning 1999. The transition amount was to be the present value of the benefit obligation at the date the standard was adopted, less the fair value of plan assets at that date, less any past service cost that was to be deferred to later periods, if the criterion regarding vesting period was met. If the transitional liability was greater than the liability which would have been recognized under the entity's previous policy for accounting for pension costs, it was required to make an *irrevocable* choice to either

1. Recognize the increase in the pension obligation immediately, with the expense included in employee benefit cost for the period; *or*
2. Amortize the transition amount over no longer than a five-year period, on the straight-line basis. Note that the five-year maximum transition would have concluded by 2004, if the entity adopted IAS 19 in 1999. The unrecognized transition amount was not to be formally included in the balance sheet, but was required to be disclosed.

If the second method were elected, and the entity had a *negative* transitional liability (that is, an asset, resulting from a surplus of pension assets over the related obligation), it was limited in the amount of such asset to present on its balance sheet to the total of any unrecognized actuarial losses plus past service cost, and the present value of economic benefits available as refunds from the plan or reductions in future contributions, with the present value determined by reference to the rate on high-quality corporate bonds. Furthermore, the amount of unrecognized transitional gain or loss as of each balance sheet date was required to have been presented, as was the amount recognized in the current period income statement.

Finally, if the second method was employed, recognition of actuarial gains (which did not include negative past service cost) was limited in two ways. If an actuarial gain was being recognized because it exceeded the 10% limit, or because the entity had elected a more rapid method of systematic recognition, then the actuarial gain was required to be recognized only to the extent the net cumulative gain exceeded the unrecognized transitional liability.

And, in determining the gain or loss on any later settlement or curtailment, the related part of the unrecognized transitional liability was required to be incorporated.

IAS 19 also stipulated that if the transitional liability was lower than the amount which would have been recognized under previous accounting rules, the adjustment was to have been taken into income immediately (i.e., amortization was not permitted).

Upon adoption of the current revised IAS 19, the reporting entity was not permitted to retrospectively compute the effect of the 10% limit on actuarial gain or loss recognition. It was clear that retrospective application would have been impracticable to accomplish and would not have generated useful information, and that was accordingly prohibited by the revised standard.

Employer's Liabilities and Assets

IAS 19 has as its primary concern the measurement of periodic expense incurred in connection with pension plans of employers. One source of dissatisfaction with the standard is its general failure to address the assets or liabilities that may be recognized on the employers' balance sheets as a consequence of expense recognition, which may include deferral of certain items (e.g., past service costs). In fact, the amounts that may find their way onto the balance sheet will often not meet the strict definition of assets or liabilities, but rather, will be "deferred charges or credits." This will consist of the cumulative difference between the amount funded and the amount expensed over the life of the plan.

Thus, IAS 19 has been criticized for not requiring, under appropriate circumstances, recognition of an additional or minimum liability when plans are materially underfunded. The point of comparison is US GAAP standard FAS 87, which does demand that this minimum liability, which results when the accumulated (accrued) benefit obligation exceeds the fair value of plan assets, and a liability in the amount of the difference is not already recorded as unfunded accrued pension cost. Under that standard, the additional minimum liability is recognized by an offset to an intangible asset up to the amount of unrecognized prior service cost. Any additional debit needed is considered a loss and is shown net of tax benefits as a separate component reducing equity. The IASB concluded that additional measures of liability were potentially confusing and did not promise to provide relevant information. Accordingly, with the exception of any liability to be accrued under IAS 37 (regarding contingencies), the decision was made to dispense with such an item.

IAS 19 does, nonetheless, require that a defined benefit liability or asset be included in the sponsor's balance sheet when certain conditions are met. Specifically, under the provisions of IAS 19, the amount recognized as a defined benefit liability in the employer's balance sheet is the net total of

1. The present value of the defined benefit obligation at the balance sheet date,
2. Any actuarial gains (less any actuarial losses) not recognized because of the "corridor" approach described elsewhere in this chapter,
3. Any past service cost not yet recognized; and
4. The fair value of plan assets as of the balance sheet date.

If this amount nets to a negative sum, it represents the defined benefit asset to be reported on the employer's balance sheet. However, the amount of asset that can be displayed, per IAS 19, is subject to a ceiling requirement.

The asset ceiling defined in IAS 19 is the lower of

1. The amount computed in the preceding paragraph, or
2. The total of
    a. Any cumulative unrecognized net actuarial losses and past service cost, and

b.   The present value of any economic benefits available in the form of refunds from the plan or reductions in future contributions to the plan, determined using the discount rate that reflects market yields at the balance sheet date on high-quality corporate bonds or, if necessary, on government bonds.

In 2002 the IASB amended IAS 19 in response to concerns raised about the perceived interaction of the deferred recognition and the asset ceiling provisions of IAS 19, and the risk that this was creating counterintuitive results. The issue affects only those entities that have, at the beginning or end of the financial reporting period, a surplus in a defined benefit plan that, based on the current terms of the plan, the entity cannot fully recover through refunds or reductions in future contributions. Such situations created financial reporting anomalies, as follows:

1.   *Gains* were being reported in the financial statements based on the occurrence of actuarial *losses* in the pension plans, or
2.   *Losses* were being reported on occurrence of actuarial *gains* in the pension plans.

More specifically, the issue was the wording of the asset ceiling provision in IAS 19. This wording, without regard to the limitation imposed by the amendment in 2002, sometimes caused, as a consequence of deferring the recognition of an actuarial loss (gain), the recognition of a gain (loss) in the income statement.

The problem occurred when an entity defers recognition of actuarial losses or past service cost in determining the amount specified in IAS 19's provision for the measurement of defined benefit liability or asset, but is required to measure the defined benefit asset at the net total of

1.   Any cumulative unrecognized net actuarial losses and past service cost, and
2.   The present value of any economic benefits available in the form of refunds from the plan or reductions in future contributions to the plan.

In particular, the cumulative unrecognized net actuarial losses and past service cost could result in the entity recognizing an increased asset because of actuarial losses or past service cost in the period. This increase in the asset would be reported as a gain in income.

To resolve this, IAS 19 was amended to prevent gains (losses) from being recognized solely as a result of the deferred recognition of past service cost or actuarial losses (gains). This was done because it was concluded that recognizing gains (losses) arising from past service cost and actuarial losses (gains) would not be representationally faithful. The solution devised in the amendment was to require the reporting entity, to ascertain the defined benefit asset, to recognize immediately the following—but only to the extent that these items arise while the defined benefit asset is determined in accordance with the asset ceiling provision limiting it to the sum of the cumulative unrecognized net actuarial losses and past service cost and the present value of any economic benefits available in the form of refunds from the plan or reductions in future contributions to the plan:

1.   The net actuarial losses of the current period and past service cost of the current period, to the extent that they exceed any reduction in the present value of the economic benefits. If there is no change or an increase in the present value of economic benefits, the entire net actuarial losses of the current period and past service cost of the current period should be recognized immediately.
2.   The net actuarial gains of the current period after the deduction of past service cost of the current period to the extent that they exceed any increase in the present value of the economic benefits. If there is no change or a decrease in the present value of

the economic benefits, the entire net actuarial gains of the current period after the deduction of past service cost of the current period should be recognized.

The foregoing applies to a reporting entity only if it has, at the beginning or end of the accounting period, a surplus in a defined benefit plan and cannot, based on the current terms of the plan, recover that surplus fully through refunds or reductions in future contributions. A surplus is an excess of the fair value of the plan assets over the present value of the defined benefit obligation. In such cases, past service cost and actuarial losses that arise in the period, the recognition of which is deferred, will increase the amount of the unrecognized net actuarial loss and past service cost determined in accordance with IAS 19. If that increase is not offset by an equal decrease in the present value of economic benefits identified also in IAS 19, there will be an increase in the net total specified by that provision and, hence, a recognized gain. The language added by the amendment prohibits the recognition of a gain in these circumstances.

The opposite effect arises with actuarial gains that arise in the period, the recognition of which is deferred under the standard, to the extent that the actuarial gains reduce cumulative unrecognized actuarial losses. The current language of IAS 19 prohibits the recognition of a loss in these circumstances.

The limitation on asset recognition—to the total of (1) any cumulative unrecognized net actuarial losses and past service cost, and (2) the present value of any economic benefits available in the form of refunds from the plan or reductions in future contributions to the plan—does not override the delayed recognition of certain actuarial losses and certain past service cost, except to the extent that the limitation on asset recognition is driven by the provision pertaining to basic computation of the defined benefit liability or asset in IAS 19. However, that limit does override the transitional option set forth by the standard (i.e., where straight-line amortization over a period not longer than five years is employed). The reporting entity must disclose any amount not recognized as an asset because of the limit stated at the beginning of this paragraph.

To illustrate this immediately previous matter, consider a defined benefit plan with the following characteristics:

Present value of the obligation	€ 550
Fair value of plan assets	(595)
	(45)
Unrecognized actuarial losses	(55)
Unrecognized past service cost	(35)
Unrecognized increase in the liability on initial adoption of IAS 19	(25)
Negative amount determined under defined benefit liability or asset definition	(160)
Present value of available future refunds and reductions in future contributions.	45
The limit is computed as follows:	
Unrecognized actuarial losses	55
Unrecognized past service cost	35
Present value of available future refunds and reductions in future contributions	45
Limit	€ 135

The limit, €135 in this example, is less than the amount determined under the basic definition of defined benefit asset, €160. Therefore, the reporting entity would recognize an asset of €135 and discloses that application of the limit had reduced the carrying amount of the asset by €25.

This amendment to IAS 19 added an appendix that provides several examples that illustrate how to apply this somewhat complex modification to the asset recognition ceiling under the standard.

Other Pension Considerations

Multiple and multiemployer plans. If an entity has more than one plan, IAS 19 provisions should be applied separately to each plan. Offsets or eliminations are not allowed unless there clearly is the right to use the assets in one plan to pay the benefits of another plan.

Participation in a multiemployer plan (to which two or more unrelated employers contribute) requires that the contribution for the period be recognized as net pension cost and that any contributions due and unpaid be recognized as a liability. Assets in this type of plan are usually commingled and are not segregated or restricted. A board of trustees usually administers these plans, and multiemployer plans are generally subject to a collective bargaining agreement. If there is a withdrawal from this type of plan and if an arising obligation is either probable or reasonably possible, the provisions of IFRS that address contingencies (IAS 37) apply.

Some plans are, in substance, a pooling or aggregation of single employer plans and are ordinarily without collective bargaining agreements. Contributions are usually based on a selected benefit formula. These plans are not considered multi-employer plans, and the accounting is based on the respective interest in the plan.

Business combinations. When an entity that sponsors a single-employer defined benefit plan is acquired and must therefore be accounted for under the provisions of IFRS 3, the purchaser should assign part of the purchase price to an asset if plan assets exceed the projected benefit obligation, or to a liability if the projected benefit obligation exceeds plan assets. The projected benefit obligation should include the effect of any expected plan curtailment or termination. This assignment eliminates any existing unrecognized components, and any future differences between contributions and net pension cost will affect the asset or liability recognized when the purchase took place.

Disclosure of Pension and Other Postemployment Benefit Costs

For defined contribution plans, IAS 19 requires only that the amount of expense included in current period earnings be disclosed. Good practice would suggest that disclosure be made of the general description of each plan, identifying the employee groups covered, and of any other significant matters related to retirement benefits that affect comparability with the previous period reported on.

For defined benefit plans, as would be expected, much more expansive disclosures are mandated. These include

1. A general description of each plan identifying the employee groups covered
2. The accounting policy regarding recognition of actuarial gains or losses
3. A reconciliation of the plan-related assets and liabilities recognized in the balance sheet, showing at the minimum

    a. The present value of wholly unfunded defined benefit obligations
    b. The present value (gross, before deducting plan assets) of wholly or partly unfunded obligations
    c. The fair value of plan assets
    d. The net actuarial gain or loss not yet recognized in the balance sheet
    e. The past service cost not yet recognized in the balance sheet
    f. Any amount not recognized as an asset because of the limitation to the present value of economic benefits from refunds and future contribution reductions
    g. The amounts which are recognized in the balance sheet

4. The amount of plan assets represented by each category of the reporting entity's own financial instruments or by property which is occupied by, or other assets used by, the entity itself
5. A reconciliation of movements (i.e., changes) during the reporting period in the net asset or liability reported in the balance sheet
6. The amount of, and location in the income statement of, the reported amounts of current service cost, interest cost, expected return on plan assets, actuarial gain or loss, past service cost, and effect of any curtailment or settlement
7. The actual return earned on plan assets for the reporting period
8. The principal actuarial assumptions used, including (if relevant) the discount rates, expected rates of return on plan assets, expected rates of salary increases or other index or variable specified in the pension arrangement, medical cost trend rates, and any other material actuarial assumptions utilized in computing benefit costs for the period. The actuarial assumptions are to be explicitly stated in absolute terms, not merely as references to other indices.

Amounts presented in the sponsor's balance sheet cannot be offset (presented on a net basis) unless legal rights of offset exist. Furthermore, even with a legal right to offset (which itself would be a rarity), unless the intent is to settle on a net basis, such presentation would not be acceptable. Thus, a sponsor having two plans, one being in a net asset position, and another in a net liability position, cannot net these in most instances.

Comprehensive example

In the following example, the various components of pension cost are reviewed in detail. Note that only a qualified actuary can compute the service cost component, which depends on numerous assumptions regarding mortality, tenure, and other factors. The remaining elements can be (but usually are not) addressed by nonactuaries, such as accountants. Amounts are keyed to summary of pension cost at end of the following discussion.

Service cost. Future compensation is considered in the calculation of the service cost component to the extent specified by the benefit formula. If part of the benefit formula, future compensation includes changes due to advancement, expected turnover of employees, inflation, etc. Indirect effects, such as predictable bonuses based on compensation levels, and automatic increases specified by the plan also need to be considered. The effect of *retroactive* amendments is included in the calculation at the point when the employer has contractually agreed to them. Service costs attributed (i.e., charged to expense) during the period increase the pension benefit obligation, since they result in additional benefits that are payable in the future.

	January 1, 2006	*2006 Service cost*
Benefit obligation based on current salary	€(1,500)	€ (90)
Effect of expected progression of salary	(400)	(24)
Actuarially determined benefit obligation	€(1,900)	€(114) (a)*

* *Component of net periodic pension cost, summarized later in this example.*

The current period service cost component is found in the actuarial report.

Interest cost. The actuarially computed benefit obligation is a discounted amount. It represents the present value, at the date of the valuation, of all benefits attributed under the plan's formula to employee service rendered prior to that date. Each year the end-of-year pension obligation becomes one year closer to the year in which the benefits attributed in prior years will begin to be paid to plan participants. Consequently, the present value of those previously attributed benefits will have increased to take into account the time value of money. This annual increment is computed by multiplying the assumed settlement discount rate times the pension obligation at the beginning of the year; this increases net periodic pension cost and the pension obligation. Since this imputed interest cost is accounted for as part of pension cost, it is not reported as interest in the financial statements, and accordingly cannot be included as interest for the purposes of optionally computing capitalized interest under IAS 23.

	January 1, 2006	*2006 Service cost*	*2006 Interest cost*
Benefit obligation based on current salary	€(1,500)	€ (90)	€(210)
Effect of expected progression of salary	(400)	(24)	(32)
Actuarially determined benefit obligation	€(1,900)	€(114) (a)*	€(152) (b)*

* *Component of net periodic pension cost, summarized later in this example*

In this example, the applicable discount rate has been assumed at 8%. The interest cost component is calculated by multiplying the start-of-the-year obligation balances by the 8% settlement rate. This amount is found in the actuarial report, although obviously readily computed.

Benefits paid. Benefits paid to retirees are deducted from the above to arrive at the end-of-the-year balance sheet amounts of the accumulated benefit obligation and the projected benefit obligation.

	January 1, 2006	*2006 Service cost*	*2006 Interest cost*	*2006 Benefits paid*	*December 31, 2006*
Benefit obligation based on current salary	€(1,500)	€ (90)	€(120)	€160	€(1,550)
Effect of expected progression of salary	(400)	(24)	(32)	--	(456)
Actuarially determined benefit obligation	€(1,900)	€(114) (a)	€(152) (b)	€160	€(2,006)

Benefits of €160 were paid to retirees during the current year. This amount is found in the report of the pension plan trustee.

Actual return on plan assets. This component is the difference between the *fair value* of the plan assets at the end of the period and the fair value of the plan assets at the beginning of the period adjusted for contributions and payments during the period. Another way to express the result is that it is the net (realized and unrealized) appreciation and depreciation of plan assets plus earnings from the plan assets for the period.

	January 1, 2006	*2006 Actual return on plan assets*	*2006 Employer funding*	*2006 Benefits paid*	*December 31, 2006*
Plan assets	€1,376	€158 (c)*	€145	€(160)	€1,519

* *Component of net periodic pension cost, summarized later in this example.*

The actual return on plan assets of €158, cash deposited with the trustee of €145, and benefits paid (€160) are amounts found in the report of the pension plan trustee. These items increase the plan assets to €1,519 at the end of the year. For purposes of reporting periodic pension cost, however, the actual return on plan assets is adjusted to the expected long-term rate (9%, which is assumed in this example and should be based on empirical data for the classes of assets held in the plan) of return on plan assets (€1,376 × 9% = €124). The difference (€158 – €124 = €34) is an actuarial gain (loss) and is deferred as a gain (loss) to be recognized, or not recognized, in future periods (as explained below).

Gain or loss. Gains (losses) result from (1) changes in plan assumptions, (2) changes in the amount of plan assets, and (3) changes in the amount of the actuarially determined benefit obligation. As discussed previously, even though these gains or losses are economic events that impact the sponsoring entity's obligations under the plan, their immediate recognition in the sponsor's financial statements is not required by IAS 19. Instead, to provide "smoothing" of the effects of short-term fluctuations, unrecognized net gain (loss) may be amortized if the deferred amount meets the criteria specified below. Unlike under the comparable US GAAP standard, however, immediate recognition is permitted under IFRS, if the reporting entity elects to do so.

Since actuarial cost methods are based on numerous assumptions (employee compensation, mortality, turnover, earnings of the pension plan, etc.), it is not unusual for one or more of these assumptions to be invalidated by changes over time. Adjustments will invariably be necessary to bring prior estimates back in line with actual events. These adjustments are known as actuarial gains (losses). The accounting issue regarding the recognition of actuarial adjustments is their timing. All pension costs must eventually be recognized as expense. Actuarial gains (losses) are not considered prior period adjustments since they result from a refinement of estimates arising from obtaining subsequent information. Thus, under APB 20, they are considered changes in an estimate to be recognized in current and future periods.

Plan asset gains (losses) result from both realized and unrealized amounts. They represent periodic differences between the actual return on assets and the expected return. The expected return is generated by multiplying the *expected long-term rate of return* by the *fair value* of plan assets as of the beginning of the reporting period. The expected rate of return is generally best determined by those having access to relevant data and an understanding of financial matters; this is often provided by the consulting actuary or investment advisor responsible for the pension fund asset management. Whatever method is used, it should be done consistently, which means from year to year for each asset class (i.e., bonds, equities), since different classes of assets may have their market-related value calculated in a different manner (i.e., fair value in one case, moving average in another case). There appears to be flexibility permitted under IFRS.

IFRS permits deferral of unrecognized gains or losses, but only to the extent that this does not exceed certain limits (defined under the parallel US GAAP requirement as a "corridor"). This limit is the *greater* of 10% of the present value of the defined benefit obligation at the end of the preceding reporting period (before deducting plan assets), or 10% of the fair value of plan assets as of the same date.

To the extent that the unrecognized net gain (loss) exceeds this limit, the *excess* over 10% is divided by the average remaining service period of active employees and included as a component of net pension costs. Average remaining life expectancies of inactive employees may be used if that is a better measure due to the demographics of the plan participants.

Net pension costs include only the expected return on plan assets, unless immediate recognition of actuarial gains and losses is elected by the reporting entity. The difference between actual and expected returns is deferred through the gain (loss) component of net pension cost. If actual return is greater than expected return, net pension cost is increased to adjust the actual return to the lower expected return. If expected return is greater than actual return, the adjustment results in a decrease to net pension cost to adjust the actual return to the higher expected return.

As noted, if the unrecognized net gain (loss) is large enough, it is amortized. Conceptually, the expected return represents the best estimate of long-term performance of the plan's investments. In any given year, however, an unusual short-term result may occur given the volatility of financial markets.

The expected long-term rate of return used to calculate the expected return on plan assets is the average rate of return expected to be earned on invested funds to provide for pension benefits included in the defined benefit pension obligation. Present rates of return and expected future reinvestment rates of return are considered in arriving at the rate to be used.

To summarize, net periodic pension cost includes a gain (loss) component consisting of *both* of the following, if applicable:

1. As a minimum, the portion of the unrecognized net gain (loss) from previous periods that exceeds the *greater* of 10% of the beginning balances of the pension obligation *or* the fair value of plan assets, amortized over the average remaining service period of active employees expected to receive benefits (or more rapidly, if so elected).
2. The difference between the expected return and the actual return on plan assets.

	January 1, 2006	2006 Return on asset adjustment	2006 Amortization	December 31, 2006
Unrecognized actuarial gain (loss)	€(210)	€34 (d)*	€2 (d)*	€(174)

* *Component of net periodic pension cost, summarized later in this example.*

The return on asset adjustment of €34 is the difference between the actual return of €158 and the expected return of €124 on plan assets. The actuarial loss at the start of the year (€210 assumed for this example) is amortized if it exceeds a limit of the larger of 10% of the pension benefit obligation at the beginning of the period (€1,900 × 10% = €190) or 10% of the fair value of plan assets (€1,376 × 10% = €138). In this example, €20 (€210 − €190) is amortized by dividing the years of average remaining service (twelve years assumed), with a result rounded to €2.

Past service cost. Past service costs are incurred when the sponsor adopts plan amendments (or a new plan, in its entirety) that increase plan benefits attributable to services rendered by plan participants in the past. Under IAS 19, these costs are to be recognized over the period until the benefits have become vested. Even though these pertain to past service, they are not handled as immediate charges.(unless immediately vested) or as corrections of prior periods' reported results. Unlike for actuarial gains or losses, IAS 19 offers no option for more rapid recognition of these costs.

Under the rare situation where benefits are reduced, resulting in negative past service cost, this too is amortized (as a reduction in periodic pension cost) over the average term until vesting.

Note that, under the corresponding US GAAP standard, prior service cost (equivalent to past service cost) may be amortized using various methods, generally over the remaining service lives (working periods) of employees at the date of the amendment to the plan. IFRS requires only that the straight-line method of amortization be used, and that this be over the vesting period. For example, if an improved benefit is granted to only employees having five years' service, the portion applicable to those workers already meeting this threshold test will be immediately expensed, while the portion applicable to those having less seniority will be amortized over the *average* term to vesting for that subgroup.

	January 1, 2006	2006 Amortization	December 31, 2006
Unrecognized prior service cost	€320	€27 (e)*	€293

* *Component of net periodic pension cost, summarized later in this example.*

Unrecognized prior service cost (€320) is amortized over the time to full vesting. In this example, that term is almost 12 years, but in practice this might be much shorter. The straight-line method must be used. These amounts are found in the actuarial report.

Transitional issues. When IAS 19 was enacted, it provided that the initial obligation was to be measured as the present value of the pension obligation, less the fair value of plan assets, less any past service cost to be amortized in later periods, as described above. When this amount exceeded what was reportable under prior GAAP used by the entity (whether an actual standard or the policy adopted by the entity in absence of definitive accounting rules), the entity had to make an irrevocable election to either immediately recognize that increased liability via a charge against earnings, or recognize the adjustment over a period of up to five years from date of adoption. A negative transition adjustment was to be recognized immediately in income.

Since IAS 19 was implemented effective 1999, all transition amounts should have been fully amortized by 2004, making this issue moot. However, to complete the current comprehensive example, the following amortization of transitional liability is included.

	January 1, 2006	2006 Amortization	December 31, 2006
Unamortized net obligation (asset) existing at IAS 19 application	€(6)	€3 (f)*	€(3)

* *Component of net periodic pension cost, summarized later in this example.*

At initial adoption of IAS 19, the "transition amount" was computed, and was being amortized using the straight-line method at a rate of €3 per year. The assumed unamortized balance at January 1, 2006, was €6 and the amortization for 2006 was €3. These amounts are found in the actuarial report.

NOTE: All such transitions should now be complete, in practice.

Summary of net periodic pension cost. The components that were identified in the above examples are summed as follows to determine the amount defined as net periodic pension cost:

		2006
Service cost	(a)	€114
Interest cost	(b)	152
Actual return on plan assets	(c)	(158)
Unrecognized gain (loss)	(d)	36
Amortization of unrecognized past service cost	(e)	27
Amortization of unrecognized net obligation (asset) existing at IAS 19 adoption	(f)	(3)
Total net periodic pension cost		€168

One possible source of confusion is the actual return on plan assets (€158) and the unrecognized gain of €36, which net to €122. The actual return on plan assets reduces pension cost. This is because, to the extent that plan assets generate earnings, those earnings help the plan sponsor subsidize the cost of providing the benefits. Thus, the plan sponsor will not have to fund benefits as they become due, to the extent that plan earnings provide the plan with cash to pay those benefits. This reduction, however, is adjusted by increasing pension cost by the difference between actual and expected return of €34 and the amortization of the excess actuarial loss of €2, for a total of €36. The net result is to include the expected return of €124 (= €158 − €34) less the amortization of the excess of €2 for a total of €122 (= €158 − €36).

In terms of reporting the results of operations, IAS 19 requires disclosure of total pension cost, with details as to the amounts of

- Current service cost
- Interest cost
- Expected return on plan assets
- Expected return on any reimbursement right recognized as an asset
- Actuarial gains and losses
- Past service cost
- The effect of any curtailment or settlement

Regarding the balance sheet, IAS 19 requires a reconciliation of pension-related assets and liabilities presented, showing

- The present value of the defined benefit pension obligation that is wholly unfunded
- The present value of the defined benefit pension obligation that is partially or fully funded, before offsetting pension assets
- The fair value of pension assets
- Net actuarial gain or loss not recognized as of the balance sheet date
- Past service cost not recognized as of the balance sheet date
- Fair value of a reimbursement right recognized as an asset
- Any other amounts recognized in the balance sheet

Reconciliation of Beginning and Ending Pension Obligation and Plan Assets

The following table summarizes the 2006 activity affecting the defined benefit pension obligation and the plan assets, and reconciles the beginning and ending balances per the actuarial report:

	Benefit obligation before salary progression	*Effect of progression of salaries and wages*	*Actuarial defined benefit obligation*	*Fair value of plan assets*
Balance, January 1, 2006	€(1,500)	€(400)	€(1,900)	€1,376
Service cost	(90)	(24)	(114) (a)	
Interest cost	(120)	(32)	(152) (b)	
Benefits paid to retired participants	160		160	(160)
Actual return on plan assets				158 (c)
Sponsor's contributions				145
Balance, December 31, 2006	€(1,550)	€(456)	€(2,006)	€1,519

Postemployment Benefits: Limited Convergence Project

In 2002, IASB undertook a limited convergence project on postemployment benefits. The stated objectives of the project did not extend to a comprehensive reexamination of the accounting for postemployment benefits—which, however, IASB believes is warranted in the near to immediate term. Rather, the goal was to build on the principles that are common to most existing national standards on benefit accounting, and to seek improvements to IAS 19 in certain specific areas. In 2004 an Exposure Draft was issued and an amendment was adopted by year-end 2004, which addresses only a few of the several topics first broached by IASB, the most important of which dealt with the reporting of actuarial gains and losses.

Under IAS 19, before this amendment, actuarial gains and losses could either be taken into income immediately, or, as was more popular with preparers of financial statements, could be deferred and later taken into income over an extended period of time. IASB had expressed its dislike for the latter approach, which is an artificial smoothing technique (albeit modeled after the very similar one under US GAAP) that is probably not conceptually logical. The amendment's solution, however, may also be subject to serious criticism.

As amended, IAS 19 now offers yet a third alternative technique for recognition of actuarial gains and losses: recognition of the entire amount of any actuarial gain or loss may be effected immediately, but outside of income, instead to be reported in a *statement of recognized gains and losses.*

In other words, for those electing this new option, actuarial gains or losses will *not* be recognized in comprehensive income (as are, for example, unrealized gains and losses on investments which are available for sale), but will nonetheless also *not* be included in net income for any period. According to this amendment, gains or losses so recognized will not later be "recycled" through earnings. Thus, actuarial gain or loss would *never* impact earnings, although these would affect retained earnings after passing through the newly designated statement of recognized gains and losses. While the mechanism for a "recycling" strategy is not obvious, the fact that this would exclude from income determination these potentially sizeable gains and losses does trouble some observers.

Additionally, the fact that this was adopted as yet a new alternative method was unsettling. As adopted, entities now have the unfettered right to choose from among three very different methods: to recognize, *in current period income*, the entire amount of any actuarial gain or loss, to recognize, *outside of income*, the entire amount of any actuarial gain or loss, or to defer and amortize actuarial gain or loss as part of pension cost (in the income statement), over an extended period of years. Those reporting entities electing to apply this new, third approach to actuarial gains and losses will permanently avoid reporting these elements of pension cost in earnings.

The amendment to IAS 19 was perhaps motivated by the desire to converge with UK GAAP, which offers essentially this option to preparers. IASB stated, in the Exposure Draft preceding this amendment, that actuarial gains and losses are economic events of the reporting period, and therefore recognizing these when they occur provides a more faithful representation of the events. On the other hand, when recognition is deferred, as is optionally the case under both US GAAP and IFRS, the information provided to users of financial statements is partial and potentially misleading. IASB noted also that the net cumulative deferred actuarial losses may result in displaying a debit item in the balance sheet that does not conform to the definition of an asset, and a net cumulative gain results in displaying a credit which is not an actual liability. Thus, it concluded that its new approach was preferable to the deferral method widely employed (but that remains an acceptable method under amended IAS 19).

The amendment also added significant new disclosure requirements to IAS 19. These are as follows:

1. Reconciliations showing the changes in plan assets and in the defined benefit obligation for the period. It was thought that this mode of reconciliaton will provide a clearer picture of the plan than the previously required reconciliation, which reported the changes in the recognized net liability or asset. The new reconciliation, which superseded the previously mandated reconciliation, will include amounts for which recognition has been deferred.

2. Information about plan assets will include

    a. Percentages that the major classes of assets held by the plan constitute of the total fair value of plan assets;
    b. Expected rates of return for each class of asset; and
    c. A description of the basis for determination of the overall expected rate of return on assets.

3. Information about the sensitivity of defined health care benefit plans to changes in medical cost trend rates. This was deemed useful by IASB because of the widely understood difficulties of assessing the effects of changes in a plan's medical cost trend rate, in part due to such complexities as the ways in which health care cost assumptions interact with caps, cost-sharing provisions, and other factors in plans. IASB concluded that the mere disclosure of a one percentage point change could be appropriate for plans operating in low-inflation environments, but would not provide useful information for plans operating in high-inflation environments.

4. Information about trends in the plan, intended to provide financial statement users with a view of the plan over time, not simply its position at the reporting date. In the absence of such information, misinterpretation of future cash flow implications of the plan can occur. The IASB requirement thus is for disclosure of five-year histories of the plan liabilities, plan assets, the plan's surplus or deficit, and experience adjustments.

5. Information about contributions to the plan, to provide insight into the entity's immediate future cash flows, beyond what can be determined from other required disclosures about the plan. The required disclosures include the employer's best estimate, as soon as this can reasonably be determined, of contributions expected to be paid to the plan during the fiscal year beginning after the balance sheet date.

6. Improved information about the nature of the plan, including all the terms of the plan that are used in the determination of the defined benefit obligation.

Other Benefit Plans

Short-term employee benefits. Per IAS 19, short-term benefits are those falling due within twelve months from the end of the period in which the employees render their services. These include wages and salaries, as well as short-term compensated absences (vacations, annual holiday, paid sick days, etc.), profit sharing and bonuses if due within twelve months after the end of the period in which these were earned, and such nonmonetary benefits as health insurance and housing or automobiles. The standard requires that these be reported as incurred. Since they are accrued currently, no actuarial assumptions or computations are needed and, since due currently, discounting is not to be applied.

Compensated absences may provide some accounting complexities, if these accumulate and vest with the employees. Under the terms of the new employee benefits standard, accumulating benefits can be carried forward to later periods when not fully consumed currently;

for example, when employees are granted two weeks' leave per year, but can carry forward to later years an amount equal to no more than six weeks, the compensated absence benefit can be said to be subject to limited accumulation. Depending on the program, accumulation rights may be limited or unlimited; and, furthermore, the usage of benefits may be defined to occur on a last-in, first-out (LIFO) basis, which in conjunction with limited accumulation rights further limits the amount of benefits which employees are likely to use, if not fully used in the period earned.

The cost of compensated absences should be accrued in the periods earned. In some cases (as when the plans subject employees to limitations on accumulation rights with or without the further restriction imposed by a LIFO pattern of usage), it will be understood that the amounts of compensated absences to which employees are contractually entitled will exceed the amount that they are likely to actually utilize. In such circumstances, the accrual should be based on the *expected* usage, based on past experience and, if relevant, changes in the plan's provisions since the last reporting period.

Example of compensated absences

Consider an entity with 500 workers, each of whom earns two weeks' annual leave, with a carryforward option limited to a maximum of six weeks, to be carried forward no longer than four years. Also, this employer imposes a LIFO basis on any usages of annual leave (e.g., a worker with two weeks' carryforward and two weeks earned currently, taking a three-week leave, will be deemed to have consumed the two currently earned weeks plus one of the carryforward weeks, thereby increasing the risk of ultimately losing the older carried-forward compensated absence time). Based on past experience, 80% of the workers will take no more than two weeks' leave in any year, while the other 20% take an average of four extra days. At the end of the year, each worker has an average of five days' carryforward of compensated absences. The amount accrued should be the cost equivalent of $[(.80 \times 0 \text{ days}) + (.20 \times 4 \text{ days})] \times 500$ workers = 400 days' leave.

Other postretirement benefits. Other postretirement benefits include medical care and other benefits offered to retirees partially or entirely at the expense of the former employer. These are essentially defined benefit plans very much like defined benefit pension plans. Like the pension plans, these require the services of a qualified actuary in order to estimate the true cost of the promises made currently for benefits to be delivered in the future. As with pensions, a variety of determinants, including the age composition, life expectancies, and other demographic factors pertaining to the present and future retiree groups, and the course of future inflation of medical care (or other covered) costs (coupled with predicted utilization factors), need to be projected in order to compute current period costs. Developing these projections requires the skills and training of actuaries; the projected pattern of future medical costs has been particularly difficult to achieve with anything approaching accuracy. Unlike most defined benefit pension plans, other postretirement benefit plans are more commonly funded on a pay-as-you-go basis, which does not alter the accounting but does eliminate earnings on plan assets as a cost offset.

Other long-term employee benefits. These are defined by IAS 19 as including any benefits other than postemployment benefits (pensions, retiree medical care, etc.), termination benefits and equity compensation plans. Examples would include sabbatical leave, "jubilee" or other long-service benefits, long-term profit-sharing payments, and deferred compensation arrangements. Executive deferred compensation plans have become common in nations where these are tax-advantaged (i.e., not taxed to the employee until paid), and these give rise to deferred tax accounting issues as well as measurement and reporting questions, as benefit plans. In general, measurement will be less complex than for defined benefit pension or other postretirement benefits, although some actuarial measures may be needed.

Reportedly for reasons of simplicity, IAS 19 decided to not provide the corridor approach to nonrecognition of actuarial gains and losses for other long-term benefits, under which (as described above) only the gain or loss in excess of a threshold level has to be recognized in the statement of operations. It also requires that past service cost (resulting from the granting of enhanced benefits to participants on a retroactive basis) and the transition gain or loss (from adoption of IAS 19) all must be reported in earnings in the period in which these are granted or occur. In other words, deferred recognition via amortization is not acceptable for these various long-term benefit programs.

For liability measurement purposes, IAS 19 stipulates that the present value of the obligation be presented on the balance sheet, less the fair value of any assets that have been set aside for settlement thereof. The long-term corporate bond rate is used here, as with defined benefit pension obligations, to discount the expected future payments to present value. As to expense recognition, the same cost elements as are set forth for pension plan expense should be included, with the exceptions that, as noted, actuarial gains and losses and past service cost must be recognized immediately, not amortized over a defined time horizon.

Termination benefits. Termination benefits are to be recognized only when the employer has demonstrated its commitment either to terminate the employee or group of employees before normal retirement date, or provide benefits as part of an inducement to encourage early retirements. Generally, a detailed, formal plan will be necessary to support a representation that such a commitment exists. According to IAS 19, the plan should, as a minimum, set forth locations, functions, and numbers of employees to be terminated; the benefits for each job class or other pertinent category; and the time when the plan is to be implemented; with inception to be as soon as possible and completion soon enough to largely eliminate the chance that any material changes to the plan will be necessary.

Since termination benefits do not confer any future economic benefits on the employing entity, these must be expensed immediately. If the payments are to fall due more than twelve months after the balance sheet date, however, discounting to present value is required (again, using the long-term corporate bond rate). Estimates, such as the number of employees likely to accept voluntary early retirement, may need to be made in many cases involving termination benefits. To the extent that accrual is based on such estimates (the possibility that greater numbers may accept, thereby triggering additional costs) further disclosure of loss contingencies may be necessary to comply with IAS 37.

Equity compensation benefits. IAS 19 included equity compensation programs in the benefits to which the standard's reporting requirements applied, when revised IAS 19 was promulgated in 1998. However, since that date the IASB has developed a comprehensive standard on share-based payments, IFRS 2, which supersedes the guidance of IAS 19. IFRS 2 is addressed in Chapter 17.

Examples of Financial Statement Disclosures

Adidas-Salomon AG, Germany
Year ended December 31, 2004

Summary of Significant Accounting Policies

Provisions for pensions and similar obligations comprise the provision obligation of the Group under defined benefit and contribution plans. The obligation under defined benefit plans is determined using the projected unit credit method in accordance with IAS 19 (revised 2000). The Group does not recognize actuarial gains or losses of defined benefit plans as income and expenses according to the corridor approach of IAS 19.92 (revised 2000) within the range of 10% of the present value of the defined benefit obligation.

Item 18. Pensions and Similar Obligations

The Group sponsors and/or contributes to various pension plans. The benefits are provided pursuant to the legal, fiscal, and economic conditions in each respective country. The provision for pensions and similar obligations consists of the following:

Pensions and Similar Obligations (€ in thousands)

	Year ending December 31	
	2004	*2003*
Defined benefit plans	100,739	94,747
Thereof: Adidas-Salomon AG	84,051	77,195
Similar obligations	10,582	10,517
Pensions and similar obligations	111,321	105,264

The actuarial valuations of defined benefit plans are made at the end of each reporting period. Similar obligations include mainly long-term liabilities under a deferred compensation plan. The funds withheld are invested by the Group on behalf of the employees in certain securities, which are presented under other long-term financial assets (see Note 13).

Pension expenses are as follows:

Pension Expenses (€ in thousands)

	Year ending December 31	
	2004	*2003*
Defined benefit plans	13,712	10,696
Thereof: Adidas-Salomon AG	9,624	8,371
Defined contribution plans	19,986	13,440
Pensions expenses	33,698	24,136

Defined Benefit Plans

The provision for pensions evolved as follows:

Provision for Defined Benefit Plans (€ in thousands)

Provision for pensions as at December 31, 2003	94,747
Currency translation differences	(36)
Pension expense	13,712
Pensions paid	(7,684)
Provision for pensions as at December 31, 2004	100,739

Most pension provisions are for employees in Germany where the actuarial assumptions for the defined benefit plans are as follows:

Actuarial Assumptions

	Year ending December 31	
	2004	*2003*
Discount rate	4.75%	5.50%
Salary increases	1.0-2.0%	1.5-3.5%
Pension increases	1.0-2.0%	1.7-2.0%

Actuarial assumptions for employee turnover and mortality are based on empirical data, the latter on the 1998 version of the mortality tables of Dr. Heubeck as in the prior year. The actuarial assumptions for other countries are not materially different.

The pension obligation consists of the following:

Provision for Defined Benefit Plans (€ in thousands)

	Year ending December 31	
	2004	*2003*
Present value of the defined benefit obligation	118,094	100,100
Unrecognized actuarial losses	(17,355)	(5,353)
Provision for pensions	100,739	94,747

On the basis of the actuarial valuations, it was not necessary to recognize actuarial gains or losses pursuant to the corridor approach of IAS 19.92 (revised 2000) in 2004 and 2003, respectively.

Pension expense attributable to the defined plans comprises

Pension Expenses for Defined Benefit Plans (€ in thousands)

| | *Year ending December 31* | |
	2004	*2003*
Current service cost	8,624	6,348
Interest cost	5,088	4,348
Pension expense	13,712	10,696

Novartis AG, Switzerland
For the year ended December 31, 2004

25. Employee Benefits

(a) Defined benefit plans

The Group has, apart from the legally required social security schemes, numerous independent pension plans. For certain Group companies, however, no independent assets exist for the pension and other long-term employee benefit obligations. In these cases the related liability is included in the balance sheet.

Defined benefit pension plans cover the majority of the Group's employees. The defined benefit obligations and related assets of all major plans are reappraised annually by independent actuaries. Plan assets are recorded at fair values. The defined benefit obligation of unfunded pension plans was $821 million at December 31, 2004 (2003: $753 million).

The following is a summary of the status of the main funded and unfunded pension and other postemployment benefit plans at December 31, 2004 and 2003:

| | Pension plans | | Other postemployment benefit plans | |
	2004	*2003*	*2004*	*2003*
		($ millions)		
Benefit obligation at beginning of the year	13,865	11,845	720	645
Service cost	351	285	24	19
Interest cost	580	559	42	40
Actuarial losses	1,401	695	91	85
Plan amendments	(41)	15	(8)	(31)
Foreign currency translation	1,204	1,256	3	2
Benefit payments	(872)	(790)	(44)	(40)
Benefit obligation at end of the year	16,488	13,865	828	720
Fair value of plan assets at beginning of the year	16,128	14,365		
Actual return on plan assets	738	916		
Foreign currency translation	1,417	1,506		
Employer contributions	207	92		
Employee contributions	52	39		
Plan amendments	(7)			
Benefit payments	(872)	(790)		
Fair value of plan assets at end of the year	17,663	16,128		
Funded status	1,175	2,263	(828)	(720)
Unrecognized past service cost	6	6	(33)	(39)
Unrecognized net actuarial losses	2,168	777	366	299
Net asset/liability in the balance sheet	3,349	3,049	(495)	(460)

The movement in the net asset and the amounts recognized in the balance sheet were as follows:

| | Pension plans | | Other postemployment benefit plans | |
	2004	2003	2004	2003
		($ millions)		
Movement in net asset/(liability)				
Net asset/(liability) in the balance sheet at the beginning of the year	3,046	2,786	(460)	(421)
Net periodic benefit costs	(198)	(54)	(75)	(63)
Employer contributions/benefit payments	207	92	44	40
Past service cost arisen in the current year	(19)	(33)	8	4
Plan amendments, net	34	(15)	(8)	(31)
Foreign currency translation	279	270	(4)	11
Net asset/(liability) in the balance sheet at the end of the year	3,349	3,046	(495)	(460)
Amounts recognized in the balance sheet				
Prepaid benefit cost	4,337	3,976		
Accrued benefit liability	(988)	(930)	(495)	(460)
Net asset/(liability) in the balance sheet	3,349	3,046	(495)	(460)

The net periodic benefit cost recorded in the income statement consisted of the following:

| | Pension plans | | | Other postemployment benefit plans | | |
	2004	2003	2002	2004	2003	2002
			($ millions)			
Components of net periodic benefit cost						
Service cost	351	285	277	24	19	14
Interest cost	580	559	552	42	40	36
Expected return on plan assets	(715)	(796)	(970)			
Employee contributions	(52)	(39)	(7)			
Recognized actuarial losses	53	72		23	8	
Recognized past service cost	(19)	(27)	9	(14)	(4)	4
Net periodic benefit cost	198	54	(139)	75	63	54
Amounts recognized in the balance sheet						
Prepaid benefit cost						
Accrued benefit liability						
Net asset/(liability) in the balance sheet						

The principal actuarial weighted-average assumptions used for calculating defined benefit plans and other postemployment benefits are as follows:

| | Pension plans | | | Other postemployment benefit plans | | |
| | 2004 | 2003 | 2002 | 2004 | 2003 | 2002 |
	%	%	%	%	%	%
Weighted-average assumptions used to determine benefit obligations at the end of the year						
Discount rate	3.8	4.3	4.5	5.8	6.3	6.8
Expected rate of salary increase	2.8	2.8	2.8			
Weighted-average assumptions used to determine net periodic pension cost for the year ended						
Discount rate	4.3	4.6	4.5	5.8	6.3	6.8
Expected return on plan assets	4.5	5.6	6.1			
Expected rate of salary increase	2.1	2.8	2.8			

The weighted average asset allocation of funded defined benefit plans at December 31, 2004 was as follows:

	Long-term target	2004	2003
	%	%	%
Equity securities	15-40	25	22
Debt securities	45-70	58	59
Real estate	0-15	8	8
Cash and other investments	0-15	9	11
Total		100	100

Strategic pension plan asset allocations are determined by the objective to achieve an investment return which, together with the contributions paid, is sufficient to maintain reasonable control over the various funding risks of the plans. Based upon current market and economic environments, actual asset allocation may periodically deviate from policy targets as determined by the plan trustees and by the Novartis pension board.

The expected future cash flows to be paid by the Group in respect of pension and other postemployment benefit plans at December 31, 2004 was as follows:

	Pension plans	Other post-employment benefit plans
	($ millions)	
Employer contributions 2005 (estimated)	179	
Expected future benefit payments		
2005	1,004	44
2006	1,005	44
2007	1,021	46
2008	1,046	47
2009	1,061	49
2010-2014	5,483	268

The health care cost trend rate assumptions for other postemployment benefits are as follows:

	2004	2003	2002
Health care cost trend rate assumptions used			
Health care cost trend rate assumed for next year	11.0%	9.0%	10.0%
Rate to which the cost trend rate is assumed to decline	4.8%	4.8%	4.8%
Year that rate reaches the ultimate trend rate	2012	2012	2006

A one-percentage-point change in the assumed health care cost trend rates compared to those used for 2004 would have the following effects:

	1% point increase	1% point decrease
	($ millions)	
Effects on total of service and interest cost components	9	(7)
Effect on postemployment benefit obligations	112	(93)

The number of Novartis AG shares held by pension and similar benefit funds at December 31, 2004, was 30.9 million shares with a market value of $1.6 billion (2003: 31.5 million shares with a market value of $1.3 billion). These funds sold 0.6 million Novartis AG shares during the year ended December 31, 2004 (2003: nil). The amount of dividends received on Novartis AG shares held as plan assets by these funds were $25 million for the year ended December 31, 2004 (2003: $22 million; 2002: $22 million).

(b) Defined contribution plans

In some Group companies employees are covered by defined contribution plans and other long-term employee benefits. The liability of the Group for these benefits is reported in other long-term employee benefits and deferred compensation and at December 31, 2004, amounts to $324 million (2003: $183 million). In 2004 contributions charged to the consolidated income statement for the defined contribution plans were $94 million (2003: $84 million; 2002: $85 million).

17 STOCKHOLDERS' EQUITY

PERSPECTIVE AND ISSUES

The IASB's *Framework* defines equity as the residual interest in the assets of an enterprise after deducting all its liabilities. Stockholders' equity is comprised of all capital contributed to the entity (including share premium, also referred to as capital paid-in in excess of par value) plus retained earnings (which represents the entity's cumulative earnings less all distributions that have been made therefrom).

IAS 1 categorizes stockholders' interests into three broad subdivisions: issued capital, reserves, and accumulated profits or losses. This standard also sets forth requirements for disclosures about the details of share capital for corporations and the various capital accounts of other types of enterprises, such as partnerships.

Equity represents an interest in the net assets (i.e., assets less liabilities) of the entity. It is not a claim on those assets in the sense that liabilities are, however. On liquidation of the business, an obligation arises for the entity to distribute any remaining assets to the shareholders, but only after the creditors are first fully paid.

Earnings are not generated by transactions in an entity's own equity (e.g., by the issuance, reacquisition, or reissuance of its common or preferred shares). Depending on the laws of the jurisdiction of incorporation, distributions to shareholders may be subject to various limitations, such as to the amount of retained (accounting basis) earnings. In other cases, limitations may be based on values not presented in the financial statements, such as the net solvency of the entity as determined on a market value basis; in such instances, IFRS-basis financial statements will not provide information needed for making such determination.

In recent years the matter of share-based payments (e.g., stock option plans and other arrangements whereby employees or others, such as vendors, are compensated via issuance of shares) has received great amounts of attention. IASB imposed a comprehensive standard, IFRS 2, which requires a fair value-based measurement of all such schemes.

A major objective of the accounting for stockholders' equity is the adequate disclosure of the sources from which the capital was derived. For this reason, a number of different paid-in capital accounts may be presented in the balance sheet. The rights of each class of shareholder must also be disclosed. Where shares are reserved for future issuance, such as under the terms of stock option plans, this fact must also be made known.

Sources of IFRS		
IFRS 2	*IAS* 1, 8, 16, 32	*IFRIC* 2

DEFINITIONS OF TERMS

Cash-settled share-based payment transaction. A share-based payment transaction in which the entity acquires goods or services by incurring a liability to transfer cash or other assets to the supplier of those goods or services for amounts that are based on the price (or value) of the entity's shares or other equity instruments of the entity.

Employees and others providing similar services. Individuals who render personal services to the entity and either (1) the individuals are regarded as employees for legal or tax purposes, (2) the individuals work for the entity under its direction in the same way as individuals who are regarded as employees for legal or tax purposes, or (3) the services rendered are similar to those rendered by employees. For example, the term encompasses all management personnel (i.e., those persons having authority and responsibility for planning, directing and controlling the activities of the entity, including nonexecutive directors).

Equity instrument. A contract that evidences a residual interest in the assets of an entity after deducting all of its liabilities, where liabilities are defined as the present obligations of the entity arising from past events, the settlement of which are expected to result in an outflow from the entity of resources embodying economic benefits (i.e., an outflow of cash or other assets of the entity).

Equity instrument granted. The right (conditional or unconditional) to an equity instrument of the entity conferred by the entity on another party, under a share-based payment arrangement.

Equity-settled share-based payment transaction. A share-based payment transaction in which the entity receives goods or services as consideration for equity instruments of the entity (including shares or share options).

Fair value. The amount for which an asset could be exchanged, a liability settled, or an equity instrument granted could be exchanged, between knowledgeable, willing parties in an arm's-length transaction.

Grant date. The date at which the entity and another party (including an employee) agree to a share-based payment arrangement, being when the entity and the counterparty have a shared understanding of the terms and conditions of the arrangement. At grant date the entity confers on the counterparty the right to cash, other assets, or equity instruments of the entity, provided the specified vesting conditions, if any, are met. If that agreement is subject to an approval process (for example, by shareholders), grant date is the date when that approval is obtained.

Intrinsic value. The difference between the fair value of the shares to which the counterparty has the (conditional or unconditional) right to subscribe or which it has the right to receive, and the price (if any) the counterparty is (or will be) required to pay for those shares.

Market condition. A condition upon which the exercise price, vesting or exercisability of an equity instrument depends that is related to the market price of the entity's equity instruments, such as attaining a specified share price or a specified amount of intrinsic value of a share option, or achieving a specified target that is based on the market price of the entity's equity instruments relative to an index of market prices of equity instruments of other entities.

Measurement date. The date at which the fair value of the equity instruments granted is measured for the purposes of this IFRS. For transactions with employees and others providing similar services, the measurement date is grant date. For transactions with parties other than employees (and those providing similar services), the measurement date is the date the entity obtains the goods or the counterparty renders service.

Reload feature. A feature that provides for an automatic grant of additional share options whenever the option holder exercises previously granted options using the entity's shares, rather than cash, to satisfy the exercise price.

Share-based payment arrangement. An agreement between the entity and another party (including an employee) to enter into a share-based payment transaction, which thereby entitles the other party to receive cash or other assets of the entity for amounts that are based on the price of the entity's shares or other equity instruments of the entity, or to receive equity instruments of the entity, provided the specified vesting conditions, if any, are met.

Share-based payment transaction. A transaction in which the entity receives goods or services as consideration for equity instruments of the entity (including shares or share options), or acquires goods or services for amounts that are based on the price of the entity's shares or other equity instruments of the entity.

Share option. A contract that gives the holder the right, but not the obligation, to subscribe to the entity's shares at a fixed or determinable price for a specified period of time.

Vest. To become an entitlement. Under a share-based payment arrangement, a counterparty's right to receive cash, other assets, or equity instruments of the entity vests upon satisfaction of any specified vesting conditions.

Vesting conditions. The conditions that must be satisfied for the counterparty to become entitled to receive cash, other assets or equity instruments of the entity, under a share-based payment arrangement. Vesting conditions include service conditions, which require the other party to complete a specified period of service, and performance conditions, which require specified performance targets to be met (such as a specified increase in the entity's profit over a specified period of time).

Vesting period. The period during which all the specified vesting conditions of a share-based payment arrangement are to be satisfied.

CONCEPTS, RULES, AND EXAMPLES

IFRS have dealt primarily with presentation and disclosure requirements relating to stockholders' equity and have yet to resolve or even address matters pertaining to the actual accounting for the various components of stockholders' equity (i.e., recognition and measurement issues). IFRS 2, which thoroughly addresses the accounting for share-based payments, was a major step forward. It should be noted that in many jurisdictions company law sets out specific requirements as regards accounting for equity, which may limit the application of IFRS.

Because of the absence of any promulgated IFRS on many details of this area, this chapter makes use of certain guidance that exists under US GAAP. The IAS 8 hierarchy requires that in the absence of a standard, the preparer should refer to the *Framework* and thereafter to national GAAP based on the same conceptual framework. In the light of the IASB's *Norwalk Agreement,* US GAAP would normally be seen as authoritative in such a case. Also, given the intent to converge US GAAP and IFRS, it is certainly possible that IFRS may formally adopt at least some of the US GAAP guidance, rather than attempt to create unique IFRS to deal with these matters.

Presentation and Disclosure Requirements under IFRS

Equity includes reserves such as statutory or legal reserves, general reserves and contingency reserves, and revaluation surplus. IAS 1 categorizes stockholders' interests in three broad subdivisions: issued capital, reserves, and accumulated profits or losses. This recently revised standard also sets forth requirements for disclosures about the details of share capital for corporations and of the various capital accounts of other types of enterprises.

Disclosures relating to share capital.

1. *The number or amount of shares authorized, issued, and outstanding.* It is required that a company disclose information relating to the number of shares authorized, issued, and outstanding. Authorized share capital is defined as the maximum number of shares that a company is permitted to issue, according to its articles of association, its charter, or its bylaws. The number of shares issued and outstanding could vary, based on the fact that a company could have acquired its own shares and is holding them as treasury stock (discussed below under reacquired shares).

2. *Capital not yet paid in.* In an initial public offering (IPO), subscribers may be asked initially to pay in only a portion of the par value, with the balance due in installments, which are known as *calls.* Thus, it is possible that on the date of the balance sheet a certain portion of the share capital has not yet been paid in. The amount not yet collected must be shown as a contra (i.e., a deduction) in the equity section, since that portion of the subscribed capital has yet to be issued. For example, while the gross amount of the stock subscription increases capital, if the due date of the final call falls on February 7, 2006, following the accounting year-end of December 31, 2005, the amount of capital not yet paid in should be shown as a deduction from stockholders' equity. In this manner, only the net amount of capital received as of the date of the balance sheet will be properly included in stockholders' equity, averting an overstatement of the entity's actual equity.

   IAS 1 requires that a distinction be made between shares that have been issued and fully paid, on the one hand, and those that have been issued but not fully paid, on the other hand. The number of shares outstanding at the beginning and at the end of each period presented must also be reconciled.

3. *Par value per share.* This is also generally referred to as legal value or face value per share. The par value of shares is specified in the corporate charter or bylaws and referred to in other documents, such as the share application and prospectus. Par value is the smallest unit of share capital that can be acquired unless the prospectus permits fractional shares (which is very unusual for commercial enterprises). In certain jurisdictions, including the United States, it is also permitted for corporations to issue no-par stock (i.e., stock that is not given any par value). In such cases, again depending on local corporation laws, sometimes a stated value is determined by the board of directors, which is then accorded effectively the same treatment as par value. IAS 1 requires disclosure of par values or of the fact that the shares were issued without par values.

    Historically, companies often issued shares at par value in cases where shares are issued immediately on incorporation or soon thereafter. This was partially due to laws, now rare, holding share owners contingently liable in the event of business failure, up to the amount of any discount from par value at the original issuance of shares. The prohibition against issuing shares at discount was thought to protect creditors and others, who could rely on aggregate par value as having been contributed in cash to the enterprise. It did not restrict any subsequent sale of the shares, however. As a practical matter, par values have had a much diminished importance as corporation laws have been modernized in many jurisdictions. Additionally, often the par values will be made trivial, such as when set at €1 or even €0.01 per share, such that the concern over an original-issuance discount is made moot, since issuance prices even at inception of a new corporation will be substantially above par value.

4. *Movements in share capital accounts during the year.* This information is usually disclosed in the financial statements or the footnotes to the financial statements, generally in a tabular or statement format, although in some circumstances merely set forth in a narrative. If a statement is presented, it is generally referred to as the Statement of Changes in Stockholders' Equity. It highlights the changes during the year in the various components of stockholders' equity. It also serves the purpose of reconciling the beginning and the ending balances of stockholders' equity, as shown in the balance sheets. Under the provisions of IAS 1, reporting entities must present either a statement showing the changes in all the equity accounts (including issued capital, reserves and accumulated profit or loss), or a statement reporting changes in equity other than those arising from transactions with, or distributions to, owners (see Chapter 3).

5. *Rights, preferences, and restrictions with respect to the distribution of dividends and to the repayment of capital.* When there is more than one class of share capital having varying rights, adequate disclosure of the rights, preferences, and restrictions attached to each such class of share capital will enhance understandability of the information provided by the financial statements.

6. *Cumulative preference dividends in arrears.* If an entity has preferred stock outstanding, and does not pay *cumulative* dividends on the preference shares annually when due, it will be required by statute to pay these arrearages in later years, before any distributions can be made on common (ordinary) shares. When there are several series of preferred shares, the individual stock indentures will spell out the relative preference order, so that, for example, senior preferred series may be paid dividends even though junior preferred stock has several years' arrearages. Al-

though practice varies, most preference shares are cumulative in nature; preference shares that do not have this feature are called *noncumulative preference shares.*

7. *Reacquired shares.* Shares that are issued but then reacquired by a company are referred to as *treasury stock.* The entity's ability to reacquire shares may be limited by its corporate charter or by covenants in its loan and/or preferred stock agreements (for example, it may be restricted from doing so as long as bonded debt remains outstanding). In those jurisdictions where the company law permits the repurchase of shares, such shares, on acquisition by the company or its consolidated subsidiary, become legally available for reissue or resale without further authorization. *Shares outstanding* refers to shares other than those held as treasury stock. That is, treasury stock does not reduce the number of shares issued, but affects the number of shares outstanding. It is to be noted that certain countries prohibit companies from purchasing their own shares, since to do so is considered as a reduction of share capital that can be achieved only with the express consent of the shareholders in an extraordinary general meeting, and then only under certain defined conditions.

IAS 1 requires that shares in the entity held in its treasury or by its subsidiaries be identified for each category of share capital and be deducted from paid-in capital. IAS 32 states that the treasury share acquisition transaction is to be reported in the statement of changes in equity. When later resold, any difference between acquisition cost and ultimate proceeds represents a change in equity, and is therefore not to be considered a gain or loss to be reported in the income statement. Accounting for treasury stock is discussed in further detail later in this chapter.

IAS 32 also specifies that the costs associated with equity transactions are to be accounted for as reductions of equity if the corresponding transaction was a share issuance, or as increases in the contra equity account when incurred in connection with treasury share reacquisitions. Relevant costs are limited to incremental costs directly associated with the transactions. If the issuance involves a compound instrument, the issuance costs should be associated with the liability and equity components, respectively, using a rational and consistent basis of allocation.

8. *Shares reserved for future issuance under options and sales contracts, including the terms and amounts.* Companies may issue stock options that grant the holder of these options rights to a specified number of shares at a certain price. A common example of a stock option is that granted under an employee stock ownership plan (ESOP). Stock options are an increasingly popular means of employee remuneration, and often top management is offered such noncash perquisites as part of its remuneration package. The options grant the holder the right to acquire shares over a defined time horizon for a fixed price, which may equal fair value at the grant date or, less commonly, at a price lower than fair value. Granting options usually is not legal unless the entity has enough authorized but unissued shares to satisfy the holders' demands, if made. If a company has shares reserved for future issuance under option plans or sales contracts, it is necessary to disclose the number of shares, including terms and amounts, so reserved. These reserved shares are not available for sale or distribution to others during the terms of the unexercised options.

IAS 32 deals with situations in which enterprise obligations are to be settled in cash or in equity securities, depending on the outcome of contingencies not under the issuer's control. In general, these should be classed as liabilities, unless the part that could require settlement in cash is not genuine, or settlement by cash or distribution of other assets is available only in the event of the liquidation of the issuer. If the optionee can demand cash, the obligation is a liability, not equity.

The accounting for stock options, which was introduced by IFRS 2, is dealt with later in this chapter. As will be seen, it presents many intriguing and complex issues.

Disclosures relating to other equity.

1. *Capital paid in excess of par value.* This is the amount received on the issuance of shares that is the excess over the par value. It is called "additional paid-in capital" in the United States, while in many other jurisdictions, including the European Union, it is referred to as "share premium." Essentially the same accounting would be required if a stated value is used in lieu of par value, where permitted.

2. *Revaluation reserve.* When a company carries property, plant, and equipment at amounts other than historical costs, as is permitted by IAS 16 (revaluation to fair value), the difference between the historical costs (net of accumulated depreciation) and the fair values is credited to the revaluation reserve.

   The standard requires that movements of this reserve during the reporting period (year or interim period) be disclosed, which is usually done in the footnotes, and this will also appear in the statement of changes in equity or the statement of recognized income and expense, where one is presented. Also, restrictions as to any distributions of this reserve to shareholders should be disclosed. Note that in some jurisdictions the directors may be empowered to make distributions in excess of recorded book capital, and this often will require a determination of fair values.

3. *Reserves.* Reserves include capital reserves as well as revenue reserves. Also, statutory reserves and voluntary reserves are included under this category. Finally, special reserves, including contingency reserves, are included herein. The use of general reserves and statutory reserves, once common or even required under company laws in many jurisdictions, is now in decline.

   Statutory reserves (or legal reserves, as they are called in some jurisdictions) are created based on the requirements of the law or the statute under which the company is incorporated. For instance, most corporate statutes in Middle Eastern countries require that companies set aside 10% of their net income for the year as a "statutory reserve," with such appropriations to continue until the balance in this reserve account equals 50% of the company's equity capital. The intent is to provide an extra "cushion" of protection to creditors, such that even significant losses incurred in later periods will not reduce the entity's net worth below zero, which would, were it to occur, threaten creditors' ability for repayment of liabilities.

   Sometimes a company's articles, charter, or bylaws may require that each year the company set aside a certain percentage of its net profit (income) by way of a contingency or general reserve. Unlike statutory or legal reserves, contingency reserves are based on the provisions of corporate bylaws. The use of general reserves is not consistent with IFRS and some national GAAP, such as that in the US.

   The standard requires that movements in these reserves during the reporting period be disclosed, along with the nature and purpose of each reserve presented within owners' equity.

4. *Retained earnings.* By definition, retained earnings represents a corporation's accumulated profits (or losses) less any distributions that have been made therefrom. However, based on provisions contained in IFRS, other adjustments are also made to the amount of retained earnings. IAS 8 requires the following to be shown as adjustments to retained earnings:

   a.   Correction of accounting errors that relate to prior periods should be reported by adjusting the opening balance of retained earnings. Comparative information should be restated, unless it is impracticable to do so.

   b.   The adjustment resulting from a change in accounting policy that is to be applied retrospectively should be reported as an adjustment to the opening balance of retained earnings. Comparative information should be restated unless it is impracticable to do so.

When dividends have been proposed but not formally approved, and hence when such intended dividends have not yet become reportable as a liability of the enterprise, disclosure is required by IAS 1. Dividends declared after the balance sheet date, but prior to the issuance of the financial statements, must be disclosed but cannot be formally recognized via a charge against retained earnings (as was sometimes done in the past, and as remains normal practice in certain jurisdictions such as the UK under national rules). Also, the amount of any cumulative preference dividends not recognized as charges against accumulated profits must be disclosed (i.e., arrearages), whether parenthetically or in the footnotes.

Classification between Liabilities and Equity

IAS 32 requires that the issuer of a financial instrument should classify the instrument, or its components, as a liability or as equity, according to the substance of the contractual arrangement on initial recognition. The crux of the issue is the differentiation between a financial liability and an equity instrument.

The standard defines a financial liability as a contractual obligation

   1.   To deliver cash or another financial asset to another enterprise, or

   2.   To exchange financial instruments with another enterprise under conditions that are potentially unfavorable.

An equity instrument, on the other hand, has been defined by the standard as any contract that evidences a residual interest in the assets of an enterprise after deducting all its liabilities.

A special situation arises in connection with cooperatives, which are member-owned organizations having capital which exhibits certain characteristics of debt, since it is not permanent in nature. IFRIC 2 addresses the accounting for members' shares in cooperatives. It holds that where a member of a cooperative has a contractual right to request redemption of shares, this does not necessarily require the shares to be classified as a liability. Members' shares are to be classified as equity if the entity has an unconditional right to refuse redemption, or if national law prohibits redemption. On the other hand, if the law prohibits redemption only conditionally (e.g., if minimum capital requirements are not maintained), this does not alter the general rule that cooperative shares are to be deemed a liability, not equity, of the entity.

IASB has also been considering the special case of shares which are puttable to the entity for a proportion of the fair value of the entity. When this right is held by the shareholder, redemption can be demanded, and under IAS 32 such shares would be classified as a liability and be measured at fair value. This creates the anomalous situation where a successful entity using historical cost would have a liability that increases every year and leaves the reporting entity with, potentially, no equity in its balance sheet, thereby causing the reporting of an increasing net deficit. This situation has been seen to occur in particular for some farming cooperatives which sell produce on behalf of members, and where a farmer must be a member to sell produce, and must also leave the cooperative venture if there is no produce to sell. The entity itself is the only market for its shares. This particular issue remains unresolved as of mid-2005 (but an already-established rule under US GAAP, FAS 150, does mandate such accounting treatment, although FASB is reportedly planning to revisit this issue.

Compound financial instruments. Increasingly, corporations issue financial instruments that exhibit attributes of both equity and liabilities. IAS 32 stipulates that an enterprise that issues such financial instruments, which are technically known as compound instruments, should classify the component parts of the financial instrument separately as equity or liability as appropriate. (For a detailed discussion on financial instruments, refer to Chapters 5 and 10.) The full fair value of the liability component(s) must be reported as liabilities, and only the residual value, at issuance, can be included as equity, according to a recent amendment to IAS 32.

Accounting for Share-Based Payments

Prior to the IASB's issuance of IFRS 2, *Share-Based Payment,* there had been no guidance under IFRS to the accounting for employee stock-based compensation or other share-based payment situations. This was an area seriously in need of attention—not merely under IFRS, which lacked any requirements, but also under most national GAAP, where (unlike in North America), the issue of stock options to employees has only recently become a common corporate practice. US GAAP had attempted to deal with this in the mid-1990s but the resulting standard was severely compromised due to strong opposition to full fair value accounting, but subsequent to the promulgation of IFRS 2 a revised US standard (FAS 123R) has largely adopted the IFRS approach.

Overview. The IASB issued its final standard in 2004 for application beginning January 1, 2005. The general principle is that all share-based payment transactions should be recognized in the financial statements, using fair value measurement, with expense recognized when the goods are received or services are rendered. Furthermore—and very importantly—the same recognition and measurement standards would apply to both public and private companies. Given the added challenge of estimating fair value for nontraded shares, this was a major point of contention among those responding to the draft standard.

In theory, transactions in which goods or services are received as consideration for equity instruments of the entity are to be measured at the fair value of the goods or services received. However, if their value cannot be determined (as the standard suggests is the case for employee services in some situations) they are to be measured with reference to the fair value of the equity instruments granted.

In the case of transactions with parties other than employees, there is a rebuttable presumption that the fair value of the goods or services received is more readily determinable. This follows logically from the fact that, in arm's-length transactions, it should be the case that management would be highly cognizant of the value it has received (in merchandise, plant assets, etc.) and that such data would not be any effort to gather and utilize. Arguments to the contrary raise basic questions about managerial performance and can rarely be given much credence.

For transactions measured at the fair value of the equity instruments granted (such as compensation transactions with employees), fair value is estimated at grant date. A point of contention here is whether grant date or exercise date is more appropriate, but the logic of the former is that the economic decision, and the employee's contractual commitment, was as of the grant date, and the accidents of timing of subsequent exercise (or, in some cases, forfeiture) are not indicative of the bargained-for value of the transaction. The grant date is when the employee accepts the commitment, not when the offer is made.

When stock is issued immediately, measurement is not generally difficult. The more problematic situation is when employees (or others) are granted options that permit exercise over a defined time horizon. The holders' ability to wait and later assess the desirability of exercising the options has value—the longer the period until the options expire, the more likely the underlying shares will increase in value, and thus the greater is the value of the option. Even if the shares are publicly traded, the value of the options will be subject to some debate. Only when the options themselves are traded (rarely the case with employee share options, which are restricted to the grantees themselves) will fair value be directly determinable by observation.

The standard holds that, to estimate the fair value of a share option where an observable market price for that option does not exist, an *option pricing model* should be used. It does not specify which particular model should be used. The entity must disclose the model used, the inputs to that model, and various other information bearing on how fair value was computed. In practice, these models are all fairly sophisticated (although various commercial software eases the computational complexities) and a number of the variables have subjective components.

One issue to be dealt with involves the tax treatment of options, which varies across jurisdictions. In most instances the tax treatment will not comply with the fair value measurement mandated under IFRS 2, and thus there will be a need for specific guidance as to the accounting for the tax effects of granting the options and of the ultimate exercise of those options, if they are not forfeited by the optionees. This is described later in this discussion.

The tax treatment of share-based payments prescribed under IFRS 2 differs from that under SFAS 123. The Basis for Conclusions of IFRS 2 notes that in jurisdictions where a tax deduction is given, such as the US, the measurement of the tax deduction does not coincide with that of the accounting deduction. Where the tax deduction is in excess of the income statement expense, the excess is taken directly to equity.

Employee stock options. For equity-settled transactions, the fundamental approach is to expense the value of stock options granted over the period during which the employee is earning the option, that is, the period until the option vests (becomes unconditional). If the options vest (become exercisable) immediately, the employee receiving the grant cannot be compelled to perform future services, and accordingly the fair value of the options is compensation in the period of the grant. More commonly, however, there will be a period (several years, typically) of future services required before the options may be exercised; in those cases, compensation is to be recognized over that vesting period. There are two practical difficulties with this: (1) estimating the value of the stock options granted (true even if vesting is immediate); and (2) allowing for the fact that not all options initially granted will ultimately vest or, if they vest, be exercised by the holders.

Measurement. IFRS 2 directs that where market prices are not available (which is virtually always the case for employee stock options, since they cannot normally be sold), the entity must estimate fair value using a valuation technique that is "consistent with generally accepted valuation methodologies for pricing financial instruments, and shall incorporate all factors and assumptions that knowledgeable, willing market participants would consider in setting the price."

Appendix B of the standard notes that all option pricing models take into account

- The exercise price of the option
- The current market price of the share
- The expected volatility of the share price
- The dividends expected to be paid on the shares
- The risk-free interest rate
- The life of the option

In essence, the grant date value of the stock option is the current market price, less the present value of the exercise price, less the dividends that will not be received during the vesting period, adjusted for the expected volatility. The time value of money, as is well understood, arises because the holder of an option is not required to pay the exercise price until the exercise date. Instead, the holder can invest his funds elsewhere, while waiting to exercise the option. According to IFRS 2, the time value of money component is determined by reference to the rate of return available on *risk-free* securities. If the stock pays a *dividend,* or is expected to pay a dividend during the life of the option, the value to the holder of the option from delaying payment of the exercise price is only the excess (if any) of the return available on a risk-free security over the return available from exercising the option today and owning the shares. The time value of money component for a divided-paying stock equals the discounted present value of the expected interest income that could be earned less the discounted present value of the expected dividends that will be forgone during the expected life of the option.

The time value associated with *volatility* represents the ability of the holder to profit from appreciation of the underlying stock while being exposed to the loss of only the option premium, and not the full current value of the stock. A more volatile stock has a higher probability of big increases or decreases in price, compared with one having lower volatility. As a result, an option on a highly volatile stock has a higher probability of a big payoff than an option on a less volatile stock, and so has a higher value relating to volatility fair value component. The longer the option term, the more likely, for any given degree of volatility, that the share price will appreciate before option expiration. Greater volatility, and longer term, each contribute to the value of the option.

Volatility is the measure of the amount by which a stock's price fluctuates during a period. It is expressed as a percentage because it relates stock price fluctuations during a period to the stock's price at the beginning of the period. Expected annualized volatility is the predicted amount that is the input to the option pricing model. This is calculated largely from the stock's historical price fluctuations.

To illustrate this basic concept, assume that the present market price of the underlying stock is €20 per share, and the option plan grants the recipient the right to purchase shares at today's market price at any time during the next five years. If a risk-free rate, such as that available on US Treasury notes having maturities of five years is 5%, then the present value of the future payment of €20 is €15.67 $\{=[€20÷(1.05)^5]\}$, which suggests that the option has a value of (€20–€15.67=) €4.33 per share before considering the value of lost dividends. If the stock is expected to pay a dividend of €.40 per share per year, the present value of the dividend stream that the option holder will forego until exercise five years hence is about €1.64, discounting again at 5%. Therefore, the *net* value of the option being granted, assuming it is expected to be held to the expiration date before being exercised, is (€4.33–€1.64=) €2.69 per share. (Although the foregoing computation was based on the full five-year life of the option, the actual requirement is to use the *expected term* of the option, which may be shorter.)

Commercial software is readily available to carry out these calculations. However, accountants must understand the theory underlying these matters so that the software can be appropriately employed and the results verified. Independent auditors, of course, have additional challenges in verifying the financial statement impacts of share-based compensation plans.

Estimating volatility does however, create special problems for unlisted or newly listed companies, since the estimate is usually based on an observation of past market movements, which are not available for unlisted or newly listed entities. The *Basis for Conclusions* says that IASB decided that, nonetheless, an estimate of volatility should still be made. Appendix B states that newly listed entities should compute volatility for whatever period this information is available and also consider volatility in the prices of companies in the same industry. Unlisted entities should consider the volatility of prices of listed entities in the same industry, or, where valuing them on the basis of a model, such as net earnings, should use the volatility of the earnings.

The IASB considered the effect of the *nontransferability* on the value of the option. The standard option pricing models have been developed to value traded options and do not take into account nontransferability. The Board came to the view that nontransferability generally led to the option being exercised early, and that this should be reflected in the expected term of the option, rather than by any explicit adjustment for nontransferability.

The likelihood of the option vesting is a function of the vesting conditions. IASB concluded that these conditions should not be factored into the value of the option, but should be reflected in calculating the number of options to be expensed. For example, if an entity granted options to 500 employees, the likelihood that only 350 would satisfy the vesting conditions should be used to determine the number of options expensed, and this should be subsequently adjusted in the light of actual experience as it unfolds.

Accounting for Employee Stock Options under IFRS 2: Valuation Models

IFRS 2 fully imposes a fair value approach to measuring the effect of stock options granted to employees. It recognizes that directly observable prices for employee options are not likely to exist, and thus that valuation models will have to be employee in most, or almost all, instances. The standard speaks to the relative strengths of two types of approaches: the venerable Black-Scholes (now called Blach-Scholes-Merton) option pricing model, designed specifically to price publicly traded European-style options (exercisable only at the expiration date) and subject to criticism as to possible inapplicability to nonmarketable American-style options; and the mathematically more challenging but more flexible lattice models, such as the binomial. IFRS 2 does not dictate choice of model and acknowledges that the Black-Scholes model may be validly applied in many situations.

To provide a more detailed examination of these two major types of options valuation approaches, several examples will now be developed.

Both valuation models (herinafter referred to as BSM and binomial) must take into account the following factors, at a minimum:

1. Exercise price of the option
2. Expected term of the option, taking into account several things including the contractual term of the option, vesting requirements, and postvesting employee termination behaviors
3. Current price of the underlying share
4. Expected volatility of the price of the underlying share
5. Expected dividends on the underlying share
6. Risk-free interest rate(s) for the expected term of the option

In practice, there are likely to be ranges of reasonable estimates for expected volatility, dividends, and option term. The closed form models, of which BSM is the most widely regarded, are predicated on a deterministic set of assumptions that remain invariant over the full term of the option. For example, the expected dividend on the shares on which options are issued must be a fixed amount each period over the full term of the option. In the real world, of course, the condition of invariability is almost never satisfied. For this reason, current thinking is that a lattice model, of which the binomial model is an example, would be preferred. Lattice models explicitly identify nodes, such as the anniversaries of the grant date, at each of which new parameter values can be specified (e.g., expected dividends can be independently defined each period).

Other features that may affect the value of the option include changes in the issuer's credit risk, if the value of the awards contains cash settlement features (i.e., if they are liability instruments). Also, contingent features that could cause either a loss of equity shares earned or reduced realized gains from sale of equity instruments earned, such as a clawback feature (for example, where an employee who terminates the employment relationship and begins to work for a competitor is required to transfer to the issuing enterprise shares granted and earned under a share-based payment arrangement.

Before presenting specific examples of accounting for stock options, simple examples of calculating the fair value of options using both the BSM and the binomial methods are provided. First, an example of the BSM, closed-form model is provided.

BSM actually computes the theoretical value of a "European" call option, where exercise can occur only at the expiration date. "American" options, which include most employee stock options, can be exercised at any time until expiration. The value of an American-style option on dividend-paying stocks is generally greater than a European-style option, since preexercise the holder does not have a right to receive dividends that are paid on the stock. (For non-dividend-paying stocks, the values of American and European options will tend to converge.) BSM ignores dividends, but this is readily dealt with, as shown below, by deducting from the computed option value the present value of expected dividend stream over the option holding period.

BSM also is predicated on constant volatility over the option term, which available evidence suggests may not be a wholly accurate description of stock price behavior. On the other hand, the reporting entity would find it very difficult, if not impossible, to compute differing volatilities for each node in the lattice model described later in this section, lacking a factual basis for presuming that volatility would increase or decrease in specific future periods.

The BSM model is

$$C \ = \ SN(d1) - Ke^{(-rt)}N(d2)$$

Where:

C	=	Theoretical call premium
S	=	Current stock price
t	=	time until option expiration
K	=	option striking price
R	=	risk-free interest rate
N	=	Cumulative standard normal distribution
e	=	exponential term (2.7183)

$$d_1 = \frac{\ln(S/k) + (r + s^2 \div 2)^t}{s\sqrt{t}}$$

d_2	=	$d_1 - s$
s	=	standard deviation of stock returns
ln	=	natural logarithm

The BSM valuation is illustrated with the following assumed facts; note that dividends are ignored in the initial calculation but will be addressed once the theoretical value is computed. Also note that volatility is defined in terms of the variability of the entity's stock price, measured by the standard deviation of prices over the past three years, which is used as a surrogate for expected volatility over the next twelve months.

Example—Determining the fair value of options using the BSM model

BSM is a closed-form model, meaning that it solves for an option price from an equation. It computes a theoretical call price based on five parameters—the current stock price, the option exercise price, the expected volatility of the stock price, the time until option expiration, and the short-term risk-free interest rate. Of these, expected volatility is the most difficult to ascertain. Volatility is generally computed as the standard deviation of recent historical returns on the stock. In the following example, the stock is currently selling at €40 and the standard deviation of prices (daily closing prices can be used, among other possible choices) over the past several years was €6.50, thus yielding an estimated volatility of €6.50/€40 = 16.25%.

Assume the following facts:

S = €40
t = 2 years
K = €45
r = 3% annual rate
s = standard deviation of percentage returns = 16.25% (based on €6.50 standard deviation of stock price compared to current €40 price)

From the foregoing data, all of which is known information (the volatility, s, is computed or assumed, as discussed above) the factors d_1 and d_2 can be computed. The cumulative standard normal variates (N) of these values must then be determined (using a table or formula), following which the BSM option value is calculated, *before the effect of dividends*. In this example, the computed amounts are

$N(d_1)$ = 0.2758
$N(d_2)$ = 0.2048

With these assumptions the value of the stock options is approximately €2.35. This is derived from the BSM as follows:

$$
\begin{aligned}
C &= SN(d_1) - Ke^{(-rt)}N(d_2) \\
&= 40(.2758) - 45(.942)(.2048) \\
&= 11.032 - 8.679 \\
&= 2.35
\end{aligned}
$$

The foregone two-year stream of dividends, which in this example are projected to be €0.50 annually, have a present value of €0.96. Therefore, the net value of this option is €1.39 (= €2.35–.96).

Example—Determining the fair value of options using the binomial model

In contrast to the BSM, the binomial model is an open form, inductive model. It allows for multiple (theoretically, unlimited) branches of possible outcomes on a "tree" of possible price movements and induces the option's price. As compared to the BSM approach, this relaxes the constraint on exercise timing. It can be assumed that exercise occurs at any point in the option period, and past experience may guide the reporting entity to make certain such assumptions (e.g., that one-half the options will be exercised when the market price of the stock reaches 150% of the strike price). It also allows for varying dividends from period to period.

It is assumed that the common (Cox, Ross, and Rubinstein) binomial model will be used in practice. To keep this preliminary example relatively simple in order to focus on the concepts involved, a single-step binomial model is provide here for illustrative purposes. Assume an option is granted of a €20 stock that will expire in one year. The option exercise price equals the stock price of €20. Also, assume there is a 50% chance that the price will jump 20% over the year and a 50% chance the stock will drop 20%, and that no other outcomes are possible. The risk-free interest rate is 4%. With these assumptions there are three basic calculations.

1. Plot the two possible future stock prices.
2. Translate these stock prices into future options values.
3. Discount these future values into a single present value.

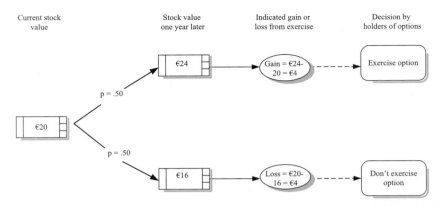

In this case, the option will only have value if the stock pricep increases, and otherwise the option would expire worthless and unexercised. In this simplistic example, there is only a 50% chance of the option having a value of (€4 ÷ 1.04 =) €3.84, and therefore the option is worth (€3.84 × .50 =) €1.92 at grant date.

The foregoing was a simplistic single-period, two-outcome model. A more complicated and realistic binomial model extends this single-period model into a randomized walk of many steps or intervals. In theory, the time to expiration can be broken into a large number of ever-smaller time intervals, such as months, weeks, or days. The advantage is that the parameter values (volatility, etc.) can then be varied with greater precision from one period to the next (assuming, or course, that there is a factual basis upon which to base these estimates). Calculating the binomial model then involves the same three calculation steps. First, the possible future stock prices are determined for each branch, using the volatility input and time to expiration (which grows shorter with each successive node in the model). This permits computation of terminal values for each branch of the tree. Second, future stock prices are translated into option values at each node of the tree. Third, these future option values are discounted and added to produce a single present value of the option, taking into account the probabilities of each series of price moves in the model.

Example—Multiperiod option valuation using the binomial model

Consider the following example of a two-period binomial model. Again, certain simplifying assumptions will be made so that a manual calculation can be illustrated (in general, computer programs will be necessary to compute option values). Eager Corp. grants 10,000 options to its employees at a time when the market price of shares is €40. The options expire in two years; expected dividends on the stock will be €0.50 per year; and the risk-free rate is currently 3%, which is not expected to change over the two-year horizon. The option exercise price is €43.

The entity's past experience suggests that, after one year (of the two-year term) elapses, if the market price of the stock exceeds the option exercise price, one-half of the options will be exercised by the holders. The other holders will wait another year to decide. If at the end of the second year—without regard to what the stock value was at the end of the first year—the market value exceeds the exercise price, all the remaining options will be exercised. The workforce has been unusually stable and it is not anticipated that option holders will cease employment before the end of the option period.

The stock price moves randomly from period to period. Based on recent experience, it is anticipated that in each period the stock may increase by €5, stay the same, or decrease by €5, with equal probability, versus the price at the period year-end. Thus since the price is €40 at grant date, one year hence it might be either €45, €40, or €35. The price at the end of the second year will follow the same pattern, based on the price when the first year ends.

Logically, holders will rather exercise their options than see them expire, as long as there is gain to be realized. Since dividends are not paid on options, holders have a motive to exercise earlier than the expiration date, which explains why historically one-half the options are exercised after one year elapses, as long as the market price exceeds the exercise price at that date, even though the exercising holders risk future market declines.

The binomial model formulation requires that each sequence of events and actions be explicated. This gives rise to the commonly seen decision tree representation. In this simple example, following the grant of the options, one of three possible events occur: either the stock price rises €5 over the next year, or it remains constant, or it falls by €5. Since these outcomes have equal *a priori* probabilities, p=1/3 is assigned to each outcome of this first year event. If the price does rise, one-half the option holders will exercise at the end of the first year, to reap the economic gain and capture the second year's dividend. The other holders will forego this immediate gain and wait to see what the stock price does in the second year before making an exercise decision.

If the stock price in the first year either remains flat or falls by €5, no option holders are expected to exercise. However, there remains the opportunity to exercise after the second year elapses, if the stock price recovers. Of course, holding the options for the second year means that no dividends will be received.

The cost of the options granted by Eager Corp., measured by fair value using the binomial model approach is computed by the sum of the probability-weighted outcomes, discounted to present value using the risk-free rate. In this example, the rate is expected to remain at 3% per year throughout the option period, but it could be independently specified for each period—another advantage the binomial model has over the more rigid BSM. The sum of these present value computations measures the cost of compensation incorporated in the option grant, regardless of what pattern of exercise ultimately is revealed, since at the grant date, using the available information about stock price volatility, expected dividends, exercise behavior and the risk-free rate, this best measures the value of what was promised to the employees.

The following graphic offers a visual representation of the model, although in practice it is not necessary to prepare such a document. The actual calculations can be made by computer program, but to illustrate the application of the binomial model, the computation will be presented explicitly here. There are four possible scenarios under which, in this example, holders will exercise the options, and thus the options will have value. All other scenarios (combinations of stock price movements over the two-year horizon) will cause the holders to allow the options to expire unexercised.

First, if the stock price goes to €45 in the first year, one-half the holders will exercise at that point, paying the exercise price of €43 per share. This results in a gain of €2 (= €45 – €43) per share. However, having waited until the first year-end, they lost the opportunity to receive the €0.50 per share dividend, so the net economic gain is only €1.50 (= €2.00 – €0.50) per share. As this occurs after one year, the present value is only €1.50 × 1.03^{-1}= €1.46 per share. When this is weighted by the probability of this outcome obtaining (given that the stock price rise to €45 in the first year has only a 1/3 probability of happening, and given further that only one-half the option holders would elect to exercise under such conditions), the actual expected value of this outcome is [(1/3)(1/2)(€1.46) =] €0.24. More formally,

$$[(1/3)(1/2)(€2.00 – €0.50)] × 1.03^{-1} = €0.2427$$

The second potentially favorable outcome to holders would be if the stock price rises to €45 the first year and then either rises another €5 the second year or holds steady at €45 during the second year. In either event, the option holders who did not exercise after the first year's stock price rise will all exercise at the end of the second year, before the options expire. If the price goes to €50 the second year, the holders will reap a gross gain of €7 (=€50 – €43) per share; if it remains constant at €45, the gross gain is only €2 per share. In either case, dividends in both years one and two will have been foregone. To calculate the compensation cost associated with these branches of the model, the first-year dividend lost must be discounted for one year, and the gross gain and the second-year dividend must be discounted for years. Also, the probabilities of the entire sequence of events must be used, taking into account the likelihood of the first year's stock price rise, the proclivity of holders to wait for a second year to elapse, and the likelihood of a second-year price rise or price stability. These computations are shown below.

For the outcome if the stock price rises again

$[(1/3)(1/2)(1/3)] \{[(€7.00) \times 1.03^{-2}] - [(€0.50) \times 1.03^{-1}] - [€0.50 \times 1.03^{-2}]\} =$
$[0.05544] \{€6.59 - €0.48 - €0.47\} = €0.31276$

For the outcome if the stock price remains stable

$[(1/3)(1/2)(1/3)] \{[(€2.00) \times 1.03^{-2}] - [(€0.50) \times 1.03^{-1}] - [€0.50 \times 1.03^{-2}]\} =$
$[0.05544] \{€1.88 - €0.48 - €0.47\} = €0.05147$

The final favorable outcome for holders would occur if the stock price holds constant at €40 the first year but rises to €45 the second year, making exercise the right decision. Note that none of the holders would exercise after the first year given that the price, €40, was below exercise price. The calculation for this sequence of events is as follows:

$[(1/3)(1/3)] \{[(€2.00) \times 1.03^{-2}] - [(€0.50) \times 1.03^{-1}] - [€0.50 \times 1.03^{-2}]\} =$
$[0.1111] \{€1.88 - €0.48 - €0.47\} = €0.10295$

Summing these values yields €0.709879 (€0.2427 + €0.31276 + €0.05147 + €0.10295), which is the expected value per optional granted. When this per-unit value is then multiplied by the number of options granted, 10,000, the total compensation cost to be recognized, €7,098.79, is derived. This would be attributed over the required service period, which is illustrated later in this section. (In the facts of this example, no vesting requirements were specified; in such cases, the employees would not have to provide future service in order to earn the right to the options, and the entire cost would be recognized upon grant.

A big advantage of the binomial model is that it can value an option that is exercisable before the end of its term (i.e., an American-style option). This is the form that employee share-based compensation arrangements normally take. IASB appears to recognize the virtues of the binomial type of model, because it can incorporate the unique features of employee stock options. Two key features that should generally be incorporated into the binomial model are vesting restrictions and early exercise. Doing so, however, requires that the reporting entity will have had previous experience with employee behaviors (e.g., gained with past employee option programs) that would provide it with a basis for making estimates of future behavior. In some instances, there will be no obvious bases upon which such assumptions can be developed.

The binomial model permits the specification of more assumptions than does the BSM, which has generated the perception that the binomial will more readily be manipulated so as to result in lower option values, and hence lower compensation costs, when contrasted to the BSM. But, this is not necessarily the case: switching from BSM to the binomial model can increase, maintain, or decrease the option's value. Having the ability to specify additional parameters, however, does probably give management greater flexibility and, accordingly, will present additional challenges for the auditors who must attest to the financial statement effects of management's specification of these variables.

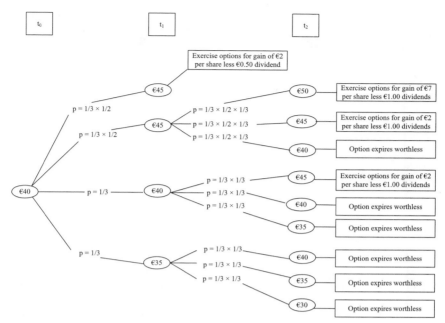

Accounting entries. Having calculated the fair value of the option at the grant date, this value then has to be expensed through the income statement by allocation over the financial years during which the option is vesting, since it is over that period that the grantee is presumably earning the related compensation. The corresponding credit is made to an equity account.

Suppose a company grants 1,000 share options with a vesting period of four years to 50 employees. The fair value of each option is determined to be €20, and the company expects, in light of past experience with employee turnover and other factors, that 75% of the options will vest. The expense (and credit to equity) in the first year will be (50,000 options x €20 x 0.75 x 0.25 =) €187,500.

At the end of the second year, the entity now considers that 80% of the options will probably vest. As with all changes in accounting estimates, the impact of this reassessment is allocated to current and future period, with no adjustment to already-concluded fiscal periods. The expense for the current (second) year is the cumulative cost based on the new parameter values, less the amount already expensed in the first year. The cumulative amount is (50,000 options x €20 × 0.80 x 0.5 =) €400,000. The year two expense therefore will be (€400,000 – €187,500 =) €212,500.

Assume that in year three there are no changes to the estimates, and the cumulative cost over the three-year period accordingly is (50,000 x €20 x 0.80 x 0.75 =) €600,000. The annual expense in year three therefore is (€600,000 – €400,000 =) €200,000.

At the end of the four-year vesting period, 41 (or 82%) of the original employees granted options are still with the company, and their options vest. The fourth year's expense (and credit to equity) takes into account the actual options vested. The cumulative cost is (50,000 x €20 x 0.82 =) €820,000 and the fourth year's expense is (€820,000 – €600,000 =) €220,000.

At some future date some or all of the options may be exercised by the remaining employees, but this will not necessarily occur. IFRS 2 takes the view that the amount credited to equity, arising from the issue of options, is *not* to be adjusted subsequently to take account of any failure to exercise the options (which is termed a forfeiture). This is consistent with the belief that the accounting for options should be a reflection of the bargain made when the option was originally agreed to. However, the entity is free to reclassify any of these amounts within equity, and where an option is exercised, the original amount recognized, plus the exercise amount, should become part of paid-in capital.

The journal entries would be

	Debit	Credit	Memorandum cumulative equity item
Year 1			
Employee remuneration	187,500		
Stock options		187,500	187,500
Year 2			
Employee remuneration	212,500		
Stock options		212,500	400,000
Year 3			
Employee remuneration	200,000		
Stock options		200,000	600,000

	Debit	Credit	Memorandum cumulative equity item
Year 4			
Employee remuneration	220,000		
Stock options		220,000	820,000

If the entity subsequently modifies the conditions of the option, then this must be reflected in the accounting. The fair value at the original grant date remains the *minimum amount to be expensed.* If the modification increases the fair value—for example, by reducing the exercise price or increasing the number of shares—the additional fair value must be expensed in the period from the modification date to the new vesting date. If the vesting conditions are changed in a way that would likely increase the probability of vesting, then this will be reflected in the number of options expected to vest. If the modification reduces the fair value, then the original fair value continues to be the basis of expensing.

If the entity cancels the option or settles it before the end of the vesting period, this should be treated as an acceleration of the vesting period, and the original fair value at grant date should be expensed over the shorter period. If a payment is made to the employee in respect of the cancellation or settlement, this is treated as a repurchase of an equity interest, and is deducted from equity. In the event that the payment exceeds the value recognized in equity, the excess is reported as an expense. If the entity settles by issuing a new option, this is treated as a modification of the original scheme and accounted for accordingly.

Nonemployee transactions. While share-based payments to nonemployees are fairly rare, they are perhaps found most commonly in connection with start-up entities which are often cash-starved and thus willing to dilute ownership in return for the provision of vital services or goods. The basic principle of IFRS 2 is that such transactions are expensed as measured by the fair value of the goods received or the services rendered. For nonemployee transactions, there is a rebuttable presumption that the value of the goods or services can be measured reliably. That fair value is measured at the date the goods are received or the services are rendered. Per IFRS 2, only "in rare cases," if the entity concludes that it cannot measure these, should the expense be measured by reference to the fair value of the instruments granted.

It should be noted that this also has a bearing on revenue recognition by the counterparty. One of the abuses noted during the late 1990s "dot-com" market bubble was that the same parcel of shares, exchanged for professional services in connection with a start-up, was valued at very little by the issuing company (which had to recognize an expense), but simultaneously at a much higher amount by the professional adviser (as revenue). If the transaction is accounted for at the fair value of the services provided, the value should be exactly the same from either party's perspective.

Cash-settled transactions. Sometimes employees will receive a variable amount of remuneration, which is based on the performance of the entity's shares, but resulting in an additional cash payment to the employee, rather than an equity instrument. This describes the issuance of the essential characteristic of various share, or stock, appreciation rights plans, or of shares that are redeemable by the company at the holder's election. The calculation of compensation expense is to be based on the underlying share option, in accordance with the above described method for equity-settled transactions, but the credit entry is to a liability account, not to equity. Another important distinction: the liability must be remeasured at each reporting date, unlike straight option grants, which are fixed in value at the date of issuance.

An entity may make an arrangement where the employee (or other counterparty) has a choice of cash or equity settlement. In this case, the entity should value the option as a compound financial instrument, and value the right to receive cash as debt, and the right to receive any additional amount as equity. IFRS 2 notes that in many cases the arrangement is structured so that the equity alternative has the same value as the cash alternative, in which case the whole amount is considered to be debt, since there is no extra value in the equity choice.

If the employee decides at the date of exercise to receive the equity alternative, the liability is transferred into equity. If the employee takes the cash alternative, the liability is extinguished. However, if a separate equity element had been established, this remains part of equity, as with other vested options that are not exercised.

In some cases the choice between cash settlement and equity settlement is in the hands of the employer. Here the standard relies on the present obligation notion similar to that used in IAS 37: where the company has a past history of making cash settlements or a stated policy of doing this (i.e., where there is a reasonable expectation of cash settlement), the transaction is considered to give rise to a liability. In the absence of such an obligation, the entity would account for the transaction as equity-settled. In the event that the entity ultimately decides to settle in cash, the cash payment is treated as a repurchase of equity.

Disclosures. IFRS 2 imposed extensive disclosure requirements, calling for an analysis of share-based payments made during the year, of their impact on earnings and financial position, and of the basis upon which fair values were measured.

Each type of share-based payment that existed during the year must be described, giving vesting requirements, the maximum term of the options, and the method of settlement (but entities that have several "substantially similar" schemes may aggregate this information). The movement (i.e., changes) within each scheme must be analyzed, including the number of share options and the weighted-average exercise price for the following:

- Outstanding at the beginning of the year
- Granted during the year
- Forfeited during the year
- Exercised during the year (plus the weighted-average share price at the time of exercise)
- Expired during the year
- Outstanding at the end of the period (plus the range of exercise prices and the weighted-average remaining contractual life).
- Exercisable at the end of the period

The entity must disclose the total expense recognized in the income statement arising from share-based payment transactions, and a subtotal of that part which was settled by the issue of equity. Where the entity has liabilities arising from share-based payment transactions, the total amount at the end of the period must be separately disclosed, as must be the total intrinsic value of those options that had vested.

The fair value methodology disclosures apply to new instruments issued during the reporting period, or old instruments modified in that time. As regards share options, the entity must disclose the weighted-average fair value, plus details of how fair value was measured. These will include the option pricing model used, the weighted-average share price, the exercise price, expected volatility, option life, expected dividends, the risk-free interest rate and any other inputs. The measurement of expected volatility must be explained, as must be the manner in which any other features of the option were incorporated in the measurement.

Where a modification of an existing arrangement has taken place, the entity should provide an explanation of the modifications, and disclose the incremental fair value and the basis on which that was measured (as above).

Where a share-based payment was made to a nonemployee, the entity should confirm that fair value was determined directly by reference to the market price for the goods or services.

If equity instruments *other than share options* were granted during the period, the number and weighted-average fair value of these should be disclosed together with the basis for measuring fair value, and if this was not market value, then how it was measured. The disclosure should cover how expected dividends were incorporated into the value and what other features were incorporated into the measurement.

Members' Shares in Cooperative Entities

Certain organizations are so-called membership organizations or cooperatives. These are often entities providing services to a group having common membership or interests, such as labor unions or university faculty and staff. Credit unions (a form of savings and loan association) are a common example of this form of organization. Other cooperatives may serve as marketing vehicles, as in the case of farmers' co-ops, or as buying organizations, as in co-ops formed by merchants in certain types of businesses, generally in order to gain economies of scale and market power in order to compete with larger merchant chains. Generally, these types of organizations will refund or rebate profits to the members in proportion to the amount of business transacted over a time period, such as a year.

Ownership in cooperatives is represented by shares. Members' shares in cooperative entities have some characteristics of equity, but also, often, characteristics of debt, since they are not permanent equity which cannot be withdrawn. Members' shares typically give the holder the right to request redemption for cash, although that right may be subject to certain limitations or restrictions, imposed by law or by the terms of the membership agreement. IFRIC 2 gives guidance on how those redemption terms should be evaluated in determining whether the shares should be classified as financial liabilities or as equity.

Under IFRIC 2, shares for which the member has the right to request redemption are normally liabilities. Even when the intent is to leave in the equity interest for a long period, such as until the member ceases business operations, this does not qualify as true equity as defined under the IASB *Framework*. However, the shares qualify as equity if

- The cooperative entity has an unconditional right to refuse redemption, or
- Local law, regulation, or the entity's governing charter imposes prohibitions on redemption.

However, the mere existence of law, regulation, or charter provisions that would prohibit redemption only if conditions (such as liquidity constraints) are met, or are not met, does not result in members' shares being treated as equity.

APPENDIX A

ILLUSTRATION OF FINANCIAL STATEMENT
PRESENTATION UNDER IFRS

This appendix provides an illustration of the treatment of equity that may be required in the financial statements.

Equity Section of Consolidated Balance Sheet

(in thousands of euros)		*2006*		*2005*
Ordinary shares				
Authorized: 10,000,000 Par value = €1				
Issued: 6,650,000		6,650		6,585
Share premium and reserves				
Share premium	12,320		12,110	
Legal reserve	665		665	
Share options granted	724		676	
Translation adjustment	(1,854)		(2,266)	
Treasury shares	(320)		(320)	
		11,535		10,865
Retained earnings		4,230		3,898
Equity of shareholders in parent company		22,415		21,348
Minority interests		360		353
Total equity		22,775		21,701

Consolidated Statement of Changes in Equity
(in thousands of euros)

	Share capital	Share premium	Legal reserve	Share options	Trans. adjustment	Treasury shares	Retained earnings	Minority interests	Total equity
Balance at 1/1/04	6,585	12,110	665	459	(3,111)	(185)	3,696	350	20,569
Net earnings							362	8	370
Dividends							(160)	(5)	(165)
Translation adjustment					845				845
Issue of share options				217					217
Acquisition of own shares						(135)			
Balance at 12/31/04	6,585	12,110	665	676	(2,266)	(320)	3,898	353	21,701
Net earnings							512	12	524
Dividends							(180)	(5)	(185)
Translation adjustment					412				412
Issue of share options				180					180
Exercise of options	65	210		(132)					143
Balance at 12/31/05	6,650	12,320	665	724	(1,854)	(320)	4,230	360	22,775

APPENDIX B

ADDITIONAL GUIDANCE UNDER US GAAP

As noted in the main body of this chapter, IFRS have to date not addressed a number of complex and interesting issues that do arise in connection with financial reporting by enterprises in many countries. Although the material in this appendix is *not authoritative*, it is being provided with the intent that it be instructive as additional guidance. Since these are matters that have not been addressed by IFRS, the treatments illustrated herein would be appropriate for application to financial statements prepared in conformity with international accounting standards, consistent with the hierarchy set forth by IAS 8.

DEFINITIONS OF US GAAP TERMS

Additional paid-in capital. Amounts received at issuance in excess of the par or stated value of capital stock and amounts received from other transactions involving the entity's stock and/or stockholders. It is classified by source.

Allocated shares. ESOP shares assigned to individual participants. These shares are usually based on length of service, compensation, or a combination of both.

Appropriation (of retained earnings). A segregation of retained earnings to communicate the unavailability of a portion for dividend distributions.

Authorized shares. The maximum number of shares permitted to be issued by a corporation's charter and bylaws.

Callable. An optional characteristic of preferred stock allowing the corporation to redeem the stock at specified future dates and at specific prices. The call price is usually at or above the original issuance price.

Cliff vesting. A condition of an option or other stock award plan which provides that the employee becomes fully vested at a single point in time.

Combination plans. Compensation plans under which employees receive two or more components, such as options and stock appreciation rights, all of which can be exercised. Thus, each component is actually a separate plan and is accounted for as such.

Committed-to-be-released shares. ESOP shares that will be allocated to employees for service performed currently. They are usually released by payment of debt service.

Compensatory plan. A stock option plan including elements of compensation that are recognized over the service period.

Compensatory stock option plans. Plans that do not meet the criteria for noncompensatory plans. Their main purpose is to provide additional compensation to officers and employees.

Constructive retirement method. Method of accounting for treasury shares that treats the shares as having been retired. The shares revert to authorized but unissued status. The stock and additional paid-in capital accounts are reduced, with a debit to retained earnings or a credit to a paid-in capital account for the excess or deficiency of the purchase cost over or under the original issuance proceeds.

Contributed capital. The amount of equity contributed by the corporation's shareholders. It consists of capital stock plus additional paid-in capital.

Convertible. An optional characteristic of preferred stock allowing the stockholders to exchange their preferred shares for common shares at a specified ratio.

Cost method. Method of accounting for treasury shares that presents aggregate cost of reacquired shares as a deduction from the total of paid-in capital and retained earnings.

Cumulative. An optional characteristic of preferred stock. Any dividends of prior years not paid to the preferred shareholders must be paid before any dividends can be distributed to the common shareholders.

Date of declaration. The date on which the board of directors votes that a dividend be paid. A legal liability (usually current) is created on this date in the case of cash, property, and scrip dividends.

Date of grant. The date on which the board of directors awards the stock to the employees in stock option plans.

Date of payment. The date on which the shareholders are paid the declared dividends.

Date of record. The date on which ownership of the shares is determined. Those owning stock on this date will be paid the declared dividends.

Deficit. A debit balance in the retained earnings account. Dividends may not generally be paid when this condition exists. Formally known as accumulated deficit.

Discount on capital stock. Occurs when the stock of a corporation is originally issued at a price below par value. The original purchasers become contingently liable to creditors for this difference.

Employee stock ownership plan (ESOP). A form of defined contribution employee benefit plan whereby the employer facilitates the purchase of shares of stock in the company for the benefit of the employees, generally by a trust established by the company. The plan may be leveraged by borrowings either from the employer-sponsor or from third-party lenders.

Fixed options. Options that grant the holder the rights to a specified number of shares at fixed prices. It is not dependent on achievement of performance targets.

Graded vesting. A vesting process whereby the employee becomes entitled to a stock-based award fractionally over a period of years.

Issued stock. The number of shares issued by the firm and owned by the shareholders and the corporation. It is the sum of outstanding shares plus treasury shares.

Junior stock. Shares with certain limitations, often as to voting rights, which are granted to employees pursuant to a performance compensation program. Such shares are generally convertible to ordinary shares on achievement of defined goals.

Legal capital. The aggregate par or stated value of stock. It represents the amount of owners' equity that cannot be distributed to shareholders. It serves to protect the claims of the creditors.

Liquidating dividend. A dividend distribution that is not based on earnings. It represents a return of contributed capital.

Measurement date. The date on which the price used to compute compensation under stock-based compensation plans is fixed.

Noncompensatory stock options. Options which, under current GAAP, do not include an element of compensation being paid to the participants. Under proposed GAAP all stock plans would include an element of compensation to be measured and allocated over the service periods of the employees.

Noncompensatory stock option plans. Plans whose primary purpose is widespread ownership of the firm among its employees and officers. They must meet four criteria (see APB 25, para 7, or the section on stock options).

No-par stock. Stock that has no par value. Sometimes a stated value is determined by the board of directors. In this case the stated value is accorded the same treatment as par value stock.

Outstanding stock. Stock issued by a corporation and held by shareholders (i.e., issued shares that are not held in the treasury).

Par value method. A method of accounting for treasury shares that charges the treasury stock account for the aggregate par or stated value of the shares acquired and charges the excess of the purchase cost over the par value to paid-in capital and/or retained earnings. A deficiency of purchase cost is credited to paid-in capital.

Participating. An optional characteristic of preferred stock whereby preferred shareholders may share ratably with the common shareholders in any profit distributions in excess of a predetermined rate. Participation may be limited to a maximum rate or may be unlimited (full).

Performance-based options. Options that are granted to employees conditional on the achievement of defined goals.

Phantom stock plan. A type of stock compensation arrangement that gives employees the right to participate in the increase in value of the company's shares (book value or market value, as stipulated in the plan) without actually being required to purchase the shares initially.

Quasi reorganization. A procedure that reclassifies amounts from contributed capital to retained earnings to eliminate a deficit in that account. All the assets and liabilities are first revalued to their current values. It represents an alternative to a legal reorganization in bankruptcy proceedings.

Retained earnings. The undistributed earnings of a firm.

Service period. The period over which a stock-based compensation award is earned by the recipient. If not otherwise defined in the plan, it is the vesting period.

Stock-based compensation. Any of a wide variety of compensation arrangements under which employees receive shares of stock, options to purchase shares, or other equity instruments, or under which the employer incurs obligations to the employees based on the price of the company's shares.

Stock options. Enables officers and employees of a corporation to purchase shares in the corporation.

Stock rights. Enables present shareholders to purchase additional shares of stock of the corporation. It is commonly used if a preemptive right is granted to common shareholders by some state corporation laws.

Suspense shares. ESOP shares that usually collateralize ESOP debt. They have not been allocated or committed to be released.

Tandem options. Compensation plans under which employees receive two or more components, such as options and stock appreciation rights, whereby the exercise of one component cancels the other(s). The accounting is based on the component that is more likely to be exercised.

Treasury stock. Shares of a corporation that have been repurchased by the corporation. This stock has no voting rights and receives no cash dividends. Some states do not recognize treasury stock. In such cases, reacquired shares are treated as having been retired.

Vesting. The process whereby the recipient of a stock-based compensation award earns the right to control or exercise the award.

CONCEPTS, RULES, AND EXAMPLES

Legal Capital and Capital Stock

Legal capital typically relates to that portion of the stockholders' investment in a corporation that is permanent in nature and represents assets that will continue to be available for the satisfaction of creditor's claims. Traditionally, legal capital was comprised of the aggregate par or stated value of common and preferred shares issued. In recent years, however, many jurisdictions have eliminated the requirement that corporate shares have a designated par or stated value. Some jurisdictions have completely eliminated the distinction between par value and the amount contributed in excess of par.

Ownership interest in a corporation is made up of common and, optionally, preferred shares. The common shares represent the residual risk-taking ownership of the corporation after the satisfaction of all claims of creditors and senior classes of equity.

Preferred stock. Preferred shareholders are owners who have certain rights superior to those of common shareholders. These rights will pertain either to the earnings or the assets of the corporation. Preferences as to earnings exist when the preferred shareholders have a stipulated dividend rate (expressed either as a dollar amount or as a percentage of the preferred stock's par or stated value). Preferences as to assets exist when the preferred shares have a stipulated liquidation value. If a corporation were to liquidate, the preferred holders would be paid a specific amount before the common shareholders would have a right to participate in any of the proceeds.

In practice, preferred shares are more likely to have preferences as to earnings than as to assets. Some classes of preferred shares may have both preferential rights, although this is rarely encountered. Preferred shares may also have the following features: participation in earnings beyond the stipulated dividend rate; a cumulative feature, affording the preferred shareholders the protection that their dividends in arrears, if any, will be fully satisfied before the common shareholders participate in any earnings distribution; and convertibility or callability by the corporation. Whatever preferences exist must be disclosed adequately in the financial statements, either on the face of the balance sheet or in the notes.

In exchange for the preferences, the preferred shareholders' rights or privileges are limited. For instance, the right to vote may be limited to common shareholders. The most important right denied to the preferred shareholders, however, is the right to participate without limitation in the earnings of the corporation. Thus, if the corporation has exceedingly large earnings for a particular period, these earnings would accrue to the benefit of the common shareholders. This is true even if the preferred stock is participating (itself a fairly uncommon feature) because even participating preferred stock usually has some upper limitation placed on its degree of participation. For example, preferred may have a 5% cumulative dividend with a further 3% participation right, so in any one year the limit would be an 8% return to the preferred shareholders (plus, if applicable, the 5% per year prior year dividends not paid).

Occasionally, as discussed in the chapter, several classes of stock will be categorized as common (e.g., Class A common, Class B common, etc.). Since there can be only one class of shares that constitutes the true residual risk-taking equity interest in a corporation, it is clear that the other classes, even though described as common stock, must in fact have some preferential status. Not uncommonly,, these preferences relate to voting rights, as when a control group holds common stock with "super voting" rights (e.g., ten votes per share). The rights and responsibilities of each class of shareholder, even if described as common, must be fully disclosed in the financial statements.

Issuance of shares. The accounting for the sale of shares by a corporation depends on whether the stock has a par or stated value. If there is a par or stated value, the amount of the proceeds representing the aggregate par or stated value is credited to the common or preferred stock account. The aggregate par or stated value is generally defined as legal capital not subject to distribution to shareholders. Proceeds in excess of par or stated value are credited to an additional paid-in capital account. The additional paid-in capital represents the amount in excess of the legal capital that may, under certain defined conditions, be distributed to shareholders. A corporation selling stock below par value credits the capital stock account for the par value and debits an offsetting discount account for the difference between par value and the amount actually received.

If there is a discount on original issue capital stock, it serves to notify the actual and potential creditors of the contingent liability of those investors. As a practical matter, corporations avoided this problem by reducing par values to an arbitrarily low amount. This reduction in par eliminated the chance that shares would be sold for amounts below par. Where corporation laws make no distinction between par value and amounts in excess of par, the entire proceeds from the sale of stock may be credited to the common stock account without distinction between the stock and the additional paid-in capital accounts. The following entries illustrate these concepts:

Facts: A corporation sells 100,000 shares of €5 par common stock for €8 per share cash.

Cash	800,000	
Common stock		500,000
Additional paid-in capital		300,000

Facts: A corporation sells 100,000 shares of no-par common stock for €8 per share cash.

Cash	800,000	
Common stock		800,000

Preferred stock will often be assigned a par value because in many cases the preferential dividend rate is defined as a percentage of par value (e.g., 5%, €25 par value preferred stock will have a required annual dividend of €1.25). The dividend can also be defined as a euro amount per year, thereby obviating the need for par values.

Stock issued for services. If the shares in a corporation are issued in exchange for services or property rather than for cash, the transaction should be reflected at the fair value of the property or services received. If this information is not readily available, the transaction should be recorded at the fair value of the shares that were issued. Where necessary, appraisals should be obtained to properly reflect the transaction. As a final resort, a valuation by the board of directors of the stock issued can be utilized. Stock issued to employees as compensation for services rendered should be accounted for at the fair value of the services performed, if determinable, or the value of the shares issued.

If shares are given by a major shareholder directly to an employee for services performed for the entity, this exchange should be accounted for as a capital contribution to the company by the major shareholder and as compensation expense incurred by the company. Only when accounted for in this manner will there be conformity with the general principle that all costs incurred by an entity, including compensation, should be reflected in its financial statements.

Issuance of stock units. In certain instances, common and preferred shares may be issued to investors as a unit (e.g., a unit of one share of preferred and two shares of common can be sold as a package). Where both of the classes of stock are publicly traded, the proceeds from a unit offering should be allocated in proportion to the relative market values of the securities. If only one of the securities is publicly traded, the proceeds should be allocated to the one that is publicly traded based on its known market value. Any excess is allocated to the other. Where the market value of neither security is known, appraisal information might be used. The imputed fair value of one class of security, particularly the preferred shares, can be based on the stipulated dividend rate. In this case, the amount of proceeds remaining after the imputing of a value of the preferred shares would be allocated to the common stock.

The foregoing procedures would also apply if a unit offering were made of an equity and a nonequity security such as convertible debentures, or of stock and rights to purchase additional shares of stock for a fixed time period.

Stock Subscriptions

Occasionally, particularly in the case of a newly organized corporation, a contract is entered into between the corporation and prospective investors, whereby the latter agree to purchase specified numbers of shares to be paid for over some installment period. These stock subscriptions are not the same as actual stock issuances, and the accounting differs.

The amount of stock subscriptions receivable by a corporation is sometimes treated as an asset on the balance sheet and is categorized as current or noncurrent in accordance with the terms of payment. However, most subscriptions receivable are shown as a reduction of stockholders' equity in the same manner as treasury stock. Since subscribed shares do not have the rights and responsibilities of actual outstanding stock, the credit is made to a stock subscribed account instead of to the capital stock accounts.

If the common stock has par or stated value, the common stock subscribed account is credited for the aggregate par or stated value of the shares subscribed. The excess over this amount is credited to additional paid-in capital. No distinction is made between additional paid-in capital relating to shares already issued and shares subscribed for. This treatment follows from the distinction between legal capital and additional paid-in capital. Where there is no par or stated value, the entire amount of the common stock subscribed is credited to the stock subscribed account.

As the amount due from the prospective shareholders is collected, the stock subscriptions receivable account is credited and the proceeds are debited to the cash account. Actual issuance of the shares, however, must await the complete payment of the stock subscription. Accordingly, the debit to common stock subscribed is not made until the subscribed shares are fully paid for and the stock is issued.

The following journal entries illustrate these concepts:

1. 10,000 shares of €50 par preferred are subscribed at a price of €65 each; a 10% down payment is received.

Cash	65,000	
Stock subscriptions receivable	585,000	
Preferred stock subscribed		500,000
Additional paid-in capital		150,000

2. 2,000 shares of no par common shares are subscribed at a price of €85 each, with one-half received in cash.

Cash	85,000	
Stock subscriptions receivable	85,000	
Common stock subscribed		170,000

3. All preferred subscriptions are paid, and one-half of the remaining common subscriptions are collected in full and subscribed shares are issued.

Cash [€585,000 + (€85,000 x 0.50)]	627,500	
Stock subscriptions receivable		627,500
Preferred stock subscribed	500,000	
Preferred stock		500,000
Common stock subscribed	127,500	
Common stock (€170,000 x 0.75)		127,500

When the company experiences a default by the subscriber, the accounting will follow the provisions of the state in which the corporation is chartered. In some jurisdictions, the subscriber is entitled to a proportionate number of shares based on the amount already paid on the subscriptions, sometimes reduced by the cost incurred by the corporation in selling the remaining defaulted shares to other stockholders. In other jurisdictions, the subscriber forfeits the entire investment on default. In this case the amount already received is credited to an additional paid-in capital account that describes its source.

Additional Paid-in Capital

Additional paid-in capital represents all capital contributed to a corporation other than that defined as par or stated value. Additional paid-in capital can arise from proceeds received from the sale of common and preferred shares in excess of their par or stated values. It can also arise from transactions relating to the following:

1. Sale of shares previously issued and subsequently reacquired by the corporation (treasury stock)
2. Retirement of previously outstanding shares
3. Payment of stock dividends in a manner that justifies the dividend being recorded at the market value of the shares distributed
4. Lapse of stock purchase warrants or the forfeiture of stock subscriptions, if these result in the retaining by the corporation of any partial proceeds received prior to forfeiture
5. Warrants that are detachable from bonds
6. Conversion of convertible bonds
7. Other gains on the company's own stock, such as that which results from certain stock option plans

When the amounts are material, the sources of additional paid-in capital should be described in the financial statements.

Examples of various transactions giving rise to (or reducing) additional paid-in capital accounts are set forth below.

Examples of Additional Paid-in Capital Transactions

Alta Vena Company issues 2,000 shares of common stock having a par value of €1, for a total price of €8,000. The following entry records the transaction:

Cash	8,000	
Common stock		2,000
Additional paid-in capital		6,000

Alta Vena Company buys back 2,000 shares of its own common stock for €10,000 and then sells these shares to investors for €15,000. The following entries record the buyback and sale transactions, respectively, assuming the use of the cost method of accounting for treasury stock:

Treasury stock	10,000	
Cash		10,000
Cash	15,000	
Treasury stock		10,000
Additional paid-in capital		5,000

Alta Vena Company buys back 2,000 shares of its own €1 par value common stock (which it had originally sold for €8,000) for €9,000 and retires the stock, which it records with the following entry:

Common stock	6,000	
Additional paid-in capital	2,000	
Retained earnings	1,000	
Cash		10,000

Alta Vena Company issues a small stock dividend of 5,000 common shares at the market price of €8 per share. Each share has a par value of €1. The following entry records the transaction:

Retained earnings	40,000	
Common stock		5,000
Additional paid-in capital		35,000

Alta Vena Company previously has recorded €1,000 of stock options outstanding as part of a compensation agreement. The options expire a year later, resulting in the following entry:

Stock options outstanding	1,000	
Additional paid-in capital		1,000

Alta Vena Company sells 2,000 of par €1,000 bonds, as well as 2,000 attached warrants having a market value of €15 each. Pro rata apportionment of the €2,000,000 cash received between the bonds and warrants results in the following entry:

Cash	2,000,000	
Discount on bonds payable	29,557	
Bonds payable		2,000,000
Additional paid-in-capital—warrants		29,557

Alta Vena's bondholders convert a €1,000 bond with an unamortized premium of €40 and a market value of €1,016 into 127 shares of €1 par common stock whose market value is €8 per share. This results in the following entry:

Bonds payable	1,000	
Premium on bonds payable	40	
Common stock		913
Additional paid-in-capital—warrants		127

Donated Capital

Donated capital should also be adequately disclosed in the financial statements. Donated capital can result from an outright gift to the corporation (e.g., a major shareholder donates land or other assets to the company in a nonreciprocal transfer) or may result when services are provided to the corporation. Under current US GAAP, such nonreciprocal transactions will be recognized as revenue in the period the contribution is received. IFRS does not, at present, address contributions or donations.

In these situations, historical cost is not adequate to reflect properly the substance of the transaction, since the historical cost to the corporation would be zero. Accordingly, these events should be reflected at fair market value. If long-lived assets are donated to the corporation, they should be recorded at their fair value at the date of donation, and the amount so recorded should be depreciated over the normal useful economic life of such assets. If donations are conditional in nature, they should not be reflected formally in the accounts until the appropriate conditions have been satisfied. However, disclosure might still be required in the financial statements of both the assets donated and the conditions required to be met.

Example of donated capital

A board member of the for-profit organization Village Social Services donates land to the organization that has a fair market value of €1 million. Village Social Services records the donation with the following entry:

Land	1,000,000	
Revenue—Donations		1,000,000

The same board member donates one year of accounting labor to Village Social Services. The fair value of services rendered is €75,000. Village Social Services records the donation with the following entry:

Salaries—accounting department	75,000	
Revenue—donations		75,000

The board member also donates one year of free rent of a local building to Village Social Services. The annual rent in similar facilities is €45,000. Village Social Services records the donation with the following entry:

Rent expense	45,000	
Revenue—donations		45,000

Finally, the board member pays off a €100,000 debt owed by Village Social Services. Village Social Services records the donation with the following entry:

Notes payable	100,000	
Revenue—donations		100,000

Following the closing of the fiscal period, the effect of all the foregoing donations will be reflected in Village Social Services' retained earnings account.

Retained Earnings

Legal capital, additional paid-in capital, and donated capital, collectively represent the contributed capital of the corporation. The other major source of capital is retained earnings, which represents the accumulated amount of earnings of the corporation from the date of inception (or from the date of reorganization) less the cumulative amount of distributions made to shareholders and other charges to retained earnings (e.g., from treasury stock transactions). The distributions to shareholders generally take the form of dividend payments, but may take other forms as well, such as the reacquisition of shares for amounts in excess of the original issuance proceeds. They key events impacting retained earnings are as follows:

- Dividends
- Certain treasury stock resales at amounts below acquisition cost
- Certain stock retirements at amounts in excess of book value
- Prior period adjustments
- Recapitalizations and reorganizations

Examples of retained earnings transactions

Baking Bread Co. declares a dividend of €84,000, which it records with the following entry:

Retained earnings	84,000	
Dividends payable		84,000

Baking Bread acquires 3,000 shares of its own €1 par value common stock for €15,000, and then resells it for €12,000. The following entries record the buyback and sale transactions, respectively, assuming the use of the cost method of accounting for treasury stock:

Treasury stock	15,000	
Cash		15,000
Cash	12,000	
Retained earnings	3,000	
Treasury stock		15,000

Baking Bread buys back 12,000 shares of its own €1 par value common stock (which it had originally sold for €60,000) for €70,000 and retires the stock, which it records with the following entry:

Common stock	12,000	
Additional paid-in capital	48,000	
Retained earnings	10,000	
Cash		70,000

Baking Bread's accountant makes a mathematical mistake in calculating depreciation, requiring a prior period reduction of €30,000 to the accumulated depreciation account, and corresponding increases in its income tax payable and retained earnings accounts. Baking Bread's income tax rate is 35%. It records this transaction with the following entry:

Accumulated depreciation	30,000	
Income taxes payable		10,500
Retained earnings		19,500

Retained earnings are also affected by action taken by the corporation's board of directors. Appropriation serves disclosure purposes and serves to restrict dividend payments but does nothing to provide any resources for satisfaction of the contingent loss or other underlying purpose for which the appropriation has been made. Any appropriation made from retained earnings must eventually be returned to the retained earnings account. It is not permissible to charge losses against the appropriation account nor to credit any realized gain to that account. The use of appropriated retained earnings has diminished significantly over the years.

An important rule relating to retained earnings is that transactions in a corporation's own stock can result in a reduction of retained earnings (i.e., a deficiency on such transactions can be charged to retained earnings) but cannot result in an increase in retained earnings (any excesses on such transactions are credited to paid-in capital, never to retained earnings).

If a series of operating losses have been incurred or distributions to shareholders in excess of accumulated earnings have been made and if there is a debit balance in retained earnings, the account is generally referred to as accumulated deficit.

Dividends

Dividends represent the pro rata distribution of earnings to the owners of the corporation. The amount and the allocation between the preferred and common shareholders is a function of the stipulated preferential dividend rate, the presence or absence of (1) a participation feature, (2) a cumulative feature, and (3) arrearages on the preferred stock, and the wishes of the board of directors. Dividends, even preferred stock dividends where a cumulative feature exists, do not accrue. Dividends become a liability of the corporation only when they are declared by the board of directors.

Traditionally, corporations were not allowed to declare dividends in excess of the amount of retained earnings. Alternatively, a corporation could pay dividends out of retained earnings and additional paid-in capital but could not exceed the total of these categories (i.e., they could not impair legal capital by the payment of dividends). Local company law obviously dictates, directly or by implication, the accounting to be applied in many of these situations. In the US, states that have adopted the Model Business Corporation Act grant more latitude to the directors. Corporations can now, in certain US jurisdictions, declare and pay dividends in excess of the book amount of retained earnings if the directors conclude that, after the payment of such dividends, the fair value of the corporation's net assets will still be a positive amount. Thus, directors can declare dividends out of unrealized appreciation, which, in certain industries, can be a significant source of dividends beyond the realized and recognized accumulated earnings of the corporation. This action, however, represents a major departure from traditional practice and demands both careful consideration and adequate disclosure.

Three important dividend dates are

1. The declaration date
2. The record date
3. The payment date

The declaration date governs the incurrence of a legal liability by the corporation. The record date refers to that point in time when a determination is made as to which specific registered stockholders will receive dividends and in what amounts. Finally, the payment date relates to the date when the distribution of the dividend takes place. These concepts are illustrated in the following example:

Example of payment of dividends

On May 1, 2004, the directors of River Corp. declare a €75 per share quarterly dividend on River Corp.'s 650,000 outstanding common shares. The dividend is payable May 25 to holders of record May 15.

May 1	Retained earnings (or Dividends)	487,500	
	Dividends payable		487,500
May 15	No entry		
May 25	Dividends payable	487,500	
	Cash		487,500

If a dividends account is used, it is closed directly to retained earnings at year-end.

Dividends may be made in the form of cash, property, or scrip, which is a form of short-term note payable. Cash dividends are either a given dollar amount per share or a percentage of par or stated value. Property dividends consist of the distribution of any assets other than cash (e.g., inventory or equipment). Finally, scrip dividends are promissory notes due at some time in the future, sometimes bearing interest until final payment is made.

Occasionally, what appear to be disproportionate dividend distributions are paid to some but not all of the owners of closely held corporations. Such transactions need to be analyzed carefully. In some cases these may actually represent compensation paid to the recipients. In other instances, these may be a true dividend paid to all shareholders on a pro rata basis, to which certain shareholders have waived their rights. If the former, the distribution should not be accounted for as a dividend but as compensation or some other expense category and included on the income statement. If the latter, the dividend should be grossed up to reflect payment on a proportional basis to all the shareholders, with an offsetting capital contribution to the company recognized as having been effectively made by those to whom payments were not made.

Property dividends. If property dividends are declared, the paying corporation may incur a gain or loss. Since the dividend should be reflected at the fair value of the assets distributed, the difference between fair value and book value is recorded at the time the dividend is declared and charged or credited to a loss or gain account.

Scrip dividends. If a corporation declares a dividend payable in scrip that is interest bearing, the interest is accrued over time as a periodic expense. The interest is not a part of the dividend itself.

Liquidating dividends. Liquidating dividends are not distributions of earnings, but rather, a return of capital to the investing shareholders. A liquidating dividend is normally recorded by the declarer through charging additional paid-in capital rather than retained earnings. The exact accounting for a liquidating dividend is affected by the laws where the business is incorporated, and these laws vary from state to state.

Stock dividends. Stock dividends represent neither an actual distribution of the assets of the corporation nor a promise to distribute those assets. For this reason, a stock dividend is not considered a legal liability or a taxable transaction.

Despite the recognition that a stock dividend is not a distribution of earnings, the accounting treatment of relatively insignificant stock dividends (defined as being less than 20 to 25% of the outstanding shares prior to declaration) is consistent with its being a real dividend. Accordingly, retained earnings are debited for the fair market value of the shares to be paid as a dividend, and the capital stock and additional paid-in capital accounts are credited for the appropriate amounts based on the par or stated value of the shares, if any. A stock dividend declared but not yet paid is classified as such in the stockholders' equity section of the balance sheet. Since such a dividend never reduces assets, it cannot be a liability.

The selection of 20 to 25% as the threshold for recognizing a stock dividend as an earnings distribution is arbitrary, but it is based somewhat on the empirical evidence that small stock dividends tend not to result in a reduced market price per share for outstanding shares. In theory, any stock dividend should result in a reduction of the market value of outstanding shares in an inverse relationship to the size of the stock dividend. The aggregate value of the outstanding shares should not change, but the greater number of shares outstanding after the stock dividend should necessitate a lower per share price. As noted, however, the declaration of small stock dividends tends not to have this impact, and this phenomenon supports the accounting treatment.

On the other hand, when stock dividends are larger in magnitude, it is observed that per share market value declines after declaration of the dividend. In such situations it would not be valid to treat the stock dividend as an earnings distribution. Rather, it should be accounted for as a split. The precise treatment depends on the legal requirements of the state of incorporation and on whether the existing par value or stated value is reduced concurrent with the stock split.

If the par value is not reduced for a large stock dividend and if state law requires that earnings be capitalized in an amount equal to the aggregate of the par value of the stock dividend declared, the event should be described as a stock split effected in the form of a dividend, with a charge to retained earnings and a credit to the common stock account for the aggregate par or stated value. When the par or stated value is reduced in recognition of the split and state laws do not require treatment as a dividend, there is no formal entry to record the split but merely a notation that the number of shares outstanding has increased and the per share par or stated value has decreased accordingly.

The concepts of small versus large stock dividends are illustrated in the following examples:

Assume that stockholders' equity for the Wasabi Corp. on November 1, 2006, is as follows:

Common stock €1 par, 100,000 shares outstanding	€100,000
Paid-in capital in excess of par	1,100,000
Retained earnings	750,000

Small stock dividend: On November 10, 2006, the directors of Wasabi Corp. declared a 15% stock dividend, or a dividend of 1.5 shares of common stock for every 10 shares held. Before the stock dividend, the stock is selling for €23 per share. After the 15% stock dividend, each original share worth €23 will become 1.15 shares, each with a value of €20 (€23/1.15). The stock dividend is to be recorded at the market value of the new shares issued, or €300,000 (15,000 new shares at the postdividend price of €20). The entries to record the declaration of the dividend and the issuance of stock (on November 30) by Wasabi Corp. are as follows:

Nov. 10	Retained earnings	€300,000	
	Stock dividends distributable		15,000
	Paid-in capital in excess of par		285,000
Nov. 30	Stock dividends distributable	15,000	
	Common stock, €1 par		15,000

Large stock dividend: In practice, US GAAP results in the par or stated value of the newly issued shares being transferred to the capital stock account from either retained earnings or paid-in capital in excess of par. To illustrate, assume that on November 10, 2006, Wasabi Corp. declares a 50% large stock dividend, a dividend of one share for every two held. Legal requirements call for the transfer to capital stock of an amount equal to the par value of the shares issued. Entries for the declaration on November 10 and the issuance of 50,000 new shares (=100,000 × .50) on November 30 are as follows:

Nov. 10	Retained earnings	50,000	
	Stock dividends distributable		50,000
	OR		
	Paid-in capital in excess of par	50,000	
	Stock dividends distributable		50,000
Nov. 30	Stock dividends distributable	50,000	
	Common stock, €1 par		50,000

Treasury Stock

Treasury stock consists of a corporation's own stock that has been issued, subsequently reacquired by the firm, and not yet reissued or canceled. Treasury stock does not reduce the number of shares issued but does reduce the number of shares outstanding, as well as total stockholders' equity. These shares are not eligible to receive cash dividends. Treasury stock is not an asset, although in some circumstances, it may be presented as an asset if adequately disclosed. Reacquired stock that is awaiting delivery to satisfy a liability created by the firm's compensation plan or reacquired stock held in a profit-sharing trust is still considered outstanding and would not be considered treasury stock. In each case, the stock would be presented as an asset with the accompanying footnote disclosure.

Three approaches exist for the treatment of treasury stock: the cost, par value, and constructive retirement methods.

Cost method. Under the cost method, the gross cost of the shares reacquired is charged to a contra equity account (treasury stock). The equity accounts that were credited for the original share issuance (common stock, paid-in capital in excess of par, etc.) remain intact. When the treasury shares are reissued, proceeds in excess of cost are credited to a paid-in capital account. Any deficiency is charged to retained earnings (unless paid-in capital from previous treasury share transactions exists, in which case the deficiency is charged to that account, with any excess charged to retained earnings). If many treasury stock purchases are made, a cost flow assumption (e.g., FIFO or specific identification) should be adopted to compute excesses and deficiencies on subsequent share reissuances. The advantage of the cost method is that it avoids identifying and accounting for amounts related to the original issuance of the shares, and is therefore the simpler more frequently used method. The cost method is most consistent with the one-transaction concept. This concept takes the view that the classification of stockholders' equity should not be affected simply because the corporation was the middle "person" in an exchange of shares from one stockholder to another. In substance, there is only a transfer of shares between two stockholders. Since the original balances in the equity accounts are left undisturbed, its use is most acceptable when the firm acquires its stock for reasons other than retirement, or when its ultimate disposition has not yet been decided.

Par value method. Under the second approach, the par value method, the treasury stock account is charged only for the aggregate par (or stated) value of the shares reacquired. Other paid-in capital accounts (excess over par value, etc.) are relieved in proportion to the amounts recognized on the original issuance of the shares. The treasury share acquisition is treated almost as a retirement. However, the common (or preferred) stock account continues at the original amount, thereby preserving the distinction between an actual retirement and a treasury share transaction.

When the treasury shares accounted for by the par value method are subsequently resold, the excess of the sale price over par value is credited to paid-in capital. A reissuance for a price below par value does not create a contingent liability for the purchaser. It is only the original purchaser who risks this obligation to the entity's creditors.

Constructive retirement method. The constructive retirement method is similar to the par value method except that the aggregate par (or stated) value of the reacquired shares is charged to the stock account rather than to the treasury stock account. This method is superior when (1) it is management's intention not to reissue the shares within a reasonable time period, or (2) the state of incorporation defines reacquired shares as having been retired.

The two-transaction concept is most consistent with the par value and constructive retirement methods. First, the reacquisition of the firm's shares is viewed as constituting a contraction of its capital structure. Second, the reissuance of the shares is the same as issuing new shares. There is little difference between the purchase and subsequent reissuance of treasury shares and the acquisition and retirement of previously issued shares and the issuance of new shares.

Treasury shares originally accounted for by the cost method can subsequently be restated to conform to the constructive retirement method. If shares were acquired with the intention that they would be reissued and it is later determined that such reissuance is unlikely (due for example, to the expiration of stock options without their exercise), it is proper to restate the transaction.

Example of accounting for treasury stock

1. 100 shares (€50 par value) that were sold originally for €60 per share are later reacquired for €70 each.
2. All 100 shares are subsequently resold for a total of €7,500.

To record the acquisition, the entry is

Cost method			Par value method			Constructive retirement method		
Treasury stock	7,000		Treasury stock	5,000		Common stock	5,000	
Cash		7,000	Additional paid-in			Additional paid-in		
			capital—common			capital—common		
			stock	1,000		stock	1,000	
			Retained earnings	1,000		Retained earnings	1,000	
			Cash		7,000	Cash		7,000

To record the resale, the entry is

Cost method			Par value method			Constructive retirement method		
Cash	7,500		Cash	7,500		Cash	7,500	
Treasury stock		7,000	Treasury stock		5,000	Common stock		5,000
Additional paid-			Additional paid-in			Additional paid-in		
in capital—			capital—common			capital—		
treasury stock		500	stock		2,500	common stock		2,500

If the shares had been resold for €6,500, the entry is

Cost method			Par value method			Constructive retirement method		
Cash	6,500		Cash	6,500		Cash	6,500	
*Retained earnings	500		Treasury stock		5,000	Common stock		5,000
Treasury stock		7,000	Additional paid-in			Additional paid-in		
			capital—common stock		1,500	capital—common		1,500
						stock		

* *"Additional paid-in capital—treasury stock" or "Additional paid-in capital—retired stock" of that issue would be debited first to the extent it exists.*

Alternatively, under the par or constructive retirement methods, any portion of or the entire deficiency on the treasury stock acquisition may be debited to retained earnings without allocation to paid-in capital. Any excesses would always be credited to an "Additional paid-in capital—retired stock" account.

The laws of some states govern the circumstances under which a corporation may acquire treasury stock and they may prescribe the accounting for the stock. For example, a charge to retained earnings may be required in an amount equal to the treasury stock's total cost. In such cases, the accounting according to state law prevails. Also, some states define excess purchase cost of reacquired (i.e., treasury) shares as distributions to shareholders that are no different in nature than dividends. In such cases, the financial statement presentation should adequately disclose the substance of these transactions (e.g., by presenting both dividends and excess reacquisition costs together in the retained earnings statement).

When a firm decides to retire the treasury stock formally, the journal entry is dependent on the method used to account for the stock. Using the original sale and reacquisition data from the illustration above, the following entry would be made:

Cost method				*Par value method*		
Common stock	5,000			Common stock	5,000	
Additional paid-in capital—common stock	1,000			Treasury stock		5,000
*Retained earnings	1,000					
Treasury stock		7,000				

* *"Additional paid-in capital—treasury stock" may be debited to the extent that it exists.*

If the constructive retirement method were used to record the treasury stock purchase, no additional entry would be necessary on formal retirement of the shares.

After the entry is made, the pro rata portion of all paid-in capital existing for that issue (i.e., capital stock and additional paid-in capital) will have been eliminated. If stock is purchased for immediate retirement (i.e., not put into the treasury) the entry to record the retirement is the same as that made under the constructive retirement method.

In the case of donated treasury stock, the intentions of management are important. If the shares are to be retired, the capital stock account is debited for the par or stated value of the shares, "Donated capital" is credited for the fair market value, and "Additional paid-in capital—retired stock" is debited or credited for the difference. If the intention of management is to reissue the shares, three methods of accounting are available. The first two methods, cost and par value, are analogous to the aforementioned treasury stock methods except that "Donated capital" is credited at the time of receipt and debited at the time of reissuance. Under the cost method, the current market value of the stock is recorded (an apparent contradiction), whereas under the par value method, the par or stated value is used. Under the last method, only a memorandum entry is made to indicate the number of shares received. No journal entry is made at the time of receipt. At the time of reissuance, the entire proceeds are credited to "Donated capital." The method actually used is generally dependent on the circumstances involving the donation and the preference of the firm.

Other Equity Accounts

There are other adjustments to balance sheet accounts that are accumulated and reflected as separate components of stockholders' equity. Under current US GAAP, these include unrealized gains or losses on available-for-sale portfolios of debt and marketable equity securities, accumulated gain or loss on translation of foreign currency-denominated financial statements, and the net loss not recognized as pension cost. The accounting for fair value changes in available-for-sale securities under IFRS (unless the "fair value option" is elected, necessitating immediate recognition through the income statement) is similar to that under US GAAP.

Convertible Preferred Stock

The treatment of convertible preferred stock at its issuance is no different from that of nonconvertible preferred. When it is converted, the book value approach is used to account for the conversion. Use of the market value approach would entail a gain or loss for which there is no theoretical justification, since the total amount of contributed capital does not change when the stock is converted. When the preferred stock is converted, the "Preferred stock" and related "Additional paid-in capital—preferred stock" accounts are debited for their original values when purchased, and "Common stock" and "Additional paid-in capital—common stock" (if an excess over par or stated value exists) are credited. If the book value of the preferred stock is less than the total par value of the common stock being issued, retained earnings is charged for the difference. This charge is supported by the rationale that the preferred shareholders are offered an additional return to facilitate their conversion to common stock. Many states require that this excess instead reduce additional paid-in capital from other sources.

Preferred Stock with Mandatory Redemption

A mandatory redemption clause requires the preferred stock to be redeemed (retired) at a specified date(s). This feature is in contrast to callable preferred stock, which is redeemed at the issuing corporation's option. When combined with a cumulative dividend preference, the mandatory redemption feature causes the preferred stock to have the characteristics of debt, especially when the stock is to be redeemed in five to ten years. The dividend payments represent interest, and redemption is the repayment of principal. However, there is one important difference, at least in the US. The dividend payments do not receive the same tax treatment as do interest payments. They are not deductible in determining taxable income.

A recent US GAAP standard, FAS 150, established the requirement that stock having mandatory redemption provisions be reported as liabilities. (It should be noted that this now conforms closely with the requirements under the international standard, IAS 32, which demands that a "substance over form" analysis be conducted and that items such as mandatorily redeemable stock be treated as debt.)

Under US GAAP, disclosure of the amounts and timing of any redemption payments for each of the five years following the balance sheet date is required.

Book Value Stock Plans

Another type of stock purchase plan, the book value plan, is intended also to be a compensation program for participating employees, although there are important secondary motives in many such plans, such as the desires to generate capital and to tie employees to the employer. Under the terms of typical book value plans, employees (or those attaining some defined level, such as manager) are given the opportunity or, in some cases, they are required to purchase shares in the company, which then must be sold back to the company on termination of employment.

Under US GAAP, if the employees participating in a nonpublic company's book value stock plan have substantive investments in the company that are at risk, the increases in book value during the period of ownership are not to be treated as compensation. However, if the employees are granted options to purchase shares at book value, compensation is to be recognized for value increases, presumably because under the latter scenario the employee has no investment at risk and is only being given an "upside" opportunity. This interpretation is also applicable to book value options granted to employees of publicly held companies.

For accounting purposes, shares issued at book value to employees are simply recorded as a normal stock sale. To the extent that book value exceeds par or stated value, additional paid-in capital accounts may also be credited.

For such plans in publicly owned companies, GAAP states that these plans are performance plans akin to stock appreciation rights, and accordingly, results in compensation expense recognition. This conclusion was reached at least in part due to pressure from the US securities regulators.

Junior Stock

Another category of stock-based compensation program involves junior stock. Typically, such shares are subordinate to normal shares of common stock with respect to voting rights, dividend rate, or other attributes, and are convertible into regular common shares if and when stipulated performance goals are achieved. Like stock appreciation rights, grants of junior stock represent a performance-based program, in contrast to fixed stock options.

An interpretation under US GAAP holds that compensation cost incurred in connection with grants of junior stock is generally to be accrued. However, compensation is to be recognized only when it is deemed to be probable (as that term is defined by the accounting literature dealing with contingencies) that the performance goals will be achieved. It may be that achievement is not deemed probable at the time the junior stock is issued, but it later becomes clear that such achievement is indeed likely. In other circumstances, the ability to convert junior stock to regular stock is dependent on the achievement of more than a single performance goal, and it is not probable that all such goals can be achieved, although some of them are deemed probable of achievement. In both scenarios, full accrual of compensation cost may be delayed until the estimated likelihood of achievement improves.

The rule specifies that the measure of compensation is derived from the comparison of the market price of ordinary common stock with the price to be paid, if any, for the junior stock. Since the junior stock will be convertible to ordinary common stock if the defined performance goals are achieved, the compensation to be received by the employees participating in the plan is linked to the value of unrestricted common shares.

Put Warrant

A detachable put warrant is occasionally issued in connection with an entity's debt. It typically can either be put back to the debt issuer for cash or exercised to acquire common stock. US GAAP holds that these instruments should be accounted for in the same manner as mandatorily redeemable preferred stock. Under provisions of the relevant standard, FAS 150, these are to be presented as liabilities. It would seem to be reasonable to analogize to IAS 32 for guidance under IFRS. Changes in the fair value of the obligation are recognized currently in earnings.

Accounting for Stock Issued to Employee Stock Ownership Plans

Increasingly, US corporations have been availing themselves of favorable tax regulations that encourage the establishment of employee stock ownership plans. Employee stock ownership plans (ESOP) are defined contribution employee benefit plans in which shares of the sponsoring entity are given to employees as additional compensation.

In brief, ESOP are created by a sponsoring corporation that either funds the plan directly (unleveraged ESOP) or, as is more often the case, facilitates the borrowing of money either directly from an outside lender (directly leveraged ESOP) or from the employer, who in turn will borrow from an outside lender (indirectly leveraged ESOP). Borrowings from outside lenders may or may not be guaranteed by the sponsor. Since effectively the only source of funds for debt repayment is future contributions by the sponsor, US GAAP requires that the ESOP's debt be considered debt of the sponsor. Depending on the reasons underlying the creation of the ESOP (estate planning by the controlling shareholder, expanding the capital base of the entity, rewarding and motivating the workforce, etc.), the sponsor's shares may be contributed to the plan in annual installments, in a block of shares from the sponsor, or shares from an existing shareholder may be purchased by the plan.

Direct or indirect borrowings by the ESOP must be reported as debt in the sponsor's balance sheet. An offset to a contra equity account, not to an asset, is also reported since the plan represents a commitment (morally, if not always legally) to make future contributions to the plan and not a claim to resources. This results in a "double hit" to the sponsor's balance sheet (i.e., the recording of a liability and the reduction of net stockholders' equity), which is often an unanticipated and unpleasant surprise. This contra equity account was called "unearned compensation" under prior accounting rules but is now referred to as "unearned ESOP shares." If the sponsor lends funds to the ESOP without a "mirror" loan from an outside lender, this loan should not be reported in the employer's balance sheet as debt, although the debit should still be reported as a contra equity account.

As the ESOP services the debt (using contributions made by the sponsor and/or dividends received on sponsor shares held by the plan) the sponsor reflects the reduction of the obligation by reducing the debt and the contra equity account on its balance sheet. Simultaneously, income and thus retained earnings will be affected as the contributions to the plan are reported in the sponsor's current results of operations. Thus, the double hit is eliminated, but net worth continues to reflect the economic fact that compensation costs have been incurred. US GAAP requires that the interest cost component be separated from the remaining compensation expense, that is, that the sponsor's income statement should reflect the true character of the expenses being incurred rather than aggregating the entire amount into a category such as "ESOP contribution."

In a leveraged ESOP, shares held serve as collateral for the debt and are not allocated to employees until the debt is retired. In general, shares must be allocated by the end of the year in which the debt is repaid; however, to satisfy the tax laws, the allocation of shares may take place at a faster pace than retirement of the principal portion of the debt.

The cost of ESOP shares allocated is measured (for purposes of reporting compensation expense in the sponsor's income statements) based on the fair value on the release date, in contrast to the actual historical cost of the shares to the plan. Dividends paid on unallocated shares (i.e., shares held by the ESOP) are reported in the sponsor's income statement as compensation cost and/or as interest expense.

Example of accounting for ESOP transactions

Assume that Intrepid Corp. establishes an ESOP, which then borrows €500,000 from Second Interstate Bank. The ESOP then purchases 50,000 shares of Intrepid no-par shares from the company; none of these shares are allocated to individual participants. The entries would be

Cash	500,000	
Bank loan payable		500,000
Unearned ESOP shares (contra equity account)	500,000	
Common stock		500,000

The ESOP then borrows an additional €250,000 from the sponsor, Intrepid, and uses the cash to purchase a further 25,000 shares, all of which are allocated to participants.

Compensation	250,000	
Common stock		250,000

Intrepid Corp. contributes €50,000 to the plan, which the plan uses to service its bank debt, consisting of €40,000 principal reduction and €10,000 interest cost. The debt reduction causes 4,000 shares to be allocated to participants at a time when the average market value had been €12 per share.

Interest expense	10,000	
Bank loan payable	40,000	
Cash		50,000
Compensation	48,000	
Additional paid-in capital		8,000
Unearned ESOP shares		40,000

Dividends of €0.10 per share are declared (only the ESOP shares are represented in the following entry, but dividends are paid equally on all outstanding shares).

Retained earnings	2,900	
Compensation	4,600	
Dividends payable		7,500

Note that in all the foregoing illustrations the effect of income taxes is ignored. Since the difference between the cost and fair values of shares committed to be released is analogous to differences in the expense recognized for tax and accounting purposes with regard to stock options, the same treatment should be applied. That is, the tax effect should be reported directly in stockholders' equity rather than in earnings.

Corporate Bankruptcy and Reorganizations

Entities operating under and emerging from protection of the bankruptcy laws. The *going concern* assumption is one of the basic postulates underlying generally accepted accounting principles (and is implicit, also, as a foundation for IFRS) and is responsible for, among other things, the historical cost convention in financial reporting. For entities that have entered bankruptcy proceedings, however, the going concern assumption will no longer be of central importance.

Traditionally, the basic financial statements (balance sheet, income statement, and statement of cash flows) presented by going concerns were seen as less useful for entities undergoing reorganization. Instead, the statement of affairs, reporting assets at estimated realizable values and liabilities at estimated liquidation amounts, was recommended for use by such organizations. In more recent years, use of the statement of affairs has not frequently been encountered in practice. In 1990, a standard was promulgated in US GAAP, setting forth certain financial reporting standards for entities undergoing, and emerging from, reorganization under the bankruptcy laws.

Under GAAP, assets are presented at estimated realizable values. Liabilities are set forth at the estimated amounts to be allowed in the balance sheet and liabilities subject to compromise are to be distinguished from those that are not. Furthermore, US GAAP requires that in both statements of income and cash flows, normal transactions be differentiated from those that have occurred as a consequence of the entity's being in reorganization. While certain allocations to the latter category are rather obvious, such as legal and accounting fees incurred, others are less clear. For example, the standard suggests that if the entity in reorganization earns interest income on funds that would normally have been used to settle obligations owed to creditors, such income will be deemed to be income arising as a consequence of the bankruptcy action.

Another interesting aspect of this standard is the accounting to be made for the emergence from reorganization (known as "confirmation of the plan of reorganization"). GAAP now provides for "fresh start" financial reporting in such instances. This accounting is similar to that applied to purchase business combinations, with the total confirmed value of the entity on its emergence from reorganization being analogous to the purchase price in an acquisition. In both cases, this total value is to be allocated to the identifiable assets and liabilities of the entity, with any excess being allocated to goodwill. In the case of entities emerging from bankruptcy, goodwill (reorganization value in excess of amounts allocable to identifiable assets) is measured as the excess of liabilities existing at the plan confirmation date, computed at present value of future amounts to be paid, over the reorganization value of assets. Reorganization value is calculated with reference to a number of factors, including forecasted operating results and cash flows of the new entity.

This standard applies only to entities undergoing formal reorganization under the bankruptcy code. Less formal procedures may still be accounted for under preexisting quasi reorganization accounting procedures.

Quasi Reorganizations

Generally, this procedure is applicable during a period of declining price levels. It is termed "quasi" since the accumulated deficit is eliminated at a lower cost and with less difficulty than a legal reorganization. Under longstanding provisions of US GAAP, the procedures in a quasi reorganization involve

1. Proper authorization from stockholders and creditors where required
2. Revaluation of assets to their current values. All losses are charged to retained earnings, thus increasing any deficit.
3. Elimination of any deficit by charging paid-in capital

    a. Additional paid-in capital to the extent it exists
    b. Capital stock when additional paid-in capital is insufficient. The par value of the stock is reduced, creating the extra additional paid-in capital to which the remaining deficit is charged.

No retained earnings may be created by a reorganization. Any excess created by the reduction of par value is credited to "Paid-in capital from quasi reorganization." Retained earnings must be dated for ten years (less than ten years may be justified under exceptional circumstances) after a quasi reorganization takes place. Disclosure similar to "since quasi reorganization of June 30, 2006" would be appropriate.

Examples of Financial Statement Disclosures

F. Hoffman-LaRoche
Period Ending December 2004

34. Equity

Share capital. As of December 31, 2004, the share capital of Roche Holding Ltd, which is the Group's parent company, consists of 160,000,000 shares with a nominal value of 1.00 Swiss franc each, as in the preceding year. The shares are bearer shares and the Group does not maintain a register of shareholders. Based on information supplied to the Group, a shareholders' group with pooled voting rights owns 50.0125% (2003: 50.0125%) of the issued shares. This is further described in Note 38. Based on information supplied to the Group, Novartis International Ltd, Basel, and its affiliates own 33.3330% (participation below 33 1/3%) of the issued shares (2003: 33.3330%).

Nonvoting equity securities (*Gennussschiene*). As of December 31, 2004, 702,562,700 nonvoting equity securities were in issue as in the preceding year. Under Swiss company law these nonvoting equity securities have no nominal value, are not part of the share capital and cannot be issued against a contribution which would be shown as an asset in the balance sheet of Roche Holding Ltd. Each nonvoting equity security confers the same rights as any of the shares to participate in the net profit and any remaining proceeds from liquidation following repayment of the nominal value of the shares and, if any, participation certificates. In accordance with the law and the Articles of Incorporation of Roche Holding Ltd, the Company is entitled at all times to exchange all or some of the nonvoting equity securities into shares or participation certificates.

Dividends. On April 6, 2004 the shareholders approved the distribution of a dividend of 1.65 Swiss francs per share and nonvoting equity security (2003: 1.45 Swiss francs) in respect of the 2003 business year. The distribution to holders of outstanding shares and nonvoting equity securities totaled 1,414 million Swiss francs (2003: 1,229 million Swiss francs) and has been recorded against retained earnings in 2004. The Board has proposed dividends for the 2004 business year of 2.00 Swiss francs per share and nonvoting equity security. This is subject to approval at the Annual General Meeting on February 28, 2005.

Own equity instruments. In 2003, following the redemption of the "LYONs II" exchange-able notes on April 20 2003 (see Note 32) and in light of the restructuring of the Group's treasury operations and debt financing, the Group carried out a comprehensive review of the arrangements whereby it covers the potential conversion obligations that may arise from its convertible debt in-struments. The Group refinanced the various instruments that cover its potential obligations to deliver nonvoting equity securities. The Group sold 11,671,933 of those nonvoting equity securi-ties that it previously held in a series of transactions, in addition to the 2,744,893 nonvoting equity securities utilized for the Disetronic transaction (see Note 3) and the 2,167,600 utilized for the conversion of the "Helveticus" bonds (see Note 32). The Group also agreed with its counter-parties to restructure its previous arrangements which used written/short put options and purchased/long call options at the same strike price, which had the combined effect of a forward purchase. By December 31 2003 all of these arrangements have been closed. In addition, in 2003 the Group purchased from various counterparties Low Exercise Price Options (LEPOs), which give the Group the right to purchase nonvoting equity securities at a low strike price.

Own equity instruments *in equivalent number of nonvoting equity securities*

	December 31, 2004	*December 31, 2003*
Nonvoting equity securities	87,386	6,448,687
Low Exercise Price Options	21,080,081	16,591,394
Forward purchases and derivative instruments	4,723,565	3,023,565
Total nonvoting equity instruments	25,891,032	26,063,646

Own equity instruments are recorded within equity at original cost of acquisition. Details of own equity instruments held at December 31, 2004 are shown in the table below. Fair values are disclosed for information purposes.

Own equity instruments: supplementary information

	Equivalent number of nonvoting equity securities	*Maturity*	*Strike price (CHF)*	*Fair value (millions of CHF)*
Nonvoting equity securities	87,386	n/a	n/a	11
Low Exercise Price Options	21,080,081	Feb. 21, 2005-Nov. 30, 2007	0.01-10.00	2,664
Derivative instruments				
Roche Option Plan	3,611,605	Feb. 26, 2009-Feb 3, 2011	77.80-129.50	92
Other options	1,111,960	Feb. 17, 2005-Apr. 24, 2006	150.00-250.00	2
Total	25,891,032			2,769

Nonvoting equity securities and Low Exercise Price Options are mainly held for the potential conversion obligations that may arise from the Group's convertible debt instruments (see Note 32). The Group's potential obligations to employees for the Roche Option Plan (see Note 12) are covered by call options that are exercisable at any time up to their maturity. The Group also holds a residual number of options that were purchased for use in the Group's previous option compen-sation scheme, which is now closed (see Note 12).

The net cash inflow from transactions in own equity instruments was 237 million Swiss francs (2003: net cash outflow of 15 million Swiss francs). Additionally in 2003 there was a net cash outflow of 1,635 million Swiss francs from the refinancing of instruments covering converti-ble debt obligations.

The Group holds none of its own shares.

Adidas-Salomon AG
Period Ending December 2004

Notes to the financial statements

21. Shareholders' Equity

In January 2004, the nominal capital of Adidas-Salomon AG was increased by €213,248 as a result of the exercise of 83,300 stock options and the issuance of 83,300 no-par-value bearer shares associated with the fifth exercise period of Tranche II (2000) and the second exercise period of Tranche III (2001) of the Management Share Option Plan (MSOP). As part of the sixth exercise period of Tranche II (2000) and the third exercise period of Tranche III (2001), the nominal capital was increased by a further €387,456 in July 2004, as a result of the exercise of 151,350 stock options and the issuance of 151,350 no-par-value bearer shares. Based on the exercise of 170,600 stock options and the issuance of 170,600 no-par value bearer shares within the scope of the seventh exercise period of Tranche II (2000) and the fourth exercise period of Tranche III (2001) as well as the first exercise period of Tranche IV (2002), the Company's nominal capital was increased by a further €436,737 in October 2004. On December 31, 2004, the nominal capital of Adidas-Salomon AG amounted to €117,399,040 and was divided into 45,859,000 no-par-value bearer shares. Capital reserves thus increased by €27,479,984.50 in 2004.

In January 2005, the nominal capital of Adidas-Salomon AG was increased by a further €207,488 as a result of the exercise of 81,050 stock options and the issuance of 81,050 no-par-value bearer shares associated with the eighth exercise period of Tranche II (2000), the fifth exercise period of Tranche III (2001) and the second exercise period of Tranche IV (2002) of the Company's share option plan. On February 18, 2005, the nominal capital of Adidas-Salomon AG amounted to €117,606,528 and is divided into 45,940,050 no-par-value bearer shares. Capital reserves thus increased by €5,363,524.50 in 2005.

Authorized Capital

Pursuant to §4 section 2 to 4 of the Articles of Association of Adidas-Salomon AG, the Executive Board shall be entitled, subject to Supervisory Board approval, to increase nominal capital until May 31, 2005.

- By issuing new shares against contributions in cash or in kind once or several times by no more than a maximum of €3,579,043.17 and, subject to Supervisory Board approval, to exclude shareholders' subscription rights (Authorized Capital III);

Until July 26, 2005

- By issuing new shares against contributions in cash once or several times by no more than €42,800,000 altogether and, subject to Supervisory Board approval, to exclude fractional shares from shareholders' subscription rights (Authorized Capital I);

Until July 14, 2009

- By issuing new shares against contributions in cash once or several times by no more than a maximum of €11,600,000 and, subject to Supervisory Board approval, to exclude shareholders' subscription rights as far as fractional shares are concerned or when issuing new shares at a price not essentially below the stock exchange price (Authorized Capital II).

Contingent Capital

As set out in §4 section 4 of the Company's Articles of Association, in the version dated January 26, 2005, the nominal capital of Adidas-Salomon AG was increased conditionally by up to €1,987,424 through the issuance of not more than 776,337 no-par-value bearer shares (Contingent Capital 1999) for the purpose of granting stock option in connection with the Management Share Option Plan to members of the executive board of Adidas-Salomon AG as well as to managing directors/senior vice presidents of its affiliated companies and to other executives of Adidas-Salomon AG and of its affiliated companies.

As a result of the exercise of 405,250 stock options and the issuance of 405,250 no-par-value bearer shares associated with three exercise periods of Tranche II (2000), three exercise periods of

Tranche III (2001) and one exercise period of Tranche IV (2002) of the stock option plan ending in January, July and October 2004, the nominal amount of Contingent Capital I at the balance sheet date amounted to €2,194,912, divided into 857,387 no-par-value bearer shares.

As a result of the exercise of 81,050 stock options and the issuance of 81,050 no-par-value bearer shares associated with the eighth exercise period of Tranche II (2000) and the fifth exercise period of Tranche III (2001) as well as the second exercise period of Tranche IV (2002) of the Management Share Option Plan in January 2005, the nominal amount of Contingent Capital I was reduced after the balance sheet date to €1,987,424, divided into 776,337 no-par-value bearer shares.

The entry of the respective changes to the Articles of Association into the Commercial Register was made on January 26, 2005.

In accordance with §4 section 6 of the Company's Articles of Association, the nominal capital is conditionally increased by up to a further €23,040,000, divided into not more than 9,000,000 no-par-value bearer shares (Contingent Capital 2001). The contingent capital increase will be implemented only to the extent that the holders of the subscription or conversion rights or the persons obligated to exercise subscription or conversion duties based on the bonds with warrants or convertible bonds, which are issued or guaranteed by the Company or a wholly owned direct or indirect subsidiary of the Company pursuant to the authorization of the Executive Board on the basis of the shareholder resolution dated May 8, 2003, make use of their subscription or conversion right or, if they are obligated to exercise the subscription or conversion rights, they meet their obligations to exercise the warrant or convert the bond. The Executive Board is authorized, subject to Supervisory Board approval, to fully suspend the shareholders' rights to subscribe the bonds with warrants and/or convertible bonds if the Executive Board has concluded following an examination in accordance with its legal duties that the issue price of the bonds with warrants and/or convertible bonds is not significantly below the hypothetical market value computed using recognized financial calculation methods. This authorization to suspend the subscriptions rights applies, however, only with respect to the bonds with warrants and/or convertible bonds with subscription or conversion rights to the shares having a pro rata amount of registered share capital totaling a maximum of €11,600,000.

The nominal value of Contingent Capital 2003 as at the balance sheet date amounted to €23,040,000, as a conversion of the bonds was not yet possible by that date. The requirements for the exercise of the conversion right, pursuant to §6 section 5(a) of the Terms and Conditions of the Convertible Bond issued by Adidas-Salomon International Finance B.V., were met on December 31, 2004, as the XERTA quotation of the Adidas-Salomon shares on at least 20 trading days within a period of 30 consecutive trading days, ending on the last trading day of this calendar year, exceeded 110% of the relevant conversion price. On February 18, 2005, the nominal value of Contingent Capital 2003 still amounts to €23,040,000, as the bondholders entitled to convert have not made us of the right to conversion of their bonds into shares.

The conversion right may be exercised during the period commencing on January 1, 2005 and ending on September 20, 2018, subject to the expiration of the conversion right according to §6 section 3 or subject to the excluded period specified in §6 section 4 of the Terms and Conditions of the Convertible Bond.

By resolution of the Annual General Meeting held on May 13, 2004, Contingent Capital II resolved upon by the Annual General Meeting of May 10, 2001, in the amount of up to €23,040,000, was canceled, as such contingent capital could no longer be used following the entry with the Commercial Register on June 26, 2003, of the cancellation of the Company's authorization to issue bonds with warrants and convertible bonds.

On the occasion of the Annual General Meeting on May 13, 2004, the shareholders resolved upon creation of a further contingent capital and the authorization to issue bonds with warrants and convertible bonds. In accordance with such new §4 section 7 of the Articles of Association, entered into the Commercial Register on July 27, 2004, the nominal capital is conditionally increased by up to a further €9,100,000, divided into not more than 3,554,687 no-par-value bearer shares. The contingent capital increase will only take place to the extent that the holders of the subscription or conversion rights or the persons obligated to exercise the subscription or conversion duties based on the bonds with warrants or convertible bonds, which are issued or guaranteed by the Company or a subsidiary of the Company pursuant the authorization of the Executive Board on the basis of the shareholder resolution dated May 13, 2004, make use of their subscription or conversion right or, if they are obligated to exercise the subscription or conversion rights, they meet their obligations to exercise the warrant or convert the bond. The Executive Board is authorized, subject to Supervisory Board approval, to fully suspend the shareholders' rights to subscribe the bonds with warrants and/or convertible bonds, if the bonds with warrants and/or convertible bonds are issued at a price which is not significantly below the market value of these bonds. The limit for subscription right exclusions of 10% of the registered stock capital according to §186 section 3 sentence 4 together with §221 section 4 sentence 2 of the German Stock Corporation Act is observed.

Acquisition of own shares

By resolution of the Annual General Meeting held on May 13, 2004, the shareholders of Adidas-Salomon AG authorized the Company to acquire its own shares in an aggregate amount up to 10% of the nominal capital for any permissible purpose until November 12, 2005. The report of the Executive Board stated in particular the following purposes for such acquisition:

- For the resale of shares against cash at a price not significantly below the stock market price of the shares with the same features.
- For the purpose of acquiring companies, parts of companies, or participations in companies.
- As consideration for the acquisition of industrial property rights such as patents, brands, names and logos of athletes, sports clubs and other third parties or for the acquisition of licenses relating to such rights.
- To meet subscription or conversion rights or conversion obligations arising from bonds with warrants and/or convertible bonds issued by the Company or any direct or indirect subsidiary of the Company
- To meet the Company's obligations arising from the Management Share Option Plan (MSOP).
- To assign to Executive Board members as compensation in the form of a stock bonus subject to the provision that a resale shall only be permitted following a retention period of at least two years from the date of assignment.

It is stipulated that the acquisition of companies or participations, industrial property rights or licenses may also be made via subsidiaries.

Distributable Profits and Dividends

Distributable profits to shareholders are determined by reference to the retained earnings of Adidas-Salomon AG and calculated under German Commercial Law.

The Executive Board of Adidas-Salomon AG recommends a dividend of €1.30 for 2004, subject to Annual General Meeting approval. The dividend for 2003 was €1.00 per share.

Currently, 45,859,000 no-par-value shares carry dividend rights. It is proposed accordingly that retained earnings of Adidas-Salomon AG as at December 31, 2004, be appropriated as follows:

Appropriation of Retained Earnings of Adidas-Salomon AG € in thousands

Retained earnings of Adidas-Salomon AG as at December 31, 2004	68,691
Less: dividend of €1.30 per share	59,617
Retained earnings carried forward	9,074

Due to the possibility to by back shares, the amount to be distributed to shareholders may change, as a result of the change in the number of shares carrying dividend rights, prior to the Annual General Meeting.

Novartis AG
For the year ended December 31, 2004

Notes to the financial statements

26. Employee share participation plans

Employee and management share participation plans can be separated into share option plans and share plans.

Share option plans. In 2004, the Board of Directors adopted the following modification to the Share Option Plans. Participants have the choice to receive their share option award in the form of share options, or restricted shares, or in equal parts in share options and restricted shares. An exchange ratio of share options to shares is set by the Board. For 2004, four share options could be exchanged for one restricted share. Shares granted have a restriction period identical to the vesting period of the share options. Executives and employees participating in the Share Option Plans were granted 792,470 shares for the Novartis Share Option Plan and 1,439,567 shares for the Novartis US ADS Incentive Plan.

Novartis Share Option Plan. Under the current plan, tradable share options are granted annually as part of the remuneration of executives and other employees, as selected by the Board's Compensation Committee. In 2004, except for Switzerland the vesting period was changed for the 2004 grants only from a two-year vesting period to a three-year vesting period and the term was changed for all grants from nine years to ten years. Each option entitles the holder to acquire one Novartis AG share at predetermined exercise price. In May 2001, the Novartis AG shares were split 40 to 1. Options granted prior to that date entitled the holder to acquire 40 Novartis AG shares per option. The figures in the tables below have been restated for grants before 2002 to reflect this change. The number of options granted depends on the performance of the individuals and the Business Unit in which they work.

| | 2004 | | 2003 | |
| | *Options* | *Weighted-average exercise price* | *Options* | *Weighted-average exercise price* |
	(millions)	*($)*	*(millions)*	*($)*
Options outstanding at January 1	21.0	44.3	11.5	43.6
Granted	4.9	46.1	9.8	36.4
Exercised	(6.3)	37.6	(0.1)	36.0
Canceled	(1.0)	37.4	(0.2)	36.0
Outstanding at December 31	18.6	48.1	21.0	44.3
Exercisable at December 31	5.0	54.6	6.0	47.8
Weighted-average fair value of options granted during the year ($)		11		15

All options were granted at an exercise price which was equal to or greater than the market price of the Group's shares at the grant date.

The following table summarizes information about share options outstanding at December 31, 2004:

| | Options outstanding | | | Options exercisable | |
Range of exercise prices	*Number outstanding* *(millions)*	*Average remaining contractual life* *(years)*	*Weighted average exercise price* *($)*	*Number exercisable* *(millions)*	*Weighted average exercise price* *($)*
35-39	0.2	2.1	37.4	0.2	37.4
40-44	9.0	7.1	43.1	0.1	42.8
45-49	0.6	4.2	45.2	0.5	45.2
50-54	7.5	7.4	52.1	2.8	54.7
55-59					
60-64	1.3	4.5	61.2	1.4	61.2
Total	18.6	6.9	48.1	5.0	54.6

Novartis US ADS Incentive Plan. The US ADS Incentive Plan was introduced in 2001 and supplements the previous US Managements ADS Appreciation Cash Plan. Under the US ADS Incentive Plan, options are granted annually on Novartis ADS at a predetermined exercise price as part of the remuneration of the US-based executives and other selected employees. As of 2004, options granted under this plan are tradable. The number of options granted depends on the performance of the individuals and of the Division/Business Unit in which they work. Options are exercisable after three years and terminate after ten years. Under the previous US Management ADS Appreciation Cash Plan, Novartis US-based employees in the USA were entitled to cash compensation equivalent to the increase in the value of Novartis ADSs compared to the market price of the ADSs at the grant date.

	2004		2003	
	ADS Options (millions)	Weighted-average Exercise price ($)	ADS Options (millions)	Weighted-average exercise price ($)
Options outstanding at January 1	40.6	37.7	23.2	39.3
Granted	9.2	46.1	20.0	36.4
Exercised	(2.4)	40.8	(0.1)	41.8
Canceled	(3.3)	38.5	(2.5)	38.0
Outstanding at December 31	44.1	39.1	40.6	37.7
Exercisable at December 31	6.3	42.5	1.2	38.8
Weighted-average fair values of options granted during the year ($)		16		17

All ADS options were granted at an exercise price which was equal to the market price of the ADS at the grant date.

The following table summarizes information about ADS options outstanding at December 31, 2004:

	ADS Options outstanding		ADS Options exercisable	
Range of exercise prices	Number outstanding (millions)	Average remaining contractual life (years)	Weighted-average exercise price ($)	Number exercisable (millions)	Weighted-average exercise price ($)
30-34	0.1	5.2	33.9	0.1	34.2
35-39	30.6	6.7	36.8	1.0	38.2
40-44	5.3	5.2	41.9	5.1	43.4
45-49	8.1	8.1	46.1	0.1	45.4
Total	44.1	6.8	39.1	6.3	42.5

Share plans

Long-Term Performance Plan. This plan is offered to selected executives. Under the Long-Term Performance Plan, participants are awarded the right to earn Novartis AG shares. Actual payouts, if any, are determined with the help of a formula which measures, among other things, Novartis' performance using economic value added relative to predetermined strategic plan targets. Additional functional objectives may be considered in the evaluation of performance. If performance is below the threshold level of the predetermined targets, no shares will be earned. During 2004 a total of 411,041 shares (2003: 507,507 shares) were granted to executives.

Leveraged Share Savings Plan. Participants under this plan can make an election to receive all or part of their annual incentive award in Novartis AG shares. Shares received under the plan are blocked for a five-year period after the grant date. At the end of the blocking period, Novartis will match the respective shares on a one-for-one basis. During 2004, 254,390 shares (2003: 279,619 shares) were granted to participants.

Swiss Employee Share Ownership Plan. The Swiss Employee Share Ownership Plan (ESOP) provides for the annual variable incentive to be delivered wholly in the form of Novartis AG shares at a fixed date at a fair market value at that date. Employees are free to sell 50% or 100% of these shares immediately. Shares received under the plan have a three-year blocking period and are matched with one share for every two shares held at the end of the blocking period. In 2004 the Swiss employees received 3,080,673 shares (2003: 3,942,687 shares) under this scheme.

Restricted Share Plan. Under the Restricted Share Plan, employees may be granted restricted share awards either as a result of a general grant or as a result of an award based on having met certain performance criteria. Shares granted under this Plan generally have a five-year vesting period. During 2004 a total of 485,609 shares (2003: 390,053 shares) were granted to executives and selected employees.

Movements in Novartis AG shares held by the Novartis Foundation for Employee Participation were as follows:

	2004 Number of shares (000)	2003 Number of shares (000)
January 1	93,300	95,072
Shares bought, net	857	1,163
Shares distributed to employees	(6,839)	(2,935)
December 31	87,318	93,300

The market value of the Novartis AG shares held by the Foundation at December 31, 2004, was €4.4 billion (2003: €4.2 billion).

Nestlé S.A.
For the year ended December 31, 2004

19. Share capital

	2004	2003
Number of registered shares of nominal value CHF 1 each	403,520,000	403,520,000
In millions of CHF	404	404

According to article 6 of the Company's Articles of Association, no natural person or legal entity may be registered as a shareholder with the right to vote for shares which it holds, directly or indirectly, in excess of 3% of the share capital. In addition, article 14 provides that, on exercising the voting rights, no shareholder, through shares owned or represented, may aggregate, directly or indirectly, more than 3% of the total share capital.

At December 31, 2004, the Share Register showed 194,554 registered shareholders. If unprocessed applications for registration and the indirect holders of shares under American Depositary Receipts are also taken into account, the total number of shareholders probably exceeds 250,000. The Company was not aware of any shareholder holding, directly or indirectly, 3% or more of the share capital.

Conditional increase in share capital. According to the Articles of Association, the share capital may be increased, though the exercise of conversion or option rights, by a maximum of CHF 10,000,000 by the issue of a maximum of 10,000,000 registered shares with a nominal value of CHF 1 each. Thus the Board of Directors has at its disposal a flexible instrument enabling it, if necessary, to finance the activities of the Company through convertible debentures or the issue of bonds with warrants.

20. Changes in equity

In millions of CHF

	Share capital	General reserve[a]	Reserve for own shares[a][b]	Special reserve	Retained earnings	Total
At January 1, 2004	404	3,934	2,458	14,041	3,616	24,453
Appropriation of profit to special reserve				757	(757)	
Profit for the year					2,844	2,844
Dividend for 2003					(2,800)	(2,800)
Movement of own shares		(161)	161			
Dividend on own shares held on the payment date of 2003 dividend					19	(19)
Dividend on own shares in respect of which the corresponding option rights were not exercised by the payment date of 2003 dividend					39	(39)
In millions of CHF						
At 31 December 2004	404	3,773	2,619	14,856	2,845	24,497

(a) The general reserve and the reserve for own shares constitute the legal reserves.
(b) See note 21

21. Reserve for own shares

At December 31, 2003, the reserve for own shares amounting to CHF 2,458 million, represented the cost of 7,830,655 freely available shares acquired by a Group company (of which, 4,336,922 shares were reserved to cover options rights granted since 2001 in favor of members of the Group's Management), as well as 665,302 shares reserved to cover option rights granted up to the year 2000, 3,524,490 shares earmarked to cover warrants attached to bond issues of an affiliated company and 3,551,694 shares held for trading purposes.

During the year, a total of 2,367,535 shares have been acquired at a cost of CHF 715 million and 1,771,498 shares have been sold for a total amount of CHF 3,573 million (including 92,972 that represented shares for which options were exercised during the year).

At December 31, 2004, 7,808,609 freely available shares were held by a Group company at an acquisition cost of CHF 28 million. The Board of Directors has decided that these shares will be earmarked for Nestlé Group companies' renumeration plans in Nestlé S.A. shares and options thereon (including the Share Plan of the Board of Directors, the Short Term Bonus-Share Plan of the Executive Board and the Management Stock Option Plan 2001 onwards, under which a total of 6,073,311 options was outstanding at December 31, 2004). As long as these shares are held by the Group company, they will be recorded in the Share Register as being without voting rights and will not rank for dividends. In addition to these, 4,262,759 shares were held for trading purposes, 572,330 shares were reserved to cover Management option rights granted before 2001 and 3,524,490 shares were earmarked to cover warrants attached to bond issues of an affiliated company. As long as the options and warrants are not exercised, or the shares sold, these shares are also recorded in the Share Register as being without voting rights and do not rank for dividends.

The total of 16,168,188 own shares held at December 31, 2004 represents 4.0% of Nestlé S.A.'s share capital.

18 EARNINGS PER SHARE

PERSPECTIVE AND ISSUES

Investors and other consumers of corporate financial information are generally anxious to identify a "shorthand" means of measuring an entity's performance, notwithstanding oft-voiced concerns that any condensed gauge of earnings inevitably runs the risk of being an incomplete, and even misleading, picture of results for the period. The accounting profession had long opposed publications of earnings per share data, because of the perceived peril of offering a distorted picture of the entity's economic performance. Nonetheless, investors in particular are devoted users of earning per share data, which is taken by many to be the single best predictor of the entity's future performance. Ultimately, recognizing that such statistics were being computed in widely varying ways and then broadly disseminated, the accounting standard setters decided to at least impose uniform practices.

The IFRS addressing earnings per share (EPS) is IAS 33. It requires that one measure—or two measures in the case of reporting entities having complex capital structures—be presented for each period for which an income statement is being reported. The principal goal in these measures is to ensure that the number of shares used in the computation(s) fully reflects the impact of dilutive securities, including those which may not be outstanding during the period, but which, if they were to become outstanding, would impact the actual future earnings available for allocation to current shareholders.

When the entity's capital structure is uncomplicated, EPS is computed by simply dividing net income (or loss) by the average number of outstanding equity shares. The computation becomes more complicated with the existence of securities that, while not presently equity shares, have the potential of causing additional equity shares to be issued in future, thereby diluting each currently outstanding share's claim to future earnings. Examples of such dilutive securities include convertible preference shares and convertible debt, as well as various options and warrants. It was long recognized that if calculated earnings per share were to ignore these potentially dilutive securities, there would be a great risk of misleading current shareholders regarding their claim to future earnings of the reporting entity.

The IFRS on EPS computations was the result of a joint international effort to refine the EPS measurements then in common use. Revised IAS 33 largely presaged the latest iteration of the requirement under US GAAP, which is set forth in FAS 128. The purpose of IAS 33 is to prescribe the ground rules for the determination and presentation of earnings per share.

As the name of the measure indicates, EPS is derived by dividing a measure of earnings by a measure of number of common shares. The standard emphasizes the denominator of the earnings per share calculation and notes that even though EPS calculations have limitations—because different accounting policies typically can be used in the determination of earnings, which is in the numerator of the equation—a consistently determined denominator enhances the consistency and meaningfulness of financial reporting.

IAS 33 states that the standard's applicability is both to enterprises whose ordinary shares or potential ordinary shares are publicly traded, and those entities that are in the process of issuing ordinary shares or potential ordinary shares in public securities markets. While IAS 33 does not define the point in the share issuance process when these requirements become effective, in practice this ambiguity has not been a source of difficulty.

Some private entities wish to report a statistical measure of performance, and often choose to use EPS as the well-understood yardstick to employ. While these entities are not required to issue EPS data, when they elect to do so they must also comply with the requirements of IAS 33.

In situations when both parent company and consolidated financial statements are presented, IAS 33 stipulates that the information called for by this standard need only be presented for consolidated information. The reason for this rule is that users of financial statements of a parent company are interested in the results of operations of the group as a whole, as opposed to the parent company on a stand-alone basis. Of course, nothing prevents the enterprise from also presenting the parent-only information, including EPS, should it choose to do so. Again, the requirements of IAS 33 would have to be met by those making such an election.

Certain changes were made to IAS 33 effective in 2005. The objective was to reduce or eliminate alternatives, redundancies and conflicts within IFRS, to address certain convergence issues, and to make selective but minor improvements. The resulting revision to IAS 33 provides additional guidance and illustrative examples on selected complex matters, including the impact of contingently issuable shares; potential common shares of subsidiaries, joint ventures or associates; participating equity instruments; written put options; purchased put and call options; and mandatorily convertible instruments. The fundamental approach to the determination and presentation of earnings per share set forth by IAS 33 was not reexamined, however. These changes are discussed in this chapter.

Sources of IFRS
IAS 33 *SIC* 24

DEFINITIONS OF TERMS

A number of terms used in a discussion of earnings per share have special meanings in that context. When used, they are intended to have the meanings given in the following definitions.

Antidilution. An increase in earnings per share or reduction in net loss per share, resulting from the inclusion of a potentially dilutive security, in EPS calculations.

Basic earnings per share. The amount of net profit or loss for the period that is attributable to each ordinary share that is outstanding during all or part of the period.

Call price. The amount at which a security may be redeemed by the issuer at the issuer's option.

Common stock. A stock that is subordinate to all other stocks of the issuer. Also known as ordinary shares.

Common stock equivalent. This expression is used under US GAAP to denote a security which, because of its terms or the circumstances under which it was issued, is in substance equivalent to common stock. There is no directly equivalent concept under IFRS.

Contingent issuance. A possible issuance of ordinary (equity) shares, for little or no consideration, that is dependent on the exercise of conversion rights, options, or warrants, and the satisfaction of certain conditions set forth in a contingent issuance, or similar arrangement.

Conversion price. The price that determines the number of ordinary (equity) shares into which a security is convertible. For example, €100 face value of debt convertible into five ordinary (equity) shares would be stated to have a conversion price of €20.

Conversion rate. The ratio of (1) the number of common shares issuable on conversion to (2) a unit of convertible security. For example, a preference share may be convertible at the rate of three ordinary shares for each preference share.

Conversion value. The current market value of the common shares obtainable on conversion of a convertible security, after deducting any cash payment required on conversion.

Diluted earnings per share. The amount of net profit for the period per share, reflecting the maximum dilutions that would have resulted from conversions, exercises, and other contingent issuances that individually would have decreased earnings per share and in the aggregate would have had a dilutive effect.

Dilution. A reduction in earnings per share or an increase in net loss per share, resulting from the assumption that convertible securities have been converted and/or that options and warrants have been exercised, or other contingent shares have been issued on the fulfillment of certain conditions. Securities that would cause such earnings dilution are referred to as dilutive securities.

Dual presentation. The presentation with equal prominence of two different earnings per share amounts on the face of the income statement: One is basic earnings per share; the other is diluted earnings per share.

Earnings per share. The amount of earnings for a period attributable to each ordinary (equity) share (common stock). For convenience, the term is used in IAS 33 to refer to either net income (earnings) per share or net loss per share. It should be used without qualifying language (e.g., diluted) only when no potentially dilutive convertible securities, options, warrants, or other agreements providing for contingent issuances of ordinary (equity) shares are outstanding.

Exercise price. The amount that must be paid for a ordinary (equity) share on exercise of a stock option or warrant.

If-converted method. A method of computing earnings per share data that assumes conversion of convertible securities as of the beginning of the earliest period reported (or at time of issuance, if later). This method was mandated under US GAAP and can be analogized to IFRS when appropriate.

Option. The right to purchase ordinary (equity) shares in accordance with an agreement upon payment of a specified amount including, but not limited to, options granted to and stock purchase agreements entered into with employees.

Ordinary shares. Those shares that are subordinate to all other stocks of the issuer. Also known as common stock.

Potential common (ordinary) shares. A financial instrument or other contract which could result in the issuance of common shares to the holder. Examples include convertible debt or preferred shares, warrants, options, and employee stock purchase plans.

Put option. Contract which gives the holder the right to have the issuer (the reporting entity) repurchase shares held, at a specified price, usually for a limited stipulated time period.

Redemption price. The amount at which a security is required to be redeemed at maturity or under a sinking-fund arrangement.

Senior security. Any security having preferential rights and which is neither an ordinary (equity) share nor a common stock equivalent (as defined above). A nonconvertible preference share is an example of a senior security.

Time of issuance. The time of issuance generally is the date when agreement as to terms has been reached and announced, even though such agreement is subject to certain further actions, such as directors' or stockholders' approval.

Treasury stock method. A method of recognizing the use of proceeds that would be obtained on exercise of options and warrants in computing earnings per share. It assumes that any proceeds would be used to purchase ordinary (equity) shares at current market prices.

Warrant. A security giving the holder the right to purchase shares of common stock in accordance with the terms of the instrument, usually on payment of a specified amount.

Weighted-average number of shares. The number of shares determined by relating (1) the portion of time within a reporting period that a particular number of shares of a certain security has been outstanding to (2) the total time in that period. For example, if 100 shares of a certain security were outstanding during the first quarter of a fiscal year and 300 shares were outstanding during the balance of the year, the weighted-average number of outstanding shares would be 250 [=(100 × 1/4) + (300 × 3/4)].

CONCEPTS, RULES, AND EXAMPLES

Simple Capital Structure

A simple capital structure may be said to exist either when the capital structure consists solely of common, or ordinary (equity), shares or when it includes no potential ordinary shares, which could be in the form of options, warrants, or other rights, that on conversion or exercise could, in the aggregate, dilute earnings per share. Dilutive securities are essentially those that exhibit the rights of debt or other senior security holders (including warrants and options) and which have the potential on their issuance to reduce the earnings per share.

Computational guidelines. In its simplest form, the EPS calculation is net income divided by the weighted-average number of common, or ordinary, shares outstanding. The objective of the EPS calculation is to determine the amount of earnings available to each ordinary share. Complexities arise because net income does not necessarily represent the earnings available to the ordinary shareholder, and a simple weighted-average of ordinary shares outstanding does not necessarily reflect the true nature of the situation. Adjustments can take the form of manipulations of the numerator or of the denominator of the formula used to compute EPS, as discussed in the following paragraphs.

Numerator. The net income figure used as the numerator in any of the EPS computations must reflect any claims against it by holders of senior securities. The justification for this reduction is that the claims of the senior securities must be satisfied before any income is available to the common, or ordinary, shareholder. These senior securities are usually in the form of preference shares, and the deduction from income is the amount of the dividend declared during the year on the preference shares. If the preference shares are cumulative, the dividend is to be deducted from income (or added to the loss), whether it is declared or not. If preference shares do not have a cumulative right to dividends and current period dividends have been omitted, such dividends should not be deducted in computing EPS. Cumulative dividends in arrears that are paid currently do not affect the calculation of EPS in the current period, since such dividends have already been considered in prior periods' EPS computations. However, the amount in arrears should be disclosed, as should all of the other effects of the rights given to senior securities on the EPS calculation.

Denominator. The weighted-average number of ordinary shares outstanding is used so that the effect of increases or decreases in outstanding shares on EPS data is related to the portion of the period during which the related consideration affected operations. The difficulty in computing the weighted-average exists because of the effect that various transactions have on the computation of ordinary shares outstanding. Although it is impossible to analyze all the possibilities, the following discussion presents some of the more common transactions affecting the number of ordinary shares outstanding. The theoretical construct set forth in these relatively simple examples can be followed in all other situations.

If a company reacquires its own shares (referred to as treasury stock) in countries where it is legally permissible to do so, the number of shares reacquired should be excluded from EPS calculations as of the date of acquisition. The same computational approach holds for the issuance of ordinary shares during the period. The number of shares newly issued is included in the computation only for the period after their issuance date. The logic for this treatment is that since the consideration for the shares was not available to the reporting entity, and hence could not contribute to the generation of earnings, until the shares were issued, the shares should not be included in the EPS computation prior to issuance. This same logic applies to the reacquired shares because the consideration expended in the repurchase of those shares was no longer available to generate earnings after the reacquisition date.

A stock dividend (bonus issue) or a stock (share) split does not generate additional resources or consideration, but it does increase the number of shares outstanding. The increase in shares as a result of a stock split or dividend, or the decrease in shares as a result of a reverse split, should be given retroactive recognition for all periods presented. Thus, even if a stock dividend or split occurs at the end of the period, it is considered effective for the entire period of each (i.e., current and historical) period presented. The reasoning is that a stock dividend or split has no effect on the ownership percentage of the common stockholder, and likewise has no impact on the resources available for productive investment by the reporting entity. As such, to show a dilution in the EPS in the period of the split or dividend would erroneously give the impression of a decline in profitability when in fact it was merely an increase in the shares outstanding due to the stock dividend or split. Furthermore, financial statement users' frame of reference is the number of shares outstanding at the balance sheet date, including shares resulting from the split or dividend, and using this in computing all periods' EPS serves to most effectively communicate to them.

IAS 33 carries this logic one step further by requiring the disclosure of pro forma (adjusted) amounts of basic and diluted earnings per share for the period in case of issue of shares with no corresponding change in resources (e.g., stock dividends or splits) occurring *after* the balance sheet date, *but before* the issuance of the financial statements. The reason given is that the nondisclosure of such transactions would affect the ability of the users of the financial statements to make proper evaluations and decisions. It is to be noted, however, that the EPS numbers as presented on the face of the income statement are not required by IAS 33 to be retroactively adjusted, as is the case under US GAAP, because such transactions do not reflect the amount of capital used to produce the net profit or loss for the period.

Complications also arise when a business combination occurs during the period. The treatment of the additional shares depends on the nature of the combination. If the business combination is recorded as a uniting of interests, the additional shares are assumed to have been issued at the beginning of the year regardless of when the combination occurred. Conversely, if the combination is accounted for as an acquisition, the shares are considered issued and outstanding as of the date of acquisition. The reason for this varied treatment lies in the income statement treatment accorded a uniting of interests (accounted for as a pooling) versus an acquisition (accounted for as a purchase). In a uniting of interests, the income of the acquired company is included in the statements for the entire year, whereas in an acquisition, the income is included only for the period after acquisition.

IAS 33 recognizes that in certain countries it is permissible for ordinary shares to be issued in partly paid form, and the standard accordingly stipulates that partly paid instruments should be included as ordinary share equivalents to the extent to which they carry rights (during the financial reporting year) to participate in dividends in the same manner as fully paid shares. Further, in the case of contingently issuable shares (i.e., ordinary shares issuable on fulfillment of certain conditions, such as achieving a certain level of profits or sales), IAS 33 requires that such shares be considered outstanding and included in the computation of basic earnings per share only when all the required conditions have been satisfied.

IAS 33 gives examples of situations where ordinary shares may be issued, or the number of shares outstanding may be reduced, without causing corresponding changes in resources of the corporation. Such examples include bonus issues, a bonus element in other issues such as a rights issue (to existing shareholders), a share split, a reverse share split, and a capital reduction without a corresponding refund of capital. In all such cases the number of ordinary shares outstanding before the event is adjusted, as if the event had occurred at the beginning of the earliest period reported. For instance, in a 5 for 4 bonus issue the number of shares outstanding prior to the issue is multiplied by a factor of 1.25. These and other situations are summarized in the tabular list that follows.

Weighted-Average (W/A) Computation	
Transaction	*Effect on W/A computation*
Common stock outstanding at the beginning of the period	Increase number of shares outstanding by the number of shares
Issuance of common stock during the period	Increase number of shares outstanding by the number of shares issued weighted by the portion of the year the common shares are outstanding
Conversion into common stock	Increase number of shares outstanding by the number of shares converted weighted by the portion of the year shares are outstanding
Company reacquires its stock	Decrease number of shares outstanding by number of shares reacquired times portion of the year outstanding
Stock dividend or split	Increase number of shares outstanding by number of shares issued or increased due to the split
Reverse split	Decrease number of shares outstanding by decrease in shares
Pooling of interest	Increase number of shares outstanding by number of shares issued
Purchase	Increase number of shares outstanding by number of shares issued weighted by the portion of year since the date of acquisition

Rights offerings are used to raise additional capital from existing shareholders. These involve the granting of rights in proportion to the number of shares owned by each shareholder (e.g., one right for each 100 shares held). The right gives the holder the opportunity to purchase a share at a discounted value, as an inducement to invest further in the entity, and in recognition of the fact that, generally, rights offerings are less costly as a means of floating more shares, versus open market transactions which involve fees to brokers. In the case of rights shares, the number of ordinary shares to be used in calculating basic EPS is the number of ordinary shares outstanding prior to the issue, multiplied by the following factor:

$$\frac{\text{Fair value immediately prior to the exercise of the rights}}{\text{Theoretical ex-rights fair value}}$$

There are several ways to compute the theoretical value of the shares on an ex-rights basis. IAS 33 suggests that this be derived by adding the aggregate fair value of the shares immediately prior to exercise of the rights to the proceeds from the exercise, and dividing the total by the number of shares outstanding after exercise.

To illustrate, consider that the entity currently has 10,000 shares outstanding, with a market value of €15 per share, when it offers each holder rights to acquire one new share at €10 for each four shares held. The theoretical value ex-rights would be given as follows:

$$\frac{(10,000 \times €15) + (2,500 \times €10)}{12,500} = \frac{€175,000}{12,500} = €14$$

Thus, the ex-rights value of the ordinary shares is €14 each.

The foregoing do not characterize all possible complexities arising in the EPS computation; however, most of the others occur under a complex structure which is considered in the following section of this chapter. The illustration below applies the foregoing concepts to a simple capital structure.

Example of EPS computation—Simple capital structure

Assume the following information:

Numerator information			*Denominator information*	
a.	Income from ordinary activities before extraordinary items	€130,000	a. Common shares outstanding 1/1/06	100,000
b.	Extraordinary loss (net of tax)	30,000	b. Shares issued for cash 4/1/06	20,000
c.	Net income	100,000	c. Shares issued in 10% stock dividend declared in July 2006	12,000
d.	6% cumulative preference shares, €100 par, 1,000 shrs. issued and outstanding	100,000	d. Shares of treasury stock purchased 10/1/06	10,000

When calculating the numerator, the claims of senior securities (i.e., preference shares) should be deducted to arrive at the earnings attributable to ordinary (equity) shareholders. In this example the preference shares are cumulative. Thus, regardless of whether or not the board of directors declares a preference dividend, holders of the preference shares have a claim of €6,000 (1,000 shares × €100 × 6%) against 2006 earnings. Therefore, €6,000 must be deducted from the numerator to arrive at the net income attributable to the holders of ordinary shares.

Note that any cumulative preference dividends in arrears are ignored in computing this period's EPS since they would have been incorporated into previous periods' EPS calculations. Also note that this €6,000 would have been deducted for noncumulative preferred only if a dividend of this amount had been declared during the period.

There may be various complications resulting from the existence, issuance, or redemption of preferred shares. Thus, if "increasing rate" preferred shares are outstanding—where contractually the dividend rate is lower in early years and higher in later years—the amount of preferred dividends in the early years must be adjusted in order to accrete the value of later, increased dividends, using an effective yield method akin to that used to amortize bond discount. If a premium is paid to preferred shareholders to retire the shares during the reporting period, this payment is treated as additional preferred dividends paid for purposes of EPS computations. Similarly, if a premium is paid (in cash or in terms of improved conversion terms) to encourage the conversion of convertible preferred shares, that payment (including the fair value of additional common shares granted as an inducement) is included in the preferred dividends paid in the reporting period, thereby reducing earnings allocable to common shares for EPS calculation purposes. Contrariwise, if preferred shares are redeemed at a value lower than carrying (book) amount—admittedly, not a very likely occurrence—that amount is used to reduce earnings available for common shareholders in the period, thereby increasing EPS.

The EPS calculations for the foregoing fact pattern follow.

Earnings per common share

On income from continuing operations before extraordinary
items = (€130,000 – €6,000) ÷ Ordinary shares outstanding   =   €1.00
On net income = (€100,000 – €6,000) ÷ Ordinary shares outstanding   =   €0.76

Note that two EPS amounts must be displayed: the EPS attributable to income (profit or loss) from continuing operations, and EPS attributable to net income. However, if income from continuing operations is not captioned on the income statement, the corresponding EPS amount is dispensed with. Only the EPS amounts relating to the parent company, in the case of consolidated (group) financial statements, must be provided.

The computation of the denominator is based on the weighted-average number of ordinary shares outstanding. Recall that use of a simple average (e.g., the sum of year-beginning and year-end outstanding shares, divided by two) is not considered appropriate because it fails to accurately give effect to various complexities. The table below illustrates one way of computing the weighted-average number of shares outstanding. Note that, had share issuances occurred mid-month, the weighted-average number of shares would have been based on the number of days elapsing between events.

Item	Number of shares actually outstanding	Fraction of the year outstanding	Shares times fraction of the year
Number of shares as of beginning of the year 1/1/06	110,000 [100,000 + 10%(100,000)]	12/12	110,000
Shares issued 4/1/06	22,000 [20,000 + 10%(20,000)]	9/12	16,500
Treasury shares purchased 10/1/06	(10,000)	3/12	(2,500)
Weighted-average number of common shares outstanding			124,000

Recall that the stock dividend declared in July is considered to be retroactive to the beginning of the year. Thus, for the period 1/1/06 through 4/1/06, 110,000 shares are considered to be outstanding. When shares are issued, they are included in the weighted-average beginning with the date of issuance. The stock dividend applicable to these newly issued shares is also assumed to have existed for the same period. Thus, we can see that of the 12,000 share dividend, 10,000 shares relate to the beginning balance and 2,000 shares to the new issuance (10% of 100,000 and 20,000, respectively). The purchase of the treasury stock requires that these shares be excluded from the calculation for the remainder of the period after their acquisition date. The figure is subtracted from the calculation because the shares were purchased from those outstanding prior to acquisition. To complete the example, we divided the previously derived numerator by the weighted-average number of common shares outstanding to arrive at EPS.

On income from continuing operations before extraordinary items =
(€130,000 – €6,000) ÷ 124,000 common shares   =   €1.00
On net income = (€100,000 – €6,000) ÷ 124,000 common shares   =   €0.76

Reporting a €0.24 loss per share (€30,000 ÷ 124,000) due to the extraordinary item is optional. The numbers computed above for the EPS based on net income are the only presentation required on the face of the income statement.

Complex Capital Structure

The computation of EPS under a complex capital structure involves all of the complexities discussed under the simple structure and many more. By definition, a complex capital structure is one that has dilutive potential common, or ordinary, shares, which are those that have the potential to be exercised and thereby reduce EPS. The effects of any antidilutive potential ordinary shares (those that increase EPS) is not to be included in the computation of diluted earnings per share. Thus, diluted EPS can never provide a more favorable impression of financial performance than does the basic EPS.

Note that a complex structure requires dual presentation of both basic EPS and diluted EPS even when the basic earnings per share is a loss per share. While previously IFRS permitted nondisclosure of diluted EPS when basic EPS was negative, under the current standard, following the Improvements Project's changes, both basic and diluted EPS must be stated, unless diluted EPS would be antidilutive.

For the purposes of calculating diluted EPS, the net profit attributable to ordinary shareholders and the weighted-average number of shares outstanding should be adjusted for the effects of all the dilutive potential ordinary shares. That is, the dilutive securities are presumed to have been converted or exercised, with common (ordinary) shares outstanding for the entire period, and with income statement effects of the dilutive securities (e.g., interest or dividends) removed from earnings. In removing the effects of dilutive securities that in fact were outstanding during the period, the associated tax effects must also be eliminated, and all consequent changes—such as employee profit-sharing contributions that are based on reported net income—must similarly be adjusted.

According to IAS 33, the numerator, representing the net profit attributable to the ordinary shareholders for the period, should be adjusted by the after-tax effect, if any, of the following items:

1. Interest recognized in the period for the convertible debt which constitutes dilutive potential ordinary shares
2. Any dividends recognized in the period for the convertible preferred shares which constitute dilutive potential ordinary shares, where those dividends have been deducted in arriving at net profit attributable to ordinary shareholders
3. Any other, consequential changes in income or expenses that would result from the conversion of the dilutive potential ordinary shares

For example, the conversion of debentures into ordinary shares will reduce interest expense which in turn will cause an increase in the profit for the period. This will have a consequential effect on contributions based on the profit figure, for example, the employer's contribution to an employee profit-sharing plan. The effect of such consequential changes on income available for common (ordinary) shareholders should be considered in the computation of the numerator of the diluted EPS ratio.

The denominator, which has the weighted number of ordinary shares, should be adjusted (increased) by the weighted-average number of ordinary shares that would have been outstanding assuming the conversion of all dilutive potential ordinary shares.

Example

To illustrate, consider Mumbai Corporation, which has 100,000 shares of ordinary shares outstanding the entire period. It also has convertible debentures outstanding, on which interest of €30,000 was paid during the year. The debentures are convertible into 100,000 shares of stock. Net income after tax (effective rate is 30%) amounts to €15,000, which is net of an employee profit-sharing contribution of €10,000, determined as 40% of after-tax income. Basic EPS is €15,000 ÷ 100,000 shares = €0.15. Diluted EPS assumes that the debentures were converted at the beginning of the year, thereby averting €30,000 of interest which, after tax effect, would add

€21,000 to net results for the year. Conversion also would add 50,000 shares, for a total of 200,000 shares outstanding. Furthermore, had operating results been boosted by the €21,000 of avoided after-tax interest cost, the employee profit sharing would have increased by €21,000 × 40% = €8,400, producing net results for the year of €15,000 + €21,000 − €8,400 = €27,600. Diluted EPS is thus €27,600 ÷ 200,000 = €0.138. Since this is truly dilutive, IFRS requires display of this amount.

Determining Dilution Effects

In the foregoing example, the assumed conversion of the convertible debentures proved to be dilutive. If it had been *antidilutive,* display of the (more favorable) diluted EPS would not be permitted under IFRS. To ascertain whether the effect would be dilutive or anti-dilutive, each potential ordinary share issue (i.e., each convertible debenture, convertible preferred, or other issuance outstanding having distinct terms) must be evaluated separately from other potential ordinary share issuances. Since the interactions among potential ordinary share issues might cause diluted EPS to be moderated under certain circumstances, it is important that each issue be considered in the order of decreasing effect on dilution. In other words, the most dilutive of the potential ordinary share issues must be dealt with first, then the next-most dilutive, and so on.

Potential ordinary shares are generally deemed to have been outstanding common shares for the entire reporting period. However, if the potential shares were only first issued, or became expired or were otherwise cancelled during the reporting period, then the related ordinary shares are deemed to have been outstanding for only a portion of the reporting period. Similarly, if potential share are exercised during the period, then for that part of the year the actual shares outstanding are included for purposes of determining basic EPS, and the potential (i.e., unexercised) shares are used in the determination of diluted EPS by deeming these to have been exercised or converted for only that fraction of the year before the exercise occurred.

To determine the sequencing of the dilution analysis, it is necessary to use a "trial and error" approach. However, options and warrants should be dealt with first, since these will not affect the numerator of the EPS equation, and thus are most dilutive in their impact. Convertible securities are dealt with subsequently, and these issues will affect both numerator and denominator, with varying dilutive effects.

Options and warrants. The exercise of options and warrants results in proceeds being received by the reporting entity. If actual exercise occurs, of course, the entity has resources which it will, logically, put to productive use, thereby increasing earnings to be enjoyed by ordinary shareholders (both those previously existing and those resulting from exercising their options and warrants). However, the presumed exercise for purposes of diluted EPS computations does not invoke actual resources being received, and earnings are not enhanced as they might have been in the case of actual exercise. If this fact were not dealt with, diluted EPS would be unrealistically depressed since the number of assumed shares would be increased but earnings would reflect the lower, actual level of investment being utilized by the entity.

Without using the terminology of the corresponding US GAAP standard, IFRS prescribes the use of the "treasury stock method" set forth in greater detail by US GAAP to deal with the hypothetical proceeds from the presumed option and warrant exercises. This method assumes that the proceeds from the option and warrant exercises would have been used to repurchase outstanding shares, at the average prevailing market price during the reporting period. This assumed repurchase of shares eliminates the need to speculate as to what productive use the hypothetical proceeds from option and warrant exercise would be put, and also reduces the assumed number of outstanding shares for diluted EPS calculation.

| **Treasury Stock Method** |
| Denominator must be increased by net dilution, as follows: |
| Net dilution = Shares issued – Shares repurchased |
| where |
| Shares issued = Proceeds received/Exercise price |
| Shares repurchased = Proceeds received/Average market price per share |

IAS 33's "shortcut" way of expressing the required use of the "treasury stock method" is as follows: "The difference between the number of ordinary shares issued and the number of ordinary shares that would have been issued at the average market price of ordinary shares during the period shall be treated as an issue of ordinary shares for no consideration."

Example

Assume the reporting entity issued 1,000 common shares to option holders who exercised their rights and paid €15,000 to the entity. During the reporting period, the average price of ordinary shares was €25. Using the proceeds of €15,000 to acquire shares at a per share cost of €25 would have resulted in the purchase of 600 shares. Thus, a net of 400 additional shares would be assumed outstanding for the year, at no net consideration to or from the entity.

In all cases where the exercise price is lower than the market price, assumed exercise will be dilutive and some portion of the shares will be deemed issued for no consideration. If the exercise price is greater than the average market price, the exercise should not be assumed since the result of this would be antidilutive.

Convertible instruments. Convertible instruments are assumed to be converted when the effect is dilutive. Convertible preferred shares will be dilutive if the preferred dividend declared (or, if cumulative, accumulated) in the current period is lower than the computed basic EPS. If the contrary situation exists, the impact of assumed conversion would be antidilutive, which is not permitted by IFRS.

Similarly, convertible debt is dilutive, and thus assumed to have been converted, if the after-tax interest, including any discount or premium amortization, is lower than the computed basic EPS. If the contrary situation exists, the assumption of conversion would be antidilutive, and thus not to be taken into account for diluted EPS computations.

While the term used under US GAAP is not explicitly employed by IAS 33, the methodology to be employed is essentially identical to the US GAAP-defined "if-converted" method. The if-converted method is used for those securities that are currently sharing in the earnings of the company through the receipt of interest or dividends as senior securities but have the potential for sharing in the earnings as ordinary shares. The if-converted method logically recognizes that the convertible security can only share in the earnings of the company as one or the other, not as both. Thus, the dividends or interest less tax effects applicable to the convertible security as a senior security are not recognized in the net income figure used to compute EPS, and the weighted-average number of shares is adjusted to reflect the conversion as of the beginning of the year (or date of issuance, if later). See the example of the if-converted method for illustration of treatment of convertible securities when they are issued during the period and therefore were not outstanding for the entire year.

Example of the if-converted method

Assume a net income of €50,000 and a weighted-average number of common shares outstanding of 10,000. The following information is provided regarding the capital structure.

1. 7% convertible debt, 200 bonds each convertible into 40 ordinary shares. The bonds were outstanding the entire year. The income tax rate is 40%. The bonds were issued at par (€1,000 per bond). No bonds were converted during the year.

2. 4% convertible, cumulative preferred stock, par €100, 1,000 shares issued and outstanding. Each preferred share is convertible into 2 common shares. The preferred shares were issued at par and were outstanding the entire year. No shares were converted during the year.

The first step is to compute the basic EPS, that is, assuming only the issued and outstanding ordinary shares. This figure is simply computed as €4.60 (€50,000 – €4,000 preferred dividends) ÷ (10,000 ordinary shares outstanding). The diluted EPS must be less than this amount for the capital structure to be considered complex and for a dual presentation of EPS to be necessary.

To determine the dilutive effect of the preferred stock, an assumption (generally referred to as the if-converted method) is made that all of the preferred stock is converted at the earliest date that it could have been during the year. In this example, the date would be January 1. (If the preferred had been first issued during the year, the earliest date conversion could have occurred would have been the issuance date.) The effects of this assumption are twofold: (1) if the preferred is converted, there will be no preferred dividends of €4,000 for the year; and (2) there will be an additional 2,000 shares of common outstanding during the year (the conversion rate is 2 for 1 on 1,000 shares of preferred). Diluted EPS is computed, as follows, reflecting these two assumptions:

$$\frac{\text{Net income}}{\substack{\text{Weighted-average of common shares outstanding} \\ + \textit{Shares issued upon conversion of preferred}}} = \frac{\text{€50,000}}{12,000 \textit{ shares}} = \text{€4.17}$$

The convertible preferred is dilutive because it reduced EPS from €4.60 to €4.17. Accordingly, a dual presentation of EPS is required.

In the example, the convertible bonds are also assumed to have been converted at the beginning of the year. Again, the effects of the assumption are twofold: (1) if the bonds are converted, there will be no interest expense of €14,000 (7% × €200,000 face value), and (2) there will be an additional 8,000 shares (200 bonds × 40 shares) of common stock outstanding during the year. One note of caution, however, must be mentioned; namely, the effect of not having €14,000 of interest expense will increase income, but it will also increase tax expense. Consequently, the net effect of not having interest expense of €14,000 is €8,400 [(1 – 0.40) × €14,000]. Diluted EPS is computed as follows, reflecting the dilutive preferred and the effects noted above for the convertible bonds.

$$\frac{\text{Net income + Interest expense (net of tax)}}{\substack{\text{Weighted-average of common shares outstanding + } \textit{Shares} \\ \textit{issued upon conversion of preferred and conversion of bonds}}} = \frac{\text{€50,000 + €8,400}}{20,000 \text{ shares}} = \text{€2.92}$$

The convertible debt is also dilutive, as it reduces EPS from €4.17 to €2.92. Together the convertible bonds and preferred reduced EPS from €4.60 to €2.92.

Contingent Issuances of Ordinary Shares

As for the computation of basic EPS, shares whose issuance is contingent on the occurrence of certain events are considered outstanding and included in the computation of diluted EPS only if the stipulated conditions have been met (i.e., the event has occurred). If as of the balance sheet date the triggering event has not occurred, issuance of the contingently issuable shares is not to be assumed.

Issuances that are dependent on certain conditions being met can be illustrated as follows. Assume that a condition or requirement exists in a contract to increase earnings over a period of time to a certain stipulated level and that, upon attainment of this targeted level of earnings, the issuance of shares is to take place. This is regarded as a contingent issuance of shares for purposes of applying IAS 33. If the condition is met as of the balance sheet date, the effect is included in basic EPS, even if the actual issuance takes place after year end—(e.g., upon delivery of the audited financial statements, per terms of the contingency agreement).

If the condition must be met and then maintained for a subsequent period, such as for a two-year period, then the effect of the contingent issuance is excluded from basic EPS, but is included in diluted EPS. In other words, the contingent shares, which will not be issued until the defined condition is met for two consecutive years, are assumed to be met for diluted EPS computation if the condition is met at the current balance sheet date. Meeting the terms of the contingency for the current period forms the basis for the expectation that the terms may again be met in the subsequent period, which would trigger the issuance of the added shares, causing dilution of EPS.

In some instances the terms of the contingent issuance arrangement make reference to share prices over a period of time extending beyond the balance sheet date. In such instances, if issuance is to be assumed for purposes of computing diluted EPS, only the prices or other data through the balance sheet date should be deemed pertinent to the computation of diluted EPS. Basic EPS is not affected, of course, since the contingent condition is not met as of the balance sheet date.

IAS 33 identifies circumstances in which the issuance of contingent shares is dependent upon meeting both future earnings and future share price threshold levels. Reference must be made to both these conditions, as they exist at the balance sheet date. If both threshold conditions are met, the effect of the contingently issuable shares is included in the computation of diluted EPS.

The standard also cites circumstances where the contingency does not pertain to market price of ordinary shares or to earnings of the reporting entity. One such example is the achievement of a defined business expansion goal, such as the opening of a targeted number of retail outlets; other examples could be the achievement of defined level of gross revenues, or development of a certain number of commercial contracts. For purposes of computing diluted EPS, the number of retail outlets, level of revenue, etc., as of the balance sheet date are to be presumed to remain constant until the expiration of the contingency period.

Example

Contingent shares will be issued at year-end 2007, with 1,000 shares issued for each retail outlet in excess of the number of outlets at the base date, year-end 2005. At year-end 2006, seven new outlets are open. Diluted EPS should include the assumed issuance of 7,000 additional shares. Basic EPS would not include this, since the contingency period has not ended and no new shares are yet required to be issued.

Contracts Which May Be Settled in Shares or for Cash

Increasingly complex financial instruments have been issued by entities in recent decades. Among these are obligations that are settleable in cash or by the issuance of shares, at the option of the debtor (the reporting entity). Thus, debt may be incurred and later settled, at the entity's option, by increasing the number of its ordinary shares outstanding, thereby diluting EPS but averting the need to disperse its resources for purposes of debt retirement.

Note that this situation differs from convertible debt, discussed above, inasmuch as it is the debtor, not the debt holder, which has the right to trigger the issuance of shares.

Per revised IAS 33, it is to be presumed that the debtor will elect to issue shares to retire this debt, if making that assumption results in a dilution of EPS. This is assumed for the calculation of diluted EPS, but is not included in basic EPS.

A similar result obtains when the reporting entity has written (i.e., issued) a call option to creditors, giving them the right to demand shares instead of cash in settlement of an obligation. Again, if dilutive, share issuance is to be presumed for diluted EPS computation purposes.

Written put options. The entity may also write put options giving shareholders the right to demand that the entity repurchase certain outstanding shares. Exercise is to be presumed if the effect is dilutive. According to IAS 33, the effect of this assumed exercise is to be calculated by assuming that the entity will issue enough new shares, at average market price, to raise the proceeds needed to honor the put option terms.

Example

> If the entity is potentially required to buy back 25,000 of its currently outstanding shares at €40 each, it must assume that it will raise the required €1,000,000 cash by selling new ordinary shares into the market. If the average market price was €35 during the reporting period, it must be assumed that €1,000,000 ÷ €35 = 28,572 shares would be issued, for a net dilution of about 3,572 net ordinary shares, which is used to compute diluted EPS.

The foregoing guidance does not apply, however, to the situation where the reporting entity holds options, such as call options on its own shares, since it is presumed that the options would only be exercised under conditions where the impact would be antidilutive. That is, the entity only would choose to repurchase its optioned shares if the option price were below market price. Similarly, if the entity held a put contract (giving it the right to sell shares to the option writer) on its own shares, it would only exercise this option if the option price were above market price. In either instance, the effect of assumed exercise would likely be antidilutive.

Computations of Basic and Diluted Earnings Per Share

Using the data presented earlier in this chapter, the complete computation of basic and diluted EPS under IAS 33 is shown in the following table:

Items	EPS on outstanding common stock (the "benchmark" EPS) Numerator	Denominator	Basic Numerator	Denominator	Diluted Numerator	Denominator
Net income	€50,000		€50,000		€50,000	
Preferred dividend	(4,000)					
Common shs. outstanding		10,000 shs.		10,000 shs.		10,000 shs.
Conversion of preferred				2,000		2,000
Conversion of bonds					8,400	8,000
Totals	€46,000 ÷	10,000 shs.	€50,000 ÷	12,000 shs.	€58,400 ÷	20,000 shs.
EPS	€4.60		€4.17		€2.92	

The preceding example was simplified to the extent that none of the convertible securities were, in fact, converted during the year. In most real situations, some or all of the securities may have been converted, and thus actual reported earnings (and basic EPS) would already have reflected the fact that preferred dividends were paid for only part of the year and/or that interest on convertible debt was accrued for only part of the year. These factors would need to be taken into consideration in developing a time-weighted numerator and denominator for the EPS equations.

Furthermore, the sequence followed in testing the dilution effects of each of several series of convertible securities may affect the outcome, although this is not always true. It is best to perform the sequential procedures illustrated above by computing the impact of each issue of potential ordinary shares from the most dilutive to the least dilutive. This rule also applies if convertible securities (for which the if-converted method will be applied) and options (for which the treasury stock approach will be applied) are outstanding simultaneously.

Finally, if some potential ordinary shares are only issuable on the occurrence of a contingency, conversion should be assumed for EPS computation purposes only to the extent that the conditions were met as of the balance sheet date. In effect, the end of the reporting period should be treated as if it were also the end of the contingency period.

No antidilution. No assumptions of conversion should be made if the effect would be antidilutive. As in the discussion above, it may be that the sequence in which the different issues or series of convertible or other instruments that are potentially ordinary shares are considered will affect the ultimate computation. The goal in computing diluted EPS is to calculate the maximum dilutive effect. The individual issues of convertible securities, options, and other items should be dealt with from the most dilutive to the least dilutive to effect this result.

Disclosure Requirements under IAS 33

1. Enterprises should present both basic EPS and diluted EPS on the face of the income statement for each class of ordinary shares that has a different right to share in the net profit for the period. Equal prominence should be given to both the basic EPS and diluted EPS figures for all periods presented.

2. Enterprises should present basic EPS and diluted EPS even if the amounts disclosed are negative. In other words, the standard mandates disclosure of not just *earnings per share,* but even *loss per share* figures.

3. Enterprises should disclose amounts used as the numerator in calculating basic EPS and diluted EPS along with a reconciliation of those amounts to the net profit or loss for the period. Disclosure is also required of the weighted-average number of ordinary shares used as the denominator in calculating basic EPS and diluted EPS along with a reconciliation of these denominators to each other.

4. a. In addition to the disclosure of the figures for basic EPS and diluted EPS, as required above, if an enterprise chooses to disclose per share amounts using a reported component of net profit, other than net profit or loss for the period attributable to ordinary shareholders, such amounts should be calculated using the weighted-average number of ordinary shares determined in accordance with the requirements of IAS 33; this will ensure comparability of the per share amounts disclosed;

    b. In cases where an enterprise chooses to disclose the above per share amounts using a component of net profit not reported as a line item in the income statement, a reconciliation is mandated by the standard, which should reconcile the difference between the component of net income used with a line item reported in the income statement; and

    c. When additional disclosure is made by an enterprise of the above per share amounts, basic and diluted per share amounts should be disclosed with equal prominence (just as basic EPS and diluted EPS figures are given equal prominence).

5. Enterprises are encouraged to disclose the terms and conditions of financial instruments or contracts generating potential ordinary shares since such terms and conditions may determine whether or not any potential ordinary shares are dilutive and, if so, the effect on the weighted-average number of shares outstanding and any consequent adjustments to the net profit attributable to the ordinary shareholders.

6. If changes (resulting from a bonus issue or share split, etc.) in the number of ordinary or potential ordinary shares occur after the balance sheet date but before issu-

ance of the financial statements, and the per share calculations reflect such changes in the number of shares, such a fact should be disclosed.

7. Enterprises are also encouraged to disclose a description of ordinary share transactions or potential ordinary share transactions other than capitalization issues and share splits, occurring after the balance sheet date that are of such importance that nondisclosure would affect the ability of the users of the financial statements to make proper evaluations and decisions.

Examples of Financial Statement Disclosures

F. Hoffman-LaRoche
Period Ending December 2004

Earnings per share and nonvoting equity security

Basic earnings per share and nonvoting equity security. For the calculation of basic earnings per share and nonvoting equity security, the number of shares and nonvoting equity securities is reduced by the weighted-average number of its own nonvoting equity securities held by the Group during the period.

| | *Continuing businesses* | | *Group* | |
	2004	*2003*	*2004*	*2003*
Net income (millions of CHF)	4,339	3,074	6,641	3,069
Number of shares (millions)	160	160	160	160
Number of nonvoting equity securities (millions)	703	703	703	703
Weighted-average number of own nonvoting equity securities held (millions)	(22)	(24)	(22)	(24)
Weighted-average number of shares and non-voting equity securities in issue used to calculate basic earnings per share (millions)	841	839	841	839
Basic earnings per share and nonvoting equity security (CHF)	5.16	3.67	7.90	3.66

Diluted earnings per share and nonvoting equity security. For the calculation of diluted earnings per share and nonvoting equity security, the net income and weighted-average number of shares and nonvoting equity securities outstanding are adjusted for the effects of all dilutive potential shares and nonvoting equity securities.

Potential dilutive effects arise from the convertible debt instruments and the employee stock option plans. If the outstanding convertible debt instruments were to be converted, this would lead to a reduction in interest expense and an increase in the number of shares which may have a net dilutive effect on the earnings per share. The exercise of outstanding vested employee stock options would have a dilutive effect. The exercise of the outstanding vested Genentech employee stock options would have a dilutive effect if the net income of Genentech is positive. The diluted earnings per share and nonvoting equity security shows the potential impacts of these dilutive effects on the earnings per share figures.

| | *Continuing businesses* | | *Group* | |
	2004	*2003*	*2004*	*2003*
Net income (millions of CHF)	4,339	3,074	6,641	3,069
Elimination of interest expense, net of tax, of convertible debt instruments, where dilutive (millions of CHF)	15	60	15	60
Increase in minority share of Group net income, net of tax, assuming all outstanding Genentech stock options exercised (millions of CHF)	(31)	(26)	(31)	(26)
Net income used to calculate diluted earnings per share (millions of CHF)	4,323	3,108	6,625	3,103

	Continuing businesses		Group	
	2004	*2003*	*2004*	*2003*
Weighted-average number of shares and nonvoting equity securities in issue (millions)	841	839	841	839
Adjustment for assumed conversion of convertible debt instruments, where dilutive (millions)	8	20	8	20
Weighted-average number of shares and nonvoting equity securities in issue used to calculate dilutive earnings per share (millions)	849	859	849	859
Diluted earnings per share and nonvoting equity security (CHF)	5.09	3.62	7.81	3.61

Mittal Steel South Africa Limited
Period Ending December 2004

	2004	*2003*
Headline earnings	4,541	1,605
Performance per ordinary share		
Attributable earnings per share (cents)		
– Basic	1,093	359
– Diluted	1,093	358
Headline earnings per share (cents)		
– Basic	1,019	360
– Diluted	1,016	359
Dividend per share (cents)		
– Interim	300	100
– Final	100	75

10. Earnings per share

Basic earnings per share is calculated by dividing earnings by the weighted-average number of ordinary shares in issue during the year. The weighted-average number of shares is calculated taking into account the shares issued as disclosed in the directors' report.

For the current year and previous period, shares under option had an effect on the adjusted weighted-average number of shares in issue as the average option price was lower than the average market price.

	Year ended December 31 2004	Six months ended December 31 2003
Attributable earnings		
Net profit attributable to ordinary shareholders (R million)	4,871	463
Basic earnings per share (cents)	1,093	104
Diluted earnings per share (cents)	1,090	103
Headline earnings		
Headline earnings (R million)	4,541	462
Basic earnings per share (cents)	1,019	104
Diluted earnings per share (cents)	1,016	103
Shares in issue		
Weighted-average number of ordinary shares in issue (million)	446	446
Weighted-average number of diluted shares (million)	447	448

HVB Group
Period Ending December 2004

Notes to the financial statements

43. Earnings per share

	2004	*2003*
Net income (loss) adjusted for minority interest (€millions)	(2,278)	(2,639)
Net income (loss) adjusted for minority interest (adjusted) (€millions)	(637)	(292)
Average number of shares	697,096,530	536,288,701
Earnings per share (adjusted)[1]	0.91	0.54
Earnings per share [2]	(3.27)	(4.92)

[1] *2004 figures adjusted for amortization of goodwill, addition to restructuring provisions, and allocation to special provisions for bad debts.*

[2] *2003 figures adjusted for amortization of goodwill, current income and expenses from Norisbank, Bank von Ernst, Bankhaus Bethmann-Mafei, and the nonscheduled items defined in the consolidated financial statements for 2003.*

Nestlé
Period Ending December 2004

Notes to the financial statements

7. Earnings per share

	2004	*2003*
Basic earnings per share in CHF	17.29	16.05
Net profit per income statement (in millions of CHF)	6,717	6,213
Weighted-average number of shares outstanding	388,448,957	387,018,429
Fully diluted earnings per share in CHF	16.96	15.92
Theoretical net profit assuming the exercise of all outstanding options and sale of all treasury shares (in millions of CHF)	6,842	15.92
Number of shares	403,520,000	403,520,000

19 INTERIM FINANCIAL REPORTING

PERSPECTIVE AND ISSUES

Interim financial reports are financial statements covering periods of less than a full fiscal year. Most commonly such reports will be for a period of three months (which are referred to as quarterly financial reports), although in some jurisdictions, tradition calls for semiannual financial reporting. The purpose of quarterly or other interim financial reports is to provide financial statement users with more timely information for making investment and credit decisions, based on the expectation that full-year results will be a reasonable extrapolation from interim performance. Additionally, interim reports can yield significant information concerning trends affecting the business and seasonality effects, both of which could be obscured in annual reports.

The basic objective of interim reporting is to provide frequent and timely assessments of an entity's performance. However, interim reporting has inherent limitations. As the reporting period is shortened, the effects of errors in estimation and allocation are magnified. The proper allocation of annual operating expenses is a significant concern. Because the progressive tax rates of most jurisdictions are applied to total annual income and various tax credits may arise, the accurate determination of interim income tax expense is often difficult. Other annual operating expenses are often concentrated in one interim period, yet benefit the entire year's operations. Examples include advertising expenses and major repairs or maintenance of equipment, which may be seasonal in nature. The effects of seasonal fluctuations and temporary market conditions further limit the reliability, comparability, and predictive value of interim reports. Because of this reporting environment, the issue of independent auditor association with interim financial reports remains problematic.

While some national standards had long existed regarding interim financial reporting—most notably in the United States where the pertinent requirements were established in 1973—IFRS on this topic developed only recently. The standard on interim financial reporting was issued in February 1998.

Two distinct views of interim reporting have been advocated, particularly by US and UK standard setters, but others believe that the distinction is less meaningful than it appears at first blush. The first view holds that the interim period is an integral part of the annual accounting period (the *integral* view), while the second views the interim period as a discrete accounting period of its own (the *discrete* view). Depending on which view is accepted, expenses would either be recognized as incurred, or would be allocated to the interim periods based on forecasted annual activity levels such as sales volume. The integral approach would require more use of estimation, and forecasts of full-year performance would be necessary antecedents for the preparation of interim reports.

Sources of IFRS
IAS 1, 8, 20, 32, 34
IASB's Framework for the Preparation and Presentation of Financial Statements

DEFINITIONS OF TERMS

Discrete view. An approach to measuring interim period income by viewing each interim period separately.

Estimated annual effective tax rate. An expected annual tax rate which reflects estimates of annual earnings, tax rates, tax credits, etc.

Integral view. An approach to measuring interim period income by viewing each interim period as an integral part of the annual period. Expenses are recognized in proportion to revenues earned through the use of special accruals and deferrals.

Interim financial report. An interim financial report refers to either a complete set of financial statements for an interim period (prepared in accordance with the requirements of IAS 1), or a set of condensed financial statements for an interim period (prepared in accordance with the requirements of IAS 34).

Interim period. A financial reporting period shorter than a full financial year (e.g., a period of three or six months).

Last-twelve-months reports. Financial reporting for the twelve-month period which ends on a given interim date.

Seasonality. The normal, expected occurrence of a major portion of revenues or costs in one or two interim periods.

Year-to-date reports. Financial reporting for the period which begins on the first day of the fiscal year and ends on a given interim date.

CONCEPTS, RULES, AND EXAMPLES

Alternative Concepts of Interim Reporting

The argument is often made that interim reporting is generically unlike financial reporting covering a full fiscal year. Two distinct views of interim reporting have developed, representing alternative philosophies of financial reporting. Under the first view, the interim period is considered to be an integral part of the annual accounting period. This view directs that annual operating expenses are to be estimated and then allocated to the interim periods based on forecasted annual activity levels, such as expected sales volume. When this approach is employed, the results of subsequent interim periods must be adjusted to reflect prior estimation errors.

Under the second view, each interim period is considered to be a discrete accounting period, with status equal to a fiscal year. Thus, no estimations or allocations that are different from those used for annual reporting are to be made for interim reporting purposes. The same expense recognition rules should apply as under annual reporting, and no special interim accruals or deferrals are to be permitted. Annual operating expenses are recognized in the interim period in which they are incurred, irrespective of the number of interim periods benefited, unless deferral or accrual would be called for in the annual financial statements.

Proponents of the integral view argue that the unique expense recognition procedures are necessary to avoid creating possibly misleading fluctuations in period-to-period results. Using the integral view results in interim earnings which are hopefully more indicative of annual earnings and, thus, useful for predictive and other decision-making purposes. Proponents of the discrete view, on the other hand, argue that the smoothing of interim results for purposes of forecasting annual earnings has undesirable effects. For example, a turning point in an earnings trend that occurred during the year may be obscured.

Yet others have noted that the distinction between the integral and the discrete approaches is arbitrary and, in fact, rather meaningless. These critics note that interim periods bear the same relationship to full years as fiscal years do to longer intervals in the life cycle of a business, and that all periodic financial reporting necessitates the making of estimates and allocations. Direct costs and revenues are best accounted for as incurred and earned, respectively, which equates a discrete approach in most instances, while many indirect costs are more likely to require that an allocation process be applied, which is suggestive of an integral approach. In short, a mix of methods will be necessary as dictated by the nature of the cost or revenue item being reported upon, and neither a pure integral nor a pure discrete approach could be utilized in practice. The IFRS on interim financial reporting, IAS 34, does, in fact, adopt a mix of the discrete and the integral views, as described more fully below.

Objectives of Interim Financial Reporting: The IASB's Perspective

The purpose of interim financial reporting is to provide information that will be useful in making economic decisions (as, of course, is the purpose of annual financial information). Furthermore, interim financial reporting is expected to provide information specifically about the financial position, performance, and change in financial position of an entity. The objective is general enough to embrace the preparation and presentation of either full financial statements or condensed information.

While accounting is often criticized for looking at an entity's performance through the rearview mirror, in fact it is well understood by standard setters that to be useful, such information must provide insights into future performance. As outlined in the objective of the IASB's standard on interim financial reporting, IAS 34, the primary, but not exclusive, purpose of timely interim period reporting is to provide interested parties (e.g., investors and creditors) with an understanding of the entity's earnings-generating capacity and its cash-flow-generating capacity, which are clearly future-oriented. Furthermore, the interim data is expected to give interested parties not only insights into such matters as seasonal volatility or irregularity, and provide timely notice about changes in patterns or trends, both as to income or cash-generating behavior, but also into such balance-sheet-based phenomena as liquidity.

In reaching the positions set forth in the standard, the International Accounting Standards Committee (IASC, which was the current IASB's predecessor) had considered the importance of interim reporting in identifying the turning points in an entity's earnings or liquidity. It was concerned that the integral approach to interim reporting can mask these turning points and thereby prevent users of the financial statements from taking appropriate actions. If this observation is correct, this would be an important reason to endorse the discrete view. In fact, the extent to which application of an integral approach masks turning points is probably related to the extent of "smoothing" applied to revenue and expense data.

It seems quite reasonable that interim reporting in conformity with the integral view, if done sensitively, could reveal turning points as effectively as would reports prepared under the discrete approach. As support for this assertion, one can consider national economic statistics (e.g., gross national product, unemployment), which are most commonly reported on seasonally adjusted bases, which is analogous to the consequence of utilizing an integral approach to interim reporting of entity financial information. Such economic data is often quite effective at highlighting turning points and is accordingly employed far more typically than is unadjusted monthly data, which would be roughly comparable to reporting under the discrete approach.

While the objectives of interim reporting are highly consistent with those of annual financial reporting, there are further concerns. These involve matters of cost and timeliness, as well as questions of materiality and measurement accuracy. In general, the conclusion is that to be truly useful, the information must be produced in a more timely fashion than is often the case with annual reports (although other research suggests that users' tolerance for delayed information is markedly declining in all arenas), and that some compromises in terms of accuracy may be warranted in order to achieve greater timeliness.

Basic Conclusions about Application of Accounting Principles to Interim Financial Reports

Although a cursory reading of the standard may give the impression that IAS 34 favors a pure discrete view, some of the examples given in Appendix 2 to IAS 34 (e.g., those explaining the accounting treatment of income taxes and employer payroll taxes, or the example which explains the application of the standard to the treatment of contingent lease payments) lead one to believe that, in fact, the IASC pursued an approach which was a combination of the discrete and the integral views.

Most noteworthy, however, is the fact that the approach adopted by IAS 34 is very different from the posture of certain leading national accounting standards, such as that imposed under US GAAP, which mandates the integral view. It is interesting to note, however, that neither standard's position is theoretically pure, in the sense that not all measures are consistent with the stated overall philosophy. Thus, the IASC's approach seems quite balanced. For example, while in IAS 34 the discrete view is endorsed for many purposes, the method of accounting for income taxes prescribed is clearly consistent with an integral view, not a discrete view.

Further, IAS 34 states that interim financial data should be prepared in conformity with accounting policies used in the most recent annual financial statements. The only exception noted is when a change in accounting principle has been adopted since the last year-end financial report was issued. The standard also stipulates that the definitions of assets, liabilities, income, and expenses for the interim period are to be identical to those applied in annual reporting situations.

While IAS 34, in many instances, is quite forthright about declaring its allegiance to the discrete view of interim financial reporting, it does incorporate a number of important exceptions to the principle. These matters are discussed in greater detail below.

Statements and Disclosures to Be Presented in Interim Financial Reports

Content of an interim financial report. Instead of repeating information previously presented in annual financial statements, interim financial reports should preferably focus on new activities, events, and circumstances that have occurred since the date of publication of the latest complete set of financial statements. IAS 34 recognizes the need to keep financial statement users informed about the latest financial condition of the reporting entity, and has thus moderated the presentation and disclosure requirements in the case of interim financial reports. Thus, in the interest of timeliness and with a sensitivity to cost considerations, and also to avoid repetition of information previously (and recently) reported, the standard allows an entity, at its option, to provide information relating to its financial position in a condensed format, in lieu of comprehensive information provided in a complete set of financial statements prepared in accordance with IAS 1. The minimum requirements as to the components of the interim financial statements to be presented (under this option) and their content are discussed later.

IAS 34 sets forth the following three important aspects of interim financial reporting:

- That the above concession (i.e., permitting presentation of condensed financial information) by the standard is not intended to either prohibit or discourage the reporting entity from presenting a complete set of interim financial statements, as defined by IAS 1;
- That even when the choice is made to present condensed interim financial statements, if an entity chooses to add line items or additional explanatory notes to the condensed financial statements, over and above the minimum prescribed by this standard, the standard does not, in any way, prohibit or discourage the addition of such extra information; and
- That the recognition and measurement guidance in IAS 34 applies equally to a complete set of interim financial statements as to condensed interim financial statements. Thus, a complete set of interim financial statements would include not only the disclosures specifically prescribed by this standard, but also disclosures required by other IFRS. For example, disclosures required by IAS 32, such as those pertaining to interest rate risk or credit risk, would need to be incorporated in a complete set of interim financial statements, in addition to the selected footnote disclosures prescribed by IAS 34.

Minimum components of an interim financial report. IAS 34 sets forth minimum requirements in relation to condensed interim financial reports. The standard mandates that the following financial statements components be presented when an entity opts for the condensed format:

- A condensed balance sheet
- A condensed income statement
- A condensed statement showing *either* all changes in equity *or* changes in equity other than those arising from capital transactions with owners and distributions to owners
- A condensed cash flow statement
- A set of selected footnote disclosures

Form and content of interim financial statements.

1. IAS 34 mandates that if an entity chooses to present the "complete set of (interim) financial statements" instead of opting for the allowed method of presenting only "condensed" interim financial statements, then the form and content of those state-

ments should conform to the requirements set by IAS 1 for a complete set of financial statements.

2.   However, if an entity opts for the condensed format approach to interim financial reporting, then IAS 34 requires that, at a minimum, those condensed financial statements include each of the headings and the subtotals that were included in the entity's most recent annual financial statements, along with selected explanatory notes, as prescribed by the standard.

It is interesting to note that IAS 34 mandates expansiveness in certain cases. The standard notes that extra line items or notes may need to be added to the minimum disclosures prescribed above, if their omission would make the condensed interim financial statements misleading. This concept can be best explained through the following illustration:

> At December 2005, an entity's comparative balance sheet had trade receivables that were considered doubtful, and hence, were fully reserved as of that date. Thus, on the face of the balance sheet as of December 31, 2005, the amount disclosed against trade receivables, net of provision, was a zero balance (and the comparative figure disclosed as of December 31, 2004, under the prior year column was a positive amount, since at that earlier point of time, that is, at the end of the previous year, a small portion of the receivable was still considered collectible). At December 31, 2005, the fact that the receivable (net of the provision) ended up being presented as a zero balance on the face of the balance sheet was well explained in the notes to the annual financial statements (which clearly showed the provision being deducted from the gross amount of the receivable that caused the resulting figure to be a zero balance that was then carried forward to the balance sheet). If at the end of the first quarter of the following year the trade receivables were still doubtful of collection, thereby necessitating creation of a 100% provision against the entire balance of trade receivables as of March 31, 2006, and the entity opted to present a condensed balance sheet as part of the interim financial report, it would be misleading in this case to disclose the trade receivables as of March 31, 2006, as a zero balance, without adding a note to the condensed balance sheet explaining this phenomenon.

3.   IAS 34 requires disclosure of earnings per share (both basic EPS and diluted EPS) on the face of the interim income statement. This disclosure is mandatory whether condensed or complete interim financial statements are presented.

4.   IAS 34 mandates that an entity should follow the same format in its interim statement showing changes in equity as it did in its most recent annual financial statements.

5.   IAS 34 requires that an interim financial report be prepared on a consolidated basis if the entity's most recent annual financial statements were consolidated statements. Regarding presentation of separate interim financial statements of the parent company in addition to consolidated interim financial statements, if they were included in the most recent annual financial statements, this standard neither requires nor prohibits such inclusion in the interim financial report of the entity.

Selected explanatory notes. While a number of notes would potentially be required at an interim date, there could clearly be far less disclosure than is prescribed under other enacted IFRS. IAS 34 reiterates that it is superfluous to provide the same notes in the interim financial report that appeared in the most recent annual financial statements, since financial statement users have access to those statements in all likelihood. To the contrary, at an interim date it would be meaningful to provide an explanation of events and transactions that are significant to an understanding of the changes in financial position and performance of the entity since the last annual reporting. In keeping with this line of thinking, it provides a list of minimum disclosures required to accompany the condensed interim financial statements, which are outlined below.

1. A statement that the same accounting policies and methods of computation are applied in the interim financial statements compared with the most recent annual financial statements, or if those policies or methods have changed, a description of the nature and effect of the change;

2. Explanatory comments about seasonality or cyclicality of interim operations;

3. The nature and magnitude of significant items affecting interim results that are unusual because of nature, size, or incidence;

4. Dividends paid, either in the aggregate or on a per share basis, presented separately for ordinary (common) shares and other classes of shares;

5. Revenue and operating result for business segments or geographical segments, whichever has been the entity's primary mode of segment reporting;

6. Any significant events occurring subsequent to the end of the interim period;

7. Issuances, repurchases, and repayments of debt and equity securities;

8. The nature and quantum of changes in estimates of amounts reported in prior interim periods of the current financial year, or changes in estimates of amounts reported in prior financial years, if those changes have a material effect in the current interim period;

9. The effect of changes in the composition of the entity during the interim period, like business combinations, acquisitions, or disposal of subsidiaries, and long-term investments, restructuring, and discontinuing operations; and

10. The changes in contingent liabilities or contingent assets since the most recent annual financial statements.

IAS 34 provides examples of the disclosures that are required. For instance, an example of an unusual item is ". . .the write-down of inventories to net realizable value and the reversal of such a write-down."

Finally, in the case of a complete set of interim financial statements, the standard allows additional disclosures mandated by other IFRS. However, if the condensed format is used, then additional disclosures required by other IFRS are *not* required.

Comparative interim financial statements. IAS 34 endorses the concept of comparative reporting, which is generally acknowledged to be more useful than is the presentation of information about only a single period. This is consistent with the position that has been taken by the accounting profession around the globe for many decades (although comparative reports are not an absolute requirement in some jurisdictions, most notably in the US). IAS 34 furthermore mandates not only comparative (condensed or complete) interim income statements (e.g., the second quarter of 2005 presented together with the second quarter of 2004), but the inclusion of year-to-date information as well (e.g., the first half of 2005 and also the first half of 2004). Thus, an interim income statement would ideally be comprised of four columns of data. On the other hand, in the case of the remaining components of interim financial statements (i.e., balance sheet, statement of cash flows, and statement of changes in stockholders' equity), the presentation of two columns of data would meet the requirements of IAS 34. Thus, the other components of the interim financial statements should present the following data for the two periods:

- The balance sheet as of the end of the current interim period and a comparative balance sheet as of the end of the immediately preceding fiscal year (*not* as of the comparable year-earlier date);

- The cash flow statement cumulatively for the current financial year to date, with a comparative statement for the comparable year-to-date period of the immediately preceding financial year; and
- The statement showing changes in equity cumulatively for the current financial year to date, with a comparative statement for the comparable year-to-date period of the immediately preceding financial year.

The following illustration should amply explain the above-noted requirements of IAS 34.

XYZ Limited presents quarterly interim financial statements and its financial year ends on December 31 each year. For the second quarter of 2006, XYZ Limited should present the following financial statements (condensed or complete) as of June 30, 2006:

1. An income statement with four columns, presenting information for the three-month periods ended June 30, 2006, and June 30, 2005; and for the six-month periods ended June 30, 2006, and June 30, 2005
2. A balance sheet with two columns, presenting information as of June 30, 2006, and as of December 31, 2005
3. A cash flow statement with two columns presenting information for the six-month periods ended June 30, 2006, and June 30, 2005
4. A statement of changes in equity with two columns presenting information for the six-month periods ended June 30, 2006, and June 30, 2006

IAS 34 recommends that, for highly seasonal businesses, the inclusion of additional income statement columns for the twelve months ending on the date of the most recent interim report (also referred to as rolling twelve-month statements) would be deemed very useful. The objective of recommending rolling twelve-month statements is that seasonality concerns would be thereby eliminated, since by definition each rolling period contains all the seasons of the year. (Rolling statements, however, cannot correct cyclicality that encompasses more than one year, such as that of secular business expansions and recessions.) Accordingly, IAS 34 encourages companies affected by seasonality to consider including these additional statements, which could result in an interim income statement comprising six or more columns of data.

Accounting Policies in Interim Periods

Consistency. The standard logically states that interim period financial statements should be prepared using the same accounting principles that had been employed in the most recent annual financial statements. This is consistent with the idea that the latest annual report provides the frame of reference that will be employed by users of the interim information. The fact that interim data is expected to be useful in making projections of the forthcoming full-year's reported results of operations makes consistency of accounting principles between the interim period and prior year important, since the projected results for the current year will undoubtedly be evaluated in the context of year-earlier performance. Unless the accounting principles applied in both periods are consistent, any such comparison is likely to be impeded.

The decision to require consistent application of accounting policies across interim periods and in comparison with the earlier fiscal year is a logical implication of the view of interim reporting as being largely a means of predicting the next fiscal year's results. It is also driven by the conclusion that interim reporting periods stand alone (rather than being merely an integral portion of the full year). To put it differently, when an interim period is seen as an integral part of the full year, it is easier to rationalize applying different accounting policies to the interim periods, if doing so will more meaningfully present the results of the portion of the full year within the boundaries of the annual reporting period. For example, deferral of certain costs at interim balance sheet dates, notwithstanding the fact that such costs could not validly be deferred at year-end, might theoretically serve the purpose of providing a more accurate predictor of full-year results.

On the other hand, if each interim period is seen as a discrete unit to be reported upon without having to serve the higher goal of providing an accurate prediction of the full-year's expected outcome, then a decision to depart from previously applied accounting principles is less easily justified. Given the IAS 34's clear preference for the discrete view of interim financial reporting, its requirement regarding consistency of accounting principles is entirely logical.

Consolidated reporting requirement. The standard also requires that, if the entity's most recent annual financial statements were presented on a consolidated basis, then the interim financial reports in the immediate succeeding year should also be presented similarly. This is entirely in keeping with the notion of consistency of application of accounting policies. The rule does not, however, either preclude or require publishing additional "parent company only" interim reports, even if the most recent annual financial statements did include such additional financial statements.

Materiality As Applied to Interim Financial Statements

Materiality is one of the most fundamental concepts underlying financial reporting. At the same time, it has largely been resistant to attempts at precise definition. Some IFRS do require that items be disclosed if material or significant, or if of "such size" as would warrant separate disclosure. For example, hitherto IAS 8 and now IAS 1 (revised), effective for periods beginning on or after January 1, 2005, require that items of income and expense which are material and relevant to explain the performance of an entity are to be separately disclosed. However, guidelines for performing an arithmetical calculation of a threshold for materiality (in order to measure "such size") is not prescribed in IAS 1, or for that matter in any other IFRS. Rather, this determination is left to the devices of each individual charged with responsibility for financial reporting.

IAS 34 advanced the notion that materiality for interim reporting purposes may differ from that defined in the context of an annual period. This follows from the decision to endorse the discrete view of interim financial reporting, generally. Thus, for example, discontinuing operations would have to be evaluated for disclosure purposes against whatever benchmark, such as gross revenue, is deemed appropriate as that item is being reported in the interim financial statements—not as it was shown in the prior year's financial statements or is projected to be shown in the current full-year's results.

The effect of the foregoing would normally be to lower the threshold level for reporting such items. Thus, it is deemed likely that some items separately set forth in the interim financials may not be so presented in the subsequent full-year's annual report that includes that same interim period.

The objective is not to mislead the user of the information by failing to include a disclosure that might appear to be material within the context of the interim report, since that is the user's immediate frame of reference. If later the threshold is raised and items previously presented are no longer deemed worthy of such attention, this is not thought to create a risk of misleading the user, in contrast to a failure to disclose an item in the interim financial statements that measured against the performance parameters of the interim period might appear significant.

Example of interim period materiality consideration

To illustrate, assume that Xanadu Corp. has gross revenues of €2.8 million in the first fiscal quarter and will, in fact, go on to generate revenues of €12 million for the full year. Traditionally, for this company's financial reporting, materiality is defined as 5% of revenues. If in the first quarter income from discontinued operations amounting to €200,000 is earned, this should be separately set forth in the quarterly financial statements since it exceeds the defined 5% threshold for materiality. If there are no other discontinued operations results for the balance of the year, it might validly be concluded that disclosure in the year-end financials may be omitted, since the €200,000 income item is not material in the context of €12 million of full year revenues. Thus, Xanadu's first quarter report might detail the discontinued operations, but that is later subsumed in continuing operations.

Recognition Issues

General concepts. The definitions of assets, liabilities, income, and expense are to be the same for interim period reporting as at year-end. These items are defined in the IASB's *Framework*. The effect of stipulating that the same definitions apply to interim reporting is to further underscore the concept of interim periods being discrete units of time upon which the statements report. For example, given the definition of assets as resources generating future economic benefits for the entity, expenditures that could not be capitalized at year-end because of a failure to meet this definition could similarly not be deferred at interim dates. Thus, by applying the same definitions at interim dates, IAS 34 has mandated the same recognition rules as are applicable at the end of full annual reporting periods.

However, while the overall implication is that identical recognition and measurement rules are to be applied to interim financial statements, there are a number of exceptions and modifications to the general rule. Some of these are in simple acknowledgment of the limitations of certain measurement techniques, and the recognition that applying those definitions at interim dates might necessitate interpretations different from those useful for annual reporting. In other cases, the standard clearly departs from the discrete view, since such departures are not only wise, but probably fully necessary. These specific recognition and measurement issues are addressed below.

Recognition of annual costs incurred unevenly during the year. It is frequently observed that certain types of costs are incurred in uneven patterns over the course of a fiscal year, while not being driven strictly by variations in volume of sales activity. For example, major expenditures on advertising may be prepaid at the inception of the campaign; tooling for new product production will obviously be heavily weighted to the preproduction and early production stages. Certain discretionary costs, such as research and development, will not bear any predictable pattern or necessary relationship with other costs or revenues.

If an integral view approach had been designated by IAS 34, there would be potent arguments made in support of the accrual or deferral of certain costs. For instance, if a major expenditure for overhauling equipment is scheduled to occur during the final interim period, logic could well suggest that the expenditure should be anticipated in the earlier interim periods of the year, if those periods were seen as integral parts of the fiscal year. Under the discrete view adopted by the standard, however, such an accrual would be seen as an inappropriate attempt to smooth the operating results over all the interim periods constituting the full fiscal year. Accordingly, such anticipation of future expenses is prohibited, unless the future expenditure gives rise to a true liability in the current period, or meets the test of being a contingency which is probable and the magnitude of which is reasonably estimable.

For example, many business entities grant bonuses to managers only after the annual results are known; even if the relationship between the bonuses and the earnings performance is fairly predictable from past behavior, these remain discretionary in nature and need not be granted. Such a bonus arrangement would not give rise to a liability during earlier interim periods, inasmuch as the management has yet to declare that there is a commitment that will be honored. (Compare this with the situation where managers have contracts specifying a bonus plan, which clearly would give rise to a legal liability during the year, albeit one which might involve complicated estimation problems. Also, a bonus could be anticipated for interim reporting purposes if it could be considered a constructive obligation, for example, based upon past practice for which the entity has no realistic alternative, and assuming that a realistic estimate of that obligation can be made).

Another example involves contingent lease arrangements. Often in operating lease situations the lessee will agree to a certain minimum or base rent, plus an amount that is tied to a variable such as sales revenue. This is typical, for instance, in retail rental contracts, such as for space in shopping malls, since it encourages the landlord to maintain the facilities in an appealing fashion so that tenants will be successful in attracting customers. Only the base amount of the periodic rental is a true liability, unless and until the higher rent becomes payable as defined sales targets are actually achieved. If contingent rents are payable based on a sliding scale (e.g., 1% of sales volume up to €500,000, then 2% of amounts up to €1.5 million, etc.), the projected level of full-year sales should not be used to compute rental accruals in the early periods; rather, only the contingent rents payable on the actual sales levels already achieved should be so recorded.

The foregoing examples were clearly categories of costs that, while often fairly predictable, would not constitute a legal obligation of the reporting entity until the associated conditions were fully met. There are, however, other examples that are more ambiguous. Paid vacation time and holiday leave are often enforceable as legal commitments, and if this is so, provision for these costs should be made in the interim financial statements. In other cases, as when company policy is that accrued vacation time is lost if not used by the end of a defined reporting year, such costs might not be subject to accrual under the discrete view. The facts of each such situation would have to be carefully analyzed to make a proper determination.

Revenues received seasonally, cyclically, or occasionally. IAS 34 is clear in stipulating that revenues such as dividend income and interest earned cannot be anticipated or deferred at interim dates, unless such practice would be acceptable under IFRS at year-end. Thus, interest income is typically accrued, since it is well established that this represents a contractual commitment. Dividend income, on the other hand, is not recognized until declared, since even when highly predictable based on past experience, these are not obligations of the paying corporation until actually declared.

Furthermore, seasonality factors should not be smoothed out of the financial statements. For example, for many retail stores a high percentage of annual revenues occur during the holiday shopping period, and the quarterly or other interim financial statements should fully reflect such seasonality. That is, revenues should be recognized as they occur.

Income taxes. The fact that income taxes are assessed annually by the taxing authorities is the primary reason for reaching the conclusion that taxes are to be accrued based on the estimated average annual effective tax rate for the full fiscal year. Further, if rate changes have been enacted to take effect later in the fiscal year (while some rate changes take effect in midyear, more likely this would be an issue if the entity reports on a fiscal year and the new tax rates become effective at the start of a calendar year), the expected effective rate should take into account the rate changes as well as the anticipated pattern of earnings to be experienced over the course of the year. Thus, the rate to be applied to interim period earnings (or losses, as discussed further below) will take into account the expected level of earnings for the entire forthcoming year, as well as the effect of enacted (or substantially enacted) changes in the tax rates to become operative later in the fiscal year. In other words, and as the standard puts it, the estimated average annual rate would "reflect a blend of the progressive tax rate structure expected to be applicable to the full year's earnings including enacted or substantially enacted changes in the income tax rates scheduled to take effect later in the financial year."

IAS 34 addresses in detail the various computational aspects of an effective interim period tax rate which are summarized in the following paragraphs.

Multiplicity of taxing jurisdictions and different categories of income. Many entities are subject to a multiplicity of taxing jurisdictions, and in some instances the amount of income subject to tax will vary from one to the next, since different laws will include and exclude disparate items of income or expense from the tax base. For example, interest earned on government-issued bonds may be exempted from tax by the jurisdiction that issued them, but be defined as fully taxable by other tax jurisdictions the entity is subject to. To the extent feasible, the appropriate estimated average annual effective tax rate should be separately ascertained for each taxing jurisdiction and applied individually to the interim period pretax income of each jurisdiction, so that the most accurate estimate of income taxes can be developed at each interim reporting date. In general, an overall estimated effective tax rate will not be as satisfactory for this purpose as would a more carefully constructed set of estimated rates, since the pattern of taxable and deductible items will fluctuate from one period to the next.

Similarly, if the tax law prescribes different income tax rates for different categories of income (such as the tax rate on capital gains which usually differs from the tax rate applicable to business income in many countries), then to the extent practicable, a separate tax rate should be applied to each category of interim period pretax income. The standard, while mandating such detailed rules of computing and applying tax rates across jurisdictions or across categories of income, recognizes that in practice such a degree of precision may not be achievable in all cases. Thus, in all such cases, IAS 34 softens its stand and allows usage of a "weighted-average of rates across jurisdictions or across categories of income" provided "it is a reasonable approximation of the effect of using more specific rates."

Tax credits. In computing an expected effective tax rate for a given tax jurisdiction, all relevant features of the tax regulations should be taken into account. Jurisdictions may provide for tax credits based on new investment in plant and machinery, relocation of facilities to backward or underdeveloped areas, research and development expenditures, levels of export sales, and so forth, and the expected credits against the tax for the full year should be given consideration in the determination of an expected effective tax rate. Thus, the tax effect of new investment in plant and machinery, when the local taxing body offers an investment credit for qualifying investment in tangible productive assets, will be reflected in those interim periods of the fiscal year in which the new investment occurs (assuming it can be forecast to occur later in a given fiscal year), and not merely in the period in which the new investment occurs. This is consistent with the underlying concept that taxes are strictly an annual phenomenon, but it is at variance with the purely discrete view of interim financial reporting.

The interim reporting standard notes that, although tax credits and similar modifying elements are to be taken into account in developing the expected effective tax rate to apply to interim earnings, tax benefits which will relate to onetime events are to be reflected in the interim period when those events take place. This is perhaps most likely to be encountered in the context of capital gains taxes incurred in connection with occasional dispositions of investments and other capital assets; since it is not feasible to project the rate at which such transactions will occur over the course of a year, the tax effects should be recognized only as the underlying events transpire.

While in most cases tax credits are to be handled as suggested in the foregoing paragraphs, in some jurisdictions tax credits, particularly those that relate to export revenue or capital expenditures, are in effect government grants. The accounting for government grants is set forth in IAS 20; in brief, grants are recognized in income over the period necessary to properly match them to the costs which the grants are intended to offset or defray. Thus, compliance with both IAS 20 and IAS 34 would necessitate that tax credits be carefully analyzed to identify those which are, in substance, grants, and then accounting for the credit consistent with its true nature.

Tax loss tax credit carrybacks and carryforwards. When an interim period loss gives rise to a tax loss carryback, it should be fully reflected in that interim period. Similarly, if a loss in an interim period produces a tax loss carryforward, it should be recognized immediately, but only if the criteria set forth in IAS 12 are met. Specifically, it must be deemed probable that the benefits will be realizable before the loss benefits can be given formal recognition in the financial statements. In the case of interim period losses, it may be necessary to assess not only whether the entity will be profitable enough in future fiscal years to utilize the tax benefits associated with the loss, but, furthermore, whether interim periods later in the same year will provide earnings of sufficient magnitude to absorb the losses of the current period.

IAS 12 provides that changes in expectations regarding the realizability of benefits related to net operating loss carryforwards should be reflected currently in tax expense. Similarly, if a net operating loss carryforward benefit is not deemed probable of being realized until the interim (or annual) period when it in fact becomes realized, the tax effect will be included in tax expense of that period. Appropriate explanatory material must be included in the notes to the financial statements, even on an interim basis, to provide the user with an understanding of the unusual relationship between pretax accounting income and the provision for income taxes.

Volume rebates or other anticipated price changes in interim reporting periods. IAS 34 prescribes that where volume rebates or other contractual changes in the prices of goods and services are anticipated to occur over the annual reporting period, these should be anticipated in the interim financial statements for periods within that year. The logic is that the effective cost of materials, labor, or other inputs will be altered later in the year as a consequence of the volume of activity during earlier interim periods, among others, and it would be a distortion of the reported results of those earlier periods if this were not taken into account. Clearly this must be based on estimates, since the volume of purchases, etc., in later portions of the year may not materialize as anticipated. As with other estimates, however, as more accurate information becomes available this will be adjusted on a prospective basis, meaning that the results of earlier periods should not be revised or corrected. This is consistent with the accounting prescribed for contingent rentals and is furthermore consistent with IAS 37's guidance on provisions.

The requirement to take volume rebates and similar adjustments into effect in interim period financial reporting applies equally to vendors or providers, as well as to customers or consumers of the goods and services. In both instances, however, it must be deemed probable that such adjustments have been earned or will occur, before giving recognition to them in the financials. This high a threshold has been set because the definitions of assets and liabilities in the IASB's *Framework* require that they be recognized only when it is probable that the benefits will flow into or out from the entity. Thus, accrual would only be appropriate for contractual price adjustments and related matters. Discretionary rebates and other price adjustments, even if typically experienced in earlier periods, would not be given formal recognition in the interim financials.

Depreciation and amortization in interim periods. The rule regarding depreciation and amortization in interim periods is more consistent with the discrete view of interim reporting. Charges to be recognized in the interim periods are to be related to only those assets actually employed during the period; planned acquisitions for later periods of the fiscal year are not to be taken into account.

While this rule seems entirely logical, it can give rise to a problem that is not encountered in the context of most other types of revenue or expense items. This occurs when the tax laws or financial reporting conventions permit or require that special allocation formulas be used during the year of acquisition (and often disposition) of an asset. In such cases, depreciation or amortization will be an amount other than the amount that would be computed based purely on the fraction of the year the asset was in service. For example, assume that convention is that one-half year of depreciation is charged during the year the asset is acquired, irrespective of how many months it is in service. Further assume that a particular asset is acquired at the inception of the fourth quarter of the year. Under the requirements of IAS 34, the first three quarters would not be charged with any depreciation expense related to this asset (even if it was known in advance that the asset would be placed in service in the fourth quarter). However, this would then necessitate charging fourth quarter operations with one-half year's (i.e., two quarters') depreciation, which arguably would distort that final period's results of operations.

IAS 34 does address this problem area. It states that an adjustment should be made in the final interim period so that the sum of interim depreciation and amortization equals an independently computed annual charge for these items. However, since there is no requirement that financial statements be separately presented for a final interim period (and most entities, in fact, do not report for a final period), such an adjustment might be implicit in the annual financials, and presumably would be explained in the notes if material (the standard does not explicitly require this, however).

The alternative financial reporting strategy, that is, projecting annual depreciation, including the effect of asset dispositions and acquisitions planned for or reasonably anticipated to occur during the year, and then allocating this ratably to interim periods, has been rejected. Such an approach might have been rationalized in the same way that the use of the effective annual tax rate was in assigning tax expense or benefits to interim periods, but this has not been done.

Inventories. Inventories represent a major category for most manufacturing and merchandising entities, and some inventory costing methods pose unique problems for interim financial reporting. In general, however, the same inventory costing principles should be utilized for interim reporting as for annual reporting. However, the use of estimates in determining quantities, costs, and net realizable values at interim dates will be more pervasive.

Two particular difficulties are addressed in IAS 34. These are the matters of determining net realizable values at interim dates and the allocation of manufacturing variances.

Regarding net realizable value determination, the standard expresses the belief that the determination of NRV at interim dates should be based on selling prices and costs to complete at those dates. Projections should therefore not be made regarding conditions which possibly might exist at the time of the fiscal year-end. Furthermore, write-downs to NRV taken at interim reporting dates should be reversed in a subsequent interim reporting period only if it would be appropriate to do so at the end of the financial year.

The last of the special issues related to inventories that are addressed by IAS 34 concerns allocation of variances at interim dates. When standard costing methods are employed, the resulting variances are typically allocated to cost of sales and inventories in proportion to the dollar magnitude of those two captions, or according to some other rational system. IAS 34 requires that the price, efficiency, spending, and volume variances of a manufacturing entity are recognized in income at interim reporting dates to the extent those variances would be recognized at the end of the financial year. It should be noted that some standards have prescribed deferral of such variances to year-end based on the premise that some of the variances will tend to offset over the course of a full fiscal year, particularly if the result of volume fluctuations due to seasonal factors. When variance allocation is thus deferred, the full balance of the variances are placed onto the balance sheet, typically as additions to or deductions from the inventory accounts. However, IAS 34 expresses a preference that these variances be disposed of at interim dates (instead of being deferred to year-end) since to not do so could result in reporting inventory at interim dates at more or less than actual cost.

Example of interim reporting of product costs

Dakar Corporation encounters the following product cost situations as part of its quarterly reporting:

- It only conducts inventory counts at the end of the second quarter and end of the fiscal year. Its typical gross profit is 30%. The actual gross profit at the end of the second quarter is determined to have been 32% for the first six months of the year. The actual gross profit at the end of the year is determined to have been 29% for the entire year.
- It determines that, at the end of the second quarter, due to peculiar market conditions, there is a net realizable value (NRV) adjustment to certain inventory required in the amount of €90,000. Dakar expects that this market anomaly will be corrected by year-end, which indeed does occur in late December.
- It suffers a decline of €65,000 in the market value of its inventory during the third quarter. This inventory value increases by €75,000 in the fourth quarter.
- It suffers a clearly temporary decline of €10,000 in the market value of a specific part of its inventory in the first quarter, which it recovers in the second quarter.

Dakar uses the following calculations to record these situations and determine quarterly cost of goods sold:

	Quarter 1	*Quarter 2*	*Quarter 3*	*Quarter 4*	*Full Year*
Sales	€10,000,000	€8,500,000	€7,200,000	€11,800,000	€37,500,000
(1-Gross profit percentage)	70%			70%	
Cost of goods, gross profit method	7,000,000		5,040,000		
Cost of goods, based on actual physical count		5,580,000[1]		8,255,000[2]	25,875,000
Temporary net realizable value decline in specific inventory [3]		90,000		(90,000)	0
Decline in inventory value with subsequent increase [4]			65,000	(65,000)	0
Temporary decline in inventory value [5]	10,000	(10,000)	0	0	0
Total cost of goods sold	€7,010,000	€5,660,000	€5,105,000	€8,100,000	€25,875,000

[1] *Calculated as [€18,500,000 sales × (1– 32% gross margin)] – €7,000,000 Quarter 1 cost of goods*
[2] *Calculated as [€37,500,000 sales × (1 – 29% gross margin)] – €17,620,000 Quarters 1-3 cost of sales*
[3] *Even though anticipated to recover, the NRV decline must be recognized.*
[4] *Full recognition of market value decline, followed by recognition of market value increase, but only in the amount needed to offset the amount of the initial decline.*
[5] *No deferred recognition to temporary decline in value.*

Example of interim reporting of other expenses

Dakar Corporation encounters the following expense situations as part of its quarterly reporting:

- Its largest customer, Festive Fabrics, has placed firm orders for the year that will result in sales of €1,500,000 in the first quarter, €2,000,000 in the second quarter, €750,000 in the third quarter, and €1,650,000 in the fourth quarter. Dakar gives Festive Fabrics a 5% rebate if Festive Fabrics buys at least €5 million of goods each year. Festive Fabrics exceeded the €5 million goal in the preceding year and was expected to do so again in the current year.
- It incurs €24,000 of trade show fees in the first quarter for a trade show that will occur in the third quarter.
- It pays €64,000 *in advance* in the second quarter for a series of advertisements that will run through the third and fourth quarters.
- It receives a €32,000 property tax bill in the second quarter that applies to the *following* twelve months.
- It incurs annual factory air filter replacement costs of €6,000 in the first quarter.
- Its management team is entitled to a year-end bonus of €120,000 if it meets a sales target of €40 million, prior to any sales rebates, with the bonus dropping by €10,000 for every million dollars of sales not achieved.

Dakar uses the following calculations to record these situations:

	Quarter 1	Quarter 2	Quarter 3	Quarter 4	Full year
Sales	€10,000,000	€8,500,000	€7,200,000	€11,800,000	€37,500,000
Deduction from sales	(75,000)[1]	(100,000)	(37,500)	(82,500)	(295,000)
Marketing expense			24,000[2]		24,000
Advertising expense			32,000[3]	32,000	64,000
Property tax expense		8,000[4]	8,000	8,000	24,000
Maintenance expense	1,500[5]	1,500	1,500	1,500	6,000
Bonus expense	30,000[6]	25,500	21,600	17,900	95,000

[1] *The sales rebate is based on 5% of the actual sales to the customer in the quarter when the sale is incurred. The actual payment back to the customer does not occur until the end of the year, when the €5 million goal is definitively reached. Since the firm orders for the full year exceed the threshold for rebates, the obligation is deemed probable and must be recorded.*

[2] *The €24,000 trade show payment is initially recorded as a prepaid expense and then charged to marketing expense when the trade show occurs.*

[3] *The €64,000 advertising payment is initially recorded as a prepaid expense and then charged to advertising expense when the advertisements run.*

[4] *The €32,000 property tax payment is initially recorded as a prepaid expense and then charged to property tax expense on a straight-line basis over the next four quarters.*

[5] *The €6,000 air filter replacement payment is initially recorded as a prepaid expense and then charged to maintenance expense over the one-year life of the air filters.*

[6] *The management bonus is recognized in proportion to the amount of revenue recognized in each quarter. Once it becomes apparent that the full sales target will not be reached, the bonus accrual should be adjusted downward. In this case, the downward adjustment is assumed to be in the fourth quarter, since past history and seasonality factors made nonachievement of the full goal unlikely until fourth quarter results were known. (Note: with other fact patterns, quarterly accruals may have differed.)*

Foreign Currency Translation Adjustments at Interim Dates

Given the IASC's adoption of the discrete view regarding interim reporting, it is not surprising that the same approach to translation gains or losses as is mandated at year-end would be adopted in IAS 34. IAS 21 prescribes rules for translating the financial statements for foreign operations into either the functional currency or the presentation currency and also includes guidelines for using historical, average, or closing foreign exchange rates. It also lays down rules for either including the resulting adjustments in income or in equity. IAS 34 requires that consistent with IAS 21, the actual average and closing rates for the interim period be used in translating financial statements of foreign operations at interim dates. In other words, the future changes to exchanges rates (in the current financial year) are not allowed to be anticipated by IAS 34.

Where IAS 21 provides for translation adjustments to be recognized in the income statement in the period it arises, IAS 34 stipulates that the same approach be applied during each interim period. If the adjustments are expected to reverse before the end of the financial year, IAS 34 requires that entities not defer some foreign currency translation adjustments at an interim date.

Adjustments to Previously Reported Interim Data

While year-to-date financial reporting is not required, although the standard does recommend it in addition to normal interim period reporting, the concept finds some expression in the standard's position that adjustments *not* be made to earlier interim periods' results. By measuring income and expense on a year-to-date basis, and then effectively backing into the most recent interim period's presentation by deducting that which was reported in earlier interim periods, the need for retrospective adjustment of information that was reported earlier is obviated. However, there may be the need for disclosure of the effects of such measurement strategies when this results effectively in including adjustments in the most current interim period's reported results.

Example of interim reporting of contingencies

Dakar Corporation is sued over its alleged violation of a patent in one of its products. Dakar settles the litigation in the fourth quarter. Under the settlement terms, Dakar must retroactively pay a 3% royalty on all sales of the product to which the patent applies. Sales of the product were €150,000 in the first quarter, €82,000 in the second quarter, €109,000 in the third quarter, and €57,000 in the fourth quarter. In addition, the cumulative total of all sales of the product in prior years is €1,280,000. Under provisions of IAS 34, Dakar cannot restate its previously issued quarterly financial results to include the following royalty expense, so instead will report the royalties expense, including that for earlier years, in the fourth quarter:

	Quarter 1	Quarter 2	Quarter 3	Quarter 4	Full year
Sales related to lawsuit	€150,000	€82,000	€109,000	€57,000	€398,000
Royalty expense	0	0	0	11,940	11,940
Royalty expense related to prior year sales	0			38,400	38,400

Accounting Changes in Interim Periods

A change in accounting policy other than one for which the transition is specified by a new standard should be reflected by restating the financial statements of prior interim periods of the current year and the comparable interim periods of the prior financial year.

One of the objectives of this requirement of IAS 34 is to ensure that a single accounting policy is applied to a particular class of transactions throughout the entire financial year. To allow differing accounting policies to be applied to the same class of transactions within a single financial year would be troublesome since it would result in "interim allocation difficulties, obscured operating results, and complicated analysis and understandability of interim period information."

Use of estimates in interim periods. IAS 34 recognizes that preparation of interim financial statements will require a greater use of estimates than annual financial statements. Appendix C to the standard provides examples of use of estimates to illustrate the application of this standard in this regard. The Appendix provides nine examples covering areas ranging from inventories to pensions. For instance, in the case of pensions, the Appendix states that for interim reporting purposes, reliable measurement is often obtainable by extrapolation of the latest actuarial valuation, as opposed to obtaining the same from a professionally qualified actuary, as would be expected at the end of a financial year. Readers are advised to read the other illustrations contained in Appendix C of IAS 34 for further guidance on the subject.

Impairment of assets in interim periods. IAS 34 stipulates that an entity should apply the same impairment testing, recognition, and reversal criteria at an interim period as it would at the end of its financial year. However, this does not mean that a detailed impairment calculation as prescribed by IAS 36 would automatically need to be used at interim periods; instead, an entity would need to review for indications of significant impairments since the date of the most recent financial year to determine whether such a calculation is required.

Interim financial reporting in hyperinflationary economies. IAS 34 requires that interim financial reports in hyperinflationary economies be prepared using the same principles as at the financial year-end. Thus, the provisions of IAS 29 would need to be complied with in this regard. IAS 34 stipulates that in presenting interim data in the measuring unit, entities should report the resulting gain or loss on the net monetary position in the interim period's income statement. IAS 34 also requires that entities do not need to annualize the recognition of the gain or loss or use estimated annual inflation rates in preparing interim period financial statements in a hyperinflationary economy.

Examples of Financial Statement Disclosures

F. Hoffman-LaRoche
Roche Group Consolidated Financial Statements
For the Period Ended June 30, 2005

1.   Accounting policies

Basis of preparation of financial statements

These financial statements are the unaudited interim consolidated financial statements (hereafter "the Interim Financial Statements") of Roche Holding Ltd., a company registered in Switzerland, and its subsidiaries (hereafter "the Group") for the six-month period ended June 30, 2005 (hereafter the "interim period"). They are prepared in accordance with International Accounting Standard 34 (IAS 34), *Interim Financial Reporting*. These Interim Financial Statements should be read in conjunction with the Consolidated Financial Statements for the year ended December 31, 2004 (hereafter the "Annual Financial Statements"), as they provide an update of previously reported information. They were approved for issue by the Board of Directors on July 19, 2005.

The accounting policies used are consistent with those used in the Annual Financial Statements, except where noted below. The presentation of the Interim Financial Statements is consistent with the Annual Financial Statements, except where noted below. Where necessary, the comparatives have been reclassified or extended from the previously reported Interim Financial Statements to take into account any presentational changes made in the Annual Financial Statements or in these Interim Financial Statements.

The preparation of the Interim Financial Statements requires management to make estimates and assumptions that affect the reported amounts of revenues, expenses, assets, liabilities, and disclosure of contingent liabilities at the date of the Interim Financial Statements. If in the future such estimates and assumptions, which are based on management's best judgment at the date of the Interim Financial Statements, deviate from the actual circumstances, the original estimates and assumptions will be modified as appropriate in the period in which the circumstances change.

The Group operates in industries where significant seasonal or cyclical variations in total sales are not experienced during the financial year. Income tax expense is recognized based upon the best estimate of the weighted-average annual income tax rate expected for the full financial year.

Changes in accounting policies

In late 2003 the International Accounting Standards Board (IASB) published a revised version of IAS 32, *Financial Instruments: Disclosure and Presentation.* A revised version of IAS 39, *Financial Instruments: Recognition and Measurement* and *Improvements to International Accounting Standards*, which makes changes to 14 existing standards. In the first quarter of 2004 the IASB published IFRS 2, *Share-Based Payment;* IFRS 3, *Business Combinations*; IFRS 4, *Insurance Contract;* IFRS 5, *Noncurrent Assets Held for Sale and Discontinued Operations*; revised versions of IAS 36, *Impairment of Assets;* and IAS 38, *Intangible Assets;* and further amendments to IAS 39. The Group adopted these effective January 1, 2005. A description of these changes and their effect on the Interim Financial Statements is given below.

The Group is currently assessing the potential impacts of the new and revised standards that will be effective from January 1, 2006.

IAS 8: Accounting Policies, Changes in Accounting Estimates and Errors. Amongst other matters the revised standard requires that changes in accounting policies that arise from the application of new or revised standards and interpretations are applied retrospectively, unless otherwise specified in the transitional requirements of the particular standard or interpretation. Previously the Group has applied all changes prospectively, unless otherwise specified in the transitional requirements.

Retrospective application means that the results of the comparative period and the opening balances of that period are restated as if the new accounting policy had always been applied. Prospective application means that the new accounting policy is only applied to the results of the current period and the comparative period is not restated.

IFRS 2: Share-Based Payment. Amongst other matters, the new standard requires that the fair value of all equity compensation plans awarded to employees be estimated at grant date and recorded as an expense over the vesting period. The expense is charged against the appropriate income statement heading. Under the Group's previous policy no expenses were recorded for equity-settled equity compensation plans. Expenses for cash-settled equity compensation plans were recorded based on the intrinsic value of the outstanding obligation as part of "other operating expenses." The standard also requires retrospective application, within certain transitional requirements. Applying the transitional requirements, a pretax expense of 197 million Swiss francs has been recorded in the interim period (98 million Swiss francs in the restated interim period of 2004). Due to the impact of the transitional requirements these amounts are not indicative of the future expenses for such plans. Expenses for cash-settled plans totaling 38 million Swiss francs in the interim period of 2004 were reclassified from "other operating expenses."

Expenses for equity compensation plans in interim results *in millions of CHF*

	Retrospective application of IFRS 2	*Previously reported as "other operating expenses"*	*Total interim 2004 (restated)*	*Total interim 2005*
Cost of sales	3	2	5	11
Marketing and distribution	9	8	17	43
Research and development	22	6	28	79
General and administration	26	22	48	64
Total operating expense	60	38	98	197

The new standard also affects the Group's effective tax rate, as deferred tax is recorded based on the expected tax benefits arising from vested awards. In the United States and many other tax jurisdictions the current equity price is used as an input to the IFRS 2 pretax expense, with any excess recognized directly in equity.

As a result of the implementation of IFRS 2, net assets on the consolidated balance sheet at December 31, 2004 were 75 million Swiss francs higher. This consists of inventories (40 million Swiss francs asset), deferred tax assets (52 million Swiss francs asset) and liabilities for cash-settled equity compensation plans (17 million Swiss francs liability).

Further information on the Group's equity compensation plans is given in Notes 5, 6, and 12 to the Annual Financial Statements.

IFRS 3: Business *Combination.* Amongst other matters, the new standard requires that amortization of goodwill cease from the date of implementation. Goodwill will continue to be tested for impairment. The standard requires prospective application. Had this standard been applied in the interim period of 2004, then goodwill amortization expenses of 282 million Swiss francs would not have been recorded. No additional impairment would have been necessary. In addition, together with IAS 38 (revised), *Intangible Assets*, this standard will typically result in more intangible assets being recognized from acquisitions than previously and consequently less goodwill will arise.

The new standard also affects the Group's effective tax rate, as no tax benefit was recorded in respect of goodwill amortization. Based on the Group's 2004 results, the Group's effective tax rate is expected to decrease by between two and three percentage points.

IAS 38 (revised): Intangible Assets. Among other matters, the revised standard will typically result in more intangible assets being recognized from in-licensing arrangements and similar research and development alliances. Previously such expenditure would be recorded as research and development expenses. The revised standard requires prospective application.

IAS 32 (revised) and IAS 39 (revised): Financial Instruments. Since the Group already fully applied the previous IAS 32 and IAS 39 on "Financial Instruments" the revised standards did not have a significant effect on the Group's results and financial position. Amongst other matters, the revised standards require that a significant *or* prolonged decline in the fair value of available-for-sale financial assets be considered as objective evidence of impairment. Under the Group's previous accounting policy, a decline in fair value of available-for sale-financial assets was considered as objective evidence of impairment where the decline was significant *and* prolonged. Consequently, the revised standards will typically result in impairment charges being recognised for available-for-sale financial assets at an earlier stage than under the previous accounting policy. The revised standards require retrospective application and this additionally resulted in a restatement of the equity conversion elements of certain of the Group's convertible debt instruments in 2004. As a result equity as at January 1, 2004, was reduced by 112 million Swiss francs and an additional pretax income of 20 million Swiss francs has been recorded for the restated interim period of 2004.

IAS 1 (revised): Presentation of Financial Statements. Amongst other matters, the revised standard permits the presentation of the result of discontinued businesses as a single amount on the face of the income statement. Additionally the revised standard requires that minority interests are included as part of the Group's equity and not as a separate category on the balance sheet. As a result of this change, and from the implementation of IFRS 2, the net accounting effect of Genentech and Chugai stock repurchases and stock options is recorded to equity and allocated to retained earnings and minority interests based on the relevant ownership percentages. Previously these entries were recorded to minority interests. The revised standard requires retrospective application and accordingly 169 million Swiss francs were reclassified from minority interests to retained earnings as at January 1, 2004.

Presentation of income statement: The new and revised standards result in significant changes to the format and content of the income statement. In addition the Group has made certain presentational changes in order to further improve comparability of results to other healthcare companies and to allow readers to make a more accurate assessment of the sustainable earnings capacity of the Group. These changes, which have been applied retrospectively, are listed below.

- "Royalties and other operating income" are shown as a separate line after "Sales."
- "Cost of sales" includes royalty expenses that are directly linked to goods sold. In the interim period this was 634 million Swiss francs (2004: 560 million Swiss francs).
- "Other operating expenses" is removed from the income statement. "Administration" is expanded to "General and administration" to additionally included in "Cost of sales."
- "Financial income" and "Financing costs" are disclosed separately on the face of the income statement.
- Capital taxes are reported as part of "General and administration" instead of "Financial income" as previously. In the interim period this was 18 million Swiss francs (2004: 12 million Swiss francs) and has been included in the "Corporate" business segment.

Restated income statement for the six months ended June 30, 2004 *in millions of CHF*

	As originally published	Discontinued business	IFRS 2	IAS 32 IAS 39	Other changes	Group restated
Sales	15,413	(887)	–	–	–	47,526
Other operating income and operating expenses	(11,853)	724	(60)	–	(12)	(11,201)
Operating profit	3,560	(163)	(60)	–	(12)	3,325
Financial and nonoperating items	727	9	–	20	12	768
Profit before taxes	4,287	(154)	(60)	20	–	4,093
Income taxes	(1,148)	42	25	(3)	–	(1,084)
Profit from continuing businesses	n/a	(112)	(35)	17	–	3,009
Profit from discontinued businesses	n/a	112	–	–	–	112
Net income	3,139	–	(35)	17	–	3,121
Attributable to						
Roche shareholders	2,920	–	(26)	17	–	2,911
Minority interests	219	–	(9)	–	–	210
Earnings per share and nonvoting equity security						
Diluted—Group (CHF)	3.41	–	(0.03)	0.02	–	3.40

Consistent with the presentation in the Annual Financial Statements:

- The business segment "Chugai OTC" results for the interim period of 2004 have been reclassified as discontinued, as this business was sold in the second half of 2004.
- A total of 22 million Swiss francs of administration and other costs that were previously allocated to the Consumer Health (OTC) business in the published 2004 interim results have been reclassified to the business segment "Corporate" within the Group's continuing business results. These items are not transferred with the sale of the business.

In addition provisions for sales returns and sales charge-backs are now classified as provisions and accrued liabilities, respectively. Previously they were reported within accounts receivable. In the December 31, 2004 balance sheet a total of 233 million Swiss francs has been reclassified from "accounts receivable" to "provisions—current" (137 million Swiss francs) and "accrued and other liabilities" (96 million Swiss francs). There was no impact on net income or equity from this reclassification.

Restated equity for January 1, 2004 *in millions of CHF*

	As originally published	IAS 1 (revised)	IFRS 2	IAS 32 IAS 39	Other changes	Group restated
Share capital	160	–	–	–	–	160
Own equity instruments	(4,583)	–	–	–	–	(4,583)
Retained earnings	30,985	–	3	(298)	169	30,859
Fair value and other reserves	(2,992)	–	–	186	–	(2,806)
Equity attributable to Roche shareholders	23,570	–	3	(112)	169	23,630
Minority interests	–	5,594	5	–	(169)	5,430
Total equity	23,570	5,594	8	(112)	–	29,060

Bayer AG
For the Period Ended June 30, 2005
Bayer Group Consolidated Statements of Income
(€) million

	2nd Quarter		1st Half	
	2004	*2005*	*2004*	*2005*
Net sales	5,890	7,053	11,682	13,757
Cost of goods sold	(3,202)	(3,811)	(6,009)	(7,353)
Gross profit	2,688	3,242	5,673	6,404
Selling expenses	(1,362)	(1,461)	(2,627)	(2,730)
Research and development expenses	(469)	(484)	(921)	(907)
General administrations expenses	(353)	(384)	(680)	(708)
Other operating income	264	405	391	789
Other operating expenses	(258)	(572)	(572)	(1,098)
Operating result (EBIT)	510	746	1,264	1,750
Income (expense) from investments in affiliated companies—net	(80)	6	(99)	4
Interest expense—net	(79)	(80)	(100)	(160)
Other non-operating expense—net	(55)	(55)	(131)	(104)
Nonoperating result	(214)	(129)	(330)	(260)
Income before income taxes	296	617	934	1,490
Income taxes	(105)	(182)	(344)	(462)
Income from continuing operations after taxes	191	435	590	1,028
Income after taxes	149	412	574	1,057
of which				
attributable to minority interest	3	6	9	(1)
attributable to Bayer AG stock holders (net income)	146	406	565	1,058
Earnings per share (€)				
From continuing operations				
Basic	0.26	0.60	0.81	1.41
Diluted	0.26	0.60	0.81	1.41
From continuing and discontinued operations				
Basic	0.20	0.56	0.77	1.45
Diluted	0.20	0.56	0.77	1.45

2004 figures restated

Bayer Group Consolidated Statements of Recognized Income and Expense
(€) million

	2nd Quarter		1st Half	
	2004	*2005*	*2004*	*2005*
Changes in fair values of hedging instruments and securities held for sale, recognized in stockholder's equity	8	(33)	18	(8)
Exchange differences on translation of foreign operations	(19)	274	186	679
Actuarial gains/losses on defined benefit obligations for pensions and other postemployment benefits	(25)	(1,183)	(25)	(1,183)
Deferred taxes on valuation adjustments offset directly against stockholders' equity	32	476	43	466
Valuation adjustments recognized directly in stockholders' equity	(4)	(466)	222	(46)
Income after taxes	149	412	574	1,057
Total income and expense recognized in the financial statements	145	(54)	796	1,011

Bayer Group Consolidated Statements of Changes in Stockholders' Equity
(€) million

Equity attributable to Bayer AG stockholders

	Capital stock and reserves of Bayer AG	Revaluation surplus	Retained earnings	Net income (loss)	Other comprehensive income (loss)	Total	Minority interest	Total stockholders' equity
December 31, 2003	4,812	0	10,479	(1,303)	(2,821)	11,167	123	11,290
Dividend payments				(365)		(365)		(365)
Allocation from retained earnings			(1,668)	1,668		0		0
Other changes in stockholders' equity					179	179	(23)	156
Taxes on transactions directly recognized in stockholders' equity					43	43		43
Net income				565		565		565
June 30, 2004	4,812	0	8,811	565	(2,599)	11,589	100	11,689
December 31, 2004	4,812	66	8,813	685	(3,544)	10,832	111	10,943
Spin off of LANXESS			(1,559)		523	(1,036)	86	(950)
Dividend payments				(402)		(402)		(402)
Allocation to retained earnings			283	(283)		0		0
Other changes in stockholders' equity					(512)	(512)	(7)	(519)
Taxes on transactions directly recognized in stockholders' equity					466	466		466
Net income				1,058		1,058		1,058
June 30, 2005	4,812	66	7,537	1,058	(3,067)	10,406	190	10,596

2004 figures restated

Notes to the Interim Report as of June 30, 2005

Accounting policies. Like the financial statements for 2004, the unaudited, consolidated financial statements for the second quarter of 2005 have been prepared according to the rules issued by the IASB, London. Reference should be made as appropriate to the notes to the 2004 statements, except as detailed below. IAS 34 (Interim Financial Reporting) has been applied in addition.

Changes in presentation in connection with the classification of assets and liabilities according to maturity as per IAS 1 and of assets held for sale and discontinued operations as per IFRS 5. The previous version of IAS 1 allowed the option of classifying assets and liabilities either according to maturity or in order of liquidity. The revised version of IAS 1, developed as part of the IASB's improvements project, prescribes classification according to maturity starting with the 2005 fiscal year.

IFRS 5, approved by the IASB on March 31, 2004, contains specific recognition principles for certain assets and liabilities held for sale and for discontinued operations. Reporting is to be based primarily on continuing operations, while assets held for sale and discontinued operations are to be stated separately in a single line item in the balance sheet, income statement and cash flow statement. The distinction between continuing and discontinued operations or assets held for sale is thus drawn differently starting on January 1, 2005, than in the financial statements as of December 31, 2004. The previous year's figures are restated accordingly.

Changes in pension accounting—application of the IAS 19 amendment. In December 2004, the IASB published an amendment to IAS 19 (Employee Benefits). The amendment introduces an additional recognition option for actuarial gains and losses arising from defined benefit plans. This option is similar to the approach provided in the UK standard FRS 17

(Retirement Benefits), which requires recognition of all actuarial gains and losses in a "statement of total recognized gains and losses" that is separate from the income statement.

Previously, in the Bayer Group statements, the net cumulative amounts of actuarial gains and losses outside of the "corridor" that were reflected in the balance sheet at the end of the previous reporting period were recognized in the income statement as income or expense, respectively, over the average remaining working lives of existing employees. This "corridor" was 10% of the present value of the defined benefit obligation or 10% of the fair value of plan assets, whichever was greater at the end of the previous year. Under the new method of pension accounting, unrealized actuarial gains and losses, instead of being gradually amortized according to the corridor methods and recognized in income, are offset in their entirety against stockholders' equity. Thus, no amortization of actuarial gains and losses is recognized in income.

Recognizing actuarial gains and losses in stockholders' equity affects the amounts of receivables and of provisions for pensions and other post-employment benefits stated in the balance sheet and also requires the recognition of deferred taxes on the resulting differences. These taxes, too, are offset against the corresponding equity items.

The Group Management Board has decided to follow the recommendation of the IASB and implement the above change as of January 1, 2005, in order to enhance the transparency of our reporting. The previous year's figures have been restated accordingly. This reporting change improves the 2004 operating result from continuing operations by €48 million and the nonoperating result by €78 million. Application of IAS 19 (revised) leads to a deferred tax expense of €50 million. In view of its immateriality to 2004 EBIT of our segments, the €48 million gain has been reflected solely in the reconciliation column of the segment table. These noncash reporting changes do not affect either gross or net cash flow. A quantitative analysis of the actuarial parameters led to an approximately €1 billion increase in pension obligations as of June 30, 2005, that was directly recognized in equity. The increase was due especially to a considerable drop in long-term interest rates in the principal countries.

Cessation of goodwill amortization. In March 2004, in connection with the issuance of IFRS 3, the IASB revised IAS 36 *(Impairment of Assets)* and IAS 38 *(Intangible Assets)*. Among the major changes is that goodwill and other intangible assets with an indefinite useful life may no longer be amortized, but must be tested annually for possible impairment. If events or changes in circumstances indicate a possible decline in value, impairment testing must be performed more frequently. Reversals of impairment losses for goodwill are prohibited. An intangible asset must be treated as having an indefinite life if it is expected to generate cash flows for the enterprise for an indefinite period of time. The revised standards apply to goodwill and other intangible assets acquired in business combinations agreed upon on or after March 31, 2004, as well as to previously acquired goodwill and other intangible assets for annual periods beginning on or after March 31, 2004.

Scope of consolidation. On June 30, 2005, the Bayer Group had a total 289 fully or proportionately consolidated companies, compared with 349 companies on December 31, 2004. The reduction is due mainly to the deconsolidation of 61 LANXESS companies.

The acquisition of the global OTC business of Roche is largely complete, resulting in the following changes in Group assets and liabilities:

OTC Acquisition[*]
(€) million

	Book value	Step-Up	Fair Value
Intangible assets	0	1,142	1,142
Goodwill	0	589	589
Property, plant and equipment	142	9	151
Inventories	96	57	153
Other acquired assets and assets and assumed liabilities	67	(22)	45

[*] *We also purchased from Roche at the end of 2004 the remaining 50% interest in the OTC joint venture in the US*

Since we have combined the sales forces, distribution function, and support functions –such as controlling –in our legal entities, it is not practicable to separately identify EBIT of the former Roche business.

Discontinued Operations. The Board of Management and Supervisory Board of Bayer AG decided in November 2003 to separated major parts of the chemicals and polymers business from the Bayer Group. The separation took place by way of a spin-off pursuant to the German Transformation Act (Umwandlungsgesetz). On January 28, 2005, the spin-off of LANXESS from Bayer AG was entered in the commercial register and thus took legal effect. It was also decided in October 2003 to divest the plasma business of the Biological Products Division of the Bayer HealthCare subgroup. This business was sold effective March 31, 2005.

Both the LANXESS business and the divested plasma business are reported as discontinued operations. This information, which is provided from the standpoint of the Bayer Group, is to be regarded as part of the reporting for the entire Group by analogy with our segment reporting and is not intended to portray either the discontinued operations or the remaining business of Bayer as separate entities. This presentation is thus in line with the principles for the reporting of discontinued operations according to IFRS 5.

Discontinued Operations
(€) million

	LANXESS 2nd Quarter		Plasma 2nd Quarter		Total Discontinued Operations 2nd Quarter	
	2004	*2005*	*2004****	*2005*	*2004****	*2005*
Net sales (external)	1,592	0	101	4	1,693	4
Operating result (EBIT)	23	0	0	(36)	23	(36)
Income (loss) after taxes	(42)	0	0	(23)	(42)	(23)
Gross cash flow*	113	0	6	6	119	6
Net cash flow*	78	0	(7)	10	71	10
Net investing cash flow	(15)	0	(2)	0	(17)	0
Net financing cash flow	(63)	0	9	(10)	(54)	(10)

	1st Half		1st Half		1st Half	
	2004	*2005***	*2004****	*2005*	*2004****	*2005*
Net sales (external)	3,070	503	193	124	3,263	627
Operating result (EBIT)	98	62	(1)	(14)	97	48
Income (loss) after taxes	(15)	38	(1)	(9)	(16)	29
Gross cash flow*	224	51	12	4	236	55
Net cash flow*	16	(80)	(39)	58	(23)	(22)
Net investing cash flow	(62)	(19)	(4)	226	(66)	207
Net financing cash flow	46	99	43	(284)	89	(185)

* *For definition see Bayer Group Key on page 2*

** *Figures for January only*

*** *2004 figures restated. Contrary to the presentation in last year's publications, activities outside the United States are now reflected in continuing operations*

Segment reporting. The spin-off of LANXESS and the acquisition of the Roche OTC business have led to a shift in the relative sizes of our businesses in terms of sales, EBIT and assets. In compliance with IAS 14 (Segment Reporting), we have therefore adjusted our segmentation effective January 1, 2005 to reflect the new Group structure.

In line with the increased importance of our Consumer Care Division, the previous Consumer Care, Diagnostics segment has been split into two reporting segments. The new Consumer Care segment comprises both our existing Consumer Care business and the OTC business acquired from Roche. Our diagnostics activities, comprising the Diabetes Care and Diagnostics divisions, are now reported as a separate segment called Diabetes Care, Diagnostics.

The Bayer CropScience subgroup was presented in the 2004 financial statements as a single segment. We are now reporting Crop Protection as a separate segment, consisting of the strategic business units Insecticides, Fungicides, Herbicides and Seed Treatment. The new Environmental

Science, BioScience segment comprises the Environmental Science and BioScience business groups.

The Bayer MaterialScience subgroup is divided for reporting purposes into the Materials and Systems segments as before.

Leverkusen, August 25, 2005

Bayer Aktiengesellschaft

The Board of Management

20 SEGMENT REPORTING

PERSPECTIVE AND ISSUES

With the rise of conglomerate businesses in the 1960s, it became clear that consolidated financial reporting, per se, might not provide enough insights to users, particularly to investors, in order to make informed economic decisions. At first merely recommended, segment reporting became required under some national GAAP by the late 1970s. Segment reporting is the disclosure of financial of information about an entity's operations in different industries or different geographic regions, and also encompasses information about the reporting entity's foreign operations and export sales, and its major customers.

Early proposals to require segment financial information were met with opposition from some preparers, who objected to the additional effort required of them, and particularly to the feared consequences of providing disclosures of sensitive data to competitors. These concerns paled, however, in comparison to the important needs of users of financial information. It became clear, however, that without the ability to understand which of an entity's major operations were making the most positive contributions to its results, users would be hindered in their ability to make intelligent investment decisions. Uncertainty results in higher capital costs, making nondisclosure a more costly (if not explicitly measured) choice than any possible loss from revealing competitively harmful information. Ultimately, the need to provide useful information to financial statement users was understood as being more important than the perceived competitive risks to the reporting entity.

The US Securities and Exchange Commission began requiring certain limited line-of-business information in registrants' annual filings in 1970, but in many instances this data was not included in the annual reports issued to stockholders. By 1974, the SEC required registrants to include some of this line-of-business information in their reports to stockholders. Later, FAS 14 was issued (in 1976), which established specific requirements under US GAAP for the disclosure of segment information in financial reports issued to stockholders. These requirements were later dropped for interim reports and for non–publicly held companies, due to complaints about cost of preparation. Under this standard, there was a rather wide range of acceptable definitions of industry segments, meaning that comparability across entities was not fully achieved.

The relevant international standard, IAS 14, was originally issued in 1981, and was closely modeled on the US standard. Thus, the range of acceptable definitions of industry segments under IFRS was also fairly broad. Subsequently, this standard was significantly revised, effective in mid-1998, by changing the method of determining reportable segments to conform more closely to how the reporting entity is actually internally managed. Eventually, standard setters in the US and elsewhere essentially conformed their standards to this new reporting philosophy, which had been pioneered by IFRS.

Under the current approach, the burden of preparing segment disclosures is lessened if the segment data captured by the entity's managerial reporting system corresponds with the standard's definitions of industry and/or geographical segments. In other cases, it will still be necessary for reporting entities to disaggregate and reaggregate data from the management information system in order to develop needed financial statement disclosures. Segment information, while recommended for all issuers of financial statements, is required only for those which have publicly traded debt or equity issues, or which are in the process of preparing a public offering.

IAS 14 offers detailed guidance on identifying business and geographical segments. The standard requires that entities refer to their organizational structure and internal reporting systems in order to identify these segments. If entities' internal segments are not geographical or products/service-based, then the entities are required to make reference to the next lower level of internal organization to identify reportable segments.

A dual presentation of segment data is required under IAS 14, addressing product/service and geographic classification schemes. One basis of segmentation is defined as primary, and the other secondary; which is designated as the primary depends on how actual management decisions are made by the entity.

Segment information should be prepared on the basis of the same accounting policies as are the financial statements of the consolidated group or entity. Disclosure requirements for the secondary segments are considerably less detailed than for the primary ones.

Sources of IFRS
IAS 14

DEFINITIONS OF TERMS

Accounting policies. Specific principles, bases, conventions, rules and practices adopted by an entity in preparing and presenting its financial statements.

Business segment. A distinguishable component of an entity that is engaged in providing a product or service or group of related products or services, and that is subject to risks and returns that are different from those of other business segments.

Cash flows. Inflows and outflows of cash and cash equivalents.

Common costs. Operating expenses incurred by the enterprise for the benefit of more than one industry segment.

Consolidated financial information. Aggregate (financial) information relating to an entity as a whole whether or not the entity has consolidated subsidiaries.

Corporate assets. Assets maintained for general corporate purposes and not used in the operations of any industry segment.

Discontinued operation. Resulting from the sale or abandonment of an operation that represents a separate, major line of business of an entity; the assets, net profit or loss, and activities can be distinguished physically, operationally, and for financial reporting purposes.

Extraordinary items. Income or expenses that arise from events or transactions that are clearly distinct from the ordinary activities of the entity and, therefore, are not expected to recur frequently or regularly.

General corporate expenses. Expenses incurred for the benefit of the corporation as a whole, which cannot be reasonably allocated to any segment.

Geographical segment. Distinguishable component of an entity engaged in operations in individual countries or groups of countries within particular geographic areas, as may be determined to be appropriate in the circumstances to reflect the nature of the entity's operations.

Identifiable assets. Those tangible and intangible assets used by an industry segment, including those the segment uses exclusively, and an allocated portion of assets used jointly by more than one segment.

Intersegment sales. Transfers of products or services, similar to those sold to unaffiliated customers, between industry segments or geographic areas of the entity.

Intrasegment sales. Transfers within an industry segment or geographic area.

Minority interest. That part of the net results of operations and of net assets of a subsidiary attributable to interests which are not owned, directly or indirectly through subsidiaries, by the parent.

Operating activities. The principal revenue producing activities of an entity and other activities that are not investing or financing activities.

Operating profit or loss. An industry segment's revenue minus all operating expenses, including an allocated portion of common costs.

Ordinary activities. Any activities which are undertaken by an entity as part of its business and such related activities in which the entity engages in furtherance of, incidental to or arising from, these activities.

Reportable segment. A business or geographical segment for which segment information is required to be disclosed.

Revenue. The gross inflow of economic benefits during a period arising in the ordinary course of business activities from sales to unaffiliated customers and from intersegment sales or transfers, excluding inflows from equity participants.

Segment accounting policies. The policies adopted for reporting the consolidated financial statements of the entity, as well as for segment reporting.

Segment assets. Operating assets employed by a segment in operating activities, whether directly attributable or reasonably allocable to the segment; these should exclude those generating revenues or expenses which are excluded from the definitions of segment revenue and segment expense.

Segment expense. Expense that is directly attributable to a segment, or the relevant portion of expense that can be allocated on a reasonable basis to a segment; it excludes interest expense, losses on sales of investments or extinguishment of debt, equity method losses of associates and joint ventures, income taxes, and corporate expenses not identified with specific segments.

Segment revenue. Revenue that is directly attributable to a segment, or the relevant portion of revenue that can be allocated on a reasonable basis to a segment, and that is derived from transactions with parties outside the enterprise and from other segments of the same entity; it excludes extraordinary items, interest and dividend income, and gains on sales of investments or extinguishment of debt.

Transfer pricing. The pricing of products or services between industry segments or geographic areas.

CONCEPTS, RULES, AND EXAMPLES

Conceptual Basis for Segmental Reporting

As business organizations have become more complex over the years, and the conglomerate form of organization (where unrelated or dissimilar operations are united within one reporting entity) has become ever more popular, it has become necessary to concede that financial statements which present the full scope of an entity's operations have declined markedly in utility. While it is certainly possible to assess the overall financial health of the reporting entity using such financial reports, it is much more difficult to evaluate management's operating and financial strategies, particularly with regard to its emphases on specific lines of business or geographic spheres of operation. For example, the extent to which operating results for a period are the consequence of the development of new products having greater potential for future growth vs. mature product lines which nonetheless still account for a majority of the entity's total sales, would be largely masked in financial statements which did not present results by business segment.

The need for the inclusion of at least some disaggregated information in general-purpose financial reports became critical by the late 1960s, and several national accounting rule-making bodies accordingly began to address this topic around that time. In the US, for example, the need for segment information was one of the first agenda items identified upon the FASB's formation in 1973. The original and long operative US requirement, FAS 14, was promulgated in 1976. A revised standard, largely (but not entirely) embracing the same approach as does the current (revised) IAS 14, was adopted as FAS 131, effective in 1998.

In the UK, the Companies Act of 1967 first mandated the disclosure of limited segment data; this requirement was expanded by later revisions of the Act, and disaggregated information was formally made part of the notes to the financial statements in 1981. A related professional accounting standard (SSAP 25) was adopted in 1990, with segments again defined either by class of business (similar to product or service areas) or by geographic location, with company management charged with the responsibility of determining which type of categorization would be most meaningful to financial statement users. As in the US, a threshold value of 10% is established for making the determination that a segment is material and thus needs to be reported on a disaggregated basis, and the criteria are virtually identical to the former US requirements under FAS 14. Information to be disclosed was also modeled on the US requirement—sales, operating results, and identifiable assets (called net assets under the UK standard, but not actually defined there).

As to IFRS, the relevant rules date from the original IAS 14 issued in 1983. The standard was reformatted, but not substantively altered, in 1995. In 1998 the IASC approved a significantly modified successor standard, revised IAS 14, which is the basis for the discussion in this chapter.

Applicability of IAS 14

In contrast to the current US standard on segment reporting (FAS 131), which affects the financial reports (including interim ones) of only publicly held companies, the *first* international standard on segment reporting was intended to be applicable to both publicly held and "other economically significant entities." While this term was undefined under IFRS, presumably it implied that all business organizations, other than those which are small, locally based, and nondiversified, were expected to apply the requirements of IAS 14. The broad sweep of this requirement understandably was not well received by smaller entities, particularly the privately held ones.

This rather vague applicability gave way, in revised IAS 14, to a rule that these disclosure requirements apply only to those entities which have publicly traded equity or debt securities, or which are in the process of issuing such securities in public markets. This essentially conformed the international rules with those of the national standard-setting bodies and limited this standard to current or prospective publicly held entities. This is not to suggest that including disaggregated information in financial statement reporting packages is not useful and potentially even cost-effective (via lower borrowing costs offered to entities having more "transparent" financial reporting) for privately held entities, and such disclosures are encouraged. If exempted entities do elect to disclose segment information, these must conform to IAS 14 in order to report in accordance with IFRS.

The philosophy underlying the segment disclosure requirements has evolved since IAS 14 was first promulgated. The original standard sought segment information for business or geographic segments having levels of revenues, profits, assets, or employment that were significant in the countries in which major operations were conducted. However, the term *significant* was not defined, and neither was a quantitative threshold set, although it was acknowledged that other standard setters had established these. For example, in the US the FASB mandated a 10% lower boundary for recognition, but level of employment was not stipulated as one of the criteria (only assets, revenues, and profits were so identified). Under original IAS 14, these remained matters of judgment.

The current IAS 14 takes a very different approach. Under this standard, the goal is to disaggregate business and geographical segments having different risk and return profiles. It sets forth a number of factors which can be used to determine whether the risks and returns do in fact vary between two or more segments. It is explicitly intended that the reporting entity's internal organization and financial reporting system be used to help in making this determination. For example, the way in which the entity is organizationally structured (by production or marketing centers) should reveal whether geographical segments are defined in terms of location of productive operations or location of customers.

It is necessary not only to define which of the business and geographical segments are reportable, but also to determine whether the business segments or the geographical segments will be the primary mode of segment reporting, with the alternative becoming the secondary mode. This depends upon whether the dominant source and nature of risk and return derives from the products and services the entity produces, or from operating in different countries or selling into different markets.

The amount of information to be disclosed for the primary segments is much greater than for the secondary segments. The standard's lack of quantitative thresholds is consistent with the decision to use the entity's internal organization and operation as the driver of the segment reporting model. Put simply: a definable portion of the business will be a segment if management behaves as if it is.

Defining Industry and Geographic Segments

Understanding what is meant by industry segments has proven to be a difficult task for many preparers and users of financial statement information. Some preparers have been inclined to define a segment in an overly broad fashion, in order to reduce the amount of disaggregated information they are required to present. However, there are certainly valid questions which can be, and have been, raised about how segments can be readily distinguished.

For one hypothetical example, consider a large manufacturer of a range of automobiles. This entity can convincingly argue that its operations represent a single business segment, while other similar enterprises might hold that a number of segments exist, such as small cars, luxury cars, sport utility vehicles, etc. Under the original IAS 14, the requirements for segment information appeared to permit liberal interpretation, so that in the foregoing example all automobile manufacturing could have been deemed a single segment, if that was the reporting entity's preference.

The current IAS 14 has defined segments in terms more consistent with internal managerial decision making. Continuing the hypothetical situation noted above, if management makes distinct decisions about the production and marketing of small cars vs. luxury cars, then those would be deemed separate segments for disclosure purposes, regardless of brand names or other artificial distinctions among the product lines. According to revised IAS 14, "an enterprise should look to its system of internal reporting to the board of directors and the chief executive officer for the purpose of identifying its business segments or geographical segments, for both its primary and secondary reporting formats...."

Characteristics of business and geographical segments. In the event that internally reported segments fail to satisfy the definitions of business and geographical segments, then the criteria in the standard are to be applied to ascertain the identities of the segments.

The standard stipulates the following factors to be considered in determining how to group products and services into business segments:

1. The nature of the products or services;
2. The nature and technology of the production processes;
3. The types of markets in which the products or services are sold;
4. Major classes of customers;
5. The distribution channels and methods for the products; and
6. A unique legislative or regulatory environment relating to part of the business, as might define banks, insurance companies, and utilities.

The following factors can be used to group geographical areas into geographical segments:

1. Proximity of operations;
2. Similarity of economic and political conditions;
3. Relationships between operations in different geographical areas;
4. Special risks associated with operations in a particular country; and
5. Underlying currency risks.

In the absence of internal organizational indicators which suffice to define business and geographical segments, the foregoing criteria should be applied in an attempt to identify primary and secondary segment formats. In that situation, the disclosure of segment data should include a statement to the effect that the externally reported segment data does not conform to that used internally, and the following three supplemental disclosures must be made for each segment which has revenue from sales to external customers amounting to 10% or more of total entity revenue from external customers:

1. Segment revenue from external customers;
2. The total carrying amount of segment assets; and
3. Capital expenditures.

Internal indications of segments are to be used whenever possible, however. The informational items to be disclosed for the segments, however they are defined, are discussed below.

Defining Reportable Segments

Reportable segments are business or geographical segments, whether identified either by internal organizational or financial reporting factors, or by application of the criteria set forth above, which meet the threshold test for becoming reportable. A segment will be reportable if a majority of its revenue is earned from sales to external customers, and furthermore

1. Its revenue from sales to external customers and from transactions with internal customers (other segments) is 10% or more of total revenue of all segments, *or*
2. Its segment result, whether profit or loss, is 10% or more of the combined result of all segments recording a profit or of all segments recording a loss, whichever is the greater in absolute monetary terms, *or*
3. Its assets are 10% or more of the total assets of all segments.

Note that the segment will be deemed reportable if any one of the three foregoing criteria are satisfied: the test is disjunctive, not conjunctive. However, since only those segments which earn a majority of revenues from external customers are subjected to this testing, those which are essentially vertically integrated will typically not be required to report as separate segments.

Segments which are too small to report separately (i.e., that fail to reach any of the foregoing 10% thresholds) may be combined, but only if in related operations. Insignificant segments cannot be merged with segments that are individually material (i.e., exceed one of the 10% thresholds) if the internal financial information is separately maintained. In other words, the quality of communication regarding defined, material segments cannot be compromised by including other, unrelated operations, even if those others are immaterial.

If the total revenue accounted for by identified segments does not aggregate to at least 75% of consolidated reporting entity revenues, the preparer must identify additional segments to report. Thus, the "miscellaneous" grouping of operating segments cannot account for 25% or more of total entity revenues.

Vertically integrated entities (e.g., where one division manufactures components that are later assembled in larger components or end products by a separate division) may either report these as separate segments, or may combine them. In many instances, the vertical integration is not complete, such that the buying segment obtains some components from other vendors, and/or the selling segment has independent customers besides its affiliate for some of its output. IAS 14 stipulates that, if the vertically integrated operations are combined for segment reporting purposes, the selling segment is to be combined with the buying segment (i.e., integrate upward), so that the buying segment defines what is reported.

The following example illustrates the three 10% tests and the 75% test.

Operating segment	Unaffiliated revenue	Intersegment revenue	Total revenue	Segment profit	Segment (loss)	Assets
A	€ 90	€ 12	€ 102	€11	€ --	€ 70
B	120	--	120	10	--	50
C	110	20	130	--	(40)	90
D	200	--	200	--	--	140
E	140	300	440	--	(100)	230
F	380	--	380	60	--	260
G	144	--	144	8	--	30
Total	€1,184	€332	€1,516	€89	€(140)	€870

NOTE: Because the €140 total segment losses exceed the €89 total segment profits, the €140 is used for the 10% test

Summary of Test Results

x = Passed test – Reportable segment

Operating segment	Revenues (10% of €1,516 = €152)	Segment loss (10% of €140 = €14	Assets (10% of €870 = €87	75% of unaffiliated revenues test
A				
B				
C		x	x	€110
D	x		x	200
E	x	x	x	140
F	x	x	x	380
G				
				830
			75% of €1,184	888
			Revenue shortfall	(58)

Note that the aggregate revenues of the reportable segments that passed the 10% tests are €58 short of providing the required coverage of 75% of unaffiliated revenues. Consequently, an additional operating segment (A, B, or G) will need to be added to the reportable segments in order to obtain sufficient coverage.

Comparative financial statements. IAS 14 provides that if a segment were deemed to be reportable in the immediate preceding period (because one or more of the aforenoted 10% thresholds had been exceeded), then even failing each of these tests in the current year would not eliminate the need to present comparable segment data currently. However, this requirement is only applicable if management believes that the segment has continuing significance; absent this, such disclosure could be eliminated. The fact that continuing disclosure is dependent upon management attitudes introduces a subjective element. This may eventually be seen as permitting nondisclosure of important information, and more objective criteria may have to be imposed at some point in time.

Furthermore, if a segment is deemed to be reportable in the current reporting period because it satisfies a relevant threshold test for the first time, the comparative prior period disclosures should be restructured to include that segment as a reportable one, notwithstanding that it did not surpass the 10% thresholds in the prior year. In establishing these two requirements, comparability was obviously a high priority.

Segment Reporting

For purposes of complying with IAS 14, segments should be defined in terms of groups of related products or services, or alternatively by types of customers to whom these are provided. It must remain a matter of judgment as to how this guideline is applied, and similar enterprises might reach different conclusions on this. For example, a manufacturer of electronic and mechanical components used in the automobile industry might market these to original equipment manufacturers (OEM) of automobiles and of heavy construction equipment, and also to aftermarket suppliers, in a number of different geographic markets (e.g., Western Europe, the former Eastern Bloc nations of Europe, and the Middle East). In presenting segment data, the entity might reach at least four distinct conclusions on how to define the segments, as follows:

1. It might argue that the entire business represents a single segment;
2. It could find that electronics and mechanical components are essentially different product lines and, thus, that there are two segments of the business;
3. It might conclude that the OEM market is generically different from the aftermarket, thus defining two different segments in another way; or

4. It could reason that automobile OEM, construction equipment OEM, and aftermarket suppliers are each distinct, thus defining three segments of the business for which information is to be disclosed.

Management judgment will continue to play a large role in financial reporting of industry segments. In reaching their decisions, however, managements should weigh the similarities and differences among the products or services, the risk characteristics of the markets, the growth potential, and the likely future importance of the segment to the entity as a whole. If some parts of the business are subject to particular or unusual regulatory oversight (such as banking typically is), this is a factor which suggests that it might constitute a separate segment for reporting purposes. The fact that a product or service line is produced in an organizationally separate unit, such as a division, may or may not be determinative; thus, internal accounting data might be usable for segment reporting, but might also first need to be reclassified in order to serve that purpose.

The determination of geographic segments is likewise subject to the application of substantial amounts of judgment. Typically, however, it will be fairly obvious in any given circumstance how the breakdown among regions should be accomplished. The only real question, in most cases, will be how much detail to present. For example, if an entity has operations in western Europe and also in former Soviet Bloc nations such as Poland, some might conclude that these are separate segments since their economic systems were so different for so long, and thus that the emerging nations of Eastern Europe present materially different risks and growth opportunities. Others might conclude that Europe is a single region, based on transportation and other logistical requirements and other criteria, especially when contrasted to North American, Latin American, and Asian geographic segments of the same business enterprise.

Disclosure Requirements

Under revised IAS 14 a rather expansive set of disclosures has been mandated. Reporting entities must determine which mode of categorization (i.e., industries or geographical area) is the primary, and which is the secondary, definition of its segment operations. The amount of detail required for the secondary segments is less than for the primary segments.

The determination of primary segmentation is based upon the dominant source of risk and return to the organization. Thus, if an entity's strategic decisions are made primarily in terms of the geographical location of either its operations (e.g., siting of manufacturing plants, sourcing materials, etc.) or its customers, then geographical segments will be the primary reporting format. If, on the other hand, decisions revolve around product or service offerings, then business segments will be the primary format.

In either case, the format not chosen as primary must be used as the secondary mode of segment reporting. Thus, a substantial amount of informative disclosure will result in either instance, although somewhat less data is provided for the secondary format than for the primary.

Primary reporting format disclosures. The following informative disclosures are mandated for each reportable segment:

1. Segment revenue, with separate disclosure of revenue derived from external customers and revenue derived from internal customers (i.e., from other segments). Also, the nature of the segment's revenue should be described, in the manner set forth in IAS 18 (i.e., separately disclosing revenues arising from sales of goods, rendering of services, interest, royalties, dividends, and from the exchange [bartering] of goods and services in each category).
2. Segment result.

3. Interest and dividend income and interest expense directly attributable to the segment or which can be reasonably allocated to the segment, separately—except that this need not be done for reportable segments whose operations are primarily of a financial nature.
4. Total assets at carrying value.
5. Segment liabilities.
6. The contingencies or commitments which can be directly attributed to a reportable segment or allocated on a reasonable basis to segments.
7. Total expenditures to acquire segment assets during the reporting period (typically referred to as capital expenditures).
8. Total depreciation and amortization expense related to segment assets and included in segment results for the reporting period.
9. The nature of any item of revenue or expense which due to size, nature, or incidence needs to be disclosed to explain performance of the segment for the period.
10. Significant noncash expenses, other than depreciation and amortization, that were deducted in arriving at segment results.
11. The segment's share of profit or loss of associates, joint ventures or other investments accounted for under the equity method, as well as the investment in that associate or joint venture.
12. A reconciliation of the information presented for reportable segments (the eleven categories above) to the amounts presented in the consolidated or enterprise-wide financial statements. In reconciling revenue, segment revenue from outsiders should be reconciled to total revenue from outside customers; segment results should be reconciled to a comparable measure of enterprise performance as well as to enterprise net income or loss; and segment liabilities should be reconciled to enterprise liabilities.

Secondary reporting format. The nature of the data presented in the secondary reporting format depends upon which of the two possible criteria determined the primary format, business or geography. If the primary disclosures were based on business segments, then the secondary, geographical, format must contain, for each segment that has sales to external customers *or* segment assets totaling 10% or more of the comparable enterprise-wide amounts

1. Segment revenue from external customers, determined by the geographical location of customer or market.
2. Total carrying amount of segment assets, determined by geographical location of the assets.
3. The total amount of capital expenditure for the period being reported on, by location of assets.

If the primary mode of reporting segment information is by geographical locations, on the other hand, then the secondary format information will be, for each business segment whose revenue from sales to external customers is 10% or more of total enterprise revenue from external customers, as follows:

1. Segment revenue from external customers.
2. Total carrying amount of segment assets.
3. The total amount of capital expenditures for the period.

Finally, if the entity defines primary segment format in terms of geographical area, based on the location of the production or service facilities, and if the markets in which the goods or services significantly differ from the location of the assets, then revenue from sales to external customers must also be reported by location of markets. The geographical markets to be identified are those whose sales to external customers is 10% or more of the corresponding enterprise total.

Other Disclosures Which May Be Necessary

Disclosures are necessary when a business or geographical segment is not deemed to be reportable because it earns a majority of its revenue from intersegment sales, yet 10% or more of entity sales to external customers is comprised of sales to external customers by this segment. This fact should be disclosed, as well as the sales revenue from external and intersegment sales generated by the segment.

The basis for determining prices for intersegment sales should be stated. This should be the same basis that the entity actually uses to recognize such transactions for internal reporting purposes. If the method has changed from the previous period, that fact should be adequately disclosed as well.

Segment disclosures are to be prepared using the same accounting principles that the entity uses for general external reporting in accordance with international accounting standards. If there have been changes in accounting policies employed at the entity level which also impact on segment informative disclosures, these should be dealt with in accordance with IAS 8. Under that standard, prior period information is restated to conform with the new principles, unless undue cost or effort would be required.

If there have been changes in accounting principles employed in determining segment disclosures, which have a material impact on the data provided to users of the financial statements, such as the method of allocating revenue and expenses to segments, the comparative prior period information should be restated to conform with the new methods utilized. This is important even when aggregate entity amounts will not have been affected by the change, since the users' understanding of segment performance may be distorted unless efforts are made to provide them with insights into these matters.

Unless it is clear from other disclosures or from the body of the financial statements themselves, the segment information should include descriptions of the activities of each reportable business segment and should also indicate the composition of each geographical segment, both for primary and secondary reporting formats. A fair amount of judgment is required in deciding on what information should be provided, but in theory, to take the geographical segment disclosure as an example, such matters as stability of currencies, political risks, and market growth expectations are all potentially useful to recipients of the data and possibly necessary to interpret the financial disclosures most meaningfully. While these are technically voluntary disclosures, in ultimately reaching a judgment as to whether the financial statements are fairly presented, the adequacy of disclosures will have to be weighed.

If an entity operates in a single business or geographical segment and therefore is not required to, and does not, report either primary or secondary segment data, that fact should be disclosed and the nature of its business segment or geographical operations should be stated. In some cases an entity will operate within a single segment, but derive revenues from a number of diverse products or services; in such instances, the new standard requires that these be described and the amounts of revenues derived from any such group of products or services which constitute 10% or more of enterprise revenue should be set forth. This clearly will require the exercise of judgment, since there will be a thin line between such disclosures and the admission that the entity, in fact, is operating in more than a single segment and thus should have made the full set of informative disclosures required by IAS 14.

Finally, if the aggregate revenue from external customers from all reportable segments totals less than 75% of the revenue reported by the entity as a whole, the standard requires that there be a general description of the nature of the remaining sources of revenue. This would normally occur when the balance of revenues are derived from a range of individually minor activities which do not constitute a single segment or group of segments. In practice, this situation will not occur very often, as the defined and reportable segments will typically add to more than the 75% threshold level.

Revisions to Definitions of Segments

Over time, an entity may determine that the definition of industry or of geographic segments needs to be revised. The effect of making such a change could be to make information presented in earlier years no longer comparable to that currently presented in the financial statements. Accordingly, at a minimum, the fact of having made this change must be disclosed, with a sufficient description so that users can appreciate the general impact that change might have had. The reasons why the change was made, such as to better reflect the way management is currently making decisions about the segments of the business, should also be stated. If reasonably determinable, the actual effect of the change should be disclosed.

As an example, the manufacturer of electronic and mechanical automobile parts used in the example below might at some point conclude that its former manner of presentation of segment data as a dichotomy between electronic and mechanical products is no longer meaningful given the growing pervasiveness of electronic components in what had previously been entirely mechanical items. Thus, the entity might determine that a more useful categorization would be by type of customer, for example, original equipment manufacturers (OEM) vs. aftermarket, since the underlying economic forces differ substantially between these. In the year of the change in presentation, the fact of the change and the logic for it should be presented, and if possible the prior period's data, which had been presented earlier on the basis of product type, should be restated on the newly adopted basis of customer class. By doing this, the users of the financial statements would be able to understand the trends affecting the segments as they are currently being defined.

Comprehensive example of segment reporting

To illustrate the expansion of reporting requirements under IAS 14, a comprehensive illustration is given below. The facts assumed are as follows, as these would have been presented in conformity with the original IAS 14:

	(All amounts in € millions)	
	Electronic components	*Mechanical components*
Net sales		
2005	345.0	228.6
2006	378.5	219.8
Operating profit		
2005	29.6	13.2
2006	36.0	8.5
Capital expenditures		
2005	12.1	3.5
2006	21.4	2.5
Identifiable assets		
2005	122.9	128.4
2006	140.2	118.5
Depreciation and amortization		
2005	13.7	15.9
2006	17.5	13.6

Unallocated (corporate) assets totaled €7.6 million in 2005 and €8.1 million in 2006. Unallocated corporate expenses equaled €3.4 million in 2005 and €4.5 million in 2006. Intersegment sales, which are made at cost, are not material in amount. Operating profit by segment is defined as third-party sales less operating expenses; corporate overhead and financing costs are excluded from segment expenses.

Revenue by geographic area is summarized below.

| | *(All amounts in € millions)* | | |
	Western Europe	*Eastern Europe*	*Middle East*
Net sales			
2005	348.8	113.4	111.7
2006	366.3	133.4	98.6
Operating profit			
2005	22.7	8.6	11.5
2006	20.6	13.9	10.0
Identifiable assets			
2005	178.4	63.2	9.7
2006	183.3	69.5	5.9

Western Europe includes primarily Germany and France, with a relatively small amount of activity in Belgium and the Netherlands. Eastern Europe includes Hungary, Poland, Slovakia and the Czech Republic. The Middle East is principally Lebanon and Syria, with a small level of activity in Egypt and Saudi Arabia. Sales in the Middle East are made almost entirely to aftermarket suppliers, whereas revenues derived from European markets are predominantly from original equipment manufacturers of automobiles and construction equipment. Approximately 12% and 14% of sales in Western Europe, for 2005 and 2006, respectively, were made to aftermarket suppliers; for Eastern European sales, the corresponding percentages were 19% and 23% for 2005 and 2006, respectively.

It is assumed that management has determined that the primary reporting format should be by business segment; the secondary reporting format, therefore, will by geographical segment. What follows is the set of required disclosures to conform with IAS 14.

Note 10. Segment information

Management has determined that the primary determinant of its decision making is the major products offered by the company, with lesser attention being based on geographical location of its customers. Accordingly, the primary disclosures, below, are based on business segment, alternatively, electronic or mechanical components, with the following secondary disclosures based on geographic location of customers.

| | *(All amounts in € millions)* | |
	Electronic components	*Mechanical components*
Net sales		
2005—In total	345.0	228.6
2005—To external customers	336.3	228.6
2005—Intersegment sales	8.7	0.0
2006—In total	378.5	219.8
2006—To external customers	371.0	219.5
2006—Intersegment sales	7.5	.3
Operating profit		
2005	29.6	13.2
2006	36.0	8.5
Interest and dividend income		
2005—Interest income	1.2	.2
2005—Dividend income	.1	0
2006—Interest income	1.1	.3
2006—Dividend income	0	0
Interest expense		
2005	1.5	1.1
2006	1.2	1.0

Identifiable assets, at net carrying amounts		
2005	122.9	128.4
2006	140.2	118.5
Segment liabilities		
2005	62.3	43.4
2006	59.6	40.1
Contingent liabilities related to contractual disputes		
2005	2.5	1.0
2006	4.4	1.2
Capital expenditures		
2005	12.1	3.5
2006	21.4	2.5
Depreciation and amortization		
2005	13.7	15.9
2006	17.5	13.6
Nonrecurring items		
2005—Revenue from government contract	6.7	0
2006—Gain from settlement of patent suit	2.3	0
Equity in income of investee		
2005	2.2	0
2006	.5	0
Investment in equity method investee		
2005	5.6	0
2006	6.9	0

Segment information is reconciled to corresponding enterprise totals in the following section:

Net sales

2005—To external customers	
Electronic components	336.3
Mechanical components	228.6
Enterprise total sales	564.9
2006—To external customers	
Electronic components	371.0
Mechanical components	219.5
Enterprise total sales	590.5

Operating profit

2005	
Electronic components	29.6
Mechanical components	13.2
Less: Unallocated corporate expenses	(3.4)
Enterprise total operating profit	39.4
2006	
Electronic components	36.0
Mechanical components	8.5
Less: Unallocated corporate expenses	(4.5)
Enterprise total operating profit	40.0

Identifiable assets, at net carrying amounts

2005	
Electronic components	122.9
Mechanical components	128.4
Unallocated corporate assets	7.6
Enterprise total assets	258.9
2006	
Electronic components	140.2
Mechanical components	118.5
Unallocated corporate assets	8.1
Enterprise total assets	266.8

Segment liabilities
2005
    Electronic components   62.3
    Mechanical components   43.4
        Enterprise total liabilities   105.7

2006
    Electronic components   59.6
    Mechanical components   40.1
        Enterprise total liabilities   99.7

Revenue by geographic area is summarized below (based on location of customers).

(All amounts in € millions)

	Western Europe	Eastern Europe	Middle East
Net sales			
2005	348.8	113.4	111.7
2006	366.3	133.4	98.6
Identifiable assets			
2005	178.4	63.2	9.7
2006	183.3	69.5	5.9
Capital expenditures			
2005	8.2	4.4	3.0
2006	12.5	5.5	5.9

Western Europe includes primarily Germany and France, with a relatively small amount of activity in Belgium and the Netherlands. Eastern Europe includes Hungary, Poland, Slovakia and the Czech Republic. The Middle East is principally Lebanon and Syria, with a small level of activity in Egypt and Saudi Arabia. Sales in the Middle East are made almost entirely to aftermarket suppliers, whereas revenues derived from European markets are predominantly from original equipment manufacturers of automobiles and construction equipment. Approximately 12% and 14% of sales in Western Europe, for 2005 and 2006, respectively, were made to aftermarket suppliers; for Eastern European sales, the corresponding percentages were 19% and 23% for 2005 and 2006, respectively.

Examples of Financial Statement Disclosures

Nestlé Group
For the Year Ended December 31, 2004

Segmental information

Segmental information is based on two segment formats: the primary format reflects the Group's management structure, whereas the secondary format is product oriented.

The primary segment format—by management responsibility and geographic area—represents the Group's management structure. The principal activity of the Group is the food business, which is managed through three geographic zones. Nestlé Waters, managed on a world-wide basis, is disclosed separately. The other activities encompass mainly pharmaceutical products as well as other food businesses, which are generally managed on a worldwide basis. The secondary segment format, representing products, is divided into six product groups (segments).

Segment results represent the contribution of the different segments to central overheads, research and development costs, and the profit of the Group. Unallocated items comprise mainly corporate expenses as well as research and development costs. Specific corporate expenses as well as specific research and development costs are allocated to the corresponding segments.

Segment assets comprise property, plant, and equipment, trade and other receivables, inventories and prepayments, and accrued income. Unallocated items represent mainly corporate and research and development assets, including goodwill. Liabilities comprise trade and other payables and accruals and deferred income. Eliminations represent intercompany balances between the different segments.

Segment assets and liabilities by management responsibilities and geographic area represent the situation at the end of the year. Assets by product group represent the annual average as this provides a better indication of the level of invested capital for management purposes.

Notes

1. **Segmental information**

    By management responsibility and geographic area

(in millions of CHF)	Sales		EBITA	
	2004	2003	2004	2003
Zone Europe	28,563	28,574	3,492	3,561
Zone Americas	27,776	27,655	4,152	4,150
Zone Asia, Oceania, and Africa	14,673	14,432	2,547	2,508
Nestlé Waters	8,039	8,066	669	782
Other activities [a]	7,718	9,252	1,744	1,537
	86,769	87,979	12,604	12,538
Unallocated items [b]			(1,634)	(1,532)
EBITA Earnings before interest, taxes and amortization of goodwill			10,970	11,006

[a] *Mainly pharmaceutical products, joint ventures managed on a worldwide basis and Eismann. 2003 comparatives include Trinks.*

[b] *Mainly corporate expenses as well as research and development costs.*

The analysis of sales by geographic area is stated by customer location. Intersegment sales are not significant.

(in millions of CHF)	Assets		Liabilities	
	2004	2003	2004	2003
Zone Europe	12,196	12,154	5,812	5,503
Zone Americas	8,913	9,643	3,223	3,205
Zone Asia, Oceania, and Africa	6,026	6,071	1,795	1,829
Nestlé Waters	4,993	5,116	1,942	2,137
Other activities [a]	3,470	3,730	1,299	1,539
	35,598	36,714	14,071	14,213
Unallocated items [b]	28,280	30,507	385	364
Eliminations	(1,501)	(1,026)	(1,501)	(1,026)
	62,377	66,195	12,955	13,551

[a] *Mainly pharmaceutical products, joint ventures managed on a worldwide basis and Eismann. 2003 comparatives include Trinks.*

[b] *Corporate and research and development assets/liabilities, including goodwill.*

(in millions of CHF)	Capital expenditure		Depreciation of property, plant, and equipment	
	2004	2003	2004	2003
Zone Europe	925	925	724	642
Zone Americas	813	739	644	674
Zone Asia, Oceania, and Africa	587	541	392	364
Nestlé Waters	558	647	415	391
Other activities [a]	285	375	206	215
	3,168	3,227	2,381	2,286
Unallocated items [b]	127	110	125	122
	3,295	3,337	2,506	2,408

[a] *Mainly pharmaceutical products, joint ventures managed on a worldwide basis and Eismann. 2003 comparatives include Trinks.*

[b] *Corporate and research and development property, plant, and equipment.*

(in millions of CHF)	Impairment of assets		Restructuring costs	
	2004	2003	2004	2003
Zone Europe	30	42	333	253
Zone Americas	29	43	28	98
Zone Asia, Oceania, and Africa	14	81	17	56
Nestlé Waters	57	55	126	182
Other activities (a)	--	1	10	9
	130	222	514	598
Unallocated items (b)			--	5
			514	603

(a) *Mainly pharmaceutical products, joint ventures managed on a worldwide basis and Eismann. 2003 comparatives include Trinks.*
(b) *Mainly corporate expenses as well as research and development costs.*

By product group

(in millions of CHF)	Sales		EBITA	
	2004	2003	2004	2003
Beverages	21,793	23,520	3,867	4,038
Milk products, Nutrition and Ice cream	23,582	23,283	2,682	2,796
Prepared dishes and cooking aids	15,878	16,068	1,924	1,884
Chocolate, confectionery, and biscuits	10,258	10,240	1,153	1,047
PetCare	9,934	9,816	1,446	1,444
Pharmaceutical products	5,324	5,052	1,532	1,329
	86,769	87,979	12,604	12,538
Unallocated items (a)			(1,634)	(1,532)
EBITA Earnings before interest, taxes and amortization of goodwill			10,970	11,006

(a) *Mainly corporate expenses as well as research and development costs.*

(in millions of CHF)	Assets	
	2004	2003
Beverages	11,452	11,237
Milk products, Nutrition and Ice cream	10,186	10,303
Prepared dishes and cooking aids	5,705	5,787
Chocolate, confectionery, and biscuits	5,033	5,208
PetCare	3,490	3,481
Pharmaceutical products	2,709	2,708
	38,575	38,724

(in millions of CHF)	Capital expenditure	
	2004	2003
Beverages	806	936
Milk products, Nutrition and Ice cream	576	421
Prepared dishes and cooking aids	250	251
Chocolate, confectionery, and biscuits	201	208
PetCare	276	254
Pharmaceutical products	69	86
	2,178	2,156
Administration, distribution, research, and development	1,117	1,181
	3,295	3,337

(in millions of CHF)	Impairment of assets		Restructuring costs	
	2004	2003	2004	2003
Beverages	59	121	186	248
Milk products, Nutrition and Ice cream	13	63	88	128
Prepared dishes and cooking aids	12	14	43	60
Chocolate, confectionery, and biscuits	22	5	152	133
PetCare	3	19	41	26
Pharmaceutical products	--	--	3	4
	109	222	513	599
Administration, distribution, research, and development	21	--	1	4
	130	222	514	603

Bayer AG
For the Year Ended December 21, 2004

Key Data by Segment

Segments

€ million	Pharmaceuticals, biological products		HealthCare Of which discontinuing operations plasma		Consumer care, diagnostics		Animal health		CropScience Crop science	
	2003	2004	2003	2004	2003	2004	2003	2004	2003	2004
Net sales (external)	4,745	4,388	613	660	3,336	3,311	790	786	5,764	5,946
- Change in €	-0.5%	-7.5%			-11.2%	-0.7%	-7.1%	-0.5%	+22.7%	+3.2%
- Change in local currencies	+11.4%	-3.4%			-0.3%	+4.6%	+4.7%	+4.5%	+32.4%	+7.1%
Intersegment sales	51	42			4	18	8	4	69	57
Other operating income	100	128			383	26	25	12	329	171
Operating result [EBIT]	(408)	302	(349)	(56)	601	400	172	157	342	492
Return on sales	(8.6)%	6.9%			18.0%	12.1%	21.8%	20.0%	5.9%	8.3%
Gross cash flow	23	405	(122)	60	648	448	144	109	860	893
Capital invested	3,001	2,934			2,891	2,609	409	392	8,033	8,386
CFROI	0.6%	14.4%			20.9%	15.6%	27.1%	25.4%	9.6%	10.6%
Net cash flow	(163)	215	(98)	(16)	719	667	226	125	1,165	778
Equity-method income (loss)	0	0			0	0	0	0	0	0
Equity-method investments	4	4			0	0	0	0	0	0
Total assets	4,632	4,581	619	621	3,207	3,096	575	554	10,745	10,820
Capital expenditures	185	134			201	161	21	25	413	209
Amortization and depreciation	555	220	227	46	300	239	32	23	749	727
Liabilities	2,279	2,067	89	134	961	1,021	207	176	2,808	2,607
Research and development expenses	964	788	44	47	209	189	72	67	725	679
Number of employees (as of December 31)	20,700	20,000	1,600	1,600	11,000	10,800	2,900	2,900	19,400	19,400

Key Data by Segment

Segments

€ million

| | MaterialScience | | | | LANXESS | | | | | |
| | Materials | | Systems | | LANXESS discontinuing operations | | Reconciliation | | Bayer Group | |
	2003	2004	2003	2004	2003	2004	2003	2004	2003	2004
Net sales (external)	2,777	3,248	4,676	5,349	5,776	6,053	703	677	28,567	29,758
- Change in €	–3.4%	+17.0%	–2.3%	+14.4%	–7.5%	+4.8%			–3.6%	+4.2%
- Change in local currencies	+5.1%	+22.1%	+6.5%	+18.8%	–1.7%	+7.8%			+5.0%	+8.2%
Intersegment sales	23	27	297	339	557	659	(1,009)	(1,146)		
Other operating income	21	32	44	96	85	64	171	275	1,158	804
Operating result [EBIT]	58	293	(455)	348	(1,290)	74	(139)	(258)	(1,119)	1,808
Return on sales	2.1%	9.0%	(9.7)%	6.5%	(22.3)%	1.2%			(3.9)%	6.1%
Gross cash flow	312	400	623	484	280	306	(26)	165	2,864	3,210
Capital invested	3,557	3,645	5,551	4,344	5,658	4,112	5,297	3,684	34,397	30,106
CFROI	8.0%	10.8%	10.3%	9.2%	4.6%	6.7%			8.1%	9.9%
Net cash flow	332	209	781	289	131	234	102	(67)	3,293	2,450
Equity-method income (loss)	1	2	(23)	(131)	0	0	(143)	(10)	(165)	(139)
Equity-method investments	16	29	703	562	0	0	147	149	870	744
Total assets	3,861	3,789	3,957	4,724	4,029	4,313	6,439	5,927	37,445	37,804
Capital expenditures	169	147	295	185	312	279	143	135	1,739	1,275
Amortization and depreciation	269	249	1,108	326	1,458	317	264	221	4,735	2,322
Liabilities	726	843	1,360	1,328	2,101	2,217	14,667	15,166	25,109	25,425
Research and development expenses	116	97	133	139	168	126	17	22	2,404	2,107
Number of employees (as of December 31)	9,100	9,100	9,200	8,800	20,500	19,700	22,600	22,300	115,400	113,000

Bayer AG
For the Year Ended December 31, 2003

Key Data by Region

Regions
€ million

	Europe		North America		Asia/Pacific	
	2003	2004	2003	2004	2003	2004
Net sales (external) – by market	12,162	12,915	8,636	8,277	4,529	4,946
Net sales (external) – by point of origin	13,518	14,454	8,763	8,434	3,913	4,254
Of which discontinuing operations	3,717	3,883	1,848	1,976	564	587
-Change in €	–2.7%	+6.9%	–4.1%	–3.8%	–2.4%	+8.7%
-Change in local currencies	–2.7%	+6.9%	+11.4%	+4.9%	+10.2%	+14.6%
Interregional sales	3,833	4,028	1876	1,900	266	239
Other operating income	812	547	64	134	84	59
Operating result [EBIT]	(267)	1,015	(1,184)	238	67	421
Of which discontinuing operations	(832)	105	(767)	(114)	(52)	58
Return on sales	(2.0)%	7.0%	(13.5)%	2.8%	1.7%	9.9%
Gross cash flow	1,483	1,731	743	836	333	416
Capital invested	20,000	16,604	9,325	7,896	2,258	2,459
CFROI	7.2%	9.5%	7.1%	9.7%	14.1%	17.6%
Equity-method income (loss)	(166)	(39)	0	(100)	1	0
Equity-method investments	452	431	412	307	2	2
Total assets	22,400	22,380	9,045	8,978	2,731	2,928
Capital expenditures	1,047	761	496	303	138	149
Amortization and depreciation	2,351	1,413	1,963	659	333	125
Liabilities	15,898	16,335	5,253	5,199	1,189	1,271
Research and development expenses	1,673	1,441	641	576	74	70
Number of employees (as of December 31)	66,700	64,800	23,300	22,300	13,900	14,100

Bayer AG
For the Year Ended December 31, 2003

Key Data by Region

Regions
€ million

	Latin America/Africa/Middle East		Reconciliation		Bayer Group	
	2003	2004	2003	2004	2003	2004
Net sales (external) – by market	3,240	3,620			28,567	29,758
Net sales (external) – by point of origin	2,373	2,616			28,567	29,758
Of which discontinuing operations	260	267			6,389	6,713
-Change in €	–8.2%	+10.2%			–3.6%	+4.2%
-Change in local currencies	+11.1%	+17.5%			+5.0%	+8.2%
Interregional sales	151	157	(6,126)	(6,324)		
Other operating income	198	64			1158	804
Operating result [EBIT]	433	364	(168)	(230)	(1,119)	1,808
Of which discontinuing operations	12	(31)			(1,639)	18
Return on sales	18.2%	13.9%			(3.9)%	6.1%
Gross cash flow	391	336	(86)	(109)	2,864	3,210
Capital invested	1,197	1,275	1,617	1,872	34,397	30,106
CFROI	31.1%	27.2%			8.1%	9.9%
Equity-method income (loss)	0	0			(165)	(139)
Equity-method investments	4	4			870	744
Total assets	1,627	2,070	1,642	1,448	37,445	37,804
Capital expenditures	58	62			1,739	1,275
Amortization and depreciation	69	56	19	69	4,735	2,322
Liabilities	675	833	2,094	1,787	25,109	25,425
Research and development expenses	16	20			2,404	2,107
Number of employees (as of December 31)	11,500	11,800			115,400	113,000

The following impairment losses were recognized on the noncurrent assets of the Bayer Group and its reporting segments:

€ million	2003	2004
Goodwill	167	20
of which LANXESS	80	20
of which Materials	--	--
of which Systems	87	--
Intangible assets, excluding goodwill	511	2
of which LANXESS	84	2
of which Materials	--	--
of which Systems	427	--
Property, plant, and equipment	1,131	46
of which LANXESS	824	46
of which Materials	--	--
of which Systems	108	--
of which Pharmaceuticals, Biological Products	199	--
Total	1,809	68
of which LANXESS	988	68
of which Materials	--	--
of which Systems	622	--
of which Pharmaceuticals, Biological Products	199	--

Substantial impairment losses were recognized in 2003, especially for the industrial business segments due to adverse economic developments.

Notes on Segment Reporting

In accordance with IAS 14 (Segment Reporting), a breakdown of certain data in the financial statements is given by segments and geographical region. The segments and regions are the same as those used for internal reporting, allowing a reliable assessment of risks and returns. The aim is to provide users of the financial statements with information regarding the profitability and future prospects of the Groups' various activities.

As of December 31, 2004, the Bayer Group comprised four subgroups with operations subdivided into divisions (HeathCare), business groups or strategic business entities (CropScience, MaterialScience and LANXESS). Their activities are aggregated into the seven reporting segments listed below according to economic characteristics, products, production processes, customer relationships, and methods of distribution.

The subgroup's activities are as follows:

Subgroup/Segment	Activities
HealthCare	
Pharmaceuticals, Biological Products	Development and marketing of prescription pharmaceuticals
Consumer Care, Diagnostics	Development and marketing of over-the-counter medications, nutritional supplements and diagnostic products for laboratory testing, near-patient testing and self-testing applications
Animal Health	Development and marketing of veterinary medicines, nutritionals and grooming products for companion animals and livestock
CropScience	
CropScience	Development and marketing of a comprehensive portfolio of fungicides, herbicides, insecticides, seed treatment products, nonagricultural applications, plant biotechnology and conventional seeds to meet a wide range of regional requirements
MaterialScience	
Materials	Production and marketing of high-quality plastics granules, methylcellulose, metallic and ceramic powders, and semifinished products.
Systems	Development, manufacturing, and marketing of polyurethanes for a wide variety of applications as well as coating and adhesive raw materials; production and marketing of basic inorganic chemicals.

LANXESS	
LANXESS	Production and marketing of synthetic and tire rubbers, polymers, basic and fine chemicals and specialty chemicals, including the development of system solutions.

In 2004, as part of the reorganization, the chemicals operations—with the exception of H.C. Starck and Wolff Walsrode—and some of the polymers operations were combined to form LANXESS. The operations of the former Bayer Polymers and Bayer Chemicals subgroups that remain in the Bayer Group continue to operate as part of the Bayer MaterialScience subgroup, which is subdivided into the Materials and Systems segments. The prior year figures have been restated to reflect these organizational changes.

The **reconciliation** eliminates intersegment items and reflects income and expenses not allocable to segments. These include in particular the Corporate Center, the service companies and sideline operations.

Business activities that Bayer has already divested or intends to divest are shown as **discontinuing operations**. For fiscal 2004 and 2003 these are the plasma business and LANXESS.

The segment data are calculated as follows:

- The intersegment and interregional sales reflect intragroup transactions effected at transfer prices fixed on an arm's-length basis.
- The return on sales is the ratio of the operating result (EBIT) to external net sales.
- The gross cash flow comprises the operating result (EBIT) plus depreciation, amortization and write-downs, minus income taxes, minus gains/plus losses on retirement of noncurrent assets, plus/minus changes in pension provisions.
- The net cash flow is the cash flow from operating activities as defined in IAS 7.
- The capital invested comprises all assets serving the respective segment that are required to yield a return on their cost of acquisition. Noncurrent assets are included at cost of cash flow return on investment acquisition or construction throughout their useful lives because the calculation of cash flow return on investment (CFROI) requires that depreciation and amortization be excluded. Interest-free liabilities are deducted. The capital invested is stated as of December 31.
- The CFROI is the ratio of the gross cash flow to the average capital invested for the year and is thus a measure of the return on capital employed.
- The equity items are those reflected in the balance sheet and income statement. They are allocated to the segments where possible. The reconciliation of the balance of equity method income and loss to the income statement line "Income (expense) from investments in affiliated companies—net" is apparent from Note [8].
- Capital expenditures, amortization and depreciation relate to intangible assets, property, plant, and equipment.
- Since financial management of Group companies is carried out centrally by Bayer AG, financial liabilities are not normally allocated directly to the respective segments. Consequently, the liabilities shown for the individual segments do not include financial liabilities. However, in connection with the spin-off of LANXESS, financial liabilities were allocated to LANXESS AG and LANXESS GmbH where this was possible and made commercial sense. Financial liabilities have therefore been recognized directly for the LANXESS segment, which we include in discontinuing operations. To reflect the LANXESS subgroup—which was split off as of January 28, 2005—in its entirety as of December 31, 2004, the relevant financial and other liabilities have been recognized under the LANXESS segment. The prior year figures have been restated accordingly. In the previous year, all financial liabilities were reflected in the reconciliation.

We use a similar procedure for segment assets. All assets allocated directly to the LANXESS subgroup as part of the spin-off are stated separately. The prior year figures have been restated and now also contain amounts recognized in the previous year in the former Polyurethanes/Coatings/Fibers, Plastics/Rubber or Chemicals segments or in the reconciliation.

21 CHANGES IN ACCOUNTING POLICIES AND ESTIMATES, AND CORRECTIONS OF ERRORS

PERSPECTIVE AND ISSUES

The information set forth in an entity's financial statements over a period of years must be comparable if it is to be of value to users of those statements. Users of financial statements usually seek to identify trends in the entity's financial position, performance, and cash flows by studying and analyzing the information contained in those statements. Thus it is imperative that, to the maximum extent possible, the same accounting policies be applied from year to year in the preparation of financial statements, and that any necessary departures from this rule be clearly disclosed.

Financial statements are impacted by the choices made from among different, acceptable accounting principles and methodologies. Companies select those accounting principles and methods that they believe depict, in their financial statements, the economic reality of their financial position, results of operations, and changes in financial position. While IASB has made great progress in narrowing the range of acceptable alternative accounting for given economic events and transactions, there remain choices (e.g., in inventory costing) that can impair the ability to compare one entity's position and results with another.

Lack of comparability among entities and within a given entity over time can result because of changes in the assumptions and estimates underlying the application of the accounting principles and methods, from changes in the details in acceptable principles made by a promulgating authority, such as an accounting standard-setting body, for other reasons. While there is no stopping the various factors causing changes to occur, it is important that changes be made only when they result in improved financial reporting, or when necessitated by imposition of new financial reporting requirements. Whatever the reason for introducing change, and hence often noncomparability, to the financial reporting process, adequate disclosures must be made so that users of the financial statements are able to comprehend the effects and compensate for them in performing financial analyses.

IAS 8 deals with accounting changes (i.e., changes in accounting estimates and changes in accounting principles) and also addresses the accounting for the correction of errors. A principal objective of IAS 8, which was last revised in 2003, is to prescribe accounting treatments and financial statement disclosures that will enhance comparability, both within an entity over a series of years, and with the financial statements of other entities.

Even though the correction of an error in financial statements issued previously is not considered an accounting change, it is discussed by IAS 8, and therefore is covered in this chapter.

In the preparation of financial statements there is an underlying presumption that an accounting principle, once adopted, should not be changed, but rather is to be uniformly applied in accounting for events and transactions of a similar type. This consistent application of accounting principles enhances the utility of the financial statements. The presumption that an entity should not change an accounting principle may be overcome only if the reporting entity justifies the use of an alternative acceptable accounting principle on the basis that it is preferable under the circumstances.

The IASB's *Improvements Project* resulted in significant changes being made to IAS 8 in 2003, with such changes becoming effective in 2005. It is now required that comparative prior period data be restated and that the earliest reported retained earnings balance be adjusted for any earlier effect of a correction of an error or of a voluntary change in accounting policy. The only exception to this rule occurs when restatement would be impracticable to accomplish.

The *Improvements Project* also resulted in some reorganization of materials in the standards, specifically moving certain guidance between IAS 1 and IAS 8. As revised, certain presentational issues have been moved to IAS 1, while guidance on accounting policies previously found in IAS 1 has been moved to IAS 8. In addition, included in revised IAS 8 is a newly established hierarchy of criteria to be applied in the selection of accounting principles.

As amended, IAS 8 incorporates the consensus formerly found in SIC 18, *Consistency—Alternative Methods*, which requires that an entity select and apply its accounting policies for a period consistently for similar transactions, other events and conditions, unless a standard or an interpretation specifically requires or permits categorization of items for which different policies may be appropriate, in which case an appropriate accounting policy shall be selected and applied consistently to each category. Simply stated, the expectation is that, absent changes in promulgated standards, or changes in the character of the transactions being accounted for, the reporting entity should continue to use accounting principles from one period to the next without change, and use them for all transactions and events within a given class or category without exception.

The term formerly used by IFRS, *fundamental error*, has been superseded by a somewhat more broadly defined term, *error*.

When IFRS are revised or new standards are developed, they often are promulgated a year or more prior to the effective date for mandatory application. Disclosure of future changes in accounting policies must be made when the reporting entity has yet to implement a new standard that has been issued but not yet come into effect. In addition, disclosure is now required of the planned date of adoption, along with an estimate of the effect of the change on the entity's financial position, except if making such an estimate requires undue cost or effort.

Sources of IFRS
IAS 8

DEFINITIONS OF TERMS

Accounting policies. Specific principles, bases, conventions, rules, and practices adopted by an entity in preparing and presenting financial statements.

Change in accounting estimate. A revision of an accounting measurement based on new information, more experience, or subsequent developments. The use of reasonable estimates is an essential part of the financial statement preparation process and does not undermine their reliability. Since uncertainties are inherent in day-to-day business activities, revisions to such accounting estimates are an acceptable practice in the accounting process.

Change in accounting principle. A switch from one generally accepted accounting principle to another generally accepted accounting principle, including the methods of applying these principles.

Comparability. The quality of information that enables users to identify similarities in and differences between two sets of economic phenomena.

Consistency. Consistency refers to conformity from period to period with unchanging policies and procedures. It enhances the utility of financial statements to users by facilitating analysis and understanding of comparative accounting data.

Cumulative effect. The difference between the beginning retained earnings balance of the year in which the change is reported and the beginning retained earnings balance that would have been reported if the new principle had been applied retrospectively for all prior periods that would have been affected.

Errors. Omission from and other misstatements of an entity's financial statements for one or more prior periods that are discovered in the current period and relate to reliable information that (1) was available when those prior period financial statements were prepared, and (2) could reasonably be expected to have been obtained and taken into account in the preparation and presentation of those financial statements. These include the effect of mathematical mistakes, mistakes in applying accounting policies, oversights or misinterpretations of facts, and fraud.

Pro forma information. Financial information that is prepared on an "as if" basis. The disclosure of required numbers computed on the assumption that certain events have transpired.

Prospective application. The method of reporting a change in an accounting policy and of recognizing the effect of a change in an accounting estimate, respectively, by (1) applying the new accounting policy to transactions, other events and circumstances occurring after the date as at which the policy is changed, and (2) recognizing and disclosing the effect of the change in the accounting estimate in the periods affected by the change.

Restatement of comparative financial information. The recasting of a prior period's balance sheet or income statement information where there has been a change in accounting policy or correction of a fundamental error.

Retrospective application. The method of reporting a change in an accounting policy and of a correction of an error, respectively, by (1) applying the new accounting policy to transactions, other events and circumstances as if that policy had always been in use, and (2) recognizing and disclosing the corrected amount(s) as if the error had never occurred.

CONCEPTS, RULES, AND EXAMPLES

Importance of Comparability and Consistency in Financial Reporting

Accounting principles—whether various national GAAP or IFRS—have long held that an important objective of financial reporting is to encourage comparability among financial statements produced by essentially similar enterprises. This is necessary to facilitate informed economic decision making by investors, creditors, regulatory agencies, vendors, customers, prospective employees, joint venturers, and others. While full comparability will not be achieved as long as alternative principles of accounting and reporting for like transactions and events remain acceptable, a driving force in developing new accounting standards has been to enhance comparability. The IASB's convergence objective is to remove alternatives both within IFRS and between IFRS and US GAAP (and, to a lesser extent, UK

GAAP), in order to arrive at a single set of international, high-quality, financial reporting rules, with few exceptions and alternatives other than those demanded by the vicissitudes among the underlying facts and circumstances of the items or transactions being accounted for.

Comparability is one of the key qualitative characteristics of financial statements identified in the IABS's *Framework*. It is similarly cited in the underlying foundational documents of various national GAAP, such as US GAAP *Statements of Financial Reporting Concepts*.

An important implication of comparability is that users be informed about the accounting policies that were employed in the preparation of the financial statements, any changes in those policies, and the effects of such changes. Disclosure of accounting policies, per se, was discussed in Chapters 2, 3, and 4; this chapter addresses the appropriate communications of *changes* in accounting policies and related matters.

Strict adherence to IFRS or any other set of standards obviously helps in achieving comparability, since a common accounting language is employed by all reporting parties. IFRS has the clear advantage, now, of being officially sanctioned as the "language of business" across the European Union, beginning in 2005, and momentum seemingly favors IFRS as more nations, from Australia to China to Russia, either converge to or simply adopt IFRS as the requirement for, at least, financial reporting by publicly held companies. While historically some accountants opposed the focus on comparability, on the grounds that uniformity of accounting removes the element of judgment needed to produce the most faithful representation of an individual company's financial position and results of operations, others have expressed concern that overemphasis on comparability might be an impediment to the development of improved accounting methods. Increasingly, however, the paramount importance of comparability is being recognized, as the current convergence efforts strongly attest.

As contrasted with comparability, consistency refers to a given reporting entity's uniform and unvarying adherence, from one period to the next, to a defined set of accounting policies and procedures. The quality of consistency enhances the utility of financial statements to users by facilitating analysis and the understanding of comparative accounting data. According to IAS 1

> the presentation and classification of items in the financial statements should be retained from one period to the next unless a significant change in the nature of the operations of the enterprise or a review of its financial statement presentation demonstrates that more relevant information is provided in a different way.

It is, however, inappropriate for an entity to continue accounting for transactions in the same manner if the policies adopted lack qualitative characteristics of relevance and reliability. Thus, if more reliable and relevant accounting policy alternatives exist, it is better for the entity to change its methods of accounting for defined classes of transactions with, of course, adequate disclosure of both the nature of the change and of its effects.

Selecting Accounting Principles

Revised IAS 8 has established a hierarchy of accounting guidance to be followed by those reporting in conformity with IFRS. This is comparable to the "hierarchy of GAAP" established under US auditing standards many years ago (reportedly soon to be replaced by guidance in the accounting literature itself), and provides a logical ordering of authoritativeness for those instances when competing and possibly conflicting guidance exists. Given the relative paucity of authoritative guidance under IFRS (which is, of course, seen as a virtue by those who prefer "principles-based" standards, vis-à-vis the more "rules-based" standards arguably exemplified by US GAAP), heavy reliance is placed on reasoning by analogy from the existing standards and from materials found in various nonauthoritative sources.

According to revised IAS 8, when an IFRS standard, or an interpretation of a standard applies to an item in the financial statements, the accounting policy or policies applied to that item are to be determined by considering the following in descending order of authoritativeness:

1. The standard itself (including any appendices that form a part of it);
2. Any relevant Interpretations;
3. Appendices that do not form a part of the standard; and
4. Implementation guidance issued in respect of the standard.

When there is not any standard or interpretation that specifically applies to an item in the financial statements or class of transaction, management must use judgment in developing and applying an accounting policy. This should result in information that is both

1. Relevant to the decision-making needs of users; and
2. Reliable in the sense that the resulting financial statements—

    a. Will represent faithfully the results and financial position of the entity;
    b. Will reflect the economic substance of transactions and other events, and not merely their legal form;
    c. Are neutral (i.e., free from bias);
    d. Are prudent; and
    e. Are complete in all material respects.

In making this judgment, management must give consideration to the following sources, in descending order:

1. The requirements and guidance in standards and in interpretations dealing with similar and related issues, and appendices and implementation guidance issued in respect of those standards;
2. The definitions, recognition criteria and measurement concepts for assets, liabilities, income and expenses set out in the *Framework*; and
3. Pronouncements of other standard-setting bodies that use a similar conceptual framework to develop accounting standards (from discussions at IASB meetings, it seems likely that people anticipate that preparers would look to US GAAP next after IFRS).
4. Other accounting literature (e.g., textbooks, handbooks, scholarly articles), and accepted industry practices, to the extent (but only to the extent) that these are consistent with the promulgated standards and interpretations cited above.

Change in Accounting Policy

A change in an accounting policy means that a reporting entity has exchanged one accounting principle for another. According to IAS 8, the term *accounting policy* includes the accounting principles, bases, conventions, rules and practices used. For example, a change in inventory costing from weighted-average to first-in, first-out would be a change in accounting policy, as would a change in accounting for borrowing costs from capitalization to immediate expensing.

An interpretation of a similar definition under US GAAP provides a meaningful framework by establishing that a change in the components used to cost a firm's inventory is a change in accounting principle. This FASB interpretation also clarified that the preferability assessment (relating to the selection of the appropriate accounting policy or principle in particular circumstances) must be made from the perspective of quality financial reporting and not from the income tax perspective.

Changes in accounting policy are permitted if

1. The change is required by a standard or an interpretation, or
2. The change in accounting principle will result in a more relevant and reliable presentation of events or transactions in the financial statements of the enterprise.

IAS 8 does not regard the following as changes in accounting policies:

1. The adoption of an accounting policy for events or transactions that differ in substance from previously occurring events or transactions; and
2. The adoption of a new accounting policy to account for events or transactions that did not occur previously or that were immaterial in prior periods

The provisions of IAS 8 are not applicable to the initial adoption of a policy to carry assets at revalued amounts, although such adoption is indeed a change in accounting policy. Rather, this is to be dealt with as a revaluation in accordance with IAS 16 or IAS 38, as appropriate under the circumstances.

Changes in accounting policy pursuant to the adoption of a standard.   When a change in an accounting policy is made consequent to the enactment of a new standard, it is to be accounted for in accordance with the transitional provisions set forth in that standard. Generally, the transitional provisions will require the restatement of comparative period information.   Nonetheless, comparative information presented for a particular prior period need not be restated if doing so is impracticable.   When the comparative information for a particular prior period is not restated, the new accounting policy is to be applied to the balances of assets and liabilities as at the beginning of the period following that one, with a corresponding adjustment made to the opening balance of retained earnings for the first period restated.   The cumulative effect as of the beginning of the earliest comparative period presented (for which restatement is applied), if any, is to be reported as an adjustment to beginning retained earnings of that period.

For example, assume that a change is adopted in 2006 and comparative 2005 financial statements are to be presented with the 2006 financial statements.   The change in accounting policy also affects previously reported 2003-2004 financial position and results of operations, but these are not to be presented in the current financial report.   Therefore, the cumulative effect (i.e., the cumulative amount of expense or income which would have been recognized in years prior to 2005) as of the beginning of 2005 must be reported as an adjustment to beginning retained earnings in 2005.

In the absence of any specific transitional provisions in a standard, a change in an accounting policy is to be applied in accordance with the requirements set forth in IAS 8 for voluntary changes in accounting policy, as described below.

When applying the transitional provisions of a standard has an effect on the current period or any prior period presented, the reporting entity is required to disclose

1. The fact that the change in accounting policy has been made in accordance with the transitional provisions of the standard, with a description of those provisions;
2. The amount of the adjustment for the current period and for each prior period presented;
3. The amount of the adjustment relating to periods prior to those included in the comparative information; and

4.   The fact that the comparative financial information has been restated, or that restatement for a particular prior period has not been made because it was impracticable.

If the application of the transitional provisions set forth in a standard may be expected to have an effect in future periods, the reporting entity is required to disclose the fact that the change in an accounting policy is made in accordance with the prescribed transitional provisions, with a description of those provisions affecting future periods.

Although the "impracticability" provision of revised IAS 8 may appear to suggest that restatement of prior periods' results could easily be avoided by preparers of financial statements, this is not an accurately drawn implication of these rules. The objective of IFRS in general, and of revised IAS 8 in particular, is to enhance the interperiod comparability of information, since doing such will assist users in making economic decisions, particularly by allowing the assessment of trends in financial information for predictive purposes. There is accordingly a general presumption that the benefits derived from restating comparative information will exceed the resulting cost or effort of doing so—and that the reporting entity would make every reasonable effort to restate comparative amounts for each prior period presented.

The standard states that applying a requirement is impracticable when the entity cannot apply it after making every reasonable effort to do so. It specifies the following as circumstances where this might be the case:

1.   Where the effects of retrospective application are not determinable (e.g., where the information is not available because it was not captured at the time)
2.   If restatement requires assumptions about what would have been management's intent at the time.
3.   When restatement requires use of estimates and it is impossible to distinguish evidence of circumstance at the time of the transaction to be revised or whether they were available at the time.

In general terms, IFRS does not permit the use of hindsight in accounting. So, for example, if an entity decided to commence reporting on a revaluation basis for property in 2006, it would need to know what an appraiser would have estimated value to be in 2005 and perhaps prior years. The fact that the property became very valuable in 2006 should be reflected in the 2006 value and not in 2005 or 2004.

In circumstances where restatement is deemed impracticable, the reporting entity will instead disclose the reason for not restating the comparative amounts.

In certain circumstances, a new standard may be promulgated with a delayed effective date. This is done, for example, when the new requirements are complex and IASB wishes to give adequate time for preparers and auditors to master the new materials. If, as of a financial reporting date, the reporting entity has not elected early adoption of the standard, it must disclose (1) the nature of the future change or changes in accounting policy; (2) the date by which adoption of the standard is required; (3) the date as at which it plans to adopt the standard; and (4) either (a) an estimate of the effect that the change(s) will have on its financial position, or (b) if such an estimate cannot be made without undue cost or effort, a statement to that effect.

Voluntary changes in accounting policies. A change in an accounting policy other than one made pursuant to the promulgation of a new standard or interpretation must, under revised IAS 8, be accounted for retrospectively. With retrospective application, the results of operations for all prior periods presented must be restated, as if the newly adopted policy had always been used. If periods *before* the earliest period being presented were also affected, then the opening balance of retained earnings for the earliest period being presented must be restated to reflect the net impact on all earlier periods.

Revised IAS 8 provides that comparative information presented for a particular prior period need not be restated if doing so would be *impracticable*. When comparative information for a particular prior period is not restated, the new accounting policy is to be applied to the balances of assets and liabilities as at the beginning of the next period, with a corresponding adjustment made to the opening balance of retained earnings for the next period. In other words, it is not acceptable to have some periods restated, interspersed among periods that were not restated. If a voluntary change is being made in 2006 and a ten-year set of comparative income statements is being presented, it is impracticable to restate, say, 2003 financial statements, then no year before 2003 can be restated, either. Instead, the opening balance of retained earnings in 2003 will have to be adjusted to reflect the impact of the change in accounting principle in all pre-2003 years.

The restatement requirement applies when an accounting policy is changed, to prior period financial statements presented in the current financial report, as well as to any other information pertaining to prior periods, such as historical summaries of financial data.

When a change in an accounting policy has an effect on the current period or any prior period presented, or may have an effect in subsequent periods, the reporting entity must disclose (1) the reasons for the change; (2) the amount of the adjustment for the current period and for each prior period presented; (3) the amount of the adjustment relating to periods prior to those presented; and (4) that comparative information has been restated, or that restatement for a particular prior period has not been made because it would require undue cost or effort.

Computing cumulative effects of changes in accounting policies. The cumulative effect of a change in policy is generally determined by first calculating income before taxes, using both the new principle and the old principle for all prior periods affected. The differences between the two computed pretax income amounts, for each prior period, is then calculated. Next, these differences are adjusted for tax effects, which may be complicated by the differing interperiod tax allocation implications of the newly adopted accounting principles. Finally, the net of tax differences for each prior period are totaled. This total represents the cumulative effect adjustment at the beginning of the current period. The cumulative effect will either be an addition to or a subtraction from the opening balance of retained earnings. (Note: this assumes no prior years' financial statements are being presented. If prior year statements are being presented, the aforementioned cumulative effect adjustment is made to the beginning retained earnings of the earliest period presented, and all periods' income statements are adjusted to reflect the newly adopted accounting policy.)

Generally, only the direct effects of the change and the related income tax effect should be included in the cumulative effect calculation (i.e., if the company changes its method of costing inventories, only the effects of the change in cost of goods sold, net of tax, are considered to be direct effects). Indirect effects, such as the effect on a profit-sharing contribution or bonus payments that would have occurred as a result of the change in net income, are not included in the cumulative effect computation unless these are to be recorded by the firm (i.e., the expense is actually incurred). For example, if a change would cause earlier years' reported earnings to be reduced, which would have, if reported timely, reduced the profit sharing contributions made to employee benefit plans, but the entity will not attempt to recover the overpayments (for various possible reasons, including legal restrictions, negative impact on employee morale, and employee withdrawals from the plan in the interim), then these adjustments must be ignored in the restatement. If the entity intends to recover excess executive bonuses, on the other hand—and assuming that there is a realistic mechanism for obtaining recoveries—then these indirect effects are to be incorporated in the restatements.

The following example illustrates the computations and disclosures necessary when voluntary changes in accounting principles are made.

Example

In 2006, the Zircon Company adopted the percentage-of-completion method of accounting for long-term construction contracts. The company had used the completed-contract method for all prior years. Assume that making this change in accounting principle is acceptable under IFRS.

The following sections present extracts from the statements of earnings and retained earnings of Zircon Company before adjusting for the effects of the change in accounting policy. Net profit for 2006 was determined under the percentage-of-completion method of accounting.

	2006	*2005*
Profit before income taxes	€120,000	€130,000
Income taxes	(20,000)	(26,000)
Net profit	100,000	104,000
Retained earnings, beginning	134,000	30,000
Retained earnings, ending	€234,000	€134,000

The effects of the change in accounting policy are presented below.

	Difference in income under the percentage-of-completion method	*Effect of the change net of income taxes*
All years prior to 2005	€20,000	€14,000
Effect for 2005	15,000	10,500
Total as of the beginning of 2006	35,000	24,500
Effect for 2006	€20,000	€14,000

Zircon Company
Extracts from Comparative Income Statement
For the years ended December 31, 2006 and 2005

	2006	*2005* *restated*
Profit before income taxes	€120,000	€145,000
Income taxes	(20,000)	(30,500)
Net profit	€100,000	€114,500

Zircon Company
Statement of Changes in Equity (Retained Earnings columns only)
For the years ended December 31, 2006 and 2005

	2006	*2005*
Retained earnings, beginning, as reported previously	€134,000	€ 30,000
Change in accounting policy, net of income taxes of €10,500 for 2006 and €6,000 for 2005 (see Note 1)	24,500	14,000
Retained earnings, beginning, as restated	158,500	44,000
Net profit for the year	100,000	114,500
Retained earnings, ending	€258,500	€158,500

Zircon Company
Extracts from Notes to the
Financial Statements

Note 1: During 2006, Zircon Company changed the accounting policy for revenue and costs for a long-term construction contract from the completed-contract method to the percentage-of-completion method, to conform with the accounting treatment of contract revenue and contract costs under IAS 11, *Construction Contracts*. This change in accounting policy has been accounted for retrospectively. The comparative financial statements for 2005 have been revised to conform to the changed policy. The effect of this change is to increase income from contracts by €20,000 in 2006 and €15,000 in 2005. Opening retained earnings for 2005 has been increased by

€14,000, which is the amount of the adjustment relating to periods prior to 2005, net of income tax effect of €6,000.

Explanation. A change in accounting policy should be applied retrospectively unless the amount of any resulting adjustment that relates to prior periods cannot be accomplished without undue cost or effort. Any resulting adjustment should be reported as an adjustment to the opening balance of retained earnings. The steps in preparing the revised financial statements and related disclosures are as follows:

1. The 2006 income statement is not adjusted, since it already reflects application of the new policy.
2. The 2005 income statement is restated as follows:

Profit from ordinary activities before income taxes, as previously reported	€130,000
Effect of the change in accounting policy	15,000
As restated	145,000
Income taxes as previous reported	26,000
Income tax effect of the change in accounting policy (€15,000 – €10,500)	4,500
As restated	30,500
Net income as restated	€114,500

3. As presented in the statement of retained earnings, the opening retained earnings for 2005 was restated to reflect an increase of €14,000, which represents the amount of adjustment related to periods prior to 2005, net of income tax effect of €6,000. The opening balance of 2006 was adjusted by €24,500, which represented the effect of the change at the beginning of 2006, net of income taxes.

In some cases, a voluntary change in accounting policy will have consequential effects. For example, other payments, such as executive bonuses, may be determined based on reported earnings, and it may be that some or all of the bonuses previously paid are, per contract, subject to adjustment if earnings are restated.

The following example illustrates the computations and disclosures necessary when a voluntary change in accounting principle is made, and there are indirect effects that can be recognized.

Example of an accounting change having effects on nondiscretionary items

InterComm, Inc. decides in 2006 to adopt the straight-line method of depreciation for plant and equipment. The straight-line method will be used for all new acquisitions as well as for previously acquired plant equipment for which depreciation had been provided using an accelerated method. Per IAS 8, this is a change to be accounted for retroactively, by restatement.

The following assumptions are being made:

1. The direct effect of the change is limited to the change in accumulated depreciation.
2. The income tax rate is a flat 40% for all years.
3. The executive incentive bonus is the only nondiscretionary item affected by the change. It is 10% of pretax accounting income. Bonus candidates are still working with Inter-Comm; additional bonus will be distributed as a consequence of the increased earnings when restatement is effected for the change in depreciation method.
4. There are 1,000,000 shares of common stock outstanding throughout the entire period affected by the change.
5. An additional 100,000 shares would be issued if all the outstanding bonds were converted to common stock. Annual interest on this bond obligation is €25,000 (net of income tax).
6. For 2005 and 2006 the income from continuing operations is given as €1,100,000 and €1,200,000 respectively, after tax. There is a discontinued operation in each year, with a net profit amounting to €100,000 for 2005 and a loss of (€35,000) for 2006.

Increase (decrease) in net income

Year	Excess of accelerated depreciation over straight-line depreciation	Direct effects of change, net of tax	Nondiscretionary item, net of tax	Adjustment to obtain pro forma amounts
Prior to 2002	€ 20,000	€ 12,000	€ (1,200)	€ 10,800
2002	80,000	48,000	(4,800)	43,200
2003	70,000	42,000	(4,200)	37,800
2004	50,000	30,000	(3,000)	27,000
2005	30,000	18,000	(1,800)	16,200
Total at beg. of 2006	€250,000	€150,000	€(15,000)	€135,000

The "excess of accelerated depreciation over straight-line depreciation" is given in this example. It is generally determined by recomputing the depreciation under the new method and obtaining the difference between the two methods. The "direct effects of change, net of tax" represents the effect of the actual change (i.e., depreciation) upon income before extraordinary items adjusted for the income tax effects. For example, in the years prior to 2002 the change in depreciation methods (from accelerated to straight-line) resulted in a €20,000 reduction in depreciation expense (or an increase in net income). The net of tax number is €12,000 because the €20,000 increase in income is reduced by €8,000 (= 40% × €20,000) increase in income tax expense.

The "nondiscretionary item, net of tax" represents the income statement items affected indirectly as a result of the change. In this case, it was stipulated that the executive incentive bonus equal to 10% of pretax accounting income was the only "nondiscretionary item" affected. Thus, in years prior to 2002, when pretax accounting income increased by €20,000, the bonus expense would have been €2,000 higher (€20,000 × 10%). This also should be computed net of income tax, and because the expense would have increased by €2,000, income taxes would have decreased by €800 (€2,000 × 40%). The net of income tax increase in expense is €1,200.

If the restatement of income will cause an adjustment to bonuses paid in prior years, then this must be addressed in the restatement. However, if bonus amounts, once computed and paid, are not subject to later adjustment (either up or down), then this should be ignored. In the present example, management has stated that the additional bonus will be paid consistent with the terms of the bonus agreements with the executives, who all remain in their positions; therefore, this should be computed as part of the restatement.

The computation for years prior to 2002 in this example is as follows:

	Increase (decrease) in net income
Decrease in depreciation expense	€20,000
Increase in income taxes attributable to reduction in depreciation expense	(8,000)
Decrease in depreciation expense, net of income tax effect	12,000
Increase in compensation expense	(2,000)
Decrease in income taxes attributable to increase in compensation expense	800
Increase in compensation expense, net of income tax effect	(1,200)
Net effect of change in prior period's depreciation	€10,800

Similar calculations are required for each of the other years.

In the present instance, assume that a five-year statistical tabulation is being presented showing the earnings for years 2002 – 2006, and also that full financials are being presented for the 2005 and 2006 years.

On the Face of the Income Statement

	2006	*2005*
Income as originally reported, after tax	€1,200,000	€1,100,000
Restatement for change in depreciation method and for consequent change to executive bonuses		
Change in depreciation from originally reported amount, net of tax		18,000
Change in executive bonuses from originally reported amount, net of tax		(1,800)
Income as restated, before discontinued operations	€1,200,000	€1,116,200
Discontinued operations (description), net of income tax	(35,000)	100,000
Net income	€1,165,000	€1,216,200

In the Notes to the Financial Statements

Note A: Change in Depreciation Method for Plant Equipment

During 2006 the company decided to change its method of computing depreciation on plant equipment from sum-of-the-years' digits (SYD) to the straight-line method. The company made the change because the straight-line method better matches revenues and cost amortization and, therefore, is a preferable accounting principle. The new method has been applied retroactively to equipment acquisitions of prior years. The effect of the change in 2006 was to increase net income by approximately €10,000. Previously reported 2005 results have been restated to reflect the retroactive change in depreciation method; this increased 2005 net income by €16,200, net of tax, and including the consequential adjustment made to executive bonuses, net of tax.

Retained earnings as of January 1, 2005, has been increased by €118,800 to reflect the changes in depreciation and in executive bonuses, net of tax, for all earlier years so affected.

The accompanying five-year earnings summary reflects changes to depreciation and to executive bonuses for all years presented.

Change in Amortization Method

Tangible or intangible long-lived assets are subject to depreciation or amortization, respectively, as set forth in IAS 16 and IAS 38. Changes in methods of amortization may be implemented in order to more appropriately recognize amortization or depreciation as an asset's future economic benefits are consumed. For example, the straight-line method of amortization may be substituted for an accelerated method when it becomes clear that the straight-line method more accurately reports the consumption of the asset's utility to the reporting entity.

While a change in amortization method would appear to be a change in accounting policy and thus subject to the requirements of IAS 8 as revised, in fact special accounting for this change is mandated by IAS 16 and IAS 38.

Under IAS 16 (as amended effective 2005), which governs accounting for property, plant, and equipment (long-lived tangible assets), a change in the depreciation method is a change in the technique used to apply the entity's accounting policy to recognize depreciation as an asset's future economic benefits are consumed. Therefore it is deemed to be a change in an accounting estimate, to be accounted for as described below. Similar guidance is found in IAS 38, pertaining to intangible assets. These standards are discussed in greater detail in Chapters 8 and 9.

The foregoing exception applies when a change is made to the method of amortizing or depreciating existing assets. A different result obtains when only newly acquired assets are to be affected by the new procedures.

When a company adopts a different method of amortization for newly acquired identifiable long-lived assets, and uses that method for all new assets of the same class without changing the method used previously for existing assets of the same class, this is to be accounted for as a change in accounting principle. No adjustment is required to comparative financial statements, nor is any cumulative adjustment to be made to retained earnings at the beginning of the current or any earlier period, since the change in principle is being applied prospectively only. In these cases, a description of the nature of the method changed and the effect on net income and related per share amounts should be disclosed in the period of the change.

Change in Accounting Estimates

The preparation of financial statements requires frequent use of estimates—for such items as asset service lives, salvage values, likely collectibility of accounts receivable, accrual of warranty costs, provision for pension costs, and so on. These future conditions and events and their effects cannot be perceived with certainty; therefore, changes in estimates will be highly likely to occur as new information and more experience is obtained. IAS 8 requires that changes in estimates be handled *currently and prospectively*. It states that, "The effect of the change in accounting estimate should be accounted for in (a) the period of change if the change affects that period only or (b) the period of change and future periods if the change affects both." For example, on January 1, 2001, a machine purchased for €10,000 was originally estimated to have a ten-year useful life, with no salvage value. On January 1, 2006 (five years after the purchase), the asset's utility is reevaluated and it is then expected to last another ten years (i.e., for a total of fifteen years). The asset is furthermore now believed to have a $1,000 salvage value at the end of its use. As a result, both the current (2006) and subsequent periods are affected by the change in periodic depreciation. The annual depreciation charge over the remaining life would be computed as follows:

$$\frac{\text{Book value of asset} - \text{Salvage value}}{\text{Remaining useful life}} = \frac{\text{€}5,000 - \text{€}1,000}{10 \text{ years}} = \text{€}400/\text{yr.}$$

An impairment affecting the cost recovery of an asset should not be handled as a change in accounting estimate but instead should be treated as a loss of the period. (See the discussions in Chapters 8 and 9.)

In some situations it may be difficult to distinguish between changes in accounting policy and changes in accounting estimates. For example, a company may change from deferring and amortizing a cost to recording it as an expense as incurred because the future benefits of the cost have become doubtful. In this instance, the company is changing its accounting principle (from deferral to immediate recognition) because of its change in the estimate of the future utility of a particular cost incurred currently.

Although IFRS do not address this matter per se, useful guidance is available by reference to the parallel standard under US GAAP, which is APB 20. That standard concluded that a change in accounting estimate that is in essence effected by a change in accounting principle should be reported as a change in accounting estimate, the rationale being that the effect of the change in accounting principle is inseparable from the effect of the change in estimate. In the example in the preceding paragraph, the company is changing its accounting principle (from cost deferral to immediate recognition) because of its change in the estimate of the future value of a particular cost. The amount of the cumulative effect would be the same as that attributable to the current or future periods.

Because the two changes are indistinguishable, in the authors' opinion changes of this type should logically be considered changes in estimates and accounted for in accordance with IAS 8. However, the changes must be clearly indistinguishable to warrant being combined. The ability to compute each element independently would preclude combining them as a single change.

Correction of Errors

Although good internal control and the exercise of due care should serve to minimize the number of financial reporting errors that occur, these safeguards cannot be expected to completely eliminate errors in the financial statements. As a result, it was necessary for the accounting profession to pro-mulgate standards that would ensure uniform treatment of accounting for error corrections.

IAS 8 deals with accounting for error corrections. Historically, that standard established the concept of a "fundamental error," and provided for both benchmark and allowed alternative approaches to effecting corrections of these errors. The IASB's *Improvements Project* has resulted in the elimination of the concept of fundamental error, and the elimination of what had been the allowed alternative treatment. Under revised IAS 8, therefore, the only permitted treatment is a prior period adjustment (subject to the exception available when this is impracticable, as described below). Prior periods must be restated to report financial position and results of operations as they would have been displayed had the error never taken place.

Errors are defined by revised IAS 8 as omissions from and other misstatements of the entity's financial statements for one or more prior periods that are discovered in the current period and relate to reliable information that (1) was available when those prior period financial statements were prepared; and (2) could reasonably be expected to have been obtained and taken into account in the original preparation and presentation of those financial statements. Errors include the effects of mathematical mistakes, mistakes in applying accounting policies, oversights or misinterpretations of facts, and the effects of fininical reporting fraud.

There is a clear distinction between errors and changes in accounting estimates. Estimates by their nature are approximations that may need revision as additional information becomes known. For example, when a gain or loss is ultimately recognized on the outcome of a contingency that previously could not be estimated reliably, this does not constitute the correction of an error and cannot be dealt with by restatement. However, if the estimated amount of the contingency had been miscomputed from data available when the financial statements were prepared, at least some portion of the variance between the accrual and the ultimate outcome might reasonably be deemed an error. An error requires that information available, which should have been taken into account, was ignored or misinterpreted.

Revised IAS 8 stipulates that the amount of the correction of an error is to be accounted for retrospectively. Subject to practicability, an error is to be corrected by either

1. Restating the comparative amounts for the prior period(s) in which the error occurred, or
2. When the error occurred before the earliest prior period presented, restating the opening balance of retained earnings for that period so that the financial statements are presented as if the error had never occurred.

As with changes in accounting policies, comparative information presented for a particular period need not be restated, if restating the information is impracticable. However, as noted earlier in this chapter, because the value ascribed to truly comparable data is high, this exception is not to be viewed as an invitation to not restate comparable periods' financial statements to remove the effects of most errors. The standard sets out what constitutes impracticability, as discussed earlier in this chapter, and this should be strictly interpreted. When comparative information for a particular prior period is not restated, the opening balance of retained earnings for the next period must be restated for the cumulative effect of the error before the beginning of that period.

Because it is to be handled retrospectively, the correction of an error—which by definition relates to one or more prior periods—is excluded from the determination of profit or loss for the period in which the error is discovered. The financial statements are presented as if the error had never occurred, by correcting the error in the comparative information for the prior period(s) in which the error occurred, unless undue cost or effort exception is invoked. The amount of the correction relating to errors that occurred in periods prior to those presented in comparative information in the financial statements is adjusted against the opening balance of retained earnings of the earliest prior period presented. This treatment is entirely analogous to that now prescribed for changes in accounting policies.

Also, any other information presented with respect to prior periods, such as historical summaries of financial data, also is to be restated, again unless restatement would require undue cost or effort.

When an accounting error is being corrected, the reporting entity is to disclose the following:

1. The nature of the error;
2. The amount of the correction for each prior period presented;
3. The amount of the correction relating to periods prior to those presented in comparative information; and
4. That comparative information has been restated, or that the restatement for a particular prior period has not been made because it would require undue cost or effort.

In practice, the major criterion for determining whether or not to report the correction of the error is the materiality of the correction. There are many factors to be considered in determining the materiality of the error correction. Materiality should be considered for each correction individually as well as for all corrections in total. If the correction is determined to have a material effect on income before taxes, net income, or the trend of earnings, it should be disclosed in accordance with the requirements set forth in the preceding paragraph.

The prior period adjustment should be presented in the financial statements as follows:

Retained earnings, 1/1/05 as reported previously	€xxx
Correction of error (description) in prior period(s) (net of €xx tax)	xxx
Adjusted balance of retained earnings at 1/1/05	xxx
Net income for the year	xxx
Retained earnings, 12/31/05	€xxx

In comparative statements, prior period adjustments should also be shown as adjustments to the beginning balances in the retained earnings statements. The amount of the adjustment on the earliest statement shall be the cumulative effect of the error on periods prior to the earliest period presented. The later retained earnings statements presented should also show a prior period adjustment for the cumulative amount as of the beginning of the period being reported on.

Example of accounting for errors under IAS 8

In 2006, the bookkeeper of Dhow Jones Corp. discovered that in 2005 the company failed to record in the accounts depreciation expense in the amount of €20,000, relating to a newly constructed building. The following presents extracts from the statement of income and retained earnings for 2006 and 2005 before correction of the error:

	2006	2005
Gross profit	€200,000	€230,000
General and administrative expenses, including depreciation	(80,000)	(80,000)
Net income from ordinary activities, before income taxes	120,000	150,000
Income taxes	(20,000)	(30,000)
Net profit	100,000	120,000
Retained earnings, beginning	150,000	30,000
Retained earnings, ending	€250,000	€150,000

Dhow Jones Corp.'s income tax rate was 20% for both years.

The following provides an illustration of the accounting treatment and presentation of financial statements under the treatment prescribed by revised IAS 8.

Dhow Jones Corp.
Extracts from Income Statement
For the years ended December 31, 2006 and 2005

	2006	2005 restated
Gross profit	€200,000	€230,000
General and administrative expenses, including depreciation	(80,000)	(100,000)
Net income from ordinary activities, before income taxes	120,000	130,000
Income taxes	(20,000)	(26,000)
Net profit	€100,000	€104,000

Dhow Jones Corp.
Statement of Changes in Equity (Retained Earnings columns only)
For the years ended December 31, 2006 and 2005

	2006	2005 restated
Retained earnings, beginning, as reported previously	€150,000	€ 30,000
Correction of error, net of income taxes of €4,000 (see Note 1)	(16,000)	--
Retained earnings, beginning, as restated	134,000	30,000
Net profit	100,000	104,000
Retained earnings, ending	€234,000	€134,000

Dhow Jones Corp.
Extracts from Notes to the Financial Statements

Note 1: The company failed to record a depreciation charge in the amount of €20,000 in 2005. The financial statements for 2005 have been restated to correct this error.

Explanation. According to revised IAS 8, the amount of correction of an error that relates to prior periods should be reported by adjusting the opening balance of retained earnings. Comparative information should be restated unless impracticable. The steps in preparing the revised financial statements and related disclosures are as follows:

1. As presented in the statement of retained earnings, the opening retained earnings was adjusted by €16,000, which represented the amount of error, €20,000, net of income tax effect of €4,000.
2. The comparative amounts in the income statement were restated as follows:

General and administrative expenses, including depreciation, before correction	€ 80,000
Amount of correction	20,000
As restated	€100,000
Income taxes before correction	€ 30,000
Amount of correction	4,000
As restated	€ 26,000

Examples of Financial Statement Disclosures

Mittal Steel South Africa Limited
For the year ended December 31, 2004

Notes to the financial statements

Change in accounting policy and early adoption of International Financial Reporting Standards (IFRS). The principal accounting policies are consistent with those applied in the previous period, except for the following:

- A change in policy to consolidate the Iscor Management Share Trust retrospectively. The effect on equity for this change is reflected in the group statement of changes in shareholders' equity. The effect on net profit for the current period is nil; and
- The accounting treatment for negative goodwill arising on the acquisition of the remaining 50% of Saldanha Steel was reexamined. It has now been established that the original interpretation of IAS 22 in 2002 for the treatment of negative goodwill was not in line with the preferred interpretation at that time. Accordingly, negative goodwill should have been amortized over the life of the Saldanha Steel plant. This change in interpretation has been corrected retrospectively.

The following financial reporting standards were adopted early:

- IFRS 2 *Share-Based Payments*
- IFRS 3 *Business Combinations*
- IFRS 4 *Insurance Contract*
- IFRS 5 *Noncurrent Assets Held for Sale and Discontinued Operations*
- IAS 36 (Revised) *Impairment of Assets*
- IAS 38 (Revised) *Intangible Assets*

The effect of the policy change and early adoption of the financial reporting standards was as follows:

	Net income Increase/(decrease)		Shareholders' equity Increase/(decrease)	
	2004 Rm	*2003 Rm*	*2004 Rm*	*2003 Rm*
Consolidation of the Iscor Management Share Trust			(36)	15
Preferred interpretation for treatment of goodwill				(2,585)
IFRS 2 Share-Based Payments	(2)			
IFRS 3 Business Combinantions				2,585
IFRS 4 Insurance Contracts*				
IFRS 5 Noncurrent Assets Held for Sale and Discontinued Operations*				
IAS 36 (Revised) Impairment of Assets*				
IAS 38 (Revised) Intangible Assets*				

* *Implementation of these standards had no effect*

22 FOREIGN CURRENCY

PERSPECTIVE AND ISSUES

International trade, always important, continues to become more prevalent, and "multinational corporations" (MNC), now comprised not only of the international giants which are household names, but also many midtier companies, are the norm. Corporations worldwide are reaching beyond national boundaries and engaging in international trade. Global economic restructuring is rampant: signings of trade pacts such as GATT, NAFTA, and the World Trade Organization (WTO) have lent further impetus to the process of internationalization. International activity by most domestic corporations has increased significantly, which means that transactions are consummated not only with independent foreign entities but also with foreign subsidiaries.

Foreign subsidiaries, associates, and branches typically handle their accounts and prepare financial statements in the respective currencies of the countries in which they are located. Thus, it is more than likely that a MNC ends up receiving, at year-end, financial statements from various foreign subsidiaries expressed in a number of foreign currencies, such as dollars, euros, pounds, lira, dinars, won, rubles, and yen. However, for users of these financial statements to analyze the MNC's foreign involvement and overall financial position and results of operations properly, foreign-currency-denominated financial statements must first be expressed in terms that the users can understand. This means that the foreign currency financial statements of the various subsidiaries will have to be translated into the currency of the country where the MNC is registered or has its major operations.

IFRS governing the translation of foreign currency financial statements and the accounting for foreign currency transactions are found primarily in IAS 21, *The Effects of Changes in Foreign Exchange Rates*. IAS 21 applies to

1. Accounting for foreign currency transactions (e.g., exports, imports, and loans) which are denominated in other than the reporting entity's functional currency
2. Translation of foreign currency financial statements of branches, divisions, subsidiaries, and other investees that are incorporated in the financial statements of an entity by consolidation, proportionate consolidation, or the equity method of accounting

IAS 21 did not address hedge accounting for foreign currency items, other than the classification of exchange differences arising from a foreign currency liability accounted for as a hedge of a net investment in a foreign entity. IAS 39 subsequently established the accounting for hedges of a net investment in a foreign entity, which closely parallels that prescribed for cash flow hedging as set forth under that standard.

As part of the IASB's *Improvements Project*, a number of changes to IAS 21 have been made, and several previously issued SICs (interpretations) have been withdrawn. Besides relocating the guidance on foreign currency derivatives to IAS 39 (without altering it, however), the major changes were to replace the current option of *reporting currency* with the twin concepts of *functional currency* (the currency in which the entity measures the items in its financial statements) and *presentation currency* (the currency in which the entity presents its financial statements). Additionally, the current freedom to choose a functional currency has been terminated; the current allowed alternative—to capitalize certain exchange differences—has been eliminated; unrestricted choice is now permitted to report in any currency; and new requirements have been imposed for the translation of comparative amounts.

Sources of IFRS	
IAS 21, 39	*SIC* 7

DEFINITIONS OF TERMS

Closing rate. This refers to the spot exchange rate (defined below) at the balance sheet date.

Conversion. The exchange of one currency for another.

Exchange difference. The difference resulting from reporting the same number of units of a foreign currency in the presentation currency at different exchange rates.

Exchange rate. This refers to the ratio for exchange between two currencies.

Fair value. The amount for which an asset could be exchanged, or a liability could be settled, between knowledgeable willing parties in an arm's-length transaction.

Foreign currency. A currency other than the functional currency of the reporting entity (e.g., the Japanese yen is a foreign currency for a US reporting entity).

Foreign currency financial statements. Financial statements that employ as the unit of measure a foreign currency that is not the presentation currency of the entity.

Foreign currency transactions. Transactions whose terms are denominated in a foreign currency or require settlement in a foreign currency. Foreign currency transactions arise when an entity (1) buys or sells on credit goods or services whose prices are denominated in foreign currency, (2) borrows or lends funds and the amounts payable or receivable are denominated in foreign currency, (3) is a party to an unperformed foreign exchange contract, or (4) for other reasons acquires or disposes of assets or incurs or settles liabilities denominated in foreign currency.

Foreign currency translation. The process of expressing in the presentation currency of the entity amounts that are denominated or measured in a different currency.

Foreign entity. When the activities of a foreign operation are not an integral part of those of the reporting entity, such a foreign operation is referred to as a foreign entity.

Foreign operation. A foreign subsidiary, associate, joint venture, or branch of the reporting entity whose activities are based or conducted in a country other than the country where the reporting entity is domiciled.

Functional currency. The currency of the primary economic environment in which the entity operates, which thus is the currency in which the reporting entity measures the items in its financial statements, and which may differ from the presentation currency in some instances.

Group. A parent company and all of its subsidiaries.

Monetary items. Money held and assets and liabilities to be received or paid in fixed or determinable amounts of money.

Net investment in a foreign operation. The amount refers to the reporting entity's interest in the net assets of that operation.

Nonmonetary items. All balance sheet items other than cash, claims to cash, and cash obligations.

Presentation currency. The currency in which the reporting entity's financial statements are presented. There is no limitation on the selection of a presentation currency by a reporting entity.

Reporting entity. An entity or group whose financial statements are being referred to. Under this standard, those financial statements reflect (1) the financial statements of one or more foreign operations by consolidation, proportionate consolidation, or equity accounting; (2) foreign currency transactions; or (3) both of the foregoing.

Spot exchange rate. The exchange rate for immediate delivery of currencies exchanged.

Transaction date. In the context of recognition of exchange differences from settlement of monetary items arising from foreign currency transactions, transaction date refers to the date at which a foreign currency transaction (e.g., a sale or purchase of merchandise or services the settlement for which will be in a foreign currency) occurs and is recorded in the accounting records.

CONCEPTS, RULES, AND EXAMPLES

Applicability of Translation Guidance Provided by Revised IAS 21

Increasingly entities carry on business transactions on a multinational, or even global, basis. Vendors and customers may be located in other nations, and transactions may be denominated in foreign currencies. Accounting for these transactions in the currency of the reporting entity (its functional currency, as defined later in this discussion) is one of the matters addressed by IAS 21.

Furthermore, many entities have foreign operations—for example, manufacturing or distribution activities conducted in foreign countries, organized as subsidiaries, joint ventures, investees, or simply as branches—and these operations will likely have a variety of transactions with the parent and other affiliated entities (capital infusions, dividends, et al.). This creates both the problem of accounting for foreign-currency-denominated transactions, as mentioned in the preceding paragraph, but also the complex process of consolidating (if a subsidiary) the foreign operation's financial statements with those of the reporting (parent) entity, or of computing the reporting entity's share of the foreign operation's earnings (if equity method accounting is applicable).

Finally, entities may, without limitation, report their financial statements in foreign currencies (e.g., a German company can elect to report UK pounds sterling—which presumably might be done if the reporting entity has a large analyst following or many shareholders in the UK). This practice would necessitate that all balances be translated into the reporting currency, and for this to occur consistently and accurately there needs to be a set of rules to be adhered to.

IAS 21 provides the needed guidance on each of these matters. Compared to the guidance under the predecessor standard (adopted in 1993), the provisions of the revised standard are somewhat simpler to grasp, particularly since certain options previously available to financial statement preparers have been eliminated. The most recent changes to IAS 21, effective in 2005, were limited as to scope, but are nonetheless very significant.

Revised IAS 21 removes all guidance on foreign currency derivatives used for hedging to IAS 39.

Classification of Foreign Operations

Prior to the most recent revisions to IAS 21, the ways in which the foreign operations were being financed and operated (i.e., in relation to the reporting entity) were important to the determination of the method to be used to translate their financial statements. Foreign operations were classified either as (1) *foreign operations* that were integral to the operations of the reporting entity or (2) foreign operations that were not integral to the operations of the reporting entity (referred to as *foreign entities*). The accounting to be applied then depended on whether the foreign branch or subsidiary was categorized as a foreign operation or foreign entity.

The significance of these classifications has been effectively eliminated by revised IAS 21, which became effective for 2005. This is now an indicator useful in determining the reporting entity's functional currency, but it is not alone determinative. Under the revised standard, each of the entities to be included in the reporting entity's financial statements are to ascertain their respective appropriate functional currencies, which then must be used to measure financial position and results of operations. Greater emphasis is now to be given to the currency of the economy that determines the pricing of the entities' transactions, rather than to the currencies in which transactions are denominated.

Functional Currency

The concept of *functional currency* is key to understanding translation of financial statements. Previously, the term "measurement currency," as first introduced by SIC 19, was more commonly employed. (SIC 19 has now been withdrawn.) Functional currency is defined as being the currency of the primary economic environment in which an entity operates. This is normally, but not necessarily, the currency in which that entity principally generates and expends cash.

In determining the relevant functional currency, an entity would give primary consideration to

1. The currency that mainly influences sales prices for goods and services, as well as the currency of the country whose competitive forces and regulations mainly determine the sales prices of the entity's goods and services, and
2. The currency that primarily influences labor, material, and other costs of providing those goods or services.

Note that the currency which influences selling prices is most often that currency in which sales prices are denominated and settled, while the currency that most influences the various input costs is normally that in which input costs are denominated and settled. There are many situations in which input costs and output prices will be denominated in or influenced by differing currencies (e.g., an entity which manufactures all of its goods in Mexico, using locally sourced labor and materials, but sells all or most of its output in Europe in euro-denominated transactions).

In addition to the foregoing, IAS 21 notes other factors which may commonly also provide evidence of an entity's functional currency. These may be deemed secondary considerations. These are

1. The currency in which funds from financing activities (i.e., from the issuance of debt and equity instruments) are generated, and
2. The currency in which receipts from operating activities are usually retained.

In making a determination of whether the functional currency of a foreign operation (e.g., a subsidiary, branch, associate, or joint venture) is the same as that of the reporting entity (parent, investor, etc.), certain additional considerations may also be relevant. These include

1. Whether the activities of the foreign operation are carried out as an extension of the reporting entity, rather than being executed more or less autonomously;
2. What proportion of the foreign operation's activities is comprised of transactions with the reporting entity;
3. Whether the foreign operation's cash flows directly impact upon the cash flows of the reporting entity, and are available for prompt remittance to the reporting entity; and
4. Whether the foreign operation is largely cash flow independent (i.e., if its own cash flows are sufficient to service its existing and reasonably anticipated debts without the injection of funds by the reporting entity).

Foreign operations are characterized as being adjuncts of the operations of the reporting entity when, for example, the foreign operation only serves to sell goods imported from the reporting entity and in turn remits all sales proceeds to the reporting entity. On the other hand, the foreign operation is seen as being essentially autonomous when it accumulates cash and other monetary items, incurs expenses, generates income and arranges borrowings, all done substantially in its local currency.

In practice, there are many gradations along the continuum between full autonomy and the state of being a mere adjunct to the reporting entity's operations. When there are mixed indications, and thus the identity of the functional currency is not obvious, judgment is required to make this determination. The selection of the functional currency should most faithfully represent the economic effects of the underlying transactions, events and conditions. According to IAS 21, however, priority attention is to be given to the identity of the currency (or currencies) that impact selling prices for outputs of goods and services, and inputs for labor and materials and other costs. The other factors noted above are to be referred to secondarily, when a clear conclusion is not apparent from considering the two primary factors.

Example

A US-based company, Majordomo, Inc., has a major subsidiary located in the UK, John Bull Co., which produces and sells goods to customers almost exclusively in EU member states. Transactions are effected primarily in euros, both for sales and, to a lesser extent, for raw materials purchases. The functional currency is determined to be euros in this instance, given the facts noted. Transactions are to be measured in euros, accordingly. For purposes of the John Bull Co.'s stand-alone financial reporting, euro-based financial data will be translated into pounds Sterling, using the translation rules set forth in revised IAS 21. For consolidation of the UK subsidiary into the financial statements of parent entity Majordomo, Inc., translation into US dollars will be required, again using the procedures defined in the standard.

Once determined, an entity's functional currency will rarely be altered. However, since the entity's functional currency is expected to reflect its most significant underlying transactions, events and conditions, there obviously can be a change in functional currency if there are fundamental changes in those circumstances. For example, if the entity's manufacturing and sales operations are relocated to another country, and inputs are thereafter sourced from that new location, this may justify changing the functional currency for that operation. When the entity's functional currency is changed, it is to apply the translation procedures applicable to the new functional currency prospectively from that date.

If the functional currency, properly determined using the aforementioned criteria, is the currency of a hyperinflationary economy, as that term is defined under IAS 29, the entity's financial statements are restated in accordance with the provisions of that standard. Revised IAS 21 stresses that an entity cannot avert such restatement by employing tactics such as adopting an alternate functional currency, such as that of its parent entity.

Monetary and Nonmonetary Items

For purposes of applying IAS 21, it is important to understand the distinction between monetary and nonmonetary items. Monetary items are those granting or imposing "a right to receive, or an obligation to deliver, a fixed or determinable number of units of currency." In contrast, nonmonetary items are those exhibiting "the absence of a right to receive, or an obligation to deliver, a fixed or determinable number of units of currency. Examples of monetary items include accounts and notes receivable; pensions and other employee benefits to be paid in cash; provisions that are to be settled in cash; and cash dividends that are properly recognized as a liability. Examples of nonmonetary items include inventories; amounts prepaid for goods and services (e.g., prepaid insurance); property, plant, and equipment; goodwill; other intangible assets; and provisions that are to be settled by the delivery of a nonmonetary asset.

Reporting Foreign Currency Transactions in the Functional Currency

Foreign currency transactions are those denominated in, or requiring settlement in, a foreign currency. These can include such common transactions as those arising from

1. The purchase or sale of goods or services in transactions where the price is denominated in a foreign currency.
2. The borrowing or lending of funds, where the amounts owed or to be received are denominated in a foreign currency; or
3. Other routine activities such as the acquisition or disposition of assets, or the incurring of settlement of liabilities, if denominated in a foreign currency.

Under the provisions of IAS 21, foreign currency transactions are to be initially recorded in the functional currency by applying to the foreign-currency-denominated amounts the spot exchange rate between the functional currency and the foreign currency at the date of the transaction. However, when there are numerous, relatively homogeneous transactions over the course of the reporting period (e.g., year), it is acceptable, and much more practical, to apply an appropriate average exchange rate. In the simplest scenario, the simple numerical average (i.e., the midpoint between the beginning and ending exchange rates) could be used. Care must be exercised to ensure that such a simplistic approach is actually meaningful, however.

If exchange rate movements do not smoothly occur throughout the reporting period, or it rates move alternately up and down over the reporting interval, rather than monotonically up or down, then a more carefully constructed, weighted-average exchange rate should be used. Also, if transactions occur in other than a smooth pattern over the period—as might be the case for products characterized by seasonal sales—then a weighted-average exchange rate might be needed if exchange rates have moved materially over the course of the reporting period. For example, if the bulk of revenues is generated in the fourth quarter, the annual average exchange rate would probably not result in an accurately translated income statement.

Example

> Continuing the preceding example, the UK-based subsidiary, John Bull, which produces and sells goods to customers almost exclusively in EU member states, also had sizeable sales to a Swiss company in 2005, denominated in Swiss francs. These occurred primarily in the fourth quarter of the year, when the Swiss franc-euro exchange rate was atypically strong. In converting these sales to the functional currency (euros), the average exchange rate in the fourth quarter was deemed to be most relevant.

Subsequent to the date of the underlying transaction, there may be a continuing need to translate the foreign currency denominated event into the entity's functional currency. For example, a purchase or sale transaction may have given rise to an account payable or an account receivable, which remains unsettled at the next financial reporting date (e.g., the following month-end). According to IAS 21, at each such balance sheet date the foreign currency *monetary* items (such as payables and receivables) are to be translated using the closing rate (i.e., the exchange rate as of the balance sheet date).

Example

> If John Bull Co. (from the preceding examples) acquires receivables denominated in a foreign currency, Swiss francs (CHF), during 2005, these are translated into the functional currency, euros, at the date of the transaction. If the CHF-denominated receivables are still outstanding at year-end, it will translate those (ignoring any allowance for uncollectibles) into euros at the year-end exchange rate. If these remain outstanding at the end of 2006 (again ignoring collectibility concerns), these will be translated into euros using the *year-end 2006* exchange rate.

To the extent that exchange rates have changed since the transaction occurred (which will likely happen), gains and losses will have to be recognized by the reporting entity, since the amount due to or from a vendor or customer, denominated in a foreign currency, is now more or less valuable than when the transaction occurred.

Example

> Assume now that John Bull Co., acquired the above-noted receivables denominated in CHF during 2005, when the CHF-euro exchange rate was CHF 1 = €.65. At year-end 2005, the rate is CHF 1 = €.61, and by year-end 2006, the euro has further strengthened to CHF 1 = €.58. Assume that John Bull acquired CHF 10,000 of receivables in mid-2005, and all remain outstanding at year-end 2006. (Again, for purposes of this example only, ignore collectibility concerns).
>
> At the date of initial recognition, John Bull records accounts receivable of €6,500, since the euro is the functional currency (translation to British pounds or US dollars—a presentation currency—will be dealt with later). At year-end 2005, these receivables equate to only €6,100, for a loss of €400, which must be recognized in the company's 2005 income statement. In effect, by holding CHF-denominated receivables while the Swiss franc declined in value against the euro, John Bull suffered a loss. The Swiss franc further weakens over 2006, so that by year-end the

CHF 10,000 of receivables will only be worth €5,800, for a further loss of €300 in 2006, which again is to be recognized currently in John Bull's results of operations.

Nonmonetary items (such as property purchased for the company's foreign operation), on the other hand, are to be translated at historical exchange rates. The actual historical exchange rate to be used, however, depends on whether the nonmonetary item is being reported on the historical cost basis, or on a revalued basis, in those instances where the latter method of reporting is permitted under IFRS. If the nonmonetary items are measured in terms of historical cost in a foreign currency, then these are to be translated by using the exchange rate at the actual historical date of the transaction. If the item has been restated to a fair value measurement, then it must be translated into the functional currency by applying the ratio of exchange rates at the date when the fair value was determined.

Example—historical cost accounting employed by reporting entity

Assume that John Bull Co. acquired machinery from a Swiss manufacturer, in a transaction denominated in Swiss francs during 2005, when the CHF-euro exchange rate was CHF 1 = €.65. The price paid was CHF 250,000. For purposes of this example, ignore depreciation. At the transaction date, John Bull Co. records the machinery at €162,500. This same amount will be presented on the year-end 2005 and 2006 balance sheets. The change in exchange rates subsequent to the transaction date will not be considered, since machinery is a nonmonetary asset.

Example—revaluation accounting employed by reporting entity

Assume again that John Bull Co. acquired machinery from a Swiss manufacturer, in a transaction denominated in CHF during 2005, when the CHF-euro exchange rate was CHF 1 = €.65. The price paid was CHF 250,000. For purposes of this example, ignore depreciation. At year-end 2005, John Bull Co. elects to use the allowed alternative method of accounting under IAS 16, and determines that the fair value of the machinery is CHF 285,000. On the entity's year-end balance sheet, this is reported at the euro equivalent of the revalued amount, using the exchange rate at the revaluation date, or (CHF 285,000 × €.61 =) €173,850. This same amount will appear on the 2006 balance sheet (assuming no further revaluation is undertaken post-2005).

If a nonmonetary asset was acquired in a foreign currency transaction by incurring debt which is to be repaid in the foreign currency (e.g., when a building for the foreign operation was financed locally by commercial debt), subsequent to the actual transaction date the translation of the asset and the related debt will be at differing exchange rates (unless rates remain unchanged, which is not likely to happen.) The result will be either a gain or a loss, which reflects the fact that a nonmonetary asset was purchased but the burden of the related obligation for future payment will vary as the exchange rates fluctuate over time, until the debt is ultimately settled—in other words, the reporting entity has assumed exchange rate risk. On the other hand, if the debt were obtained in the reporting (parent) entity's home country or were otherwise denominated in the buyer's functional currency, there would be no exchange rate risk and no subsequent gain or loss resulting from such an exposure.

Example

Assume now that John Bull Co. acquired machinery from a Swiss manufacturer, in a transaction denominated in CHF during 2005, when the CHF-euro exchange rate was CHF 1 = €.65. The price paid was CHF 250,000. For purposes of this example, ignore depreciation. At the transaction date, John Bull Co. records the machinery at €162,500. This same amount will be presented on the year-end 2005 and 2006 balance sheets. The change in exchange rates subsequent to the transaction date will not be considered, since machinery is a nonmonetary asset.

However, the purchase of the machinery was effected by signing a 5-year note, payable in Swiss francs. Assume for simplicity the note is nonamortizing (i.e., due in full at maturity). The note is recorded, at transaction date, as a liability of €162,500. However, at year-end 2005, since the euro has strengthened, the obligation is only €152,500, for an exchange gain of €10,000. This is reported in current results of operations.

At year-end 2006, this obligation has a euro value of only €145,000, and thus a further gain of €7,500 is realized by John Bull Co. for financial reporting purposes.

Had the machinery been acquired for a euro-denominated obligation of €162,500, this would remain at that amount until ultimately retired. In this alternative case, the Swiss machinery manufacturer, not the British customer (whose functional currency is the euro), accepted exchange rate risk, and John Bull Co. will report no exchange rate gain or loss.

Other complications can arise, also, when accounting for transactions executed in a foreign currency. IAS 21 identifies circumstances where the carrying amount of an item is determined by comparing two or more amounts, as when inventory is to be presented at the lower of cost or net realizable value, consistent with the requirements of IAS 2. Another cited example pertains to long-lived assets, which must be reviewed for impairment, per IAS 36. In situations such as these (i.e., where the asset is nonmonetary and is measured in a foreign currency) the carrying amount in terms of functional currency is determined by comparing

1. The cost or carrying amount, as appropriate, translated at the exchange rate at the date when that amount was determined (i.e., the rate at the date of the transaction for an item measured in terms of historical cost, or the date of revaluation if the item were restated under relevant IFRS); and

2. The net realizable value or recoverable amount, as appropriate, translated at the exchange rate at the date when *that* value was determined (which would normally be the closing rate at the balance sheet date).

Note that by comparing translated amounts that are determined using exchange rate ratios as of differing dates, the actual effect of performing the translation will reflect two economic phenomena; namely, the IFRS-driven lower of cost or fair value comparison (or equivalent), and the changing exchange rates. The effect may be that an impairment loss is to be recognized in the functional currency when it would not have been recognized in the foreign currency, or the opposite relationship may hold (and, of course, there could be impairments in either case, albeit for differing amounts).

Example

John Bull Co. acquired raw materials inventory from a Swiss manufacturer, in a transaction denominated in CHF during 2005, when the CHF-euro exchange rate was CHF 1 = €.65. The price paid was CHF 34,000. At year-end, when the exchange rate was CHF 1 = €.61, the net realizable value of the inventory, which was still on hand, was CHF 32,000. Applying the IAS 21 requirements, it is determined (1) that the purchase cost in euros was (CHF 34,000 × .65 =) €22,100; and (2) that NRV at the balance sheet date is CHF 32,000 × .61 =) €19,520. A lower of cost or realizable value impairment adjustment is reported equal to (€22,100 – €19,520 =) €2,580.

See below for another example, where a NRV loss is called for even though NRV in the foreign currency is greater than cost, due to the interaction of exchange rate changes and NRV movements.

Translation of Foreign Operations and Foreign Entities

As noted, revised IAS 21, which became effective in 2005, diminishes the importance of distinguishing between *integral foreign operations* and *foreign entities,* which under earlier versions of the standard were central to determining how to translate foreign entity (e.g., subsidiary) financial statements. These requirements are now included among the secondary indicators to be used in determining an entity's functional currency.

As a consequence of this change, there is no longer a meaningful distinction between integral foreign operations and foreign entities. All entities that were previously classified as integral foreign operations now will have the same functional currency as their respective reporting entities (e.g., parent entities) have. For example, if a British subsidiary is integral to the operations of its US parent entity, the US dollar would be its functional currency.

Under the revised standard, only a single translation method can be used for foreign operations, and this is the same method that is applicable to foreign entities. Specifically, the reporting entity is required to translate the assets and liabilities of its foreign operations and foreign entities at the closing (balance sheet date) rate, and required to translate income and expenses at the exchange rates at the dates of the transactions (or at the average rate for the period, if this offers a reasonable approximation of actual transaction date rates).

Furthermore, IAS 21 now permits the reporting entity to present its financial statements in any currency (or currencies) that it chooses to use. This guideline applies whether the reporting unit is a stand-alone entity, a parent preparing consolidated financial statements, or a parent company, an investor, or a venturer preparing separate financial statements, as permitted under IAS 27.

As noted previously, sometimes an adjustment may be required to reduce the carrying amount of an asset in the financial statements of the reporting entity even though such an adjustment was not necessary in the separate, foreign currency based financial statements of the foreign operation. This stipulation of IAS 21 can best be illustrated by the following case study.

Example

Inventory of merchandise owned by a foreign operation of the reporting entity is being carried by the foreign operation at 3,750,000 SR (Saudi riyals) on its balance sheet. Suppose that the exchange rate fluctuated from 3.75 SR = 1 US dollar at September 15, 2005, when the merchandise was bought, to 4.25 SR = 1 US dollar at December 31, 2005 (i.e., the balance sheet date). The translation of this item into the functional currency will necessitate an adjustment to reduce the carrying amount of the inventory to its net realizable value if this value when translated into the functional currency is lower than the carrying amount translated at the rate prevailing on the date of purchase of the merchandise.

Although the net realizable value, which in terms of Saudi riyals is 4,000,000 (SR), is higher than the carrying amount in Saudi riyals (i.e., 3,750,000 SR) when translated into the functional currency (i.e., US dollars) at the balance sheet date, the net realizable value is lower than the carrying amount (translated into the functional currency at the exchange rate prevailing on the date of acquisition of the merchandise). Thus, on the financial statements of the foreign operation the inventory would not have to be adjusted. However, when the net realizable value is translated at the closing rate (which is 4.25 SR = 1 US dollar) into the functional currency, it will require the following adjustment:

1. Carrying amount translated at the exchange rate on September 15, 2005 (i.e., the date of acquisition) = SR 3,750,000 @ 3.75 SR to 1 US dollar = $1,000,000.
2. Net realizable value translated at the closing rate = SR 4,000,000 @ 4.25 SR to 1 US dollar = $941,176.
3. Adjustment needed = $1,000,000 – $941,176 = $58,824.

Conversely, IAS 21 further stipulates that an adjustment that already exists on the financial statements of the foreign operation may need to be reversed in the financial statements of the reporting entity. To illustrate this point, the facts of the example above are repeated, with some variation, below.

Example

All other factual details remaining the same as the preceding example; it is now assumed that the inventory, which is carried on the books of the foreign operation at Saudi riyals (SR)

3,750,000, instead has a net realizable value of SR 3,250,000 at year-end. Also assume that the exchange rate fluctuated from SR 3.75 = 1 US dollar at the date of acquisition of the merchandise to SR 3.00 = 1 US dollar on the balance sheet date.

Since in terms of Saudi riyals, the net realizable value on the balance sheet date was lower than the carrying value of the inventory, an adjustment must have been made on the balance sheet of the foreign operation (in Saudi riyals) to reduce the carrying amount to the lower of cost or net realizable value. In other words, a contra asset account (i.e., a lower of cost or market reserve) representing the difference between the carrying amount (SR 3,750,000) and the net realizable value (SR 3,250,000) must have been created on the books of the foreign operation.

On translating the financial statements of the foreign operation into the functional currency, however, it is noted that due to the fluctuation of the exchange rates the net realizable value when converted to the functional currency [SR 3,250,000 (@ 3.00 SR = 1 US dollar) = $1,083,333] is no longer lower than the translated carrying value which is to be converted at the exchange rate prevailing on the date of acquisition of the merchandise [SR 3,750,000 (@ SR 3.75 = 1 US dollar) = $1,000,000].

Thus, a reversal of the adjustment (for lower of cost or market) is required on the financial statements of the reporting entity, upon translation of the financial statements of the foreign operation.

IAS 21 Financial Statement Translation Method in Greater Detail

Over the years, various national and international accounting standard-setting regimes, subscribing to various philosophies, have attempted to deal with the task of translating the financial statements of foreign operations or entities. No one methodology has been fully satisfactory in accomplishing the objectives of financial reporting for the parent or other reporting entity, and there remains a good deal of confusion among users of the financial statements regarding these matters. IAS 21 embraced one (of four) popular approaches, a method that was commonly known as the *current rate* method, as its prescribed methodology.

Under revised IAS 21, which maintains the fundamental approach of its predecessor standard, there are two sets of translation requirements. The first of these deals with translation of foreign currency *transactions* by each individual entity, which may also be part of reporting group (e.g., consolidated parent and subsidiaries). This requires that all transactions and balances be translated into the individual entities' functional currencies. The second set of requirements is for the translation of entities' financial statements (e.g., those of subsidiaries) into that of the reporting entity (e.g., the parent) into the presentation currency. These matters are addressed in turn in the following paragraphs.

Conversion of foreign currency transactions and balances into functional currency. As discussed above, conversion of balance sheet items into functional currency is driven by the basic determination of monetary and nonmonetary items, with the former being translated at current (balance sheet reporting date) exchange rates, and the latter being translated at historical rates. This method would be used when the foreign currency transactions are being directly entered into by the reporting entity, or by what under former IAS 21 were deemed to be integrated or nonautonomous operations of the reporting entity.

For example, branch sales offices or production facilities of a large, integrated operation would qualify for this treatment (e.g., the European field operation of a US corporation, which is principally supplied by the home office but which occasionally also enters into local currency transactions). Since most (but not all) of its sales are US dollar denominated, and most of its costs, including merchandise, are the result of US transactions, the application of the previously mentioned criteria would conclude that the functional currency of the European sales office is the US dollar, and translation of foreign currency denominated assets and liabilities, and transactions would follow the monetary/nonmonetary distinction noted above.

In general, translation of nonmonetary items (inventory, plant assets, etc.) is done by applying the historical exchange rates. The historical rates usually are those in effect when the asset was acquired or (less often) when the nonmonetary liability was incurred, but if there was a subsequent revaluation, if this is permitted under IFRS, then the exchange rate reference date is that of the most recent revaluation.

If there is a revaluation, the translation adjustment follows the treatment accorded to the related nonmonetary item. Thus, if the revaluation creates a gain or loss recognized in income (e.g., from applying lower of cost or realizable value for inventory), the translation effect is likewise taken into income. If, on the other hand, the gain or loss from revaluation is required under IFRS to be reported directly in equity (e.g., from revaluation of plant assets, or from fair value adjustments made to available-for sale-securities investments), then the associated translation effect is also to be included directly in equity.

Net investment in foreign operation. A special rule applies to a net investment in a foreign operation. According to revised IAS 21, when the reporting entity has a monetary item that is receivable from or payable to a foreign operation for which settlement is neither planned nor likely to occur in the foreseeable future, this is, in substance, a part of the entity's net investment in its foreign operation. This item should be accounted for as follows:

1. Exchange differences arising from translation of monetary items forming part of the net investment in the foreign operations should be reflected in income in the *separate* financial statements of the reporting entity (investor/parent) and in the separate financial statements of the foreign operations, *but*
2. In the consolidated financial statements which include the investor/parent and the foreign operations, the exchange difference should be recognized initially in equity as a separate component, but eventually taken into income upon disposition of the foreign operation.

Note that when a monetary item is a component of a reporting entity's net investment in a foreign operation and it is denominated in the functional currency of the reporting entity, an exchange difference arises only in the foreign operation's individual financial statements. Conversely, if the item is denominated in the functional currency of the foreign operation, an exchange difference arises only in the reporting entity's separate financial statements.

Translation of financial statements. The other requirements and procedures under IAS 21 pertain to translating foreign currency denominated financial statements, rather than accounting for specific transactions executed in foreign currencies. The most commonly encountered need for this is when the parent entity is preparing consolidated financial statements, and one or more of the subsidiaries have reported in their respective currencies. The same need presents itself if an investee or joint venture's financial information is to be incorporated via the proportionate consolidation or the equity methods of accounting.

As noted above, under IAS 21 the method used for financial statement translation is essentially what is commonly called the *current rate* method.

Under the current rate method (which is also the primary method mandated under US GAAP), all assets and liabilities, both monetary and nonmonetary, are translated at the closing (balance sheet date) rate, which simplifies the process compared to all other historically advocated methods. More importantly, this more closely corresponds to the viewpoint of financial statement users, who tend to relate to currency exchange rates in existence at the balance sheet date, rather than to the various specific exchange rates that may have applied in prior months or years.

However, financial statements of preceding years should be translated at the rate(s) appropriately applied when these translations were first performed, (i.e., these are *not* to be updated to current closing or average rates). This rule applies because it would cause great confusion to users of financial statements if amounts once reported (when current) were now all restated even though no changes were being made to the underlying data, and of course the underlying economic phenomena, now one or more years in the past, cannot have changes since initially reported upon.

The theoretical basis for the current rate method is the "net investment concept," wherein the foreign entity is viewed as a separate entity that the parent invested into, rather than being considered as part of the parent's operations. Information provided about the foreign entity retains the internal relationships and results created in the foreign environments (economic, legal, and political) in which the entity operates. This approach works best, of course, when foreign-denominated debt is used to purchase the assets that create foreign-denominated revenues; these assets thus serve as a hedge against the effects caused by changes in the exchange rate on the debt. Any excess (i.e., net) assets will be affected by this foreign exchange risk, and this is the effect that is recognized in the parent company's balance sheet, as described below.

The following rules should be used in translating the financial statements of a foreign entity:

1. All assets and liabilities in the current year-end balance sheet, whether monetary or nonmonetary, should be translated at the closing rate.
2. Income and expense items in the current statement of income should be translated at the exchange rates at the dates of the transactions, except when the foreign entity reports in a currency of a hyperinflationary economy (as defined in IAS 29), in which case they should be translated at the closing rates.
3. All resulting exchange differences should be classified as a separate component of equity of the reporting entity until disposal of the net investment in a foreign entity.
4. All assets and liabilities in *prior period* balance sheets, being presented currently (e.g., as comparative information) whether monetary or nonmonetary, are translated at the exchange rates in effect as of those respective balance sheet dates.
5. Income and expense items in *prior period* statements of income, being presented currently (e.g., as comparative information), are translated at the exchange rates as of the dates of the original transactions (or averages, where appropriate).

Guidance Applicable to Special Situations

Minority interests. When a foreign entity is consolidated, but it is not wholly owned by the reporting entity, there will be minority interest reported in the consolidated balance sheet. IAS 21 requires that the accumulated exchange differences resulting from translation and attributable to the minority interest be allocated to and reported as minority interest instead of as a separate component of equity.

Goodwill arising on acquisition of a foreign entity. Any goodwill arising on the acquisition of a foreign entity should be treated as either

1. An asset of the foreign entity and translated at the closing rate, or
2. An asset of the reporting entity which is either already expressed in the functional currency or is converted to the functional currency, such as nonmonetary items that are carried at historical costs and translated at the exchange rate on the date of the transaction in accordance with IAS 21.

Note that under IFRS 3, negative goodwill can no longer be recognized (as any net excess of fair value of net acquired assets over cost is to be taken immediately into income). However, unless the reporting entity elects to retrospectively adopt IFRS 3, negative goodwill from earlier "bargain purchase" acquisitions may remain to be amortized to income over the lives of acquired assets. (See discussion in Chapter 11 for details.)

Fair value adjustments to carrying amount of assets and liabilities arising on acquisition of a foreign entity. IAS 21 prescribes the same treatment for this as for goodwill arising on acquisition of a foreign entity (discussed above).

Exchange differences arising from elimination of intragroup balances. While incorporating the financial statements of a foreign entity into those of the reporting entity, normal consolidation procedures such as elimination of intragroup balances and transactions are undertaken as required by IAS 27 and IAS 31. However, IAS 21 requires that exchange differences arising from intragroup monetary items should not be eliminated against corresponding amounts arising on other intragroup balances. This is because monetary items represent commitments to convert one currency into another and expose the reporting entity to a gain or loss through currency fluctuations. Thus, on consolidation, such exchange differences would continue to be recognized either as income or expense, or if they arise from exceptional circumstances described in IAS 21, they should be classified as equity until the disposal of the net investment.

Different reporting dates. When reporting dates for the financial statements of a foreign entity and those of the reporting entity differ, the foreign entity normally switches and prepares financial statements with reporting dates coinciding with those of the reporting entity. However, sometimes this may not be practicable to do. Under such circumstances IAS 27 allows the use of financial statements prepared as of different dates, provided that the difference is no more than three months. In such a case, the assets and liabilities of the foreign entity should be translated at the exchange rates prevailing on the balance sheet date of the foreign entity. Adjustments should be made for any significant movements in exchange rates between the balance sheet date of the foreign entity and that of the reporting entity in accordance with the provisions of IAS 27 and IAS 28 relating to this matter.

Disposal of a foreign entity. Any cumulative exchange differences are to be carried as a separate component of equity until the disposal of the foreign entity. The standard prescribes the treatment of the cumulative exchange differences account on the disposal of the foreign entity. This balance, which has been deferred, should be recognized as income or expense in the same period in which the gain or loss on disposal is recognized.

Disposal has been defined to include a sale, liquidation, repayment of share capital, or abandonment of all or part of the entity. Normally, payment of dividends would not constitute a repayment of capital. However, in rare circumstances, it does; for instance, when an entity pays dividends out of capital instead of accumulated profits, as defined in the companies' acts of certain countries, such as the United Kingdom, this would constitute repayment of capital. In such circumstances, obviously, dividends paid would constitute a disposal for the purposes of this standard.

IAS 21 further stipulates that in the case of a partial disposal of an interest in a foreign entity, only a proportionate share of the related accumulated exchange differences is recognized as a gain or a loss. A write-down of the carrying amount of the foreign entity does not constitute a partial disposal, and thus the deferred exchange differences carried forward as part of equity would not be affected by such a write-down.

Comprehensive example of the practical application of the current rate method

Assume that a US company has a 100%-owned subsidiary in Germany that began operations in 2005. The subsidiary's operations consist of utilizing company-owned space in an office building. This building, which cost five million euros, was financed primarily by German banks, although the parent did invest two million euros in the German operation. All revenues and cash expenses are received and paid in euros. The subsidiary also maintains its books and records in euros.

The financial statements of the German subsidiary are to be translated for incorporation into the US parent's financial statements. The subsidiary's balance sheet at December 31, 2005, and its combined statement of income and retained earnings for the year ended December 31, 2005, are presented below in euros.

German Company
Balance Sheet
at December 31, 2005
(000 omitted)

Assets		*Liabilities and stockholders' equity*	
Cash	€ 500	Accounts payable	€ 300
Note receivable	200	Unearned rent	100
Land	1,000	Mortgage payable	4,000
Building	5,000	Common stock	400
Accumulated depreciation	(100)	Additional paid-in capital	1,600
		Retained earnings	200
		Total liabilities and	
Total assets	€6,600	stockholders' equity	€6,600

German Company
Combined Statement of Income and Retained Earnings
for the Year Ended December 31, 2005
(000 omitted)

Revenues	€2,000
Operating expenses (including depreciation expense of €100)	1,700
Net income	300
Add retained earnings, January 1, 2005	--
Deduct dividends	(100)
Retained earnings, December 31, 2005	€ 200

Various *assumed* exchange rates for 2005 are as follows:

€1 = $0.90 at the beginning of 2005 (when the common stock was issued and the land and building were financed through the mortgage)
€1 = $1.05 weighted-average for 2005
€1 = $1.10 at the date the dividends were declared and the unearned rent was received
€1 = $1.20 at the end of 2005

The German company's financial statements must be translated into US dollars in terms of the provisions of IAS 21 (i.e., by the current rate method). This translation process is illustrated below.

German Company
Balance Sheet Translation
at December 31, 2005
(000 omitted)

Assets	*Euros*	*Exchange rates*	*US dollars*
Cash	€ 500	1.20	$ 600
Accounts receivable	200	1.20	240
Land	1000	1.20	1,200
Building (net)	4,900	1.20	5,880
Total assets	€6,600		$7,920

Liabilities and stockholders' equity

	Euros	Exchange rates	US dollars
Accounts payable	€ 300	1.20	$ 360
Unearned rent	100	1.20	120
Mortgage payable	4000	1.20	4,800
Common stock	400	0.90	360
Additional paid-in capital	1600	0.90	1,440
Retained earnings	200	(see income statement)	205
Cumulative exchange difference (translation adjustments)	--	--	635
Total liabilities and stockholders' equity	€6,600		$7,920

German Company
Combined Income and Retained Earnings Statement Translation
for the Year Ended December 31, 2005
(000 omitted)

	Euros	*Exchange rates*	*US dollars*
Revenues	€2,000	1.05	$2,100
Expenses (including €100 depreciation expense)	1,700	1.05	1,785
Net income	300		315
Add retained earnings, January 1	--	--	--
Deduct dividends	(100)	1.10	(110)
Retained earnings, December 31	€ 200		$ 205

German Company
Statement of Cash Flows
for the Year Ended December 31, 2005
(000 omitted)

	Euros	*Exchange rates*	*US dollars*
Operating activities			
Net income	€ 300	1.05	$ 315
Adjustments to reconcile net income to net cash provided by operating activities:			
Depreciation	100	1.05	105
Increase in accounts receivable	(200)	1.05	(210)
Increase in accounts payable	300	1.05	315
Increase in unearned rent	100	1.10	110
Net cash provided by operating activities	600		635
Investing activities			
Purchase of land	(1,000)	0.90	(900)
Purchase of building	(5,000)	0.90	(4,500)
Net cash used by investing activities	(6,000)		(5,400)
Financing activities			
Common stock issue	2,000	0.90	1,800
Mortgage payable	4,000	0.90	3,600
Dividends paid	(100)	1.10	(110)
Net cash provided by financing	5,900		5,290
Effect on exchange rate changes on cash	N/A		75
Increase in cash and equivalents	500		600
Cash at beginning of year	--		--
Cash at end of year	€ 500	1.20	$ 600

The following points should be noted concerning the current rate method:

1.   All assets and liabilities are translated using the current exchange rate at the balance sheet date (€1 = $1.20). All revenues and expenses should be translated at the rates in effect when these items are recognized during the period. Due to practical considera-

tions, however, weighted-average rates can be used to translate revenues and expenses (€1 = $1.05).

2. Stockholders' equity accounts are translated by using historical exchange rates. Common stock was issued at the beginning of 2005 when the exchange rate was €1 = $0.90. The translated balance of retained earnings is the result of the weighted-average rate applied to revenues and expenses and the specific rate in effect when the dividends were declared (€1 = $1.10).

3. Cumulative exchange differences (translation adjustments) result from translating all assets and liabilities at the current rate, while stockholders' equity is translated by using historical and weighted-average rates. The adjustments have no direct effect on cash flows; however, changes in exchange rate will have an indirect effect on sale or liquidation. Prior to this time, the effect is uncertain and remote. Also, the effect is due to the net investment rather than the subsidiary's operations. For these reasons the translation adjustments balance is reported as a separate component in the stockholders' equity section of the US company's consolidated balance sheet. This balance essentially equates the total debits of the subsidiary (now expressed in US dollars) with the total credits (also in dollars). It may also be determined directly, as shown next, to verify the translation process.

4. The cumulative exchange differences (translation adjustments) credit of $635 is calculated as follows:

Net assets at the beginning of 2005 (after common stock was issued and the land and building were acquired through mortgage financing)	€2,000 (1.20 – 0.90)	=	$600 credit
Net income	€ 300 (1.20 – 1.05)	=	45 credit
Dividends	€ 100 (1.20 – 1.10)	=	10 debit
Exchange difference (translation adjustment)			$635 credit

5. Since the translation adjustments balance that appears as a separate component of stockholders' equity is cumulative in nature, the change in this balance during the year should be disclosed in the financial statements. In the illustration, this balance went from zero to $635 at the end of 2005. The analysis of this change was presented previously.

In addition to the foregoing transactions, assume that the following occurred during 2006:

German Company
Balance Sheet
December 31
(000 omitted)

	2006	2005	*Increase/(decrease)*
Assets			
Cash	€1,000	€ 500	€500
Accounts receivable	--	200	(200)
Land	1,500	1,000	500
Building (net)	4,800	4,900	(100)
Total assets	€7,300	€6,600	€700
Liabilities and stockholders' equity			
Accounts payable	€ 500	€ 300	€200
Unearned rent	--	100	(100)
Mortgage payable	4,500	4,000	500
Common stock	400	400	--
Additional paid-in capital	1,600	1,600	--
Retained earnings	300	200	100
Total liabilities and stockholders' equity	€7,300	€6,600	€700

Wiley IFRS 2006

German Company
Combined Statement of Income and Retained Earnings
for the Year Ended December 31, 2006
(000 omitted)

Revenues	€2,200
Operating expenses (including depreciation expense of €100)	1,700
Net income	500
Add: Retained earnings, Jan. 1, 2006	200
Deduct dividends	(400)
Retained earnings, Dec. 31, 2006	€ 300

Exchange rates were:

€1 = $1.20 at the beginning of 2006
€1 = $1.16 weighted-average for 2006
€1 = $1.08 at the end of 2006
€1 = $1.10 when dividends were paid in 2006 and land bought by incurring mortgage

The translation process for 2006 is illustrated below.

German Company
Balance Sheet Translation
at December 31, 2006
(000 omitted)

Assets	*Euros*	*Exchange rates*	*US dollars*
Cash	€1,000	1.08	$1,080
Land	1,500	1.08	1,620
Building	4,800	1.08	5,184
Total assets	€7,300		$7,884
Liabilities and stockholders' equity			
Accounts payable	€ 500	1.08	$ 540
Mortgage payable	4,500	1.08	4,860
Common stock	400	0.90	360
Addl. paid-in capital	1,600	0.90	1,440
Retained earnings	300	(see income statement)	345
Cumulative translation adjustments	--		339
Total liabilities and stockholders' equity	€7,300		$7,884

German Company
Combined Income and Retained Earnings Statement Translation
for the Year Ended December 31, 2006
(000 omitted)

	Euros	*Exchange rates*	*US dollars*
Revenues	€2,200	1.16	$2,552
Operating expenses (including depreciation of €100)	1,700	1.16	1,972
Net income	500	1.16	580
Add: Retained earnings 1/1/05	200	--	205
Less: Dividends	(400)	1.10	(440)
Retained earnings 12/31/05	€ 300		$ 345

German Company
Statement of Cash Flows
for the Year Ended December 31, 2006
(000 omitted)

	Euros	*Exchange rates*	*US dollars*
Operating activities			
Net income	€ 500	1.16	$ 580
Adjustments to reconcile net income to net cash provided by operating activities:			
Depreciation	100	1.16	116
Decrease in accounts receivable	200	1.16	232
Increase in accounts payable	200	1.16	232
Decrease in unearned rent	(100)	1.16	(116)
Net cash provided by operating activities	900		1,044
Investing activities			
Purchase of land	(500)	1.10	(550)
Net cash used by investing activities	(500)		(550)
Financing activities			
Mortgage payable	500	1.10	550
Dividends	(400)	1.10	(440)
Net cash provided by financing activities	100		110
Effect of exchange rate changes on cash	N/A		(124)
Increase in cash and equivalents	500		480
Cash at beginning of year	500		600
Cash at end of year	€1,000	1.08	$1,080

Using the same mode of analysis that was presented before, the total exchange differences (translation adjustment) attributable to 2006 would be computed as follows:

Net assets at January 1, 2006	€2,200 (1.08 − 1.20)	=	$264 credit
Net income for 2006	€500 (1.08 − 1.16)	=	40 credit
Dividends for 2006	€400 (1.08 − 1.10)	=	8 debit
Total			$296 credit

The balance in the net exchange differences (translation adjustment) account at the end of 2006 would be $339 ($635 from 2005 less $296 from 2006).

6. Use of the equity method by the US company in accounting for the subsidiary would result in the following journal entries based on the information presented above:

	2005		*2006*	
Original investment				
Investment in German subsidiary	1,800*		--	
Cash		1,800		--

* *[$0.90 × common stock of €400 plus additional paid-in capital of €1,600]*

Earnings pickup				
Investment in German subsidiary	315*		580**	
Equity in subsidiary income		315		580

* *[$1.05 × net income of €300]*
** *[$1.16 × net income of €500]*

	2005		*2006*	
Dividends received				
Cash	110*		440**	
Investment in German subsidiary		110		440

Exchange difference (translation adjustments)	*2005*		*2006*	
Investment in German subsidiary	635			
Translation adjustments		635		
Translation adjustments			296	
Investment in German subsidiary				296

*   *[$1.10 × dividend of €100]*
** *[$1.10 × dividend of €400]*

Note that the stockholders' equity of the US company should be the same whether or not the German subsidiary is consolidated (per IAS 28). Since the subsidiary does not report the translation adjustments on its financial statements, care should be exercised so that it is not forgotten in application of the equity method.

7. If the US company disposes of its investment in the German subsidiary, the translation adjustments balance becomes part of the gain or loss that results from the transaction and must be eliminated. For example, assume that on January 2, 2007, the US company sells its entire investment for €3,000. The exchange rate at this date is €1 = $1.08. The balance in the investment account at December 31, 2006, is $2,484 as a result of the entries made previously.

	Investment in German Subsidiary	
1/1/05	1,800	
	315	110
	635	
1/1/06	2,640	
	580	440
		296
12/31/06	2,484	

The following entries would be made to reflect the sale of the investment:

Cash (€3,000 × $1.08)	3,240	
Investment in German subsidiary		2,484
Gain from sale of subsidiary		756
Translation adjustments	339	
Gain from sale of subsidiary		339

If the US company had sold a portion of its investment in the German subsidiary, only a proportionate share of the translation adjustments balance (cumulative amount of exchange differences) would have become part of the gain or loss from the transaction. To illustrate, if 80% of the German subsidiary was sold for €2,500 on January 2, 2006, the following journal entries would be made:

Cash (€2,500 × $1.08)	2,700.00	
Investment in German subsidiary (0.8 × $2,484)		1,987.20
Gain from sale of subsidiary		712.80
Cumulative exchange difference (translation adjustments) (0.8 × $339)	271.20	
Gain from sale of subsidiary		271.20

Translation of Foreign Currency Transactions in Further Detail

According to IAS 21, a foreign currency transaction is a transaction that is "denominated in or requires settlement in a foreign currency." Denominated means that the amount to be received or paid is fixed in terms of the number of units of a particular foreign currency, regardless of changes in the exchange rate.

From the viewpoint of a US company, for instance, a foreign currency transaction results when it imports or exports goods or services to a foreign entity or makes a loan involving a foreign entity and agrees to settle the transaction in currency other than the US dollar (the presentation currency of the US company). In these situations, the US company has "crossed currencies" and directly assumes the risk of fluctuating exchange rates of the foreign currency in which the transaction is denominated. This risk may lead to recognition of foreign exchange differences in the income statement of the US company. Note that exchange differences can result only when the foreign currency transactions are denominated in a foreign currency.

When a US company imports or exports goods or services and the transaction is to be settled in US dollars, the US company will incur neither gain nor loss because it bears no risk due to exchange rate fluctuations. The following example illustrates the terminology and procedures applicable to the translation of foreign currency transactions.

Assume that a US company, an exporter, sells merchandise to a customer in Germany on December 1, 2005, for €10,000. Receipt is due on January 31, 2006, and the US company prepares financial statements on December 31, 2005. At the transaction date (December 1, 2005), the spot rate for immediate exchange of foreign currencies indicates that €1 is equivalent to $1.18.

To find the US dollar equivalent of this transaction, the foreign currency amount, €10,000, is multiplied by $1.18 to get $11,800. At December 1, 2005, the foreign currency transaction should be recorded by the US company in the following manner:

Accounts receivable—Germany	11,800	
Sales		11,800

The accounts receivable and sales are measured in US dollars at the transaction date using the spot rate at the time of the transaction. While the accounts receivable is measured and reported in US dollars, the receivable is denominated or fixed in euros.

Foreign exchange gains or losses may occur if the spot rate for euros changes between the transaction date and the date of settlement (January 31, 2005). If financial statements are prepared between the transaction date and the settlement date, all receivables and payables that are denominated in a currency different than that in which payment will ultimately be received or paid (the euro) must be restated to reflect the spot rates in existence at the balance sheet date.

Assume that on December 31, 2005, the spot rate for euros is €1 = $1.20. This means that the €10,000 are now worth $12,000 and that the accounts receivable denominated in euros should be increased by $200. The following journal entry would be recorded as of December 31, 2005:

Accounts receivable—Germany	200	
Foreign currency exchange difference		200

Note that the sales account, which was credited on the transaction date for $11,800, is not affected by changes in the spot rate. This treatment exemplifies what may be called a two-transaction viewpoint. In other words, making the sale is the result of an operating decision, while bearing the risk of fluctuating spot rates is the result of a financing decision. Therefore, the amount determined as sales revenue at the transaction date should not be altered because of a financing decision to wait until January 31, 2006, for payment of the account.

The risk of a foreign exchange transaction loss can be avoided either by demanding immediate payment on December 1 or by entering into a forward exchange contract to hedge the exposed asset (accounts receivable). The fact that the US company in the example did not act in either of these two ways is reflected by requiring the recognition of foreign currency exchange differences (transaction gains or losses) in its income statement (reported as financial or nonoperating items) in the period during which the exchange rates changed.

This treatment has been criticized, however, because both the unrealized gain and/or loss are recognized in the financial statements, a practice that is at variance with traditional

GAAP. Furthermore, earnings will fluctuate because of changes in exchange rates and not because of changes in the economic activities of the entity.

On the settlement date (January 31, 2006), assume that the spot rate is €1 = $1.17. The receipt of €10,000 and their conversion into US dollars would be journalized in the following manner:

Foreign currency	11,700	
Foreign currency transaction loss	300	
Accounts receivable—Germany		12,000
Cash	5,100	
Foreign currency		5,100

The net effect of this foreign currency transaction was to receive $11,700 from a sale that was measured originally at $11,800. This realized net foreign currency transaction loss of $100 is reported on two income statements: a $200 gain in 2005 and a $300 loss in 2006. The reporting of the gain or loss in two income statements causes a temporary difference between pretax accounting and taxable income. This results because the transaction loss of $100 is not deductible until 2006, the year the transaction was completed or settled. Accordingly, interperiod tax allocation is required for foreign currency transaction gains or losses.

Losses from Severe Currency Devaluation or Depreciation

IAS 21 requires recognition of exchange differences as income or expense in the period in which they arise, as illustrated in the foregoing example. Previously, there had been an allowed alternative treatment for certain losses incurred due to effects of exchange rate changes on foreign-denominated obligations associated with asset acquisition. This allowed alternative treatment resulted in capitalization of the loss. However, revised IAS 21 removed the limited option in the previous version of IAS 21 to capitalize exchange differences resulting from a severe devaluation or depreciation of a currency against which there is no means of hedging. Under the current standard, such exchange differences must be uniformly recognized in profit or loss.

Disclosure Requirements

A number of disclosure requirements have been prescribed by IAS 21. Primarily, disclosure is required of the amounts of exchange differences included in net income or loss for the period, exchange differences that are included in the carrying amount of an asset, and those that are classified as equity along with a reconciliation of the beginning and ending balance in the cumulative exchange difference account carried as part of the equity.

When there is a change in classification of a foreign operation, disclosure is required as to the nature of the change, reason for the change, and the impact of the change on the current and each of the prior years presented. When the presentation currency is different from the currency of the country of domicile, the reason for this should be disclosed, and in case of any subsequent change in the presentation currency, the reason for making this change should also be disclosed. An entity should also disclose the method selected to translate goodwill and fair value adjustments arising on the acquisition of a foreign entity. Disclosure is encouraged of an entity's foreign currency risk management policy.

The following additional disclosures are required:

- When the functional currency is different from the currency of the country in which the entity is domiciled, the reason for using a different currency;
- The reason for any change in functional currency or presentation currency; and

- When financial statements are presented in a currency other than the entity's functional currency, the reason for using a different presentation currency, and a description of the method used in the translation process.
- When financial statements are presented in a currency other than the functional currency, an entity should state the fact that the functional currency reflects the economic substance of underlying events and circumstances;
- When financial statements are presented in a currency other than the functional currency, and the functional currency is the currency of a hyperinflationary economy, an entity should disclose the closing exchange rates between functional currency and presentation currency existing at the date of each balance sheet presented;
- When additional information not required by IAS is displayed in financial statements and in a currency other than presentation currency, as a matter of convenience to certain users, an entity should
  - Clearly identify such information as supplementary information;
  - Disclose the functional currency used to prepare the financial statements and the method of translation used to determine the supplementary information displayed;
  - Disclose the fact that the functional currency reflects the economic substance of the underlying events and circumstances of the entity and the supplementary information is displayed in another currency for convenience purposes only; and
  - Disclose the currency in which supplementary information is displayed.

Hedging a Net Investment in a Foreign Entity or Specific Transactions

Hedging a net investment. While IAS 21 did not address hedge accounting for foreign currency items other than classification of exchange differences arising on a foreign currency liability accounted for as a hedge of a net investment in a foreign entity, IAS 39 has established accounting requirements which largely parallel those for cash flow hedges. (Cash flow hedging is discussed in Chapter 10.) Specifically, IAS 39 states that the portion of the gain or loss on the hedging instrument that is determined to be an effective hedge is to be recognized directly in equity via the statement of changes in equity, whereas the ineffective portion of the hedge is to be either recognized immediately in results of operations if the hedging instrument is a derivative instrument, or else reported directly in equity if the instrument is not a derivative.

The gain or loss associated with an effective hedge is reported similar to foreign currency translation gain or loss, as an additional equity account. In fact, if the hedge is fully effective (which is rarely achieved in practice, however) the hedging gain or loss will be equal in amount and opposite in sign to the translation loss or gain.

In the examples set forth earlier in this chapter (see page 762), which illustrated the accounting for a foreign (German) operation of a US company, the cumulative translation gain as of year-end 2005 was reported as $635,000. If the US entity had been able to enter into a hedging transaction that was perfectly effective (which would most likely have involved a series of currency forward contracts), the net loss position as of that date would have been $635,000. If this were reported in stockholders' equity, as required under IAS 39, it would have served to exactly offset the cumulative translation gain at that point in time.

It should be noted that under the translation methodology prescribed by IAS 21 the ability to precisely hedge the net (accounting) investment in the German subsidiary would have been very remote, since the cumulative translation gain or loss is determined by both the changes in exchange rates since the common stock issuances of the subsidiary (which occurred at discrete points in time and thus could conceivably have been hedged), as well as the changes in the various periodic increments or decrements to retained earnings (which having occurred throughout the years of past operations, would involve a complex array of exchange rates, making hedging very difficult to achieve). As a practical matter, hedging the net investment in a foreign subsidiary would serve a very limited economic purpose at best. Such hedging is more often done to avoid the potentially embarrassing impact of changing exchange rates on the reported results of operations and financial position of the parent company, which may be important to management, but rarely connotes real economic performance over a longer time horizon.

Notwithstanding the foregoing comments, it is possible for a foreign currency transaction to act as an economic hedge against a parent's net investment in a foreign entity if

1. The transaction is designated as a hedge.
2. It is effective as a hedge.

To illustrate, assume that a US parent has a wholly owned British subsidiary which has net assets of £2 million. The US parent can borrow £2 million to hedge its net investment in the British subsidiary. Assume further that the British pound is the functional currency and that the £2 million liability is denominated in pounds. Fluctuations in the exchange rate for pounds will have no net effect on the parent company's consolidated balance sheet because increases (decreases) in the translation adjustments balance due to the translation of the net investment will be offset by decreases (increases) in this balance due to the adjustment of the liability denominated in pounds.

Hedging transactions. It may be more important for managers to hedge specific foreign currency denominated transactions, such as merchandise sales or purchases which involve exposure for the time horizon over which the foreign currency denominated receivable or payable remains outstanding. For example, consider the illustration set forth earlier in this chapter (see page 769), which discussed the sale of merchandise by a US entity to a German customer, denominated in euros, with the receivable being due some time after the sale. During the period the receivable remains pending, the creditor is at risk for currency exchange rate changes that might occur, leading to exchange rate gains or losses, depending on the direction the rates move. The following discussion sets forth the possible approach that could have been taken (and the accounting therefore) to reduce or eliminate this risk.

In the example, the US company could have entered into a forward exchange contract on December 1, 2005, to sell €10,000 for a negotiated amount to a foreign exchange broker for future delivery on January 31, 2006. Such a forward contract would be a hedge against the exposed asset position created by having an account receivable denominated in euros. The negotiated rate referred to above is called a futures or forward rate. This instrument would qualify as a derivative under IAS 39.

In most cases, this futures rate is not identical to the spot rate at the date of the forward contract. The difference between the futures rate and the spot rate at the date of the forward contract is referred to as a discount or premium. Any discount or premium must be amortized over the term of the forward contract, generally on a straight-line basis. The amortization of discount or premium is reflected in a separate revenue or expense account, not as an addition or subtraction to the foreign currency transaction gain or loss amount. It is important to observe that under this treatment, no net foreign currency transaction gains or losses result if assets and liabilities denominated in foreign currency are completely hedged at the transaction date.

To illustrate a hedge of an exposed asset, consider the following additional information for the German transaction.

> On December 1, 2005, the US company entered into a forward exchange contract to sell €10,000 on January 31, 2006, at $1.14 per euro. The spot rate on December 1 is $1.12 per euro.

The journal entries that reflect the sale of goods and the forward exchange contract appear as follows:

Sale transaction entries			Forward exchange contract entries (futures rate €1 = $1.14)		
12/1/05 (spot rate €1 = $1.12)			Due from exchange broker	11,400	
Accounts receivable—Germany	11,200		Due to exchange broker		11,200
Sales		11,200	Premium on forward contract		200
12/31/05 (spot rate €1 = $1.15)			Foreign currency transaction loss	300	
Accounts receivable—Germany	300		Due to exchange broker		300
Foreign currency transaction			Premium on forward contract	100	
gain		300	Financial revenue		
			($100 = $200/2 months)		100
1/31/06 (spot rate €1 = $1.17)					
Foreign currency	11,700		Due to exchange broker	11,500	
Accounts receivable—			Foreign currency		11,700
Germany		11,500	Foreign currency transaction loss	200	
Foreign currency transaction					
gain		200			
			Cash	11,400	
			Due from exchange broker		11,400
			Premium on forward contract	100	
			Financial revenue		100

The following points should be noted from the entries above:

1. The net foreign currency transaction gain or loss is zero. The account "Due from exchange broker" is fixed in terms of US dollars, and this amount is not affected by changes in spot rates between the transaction and settlement dates. The account "Due to exchange broker" is fixed or denominated in euros. The US company owes the exchange broker €10,000, and these must be delivered on January 31, 2006. Because this liability is denominated in euros, its amount is determined by spot rates. Since spot rates change, this liability changes in amount equal to the changes in accounts receivable because both of the amounts are based on the same spot rates. These changes are reflected as foreign currency transaction gains and losses that net out to zero.
2. The premium on forward contract is fixed in terms of US dollars. This amount is amortized to a financial revenue account over the life of the forward contract on a straight-line basis.
3. The net effect of this transaction is that $11,400 was received on January 31, 2006, for a sale originally recorded at $11,200. The $200 difference was taken into income via amortization.

Interpretations on Currency Transactions as Derivatives

The IASC's IAS 39 Implementation Guidance Committee (IGC) has addressed a few issues that pertain to translation of financial statements and foreign currency transactions. It has considered whether a currency swap that requires an exchange of different currencies of equal fair values at inception is a derivative, and has ruled that indeed it is. The IGC finds that the definition of a derivative instrument includes such currency swaps because the initial exchange of currencies of equal fair values does not result in an initial net investment in the contract, but instead, is an exchange of one form of cash for another form of cash of equal value. Such a contract has underlying variables (the foreign exchange rates) and will be settled at a future date. Thus, the criteria for being defined as a derivative financial instrument are all met.

The IGC offers an illustration similar to the following to demonstrate how such a swap works. Assume that Axis Corp. and Basic GmbH enter into a five-year fixed-for-fixed currency swap on euros and US dollars. The current spot exchange rate is 1 euro per dollar.

The five-year interest rate in the United States is presently 8%, while the five-year interest rate in euro countries is 6%. At the initiation of the swap, Axis pays 20 million euros to Basic, which in return pays $20 million to Axis. During the life of the swap, Axis and Basic make periodic interest payments to each other gross (i.e., without netting). Basic pays 6% per year on the 20 million euros it has received (1.2 million euros per year), while Axis pays 8% per year on the 20 million dollars it has received ($1.6 million per year). At the termination of the swap, the two parties again exchange the original principal amounts.

The IGC has also noted that certain foreign currency denominated transactions can involve embedded derivative instruments. It illustrates this concept with an example of a supply contract that provides for payment in a currency other than (1) the currency of the primary economic environment of either party to the contract and (2) the currency in which the product is routinely priced in international commerce. This arrangement contains an implicit embedded derivative that should be separated under IAS 39.

In the IGC's example, a Norwegian company agrees to sell oil to a company in France. The oil contract is denominated in Swiss francs, although oil contracts are routinely denominated in US dollars in international commerce. Importantly, neither company carries out any significant activities in Swiss francs. In this case, the Norwegian company regards the supply contract as a host contract with an embedded foreign currency forward to purchase Swiss francs. The French company regards the supply contract as a host contract with an embedded foreign currency forward to sell Swiss francs. Each company includes fair value changes on the currency forward in net profit or loss unless the reporting entity designates it as a cash flow hedging instrument, if doing so would be appropriate under the circumstances.

Examples of Financial Statement Disclosures

Bayer Aktiengesellschaft
Bayer Corporation
December 31, 2004

Foreign currency translation

In the financial statements of the individual consolidated companies, foreign currency receivables and payables are translated at closing rates, irrespective of whether they are exchange-hedged. Forward contracts that, from an economic point of view, serve as a hedge against fluctuations in exchange rates are stated at fair value.

The majority of consolidated companies outside the euro zone are to be regarded as foreign entities since they are financially, economically, and organizationally autonomous. Their functional currencies according to IAS 21 (*The Effects of Changes in Foreign Exchange Rates*) are thus the respective local currencies. The assets and liabilities of these companies are therefore translated at closing rates, income and expense items at average rates for the year.

Where the operations of a company outside the euro zone are integral to those of Bayer AG, the functional currency is the euro. Property, plant, and equipment, intangible assets, investments in affiliated companies and other securities included in investments are translated at the historical exchange rates on the dates of addition, along with any relevant amortization, depreciation and write-downs. All other balance sheet items are translated at closing rates. Income and expense items (except amortization, depreciation, and write-downs) are translated at average rates for the year.

Companies operating in hyperinflationary economies prepare their statements in hard currency and thus, in effect, by the temporal method described above.

Exchange differences arising from the translation of foreign companies' balance sheets are shown in a separate stockholders' equity item.

In case of divestiture, the respective exchange differences are reversed and recognized in income.

The exchange rates for major currencies against the euro varied as follows:

€1		Closing rate		Average rate	
		2003	*2004*	*2003*	*2004*
Argentina	ARS	3.70	4.05	3.33	3.66
Brazil	BRL	3.66	3.62	3.47	3.64
UK	GBP	0.70	0.71	0.69	0.68
Japan	JPY	135.05	139.65	130.96	134.40
Canada	CAD	1.62	1.64	1.58	1.62
Mexico	MXN	14.18	15.23	12.22	14.04
Switzerland	CHF	1.56	1.54	1.52	1.54
USA	USD	1.26	1.36	1.13	1.24

Nokia Corporation
December 31, 2004

Foreign Group companies

In the consolidated accounts all items in the profit and loss accounts of foreign subsidiaries are translated into euro at the average foreign exchange rates for the accounting period. The balance sheets of foreign Group companies are translated into euro at the year-end foreign exchange rates with the exception of goodwill arising on the acquisition of a foreign company, which is translated to euro at historical rates. Differences resulting from the translation of profit and loss account items at the average rate and the balance sheet items at the closing rate are also treated as an adjustment affecting consolidated shareholders' equity. On the disposal of all or part of a foreign Group company by sale, liquidation, repayment of share capital or abandonment, the cumulative amount or proportionate share of the translation difference is recognized as income or as expense in the same period in which the gain or loss on disposal is recognized.

Foreign currency hedging of net investments

The Group also applies hedge accounting for its foreign currency hedging on net investments. Qualifying hedges are those properly documented hedges of the foreign exchange rate risk of foreign-currency-denominated net investments that meet the requirements set out in IAS 39. The hedge must be effective both prospectively and retrospectively.

The Group claims hedge accounting in respect of forward foreign exchange contracts, foreign-currency-denominated loans, and options, or option strategies, which have zero net premium or a net premium paid, and where the terms of the bought and sold options within a collar or zero premium structure are the same.

For qualifying foreign exchange forwards the change in fair value that reflects the change in spot exchange rates is deferred in shareholders' equity. The change in fair value that reflects the change in forward exchange rates less the change in spot exchange rates is recognized in the profit and loss account. For qualifying foreign exchange options the change in intrinsic value is deferred in shareholders' equity. Changes in the time value are at all times taken directly to the profit and loss account.

If a foreign-currency-denominated loan is used as a hedge, all foreign exchange gains and losses arising from the transaction are recognized in shareholders' equity. Accumulated fair value changes from qualifying hedges are released from shareholders' equity into the profit and loss account only if the legal entity in the given country is sold or liquidated.

23 RELATED-PARTY DISCLOSURES

PERSPECTIVE AND ISSUES

Transactions between enterprises that are considered *related parties* (as defined by IAS 24) must be adequately disclosed in financial statements of the reporting entity. Such disclosures have long been a common feature of financial reporting, and most national accounting standard-setting bodies have imposed similar mandates. The rationale for compelling these disclosures is based upon the concern that entities which are related to each other, whether by virtue of an ability to control or to exercise significant influence (both as defined under IFRS) usually have leverage in the setting of prices to be charged. If these events and transactions were simply mingled with transactions conducted on normal arm's-length terms with customers or vendors, the users of the financial statements would likely be impeded in their ability to project future earnings and cash flow for the entity. Thus, in order to ensure transparency, reporting entities are required to disclose the nature, type, and components of transactions with related parties.

IAS 24 addresses the related-party issue and prescribes extensive disclosures. This standard became effective in 1986 and was revised effective 2005, as part of IASB's *Improvements Project.*

Although IAS 24 states "related-party relationships are a normal feature of commerce and business," it nevertheless recognizes that a related-party relationship could have an effect on the financial position and operating results of the reporting entity, due to the possibility that transactions with related parties may not be effected at the same amounts as are those between unrelated parties. For that reason, extensive disclosure of such transactions is deemed necessary to convey a full picture of the entity's position and results of operations.

While IAS 24 has been operative for almost two decades, it is commonly observed that related-party transactions are still not being disclosed properly in all instances. This is due in part, perhaps, to the perceived sensitive nature of such disclosures. As a consequence, even when a note to financial statements that is captioned "related-party transactions" is presented, it is often fairly evident that the full gamut of disclosures as required by IAS 24 have not been included. There seems to be particular resistance to reporting certain types of related-party transactions, such as loans to directors, key management personnel, or close members of the executives' families. Presumably, these deficiencies will occur less frequently over time, and as independent auditors become more familiar with IFRS requirements.

IAS 1 demands, as a prerequisite to asserting that financial statements have been prepared in conformity with IFRS, that there be *full compliance* with all IFRS. This requirement pertains to all recognition and measurement standards, and extends to the disclosures to be made as well. As a practical matter, it becomes incumbent upon the auditors to ascertain whether disclosures, including related-party disclosures, comply with IFRS when the financial statements represent such to be the case.

Related-party disclosures are prescribed by most national GAAP, including US GAAP. The US GAAP counterpart of IAS 24 is FAS 57, which was issued in 1982. While there are some differences between the US standard and IAS 24, in general these two standards could be considered similar to each other.

Sources of IFRS
IAS 1, 5, 8, 24, 27, 28, 30

DEFINITIONS OF TERMS

Close members of the family of an individual. For the purpose of IAS 24, close members of the family of an individual are defined as "those that may be expected to influence, or be influenced by, that person in their dealings with the entity." The following may be considered close members of the family: an individual's domestic partner and children, children of the individual's domestic partner, and dependents of the individual or the individual's domestic partner.

Compensation. Compensation encompasses all employee benefits (as defined in IAS 19) and also includes share-based payments as envisaged in IFRS 2. Employee benefits include all forms of consideration paid in exchange for services rendered to the entity. It also includes such consideration paid on behalf of a parent of the entity in respect to activities of the entity. Compensation thus includes short-term employee benefits (such as wages, salaries, paid annual leave), postemployment benefits (such as pensions), other long-term benefits (such as long-term disability benefits), termination or end-of-service benefits, and share-based payments.

Control. An entity is considered to have the ability to control another entity if it has the power to govern the financial and operating policies of the other entity so as to obtain benefits from its activities.

Joint control. An entity is considered to be jointly in control with another entity if they contractually agree to share control over an economic activity.

Key management personnel. IAS 24 defines key management personnel as "those persons having authority and responsibility for planning, directing, and controlling the activities of the reporting entity, including directors (whether executive or otherwise) of the entity."

Related party. Entities are considered to be related parties when one of them either (1) has the ability to control the other entity, (2) can exercise significant influence over the other entity in making financial and operating decisions, (3) has joint control over the other, (4) is a joint venture in which the other entity is a joint venturer, (5) functions as key management personnel of the other entity, or (6) is a close family member of any individual having the ability to control or influence the entity or is a key management member thereof.

Related-party transactions. Related-party transactions are dealings between related parties involving transfer of resources or obligations between them, regardless of whether a price is charged for the transactions.

Significant influence. For the purposes of this standard, an entity is considered to possess the ability to exercise significant influence over another entity if it participates in, as opposed to controls, the financial and operating policy decisions of that other entity.

CONCEPTS, RULES, AND EXAMPLES

The Need for Related-Party Disclosures

For strategic or other reasons, entities sometimes will carry out certain aspects of their business activity through associates or subsidiaries. For example, in order to ensure that it has a guaranteed supply of raw materials, an entity may decide to purchase a portion of its requirements (of raw materials) through a subsidiary or, alternatively, will make a direct investment in its vendor. In this way, the entity might be able to control or exercise significant influence over the financial and operating decisions of its major supplier (the investee), including insuring a source of supply and, perhaps, affecting the prices charged. Such related-party relationships and transactions are thus a normal feature of commerce and business, and need not suggest any untoward behavior.

A related-party relationship could have an impact on the financial position and operating results of the reporting enterprise because

1. Related parties may enter into certain transactions with each other which unrelated parties may not normally want to enter into (e.g., uneconomic transactions).
2. Amounts charged for transactions between related parties may not be comparable to amounts charged for similar transactions between unrelated parties (either higher or lower prices than arm's-length).
3. The mere existence of the relationship may sometimes be sufficient to affect the dealings of the reporting entity with other (unrelated) parties. (For instance, an entity may stop purchasing from its major supplier on acquiring a subsidiary which is a competitor of its [erstwhile] major supplier.)
4. Transactions between entities would not have taken place if the related-party relationship had not existed. For example, a company sells its entire output to an associate at cost. It might not have survived but for these related-party sales to the associate, since it does not have enough business with arm's-length customers for the kind of goods it deals in.
5. The existence of related-party relationships may result in certain transactions not taking place, which otherwise would have. Thus, even absent actual transactions with related entities, the mere fact that these exist could be material information from the viewpoints of various users of financial statements, including current and potential vendors, customers, and employees.

Because of peculiarities such as these, which often distinguish related-party transactions from those with unrelated entities, accounting standards (including IFRS) have almost universally mandated financial statement disclosure of such transactions. Disclosures of related-party transactions in financial statements is a means of conveying the message to users of financial statements that certain related-party relationships exist as of the date of the financial statements, or certain transactions were consummated with related parties during the period which the financial statements cover, and the financial impacts of these related-party transactions have been incorporated in the financial statements being presented. Since related-party transactions could have an effect on the financial position and operating results of the reporting entity, disclosure of such transactions would be prudent based on the increasingly cited principle of transparency (in financial statements). Only if such information is disclosed to them can the users of financial statements make informed decisions.

Scope of the Standard

IAS 24 is to be applied in dealing with related parties and transactions between a reporting entity and its related parties. The requirements of this standard apply to the financial statements of each reporting entity. IAS 24 sets forth disclosure requirements only; it does not prescribe the accounting for related-party transactions, nor does it address the measurements to be applied in the instance of such transactions. Thus, related-party transactions are reported at the nominal values ascribed to them, and are not subject to interpretation for financial reporting purposes.

IAS 24 is to be employed in determining the existence of related-party transactions and balances; identifying the ending balances between related parties; concluding on whether disclosures are required under the circumstances; and determining the content of such disclosures.

Related-party disclosures are required not only in the consolidated (group) financial statements, but also in the separate financial statements of the parent entity or a venturer or investor. In separate statements any intragroup transactions and balances must be disclosed in the related-party note, although these will be eliminated in consolidated financial reports.

Applicability

The requirements of the standard should be applied to related parties as set forth below. A party is related to an entity if

1. It controls (directly or indirectly through intermediaries) or is controlled by, or is under common control with the reporting entity. Examples include a parent company, subsidiaries, and fellow subsidiaries of a common parent.
2. It has an interest in the entity giving it significant influence.
3. It has joint control over the entity.
4. It is an associate of the reporting entity, as defined in IAS 28;
5. It is a party who is a member of key management personnel of the entity or its parent.
6. It is a close family member of those having control over the entity or those who are members of the key management team of the entity.
7. It is an entity that is controlled, jointly controlled or significantly influenced by, or for which significant voting power in such entity resides with (directly or otherwise) any individual who is a key management member or a close family member of those having control or serving in a key management role.
8. It is a postemployment benefit plan for the benefit of the employees of the entities, or of any entity that is a related party of the reporting entity.

Close family members. IAS 24 defines these as persons who would be expected to be able to exert influence over, or be influenced by, the individual who has control over the reporting entity or serves in a key management capacity with the reporting entity. It includes domestic partners and children, children of the domestic partner, and dependants of the individual or his/her domestic partner. Transactions with any such persons would be subject to IAS 24 disclosure requirements.

Substance over Form

The standard clarifies that in applying the deeming provisions of IAS 24 to each possible related-party relationship, consideration should be given to the substance of the relationship and not merely to the legal form. Thus, certain relationships might not rise to the level of related parties for purpose of necessitating disclosure under the provisions of IAS 24, Examples of such situations follow:

1. Two entities having only a common director or other key management personnel, notwithstanding the specific requirements of IAS 24 above.
2. Certain agencies, entities, or departments which play a role in the day-to-day business of the entity (even if they participate in its decision-making process). For example
    a. Providers of finance (e.g., banks and creditors)
    b. Trade unions
    c. Public utilities
    d. Government departments and agencies
3. Entities upon which the reporting entity may be economically dependent, due to the volume of business the entity transacts with them. For example
    a. A single customer;
    b. A major supplier;
    c. A franchisor;
    d. A distributor; or
    e. A general agent.
4. Two venturers, simply because they share joint control over a joint venture.

Significant Influence

The existence of the ability to exercise significant influence is an important concept in relation to this standard. It is one of the two criteria stipulated in the definition of a related party, which when present would, for the purposes of this standard, make one party related to another. In other words, for the purposes of this standard, if one party is considered to have the ability to exercise significant influence over another, then by virtue of this requirement of the standard, the two parties are considered to be related.

The existence of the ability to exercise significant influence may be evidenced in one or more of the following ways:

1. By representation on the board of directors of the other enterprise;
2. By participation in the policy-making process of the other enterprise;
3. By having material intercompany transactions between two enterprises;
4. By interchange of managerial personnel between two enterprises; or
5. By dependence on another enterprise for technical information.

Significant influence may be gained through agreement or statute or share ownership. Under the provisions of IAS 24, similar to the presumption of significant influence under IAS 28, an enterprise is deemed to possess the ability to exercise significant influence if it directly or indirectly through subsidiaries holds 20% or more of the voting power of another enterprise (unless it can be clearly demonstrated that despite holding such voting power the investor does not have the ability to exercise significant influence over the investee). Conversely, if an enterprise, directly or indirectly through subsidiaries, owns less than 20% of the voting power of another enterprise, it is presumed that the investor does not possess the ability to exercise significant influence (unless it can be clearly demonstrated that the investor does have such an ability despite holding less than 20% of the voting power). Further, while explaining the concept of significant influence, IAS 28 also clarifies that "a substantial or majority ownership by another investor does not *necessarily* preclude an investor from having significant influence" (emphasis added).

In the authors' opinion, by defining the term "related party" to include the concepts of control and significant influence, and by further broadening the definition to cover not just direct related-party relationships, but even indirect ones like those with "close members of the family of an individual," the IASB intended to cast a wide net, in order to cover related-party transactions which would sometimes not be considered such. This makes disclosures under this standard somewhat subjective, and the related-party issue itself a more contentious one, since it lends itself to aggressive interpretations by the reporting entity. This obviously could have a significant bearing on the related-party disclosures flowing from these interpretations.

Financial Statement Disclosures

IAS 24 recognizes that in many countries certain related-party disclosures are prescribed by law. In particular, transactions with directors, because of the fiduciary nature of their relationship with the enterprise, are mandated financial statement disclosures in some jurisdictions. In fact, corporate legislation in some countries goes further and requires certain disclosures which are even more stringent than the disclosure requirements under IAS 24, or under most national GAAP.

For example, under the Companies Act of a certain nation, in addition to the usual disclosures pertaining to related-party transactions, companies are required to disclose not just year-end balances that are due to or due from directors or certain other related parties, but are also required to disclose the highest balances for the period (for which financial statements are presented) which were due to or due from them to the corporate entity. In the authors' opinion, such a requirement is appropriate, since absent this disclosure balances at year-end can be "cleaned up" (e.g., via short-term bank borrowings) and the artificially low amounts reported can provide a misleading picture to financial statement users regarding the real magnitude of such transactions and balances.

For example, an enterprise which has advanced large sums of money to its directors could make arrangements for the directors to repay the loans to the enterprise a few days before the last day of the reporting period and agree to loan back to those directors these amounts shortly after the first day of the next reporting period. This type of practice, which is often referred to as "window dressing," can cause the financial statements and associated notes to be somewhat misleading while nonetheless compliant with the pertinent financial reporting requirements. Under IAS 24, it does not appear that such amounts of loans to directors (despite being material) would need to be disclosed, since none of them were actually outstanding at the end of the reporting period. As noted, however, disclosure of not just outstanding balances at the end of the reporting period, but also the highest balance(s) due to or due from related parties during the period, or the time-weighted average balance, would improve the quality of information disclosed. There is nothing in IAS 24 that prohibits this supplemental disclosure.

It should be noted that under IAS 30, banks and similar financial institutions are specifically required to make this additional disclosure (for a detailed discussion of disclosures of related-party transactions in the case of banks and similar financial institutions, see Chapter 24), thus confirming the usefulness of such disclosures, albeit in the limited context of financial institutions. There is thus clear precedent for disclosing ranges or average balances outstanding from or to related parties, even absent a material year-end balance.

IAS 24 provides examples of situations where related-party transactions may lead to disclosures by a reporting entity in the period that they affect.

- Purchases or sales of goods (finished or unfinished, meaning work in progress)

- Purchases or sales of property and other assets
- Rendering or receiving of services
- Agency arrangements
- Leasing arrangement
- Transfer of research and development
- License agreements
- Finance (including loans and equity participation in cash or in kind)
- Guarantees and collaterals
- Settlement of liabilities on behalf of the entity or by the entity on behalf of another party.

The foregoing should not be considered an exhaustive list of situations requiring disclosure. As very clearly stated in the standard, these are only "examples of situations . . . which may lead to disclosures." In practice, many other situations are encountered which would warrant disclosure. For example, a contract for maintaining and servicing computers, entered into with a subsidiary company, would need to be disclosed by the reporting entity in parent company financial statements.

Disclosure of Parent-Subsidiary Relationships

IAS 24 requires disclosure of relationships between parent and subsidiaries irrespective of whether there have been transactions between the related parties. The name of the parent entity must be provided in the subsidiary's financial statement disclosures; if the ultimate controlling party is a different entity, its name must be disclosed. One reason for this requirement is to enable users of the reporting entity's financial statements to seek out the financial statements of the parent or ultimate controlling party. If neither of these produces financial statements, IAS 24 provides that the name of the "next most senior parent" that produces financial statements must be stated, in addition. These requirements are in addition to those set forth by IAS 27, IAS 28, and IAS 31.

To illustrate this point, consider the following example:

> Company A owns 25% of Company B, and by virtue of share ownership of more than 20% of the voting power, would be considered to possess the ability to exercise significant influence over Company B. During the year, Company A entered into an agency agreement with Company B; however, no transactions took place during the year between the two companies based on the agency contract. Since Company A is considered a related party to Company B by virtue of the ability to exercise significant influence, rather than control (i.e., there is not a parent-subsidiary relationship), no disclosure of this related-party relationship would be needed under IAS 24. In case, however, Company A owned 51% or more of the voting power of Company B and thereby would be considered related to Company B on the basis of control, disclosure of this relationship would be needed, irrespective of whether any transactions actually took place between them.

Disclosures to Be Provided

Per IAS 24, if there have been transactions between related parties, the reporting entity should disclose

1. The nature of the related-party transaction, and
2. Information about transactions and outstanding balances necessary to understand the potential effect of the relationship on the financial statements. At a minimum the following disclosure shall be made:

   a. The amount of the transaction
   b. Amount of outstanding balances and their terms and conditions, including whether they are secured and details of any guarantees given or received;

3. Provision for doubtful debts related to the amount of the outstanding balances;
4. Any expense recognized during the period in respect of bad or doubtful debts due from the related parties.

The disclosures required are to be made *separately* for each of the following categories:

1. The parent;
2. Entities with joint control or significant influence over the entity;
3. Subsidiaries;
4. Associates
5. Joint venture in which the entity is a venturer;
6. Key management personnel of the entity or its parent; and
7. Other related parties.

Arm's-length transaction price assertions. The assertion that related-party transactions were made at terms that are normal or that the related-party transactions are at arm's-length can be made only if it can be supported. The default presumption is that related-party transactions are not necessarily conducted on arm's-length terms, however.

Thus, for example, when an entity purchases raw materials amounting to €5 million from an associated company, these are at normal commercial terms (which can be supported, e.g., by competitive bids), and these purchases account for 75% of its total purchases for the year, the following disclosures would seem appropriate:

> During the year, purchases amounting to €5 million were made from an associated company. These purchases were made at normal commercial terms, at prices equivalent to those offered by competitive unrelated vendors. At December 31, 2005, the balance remaining outstanding and owed to this associated company amounted to € 2.3 million.

Note that the obtaining of sufficient competent evidence to support an assertion that terms, including prices, for related-party transactions were equivalent to those which would have prevailed for transactions with unrelated parties may be difficult. For example, if the reporting entity formerly purchased from multiple unrelated vendors but, after acquiring a captive source of supply, moves a large portion of its purchases to that vendor, even if prices are the same as had been formerly negotiated with the many unrelated suppliers, this might not warrant an assertion such as the above. The reason is that, with 75% of all purchases being made with this single, related-party supplier, it might not be valid to compare those prices with the process previously negotiated with multiple vendors each providing only a smaller fraction of the reporting entity's needs. Had a large (almost single-source) supply arrangement been executed with any one of the previous suppliers, it might have been possible to negotiate a lower schedule of prices, making comparison of former prices paid for small purchases inapplicable to support this assertion.

Aggregation of disclosures. IAS 24 requires that items of a similar nature may be disclosed in the aggregate. However, when separate disclosure is necessary for an understanding of the effects of the related-party transactions on the financial statements of the reporting entity, aggregation would not be appropriate.

A good example of the foregoing is an aggregated disclosure of total sales made during the year to a number of associated companies, instead of separately disclosing sales made to each associated company. On the other hand, an example of separate disclosure (as opposed to aggregated disclosure) is the disclosure of year-end balances due from various related parties disclosed by category (e.g., advances to directors, associated companies, etc.). In the latter case, it makes sense to disclose separately by categories of related parties, instead of aggregating all balances from various related parties together and disclosing, say, the total amount due from all related parties as one amount, since the character of the transactions could well be at variance, as might be the likelihood of timely collection. In fact, separate disclosure in this case seems necessary for an understanding of the effects of related-party transactions on the financial statements of the reporting entity.

IAS 24 specifically cites other IAS which also establish requirements for disclosures of related-party transactions. These include

- IAS 27, which requires disclosure of a listing of significant subsidiaries
- IAS 28, which requires disclosure of a listing of significant associates
- IAS 8, which requires disclosure of exceptional items (i.e., those that are of such size, nature, or incidence that their disclosure is relevant to explain the performance of the enterprise) that arise in transactions with related parties

Compensation. A controversial topic is the disclosure of details regarding management compensation. In some nations, such disclosures (at least for the upper echelon of management) are required, but in other instances these are secrets closely kept by the reporting entities. As part of the deliberations resulting in the revision effective 2005, the IASB considered deleting these disclosures, given privacy and other concerns, and the belief that other "approval processes" (i.e., internal controls) regulated these arrangements, which therefore would not be subject to frequent abuse. However, these disclosures were maintained in the revised standard because these are deemed relevant for decision making by statement users and are clearly related-party transactions.

The reporting entity is required to disclose key management personnel compensation in total and for each of the following categories:

- Short-term employee benefits;
- Postemployment benefits;
- Other long-term benefits;
- Terminal benefits, and
- Share-based payment.

Examples of Financial Statement Disclosures

Novartis AG
For the year ended December 31, 2004

Major Shareholders and Related-Party Transactions

7.B. Related-Party Transactions

We have formed certain foundations for the purpose of advancing employee welfare, employee share participation, research and charitable contributions. The charitable foundations foster health care and social development in rural countries. The foundations are autonomous, and their boards are responsible for administering the foundations in accordance with the foundations' purpose and applicable law.

The employee share participation foundation has not been included in our consolidated financial statements prepared under IFRS, as SIC Interpretation 12, as issued by the Standing Interpretations Committee exempts postemployment and equity compensation plans from its scope. The total assets of this foundation, as of December 31, 2004, included 87.3 million of our shares with a market value of approximately $4.4 billion. As of December 31, 2003, the assets included 93.3 million of our shares with a market value of approximately $4.2 billion. As of December 31, 2002, the assets included 95.1 million of our shares with a fair market value of $3.4 billion. This foundation has been consolidated with our financial statements under US GAAP, and is included as a reconciling item in the US GAAP reconciliation.

In 2004 we granted short-term loans totaling $713 million to the employee welfare and other foundations and received short-term loans totaling $16 million from them. In 2003 we granted short-term loans totaling $651 million to the employee welfare and other foundations and received short-term loans totaling $8 million from them. In 2002, we granted short-term loans totaling $623 million to these foundations and received short-term loans totaling $2 million from them, nor any beneficial owner known to us holds more than 2% of our shares.

Notes to the financial statements

27. Related parties

The Novartis Group has formed certain foundations with the purpose of advancing employee welfare, employee share participation, employee education, research, and charitable contributions. The charitable foundations foster health care and social development in rural countries. Each of these foundations is autonomous and its board is responsible for its respective administration in accordance with the foundation's purpose and applicable law.

The Novartis Foundation for Employee Participation has not been included in the consolidated financial statements prepared under IFRS, as Interpretation 12 of the Standing Interpretations Committee exempts postemployment and equity compensation plans from its scope. The total assets of this Foundation as of December 31, 2004, included 87.3 million shares of Novartis AG with a market value of $4.4 billion. As of December 31, 2003, the assets included 93.3 million Novartis shares with a market value of $4.2 billion. This Foundation is consolidated under US GAAP and is included as a reconciling item in the US GAAP reconciliation.

In 2004, the Group made short-term deposits totaling $713 million with the above mentioned foundations and received short-term loans totaling $16 million from them. In 2003, the Group made short-term deposits totaling $651 million with the foundations and received short-term loans totaling $8 million from them.

In addition, there are approximately fifteen other foundations that were established for charitable purposes that have not been consolidated, as the Group does not receive a benefit therefrom. As of December 31, 2004, these foundations held approximately 6.1 million shares of Novartis, with a cost of approximately $35 million.

See notes 5, 10, 25, 26 and 28 to the consolidated financial statements for disclosure of other related-party transactions and balances.

Clariant International Ltd.
Period ending December 2004

Related-party transactions

Clariant maintains business relationships with mainly two groups of related parties. One group consists of the associated companies, where the most important ones are described in Note 4. The most important business with these companies is the purchase of services by Clariant (e.g., energy, rental of land and buildings) in Germany. In addition to this, Clariant exchanges services and goods with parties which are associated companies (i.e., in which Clariant holds a stake of between 20% and 50%). The pricing of all exchanges of goods and services with these parties is at arm's length.

The second group of related parties include the Board of Directors (nonexecutive members) and Board of Management. More information on the relationship with the Board of Directors is given in the chapter on corporate governance.

Income and expense		
CHF (million)	*2004*	*2003*
Income from the sale of goods to related parties	49	39
Income from the rendering of services to related parties	21	20
Expense from the purchase of goods from related parties	(17)	(26)
Expense from the purchase of services from related parties	(378)	(435)
Payables, receivables, and loans	*12/31/2004*	*12/31/03*
Receivables from related parties	11	8
Payables to related parties	40	53
Loans to related parties	1	0

CHF (millions)	*2004*	*2003*
Transactions with Board of Management		
Salaries and other short-term benefits	4	6
Termination benefits	4	8
Postemployment benefits	1	2
Share-based payments	1	1
Total	10	17

	12/31/2004	*12/31/03*
Number of granted shares	33,347	42,973
Bumber of granted options	49,326	41,370

Transactions with Board of Directors (nonexecutive members) CHF (million)	*2004*	*2003*
Cash compensation	600	600
Total	600	600
Number of shares allocated	18,406	18,979

There were no outstanding loans by the Group to any members of the Board of Directors or Board of Management.

Nokia Group
Period ending December 2003

Nokia Pension Foundation is a separate legal entity that manages and holds in trust the assets for the Group's Finnish employee benefit plans; these assets include 0.03% of Nokia's shares. In 2002 Nokia Pension Foundation was the counterparty to equity swap agreements with the Group. The equity swaps were entered into to hedge part of the company's liability relating to future social security cost on stock options. During 2003, all outstanding transactions were terminated and no new ones were entered into. During 2002 new transactions were entered into and old ones terminated based on the hedging need. The transactions and terminations were executed on standard commercial terms and conditions.

The notional amount of the equity swaps outstanding at December 31, 2002, was EUR 12 million and the fair value EUR 0 million. At December 31, 2003, the Group had no contribution payment liability to Nokia Pension Foundation (EUR 14 million in 2002 included in accrued expenses).

At December 31, 2003, the Group had borrowings amounting to EUR 64 million (EUR 66 million in 2002) from Nokia Unterst utzungskasse GmbH, the Group's German pension fund, which is a separate legal entity.

The group recorded net rental expense of EUR 2 million in 2003 (EUR 2 million in 2002 and EUR 4 million in 2001) pertaining to a sale-leaseback transaction with the Nokia Pension Foundation involving certain buildings and a lease of the underlying land.

There were no loans granted to top management at December 31, 2003 or 2002.

F. Hoffmann-LaRoche Ltd.
Period ending December 2004

Controlling shareholders. The share capital of Roche Holding Ltd., which is the Group's parent company, consists of 160,000,000 bearer shares. Based on information supplied by a shareholders' group with pooled voting rights, comprising Ms. Vera Michalski-Hoffmann, Ms. Maja Hoffmann, Mr. André S. Hoffmann, Dr. Andreas Oeri, Ms. Sabine Duschmalé-Oeri, Ms. Catherine Oeri, Ms. Beatrice Oeri, and Ms. Maja Oeri, that group holds 80,020,000 shares as in the preceding year, which represents 50.01% of the issued shares. This figure does not include any shares without pooled voting rights that are held outside this group by individual members of the group.

Mr. André S. Hoffmann and Dr. Andreas Oeri are members of the Board of Directors of Roche Holding Ltd. and in this capacity receive an annual remuneration of 300 thousand Swiss francs. In addition, Mr. Hoffmann and Dr. Oeri receive 20 thousand Swiss francs and 10 thousand Swiss francs respectively for their time and expenses related to their membership of Board committees. Until his retirement at the Annual General Meeting on April 6, 2004, Dr. Fritz Gerber was a member of the above mentioned shareholders' group and was also a member of the Board of Directors of Roche Holding Limited. For the period until April 6, 2004, Dr. Gerber received a remuneration of 75 thousand Swiss francs and a pension of 396 thousand Swiss francs.

There were no other transactions between the Group and the individual members of the above shareholders' group.

Subsidiary and associated companies. A listing of the major Group subsidiaries and associated companies is included in Note 41. Transactions between the parent company and its subsidiaries and between subsidiaries are eliminated on consolidation.

Transactions between the Group and its associated companies in millions of CHF.

	2004	*2003*
Income statement		
Income from the sale of goods or supply of services	–	4
Expenses for the purchase of goods or supply of services	–	(21)
Milestone and other upfront payments	–	(11)
Balance sheet	–	1
Trade accounts receivable	–	–
Trade accounts payable	–	–

Key management personnel. Members of the Board of Directors of Roche Holding Ltd. receive an annual remuneration and payment for their time and expenses related to their membership of Board committees. Total payments to nonexecutive directors in 2004 for this remuneration and expenses were 3 million Swiss francs (2003: 3 million Swiss francs). Payments to Dr. Franz B. Humer, who is also a member of the Executive Committee, are included in the figures for the Executive Committee below.

Members of the Executive Committee received total remuneration as shown in the table below.

Remuneration of members of the Executive Committee (in millions of CHF)

	2004	*2003*
Salary	12	13
Bonuses	5	4
Total cash remuneration paid	17	17
Options awarded (equivalent number of nonvoting equity securities)	147,815	226,482
Pension and social insurance contributions paid by the Group	8	6

24 SPECIALIZED INDUSTRIES

BANKS AND SIMILAR FINANCIAL INSTITUTIONS

PERSPECTIVE AND ISSUES

Disclosure requirements relating to financial statements of banks and similar financial institutions are contained in IAS 30. A broad definition of the term "bank" has been given by IAS 30 and covers all those enterprises (whether the word bank is included in their name or not)

1. Which are financial institutions
2. Whose principal activities are to accept deposits and borrow money with the intention of lending and investing
3. Which are within the scope of banking and similar legislations

Since banks' operations differ in many material respects from other commercial enterprises and liquidity and solvency is of paramount importance, their financial reporting inevitably will be somewhat specialized in nature. In recognition of their special needs, IAS 30 lays down a number of disclosure requirements. Some of these disclosures may seem unusual from the standpoint of other commercial enterprises and may be perceived by users of the banks' financial statements as excessive or superfluous; however, these disclosures have been made mandatory for banks, keeping in view the special characteristics of banks' operations and the role they play in maintaining public confidence in the monetary system of the country through their close relationship with regulatory authorities (such as the country's central bank) and the government. Further, a bank is exposed not only to liquidity risks but even risks arising from currency fluctuations, interest rate movements, changes in market prices, and counterparty failure. These risks are associated not only with assets and liabilities, which are recognized on a bank's balance sheet, but also with off-balance-sheet items. Thus, certain disclosure requirements as outlined by IAS 30 relate to off-balance-sheet items as well.

The development of IAS 30 took about ten years, an inordinate amount of time when contrasted to other standards produced by the former IASC. This was partly because of IASC's efforts to obtain input from bankers worldwide, and partly due to the regulated nature of the banking industry, which adds to the complexity of imposing uniform disclosure requirements across national boundaries.

Although IAS 30 applies exclusively to financial statements of banks and similar financial institutions, it does not, of itself, define all the disclosures required by those entities. They must also conform to the disclosure requirements of standards such as IAS 24 (related parties), IAS 19 (segment reporting), IAS 32 and IAS 39 (both dealing with financial instruments). Furthermore, IAS 7 incorporates special provisions that are applicable to financial institutions, and its appendix illustrates the use of the direct method by financial institutions.

Apart from minor revisions necessitated by the enactment of new standards, IAS 30 remained intact since its promulgation, but will be withdrawn when IFRS 7 (below) becomes effective in 2007. The most recent changes to IAS 30 were limited to revising the wording of the standard to conform it to amendments adopted to other standards; also, several paragraphs in the standard were deleted as consequential amendments to the IASB's *Improvements Project*.

Over the past half-decade the IASB (first, the IASC) came to recognize that there was the need to update and conform IAS 30 to the many standards produced since its issuance. In 1999, a project to do this was started by the IASC, and a steering committee was appointed in 2000 for that purpose. After much work, in December 2002 the IASB concluded that it would be impractical to incorporate the proposals into IAS 32 in time to be applied in 2005 (when the EU member states planned to adopt IFRS for the first time). Hence, IASB determined that a separate Exposure Draft, which would replace the financial risk disclosures in IAS 32 and IAS 30 and would be made effective after 2005, should be developed.

An Exposure Draft of this replacement standard was produced in 2004 and the final standard, IFRS 7, was published in mid-2005. IFRS 7 will not become mandatorily effective until 2007, although earlier application is encouraged.

Since this edition of *Wiley IFRS* will be used by readers in preparing 2005 and, perhaps 2006 financial statements, the IAS 30 materials have been retained in their entirety. This chapter also details the requirements under IFRS 7.

Sources of IFRS	
IAS 1, 7, 16, 18, 24, 30, 32, 37, 39	*IFRS* 7

CONCEPTS, RULES, AND EXAMPLES

Accounting Policies Disclosure Requirements under IAS 30

IAS 1, which applies to financial statements of all commercial, industrial, and business enterprises in general (which includes banks and similar financial institutions as well), requires that disclosure be made of all significant accounting policies that were adopted in the preparation and presentation of an entity's financial statements. To comply with that standard and also in recognition of the differences between financial institutions and other commercial enterprises, disclosures by banks were later prescribed by IAS 30. The intention was to enable users of banks' financial statements to better understand the basis of preparation of those financial statements. Specifically, disclosure of the following accounting policies is prescribed by IAS 30:

1. The accounting policy setting forth the recognition of the principal types of income. An example of this disclosure follows:

    "Interest income and loan commitment fees are recognized on a time proportion basis[*] taking into account the principal outstanding and the rate applicable. Other fee income is recognized when due."

    [*] *IAS 18 specifically requires that interest income be recognized on a time proportion basis.*

2. Accounting policies relating to the valuation of investments and dealing securities. An illustration follows:

    Example of accounting policy relating to valuation of investments

    Trading investments. Trading investments are carried at fair values with any gain or loss arising from changes in fair values being taken to the Income Statement.

    NOTE: Before amendment (consequential to the enactment of IAS 39), IAS 30 mandated that banks disclose market values of dealing securities and marketable investment securities if these values were different from their carrying amounts in the financial statements. In order not to be inconsistent with the requirements of IAS 39 (and to be consistent with the evolving emphasis on fair value accounting), the amended IAS 30 requires disclosure of fair values of each class of its financial assets and liabilities.

3. Accounting policy explaining the distinction between transactions and events that result in the recognition of assets and liabilities on the balance sheet versus those that give rise to contingencies and commitments, including off-balance-sheet items. An example follows:

Example of accounting policy relating to off-balance-sheet items

Commitments. Undrawn lending facilities, such as lines of credit extended to customers, that are irrevocable according to agreements with customers (and cannot be withdrawn at the discretion of the bank), are disclosed as commitments rather than as loans and advances to customers. If, and to the extent, the facilities are utilized by customers before year-end, these will be reported as actual loans and advances.

4. Accounting policy that outlines the basis for the determination of

    a. The provision for possible losses on loans and advances
    b. Write-off of uncollectable loans and advances

    Example of accounting policies (adapted from published financial statements)

    Impairment of loans and advances. Loans and advances are reviewed periodically at each balance sheet date to determine whether there is objective evidence of impairment. If there is evidence of such impairment, it is to be estimated as set forth below.

    a. In case of "originated loans and advances" based on the present value of the expected cash flows discounted at the instrument's original effective interest rate.
    b. In case of other "loans and advances" specific allowances are provided against those loans and advances that are *identified as impaired* based on reviews of the outstanding balances and in case of *portfolios of similar loans and advances* the expected cash flows which are estimated based on previous experience taking into consideration the credit rating of the underlying customers and their payment history and are discounted at original effective interest rates.

    In subsequent years if the impairment losses reverse the provisions is written back to the income statement.

5. Accounting policy explaining the basis for determining and setting aside amounts toward general banking risks and the accounting treatment accorded to this reserve.

    Regulatory bodies, such as the central bank of the country in which the bank is incorporated, or local legislation may require or allow a bank to set aside amounts for general banking risks, including future losses or other unforeseeable risks or even reserves for contingencies over and above accruals required by IAS 37. It would not be proper to allow banks to charge these additional reserves to the income statement, as this would distort the true financial position of the bank. Thus, IAS 30 requires that the above mentioned reserves be appropriated out of the retained earnings and be separately disclosed as such. An example is

    Note 1. Statutory Reserves

    As required by the Companies Commercial Code of Nation XYZ, and in accordance with the bank's articles of association, 10% of the net income for the year is set aside as a statutory reserve annually. Such appropriations of net income are to continue until the balance in the statutory reserve equals 50% of the bank's paid-up capital.

Preparation and Presentation of Banks' Financial Statements

The following ground rules have been established by IAS 30 for the preparation and presentation of the financial statements of banks:

1. The income statement of a bank should be presented in a manner that groups income and expenses by nature and discloses the amounts of the principal types of in-

come and expenses. This principle has been further elucidated by the standard as follows:

a. Disclosures in the income statement or in the footnotes should include, but are not limited to, the following items:

  (1) Interest and similar income
  (2) Interest expense and similar charges
  (3) Dividend income
  (4) Fee and commission income
  (5) Fee and commission expense
  (6) Gains less losses arising from dealing securities
  (7) Gains less losses arising from investment securities
  (8) Gains less losses arising from dealing in foreign currencies
  (9) Other operating income
  (10) Losses on loans and advances
  (11) General and administrative expenses
  (12) Other operating expenses

  These disclosures, to be incorporated into the bank's income statement, are of course in addition to disclosure requirements of other international accounting standards.

b. Separate disclosure of the principal types of income and expenses as above is essential in order that users of the bank's financial statements can assess the performance of the bank.

c. To enhance financial statement transparency, IAS 30 prohibits the offsetting of income and expense items, except those relating to hedges and to assets or liabilities wherein the legal right of setoff exists and the offsetting represents the expectation as to the realization or settlement of the asset or liability. In case income and expense items were allowed to be offset, it would prevent users from assessing the return on particular classes of assets; this, in a way, would restrict users of financial statements in their assessment of the performance of the bank.

d. The following income statement items are, however, allowed to be presented on a net basis:

  (1) Gains or losses from dealings in foreign currencies
  (2) Gains or losses from disposals of investment securities
  (3) Gains or losses from disposals and changes in the carrying amount of dealing securities

Example of bank financial reporting

ABC Banking Corporation
Statement of Income
For the Years Ended December 31, 2005 and 2004

	2005	*2004*
Operating income		
Interest income	€400,000	€380,000
Interest expense	(205,000)	(200,000)
Net interest income	195,000	180,000
Net income from trading securities	2,000	2,000
Net gain from dealings in foreign currencies	14,000	10,000
Net gain from disposal of available-for-sale investments	20,000	13,000

	2005	*2004*
Fees and commission	50,000	40,000
Other operating income	8,000	8,000
	289,000	253,000
Operating expenses		
Provision for losses on loans and advances	70,000	50,000
Provision for impairment of investments	1,000	1,000
	71,000	51,000
Profit from operations	218,000	202,000
Other income	9,000	8,000
	227,000	210,000
General and administration expenses	80,000	75,000
Depreciation on property and equipment	11,000	10,000
Provision for taxation	6,000	6,000
Net income for the year	€130,000	€119,000

2. The balance sheet of a bank should group assets and liabilities by nature and list them in the order of their respective liquidity. This is explained further by the standard as follows:

   a. Disclosure of the grouping of assets and liabilities by their nature and listing them by their respective liquidity is illustrated by the standard. These are to be made either on the face of the balance sheet or in the footnotes. The following disclosures are prescribed with a provision that disclosures should include but are not limited to:

Assets	**Liabilities**
Cash and balances with the central bank	Deposits from other banks
Treasury bills and other bills eligible for rediscounting with the central bank	Other money market deposits
Government and other securities held for dealing purposes	Amounts owed to other depositors
	Certificates of deposits
Placements with, and loans and advances to, other banks	Promissory notes and other liabilities evidenced by paper
Other money market placements	Other borrowed funds
Loans and advances to customers	
Investment securities	

   These disclosures, to be incorporated into the bank's income statement, are of course in addition to disclosure requirements of other international accounting standards.

   b. Grouping the assets and liabilities by nature does not pose a problem and, in fact, is probably the most logical way of combining financial statement items for presentation on the bank's balance sheet. For instance, deposits with other banks and loans/advances to other banks are combined and presented as a separate line item on the asset side of a bank's balance sheet and referred to as placements with other banks. These items would, however, be presented differently on financial statements of other commercial enterprises since deposits with banks in those instances would be combined with other cash and bank balances, and loans to banks would probably be classified as investments. On the other hand, balances with other banks are not combined with balances with other parts of the money market, even though by nature they are placements with other financial institutions, since this gives a better understanding of the bank's relations with and dependency on other banks versus other constituents of the money market.

c. Listing of assets by liquidity could be considered synonymous with listing of liabilities by maturity, since maturity is a measure of liquidity in case of liabilities. For instance, certificates of deposits are liabilities of banks and have contractual maturities of perhaps, one month, three months, six months, and one year. Similarly, there are other bank liabilities, such as promissory notes, that may not be due, perhaps, for another three years from the balance sheet date. Thus, a relative maturity analysis would suggest that the certificates of deposit be listed on the bank's balance sheet before or above the promissory notes since they would mature earlier. Similarly, assets of a bank could be analyzed based on their relative liquidity, and those assets that are more liquid than others (i.e., will convert into cash faster than others) should be listed on the balance sheet above the others. Thus, cash balances and balances with the central bank are usually listed above other assets on the balance sheets of all banks, being relatively more liquid than other assets.

d. Offsetting of assets against liabilities, or vice versa, is generally not allowed unless a legal right of setoff exists and the offsetting represents the expectation as to the realization or settlement of the asset or liability. This is true even in the case of other enterprises; IAS 1, which applies to all entities reporting in accordance with IAS, including banks, contains similar provisions.

e. The now superseded IAS 25 had provided that entities not normally distinguishing between current and long-term investments in their balance sheets were nevertheless to make such a distinction for measurement purposes. Under IAS 39, the current versus long-term distinction is no longer important, but it will instead be necessary to assign all such investments to the trading, available-for-sale, or held-to-maturity portfolios. IAS 30 stipulates that banks must disclose the market value of investments in securities if different from the carrying values in the financial statements. Since both trading and available-for-sale securities are carried in the balance sheet at fair value, this added disclosure requirement now only impacts held to maturity securities, which are maintained at amortized cost.

Example

ABC Banking Corporation
Balance Sheet
As at December 31, 2005 and 2004

	2005	2004
Assets		
Cash and balances with central bank	€ 480,000	€ 370,000
Placements with other banks	3,685,000	2,990,000
Portfolio held for trading	8,286,000	6,786,000
Nontrading investments	364,000	26,000
Loans and advances, net	40,000	28,000
Investment property	358,000	283,000
Property and equipment, net	90,000	89,000
Other assets	55,000	44,000
Total assets	13,358,000	10,616,000
Liabilities and Shareholders' Equity		
Liabilities:		
Due to banks	2,187,000	998,000
Customer deposits	8,040,000	6,536,000
Long-term loan from government	1,300,000	1,380,000
Other liabilities	108,000	96,000
Total liabilities	€11,635,000	€ 8,930,000
Shareholders' Equity:		
Share capital	€ 1,250,000	€ 1,250,000
Statutory reserve	73,000	60,000
Contingency reserve	29,000	12,000
General reserve	325,000	325,000
Retained earnings	46,000	39,000
Total shareholders' equity	€ 1,723,000	€ 1,686,000
Total liabilities and shareholders' equity	€13,358,000	€10,616,000
Commitments and contingent liabilities	€15,300,000	€12,100,000

Cash Flow Statement for Banks and Other Financial Institutions

Cash flow statements are an integral part of financial statements. Every entity is required to present a cash flow statement in accordance with the provisions of IAS 7.

Although the general requirements of IAS 7 are common to all entities, the standard does contain special provisions that are applicable only to financial institutions. These specific provisions deal with reporting of certain cash flows on a "net basis." The following cash flows are to be reported on a net basis:

1. Cash receipts and payments on behalf of customers when the cash flows reflect the activities of the customer rather than those of the enterprise; the standard refers to "the accepting and repayment of demand deposits of a bank"
2. Cash receipts and payments for the acceptance and repayment of deposits with a fixed maturity date
3. The placement of deposits with and withdrawal of deposits from other financial institutions
4. Cash advances and loans made to customers and the repayment of those advances and loans

The appendix to IAS 7 (see the discussion below) illustrates the application of the standard to financial institutions preparing cash flow statements under the direct method (for a more detailed discussion of cash flow statements, see Chapter 4).

Example of cash flow statement for banks

Community Bank
Consolidated Statement of Cash Flows
For the Year Ended December 31, 2005
(€000)

Cash flows from operating activities:		
Interest and commission receipts	€28,447	
Interest payments	(23,463)	
Recoveries on loans previously written off	237	
Cash payments to employees and suppliers	(997)	
Operating profit before changes in operating assets	4,224	
(Increase) decrease in operating assets:		
Placements with other banks	(650)	
Deposits with Central bank for regulatory purposes	234	
Funds advanced to customers	(288)	
Net increase in credit card receivables	(360)	
Interest receivable	(120)	
Increase (decrease) in operating liabilities:		
Deposits from customers	600	
Balances due to other banks	(200)	
Net cash from operating activities before income tax	3,440	
Income taxes paid	(100)	
Net cash from operating activities		3,340
Cash flows from investing activities:		
Proceeds from disposal of subsidiary Y	50	
Dividends received	200	
Interest received	300	
Proceeds from sales of nontrading securities	1,200	
Purchase of investment property	(600)	
Purchase of property, plant, and equipment	(500)	
Net cash from investing activities		650
Cash flows from financing activities:		
Issuance of equity capital	1,000	
Issue of preference shares by subsidiary undertaking	800	
Dividends paid	(1,600)	
Net cash from financing activities		200
Effects of exchange rate changes on cash and cash equivalents		600
Net increase in cash and cash equivalents		4,790
Cash and cash equivalents at beginning of period		4,050
Cash and cash equivalents at end of period		€8,840

Disclosure Requirements for Banks and Similar Institutions

Contingencies and commitments including off-balance-sheet items. Contingent liabilities are *possible obligations* that arise from past events whose existence will be confirmed only by the ultimate outcome of one or more uncertain future events that are not wholly within the control of the enterprise. Contingent liabilities could also be *present obligations* that arise from past events but are not recognized either because it is not probable that an outflow of resources will be required or because the amount of the obligation cannot be measured reliably. Generally, the accounting for and disclosure of provisions and contingent liabilities has been addressed by IAS 37. Exceptions have been made in certain cases; for instance, liabilities of life insurance companies arising from insurance policies issued by them and other entities, such as retirement benefit plans, have been specifically excluded from the scope of IAS 37. However specific contingent liabilities relating to the banking industry (see list below) are required to be disclosed in accordance with the provisions of

IAS 30, since provisions or contingent liabilities of banking or similar financial institutions have not specifically been excluded from the purview of IAS 37.

This means that the general principles of recognizing provisions or disclosing contingent liabilities as set forth in IAS 37 will differ for the banking industry compared to other commercial enterprises. This has raised some eyebrows, and for good reason. The often asked questions on this issue are the following: If the general principles of disclosure of contingent liabilities as set out in IAS 37 are equally applicable to banks and other similar institutions as they are applicable to other commercial enterprises, then why does IAS 30 still address this area? Is it a case of redundancy or is it there for a purpose that is not obvious? These queries are amply clarified by IAS 30, Paragraph 27, which states

> *...This standard is of particular relevance to banks because banks often engaged in transactions that lead to contingent liabilities and commitments, some revocable and others irrevocable, which are frequently significant in amount and substantially larger than those of other commercial enterprises.*

The disclosures required in this regard are the following:

1. The nature and amount of commitments to extend credit that are irrevocable because they cannot be withdrawn at the discretion of the bank without incurring significant penalty or expenses
2. The nature and amount of contingencies and commitments arising from off-balance-sheet items, including those relating to

   a. Direct credit substitutes, which include general guarantees of indebtedness, bank acceptances, and standby letters of credit, which serve as financial backup for loans and securities
   b. Transaction-related contingencies, which include performance bonds, bid bonds, warranties, and standby letters of credit related to particular transactions
   c. Trade-related contingencies, which are self-liquidating and short-term trade-related contingencies arising from the movement of goods, such as documentary credit wherein the underlying goods are used as security for the bank credit (sometimes referred to as trust receipts, or simply as TR)
   d. Sales and repurchase agreements that are not reflected or recognized on the bank's balance sheet
   e. Interest and foreign exchange rate related items, which include items such as options, futures, and swaps
   f. Other commitments, including other off-balance-sheet items such as revolving underwriting facilities and note issuance facilities

It is important for the users of the bank's financial statements to be cognizant about the contingencies and irrevocable commitments because these may have an effect in the future on the liquidity and solvency of the bank. For instance, undrawn facilities, to which the bank is irrevocably committed, could serve as a good example of what could happen to a bank's liquidity position if a majority of the customers utilize them at the same time, for example, when there is a sudden shortage of funds in the market, due to economic reasons or otherwise. Thus, disclosing such irrevocable commitments and contingencies, in the footnotes or elsewhere, is of paramount importance to the user of the bank's financial statements.

Also, off-balance-sheet items, such as letters of credit (LC), guarantees, acceptances, and so on, constitute an important part of the bank's business and thus should be disclosed in the financial statements, since without knowing about the magnitude of such items, a fair evaluation of the bank's financial position is not possible (mostly because it adds significantly to the level of business risk the bank is exposed to at any given point of time).

Certain items that are typically not included in the balance sheet are commonly referred to as memoranda accounts, and less frequently are called contra items. These are often interrelated items which are both contingent assets and contingent liabilities, such as bills held for collection for customers, that if and when collected will in turn be remitted to the customer and not retained by the bank. The logic is that since the asset and liability both have contingent aspects, and since the bank is effectively only acting as an agent on behalf of a customer, it is valid to exclude both elements from the statement of financial condition. The existence of such items, however, generally must be disclosed even if not formally recognized.

Example of disclosure of contingencies and commitments

	2005	*2004*
At December 31, 2005 and 2004, the contingent liabilities and commitments were the following (in thousands of euros):		
Letters of credit	€10,000	€ 9,000
Guarantees	11,000	8,000
Acceptances	12,000	11,000
Bills for collection	13,000	12,000
Commitments under undrawn lines of credit	15,000	12,000
	€61,000	€52,000

Illustrative Extracts from Published Financial Statements

UBS Group Financial Statements
December 31, 2004

Notes to the financial statements

Note 25. Commitments and contingent liabilities

The Group utilizes various lending-related financial instruments in order to meet the financial needs of its customers. The Group issues commitments to extend credit, standby and other letters of credit, guarantees, commitments to enter into repurchase agreements, note issuance facilities and revolving underwriting facilities. Guarantees represent irrevocable assurances, subject to the satisfaction of certain conditions, that the Group will make payment in the event that the customer fails to fulfill its obligation to third parties. The Group also enters into commitments to extend credit in the form of credit lines which are available to secure the liquidity needs of our customers, but not yet drawn upon by them, the majority of which range in maturity from 1 month to 5 years. The contractual amount of these instruments is the maximum amount at risk for the Group if the customer fails to meet its obligations. The risk is similar to the risk involved in extending loan facilities and is monitored with the same risk control processes and specific credit risk policies. For the years ended December 31, 2004, 2003, and 2002, the Group recognized a CHF 31 million credit loss expense, CHF 23 million credit loss recovery, and CHF 13 million credit loss expense, respectively, related to obligations incurred for contingencies and commitments. The Group generally enters into subparticipations to mitigate the risks from the Group's commitments and contingencies. A subparticipation is an agreement with another party to fund a portion of the credit facility and to take a share of the loss in the event that the borrower fails to fulfill its obligations. The Group retains the contractual relationship with the borrower and the subparticipant has only an indirect relationship with the borrower. The Group will only enter into subparticipation agreements with banks whose rating is at least equal to or higher than that of the borrower.

CHF million	12/31/04	12/31/03
Contingent liabilities		
Credit guarantees and similar instruments[1]	10,252	10,832
Subparticipations	(621)	(765)
Total	9,631	10,067
Performance guarantees and similar instruments[2]	2,536	2,760
Subparticipations	(415)	(276)
Total	2,121	2,484
Irrevocable commitments and documentary credits	2,106	1,971
Subparticipations	(272)	(373)
Total	1,834	1,598
Gross contingent liabilities	14,894	15,563
Subpartcipations	(1,308)	(1,414)
Net contingent liabilities	13,586	14,149
Irrevocable commitments		
Undrawn irrevocable credit facilities	53,168	46,623
Subparticipations	(7)	(235)
Total	53,161	46,388
Liabilities for calls on shares and other equities	19	337
Gross irrevocable commitments	53,187	46,960
Subparticipations	(7)	(235)
Net irrevocable commitments	53,180	46,725
Gross commitments and contingent liabilities	68,081	62,523
Subparticipations	(1,315)	(1,649)
Net commitments and contingent liabilities	66,766	60,874
Market value guarantees in form of written put options	352,509	218,638

[1] *Credit guarantees in the form of bills of exchange and other guarantees, including guarantees in the form of irrevocable letters of credit, endorsements liabilities from bills rediscounted, advance payment guarantees and similar facilities.*

[2] *Bid bonds, performance bonds, builders' guarantees, letters of indemnity, other performance guarantees in the form of irrevocable letters of credit and similar facilities.*

As part of its trading and market-making activities, UBS writes put options on a broad range of underlyings. For writing put options, UBS receives a premium, which is recognized as negative replacement value on the balance sheet. The contract volume of a written put option, which is the number of units of the underlying multiplied by the exercise price per unit, is considered a market price guarantee issued, because the option holder is entitled to make UBS purchase the underlying at the stated exercise price. The fair value of all written put options is recognized on the balance sheet as negative replacement value, which is significantly lower than the underlying total contract volume that represents the maximum potential payment UBS could be required to make upon exercise of the puts. The exposure from writing put options is managed through UBS's standard risk management process at a level that is within the set risk limits. Accordingly, neither the underlying total contract volume nor the negative replacement value are indicative of the actual risk exposure arising from written put options.

Maturities of Assets and Liabilities

Information about maturities of assets and liabilities is the most important disclosures required of banks, since it gives users a concise picture of the bank's liquidity. Well managed banks typically exhibit closely aligned maturities of assets, such as loans and investments, and liabilities, such as time deposits. To the extent these are mismatched, it not only raises a liquidity (or even solvency) question, but also in periods of changing interest rates it places the bank at risk of having its normal "spread" (the difference between interest earned and interest paid) become diminished or turn negative.   Since even an otherwise healthy institution, having positive net worth, can have mismatches in some of the maturities, potential problems are identified through the schedule of asset and liability maturities which would not otherwise be apparent from the financial statements.

Maturity groupings applied to assets and liabilities differ from bank to bank, and IAS 30 does not prescribe the periods but only gives examples of periods that are used in practice, as follows:

1. Up to one month
2. From one month to three months
3. From three months to one year
4. From one year to five years
5. From five years and above

It is imperative that the maturity periods adopted by a bank should be the same for assets and liabilities. This ensures that the maturities are matched and brings to light dependency, if any, on other sources of liquidity.

Maturities could be expressed in more than one way, for instance, by remaining period to the repayment date or by the original period to the repayment date. IAS 30 recommends that the maturity analysis of assets and liabilities be presented by the remaining period to the repayment date, as this provides the best basis to evaluate the liquidity of the bank.

In some countries time deposits could be withdrawn even on demand, and advances given by the bank may be repayable on demand, in which case, maturities according to the contractual dates should be used for the purposes of this analysis since it reflects the liquidity risks attaching to the bank's assets and liabilities.

Certain assets do not have a contractual maturity date. In all such cases the period in which these assets are assumed to mature is usually taken to be the expected date on which the assets will be realized. For instance, in the case of fixed assets that have no maturity date as such, as in the case of a certificate of deposit, the authors are of the opinion that their remaining useful lives as of the balance sheet date could be used as a measure of the maturity profile of these assets.

Example of disclosure of maturities of assets and liabilities

The maturity profile of assets and liabilities at December 31, 2005, was as follows:

	(€ in thousands)			
	Up to 3 months	*3 months to 1 year*	*1 year to 5 years*	*Over 5 years*
Assets				
Cash and short-term funds	€ 10,157	€ --	€ --	€ --
Deposits with banks	298,771	--	--	--
Investments—available-for-sale	101,013	--	--	--
Trading investments	113,109	76,173	--	--
Investments—held-to-maturity	--	--	--	284,281
Accrued interest and other assets	9,919	18,681	2,150	--
Investment property	--	--	366,259	--
Fixed assets	--	--	--	57,997
Total assets	€532,969	€ 94,854	€368,409	€ 342,278
Liabilities				
Deposits from banks	€105,492	€ 18,400	€ --	€ --
Customer deposits	36,062	1,033	130,127	--
Accrued interest and other payable	38,882	9,952	30,865	--
Medium-term facilities	--	250,000	330,000	--
Total liabilities	€180,436	€279,385	€490,992	€ --

Concentration of Assets, Liabilities and Off-Balance-Sheet Items

Banks are required to disclose any significant concentrations of its assets, liabilities, and off-balance-sheet items. Such disclosures are a means of identification of potential risks, if any, that are inherent in the realization of the assets and liabilities (the funds available) to the bank.

Concentration of assets, liabilities, and off-balance-sheet items could be disclosed in the following ways:

1. By geographical areas such as individual countries, group of countries, or regions within a country
2. By customer groups such as governments, public authorities, and commercial enterprises
3. By industry sectors such as real estate, manufacturing, retail, and financial
4. Other concentrations of risk that are appropriate in the circumstances of the bank

Example of disclosure of concentration of assets, liabilities, and off-balance-sheet items

	2005			2004		
	Assets	Liabilities	Off-balance-sheet	Assets	Liabilities	Off-balance-sheet
Geographical region						
North America	€ 679,829	€ 26,103	€ 57,479	€ 681,958	€ 86,267	€ 146,099
Europe	662,259	778,470	621,316	574,699	662,690	1,117,110
Middle East	93,003	184,485	114,984	71,328	216,486	98,236
Other	279	--	--	10,525	370	198,138
Total	€1,395,370	€989,058	€793,779	€1,338,510	€965,813	€1,559,583
Industry sector						
Banking and finance	€ 314,563	€866,483	€715,141	€ 482,874	€846,513	€1,484,248
Food processing	40,535	--		40,777	--	--
Luxury merchandise	336,966	3,797	11,811	224,829	--	1,649
Retail	356,879	--	--	315,554	--	--
Real estate	96,743	--	63,871	68,744	--	72,947
Manufacturing and services	153,151	--	--	124,366	--	--
Other	96,533	118,779	2,956	81,366	119,300	739
Total	€1,395,370	€989,058	€793,779	€1,338,510	€965,813	€1,559,583

(€ in thousands)

Losses on Loans and Advances

Loans and advances to customers may sometimes become uncollectable, and in those circumstances the bank would have to suffer losses on loans, advances, and other credit facilities. The amount of losses that are specifically identified and the potential losses not specifically identified should both be recognized as expenses and deducted from the carrying amount of the loans and advances. The assessment of these losses is dependent on management judgment and it is essential that it should be applied consistently from one period to another. Any amounts are set aside in excess of the foregoing provision for losses on loans and advances, if required by local circumstances or legislation, should be treated as an appropriation of retained earnings and are not to be included in the determination of net profit or loss for the period. Similarly, any credits resulting in the reduction of such amounts are to be credited to retained earnings.

A number of disclosure requirements are prescribed by IAS 30 in this regard, as summarized below.

1. The accounting policy describing the basis on which uncollectible loans and advances are recognized as an expense and written off.

2. Details of movements in the provision for losses on loans and advances during the period: These details should include the amount recognized as an expense in the period on account of losses on loans and advances, the amount charged in the period for loans and advances written off, and the amount credited in the period resulting from the recovery of the amounts previously written off.

3. The aggregate amount of the provision for losses on loans and advances at the balance sheet date.

Example of disclosure of loans and advances

	2005	*2004*
Balance, beginning of the year	€500,000	€400,000
Provision during the year—against specific advances	50,000	50,000
Written off during the year	(10,000)	(20,000)
Balance, end of the year	€540,000	€430,000

Illustrative Extracts from Published Financial Statements

UBS Group Financial Statements
December 31, 2004

Notes to the financial statements

Note 9a. Due from banks and loans

By type of exposure

CHF million	*12/31/04*	*12/31/03*
Banks[1]	35,520	32,024
Allowance for credit losses	(256)	(284)
Net due from banks	35,264	31,740
Loans		
Residential mortgages	117,731	109,980
Commercial mortgages	18,950	19,162
Other loans	98,081	86,829
Subtotal	234,762	215,971
Allowance for credit losses	(2,375)	(3,292)
Net loans	232,387	212,679
Net due from banks and loans	267,651	244,419

[1]   *Includes due from banks from industrial holdings in the amount of CHF 764 million*

By geographic region (based on the location of the borrower)

CHF million	*12/31/04*	*12/31/03*
Switzerland	152,433	152,358
Rest of Europe/Africa/Middle East	45,712	43,842
Americas	61,751	42,653
Asia/Pacific	10,386	9,142
Subtotal	270,282	247,995
Allowance for credit losses	(2,631)	(3,576)
Net due from banks and loans	267,651	244,419

By type of collateral

CHF million	*12/31/04*	*12/31/03*
Secured by real estate	138,692	130,740
Collateralized by securities	38,872	28,062
Guarantees and other collateral	18,973	18,295
Unsecured	73,745	70,898
Subtotal	270,282	247,995
Allowance for credit losses	(2,631)	(3,576)
Net due from banks and loans	267,651	244,419

UBS Group Financial Statements
December 31, 2004

Notes to the financial statements

Note 9b. Allowances and provisions for credit losses

CHF million	Specific allowances and provisions	Collective loan loss provision	Total 12/31/04	Total 12/31/03[2]
Balance at the beginning of the year[1]	3,692	262	3,954	5,232
Write-offs	(854)	(3)	(857)	(1,436)
Recoveries	59	--	59	87
Increase/(decrease) in credit loss allowance and provision	(251)	(25)	(276)	72
Foreign currency translation and other adjustments	(30)	(27)	3	(1)
Balance at the end of the year	2,676	207	2,883	3,954

CHF million	12/31/04	12/31/03
As a reduction of due from banks	256	284
As a reduction of loans	2,375	3,292
As a reduction of other balance sheet positions	41	88
Subtotal	2,672	3,664
Included in other liabilities related to commitments and contingent liabilities	211	290
Total allowances and provisions for credit losses	2,883	3,954

[1] *Includes country provisions of CHF 183 million and CHF 262 million at December 31, 2004, and December 31, 2003, respectively.*

[2] *Restated to reflect transfers of allowances and provisions for OTC derivatives to the trading portfolio as a reduction of fair value, following the revised treatment of OTC derivatives credit losses.*

UBS Group Financial Statements
December 31, 2004

Notes to the financial statements

Note 9c. Impaired due from banks and loans

CHF million	12/31/04	12/31/03
Total gross impaired due from banks and loans[1,2]	4,861	7,209
Allowance for impaired due from banks	239	245
Allowance for impaired loans	2,266	3,213
Total allowances for credit losses related to impaired due from banks and loans	2,505	3,458
Average total gross impaired due from bank and loans[3]	6,038	8,594

[1] *All impaired due from banks and loans have a specific allowance for credit losses.*

[2] *Interest income on impaired due from banks and loans was CHF 172 million for 2004 and CHF 279 million for 2003.*

[3] *Average balances were calculated from quarterly data.*

CHF million	12/31/04	12/31/03
Total gross impaired due from banks and loans	4,861	7,209
Estimated liquidation proceeds of collateral	1,758	2,465
Net impaired due from banks and loans	3,103	4,477
Specific allowances and provisions	2,505	3,458

UBS Group Financial Statements
December 31, 2004

Notes to the financial statements

Note 9d. Nonperforming due from banks and loans

A loan (included in due from banks or loans) is classified as nonperforming (1) when the payment of interest, principal, or fees is overdue by more than 90 days and there is no firm evidence that they will be made good by later payments or the liquidation of collateral; (2) when insolvency proceedings have commenced; or (3) when obligations have been restructured on concessionary terms.

CHF million	12/31/04	12/31/03
Total gross nonperforming due from banks and loans	3,696	4,901
Total allowances for credit losses related to nonperforming due from banks and loans	2,264	2,764
Average total gross nonperforming due from banks and loans[1]	4,338	5,410

[1] *Average balances are calculated from quarterly data.*

CHF million	12/31/04	12/31/03
Nonperforming due from banks and loans at the beginning of the year	4,901	6,000
Net additions/(reductions)	(496)	317
Write-offs and disposals	(709)	(1,416)
Nonperforming due from banks and loans at the end of the year	3,696	4,901

By type of exposure

CHF million	12/31/04	12/31/03
Banks	242	253
Loans		
Mortgages	1,011	1,470
Other	2,443	3,178
Total loans	3,454	4,648
Total nonperforming due from banks and loans	3,696	4,901

By geographic region (based on the location of the borrower)

CHF million	12/31/04	12/31/03
Switzerland	2,772	4,012
Rest of Europe/Africa/Middle East	607	488
Americas	220	366
Asia/Pacific	97	35
Total nonperforming due from banks and loans	3,696	4,901

Related-Party Transactions

Parties are considered to be related if one has the ability to control the other or exercise significant influence over the other in making financial and operating decisions. IAS 24 requires that related-party transactions be disclosed. When a bank has entered into transactions with related parties, the nature of the relationship (e.g., director, shareholder, etc.), as well as information about the transactions and the outstanding balances should be disclosed. The disclosures to be made include the bank's lending policy to related parties and, in respect of related-party transactions, the amount included in or the proportion of

1. Each of loans and advances, deposits and acceptances, and promissory notes; disclosures may include the aggregate amounts outstanding at the beginning and end of the year as well as changes in these accounts during the year
2. Each of the principal types of income, interest expense, and commissions paid
3. The amount of the expense recognized in the period for the losses on loans and advances and the amount of the provision at the balance sheet date
4. Irrevocable commitments and contingencies and commitments from off-balance-sheet items

Example of related-party disclosures

Note 5. Related-party transactions

The bank has entered into transactions in the ordinary course of business with certain related parties, such as shareholders holding more than 20% equity interest in the bank and with certain directors of the bank.

At December 31, 2005 and 2004, the following balances were outstanding in the aggregate in relation to those related-party transactions:

	2005	*2004*
Loans and advances	€2,000,000	€1,800,000
Customer deposits	750,000	600,000
Guarantees	3,000,000	1,500,000

For the years ended December 31, 2005 and 2004, the following income and expense items are included in the aggregate amounts arising from the above-related transactions:

	2005	*2004*
Interest income	€300,000	€270,000
Interest expense	40,000	35,000
Commissions	60,000	30,000

Illustrative Extracts from Published Financial Statements

UBS Group Financial Statements
December 31, 2004

Notes to the financial statements

Note 33. Related parties

The Group defines related parties as Associated companies, private equity investees, the Board of Directors, the Group Executive Board, close family members, and enterprises which are controlled by these individuals through their majority shareholding or their role as chairman and/or CEO in those companies. This definition is based on the requirements of the "Directive on Information Relating to Corporate Governance: issued by the SWX Swiss Exchange and effective from July 1, 2002, for all listed companies in Switzerland.

  1. **Remuneration and equity holdings**

The executive members of the Board of Directors have top-management employment contracts and receive pension benefits upon retirement. Total remuneration to the executive members of the Board of Directors and Group Executive Board recognized in the income statement including cash, shares, and accrued pension benefits amounted to CHF 165.3 million in 2004, CHF 144.6 million in 2003 and CHF 131.8 million in 2002. Total compensation numbers exclude merger-related retention payments for the two ex-PaineWebber executives of CHF 21.1 millions (USD 17.0 million) in 2003 and CHF 20.6 million (USD 14.9 million) in 2002. These retention payments were committed to at the time of the merger in 2000 and fully disclosed at the time. No additional payments were due in 2004.

The external members of the Board of Directors do not have employment or service contracts with UBS, and thus are not entitled to benefits upon termination of their service on the Board of Directors. Total fees paid to these individuals for their services as external board members amounted to CHF 5.7 million in 2004, CHF 5.4 million in 2003, and CHF 3.5 million in 2002.

The number of long-term stock options outstanding to the executive members of the Board of Directors and Group Executive Board from equity participation plans was 6,004,997 (equivalent tot the same number of shares) at December 31, 2004, 6,218,011 options (equivalent to the same number of shares) and 120,264 warrants (equivalent to 7,214 shares) at December 31, 2003, and 5,410,172 options (equivalent to the same number of shares) and 24,558,529 warrants (equivalent to 1,473,217 UBS shares) at December 31, 2002. These plans are further explained in Note 32, Equity Participation Plans.

The total number of shares held by members of the Board of Directors, the Group Executive Board, and parties closely linked to them was 3,506,610 at December 31, 2004, 3,150,217 at December 31, 2003, and 2,139,371 at December 31, 2002. No member of the Board of Directors or Group Executive Board is the beneficial owner of more than 1% of the Group's shares at December 31, 2004.

2. **Loans and advances to Board of Directors and senior executives**

The outstanding balance of loans to the members of the Board of Directors, the Group Executive Board, and close family members amounted to CHF 15.8 million at December 31, 2004, and CHF 25.2 million at December 31, 2003. Executive members of the Board and GEB members have been granted loans, fixed advances and mortgages at the same terms and conditions that are available to other employees, based on terms and conditions granted to third parties adjusted for reduced credit risk. In 2002, a thorough review of outstanding loans to senior executives was performed to ensure compliance with the US Sarbanes-Oxley Act of 2002. Nonexecutive Board members are granted loans and mortgages at general market conditions.

3. **Loans to significant associated companies**

CHF million	12/31/04	12/31/03
Balance at the beginning of the year	63	40
Additions	38	48
Reductions	(36)	(25)
Balance at the end of the year	65	63

All loans to associated companies are transacted at arm's length. At December 31, 2004 and 2003, there were commitments and contingent liabilities to significant associated companies of CHF 55 million and CHF 14 million, respectively. In addition, the Group routinely receives services from associated companies at arm's-length terms. For the years ended December 31, 2004, December 31, 2003, and December 31, 2002, the amount paid to significant associates for these services was CHF 248 million, CHF 106 million and CHF 60 million, respectively. Fees reeived for services provided to associated companies for the years ended December 31, 2004, December 31, 2003, and December 31, 2002 was CHF 180 million, CHF 122 million and CHF 2 million, respectively.

During 2003, UBS sold its VISA acquiring business to Telekurs Holding AG, an associated company. UBS realized a CHF 90 million gain from this divestment.

Note 36 provides a list of significant associates.

4. **Loans to private equity investees**

CHF million	12/31/04	12/31/03
Balance at the beginning of the year	366	338
Additions	46	153
Reductions	(222)	(125)
Balance at the end of the year	190	366

At December 31, 2004, and December 31, 2003, there were commitments and contingent liabilities to private equity companies of CHF 36 million and CHF 23 million, respectively. In addition, the Group purchased services from private equity companies at arm's-length terms for the years ended December 31, 2004, December 31, 2003, and December 31, 2002, in the amount of CHF 0 million, CHF 14 million and CHF 116 million, respectively.

5. **Other related-party transactions**

During 2004 and 2003, UBS entered into the following transactions at arm's length with companies whose Chairman and/or CEO is an external member of the Board of Directors of UBS or of which an external director is a controlling shareholder.

In 2004 and 2003, these companies included Bertarelli & Cie (Switzerland), Kedge Capital Partners Ltd. (Jersey), J Sainsbury plc. (UK), Serono Group (Switzerland), Team

Alinghi (Switzerland), Unisys Corporation (USA. In addition to those mentioned, related parties in 2004 also included BMW Group (Germany) and Stadler Rail Group (Switzerland). In 2003, related parties also included Sika AG (Switzerland).

Other related party transactions
CHF million

	12/31/04	*12/31/03*
Goods sold and services provided by related parties to UBS	34	43
Services provided to related parties by UBS (fees received)	10	7
Loans granted to related parties by UBS[1]	294	79

[1] In 2004, includes loans, guarantees, and contingent liabilities of CHF 32 million and unused committed facilities of CHF 262 million but excludes unused uncommitted working capital facilities and unused guarantees of CHF 110 million. In 2003, includes loans, guarantees, contingent liabilities and committed credit facilities of CHF 58.5 million, but excludes uncommitted working capital facilities of CHF 119.5 million.

As part of its sponsorship of Team Alinghi, defender for the "America's Cup 2007," UBS paid CHF 8.5 million (EUR 5.5 million) as a sponsoring fee for the UBS Trophy in New Port, RI, USA. Team Alinghi's controlling shareholder is UBS board member Ernesto Bertarelli.

UBS also engages in trading and risk management activities (e.g., swaps, options, forwards) with related parties. These transactions may give rise to credit risk either for UBS or for a related party towards UBS. As part of its normal course of business, UBS is also a market maker in equity and debt instruments and at times may hold positions in instruments of related parties.

Disclosure of General Banking Risks

Based on local legislation or circumstances, a bank may need to set aside a certain amount each year for general banking risks, including future losses or other unforeseeable risks, in addition to the provision for losses on loans and advances explained earlier. The bank may also be required to earmark a certain amount each year as a contingency reserve, over and above the amounts accrued under IAS 10. All such amounts set aside should be treated as appropriations of retained earnings, and any credits resulting from the reduction of such amounts should be returned directly to retained earnings and not included in determination of net income or loss for the year.

Disclosure of Assets Pledged as Security

If the bank is required by law or national custom to pledge assets as security to support certain deposits or other liabilities, the bank should then disclose the aggregate amount of secured liabilities and the nature and carrying amount of the assets pledged as security.

Illustrative Extracts from Published Financial Statements

UBS Group Financial Statements
December 31, 2004

Notes to the financial statements

Note 27. Pledged assets

Assets are pledged as collateral for collateralized credit lines with central banks, loans from central mortgage institutions, deposit guarantees for savings banks, security deposits relating to stock exchange membership and mortgages on the Group's property. No financial assets are pledged for contingent liabilities. The following table shows additional information about assets pledged or assigned as security for liabilities and assets subject to reservation of title for the years ended December 31, 2004, and December 31, 2003.

CHF million	Carrying amount 12/31/04	Related liability 12/31/04	Carrying amount 12/31/03	Related liability 12/31/03
Mortgage loans	175	60	428	209
Securities	193,028	131,462	157,639	121,984
Property and equipment	320	--	--	--
Total pledged assets	193,523	131,522	158,067	122,193

Disclosure of Trust Activities

If a bank is holding in trust, or in any other fiduciary capacity, assets belonging to others, those assets should not be included on the bank's financial statements since they are being held on behalf of third parties such as trusts and retirement funds. If a bank is engaged in significant trust activities, this deserves disclosure of the fact and an indication of the extent of those trust activities. Such disclosure will take care of any potential liability in case the bank fails in its fiduciary capacity. The safe custody services that banks offer are not part of these trust activities.

Illustrative Extracts from Published Financial Statements

UBS Group Financial Statements
December 31, 2004

Notes to the financial statements

Note 24. Fiduciary transactions

Fiduciary placement represents funds which customers have instructed the Group to place in foreign banks. The Group is not liable to the customer for any default by the foreign bank nor do creditors of the Group have a claim on the assets placed.

CHF million	12/31/04	12/31/03
Placements with third parties	39,588	37,851
Fiduciary credits and other fiduciary financial transactions	57	74
Total fiduciary transactions	39,645	37,925

The Group also acts in its own name as trustee or in fiduciary capacities for the account of third parties. The assets managed in such capacities are not reported on the balance sheet unless they are invested with UBS. UBS earns commission and fee income from such transactions and assets. These activities potentially expose UBS to liability risks in cases of gross negligence with regard to noncompliance with its fiduciary and contractual duties. The risks associated with this business are covered by the standard UBS risk framework.

Replacement for IAS 30: IFRS 7

When IAS 30 was promulgated, many of the now-extant standards (most importantly, those addressing accounting for financial instruments, IAS 32 and IAS 39) had yet to be issued, and banking, as an important highly regulated industry with worldwide impact, was perhaps uniquely in need of standardized financial reporting guidance. However, by the late 1990s, many began to note that IAS 30 was in need of an overhaul, since there were growing instances of redundancies with other later standards, and in some particulars, a need for new or expanded coverage. Also, fundamental changes had been taking place in the financial services industries, and in the way in which financial institutions were managing their activities and their risk exposures.

The IASC added a project to its agenda to revise IAS 30 in 1999, and in 2000, appointed a steering committee for that purpose, including representatives of financial institutions, auditors, and bank and securities regulators. IASB, after its creation, endorsed that undertaking and continued to use that steering committee, which has been expanded to include analysts and nonfinancial institutions, as an advisory group. It subsequently became clear that the project should also consider disclosure and presentation issues that arise for all types of entities that engage in deposit taking, lending, or securities activities, whether or not regulated and supervised as banks. This was because, since IAS 30 was first released, there had been widespread dismantling of regulatory barriers in many countries, and increasing competition between banks and nonbank financial services firms and conglomerates in providing the same types of financial services. This, in turn, made it inappropriate to limit the scope of this project to banks and similar financial institutions.

At the inception of this project it was expected that three types of changes to the existing requirements of IAS 30 would be considered. The first would be to eliminate apparent redundancies between IAS 30 and other, mostly subsequent, standards. For example, the guidance in IAS 30 on the offsetting of assets and liabilities was duplicative of that subsequently incorporated into IAS 1 and IAS 32. The disclosures about fair values were later addressed globally by IAS 32, as were matters pertaining to the disclosure of maturities of assets and liabilities. Related-parties disclosures are set forth by IAS 24, and information regarding concentrations of credit risk is required by IAS 32. Finally, the guidance on loan loss recognition in IAS 30 may have been made superfluous due to later issuance of IAS 39.

A second category of revisions were to be made in order to bring the existing requirement under IAS 30 up to date. According to IASB, financial services industry representatives had been positive about the guidance in IAS 30 relative to balance sheet and income statement presentation, but believed that further guidance would eliminate remaining differences across countries in reporting formats which result in costs for financial institutions operating in several jurisdictions and difficulties for users in comparing financial statements across countries. Thus, some saw the need for further detailed guidance, which could reduce or eliminate remaining variations.

Finally, a third category of changes to IAS 30 were to be undertaken to enhance the quality of disclosures. Two key areas cited were

1. Disclosures supplementing the balance sheet and income statement, and
2. Risk exposure information

The IASB decided that it was impracticable to incorporate the above proposals into IAS 32 for completion in time for the 2005 transition to IFRS by EU member state publicly held companies, and instead opted to develop a separate Exposure Draft that would replace the financial disclosure requirements in both IAS 32 and IAS 30. This effort has been brought to fruition with the promulgation of IFRS 7, which is mandatorily effective in 2007.

IFRS 7 Requirements in Detail

IFRS 7 supersedes, when fully implemented, the disclosure requirements in IAS 32 and IAS 30 in its entirety. IFRS 7 is covered in Chapter 5.

APPENDIX A

EXAMPLE BANK SIGNIFICANT ACCOUNTING POLICIES

UBS Group Financial Statements
December 31, 2004

Notes to the financial statements

Note 1. Summary of significant accounting policies

1. **Basis of accounting**

    UBS AG and subsidiaries ("UBS" or the "Group") provide a broad range of financial services including advisory services, underwriting, financing, market making, asset management, brokerage, and retail banking on a global level. The Group was formed on June 29, 1998, when Swiss Bank Corporation and Union Bank of Switzerland merged. The merger was accounted for using the uniting of interests method of accounting.

    The consolidated financial statements of UBS (the "Financial Statements") are prepared in accordance with International Financial Reporting Standards (IFRS), issued by the International Accounting Standards Board (IASB), and stated in Swiss francs (CHF), the currency of the country in which UBS AG is incorporated. On February 3, 2005, the Board of Directors approved them for issue.

2. **Use of estimates in the preparation of Financial Statements**

    In preparing the Financial Statements, management is required to make estimates and assumptions that affect reported income, expenses, assets, liabilities, and disclosure of contingent assets and liabilities. Use of available information and application of judgment are inherent in the formation of estimates. Actual results in the future could differ from such estimates and the differences may be material to the Financial Statements.

3. **Consolidation**

    The Financial Statements comprise those of the parent company (UBS AG), its subsidiaries and certain special-purpose entities, presented as a single economic entity. The effects of intragroup transactions are eliminated in preparing the Financial Statements. Subsidiaries and special-purpose entities which are directly or indirectly controlled by the Group are consolidated, with the exception of certain employee benefit trusts (see also section 28). Subsidiaries acquired are consolidated from the date control is transferred to the Group. Subsidiaries to be divested are consolidated up to the date of disposal. Temporarily controlled entities that are acquired and held with a view to their subsequent disposal are recorded as financial investments.

    Assets held in an agency or fiduciary capacity are not assets of the Group and are not reported in the Financial Statements. Equity and net income attributable to minority interests are shown separately in the balance sheet and income statement, respectively.

    Investments in associates in which UBS has a significant influence are accounted for under the equity method of accounting. Significant influence is normally evidenced when UBS owns 20% or more of a company's voting rights. Investments in associates are initially recorded at cost and the carrying amount is increased or decreased to recognize the Group's share of the investee's profits or losses after the date of acquisition. Investments in associates for which significant influence is intended to be temporary because the investments are acquired and held exclusively with a view to their subsequent disposal are recorded as financial investments.

    The Group sponsors the formation of entities, which may or may not be directly or indirectly owned subsidiaries, for the purpose of asset securitization transactions and structured debt issuance, and to accomplish certain narrow and well-defined objectives. These companies may acquire assets directly or indirectly from UBS or its affiliates. Some of these companies are bankruptcy-remote entities whose assets are not available to satisfy the claims of creditors of the Group or any of its subsidiaries. Such companies are consolidated in the Group's financial statements when the substance of the relationship between the Group and the company indicates that the company is controlled by the Group. Certain transactions of consolidated entities meet the criteria for derecognition of financial assets, (see section 4 below). These transactions do not affect the consolidation status of an entity.

4. **Derecognition**

UBS enters into transactions where it transfers assets recognized on its balance sheet, but retains either all risks and rewards of the transferred assets or a portion of them. If all or substantially all risks and rewards are retained, the transferred assets are not derecognized from the balance sheet. Transfers of assets with retention of all or substantially all risks and rewards include, for example, securities lending and repurchase transactions described under paragraphs 6 and 7 below. Another example of a transaction where all risks and rewards are retained is where assets are sold to a third party with a concurrent total rate of return swap on the transferred assets. These types of transactions are accounted for as secured financing transactions similar to repurchase agreements.

In transactions where UBS neither retains nor transfers substantially all the risks and rewards of ownership of a financial asset, it derecognizes the asset if control over the asset is lost. The rights and obligations retained in the transfer are recognized separately as assets and liabilities as appropriate. In transfers where control over the asset is retained, the Group continues to recognize the asset to the extent of its continuing involvement, determined by the extent to which it is exposed to changes in the value of the transferred asset.

In certain transactions, UBS retains rights to service a transferred financial asset for a fee. The transferred asset is derecognized in its entirety, if it meets the derecognition criteria. An asset or liability is recognized for the servicing rights, depending on whether the servicing fee is more than adequate to cover servicing expenses (asset) or is less than adequate for performing the servicing (liability).

5. **Securitizations**

UBS securitizes various consumer and commercial financial assets, which generally results in the sale of these assets to special-purpose entities, which in turn issue securities to investors. Interests in the securitized financial assets may be retained in the form of senior or subordinated tranches, interest-only strips, or other residual interests ("retained interests"). Retained interests are primarily recorded in Trading portfolio assets and carried at fair value. Gains or losses on securitization depend in part on the carrying amount of the transferred financial assets, allocated between the financial assets derecognized and the retained interests based on their relative fair values at the date of the transfer. Gains or losses on securitization are recorded in Net trading income.

6. **Securities borrowing and lending**

Securities borrowing and securities lending transactions are generally entered into on a collateralized basis, with securities predominantly advanced or received as collateral. Transfer of the securities themselves, whether in a borrowing/lending transaction or as collateral, is not reflected on the balance sheet unless the risks and rewards of ownership are also transferred. If cash collateral is advanced or received, securities borrowing and lending activities are recorded at the amount of cash collateral advanced (Cash collateral on securities borrowed) or received (Cash collateral on securities lent).

UBS monitors the market value of the securities borrowed and lent on a daily basis and provides or requests additional collateral in accordance with the underlying agreements.

Fees and interest received or paid are recognized on an accrual basis and recorded as interest income or interest expense.

7. **Repurchase and reverse repurchase transactions**

Securities purchased under agreements to resell (reverse repurchase agreements) and securities sold under agreements to repurchase (repurchase agreements) are generally treated as collateralized financing transactions. In reverse repurchase agreements, the cash advanced, including accrued interest, is recognized on the balance sheet as Reverse repurchase agreements. In repurchase agreements, the cash received, including accrued interest, is recognized on the balance sheet as Repurchase agreements.

Securities received under reverse repurchase agreements and securities delivered under repurchase agreements are not recognized on or derecognized from the balance sheet, unless control of the contractual rights that comprise these securities is obtained or relinquished. UBS monitors the market value of the securities received or delivered on a daily basis and provides or requests additional collateral in accordance with the underlying agreements.

Interest earned on reverse repurchase agreements and interest incurred on repurchase agreements is recognized as interest income or interest expense over the life of each agreement.

The Group offsets reverse repurchase agreements and repurchase agreements with the same counterparty for transactions covered by legally enforceable master netting agreements when net or simultaneous settlement is intended.

8. **Segment reporting**

UBS's financial businesses are organized on a worldwide basis into four Business Groups and the Corporate Center. Wealth Management & Business Banking is segregated into two segments, Wealth Management and Business Banking Switzerland. The Corporate Center also consists of two segments, Private Banks & GAM and Corporate Functions. The Industrial Holdings segment holds all industrial operations controlled by the Group. In total, UBS now reports eight business segments.

Segment income, segment expenses, and segment performance include transfers between business segments and between geographical segments. Such transfers are conducted at arm's length.

9. **Foreign currency translation**

Foreign currency translations are recorded at the rate of exchange on the date of the transaction. At the balance sheet date, monetary assets and liabilities denominated in foreign currencies are reported using the closing exchange rate. Exchange differences arising on the settlement of transactions at rates different from those at the date of the transaction, and unrealized foreign exchange differences on unsettled foreign currency monetary assets and liabilities are recognized in the income statement.

Unrealized exchange differences on nonmonetary financial assets (investments in equity instruments) are a component of the change in their entire fair value. For a nonmonetary financial asset classified as held for trading, unrealized exchange differences are recognized in the income statement. For nonmonetary financial investments, which are classified as available-for-sale, unrealized exchange differences are recorded directly in shareholders' equity until the asset is sold.

When preparing consolidated financial statements, assets and liabilities of foreign entities are translated at the exchange rates at the balance sheet date, while income and expense items are translated at weighted-average rates for the period.

Differences resulting from the use of closing and weighted-average exchange rates and from revaluing a foreign entity's opening net asset balance at closing rate are recognized directly in foreign currency translation within shareholders' equity.

10. **Cash and cash equivalents**

Cash and cash equivalents consist of cash and balances with central banks, balances included in due from banks that mature in less than three months, and money market paper included in trading portfolio assets and financial investments.

11. **Fee income**

UBS earns fee income from a diverse range of services it provides to its customers. Fee income can be divided into two broad categories: Income earned from services that are provided over a certain period of time, for which customers are generally billed on an annual or semiannual basis, and income earned from providing transaction-type services. Fees earned from services that are provided over a certain period of time are recognized ratably over the service period. Fees earned from providing transaction-type services are recognized when the service has been completed. Fees or components of fees that are performance linked are recognized when the performance criteria are fulfilled.

The following fee income is predominantly earned from services that are provided over a period of time: investment fund fees, fiduciary fees, custodian fees, portfolio and other management and advisory fees, insurance-related fees, credit-related fees, and commission income. Fees predominantly earned from providing transaction-type services include underwriting fees, corporate finance fees, and brokerage fees.

12. **Determination of fair value**

The determination of fair values of financial assets and financial liabilities is based on quoted market prices or dealer price quotations for financial instruments traded in active markets. For all other financial instruments fair value is determined by using valuation techniques. Valuation techniques include net present value techniques, the discounted cash flow method, comparison to similar instruments for which market observable prices exist, and valuation models. UBS uses widely recognized valuation models for determining fair value of common and more simple financial instruments like options and interest rate and currency swaps. For these financial instruments, inputs into models are market observable.

For more complex instruments, UBS uses proprietary models, which usually are developed from recognized valuation models. Some or all of the inputs into these models may not be market observable, and are derived from market prices or rates, or estimated based on assumptions. When entering into a transaction, the financial instrument is initially recognized at the transaction price, which is the best indicator of fair value, although the value obtained from the valuation model may differ from the transaction price. This initial difference, usually an increase, in fair value indicated by valuation techniques is recognized in income depending upon the individual facts and circumstances of each transaction and not later than when the market data becomes observable.

The value produced by a model or other valuation technique is adjusted to allow for a number of factors as appropriate, because valuation techniques cannot appropriately reflect all factors market participants take into account when entering into a transaction. Valuation adjustments are recorded to allow for model risks, bid-ask spreads, liquidity risks, as well as other factors. Management believes that these valuation adjustments are necessary and appropriate to fairly state financial instruments carried at fair value on the balance sheet.

13. **Trading portfolio**

Trading portfolio assets consist of money market paper, other debt instruments, including traded loans, equity instruments, precious metals, and commodities which are owned by the Group ("long" positions). Trading portfolio liabilities consist of obligations to deliver trading securities such as money market paper, other debt instruments and equity instruments which the Group has sold to third parties but does not own ("short" positions).

The trading portfolio is carried at fair value. Gains and losses realized on disposal or redemption and unrealized gains and losses from changes in the fair value of trading portfolio assets or liabilities are reported as net trading income. Interest and dividend income and expense on trading portfolio assets or liabilities are included in interest and dividend income or interest and dividend expense, respectively.

The Group uses settlement date accounting when recording trading portfolio transactions. It recognizes from the date the transaction is entered into (trade date) any unrealized profits and losses arising from revaluing that contract to fair value in the income statement. Subsequent to the trade date, when the transaction is consummated (settlement date) a resulting financial asset or liability is recognized on the balance sheet at the fair value of the consideration given or received plus or minus the change in fair value of the contract since the trade date. When the Group becomes party to a sales contract of a financial asset classified in its trading portfolio, it derecognizes the asset on the day of its transfer.

14. **Financial instruments designated as held at fair value through profit and loss**

UBS has a substantial portion of its compound debt instruments classified as held at fair value through profit and loss.

These liabilities are presented in a separate line on the face of the balance sheet. A small amount of financial assets has also been classified as held at fair value through profit and loss, and they are likewise presented in a separate line. A financial instrument may be designated at inception as held at fair value through profit and loss and can subsequently not be changed.

The fair value designation was made possible as part of the transition to the revised IAS 39, which UBS adopted on January 1, 2004. The Group designated approximately CHF 35.3 billion of existing compound debt instruments as held at fair value through profit and loss at January 1, 2004. All fair value changes related to financial instruments held at fair value through profit and loss are recognized in Net trading income.

15. **Derivative instruments and hedging**

All derivative instruments are carried at fair value on the balance sheet and are reported as positive or negative replacement values. Where the Group enters into derivatives for trading purposes, realized and unrealized gains and losses are recognized in net trading income.

The Group also uses derivative instruments as part of its asset and liability management activities to manage exposures to interest rate, foreign currency, and credit risks, including exposures arising from forecast transactions. The Group applies either fair value or cash flow hedge accounting when transactions meet the specified criteria to obtain hedge accounting treatment.

At the time a financial instrument is designated as a hedge, the Group formally documents the relationship between the hedging instruments(s) and hedged item(s). Documentation includes its risk management objectives and its strategy in undertaking the hedge transaction, together with the methods that will be used to assess the effectiveness of the hedging relationship. Accordingly, the Group formally assesses, both at the inception of the hedge and on an ongoing basis, whether the hedging derivatives have been "highly effective" in offsetting changes in the fair value or cash flows of the hedged items. A hedge is normally regarded as highly effective if, at inception and throughout its life, the Group can expect, and actual results indicate, that changes in the fair value or cash flows of the hedged item are effectively offset by the changes in the fair value or cash flows of the hedging instrument, and actual results are within a range of 80% to 125%. In the case of hedging a forecast transaction, the transaction must have a high probability of occurring and must present an exposure to variations in cash flows that could ultimately affect reported net profit or loss. The Group discontinues hedge accounting when it is determined that: a derivative is not, or has ceased to be, highly effective as a hedge; when the derivative expires, or is sold, terminated, or exercised; when the hedged item matures or is sold or repaid; or when a forecast transaction is no longer deemed highly probable.

Hedge ineffectiveness represents the amount by which the changes in the fair value of the hedging derivative differ from changes in the fair value of the hedged item or the amount by which changes in the cash flow of the hedging derivative differ from changes (or expected changes) in the cash flow of the hedged item. Such gains and losses are recorded in current period earnings in net trading income, as are gains and losses on components of a hedging derivative that are excluded from assessing hedge effectiveness.

For qualifying fair value hedges, the change in fair value of the hedging derivative is recognized in net profit and loss. Those changes in fair value of the hedged item which are attributable to the risks hedged with the derivative instrument are reflected in an adjustment to the carrying value of the hedged item, which is also recognized in net profit or loss. If the hedge relationship is terminated for reasons other than the derecognition of the hedged item, the difference between the carrying value of the hedged item at that point and the value at which it would have been carried had the hedge never existed (the "unamortized fair value adjustment"), is, in the case of interest-bearing instruments, amortized to net profit or loss over the remaining term of the original hedge, while for noninterest-bearing instruments that amount is immediately recognized in earnings. If the hedged instrument is derecognized, (e.g., is sold or repaid), the unamortized fair value adjustment is recognized immediately in net profit and loss.

A fair value gain or loss associated with the effective portion of a derivative designated as a cash flow hedge is recognized initially in shareholders' equity. When the cash flows that the derivative is hedging materialize, resulting in income or expense, then the associated gain or loss on the hedging derivative is simultaneously transferred from shareholders' equity to the corresponding income or expense line item.

If a cash flow hedge for a forecast transaction is deemed to be no longer effective, or the hedge relationship is terminated, the cumulative gain or loss on the hedging derivative previously reported in shareholders' equity remains in shareholders' equity until the committed or forecast transaction occurs, at which point it is transferred from shareholders' equity to the income statement.

Derivative instruments transacted as economic hedges but not qualifying for hedge accounting are treated in the same way as derivative instruments used for trading purposes, (i.e., realized and unrealized gains and losses are recognized in net trading income). In particular, the Group has entered into economic hedges of credit risk within the loan portfolio using credit default swaps to which it cannot apply hedge accounting. In the event that the Group recognizes an impairment on a loan that is economically hedged in this way, the impairment is recognized in credit loss expense whereas any gain on the credit default swap is recorded in net trading income—see Note 23 for additional information.

A derivative may be embedded in a "host contract." Such combinations are known as compound instruments and arise predominantly from the issuance of certain structured debt instruments. If the host contract is not carried at fair value with changes in fair value reported in net profit or loss, the embedded derivative is separated from the host contract and accounted for as a stand-alone derivative instrument at fair value if, and only if, the economic characteristics and risks of the embedded derivative are not closely related to the economic characteristics and risks of the host contract and the embedded derivative actually meets the definition of a derivative.

16. **Loans**

Loans include loans originated by the Group where money is provided directly to the borrower, participation in a loan from another lender, and purchased loans that are not quoted in an active market and for which no intention of immediate or short-term resale exists. Originated and purchased loans which are intended to be sold in the short term are recorded as trading portfolio assets.

Loans are recognized when cash is advanced to borrowers. They are initially recorded at fair value, which is the cash given to originate the loan, including any transaction costs, and are subsequently measured at amortized cost using the effective interest rate method.

Interest on loans is included in interest earned on loans and advances and is recognized on an accrual basis. Fees and direct costs relating to loan origination, refinancing or restructuring, and to loan commitments are deferred and amortized to interest earned on loans and advances over the life of the loan using the straight-line method which approximates the effective interest rate method. Fees received for commitments which are not expected to result in a loan are included in credit-related fees and commissions over the commitment period. Loan syndication fees where UBS does not retain a portion of the syndicated loan are credited to commission income.

17. **Allowance and provision for credit losses**

An allowance for credit losses is established if there is objective evidence that the Group will be unable to collect all amounts due on a claim according to the original contractual terms or the equivalent value. A "claim" means a loan, a commitment such as a letter of credit, a guarantee, a commitment to extend credit, or other credit product.

An allowance for credit losses is reported as a reduction of the carrying value of a claim on the balance sheet, whereas for an off-balance-sheet item such as a commitment, a provision for credit loss is reported in other liabilities. Additions to the allowances and provisions for credit losses are made through credit loss expense.

Allowances and provisions for credit losses are evaluated at a counterparty-specific level based on the following principles:

Counterparty-specific: a claim is considered impaired when management determines that it is probable that the Group will not be able to collect all amounts due according to the original contractual terms or the equivalent value.

Individual credit exposures are evaluated based upon the borrower's character, overall financial condition, resources, and payment record; the prospects for support from any financially responsible guarantors; and, where applicable, the realizable value of any collateral.

The estimated recoverable amount is the present value, using the loan's original effective interest rate, of expected future cash flows, which may result from restructuring or liquidation. Impairment is measured and allowances for credit losses are established for the difference between the carrying amount and the estimated recoverable amount.

Upon impairment, the accrual of interest income based on the original terms of the claim is discontinued, but the increase of the present value of impaired claims due to the passage of time is reported as interest income.

All impaired claims are reviewed and analyzed at least annually. Any subsequent changes to the amounts and timing of the expected future cash flows compared to the prior estimates will result in a change in the allowance for credit losses and be charged or credited to credit loss expense.

An allowance for an impairment is reversed only when the credit quality has improved such that there is reasonable assurance of timely collection of principal and interest in accordance with the original contractual terms of the claim agreement.

A write-off is made when all or part of a claim is deemed uncollectible or forgiven. Write-offs are charged against previously established allowances for credit losses or directly to credit loss expense and reduce the principle amount of a claim. Recoveries in part or in full of amounts previously written off are credited to credit loss expense.

A loan is classified as nonperforming when the payment of interest, principal or fees is overdue by more than 90 days and there is no firm evidence that they will be made good by later payments or the liquidation of collateral, or when insolvency proceedings have commenced, or when obligations have been restructured on concessionary terms.

Collectively: all loans for which no impairment is identified on a counterparty-specific level are grouped into economically homogeneous portfolios to collectively assess whether impairment exists within a portfolio. Allowances from collective assessment of impairment are recognized as credit loss expense and result in an offset to the loan position. As the allowance cannot be allocated to individual loans, interest is accrued on all loans according to contractual terms.

Where, in management's opinion, it is probable that some claims may be affected by systemic crisis, transfer restrictions, or nonenforceability, country allowances and provisions for probable losses are established. They are based on country-specific scenarios, taking into consideration the nature of the individual exposures, but excluding those amounts covered by counterparty-specific allowances and provisions. Such country allowances and provisions are part of the collectively assessed loan loss allowances and provisions.

18. **Financial investments**

Financial investments are classified as available-for-sale and recorded on a settlement date basis. Available-for-sale financial investments are instruments which, in management's opinion, may be sold in response to or in anticipation of needs for liquidity or changes in interest rates, foreign exchange rates or equity prices. Financial investments consist of money market paper, other debt instruments, and equity instruments, including private equity investments.

Available-for-sale financial investments are carried at fair value. Unrealized gains or losses on available-for-sale investments are reported in shareholders' equity, net of applicable income taxes, until such investments are sold, collected, or otherwise disposed of, or until such investment is determined to be impaired. On disposal of an available-for sale investment, the accumulated unrealized gain or loss included in shareholders' equity is transferred to net profit or loss for the period and reported in other income. Gains and losses on disposal are determined using the average cost method.

Interest and dividend income on available-for-sale financial investments is included in Interest and dividend income from financial investments.

If an available-for-sale investment is determined to be impaired, the cumulative unrealized loss previously recognized in Shareholders' equity is included in net profit or loss for the period and reported in Other income. A financial investment is considered impaired if its cost exceeds the recoverable amount. For nonquoted equity investments, the recoverable amount is determined by applying recognized valuation techniques. The standard method applied is based on the multiple of earnings observed in the market for comparable companies. Management may adjust valuations determined in this way based on its judgment. For quoted financial investments, the recoverable amount is determined by reference to the market price. They are considered impaired if objective evidence indicates that the decline in market price has reached such a level that recovery of the cost value cannot be reasonably expected within the foreseeable future.

19. **Property and equipment**

Property and equipment includes own-used properties, investment properties, leasehold improvements, IT, software and communication, plant and manufacturing equipment, and other machines and equipment.

Own-used property is defined as property held by the Group for use in the supply of services or for administrative purposes, whereas investment property is defined as property held to earn rentals and/or for capital appreciation. If a property of the Group includes a portion that is own-used and another portion that is held to earn rentals or for capital appreciation, the classification is based on whether or not these portions can be sold separately. If the portions of the property can be sold separately, they are accounted for as own-used property and investment property. If the portions cannot be sold separately, the whole property is classified as own-used property unless the portion used by the bank is minor. The classification of property is reviewed on a regular basis to account for major changes in its usage.

Leasehold improvements are investments made to customize buildings and offices occupied under operating lease contracts to make them suitable for the intended purpose. The present value of estimated reinstatement costs to bring a lease property into its original condition at the end of the lease, if required, is capitalized as part of the total leasehold improvements costs. At the same time, a corresponding liability is recognized to reflect the obligation incurred. Reinstatement costs are recognized in profit and loss through depreciation of the capitalized leasehold improvements over their estimated useful life.

Software development costs are capitalized when they meet certain criteria relating to identifiability, it is probable that future economic benefits will flow to the enterprise, and the cost can be measured reliably. Internally developed software meeting these criteria and purchased software are classified within IT, software and communication.

Plant and manufacturing equipment include primarily thermal and hydro power plants and power transmission grids and equipment. The useful life is estimated based on the economic utilization of the asset, or for power plants on the end of operating life.

With the exception of investment properties, Property and equipment is carried at cost less accumulated depreciation and accumulated impairment losses. Property and equipment is periodically reviewed for impairment.

Property and equipment is depreciated on a straight-line basis over its estimated useful life as follows:

Properties, excluding land	Not exceeding 50 years
Leasehold improvements	Residual lease term, but not exceeding 10 years
Other machines and equipment	Not exceeding 10 years
IT, software and communication	Not exceeding 5 years
Plant and manufacturing equipment:	
Power plants	25 to 80 years
Transmission grids and equipment	15 to 40 years

Property formerly own-used or leased to third parties under an operating lease, which the Group has decided to dispose of, and foreclosed property are defined as properties held for resale and recorded in Other assets. They are carried at the lower of cost or recoverable value.

Investment property is carried at fair value with changes in fair value recognized in the income statement in the period of change. UBS employs internal real estate experts who determine the fair value of investment property by applying recognized valuation techniques. In cases where prices of recent market transactions of comparable properties are available, fair value is determined by reference to these transactions.

20. **Goodwill and other intangible assets**

Goodwill represents the excess of the cost of an acquisition over the fair value of the Group's share of net identifiable assets of the acquired entity at the date of acquisition. Other intangible assets are comprised of separately identifiable intangible items arising from acquisitions and certain purchased trademarks and similar items.

Goodwill and other intangible assets are recognized on the balance sheet at cost determined at the date of acquisition and are amortized using the straight-line method over their estimated useful economic life, not exceeding 20 years. At each balance sheet date, goodwill and other intangible assets are reviewed for indications of impairment or changes in estimated future benefits. If such indications exist, an analysis is performed to assess whether the carrying amount of goodwill or other intangible assets is fully recoverable. A write-down is made if the carrying amount exceeds the recoverable amount.

With the introduction of IFRS 3, *Business Combinations,* goodwill acquired in business combinations entered into after March 31, 2004, is not amortized, but tested annually for impairment. The impairment test is conducted at the segment level as reported in Note 2. The segment has been determined as the cash generating unit for impairment testing purposes as this is the level at which the performance of an investment is reviewed and assessed by management. During 2004, UBS recorded goodwill of CHF 631 million from business combinations entered into after March 31, 2004.

Intangible assets are classified into two categories: infrastructure, and customer relationships, contractual rights and other. Infrastructure includes one intangible asset recognized in connection with the acquisition of PaineWebber Group, Inc. Customer relationships, contractual rights and other include customer relationship intangibles from acquisition of financial services businesses as well as from the acquisition of Motor-Columbus, where other contractual rights from delivery and supply contracts were identified. These contractual rights are amortized over the remaining contract terms, which are up to 25 years. The most significant contract, however, is amortized over its remaining contract life of seven years, which is the shortest remaining life of all contractual rights recognized.

21. **Income taxes**

Income tax payable on profits is recognized as an expense based on the applicable tax laws in each jurisdiction in the period in which profits arise. The tax effects of income tax losses available for carryforward are recognized as a deferred tax asset if it is probable that future taxable profit will be available against which those losses can be utilized.

Deferred tax liabilities are recognized for temporary differences between the carrying amounts of assets and liabilities in the balance sheet and their amounts as measured for tax purposes, which will result in taxable amounts in future periods.

Deferred tax assets are recognized for temporary differences which will result in deductible amounts in future periods, but only to the extent it is probable that sufficient taxable profits will be available against which these differences can be utilized. Deferred tax assets and liabilities are measured at the tax rates that are expected to apply in the period in which the asset will be realized or the liability will be settled based on enacted rates.

Current as well as deferred tax assets and liabilities are offset when they arise from the same tax reporting group and relate to the same tax authority and when the legal right to offset exists.

Current and deferred taxes are recognized as income tax benefit or expense except for (1) deferred taxes recognized or disposed of upon the acquisition or disposal of a subsidiary, and (2) unrealized gains or losses on available-for-sale investments and changes in fair value of derivative instruments designated as cash flow hedges, which are recorded net of taxes in Net gains or losses not recognized in the income statement within Shareholders' equity.

22. **Debt issued**

Debt issued is initially measured at fair value, which is the consideration received, net of transaction costs incurred. Subsequent measurement is at amortized cost, using the effective interest rate method to amortize cost at inception to the redemption value over the life of the debt.

Compound debt instruments that are related to non-UBS AG equity instruments, foreign exchange, credit instruments or indices are considered structured instruments. If such instruments have not been designated at fair value through profit and loss, the embedded derivative is separated from the host contract and accounted for as a stand-alone derivative if the criteria for separation are met. The host contract is subsequently measured at amortized cost. For most of its structured debt instruments, UBS has designated them as held at fair value through profit and loss; see section 14.

Debt instruments with embedded derivatives that are related to UBS AG shares or to a derivative instrument that has UBS AG shares as underlying are separated into a liability and an equity component at issue date, if they require physical settlement. Initially, a portion of the net proceeds from issuing the compound debt instrument is allocated to the equity component based on its fair value. The determination of fair value is generally based on quoted market prices for UBS debt instruments with comparable terms. The liability component is subsequently measured at amortized cost. The remaining amount is allocated to the equity component and reported in share premium account. Subsequent changes in fair value of the separated equity component are not recognized. However, if the combined instrument or the embedded derivative related to UBS AG shares is cash settled or if it contains a settlement alternative, then the separated derivative is accounted for as a trading instrument with changes in fair value recorded in income or the entire compound instrument is designated as held at fair value through profit and loss.

It is the Group's policy to hedge the fixed interest rate risk on debt issues (except for certain subordinated long-term note issues; see Note 30a) and apply fair value hedge accounting. When hedge accounting is applied to fixed rate debt instruments, the carrying values of debt issues are adjusted for changes in fair value related to the hedged exposure rather than carried at amortized cost. See 15 Derivative instruments and hedging for further discussion.

Own bonds held as a result of market making activities or deliberate purchases in the market are treated as a redemption of debt. A gain or loss on redemption is recorded depending on whether the repurchase price of the bond was lower or higher than its carrying value. A subsequent sale of own bonds in the market is treated as reissuance of debt.

Interest expense on debt instruments is included in interest on debt issued.

23.   **Treasury shares and contracts on UBS shares**

UBS AG shares held by the Group are classified in shareholders' equity as treasury shares and accounted for at weighted-average cost. The difference between the proceeds from sales of Treasury shares and their costs (net of tax, if any) is classified as Share premium.

Contracts that require physical settlement in UBS AG shares are classified as shareholders' equity and reported as share premium. Upon settlement of such contracts the proceeds received less cost (net of tax, if any), are reported as share premium.

Contracts on UBS AG shares that require net cash settlement or provide for a choice of settlement are classified as trading instruments, with the changes in fair value reported in the income statement.

An exception to this treatment is physically settled written put options and forward share purchase contracts, including contracts where physical settlement is a settlement alternative. In both cases the present value of the obligation to purchase own shares in exchange for cash is transferred out of Shareholders' equity and recognized as a liability at inception of a contract. The liability is subsequently accreted, using the effective interest rate method, over the life of the contract to the nominal purchase obligation by recognizing interest expense. Upon settlement of a contract, the liability is derecognized and the amount of equity originally transferred to liability is reclassified within Shareholders' equity to treasury shares. The premium received for writing put options is recognized directly in Share premium.

24.   **Retirement benefits**

UBS sponsors a number of retirement benefit plans for its employees worldwide. These plans include both defined benefit and defined contribution plans and various other retirement benefits such as postemployment medical benefits. Contributions to defined contribution plans are expensed when employees have rendered services in exchange for such contributions, generally in the year of contribution.

The Group uses the projected unit credit actuarial method to determine the present value of its defined benefit plans and the related service cost and, where applicable, past service cost.

The principal actuarial assumptions used by the actuary are set out in Note 31.

The Group recognizes a portion of its actuarial gains and losses as income or expense if the net cumulative unrecognized actuarial gains and losses at the end of the previous reporting period exceeded the greater of

   a.   10% of present value of the defined benefit obligation at that date (before deducting plan assets); and
   b.   10% of the fair value of any plan assets at that date.

The unrecognized actuarial gains and losses exceeding the greater of the two values are recognized in the income statement over the expected average remaining working lives of the employees participating in the plans.

If an excess of the fair value of the plan assets over the present value of the defined benefit obligation cannot be recovered fully through refunds or reductions in future contributions, no gain is recognized solely as a result of deferral of an actuarial loss or past service cost in the current period or no loss is recognized solely as a result of deferral of an actuarial gain in the current period.

25.   **Equity participation plans**

UBS provides various equity participation plans in the form of stock plans and stock option plans. UBS generally uses the intrinsic value method of accounting for such awards. Consequently, compensation expense is measured as the difference between the quoted market price of the stock at the grant date less the amount, if any, that the employee is required to pay, or by the excess of stock price over option strike price, if any. The Group's policy is to recognize compensation expense for equity awards in the performance year.

26. **Earnings per share (EPS)**

Basic earnings per share is calculated by dividing the net profit or loss for the period attributable to ordinary shareholders by the weighted-average number of ordinary shares outstanding during the period.

Diluted earnings per share is computed using the same method as for basic EPS, but the determinants are adjusted to reflect the potential dilution that could occur if options, warrants, convertible debt securities or other contracts to issue ordinary shares were converted or exercised into ordinary shares.

27. **Changes in accounting policies and comparability**

Financial instruments

On January 1, 2004, UBS adopted revised IAS 32, *Financial Instruments: Disclosure and Presentation,* and revised IAS 39, *Financial Instruments: Recognition and Measurement,* which were applied retrospectively to all financial instruments affected within the context of the two standards with the exception of the guidance relating to derecognition of financial assets and liabilities and, in part, recognition of Day 1 profit and loss, which were applied prospectively. As a result of adopting the revised standards, UBS has restated prior period comparative information.

Revised IAS 32 amended the accounting for certain derivative contracts linked to an entity's own shares. Physically settled written put options and forward purchase contracts with UBS shares as underlying are recorded as liabilities; see section 23. UBS currently has physically settled written put options linked to own shares that are now accounted for as liabilities. Liabilities of CHF 96 million at December 31, 2004, and CHF 49 million at December 31, 2003, were debited to Shareholders' equity due to written options. The impact on the income statement of all periods presented is insignificant. All other existing derivative contracts linked to own shares are accounted for as derivative instruments and are carried at fair value on the balance sheet under Positive replacement values or Negative replacement values.

Revised IAS 32 provides that netting is permitted only if, in addition to all other netting conditions, normal settlement is intended to take place on a net basis. In general, that condition is not met for derivative instruments and therefore replacement values are now reported on a gross basis. In the December 31, 2003 balance sheet, replacement values of CHF 165,050 million that were previously offset are now reported gross.

Revised IAS 39 permits any financial instrument to be designated at inception, or at adoption of revised IAS 39, as carried at fair value through profit and loss. Upon adoption of revised IAS 39, UBS made that designation for the majority of its compound instruments issued. Previously, UBS separated the embedded derivative from the host contract and accounted for the separated derivative as a trading instrument. The amounts are now included on the balance sheet within the line item Financial liabilities designated at fair value, with amounts of CHF 65,756 million at December 31, 2004, and CHF 35,286 million at December 31, 2003, being reported in that new line. Also, at December 31, 2004, assets in the amount of CHF 653 million are reported in the new line Financial assets designated at fair value. At December 31, 2003, no financial assets were designated as held at fair value.

The guidance governing recognition and derecognition of a financial asset is considerably more complex under revised IAS 39 than previously and requires a multistep decision process to determine whether derecognition is appropriate.

See section 4 for a discussion of the accounting policies regarding derecognition. As a result, certain transactions are now accounted for as secured financing transactions instead of purchases or sales of trading portfolio assets with an accompanying swap derivative. The provisions of this guidance were applied prospectively as of January 1, 2004.

The effect of restating the income statement due to the adoption of revised IAS 32 and 39 on the comparative prior periods is a reduction of net profit by CHF 82 million for 2003 and a reduction of CHF 24 million for 2002.

Investment properties

Effective January 1, 2004, UBS changed its accounting policy for investment property from historical cost less accumulated depreciation to the fair value model. All changes in the fair value of investment property are now recognized in the income statement, and depreciation expense is no longer recorded. Investment property is defined as property held exclusively to earn rental income and benefit from appreciation in value. Fair value of investment property is determined by appropriate valuation techniques employed in the real estate industry, taking into account the specific circumstances for each item. This change required restatement of the 2003 and 2002 comparative financial years. The effects of the restatement were a reduction of net profit by CHF 64 million in 2003, and an increase of net profit by CHF 19 million in 2002.

Credit losses incurred on OTC derivatives

Effective January 1, 2004, the method of accounting for credit losses incurred on over-the-counter (OTC) derivatives has been changed. All such credit losses are now reported in net trading income and are no longer reported in credit loss expense. This change did not affect net profit or earnings per share results. It did, however, affect segment reporting, as losses reported as credit loss expense were previously deferred over a three-year period in the Business Group segment reporting, whereas under the changed method of accounting, losses in trading income are not subject to such a deferral. In the segment report, therefore, losses on OTC derivatives are now reported as they are incurred. This change in accounting method affected, to a minor extent, certain balance sheet lines at December 31, 2003, which have been restated to conform to the current year presentation. The changed method of accounting had the following impact on the performance before tax of our Business Groups: In 2003, it reduced Wealth Management & Business Banking's pretax performance by CHF 8 million. It raised the Investment Bank's by CHF 37 million while Corporate Functions' fell by CHF 29 million. In 2002, the changed method lowered the Investment Bank's pretax performance by CHF 28 million and raised Corporate Functions' by CHF 28 million.

Segment reporting

On July 1, 2004, UBS purchased an additional 20% interest in Motor-Columbus AG, which increased its overall ownership stake to 55.6%. Motor-Columbus has been consolidated as of July 1, 2004, when UBS gained control over the company. Due to its size and nature of business—production, distribution, and trading of electricity—a new business segment, Industrial Holdings, was added, in which Motor-Columbus is reported.

As at January 1, 2003, the five private label banks (three of which were subsequently merged into one bank) owned by UBS were transferred out of Wealth Management & Business Banking into Corporate Center. At the same time, GAM was transferred out of Global Asset Management into Corporate Center. The two businesses formed the Private Banks & GAM segment, whereas the remainder of Corporate Center is reported as the Corporate Functions segment. Also, Wealth Management & Business Banking is reported as two segments, Wealth Management and Business Banking Switzerland. As at January 1, 2002, Wealth Management USA was separated from Investment Bank and became a stand-alone business group.

Note 2 to these Group financial statements reflects the new segment reporting structure. In all applicable instances, prior period comparative amounts of the affected business groups have been restated to conform to the current year presentation.

Business combinations

On April 1, 2004, UBS adopted IFRS 3, *Business Combinations*, for all business combinations entered into after March 31, 2004. Subsequent to the adoption of the new standard, UBS has entered into and completed a number of business combinations that were all accounted for under the new standard. The most significant change under the new standard is that goodwill is no longer amortized over its estimated useful life but instead tested annually for impairment. Accordingly, no amortization expense has been recognized for goodwill of CHF 631 million recognized on the balance sheet related to business combinations entered into after April 1, 2004. Intangible assets may be assigned an indefinite useful life, if supportable based on facts and circumstances. These intangibles are not amortized, but tested periodically for impairment.

In a step acquisition, where control over a subsidiary is achieved in stages, or where additional shares of a subsidiary are purchased from minority owners, all assets and liabilities of that entity, excluding goodwill, are remeasured to fair value as of the acquisition date of the latest share transaction. The revaluation difference on the existing ownership interest from the carrying value to the newly established fair value is recorded directly in Shareholders' Equity. As a consequence of remeasuring all assets and liabilities to fair value, minority interests are also carried at fair value of net assets excluding goodwill. Previously, only the percentage of assets and liabilities was increased to fair value by which the ownership interest was increased. Existing ownership interests were kept at their carryover basis. Other relevant changes in accounting for business combinations are that liabilities incurred for restructuring and integration of newly acquired businesses must be expensed as incurred, unless they were a preacquisition contingency of the acquired business. Previously, liabilities incurred for restructuring and integration could be recognized in purchase accounting, if they met certain criteria, increasing goodwill recognized. Contingent liabilities of an acquired business have to be recognized on the balance sheet at their fair value in purchase accounting, if fair value is determinable. Previously, contingent liabilities were not recognized.

The accounting for business combinations entered into before March 31, 2004, was not affected by the new standard.

Amended IAS 19, *Employee Benefits*

UBS adopted in 2002 the amended standard IAS 19, *Employee Benefits*. The amendments introduce an asset ceiling provision that applies for defined benefit plans that have a surplus of plan assets over benefit obligations. The implementation of the amended standard had no material impact.

Change in treatment of corporate client assets

Effective January 1, 2004, UBS reclassified corporate client assets of Business Banking Switzerland (except for pension funds) to exclude them from invested assets. This change was made because UBS has a minimal advisory role for such clients and asset flows are often driven more by liquidity requirements than pure investment reasons. This change reduced invested assets at December 31, 2003, by approximately CHF 76 billion and increased net new money for 2003 by CHF 7.5 billion.

28. **International financial reporting standards to be adopted in 2005**

IASB Improvements Project

In December 2003, the IASB issued 15 revised International Accounting Standards under it Improvement Project in an attempt to clarify language, to remove inconsistencies, and to achieve convergence with other accounting standards, notably US GAAP. All revised standards are effective for financial years beginning on or after January 1, 2005. Two of these 15 improved standards, IAS 32 and IAS 39, were adopted early at the beginning of 2004. Two of the remaining 13 improved standards will have a significant impact on UBS, which are IAS 27, *Consolidated and Separate Financial Statements* and IAS 28, *Investments in Associates*.

IAS 27 has been amended to eliminate the exemption from consolidating a subsidiary where control is exercised temporarily. UBS has several private equity investments where it owns a controlling interest, which are classified and accounted for as Financial investments available-for-sale, which will be required to be consolidated. UBS will adopt IAS 27 on January 1, 2005, with retrospective restatement of comparative prior years 2004 and 2003. The effect of the adoption and consolidating these investments will be as follows: At January 1, 2003, equity including minority interests are reduced by CHF 723 million, representing the difference between the carrying value as Financial investments available-for-sale and the value on a consolidated basis. Consolidation will lead to recognition of total assets in the amount of CHF 1.7 billion and CHF 2.9 billion at December 31, 2004 and 2003, respectively. Significant balance sheet line items affected will include Property and equipment, Intangible assets, Goodwill and Other assets. These investments generated additional income of CHF 3.8 billion and CHF 4.1 billion in 2004 and 2003, respectively, and additional net profit of CHF 92 million and CHF 86 million in 2004 and 2003, respectively.

IAS 28 has been amended in the same way as IAS 27 to eliminate the exemption from equity method accounting for investments that are held exclusively for disposal. UBS will adopt the IAS 28 amendment on January 1, 2005, with retrospective restatement of comparative prior years 2004 and 2003. Certain private equity investments where UBS has a significant influence will be equity accounted for commencing January 1, 2005. Applying the equity method of accounting for these investments will have the following effects: At January 1, 2003, equity is debited by CHF 266 million, representing the difference between the carrying value as Financial investments available-for-sale versus the value on an equity method basis. The carrying value of these equity method investments will be CHF 248 million and CHF 393 million at December 31, 2004 and 2003, respectively, which includes equity in losses of CHF 55 million and gains of CHF 10 million recognized in the income statement in 2004 and 2003, respectively. When accounted for as Financial investments, gains on sale recognized were CHF 70 million in 2004 and CHF 34 million in 2003.

In 2005, these entities, along with all other investments made by the Private Equity business unit, will be reclassified from the Investment Bank segment to the Industrial Holdings segment. In addition, seven of the newly consolidated investments held at January 1, 2003, were sold during 2003 and 2004 and will be presented as discontinued operations in the restated comparative prior periods in accordance with IFRS 5 which is discussed below. Gain on sale in the amount of CHF 90 million and CHF 194 million have been reported related to private equity investments sold in 2004 and 2003, respectively. On a restated basis, the net profit from discontinued operations related to these entities will be CHF 145 million and CHF 186 million in 2004 and 2003, respectively.

UBS also has employee benefit trusts that are used in connection with share-based payment arrangements and deferred compensation schemes. In connection with the issuance of IFRS 2, the IFRIC amended SIC 12, *Consolidation—Special Purpose Entities*, an interpretation of IAS 27, to eliminate the scope exclusion for equity compensation plans. Therefore, pursuant to the criteria set out in SIC 12, and entity that controls an employee benefit trust (or similar entity) set up for the purposes of a share-based payment arrangement will be required to consolidate that trust.

Consolidating these trusts will have the following effects: At January 1, 2003, no adjustment to opening retained earnings is made as assets and liabilities of the trust are equal. Consolidation will lead to recognition of total assets in the amount of CHF 1.1 billion and CHF 1.3 billion and liabilities of CHF 1.1 billion and CHF 1.3 billion at December 31, 2004 and 2003, respectively. The amount of treasury shares will increase by CHF 2,029 million and CHF 1,474 million at December 31, 2004, and 2003, respectively. The weighted-average number of treasury shares held by these trusts was 22,995,954 in 2004 and 30,792,147 in 2003, thus decreasing the numerator to calculate basic earnings per share. The reduction in weighted-average shares outstanding will increase the basic earnings per share, but have no impact on diluted earnings per share, as the additional treasury shares will be fully added back for calculating diluted earnings per share.

All other revised standards under the Improvement Project will primarily affect presentation and disclosure, but not recognition and measurement of assets and liabilities, and will therefore not have a material impact on the financial statements. The two most significant presentation differences relate to minority interests and earnings per share. Beginning 2005, Net profit and Equity will be presented including minority interests. Net profit will be allocated to net profit attributable to UBS shareholders and attributable to minority interests on the face of the income statement.

Earnings per share will continue to be presented based on net profit attributable to UBS shareholders, but will be allocated to earnings per share from continuing operations and from discontinued operations.

IFRS 2, *Share-Based Payment*

In February 2004, the IASB issued IFRS 2, *Share-Based Payment*, which requires share-based payments made to employees and nonemployees to be recognized in the financial statements based on the fair value of these awards measured at the date of grant. UBS will adopt the new standard on January 1, 2005, and fully restate the two comparative prior years. In accordance with IFRS 2, UBS will apply the new requirements of the standard to all prior period awards that impact income statements commencing 2003. This includes all unvested equity settled awards and all outstanding cash settled awards at January 1, 2003. The effects of restatement are as follows: The opening balance of retained earnings at January 1, 2003, will be credited by CHF 559 million. Additional compensation expense of zero and CHF 558 million will be recognized in 2004 and 2003, respectively. The change in compensation expense is attributable to the first-time recognition of compensation expense for the fair value of share options, as well as the recognition of expense for share awards over the vesting period. Previously, share awards were recognized as compensation expense in the performance year, which is generally the year prior to grant. The reason for the zero impact in 2004 is that a significantly higher amount of bonus payments were made in the form of restricted stock rather than cash. The reversal of compensation expense attributable to these share payments offset the effect from recognizing options at fair value and share awards made prior to 2004 over the vesting period.

UBS will introduce a new valuation model to determine the fair value of share options granted in 2005 and later. Share options granted in 2004 and earlier will not be affected by this change in valuation model. As part of the implementation of IFRS 2, UBS thoroughly reviewed the option valuation model employed in the past by comparing it to alternative models. As a result of this review, a valuation model was identified that better reflects the exercise behavior of employees and the specific terms and conditions under which the share options are granted. Concurrent with the introduction of the new model, UBS will use implied instead of historic volatility as input into the new model.

IFRS 3, *Business Combinations*, IAS 36, *Impairment of Assets* and IAS 38, *Intangible Assets*

On March 31, 2004, the IASB issued IFRS 3, *Business Combinations*, revised IAS 36, *Impairment of Assets*, and revised IAS 38, *Intangible Assets*. UBS adopted the standards on April 1, 2004. Under the transitional requirements of IFRS 3, goodwill recognized in business combinations after March 31, 2004, will no longer be amortized over its estimated useful life but be tested annually for impairment. Goodwill existing at March 31, 2004, will cease to be amortized as of January 1, 2005, and reviewed annually for impairment. UBS recorded goodwill amortization expense of CHF 713 million in 2004 and CHF 756 million in 2003. Intangible assets acquired in a business combination must be recognized separately from goodwill, if they meet the recognition criteria. UBS will reclassify the trained workforce intangible recognized in connection with the acquisition of PaineWebber with a book value of CHF 1,010 million to Goodwill at January 1, 2005.

IFRS 4, *Insurance Contracts*

On March 31, 2004, the IASB issued IFRS 4, *Insurance Contracts*. The standard applies to all insurance contracts written and to reinsurance contracts held. It requires that insurance contracts that include a deposit component are separated into the deposit and the insurance component. UBS will adopt the new standard as of January 1, 2005, and apply it to its insurance contracts. The new standard will not have a material effect on the financial statements.

*IFRS 5, **Noncurrent Assets Held for Sale and Discontinued Operations***

On March 31, 2004, the IASB issued IFRS 5, *Noncurrent Assets Held for Sale and Discontinued Operations*. The standard requires that noncurrent assets or disposal groups be classified as held for sale if their carrying amount is recovered principally through a sale transaction rather than through continuing use. Such assets are measured at the lower of carrying amount and fair value less costs to sell and are classified separately from other assets in the balance sheet. Netting of assets and liabilities is not permitted. Discontinued operations are presented on the face of the income statement as a single amount comprising the total of the net profit or loss of discontinued operations and the after-tax gain or loss recognized on the sale or the measurement to fair value less costs to sell of the net assets constituting the discontinued operations.

IFRS 5 provides certain criteria to be met for a component of an entity to be defined as a discontinued operation. Certain private equity investments meet this definition and will be reclassified as discontinued operations. UBS will adopt the new standard on January 1, 2005, and restate comparative prior years 2004 and 2003. While the impact on the financial statements will not be material, the income statement will be divided into two sections; net income from continuing operations and net income from discontinued operations.

APPENDIX B
EXAMPLE BANK FINANCIAL STATEMENTS
UBS Group Financial Statements
December 31, 2004

UBS Income Statement

CHF million, except per share data

		For the year ended			% change from
	Note	*12/31/04*	*12/31/03*	*12/31/02*	*12/31/03*
Operating income					
Interest income	3	39,398	40,159	39,963	(2)
Interest expense	3	(27,538)	(27,860)	(29,417)	(1)
Net interest income		11,860	12,299	10,546	(4)
Credit loss (expense)/recovery		276	(72)	(115)	--
Net interest income after credit loss expense		12,136	12,227	10,431	(1)
Net fee and commission income	4	19,416	17,345	18,221	12
Net trading income	3	4,972	3,756	5,451	32
Other income	5	897	462	4	94
Income from industrial holdings		3,648	--	--	--
Total operating income		41,069	33,790	34,107	22
Operating expenses					
Personnel expenses	6	18,515	17,231	18,524	7
General and administrative expenses	7	6,703	6,086	7,072	10
Depreciation of property and equipment	14	1,352	1,353	1,514	--
Amortization of goodwill and other intangible assets	15	964	943	2,460	2
Goods and materials purchased		2,861	--	--	--
Total operating expenses		30,395	25,613	29,570	19
Operating profit before tax and minority interests		10,674	8,177	4,537	31
Tax expense	21	2,135	1,593	676	34
Net profit before minority interests		8,539	6,584	3,861	30
Minority interests	22	(450)	(345)	(331)	30
Net profit		8,089	6,239	3,530	30
Basic earnings per share (CHF)	8	7.68	5.59	2.92	37
Diluted earnings per share (CHF)	8	7.47	5.48	2.87	36

Balance Sheet

CHF million

				% change from
	Note	*12/31/04*	*12/31/03*	*12/31/03*
Assets				
Cash and balances with central banks		6,036	3,584	68
Due from banks	9	35,264	31,740	11
Cash collateral on securities borrowed	10	220,242	213,932	3
Reverse repurchase agreements	10	357,164	320,499	11
Trading portfolio assets	11	370,259	341,013	9
Trading portfolio assets pledged as collateral	11	159,115	120,759	32
Positive replacement values	23	284,577	248,206	15
Financial assets designated at fair value		653	--	--
Loans	9	232,387	212,679	9
Financial investments	12	5,049	5,139	(2)
Accrued income and prepaid expenses		5,876	6,218	(6)
Investments in associates	13	2,247	1,616	50
Property and equipment	14	8,736	7,683	14
Goodwill and other intangible assets	15	12,149	11,529	5
Other assets	16, 21	34,850	25,459	37
Total assets		1,734,784	1,550,056	12

CHF million	Note	12/31/04	12/31/03	% change from 12/31/03
Liabilities				
Due to banks	17	118,901	127,012	(6)
Cash collateral on securities lent	10	61,545	53,278	16
Repurchase agreements	10	422,587	415,863	2
Trading portfolio liabilities	11	171,033	143,957	19
Negative replacement values	23	303,712	254,768	19
Financial liabilities designated at fair value	18	65,756	35,286	86
Due to customers	17	376,083	346,633	8
Accrued expenses and deferred income		14,685	13,673	7
Debt issued	18	117,828	88,843	33
Other liabilities	19, 20, 21	42,342	31,360	35
Total liabilities		1,694,472	1,510,673	12
Minority interests	22	5,334	4,073	31
Shareholders' equity				
Share capital		901	946	(5)
Share premium account		7,348	6,935	6
Net gains/(losses) not recognized in the income statement, net of tax		(1,644)	(983)	(67)
Revaluation reserve from step acquisitions		90	--	--
Retained earnings		37,455	36,641	2
Equity classified as obligation to purchase own shares		(96)	(49)	(96)
Treasury shares		(9,076)	(8,180)	(11)
Total shareholders' equity		34,978	35,310	(1)
Total liabilities, minority interests, and shareholders' equity		1,734,784	1,550,056	12

Statement of Changes in Equity

CHF million	For the year ended		
	12/31/04	12/31/03	12/31/02
Issued and paid-up share capital			
Balance at the beginning of the year	946	1,005	3,589
Issue of share capital	2	2	6
Capital repayment by par value reduction[1]			(2,509)
Cancellation of second trading line treasury shares (2001 Program)			(81)
Cancellation of second trading line treasury shares (2002 Program)		(61)	
Cancellation of second trading line treasury shares (2003 Program)	(47)		
Balance at the end of the year	901	946	1,005
Share premium			
Balance at the beginning of the year, restated	6,935	12,641	14,408
Premium on shares issued and warrants exercised	379	92	157
Net premium/(discount) on treasury share and own equity derivative activity	26	(330)	285
Employee stock option plan	8		
Cancellation of second trading line treasury shares (2001 Program)			(2,209)
Cancellation of second trading line treasury shares (2002 Program)		(5,468)	
Balance at the end of the year	7,348	6,935	12,641
Net gains/(losses) not recognized in the income statement, net of taxes			
Foreign currency translation			
Balance at the beginning of the year	(1,644)	(849)	(769)
Movements during the year	(818)	(795)	(80)
Subtotal—balance at the end of the year	(2,462)	(1,644)	(849)

	For the year ended		
	12/31/04	*12/31/03*	*12/31/02*
Net unrealized gains/(losses) on available-for-sale investments, net of taxes			
Balance at the beginning of the year	805	946	1,035
Net unrealized gains/(losses) on available-for-sale investments	474	(108)	(144)
Impairment charges reclassified to the income statement	192	285	635
Realized gains reclassified to the income statement	(353)	(340)	(600)
Realized losses reclassified to the income statement	22	22	20
Subtotal—balance at the end of the year	1,140	805	946
Change in fair value of derivative instruments designated as cash flow hedges, net of taxes			
Balance at the beginning of the year	(144)	(256)	(459)
Net unrealized gains/(losses) on the revaluation of cash flow hedges	(223)	116	(11)
Net realized (gains)/losses reclassified to the income statement	45	(4)	214
Subtotal—balance at the end of the year	(322)	(144)	(256)
Balance at the end of the year	(1,644)	(983)	(159)
Revaluation reserve from step acquisitions, net of taxes			
New acquisitions	90		
Balance at the end of the year	90		
Retained earnings			
Balance at the beginning of the year, restated	36,641	32,700	29,103
Net profit for the year	8,089	6,239	3,597
Dividends paid[1]	(2,806)	(2,298)	
Cancellation of second trading line treasury shares (2003 program)[2]	(4,469)		
Balance at the end of the year	37,455	36,641	32,700
Equity classified as obligation to purchase own shares			
Balance at the beginning of the year, restated	(49)	(104)	
Net movements	(47)	55	(104)
Balance at the end of the year	(96)	(49)	(104)
Treasury shares, at cost			
Balance at the beginning of the year	(8,180)	(7,131)	(3,377)
Acquisitions	(8,813)	(8,424)	(8,313)
Disposals	3,401	1,846	2,269
Cancellation of second trading line treasury shares (2001 program)			2,290
Cancellation of second trading line treasury shares (2002 program)		5,529	
Cancellation of second trading line treasury shares (2003 program)	4,516		
Balance at the end of the year	(9,076)	(8,180)	(7,131)
Total shareholders' equity	34,978	35,310	38,952

[1] On July 10, 2002, UBS made a distribution of CHF 7.00 per share to shareholders which reduced the par value from CHF 2.80 to CHF 0.80 per share. Dividends of CHF 2.00 per share and CHF 2.60 per share were paid on April 23, 2003, and April 20, 2004, respectively

[2] The cancellation of second trading line treasury shares is now made against retained earnings. In prior years it was made against the share premium amount.

Shares issued

Number of shares	12/31/04	For the year ended 12/31/03	12/31/02	% change from 12/31/03
Balance at the beginning of the year	1,183,046,764	1,256,297,678	1,281,717,499	(6)
Issue of share capital	3,293,413	2,719,166	3,398,869	21
Cancellation of second trading line treasury shares (2001 program)			(28,818,690)	
Cancellation of second trading line treasury shares (2002 program)		(75,970,080)		
Cancellation of second trading line treasury shares (2003 program)	(59,482,000)			
Balance at the end of the year	1,126,858,177	1,183,046,764	1,256,297,678	(5)

Treasury shares		For the year ended		% change from
Number of shares	12/31/04	12/31/03	12/31/02	12/31/03
Balance at the beginning of the year	111,360,692	97,181,094	41,254,951	15
Acquisitions	96,139,004	116,080,976	110,710,741	(17)
Disposals	(44,492,725)	(25,931,298)	(25,965,908)	(72)
Cancellation of second trading line treasury shares (2001 program)			(28,818,690)	
Cancellation of second trading line treasury shares (2002 program)		(75,970,080)		100
Cancellation of second trading line treasury shares (2003 program)	(59,482,000)			
Balance at the end of the year	103,524,971	111,360,692	97,181,094	(7)

During the year a total of 59,482,000 shares acquired under the second trading line buyback program 2003 were canceled. On December 31, 2004, a maximum of 3,533,012 shares can be issued against the exercise of options from former PaineWebber employee option plans. These shares are shown as conditional share capital in the UBS AG (Parent Bank) disclosure. Out of the total number of 103,524,971 treasury shares, 39,935,094 shares (CHF 3,543 million) have been repurchased for cancellation. The Board of Directors will propose to the Annual General Meeting on April 21, 2005, to reduce the outstanding number of shares and the share capital by the number of shares purchased for cancellation. All issued shares are fully paid.

Statement of Cash Flows

CHF million

	For the year ended		
	12/31/04	12/31/03	12/31/02
Cash flow from/(used in) operating activities			
Net profit	8,089	6,239	3,530
Adjustments to reconcile net profit to cash flow from/(used in) operating activities			
Noncash items included in net profit and other adjustments:			
Depreciation of property and equipment	1,352	1,353	1,514
Amortization of goodwill and other intangible assets	964	943	2,460
Credit loss expense/(recovery)	(276)	72	115
Equity in income of associates	(65)	(123)	(7)
Deferred tax expense/(benefit)	3	489	(511)
Net loss/(gain) from investing activities	(475)	(63)	986
Net loss/(gain) from financing activities	1,203	115	(446)
Net (increase)/decrease in operating assets:			
Net due from/to banks	(11,679)	42,921	(22,382)
Reverse repurchase agreements and cash collateral on securities borrowed	(42,975)	(101,381)	(944)
Trading portfolio and net replacement values	(19,834)	(52,197)	22,427
Loans/due to customers	10,035	38,638	(11,446)
Accrued income, prepaid expenses, and other assets	(6,927)	(16,100)	2,875
Net increase/(decrease) in operating liabilities:			
Repurchase agreements and cash collateral on securities lent	14,991	65,413	4,791
Accrued expenses and other liabilities	19,032	18,183	(4,754)
Income taxes paid	(1,336)	(1,104)	(572)
Net cash flow from/(used in) operating activities	(27,898)	3,403	(2,364)

	For the year ended		
	12/31/04	*12/31/03*	*12/31/02*
Cash flow from/(used in) investing activities			
Investments in subsidiaries and associates	(2,511)	(428)	(60)
Disposal of subsidiaries and associates	800	834	984
Purchase of property and equipment	(1,149)	(1,376)	(1,763)
Disposal of property and equipment	704	123	67
Net (investment in)/divestment of financial investments	686	2,317	2,153
Net cash flow from/(used in) investing activities	(1,470)	1,470	1,381
Cash flow from/(used in) financing activities			
Net money market paper issued/(repaid)	21,379	(14,737)	(26,206)
Net movements in treasury shares and own equity derivative activity	(4,999)	(6,810)	(5,605)
Capital issuance	2	2	6
Capital repayment by par value reduction			(2,509)
Dividends paid	(2,806)	(2,298)	
Issuance of long-term debt, including financial liabilities designated at fair value	51,211	23,644	17,132
Repayment of long-term debt, including financial liabilities designated at fair value	(24,717)	(13,615)	(14,911)
Increase in minority interests[1]	102	755	0
Dividend payments to/purchase from minority interests	(332)	(278)	(377)
Net cash flow from/(used in) financing activities	39,840	(13,337)	(32,470)
Effects of exchange rate differences	(1,052)	(524)	(462)
Net increase/(decrease) in cash equivalents	9,420	(8,988)	(33,915)
Cash and cash equivalents, beginning of the year	73,356	82,344	116,259
Cash and cash equivalents, end of the year	82,776	73,356	82,344
Cash and cash equivalents comprise:			
Cash and balances with central banks	6,036	3,584	4,271
Money market paper[2]	45,409	40,599	46,183
Due from banks maturing in less than three months	31,331	29,173	31,890
Total	82,776	73,356	82,344
Significant noncash investing and financing activities			
Hyposwiss, Zurich, deconsolidation			
Financial investments			53
Property and equipment			18
Debt issued			63
Hirslanden Holding AG, Zurich, deconsolidation			
Financial investments			3
Property and equipment			718
Goodwill and other intangible assets			15
Consolidation of special-purpose entities			
Debt issued			2,322
Provision for reinstatement costs			
Property and equipment		137	
Motor-Columbus, Baden, from valuation at equity to full consolidation			
Financial investments	644		
Investments in associates	261		
Property and equipment	2,083		
Goodwill and other intangible assets	1,194		
Debt issued	727		
Minority interests	1,742		
Investment funds transferred to other liabilities according to IAS 32			
Minority interests	336		

[1] *Includes issuance of trust preferred securities of CHF 372 million for the year ended December 31, 2003.*
[2] *Money market paper is included in the balance sheet under trading portfolio assets and financial investments. CHF 13,247 million, CHF 6,430 million, and CHF 10,475 million more were pledged at December 31, 2004, December 31, 2003, and December 31, 2002, respectively.*

Cash paid for interest during 2004 was CHF 18,614 million.

APPENDIX C

EXAMPLE BANK FINANCIAL INSTRUMENTS DISCLOSURES

UBS Group Financial Statements
December 31, 2004

Notes to the financial statements

Note 10. Securities borrowing, securities lending, repurchase and reverse repurchase agreements

The Group enters into collateralized reverse repurchase and repurchase agreements and securities borrowing and securities lending transactions that may result in credit exposure in the event that the counterparty to the transaction is unable to fulfill its contractual obligations. The Group controls credit risk associated with these activities by monitoring counterparty credit exposure and collateral values on a daily basis and requiring additional collateral to be deposited with or returned to the Group when deemed necessary.

Balance sheet assets

CHF million	Cash collateral on securities borrowed 12/31/04	Reverse repurchase agreements 12/31/04	Cash collateral on securities borrowed 12/31/03	Reverse repurchase agreements 12/31/03
By counterparty:				
Banks	167,567	243,890	172,783	237,148
Customers	52,675	113,274	41,149	83,351
Total	220,242	357,164	213,932	320,499

Balance sheet liabilities

CHF million	Cash collateral on securities lent 12/31/04	Repurchase agreements 12/31/04	Cash collateral on securities lent 12/31/03	Repurchase agreements 12/31/03
By counterparty:				
Banks	40,580	252,151	39,587	263,905
Customers	20,965	170,436	13,691	151,958
Total	61,545	422,587	53,278	415,863

Under reverse repurchase and securities borrowing arrangements, the Group obtains securities on terms that permit it to repledge or resell the securities to others. Amounts on such terms as at December 31, 2004, and December 31, 2003, were are follows:

CHF million	12/31/04	12/31/03
Securities received under reverse repurchase and/or securities borrowing arrangements which can be repledged or resold	949,570	827,602
Thereof repledged/transferred to others in connection with financing activities or to satisfy commitments under short sale transactions	639,865	593,049

Note 11. Trading portfolio

The Group trades in debt instruments (including money market paper and tradeable loans), equity instruments, precious metals, commodities and derivatives to meet the financial needs of its customers and to generate revenue. Note 23 provides a description of the various classes of derivatives together with the related notional amounts, while Note 10 provides further details about cash collateral on securities borrowed and lent and repurchase and reverse repurchase agreements.

CHF million	12/31/04	12/31/03
Trading portfolio assets		
Money market paper	44,842	40,003
Thereof pledged as collateral with central banks	4,706	6,208
Thereof pledged as collateral and can be repledged or resold by counterparty	12,580	--

	12/31/03	12/31/02
Debt instruments		
Swiss government and government agencies	776	1,011
US Treasury and government agencies	92,330	92,250
Other government agencies	79,340	69,755
Corporate listed	140,500	152,413
Other unlisted	35,646	8,457
Total	348,592	323,886
Thereof pledged as collateral	147,525	130,093
Thereof can be repledged or resold by counterparty	120,317	104,402
Equity instruments		
Listed	90,594	64,116
Unlisted	18,119	10,507
Total	108,713	74,623
Thereof pledged as collateral	27,140	16,426
Thereof can be repledged or resold by counterparty	26,218	16,357
Traded loans	16,077	12,650
Precious metals, commodities[1]	11,150	10,610
Total trading portfolio assets	529,374	461,772
Trading portfolio liabilities		
Debt instruments		
Swiss government and government agencies	511	586
US Treasury and government agencies	54,848	52,377
Other government agencies	49,512	38,369
Corporate listed	27,413	13,537
Other unlisted	2,600	10,851
Total	134,884	115,720
Equity instruments	36,149	28,237
Total trading portfolio liabilities	171,033	143,957

[1] *Commodities basically consist of energy*

Note 12. Financial investments (available for sale)

CHF million	12/31/04	12/31/03
Money market paper	567	596
Other debt instruments		
Listed	261	189
Unlisted	21	72
Total	282	261
Equity investments		
Listed	504	387
Unlisted	687	630
Total	1,191	1,017
Private equity investments	3,009	3,265
Total financial investments	5,049	5,139
Thereof eligible for discount at central banks	86	196

The following tables show the unrealized gains and losses not recognized in the income statement for the years ended 2004 and 2003.

CHF million	Fair value	*Unrealized gains/losses not recognized in the income statement*				
		Gross gains	Gross losses	Net, before tax	Tax effect	Net, after tax
December 31, 2004						
Money market paper	567	0	0	0	0	0
Debt securities issued by the Swiss national government and agencies	10	1	0	1	0	1
Debt securities issued by Swiss local governments	20	1	0	1	0	1
Debt securities issued by US Treasury and agencies	0	0	0	0	0	0
Debt securities issued by foreign governments and official institutions	40	0	0	0	0	0
Corporate debt securities	140	7	(4)	3	0	3
Mortgage-backed securities	72	0	0	0	0	0
Other debt securities	0	0	0	0	0	0
Equity securities	1,191	455	(5)	450	(83)	367
Private equity investments	3,009	979	(44)	935	(89)	846
Total	5,049	1,443	(53)	1,390	(172)	1,218

CHF million	Fair value	*Unrealized gains/losses not recognized in the income statement*				
		Gross gains	Gross losses	Net, before tax	Tax effect	Net, after tax
December 31, 2003							0
Money market paper	596	0	0	0	0	2
Debt securities issued by the Swiss national government and agencies	14	2	0	2	0	0
Debt securities issued by Swiss local governments	25	0	0	0	0	0
Debt securities issued by US Treasury and agencies	0	0	0	0	0	0
Debt securities issued by foreign governments and official institutions	54	0	0	0	0	0
Corporate debt securities	156	3	(8)	(5)	(1)	(6)
Mortgage-backed securities	0	0	0	0	0	0
Other debt securities	12	0	0	0	0	0
Equity securities	1,017	296	(7)	289	(58)	231
Private equity investments	3,265	781	(216)	565	0	565
Total	5,139	1,082	(231)	851	(59)	792

The unrealized losses not recognized in the income statement are considered to be temporary on the basis that the investments are intended to be held for a period of time sufficient to recover their cost, and UBS believes that the evidence indicating that the cost of the investments should be recoverable within a reasonable period of time outweighs the evidence to the contrary. This includes the nature of the investments, valuations and research undertaken by UBS, the current outlook for each investment, offers under negotiation at favorable prices, and the duration of the unrealized losses.

The following table shows the duration of unrealized losses not recognized in the income statement for the year ended 2004:

	Fair Value			Unrealized Losses		
CHF million	*Investments with unrealized loss less than 12 months*	*Investments with unrealized loss more than 12 months*	*Total*	*Investments with unrealized loss less than 12 months*	*Investments with unrealized loss more than 12 months*	*Total*
December 31, 2004						
Money market paper	0	0	0	0	0	0
Debt securities issued by the Swiss national government and agencies	0	0	0	0	0	0
Debt securities issued by Swiss local governments	0	0	0	0	0	0
Debt securities issued by US Treasury and agencies	0	0	0	0	0	0
Debt securities issued by foreign governments and official institutions	0	0	0	0	0	0
Corporate debt securities	0	0	0	0	(4)	(4)
Mortgage-backed securities	0	0	0	0	0	0
Other debt securities	0	0	0	0	0	0
Equity securities	1	24	25	(1)	(4)	(5)
Private equity investments	424	82	506	(5)	(39)	(44)
Total	425	106	531	(6)	(47)	(53)

Contractual maturities of the investments in debt instruments[1]

	Within 1 year		1-5 years		5-10 years		Over 10 years	
CHF million, except percentages	*Amount*	*yield (%)*	*Amount*	*yield (%)*	*Amount*	*yield (%)*	*Amount*	*yield (%)*
December 31, 2004								
Swiss national government and agencies	1	5.50	2	4.29	6	3.80	1	4.00
Swiss local governments	10	3.97	10	4.14	0	0.00	0	0.00
Foreign governments and official institutions	36	2.13	4	1.25	0	0.00	0	0.00
Corporate debt securities	57	2.74	50	2.92	0	0.00	33	0.00
Mortgage-backed securities	3	2.50	0	0.00	5	3.21	64	4.36
Other debt securities	0	0.00	0	0.00	0	0.00	0	0.00
Total fair value	107		66		11		98	

[1] *Money market papers have contractual maturities of less than one year.*

Proceeds from sales and maturities of investment securities available for sale, excluding private equity, were as follows:

CHF million	*12/31/04*	*12/31/03*
Proceeds	277	1,379
Gross realized gains	49	112
Gross realized losses	(4)	(23)

Note 29. Financial instruments—Risk position

This section presents information about UBS's exposure to and its management and control of risks, in particular the primary risks associated with its use of financial instruments.

- Market risk (part a) is exposure to market variables such as interest rates, exchange rates and equity markets
- Credit risk (part b) is the risk of loss resulting from client or counterparty default and arises on credit exposure in all forms, including settlement risk
- Liquidity and funding risk (part c) is the risk that UBS is unable to meet its payment obligations when due, or that it is unable, on an ongoing basis, to borrow funds in the market on an unsecured, or even secured basis at an acceptable price to fund actual or proposed commitments.
- Part (d) presents and explains the Group's regulatory capital position

Sections (a) to (d) generally refer only to UBS's financial businesses, while section (e) covers the financial instruments risk positions of the industrial holding Motor-Columbus through its operating subsidiary Atel. The tables in this note which are based on risk information include only the financial businesses of the Group. Those which present an analysis of the whole balance sheet include the positions of Motor-Columbus.

It should be noted that, in management's view, any representation of risk at a specific date offers only a snapshot of the risks taken, since both trading and nontrading positions can vary significantly on a daily basis, because they are actively managed. As such, it may not be representative of the level of risk at other times.

(a) Market risk
(i) Overview

Market risk is the risk of loss arising from movements in market variables including observable variables such as interest rates, exchange rates, and equity markets, and others which may be only indirectly observable such as volatilities and correlations. The risk of price movements on securities and other obligations in tradable form resulting from general credit and country risk factors and events specific to individual issuers is also considered market risk.

Market risk is incurred in UBS primarily through trading activities which are centered in the Investment Bank but also arise, to a much lesser extent, in the wealth management businesses. It arises from market making, client facilitation and proprietary positions in equities, fixed income and interest rate products, foreign exchange and, to a lesser extent, precious metals and energy.

Additionally, Group Treasury assumes material nontrading market risk positions that arise from its balance sheet and capital management activities. There are also smaller nontrading market risk positions, predominantly interest rate risks, in the other Business Groups.

Each Business Group has a Chief Risk Officer (CRO), reporting functionally to the Group CRO, responsible for independent risk control of market risk.

Market risk authority, including both approval of market risk limits and approval of market risks in large or complex transactions and securities underwritings, is exercised by the chairman's office and the GEB and is further delegated on an ad personam basis to the Group CRO and market risk officers within the Business Groups.

Market risk measures and controls are applied to all trading activities, to foreign exchange, precious metal and energy exposures wherever they arise, and to interest rate risk in the banking books of all Business Groups including Group Treasury and the independent private banks.

The principal portfolio risk measures and limits on market risk are Value at Risk (VaR) and stress loss. VaR is an estimate of the potential loss on the current portfolio from adverse market movements, based on historical market movements, assuming a specified time horizon before positions can be adjusted (holding period), and expressed as the maximum potential loss that, with a specified level of confidence (probability), will not be exceeded. Stress loss is assessed against a set of forward-looking scenarios, using stress moves in market variables, which are regularly reviewed. Complementary controls are also applied where appropriate, to prevent undue concentrations, taking into account variations in price volatility and market depth and liquidity. They include controls on exposure to individual market risk variables, such as individual interest or exchange rates, and on positions in the securities of individual issuers (issuer risk).

(ii) Interest rate risk

Interest rate risk is the risk of loss resulting from changes in interest rates. It is controlled primarily through the limit structure described in (a)(i) above. Exposure to interest rate movements can be expressed for all interest rate sensitive positions, whether marked to market or subject to amortized cost accounting, as the impact on their fair values of a one-basis-point (0.01%) change in interest rates. This sensitivity, analyzed by time band, is set out below. Interest rate sensitivity is one of the inputs to the VaR model.

The table sets out the extent to which UBS was exposed to interest rate risk at December 31, 2004 and 2003. It shows the net impact of a one-basis-point (0.01%) increase in market interest rates across all time bands on the fair values of interest rate sensitive positions, both on- and off-balance-sheet. The impact of such an increase in interest rates depends on UBS's net asset or net liability position in each category, currency and time band in the table. A negative amount in the table reflects a potential reduction in fair value, while a positive amount reflects a potential increase in fair value.

Interest rate sensitivity position[1]

CHF thousand gain/(loss) per basis point increase		Interest rate sensitivity by time bands at 12/31/04					
		Within 1 month	*1 to 3 months*	*3 to 12 months*	*1 to 5 years*	*Over 5 years*	*Total*
CHF	Trading	65	69	(83)	24	120	195
	Nontrading	(203)	(13)	(313)	(3,575)	(2,641)	(6,745)
USD	Trading	49	(236)	(1,184)	836	127	(358)
	Nontrading	30	(158)	(121)	(2,010)	(2,472)	(4,731)
EUR	Trading	192	(276)	342	(356)	(814)	(922)
	Nontrading	(8)	1	(22)	(180)	(200)	(409)
GBP	Trading	(19)	52	60	(380)	(32)	(319)
	Nontrading	(1)	(7)	(34)	(290)	270	(62)
JPY	Trading	(17)	630	(562)	(1,804)	781	(972)
	Nontrading	(1)	1	(1)	(4)	(1)	(6)
Other	Trading	75	(121)	(8)	5	145	96
	Nontrading	(1)	1	1	(1)	(2)	(2)

CHF thousand gain/(loss) per basis point increase		Interest rate sensitivity by time bands at 12/31/03					
		Within 1 month	*1 to 3 months*	*3 to 12 months*	*1 to 5 years*	*Over 5 years*	*Total*
CHF	Trading	19	(185)	(6)	311	(91)	48
	Nontrading	(38)	(99)	(359)	(4,288)	(3,587)	(8,371)
USD	Trading	(17)	(690)	(638)	(941)	1,190	(1,096)
	Nontrading	50	(55)	(92)	(2,213)	(1,702)	(4,012)
EUR	Trading	(84)	(206)	393	(1,018)	649	(261)
	Nontrading	4	6	(21)	(131)	(196)	(338)
GBP	Trading	24	31	131	(736)	536	(14)
	Nontrading	0	(10)	(55)	(40)	481	376
JPY	Trading	59	(326)	(34)	410	(273)	(164)
	Nontrading	(4)	3	(1)	(5)	(2)	(9)
Others	Trading	(43)	22	80	(454)	335	(70)
	Nontrading	(1)	0	(6)	(1)	(3)	(11)

Positions shown as "trading" are those which contribute to market risk regulatory capital (i.e., those considered "trading book") for regulatory capital purposes (see section d.). "Nontrading" includes all other interest rate sensitive assets and liabilities including derivatives designated as hedges for accounting purposes (as explained in Note 23) and off-balance-sheet commitments on which an interest rate has been fixed. This distinction differs somewhat from the accounting classification of trading and nontrading assets and liabilities.

Details of money market paper and debt instruments defined as trading portfolio for accounting purposes are included in Note 11 and of debt instruments defined as financial investments for accounting purposes in Note 12. Details of derivatives are shown in Note 23, but it should be noted that interest rate risk arises not only on interest rate contracts but also on other forwards, swaps and options, in particular, on forward foreign exchange contracts. Off-balance-sheet commitments on which an interest rate has been fixed are primarily forward starting fixed-term loans.

Trading

The major part of this risk arises in the Investment Bank's Fixed Income Rates and Currencies business.

Nontrading

Interest rate risk is inherent in many of UBS's businesses and arises from factors such as differences in timing between contractual maturity or repricing of assets, liabilities and derivative instruments.

Most nontrading interest rate risk is captured at the point of business origination and transferred to a risk management unit—primarily the Cash and Collateral Trading unit of the Investment Bank or Group Treasury—where it is managed within the market risk limits described in (a)(i). The margin risks embedded in retail products remain with, and are subject to additional analysis and control by, the originating business units.

Many client products have no contractual maturity date or directly market-linked rate. Their interest rate risk is transferred on a pooled basis through "replication" portfolios—portfolios of revolving transactions between the originating business unit and Group Treasury at market rates designed to approximate their average cash flows and repricing behavior. The structure and parameters of the replication portfolios are set in accordance with long-term observations of market and client behavior, and are reviewed periodically.

Interest rate risk also arises from balance sheet items such as the financing of bank property and investments in equity of associated companies, and from the investment of the Group's equity. The risk on these items is also transferred to Group Treasury, through replicating portfolios designed to approximate the desired funding or investment profile.

The Group's equity is invested at longer-term fixed interest rates in CHF, USD, EUR, and GBP with an average duration of between three and four years, in line with strategic investment targets set by the Group Executive Board (GEB). These investments account for CHF 12.6 million of the nontrading interest rate sensitivity, with CHF 6.6 million arising in CHF, CHF 5.0 million in USD and the remainder in EUR and GBP. The interest rate sensitivity of these investments is directly related to the chosen investment duration and it should be recognized that, although investing in significantly shorter maturities would lead to a reduction in apparent interest rate sensitivity, it would lead to higher volatility in interest earnings.

(iii) Currency risk

Currency risk is the risk of loss resulting from changes in exchange rates.

Trading

UBS is an active participant in currency markets and carries currency risk from these trading activities, conducted primarily in the Investment Bank. These trading exposures are subject to VaR, stress and concentration limits as described in (a)(i). Details of foreign exchange contracts, most of which arise from trading activities and contribute to currency risk, are shown in Note 23.

Nontrading

UBS's reporting currency is the Swiss franc but its assets, liabilities, income and expense are denominated in many currencies, with significant amounts in USD, EUR, and GBP, as well as CHF.

Reported profits or losses are exchanged monthly into CHF, reducing volatility in the Group's earnings from subsequent changes in exchange rates. Group Treasury also, from time to time, proactively hedges significant expected foreign currency earnings/costs (mainly USD, EUR, and GBP) within a time horizon of one year, in accordance with the instructions of the GEB and subject to its VaR limit. Economic hedging strategies employed include a cost-efficient option strategy, providing a safety net against unfavorable currency fluctuations while preserving upside potential.

The Group's equity is invested in a diversified portfolio broadly reflecting the currency distribution of its risk-weighted assets in CHF, USD, EUR and GBP. This creates structural foreign currency exposures, the gains or losses on which are recorded through equity, leading to fluctuations in UBS's capital base in line with the fluctuations in risk-weighted assets, thereby protecting the BIS Tier 1 capital ratio.

At December 31, 2004, the largest combined trading and nontrading currency exposures against the Swiss franc were in USD (short USD 224 million), EUR (short EUR 664 million) and

GBP (long GBP 221 million). At December 31, 2003 the largest exposures were in USD (short USD 723 million), EUR (long EUR 71 million and GBP (short GBP 40 million).

(iv) Equity risk

Equity risk is the risk of loss resulting from changes in the levels of equity indices and values of individual stocks.

The Investment Bank is a significant player in major equity markets and carries equity risk from these activities. These exposures are subject to VaR, stress and concentration limits as described on (a)(i), and, in the case of individual stocks, to issuer risk controls as described in (a)(v).

Details of equities defined as trading portfolio for accounting purposes are given in Note 11. Details of equity derivatives contracts (on indices and individual equities), which arise primarily from the Investment Bank's trading activities, are shown in Note 23.

(v) Issuer risk

The values of tradable assets—equities, bonds, and other debt instruments (including money market paper and tradable loans) held for trading—are affected by factors specific to individual issuers as well as general market moves. This can include short-term factors influencing price but also more fundamental causes including severe financial deterioration.

As an active trader and market maker in equities, bonds, and other securities, the Investment Bank holds positions in tradable assets, which are not only included in VaR, but are also subject to concentration limits on exposure to individual issuers. This includes both exposures arising from physical holdings, and exposures from derivatives based on such assets.

(b) Credit risk

Credit risk represents the loss which UBS would suffer if a client or counterparty failed to meet its contractual obligations. It is inherent in traditional banking products—loans, commitments to lend and other contingent liabilities, such as letters of credit—and in traded products—derivative contracts, such as forwards, swaps and options, and repo and securities borrowing and lending transactions. Some of these products are accounted for on an amortized cost basis while others are recorded in the financial statements at fair value. Banking products are generally carried at amortized cost, but loans which have been originated by the Group for subsequent syndication or distribution through the cash markets, are carried at fair value. Within traded products, OTC derivatives are carried at fair value, while repos and securities borrowing and ending transactions are accounted for on an amortized cost basis. Regardless of the accounting treatment, all banking and traded products are controlled under the same credit risk framework.

All Business Groups taking material credit risk have independent credit risk control functions headed by Chief Credit Officers (CCOs) reporting functionally to the Group CCO. They are responsible for the independent control of credit risk including counterparty ratings and credit risk assessment. Credit risk authority, including authority to establish allowances and provisions and credit valuation adjustments for impaired claims, is exercised by the Chairman's Office and the GEB and is further delegated on an *ad personam* basis to the Group CCO and to credit officers within the Business Groups.

For credit control purposes, credit exposure is measured for banking products as the face value amount. For traded products, credit exposure is measured as the current replacement value of contracts plus potential future changes in replacement value, taking account of master netting agreements with individual counterparties where they are considered enforceable in insolvency. UBS is an active user of credit derivatives to hedge credit risk on individual names and on a portfolio basis in banking and traded products. In line with general market trends, UBS has also entered into bilateral collateral agreements with market participants to mitigate credit risk on OTC derivatives. Individual hedges and collateral arrangements are reflected in our internal credit exposure measurement, and credit limits are applied on this basis.

In the table, the amounts shown as credit exposure differ somewhat from the internal credit view. For banking products, they are based on the accounting view, which, for example, does not reflect risk reduction resulting from credit hedges and collateral received, but does include cash collateral posted by UBS against negative replacement values on derivatives. For traded products, positive and negative replacement values are shown net only where permitted for regulatory capital purposes (consistent with the table in part d Capital Adequacy), and potential future exposure is not included. This in turn differs from the accounting treatment of traded products in several respects. OTC derivatives are represented on the balance sheet by positive and negative replacement values, which are netted only if the cash flows will actually be settled net, which is not generally the case—for details see Note 23. Securities borrowing and lending transactions are represented on the balance sheet by the gross values of cash collateral placed with or received from counterparties while repos/reverse repos are represented by the gross amounts of the forward commitments—for details see Note 10—the credit exposure generally being only a small percentage of these balance sheet amounts.

Breakdown of credit exposure

Amounts for each product type are shown gross before allowances and provisions.

CHF million	12/31/04	12/31/03
Banking products		
Loans to customers and due from banks[1]	269,518	247,995
Contingent liabilities (gross—before participations)[2]	14,894	15,563
Undrawn irrevocable commitments (gross—before participations)[2]	53,168	45,623
Traded products[3]		
Derivatives positive replacement values (before collateral but after netting)[4]	78,317	84,334
Securities borrowing and lending, repos and reverse repos[5, 6]	24,768	30,833
Allowances and provisions[7]	(2,883)	(3,954)
Total credit exposure net of allowances and provisions[8]	437,782	421,394

[1] *Positions in Industrial Holdings are excluded.*
[2] *See Note 9a—Due from Banks and Loans for further information.*
[3] *See Note 25—Commitments and Contingent Liabilities for further information.*
[4] *Does not include potential future credit exposure arising from changes in value of products with variable value. Potential future credit exposure is however included in internal measures of credit exposure for risk management and control purposes.*
[5] *Replacement values are shown net where netting is permitted for regulatory capital purposes. See also Note 23—Derivative Instruments for further information.*
[6] *This figure represents the difference in value between the cash or securities lent or given as collateral to counterparties, and the value of cash or securities borrowed or taken as collateral from the same counterparties under stock borrow/lend and repo/reverse repo transactions.*
[7] *See note 10—Securities Borrowing, Securities Lending, Repurchase and Reverse Repurchase Agreements for further information about these types of transactions.*
[8] *See Note 9b—Allowances and Provisions for Credit Losses for further information.*

UBS manages and controls concentrations of credit risk wherever they are identified, in particular to individual counterparties and groups, and to industries and countries. UBS sets limit on its credit exposure to both individual counterparties and counterparty groups. Concentrations of credit risk exist if clients are engaged in similar activities, or are located in the same geographic region or have comparable economic characteristics such that their ability to meet contractual obligations would be similarly affected by changes in economic, political, or other conditions. Stress measures are applied to assess the impact of variations in default rates and asset values, taking into account risk concentrations in each portfolio. Stress loss limits are applied where considered necessary, including limits on credit exposure to all but the best-rated countries. With the exceptions of private households (CHF 135,397 million), banks and financial institutions (CHF 75,311 million), and real estate and rentals in Switzerland (CHF 11,466 million), there are no material concentrations of loans at December 31, 2004, and the vast majority of those to private households and to real estate and rentals are secured. Derivatives exposure is predominantly to investment grade banks and financial institutions.

Impaired claims

UBS classifies a claim as impaired if it considers that it will suffer a loss on that claim as a result of the obligor's inability to meet its commitments (including interest payments, principal repayments or other payments due, for example on a derivative product or under a guarantee) according to the contractual terms, and after realization of any available collateral. Loans are further classified as nonperforming where payment of interest, principal, or fees is overdue by more than 90 days and there is no firm evidence that they will be made good by later payments or when insolvency proceedings have commenced or obligations have been restructured on concessionary terms.

The recognition of impairment in the financial statements depends on the accounting treatment of the claim. For products accounted for on an amortized cost basis, impairment is recognized through the creation of a provision or allowance, which is charged to the income statement as credit loss expense. Allowances or provisions are determined such that the carrying values of impaired claims are consistent with the principles of IAS 39. For products recorded at fair value, impairment is recognized through a credit valuation adjustment, which is charged to the income statement through the net trading income line.

UBS also assesses portfolios of claims with similar credit risk characteristics for collective impairment in accordance with IAS 39 (amortized cost products only). A portfolio is considered impaired on a collective basis if there is objective evidence to suggest that it contains impaired obligations but the individual impaired items cannot yet be identified.

For further information about accounting policy for allowances and provisions for credit losses see Note 1q. For the amounts of allowance and provision for credit losses and amounts of impaired and nonperforming loans, see Note 9 b, c, and d. It should be noted that allowance and provisions for collective impairment are included in the total of allowances and provisions in the table on the previous page, and in Notes 9a and 9b, but that portfolios against which collective loan loss provisions have been established are not included in the totals of impaired loans in Note 9c.

The occurrence of credit losses is erratic in both timing and amount and those that arise usually relate to transactions entered into in previous accounting periods. In order to reflect the fact that future credit losses are implicit in the current portfolio, and to encourage risk-adjusted pricing for products carried at amortized cost, UBS uses the concept of "expected loss" for management purposes. Expected loss is a forward looking, statistically based concept which is used to estimate the annual costs that will arise, on average over time, from positions in the current portfolio that become impaired. It is derived from the probability of default (given by the counterparty rating), current and likely future exposure to the counterparty and the likely severity of the loss should default occur. Note 2a includes two tables: the first shows credit loss expense, as recorded in the financial statements, for each Business Group; the second reflects an "adjusted expected credit loss" for each Business Group, which is the expected credit loss on its portfolio, plus the difference between Credit loss expense and expected credit loss, amortized over a three-year period. The difference between the total of these adjusted expected credit loss figures and the credit loss expense recorded at Group level for financial reporting is reported in Corporate Functions.

(c) Liquidity risk

UBS's approach to liquidity management is to ensure, as far as possible, that it will always have sufficient liquidity to meet its liabilities when due, without compromising its ability to respond quickly to strategic market opportunities. A centralized approach is adopted, based on an integrated framework incorporating the assessment of expected cash flows and the availability of high-grade collateral that could be used to secure additional funding if required. The liquidity position is assessed and managed under a variety of scenarios, giving due consideration to stress factors. Scenarios encompass not only normal market conditions but also stressed conditions, including both UBS-specific and general market crises. The impact on both trading and client businesses is considered, taking account of potential collateral with which funds might be raised, and the possibility that customers might seek to withdraw funds or draw down unutilized committed credit lines.

The breakdown by contractual maturity of assets and liabilities, which is the basis of the "normal market conditions" scenario, at December 31, 2004, is shown in the table below.

Maturity analysis of assets and liabilities

CHF billion	On demand	Subject to notice[1]	Due within 3 mths	Due between 3 and 12 mths	Due between 1 and 5 years	Due after 5 years	Total
Assets							
Cash and balances with central banks	6.0						6.0
Due from banks	20.0	0.4	10.5	1.1	2.1	1.2	35.3
Cash collateral on securities borrowed	0.0	186.0	32.0	2.1	0.1	0.0	220.2
Reverse repurchase agreements	0.0	49.6	255.0	46.0	5.5	1.1	357.2
Trading portfolio assets[2]	370.3	0.0	0.0	0.0	0.0	0.0	370.3
Trading portfolio assets pledged as collateral	159.1	0.0	0.0	0.0	0.0	0.0	159.1
Positive replacement values[2]	284.6	0.0	0.0	0.0	0.0	0.0	284.6
Financial assets designated at fair value	0.7	0.0	0.0	0.0	0.0	0.0	0.7
Loans	23.1	35.8	47.3	30.2	79.6	16.4	232.4
Financial investments	4.1	0.0	0.6	0.1	0.2	0.1	5.1
Accrued income and prepaid expenses	5.9	0.0	0.0	0.0	0.0	0.0	5.9
Investments in associates	0.0	0.0	0.0	0.0	0.0	2.4	2.4
Property and equipment	0.0	0.0	0.0	0.0	0.0	8.7	8.7
Goodwill and other intangible assets	0.0	0.0	0.0	0.0	0.0	12.1	12.1
Other assets	15.6	19.2	0.0	0.0	0.0	0.0	34.8
Total 12/31/04	889.4	291.0	345.4	79.5	87.5	42.0	1,734.8
Total 12/31/03	832.4	260.6	271.2	82.6	72.2	31.1	1,550.1
Liabilities							
Due to banks	30.8	6.5	77.8	1.5	1.9	0.4	118.9
Cash collateral on securities lent	0.0	51.7	9.8	0.0	0.0	0.0	61.5
Repurchase agreements	0.0	20.2	363.2	37.8	1.2	0.2	422.6
Trading portfolio liabilities[2]	171.0	0.0	0.0	0.0	0.0	0.0	171.0
Negative replacement values[2]	303.7	0.0	0.0	0.0	0.0	0.0	303.7
Financial liabilities designated at fair value	0.0	0.0	2.3	9.0	45.4	8.1	65.8
Due to customers	119.1	112.0	135.4	5.2	1.5	2.9	376.1
Accrued expenses and deferred income	14.7	0.0	0.0	0.0	0.0	0.0	14.7
Debt issued	0.0	0.0	74.9	12.1	5.0	25.8	117.8
Other liabilities	20.3	22.1	0.0	0.0	0.0	0.0	42.4
Total 12/31/04	659.6	212.5	663.4	65.6	56.0	37.4	1,694.5
Total 12/31/03	795.0	138.0	338.5	130.4	36.5	22.3	1,510.7

[1] *Deposits without a fixed term, on which notice of withdrawal or termination has not been given (such funds may be withdrawn by the depositor or repaid by the borrower subject to an agreed period of notice which can be from 7 days to 6 months).*

[2] *Trading and derivative positions are shown within "on demand" which management believes most accurately reflects the short-term nature of trading activities. The contractual maturity of the instruments may however extend over significantly longer periods.*

(d) Capital adequacy

The adequacy of UBS's capital is monitored using, among other measures, the rules and ratios established by the Basel Committee on Banking Supervision ("BIS rules/ratios"). The BIS ratios compare the amount of the Group's eligible capital (in total and Tier 1) with the total of risk-weighted assets (RWA).

While UBS monitors and reports its capital ratios under BIS rules, it is the rules established by the Swiss regulator, the EBK, which ultimately determine the regulatory capital required to underpin its business, and these rules, on balance, result in higher RWA than the BIS rules. As a result, UBS's ratios are lower when calculated under the EBK regulations than under the BIS rules.

BIS eligible capital

BIS eligible capital consists of two parts: Tier 1 capital comprises share capital, share premium, retained earnings including current year profit, foreign currency translation and minority interests less accrued dividends, net long positions in own shares and goodwill. Certain adjustments are made to IFRS-based profit and reserves, in line with BIS recommendations, as prescribed by the EBK. Tier 2 capital includes subordinated long-term debt. Tier 1 capital is required to be at least 4% and total eligible capital at least 8% of RWA.

BIS risk-weighted assets (RWA)

Total RWAs are made up of three elements—credit risk, other assets, and market risk, each of which is described below.

The credit risk component consists of on- and off-balance-sheet claims, measured according to regulatory formulae outlined below, weighted according to type of counterparty and collateral at 0%, 20%, 50%, or 100%. The least risky claims, such as claims on OECD governments and claims collateralized by cash, are weighted at 0%, meaning that no capital support is required, while the claims deemed most risky, including unsecured claims on corporate and private customers, are weighted at 100%, meaning that 8% capital support is required.

Securities not held for trading are included as claims, based on the net long position in the securities of each issuer, including both physical holdings and positions derived from other transactions such as options. UBS's investment in Motor-Columbus is treated for regulatory capital purposes as a position in a security not held for trading.

Claims arising from derivatives transactions include two components: the current positive replacement value and "add-ons" to reflect their potential future exposure. Where UBS has entered into a master netting agreement which is accepted by the EBK as being legally enforceable in insolvency, positive and negative replacement values with individual counterparties can be netted and therefore the on-balance-sheet component of RWAs for derivatives transactions shown in the table on the next page (positive replacement values) is less than the balance sheet value of positive replacement values. The add-ons component of the RWAs is shown in the table on the next page under off-balance-sheet exposures and other positions—forward and swap contracts, and purchased options.

Claims arising from contingent commitments and irrevocable facilities granted are converted to credit equivalent amounts based on specified percentages of nominal value.

There are other types of assets, most notably property and equipment and intangibles, which, while not subject to credit risk, represent a risk to the bank in respect of their potential for write-down and impairment and which therefore require capital underpinning.

Capital is required to support market risk arising in all foreign exchange, precious metals and commodity (including energy) positions, and all positions held for trading in interest rate instruments and equities, including risks on individual equities, and traded debt obligations such as bonds. UBS computes this risk using a Value at Risk (VaR) model approved by the EBK, from which the market risk capital requirement is derived. Unlike the calculations for credit risk and other assets, this produces the capital requirement itself rather than the RWA amount. In order to compute a total capital ratio, the market risk capital requirement is therefore converted to a "RWA equivalent" (shown in the table below as market risk positions) such that the capital requirement is 8% of this RWA equivalent, (i.e., the market risk capital requirement is multiplied by 12.5).

Risk-weighted assets (BIS)

CHF million	Exposure 12/31/04	Risk-weighted amount 12/31/04	Exposure[1] 12/31/03	Risk-weighted amount 12/31/03
Balance sheet assets				
Due from banks and other collateralized lendings[2]	556,947	7,820	531,093	8,565
Net positions in securities[3, 4]	8,227	6,914	7,277	6,182
Positive replacement values[5]	78,317	17,121	84,334	22,324
Loans, net of allowances for credit losses and other collateralized lendings[2]	429,186	164,620	359,154	153,537
Accrued income and prepaid expenses	5,790	3,573	6,218	4,284
Property and equipment	8,772	8,772	9,611	9,611
Other assets	32,725	8,949	24,918	7,673
Off-balance-sheet exposures				
Contingent liabilities	14,894	7,569	15,563	8,167
Irrevocable commitments	53,187	11,764	46,960	6,863
Forward and swap contracts[6]	14,419,106	8,486	11,746,880	4,710
Purchased options[6]	2,306,605	386	1,183,708	1,716
Market risk positions[7]		18,151		18,269
Total risk-weighted assets		264,125		251,901

[1] Prior year numbers have been adjusted to conform with current year's presentation.
[2] Includes gross securities borrowing and reverse repo exposure, as well as traded loans which are included in trading assets. These positions have not been included in the market risk position.
[3] Includes security positions which are not included in the market risk position, including Motor-Columbus, which is not consolidated for capital adequacy purposes.
[4] Excluding positions in the trading book, which are included in market risk positions.
[5] Represents the mark to market vlues of forward and swap contracts and purchased options, where positive but after netting where applicable.
[6] Represents the "add-ons" for these contracts.
[7] Regulatory capital adequacy requirements for market risk, calculated using the approved value at risk model multiplied by 17.5 to give the "risk-weighted asset equivalent".

BIS capital ratios

	Capital CHF million 12/31/04	Ratio % 12/31/04	Capital CHF million 12/31/03	Ratio % 12/31/03
Tier 1	31,051	11.8	29,765	11.8
Of which hybrid Tier 1	2,963	1.1	3,224	1.3
Tier 2	4,815	1.8	3,816	1.5
Total BIS	35,866	13.6	33,581	13.3

The Tier 1 capital includes CHF 2,963 million (USD 2,600 million) in trust preferred securities at December 31, 2004, and CHF 3,224 million (USD 2,600 million) at December 31, 2003.

(e) Financial instruments risk position in Motor-Columbus

The Atel Group, the operating arm of Motor-Columbus, is exposed to electricity price risk, interest rate risk, currency risk, credit risk, and other business risks.

Risk limits are allocated to individual risk categories and compliance with these limits is continuously monitored, the limits being periodically adjusted in the broad context of the company's overall risk capacity.

A risk policy has been established and is monitored by a risk committee composed of executive management. It was approved by the Board of Directors of Atel and is reviewed and ratified by them annually. The policy sets out the principles for Atel's business. It specifies requirements for entering into, measuring, managing and limiting risk in its business and the organization and responsibilities of risk management. The objective of the policy is to provide a reasonable balance between the business risks entered into and Atel's earnings and risk bearing shareholders' equity.

A financial risk policy sets out the context of financial risk management in terms of content, organization and systems, with the objective of reducing financial risk, balancing the costs of hedging and the risks assumed. The responsible units manage their financial risks within the framework of this policy and limits defined for their area.

Energy price risk

Price risks in the energy business arise from, among others, price volatility, changing market prices and changing correlations between markets and products. Derivative financial instruments are used to hedge underlying physical transactions, subject to the risk policy.

Interest rate risk

Interest rate swaps are permitted to hedge capital markets interest rate exposure, with changes in fair value being reported in the income statement.

Currency risks

To minimize currency risk, Atel tries to offset operating income and expenses in foreign currencies. Any surplus is hedged through currency forwards and options within the framework of the financial risk policy.

Net investment in foreign subsidiaries is also subject to exchange rate movements, but differences in inflation rates tend to cancel out these changes over the longer tem and for this reason Atel does not hedge investment in foreign subsidiaries.

Credit risk

Credit risk management is based on assessment of the creditworthiness of new contracting parties before entering into any transaction, giving rise to credit exposure, and continuous monitoring of creditworthiness and exposures thereafter. In the energy business, Atel only enters into transactions leading to credit exposure with counterparties that fulfill the criteria laid out in the risk policy. Concentration risk is minimized by the number of customers and their geographical distribution.

Financial assets reported in the balance sheet represent the maximum loss to Atel in the event of counterparty default at the balance sheet date.

Note 30. Fair value of financial instruments

30a Fair value of financial instruments

The following table presents the fair value of financial instruments, including those not reflected in the financial statements at fair value. It is accompanied by a discussion of the methods used to determine fair value for financial instruments.

CHF billion	Carrying value 12/31/04	Fair value 12/31/04	Unrealized gain/(loss) 12/31/04	Carrying value 12/31/03	Fair value 12/31/03	Unrealized gain/(loss) 12/31/03
Assets						
Cash and balances with central banks	6.0	6.0	0.0	3.6	3.6	0.0
Due from banks	35.3	35.3	0.0	31.7	31.7	0.0
Cash collateral on securities borrowed	220.2	220.2	0.0	213.9	213.9	0.0
Reverse repurchase agreements	357.1	357.1	0.0	320.5	320.5	0.0
Trading portfolio assets	370.3	370.3	0.0	341.0	341.0	0.0
Trading portfolio assets pledged as collateral	159.1	159.1	0.0	120.8	120.8	0.0
Positive replacement values	284.6	284.6	0.0	248.2	248.2	0.0
Financial assets designated at fair value	0.7	0.7	0.0	0.0	0.0	0.0
Loans	232.4	233.8	1.4	212.7	214.0	1.3
Financial investments	5.0	5.0	0.0	5.1	5.1	0.0
Liabilities						
Due to banks	118.9	118.9	0.0	127.0	127.0	0.0
Cash collateral on securities lent	61.5	61.5	0.0	53.3	53.3	0.0
Repurchase agreements	422.6	422.6	0.0	415.9	415.9	0.0
Trading portfolio liabilities	171.0	171.0	0.0	144.0	144.0	0.0
Negative replacement values	303.7	303.7	0.0	254.8	254.8	0.0

CHF billion	Carrying value 12/31/04	Fair value 12/31/04	Unrealized gain/(loss) 12/31/04	Carrying value 12/31/03	Fair value 12/31/03	Unrealized gain/(loss) 12/31/03
Financial liabilities designated at fair value	65.8	65.8	0.0	35.3	35.3	0.0
Due to customers	376.1	376.1	0.0	346.6	346.6	0.0
Debt issued	117.8	118.9	(1.1)	88.8	90.0	(1.2)
Subtotal			0.3			0.1
Unrealized gains and losses recorded in shareholders' equity before tax on						
Financial investments			1.4			0.8
Derivative instruments designated as cash flow hedges			(0.4)			(0.2)
Net unrealized gains and losses not recognized in the income statement			1.3			0.7

Fair value is the amount for which an asset could be exchanged, or a liability settled, between knowledgeable, willing parties in an arm's-length transaction. For financial instruments carried at fair value, market prices or rates are used to determine fair value where an active market exists (such as recognized stock exchange), as it is the best evidence of the fair value of a financial instrument.

Market prices are not, however, available for a significant number of the financial assets and liabilities held and issued by UBS. Therefore, where no active market price or rate is available, fair values are estimated using present value or other valuation techniques, using inputs based on market conditions existing at balance sheet dates.

Valuation techniques are generally applied to OTC derivatives, unlisted trading portfolio assets and liabilities, and unlisted financial investments. The most frequently applied pricing models and valuation techniques include forward pricing and swap models using present value calculations, option models such as the Black-Scholes model or generalizations of it, and credit models such as default rate models or credit spread models.

The values derived from applying these techniques are significantly affected by the choice of valuation model used and the underlying assumptions made concerning factors such as the amounts and timing of future cash flows, discount rates, volatility, and credit risk.

The following methods and significant assumptions have been applied in determining the fair values of financial instruments presented in the above table, both for financial instruments carried at fair value, and those carried at cost (for which fair values are provided as a comparison):

a. Trading portfolio assets and liabilities, trading portfolio assets pledged as collateral, financial assets and liabilities designated at fair value, derivatives, and other transactions undertaken for trading purposes are measured at fair value by reference to quoted market prices when available. If quoted market prices are not available, then fair values are estimated on the basis of pricing models, or other recognized valuation techniques. Fair value is equal to the carrying amount for these items;

b. Financial investments classified as available-for-sale are measured at fair value by reference to quoted market prices when available. If quoted market prices are not available, then fair values are estimated on the basis of pricing models or other recognized valuation techniques. Fair value is equal to the carrying amount for these items, and unrealized gains and losses, excluding impairment writedowns, are recorded in Shareholders' equity until an asset is sold, collected or otherwise disposed of;

c. The carrying amount of liquid assets and other assets maturing within 12 months is assumed to approximate their fair value. This assumption is applied to liquid assets and the short-term elements of all other financial assets and financial liabilities;

d. The fair value of demand deposits and savings accounts with no specific maturity is assumed to be the amount payable on demand at the balance sheet date;

e. The fair value of variable rate financial instruments is assumed to be approximated by their carrying amounts and, in the case of loans, does not, therefore, reflect changes in their credit quality, as the impact of credit risk is recognized separately by deducting the amount of the allowance for credit losses from both carrying and fair values;

f. The fair value of fixed-rate loans and mortgages carried at amortized cost is estimated by comparing market interest rates when the loans were granted with current market rates offered on similar loans. Changes in the credit quality of loans within the portfolio are not taken into account in determining gross fair values, as the impact of credit risk is recognized separately by deducting the amount of the allowance for credit losses from both carrying and fair values.

Where applicable, for the purposes of the fair value disclosure on the previous page, the interest accrued to date on financial instruments is included in the carrying value of the financial instruments.

These valuation techniques and assumptions provide a consistent measurement of fair value for UBS's assets and liabilities as shown in the table. However, because other institutions may use different methods and assumptions when estimating fair value using a valuation technique, and when estimating the fair value of financial instruments not carried at fair value, such fair value disclosures cannot necessarily be compared from one financial institution to another.

The table does not reflect the fair values of nonfinancial assets and liabilities such as property, equipment, goodwill, prepayments, and noninterest accruals.

Substantially all of UBS's commitments to extend credit are at variable rates. Accordingly, UBS has no significant exposure to fair value fluctuations resulting from interest rate movements related to these commitments.

The fair values of UBS's fixed-rate loans, long- and medium-term notes and bonds issued are predominantly hedged by derivative instruments, mainly interest rate swaps, as explained in Note 23. The interest rate risk inherent in balance sheet positions with no specific maturity is also hedged with derivative instruments based on management's view on the effective interest repricing date of the products.

Derivative instruments used for hedging are carried on the balance sheet at fair values, which are included in the positive or negative replacement values in the table. When the interest rate risk on a fixed-rate financial instrument is hedged with a derivative in a fair value hedge, the fixed-rate financial instrument (or hedged portion thereof) is reflected in the table at fair value only in relation to the interest rate risk, not the credit risk, as explained in f. Fair value changes are recorded in net profit. The treatment of derivatives designated as cash flow hedges is explained in Note 1o. The amount shown in the table as "Derivative instruments designated as cash flow hedges" is the net change in fair values on such derivatives that is recorded in Shareholders' equity and not yet transferred to income or expense.

30b Determination of fair values from quoted market prices or valuation techniques

For trading portfolio securities and financial investments which are listed or otherwise traded in an active market, for exchange traded derivatives, and for other financial instruments for which quoted prices in an active market are available, fair value is determined directly from those quoted market prices.

For financial instruments which do not have directly available quoted market prices, fair values are estimated using valuation techniques, or models, based wherever possible on assumptions supported by observable market prices or rates existing at the balance sheet date. This is the case for the majority of OTC derivatives, most unlisted instruments, and other items which are not traded in active markets.

For a small portion of financial instruments, fair values cannot be obtained directly from quoted market prices, or indirectly using valuation techniques or models supported by observable market prices or rates. This is generally the case for private equity investments in unlisted securities, and for certain exotic or structured financial instruments. In these cases fair value is estimated indirectly using valuation techniques or models for which the inputs are reasonable assumptions, based on market conditions.

The following table presents the valuation methods used to determine fair values of financial instruments carried at fair value:

CHF billion	*Quoted market price*	*Valuation techniques— market observable inputs*	*Valuation techniques— nonmarket observable inputs*	*Total*
Trading portfolio assets	209.6	159.7	1.0	370.3
Trading portfolio assets pledged as collateral	156.0	3.1	0.0	159.1
Positive replacement values	6.2	265.2	13.2	284.6
Financial assets designated at fair value	0.7	0.0	0.0	0.7
Financial investments	1.1	0.4	3.5	5.0
Total assets	373.6	428.4	17.7	819.7
Trading portfolio liabilities	161.3	9.7	0.0	171.0
Negative replacement values	9.8	270.1	23.8	303.7
Financial liabilities designated at fair value	0.0	65.8	0.0	65.8
Total liabilities	171.1	345.6	23.8	540.5

30c Sensitivity of fair values to changing significant assumptions to reasonably possible alternatives

Included in the fair value of financial instruments carried at fair value on the balance sheet are those estimated in full or in part using valuation techniques based on assumptions that are not supported by observable market prices or rates. Models used in these situations undergo an internal validation process before they are certified for use. Any related model valuation uncertainty is quantified, and deducted from the fair values produced by the models. Based on the controls and procedural safeguards we employ, management believes the resulting estimated fair values recorded in the balance sheet and the changes in fair values recorded in the income statement are reasonable, and are the most appropriate at the balance sheet date.

The potential effect of using reasonably possible alternative assumptions as inputs to valuation models from which the fair values of these financial instruments are determined has been quantified as a reduction of approximately CHF 579 million using less favorable assumptions, and an increase of approximately CHF 927 million using more favorable assumptions.

The determination of reasonably possible alternative assumptions is itself subject to considerable judgment, but for this purpose was determined using the same technique as for the model valuation adjustments. This was based on increasing and decreasing the confidence level applied to determine the original model valuation adjustments. The resulting effect on fair values reflects the application of less favorable and more favorable assumptions. In changing the assumptions it was assumed that the impact of correlation between different financial instruments and models is minimal.

30d Changes in fair value recognized in profit or loss during the period which were estimated using valuation techniques

Total net trading income for the year ended December 31, 2004, was CHF 4,972 million, which represents the net result from a range of products traded across different business activities, including the effect of foreign currency translation, and including both realized and unrealized income. Unrealized income is determined from changes in fair values, using quoted prices in active markets when available, and is otherwise estimated using valuation techniques.

Included in the unrealized portion of Net trading income are net losses from changes in fair values of CHF 7,123 million on financial instruments for which fair values were estimated using valuation techniques. These valuation techniques included models such as those described above, which range from relatively simple models with market observable inputs, to those which are more complex and require the use of assumptions or estimates based on market conditions.

Net trading income is often generated in transactions involving several financial instruments, or subject to hedging or other risk management techniques, which may result in different portions of the transaction being priced using different methods.

Consequently, the changes in fair value recognized in profit or loss during the period which were estimated using valuation techniques represent only a portion of net trading income, and in many cases these amounts were offset by other financial instruments or transactions, which were priced in active markets using quoted market prices or rates, or in which have been realized. The amount of such income in the current year, including the effect of foreign currency translation on unrealized transactions, was a gain of CHF 12,095 million.

Changes in fair value estimated using valuation techniques are also recognized in net profit, in situations of unrealized impairments on financial investments available-for-sale. The total of such impairment amounts recognized in net profit during the period was CHF 218 million.

30e Continuing involvment in assets that have been transferred

The following table presents details of assets which have been sold or otherwise transferred, but which continue to be recognized, either in full or to the extent of UBS's continuing involvment:

	Continued asset recognition in full	
CHF billion	*Total assets*	*Associated liability*
Nature of transaction		
Securities lending agreements	37.3	13.8
Repurchase agreements	121.8	117.6
Other collateralized securities trading	2.9	2.1
Total 12/31/04	162.0	133.5

The assets in the above table continue to be recognized to the extent shown, due to transactions which do not qualify for derecognition of the assets from the balance sheet. Derecognition criteria are discussed in more detail in Notes 1d and aa.

In each situation of continued recognition, whether in full, or to the extent of continuing involvement, UBS retains the risks of the relevant portions of the retained assets. These include credit risk, settlement risk, country risk, and market risk. In addition, the nature of an associated transaction which gives rise to the continued involvement may modify existing risks, or introduce risks such as a credit exposure to the counterparty to the associated transaction.

The majority of retained assets relate to repurchase agreements and securities lending agreements. Repurchase agreements are nearly always concluded with debt instruments, such as bonds, notes or money market paper; the majority of securities lending agreements are concluded with shares, and the remainder typically with bonds and notes. Both types of transactions are transacted using standard agreements employed by financial market participants, and are undertaken with counterparties subject to UBS's normal credit approval processes. The resulting credit exposures are controlled by daily monitoring and collateralization of the positions. The amounts for repurchase agreements and securities lending agreements are shown in the above table.

A small portion of retained assets relate to transactions in which UBS has transferred assets, but continues to have involvement in the transferred assets, for example through providing a guarantee, writing put options, acquiring call options, or entering into a total return swap or other type of swap linked to the performance of the asset. If control is retained due to these types of associated transactions, UBS continues to recognize the transferred asset in its entirety, otherwise to the extent of its continuing involvement.

In particular, transactions involving the transfer of assets in conjunction with entering into a total rate of return swap are accounted for as secured financing transactions, instead of sales of trading portfolio assets with an accompanying swap derivative. These transactions are included in the above table within Trading portfolio assets.

Note 23. Derivative instruments

A derivative is a financial instrument, the value of which is derived from the value of another ("underlying") financial instrument, an index, or some other variable. Typically, the underlying is a share, commodity or bond price, an index value, or an exchange or interest rate.

The majority of derivative contracts are negotiated as to amount ("notional"), tenor and price between UBS and its counterparties, whether other professionals or customers (OTC). The rest are standardized in terms of their amounts and settlement dates and are bought and sold in organized markets (exchange traded).

The "notional" amount of a derivative is generally the quantity of the underlying instrument on which the derivative contract is based and is the basis upon which changes in the value of the contract are measured. It provides an indication of the underlying volume of business transacted by the Group but does not provide any measure of risk.

Derivative instruments are carried at fair value, shown in the balance sheet as separate totals of positive replacement values (assets) and negative replacement values (liabilities). Positive replacement values represent the cost to the Group of replacing all transactions with a fair value in the Group's favor if all the relevant counterparties of the Group were to default at the same time, assuming transactions could be replaced instantaneously. Negative replacement values represent the cost to the Group's counterparties of replacing all their transactions with the Group with a fair value in their favor if Group were to default. Positive and negative replacement values on different transactions are only netted if the transactions are with the same counterparty and the cash flows will be settled on a net basis. Changes in replacement values of derivative instruments are recognized in trading income unless they qualify as hedges for accounting purposes, as explained in Note 1 Summary of Significant Accounting Policies, section (o), Derivative instruments and hedging.

Types of derivatives

The Group uses the following derivative financial instruments for both trading and hedging purposes:

Forwards and futures are contractual obligations to buy or sell financial instruments or commodities on a future date at a specified price. Forward contracts are tailor-made agreements that are transacted between counterparties in the over-the-counter (OTC) market, whereas futures are standardized contracts transacted on regulated exchanges.

Swaps are transactions in which two parties exchange cash flows on a specified notional amount for a predetermined period. Most swaps are traded OTC. The major types of swap transaction undertaken by the Group are as follows:

- Interest rate swap contracts generally entail the contractual exchange of fixed- and floating-rate interest payments in a single currency, based on a notional amount and an interest reference rate (e.g., LIBOR).
- Cross-currency swaps involve the exchange of interest payments based on two different currency principal balances and reference interest rates and generally also entail exchange of principal amounts at the start and/or end of the contract.
- Credit default swaps (CDS) are the most common form of credit derivative, under which the party buying protection makes one or more payments to the party selling protection in exchange for an undertaking by the seller to make a payment to the buyer following a credit event (as defined in the contract) with respect to a third party. Settlement following a credit event may be a net cash amount, or cash in return for physical delivery of one or more obligations of the credit entity (as defined in the contract) and is made regardless of whether the protection buyer has actually suffered a loss. After a credit event and settlement, the contract is terminated.
- Total rate of return swaps give the total return receiver exposure to all of the cash flows and economic benefits and risks of an underlying asset, without having to own the asset, in exchange for a series of payments, often based on a reference interest rate (e.g., LIBOR). The total return payer has an equal and opposite position.

Options are contractual agreements under which, typically, the seller (writer) grants the purchaser the right, but not the obligation, either to buy (call option) or sell (put option) by or at a set date, a specified quantity of a financial instrument or commodity at a predetermined price. The purchaser pays a premium to the seller for this right. Options involving more complex payment structures are also transacted. Options may be traded OTC or on a regulated exchange, and may be traded in the form of a security (warrant).

Derivatives transacted for trading purposes

Most of the Group's derivative transactions relate to sales and trading activities. Sales activities include the structuring and marketing of derivative products to customers to enable them to take, transfer, modify, or reduce current or expected risks. Trading includes market-making, positioning and arbitrage activities. Market-making involves quoting bid and offer prices to other market participants with the intention of generating revenues based on spread and volume. Positioning means managing market risk positions with the expectation of profiting from favorable movements in prices, rates, or indices. Arbitrage activities involve identifying and profiting from price differentials between the same product in different markets or the same economic factor in different products.

Derivatives transacted for hedging purposes

The Group enters into derivative transactions for the purposes of hedging assets, liabilities, forecast transactions, cash flows, and credit exposures. The accounting treatment of hedge transactions varies according to the nature of the instrument hedged and whether the hedge qualifies as such for accounting purposes.

Derivative transactions may qualify as hedges for accounting purposes if they are fair value hedges or cash flow hedges. These are described under the corresponding headings below. The Group's accounting policies for derivatives designated and accounted for as hedging instruments are explained in Note 1o, Derivative instruments and hedging, where terms used in the following section are explained.

The Group also enters into derivative transactions which provide economic hedges for credit risk exposures but do not meet the requirements for hedge accounting treatment: the Group uses CDs as economic hedges for credit risk exposures in the loan and traded product portfolios but cannot apply hedge accounting to such positions.

Fair value hedges

The Group's fair value hedges principally consist of interest rate swaps that are used to protect against changes in the fair value of fixed-rate long-term debt due to movements in market interest rates. For the year ended December 31, 2004, the Group recognized a net gain of CHF 22 million and in 2003 a net gain of CHF 21 million, representing the ineffective portions, as defined in Note 1o, of fair value hedges. The fair values of outstanding derivatives designated as fair value hedges were a CHF 438 million net positive replacement value at December 31, 2004 and a CHF 797 million net positive replacement value at December 31, 2003.

Cash flow hedges of forecast transactions

The Group is exposed to variability in future interest cash flows on nontrading assets and liabilities which bear interest at variable rates or which are expected to be re-funded or reinvested in the future. The amounts and timing of future cash flows, representing both principal and interst flows, are projected for each portfolio of financial assets and liabilities, based on their contractual terms and other relevant factors including estimates of prepayments and defaults. The aggregate principal balances and interest cash flows across all portfolios over time form the basis for identifying the nontrading interest rate risk of the Group, which is hedged with interest rate swaps, the maximum maturity of which is twenty-two years.

The schedule of forecast principal balances on which the expected interest cash flows arise as at December 31, 2004, is as follows:

CHF billion	< 1 year	1–3 years	3–5 years	5–10 years	Over 10 years
Cash inflows (assets)	135	255	180	153	8
Cash outflows (liabilities)	88	142	87	91	72
Net cash flows	47	113	93	62	(64)

Gains and losses on the effective portions of derivatives designated as cash flow hedges of forecast transactions are initially recorded in Shareholders' equity as Gains/losses not recognized in the income statement and are transferred to current period earnings when the forecast cash flows affect net profit or loss. The gains and losses on ineffective portions of such derivatives are recognized immediately in the income statement. In 2004, a gain of CHF 13 million was recognized due to hedge ineffectiveness, whereas in 2003 and 2002 no gains or losses from hedge ineffectiveness arose.

As at December 31, 2004 and 2003, the fair values of outstanding derivatives designated as cash flow hedges of forecast transactions was a CHF 818 million net negative replacement value and a CHF 871 million net negative replacement value, respectively. Swiss franc hedging interest rate swaps terminated during 2003 had a positive replacement value of CHF 867 million. No interest rate swaps designated as cash flow hedges were terminated during 2004. At year-end 2004, unrecognized income of CHF 501 million associated with these swaps has remained deferred in Shareholders' equity. It will be removed from equity when the hedged cash flows impact net profit or loss. Amounts reclassified from Realized gains/losses not recognized in the income statement to current period earnings due to discontinuation of hedge accounting were a CHF 304 million net gain in 2004 and a CHF 7 million net gain in 2003. These amounts were recorded in net interest income.

Risks of derivative instruments

Derivative instruments are transacted in many trading portfolios, which generally include several types of instruments, not just derivatives. The market risk of derivatives is managed and controlled as an integral part of the market risk of these portfolios. The Group's approach to market risk is described in Note 29, Financial Instruments Risk Position, part a, Market risk.

Derivative instruments are transacted with many different counterparties, most of whom are also counterparties for other types of business. The credit risk of derivatives is managed and controlled in the context of the Group's overall credit exposure to each counterparty. The Group's approach to credit risk is described in Note 29, Financial Instruments Risk Position, part b, Credit risk. It should be noted that although the positive replacement values shown on the balance sheet can be an important component of the Group's credit exposure, the positive replacement values for any one counterparty are rarely an adequate reflection of the Group's credit exposure on its derivatives business with that counterparty. This is because, on the one hand, replacement values can increase over time ("potential future exposure"), while on the other hand, exposure may be mitigated by entering into master netting agreements and bilateral collateral arrangements with counterparties. Both the exposure measures used by the Group internally to control credit risk and the capital requirements imposed by regulators reflect these additional factors. In Note 29, part b, Credit risk, the derivatives positive replacement values shown under traded products, and in Note 29, part d, Capital adequacy, the positive replacement values shown under balance sheet assets are lower than those shown in the balance sheet and in the tables on the next two pages because they reflect legally enforceable close-out netting arrangements. Conversely, there are additional capital requirements shown in Note 29, part d, Capital adequacy under off-balance-sheet and other positions as forward and swap contracts and purchased options, which reflect the additional potential future exposure.

As at December 31, 2004

CHF million	Within 3 months PRV[1]	Within 3 months NRV[2]	3 – 12 months PRV	3 – 12 months NRV	1 – 5 years PRV	1 – 5 years NRV	Over 5 years PRV	Over 5 years NRV	Total PRV	Total NRV	Total notional amount CHF bn
Interest rate contracts											
Over the counter (OTC) contracts											
Forward contracts	440	495	112	144	58	34	90	166	700	839	843.6
Swaps	4,305	4,002	11,015	11,921	65,419	64,487	76,470	75,287	157,209	155,697	9,871.0
Options	806	722	1,845	2,239	6,553	8,292	5,942	6,479	15,146	17,732	1,181.4
Exchange-traded contracts[3]											
Futures											2,073.0
Options	86	87	133	103	5	5			224	195	817.9
Total	5,637	5,306	13,105	14,407	72,035	72,818	82,502	81,932	173,279	174,463	14,786.9
Credit derivative contracts											
Over the counter (OTC) contracts											
Credit default swaps	7	10	51	99	3,819	5,409	2,401	1,501	6,278	7,019	639.2
Total rate of return swaps	31	15	57	69	433	1,076	376	272	897	1,432	27.1
Total	38	25	108	168	4,252	6,485	2,777	1,773	7,175	8,451	666.3
Foreign exchange contracts											
Over the counter (OTC) contracts											
Forward contracts	3,496	4,585	807	1,316	186	449	68	240	4,557	6,590	355.6
Interest and currency swaps	27,587	28,094	15,101	14,907	20,897	15,484	7,189	7,240	70,774	65,725	2,811.4
Options	2,224	2,202	2,809	2,553	508	503	4	4	5,545	5,262	559.2
Exchange-traded contracts[3]											
Futures											2.9
Options	9	9	81	79	11	10			101	98	5.9
Total	33,316	34,890	18,798	18,855	21,602	16,446	7,261	7,484	80,977	77,675	3,735.0
Precious metals contracts											
Over the counter (OTC) contracts											
Forward contracts	130	113	150	201	447	192	9	24	736	530	13.5
Options	156	115	281	251	683	615	34	28	1,154	1,009	43.4
Exchange-traded contracts[3]											
Futures											0.8
Options	215	237	195	259	18	33			428	529	2.5
Total	501	465	626	711	1,148	840	43	52	2,318	2,068	60.2

CHF million	Within 3 months PRV[1]	Within 3 months NRV[2]	3 – 12 months PRV	3 – 12 months NRV	1 – 5 years PRV	1 – 5 years NRV	Over 5 years PRV	Over 5 years NRV	Total PRV	Total NRV	Total notional amount CHF bn
Equity/index contracts											
Over the counter (OTC) contracts											
Forward contracts	795	506	572	419	1,912	928	129	24	3,408	1,877	103.6
Options	2,017	7,807	2,057	7,245	7,367	16,290	455	2,144	11,896	33,486	223.6
Exchange-traded contracts[3]											
Futures											8.1
Options	1,212	1,040	947	1,142	1,711	1,979	98	109	3,968	4,270	401.6
Total	4,024	9,353	3,576	8,806	10,990	19,197	682	2,277	19,272	39,633	736.9
Commodity contracts											
Over the counter (OTC) contracts											
Forward contracts	338	343	519	491	420	379			1,277	1,213	35.4
Options	76	73	85	79	118	57			279	209	4.7
Total	414	416	604	570	538	436	0	0	1,556	1,422	40.1
Total derivative instruments	43,930	50,455	36,817	43,517	110,565	116,222	93,265	93,518	284,577	303,712	

1 PRV: Positive Replacement Value.
2 NRV: Negative Replacement Value.
3 Exchange-traded products include proprietary trades only.

As at December 31, 2003

CHF million	Within 3 months PRV[1]	Within 3 months NRV[2]	3 – 12 months PRV	3 – 12 months NRV	1 – 5 years PRV	1 – 5 years NRV	Over 5 years PRV	Over 5 years NRV	Total PRV	Total NRV	Total notional amount CHF bn
Interest rate contracts											
Over the counter (OTC) contracts											
Forward contracts	424	586	258	312	71	130	5	4	758	1,032	1,128.4
Swaps	3,831	4,383	8,698	5,991	64,216	65,075	52,019	50,517	128,764	125,971	8,065.4
Options	464	978	868	992	4,636	5,967	4,223	5,334	10,241	13,271	815.4
Exchange-traded contracts[3]											
Futures											243.7
Options	7	9	2	8					9	17	63.4
Total	4,726	5,961	9,826	7,303	68,973	71,172	56,247	55,855	139,772	140,291	10,316.3
Credit derivative contracts											
Over the counter (OTC) contracts											
Credit default swaps	109	102	39	61	3,443	3,536	1,928	1,880	5,519	5,579	289.3
Total rate of return swaps	27	2	29	576	197	470	112	305	365	1,353	12.0
Total	136	104	68	637	3,640	4,006	2,040	2,185	5,884	6,932	301.3

| CHF million | Term to maturity | | | | | | | | | | Total notional amount CHF bn |
| | Within 3 months | | 3 – 12 months | | 1 – 5 years | | Over 5 years | | Total | | |
	PRV[1]	NRV[2]	PRV	NRV	PRV	NRV	PRV	NRV	Total PRV	Total NRV	
Foreign exchange contracts											
Over the counter (OTC) contracts											
Forward contracts	3,045	3,879	1,978	2,573	161	317	15	12	5,199	6,781	298.4
Interest and currency swaps	24,929	25,242	14,258	12,428	17,780	14,394	6,002	5,250	62,969	57,314	2,254.4
Options	3,232	3,348	3,211	2,550	513	356	9	1	6,965	6,255	576.8
Exchange-traded contracts[3]											
Futures											5.0
Options	3	3	119	116	3	4			122	119	13.2
Total	31,209	32,472	19,566	17,667	18,454	15,067	6,026	5,263	75,255	70,469	3,147.8
Precious metals contracts											
Over the counter (OTC) contracts											
Forward contracts	246	247	377	305	333	270	18	23	974	845	15.9
Options	304	193	308	386	668	629	116	54	1,396	1,262	35.1
Exchange-traded contracts[1]											
Futures											1.1
Options	9	40	21	63	3	4			33	107	2.3
Total	559	480	706	754	1,004	903	134	77	2,403	2,214	54.4
Equity/index contracts											
Over the counter (OTC) contracts											
Forward contracts	509	529	763	583	917	449	1,408	501	3,597	2,062	57.9
Options	1,841	2,783	3,482	7,847	11,111	13,646	1,328	4,560	17,762	28,841	213.8
Exchange-traded contracts[3]											
Futures											8.6
Options	708	858	892	1,363	883	768	54	117	2,537	3,106	62.6
Total	3,058	4,175	5,137	9,793	12,911	14,863	2,790	5,178	23,896	34,009	342.9
Commodity contracts											
Over the counter (OTC) contracts											
Forward contracts	206	181	456	424	93	42			755	647	10.6
Options	168	153	73	53			0	0	241	206	1.6
Total	374	334	529	477	93	42	0	0	996	853	12.2
Total derivative instruments	40,062	43,526	35,832	36,631	105,075	106,053	67,237	68,558	248,206	254,768	

1 PRV: Positive Replacement Value.
2 NRV: Negative Replacement Value.
3 Exchange-traded products include proprietary trades only.

ACCOUNTING AND REPORTING BY RETIREMENT BENEFIT PLANS

PERSPECTIVE AND ISSUES

IAS 26 sets out the form and content of the general-purpose financial reports of retirement benefit plans. This standard deals with accounting and reporting to all participants of a plan as a group, and not with reports which might be made to individuals about their particular retirement benefits. The standard applies to

- Defined contribution plans where benefits are determined by contributions to the plan together with investment earnings thereon; and
- Defined benefit plans where benefits are determined by a formula based on employees' earnings and/or years of service.

IAS 26 may be compared to IAS 19. The former addresses the financial reporting considerations for the benefit plan itself, as the reporting entity, while the latter deals with employers' accounting for the cost of such benefits as they are earned by the employees. While these standards are thus somewhat related, there will not be any direct interrelationship between amounts reported in benefit plan financial statements and amounts reported under IAS 19 by employers.

IAS 26 became effective for financial statements of retirement benefit plans in 1988. While IAS 19 has been revised twice, IAS 26 has never been revised by the IASC. It was, however, reformatted in 1994 to bring it in line with the current IASC practice. There are no current plans to address this topic again.

Sources of IFRS
IAS 26

DEFINITIONS OF TERMS

Actuarial present value of promised retirement benefits. The present value of the expected future payments by a retirement benefit plan to existing and past employees, attributable to the service already rendered.

Defined benefit plans. Retirement benefit plans whereby retirement benefits to be paid to plan participants are determined by reference to a formula usually based on employees' earnings and/or years of service.

Defined contribution plans. Retirement benefit plans whereby retirement benefits to be paid to plan participants are determined by contributions to a fund together with investment earnings thereon.

Funding. The transfer of assets to a separate entity (distinct from the employer's enterprise), the "fund," to meet future obligations for the payment of retirement benefits.

Net assets available for benefits. The assets of a retirement benefit plan less its liabilities other than the actuarial present value of promised retirement benefits.

Participants. The members of a retirement benefit plan and others who are entitled to benefits under the plan.

Retirement benefit plans. Formal or informal arrangements based upon which an enterprise provides benefits for its employees on or after termination of service, which are usually referred to as "termination benefits." These could take the form of annual pension payments or lump-sum payments. Such benefits, or the employer's contributions towards them, should however be determinable or possible of estimation in advance of retirement, from the provisions of a document (i.e., based on a formal arrangement) or from the enterprise's practices (which is referred to as an informal arrangement).

Vested benefits. Entitlements, the rights to which, under the terms of a retirement benefit plan, are not conditional on continued employment.

CONCEPTS, RULES, AND EXAMPLES

Scope

IAS 26 should be applied in accounting and reporting by retirement benefit plans. The terms of a retirement plan may require that the plan present an annual report; in some jurisdictions this may be a statutory requirement. IAS 26 does not establish a mandate for the publication of such reports by retirement plans. However, if such reports are prepared by a retirement plan, then the requirements of this standard should be applied to them.

IAS 26 regards a retirement benefit plan as a separate entity, distinct from the employer of the plan's participants. It is noteworthy that this standard also applies to retirement benefit plans that have sponsors other than employer (e.g., trade associations or groups of employers). Furthermore, this standard deals with accounting and reporting by retirement benefit plans to all participants as a group; it does not deal with reports to individual participants with respect to their retirement benefit entitlements.

The standard applies the same basis of accounting and reporting to informal retirement benefit arrangements as it applies to formal retirement benefit plans. It is also worthy of mention that this standard applies whether or not a separate fund is created and regardless of whether there are trustees. The requirements of this standard also apply to retirement benefit plans with assets invested with an insurance company, unless the contract with the insurance company is in the name of a specified participant or a group of participants and the responsibility is solely of the insurance company.

Defined Contribution Plans

Retirement benefit plans are usually described as being either defined contribution or defined benefit plans. When the quantum of the future benefits payable to the retirement benefit plan participants is determined by the contributions paid by the participants' employer, the participants, or both, together with investment earnings thereon, such plans are defined contribution plans. Defined benefit plans, by contrast, promise certain benefits, often determined by formulae which involve factors such as years of service and salary level at the time of retirement, without regard to whether the plan has sufficient assets; thus the ultimate responsibility for payment (which may be guaranteed by an insurance company, the government or some other entity, depending on local law and custom) remains with the employer. In rare circumstances, a retirement benefit plan may contain characteristics of both defined contribution and defined benefit plans; such a hybrid plan is deemed to be a defined benefit plan for the purposes of this standard.

IAS 26 requires that the report of a defined contribution plan contain a statement of the net assets available for benefits and a description of the funding policy. In preparing the statement of the net assets available for benefits, the plan investments should be carried at fair value, which for marketable securities would be market value. In case an estimate of fair value is not possible, disclosure is required of the reason as to why fair value has not been used. As a practical matter, most plan assets will have determinable market values, since the plans' trustees' discharge of their fiduciary responsibilities will generally mandate that only marketable investments be held.

An example of a statement of net assets available for plan benefits, for a defined contribution plan, is set forth below.

XYZ Defined Contribution Plan
Statement of Net Assets Available for Benefits
December 31, 2005
(€000)

Assets
Investments at fair value

US government securities	€ 5,000
US municipal bonds	3,000
US equity securities	3,000
Non-US equity securities	3,000
US debt securities	2,000
Non-US corporate bonds	2,000
Others	1,000
Total investments	19,000

Receivables

Amounts due from stockbrokers on sale of securities	15,000
Accrued interest	5,000
Dividends receivable	2,000
Total receivables	22,000

Cash	5,000
Total assets	€46,000

Liabilities
Accounts payable

Amounts due to stockbrokers on purchase of securities	€10,000
Benefits payable to participants—due and unpaid	11,000
Total accounts payable	21,000

Accrued expenses	11,000
Total liabilities	€32,000
Net assets available for benefits	€14,000

Defined benefit plans. When amounts to be paid as retirement benefits are determined by reference to a formula, usually based on employees' earnings and/or years of service, such retirement benefit plans are defined benefit plans. The key factor is that the benefits are fixed or determinable, without regard to the adequacy of assets which may have been set aside for payment of the benefits. This contrasts to the defined contribution plans approach, which is to provide the workers, upon retirement, with the amounts which have been set aside, plus or minus investment earnings or losses which have been accumulated thereon, however great or small that amount may be.

The standard requires that the report of a defined benefit plan should contain **either**

1. A statement that shows

    a. The net assets available for benefits;
    b. The actuarial present value of promised retirement benefits, distinguishing between vested and nonvested benefits; and
    c. The resulting excess or deficit;

or

2. A statement of net assets available for benefits including *either*

    a. A note disclosing the actuarial present value of promised retirement benefits, distinguishing between vested and nonvested benefits; or
    b. A reference to this information in an accompanying actuarial report.

IAS 26 recommends, but does not mandate, that in each of the three formats described above, a trustees' report in the nature of a management or directors' report and an investment report may also accompany the statements.

The standard does not make it incumbent upon the plan to obtain annual actuarial valuations. If an actuarial valuation has not been prepared on the date of the report, the most recent valuation should be used as the basis for preparing the financial statement. The date of the valuation used should be disclosed. Actuarial present values of promised benefits should be based either on current or projected salary levels; whichever basis is used should be disclosed. The effect of any changes in actuarial assumptions that had a material impact on the actuarial present value of promised retirement benefits should also be disclosed. The report should explain the relationship between actuarial present values of promised benefits, the net assets available for benefits and the policy for funding the promised benefits.

As in the case of defined contribution plans, investments of a defined benefit plan should be carried at fair value, which for marketable securities, would be market value.

The following are examples of the alternative types of reports prescribed for a defined benefit plan:

ABC Defined Benefit Plan
Statement of Net Assets Available for Benefits, Actuarial Present Value of Accumulated
Retirement Benefits and Plan Excess or Deficit
December 31, 2005
(€000)

1. Statement of Net Assets Available for Benefits

Assets	
Investments at fair value	
US government securities	€ 50,000
US municipal bonds	30,000
US equity securities	30,000
Non-US equity securities	30,000
US debt securities	20,000
Non-US corporate bonds	20,000
Others	10,000
Total investments	€190,000
Receivables	
Amounts due from stockbrokers on sale of securities	150,000
Accrued interest	50,000
Dividends receivable	20,000
Total receivables	220,000
Cash	50,000
Total assets	€460,000
Liabilities	
Accounts payable	
Amounts due to stockbrokers on purchase of securities	€100,000
Benefits payable to participants–due and unpaid	110,000
Total accounts payable	210,000
Accrued expenses	110,000
Total liabilities	320,000
Net assets available for benefits	€140,000

2. Actuarial present value of accumulated plan benefits

Vested benefits	€100,000
Nonvested benefits	20,000
Total	€120,000

3. Excess of net assets available for benefits over actuarial present value of accumulated plan benefits

	€ 20,000

ABC Defined Benefit Plan
Statement of Changes in Net Assets Available for Benefits
December 31, 2005
(€000)

Investment income	
Interest income	€ 40,000
Dividend income	10,000
Net appreciation (unrealized gain) in fair value of investments	10,000
Total investment income	60,000
Plan contributions	
Employer contributions	50,000
Employee contributions	50,000
Total plan contributions	100,000
Total additions to net asset value	160,000
Plan benefit payments	
Pensions (annual)	30,000
Lump sum payments on retirement	30,000
Severance pay	10,000
Commutation of superannuation benefits	15,000
Total plan benefit payments	85,000
Total deductions from net asset value	85,000
Net increase in asset value	75,000
Net assets available for benefits	
Beginning of year	65,000
End of year	€140,000

Additional Disclosures

IAS 26 requires that the reports of a retirement benefit plan, both defined benefit plans and defined contribution plans, should also contain the following information:

1. A statement of changes in net assets available for benefits;
2. A summary of significant accounting policies; and
3. A description of the plan and the effect of any changes in the plan during the period.

Reports provided by retirement benefits plans may include the following, if applicable:

1. A statement of net assets available for benefits disclosing

   a. Assets at the end of the period suitably classified;
   b. The basis of valuation of assets;
   c. Details of any single investment exceeding either 5% of the net assets available for benefits or 5% of any class or type of security;
   d. Details of any investment in the employer; and
   e. Liabilities other than the actuarial present value of promised retirement benefits;

2. A statement of changes in net assets available for benefits showing the following:

   a. Employer contributions;
   b. Employee contributions;
   c. Investment income such as interest and dividends;
   d. Other income;
   e. Benefits paid or payable (analyzed, for example, as retirement, death and disability benefits, and lump-sum payments);
   f. Administrative expenses;
   g. Other expenses;
   h. Taxes on income;

    i.   Profits and losses on disposal of investments and changes in value of investments; and

    j.   Transfers from and to other plans;

3. A description of the funding policy;

4. For defined benefit plans, the actuarial present value of promised retirement benefits (which may distinguish between vested benefits and nonvested benefits) based on the benefits promised under the terms of the plan, on service rendered to date and using either current salary levels or projected salary levels. This information may be included in an accompanying actuarial report to be read in conjunction with the related information; and

5. For defined benefit plans, a description of the significant actuarial assumptions made and the method used to calculate the actuarial present value of promised retirement benefits.

According to the standard, since the report of a retirement benefit plan contains a description of the plan, either as part of the financial information or in a separate report, it may contain the following:

1. The names of the employers and the employee groups covered;

2. The number of participants receiving benefits and the number of other participants, classified as appropriate;

3. The type of plan—defined contribution or defined benefit;

4. A note as to whether participants contribute to the plan;

5. A description of the retirement benefits promised to participants;

6. A description of any plan termination terms; and

7. Changes in items 1. through 6. during the period covered by the report.

Furthermore, it is not uncommon to refer to other documents that are readily available to users and in which the plan is described, and to include only information on subsequent changes in the report.

AGRICULTURE

PERSPECTIVE AND ISSUES

Over most of its existence, the former IASC was focused on the task of developing or endorsing existing standards that are pertinent to general-purpose financial reporting. In the more recent of those years, completion of the core set of standards, which too was oriented toward general-purpose financial statement needs, was of paramount importance. The special needs of individual industries, of necessity, received very little attention during this period.

However, the IASC was able, before its existence ended when the restructuring (described in Chapter 1) took place and IASB became the standard-setting body, to complete its project on accounting for agricultural activities. This was a major project having widespread implications, particularly for those many nations which rely heavily on their agricultural sectors.

Agriculture, the first set of specialized financial reporting issues to be given a comprehensive financial reporting model (banking was given only expanded disclosure rules), received a great deal of attention from IASC. When the IASC's draft statement of position was issued, it marked the first real attention paid to one of the world's most prominent economic activities by any of the accounting rule-making bodies. For developing nations, agriculture is indeed disproportionately significant, and given the IASC's role in establishing financial reporting standards for those nations, the focus on agriculture was perhaps to be expected.

IAS 41, *Agriculture,* was effective for financial statements covering periods beginning on or after January 1, 2003.

Sources of IFRS
IAS 41

DEFINITIONS OF TERMS

Active market. Market for which all these conditions exist: the items traded within the market are homogeneous; willing buyers and sellers can normally be found at any time; and prices are available to the public.

Agricultural activity. Managed biological transformation of biological assets into agricultural produce for sale, consumption, further processing, or into other biological assets.

Agricultural land. Land used directly to support and sustain biological assets in agricultural activity; the land itself is not a biological asset, however.

Agricultural produce. The harvested product of the enterprise's biological assets awaiting sale, processing, or consumption.

Bearer biological assets. Those which bear agricultural produce for harvest. The biological assets themselves are not the primary agricultural produce, but rather are self-regenerating (such as sheep raised for wool production; fruit trees).

Biological assets. Living plants and animals controlled by the enterprise as a result of past events. Control may be through ownership or through another type of legal arrangement.

Biological transformation. The processes of growth, degeneration, production and procreation, which cause qualitative and quantitative changes in living organisms and the generation of new assets in the form of agricultural produce or additional biological assets of the same class.

Carrying amount. Amount at which an asset is recognized in the balance sheet after deducting any accumulated depreciation or amortization and accumulated impairment losses thereon.

Consumable biological assets. Those which are to be harvested as the primary agricultural produce, such as livestock intended for meat production, annual crops, and trees to be felled for pulp.

Fair value. The amount for which an asset could be exchanged or a liability settled between knowledgeable, willing parties in an arm's-length transaction.

Group of biological assets. A herd, flock, etc., that is managed jointly to ensure that the group is sustainable on an ongoing basis, and is homogeneous as to both type of animal or plant and activity for which the group is deployed.

Harvest. The detachment of agricultural produce from the biological asset, the removal of a living plant from agricultural land for sale and replanting, or the cessation of a biological asset's life processes.

Immature biological assets. Those that are not yet harvestable or able to sustain regular harvests.

Mature biological assets. Those which are harvestable or able to sustain regular harvest. Consumable biological assets are mature when they have attained harvestable specifications; bearer biological assets are mature when they are able to sustain regular harvests.

Net realizable value. Estimated selling price in the ordinary course of business, less the estimated costs of completion and the estimated costs necessary to make the sale.

CONCEPTS, RULES, AND EXAMPLES

Background

Historically, agricultural activities received scant, if any, attention from the world's accounting standard setters. This may have been due to the fact that the major national and international accounting standard setters have been those of the US and the UK, whose economies are far less dependent upon agriculture than those of many lesser-developed nations of the world. The IASC, in seeking to become the world's preeminent accounting standard setter, has until very recently had its greatest impact on the financial reporting standards of the developing nations, many of which have adopted IAS as a whole, and many more of which have based their respective national standards on the IAS. Perhaps because of the IASC's sensitivity to this constituency, its agriculture project, begun some five years ago, received a good deal of serious attention. The culmination of this lengthy project, the newly issued standard IAS 41, is by far the most comprehensive addressing of this financial reporting topic ever undertaken.

The earlier exclusion of agriculture from most established accounting and financial reporting rules can best be understood in the context of certain unique features of the industry. These include biological transformations (growth, procreation, production, degeneration) which alter the very substance of the biological assets; the wide variety of characteristics of the living assets which challenge traditional classification schemes; the nature of management functions in the industry; and the predominance of small, closely held ownership. On the other hand, since in many nations agriculture is a major industry, in some cases accounting for over 50% of gross national product, logic would suggest that comprehensive systems of financial reporting for business enterprises cannot be deemed complete while excluding so large a segment of the economy.

In the past, the general lack of urgency in dealing with this subject has been abetted by the fact that much of agriculture is controlled by closely held or family held businesses, with few, if any, outside owners who might have demanded formal financial statements prepared in accordance with agreed-upon accounting principles. Also, grantors of farm credit have historically looked to the character of the borrower, usually a longtime resident with deep roots in the community, rather than to financial statements. While some of these factors continue to be valid, the IASC concluded that the time had long since arrived to give financial reporting concerns their due attention.

In the realm of previously established international accounting standards, most of the rules which logically could have addressed agricultural issues (IAS 2 on inventories; IAS 16 on plant, property, and equipment; and IAS 18 on revenue recognition) deliberately excluded most or all agriculture-related applications. A review of published financial statements for agriculture-related enterprises would have revealed the consequences of this neglect: a wide range of methods and principles have been applied to such businesses as forest products, livestock, and grain production.

For example, some forest products companies have accounted for timberlands at original cost, charging depreciation only to the extent of net harvesting, with reforestation costs charged to expense as incurred. Others in the same industry capitalized reforestation costs and even carrying costs, and charged depletion on a units-of-production basis. Still others have been valuing forest lands at the net present value of expected future cash flows. This wide disparity obviously has impaired users' ability to gauge the relative performance of enterprises operating within a single industry group, hindering investment and other decision making by them.

For this reason, the IASC concluded in the mid-1990s that excluding agriculture from the scope of IAS was no longer appropriate. At the same time, it also accepted the need for a relatively simple, uniform, and coherent set of principles applicable to this industry group because of the preponderance of small, less sophisticated businesses. The IASC concluded that embracing fair value in addition to, or instead of, the historical cost model, which had already been applied by existing IAS (e.g., to plant and equipment and to investments), offered the best solution to this problem. The new standard will apply only to biological assets, as those are the aspects of agriculture that have unique characteristics; the accounting for assets such as inventories and plant and equipment will be guided by such existing standards as IAS 2 and 16. In other words, once the biological transformation process is complete (e.g., when grain is harvested, animals are slaughtered, or trees are cut down), the specialized accounting principles imposed on agriculture will cease to apply.

Defining Agriculture

Agriculture is to be defined as essentially the management of the biological transformation of plants and animals to yield produce for consumption or further processing. The term agriculture encompass livestock, forestry, annual and perennial cropping, orchards, plantations, and aquiculture. Agriculture is distinguished from "pure exploitation," where resources are simply removed from the environment (e.g., by fishing or deforestation) without management initiatives such as operation of hatcheries, reforestation, or other attempts to manage their regeneration. IAS 41 does not apply to pure exploitation activities, nor does it apply to agricultural produce, which is harvested and is thus a nonliving product of the biological assets. The standard furthermore does not govern accounting for agriculture produce which is incorporated in further processing, as occurs in integrated agribusiness enterprises that involve activities which are not unique to agriculture.

IAS 41 sets forth a three-part test or set of criteria for agricultural activities. First, the plants or animals which are the object of the activities must be alive and capable of transformation. Second, the change must be managed, which implies a range of activities (e.g., fertilizing the soil and weeding in the case of crop growing; feeding and providing health care in the instance of animal husbandry; etc.). Third, there must be a basis for the measurement of change, such as the ripeness of vegetables, the weight of animals, circumference of trees, and so forth. If these three criteria are all satisfied, the activity will be impacted by the financial reporting requirements imposed by IAS 41.

Biological assets are the principal assets of agricultural activities, and they are held for their transformative potential. This results in two major types of outcomes: the first may involve asset changes—as through growth or quality improvement, degeneration, or procreation. The second involves the creation of separable products initially qualifying as agricultural produce. The management of the biological transformation process is the distinguishing characteristic of agricultural activities.

Biological assets often are managed in groups, as exemplified by herds of animals, groves of trees, and fields of crops. To be considered a group, however, the components must be homogeneous in nature and there must further be homogeneity in the activity for which the group is deployed. For example, cherry trees maintained for their production of fruit are not in the same group as cherry trees grown for lumber.

IAS 41 applies to forests and similar regenerative resources excluded from IAS 16; producers' inventories of livestock, agriculture, and forest products, including those excluded from IAS 2, to the extent they are to be measured at net realizable value; and natural increases in herds and agricultural and forest products excluded from IAS 18. It also addresses financial statement presentation and disclosure (the primary province of IAS 1 revised). Furthermore, it establishes that, unless explicit exclusions are provided, all international accounting standards are meant to apply equally to agriculture.

Basic Principles of IAS 41: Fair Value Accounting Is Necessary

IAS 41 applies to all enterprises which undertake agricultural activities. Animals or plants are to be recognized as assets when it is probable that the future economic benefits associated with the asset will flow to the reporting entity, and when the cost or value to the enterprise can be measured reliably. There is a strong presumption that any enterprise entering into agricultural activities on a for-profit basis will have an ability to measure cost and/or fair value. The new standard also governs the initial measurement of agricultural produce, which is the end product of the biological transformation process; it furthermore guides the accounting for government grants pertaining to agricultural assets.

The most important feature of the new standard is the requirement that biological assets are to be measured at each balance sheet date at their respective fair values. This departure from historical cost is the most significant facet of IAS 41, and is one which has generated a good deal of debate during the drafting and exposure draft stages. The imperative to deploy fair value accounting springs from the fact that there are long production periods for many crops (an extreme being forests under management for as long as thirty years before being harvested) and, even more typically, for livestock. In the absence of fair value accounting with changes in value being reported in operating results, the entire earnings of a long-term production process might only be reported at lengthy intervals, which would not faithfully represent the underlying economic activities being carried out. This is entirely analogous to long-term construction projects, for which percentage-of-completion accounting is commonly prescribed, for very similar reasons.

Historical cost based accounting, with revenue to be recognized only upon ultimate sale of the assets, would often result in a gross distortion of reported results of operations, with little or no earnings being reflected in some periods, or even losses being reported to the extent that production expenses are not inventoried. Other periods—when trees are harvested, for example—would reflect substantial reported profits. Thus, the use of historical costs based on completed transactions is no longer deemed meaningful in the case of agricultural activities.

Not only are such periodic distortions seen as being misleading, but it also has been concluded that each stage of the biological transformation process has significance. Each stage (growth, degeneration, procreation, and production) is now seen as contributing to the expected economic benefits to be derived from the biological assets. Unless a fair value model were employed for financial reporting, there would be a lack of explicit recognition (in effect, no matching) of the benefits associated with each of these discrete events. Furthermore, this recognition underlines the need to apply the same measurement concept to each stage in the life cycle of the biological assets; for example, for live weight change, fleece weight change, aging, deaths, lambs born, and wool shorn, in the case of a flock of sheep.

The obvious argument in favor of historical cost based measures derives from the superior reliability of that mode of measurement. With completed transactions, there is no imprecision due to the inherently subjective process of making or obtaining fair value assessments. By contrast, superior relevance is the strongest argument for current value measurement schemes. The IASC evaluated various measures, including current cost and net realizable value, as well as market value, as alternatives to historical cost, but ultimately identified fair value (ironically, the one approach not addressed in the IASC's seminal document, the *Framework for the Preparation and Presentation of Financial Statements)* as having the best combination of attributes for the determination of agriculture-related earnings. The IASC was particularly influenced by the market context in which agriculture takes place and the transformative characteristics of biological assets, and it concluded that fair value would offer the best balance of relevance, reliability, comparability, and understandability.

The IASC also concluded that annual determinations of fair value would be necessary to properly portray the combined impact of nature and financial transactions for any given reporting period. Less frequent measurements were rejected because of the continuous nature of biological transformations, the lack of direct correlation between financial transactions and the different outcomes arising from biological transformation (thus, the former could not serve as surrogate indicators of the latter during off periods), the volatilities which often characterize natural and market environments affecting agriculture, and the fact that market-based measures are in fact readily available.

The idea of maintaining historical cost as an allowed alternative was rejected, essentially because historical cost is not viewed as meaningful in the context of biological assets, but also due to concerns about the extreme lack of comparability that would result from permitting two so disparate methodologies to coexist. Notwithstanding the fact that historical cost is rejected as being meaningful in this context, the IASC agreed that an exception should exist for those circumstances when fair value cannot be reliably estimated. In such instances, historical costs will continue to be employed instead.

Determining Fair Values

The primary determinant of fair value is market value, just as it is for financial instruments having active markets (as defined in IAS 32, discussed at length in Chapter 5). The required use of "farm gate" market prices will reflect both the "as is" and "where is" attributes of the biological assets. That is, the value is meant to pertain to the assets as they exist, where they are located, in the condition they are in as of the measurement (balance sheet) date. They are not hypothetical values, as for instance hogs when delivered to the slaughterhouse. Where these "farm gate" prices are not available, market values will have to be reduced by transaction costs, including transport, to arrive at net market values which would equate to fair values as intended by IAS 41.

In the case of products for which market values might not be readily available, other approaches to fair value determination will have to be employed. This is most likely to become an issue where market values exist but, due to market imperfections, are not deemed to be useful. For example, when access to markets is restricted or unduly influenced by temporary monopoly or monopsony conditions, or when no market actually exists as of the balance sheet date, alternative measures will be called for. In such circumstances, it might be necessary to refer to such indicators as the most recent market prices for the class of asset at issue, market prices for similar assets (e.g., different varieties of the same crop), sector benchmarks (e.g., relating value of a dairy farm to the kilograms of milk solids or fat produced), net present value of expected future cash flows discounted at a risk-class rate, or net realizable values for short-cycle products for which most growth has already occurred. Last and probably least useful would be historical costs, which might be particularly suited to biological assets that have thus far experienced little transformation.

One practical problem arises when an indirect method of valuation implicitly values both the crop and the land itself, taken together as a whole. IAS 41 indicates that such valuations must be allocated to the different assets to give a better indication of the future economic benefits each will confer. If a combined market price, for example, can be obtained for the land plus the immature growing crops situated thereon, and a quotation for the land alone can also be obtained, this will permit a fair value assessment of the immature growing crops (while the land itself will generally be presented on the balance sheet at cost, not fair value, under IAS 16). Another technique would involve the subdivision of the assets into classes based on age, quality, or other traits, and the valuation of each subgroup by reference to market prices. While these methods may involve added effort, IAS 41 concludes that the usefulness of the resulting financial statements will be materially enhanced if this is done.

Increases in fair value due to the growth of the biological asset is only one-half of the accounting equation, of course, since there will normally have been cost inputs incurred to foster the growth (e.g., applications of fertilizer to the fields, etc.). Under the provisions of IAS 41, costs of producing and harvesting biological assets are to be charged to expense as incurred. This is necessary, since if costs were added to the assets' carrying value (analogous to interest on borrowings in connection with long-term construction projects) and the assets were then also adjusted to fair value, there would be risk of double-counting cost or value increases. As mandated, however, value increases due to either price changes or growth, or both, will be taken into current income, where costs of production will be appropriately matched against them, resulting in a meaningful measure of the net result of periodic operations.

Recognition of Changes in Biological Assets

When the IASC's agriculture project was undertaken, the presumption was that changes resulting from fluctuations in fair value were generically distinct from physical changes due to growth and other natural phenomena. Accordingly, the 1996 DSOP proposed that the change in carrying amounts for a group of biological assets would be so allocated. The original intent was to have the former, which corresponds to revaluations of plant and equipment assets under the alternative treatment permitted by IAS 16, reported directly in equity, while the latter would be included in current period operating results. However, even if this bifurcation strategy was conceptually sound, the practical difficulties of allocating such value changes soon became obvious.

By the time the Exposure Draft, E65, was issued, the IASC's position had shifted to the inclusion of both of these value changes in current period results of operations. The draft did urge separate disclosure of the fair value changes and the effects of growth, either on the face of the income statement or in the notes thereto; this was not to be made an actual requirement. The final standard, IAS 41, has dropped this suggestion entirely, probably because it would have proven to be unpopular and therefore rarely complied with.

The actual recognition and measurement requirements of IAS 41 are as follows:

1. Biological assets are to be measured at their fair value, less estimated point-of-sale costs, except where fair value cannot be measured reliably. In the latter instance, historical cost is to be used.

2. Agricultural produce harvested from an enterprise's biological assets should be measured at fair value less estimated point-of-sale costs at the point of harvest. That amount effectively becomes the cost basis, to which further processing costs may be added, as the conditions warrant, with accounting thereafter guided by IAS 2, *Inventories,* or other applicable standard.

3. The presumption is that fair value can be measured reliably for a biological asset. That presumption can be rebutted, only at the time of initial recognition, for a biological asset for which market-determined prices or values are not available and for which alternative estimates of fair value are determined to be clearly unreliable. Once the fair value of such a biological asset becomes reliably measurable, it must be measured at its fair value less estimated point-of-sale costs.

4. If an active market exists for a biological asset or for agricultural produce, the quoted price in that market is the appropriate basis for determining the fair value of that asset. If an active market does not exist, however, the reporting entity should

use market-determined prices or values, such as the most recent market transaction price, when available.

5. Under certain circumstances, market-determined prices or values may not be available for an asset, as it exists in its current condition. In these circumstances, the entity should use the present value of expected net cash flows from the asset discounted at a current market-determined pretax rate, in determining fair value.

6. The gain or loss which is reported upon initial recognition of biological assets, and also those arising from changes in fair value less estimated point-of-sales costs, should be included in net profit or loss for the period in which the gain or loss arises. That is, these are reported in current period results of operations, and not taken directly into equity.

7. The gain or loss arising from the initial recognition of agricultural produce should be included in net profit or loss for the period in which it arises.

8. Land is to be accounted for under IAS 16, *Property, Plant, and Equipment,* or IAS 40, *Investment Property,* as is appropriate under the circumstances. Biological assets that are physically attached to land are recognized and measured at their fair value less estimated point-of-sales costs, separately from the land.

9. If the entity receives an unconditional government grant related to a biological asset measured at its fair value less estimated point-of-sales costs, the grant should be recognized as income when it first becomes receivable. If the grant related to a biological asset measured at its fair value less estimate point-of-sale costs is conditional, including grants which require an entity not to engage in specified agricultural activity, the grant should be recognized in income when the conditions attaching to it are first met.

10. For government grants pertaining to biological assets which are measured at cost less accumulated depreciation and any accumulated impairment losses, IAS 20, *Accounting for Government Grants and Disclosure of Government Assistance,* should be applied. (See Chapter 26.)

11. Some contracts for the sale of biological assets or agricultural produce are not within the scope of IAS 39, *Financial Instruments: Recognition and Measurement,* because the reporting entity expects to deliver the commodity, rather than settle up in cash. Under IAS 41, such contracts are to be measured at fair value until the biological assets are sold or the produce is harvested.

Agricultural Produce

Agricultural produce is distinguished from biological assets and is not to be measured at fair value other than at the point of harvest, which is the point where biological assets become agricultural produce. For example, when crops are harvested they become agricultural produce and are initially valued at the fair value as of the date of harvest, at the location of harvest (i.e., the value of harvested crops at a remote point of delivery would not be a pertinent measure). If there has been a time interval between the last valuation and the harvest, the value as of the harvest date should be determined or estimated; any increase or decrease since the last valuation would be taken into earnings.

Financial Statement Presentation

Balance sheet. Official thinking about the level of detail required when the reporting entity has biological assets has evolved since the DSOP first issued. At that time, it was suggested that biological assets should be set forth as a distinct class of assets, being part of neither current nor noncurrent assets. By the time the Exposure Draft was issued, inclusion of biological assets in current and noncurrent assets, as appropriate, either in the aggregate or by major groups of biological assets, was proposed. The ED furthermore encouraged that biological assets be categorized according to class of animal or plant, nature of activities (e.g., being maintained for harvesting or as breeding stock), and the maturity or immaturity for the intended purpose. It suggested that if the plant or animal is being maintained for consumption (to be harvested, etc.), maturity would be gauged by attainment of harvestable specifications. If the plant or animal is for bearing purposes, the maturity criterion would be the attainment of sufficient maturity to sustain economic harvests.

When IAS 41 was promulgated, however, it only established a requirement that the carrying amount of biological assets be presented separately on the face of the balance sheet (i.e., not included with other, nonbiological assets). Preparers were encouraged to describe the nature and stage of production of each group of biological assets in narrative format in the notes to the financial statements, optionally quantified. Consumable biological assets are to be differentiated from bearer assets, with further subdivisions into mature and immature subgroups for each of these broad categories. The purpose of these disclosures is to give the users of the financial statements some insight into the timing of future cash flows, since the mature subgroups will presumably be realized through market transactions in the near future, and the pattern of cash flows resulting from bearer assets differs from those deriving from consumables.

Income statement. The changes in fair value should be presented on the face of the income statement, ideally broken down between groups of biological assets. However, group level detail may be reserved to the notes to the financial statements.

Also, while separate disclosure of the components of fair value change (i.e., that due to growth and that due to price changes) had been encouraged in the exposure draft, this is no longer being promoted, while of course not being prohibited either. Clearly, the change in fair value which is a consequence of price changes (whether general inflation or specific changes in the market prices of given commodities, such as wheat, due to factors such as the expectations regarding the harvest) is generically distinct from the growth which has occurred during the period being reported on. Distinguishing between these two factors would be important in making the financial reporting process more meaningful, and several examples of how this dichotomizing of fair value changes can be accomplished and presented in the financial statements was included in the Exposure Draft preceding IAS 41's issuance.

IAS 1 permits the presentation of expenses in accordance with either a natural classification (e.g., materials purchases, depreciation, etc.) or a functional basis (cost of sales, administrative, selling, etc.). The draft statement on agriculture had urged that the natural classification of income and expenses be adopted for the income statement. Sufficient detail is to be included in the face of the income statement to support an analysis of operating performance. However, these are recommendations, not strict requirements.

Disclosures. IAS 41 establishes new disclosure requirements for biological assets measured at cost less any accumulated depreciation and any accumulated impairment losses (i.e., for those exceptional biological assets which are **not** being carried at fair value). The new disclosures are as follows:

1. A separate reconciliation of changes in the carrying amount of those biological assets
2. A description of those biological assets
3. An explanation of why fair value cannot be measured reliably
4. A statement of the range of estimates within which fair value is highly likely to lie (if this is possible to give)
5. The amount of any gain or loss recognized on disposal of the biological assets

6. The depreciation method used
7. The useful lives or the depreciation rates used; and
8. The gross carrying amount and the accumulated depreciation at the beginning and end of the reporting period.

In addition to the foregoing, these disclosures are required

1. If the fair value of biological assets previously measured at cost less any accumulated depreciation and any accumulated impairment losses subsequently becomes reliably measurable, the reporting entity must disclose a description of the biological assets, and explanation of how fair value has become reliably measurable, and the effect of the change in accounting method; and
2. Information about any significant decreases in the expected level of government grants related to agricultural activity covered by IAS 41.

The normally anticipated disclosures regarding the nature of operations, which are necessary to comply with IAS 1, also apply to entities engaging in biological and agricultural operations. These disclosures could incorporate, either in narrative form or as quantified terms, information about the groups of biological assets, the nature of activities regarding each of these groups, the maturity or immaturity for intended purposes of each group, the relative significance of different groups by reference to nonmonetary amounts (e.g., numbers of animals, acres of trees) dedicated to each, and nonfinancial measures or estimates of the physical quantities of each groups of assets at the balance sheet date and the output of agricultural produce during the reporting period.

Good practice, necessary to make the financial statements meaningful for users, would dictate that disclosures be made of the measurement bases used to derive fair values; whether an independent appraiser was utilized; where relevant, the discount rate employed to compute net present values, along with the number of years' future cash flows assumed; additional details about the changes in fair value from the prior period, where needed; any restrictions on title and any pledging of biological assets as security for liabilities; commitments for further development or acquisitions of biological assets; specifics about risk management strategies employed by the entity (note that the use of hedging is widespread; the futures market, now heavily employed to control financial risks, was developed originally for agricultural commodities); and activities which are unsustainable, along with estimated dates of cessation of those activities. Other possible disclosures include the carrying amount of agricultural land (at either historical cost or revalued amount) and of agricultural produce (governed by IAS 2, and subject to separate classification in the balance sheet).

Agricultural Land

Agricultural land is not deemed a biological asset; thus, the principles espoused in IAS 41 for biological and agricultural assets do not apply to land. The requirements of IAS 16, which are applicable to other categories of plant, property, and equipment, apply equally to agricultural land. The use of the allowed alternative method (i.e., revaluation), particularly for land-based systems such as orchards, plantations, and forests, where the fair value of the biological asset was determined from net realizable values which included the underlying land, would be logical and advisable, but is not actually a requirement. It would also enhance the usefulness of the financial statements if land held by entities engaged in agricultural activities is further classified in the balance sheet according to specific uses. Alternatively, this information can be conveyed in the notes to the financial statements.

Intangible Assets Related to Agriculture

Under IAS 38, intangible assets may be carried at cost (the benchmark treatment) or at revalued amounts (the allowed alternative treatment), but only to the extent that active markets exist for the intangibles. In general, it is not expected that such markets will exist for commonly encountered classes of intangible assets. On the other hand, agricultural activities are expected to frequently involve intangibles such as water rights, production quotas, and pollution rights, and it is anticipated that for these intangibles active markets may in fact exist.

To enhance the internal consistency of financial statements of entities engaged in biological and agriculture operations, if intangibles which pertain to the entity's agricultural activities have active markets, these should be presented in the balance sheet at their fair values. This is not, however, an actual requirement.

Government Grants

IAS 20 addresses the accounting for government grants, whether received with conditions attached or not, and whether received in cash or otherwise. As noted above, IAS 41 effectively amends this in the case of reporting by entities an unconditional government grant related to a biological asset measured at its fair value less estimated point-of-sale costs. It also provides that, for grants which are conditional, recognition in income will occur when there is reasonable assurance that the conditions have been met. If conditional grants are received before the conditions have been met, the grant should be recognized as a liability, not as revenue. For grants received in the form of nonmonetary assets, fair value is to be assessed in order to account for the grant. IASB intends to replace or amend IAS 20 (see discussion in Chapter 26).

EXTRACTIVE INDUSTRIES

Sources of IFRS
IFRS 6

DEFINITIONS OF TERMS

Exploration and evaluation assets. Exploration and evaluation expenditures recognized as assets in accordance with the reporting entity's accounting policy.

Exploration and evaluation expenditures. Expenditures incurred by a reporting entity in connection with the exploration for and evaluation of mineral resources, before the technical feasibility and commercial viability of extracting a mineral resource have been demonstrated.

Exploration for and evaluation of mineral resources. The search for mineral recources, including minerals, oil, natural gas, and similar nonregenerative resources after the entity has obtained legal rights to explore in a specific area, as well as the determination of the technical feasibility and commercial viability of extracting the mineral resource.

CONCEPTS, RULES AND EXAMPLES

Background. Before its demise, the IASC had begun to direct its attention to financial reporting needs of specialized industries. Among those deemed worthy of such attention were certain extractive industries, which were seen as having significant financial accounting and reporting issues, and as being disproportionately relevant to the economies of the lesser-developed nations, with which IFRS has historically had the greatest influence. In particular, it had focused on those industries most often operating internationally, thereby exerting significant economic influence worldwide. The accounting and reporting practices by companies in those industries were seen as being unusually diverse, and often varying significantly from those of entities in other types of industries. It was perceived that these conditions would make within-industry and across-industry comparisons difficult for users of the financial statements.

This effort yielded a major Issues Paper in 2000, with the expectation that definitive standards would be promulgated as early as 2002. When the IASB succeeded the IASC, however, this project received reduced attention, with the Improvements Project (which subsequently resulted in over a dozen new or amended standards at year-end 2003) and the Convergence Projects being of greater immediate concern.

In mid-2001 IASB signaled that this project would not take priority on its technical agenda, and by late 2002 it was stated that it would not be feasible to timely complete a comprehensive project for the mass adoption of IFRS by the EU in 2005. Subsequently, in early 2004, IASB asked a group of staff from the national standard setters in Australia, Canada, Norway, and South Africa (each of which have important mining industries) to undertake research that would build on the results of the Issues Paper and the responses that it had generated. The goal is to develop proposals for standard-setting projects; the panel is in the process of being established as of late 2004.

As presently envisioned, the research project will consider all issues associated with accounting for "upstream" extractive activities. Specifically, this will address the treatment of

1. Reserves/resources—which will include determining whether

    a. Reserves/resources can or should be recognized as assets on the balance sheet;
    b. Predevelopment costs incurred following the discovery of reserves/resources should be capitalized or expensed if reserves/resources are not recognized;
    c. Predevelopment costs incurred prior to the discovery of reserves/resources should be capitalized or expensed; and
    d. Reserves/resources information should be disclosed—and if so, what information.

2. Other issues identified in the Issues Paper and implementation issues arising from the application of IFRS by entities conducting extractive activities.

The work plan is for the project team to produce a discussion document, incorporating the IASB's preliminary views regarding accounting for extractive activities, to be published in 2005.

Meanwhile, in early 2004, IASB issued ED 6, which proposed an interim solution, designed to facilitate compliance with IFRS by entities reporting exploration and evaluation assets, without making substantial changes to existing accounting practices. In this regard, ED 6 was similar to IFRS 4, *Insurance Contracts*, discussed later in this chapter. In mid-2005, this culminated with the issuance of IFRS 6, *Exploration for and Evaluation of Mineral Resources*, detailed below.

The reasons cited by IASB for the development of an interim standard addressing exploration for and evaluation of mineral resources were as follows:

1. There are no IFRS that specifically address the exploration for and evaluation of mineral resources, which are excluded from the scope of IAS 38. Furthermore, mineral rights and mineral resources such as oil, natural gas and similar nonregenerative resources are excluded from the scope of IAS 16. Accordingly, a reporting entity having such assets and activities is required to determine accounting policies for such expenditures in accordance with IAS 8.

2. There are alternative views on how the exploration for and evaluation of mineral resources and, particularly, the recognition of exploration and evaluation assets should be accounted for under IFRS.

3. Accounting practices for exploration and evaluation expenditures under various national GAAP standards are diverse and often differ from practices in other sectors for items that may be considered similar (e.g., the accounting practices for research costs under IAS 38).

4. Exploration and evaluation expenditures represent a significant cost to entities engaged in extractive activities.

5. While relatively few entities incurring exploration and evaluation expenditures report under IFRS at present, many more are expected to do so beginning in 2005.

IFRS 6 in Greater Detail

As proposed and then enacted, IFRS 6 sets forth a set of generalized principles that define the main issues for reporting entities that have activities involving the exploration for and evaluation of mineral resources. These principles are as follows:

1. IFRS will fully apply to these entities, except when they are specifically excluded from the scope of a given standard.

2. Reporting entities may continue employing their existing accounting policies to account for exploration and evaluation assets, but any change in accounting will have to qualify under the criteria set forth by IAS 8.

3. A reporting entity that recognizes exploration and evaluation assets will need to assess them for impairment annually, in accordance with IAS 36. However, the entity may conduct the assessment at the level of "a cash-generating unit for exploration and evaluation assets," rather than the level otherwise required by IAS 36. As set forth by IFRS 6, this is a higher level of aggregation than would have been the case under a strict application of the criteria in IAS 36.

Thus, according to IFRS 6, entities that have assets used for exploration and evaluation of mineral resources are to report under IFRS, but certain assets may be subject to alternative measurement requirements. However, adoption of new, specialized requirements will be optional, at least at this time.

Cash-generating units for exploration and evaluation assets. Perhaps the most significant aspect of IFRS 6 concerns its establishment of unique definition of cash-generating units permitted to be used for impairment testing. It has created a different level of aggregation for mineral exploration and evaluation assets, when compared to all other assets subject to impairment considerations under IAS 36. The reason for this distinction, according to the Exposure Draft, is that IASB was concerned that requiring entities to use the standard definition of a cash-generating unit, as set forth by IAS 36, when assessing exploration and evaluation assets for impairment might have negated the effects of the other aspects of the proposal, thereby resulting in the inappropriate recognition of impairment losses under certain circumstances. Specifically, IASB was of the opinion that the standard definition of a cash-generating unit could cause there to be uncertainty about whether the reporting entity's existing accounting policies were consistent with IFRS, because exploration and evaluation assets would often not be expected to

1. Be the subject of future cash inflow and outflow projections relating to the development of the project, on a reasonable and consistent basis, without being heavily discounted because of uncertainty and lead times;

2. Have a determinable net selling price; or
3. Be readily identifiable with other assets that generate cash inflows as a specific cash-generating unit.

In the IASB's view, the implications of the foregoing matters were that an exploration and evaluation asset would often be deemed to be impaired, inappropriately, if the IAS 36 definition of a cash-generating unit was applied without at least the potential for modification.

Given the foregoing concern, in the draft standard the IASB had proposed a unique definition of a cash-generating unit for exploration and evaluation assets. The cash-generating unit for exploration and evaluation assets was to be the cash-generating unit that represents the smallest identifiable group of assets that, together with exploration and evaluation assets, generates cash inflows from continuing use to which impairment tests were applied by the entity under the accounting policies applied for its most recent annual financial statements. The entity would be permitted to elect, under the proposed rules, to apply either the IAS 36 definition of a cash-generating unit, or the special definition above. The election would have to be made when the proposed IFRS was first applied. Beyond the choice of definition of the cash-generating unit, the mechanics of the impairment test itself would be as set forth at IAS 36.

During the development of IFRS 6, IASB expressed concern that the availability of a choice in defining cash generating-units might impair the reliability and relevance of financial statements. To limit this risk, it proposed that a cash-generating unit for exploration and evaluation assets could be no larger than a segment, as defined by IAS 14.

As adopted, IFRS 6 mandates the proposed approach to impairment testing. Specifically, the standard provides that the reporting entity is to determine an accounting policy for allocating exploration and evaluation assets to cash-generating units or groups of cash-generating units for the purpose of assessing those assets for impairment as that need arises. Accordingly, each cash-generating unit or group of units to which an exploration and evaluation asset is allocated is not to be larger than a segment based on either the entity's primary or secondary reporting format, determined in accordance with IAS 14. The level identified by the entity for the purposes of testing exploration and evaluation assets for impairment can comprise one or more cash-generating units.

IFRS 6 provides that exploration and evaluation assets are to be assessed for impairment when facts and circumstances suggest that the carrying amount of an exploration and evaluation asset might exceed the recoverable amount, as with other impairment testing prescribed by IAS 36. When facts and circumstances indicate that the carrying amount might exceed the respective recoverable amount, the reporting entity is required to measure, present, and disclose any resulting impairment loss in accordance with IAS 36, with the exception that the extent of aggregation may be greater than for other assets.

In addition to the criteria set forth in IAS 36, IFRS 6 identifies certain indications that impairment may have occurred regarding the exploration and evaluation assets. It states that one or more of the following facts and circumstances indicate that the reporting entity should test exploration and evaluation assets for impairment:

1. The period for which the entity has the right to explore in the specific area has expired during the period or will expire in the near future, and is not expected to be renewed.
2. Substantive expenditure by the entity on further exploration for and evaluation of mineral resources in the specific area is neither budgeted nor planned.
3. Exploration for and evaluation of mineral resources in the specific area have not resulted in the discovery of commercially viable quantities of mineral resources, and

accordingly the reporting entity decided to discontinue such activities in the specific area.

4. Sufficient data exist to suggest that, although a development in the specific area is likely to proceed, the carrying amount of the exploration and evaluation asset is unlikely to be recovered in full from successful development or by sale.

If testing identifies impairment, the consequent adjustment of carrying amounts to the lower, impaired value results in a charge to current operating results, just as described by IAS 36 (discussed in Chapter 8).

Assets subject to this categorization. IFRS 6 provides a listing of assets that would fall within the definition of exploration and evaluation expenditures, which are identical to what had been earlier proposed. These assets are those that are related to the following activities:

1. Acquisition of rights to explore;
2. Topographical, geological, geochemical, and geophysical studies;
3. Exploratory drilling;
4. Trenching;
5. Sampling; and
6. Activities in relation to evaluating technical feasibility and commercial viability of extracting a mineral resource.

The qualifying expenditures *exclude* those that are incurred in connection with the development of a mineral resource once technical feasibility and commercial viability of extracting a mineral resource have been established, and any administration and other general overhead costs.

Availability of cost or revaluation models. Consistent with IAS 16, IFRS 6 requires initial recognition of exploration and evaluation assets based on actual cost, but subsequent recognition can be effected under either the historical cost model or the revaluation model. The standard does not offer guidance regarding accounting procedures, but it is presumed that those set forth under IAS 16 would be applied (e.g., regarding recognition of impairment and recoveries of previously recognized impairments). (See discussion in Chapter 8.)

Financial statement classification. IFRS 6 provides that the reporting entity is to classify exploration and evaluation assets as tangible or intangible according to the nature of the assets acquired, and apply the classification consistently. It notes that certain exploration and evaluation assets, such as drilling rights, have traditionally been considered intangible assets, while other assets have historically been identified as tangible (such as vehicles and drilling rigs). The standard states that, to the extent that a tangible asset is consumed in developing an intangible asset, the amount reflecting that consumption (that would otherwise be reported as depreciation) becomes part of the cost of the intangible asset. Using a tangible asset to develop an intangible asset, however, does not warrant classifying the tangible asset as an intangible asset.

In the balance sheet, exploration and evaluation assets are to be set forth as a separate class of long-lived assets.

IFRS 6 only addresses exploration and evaluation. It holds that once the technical feasibility and commercial viability of extracting a mineral resource has been demonstrated, exploration and evaluation assets are no longer to be classified as such. At that point, the exploration and evaluation assets are to be assessed for impairment, and any impairment loss recognized, before reclassification as operating or other asset classes.

Disclosure requirements under IFRS 6. A reporting entity is required to disclose information that identifies and explains the amounts recognized in its financial statements that pertain to the exploration for and evaluation of mineral resources. This could be accomplished by disclosing

1. Its accounting policies for exploration and evaluation expenditures, including the recognition of exploration and evaluation assets.
2. The amounts of assets, liabilities, income, and expense (and, if a cash flow statement using the direct method is presented, cash flows) arising from the exploration for and evaluation of mineral resources.

The Exposure Draft also proposed that the mandatory disclosures identify the level at which the entity assesses exploration and evaluation assets for impairment. While this is not set forth in IFRS 6, it is obviously a good practice, and is therefore strongly recommended by the authors.

The IASC Issues Paper

As discussed above, IFRS 6 addresses only a limited range of issues arising in the accounting for entities involved in mineral production. The full scope of the issues to be ultimately addressed can be appreciated from a review of the various preliminary documents produced by IASC/IASB dealing with this important group of financial reporting matters.

The IASC's 2000 Issues Paper directs attention to the upstream activities of mining and petroleum producers, defined as consisting of exploration and production. These exclude "downstream" activities such as refining, marketing, and transportation, which would continue to be governed by other relevant international standards, such as IAS 2 and IAS 16.

It set forth in vast detail the accounting practices found in the mining and petroleum industries, discussing the strengths and weaknesses of each of the alternative methods.

Key issues. The Issues Paper identified a number of key financial reporting issues that must be resolved. These include the following items:

1. Which costs of finding, acquiring, and developing mineral reserves should be capitalized;
2. How capitalized costs should be depreciated (amortized);
3. The extent to which quantities and values of mineral reserves, rather than costs, should impact upon recognition, measurement, and disclosure; and
4. How to define, classify, and measure mineral reserves.

With regard to cost recognition, the two most popular methods, "full costing" and "successful efforts," are seen as representing the two ends of a continuum. Under full cost accounting, all costs incurred in searching for, acquiring, and developing mineral reserves in a large cost center, such as a country or continent, are capitalized as part of the cost of whatever reserves have been found, even though a specific cost was incurred in a failed effort. The underlying theory is that entities in such industries know that many "dry holes" must be drilled (to use the oil exploration industry as an example) to find one producing well, and accordingly are cognizant of the fact that all such costs are actually the necessary costs of developing successful wells. Full cost accounting is used by many midsize to small petroleum enterprises, but rarely has been employed by mining enterprises.

On the other hand, under successful efforts accounting (which is used by most large oil and gas companies and by some mining enterprises), costs that lead directly to finding mineral reserves are capitalized, while costs that do not lead directly to mineral reserves are charged to expense. The concept here is not so much that costs associated with unsuccessful efforts are rightfully charged to current expense, but rather, from a practical perspective, given that many projects are ongoing at any time (which is particularly true for the larger entities), essentially the same result will occur with less complicated accounting, if only costs associated with successful ventures are capitalized and amortized. In other words, the matching objective is met equally well, in these situations, by use of the less burdensome successful efforts method of accounting.

According to the IASC paper, many mining enterprises use an accounting method which lies between the extremes of the full costing and successful efforts methods. Other entities use various hybrid methods, adding to the difficulty of establishing a taxonomy of accounting methods. Imposing a uniform methodology is thus seen as being a pressing need.

A third major approach to cost capitalization is the "area-of-interest" method. According to the IASC paper, some view the area-of-interest concept (sometimes also referred to as the "project method") as a variation on the successful efforts method of accounting, while others see it as a version of full cost accounting applied on an area-of-interest basis. Under the area-of-interest approach, all costs that relate directly to an area of interest or that can be logically allocated to the area of interest are recorded as belonging to that area. That is, prospecting costs, mineral acquisition costs, exploration costs, appraisal costs, and development costs are associated with an individual geological area that has features that are conducive to a coordinated, unified search program and that has been identified as being a favorable environment for the presence of, or known to contain, a mineral deposit. These costs would be accumulated and deferred for each area of interest, to be depreciated as the reserves from that area of interest are produced.

The area-of-interest approach is believed to be fairly commonly employed in the mining industry, although the precise extent of its usage remains under debate. Some studies cited by IASC suggest that this method is the most commonly used way to account for costs— more so than either the successful efforts or full cost methods. Thus, while the area-of-interest approach is not one which is set forth in most textbooks (which typically only cite the successful efforts and full costing approaches), it may have great currency in actual usage.

Probably the other issue which is most important and central to this project is whether financial reporting is to be based on traditional historical costs, or on a fair value approach, driven by estimates of actual mineral reserves on hand and expected final selling prices therefore. The latter approach has been advocated for decades (in the US, the SEC's proposed "reserve recognition accounting," which was ultimately not adopted, was one such attempt). While many coherent arguments can be made for fair value accounting for mineral reserves, persistent questions about reliability (both of quantity estimates and of selling price projections) have ultimately prevented abandonment of historical cost-based methods. However, fair value data has been widely incorporated into supplemental disclosures (such as those required under SEC rules in the US).

Steering Committee's views. The Steering Committee developed tentative views on many of the major issues set out in the Issues Paper. In some cases, these address only the basic issues and do not extend to the subissues associated with a given basic issue. These views are tentative and will be revisited in light of comment letters received, and thus may change markedly as the research continues.

The Steering Committee's tentative views have been summarized as follows in the Issues Paper:

1. An International Accounting Standard on financial reporting in the extractive industries is needed.
2. IASC should develop a single IAS with common standards for both the mining and petroleum industries, but with separate requirements or guidance for mining or petroleum, as necessary, to address industry-specific issues.

3. The IAS should be restricted to upstream activities (exploration for, and development and production of, minerals).

4. Information about reserve quantities and values, and changes in them, is a key indicator of the performance of an extractive industries enterprise.

5. The primary financial statements of an extractive industries enterprise should be based on historical costs, not on estimated reserve values.

6. Information about reserve quantities and values, and changes in them, should be disclosed as supplemental information.

7. The Steering Committee favors adoption of a method of accounting more consistent with the successful efforts concept than with other concepts (such as full costing or area-of-interest accounting).

8. All preacquisition prospecting and exploration costs should be charged to expense when incurred, and not deferred to future periods.

9. All direct and incidental property acquisition costs should be initially recognized as an asset.

10. All postacquisition exploration and appraisal costs should be initially recognized as an asset, pending the determination of whether commercially recoverable reserves have been found.

11. Some limit should be imposed if postacquisition exploration and appraisal costs are deferred, pending determination of whether commercially recoverable reserves have been found.

12. All development costs should be recognized as an asset.

13. Construction costs that relate to a single mineral cost center should be capitalized as part of the capitalized costs of that cost center (normally to be depreciated on a unit-of-production basis if the life of the assets is coincident with the life of the mineral reserves, or on a straight-line basis if the economic life is less than the life of the reserves). Construction costs that relate to more than one mineral cost center should be accounted for in the same way as other property, plant, and equipment under IAS 16, (normally depreciated on a time basis).

14. Postproduction exploration and development costs should be treated in the same way as any other exploration or development costs.

15. Both the benchmark (immediate expensing) and allowed alternative (capitalization and amortization) treatments of borrowing costs contained in IAS 23 should be permitted.

16. Overhead cost should be attributed to the relevant phase of operations (prospecting, acquisition, exploration, valuation, development, and construction) and further identified with a specific prospect, property, or area of interest. The overhead cost should be capitalized if, and only if, the indirect costs of that phase of operations are capitalized for that specific prospect, property, or area of interest.

17. The Steering Committee does not favor cost reinstatement (reversing a prior period expense recognition in a subsequent period in which information becomes available that commercially recoverable reserves have been discovered).

18. Costs should be accumulated by area of interest or geological units smaller than an area of interest (e.g., the field or the mine).

19. Use unit-of-production depreciation for all capitalized preproduction costs with two exceptions

   a. Use straight-line depreciation for capitalized construction costs that serve a single mineral cost center, if the economic life of the asset is less than the life of the reserves, and

b.   Follow IAS 16 for capitalized construction costs that serve two or more cost centers (sometimes called service assets).

20.   Changes in reserve estimates should be reflected prospectively; that is, included in the determination of net profit or loss in the period of the change and future periods, consistent with the requirements of IAS 8.

21.   IAS 37 should be applied without modification to the recognition of removal and restoration costs and obligations in the extractive industries.

22.   If the amount of a provision is part of the cost of acquiring the asset, it is recognized as such and is included in the depreciable amount of the asset.

23.   The cost relating to a provision necessitated by production activities after an asset is installed should be capitalized as an additional cost of acquiring the asset, if the cost provides incremental future economic benefits.

24.   If the cost associated with a provision was initially capitalized, changes in the estimated amount of the provision should be recognized is subsequent periods as an adjustment to the carrying amount of the asset.

25.   IAS 36 should be applied without modification to account for impairments of assets in the extractive industries.

26.   Impairment of capitalized preproduction costs should be assessed based on proved and probable reserves.

27.   An impairment test cannot be applied to deferred preproduction costs whose outcome is unknown. The Steering Committee favors some type of limit if preproduction costs are deferred, pending determination of whether commercially recoverable reserves are found.

28.   The general provisions of IAS 18 should apply to enterprises in the extractive industries, and IAS 18 should be amended to eliminate the scope exclusion.

29.   Revenue received prior to the production phase should be recognized as revenue to other income, not as a reduction of capitalizable costs.

30.   Royalties paid in cash, royalties paid in kind, and severance taxes should all be included in the producer's gross revenue and deducted as an expense.

31.   Inventories of minerals should be measured at historical cost, even if those minerals have quoted market prices in active markets with a short time between production and sale and insignificant costs to be incurred beyond the point of production, and the enterprise intends to sell those minerals in that market.

32.   All members of the Steering Committee favor disclosure of reserve quantities. The Steering Committee is divided regarding disclosure of reserve values, however.

33.   Proved and probable reserves should be disclosed separately, and within proved reserves disclosure should be made separately of proved developed and proved undeveloped reserves.

ACCOUNTING FOR INSURANCE CONTRACTS

Background

Before the IASC ceased existence, it undertook a major project to address the accounting for insurance contracts, a subject that has proven to be challenging for many of the national accounting standard setters as well. The objective of this project was to address only accounting for insurance contracts rather than all the various complex aspects of accounting by insurance companies. The process involved the development of an extensive Issues Paper, which was published in late 1999, a Draft Statement of Principles published in 2001, and the draft pronouncement, ED 5, in mid-2003. The final standard on the portions of the project (what came to be referred to as Phase I) covered in ED 5 was issued in early 2004 as IFRS 4, *Insurance Contracts*. It is effective for periods beginning in 2005, when European adoption of IAS (by publicly held companies) will be required.

IFRS 4 addresses the financial reporting for insurance contracts by any entity that issues these contracts—not merely insurance companies. It applies to insurance contracts issued, reinsurance contracts held, and financial instruments issued with a discretionary participation feature.

The more comprehensive—and thus difficult—Phase II of the IASB's insurance project will address the actual accounting for insurance contracts. This project has been dormant, but with the naming of an advisory group in late 2004 it is expected to receive renewed attention and has been identified as a high-priority project by IASB, with a goal of an Exposure Draft by mid-2005.

In Phase II, the IASB will be attempting to address basic questions regarding model and measurement. It wishes to determine whether a single financial accounting model would be appropriate for all insurance contracts, and what that model should be based upon. For example, alternatives could include direct measurements of assets and liabilities—a balance sheet orientation—or a deferral and matching approach—which would emphasize the income statement and periodic performance assessment. Given the IASB's current concern with revenue recognition issues, this is a fundamental matter that has to be resolved.

Measurement will inevitably raise once again the debate between historical (transaction) costing and fair value accounting. The move toward fair value assessments for financial instruments over the past few years suggests that insurance contracts could reasonably be subjected to a fair value approach as well. Given the complex nature of many insurance contracts (with various embedded guarantees and options), this could prove a daunting task.

The Phase II efforts will also eventually address discounting (which is inconsistently applied throughout IFRS, as it is under various national GAAP, as well), the interaction between asset and liability measurements, risk and service adjustments, accounting for policy acquisition costs, participation rights, and other matters. These issues are noted later in the following discussion.

Sources of IFRS
IFRS 4

Insurance Contracts

An insurance contract is an arrangement under which one party (the insurer) accepts significant insurance risk by agreeing with another party (the policyholder) to compensate the policyholder or other beneficiary if a specified uncertain future event (the insured event) adversely affects the policyholder or other beneficiary (other than an event that is only a change in one or more of a specified interest rate, security price, commodity price, foreign exchange rate, index of prices or rates, a credit rating or credit index, or similar variable—which would continue to be accounted for under IAS 39 as derivative contracts). A contract creates sufficient insurance risk to qualify as an insurance contract only if there is a reasonable possibility that an event affecting the policyholder or other beneficiary will cause a significant change in the present value of the insurer's net cash flows arising from that contract. In considering whether there is a reasonable possibility of such significant change, it is necessary to consider the probability of the event and the magnitude of its effect. Also, a contract that qualifies as an insurance contract at inception or later remains an insurance contract until all rights and obligations are extinguished or expire. If a contract did not qualify as an insurance contract at inception, it should be subsequently reclassified as an insurance contract if, and only if, a significant change in the present value of the insurer's net cash flows becomes a reasonable possibility.

A range of other arrangements, which share certain characteristics with insurance contracts, would be excluded from any imposed insurance contracts accounting standard, since they are dealt with under other IAS. These include financial guarantees (including credit insurance) measured at fair value; product warranties issued directly by a manufacturer, dealer or retailer; employers' assets and liabilities under employee benefit plans (including equity compensation plans); retirement benefit obligations reported by defined benefit retirement plans; contingent consideration payable or receivable in a business combination; and contractual rights or contractual obligations that are contingent on the future use of, or right to use, a nonfinancial item (for example, certain license fees, royalties, lease payments, and similar items).

The standard developed during Phase I of the IASB's insurance project, IFRS 4, applies to all insurance contracts, including reinsurance. Thus, the standard will not relate only to insurance companies, strictly defined. However, it will not apply to other assets and liabilities of issuers of insurance contracts, although other IFRS will apply. Insurance assets and liabilities will be subject to recognition when contractual rights and obligations, respectively, are created under the terms of the contract. When these no longer exist, derecognition will take place.

IFRS 4 does not apply to product warranties issued directly by a manufacturer, dealer or retailer; employers' assets and liabilities under employee benefit plans and retirement benefit obligations reported by defined benefit retirement plans; contractual rights or obligations that are contingent on the future use of or right to use a nonfinancial item, as well as lessee's residual value guarantees on finance leases; financial guarantees entered into or retained on transferring financial assets or financial liabilities within the scope of IAS 39; contingent consideration payable or receivable in a business combination; or direct insurance contracts that an entity holds as a policyholder.

Recognition and Measurement of Insurance Liabilities under IFRS 4

Insurance risk. IFRS 4 sets forth the accounting and financial reporting requirements which will now be applicable to all insurance contracts (including reinsurance contracts) that are issued by the reporting entity, and to reinsurance contracts that the reporting entity holds, except for specified contracts which are covered by other IFRS. IFRS 4 does not apply to other assets and liabilities of an insurer (e.g., financial assets and financial liabilities which are addressed by IAS 39), nor does it address accounting or financial reporting by policyholders. The standard uses the term "insurer" to denote the party accepting liability as an insurer, whether or not the entity is legally or statutorily an insurance company.

IFRS 4 replaces what had been an indirect definition of an insurance contract under IAS 32 with a positive definition based on the transfer of significant insurance risk from the policyholder to the insurer. This definition covers most motor, travel, life, annuity, medical, property, reinsurance, and professional indemnity contracts. Some catastrophe bonds and weather derivatives would also qualify, as long as payments are linked to a specific climatic or other insured future event that would adversely affect the policyholder. On the other hand, policies that transfer no significant insurance risk—such as some savings and pensions plans—will be deemed financial instruments, addressed by IAS 39, regardless of their legal form. IAS 39 also applies to contracts that principally transfer financial risk, such as credit derivatives and some forms of financial reinsurance.

There may be some difficulty in classifying the more complex products (including certain hybrids). To facilitate this process, IASB has explained that insurance risk will be deemed *significant* only if an insured event could cause an insurer to pay significant additional benefits in *any* scenario, apart from a scenario that lacks commercial substance (which in the Exposure Draft preceding IFRS 4 was denoted as a "plausible" event). As a practical matter, reporting entities should compare the cash flows from (1) the occurrence of the insured event against (2) all other events. If the cash flows under the former are significantly larger than under the latter, significant insurance risk is present.

For example, when the insurance benefits payable upon death are significantly larger than the benefits payable upon surrender or maturity, there is significant insurance risk. The significance of the additional benefits is to be measured irrespective of the probability of the insured event, if the scenario has commercial substance. Reporting entities have to develop internal quantitative guidance to ensure the definition is applied consistently throughout the entity. To qualify as significant, the insurance risk also needs to reflect a *preexisting* risk for the policyholder, rather than having arisen from the terms of the contract.

This requirement would specifically exclude from the cash flow comparison features such as waivers of early redemption penalties within investment plans or mortgages in the event of death. Since it is the contract itself that brought the charges into place, the waiver does not represent an additional benefit received for the transfer of a preexisting insurance risk.

The application of this IFRS 4 definition is expected to cause the redesignation of a significant fraction of existing insurance contracts as investment contracts. In other situations, the impact could be the opposite. For example, a requirement to pay benefits **earlier** if an insured event occurs could make a contract insurance; this means that many pure endowment contracts are likely to meet the definition of insurance. All told, insuring entities will need to set clear, consistent, and justifiable contract classification criteria and rigorously apply these.

Adequacy of insurance liabilities. IFRS 4 imposes a *liability adequacy test*, which requires that at each reporting (i.e., balance sheet) date the "insurer" must assess whether its recognized insurance liabilities are adequate, using then-current estimates of future cash flows under the outstanding insurance contracts. If as a result of that assessment it is determined that the carrying (i.e., book) amount of insurance liabilities (less related deferred acquisition costs and related intangible assets, if appropriate—see discussion below) is insufficient given the estimated future cash flows, the full amount of such deficiency must be reported currently in earnings.

The standard defines minimum requirements for the adequacy test that is to be applied to the liability account. These minimum requirements are that

1. The test considers the current estimates of all contractual cash flows, and of such related cash flows as claims handling costs, as well as cash flows that will result from embedded options and guarantees.
2. If the test shows that the liability is inadequate, the entire deficiency is recognized in profit or loss.

In situations where the insuring entity's accounting policies do not require a liability adequacy test, or provides for a test that does not meet the minimum requirements noted above, then the entity is required under IFRS 4 to

1. Determine the carrying amount of the relevant insurance liabilities, less the carrying amount of
   a. Any related deferred acquisition costs; and
   b. Any related intangible assets, such as those acquired in a business combination or portfolio transfer.

2. Determine whether the carrying amount of the relevant net insurance liabilities is less than the carrying amount that would be required if the relevant insurance liabilities were within the scope of IAS 37.

The IAS 37-based amount is the required minimum liability to be presented. Therefore, if the current carrying amount is less, the insuring entity must recognize the entire shortfall in current period earnings. The corresponding credit to this loss recognition will either decrease the carrying amount of the related deferred acquisition costs or related intangible assets or increase the carrying amount of the relevant insurance liabilities, or both, dependent upon the facts and circumstances.

In applying the foregoing procedures, any related reinsurance assets are not considered, because an insuring entity accounts for these separately, as noted later in this discussion.

If an insuring entity's liability adequacy test meets the minimum requirements set forth above, this test is applied at the level of aggregation specified above. On the other hand, if the liability adequacy test does not meet the stipulated minimum requirements, the comparison must instead be made at the level of a portfolio of contracts that are subject to broadly similar risks and which are managed together as a single portfolio.

For purposes of comparing the recorded liability to the amount required under IAS 37, it is acceptable to reflect future investment margins only if the carrying (i.e., book) amount of the liability also reflects those same margins. Future investment margins are defined under IFRS 4 as being employed if the discount rate used reflects the estimated return on the insuring entity's assets, or if the returns on those assets are projected at an estimated rate of return, and discounted at a different rate, with the result included in the measurement of the liability. There is a rebuttable presumption that future investment margins should not be used, however, although exceptions (see below) can exist.

Impairment testing of reinsurance assets. When an insuring entity obtains reinsurance (making it the *cedant*), an asset is created in its financial statements. As with other assets, the reporting entity must consider whether an impairment has occurred as of the reporting (balance sheet) date. Under IFRS 4, a reinsurance asset is impaired only when there is objective evidence that the cedant may not receive all amounts due to it under the terms of the contract, as a consequence of an event that occurred after initial recognition of the reinsurance asset, and furthermore the impact of that event is reliably measurable in terms of the amounts that the cedant will receive from the reinsurer.

When the reinsurance asset is found to be impaired, the carrying value is adjusted downward and a loss is recognized in current period earnings for the full amount.

Selection of accounting principles. IFRS requires certain accounting practices to be adopted with regard to insurance contracts, but also allows other, existing procedures to remain in place under defined conditions. An insuring entity may, under provisions of IFRS 4, change accounting policies for insurance contracts only if such change makes the financial statements more relevant to the economic decision-making needs of users and no less reliable, or more reliable and no less relevant to those needs. Relevance and reliability are to be assessed by applying the criteria set forth in IAS 8.

To justify changing its accounting policies for insurance contracts, an insuring entity must demonstrate that the change brings its financial statements nearer to satisfying the criteria of IAS 8, but the change does not necessarily have to achieve full compliance with those criteria. The standard addresses changes in accounting policies in the context of current interest rates; continuation of existing reporting practices; prudence; future investment margins; and "shadow accounting." These are discussed in the following paragraphs.

Regarding interest rates, IFRS 4 provides that an insuring entity is permitted, although it is not required, to change its accounting policies such that it remeasures designated insurance liabilities to reflect current market interest rates, and recognizes changes in those liabilities in current period earnings. It may also adopt accounting policies that require other current estimates and assumptions for the designated liabilities. IFRS 4 permits an insuring entity to change its accounting policies for designated liabilities, without consistently applying those policies to all similar liabilities, as the requirements under IAS 8 would suggest. If the insuring entity designates liabilities for this policy choice, it must continue to apply current market interest rates consistently in all periods to all these liabilities until they are later eliminated.

An unusual feature of IFRS 4 is that it offers affected reporting entities the option to continue with their existing accounting policies. Specifically, an insuring entity is allowed to continue the following practices if in place prior to the effective date of IFRS 4:

1. Measuring insurance liabilities on an *undiscounted* basis.
2. Measuring contractual rights to future investment management fees at an amount that exceeds their fair value as implied by a comparison with current fees charged by other market participants for similar services. It is likely that the fair value at inception of those contractual rights equals the origination costs paid, unless future investment management fees and related costs are out of line with market comparables.
3. Employing nonuniform accounting policies for the insurance contracts (and related deferred acquisition costs and intangible assets, if any) of subsidiaries, except as permitted by the above-noted interest provision. If those accounting policies are not uniform, the insuring entity may change them if the change does not make the accounting policies more diverse, and also satisfies the other requirements of the standard.

The concept of *prudence*, as set forth in IFRS 4, is meant to excuse an insuring entity from a need to change its accounting policies for insurance contracts in order to eliminate excessive prudence (i.e., conservatism). However, if the insuring entity already measures its insurance contracts with sufficient prudence, it is not permitted to introduce additional prudence following adoption of IFRS 4.

The matter of *future investment margins* requires some explanation. Under IFRS 4 it is clearly preferred that the measurement of insurance contracts should not reflect future investment margins, but the standard does not require reporting entities to change accounting policies for insurance contracts to eliminate future investment margins. On the other hand, adopting a policy that would reflect this is presumed to be improper (the standard states that there is a rebuttable presumption that the financial statements would become less relevant and reliable if an accounting policy that reflects future investment margins in the measurement of insurance contracts is adopted, unless those margins affect the contractual payments). The standard offers two examples of accounting policies that reflect those margins. The first is using a discount rate that reflects the estimated return on the insurer's assets, while the second is projecting the returns on those assets at an estimated rate of return, discounting those projected returns at a different rate and including the result in the measurement of the liability.

IFRS 4 states that the insuring entity could possibly overcome this rebuttable presumption if the other components of a change in accounting policies increase the relevance and reliability of its financial statements sufficiently to outweigh the decrease in relevance and reliability caused by the inclusion of future investment margins. As an example, it cites the situation where the existing accounting policies for insurance contracts involve excessively prudent (i.e., conservative) assumptions set at inception, and a statutory discount rate not directly referenced to market conditions, and ignore some embedded options and guarantees.

This entity might make its financial statements more relevant and no less reliable by switching to a comprehensive investor-oriented basis of accounting that is widely used and involves current estimates and assumptions; a reasonable (but not excessively prudent) adjustment to reflect risk and uncertainty; measurements that reflect both the intrinsic value and time value of embedded options and guarantees; and a current market discount rate, even if that discount rate reflects the estimated return on the insuring entity's assets.

The actual ability to overcome IFRS 4's rebuttable presumption is fact dependent. Thus, in some measurement approaches, the discount rate is used to determine the present value of a future profit margin, which is then attributed to different periods using a formula. In such approaches, the discount rate affects the measurement of the liability only indirectly, and the use of a less appropriate discount rate has a limited or no effect on the measurement of the liability at inception. In yet other approaches, the discount rate determines the measurement of the liability directly, and because the introduction of an asset-based discount rate has a more significant effect, it is highly unlikely that an insurer could overcome the rebuttable presumption noted above.

Finally, there is the matter of *shadow accounting*. According to IFRS 4, an insurer is permitted, but not required, to change its accounting policies so that a recognized but unrealized gain or loss on an asset affects those measurements in the same way that a realized gain or loss does. This is because, under some accounting models, realized gains or losses on an insurer's assets have a direct effect on the measurement of some or all of (1) its insurance liabilities, (2) related deferred acquisition costs, and (3) related intangible assets. IFRS 4 provides that the related adjustment to the insurance liability (or deferred acquisition costs or intangible assets) may be recognized in equity if, and only if, the unrealized gains or losses are recognized directly in equity.

Unbundling. Specific requirements pertain to *unbundling* of elements of insurance contracts, and dealing with embedded derivatives, options and guarantees.

Unbundling refers to the accounting for components of a contract as if they were separate contracts. Some insurance contracts consist of an insurance component and a deposit component. IFRS 4 in some cases requires the reporting entity to unbundle those components, and in other fact situations provides the entity with the option of unbundled accounting. Specifically, unbundling is *required* if both the following conditions are met:

1. The insuring entity can measure the deposit component (inclusive of any embedded surrender options) separately, *and*
2. The insuring entity's accounting policies do not otherwise require it to recognize all obligations and rights arising from the deposit component.

On the other hand, unbundling is permitted, but not required, if the insuring entity can measure the deposit component separately but its accounting policies require it to recognize all obligations and rights arising from the deposit component, regardless of the basis used to measure those rights and obligations.

Unbundling is actually prohibited if an insuring entity cannot measure the deposit component separately.

If unbundling is applied to a contract, the insuring entity applies IFRS 4 to the insurance component of the contract, while using IAS 39 to account for the deposit component of that contract.

Recognition and measurement. IFRS 4 prohibits the recognition of a liability for any provisions for possible future claims, if those claims arise under insurance contracts that are not in existence at the reporting date. Catastrophe and equalization provisions are thus prohibited, because they do not reflect loss events that have already occurred and, therefore, recognition would be inconsistent with IAS 37. Loss recognition testing is required for losses already incurred at each balance sheet date, as described above. An insurance liability (or a part of an insurance liability) is to be removed from the balance sheet only when it is extinguished (i.e., when the obligation specified in the contract is discharged or canceled or expires).

In terms of display, offsetting of reinsurance assets against the related insurance liabilities is prohibited, as is offsetting of income or expense from reinsurance contracts against the expense or income from the related insurance contracts.

Discretionary participation features in insurance contracts. Insurance contracts sometimes contain a discretionary participation feature, as well as a guaranteed element. (That is, some portion of the return to be accrued to policyholders is at the discretion of the insuring entity.) Under the provisions of IFRS 4, the issuer of such a contract may, but is not required to, recognize the guaranteed element separately from the discretionary participation feature. If the issuer does not recognize them separately, it must classify the entire contract as a liability. If, on the other hand, the issuer classifies them separately, it will classify the guaranteed element as a liability. If the entity recognizes the discretionary participation feature separately from the guaranteed element, the discretionary participation feature can be classified either as a liability or as a separate component of equity; the standard does not specify how the decision should be reached. In fact, the issuer may even split that feature into liability and equity components, if a consistent accounting policy is used to determine that split.

When there is a discretionary participation feature which is reported in equity, the reporting entity is permitted to recognize all premiums received as revenue, without separating any portion that relates to the equity component. Changes in the guaranteed element and in the portion of the discretionary participation feature classified as a liability are to be reported in earnings, while changes in the part of the discretionary participation feature classified as equity are to be accounted for as an allocation of earnings, similar to how minority interest is reported.

If the contract contains an embedded derivative within the scope of IAS 39, that standard must be applied to that embedded derivative.

Disclosure. Under the provisions of IFRS 4, insuring entities must disclose information that identifies and explains the amounts in its financial statements arising from insurance contracts. This is accomplished by disclosure of accounting policies for insurance contracts and related assets, liabilities, income and expense; of recognized assets, liabilities, income and expense (and, if it presents its cash flow statement using the direct method, cash flows) arising from insurance contracts. Additionally, if the insuring entity is a cedant, it must also disclose gains and losses recognized in profit or loss on buying reinsurance; and, if the cedant defers and amortizes gains and losses arising on buying reinsurance, the amortization for the period and the amounts remaining unamortized at the beginning and end of the period.

Disclosure is also required of the process used to determine the assumptions that have the greatest effect on the measurement of the recognized amounts described above. When practicable, quantified disclosure of those assumptions is to be presented as well. The effect of changes in assumptions used to measure insurance assets and insurance liabilities is required, reporting separately the effect of each change that has a material effect on the financial statements.

Finally, reconciliation of changes in insurance liabilities, reinsurance assets and, if any, related deferred acquisition costs are mandated by IFRS 4.

Regarding the amount, timing and uncertainty of cash flows, the entity is required to disclose information that helps users to understand these matters as they result from insurance contracts. This is accomplished if the insuring entity discloses its objectives in managing risks arising from insurance contracts and its policies for mitigating those risks.

Phase II of the IASB Insurance Project

The bulk of the materials contained in the DSOP on insurance, issued by the IASC in 2001 will, if endorsed by IASB, become part of the standard(s) to be developed in Phase II of the Insurance Project. IASB is currently anticipating the production of an Exposure Draft in 2005; the timetable for the promulgation of a final standard has not yet been established. However, it is expected that a new standard would have an effective date for year-ends after 2005. While it is far too early to surmise what conclusions may ultimately be reached, the major issues set forth in the DSOP will be summarized.

The 2001 DSOP had proposed that while IAS 39 remains in place, insurance liabilities and insurance assets should be measured at entity-specific value. *Entity-specific value* would represent the value of an asset or liability to the enterprise that holds it, and could reflect factors that are not available (or not relevant) to other market participants. In particular, the entity-specific value of an insurance liability is the present value of the costs that the enterprise will incur in settling the liability with policyholders or other beneficiaries in accordance with its contractual terms over the life of the liability.

The DSOP concluded that when (and if) a successor standard to IAS 39 introduces fair value measurement for the substantial majority of financial assets and liabilities, IASB should consider introducing fair value measurement for all insurance liabilities and insurance assets. Fair value is the amount for which an asset could be exchanged or a liability settled between knowledgeable, willing parties in an arm's-length transaction. In particular, the fair value of a liability is the amount that the enterprise would have to pay a third party at the balance sheet date to take over the liability.

IASB reportedly favors an asset and liability model that requires an entity to identify and measure directly individual assets and liabilities arising from insurance contracts rather than deferrals of inflows and outflows. Under that model, insurance contract assets and liabilities would be measured at fair value (which involves discounting), except that entity-specific assumptions and information could still be used to determine fair value if market-based information were not available; and the estimated fair value of an insurance liability could be no less than the entity would charge to accept new contracts with identical terms and remaining term from new policyholders.

The move to a pure fair value model for financial instruments, long advocated, has been vehemently opposed by certain segments (such as banking), and thus it is problematic whether this can be adopted in the near or intermediate term. Pending resolution of the fair value accounting issue, the IASB has largely focused its attention at insurance contract accounting matters that transcend this concern. It has considered whether the starting point for measuring insurance assets and insurance liabilities should be the expected present value of all future preincome tax cash flows arising from the contractual rights and contractual obligations associated with the closed book of insurance contracts.

Also addressed was whether cash flows arising from the contractual rights and obligations associated with the closed book of insurance contracts should include cash flows from future renewals only to the extent that their inclusion would increase the measurement of the insurer's liability, or alternatively to the extent that policyholders hold uncancelable renewal options that are potentially valuable to them. (A renewal option is potentially valuable only if there is a reasonable possibility that it will significantly constrain the insurer's ability to reprice the contract at rates that would apply for new policyholders who have similar characteristics to the holder of the option.) No decisions have been made on these issues.

The IASB did, however, conclude as working hypotheses that, in determining entity-specific value, each cash flow scenario used to determine expect presented value should be based on reasonable, supportable, and explicit assumptions that reflect all the future events, including statutory and technological changes, that may affect future cash flows from the closed book of existing insurance contracts included in the scenario. Inflation is addressed by estimating discount rates and cash flows both consistently in either real or in nominal terms. All entity-specific future cash flows that would arise in that scenario for the current insurer must be included, even cash flows that would not arise for other market participants if they took over the current insurer's rights and obligations under the insurance contract.

However, future cash flows for the following items would not be included in determining the expected present value of future pretax cash flows arising from the closed book of insurance contracts: income tax payments and receipts; cash flows arising from future insurance contracts; payment to and from reinsurers; investment returns from current or future investments (except for certain performance-linked contracts); and cash flows between different components of the reporting entity.

Furthermore, market assumptions would need to be consistent with current market prices and other market derived data, unless there is reliable and well-documented evidence that current market experience trends will not continue. This evidence would exist only if a single objectively identifiable event causes severe and short-lived disruption to market prices, in which case the assumptions would be based on this reliable evidence. Nonmarket assumptions would have to be consistent with the just-noted market assumptions, and with the most recent financial budgets and forecasts that have been approved by management. If budgets and forecasts are not current and not intended as neutral estimates of future events, the insurer would need to adjust those assumptions. If the budgets and forecasts are deterministic, rather than stochastic (i.e., based on probability distributions on the occurrence of future events), the entire package of scenarios should be consistent with the budgets and forecasts.

IASB concluded that if fair value were not observable directly in the market, it would have to be estimated as just stated, except that it would not reflect entity-specific future cash flows that would arise for other market participants if they took over the current insurer's rights and obligations under the insurance contract, and any contrary data indicating that market participants would not use the same assumptions as the insurer, fair value would have to reflect that market information.

It was decided that the entity-specific value of an insurance liability should not reflect the insurer's own credit standing. This decision was taken not because of any conceptual disagreement, but rather because this raises wider issues that will be dealt with in a separate context.

Another tentative conclusion was that until rights to recoveries qualify for recognition as an asset, the insurer should include potential recoveries from salvage and subrogation in estimated future cash flows from existing insurance contracts and not recognize those rights as separate assets. The rights would qualify as an asset only when

1. The insurer controls those rights as a result of past events,
2. It is probable that the economic benefits associated with those rights will flow to the insurer, and
3. The insurer can measure those rights reliably.

An insurer would then measure those rights at entity-specific values if insurance liabilities are measured at entity-specific value, and at fair values if insurance liabilities are measured at fair value (which has yet to be resolved).

Either the entity-specific or the fair value of insurance liabilities and assets would have to reflect risk and uncertainty—preferably in the cash flows, or alternatively in the discount rate(s), which are mutually exclusive techniques. Estimates under either approach would reflect the market's risk preferences, inferred from observable market data, using consistent methodology over time. Changes in the inferred level of risk preferences would be made only in response to observable market data. The risk of changes in exchange rates would only be taken into account when future cash inflows and outflows are denominated in more than a single currency.

Several tentative decisions were made regarding the discount rate to be applied to projected future cash flows. The starting point for determining the discount rate for insurance liabilities and insurance assets would be the pretax market yield at the balance sheet date on risk-free assets. It would be adjusted to reflect risks not reflected in the cash flows from the insurance contracts. The currency and timing of the cash flows from the risk-free assets— those having readily observable market prices whose cash flows are least variable for a given maturity and currency—would be consistent with the currency and timing of the cash flows from the insurance contracts. Estimated cash flows in foreign currency are discounted using the appropriate discount rate for the foreign currency, with the resulting present value being translated into the measurement currency using the spot rate at the reporting date. Special rules would apply to reinsurance situations.

A reinsurance contract would be defined as an insurance contract issued by one insurer (the reinsurer) to indemnify another insurer (the cedant) against losses on an insurance contract issued by the cedant. Reinsurers and cedants would have to apply all the recognition, derecognition and measurement requirements in the principles set forth in the DSOP to all reinsurance contracts. If a reinsurance transaction would not qualify for derecognition of the related direct insurance liability, a cedant should present: an insurance asset arising under reinsurance contracts as an asset, not as a deduction from the related direct insurance liability; and reinsurance premiums as an expense and the reinsurer's share of claim expense as income.

IASB concluded that policyholders would measure contractual rights and obligations as follows:

1. Prepaid insurance premiums at amortized cost, adjusted for any impairment or uncollectibility;
2. Virtually certain reimbursements of expenditures required to settle a recognized provision at the present value of the reimbursement but not more than the amount of the recognized provision; and
3. Valid claims for an insured event that has already occurred at the present value of the expected future receipts under the claim, but if it is not virtually certain that the insurer will accept the claim, the claim is a contingent asset and would, under IAS 37, not be recognized as an asset.

The 2001 DSOP argued that insurers should be required to account for investment property at fair value, plant assets at revalued amounts, and deferred tax assets and liabilities at discounted values, but the IASB rejected these positions and will not prohibit accounting for investment property at cost and plant assets at amortized cost. It will not endorse the discounting of deferred tax assets and liabilities (prohibited by IAS 12) at this time. Certain of the illustrations in the DSOP were found objectionable and accordingly will not be included in the final standard.

IASB may continue its discussion on several key topics, including

1. Whether the measurement objective for insurance contracts should be measured at entity-specific value, fair value, or some other basis;

2. The possible implications of the proposed approach for other long-term contracts such as investment management contracts, bank core deposits, credit card receivables, prepayable mortgages, mortgage servicing rights, construction contracts, long-term supply contracts, and customer loyalty programs;

3. The criteria that should be used to determine when it is appropriate to include the additional cash flows;

4. The possible implications of this approach for the recognition of gains at the inception of an insurance contract; and

5. Whether an insurer should report, as a separate asset or as a reduction of the liability, the debit that could result from the expected present value (probability-weighted and risk-adjusted) of the additional cash flows.

Two alternative performance reporting models are under consideration by IASB for insurance enterprises. The traditional insurance reporting model separates underwriting and investing and financing activities, while the alternative reporting model developed by the Insurance Steering Committee would report three components of performance: profit or loss from new business, ongoing profit or loss from prior years' business, and profit or loss from investing and financing activities

The two approaches are illustrated as follows:

Income statement: Traditional insurance reporting model

Premiums earned	xxx
Claims incurred	(xxx)
Amortization of acquisition costs	(xxx)
Maintenance costs	xxx
Profit (loss)—underwriting business	xxx
Investing and financing activities:	
Investment income	xxx
Net profit (loss)	xxx

Income statement: Steering Committee reporting model

New business—new policyholders:	
EPV of premiums	xxx
EPV of claims	(xxx)
Provision for risk and uncertainty	xxx
EPV of maintenance costs	(xxx)
Acquisition costs	(xxx)
Profit (loss)—new business	xxx
Previous years' business:	
Changes in estimates/assumptions	xxx
Release of risk	xxx
Change in adjustment for risk and uncertainty	xxx
Profit (loss)—insurance business	xxx
Investing and financing activities:	
Unwinding of discount—insurance provisions	(xxx)
Effect of changes in discount rate	xxx
Return on investments	xxx
Profit (loss)—investing and financing activities	xxx
Net profit (loss)	xxx

The alternative approaches to performance reporting differ not only in presentation format but—more fundamentally—with respect to when profit or loss from insurance contracts should be recognized. The traditional model is a deferral and matching approach. The Steering Committee proposal is to recognize more profit or loss at the time the contract is entered into. Reportedly, IASB has made no tentative decisions on this fundamental question.

25 INFLATION AND HYPERINFLATION

PERSPECTIVE AND ISSUES

While the use of fair value as a measurement attribute for purposes of financial statement display has become increasingly popular in recent years, accounting principles—both national GAAP and IFRS—still remain largely grounded in historical costing. In periods of price stability, this does not do much of a disservice to understanding the reporting entity's financial position and results of operations. However, in times of price instability—or, in the case of long-lived assets, even in periods of modest changes in prices over long stretches of time—financial reporting can be distorted. Over many decades, a wide variety of solutions to this problem have been proposed, and, in certain periods of rampant inflation, some of these have even been put into practice. The now-withdrawn international standard, IAS 15, was one such attempt to neutralize the effects of changing prices on the financial statements.

Popular interest in alternative techniques of inflation accounting (as the various methods are all called) declined markedly once price stability was restored since the highly inflationary years of the 1970s and early 1980s. Most of the financial reporting standards adopted (including those in the US, the UK, and under IFRS) have either been revoked, made optional, or fallen into broad disuse during this time. As part of the IASB's Improvements Project, IAS 15, the standard on inflation accounting, compliance with which was reduced to voluntary status over a decade ago, was officially withdrawn, effective 2005.

While the standard has been withdrawn, it does remain on record as one highly evolved set of guidance that entities can utilize should the decision be made to present supplementary financial statements on a basis which removes the effects of cost changes. For reporting entities electing to present inflation adjusted financial statements, this will continue to be pertinent guidance. Thus, although presentation of inflation adjusted financial statements is no longer required, for entities choosing to present such financial data, this guidance continues to be pertinent.

IAS 29, which has *not* been withdrawn, addresses financial reporting in hyperinflationary economies. While, in general, this applies the same principles as are employed in general price level accounting, the objective is to convert the financial statements of entities operating under conditions which render unadjusted financial statement of little or no value into meaningful measures of position and performance. Fortunately, over recent years there have been very few nations suffering from hyperinflation (certain South American nations are the major exception), but as with more moderate inflationary cycles, these have hardly disappeared from the economic horizon. Since there is some current need for this guidance, and the possibility of more need over time, this will also be explained in some detail in the present chapter. It should be noted that the withdrawal of IAS 15 had no bearing on the status of IAS 29.

Sources of IFRS
IAS 29

DEFINITIONS OF TERMS

Common dollar reporting. Synonymous with general price level or constant dollar financial reporting.

Constant dollar accounting. An accounting model that treats dollars of varying degrees of purchasing power essentially in the manner that foreign currencies are treated; dollars are translated into current purchasing power units and presented in restated financial statements. Constant dollar accounting converts all nonmonetary assets and equities from historical to current dollars by applying an index of general purchasing power. Specific value changes are ignored, and thus there are no holding gains or losses recognized. Monetary items are brought forward without adjustment, and these accounts (cash, claims to fixed amounts of cash, and obligations to pay fixed amounts of cash) therefore do give rise to purchasing power gains or losses. Constant dollar accounting does not attempt to address value changes.

Current cost accounting. An accounting model that attempts to measure economic values and changes therein, whether or not realized in the traditional accounting sense. In current cost accounting financial statements, nonmonetary items are reflected at current value amounts, measured variously by replacement cost, exit value, fair market value, net present value, or by other methodologies. Current cost based statements of earnings will report as operating income the amount of resources that are available for distribution (to shareholders and others) without impairing the entity's ability to replace assets as they are sold or consumed in the operation of the business. Holding gains may or may not also be reportable as a component of income, although these are never deemed to be distributable unless the entity is liquidating itself. In a pure current cost accounting system, no purchasing power gains or losses are given recognition, but hybrid models have been proposed under US GAAP and IAS, which do recognize these as well as specific price changes.

Distributable (replicatable) earnings. The amount of resources that could be distributed (e.g., by dividends to shareholders) from the current period's earnings without impairing the entity's operating capacity vs. its level at the beginning of the period. This parallels the classic definition of economic income. It is generally conceded that current cost would provide the best measure of distributable earnings. Traditional historical cost based financial reporting, on the other hand, does not attempt to measure economic income, but rather, seeks to match actual costs incurred against revenues generated; the result in many cases is that this measure of income will exceed real economic earnings.

Economic value. The ideal measure of current value/current cost; also known as deprival value. In practice, surrogate measures are often used instead.

Excess of specific price changes over general price level increase. A measure first introduced by the US GAAP standard on inflation accounting (FAS 33) and usable under IAS 15 as well. This is the amount of increase in current cost of inventories and plant assets, in excess of the increase that would have occurred during the period had the change in values been at the rate of change of a broad-based market basket of goods and services.

Exit value. Also known as net realizable value, this is the measure of the resources that could be obtained by disposing of a specified asset, often for scrap or salvage value. Valuing assets at exit value is not generally valid as a measure of current cost, since value in use usually exceeds exit value, and most assets held by the enterprise will not be disposed of; however, for assets that are not to be replaced in the normal course of business, exit value may be a meaningful measure.

Fair value. Fair market value, or market value. For certain specialized properties, such as natural resources, this may be the most meaningful measure of current cost.

Fair value accounting. A now obsolete term which implies current cost or current value financial reporting.

Gains/losses on net monetary items. Synonymous with general purchasing power gains and losses.

Gearing adjustment. A term used in the proposed British inflation accounting standard, which reflects the conclusion that if an entity is financed externally (i.e., by debt), it may not need to retain resources in an amount equal to the replacement cost of goods sold and of depreciation in order to maintain existing productive capacity; sufficient borrowed funds must, however, continue to be available so that the existing degree of financial leverage (gearing) can be maintained in the future. This adjustment was not addressed by IAS 15.

Holding gains/losses. In general, the increase or decrease in the current cost of nonmonetary assets (plant assets and inventories, for the most part) during a period. Notwithstanding the gain/loss terminology, such items are not generally recognized as part of income but rather as part of stockholders' equity, although practice varies. Holding gains are not distributable to shareholders without impairing operating capacity. In some models, only the excess of specific price changes over general price level changes are deemed to be holding gains/losses.

Hyperinflation. The condition in an economy in which there is such extreme inflation that historical cost financial statements become meaningless; characterized by a general aversion of the population to holding monetary assets, the conducting of business in ways that provide some protection against inflation, such as denominating transactions in a stable foreign currency or indexing to compensate for price changes, and a cumulative inflation rate over three years approaching 100%.

Inventory profits. The overstatement of income resulting from charging cost of sales at historical levels instead of at replacement costs; during periods of rapid inflation, historical cost based income will exceed real, economic earnings (distributable or replicatable earnings); this is partly the result of inventory profits. Not all entities are affected similarly. Those using LIFO costing will be less severely affected, and entities having faster inventory turnover will also have less inventory profits.

Monetary items. Claims to, or obligations to pay, fixed sums of cash or its equivalent. Examples are accounts receivable and accounts payable. If constant dollar accounting is employed, net monetary assets or liabilities will create purchasing power gains or losses in periods of changing general prices, since such fixed claims to cash or obligations to pay cash gain or lose value as the general purchasing power of the currency grows or shrinks.

Net present value. The future cash flows that will be generated by operation of an asset, discounted by a relevant factor such as the opportunity cost of capital, to an equivalent present value amount. This is a surrogate measure for economic value (deprival value) that is useful in certain circumstances (e.g., determining the future net cash flow of income producing real estate). For other assets, such as machinery, this is difficult to compute because future cash flows are difficult to forecast and because the assets are part of integrated processes generating cash flows that cannot be attributed to each component.

Net realizable value. Generally used in accounting to denote the amount that could be realized from an immediate disposition of an asset; also known as exit value. Net realizable value is sometimes used for current costing purposes if the asset in question is not intended to be held beyond a brief period.

Nonmonetary items. Items that are not claims to, or obligations to pay fixed sums of cash or its equivalent. Examples are inventories and plant assets. When constant dollar accounting is employed, all nonmonetary items are adjusted to current dollar equivalents by application of a general measure of purchasing power changes. If current cost accounting is employed, nonmonetary items are recorded at current economic values (measured by replacement cost, deprival value, etc.); nonmonetary equity accounts may be explicitly adjusted or the necessary balancing amounts can be imputed. Holding gains and losses result from applying current cost measures to nonmonetary items.

Price level accounting. See constant dollar accounting.

Purchasing power accounting. See constant dollar accounting.

Purchasing power gains/losses. The economic benefit or detriment that results when an entity has claims to fixed amounts of cash (monetary assets) or has obligations to pay fixed sums (monetary liabilities) during periods when the general purchasing power of the monetary unit is changing. An excess of monetary assets over monetary liabilities coupled with rising prices results in a purchasing power loss; an excess of monetary liabilities results in a gain. These are reversed if prices are declining.

Realized holding gains/losses. Holding gains/losses can be realized or unrealized. If an appreciated item of inventory is sold, the holding gain is realized; if unsold at period end, it is unrealized. Historical cost based accounting does not recognize unrealized holding gains/losses (with some exceptions), and realized holding gains/losses are merged with other operating income and not given separate recognition. Use of the term holding gain/loss was prohibited by the US GAAP inflation accounting standard and was not addressed by the now-withdrawn IAS 15.

Recoverable amount. The amount that could be obtained either from the continued use of an asset (the net present value of future cash flows) or from its disposal (exit or net realizable value).

Replacement cost. The lowest cost that would be incurred to replace the service potential of an asset in the normal course of the business.

Replicatable earnings. See distributable earnings.

Reproduction cost. The cost of acquiring an asset identical to the one presently in use. The distinction between reproduction cost and replacement cost is that operating efficiencies and technological changes may have occurred and the nominally identical asset would have a different productive capacity. Typically, replacement costs are lower than reproduction costs, and use of the latter would tend to overstate the effects of inflation.

Unrealized holding gains/losses. Holding gains or losses that have yet to be realized through an arm's-length transaction.

Value in use. Also known as value to the business, this is defined as the lesser of current cost or net recoverable amount.

INFLATION ADJUSTED FINANCIAL REPORTING

CONCEPTS, RULES, AND EXAMPLES

Historical Review of Inflation Accounting

Accounting practice today, on virtually a worldwide basis, relies heavily on the historical cost measurement strategy, whereby resources and obligations are given recognition as assets and liabilities, respectively, at the original (dollar, yen, etc.) amount of the transaction from which they arose. Once recorded, these amounts are not altered to reflect changes in value, except to the limited extent that various national GAAP standards or IFRS require recognition of impairments (e.g., lower of cost or fair value for inventories, etc.). Most long-lived assets such as buildings are amortized against earnings on a rational basis over their estimated useful lives, while short-lived assets are expensed as physically consumed. Liabilities are maintained at cost until paid off or otherwise discharged.

It is useful to recall that before the historical cost model of financial reporting achieved nearly universal adoption, various alternative recognition and measurement approaches were experimented with. Fair value accounting was in fact widely employed in the nineteenth and early twentieth centuries, and for some regulatory purposes (especially in setting utility service prices, where regulated by governmental agencies) remained in vogue until somewhat more recently. The retreat from fair value accounting was, in fact, due less to any inherent attractiveness of the historical cost model than to negative reaction to abuses in fair value reporting. This came to a climax during the 1920s in much of the industrialized world, when prosperity and inflation encouraged overly optimistic reflections of values, much of which were reversed after the onset of the worldwide Great Depression.

Most of what are known as generally accepted accounting principles (GAAP) were developed after the crash of 1929. The more important of the basic postulates, which underlie most of the historical cost accounting principles, include the realization concept, the stable currency assumption, the matching concept, conservatism (or prudence), and historical costing. Realization means that earnings are not recognized until a definitive event, involving an arm's-length transaction in most instances, has occurred. Stable currency refers to the presumption that a €1,000 machine purchased today is about the same as a €1,000 machine purchased twenty years ago, in terms of real productive capacity. The matching concept has come to suggest a quasi-mechanical relationship between costs incurred in prior periods and the revenues generated currently as a result; the net of these is deemed to define earnings. Conservatism, among other things, implies that all losses be provided for but that gains not be anticipated, and is often used as an argument against fair value accounting. Finally, the historical costing convention was adopted as the most objectively verifiable means of reporting economic events.

The confluence of these underlying postulates has served to make historical cost based accounting, as it has been practiced for the past sixty years, widely supported. Even periods of rampant inflation, as the Western industrialized nations experienced during the 1970s, has not seriously diminished enthusiasm for this model, despite much academic research and the fairly sophisticated and complete alternative financial reporting approaches proposed in the United Kingdom and the United States and a later international accounting standard that built on those two recommendations. All of these failed to generate wide support and have largely been abandoned, being relegated to suggested supplementary information status, with which very few reporting enterprises comply.

What should accounting measure? Accounting was invented to measure economic activity in order to facilitate it. It is an information system, the product of which is used by one or more groups of decision makers: managers, lenders, investors, even current and prospective employees. In common with other types of decision-relevant data, financial statements can be evaluated along a number of dimensions, of which relevance and objectivity are frequently noted as being the most valuable. Information measured or reported by accounting systems should be, on the one hand, objective in the sense that independent observers will closely agree that the information is correct, and on the other hand, the information should be computed and reported in such as way that its utility for decision makers is enhanced.

Objectivity has become what one critic called an occupational distortion of the accounting profession. While objectivity connotes a basic attitude of unprejudiced fairness that should be highly prized, it has also come to denote an excessive reliance on completed cash transactions as a basis for recording economic phenomena. However, objectivity at the cost of diminished relevance may not be a valid goal. It has been noted that "relevance is the more basic of the virtues; while a relevant valuation may sometimes be wrong, an irrelevant one can never be of use, no matter how objectively it is reached." Both the FASB in the United States and the IASB in the international arena have published conceptual framework documents which support the notion that more relevant information, even if necessitating a departure from the historical costing tradition, could be more valuable to users of financial statements.

Why inflation undermines historical cost financial reporting. Actual and would-be investors and creditors, as well as entity managers and others, desire accounting information to support their decision-making needs. Financial statements that ignore the effects of general price level changes as well as changes in specific prices are inadequate for several reasons.

1. Reported profits often exceed the earnings that could be distributed to shareholders without impairing the entity's ability to maintain the present level of operations, because inventory profits are included in earnings and because depreciation charges are not adequate to provide for asset replacements.
2. Balance sheets fail to reflect the economic value of the business, because plant assets and inventories, especially, are recorded at historical values which may be lower than current fair values or replacement costs.
3. Future earnings prospects are not easily projected from historical cost based earnings reports.
4. The impact of changes in the general price level on monetary assets and liabilities is not revealed, yet can be severe.
5. Because of the foregoing deficiencies, future capital needs are difficult to forecast, and in fact may contribute to the growing leveraging (borrowing) by many enterprises, which adds to their riskiness.
6. Distortions of real economic performance lead to social and political consequences ranging from suboptimal capital allocations to ill-conceived tax policies and public perceptions of corporate behavior.

Example

A business starts with one unit of inventory, which cost €2 and which at the end of the period is sold for €10 at a time when it would cost €7 to replace that very same unit on the display shelf. Traditional accounting would measure the earnings of the entity at €10 − €2 = €8, although clearly the business is only €3 "better off" at the end of the period than at the beginning, since real economic resources have only grown by €3 (after replacing the unit sold there is only that amount of extra resource available). The illusion that there was profit of €8 could readily destroy the entity if, for example, dividends of more than €3 were withdrawn or if fiscal policy led to taxes of more than €3 on the €8 profit.

On the other hand, if the financial report showed only €3 profit for the period, there could be several salutary effects. Owners' expectations for dividends would be tempered, the entity's real capital would more likely be preserved, and projections of future performance would be more accurate, although projections must always be fine-tuned since the past will never be replicated precisely.

The failure of the historical cost balance sheet to reflect values is yet another major deficiency of traditional financial reporting. True, accounting was never intended to report values per se, but the excess of assets over liabilities has always been denoted as net worth, and to many that clearly connotes value. Similarly, the alternative titles for the balance sheet, statement of financial position and statement of financial condition, strongly suggest value to the lay reader. The confusion largely stems from a failure to distinguish *realized* from *unrealized* value changes; if this distinction were carefully maintained, the balance sheet could be made more useful while remaining true to its traditions.

Evolving use of the financial statements. The traditional balance sheet was the primary, even the only, financial statement presented during much of accounting's history. However, beginning during the 1960s, the income statement achieved greater importance, partly because users came to realize that the balance sheet had become the repository for unmatched costs, deferred debits and credits, and other items that bore no relationship to real economic assets and obligations. In the aggressive and high-growth 1960s and early 1970s, the focus was largely on summary measures of enterprise performance, such as earnings per share, which derived from the income statement. During this era, the matching concept became the key underlying postulate that drove new accounting rules.

As a result of a series of unpleasant economic events, including numerous credit crunches and recessions in the 1970s and 1980s, the focus substantially shifted back to the balance sheet. Partly in response, the major accounting standard-setting bodies developed conceptual standards that urged the elimination of some of the items previously found on balance sheets that were not really either assets or liabilities. Some of these were the leftovers from double entry bookkeeping, which was oriented toward achieving income statement goals; an example is the interperiod tax allocations that resulted in the reporting of ever-growing deferred tax liabilities that were never going to be paid. While the tension between achieving a meaningful balance sheet and an accurate income statement is inherent in the accounting model in use for almost 500 years, accountants are learning that improvements in both can be achieved. Inflation adjusted accounting can contribute to this effort, as will be demonstrated.

General vs. specific price changes. An important distinction to be understood is that between general and specific price changes, and how the effects of each can be meaningfully reported on in financial statements. Changes in specific prices, as with the inventory example above, should not be confused with changes in the general level of prices, which give rise to what are often referred to as purchasing power gains or losses, and result from holding net monetary assets or liabilities during periods of changing general prices. As most consumers are well aware, during periods of general price inflation, holding net monetary assets typically results in experiencing a loss in purchasing power, while a net liability position leads to a gain, as obligations are repaid with "cheaper" dollars. Among other effects, prolonged periods of general price inflation motivates entities to become more leveraged (more indebted to others) because of these purchasing power gains, although in reality creditors are aware of this and adjust interest rates to compensate.

Specific prices may change in ways that are notably different from the trend in overall prices, and they may even move in opposite directions. This is particularly true of basic commodities such as agricultural products and minerals, but may also be true of manufactured goods, especially if technological changes have great influence. For example, even during the years of rampant inflation during the 1970s some commodities, such as copper, were dropping in price, and certain goods, such as computer memory chips, were also declining even in nominal prices. For entities dealing in either of these items, holding inventories of these *nonmonetary* goods (usually a hedge against price inflation) would have produced large economic losses during this time. Thus, not only the changes in general prices, but also the changes in specific prices, and very important, the interactions between these can have major effects on an enterprise's real wealth. Measurement of these phenomena should be within the province of accounting.

Experiments and proposals for inflation accounting. Over the past fifty years there have been a number of proposals for pure price level accounting, financial reporting that would be sensitive to changes in specific prices, and combinations of these. There have been proposals (academic proposals) for comprehensive financial statements that would be adjusted for inflation, as well as for supplemental disclosures that would isolate the major inflation effects without abandoning primary historical cost based statements (generally, the professional proposals and regulatory requirements were of this type). To place the former requirements of the now-withdrawn standard IAS 15 in context, a number of its more prominent predecessors will be reviewed in brief.

Price level accounting concepts and proposals. At its simplest, price level accounting views any given currency at different points in time as being analogous to different currencies at the same point in time. That is, 1955 US dollars have the same relationship to 2006 dollars as 2006 Swiss francs have to 2006 dollars. They are "apples and oranges" and cannot be added or subtracted without first being converted to a common measuring unit. Thus, "pure" price level accounting is held to be within the mainstream historical cost tradition and is merely a translation of one currency into another for comparative purposes. A broadly based measure of all prices in the economy should be used in accomplishing this (often, a consumer price index of some sort is employed).

Consider a simple example. Assume that the index of general prices was as follows:

January 1, 1985	65
January 1, 1997	100
January 1, 2006	182
December 31, 2006	188

Also assume the following items selected from the December 31, 2006 balance sheet:

	Historical cost	*Price level adjusted cost*
Cash	€ 50,000	€ 50,000
Inventories (purchased 1/1/06)	350,000	
x 188/182		361,538
Land (acquired 1/1/85)	500,000	
x 188/65		1,446,154
Machinery (purchased 1/1/97)	300,000	
x 188/100		564,000
Accumulated depreciation	(200,000)	
x 188/100		(376,000)
Book value of assets	€1,000,000	€2,045,692
Less monetary liabilities	(500,000)	(500,000)
Net assets	€ 500,000	€1,545,692

In the foregoing, all nonmonetary items were adjusted to "current dollars" using the same index of general prices. This is not based on the notion that items such as inventory and machinery actually experienced price changes of that magnitude, but on the idea that converting these to current dollars is a process akin to converting foreign currency denominated financial statements. The implication is that the historical cost balance sheet, showing net assets of €500,000, is equivalent to a balance sheet that reports some items in German marks, some in French francs, some in Italian lira, and so on. The price level adjusted balance sheet, by contrast, is deemed to be equivalent to a balance sheet in which all items have been translated into dollars.

This analogy is a weak one, however. Not only are such statements essentially meaningless, they can also be misleading from a policy viewpoint. For example, during a period of rising prices, an entity holding more monetary assets than monetary liabilities will report an economic loss due to the decline in the purchasing power of its net monetary assets. Nonmonetary assets, of course, are adjusted for price changes and thus appear to be immune from purchasing power gains or losses. The implication is that holding nonmonetary assets is somehow preferable to holding monetary assets.

In the foregoing example, the net monetary liabilities at year-end are €500,000 – €50,000 = €450,000. Assuming the same net monetary liability position at the beginning of 2006, the gain experienced by the entity (due to owning monetary debt during a period of depreciating currency) would be given as

$$(\text{€}450,000 \times 188/182) - \text{€}450,000 = \text{€}14,835$$

This suggests that the entity has experienced a gain, at the obvious expense of its creditors, which have incurred a corresponding loss, in the amount of €14,835. This fails entirely to recognize that creditors may have demanded an inflation adjusted rate of return based on actual past and anticipated future inflationary behavior of the economy; if this were addressed in tandem with the computed purchasing power gain, a truer picture would be given of the real wisdom of the entity's financial strategy.

Furthermore, the actual price level protection afforded by holding investments in nonmonetary assets is a function of the changes in their specific values. If the replacement value of the inventory had declined, for example, during 2005, having held this inventory during the year would have been an economically unwise maneuver. Land that cost €500,000 might, due to its strategic location, now be worth €2.5 million, not the indicated €1.4 million, and the machinery might be obsolete due to technological changes, and not worth the approximately €190,000 suggested by the price level adjusted book value. In fairness, of course, the advocates of price level accounting do not claim that these adjusted amounts represent *values*. However, the utility of these adjusted balance sheet captions for decision makers is difficult to fathom and the potential for misunderstanding is great.

US and UK proposals. A number of proposals have been offered over the years for either replacing traditional financial statements with price level adjusted statements, or for including supplementary price level statements in the annual report to shareholders. In the United States, the predecessor of the current accounting standard setter, the Accounting Principles Board, proposed supplementary reporting in 1969; no major publicly held corporation complied with this request, however. The FASB made a similar proposal in 1974 and might have succeeded in imposing this standard had not the US securities market watchdog, the SEC, suggested instead that a current value approach be developed. (Later the SEC did impose a replacement costing requirement on large companies, and the FASB followed with its own version a few years thereafter.)

In the United Kingdom a similar course of events occurred. After an early postwar recommendation (not implemented) that there be earnings set aside for asset replacements, a late-1960s proposal for supplementary price level adjusted reporting was made, followed a few years later by a more comprehensive constant dollar recommendation. As happened in the United States at about the same time, what appeared to be a private sector juggernaut favoring price level adjustments was derailed by governmental intervention. A Royal Commission, established in 1973, eventually produced the Sandilands report, supporting current value accounting and not addressing the reporting of purchasing power gains or losses at all. This marked the end of British enthusiasm for general price level adjusted financial statements. Even a fairly complex later proposal (ED 18) made in 1977 did not incorporate any measure of purchasing power gains or losses, although it did add some novel embellishments to what basically was a current value model.

Other European nations have never been disposed favorably toward general price level accounting, with the exception of France. However, Latin American nations, having dealt with virtually runaway inflation for decades, have generally welcomed this type of financial reporting and in some cases have required it, even for some tax purposes. While price level adjustments are no more logical in Brazil, for example, than in the United States, since specific prices are changing, often at widely disparate rates, the role of accounting in those nations, serving as much more of an adjunct to the countries' respective tax collection and macroeconomic policy efforts than in European or other Western nations, has tended to encourage support for this approach to accounting for changing prices.

Current value models and proposals. By whatever name it is referred to, current value (replacement cost, current cost) accounting is really based on a wholly different concept than is price level (constant dollar) accounting. Current value financial reporting is far more closely tied to the original intent of the accounting model, which is to measure enterprise economic wealth and the changes therein from period to period. This suggests essentially a "balance sheet orientation" to income measurement, with the difference between net worth (as measured by current values) at year beginning and year-end being, after adjustment for capital transactions, the measure of income or loss for the intervening period. How this is further analyzed and presented in the income statement (as realized and unrealized gains and losses) or even whether some of these changes even belong in the income statement (or instead, are reported in a separate statement of movements in equity, or are taken directly into equity) is a rather minor bookkeeping concern.

Although the proliferation of terminology of the many competing proposals can be confusing, four candidates as measures of current value can readily be identified: economic value, net present value, net realizable value (also known as exit value), and replacement cost (which is a measure of entry value). A brief explanation will facilitate the discussion of the IAS requirements later in this chapter.

Economic value is usually understood to mean the equilibrium fair market value of an asset. However, apart from items traded in auction markets, typically only securities and raw commodities, direct observation of economic value is not possible.

Net present value is often suggested as the ideal surrogate for economic value, since in a perfect market values are driven by the present value of future cash flows to be generated by the assets. Certain types of assets, such as rental properties, have predictable cash flows and in fact are often priced in this manner. On the other hand, for assets such as machinery, particularly those that are part of a complex integrated production process, determining cash flows is difficult.

Net realizable values (NRV) are more familiar to most accountants, since even under existing US, UK, and international accounting standards, there are numerous instances when references to NRV must be made to ascertain whether asset write-downs are to be required. NRV is a measure of "exit values" since these are the amounts that the organization would realize on asset disposition, net of all costs; from this perspective, this is a conservative measure (exit values are lower than entry values in almost all cases, since transactions are not costless), but also is subject to criticism since under the going concern assumption it is not anticipated that the enterprise will dispose of all its productive assets at current market prices, indeed, not at any prices, since these assets will be retained for use in the business.

The biggest failing of this measure, however, is that it does not assist in measuring economic income, since that metric is intended to reveal how much income an entity can distribute to its owners, and so on, while retaining the ability to replace its productive capacity as needed. In general, an income measure based on exit values would overstate earnings (since depreciation and cost of sales would be based on lower exit values for plant assets and inventory) when compared with an income measure based on entry values. Thus, while NRV is a familiar concept to many accountants, this is not the ideal candidate for a current value model.

Replacement cost is intended as a measure of entry value and hence of the earnings reinvestment needed to maintain real economic productive capacity. Actually, competing proposals have engaged in much hairsplitting over alternative concepts of entry value, and this deserves some attention here. The simplest concept of replacement value is the cost of replacing a specific machine, building, and so on, and in some industries it is indeed possible to determine these prices, at least in the short run, before technology changes occur. However, in many more instances (and in the long run, in all cases) exact physical replacements are not available, and even nominally identical replacements offer varying levels of productivity enhancements that make simplistic comparisons distortive.

As a very basic example, consider a machine with a cost of €40,000 that can produce 100 widgets per hour. The current price of the replacement machine is €50,000, that superficially suggests a specific price increase of 25% has occurred. However, on closer examination, it is determined that while nominally the same machine, some manufacturing enhancements have been made (e.g., the machine will require less maintenance, will require fewer labor inputs, runs at a higher speed, etc.) which have altered its effective capacity (considering reduced downtime, etc.) to 110 widgets per hour. Clearly, a naive adjustment for what is sometimes called "reproduction cost" would overstate the machine's value on the balance sheet and overstate periodic depreciation charges, thereby understating earnings. A truer measure of the replacement cost of the service potential of the asset, not the physical asset itself, would be given as

$$€40,000 \times (50,000/40,000) \times 100/110 = €45,454$$

That is, the service potential represented by the asset in use has a current replacement cost of €45,454, considering that a new machine costs 25% more but is 10% more productive.

Consider another example: An integrated production process uses machines A and B, which have reproduction costs today of €40,000 and €45,000, respectively. However, management plans to acquire a new type of machine, C, which at a cost of €78,000 will replace both machines A and B and will produce the same output as its predecessors. The combined reproduction cost of €85,000 clearly overstates the replacement cost of the service potential of the existing machines in this case, even if there had been no technological changes affecting machines A and B.

Some, but not all, proposals that have been made in academia over the past sixty years, and by standards setters and regulatory authorities over the past twenty-five years, have understood the foregoing distinctions. For example, the US SEC requirements of the mid-1970s called for measures of the replacement cost of productive capacity, which clearly implied that productivity changes had to be factored in. The subsequent private sector rules issued by FASB seemed to redefine what the SEC had mandated to highlight its own current cost requirement; in essence, the FASB's current costs were nothing other than the SEC's replacement costs. Other proposals have been more ambiguous, however. Furthermore, measuring the impact of technological change adds vastly to the complexity of applying replacement cost measures, since raw replacement costs (known as reproduction costs) are often easily obtained (from catalog prices, etc.), but productivity adjustments must be ascertained by carefully evaluating advertising claims, engineering studies, and other sources of information, which can be a complex and costly process.

Limitations on replacement cost. While entry value is clearly the most logical of the alternative measures discussed thus far, under certain circumstances one of the other candidates would be preferable as a measure to use in current cost financial reporting. For example, consider a situation in which the value in use (economic value or net present value of future cash flows) is lower than replacement cost, due to changing market conditions affecting pricing of the entity's output. In such a circumstance, although the enterprise may continue to use the machines on hand and to sell the output profitably, it would not contemplate replacement of the asset, instead viewing it as a cash cow. If current cost financial statements were to be developed that incorporated depreciation based on the replacement cost of the machine, earnings would be understated, since actual replacement is not to be provided for. A number of other hypothetical circumstances could also be presented; the end result is that a series of decision rules can be developed to guide the selection of the best measure of current cost. These are summarized in the following table, where NRC stands for net replacement cost, which is synonymous with current cost; NRV is net realizable value or exit value; and EV is the same as net present value.

Conditions	Value to the business
EV > NRC > NRV	NRC
NRC > EV > NRV	EV
NRC > NRV > EV	NRV
EV > NRV > NRC	NRC
NRV > EV > NRC	NRC
NRV > NRC > EV	NRC

Measuring Income under the Replacement Cost Approach

There are two reasons to employ replacement cost accounting: (1) to compute a measure of earnings that can probably be replicated on an ongoing basis by the enterprise and approximates real economic wealth creation, and (2) to present a balance sheet that presents the economic condition of the entity at a point in time. Of these, the first is by far the more important objective, since decision makers' use of financial statements is largely oriented toward the future operations of the business, in which they are lenders, owners, managers, or employees.

Given the foregoing, the principal use of replacement cost information will be to assist in computing current period earnings on a true economic basis. The income statement items which on the historical cost basis are most distortive, in most cases, are depreciation and cost of sales. Historical cost depreciation can be based on asset prices that are ten to forty years old, during which time even modest price changes can compound to very sizable misrepresentations. Cost of sales will not typically suffer from compounding over such a long period, since turnover for most businesses will be in a matter of months (although this can be greatly distorted if low LIFO inventory costs are released into cost of sales), but since cost of sales will account for a much larger part of the entity's total costs than does depreciation, it can still have a major impact.

Thus, current cost/replacement cost/current value earnings are typically computed by adjusting historical cost income by an allowance for replacement cost depreciation and cost of sales. Typically, these two adjustments will effectively derive a modified earnings amount that closely approximates economic earnings. This modified amount can be paid out as dividends or otherwise disbursed, while leaving the enterprise with the ability to replace its productive capacity and continue to operate at the same level as it had been. (This does not, however, address the matter of purchasing power that may have been gained or lost by holding net monetary assets or liabilities during the period, which requires yet another computation.)

Determining current costs. In practice, replacement costs are developed by applying one or more of four principal techniques: indexation, direct pricing, unit pricing, and functional pricing. Each has advantages and disadvantages, and no single technique will be applicable to all fact situations and all types of assets. The following are useful in determining current costs of plant assets.

Indexation is accomplished by applying appropriate indices to the historical cost of the assets. Assuming that the assets in use were acquired in the usual manner (bargain purchases and other such means of acquisition will thwart this effort, since any index when applied to a nonstandard base will result in a meaningless adjusted number) and that an appropriate index can be obtained or developed (which incorporates productivity changes as well as price variations), this will be the most efficient approach to employ. For many categories of manufactured goods, such as machinery and equipment, this technique has been widely used with excellent results. One concern is that many published indices actually address only reproduction costs, and if not adjusted further, the likely outcome will be that costs are overstated and adjusted earnings will be artificially depressed.

Direct pricing, as the name suggests, relies on information provided by vendors and others having data about the selling prices of replacement assets. To the extent that these are list prices that do not reflect actual market transactions, these must be adjusted, and the same concern with productivity enhancements mentioned with reference to indexation must also be addressed. Since many enterprises are in constant, close contact with their vendors, obtaining such information is often straightforward, particularly with regard to machinery and other equipment.

Unit pricing is the least commonly employed method but can be useful when estimating the replacement cost of buildings. This is the bricks-and-mortar approach, which relies on statistical data about the per unit cost of constructing various types of buildings and other assets. For example, construction cost data may suggest that single-story light industrial buildings in cold climates (e.g., Europe) with certain other defined attributes may have a current cost of €47 per square foot, or that a first-class high-rise urban hotel in England has a construction cost of €125,000 per room. By expanding these per unit costs to the scale of the enterprise's facilities, a fairly accurate replacement cost can be derived. There are complications; for example, costs are not linearly related to size of facility due to the presence of fixed costs, but these are widely understood and readily dealt with. Unit pricing is typically not meaningful for machinery or equipment, however.

Functional pricing is the most difficult of the four principal techniques and is best reserved for highly integrated production processes, such as refineries and chemical plants, where attempts to price individual components would be exceptionally difficult. For example, a plant capable of producing 400,000 tons of polyethylene annually could be priced as a unit by having an engineering estimate made of the cost to construct similar capacity in the current environment. Clearly, this is not a merely mechanical effort, as indexation in particular is likely to be, but demands the services of a skilled estimator. Technological issues are neatly avoided since the focus is on creating a new plant with defined output capacity, using whatever mix of components would be most cost-effective. This technique has been widely employed in actual practice.

Inventory costing problems. For a merchandising concern, direct pricing is likely to be an effective technique to assist in developing cost of sales on a current cost basis. Manufacturing firms, on the other hand, will need to build up replacement cost basis cost of goods manufactured and sold by separately analyzing the cost behavior of each major cost element (e.g., labor contracts, overhead expenses, and raw materials prices). It is unlikely that these will have experienced the same price movements, and therefore an averaging approach would not be sufficiently accurate. Also, as product mix changes over time, the entity may be subject to varying influences from one period to the next. Finally, the inventory costing method used (e.g., LIFO vs. FIFO) will affect the extent of adjustment to be made, with (assuming that costs trend upward over time) relatively greater adjustments made to cost of sales determined on the FIFO basis, since relatively older costs are included in the GAAP income statement.

Whatever assortment of methods is used, the end product is a restated inventory of plant assets, depreciation on which must then be computed. For the current cost earnings data to be comparable with the historical cost financial statements, it is usually recommended that no other decisions be superimposed. For example, no changes in asset useful lives should be made, for to do so would exacerbate or ameliorate the impact of the replacement cost depreciation and make interpretation very difficult for anyone not intimately familiar with the company. Some ancillary costs may need to be adjusted in computing cost of sales and depreciation on the revised basis. For example, if the only replacement machines available will reduce the need for skilled labor, the (higher) replacement cost depreciation should be reduced by related cost savings, if accurately predictable. There are literally scores of similar issues to be addressed, and indeed entire volumes have been written providing detailed guidance on how to apply current cost measures.

Examples of current costing adjustments to depreciation and cost of sales

Example 1

Hapsburg Corp. is a wholesale distributor for a single product. For 2006, the company reports sales of €35,000,000, representing sales of 600,000 units of its single product. The traditional income statement reports cost of sales as follows:

	(000 omitted)
Beginning inventory	€ 8.8
Purchases, net	25.7
Ending inventory	(6.5)
Cost of goods sold	€28.0

Reference to purchase orders reveals the fact that product cost early in 2006 was €42 per unit and was €55 per unit late in December of that year. The company employs FIFO accounting.

Since there is no evidence presented to the effect that net realizable value of the product is below current replacement cost, current cost can be used without modification.

Beginning current cost	€42.0
Ending current cost	€55.0
Average	€48.5

Total cost of sales for the period, on a replacement cost basis, is therefore €48.5 x 600,000 units = €29,100,000.

Example 2

In the following example, deprival value is, for one product line, better measured by net realizable value than by replacement cost. The company, St. Ignatz Mfg. Co., manufactures and sells two products, A and B. Product A has been a declining item for several years, and management now believes that it must close this line due to the shrinking market share, which will not support higher costs. St. Ignatz will continue to produce Product B and may possibly expand into new products in the future.

Company records show the following results in 2006:

	(000,000 omitted)		
	Product A	*Product B*	*Total*
Sales	€19.5	€40.5	€60.0
Cost of sales			
Beginning inventory	12.5	6.8	
Purchases	8.7	20.0	
Ending inventory	(3.0)	(5.4)	
Cost of sales	18.2	21.4	39.6
Gross profit	€ 1.3	€19.1	20.4
All other expenses			(18.8)
Net income			€ 1.6

The company's manufacturing records show the following data:

Current costs, beginning of year	€52.0	€75.0
Current costs, ending of year	€63.0	€79.0
Current costs, average	€57.5	€77.0

Sales in 2006 comprised 390,000 units of Product A and 540,000 units of Product B. Management believes that the market for Product A cannot support further price increases, and thus the remaining inventory will probably be sold at a loss. Selling expenses are estimated at €6 per unit.

Product A has a recoverable value lower than current manufacturing costs. The net recoverable amount is given by the selling price per unit less selling expenses: €50 − €6 = €44 per unit. Current cost of sales is €44 x €390,000 = €17,160,000. Note that recoverable amount, not replacement cost, is used.

Product B has an average current cost of €77 per unit, so 2006 cost of sales on a current cost basis is €77 x €540,000 = €41,580,000.

Total cost of sales on the current cost basis is therefore €17,160,000 + €41,580,000 = €58,740,000.

Example 3

Jacquet Corp. reports depreciation of €16,510 for 2006 in its historical cost based financial statements prepared on the basis of GAAP. A summary of plant assets reveals the following:

Asset class	*Total depreciable cost**	*Useful life (yr.)*	*Depreciation rate (%)***
A	€24,000	8	12 1/2
B	50,000	10	10
C	45,000	12	8 1/3
D	60,000	15	6 2/3
E	19,000	25	4

   * *Depreciable cost is historical cost less salvage value.*
  ** *Depreciation rate is 1/useful life.*

Management employs appraisals and other methods, including information from vendors and indices, to develop current cost data as shown below.

Asset class	*1/1/06*	*Current costs 12/31/06*	*Average*
A	€28,000	€31,000	€29,500
B	56,000	60,000	58,000
C	55,000	60,000	57,500
D	62,000	68,000	65,000
E	30,000	33,000	31,500

From this information the current cost depreciation for the year 2006 can be computed as follows:

Asset class	Depreciation rate (%)	Average current cost	Depreciation
A	12 1/2	€29,500	€ 3,687.5
B	10	58,000	5,800.0
C	8 1/3	57,500	4,792.0
D	6 2/3	65,000	4,333.0
E	4	31,500	1,260.0
			€19,872.5

Note that the replacement cost basis depreciation for the year is €3,362.50 greater than was the historical cost depreciation.

Purchasing power gains or losses in the context of current cost accounting. Thus far, general price level (or purchasing power or constant dollar) accounting has been viewed as a reporting concept totally separate from current value (or current cost or replacement cost) accounting. As noted, advocates of price level adjustments have argued that these are not attempts to measure value, as current cost accounting is, but merely to "translate" old dollars into current dollars. For their part, advocates of current value accounting have generally been more focused on deriving a measure of the "replicatable" economic earnings of the enterprise, usually with no mention of the fact that changing specific prices of productive assets exist against a backdrop of changing general price levels.

In fact, the FASB requirements imposed in the late 1970s (and made optional in the 1980s for lack of interest) attempted to measure both general and specific price changes. That standard included a requirement for reporting purchasing power gains or losses, as well as for stating the amount of adjustment for current cost depreciation and cost of sales. The IASC had imposed a somewhat similar requirement in the former IAS 15, albeit with less specificity. Although IAS 15 has been withdrawn, any entity that reports on an IAS-compliant basis and desires to report the effects of changing prices would be well-served to apply procedures set forth in IAS 15, supplemented as necessary by guidance under US GAAP.

Former Requirements under IAS 15

The experience of the international accounting standard that was designed to reveal the effects of inflation is very similar to the experiences in the United States and the United Kingdom. That is, while there was a great clamor, primarily from the financial analyst community, in favor of this supplementary financial reporting model, once it was mandated there was a noticeable decline in interest. It would appear that analysts much prefer to develop their own estimates of the impact of inflation on the companies they follow and may have an inherent distrust of management-supplied data. As for management, it generally argued that such information was useless before the standard was imposed, which at the time seemed to be self-serving posturing in the hope that an expensive new mandate could be averted.

As in the United States, after a few years of mandatory presentation of supplementary inflation adjusted information (IAS 15 was imposed in 1981), the IASC announced in 1989 that presentation would no longer be required to comply with the standard, although it would still be encouraged. This status continued until the Improvements Project determined to eliminate the guidance entirely.

Alternative approaches permitted. The standard was intended to require certain supplementary current value and constant dollar information. A great deal of latitude was given to entities, which could choose from among a range of supportable methods to accomplish this directive. As the standard notes, the two main methods are intended to (1) recognize income after the general purchasing power of shareholders' equity has been maintained (price level accounting), and (2) recognize income after the operating capacity of the enterprise is maintained (current value accounting, which may or may not also include adjustments related to the general price level).

General purchasing power approach. IAS 15 did not stipulate what index was to be used to measure the change in the general level of prices but did identify depreciation and cost of sales as being subject to adjustment. It also noted the need to measure the effect of changing prices on net monetary items held.

Current cost approach. IAS 15 acknowledged the existence of various methods, with replacement cost being identified as the principal measurement strategy, subject to the caveat that when replacement cost was found to be higher than both net realizable value and present value, replacement value was not to be used. Instead, the higher of net realizable value and present value would denote current value, as explained earlier in this chapter. Replacement costs were said to be found in information about current acquisitions of new or used assets of similar productive capacities or service potentials. Specific price indices were also favorably noted as sources of current cost data. Briefly stated, net realizable value is generally a representation of net current selling price (i.e., exit value), while present value is the discounted amount of future receipts attributable to the asset.

IAS 15 had discussed, at some length, the need to determine an adjustment for the effects of changing prices on net monetary items, including long-term debt, but suggested that some current cost methods (which it did not name) may not need to address this separately. In particular, the discussion in IAS 15 alluded to the argument (made explicitly in the British proposal of the 1970s but not otherwise enacted in any standards) that since depreciable assets in particular are often acquired at least in part in exchange for monetary debt, the gross replacement cost adjustment exaggerates the negative effect on earnings and that this is moderated to the extent leveraging is used.

In fact, one can make this argument, but as noted earlier in the chapter, to do so assumes that added borrowing in periods of rising prices is "costless" in the sense that no premium is added by lenders to compensate for either (1) the borrowers' greater riskiness as they become more leveraged, or (2) for the loss to be incurred on repayment of the debt in devalued currency. It is not likely that in the long run lenders will go uncompensated for either of these, and therefore to offset the higher charges for depreciation and cost of sales by the fraction to be borne by the lenders may be imprudent.

Minimum disclosures that had been required by IAS 15. The disclosures which were first required, then later made optional, under now-withdrawn IAS 15 included the following:

1. The amount of adjustment to, or the adjusted amount of, depreciation of property, plant, and equipment
2. The amount of adjustment to, or the adjusted amount of, cost of sales
3. The adjustments relating to monetary items, the effect of borrowing, or equity interests when such adjustments have been taken into account in determining income under the (inflation) accounting method adopted
4. The overall effect on results of the adjustments described above, as well as any other items reflecting the effects of changing prices
5. If a current cost method is used, the current cost of property, plant, and equipment and of inventories should be disclosed.
6. There should be a description of the methods used to compute the foregoing items.

Example of disclosure consistent with IAS 15

DeKalb Thermodynamics Inc.
Statements of Income from Continuing Operations
Year Ended December 31, 2005

	As reported in primary statements	Adjusted for general inflation	Adjusted for changes in specific prices (current costs)
Net sales and other revenue	€253,000	€253,000	€253,000
Cost of goods sold	€197,000	€204,384	€205,408
Depreciation and amortization	10,000	14,130	19,500
Other operating expense	20,835	20,835	20,835
Interest expense	7,165	7,165	7,165
Provision for income taxes	9,000	9,000	9,000
	€244,000	€255,514	€261,908
Income (loss) from continuing operations	€ 9,000	€ (2,514)	€ (8,908)
Gain from decline in purchasing power of net amounts owed		€ 7,729	€ 7,729
Increase in specific prices (current costs) of inventories and property, plant, and equipment held during the year			€ 24,608
Effect of general price level increase			18,959
Excess of increase in specific prices over increase in general price level			€ 5,649

NOTE: Current costs are determined by consulting current prices posted for plant assets, net of applicable discounts, and by reference to indexed or replacement costs adjusted for productivity increases. The gain on purchasing power change is determined by reference to the consumer price index for all urban consumers.

The Improvements Project concluded that IAS 15 was no longer needed and should be withdrawn. The IASB stated that, "…the Board does not believe that entities should be required to disclose information that reflects the effects of changing prices in the current economic environment." In the authors' view, for those (few) entities which believe that inflation adjusted financial reporting continues to serve a useful purpose, the guidance in IAS 15 and in the foregoing discussion of this chapter continue to be germane.

FINANCIAL REPORTING IN HYPERINFLATIONARY ECONOMIES

CONCEPTS, RULES, AND EXAMPLES

Hyperinflation and Financial Reporting

Hyperinflation is a condition that is difficult to define precisely, as there is not a clear demarcation between merely rampant inflation and true hyperinflation. However, in any given economic system, when the general population has so lost faith in the stability of the local economy that business transactions are commonly either denominated in a stable reference currency of another country, or are structured to incorporate an indexing feature intended to compensate for the distortive effects of inflation, this condition may be present. As a benchmark, when cumulative inflation over three years approaches or exceeds 100%, it must be conceded that the economy is suffering from hyperinflation.

Hyperinflation is obviously a major problem for any economy, as it creates severe distortions and, left unaddressed, results in uncontrolled acceleration of the rate of price changes, ending in inevitable collapse as was witnessed in post–World War I Germany. From a financial reporting perspective, there are also major problems, since even over a brief interval such as a year or even a quarter, the income statement will contain transactions with such a variety of purchasing power units that aggregation becomes meaningless, as would adding dollars, francs, and marks. This is precisely the problem discussed earlier in this chapter, but raised to an exponential level.

In a truly hyperinflationary economy, users of financial statements are unable to make meaningful use of such statements unless they have been recast into currency units having purchasing power defined by prices at or near the date of the statements. Unless this common denominator is employed, the financial statements are too difficult to interpret for purposes of making management, investing, and credit decisions. Although some sophisticated users, particularly in those countries where hyperinflation has been endemic, such as some of the South American nations, including Brazil and Argentina, and for certain periods nations such as Israel, are able to apply rules of thumb to cope with this problem, in general modifications must be made to general-purpose financial statements if they are to have any value.

Under international accounting standards, if hyperinflation is deemed to characterize the economy, a form of price level accounting must be applied to the financial statements to conform to generally accepted accounting principles. IAS 29 requires that all the financial statements be adjusted to reflect year-end general price levels, which entails applying a broad-based index to all nonmonetary items on the balance sheet and to all transactions reported in the income statement and the cash flow statement.

Restating Historical Cost Financial Statements under Hyperinflation Conditions

The precise adjustments to be made depend on whether the financial reporting system is based on historical costs or on current costs, as those terms were described in the now-withdrawn IAS 15 and explained earlier in this chapter. Although in both cases the goal is to restate the financial statements into the measuring unit that exists at the balance sheet date, the mechanics will vary to some extent.

If the financial reporting system is based on historical costing, the process used to adjust the balance sheet can be summarized as follows:

1. Monetary assets and liabilities are already presented in units of year-end purchasing power and receive no further adjustment. (See the appendix for a categorization of different assets and liabilities as to their status as monetary or nonmonetary.)

2. Monetary assets and liabilities that are linked to price changes, such as indexed debt securities, are adjusted according to the terms of the contractual arrangement. This does not change the characterization of these items as monetary, but it does serve to reduce or even eliminate the purchasing power gain or loss that would have otherwise been experienced as a result of holding these items during periods of changing general prices.

3. Nonmonetary items are adjusted by applying a ratio of indices, the numerator of which is the general price level index at the balance sheet date and the denominator of which is the index as of the acquisition or inception date of the item in question. For some items, such as plant assets, this is a straightforward process, while for others, such as work in process inventories, this can be more complex.

4. Certain assets cannot be adjusted as described above, because even in nominally historical cost financial statements these items have been revised to some other basis, such as fair value or net realizable amounts. For example, under the allowed alternative method of IAS 16, plant, property, and equipment can be adjusted to fair value. In such a case, no further adjustment would be warranted, assuming that the adjustment to fair value was made as of the latest balance sheet date (although IAS 16 only demands that this be done at least every three years). If the latest revaluation was as of an earlier date, the carrying amounts should be further adjusted

to compensate for changes in the general price level from that date to the balance sheet date, using the indexing technique noted above.

5. Consistent with the established principles of historical cost accounting, if the restated amounts of nonmonetary assets exceed the recoverable amounts, these must be reduced appropriately. This can easily occur, since (as discussed earlier in this chapter) specific prices of goods will vary by differing amounts, even in a hyperinflationary environment, and in fact some may decline in terms of current cost even in such cases, particularly when technological change occurs rapidly. Since the application of price level accounting, whether for ordinary inflation or for hyperinflation, does not imply an abandonment of historical costing, being a mere translation into more timely and relevant purchasing power units, the rules of that mode of financial reporting still apply. Generally accepted accounting principles require that assets not be stated at amounts in excess of realizable amounts, and this constraint applies even when price level adjustments are reflected.

6. Equity accounts must also be restated to compensate for changing prices. Paid-in capital accounts are indexed by reference to the dates when the capital was contributed, which are usually a discrete number of identifiable transactions over the life of the enterprise. Revaluation accounts, if any, are eliminated entirely, as these will be subsumed in restated retained earnings. The retained earnings account itself is the most complex to analyze and in practice is often treated as a balancing figure after all other balance sheet accounts have been restated. However, it is possible to compute the adjustment to this account directly, and that is the recommended course of action, lest other errors go undetected. To adjust retained earnings, each year's earnings should be adjusted by a ratio of indices, the numerator being the general price level as of the balance sheet date, and the denominator being the price level as of the end of the year for which the earnings were reported. Reductions of retained earnings for dividends paid should be adjusted similarly.

7. IAS 29 addresses a few other special problem areas. For example, the standard notes that borrowing costs typically already reflect the impact of inflation (more accurately, interest rates reflect inflationary expectations), and thus it would represent a form of double counting to fully index capital asset costs for price level changes when part of the cost of the asset was capitalized interest, as defined in IAS 23 as an allowed alternative method. As a practical matter, interest costs are often not a material component of recorded asset amounts, and the inflation-related component would only be a fraction of interest costs capitalized. However, the general rule is to delete that fraction of the capitalized borrowing costs which represents inflationary compensation, since the entire cost of the asset will be indexed to current purchasing units.

To restate the current period's income statement, a reasonably accurate result can be obtained if revenue and expense accounts are multiplied by the ratio of end-of-period prices to average prices for the period. Where price changes were not relatively constant throughout the period, or when transactions did not occur ratably, as when there was a distinct seasonal pattern to sales activity, a more precise measurement effort might be needed. This can be particularly important when a devaluation of the currency took place during the year.

While IAS 29 addresses the cash flow statement only perfunctorily (its issuance was prior to the revision of IAS 7), this financial statement must also be modified to report all items in terms of year-end purchasing power units. For example, changes in working capital accounts, used to convert net income into cash flow from operating activities, will be altered to reflect the real (i.e., inflation adjusted) changes.

To illustrate, if beginning accounts receivable were €500,000 and ending receivables were €650,000, but prices rose by 40% during the year, the apparent €150,000 increase in receivables (which would be a use of cash) is really a €50,000 decrease [(€500,000 x 1.4 = €700,000) – €650,000], which in cash flow terms is a source of cash. Other items must be handled similarly. Investing and financing activities should be adjusted on an item-by-item basis, since these are normally discrete events that do not occur ratably throughout the year.

In addition to the foregoing, the adjusted income statement will report a gain or loss on net monetary items held. As an approximation, this will be computed by applying the change in general prices for the year to the average net monetary assets (or liabilities) outstanding during the year. If net monetary items changed materially at one or more times during the year, a more detailed computation would be warranted. In the income statement, the gain or loss on net monetary items should be associated with the adjustment relating to items that are linked to price level changes (indexed debt, etc.) as well as with interest income and expense and foreign exchange adjustments, since theoretically at least, all these items contain a component that reflects inflationary behavior.

Restating Current Cost Financial Statements under Hyperinflation Conditions

If the financial reporting system is based on current costing (as described earlier in the chapter), the process used to adjust the balance sheet can be summarized as follows:

1. Monetary assets and liabilities are already presented in units of year-end purchasing power and receive no further adjustment. (See the appendix for a categorization of different assets and liabilities as to their status as monetary or nonmonetary.)
2. Monetary assets and liabilities that are linked to price changes, such as indexed debt securities, are adjusted according to the terms of the contractual arrangement. This does not change the characterization of these items as monetary, but it does serve to reduce or even eliminate the purchasing power gain or loss that would have otherwise been experienced as a result of holding these items during periods of changing general prices.
3. Nonmonetary items are already stated at year-end current values or replacement costs and need no further adjustments. Issues related to recoverable amounts and other complications associated with price level adjusted historical costs should not normally arise.
4. Equity accounts must also be restated to compensate for changing prices. Paid-in capital accounts are indexed by reference to the dates when the capital was contributed, which are usually a discrete number of identifiable transactions over the life of the enterprise. Revaluation accounts are eliminated entirely, as these will be subsumed in restated retained earnings. The retained earnings account itself will typically be a "balancing account" under this scenario, since detailed analysis would be very difficult, although certainly not impossible, to accomplish.

The current cost income statement, absent the price level component, will reflect transactions at current costs as of the transaction dates. For example, cost of sales will be comprised of the costs as of each transaction date (usually approximated on an average basis). To report these as of the balance sheet date, these costs will have to be further inflated to year-end purchasing power units, by means of the ratio of general price level indices, as suggested above.

In addition to the foregoing, the adjusted income statement will report a gain or loss on net monetary items held. This will be similar to that discussed under the historical cost reporting above. However, current cost income statements, if prepared, already will include the net gain or loss on monetary items held, which need not be computed again.

To the extent that restated earnings differ from earnings on which income taxes are computed, there will be a need to provide more or less tax accrual, which will be a deferred tax obligation or asset, depending on the circumstances.

Comparative Financial Statements

Consistent with the underlying concept of reporting in hyperinflationary economies, all prior-year financial statement amounts must be updated to purchasing power units as of the most recent balance sheet date. This will be a relatively simple process of applying a ratio of indices of the current year-end price level to the year earlier price level.

Other Disclosure Issues

IAS 29 requires that when the standard is applied, the fact that hyperinflation adjustments have been made be noted. Furthermore, the underlying basis of accounting, historical cost or current cost, should be stipulated, as should the price level index that was utilized in making the adjustments.

Economies Which Cease Being Hyperinflationary

When application of IAS 29 is discontinued, the amounts reported in the last balance sheet that had been adjusted become, effectively, the new cost basis. That is, previously applied adjustments are not reversed, since an end to a period of hyperinflation generally means only that prices have plateaued, not that they have deflated to earlier levels.

Revisions to IAS 29

Certain consequential amendments were made to IAS 29 due to the withdrawal of IAS 15. The most important of these was to conform to the new requirements incorporated into revised IAS 21. This stipulates that the results of operations and financial position of an entity whose functional currency is the currency of a hyperinflationary economy is to be translated into a different presentation currency using the following procedures:

1. All amounts (i.e., assets, liabilities, equity items, income items and expense items, including comparatives) are to be translated at the closing rate at the date of the most recent balance sheet, except that
2. When amounts are being translated into the currency of a nonhyperinflationary economy, comparative amounts shall be those that were presented as current year amounts in the relevant prior year financial statements (i.e., not adjusted for either subsequent changes in the price level or subsequent changes in exchange rates).

Revised IAS 21 further requires that, when the functional currency of an entity is the currency of a hyperinflationary economy, its financial statements are to be restated under IAS 29, before the translation method set out in IAS 21 is applied, except for comparative amounts that are being translated into a currency of a nonhyperinflationary economy. When the economy ceases to be hyperinflationary and the entity no longer restates its financial statements in accordance with IAS 29, the financial statements will use the amounts restated to the price level at the date the entity ceased restating its financial statements as the historical costs for translation into the presentation currency.

Beyond the changes already adopted, IFRIC has proposed an Interpretation of IAS 29 to address differentiating between monetary and nonmonetary items. IAS 29 requires that when an entity identifies the existence of hyperinflation in the economy of its functional currency it must restate its financial statements for the effects of inflation. The restatement approach distinguishes between monetary and nonmonetary items, but in practice it has been noted there is uncertainty about how to restate the financial statements for the first time, particularly with regard to deferred tax balances and comparatives.

The Draft Interpretation would require that, in the first year that an entity identifies the existence of hyperinflation, it would start applying IAS 29 as if it had always applied that standard. Therefore, it must recreate an opening balance sheet at the beginning of the earliest annual accounting period presented in the restated financial statements, for the first year it applies IAS 29.

The Draft Interpretation also states that if detailed records of the acquisition dates for items of property, plant, and equipment are not available or are not capable of estimation, the reporting entity should use an independent professional assessment of the fair value of the items as the basis for restatement. Likewise, if a general price index is not available, it may be necessary to use an estimate based on the changes in the exchange rate between the functional currency and a relatively stable foreign currency, for example, when the entity restates its financial statements.

As of mid-2005, this draft remains outstanding.

APPENDIX

MONETARY VS. NONMONETARY ITEMS

Item	Monetary	Nonmonetary	Requires analysis
Cash on hand, demand deposits, and time deposits	x		
Foreign currency and claims to foreign currency	x		
Securities			
Common stock (passive investment)		x	
Preferred stock (convertible or participating) and convertible bonds			x
Other preferred stock or bonds	x		
Accounts and notes receivable and allowance for doubtful accounts	x		
Mortgage loan receivables	x		
Inventories		x	
Loans made to employees	x		
Prepaid expenses			x
Long-term receivables	x		
Refundable deposits	x		
Advances to unconsolidated subsidiaries	x		
Equity in unconsolidated subsidiaries		x	
Pension and other funds			x
Property, plant, and equipment and accumulated depreciation		x	
Cash surrender value of life insurance	x		
Purchase commitments (portion paid on fixed-price contracts)		x	
Advances to suppliers (not on fixed-price contracts)	x		
Deferred income tax charges	x		
Patents, trademarks, goodwill, and other intangible assets		x	
Deferred life insurance policy acquisition costs	x		
Deferred property and casualty insurance policy acquisition costs		x	
Accounts payable and accrued expenses	x		
Accrued vacation pay			x
Cash dividends payable	x		
Obligations payable in foreign currency	x		
Sales commitments (portion collected on fixed-price contracts)		x	
Advances from customers (not on fixed-price contracts)	x		
Accrued losses on purchase commitments	x		
Deferred revenue			x
Refundable deposits	x		
Bonds payable, other long-term debt, and related discount or premium	x		
Accrued pension obligations			x
Obligations under product warranties		x	
Deferred income tax obligations	x		
Deferred investment tax credits		x	
Life or property and casualty insurance policy reserves	x		
Unearned insurance premiums		x	
Deposit liabilities of financial institutions	x		

26 GOVERNMENT GRANTS

PERSPECTIVE AND ISSUES

Government grants or other types of assistance, where provided, are usually intended to encourage entities to embark on activities that they would not have otherwise undertaken. Government assistance, according to the standard, is action by the government aimed at providing economic benefits to some constituency by subsidizing entities that will provide them with jobs, services, or goods that might not otherwise be available or available at a desired cost. A government grant, on the other hand, is government assistance that entails the transfer of resources in return for compliance, either past or future, with certain conditions relating to the enterprise's operating activities, such as for remediating a polluted plant site. However, there is a wide range of government interventions and interactions with business in countries using IFRS, and this is an area of accounting where the IASB is expected to expand its literature significantly in the near term.

The current standard, IAS 20, was promulgated in 1982 and has remained intact since then. Although accepted by IOSCO as a "core standard" in its present form, it has been subject to wide criticism, particularly in Australia where accountants believe that national GAAP is superior, but nonetheless is scheduled to be replaced by IASB by 2006. Accounting for grants as a deferred credit is considered to be inconsistent with the IASB's *Framework,* and reducing the carrying value of assets by a grant is not accepted by some. The Board had taken the view that it should await finalization of a general standard on revenue recognition before undertaking an overhaul of IAS 20. However, the need to deal with the grant of emission rights has persuaded the Board to carry out a short-term change by harmonizing IAS 20 with the government grant rules in IAS 41.

Another important gap in the literature is the absence of any guidance on accounting for service concessions, which occurs relatively frequently in Europe, where government assets may be operated by commercial entities. IFRIC is working on a related series of interpretations in this area.

Until it is revised, however, IAS 20 provides authoritative guidance on financial statement presentation for all entities enjoying government assistance, with additional guidance to be found in IAS 41, which is, however, at the moment restricted to agriculture. IAS 20 deals with the accounting treatment and disclosure of government grants and the disclosure requirements of government assistance. Depending on the nature of the assistance given and the associated conditions, government assistance could be of many types, including grants, forgivable loans, and indirect or nonmonetary forms of assistance, such as technical advice.

It is interesting to note that there is no equivalent standard under US GAAP, where, according to some IASB members, equivalent transactions do not take place.

Sources of IFRS
IAS 20, 41   *SIC* 10

DEFINITIONS OF TERMS

Fair value. The amount for which an asset could be exchanged between a knowledgeable, willing buyer and a knowledgeable, willing seller in an arm's-length transaction.

Forgivable loans. Those loans which the lender undertakes to waive repayment of under certain prescribed conditions.

Government. For the purposes of IAS 20, the term government refers not only to a government (of a country), as is generally understood, but also to government agencies and similar bodies whether local, national, or international.

Government assistance. Government assistance is action by government aimed at providing an economic benefit to an enterprise or group of enterprises qualifying under certain criteria. It includes a government grant and also includes other kinds of nonmonetary government assistance such as providing, at no cost, legal advice to an entrepreneur for setting up a business in a free trade zone. It excludes benefits provided indirectly through action affecting trading conditions in general; for example, laying roads that connect the industrial area in which an enterprise operates to the nearest city or imposing trade constraints on foreign companies in order to protect domestic entrepreneurs in general.

Government grants. A government grant is a form of a government assistance that involves the transfer of resources to an enterprise in return for past or future compliance (by the enterprise) of certain conditions relating to its operating activities. It excludes

- Those forms of government assistance that cannot reasonably be valued, and
- Transactions with governments that cannot be distinguished from the normal trading transactions of the enterprise.

Grants related to assets. Those government grants whose primary condition is that an enterprise qualifying for them should acquire (either purchase or construct) a long-term asset or assets are referred to as "grants related to assets." Subsidiary conditions may also be attached to such a grant. Examples of subsidiary conditions include specifying the type of long-term assets, location of long-term assets, or periods during which the long-term assets are to be acquired or held.

Grants related to income. Government grants, other than those related to assets, are grants related to income.

CONCEPTS, RULES AND EXAMPLES

Scope

IAS 20 deals with the accounting treatment and disclosure requirements of grants received by enterprises from a government. It also mandates disclosure requirements of other forms of government assistance.

The standard specifies certain exclusions. In addition to the four exclusions contained within the definitions of the terms "government grant" and "government assistance," IAS 20 *excludes* the following from the purview of the standard:

1. Special problems arising in reflecting the effects of changing prices on financial statements or similar supplementary information;
2. Government assistance provided in the form of tax benefits (including income tax holidays, investment tax credits, accelerated depreciation allowances and concessions in tax rates); and
3. Government participation in the ownership of the enterprise.
4. Government grants covered by IAS 41.

The rationale behind excluding items 1. and 2. above seems fairly obvious (i.e., they are covered by other international accounting standards); IAS 29 addresses accounting in hyperinflationary conditions, while tax benefits are dealt with by IAS 12. The reason for excluding item 3. above, however, has been the subject of some controversy and conjecture.

Authorities on the subject have offered different opinions as plausible reasons for specifically excluding "government participation in the ownership of the enterprise" from the scope of IAS 20. According to one school of thought, participation in ownership of an enterprise is normally in anticipation of a return on the investment while government assistance is provided with an economic cause in mind, for example, the public interest or public policy. Thus, when the government invests in the equity of an enterprise (with the intention of encouraging the enterprise to undertake a line of business that it would normally not have embarked on), such government participation in ownership of the enterprise would *not qualify* as a government grant under this standard.

Government Grants

Government grants are assistance provided by government by transfer of resources (either monetary or nonmonetary) to enterprises. In order to qualify as a government grant, in strict technical terms, it is a prerequisite that the grant should be provided by the government to an enterprise in return for past or future compliance with conditions relating to the operating activities of the enterprise.

For years, it has been unclear whether the provisions of IAS 20 would apply even to government assistance aimed at encouraging or supporting business activities in certain regions or industry sectors, since related conditions may not specifically relate to the operating activities of the enterprise. Examples of such grants are: government grants which involve transfer of resources to enterprises to operate in a particular area (i.e., an economically backward area) or a particular industry (i.e., an agriculture-based industry that due to its low profitability may not be a popular choice of entrepreneurs). The Standing Interpretations Committee's interpretation, SIC 10, has clarified that "the general requirement to operate in certain regions or industry sectors in order to qualify for the government assistance constitutes such a condition in accordance with IAS 20." This has set to rest the confusion as to whether or not such government assistance does fall within the definition of government grants and thus the requirements of IAS 20 apply to them as well.

Recognition of Government Grants

Criteria for recognition. Government grants are provided in return for past or future compliance of certain conditions. Thus grants should not be recognized until there is *reasonable assurance* that both

1. The enterprise will comply with the conditions attaching to the grant; and
2. The grant(s) will be received.

Some specific issues relating to recognition and treatment of government grants are considered below.

Firstly, the receipt of the grant does not provide any assurance that, in fact, the conditions attaching to the grant have been or will be complied with by the enterprise. Thus, both conditions are equally important and the enterprise should have reasonable assurance with respect to the two conditions before a grant could be recognized.

Secondly, the term "reasonable assurance" has not been defined in this standard. However, one of the recognition criteria for income under the IASC's *Framework* is existence of "sufficient degree of certainty." Furthermore, under IAS 18, revenue is recognized only when it is probable that economic benefits will flow to the enterprise. Thus, the criterion of reasonable assurance could possibly be interpreted as *probable*. Comparing this with the criterion for the recognition of contingent gains under IAS 37, it appears that there the criterion has been made more stringent than the above criterion for recognition of a government grant. In the case of recognition of a government grant, it seems the criterion has been relaxed to a degree lower than virtually certain—it has been pegged at the reasonable assurance level. However, under IAS 37 contingent gains could be recognized if, and only if, realization was virtually certain.

Thirdly, under IAS 20 a forgivable loan from a government is treated as a government grant when there is reasonable assurance that the enterprise will meet the terms of forgiveness of the loan. Thus, on receiving a forgivable loan from a government and on fulfilling the criterion of reasonable assurance with respect to meeting the terms of forgiveness of the loan, an enterprise would normally recognize the government grant. Some authorities on the subject have suggested that the grant would be recognized when the loan is forgiven and not when the forgivable loan is received. Under IAS 20 it is fairly obvious that "a forgivable loan from the government is treated as a grant when there is reasonable assurance that the enterprise will meet the terms for forgiveness of the loan" (emphasis added). In the authors' opinion, this implies that the recognition of the grant is to be made at the point of time when the forgivable loan is granted, as opposed to the point of time when it is actually forgiven.

Once a grant has been recognized, IAS 20 clarifies that any related contingency would be treated in accordance with IAS 37. Contingent assets and liabilities, as these are defined under IFRS, are not subject to formal recognition, although disclosure is acceptable and often useful.

Recognition period. Two broad approaches with respect to the accounting treatment of government grants have been discussed by the standard: the "capital approach" and the "income approach." The standard clearly does *not* support the capital approach, which advocates crediting a grant directly to the shareholders' equity. Endorsing the income approach, the standard lays down the rule for recognition of government grants as follows: Government grants should be recognized as income, on a systematic and rational basis, over the periods necessary to match them with the related costs. As a corollary, and by way of abundant precaution, the standard reiterates that government grants should *not* be credited directly to shareholders' interests.

The standard established rules for recognition of grants under different conditions. These are explained through numerical examples as follows:

1. Grants in recognition of specific costs are recognized as income over the same period as the relevant expense.

To illustrate this rule, let us consider the following example:

> An enterprise receives a grant of €30 million to defray environmental costs over a period of five years. Environmental costs will be incurred by the enterprise as follows:

Year	*Costs*
1	€1 million
2	€2 million
3	€3 million
4	€4 million
5	€5 million

Total environment costs will equal €15 million, whereas the grant received is €30 million.

Applying the principle outlined in the standard for recognition of the grant, that is, recognizing the grant as income "over the period which matches the costs" and using a "systematic and rational basis" (in this case, sum-of-the-years' digits amortization), the total grant would be recognized as follows:

Year	*Grant recognized*
1	€30 * (1/15) = € 2 million
2	€30 * (2/15) = € 4 million
3	€30 * (3/15) = € 6 million
4	€30 * (4/15) = € 8 million
5	€30 * (5/15) = €10 million

2. Grants related to depreciable assets are usually recognized as income over the periods and in the proportions in which depreciation on those assets is charged.

The following example will illustrate the above rule:

> An enterprise receives a grant of €100 million to purchase a refinery in an economically backward area. The enterprise has estimated that such a refinery would cost €200 million. The secondary condition attached to the grant is that the enterprise should hire labor locally (i.e., from the economically backward area where the refinery is located) instead of employing workers from other parts of the country. It should maintain a ratio of 1:1 (local workers : workers from outside) in its labor force for the next five years. The refinery is to be depreciated using the straight-line method over a period of ten years.
>
> The grant will be recognized over a period of ten years. In each of the ten years, the grant will be recognized in proportion to the annual depreciation on the refinery. Thus, €10 million will be recognized as income in each of the ten years. With regard to the secondary condition of maintenance of the ratio of 1:1 in the labor force, this contingency would need to be disclosed in the footnotes to the financial statements for the next five years (during which period the condition is in force) in accordance with disclosure requirements of IAS 37.

3. Grants related to nondepreciable assets may also require the fulfillment of certain obligations and would then be recognized as income over periods which bear the cost of meeting the obligations.

To understand this rule, let us consider the following case study:

> ABN Inc. was granted 1000 acres of land, on the outskirts of the city, by a local government authority. The condition attached to this grant was that ABN Inc. should clean up this land and lay roads by employing laborers from the village in which the land is located. The government has fixed the minimum wage payable to the workers. The entire operation will take three years and is estimated to cost €60 million. This amount will be spent as follows: €10 million each in the first and second years and €40 million in the third year. The fair value of this land is presently €120 million.
>
> ABN Inc. would need to recognize the fair value of the grant over the period of three years in proportion to the cost of meeting the obligation. Thus, €120 million will be recognized as follows:

Year	*Grant recognized*
1	€120 * (10/60) = €20 million
2	€120 * (10/60) = €20 million
3	€120 * (40/60) = €80 million

4. Grants are sometimes received as part of a package of financial or fiscal aids to which a number of conditions are attached.

When different conditions attach to different components of the grant, the terms of the grant would have to be evaluated in order to determine how the various elements of the grant would be earned by the enterprise. Based on that assessment, the total grant amount would then be apportioned.

For example, an enterprise receives a consolidated grant of €120 million. Two-thirds of the grant is to be utilized to purchase a college building for students from third-world or developing countries. The balance of the grant is for subsidizing the tuition costs of those students for four years from the date of the grant.

The grant would first be apportioned as follows:

Grant related to assets   (2/3) = €80 million, and
Grant related to income (1/3) = €40 million

The grant related to assets would be recognized in income over the useful life of the college building, for example, ten years, using a systematic and rational basis. Assuming the college building is depreciated using the straight-line method, this portion of the grant (i.e., €80 million) would be recognized as income over a period of ten years at €8 million per year.

The grant related to income would be recognized over a period of four years. Assuming that the tuition subsidy will be offered evenly over the period of four years, this portion of the grant (i.e., €40 million) would be taken to income over a period of four years at €10 million per year.

5. A government grant that becomes receivable as compensation for expenses or losses already incurred or for the purpose of giving immediate financial support to the enterprise with no future related costs should be recognized as income of the period in which it becomes receivable.

Sometimes grants are awarded for the purposes of giving immediate financial support to an enterprise, for example, to revive a commercial insolvent business (referred to as "sick unit" in third-world countries). Such grants are not given as incentives to invest funds in specified areas or for a specified purpose from which the benefits will be derived over a period of time in the future. Instead such grants are awarded to compensate an enterprise for losses incurred in the past. Thus, they should be recognized as income in the period in which the enterprise becomes eligible to receive such grants.

A grant may be awarded to an enterprise to compensate it for losses incurred in the past for operating out of an economically backward area that has been hit by an earthquake recently. During the period the enterprise operated in that area, the area experienced an earthquake and thus the enterprise incurred massive losses. Such a grant received by the enterprise should be recognized as income in the year in which the grant becomes receivable. Under IAS 20, when losses suffered were extraordinary in nature, the grant would potentially need to be presented as an extraordinary item in the financial statements. However, extraordinary item classification has been eliminated by revised IAS 1 and may no longer be employed.

Nonmonetary Grants

A government grant may not always be given in cash or cash equivalents. Sometimes a government grant may take the form of a transfer of a nonmonetary asset, such as grant of a plot of land or a building in a remote area. In these circumstances the standard prescribes the following optional accounting treatments:

1. To account for both the grant and the asset at the fair value of the nonmonetary asset, or
2. To record both the asset and the grant at a "nominal amount."

Presentation of Grants Related to Assets

Presentation on the balance sheet. Government grants related to assets, including nonmonetary grants at fair value, should be presented in the balance sheet in either of the two ways

1. By setting up the grant as deferred income, or
2. By deducting the grant in arriving at the carrying amount of the asset.

To understand this better, let us consider the following case study:

Natraj Corp. received a grant related to a factory building which it bought in 2004. The total amount of the grant was €3 million. Natraj Corp. purchased the building from an industrialist identified by the government. The factory building was located in the slums of the city and was to be repossessed by a government agency from the industrialist, in case Natraj Corp. had not purchased it from him. The factory building was purchased for €9 million by Natraj Corp. The useful life of the building is not considered to be more than three years mainly because it was not properly maintained by the industrialist.

Under Option 1: Set up the grant as deferred income.

- The grant of €3 million would be set up initially as deferred income in 2004.
- At the end of 2004, €1 million would be recognized as income and the balance of €2 million would be carried forward in the balance sheet.
- At the end of 2005, €1 million would be taken to income and the balance of €1 million would be carried forward in the balance sheet.
- At the end of 2006, €1 million would be taken to income.

Under Option 2: The grant will be deducted from carrying value.

The grant of €3 million is deducted from the gross book value of the asset to arrive at the carrying value of €6 million. The useful life being three years, annual depreciation of €2 million per year is charged to the income statement for the years 2004, 2005, and 2006.

The effect on the operating results is the same whether the first or the second option is chosen.

Under the second option, the grant is indirectly recognized in income through the reduced depreciation charge of €1 million per year, whereas under the first option, it is taken to income directly.

Presentation in the cash flow statement. When grants related to assets are received in cash, there is an inflow of cash to be shown under the investing activities section of the cash flow statement. Furthermore, there would also be an outflow resulting from the purchase of the asset. IAS 20 specifically requires that both these movements should be shown separately and not be netted. The standard further clarifies that such movements should be shown separately regardless of whether or not the grant is deducted from the related asset for the purposes of the balance sheet presentation.

Presentation of Grants Related to Income

The standard allows a free choice between two presentations.

Option 1: Grant presented as a credit in the income statement, either separately or under a general heading other income

Option 2: Grant deducted in reporting the related expense

The standard does not show any bias towards any one option. It acknowledges the reasoning given in support of each approach by its supporters. The standard considers both methods as acceptable. However, it does recommend disclosure of the grant for a proper understanding of the financial statements. The standard recognizes that the disclosure of the effect of the grants on any item of income or expense may be appropriate.

Repayment of Government Grants

When a government grant becomes repayable, for example, due to nonfulfillment of a condition attaching to it, it should be treated as a change in estimate, under IAS 8, and accounted for prospectively (as opposed to retrospectively).

Repayment of a grant related to income should

1. First be applied against any unamortized deferred income (credit) set up in respect of the grant, and
2. To the extent the repayment exceeds any such deferred income (credit), or in case no deferred credit exists, the repayment should be recognized immediately as an expense.

Repayment of a grant related to an asset should be

1. Recorded by increasing the carrying amount of the asset or reducing the deferred income balance by the amount repayable, and
2. The cumulative additional depreciation that would have been recognized to date as an expense in the absence of the grant should be recognized immediately as an expense.

When a grant related to an asset becomes repayable, it would become incumbent upon the enterprise to assess whether any impairment in value of the asset (to which the repayable grant relates) has resulted. For example, a bridge is being constructed through funding from a government grant and during the construction period, because of nonfulfillment of the terms of the grant, the grant became repayable. Since the grant was provided to assist in the construction, it is possible that the enterprise may not be in a position to arrange funds to complete the project. In such a circumstance, the asset is impaired and may need to be written down to its recoverable value, in accordance with IAS 36.

Government Assistance

Government assistance includes government grants. IAS 20 deals with both accounting and disclosure of government grants and disclosure of government assistance. Thus government assistance comprises government grants and other forms of government assistance (i.e. those not involving transfer of resources).

Excluded from the government assistance are certain forms of government benefits that cannot reasonably have a value placed on them, such as free technical or other professional advice. Also excluded from government assistance are government benefits that cannot be distinguished from the normal trading transactions of the enterprise. The reason for the second exclusion is obvious: although the benefit cannot be disputed, any attempt to segregate it would necessarily be arbitrary.

Loans at zero or low interest are a form of government assistance. They should not have a value attributed to them in the financial statements, since the benefit could only be quantified by imputing interest costs, which is arbitrary. Thus, an enterprise that is currently benefiting from such assistance (e.g., in the form of low interest), but is likely to borrow funds in the near future at commercial rates of interest, would need to disclose when the full interest is going to commence.

Disclosures

The following disclosures are prescribed:

1. The accounting policy adopted for government grants, including the methods of presentation adopted in the financial statements;
2. The nature and extent of government grants recognized in the financial statements and an indication of other forms of government assistance from which the enterprise has directly benefited; and
3. Unfulfilled conditions and other contingencies attaching to government assistance that has been recognized.

Expected Changes to IAS 20

There has been general and widespread dissatisfaction with IAS 20 for many years. The IASB decided in 2004 that IAS 20 should be amended by replacing its rules with those set forth in IAS 41, *Agriculture*. The agriculture standard embraced the basic concept that government grants are income (not either a capital contribution or a reduction of the cost of acquiring an asset). IAS 41 distinguishes between unconditional and conditional grants: unconditional grants are taken directly to income when received or receivable, while conditional grants are taken to income when the conditions have been met. The conditions might relate to operating in a particular area for a specific period, in which case the grant is income at the end of the period, unless it becomes unconditional on a proportional or other basis. A condition is a stipulation that entitles government to the return of the granted resources if a specified future event that is not presently regarded as remote either occurs or does not occur. IASB determined that the definition should refer to the condition having commercial substance (i.e., in order to exclude routine or normal trading transactions).

IASB staff recommended that an entity should recognize a government grant as an asset at the earlier of having an unconditional right to receive the government grant without conditions attached to its retention, or actually receiving the government grant.

While this tentative solution was not the preferred solution, it was nonetheless agreed that further development is outside the scope of a short-term convergence project. IASB agreed not to provide guidance on whether an asset and liability would be recognized when a repayment clause is attached to a condition, or whether no asset should be recognized at all until the grant is fully nonrepayable.

It is expected that revised IAS 20 will hold that an asset acquired in connection with a government grant should be tested for impairment on initial recognition. Any liability recognized in relation to the grant is to be considered part of the cash-generating unit.

The Board also identified a conflict between IAS 20 and IAS 39. IAS 20 does not take account of low-interest or interest-free loans, or of the effect of government guarantees, while IAS 39 says liabilities should be measured at fair value, which implies at market rates of interest. The IAS 20 exclusion will accordingly be removed when the standard is revised so that IAS 39 will apply.

An Exposure Draft was promised for 2004 but, as of mid-2005, has not been forthcoming.

Emission Rights

Beginning in 2005, a number of countries are proposing to implement emission reduction incentives. These are generally based on the notion that an enterprise will be given pollution allowances up to its current levels. It can either reduce pollution and sell its allowances or, if it increases the pollution it produces, it must buy further allowances in the market. Each year the entity will have to surrender allowances appropriate to the volume of its polluting emissions.

IFRIC issued a Draft Interpretation (DI Emission Rights) in 2003, which proposed that the pollution allowance should be recognized as an intangible asset at fair value. Any difference between fair value and the amount paid would be treated as a government grant. An entity that made emissions that would require it to give up allowances should create a provision as the emissions are made. Comment letters pointed out that the changes in fair value of the allowance would flow to equity, while the changes in the provision amount would flow through the income statement. As a consequence, IFRIC proposed to the IASB that IAS 38, *Intangible Assets*, should be amended to permit pollution allowances to be treated as akin to a currency, with fair value changes going to income. The IASB agreed with this proposed solution, but IFRIC decided not to proceed at the time.

IFRIC did later issue an interpretation, IFRIC 3, *Emission Rights*, in late 2004, to have become effective in early 2005. However, in June 2005 this interpretation was withdrawn.

The now-withdrawn IFRIC 3 dealt with the required accounting by participants in "cap and trade schemes" that are already operational. It concluded that a cap and trade scheme gives rise to: (1) an asset for allowances held; (2) a government grant; and (3) a liability for the obligation to deliver allowances equal to emissions that have been made. These were to be recorded individually, not presented as a net asset or liability.

IFRIC 3 also held that allowances, whether issued by government or purchases, were to be treated as intangible assets, in accordance with IAS 38. It stated that allowances that were issued for less than fair value were to be measured initially at fair value. If issued for less than fair value, the difference between the amount paid and fair value was to be accounted for as a government grant, within the scope of IAS 20.

IFRIC 3 stipulated that, initially, the grant was to have been recognized as deferred income in the balance sheet, and then taken into income on a systematic basis over the compliance period for which the allowances had been issued, regardless of whether the allowances were held or sold.

Furthermore, it stated that, as emissions would later be made, a liability was to be recognized for the obligation to deliver allowances equal to emissions made. This liability was to have been treated as a provision in accordance with IAS 37, measured at the best estimate of the expenditure required to settle the present obligation at the balance sheet date. This would usually be the present market price of the number of allowances required to cover emissions made up to the balance sheet date.

The existence or requirements of an emission rights scheme could cause a reduction in the cash flows expected to be generated by certain assets. In such instances, IFRIC 3 would have directed that such a reduction be understood as an indication that those assets may be impaired and thus trigger a test for impairment under IAS 36.

IASB considered amending IAS 38 to create a category of intangible to be measured at fair value, with changes recognized currently in results of operations. It also was attempting to address an EFRAG proposal dealing with hedge accounting as a mechanism for dealing with supposed mismatching created under IFRIC 3. As of mid-2005, no actions have resulted. However, EFRAG recommended that IFRIC 3 not be endorsed for use by EU companies, and the urgency responsible for the issuance of this interpretive guidance had abated. Accordingly, the interpretation was withdrawn; this was explained as being done in recognition that the markets for emission rights had not developed as quickly as expected and that further development work, to ease the asset/liability mismatching concern, would be required.

Service Concessions

Government involvement directly with business is much more common in Europe than in North America, and European adoption of IFRS has created a need to expand the IFRS literature to address a number of such involvements. The service concession, particularly common in France, occurs when a commercial entity operates a commercial asset which is owned by, or has to be transferred to, a local, regional, or national government organization. The most famous example of this is perhaps the Channel Tunnel, linking England and France. This was built by a commercial entity which has a concession to operate it for a period of years, at the end of which the asset reverts to the British and French governments. A more mundane example would be companies that erect bus shelters free of charge in municipalities, in return for the right to advertise on them for a period of time.

The IFRIC has been working on the accounting for service concession since 2003. Its analysis has led it to believe that there are two broad models that apply. Their analysis talks about the "grantor" (the organization making the concession available, e.g., the British and French governments regarding the Channel Tunnel) and the "operator" (the entity that operates the concession, e.g., Eurotunnel plc for the Channel Tunnel). In all cases it is assumed that the grantor retains the residual interest in the central asset or group of assets so the grantor would (if it publishes a balance sheet) account for the tangible asset, while the operator would report either an intangible or a financial asset. The operator has a financial asset, under what the IFRIC styles the *receivables model*, which is where the grantor has a responsibility to pay the operator for the services. The operator has an intangible asset when it receives payments directly from the users of the asset (e.g., motorway tolls from motorists).

As of mid-2005, three draft IFRIC interpretations dealing with service concessions remain outstanding.

27 FIRST-TIME ADOPTION OF INTERNATIONAL FINANCIAL REPORTING STANDARDS

PERSPECTIVE AND ISSUES

When a reporting entity prepares its financial statements in accordance with international accounting standards for the first time, a number of implementation questions will need to be addressed and resolved. IASB's predecessor standard setter, IASC, had provided only limited guidance on this matter, which was set forth in SIC 8. This was superseded by a more comprehensive standard, IFRS 1, *First-Time Adoption of IFRS.* IFRS 1 differs in several important respects from SIC 8.

With many countries mandating adoption of IFRS in 2005 (e.g., all publicly held entities in the 25 EU member states), first-time adopters have learned that this is more than a mere mechanical exercise, requiring significant effort and time to accomplish correctly. Global players such as Australia and Russia, which have decided to adopt IFRS as their respective national GAAP, will also need to gain a thorough insight into the various implementation aspects of IFRS 1 when adoption becomes effective. The fact that the EU has defined certain "carve outs" from IAS 39 only adds to the confusion surrounding IFRS adoption, and as of mid-2005 the full implications, including auditors' ability to certify financial statements not fully complying with IFRS, have yet to be completely understood.

While truly universal adoption of IFRS is not yet imminent, events are moving very rapidly, as even the US standard setter, the FASB, is now committed to "convergence" with IFRS, and several new US rules, clearly modeled on IFRS, were promulgated in late 2004 and early 2005. Many more countries in Eastern Europe, South Asia, and the Far East are planning to be included in the growing list of new converts to IFRS. It is within this context that IASB decided to promulgate a standard on this subject as its *maiden* pronouncement, notwithstanding the existing guidance on this topic (SIC 8).

Sources of IFRS
IFRS 1
IASB Framework for the Preparation and Presentation of Financial Statements

DEFINITIONS OF TERMS

Date of transition to IFRS. This refers to the beginning of the earliest period for which an entity presents full comparative information under IFRS in its "first IFRS financial statements" (defined below).

Deemed cost. An amount substituted for "cost" or "depreciated cost" at a given date. In subsequent periods, this value is used as the basis for depreciation or amortization.

Fair value. The amount for which an asset could be exchanged, or a liability settled, between knowledgeable, willing parties in an arm's-length transaction.

First IFRS financial statements. The first annual financial statements in which an entity adopts IFRS by making an explicit and unreserved statement of compliance with IFRS.

First-time adopter (of IFRS). An entity is referred to as a first-time adopter in the period in which it presents its first IFRS financial statements.

International financial reporting standards (IFRS). The standards issued by the International Accounting Standards Board (IASB); more generally, the term connotes the currently outstanding standards (IFRS), the interpretations issued by the International Financial Reporting Interpretations Committee (IFRIC), all previous standards (IAS) issued by the predecessor International Accounting Standards Committee (IASC), and the interpretations issued by the IASC's Standards Interpretations Committee (SIC).

Opening IFRS balance sheet. The balance sheet prepared in accordance with the requirements of IFRS 1 as of the "date of transition to IFRS." IFRS 1 only requires that a first-time adopter *prepare* an opening balance sheet, but it is not required to *present* an opening balance sheet; thus, whether or not this balance sheet is *published* along with the "first IFRS financial statements," this would still be considered to be the entity's opening IFRS balance sheet.)

Previous GAAP. This refers to whatever basis of accounting (e.g., national standards) a first-time adopter used immediately prior to IFRS adoption.

Reporting date. The end of the latest period covered by financial statements or by an interim financial report.

CONCEPTS, RULES AND EXAMPLES

Background

IFRS 1 was issued by the IASB in June 2003, superseding SIC 8. Certain aspects of SIC 8 were considered difficult to implement by first-time adopters (of IFRS). The principal concerns were

1. The requirement that all standards be applied by the first-time adopter with full retrospective application, and
2. The rule that a first-time adopter was expected to apply different versions of IFRS in those instances where new versions of a standard had been introduced during the periods covered by the first set of financial statements prepared under IFRS.

The main differences between the requirements of IFRS 1 and the provisions of SIC 8 may be summarized as follows:

- While SIC 8 mandated retrospective application, IFRS 1 requires retrospective application in a majority of instances, with *targeted exemptions* in certain cases and *prohibitions* against retrospective application in certain other instances;
- IFRS 1 clarifies certain issues that SIC 8 had either not categorically addressed or had failed to explain in adequate detail. For instance, SIC 8 had not explicitly stated whether a first-time adopter should use hindsight in the retrospective application of the various standards (IFRS) and also whether the "transitional provisions" of the individual IAS were to be considered as well. These matters have now been clarified by IFRS 1; and
- IFRS 1 mandates new disclosures that were not required under SIC 8.

Scope and applicability of the new standard. IFRS 1 applies to an entity that presents its first IFRS financial statements. It specifies the requirements that an entity must follow when it first adopts IFRS as the basis for preparing its general-purpose financial statements. IFRS 1 refers to these entities as *first-time adopters.* Since specific requirements apply to the financial statements of first-time adopters, the narrowly delimited definition of *first IFRS financial statements* must be carefully reviewed.

Per IFRS 1, an entity must apply the standard in its first IFRS financial statements and in *each interim financial report* it presents under IAS 34 for a part of the period covered by its first IFRS financial statements. For example, if 2006 is the first annual period for which IFRS financial statements are being prepared, the quarterly or semiannual statements for 2006, if presented, must also comply with IFRS.

According to the standard, an entity's first IFRS financial statements refer to the first annual financial statements in which the entity adopts IFRS by making an *explicit and unreserved statement* (in the financial statements) of compliance with IFRS. IFRS-compliant financial statements presented in the current year would qualify as first IFRS financial statements if the reporting entity presented its most recent previous financial statements

- Under national GAAP or standards that were inconsistent with IFRS in all respects;
- In conformity with IFRS in all respects, but without an explicit and unreserved statement to that effect;
- With a categorical statement that the financial statements complied with certain IFRS, but not with all applicable standards;
- Under national GAAP or standards that differ from IFRS but using some individual IFRS to account for items which were not addressed by its national GAAP or other standards;
- Under national GAAP or standards, but with a reconciliation of selected items to amounts determined under IFRS.

Other examples of situations where an entity's current year's financial statements would qualify as first IFRS financial statements are

- Where the entity prepared financial statements in the previous period under IFRS but the financial statements were identified as being "for internal use only" and were not made available to the entity's owners or any other external users;
- Where IFRS-compliant financial reporting was produced in earlier years, with explicit and unreserved statement of this fact, but national GAAP, not IFRS, was used in the period immediately preceding the preparation of the current year's first IFRS financial statements;
- Where the entity prepared a reporting package in the previous period under IFRS for consolidation purposes without preparing a complete set of financial statements as mandated by IAS 1; and

- Where the entity did not present financial statements for the previous periods at all.

The following example would help illustrate the implications of this requirement of the standard.

> Excellent Inc., incorporated in Mysteryland, is a progressive multinational corporation that has always presented its financial statements under the national GAAP of the country of incorporation, with additional disclosures made in its footnotes. The supplementary data included value-added statements and a reconciliation of major items on its balance sheet to International Financial Reporting Standards (IFRS). Excellent Inc. has significant borrowings from international financial institutions, and these have certain restrictive financial covenants—such as a defined upper limit on the ratio of external debt to equity, and minimum annual return on investments. In order to monitor compliance with these covenants, Excellent Inc. also prepared a separate set of financial statements in accordance with IFRS, but these were never made available to the international financial institutions or to the shareholders of Excellent Inc.
>
> With the growing global acceptance that IFRS had been receiving in recent years, the finance minister of Mysteryland attempted to have the country adopt IFRS as its national GAAP, but this was blocked by the standard setters of his country. Mysteryland's accession to membership in the WTO is being planned for 2006, and the country is taking steps to be recognized as a global economic player. Mysteryland was invited to participate in the World Economic Forum, and to publicize his country's commitment to globalization, the finance minister announces at this event that his country would adopt IFRS as its national GAAP beginning in 2005. This announcement was subsequently ratified by Mysteryland's parliament (and later by its national standard-setting body) and thus it was publicly announced that IFRS would be adopted as the country's national GAAP from 2005.
>
> Excellent Inc. had always presented its financial statements under its national GAAP but had also voluntarily provided a reconciliation of major items on its balance sheet to IFRS in its footnotes, and "for internal purposes" had also prepared a separate set of financial statements under IFRS. Despite these previous overtures towards IFRS compliance, in the year 2005—when Excellent Inc. moves to IFRS as its national GAAP and presents its financial statements to the outside world under IFRS, with an explicit and unreserved statement that these financial statements comply with IFRS—it will nonetheless be considered a first-time adopter and will have to comply with the requirements of IFRS 1.

Exceptions to the "first-time adopter" rule. If an entity's financial statements in the previous year contained an explicit and unreserved statement of compliance with IFRS, but in fact did not fully comply with all aspects of IFRS, such an entity would *not* be considered a first-time adopter for the purposes of IFRS 1 in the current year. The disclosed or undisclosed departures from IFRS in previous year's financial statements of this entity would be treated as an "error" under IFRS 1, which warrants correction made in this manner prescribed by IAS 8. IFRS 1 identifies three situations in which IFRS 1 would *not* apply. These exceptions are as follows:

1. When an entity presented its financial statements in the previous year that contained an explicit and unreserved statement of compliance with IFRS, and its auditors qualified their report on those financial statements;
2. When an entity in the previous year presented its financial statements under national requirements (i.e., its national GAAP) along with another set of financial statements that contained an explicit or unreserved statement of compliance with IFRS, and in the current year it discontinues this practice of presenting under its national GAAP and presents only under IFRS; and
3. When an entity in the previous year presented its financial statements under national requirements (its national GAAP) and those financial statements contained (improperly) an explicit and unreserved statement of IFRS compliance.

Opening IFRS balance sheet. At the *date of transition to IFRS,* the reporting entity is required to prepare an opening IFRS balance sheet. This opening IFRS balance sheet serves as the starting point for the entity's accounting under IFRS. The requirement under IFRS 1 is to *prepare* an opening balance sheet, which does not mean that the opening IFRS balance sheet must also be *presented* in the entity's first IFRS financial statements. In fact, it is likely that most entities will not make such a presentation, although some selected elements might be incorporated into various footnote explanations.

As defined in Appendix A to IFRS 1, *date of transition to IFRS* refers to *the beginning of the earliest period for which an entity presents full comparative information under IFRS in its first IFRS financial statements.* Thus the date of transition to IFRS depends on two factors: first, the date of adoption of IFRS and second, the number of years of comparative information that the entity decides to present along with the financial information of the year of adoption. The following illustration will clarify this point:

> Adaptability Inc. presented its financial statements, under its previous GAAP, on a calendar year basis. The most recent such financial statements it presented were as of December 31, 2004. Adaptability Inc. decided to adopt IFRS as at December 31, 2005, and to present comparative information for the year 2004. Thus, the beginning of the earliest period for which the entity should present full comparative information would be January 1, 2004. Accordingly, the opening IFRS balance sheet for purposes of compliance with IFRS 1 would be that as of January 1, 2004 (equivalent to the year-end 2003 balance sheet).

> Alternatively, if Adaptability Inc. decided (or was required, e.g., by the stock listing authorities) to present two-year comparative information (i.e., for both 2004 and 2003), then the beginning of the earliest period for which the entity would present full comparative information would be January 1, 2003 (equivalent to the year-end 2002 balance sheet). Accordingly, the opening IFRS balance sheet for purposes of compliance with IFRS 1 would be that as of January 1, 2003.

Adjustments required in preparing the opening IFRS balance sheet (or in transition from previous GAAP to IFRS as of the first-time adoption). In preparing the opening IFRS balance sheet, an entity should apply the following four rules, except in cases where IFRS 1 grants targeted exemptions and prohibits retrospective application:

1. *Recognize* all assets and liabilities whose recognition is required under IFRS;
    It is expected that many companies will recognize additional assets and liabilities under IFRS reporting, when compared with the national GAAP formerly employed. Areas which may result in this effect include

    -   Defined benefit pension plans
    -   Deferred taxation
    -   Assets and liabilities under finance leases
    -   Provisions where there is a legal or construction obligation
    -   Derivative financial instruments
    -   Acquired intangible assets
    -   Share-based payments (per new standard IFRS 2)

2. *Derecognize* items as assets or liabilities if IFRS do not permit such recognition;
    Some assets and liabilities recognized under a company's previous (national) GAAP will have to be derecognized. For example

    -   Provisions where there is no legal or constructive obligation (e.g., general reserves)
    -   Internally generated intangible assets
    -   Deferred tax assets where recovery is not probable

3. *Reclassify* items that it recognized under previous GAAP as one type of asset, liability, or component of equity, but are a different type of asset, liability, or component of equity under IFRS.

   Assets and liabilities that might be reclassified to conform to IFRS include

   • Investments accounted for in accordance with IAS 39
   • Certain financial instruments previously classified as equity
   • Any assets and liabilities that have been offset where the criteria for offsetting in IRS are not met—for example, the offset of an insurance recovery against a provision
   • Noncurrent assets held-for-sale (per new standard IFRS 5)

4. *Measure* all recognized assets and liabilities according to principles set forth in IFRS.

   Assets and liabilities that might have to be measured differently include

   • Receivables (IAS 18)
   • Employee benefit obligations (IAS 19)
   • Deferred taxation (IAS 12)
   • Financial instruments (IAS 39)
   • Provisions (IAS 37)
   • Impairments of property, plant, and equipment, and intangible assets (IAS 36)
   • Assets held for disposal (under IFRS 5)
   • Share-based payments (per IFRS 2)

The following comprehensive example illustrates the practical application of the four rules outlined above:

Situation

ABC Corp. presented its financial statements under the national GAAP of XYZ country through 2004. It adopted IFRS from 2005 and is required to prepare an opening IFRS balance sheet as at January 1, 2004. In preparing the IFRS opening balance sheet, ABC Corp. noted the following:

Under its previous GAAP, ABC Corp. had deferred training costs of $250,000 and had classified proposed dividends of $400,000 as a current liability. Furthermore, it had not made a provision for warranty of $100,000 in the financial statements since the concept of "constructive obligation" was not recognized under its previous GAAP. Finally, in arriving at the amount to be capitalized as part of costs necessary to bring an asset to its working condition, ABC Corp. had not included professional fees of $50,000 paid to architects at the time when the building it presently occupies as its home office was being constructed.

Solution

In order to prepare the opening IFRS balance sheet at January 1, 2004, ABC Corp. would need to make the following adjustments to its balance sheet at December 31, 2003, presented under its previous GAAP:

1. IAS 38 does not allow training costs to be deferred whereas ABC Corp.'s previous GAAP allowed this treatment. Thus, $250,000 of such deferred costs should be *derecognized* (expensed) under IFRS;

2. IAS 37 requires recognition of a provision for warranty but ABC Corp.'s previous GAAP did not allow a similar treatment. Thus, a provision for warranty of $100,000 should be *recognized* under IFRS;

3. IAS 10 does not allow proposed dividends to be recognized as a liability, instead they are to be included in footnotes. ABC Corp.'s previous GAAP allowed proposed dividends to be treated as a current liability. Therefore, proposed dividends of $400,000 should be *eliminated* from current liability and just disclosed in footnotes; and

4. IAS 16 requires all directly attributable costs of bringing an asset to its working condition for its intended use to be capitalized as part of the carrying cost of property, plant, and equipment. Thus $50,000 of architects' fees should be capitalized as part of (i.e., used in the *measurement* of) property, plant, and equipment under IFRS.

Accounting policies. IFRS 1 stipulates that in preparing an opening IFRS balance sheet the first-time adopter is to use the same accounting policies as it has used throughout all periods presented in its first IFRS financial statements. Furthermore, the standard requires that those accounting policies must comply with each IFRS effective at the "reporting date" (as explained below) for its first IFRS financial statements, except under certain defined circumstances wherein the entity claims targeted exemptions from retrospective application of IFRS, or is prohibited by IFRS from applying IFRS retrospectively (both concepts are discussed below). In other words, a first-time adopter should consistently apply the same accounting policies throughout the periods presented in its first IFRS financial statements and these accounting policies should be based on "latest version of the IFRS" effective at the reporting date. (The rationale for this is discussed later in this section.)

If a new IFRS has been issued on the reporting date, but application is not yet mandatory, although reporting entities have been encouraged to apply it before the effective date, the first-time adopter is permitted, but not required, to apply it as well.

Reporting period. "Reporting date" for an entity's first IFRS financial statements refers to the end of the latest period covered by the annual financial statements or interim financial statements, if any, that the entity presents under IAS 34 for the period covered by its first IFRS financial statements. This is illustrated in the following examples:

Example 1: Xodus Corp. presents its first annual financial statements under IFRS for the calendar year 2005, which include an explicit and unreserved statement of compliance with IFRS. It also presents full comparative financial information for the calendar year 2004. In this case, the latest period covered by these annual financial statements would end on December 31, 2005, and the *reporting date* for the purposes of IFRS 1 is December 31, 2005 (presuming the entity does not present financial statements under IAS 34 for interim periods within calendar year 2005).

Example 2: Alternatively, if Xodus Corp. decides to present its first IFRS interim financial statements for the six months ended June 30, 2005, in addition to the first IFRS annual financial statements for the year ended December 31, 2005, the *reporting date* may no longer be December 31, 2005; it is dependent upon how the interim financial statements are prepared. If the interim financial statements for the six months ended June 30, 2005 were prepared in accordance with IAS 34, then the reporting period would be June 30, 2005 (instead of December 31, 2005). If however, the interim financial statements for the six months ended June 30, 2005, were not prepared in accordance with IAS 34, then the reporting date would continue to be December 31, 2005 (and not June 30, 2005).

Rationale for using the "current version of IFRS." With the passage of time IFRS have been revised or amended several times and in some instances the current version of IFRS is vastly different from the earlier versions that were either superseded or amended. IFRS 1 requires a first-time adopter to use the current version of IFRS, without considering the superseded or amended versions. This obviates the need to identify varying iterations of the standards that would have guided the preparation of the entity's financial statements at each prior reporting date, which would have been a very time-consuming and problematic task. This means that the comparative financial statements accompanying the first IFRS compliant reporting may differ—perhaps materially—from what would have been presented in those earlier periods had the entity commenced reporting consistent with IFRS at an earlier point in time.

It should be noted that IASB's original thinking on this matter was different. Under ED 1, the draft standard that preceded the issuance of IFRS 1, the first-time adopter would have had an option to elect application of IFRS *as if it had always applied IFRS* (i.e., from inception). To actualize this, the first-time adopter would have had to consider the possibly several different versions of IFRS promulgated over the period of time culminating with the date of its actual adoption of IFRS.

In reaching its conclusion to eliminate this proposed optional methodology, the IASB took into account the following factors:

- The methodology in the final standard enhances "comparability," since the information in a first-time adopter's first financial statements is prepared on a consistent basis over time, on a basis that comports with the users' current frame of reference;
- The adopted approach gives users comparative information prepared using later versions of IFRS that the Board regards as superior to superseded versions; and
- It avoids having financial statement preparers incur unnecessary costs.

Additionally, in reaching its decision on this matter IASB relied upon basic concepts enshrined in its *Framework*. The *Framework* sets out four qualitative characteristics that make information in financial statements meaningful for users, one of which is *comparability*. In setting the earlier rule, that a first-time adopter should comply with the same Standards as an entity that already applied IFRS, SIC 8 had sought to achiever comparability between a first-time adopter of IFRS and entities that had already been using IFRS.

The IASB took a different stand on this issue, however. It ruled that not only was it more important to establish a basis for future comparability within a first-time adopter's first IFRS financial statements, but also it was vital that comparability between different entities adopting IFRS for the first time be facilitated. Thus the IASB changed its approach in IFRS 1 (vis-à-vis the IASC's stand in SIC 8) and ruled that a first-time adopter of IFRS would need to apply the current version of IFRS as opposed to the historical versions of IFRS that were applicable from time to time. According to the IASB, it is more important to achieve comparability over time within a first-time adopter's first IFRS financial statements and between different entities adopting IFRS for the first time at a given date; achieving comparability between first-time adopter and entities that already apply IFRS is at best only a secondary objective.

To illustrate, consider the following example.

> According to a previous version of the standard relating to property, plant, and equipment (IAS 16), under the allowed alternative treatment, when property was revalued, the fair value was its market value *for existing use*. Subsequently, this aspect of IAS 16 was revised in order to conform to the guidance in IAS 22; now the standard stipulates that when property, plant, and equipment is revalued, the market value should be fair value, which is the amount for which it can be exchanged between knowledgeable, willing parties in an arm's-length transaction, without restricting the definition of fair value to market value for *existing use*.

> This difference in terminology could have a significant impact. In some cases, the valuation of the property would differ if successive versions of the IFRS were applied for different time periods. Consider the case of land and building that is presently being used as a factory building by an entity that is contemplating a change from national GAAP to IFRS. According to the earlier version of IAS 16, the fair value would be based on its market value for *existing use* whereas, under the revised version of IAS 16, that restriction having being removed, the market value would be its fair value (i.e., "the amount for which it can be exchanged between knowledgeable, willing parties in an arm's-length transaction"). Thus, if the intention of the entity is to convert the factory building at a later date into a shopping mall, then its market value might be quite different (compared to a case where there is no such plan of change in *existing use*) since it would be a valuation driven by the market value of the property based on its *intended use* (as opposed to its *existing use*).

Transitional provisions in other IFRS. Certain IFRS set forth transitional provisions that are meant to facilitate transition to those particular new standards. These transitional provisions, in some cases, permit entities adopting a new standard to deviate from the provisions of other existing standards to an extent, usually in cases when retrospective application of those standards would make it cumbersome to apply the new standard.

IFRS 1 concluded that the transitional provisions in other IFRS were intended to apply to situations where changes in accounting policies were being made by an entity that already reported under IFRS, and thus those standards provide the transitional provisions that were not specifically designed to apply to first-time adopters. IFRS 1 therefore does not permit first-time adopters to invoke transition provisions in other IFRS (although IFRS 1 itself does create certain exceptions, explained below). If this clarification had not been provided in IFRS 1, there could have been confusion in applying certain IFRS that have transitional provisions, as to whether the first-time adopters would need to apply those provisions as well.

Targeted exemptions from other IFRS. In a dramatic change of approach from what had been proposed in ED 1, IFRS 1 allows a first-time adopter to elect to use one or more targeted exemptions. In response to the original draft, many commentators disagreed with ED 1's proposed approach of granting a first-time adopter permission to use either all or none of the exemptions. The IASB thus abandoned the proposed requirement that advocated an "all-or-nothing" approach to exemptions.

Under IFRS 1, a first-time adopter of IFRS may elect to use exemptions from the general measurement and restatement principles in one or more of the following instances:

- Business combinations that occurred before the date of transition to IFRS;
- Assets (property, plant, and equipment, intangible assets, and investment property) measured at fair value or revalued under previous GAAP;
- Employee benefits;
- Cumulative translation differences;
- Compound financial instruments; and
- Assets and liabilities of subsidiaries, associates, and joint ventures at the date of transition to IFRS.

The application of these targeted exemptions is explained in detail below.

Business combinations. IFRS 1 exempts the first-time adopter from mandatory retrospective application in the case of business combinations that occurred before the date of transition to IFRS. That is, requirements under IAS 22 (the standard in effect when IFRS 1 was promulgated) can be applied in accounting for combinations that occurred before the first reporting under IFRS, but need not do so. Thus, under IFRS 1, an entity may elect to use previous national GAAP accounting relating to such business combinations. The IASB provided this exemption because, if retrospective application of IAS 22 had been made obligatory, it could have forced entities to make subjective estimates (or educated guesses) about conditions that supposedly prevailed at the dates of past business combinations. This would have particularly been the case where data from past business combinations had not been preserved. The use of such estimates or guesses could have adversely affected the relevance and reliability of the financial statements and was thus seen as a situation to be avoided.

In evaluating responses to ED 1, the IASB concluded that notwithstanding the fact that restatement of past business combinations to conform with IFRS is conceptually preferable, a pragmatic assessment of cost versus benefit weighed in favor of *permitting* but *not requiring* restatement. However, the IASB did place an important limitation on this election: if a first-time adopter restates *any* business combination, it must restate *all* business combinations that took place subsequent to the date of that restated combination transaction. First-time adopters cannot "cherry pick" among past business combinations to apply IFRS opportunistically to certain of them.

For instance, if BBB Inc., a first-time adopter, did not seek this exemption, instead opted to apply IFRS 3 (which replaced the former standard, IAS 22, in 2004) retrospectively, and restated a major business combination that took place two years ago, then, under this requirement of IFRS 1, BBB Inc. is required to restate all business combinations that took place subsequent to the date of this major business combination to which it applied IFRS 3 retrospectively. Earlier combinations would not have to be restated.

If the entity employs the exemption under IFRS 1 and does not apply IFRS 3 retrospectively to a past business combination, it must observe these rules.

1. The first-time adopter should preserve the same classification (an *acquisition* or a *uniting of interests*) as was applied in its previous GAAP financial statements.

2. The first-time adopter should recognize all assets and liabilities at the date of transition to IFRS that were acquired or assumed in a past business combination, except

   a. Certain financial assets and financial liabilities that were derecognized under its previous GAAP; and

   b. Assets (including goodwill) and liabilities that were not recognized in the acquirer's consolidated balance sheet under previous GAAP and also would not qualify for recognition under IFRS in the separate balance sheet of the acquiree.

   Any resulting change should be recognized by the first-time adopter in retained earnings (or another component of equity, if appropriate) unless the change results from the recognition of an intangible asset that was previously incorporated within goodwill.

3. The first-time adopter should derecognize (exclude) from its opening IFRS balance sheet any item recognized under previous GAAP that does not qualify for recognition, either as an asset or liability, under IFRS. The resulting change from this derecognition should be accounted by the first-time adopter as follows: first, if the first-time adopter had classified a past business combination as an acquisition and recognized as an intangible asset an item that does not qualify for recognition as an asset under IAS 38, it should reclassify that item (and any related deferred tax and minority interests) as part of goodwill (unless it deducted goodwill from equity, instead of presenting it as an asset, under its previous GAAP); and second, the first-time adopter should recognize all other resulting changes in retained earnings.

4. In cases where IFRS require subsequent measurement of some assets and liabilities on a basis other than original cost, such as fair value, the first-time adopter should measure these assets and liabilities on that basis in its opening IFRS balance sheet, even if these assets and liabilities were acquired or assumed in a past business combination. Any resulting change in the carrying amount should be recognized by the first-time adopter in retained earnings (or another component of equity, if appropriate), instead of as an adjustment to goodwill.

5. Subsequent to the business combination, the carrying amount under previous GAAP of assets acquired and liabilities assumed in the business combination should be treated as their *deemed cost* under IFRS at that date. If IFRS require a cost-based measurement of those assets and liabilities at a later date, deemed cost should be used instead (e.g., as the basis for cost-based depreciation or amortization from the date of the business combination).

6. If assets acquired or liabilities assumed were not recognized in a past business combination under the previous GAAP, the first-time adopter should recognize and

measure them in its consolidated balance sheet on the basis that IFRS would require in the separate balance sheet of the acquiree.

7. The carrying amount of goodwill in the opening IFRS balance sheet should be its carrying amount under previous GAAP at the date of transition to IFRS, after the following adjustments:

   a. The carrying amount of goodwill should be increased due to a reclassification that would be needed for an intangible asset recognized under previous GAAP but which does not qualify as an intangible asset under IAS 38. Similarly, the carrying amount of goodwill should be decreased due to inclusion of an intangible asset as part goodwill under previous GAAP but which requires separate recognition under IFRS.

   b. If the purchase consideration of a past business combination was based on a contingency which was resolved prior to the date of transition to IFRS, and a reliable estimate of the adjustment relating to the contingency can be made and it is probable that a payment will be made, the first-time adopter should adjust the carrying amount of goodwill by that amount. Similarly, if a previously recognized contingency can no longer be measured reliably, or its payment is no longer probable, the first-time adopter should adjust the carrying amount of goodwill accordingly.

   c. Whether or not there is evidence of impairment of goodwill, the first-time adopter should apply IAS 36 in testing goodwill for impairment, if any, and should recognize the resulting impairment loss in retained earnings (or, if so required by IAS 36, in revaluation surplus).

   The impairment test should be based on conditions at the date of transition to IFRS.

8. No other adjustments are permitted by IFRS 1 to the carrying amount of goodwill at the date of transition to IFRS. Thus, adjustments such as the following *cannot* be made:

   a. Excluding in-process research and development acquired in that business combination,

   b. Adjusting previous amortization of goodwill, or

   c. Reversing adjustments to goodwill that IFRS 3 would not permit but which were appropriately made under previous GAAP.

9. If under its previous GAAP a first-time adopter did not consolidate a subsidiary acquired in a business combination (i.e., because the parent did not treat it as a subsidiary under previous GAAP), the first-time adopter should adjust the carrying amounts of the subsidiary's assets and liabilities to the amounts that IFRS would require in the subsidiary's separate balance sheet. The deemed cost of goodwill would be equal to the difference at the date of transition to IFRS between the parent's interest in those adjusted carrying amounts and the cost in the parent's separate financial statements of its investment in the subsidiary.

10. The above adjustments to recognized assets and liabilities should also flow through to minority interests and deferred assets.

IFRS 1 states that these exemptions for past business combinations also apply to past acquisitions of investments in associates and in joint ventures. Furthermore, the date chosen for electing to apply IFRS 3 retrospectively to past business combinations applies equally to all such investments.

Fair value or revaluation as deemed cost. An entity may elect to measure an item of property, plant, and equipment at fair value at the date of its transition to IFRS and use the fair value as its deemed cost at that date. A first-time adopter may elect to use a previous GAAP revaluation of a item of property, plant, and equipment at, or before, the date of transition to IFRS as deemed costs at the date of revaluation if the revaluation amount, when determined, was broadly comparable to either fair value or cost (or depreciated cost under IFRS adjusted for changes in general or specific price index).

These elections are equally available for investment property measured under the cost model and intangible assets that meet the recognition criteria and the criteria for revaluation (including the existence of an active market).

If a first-time adopter has established a deemed cost under the previous GAAP for any of its assets or liabilities by measuring them at their fair values at a particular date because of the occurrence of an event such as privatization or an initial public offering (IPO), it is allowed to use such an event-driven fair value as deemed cost for IFRS at the date of that measurement.

Employee benefits. Under IAS 19 an entity may have unrecognized actuarial gains or losses when it uses the corridor approach defined under that standard. Prior GAAP may not have provided similar treatment, however. Retrospective application of IAS 19 would necessitate splitting the cumulative gains and losses, from inception of the plan until the date of transition to IFRS, into a recognized and an unrecognized portion. This would necessitate an enormously complicated analysis in some situations.

IFRS 1 allows a first-time adopter to elect to recognize all cumulative actuarial gains and losses at the date of transition to IFRS, even if it uses the corridor approach for subsequent actuarial gains or losses. IFRS 1 does mandate, however, that if an election is made for one employee benefit plan, it should apply to all other employee plans of that reporting entity.

Cumulative translation differences. IAS 21 requires an entity to classify certain translation differences as a separate component of equity, and upon disposal of the foreign operation to transfer the cumulative translation difference relating to the foreign operation to the income statement as part of the gain or loss on disposal.

A first-time adopter is exempted from a transfer of the cumulative translation adjustment that existed on the date of transition to IFRS. If it elects this exemption, the cumulative translation adjustment for all foreign operations would be deemed to be zero at the date of transition to IFRS. The gain or loss on subsequent disposal of any foreign operation should exclude translation differences that arose before the date of transition to IFRS, but would include all subsequent translation adjustments.

Compound financial instruments. If an entity has issued a compound financial instrument, such as a convertible debenture, IAS 32 requires that at inception, it should split and separate the liability component of the compound financial instrument from equity. If the liability portion no longer is outstanding at the date of adoption of IFRS, a retrospective and literal application of IAS 32 would require separating two portions of equity. The first portion, which is in retained earnings, represents the cumulative interest accreted on the liability component. The other portion represents the original equity component of the instrument, and would be in paid-in capital.

IFRS 1 exempts a first-time adopter from this split accounting if the former liability component is no longer outstanding at the date of transition to IFRS.

Assets and liabilities of subsidiaries, associates, and joint ventures. IFRS 1 discusses exemptions under two circumstances.

1. If a subsidiary becomes a first-time adopter later than its parent, the subsidiary must, in its separate (stand-alone) financial statements, measure its assets and liabilities at either

a. The carrying amounts that would be included in its parent's consolidated financial statements, based on its parent's date of transition to IFRS (if no adjustments were made for consolidation procedures and for the effect of the business combination in which the parent acquired the subsidiary), or

b. The carrying amounts required by the other provisions of IFRS 1, based on subsidiary's date of transition to IFRS.

2. If a reporting entity becomes a first-time adopter after its subsidiary (or associate or joint venture) does, the entity is required, in its consolidated financial statements, to measure the assets and liabilities of the subsidiary (or associate or joint venture) at the same carrying amounts as in the separate (stand-alone) financial statements of the subsidiary (or associate or joint venture), after adjusting for consolidation and equity accounting adjustments and for effects of the business combination in which an entity acquired the subsidiary. In a similar manner, if a parent becomes a first-time adopter for its separate financial statements earlier or later than for its consolidated financial statements, it shall measure its assets and liabilities at the same amounts in both financial statements, except for consolidation adjustments.

Exceptions to retrospective application of other IFRS. IFRS 1 *prohibits* retrospective application of certain aspects of other IFRS. These relate to

1. **Derecognition of financial assets and financial liabilities.** If a first-time adopter derecognized financial assets or financial liabilities under its previous GAAP in a financial year prior to January 1, 2001, it should not rerecognize those assets and liabilities under IFRS.

    However, a first-time adopter should recognize all derivatives and other interests retained after derecognition and still existing, and consolidate all special-purpose entities (SPE) that it controls at the date of transition to IFRS (even if the SPE existed before the date of transition to IFRS or hold financial assets or financial liabilities that were derecognized under previous GAAP).

2. **Hedge accounting.** A first-time adopter is required, at the date of transition to IFRS, to measure all derivatives at fair value and eliminate all deferred losses and gains on derivatives that were reported under its previous GAAP.

    However, a first-time adopter is not permitted to reflect a hedging relationship in its opening IFRS balance sheet if it does not qualify for hedge accounting under IAS 39. But if an entity designated a net position as a hedged item under its previous GAAP, it may designate an individual item within that net position as a hedged item under IFRS, provided it does so prior to the date of transition to IFRS. Transitional provisions of IAS 39 apply to hedging relationships of a first-time adopter at the date of transition to IFRS.

3. **Estimates.** An entity's estimates under IFRS at the date of transition to IFRS should be consistent with estimates made for the same date under its previous GAAP, unless there is objective evidence that those estimates were in error, as that term is defined under IFRS.

    Any information an entity receives after the date of transition to IFRS about estimates it made under previous GAAP should be treated by it as a *nonadjusting* event after the balance sheet date, and accorded the treatment prescribed by IAS 10 (i.e., by making disclosure in footnotes as opposed to actual adjustment of items in the financial statements).

Presentation and disclosure.

1. A first-time adopter should present at least one year of comparative financial statement information. If an entity also presents historical summaries of selected data for periods prior to the first period that it presents full comparative information under IFRS, and IFRS does not require the summary data to be in compliance with IFRS, such data should be labeled prominently as not being in compliance with IFRS and also disclose the nature of the adjustment that would make that data IFRS-compliant.

2. A first-time adopter should explain how the transition to IFRS affected its reported financial position, financial performance, and cash flows. In order to comply with the above requirement, reconciliation of equity and profit and loss as reported under previous GAAP to IFRS should be included in the entity's first IFRS financial statements.

3. If an entity uses fair values in its opening IFRS balance sheet as deemed cost for an item of property, plant, and equipment, an investment property or an intangible asset, then disclosure is required for each line item in the opening IFRS balance sheet of the aggregate of those fair values and of the aggregate adjustments made to the carrying amounts reported under previous GAAP.

4. If an entity presents an interim financial report under IAS 34 for a part of the period covered by its first IFRS financial statements, in addition to disclosures made under IAS 34 the first-time adopter should present a reconciliation of the equity and profit and loss under previous GAAP for the comparable interim period to its equity and profit and loss under IFRS.

It is anticipated, and recommended, that transition-period disclosures be presented as a complete package, covering

- A full set of restated financial statements (balance sheets, income statements, cash flow statements, and statements of changes in shareholders' equity);
- Notes explaining the restatement, including reconciliations from previously reported amounts to restated amounts under IFRS; and
- Notes on the accounting policies to be applied under IFRS and applied at transition

Additional footnote detail in the annual financial statements for the first year IFRS is applied may also be useful. At a minimum, however, to provide a thorough understanding of the transition, it will be advisable to identify all the relevant factors considered by the preparer (the reporting entity) in converting to IFRS, in the transition disclosure package itself.

Consequential amendments to other IFRS. IFRS 1 amended IAS 39 with respect to recognition of derivatives or other retained interests (such as servicing rights or liabilities) and special-purpose entities (SPE) controlled by the transferor. Specifically, the first-time adopter is required to

1. Recognize all derivatives and other interests, such as servicing rights or servicing liabilities, retained after the derecognition transaction and still existing at the date of transition to IFRS; and

2. Consolidate all special-purpose entities (SPE) that it controls at the date of transition to IFRS, even if the SPE existed before the date of transition to IFRS or hold financial assets or financial liabilities that were derecognized under previous GAAP.

Effective date. An entity is to apply IFRS 1 if its first IFRS financial statements are for periods beginning on or after January 1, 2004. Earlier application is encouraged.

If an entity's first IFRS financial statements are for periods beginning before January 1, 2004, and it applies IFRS 1 instead of SIC 8, it must disclose that fact.

Areas of likely differences from predecessor national GAAP. While the extent to which first-time IFRS-compliant financial statements will differ from the former presentation under national GAAP depends entirely on which national GAAP was previously applied (since IFRS is most similar to US GAAP and UK GAAP, and dissimilar from certain other national standards, including many EU nations' prior GAAP), the following summarizes what are likely to be the more complex areas.

1. The use of revaluation for fixed assets, intangibles, and investment property under IFRS differs from that permitted under the various national GAAP. In fact, a strict historical cost requirement is more commonly found, so that revaluation of fixed assets is not permitted. The fair value approach to investment property, imposed by revised IAS 40, is new for even those previously familiar with IAS, and at variance with national GAAP, in the main.

2. The "fair value" override permitted under IFRS (and also under UK GAAP), is intended to place the ultimate objective of financial reporting above any specific measurement rules imposed under the standards, thus offering preparers (and their auditors) the right to contravene specific IFRS requirements when necessary in order to better reflect the truth in the financial statements. While a somewhat similar option exists for US reporting (found in US professional ethical standards, however, not in US GAAP), this is very rarely invoked (and not generally permitted by the SEC, notwithstanding the profession's endorsement), and is also very rare under European GAAP. Where used, it generally has been achieved by variations in the informative disclosures, and not by applying alternative measures to transactions and balances. It is too early to predict if, and to what extent, preparers and their auditors may seek to draw upon this permission to depart from strict application of IFRS.

3. The requirements for first-time adoption, under IFRS 1, make conversion a process that will require full retrospective application of current IFRS standards. This undertaking will be arduous, which creates some risk of misapplication, etc. For example, for standards which have been revised over the past several years, there will be confusion about whether the requirements should be the current ones or those in effect historically from time to time.

4. The reporting of extraordinary items is now barred under IFRS, but still receives varying treatment under different national GAAP (e.g., elimination of negative goodwill is extraordinary item under US GAAP). Depending on past experience, preparers may have greater or lesser difficulties in finding the appropriate "home" for charges and credits that would otherwise have been deemed extraordinary.

5. Cash flow statements prepared in compliance with IFRS offer certain alternatives, for reporting items such as dividends and interest, that are not permitted under US GAAP and may vary from some or all European national GAAP. The election among alternatives should be communicated to users, if the impact is material.

6. Changes in accounting policies require the restatement of comparative financial statements, while some national GAAP, including that of the US, require reporting in the current period a cumulative charge or credit for the change, perhaps with required pro forma disclosures for the prior comparative periods.

7. Special-purpose entities (now called variable interest entities in the US) now face strict consolidation rules under US GAAP, with somewhat less strict rules under IFRS, and yet less strict requirements under some national GAAP and no rules at

all, in some cases). Adopters of IFRS will have to determine which previously non-consolidated SPEs might now have to be consolidated in the beneficiary's financial statements, and this might be accomplished with varying degrees of precision.

8. Consolidation rules are strict under US GAAP, and similarly strict under IFRS (i.e., very few exceptions to mandatory consolidation of majority owned subsidiaries), but under some national GAAP there were less stringent requirements which permitted the nonconsolidation of nonhomogeneous subsidiaries.

9. Reporting the currency effects of the consolidation of foreign subsidiaries varies. Both IFRS and US GAAP require (in almost all instances) that balance sheet translation be at the current rate, income statement at transaction date rates, and effect of net translation be reported in the equity section of the balance sheet. Other national GAAP use various methods, some of which reported translation in income statement.

10. Some business combinations are still being accounted for as unitings (poolings) of interest under national GAAP, while this method is banned under US GAAP and now also under IFRS. Poolings subsequent to elimination of this method under IFRS will have to be restated as purchases.

11. National GAAP treatment of goodwill (that is, whether to amortize, and over what period) varies; IFRS now largely conforms to US GAAP requirement that no amortization be recognized, but that impairment testing be done every year. Restatement to IFRS will thus have to adjust for prior purchase business combinations.

12. National GAAP treatment of negative goodwill varies, but some still permit deferred recognition in income, while under IFRS (which has been largely conformed to US GAAP), net negative goodwill receives income statement recognition at the acquisition date.

13. Long-term construction contract accounting varies under national GAAP, and some do not permit percentage-of-completion method to be used in any circumstances. IFRS requires percentage-of-completion method (US GAAP generally does also, with some exceptions).

14. Pension accounting requirements vary considerably among the European nations. Besides the diversity of requirements, this is a complex area, making transition to IFRS quite challenging. US GAAP and IFRS are similar to each other, and both are more strict (in terms of reporting pension obligations on employers' financial statements) than some national GAAP.

15. Similar to pension accounting is the area of other postemployment benefits. OPEB reporting rules are similar under US GAAP and IFRS, but other national GAAP rules are vague, meaning that there are many variations in interpretation of the expense accrual requirements. Upon adopting IFRS, it is likely that additional liabilities may have to be reported by these entities.

16. The rules governing accounting for internally developed assets vary considerably. IFRS requires expensing of research expenses, but requires capitalization of development expenditures. In contrast, US GAAP requires expensing of both research and development expense as incurred. National GAAP do vary, but in some cases even internally constructed tangible assets must be expensed, in addition to research and development costs.

17. Capital lease accounting by lessee and lessor varies across national GAAP, while under US GAAP and IFRS the financial reporting considerations are similar. Entities first adopting IFRS will have to determine if leased assets need to be capitalized, with the associated debt obligation shown as liabilities.

18. Impairment of long-lived assets is accounted for under various methodologies across national GAAP. Reversals of previously recognized write-downs are permitted by IFRS under certain circumstances, while this is not necessarily permitted under other GAAP. (US GAAP does not permit this.)

19. Interest capitalization on long-term construction projects varies across national GAAP. This is merely optional under IFRS (but is required under US GAAP).

20. The fair value option is new for accounting for investment property under IFRS, but under national GAAP use of depreciated historical cost is more likely required. (US GAAP also requires cost-based accounting for nonsecurities investments.) Entities adopting fair value reporting upon conversion to IFRS will have some issues in making determinations of fair values at historical dates.

21. Agricultural (biological) activities are accounted for by fair value method under IFRS, whereas national GAAP generally requires application of historical cost-based methods, as is also true under US GAAP.

22. Accounting for derivatives and hedging activities are very similar under current US GAAP and IFRS, but most national GAAP have not yet adapted fair value accounting for derivatives, so much of this was "off the books" under prior standards. Conversion to IFRS reporting will force these derivatives onto the balance sheets of the reporting entities.

23. Recognition of restructuring obligations varies across national GAAP. Under US GAAP, which is strictest now that liability definition must be met, relatively less of these accruals can be made.

24. Deferred tax provisions may be based on older, income statement-oriented matching concept, under some national GAAP standards. This contrasts with the more modern, balance sheet–oriented IFRS and US GAAP liability method approach to deferred tax accounting. There may also be differences from the IFRS comprehensive allocation method (UK GAAP, until recently, used the partial allocation approach).

25. Classification of financial instruments as debt or equity varies across national GAAP. Recent US GAAP has expanded need to consider some nominal equity instruments as debt, and IFRS has been consistently strict on this matter. Other national GAAP still permit equity classification for instruments having certain features of debt. Upon conversion to IFRS, these balance sheets may show reduction in equity, increase in debt, as a consequence.

26. Requirements concerning the reporting of discontinued operations vary. Some standards have no requirements for this at all, in contrast to US GAAP and IFRS requirements. Adoption of IFRS may necessitate reclassification of these items within the preparer's income statement.

APPENDIX A

DISCLOSURE CHECKLIST

This checklist provides a reference to the disclosures common to the financial statements of entities that are complying with International Financial Reporting Standards (IFRS), including those set forth by the International Accounting Standards (IAS) promulgated by the IASC earlier. These disclosures are set forth by IFRS/IAS and IFRIC/SIC and are effective for periods beginning after December 31, 2005. Changes which have been proposed but which have not been promulgated are not addressed in this checklist. Superseded disclosures have also been excluded.

DISCLOSURE CHECKLIST INDEX

General

A. Identification of Financial Statements and Basis of Reporting
B. Compliance with International Financial Reporting Standards
C. Changes in Accounting Policies, Changes in Accounting Estimates and Errors
D. Related-Party Disclosures
E. Contingent Liabilities and Contingent Assets
F. Events After the Balance Sheet Date
G. Comparative Information
H. Going Concern
I. Current/Noncurrent Distinction
J. Uncertainties
K. Judgments and Estimations
L. First-Time Adoption of IFRS
M. Share-Based Payment
N. Insurance Contracts

Balance Sheet

A. Minimum Disclosures on the Face of the Balance Sheet
B. Additional Line Items on the Face of the Balance Sheet
C. Further Subclassifications of Line Items Presented
D. Inventories
E. Property, Plant, and Equipment (PP&E)
F. Intangible Assets
G. Other Long-Term Assets (Consolidated Financial Statement & Investment in Subsidiaries)
H. Investments in Associates
I. Investments in Joint Ventures
J. Investment Property
K. Financial Instruments
L. Provisions
M. Deferred Tax Liabilities and Assets
N. Employee Benefits—Defined Benefit Pension and Other Postretirement Benefit Programs
O. Employee Benefits—Other Benefit Plans
P. Leases—from the Standpoint of a Lessee
Q. Leases—from the Standpoint of a Lessor
R. Lease—Substance of the Transaction Involving the Legal Form
S. Stockholders' Equity

Income Statement

A. Minimum Disclosures on the Face of the Income Statement
B. Investment Property
C. Income Taxes
D. Extraordinary Items

E.   Noncurrent Assets Held for Sale and Discontinued Operations
F.   Segment Data
G.   Construction Contracts
H.   Foreign Currency Translation
I.   Business Combinations
J.   Earnings Per Share
K.   Dividends Per Share
L.   Impairments of Assets

Cash Flow Statement

A.   Basis of Presentation
B.   Format
C.   Additional Recommended Disclosures

Statement of Changes in Equity

A.   Statement of Changes in Equity

Notes to the Financial Statements

A.   Structure of the Notes
B.   Accounting Policies
C.   Service Concession Arrangements

Interim Financial Statements

A.   Minimum Components of an Interim Financial Report
B.   Form and Content of Interim Financial Statements
C.   Selected Explanatory Notes

Disclosures for Banks and Similar Financial Institutions (IAS 30)

A.   Income Statement
B.   Balance Sheet
C.   Contingencies and Commitments Including Off-Balance-Sheet Items
D.   Maturities of Assets and Liabilities
E.   Concentrations of Assets and Liabilities
F.   Losses on Loans and Advances
G.   General Banking Risks
H.   Assets Pledged as Security
I.   Related-Party Transactions
J.   Trust Activities

Insurance Contracts

Agriculture

A.   General
B.   Additional Disclosure for Biological Assets Where Fair Value Cannot Be Measured Reliably
C.   Government Grants

Exploration for and Evaluation of Mineral Resources

GENERAL

A.   **Identification of Financial Statements and Basis of Reporting**

1.   The financial statements should be identified clearly and distinguished from other information in the same published document. In addition, the following information shall be displayed prominently, and repeated when it is necessary for a proper understanding of the information presentation:

a. Name of the entity whose financial statements are being presented, or other means of identification, and any change in that information from the preceding balance sheet;

b. Disclosure whether the financial statements cover the individual entity or a group of entities;

c. The accounting policies, including measurement bases and other policies necessary to an understanding of the financial statements;

d. Presentation currency as defined in IAS 21;

e. When presentation currency differs from functional currency, state this fact;

f. Level of rounding used in presentation of the figures in the financial statements;

g. Balance sheet date or the period covered by the financial statements, whichever is appropriate to that component of financial statement.

h. Identify each component of the financial statements.

(IAS 1, Paras 44, 46 & 108; IAS 21, Para 53)

2. An entity shall disclose the following, if not disclosed elsewhere in information published in the financial statements:

a. Entity's country of incorporation, domicile and legal form;

b. Address of its registered office or principal place of business if different from the registered office;

c. Name of the reporting entity's parent and the ultimate parent of the group;

d. Description of the nature of the entity's operations and its principal activities;

(IAS 1, Para 126)

B. Compliance with International Financial Reporting Standards

1. Financial statement shall present fairly the financial position, financial performance and the cash flows of the entity. Fair presentation requires the faithful presentation of the transactions, other events, and condition in accordance with the definitions and recognition criteria for assets, liabilities, income and expenses set out in the framework. The application of IFRS, with additional disclosure when necessary, is presented to result in financial statements that achieve a fair presentation.

(IAS 1, Para 13)

2. An entity whose financial statements comply with IFRS shall make an explicit and unreserved statement of such compliance in the notes. Financial statements shall not be described complying with IFRS unless they comply with all the requirements of IFRS.

(IAS 1, Para 14)

3. In extremely rare circumstances in which management concludes that compliance with a requirement in a Standard or an Interpretation would be so misleading that it would conflict with the objective of financial statements set out in the Framework, the entity shall depart from that requirement in the manner set out in IAS 1, paragraph 18 (see below) if the relevant regulatory framework requires, or otherwise does not prohibit, such a departure.

(IAS 1, Para 17)

4. When an entity departs from a requirement of a Standard or an Interpretation in accordance with IAS 1, paragraph 17, it shall disclose

a. That management has concluded that the financial statements present fairly the entity's financial position, financial performance and cash flows;

b. That it had complied with applicable Standards and Interpretations, except that it had departed from a particular requirement to achieve a fair presentation;

c. The title of the Standard or Interpretation from which the entity has departed, the nature of the departure, including the treatment that the Standard or Interpretation would require, the reason why the treatment would be so misleading in the circumstances that it would conflict with the objective of financial statements set out in the Framework, and the treatment adopted; and

    d.   For each period presented, the financial impact of the departure on each item in the financial statements that would have been reported in complying with the requirement.

(IAS 1, Para 18)

5.   When an entity has departed from a requirement of a Standard or an Interpretation in a prior period, and that departure affects the amounts recognized in the financial statements for the current period, it shall make the disclosures set out in IAS 1, Paras 18(c) and (d).

(IAS 1, Para 19)

6.   When in extremely rare circumstances in which management concludes that compliance with a requirement of the Standard or Interpretation would be misleading and that it would conflict with the objective of the financial statements set out in the Framework, but the regulatory framework prohibits departure from the requirement, the entity shall, to the maximum extent possible, reduce the perceived misleading aspects of compliance by disclosing the following:

    a.   The title of the Standard of Interpretation in question, the nature of the requirement, and the reason why the management has concluded that complying with the requirement is so misleading in the circumstances that it conflicts with the objective of the financial statement se out in the Framework; and

    b.   For each period presented, the adjustment to each item of the financial statements that the management has concluded would be necessary to achieve a fair presentation.

(IAS 1, Para 21)

C.   Changes in Accounting Policies, Changes in Accounting Estimates and Errors

1.   When initial application of a Standard or an Interpretation has an effect on the current period or any prior period, would have such an effect except that is impracticable to determine the amount of the adjustment, or might have an effect on future periods, an entity shall disclose

    a.   The title of the Standard or Interpretation;

    b.   When applicable, that the change in accounting policy is made in accordance with its transitional provisions;

    c.   The nature of change in accounting policy;

    d.   When applicable, a description of the transitional provisions;

    e.   When applicable, the transitional provisions that might have an effect on future periods;

    f.   For current period and each prior period presented, to the extent practicable, the amount of the adjustment

        (1)   For each financial statement line item affected; and

        (2)   If IAS 33, *Earnings per Share,* applies to the entity, for basic and diluted earnings per share;

    g.   The amount of the adjustment relating to periods before those presented, to the extent practicable; and

    h.   If retrospective application required by IAS 8, paragraph 19(a) or (b) is impracticable for a particular prior period, or for periods before those presented, the circumstances that led to the existence of that condition and a description of how and from when the change in accounting policy has been applied.

(Financial statements of subsequent periods need not repeat these disclosures.)

(IAS 8, Para 28)

2.   When a voluntary change in accounting policy has an effect on the current period or any prior period, would have an effect on that period except that it is impracticable to determine the amount of the adjustment, or might have an effect on future periods, an entity shall disclose

    a.   The nature of change in accounting policy;

    b.   The reasons why applying the new accounting policy provides reliable and more relevant information;

c. For the current period and each prior period presented, to the extent practicable, the amount of the adjustment

(1) For each financial statement line item affected; and

(2) If IAS 33 applies to the entity, for basic and diluted earning per share;

d. The amount of the adjustment relating to periods before those presented, the circumstances that led to the existence of that condition and description of how and from when the change in accounting policy has been applied.

e. If retrospective application is impracticable for a particular prior period, or for periods before those presented, the circumstances that led to the existence of that condition and a description of how and from when the change in accounting policy has been applied.

(Financial statements of subsequent periods need not repeat these disclosures.)

(IAS 8, Para 29)

3. When an entity has applied a new Standard or Interpretation that has been issued but is not yet effective, the entity shall disclose

a. This fact; and

b. Known or reasonably estimable information relevant to assessing the possible impact that application of the new Standard or Interpretation will have on entity's financial statements in the period of application.

(IAS 8, Para 30)

4. An entity shall disclose the nature and amount of a change in an accounting estimate that has an effect in the current period or is expected to have an effect in future periods when it is impracticable to estimate that effect.

(IAS 8, Para 39)

5. If the amount of the effect in future periods is not disclosed because estimating it is impracticable, an entity shall disclose the fact.

(IAS 8, Para 40)

6. In correcting material prior period errors, as outlined in IAS 1, paragraph 42, an entity shall disclose the following:

a. The nature of the prior period error;

b. For each prior period presented, to the extent practicable, the amount of correction;

(1) For each financial statement line item affected;

(2) If IAS 33 applies to the entity, for basic and diluted earnings per share;

c. The amount of correction at the beginning of the earliest prior period presented; and

d. If retrospective restatement is impracticable for a particular prior period, the circumstances that led to the existence of that condition and description of how and from when the error has been corrected.

(Financial statements of the subsequent periods need not repeat these disclosures.)

(IAS 1, Para 49)

7. A prior period error shall be corrected by retrospective restatement except to the extent that it is impractical to determine either the period-specific effects or the cumulative effect of the error.

(IAS 8, Para 43)

8. When it is impracticable to determine the period-specific effects of an error on comparative information for one or more prior periods presented, the entity shall restate the opening balances of assets, liabilities and equity for the earliest period for which retrospective restatement is practical.

(IAS 8, Para 44)

9. When it is impracticable to determine the cumulative effect, at the beginning of the current period, of an error on all prior periods, the entity shall restate the comparative information to correct the error prospectively from the earliest date practicable.

(IAS 8, Para 45)

D. Related-Party Disclosures

1. Relationships between parents and subsidiaries shall be disclosed irrespective of whether there have been transactions between those related parties. An entity shall disclose the name of the entity's parent and, if different, the ultimate controlling party. If neither the entity's parent nor the ultimate controlling party produces financial statements available for public use, the name of the next most senior parent that does so shall also be disclosed.

(IAS 24, Para 12)

2. If there have been transactions between related parties, an entity shall disclose the nature of the related-party relationship as well as the information about the transactions and outstanding balances necessary for an understanding of the potential effect of the relationship on the financial statements. These disclosure requirements are in addition to the requirements in IAS 24, paragraph 16 to disclose key management personnel compensation. At a minimum, disclosure shall include

    a. The amount of the transactions;
    b. The amount of outstanding balances; and

        (1) Their terms and conditions, including whether they are secured, and the nature of the consideration to be provided in settlement; and
        (2) Details of any guarantees given or received;

    c. Provisions for doubtful debt related to the amount of outstanding balances; and
    d. The expense recognized during the period in respect of bad or doubtful debts due from related parties.

        The disclosure required by above paragraph shall be made separately for each of the following categories:

        (1) The parent;
        (2) Entities with joint control or significant influence over the entity;
        (3) Subsidiaries;
        (4) Associates;
        (5) Joint ventures in which the entity is a venturer;
        (6) Key management personnel of the entity or its parent; and
        (7) Other related parties.

(IAS 24, Paras 17 & 18)

3. Aggregation of items of similar nature is permitted, unless separate disclosure is needed for an understanding of the effects of the related-party transactions on the financial statements of the reporting entity.

(IAS 24, Para 22)

4. An entity shall disclose key management personnel compensation in total and for each of the following categories:

    a. Short-term employee benefits;
    b. Postemployment benefits;
    c. Other long-term benefits;
    d. Termination benefits; and
    e. Share-based payments

(IAS 24, Para 16)

E. Contingent Liabilities and Contingent Assets

1. An entity should disclose for each class of contingent liability, unless the possibility of any outflow in settlement is remote, a brief description of the nature of the contingent liability. If practicable, an entity should also disclose an estimate of its financial effects, an indication of the uncertainties relating to the amount or timing of the outflow, and the possibility of any reimbursement.

    (IAS 37, Para 86)

2. An entity should show a brief description of the nature of the contingent assets at the balance sheet date, where an inflow of economic benefits is probable. Where practical, an estimate of the financial effect should be disclosed.

    (IAS 37, Para 89)

3. Where an entity does not disclose any information required by IAS 37, para 86, and IAS 37, para 89, because it is not practical to do so, that fact should be disclosed.

    (IAS 37, Para 91)

    a. When provisions and contingent liabilities arise from a single event, the relationship between the provision and the contingent liability should be made clear.

    (IAS 37, Para 38)

    b. Disclose contingencies arising from postemployment benefit obligations and termination benefits.

    (IAS 19, Paras 125 & 141)

4. In extremely rare circumstances, if disclosures of some or all of the information required by IAS 37, para 89, would prejudice seriously the position of the entity in a dispute with other parties, on the subject matter of the contingent liability or contingent asset, an entity need not disclose such information. Instead, in such cases it should disclose the general nature of the dispute, along with the fact that, and reason why, the information has not been disclosed by the entity.

    (IAS 37, Para 92)

F. Events After the Balance Sheet Date

1. When nonadjusting events after the balance sheet date are so significant that nondisclosure would affect the ability of the users of the financial statements to make proper evaluations and decisions, an entity should disclose the nature of the event and an estimate of its financial effect. Such disclosure is required for each significant category of nonadjusting post-balance-sheet event. If such an estimate is not possible, a statement to that effect should be made.

    (IAS 10, Para 21)

2. The date when the financial statements were authorized for issue and who gave the authorization should be disclosed by an entity. If the entity's owners or others have the power to amend the financial statements after issuance, the entity should disclose that fact.

    (IAS 10, Para 17)

3. If an entity receives information after the balance sheet date that existed at the balance sheet date, the entity should update the disclosures that relate to these conditions, based on the new information received.

    (IAS 10, Para 19)

4. In respect of loans classified as current liabilities, if the following events occur between the balance sheet date and the date financial statements are authorized for issue, those events qualify for disclosures of nonadjusting events in accordance with IAS 10, *Events After the Balance Sheet Date*

    a. Refinancing on a long-term basis;

    b.   Rectification of a breach of a long-term loan agreement; and

    c.   The receipt from the lender of a period of grace to rectify a breach of a long-term loan agreement ending at least twelve months after the balance sheet date.

(IAS 1, Para 67)

5.   Disclose income tax consequences of dividends proposed or declared after the balance sheet date; if payable at a rate different than normal due to being paid out as dividends, disclose nature of income tax effects and estimated amount.

(IAS 12, Paras 81 & 82)

G.   Comparative Information

1.   In the case of provisions, comparative information is not required for the reconciliation of carrying amount at the beginning and end of the period.

(IAS 37, Para 84)

2.   Except when a Standard or an Interpretation permits or requires otherwise, comparative information shall be disclosed in respect of the previous period for all amounts reported in the financial statements. Comparative information shall be included for narrative and descriptive information when it is relevant to an understanding of the current period's financial statements.

(IAS 1, Para 36)

3.   When the presentation and classification of items in the financial statements is amended, comparative amounts should be reclassified unless the reclassification is impracticable. When comparative amounts are reclassified, an entity shall disclose

    a.   The nature of the reclassification;

    b.   The amount of each item or class of items that is reclassified; and

    c.   The reason for the reclassification.

(IAS 1, Para 38)

4.   When it is impracticable to reclassify comparative amounts, an entity shall disclose

    a.   The reason for nonreclassifying the amounts; and

    b.   The nature of the adjustment that would have been made if the amounts had been reclassified.

(IAS 1, Para 39)

H.   Going Concern

1.   When management is aware in making its assessment of material uncertainties related to events or conditions which may cast significant doubt upon the entity's ability to continue as a going concern, those uncertainties should be disclosed. When the financial statements are not prepared on a going concern basis, that fact should be disclosed, together with the basis on which the financial statements are prepared and the reason why the entity is not considered to be a going concern.

(IAS 1, Para 23)

I.   Current/Noncurrent Distinction

1.   An entity shall present current and noncurrent assets, and current and noncurrent liabilities, as separate classifications on the face of the balance sheet except when a presentation based on liquidity provides information that is reliable and more relevant. When that exception applies, all assets and liabilities shall be presented broadly in order of liquidity.

(IAS 1, Para 51)

2.   Whether an entity chooses a classified presentation of the balance sheet with current/noncurrent distinction, or it presents an unclassified balance sheet, it should disclose, for each asset and liability item that combines amounts expected to be recovered or settled

both before and after twelve months from the balance sheet date, the amount expected to be recovered or settled after more than twelve months.

(IAS 1, Para 52)

3. For some entities, such as financial institutions, a presentation of assets and liabilities in increasing or decreasing order of liquidity provides information that is reliable and more relevant than a current/noncurrent presentation because the entity does not supply goods or services within a clearly identifiable operating cycle.

(IAS 1, Para 54)

4. If an entity declares dividends to equity shareholders after the balance date, the entity shall not recognize those dividends as a liability at the balance sheet date.

(IAS 10, Para 12)

J.   Uncertainties

1. Entities are encouraged to disclose, outside the financial statements, a financial review by management, setting forth information about the principal uncertainties they face. Such a report may provide a review of

   a.   The main factors that influence and determine financial performance, including changes in environment in which the entity operates, the entity's response to those changes and their effect;

   b.   The entity's sources of funding and its target ratio of liabilities to equity;

   c.   The entity's resources not recognized on the balance sheet.

(IAS 1, Para 9)

K.   Judgments and Estimations

1. An entity shall disclose, in the summary of significant accounting policies or other notes, the judgments, apart from those involving estimations, management has made in the process of applying the entity's accounting policies that have the most significant effect on the amounts recognized in the financial statements.

(IAS 1, Para 113)

2. An entity shall disclose in the notes information about the key assumptions concerning the future, and other key sources of estimation uncertainty at the balance sheet date, that have a significant risk of causing a material adjustment to the carrying amounts of assets and liabilities within the next financial year. In respect of those assets and liabilities, the notes shall include details of their nature and their carrying amount as at the balance sheet date.

(IAS 1, Para 116)

L.   First-Time Adoption of IFRS

1. IFRS 1 does not exempt a first-time adopter from the presentation and disclosure requirements of other IFRS—thus a first-time adopter should provide all disclosures required by other IFRS.

(IFRS 1, Para 35)

2. An entity's first IFRS financial statements shall include at least one year of comparative information under IFRS.

(IFRS 1, Para 36)

3. If an entity presents historical summaries of selected data for periods before the first period for which it presents full comparative information under IFRS, or if it presents comparative information under previous GAAP as well as comparative information required by IFRS 1, then it shall

    a.   Label the previous GAAP information prominently as not being prepared under IFRS; and

    b.   Disclose the nature of the main adjustments that would be required to make it comply with IFRS (quantifying those adjustments is not required).

(IFRS 1, Para 37)

4.   A first-time adopter shall present reconciliation (of equity and profit or loss presented under previous GAAP to corresponding amounts presented under IFRS) to explain how the transition from previous GAAP to IFRS affected its reported financial position, financial performance and cash flows.

(IFRS 1, Para 38)

    a.   First-time IFRS financial statements should include reconciliations of equity under prior GAAP and IFRS as of date of transition and end of most recently presented financial statements under prior GAAP.

    b.   First-time IFRS financial statements should include reconciliations of results of operations under prior GAAP and IFRS for the most recently presented financial statements under prior GAAP.

    c.   If any impairment losses were recognized or reversed for first time in preparing opening IFRS balance sheet, the IAS 36 disclosures that would have been required if these would have been recognized in the period beginning with the transition date should be disclosed.

(IFRS 1, Para 39)

5.   If an entity did not present financial statements for previous periods, its first IFRS financial statements shall disclose that fact.

(IFRS 1, Para 43)

6.   If an entity uses fair values in its opening IFRS balance sheet as deemed costs for items of property, plant, and equipment, investment property or intangible assets, then its opening IFRS balance sheet shall disclose, for each line item (in the opening balance sheet)

    a.   The aggregate of those fair values; and

    b.   The aggregate adjustment to the carrying amounts reported under previous GAAP.

(IFRS 1, Para 44)

7.   If a first-time adopter presents interim financial reports under IAS 34 for part of the period covered by its first IFRS financial statements, it shall

    a.   Present reconciliation of equity and profit or loss under previous GAAP at the end of an interim period to corresponding amounts under IFRS at a comparable date (this reconciliation is in addition to the reconciliation required to be presented in 4. above)

(IFRS 1, Para 45)

    b.   If a first-time adopter in its most recent annual financial statements under previous GAAP did not disclose information material to an understanding of the current interim period, its interim financial report shall disclose that information or include a cross-reference to another published document that includes it.

(IFRS 1, Para 46)

M. Share-Based Payment

1.   An entity shall disclose information that enables users of the financial statements to understand the nature and extent of share-based payment arrangements that existed during the period.

(IFRS 2, Para 44)

2. The entity shall disclose at least the following:

   a. A description of each type of share-based payment arrangement at any time during the period, including the general terms and condition of each arrangement, such as vesting requirement, the maximum term of options granted, and the method of settlement. An entity having similar type of share-based payment arrangements shall aggregate this information unless separate disclosure is required to satisfy the principle in IFRS 2, paragraph 44.

   b. The number and weighted-average exercise prices of share options for each of the following group of options:

      (1) Outstanding at the beginning of the period;
      (2) Granted during the period;
      (3) Forfeited during the period;
      (4) Exercised during the period;
      (5) Expired during the period;
      (6) Outstanding at the end of the period; and
      (7) Exercisable at the end of the period.

   c. If share options exercised during the period, the weighted-average prices at the date of exercise. If share options exercised regularly during the period, than the entity may disclose weighted-average share price during the period.

   d. For share options outstanding at the end of the period, the range of the prices and weighted-average remaining contractual life. If the range of the prices is wide, the outstanding options shall be divided into ranges that are meaningful for assessing the number and timing of additional shares that may be issued and the cash that may be received upon exercise of those options.

   (IFRS 2, Para 45)

3. An entity shall disclose information that enables users of the financial statements to understand how the fair value of the goods and services received, or the fair value of the equity instruments granted, during the period was determined.

   (IFRS 2, Para 46)

4. If the entity has measured the fair value of goods or services received as consideration for equity instruments of the entity indirectly, by reference to the fair value of the equity instruments granted, to give to the principle in IFRS 2, paragraph 46, the entity shall disclose at least the following:

   a. For share options granted during the period, the fair value at the measurement date and how that fair value was measured, including

      (1) The option pricing model used and the inputs to that model, including the weighted average share price, exercise price, expected volatility, option life, expected dividend and risk-free interest rate and any other inputs to the model, including the method used and assumptions made to incorporate the effects of expected early exercise;

      (2) How expected volatility was determined, including an explanation of the extent to which expected volatility was based on historical volatility; and

      (3) Whether and how any other features of the option grant were incorporated into the measurement of fair value, such as market condition.

   b. For other equity instruments granted during the period, the number and the weighted-average fair value of those equity instruments at the measurement, and information on how that fair value was measured, including

      (1) If fair value was not measured on the basis of an observable market price, how it was determined;

      (2) Whether and how expected dividends were incorporated into the measurement of fair value; and

        (3)   Whether and how any other features of the equity instruments granted were incorporated into the measurement of fair value.

    c.   For share-based payment arrangements that were modified during the period

        (1)   An explanation of those modifications;

        (2)   The incremental fair value granted (as a result of those modifications); and

        (3)   Information on how the incremental fair value granted was measured, consistently with the requirements set out in a. and b. above, where applicable.

(IFRS 2, Para 47)

5.   If the entity has directly measured the fair value of the goods and services received during the period, the entity shall disclose how that fair value was determined.

(IFRS 2, Para 48)

    a.   If the assumption that fair value of goods or services exchanged for shares, other than employee services, can be measured has been rebutted, this must be stated together with an explanation.

(IFRS 2, Para 49)

6.   An entity shall disclose information that enables users of the financial statements to understand the effect of share-based payment transaction on the entity's profit or loss of the period and on its financial position.

(IFRS 2, Para 50)

7.   To give effect to IFRS 2, paragraph 50, the entity shall disclose at least the following:

    a.   The total expenses recognized for the period arising from share-based payment transactions in which goods or services received did not qualify for recognition as assets and hence were recognized immediately as an expense, including separate disclosure of that portion of the total expense that arises from transactions accounted for as equity-settled share-based payment transaction;

    b.   For liabilities arising from share-based payment transaction

        (1)   The total carrying amount at end of the period; and

        (2)   The total intrinsic value at the end of the period of liabilities for which the counterparty's right to cash or other assets had vested by the end of the period.

(IFRS 2, Para 51)

8.   If the information required to be disclosed by this IFRS does not satisfy the principles in IFRS 2, paragraphs 44, 46, and 50, the entity shall disclose such additional information as is necessary to satisfy them.

(IFRS 2, Para 52)

N. Insurance Contracts

1.   An insurer shall disclose information that identifies and explains the amount in its financial statements arising from insurance contracts.

(IFRS 4, Para 36)

2.   To comply with IFRS 4, paragraph 36, an insurer shall disclose

    a.   Its accounting policies for insurance contracts and related assets and liabilities, income and expense;

    b.   The recognized assets, liabilities, income and expense (and, if it presents its cash flow statement using the direct method, cash flows) arising from insurance contracts. Furthermore, if the insurer is a cedant, it shall disclose

        (1)   Gains and losses recognized in profit or loss on buying reinsurance;

> (2) If the cedant differs and amortizes gains and losses arising on buying reinsurance, the amortization for the period and the amounts remaining unamortized at the beginning and at the end of the period.

    c. The process used to determine the assumptions that have the greatest effect on the measurement of the recognized amounts described in b. When practicable, an insurer shall also give quantified disclosures of those assumptions.

    d. The effect of changes in assumption used to measure insurance assets and insurance liabilities, showing separately the effect of each change that has a material effect on the financial statements.

    e. Reconciliation of changes in insurance liabilities, reinsurance assets and if any, related deferred acquisition costs.

(IFRS 4, Para 37)

3. An insurer shall give the information to understand the amount, timing and uncertainty of future cash flows from insurance contracts.

(IFRS 4, Para 38)

4. To comply with IFRS 4, paragraph 38, an insurer shall disclose

    a. Its objectives in managing risks arising from insurance contracts and its policies for mitigating those risks.

    b. Those terms and conditions of insurance contracts that have a material effect on the amount, timing, and uncertainty of the insurer's future cash flows.

    c. Information about insurance risk (both before and after risk mitigation by reinsurance), including information about

> (1) The sensitivity of profit or loss and equity to changes in variables that have material effect on them;
>
> (2) Concentrations of insurance risk;
>
> (3) Actual claims compared with previous estimates (i.e., claim development). The disclosure about claims development shall go back to the period when the earliest material claim arose for which there is still uncertainty about the amount and timing of the claims payment, but need not go back more than ten years. An insurer need not disclose this information for claims for which uncertainty about the amount and timing of claims payments is typically resolved within one year.

    d. The information about interest rate risk and credit risk that IAS 32 would require if the insurance contracts were within the scope of IAS 32.

    e. Information about exposures to interest rate risk or market risk under embedded derivatives contained in a host insurance contract if the insurer is not required to, and does not, measure the embedded derivatives at fair value.

(IFRS 4, Para 39)

5. An entity need not apply the disclosure requirements in this IFRS to comparative information that relates to the annual period beginning before January 1, 2005, except for the disclosure required by IFRS 4, paragraph 37(a) and (b) about accounting policies, and recognized assets, liabilities, income and expense (and cash flow if direct method is used).

(IFRS 4, Para 42)

6. If it is impracticable to apply a particular requirement to comparative information that relates to annual periods beginning January 1, 2005, an entity shall disclose that fact. Applying the liability adequacy test to such comparative information might sometimes be impracticable, but it is highly unlikely to be impracticable to apply other requirements to such comparative information.

(IFRS 4, Para 43)

7. When an entity first applies this IFRS and if it is impracticable to prepare information about claim development that occurred before the beginning of the earliest period for which an en-

tity presents full comparative information that complies with this IFRS, the entity shall disclose this fact.

(IFRS 4, Para 44)

BALANCE SHEET

A. Minimum Disclosures on the Face of the Balance Sheet

1. The face of the balance sheet should include, as a minimum, the following categories:

    a. Property, plant, and equipment;
    b. Investment property;
    c. Intangible assets;
    d. Financial assets (excluding amounts shown under e., h., and .i;
    e. Investments accounted for using the equity method;
    f. Biological assets;
    g. Inventories;
    h. Trade and other receivables;
    i. Cash and cash equivalents;
    j. Trade and other payables;
    k. Provisions;
    l. Financial liabilities (excluding amounts shown under j. and k.);
    m. Liabilities and assets for current tax;
    n. Deferred tax liabilities and deferred tax assets;
    o. Minority interest; and
    p. Issued capital and reserves.

    (IAS 1, Para 68)

2. The face of the balance sheet shall include line items that present the following amounts;

    a. The total of assets classified as held for sale and assets included in disposal groups classified as held for sale in accordance with IFRS 5, *Noncurrent Assets Held for Sale and Discontinued Operations*, and
    b. Liabilities included in disposal groups classified as held for sale in accordance with IFRS 5.

    (IAS 1, Para 68A)

B. Additional Line Items on the Face of the Balance Sheet

1. Additional line items, headings and subtotals should be presented on the face of the balance sheet when an IAS requires it, or when such presentation is necessary to present fairly the entity's financial position.

    (IAS 1, Para 69)

C. Further Subclassifications of Line Items Presented

1. An entity shall disclose either on the face of the balance sheet or in the notes further subclassifications of the line items presented, classified in a manner appropriate to the entity's operations. The detail provided in subclassifications depends on the requirement of IFRS and on the size, nature, and function of the amounts involved.

    (IAS 1, Paras 74 & 75)

D. Inventories

1. The accounting policies and the cost formula used in inventory valuation.

    (IAS 2, Para 36[a])

2. Total carrying amount and the breakdown of the carrying amount by appropriate subclassifications, such as merchandise, production supplies, work in progress, and finished goods.

    (IAS 2, Paras 36[b] & 37)

3. Carrying amount of inventories at fair value less cost to sell.

(IAS 2, Para 36[c])

4. Carrying amount of inventories pledged as securities.

(IAS 2, Para 36[h])

5. The amount of any reversal of any write-down that is recognized as a reduction in the amount of inventories recognized as expense in the period in accordance with paragraph 34.

(IAS 2, Para 36 [f])

6. The financial statement shall disclose

   a. The amount of inventories recognized as an expense during the period.

(IAS 2, Para 36(d))

7. When inventories are sold, the carrying amount of those inventories shall be recognized as an expense in the period in which the related revenue is recognized. The amount of any write-down of inventories to net realizable value and all losses of inventories shall be recognized as an expense in the period the write-down or loss occurs. The amount of any reversal of any write-down of inventories arising from an increase in net realizable value shall be recognized as a reduction in the amount of inventories recognized as an expense in the period in which the reversal occurs.

(IAS 2, Para 34)

8. The financial statement shall disclose

   a. The amount of any write-down of inventories recognized as an expense in the period in accordance with paragraph 34;
   b. The circumstances or events that led to the reversal of a write-down of inventories in accordance with paragraph 34.

(IAS 2, Paras 36[e] & [g])

E. Property, Plant, and Equipment (PP&E)

1. In respect of each class (i.e., groupings of assets of a similar nature and use) of PP&E, the following disclosures are required:

   a. Measurement basis/bases used for the determination of the gross carrying amount; if more than one basis has been employed, then also the gross carrying amount determined in accordance with that basis in each category;
   b. The depreciation method(s) used;
   c. Either the useful lives or the depreciation rates used;
   d. The gross carrying amount and the accumulated depreciation at the beginning and the end of the period;
   e. A reconciliation of the carrying amount at the beginning and the end of the period disclosing

      (1) Additions;
      (2) Disposals;
      (3) Acquisitions by means of business combinations;
      (4) Increases/decreases resulting from revaluations and from impairment losses recognized or reversed directly in equity (if any);
      (5) Impairment losses recognized in the income statement (if any);
      (6) Impairment losses reversed in the income statement (if any);
      (7) Depreciation;
      (8) Net exchange differences arising from translation of financial statements of a foreign entity (in accordance with IAS 21); and
      (9) Other changes, if any.

(IAS 16, Para 73)

2. Additional disclosures to be made include the following:

    a. The existence and amount of restrictions on title, and PP&E pledged as security for liabilities;
    b. If it is not disclosed separately on the face of the income statement, the amount of compensation from third parties for items of P&PE that were impaired, lost or given up that is included in profit or loss;
    c. The amount of expenditures in respect of PP&E in the course of construction; and
    d. The amount of outstanding commitments for acquisition of PP&E.

    (IAS 16, Para 74)

3. In case items of PP&E are stated at revalued amounts, disclose the following information:

    a. The effective date of revaluation;
    b. Whether an independent party prepared the valuation;
    c. The methods and significant assumptions applied in estimating the item's fair value;
    d. The extent to which the item's fair value was determined directly by reference to observable prices in an active market or in a recent market transaction at arm's length or were estimated using other valuation techniques;
    e. The carrying amount of each class of PP&E that would have been included in the financial statements had the assets been carried under the benchmark treatment; and
    f. The revaluation surplus, including the movement for the period in that account and disclosure of any restrictions on the distribution of the balance in the revaluation surplus account to shareholders.

    (IAS 16, Para 77)

4. An entity should disclose information on impaired property, plant, and equipment under IAS 36 in addition to information required under IAS 16, para 73[e] (iv to vi)

    (IAS 16, Para 78)

5. Other recommended disclosures

    a. The carrying amount of temporarily idle PP&E;
    b. The gross carrying amount of fully depreciated PP&E still in use;
    c. The carrying amount of PP&E retired from active use and held for sale; and
    d. In cases where items of PP&E are carried at cost model the fair value of PP&E if it is materially different from the carrying amount.

    (IAS 16, Para 79)

F. Intangible Assets

1. In the case of each class of intangible assets, distinguishing between internally generated intangible assets and other intangible assets, the financial statements should disclose

    a. The useful lives of the amortization rates used;
    b. The amortization methods used;
    c. The gross carrying amount and the accumulated amortization (aggregated with accumulated impairment) at the beginning and at the end;
    d. The line item(s) of the income statement in which the amortization of intangible assets is included;
    e. A reconciliation of the carrying amount at the beginning and the end of the period showing:

        (1) Additions, indicating separately those from internal development and through business combinations;
        (2) Retirements and disposals;
        (3) Increases or decreases resulting from revaluations and from impairment losses recognized or reversed directly in equity (if any);
        (4) Impairment losses recognized in income statement (if any);
        (5) Impairment losses reversed in the income statement (if any);

      (6)   Amortization recognized;

      (7)   Net exchange differences arising on translation of financial statements of a foreign entity; and

      (8)   Other changes in carrying amount.

(IAS 38, Para 118)

2.   Additional disclosures with respect to intangibles are the following:

   a.   An intangible asset assessed as having an indefinite useful life, the carrying amount of that asset and the reasons supporting the assessment of an indefinite useful life. In giving these reasons, the entity shall describe the factor(s) that play a significant role in determining that the asset has an indefinite useful life.

   b.   In the case of an individual intangible asset that is material to the financial statements as a whole, a description, the carrying amount, and the remaining amortization period;

   c.   In the case of intangible assets acquired by way of a government grant and initially recognized at fair value: the fair value initially recognized for these assets, their carrying amounts, and whether they are carried under the benchmark treatment or the allowed alternative treatment for subsequent measurements;

   d.   The existence and the carrying amount of intangible assets pledged as security for liabilities; and

   e.   The amount of commitments for the acquisition of intangible assets.

(IAS 38, Para 122)

3.   In the case of intangible assets carried under the allowed alternative method (i.e., at revalued amounts), the following disclosures are prescribed:

   a.   By class of intangible assets: the effective date of the revaluation, the carrying amount of revalued intangible assets carried under the benchmark treatment (i.e., at cost less accumulated amortization); and

   b.   The quantum of revaluation surplus that relates to intangible assets at the beginning and the end of the period, indicating the changes during the period and any restrictions on the distributions of the balance to shareholders.

   c.   The methods and significant assumptions applied in estimating the assets' fair values.

(IAS 38, Para 124)

4.   The financial statements should disclose the aggregate amount of research and development expenditure recognized as an expense during the period.

(IAS 38, Para 126)

5.   Provide a reconciliation of goodwill carrying value, showing gross carrying amount and any impairment loss, as of beginning of period; any additions; any adjustments arising from recognition of deferred taxes subsequent to acquisition date; disposals; impairment losses during period; net exchange differences during period; other changes; and gross carrying amount and any impairment loss as of end of period.

(IFRS 3, Para 75)

G. Other Long-Term Assets (Consolidated Financial Statement and Investment in Subsidiaries)

1.   The following items should be disclosed separately:

   a.   The names of any entity in which more than one-half of the voting power is owned, directly or indirectly through subsidiaries, but which, because of the absence of control, are not subsidiaries.

(IAS 27, Para 40(d))

2.   A parent need not present consolidated financial statement if and only if

   a.   The parent is itself a wholly owned subsidiary, or is a partially owned subsidiary of another entity and its other owners, including those not otherwise entitled to vote, have been informed about, and do not object to, the parent not presenting consolidated financial statement;

b. The parent's debt or equity instrument is not traded in a public market (a domestic or foreign exchange or an over the counter market, including local and regional markets);

c. The parent did not file, nor is it in the process of filing, its financial statements with a securities commission or other regulatory organization for purpose of issuing any class of instruments in a public market; and

d. The ultimate or any intermediate parent of the parent produces consolidated financial statement available for public use that comply with IFRS

(IAS 27, Para 10)

3. Consolidated financial statement shall be prepared using uniform accounting policies for like transactions and other events in similar circumstances.

(IAS 27, Para 28)

4. The following disclosures shall be made in consolidated financial statements:

a. The nature of the relationship between the parent and the subsidiary, when the parent does not own, directly or indirectly through subsidiaries, more than one-half of the voting power;

b. The reasons why the ownership, of more than half of the voting power of an investee does not constitute control;

c. The reporting date of the financial statements of a subsidiary when such financial statements are used to prepare consolidated financial statements and are of a reporting date of for a period that is different from that of the parent, and the reason for using the different reporting date or period.

d. The nature and extent of any significant restrictions (e.g., resulting from borrowing arrangements or regulatory requirements) on the ability of subsidiaries to transfer funds to the parent in the form of cash dividends or to repay loans or advances.

(IAS 27, Para 40)

5. When separate financial statements are prepared for a parent that, in accordance with IAS 27, paragraph 10, elects not to prepare consolidated financial statements, those separate financial statements shall disclose

a. The fact that the financial statements are separate financial statements; that the exemption from consolidation has been used; the name and country of incorporation or residence of the entity whose consolidated financial statements that comply with International Financial Reporting Standards have been produced for public use; and the address where those consolidated financial statements are obtainable;

b. A list of significant investments in subsidiaries; jointly controlled entities and associates, including the name, country or incorporation or residence, proportion of ownership interest, and, if different, proportion of voting power held; and

c. A description of the method used to account for the investments listed under b.

(IAS 27, Para 41)

6. When a parent (other than a parent covered by paragraph 41), venturer with an interest in a jointly controlled entity or an investor in an associate prepares separate financial statements, those separate financial statements shall disclose

a. The fact that the statements are separate financial statements and the reasons why those statements are prepared if not required by law;

b. A list of significant investments in subsidiaries, jointly controlled entities and associates, including the name, country of incorporation or residence, proportion of ownership interest and, if different, proportion of voting power held;

c. A description of a method used to account for the investments listed under b.; and shall identify the financial statements prepared in accordance with IAS 27, paragraph 9, IAS 28 and IAS 31 to which they relate.

(IAS 72, Para 42)

H. Investments in Associates

1. Investments in associates accounted for using the equity method should be classified as noncurrent assets and separately set forth in the balance sheet. The investor's share of profit or losses of such investments should be disclosed as separate item in the income statement.

(IAS 28, Para 38)

2. The fact that investor's share of investee's carrying value includes amount analogous to goodwill, and any accumulated impairment, should be stated.

(IAS 28, Para 23)

3. The following disclosures shall be made:

   a. The fair value of investments in associates for which there are published price quotations;
   b. Summarized financial information of associates, including the aggregated amounts of assets, liabilities, revenues, and profit or loss;
   c. The reasons why the presumption that an investor does not have significant influence is overcome if the investor holds, directly or indirectly though subsidiaries, less than 20% of the voting or potential voting power of the investee but concludes that it has significant influence;
   d. The reasons why the presumption that an investor has significant influence is overcome if the investor holds, directly or indirectly through subsidiaries, 20% or more of the voting or potential voting power of the investee but concludes that it does not have significant influence;
   e. The reporting date of the financial statements of an associate, when such financial statements are used in applying the equity method and are as of a reporting date or for a period that is different from that of the investor, and the reason for using different reporting date or different period;
   f. The nature and extent of any significant restrictions on the ability of associates to transfer funds to the investor in the form of cash dividends, or repayments of loans or advances;
   g. The unrecognized share of losses of an associate, both for the period and cumulatively, if an investor has discontinued recognition of its share of losses of an associate;
   h. The fact that an associate is not accounted for using the equity method;
   i. Summarized financial information of associates, either individually or in groups, that are not accounted for using the equity method, including the amounts of total assets, total liabilities, revenues and profit or loss.

(IAS 28, Para 37)

4. The investor's share of changes recognized directly in the associate's equity shall be recognized directly.

(IAS 28, Para 39)

5. In accordance with 37 Provisions, Contingent Liabilities, and Contingent Assets, the investor shall disclose

   a. Its share of the Contingent liabilities of an associate incurred jointly with other investors; and
   b. Those contingent liabilities that arise because that investor is severally liable for all or part of the liabilities of the associate.

(IAS 28, Para 40)

I. Investments in Joint Ventures

1. The venturer is to disclose a listing and description of interests in significant joint ventures and proportions held in each, and aggregate current assets, noncurrent assets, current liabilities, noncurrent liabilities, income and expense related to interests in joint ventures.

(IAS 31, Para 56)

2.   Separately from other contingent liabilities, disclose contingent liabilities arising from interest in joint ventures and share in each incurred jointly with other venturers; shares in contingent liabilities of the joint ventures themselves for which there are contingent obligations; and contingent liabilities arising in connection with contingent liability for obligations of the other venturers.

(IAS 31, Para 54)

3.   Separately from other commitments, disclose capital commitments arising in connection with joint obligations with other venturers, and share of capital commitments of the joint ventures themselves.

(IAS 31, Para 55)

J.   Investment Property

1.   In certain cases investment property will be property that is owned by the reporting entity and leased to others under operating-type lease arrangements. The disclosure requirement set forth in IAS 17 continue unaltered by IAS 40. (In addition IAS 40 stipulates a number of new disclosure requirements set out below.)

(IAS 40, Para 74)

2.   An entity shall disclose

a.   Whether it applies the fair value model or cost model.

b.   If it applies fair value model, whether and in what circumstances the property held under operating leases are classified and accounted for as investment property.

c.   When classification is difficult, an entity that holds an investment property will need to disclose the criteria used to distinguish investment property from owner-occupied property and from property held for sale in the ordinary course of business.

d.   The method and any significant assumptions that were used in ascertaining the fair values of the investment properties are to be disclosed as well. Such disclosure should also include a statement about whether the determination of fair value was supported by market evidence or it relied heavily on other factors (which the entity needs to disclose as well) due to the nature of the property and the absence of comparable market data;

e.   If investment property has been revalued by an independent valuer having recognized and relevant qualifications and who has recent experience with properties having similar characteristics of location and type, the extent to which the fair value of investment property is based on valuation by such an independent valuer, if there is no such valuation, the fact should be disclosed as well;

f.   The amounts recognized in profit or loss for

(1) Rental income from investment property;

(2) Direct operating expenses including repairs and maintenance arising from investment property that generated rental income during the period;

(3) Direct operating expenses including repairs and maintenance arising from investment property that did not generate rental income during the period; and

(4) The cumulative change in fair value recognized in profit or loss on a sale of investment property from a pool of assets in which the cost model is used.

g.   The existence and the amount of any restrictions which may potentially affect the reliability of investment property or the remittance of income and proceeds from disposal to be received; and

h.   Material contractual obligations to purchase or build investment property or for repairs, maintenance, or improvements thereto.

(IAS 40, Para 75)

3.   Disclosure applicable to investment property measured using the fair value model

a.   In addition to the disclosures outlined in IAS 40, para 76, the standard requires that an entity that uses the fair value model should also disclose a reconciliation to be presented of the carrying amount of investment property, from business combinations, and those derived from capitalized expenditures. It will also identify assets classified as held for sale or included in a disposal group classified as held for sale in accordance with IFRS 5 and other disposals, gains, or losses from fair value adjustment, the net exchange differences, if any, arising from the translation of the financial statements of a foreign entity, transfers to and from inventories and owner-occupied properties and any other movements. *(It will not be required that comparative reconciliation data be presented for prior periods.)*

    b.   Under exceptional circumstances, due to lack of reliable fair value, when an entity measures investment property using the cost model under IAS 16, the above reconciliation should disclose amounts separately for that investment property from amounts relating to other investment property. In addition, an entity should also disclose

        (1)   A description of such a property,

        (2)   An explanation of why fair value cannot be reliably measured,

        (3)   If possible, the range of estimates within which fair value is highly likely to lie, and

        (4)   On disposal of such an investment property, the fact that the entity has disposed of investment property not carried at fair value along with its carrying amount at the time of disposal and the amount of gain or loss recognized.

(IAS 40, Paras 76 & 78)

    4.   Disclosures applicable to investment property measured using the cost model

        a.   In addition to the disclosure requirements outlined in IAS 40, para 75, the standard requires that an entity that applies the cost model should also disclose: the depreciation methods used, the useful lives or the depreciation rates used, and the gross carrying amount and the accumulated depreciation (aggregated with accumulated impairment losses) at the beginning and end of the period. It should also disclose a reconciliation of the carrying amount of investment property at the beginning and the end of the period showing the following details: additions resulting from acquisitions, those resulting from business combinations, and those deriving from capitalized expenditures subsequent to the property's initial recognition. It should also disclose disposals, depreciation, impairment losses recognized and reversed, the net exchange differences, if any, arising from the translation of the financial statements of a foreign entity, transfers to and from inventories and owner-occupied properties, and any other movements.

        b.   The fair value of investment property carried under the cost model should also be disclosed. In exceptional cases, when the fair value of the investment property cannot be reliably estimated, the entity should also disclose

        (1)   A description of such property,

        (2)   An explanation of why fair value cannot be reliably measured, and

        (3)   If possible, the range of estimates within which fair value is highly likely to lie.

(IAS 40, Para 79)

K. Financial Instruments

    1.   Mandatory disclosures

        a.   For each class of either financial asset, financial liability or equity instrument, whether recognized in the balance sheet or not, disclose the following:

        (1)   Information concerning the extent and nature of the instrument, including significant terms and conditions which may affect the amount, timing, or certainty of future cash flows; and

        (2)   The accounting policies and methods used to account for the instruments, including relevant criteria for recognition and the basis of measurement employed.

(IAS 32, Para 60)

b. For each class of either financial asset or financial liability, whether recognized in the balance sheet or not, disclose the following information about exposure to interest rate risk:

(1) The dates of contractual repricing or maturity, whichever comes first; and

(2) The effective interest rates, if applicable.

(IAS 32, Para 67)

c. For each class of financial asset, whether recognized in the balance sheet or not, disclose the following information about exposure to credit risk:

(1) The amount which represents the maximum credit risk exposure as of the balance sheet date, without regard to any collateral held, should the other party fail to perform under the terms of the instrument; and

(2) Any significant concentrations of credit risk.

(IAS 32, Para 76)

d. For each class of financial assets and financial liabilities, an entity shall disclose the fair value of that class of assets and liabilities in a way that permits it to be compared with the corresponding carrying amount in the balance sheet.

(IAS 32, Para 86)

e. If investments in unquoted equity instruments or derivatives linked to such equity instruments are measured at cost because their fair value cannot be measured reliably, that fact shall be disclosed together with the description of the financial instruments, their carrying amount, an explanation of why fair value cannot be measured reliably, and if possible, the range of estimates within which the fair value is highly likely to lie. Furthermore, if financial assets whose fair value previously could not be reliably measured are sold, that fact, the carrying amount of such financial assets at the time of sale and the amount of gain or loss recognized shall be disclosed.

(IAS 32, Para 90)

f. Some financial assets and financial liabilities contain a discretionary participation feature as described in IFRS 4, *Insurance Contracts*. If an entity cannot measure reliably the fair value of that feature, the entity shall disclose that fact together with a description of the contract, its carrying amount, an explanation of why fair value cannot be measured reliably and, if possible, the range of estimates within which the fair value is highly likely to lie.

(IAS 32, Para 91A)

g. An entity shall disclose

(1) The methods and significant assumptions applied in determining fair values of financial assets and financial liabilities separately for significant classes of financial assets and financial liabilities.

(2) Whether fair values of financial assets and liabilities are determined directly, in full or in part, by reference to published price quotations in an active market or are estimated using a valuation technique.

(3) Whether its financial statements include financial instruments measured at fair values that are determined in full or in part using a valuation technique based on assumptions that are not supported by observable market prices or rates. If changing any such assumption to a reasonably possible alternative would result in a significantly different fair value, the entity shall state this fact and disclose the effect on the fair value of a range of reasonably possible alternative assumptions. For this purpose, significance can be judged with respect to profit or loss and total assets or total liabilities.

(4) The total amount of the change in fair value estimated during a valuation technique that was recognized in profit or loss during the year.

(IAS 32, Para 92)

h. An entity should disclose its financial risk management objectives and policies, including its policy for hedging each major type of forecasted transaction for which hedge accounting is used.

(IAS 32, Para 56)

i. The financial statements should include **all** of the following additional disclosures relating to hedging:

   (1) A description of the entity's financial risk management objectives and policies, including its policy for hedging each major type of forecasted transaction;

   (2) Disclosure of the following separately for designated fair value hedges, cash flow hedges, and hedges of a net investment in a foreign entity:

   (a) A description of the hedge;

   (b) A description of the financial instruments designated as hedging instruments for the hedge and their fair values at the balance sheet date;

   (c) The nature of the risks being hedged; and

   (d) For hedges of forecasted transactions, the periods in which the forecasted transactions are expected to occur, when they are expected to enter into the determination of net profit or loss, and a description of any forecasted transaction for which hedge accounting had previously been used but that is no longer expected to occur; and

   (3) If a gain or loss on derivative and nonderivative financial assets and liabilities designated as hedging instruments in cash flow hedges has been recognized directly in equity, to disclose the following:

   (a) The amount that was so recognized in equity during the current period;

   (b) The amount that was removed from equity and reported in net profit or loss for the period; and

   (c) The amount that was removed from equity and added to the initial measurement of the acquisition cost or other carrying amount of the asset or liability in a hedged forecasted transaction during the current period.

(IAS 32, Para 58 & 59)

j. For each class of financial assets and financial liabilities, an entity shall disclose information about its exposure to interest rate risk, including

   (1) Contractual repricing or maturity dates, whichever are earlier; and

   (2) Effective interest rates, when applicable

(IAS 32, Para 67)

k. Information about exposure to future changes in prevailing interest rates.

(IAS 32, Para 68)

l. Optionally, information about expected repricing or maturity dates, when different than contractual dates, can be provided.

(IAS 32, Para 70)

m. Identify which financial assets and liabilities are exposed to fair value interest rate risk; cash flow interest risk, or not directly exposed to risk at all.

(IAS 32, Para 71)

n. For each class of financial assets and other credit exposures, an entity shall disclose information about its exposure to credit risk, including

   (1) The amount that best represents its maximum credit exposure at the balance sheet date, without taking account of the fair value of any collateral, in the event of other parties failing to perform their obligations under financial instruments; and

   (2) Significant concentration of credit risk.

(IAS 32, Para 76)

o.   For each class of financial asset and liability (unless excepted by IAS 32, para 90), disclose the fair value of that class in a manner that facilitates comparison to carrying values in the financial statements.

(IAS 32, Para 86)

p.   For fair value disclosures, grouping and offsets (if any) should follow that in the financial statements.

(IAS 32, Para 89)

q.   For investments measured at cost, as permitted by IAS 39 when fair value cannot be assessed, disclose that fact together with a description of the instruments (e.g., unlisted stocks). If such instruments are sold, identify that event and the carrying amount of the financial asset at the date of sale, and gain or loss recognized, must be disclosed.

(IAS 32, Para 90)

r.   Disclosure required of methods and significant assumptions used in determining the fair values of financial assets and liabilities, by major classification; whether fair values were determined directly by reference to published prices in active markets, or were estimated using a valuation technique; whether, if valuation techniques were used, these were based in part on assumptions that would not be supported by observable market data and, if so, the effect of such assumptions on the fair values; and the total amount of change in fair value recognized in the current period's results of operations that derived from such valuation technique.

(IAS 32, Para 92)

s.   Other disclosures

(1)   An entity may have either transferred a financial asset or entered into the type of arrangement as described in IAS 39, paragraph 19, in such a way that the arrangement does not qualify as a transfer of a financial asset. If the entity either continues to recognize all of the asset or continues to recognize the asset to the extent of entity's continuing involvement, it shall disclose for each class of financial asset

(a)   The nature of the assets;
(b)   The nature of the risks and rewards to which the entity remains exposed;
(c)   When the entity continues to recognize all of the asset, the carrying amounts of the asset and of the associated liability; and
(d)   When the entity continues to recognize the asset to the extent of its continuing involvement, the total amount of the asset, the amount of the asset that the entity continues to recognize, and the carrying amount of associated liability.

(2)   An entity shall disclose the carrying amount of financial assets pledged as collateral for liabilities, the carrying amount of financial assets pledged as collateral for contingent liabilities and any material terms and conditions relating to assets pledged as collateral.

(3)   When an entity has accepted collateral that it is permitted to sell or repledge in the absence of default by the owner of the collateral, it shall disclose

(a)   The fair value of the collateral accepted (financial and nonfinancial assets);
(b)   The fair value of any such collateral sold or pledged and whether the entity has an obligation to return it; and
(c)   Any material terms and conditions associated with its use of this collateral.

(4)   If an entity has issued an instrument that contains both a liability and an equity component and the instrument has multiple embedded derivative features whose values are independent, it shall disclose existence of those features and the effective interest rate on the liability component.

(5)   An entity shall disclose the carrying amount of financial assets and financial liabilities that

(a) Are classified as held for trading; and

(b) Were, upon initial recognition, designated by the entity as financial assets and financial liabilities at fair value through profit or loss.

(6) If an entity has designated a financial liability as at fair value through profit or loss, it shall disclose

(a) The amount of change in its fair value that is not attributable to changes in a benchmark interest rate; and

(b) The difference between its carrying amount and the amount the entity would be contractually required to pay at maturity to the holder of the obligation.

(7) If the entity has reclassified a financial asset as one measured at cost or amortized cost rather than at fair value, it shall disclose the reason for that reclassification.

(8) An entity shall disclose material items of income, expense and gains and losses resulting from financial assets and liabilities, whether included in profit or loss or as a separate component of an equity. For this purpose disclosure shall include at least the following items:

(a) Total interest income and the total interest expense for financial assets and financial liabilities that are not at fair value through profit or loss;

(b) For available-for-sale financial assets, the amount of any gain or loss recognized directly in equity during the period and the amount that was removed from equity and recognized in profit or loss for the period; and

(c) The amount of interest income accrued on impaired financial assets in accordance with IAS 39.

(9) An entity shall disclose the nature and amount of an impairment loss recognized in profit or loss for a financial asset, separately for each significant class of financial asset.

(10) With respect to any defaults of principal, interest, sinking fund or redemption provisions during the period on loans payable recognized as at the balance sheet date, and any other breaches during the period of loan agreements when those breaches can permit the lender to demand repayment (except for breaches that are remedied, or in response to which the terms of the loan are renegotiated, on or after the balance sheet date), an entity shall disclose

(a) Details of those breaches;

(b) The loans recognized as at the balance sheet date in respect of the loans payable on which the breaches occurred; and

(c) With respect to amounts disclosed under (b), whether the default has been remedied or the terms of the loans payable renegotiated before the date the financial statements were authorized for issue.

(IAS 32, Para 94)

L. Provisions

1. For each class of provision:

   a. The carrying amount at the beginning and end of the period;

   b. Exchange differences from translation of foreign entities' financial statements;

   c. Additional provisions made during the current period, including increases to existing provisions;

   d. Amounts utilized (i.e., incurred and charged against the provision) during the period;

   e. Unused amounts reversed during the period; and

   f. The increase during the period in the discounted amount resulting from the passage of time and the effect of any change in discount rate.

(Comparative information is not required.)

(IAS 37, Para 84)

2. For each class of provision an entity should disclose the following:

   a. A brief description of the nature of the obligation and the expected timing of resulting outflows of economic benefits;
   b. An indication of any uncertainties about the amount or timing of those outflows. Where necessary, disclosure of major assumptions made concerning future events; and
   c. The amount of any expected reimbursement, disclosing any asset that has been recognized for that expected reimbursement.

   (IAS 37, Para 85)

3. Unless the possibility of any outflow in settlement is remote, an entity shall disclose for each class of contingent liability at the balance sheet date a brief description of the nature of contingent liability and, where practicable

   a. An estimate of its financial effect;
   b. An indication of the uncertainties relating to the amount or timing of any outflow; and
   c. The possibility of any reimbursement.

   (IAS 37, Para 86)

4. Where an inflow of economic benefits is probable, an entity shall disclose a brief description of the nature of the contingent assets at the balance sheet date, and where practicable, an estimate of their financial effect, measured using the principles set out in IAS 37, paragraphs 36-52.

   (IAS 37, Para 89)

5. In *extremely rare circumstances,* if some or all disclosures as outlined in IAS 37, paragraphs 84 and 85, are expected to prejudice seriously the position of the entity in a dispute with other parties, an entity need not disclose such information. Instead, it should disclose the general nature of the dispute, along with the fact that, and reason why, the information has not been disclosed.

   (IAS 37, Para 92)

M. Deferred Tax Liabilities and Assets

1. The following shall be disclosed separately:

   a. The aggregate current and deferred tax relating to items that are charged or credited to equity;
   b. An explanation of the relationship between tax expense (income) and accounting profit in either or both of the following forms:
      (1) A numerical reconciliation between tax expense (income) and accounting profit multiplied by the applicable tax rate(s) is (are) computed; or
      (2) A numerical reconciliation between average effective tax rate and the applicable tax rate, disclosing also the basis on which the applicable tax rate is computed;
   c. An explanation of changes in the applicable tax rate(s) compared to the previous accounting period;
   d. The amount (and expiration date, in any) of deductible temporary differences, unused tax losses, and unused tax credits for which no deferred tax asset is recognized in the balance sheet;
   e. The aggregate amount of temporary differences associated with investments in subsidiaries, branches and associates and interests in joint ventures, for which deferred tax liabilities have not been recognized.
   f. In respect of each temporary difference, and in respect of each type of unused tax credits
      (1) The amount of deferred tax assets and liabilities recognized in the balance sheet for each period presented;

    (2) The amount of deferred tax income or expense recognized in the income statement, if this is not apparent from changes in the amounts recognized in the balance sheet for each period presented;

    (3) In respect of discontinued operations, the tax expense relating to

        (a) The gain or loss on discontinuance; and

        (b) The profit or loss from the ordinary activities of the discontinued operation for the period, together with the corresponding amounts for each prior period presented; and

  g. The amount of income tax consequences of dividends to shareholders of the entity that were proposed or declared before the financial statements were authorized for issue, but are not recognized as a liability in the financial statements.

(IAS 12, Para 81)

2. An entity shall disclose the amount of deferred tax asset and the nature of the evidence supporting its recognition, when

  a. The utilization of the deferred tax asset is dependent on future taxable profits in excess of the profits arising from the reversal of existing taxable temporary differences; and

  b. The entity has suffered a loss in either the current or preceding period in the jurisdiction to which the deferred tax relates.

(IAS 12, Para 82)

3. In the circumstances described in paragraph set out below, an entity shall disclose the nature of the potential income tax consequences that would result from the payment of dividends to its shareholders. In addition, the entity shall disclose the amounts of the potential income tax consequences not practically determinable. In some jurisdictions, income taxes are payable at a higher or lower rate if part or all of the net profit or retained earnings is paid out as a dividend to shareholders of the entity. In these circumstances, current and deferred tax assets and liabilities are measured at the tax rate applicable to undistributed profits.

(IAS 12, Para 82A & 52A)

4. Current tax assets and tax liabilities should not be offset unless there is a legally enforceable right of offset and the entity intends to settle on a net basis, or to realize the asset and settle the liability simultaneously.

(IAS 12, Para 71)

5. Deferred tax assets and tax liabilities relating to different jurisdictions should be presented separately.

(IAS 12, Para 74)

6. Deferred tax assets and tax liabilities relating to different entities in a group which are taxed separately by the taxation authorities should not be offset unless there is a legally enforceable right of offset.

(IAS 12, Para 74)

7. When utilization of deferred tax assets is dependent upon future profitability in excess of amounts from the reversals of taxable temporary differences, and the entity has incurred losses in either the current or preceding period, the amount of deferred tax asset should be disclosed together with the nature of any evidence of its realizability.

(IAS 12, Para 82)

N. Employee Benefits—Defined Benefit Pension and Other Postretirement Benefit Programs

  1. The entity's accounting policy for recognizing actuarial gains and losses.

  2. A general description of the types of plans in use.

  3. A reconciliation of the assets and liabilities recognized in the balance sheet, at a minimum presenting

a. The present values, as of the balance sheet dates, of wholly unfunded defined benefit obligations;
b. The present values, as of the balance sheet dates, before any deduction for fair value of plan assets, of defined benefit obligations that are wholly or partially funded;
c. The fair value of plan assets as of the balance sheet dates;
d. Net actuarial gains or losses excluded from the balance sheets;
e. Past service costs not yet recognized in the balance sheets;
f. Any amounts not recognized as assets due to application of IAS 19, para 58(b); and
g. The fair value of reimbursement rights recognized as assets, together with explanation of linkage to related obligations;
h. The amounts recognized in the balance sheets.

4. The amounts included in the fair value of plan assets for

a. Each category of the reporting entity's own financial instruments; and
b. Any property occupied by, or other assets used by, the reporting entity.

5. A reconciliation showing changes during the period in the net liability (or asset) recognized in the balance sheets, identifying carrying amount at beginning of period, exchange differences, liabilities assumed through business combinations expense recognized during the period, contributions paid, and carrying amount at the end of the period.

6. The total expense recognized in the income statements, for each of the following cost components, identifying the line item(s) of the income statement in which these are included:

a. Current service cost;
b. Interest cost;
c. Expected return on plan assets;
d. Expected return on recognized reimbursement rights;
e. Actuarial gains or losses;
f. Past service cost; and
g. The effects of any curtailments or settlements.

7. The actual return on plan assets; and
8. The principal actuarial assumptions used as of the balance sheet dates, including, where applicable (to be disclosed in absolute, not relative, terms)

a. The discount rates;
b. The expected rates of return on any plan assets for the periods presented in the financial statements;
c. The expected rates of return on recognized reimbursement rights;
d. The expected rates of salary increases (and/or changes in an index or other variable specified in the formal or constructive terms of a plan as the basis for future benefit increases);
e. Medical cost trend rates; and
f. Any other material actuarial assumptions used.

(IAS 19, Para 120)

O. Employee Benefits—Other Benefit Plans

1. For defined contribution pension plans and similar arrangements, the amount recognized as expense for the period being reported upon must be disclosed.

(IAS 19, Para 46)

2. For long-term compensated absences, long-term disability plans, profit sharing or bonus arrangements or deferred compensation plans payable more than twelve months after the end of the period in which benefits are earned, and similar types of benefit plans, any disclosures which would be mandated by other international standards, such as IAS 8 and IAS 24 (there being no specific disclosures required by IAS 19).

(IAS 19, Para 131)

3. For termination benefits, disclosures mandated for contingencies by IAS 10, as well as other disclosures which may be required under other international accounting standards such as IAS 8 and IAS 24.

(IAS 19, Paras 141-143)

4. For short-term employee benefits, such as short-term compensated absences and profit sharing or bonus arrangements to be paid within twelve months after the end of the period in which the employees render the related services, any disclosures which would be required by other international accounting standards, such as IAS 24, must be made.

(IAS 19, Para 23)

P. Leases—from the Standpoint of a Lessee

1. For finance leases

   In addition to requirements of IAS 32, the revised IAS 17, para 23, mandates the following disclosures for lessees under finance leases:

   a. For each class of asset, the net carrying amount at balance sheet date;
   b. A reconciliation between the total of minimum lease payments at the balance sheet date, and their present value. In addition, an entity should disclose the total of the minimum lease payments at the balance sheet date, their present value, for each of the following periods:

      (1) Due in one year or less,
      (2) Due in more than one but no more than five years, and
      (3) Due in more than five years.

   c. Contingent rents included in profit or loss for the period.
   d. The total of minimum sublease payments to be received in the future under noncancelable subleases as of the balance sheet date.
   e. A general description of the lessee's significant leasing arrangements including, but not necessarily limited to the following:

      (1) The basis for determining contingent rentals;
      (2) The existence and terms of renewal or purchase options and escalation clauses; and
      (3) Restrictions imposed by lease arrangements such as on dividends or assumptions of further debt or further leasing.

(IAS 17, Para 31)

2. For operating leases, including those arising from sale-leaseback transactions

   Lessees should, in addition to the requirements of IAS 32, make the following disclosures for operating leases:

   a. Total of the future minimum lease payments under noncancelable operating leases for each of the following periods:

      (1) Due in one year or less;
      (2) Due in more than one year but no more than five years; and
      (3) Due in more than five years.

   b. The total of future minimum sublease payments expected to be received under noncancelable subleases at the balance sheet date;
   c. Lease and sublease payments included in profit or loss for the period, with separate amounts of minimum lease payments, contingent rents, and sublease payments;
   d. A general description of the lessee's significant leasing arrangements including, but not necessarily limited to the following:

      (1) The basis for determining contingent rentals,
      (2) The existence and terms of renewal or purchase options and escalation clauses, and
      (3) Restrictions imposed by lease arrangements such as on dividends or assumption of further debt or on further leasing.

(IAS 17, Para 35)

Q. Leases—from the Standpoint of a Lessor

1. For finance leases

    Lessors under finance leases are required to disclose, in addition to disclosures under IAS 32, the following:

    a. A reconciliation between the total gross investment in the lease at the balance sheet date, and the present value of minimum lease payments receivable as of the balance sheet date, categorized into

        (1) Those due in one year or less;
        (2) Those due in more than one year but not more than five years; and
        (3) Those due beyond five years.

    b. Unearned finance income.
    c. The accumulated allowance for uncollectible minimum lease payments receivable.
    d. Total contingent rentals included in income.
    e. A general description of the lessor's significant leasing arrangements.

    (IAS 17, Para 47)

2. For operating leases

    For lessors under operating leases the following expanded disclosures are prescribed:

    a. Future minimum lease payments under noncancelable operating leases, in the aggregate and classified into

        (1) Those due in no more than one year;
        (2) Those due in more than one but not more than five years; and
        (3) Those due in more than five years.

    b. Total contingent rentals included in income for the period.
    c. A general description of leasing arrangements to which it is a party.

    (IAS 17, Para 56)

R. Lease—Substance of the Transaction Involving the Legal Form

1. All aspects of an arrangement that does not, in substance, involve a lease under IAS 17 should be considered in determining the appropriate disclosures that are necessary to understand the arrangement and the accounting treatment adopted. An entity should disclose the following in **each period** that an arrangement exists:

    a. A description of the arrangement including

        (1) The underlying asset and any restrictions on its use;
        (2) The life and other significant terms of the arrangement;
        (3) The transactions that are linked together, including any options; and

    b. The accounting treatment applied to any fee received;
    c. The amount of fees recognized as income in the period; and
    d. The line item of the income statement in which the fee income is included.

    (SIC 27, Para 10)

2. The disclosures required in accordance with SIC 27, paragraph 10, above, should be provided individually for each arrangement or in aggregate for each class of arrangement. (A "class" is a grouping of arrangements with underlying assets of a similar nature [e.g., power plants]).

    (SIC 27, Para 11)

S. Stockholders' Equity

1. The following disclosures should be made by an entity either on the face of the balance sheet or in the notes:

    a. For each class of share capital

      (1)   The number of shares authorized;

      (2)   The number of shares issued and fully paid, and issued but not fully paid;

      (3)   Par value per share, or the fact that the shares have no par value;

      (4)   A reconciliation of the number of shares outstanding at the beginning of the year to the number of shares outstanding at the end of the year;

      (5)   The rights, preferences and restrictions attaching to each class of shares, including restrictions on the distribution of dividends and the repayment of capital;

      (6)   Shares reserved for future issuance under options and sales contracts, including terms and amounts; and

      (7)   Shares held by the entity itself or by subsidiaries or associates of the entity;

   b.   For reserves within the owners' equity, a description, nature, and purpose of each reserve;

(IAS 1, Para 76)

2.   An entity without share capital, such as a partnership, should disclose information equivalent to that required above, showing movements during the year in each category of equity interest and the rights, preferences, and restrictions attaching to each category of equity interest.

(IAS 1, Para 77)

3.   Treasury shares require the following disclosures:

   a.   The amount of reductions to equity for treasury shares should be disclosed separately. This disclosure could be either on the face of the balance sheet or in the notes to the financial statements.

   b.   Where the entity, or its subsidiary, reacquires its own shares from parties able to control or exercise significant influence over the entity, this should be disclosed as a related-party transaction under IAS 24.

(IAS 32, Para 34)

4.   Transaction costs of issuing equity instruments or of acquiring them should be accounted for as a deduction from equity and separately disclosed. The related income taxes recognized directly in equity should also be included in the disclosure of the aggregate amount of current and deferred income tax credited or charged to equity.

(IAS 32, Para 35)

INCOME STATEMENT

A. Minimum Disclosures on the Face of the Income Statement

1.   Minimum disclosures on the face of the income statement should include the following:

   a.   Revenue;

   b.   Finance costs;

   c.   Share of profits and losses of associates and joint ventures accounted for using the equity method;

   d.   Tax expense;

   e.   A single amount which will include (1) posttax profit/loss of discontinued operation and posttax gain or loss recognized on the measurement to fair value less costs to sell or on the disposal of the assets or disposal groups constituting the discontinued operation; and

   f.   Net profit or loss for the period.

(IAS 1, Para 81)

2.   The following items shall be disclosed on the face of the income statement as allocations of the profit and loss for the period:

   a.   Profit and loss attributable to minority interest; and

   b.   Profit or loss attributable to equity shareholders of the parent.

(IAS 1, Para 82)

3. Additional line items, headings and subtotals should be presented on the face of the income statement when required by an IAS or when such a presentation is necessary in order to fairly present the entity's financial performance.

(IAS 1, Para 83)

B. Investment Property

1. Amounts included in income statement for

   a. Rental income from investment property;
   b. Direct operating expenses (including repairs and maintenance) arising from investment property that is the source of the rental income during the period; and
   c. Direct operating expenses (including repairs and maintenance) arising from investment property that did not generate rental income for the period.
   d. Cumulative change in fair value recognized in profit or loss on sale of investment property from pool of assets in which the cost model is used into a pool in which fair value model is used.

(IAS 40, Para 75f)

2. In the case of investment property carried under the fair value model, as part of the reconciliation of the carrying amount of the investment at the beginning and the end of the period, the entity should disclose the following:

   a. Additions, comprising additions from acquisitions and from subsequent expenditure recognized in the carrying amount of an asset;
   b. Additions following from acquisitions through business combination;
   c. Assets held for sale or included in a disposal group held for sale in accordance with IFRS 5 and any other disposal;
   d. Net profit or losses incurred from fair value adjustment;
   e. Exchange differences arising on the translation of financial statements into a different presentation currency of the reporting entity;
   f. Transfers to and from inventories and owner-occupied property; and
   g. Any other changes.

(IAS 40, Para 76)

3. In the case of investment property carried under the cost model, as part of the reconciliation of the carrying amount of the investment at the beginning and at the end of the period, the depreciation, the amount of impairment losses recognized and reversed and the net exchange differences arising from the translation of the financial statements of a foreign entity and any additions resulting from acquisitions and from subsequent expenditure recognized as an asset and from acquisitions through business combinations and assets classified as held for sale or included in a disposal group classified as held for sale in accordance with IAS 36, transfers to and from inventories and owner-occupied property and other changes.

(IAS 40, Para 79d)

C. Income Taxes

1. Tax expense related to profit or loss from ordinary activities should be presented on the face of the income statement.

(IAS 12, Para 77)

2. The major components of tax expense should be presented separately. These commonly would include the following:

   a. Current tax expense;
   b. Any adjustments recognized in the period for current tax of prior periods;
   c. The amount of deferred tax expense relating to the origination and the reversal of timing differences;

d.   The amount of deferred tax expense relating to changes in tax rates or the imposition of new taxes;

e.   The amount of deferred tax expense or benefit relating to changes in tax rates or the imposition of new taxes;

f.   The amount of the benefit arising from a previously unrecognized tax loss, tax credit, or temporary difference of a prior period that is used to reduce current taxes;

g.   The amount of a benefit from a previously unrecognized tax loss, tax credit, or temporary difference of a prior period that is used to reduce deferred taxes;

h.   Deferred tax expense related to a write-down of a deferred tax asset or the reversal of a write-down; and

i.   The amount of tax expense relating to changes in accounting policies and correction of fundamental errors, accounted for consistent with the allowed alternative method under IAS 8.

(IAS 12, Paras 79 & 80)

3.   The following items also require separate disclosure:

a.   Tax expense relating to items which are charged or credited to equity;

b.   Tax expense relating to extraordinary items;

c.   An explanation of the relationship between tax expense or benefit and accounting profit or loss either (or both) as

(1)   A numerical reconciliation between tax expense or benefit and the product of accounting profit or loss times the applicable tax rate(s), with disclosure of how the rate(s) was determined; or

(2)   A numerical reconciliation between the average effective tax rate and the applicable rate, also with disclosure of how the applicable rate was determined.

d.   An explanation of changes in the applicable tax rates vs. the prior period;

e.   The amount and expiration date of deductible temporary differences, and unused tax losses and tax credits for which no deferred tax asset has been recognized;

f.   Aggregate temporary differences associated with investments in subsidiaries, branches, and associates, and interests in joint ventures, for which deferred tax liabilities have not been recognized;

g.   For each type of temporary difference, and for each type of unused tax loss or unused credit, the amount of deferred tax asset and liability recognized in the balance sheet and the amount of deferred tax expense or benefit recognized in the income statement, unless otherwise apparent from changes in the balance sheet accounts; and

h.   With regard to discontinued operations, the tax expense relating to the gain or loss on discontinuance and the tax expense on the profit or loss from ordinary activities of the discontinued operation.

i.   Amount of income tax on dividend that was declared or proposed before the financial statements are authorized for issue but are not recognized as a liability in the financial statements.

(IAS 12, Para 81)

D.   Extraordinary Items

1.   An entity shall not designate any item of income and expense as being an extraordinary item, either on the face of the income statement or in the notes.

(IAS 1, Para 85)

E.   Noncurrent Assets Held for Sale and Discontinued Operations

1.   An entity shall present and disclose information that enables users of the financial statements to evaluate the financial effects of discontinued operations and disposals of noncurrent assets (or disposal groups).

(IFRS 5, Para 30)

2. An entity shall disclose

    a. A single amount on the face of the income statement comprising the total of

        (1) The posttax profit or loss of discontinuing operations; and;

        (2) The posttax gain or loss recognized on the measurement to fair value less costs to sell or on the disposal of the assets or disposal group(s) constituting the discontinued operation.

    b. An analysis of the single amount in a. into

        (1) The revenue, expenses and pretax profit or loss of discontinued operations;

        (2) The related income tax expense as required by IAS 12, paragraph 81(h);

        (3) The gain or loss recognized one the measurement to fair value less costs to sell or on the disposal of the assets or disposal group(s) constituting the discontinued operation; and

        (4) The related income tax expense as required by IAS 12, paragraph 81(h). The analysis may be presented in the notes or on the face of the income statement. If it is presented on the face of the income statement it shall be presented in a section identified as relating to discontinued operations (i.e., separately from continuing operations). The analysis is not required for disposal groups that are newly acquired subsidiaries that meet the criteria to be classified as held for sale on acquisition.

    c. The net cash flows attributable to the operating, investing, and financing activities of discontinued operations. These disclosures may be presented either in the notes or on the face of the financial statements. These disclosures are not required for disposal groups that are newly acquired subsidiaries that meet the criteria to be classified as held for sale on acquisition.

(IFRS 5, Para 33)

3. An entity shall represent the disclosures in IFRS 5, paragraph 33 for prior period presented in the financial statements so that the disclosures relate to all operations that have been discontinued by the balance sheet date for the latest period presented.

(IFRS 5, Para 34)

4. An entity shall present a noncurrent asset classified as held for sale and the assets of a disposal group classified as held for sale separately from other assets in the balance sheet. The liabilities of the disposal group classified as held for sale shall be presented separately from other liabilities in the balance sheet. Those assets and liabilities shall not be offset and presented as a single amount. The major classes of assets and liabilities classified as held for sale shall be separately disclosed either on the face of the balance sheet or in the notes. An entity shall present separately any cumulative income or expense recognized directly as equity relating to a noncurrent asset classified as held for sale.

(IFRS 5, Para 38)

5. If the disposal group is a newly acquired subsidiary that meets the criteria to be classified as held for sale on acquisition, disclosure of the major classes of assets and liabilities is not required.

(IFRS 5, Para 39)

6. An entity shall not reclassify or represent amount presented for noncurrent assets or for the assets and liabilities of disposal groups classified as held for sale in the balance sheet for prior periods to reflect the classification in the balance sheet for the latest period presented.

(IAS 5, Para 40)

7. An entity shall disclose the following information in the notes in the period in which a noncurrent asset (disposal group) has been either classified as held for sale or sold:

a. A description of the noncurrent asset (or disposal group);

b. A description of the facts and circumstances of the sale, or leading to the expected disposal, the expected manner and timing of that disposal;

c. The impairment gain or loss recognized in accordance with IFRS 5, and if not separately presented on the face of the income statement, the caption in the income statement that includes that gain or loss;

d. If applicable, the segment in which the noncurrent asset (or disposal group) is presented in accordance with IAS 14, *Reporting Financial Information by Segment.*

(IFRS 5, Para 41)

8. If, as per IFRS 5, an entity changes to the plan of sale, it shall disclose, in the period of the decision to change the plan to sell the noncurrent asset (or disposal group), a description of the facts and circumstances leading to the decision and the effect of the decision on the results of operations for the period and any prior periods presented.

(IFRS 5, Para 42)

F. Segment Data

1. For each reportable segment based on the entity's primary reporting format

   a. Segment revenue, with revenue from external customers distinguished from revenue from transactions with other segments;

   (IAS 14, Para 51)

   b. Segment results (net profit or loss if this is computable without making arbitrary allocations; an other measure, such as gross margin, in other instances), with an indication if accounting policies other than those adopted for consolidated financial reporting have been employed;

   (IAS 14, Para 52)

   c. Total carrying values for segment assets;

   (IAS 14, Para 55)

   d. Total liabilities;

   (IAS 14, Para 56)

   e. Total cost incurred during the period being reported upon for acquisitions of segment assets expected to be used for greater than one period (i.e., plant assets and intangibles), determined on an accrual (not cash) basis;

   (IAS 14, Para 57)

   f. Total depreciation and amortization expense of segment assets during the period;

   (IAS 14, Para 58)

   g. (Optional but recommended) The nature and amounts of any items of segment revenue or expense that are of such size, nature, or incidence as to be relevant to explain performance;

   (IAS 14, Para 59)

   h. Total amounts of significant noncash expenses other than depreciation and amortization (this may be omitted if the segment cash flow data encouraged by IAS 7 is provided, however);

   (IAS 14, Para 61)

   i. The aggregate of the entity's share of the net profit or loss of associates, joint ventures, or other equity method investments, if substantially all the associates' operations are within the single segment, and, if so, the aggregate amount of the investments in those associates;

   (IAS 14, Paras 64 & 66)

j.   The amount of impairment losses recognized in the income statement and, separately, directly in equity; and the amount of reversals of impairments, also separately recognized in the income statement and directly in equity;

(IAS 36, Para 129)

k.   Disclose by segment if the amount of impairment or reversal of impairment is material to the financial statements taken as a whole information regarding the segment to which the asset belongs or the cash-generating unit;

(IAS 36, Para 130)

l.   A reconciliation between the information provided by segment and the aggregated information presented in the consolidated or entity financial statements (e.g., segment revenues from external customers reconciled to total revenues; segment results to the same measurement item on an entity-wide basis, etc.).

(IAS 14, Para 67)

m.   If the primary format for segment disclosures is based on geography, if the disclosures were by asset location, disclose revenues from sales to external customers by geographic area. Conversely, if primary disclosures are based on customer locations, disclose supplementally asset locations by segment, as well as capital expenditures for property, plant, and equipment and for intangibles by segment.

(IAS 14, Para 72)

2.   For each reportable segment based on the entity's secondary reporting format

a.   If the primary reporting format is business segments, then the following should be presented:

(1)   Segment revenue from external customers by geographical area based on location of customers, for each geographical segment whose revenues from external customers is 10% or greater of total entity revenues from external customers;

(2)   Total carrying amount of segment assets by geographical location of assets, for each geographical segment whose segment assets are 10% or greater of total assets; and

(3)   The total cost incurred during the period to acquire segment assets expected to be used for more than one period, by geographical location of assets, for each geographical segment whose segment assets are 10% or greater of total assets.

(IAS 14, Para 69)

b.   If the primary reporting format is geographical segments (whether based on location of assets or of customers), the following should be reported for each business segment whose revenue from external customers is 10% or greater of total entity revenue from external customers, **or** whose segment assets are 10% or greater of total assets of all segments:

(1)   Segment revenues from external customers;

(2)   Total carrying amounts of segment assets; and

(3)   Total cost incurred during the period to acquire segment assets expected to be used for more than one period.

(IAS 14, Para 70)

c.   If the primary reporting format is geographical segments based on location of assets, and if location of customers differs from location of assets, then the entity should also report revenues from external customers for each customer-based geographical segment whose revenue from external customers is 10% or greater of total entity revenue from external customers.

(IAS 14, Para 71)

    d.   If the primary reporting format is geographical segments based on location of customers, and if location of customers differs from location of assets, then the entity should also report the following for each asset-based geographical segment whose revenue from external customers or segment assets is 10% or greater of total entity revenue from external customers or consolidated assets, respectively:

        (1)   Total carrying amount of segment assets by geographical location; and

        (2)   Total cost incurred during the period to acquire segment assets expected to be used for more than one period.

(IAS 14, Para 72)

3.   If a business or geographical segment is not reportable because a majority of revenues are from sales to other segments, but nevertheless revenues from external customers are 10% or greater of total entity revenues, this fact should be disclosed and the amounts of revenues from external customers and from other segments must be stated.

(IAS 14, Para 74)

4.   The bases of pricing intersegment transfers, and changes therein, should be disclosed.

(IAS 14, Para 75)

5.   Changes in accounting policies for segment reporting having material effects on segment information should be disclosed, and prior period segment presented as comparative data should be restated, unless impracticable to do so. Disclosures should include description and nature of change, reasons for making the change, whether comparative data has been restated or the fact that it was impracticable to do so, and the financial effect of the change, if reasonably determinable. If segment definitions have changed and prior period data has not been restated, then the current period data should be prepared and presented under both the old and the new classification schemes, so that comparability will be preserved.

(IAS 14, Para 76)

6.   The types of products and services included in each reportable business segment, and the composition of each reported geographical segment, both primary and secondary, should be disclosed unless otherwise reported in the financial statements.

(IAS 14, Para 81)

G. Construction Contracts

1.   An entity which accounts for construction contracts in accordance with IAS 11 should disclose the following in its financial statements:

    a.   The amount of contract revenue recognized as revenue in the period;

    b.   The methods used to determine the contract revenue recognized in the period; and

    c.   The methods used to determine the stage of completion for contracts in progress.

(IAS 11, Para 39)

2.   Each of the following should be disclosed for the contracts in progress:

    a.   The aggregate amount of costs incurred and recognized profits (net of any recognized losses) to date;

    b.   The amount of advances received; and

    c.   The amount of retentions.

(IAS 11, Para 40)

3.   On the balance sheet, present gross amounts due from customers as an asset, and gross amounts due to customers for contract work as a liability.

(IAS 11, Para 42)

H. Foreign Currency Translation

1.   Disclosure is required of the following:

a.   The amount of exchange differences included in net profit or loss for the period;

b.   Net exchange differences classified as a separate component of equity, and a reconciliation of the amount of such exchange differences at the beginning and the end of the period.

(IAS 21, Para 52)

2.   If the reporting currency is different from the currency of the country in which the entity is domiciled, disclosure is required of the following:

a.   The reason for using a different currency; and

b.   The reason for any change in the reporting currency.

(IAS 21, Para 53)

3.   When there is a change in classification of a significant foreign operation, the following disclosures are required:

a.   The nature of the change; and

b.   The reason for the change;

(IAS 21, Para 54)

4.   When an entity presents its financial statements in a currency that is different from its functional currency, it shall describe the financial statements as complying with IFRS only if they comply with all the requirements of each applicable Standard and each applicable Interpretation of those Standards including the translation method.

(IAS 21, Para 55)

5.   When an entity displays its financial statements or other financial information in a currency that is different from either its functional currency or its presentation currency and the requirements of IAS 21, paragraph 21 are not met, it shall

a.   Clearly identify the information as supplementary information to distinguish it from the information that complies with IFRS;

b.   Disclose the currency in which the supplementary information is displayed; and

c.   Disclose the entity's functional currency and the method of translation used to determine the supplementary information.

(IAS 21, Para 57)

I. Business Combinations

1.   An acquirer shall disclose information that enables users of its financial statements to evaluate the nature and financial effect of business combinations that were effected

a.   During the period;

b.   After the balance sheet date but before the financial statements are authorized for issue.

(IFRS 3, Para 66)

2.   The acquirer shall disclose the following information for each business combination that was effected during the period:

a.   The names and descriptions of the combining entities or businesses;

b.   The acquisition date;

c.   The percentage of voting equity acquired;

d.   The cost of combination and a description of the components of that cost, including any costs directly attributable to combination. When equity instruments are issued or issuable as part of the cost, the following shall be disclosed:

(1)   The number of equity instruments issued or issuable; and;

(2)   The fair value of those instruments and the basis for determining the fair value; if a published price does not exist for the instruments at the date of the exchange, the

significant assumptions used to determine fair value shall be disclosed. If a published price exists at a date of exchange but was not used as the basis for determining the cost of combination, that fact shall be disclosed together with: the reasons the published price was not used; the method and significant assumptions used to attribute a value to the equity instruments; and the aggregate amount of the difference between the value attributed to, and the published price of, the equity instruments.

e. Details of any operations the entity has decided to dispose of as a result of the combination.

f. The amounts recognized at the acquisition date for each class of the acquiree's assets, liabilities and contingent liabilities and, unless disclosure should be impracticable, the carrying amounts of each of these classes, determined in accordance with IFRS, immediately before the combination. If such disclosure would be impracticable, that fact should be disclosed, together with an explanation of why this is the case.

g. The amount of any excess recognized in profit or loss in accordance with IFRS 3, paragraph 56, and the line item in the income statement in which the excess is recognized.

h. A description of the factors that contributed to a cost that results in the recognition of goodwill, a description of each intangible asset that was not recognized separately from goodwill and an explanation of why the intangible asset's fair value could not be measured reliably, or a description of the nature of any excess recognized in profit or loss in accordance with IFRS 3.

i. The amount of the acquiree's profit or loss since the acquisition date included in the acquirer's profit or loss of the period, unless disclosure would be impracticable, that fact shall be disclosed, together with an explanation of why this is the case.

(IFRS 3, Para 67)

3. The information required to be disclosed by IFRS 3, paragraph 67, shall be disclosed in aggregate for business combinations effected during the reporting period that are individually immaterial.

(IFRS 3, Para 68)

4. If the initial accounting for a business combination that was effected during the period was determined only provisionally described in IFRS 3, paragraph 62, the fact should be also disclosed together with an explanation of why this is the case.

(IFRS 3, Para 69)

5. To give effect to the principle in IFRS 3, paragraph 66(a), the acquirer shall disclose the following information, unless such disclosure should be impracticable:

a. The revenues of the combined entity for the period as though the acquisition date for all business combinations effected during the period had been the beginning of that period.

b. The profit or loss of the current entity for the period as though the acquisition date for all business combinations effected during the period had been the beginning of the period. If disclosure of this information is impracticable, the fact shall be disclosed, together with an explanation of why this is the case.

(IFRS 3, Para 70)

6. To give effect to the principle in IFRS 3, paragraph 66(b), the acquirer shall disclose the information required by IFRS 3, paragraph 67, for each business combination effected after the balance sheet date but before the financial statements are authorized, for issue, unless such disclosure would be impracticable. If disclosure of any of this information would be impracticable, the fact shall be disclosed together with an explanation of why this is the case.

(IFRS 3, Para 71)

7. An acquirer shall disclose information that enables its users to evaluate the financial effects of gains, losses, error corrections, and other adjustments recognized in the current period that relate to business combinations that were effected in the current or in previous periods.

(IFRS 3, Para 72)

8. To give effect to the principle in IFRS 3, paragraph 72, the acquirer shall disclose the following information:

   a. The amount and an explanation of any gain or loss recognized in the current period that

      (1) Relates to the identifiable assets acquired or liabilities or contingent liabilities assumed in a business combination that was effected in the current or the previous period; and

      (2) Is of such size and nature or incidence that disclosure is relevant to an understanding of the combined entity's financial performance.

   b. If the initial accounting for a business combination that was effected in the immediately preceding period was determined only provisionally at the end of that period, the amounts and explanations of the adjustments to the provisional values recognized during the current period.

   c. The information about error corrections required to be disclosed by IAS 8 for any of the acquiree's identifiable assets, liabilities or contingent liabilities, or changes in the values assigned to those items, that acquirer recognizes during the current period in accordance with IFRS 3, paragraphs 63 and 64.

(IFRS 3, Para 73)

9. An entity shall disclose information to evaluate the changes in the carrying amount of goodwill during the period.

(IFRS 3, Para 74)

10. To give effect to the principle in IFRS 3, paragraph 74, the entity shall disclose a reconciliation of the carrying amount of goodwill at the beginning and the end of the period, showing separately

    a. The gross amount and accumulated impairment losses at the beginning of the period;

    b. Additional goodwill recognized during the period except goodwill included in a disposal group that, on acquisition, meets the criteria to be classified as held for sale in accordance with IFRS 5;

    c. Adjustments resulting from the subsequent recognition of deferred tax assets during the period in accordance with IFRS 3, paragraph 65;

    d. Goodwill included in disposal group classified as held for sale in accordance with IFRS 5 and goodwill derecognized during the period without having been previously included in a disposal group classified for sale;

    e. Impairment losses recognized during the period in accordance with IAS 36;

    f. Net exchange differences arising during the period in accordance with IAS 21, *The Effects of Changes in Foreign Exchange Rates*;

    g. Any other changes in the carrying amount during the period.

(IFRS 3, Para 75)

11. An entity shall disclose information about the recoverable amount and impairment of goodwill in accordance with IAS 36 in addition to the information required to be disclosed by IFRS 3, paragraph 75(5).

(IFRS 3, Para 76)

12. An entity shall disclose such additional information as is necessary to satisfy the objectives set out in IFRS 3, paragraphs 66, 72, and 74 if it is not able to satisfy these objectives under any situation.

(IFRS 3, Para 77)

13. All required disclosures concerning business acquisitions occurring during the period are also to be made for those occurring after the balance sheet date.

(IFRS 3, Para 66)

14. Business disposals during the period require disclosure of total consideration; the portion of total consideration received in cash or equivalents; the amount of cash or equivalents that was in the disposed-of operation; and the amount of assets and liabilities other than cash or equivalents, summarized by major categories.

(IAS 7, Para 40)

J. Earnings Per Share

1. Entities should present both basic EPS and diluted EPS on the face of the income statement for each class of ordinary shares that has a different right to share in the net profit for the period. Equal prominence should be given to both the basic EPS and diluted EPS figures for all periods presented.

(IAS 33, Para 66)

2. Entities should present basic EPS and diluted EPS even if the amounts disclosed are negative.

(IAS 33, Para 69)

3. Where relevant, EPS from continuing operations should be presented also.

(IAS 33, Para 66)

4. Entities should disclose amounts used as the numerator in calculating basic EPS and diluted EPS along with a reconciliation of those amounts to the net profit or loss for the period. Disclosure is also required of the weighted-average number of ordinary shares used as the denominator in calculating basic EPS and diluted EPS along with a reconciliation of these denominators to each other.

(IAS 33, Paras 70[a] & 70[b])

5. a. In addition to the disclosure of the figures for basic EPS and diluted EPS, as required above, if an entity *chooses to disclose* per share amounts using a reported component of net profit, other than net profit or loss for the period attributable to ordinary shareholders, such amounts should be calculated using weighted-average number of ordinary shares determined in accordance with the requirements of IAS 33; this will ensure comparability of the per share amounts disclosed;

   b. In cases where an entity chooses to disclose the above per share amounts using a component of net profit not reported as a line item in the income statement, a reconciliation is mandated by the standard, which should reconcile the difference between the component of net income used with a line item reported in the income statement; and

   c. When additional disclosure is made by an entity of the above per share amounts, basic and diluted per share amounts should be disclosed with equal prominence (just as basic EPS and diluted EPS figures are given equal prominence).

(IAS 33, Para 73)

6. Entities are encouraged to disclose the terms and conditions of financial instruments or contracts generating potential ordinary shares, since such terms and conditions may determine whether or not any potential ordinary shares are dilutive and, if so, the effect on the weighted-average number of shares outstanding and any consequent adjustments to the net profit attributable to the ordinary shareholders.

(IAS 33, Para 72)

7. If changes (resulting from bonus issue or share split etc.) in the number of ordinary or potential ordinary shares occur, after the balance sheet date but before issuance of the financial statements, and the per share calculations reflect such changes in the number of shares, such a fact should be disclosed.

(IAS 33, Para 70[d])

8. An entity shall disclose the instruments (including contingently issuable shares) that could potentially dilute basic earnings per share in the future, but were not included in the calculation of diluted earnings per share because they are antidilutive for the period(s) presented.

(IAS 33, Para 70[c])

K. Dividends Per Share

1. An entity should disclose, either on the face of the income statement or in the notes, the amount of dividends per share, declared or proposed, for the period covered by the financial statements.

(IAS 1, Para 95)

L. Impairments of Assets

1. For each class of assets, the financial statements should disclose:

   a. The amount of impairment losses recognized in the income statement during the period and the line item(s) of the income statements in which those impairment losses are included;

   b. The amount of reversals of impairment losses recognized in the income statement during the period and the line item(s) of the income statement in which those impairment losses are reversed;

   c. The amount of impairment losses recognized directly in equity during the period; and

   d. The amount of reversals of impairment losses recognized directly in equity during the period.

(IAS 36, Para 126)

2. If impairment loss for an asset or a cash-generating unit is recognized or reversed during the period and is **material** to the financial statements as a whole, an entity should disclose

   a. Events and circumstances that led to the recognition or reversal of the impairment loss;

   b. Amount of the impairment loss recognized or reversed;

   c. For an individual asset, its nature and the primary reportable segment to which it belongs, based on the entity's primary format (as defined in IAS 14, if that IAS applies to the entity);

   d. For a cash-generating unit, a description of the cash-generating unit, the amount of the impairment loss recognized or reversed by the class of assets and by the reportable segment based on the entity's primary format (as defined by IAS 14, if that IAS applies to the entity) and if the aggregation of assets for identifying the cash-generating unit has changed since the previous estimate of the cash-generating unit's recoverable amount (if any), the entity should describe the current and former manner of aggregating assets and the reasons for the change;

   e. Whether the recoverable amount of the asset (cash-generating unit) is its net selling price or its value in use;

   f. The basis used to determine net selling price (such as with reference to an active market or any other manner) in case the recoverable amount is net selling price; and

   g. If recoverable amount is value in use, the discount rate(s) used in the current estimate and previous estimate (if any) of value in use.

(IAS 36, Para 130)

3. If impairment losses recognized (reversed) during the period are **material** in aggregate to the financial statements of the entity as a whole, an entity should disclose a brief description of the following:

   a. The main classes of assets affected by impairment losses (reversals of impairment losses) for which no information is disclosed under IAS 36, para 117); and

   b. The main events and circumstances that led to the recognition (reversal) of these impairment losses for which no information is disclosed under IAS 36, para 117).

(IAS 36, Para 131)

4. If any portion of goodwill acquired in a business combination effected during the current period was not allocated to a cash-generating unit at the balance sheet date, per IAS 36, para 84, the amount of the unallocated goodwill is to be disclosed, with an explanation of why it remains unallocated.

(IAS 36, Para 133)

5. For each cash-generating unit with material amounts of indefinite-life intangibles or goodwill

   a. Disclose the carrying amount of goodwill; the carrying amount of indefinite life intangibles; the basis on which recoverable amounts were determined.
   b. If the recoverable amounts were based on value in use, describe key assumptions made by management affecting the cash flow projections, management's approach to value determination for each key assumption, the period over which cash flows were projected with an explanation, as necessary, for projections over greater than five years, and the growth rate used to project cash flows, with explanations for any that exceed the entity's historical long-term growth rate.
   c. If the recoverable amounts were based on fair value less costs to sell, disclose methodology used to determine such amounts where not based on observable market data; describe each key assumption and management's approach to determining values assigned to key assumptions.
   d. When reasonably possible change in a key assumption could cause carrying value of cash-generating unit to exceed recoverable amount, disclose the amount by which aggregate recoverable amounts exceed carrying values, the value(s) assigned to key assumption(s), and the amount by which the value assigned to assumption(s) would need to change to cause recoverable amounts to equal carrying amounts.

(IAS 36, Para 134)

6. Compensation from third parties for items of property, plant, and equipment that were impaired, lost, or given up shall be included in profit or loss when the compensation becomes receivable.

(IAS 16, Para 65)

CASH FLOW STATEMENT

A. Basis of Presentation

1. A cash flow statement (CFS) should be prepared in accordance with IAS 7 and presented as an integral part of an entity's financial statements for each period for which the financial statements are presented.

(IAS 7, Para 1)

2. The CFS should report cash flows during the period, classified by

   a. Operating activities;
   b. Investing activities; and
   c. Financing activities.

(IAS 7, Para 10)

B. Format

1. Cash flows from operating activities should be reported using either

   a. The direct method, under which major classes of gross cash receipts and gross cash payments are disclosed; **or**
   b. The indirect method, wherein net profit or loss for the period is adjusted for the following:

      (1) The effects of noncash transactions;
      (2) Any deferrals or accruals of past or future operating cash receipts or payments; and
      (3) Items of income or expense related to investing or financing cash flows.

(IAS 7, Para 18)

2. An entity should generally report (separately) major gross cash receipts and payments from investing and financing activities.

(IAS 7, Para 21)

3. Under the following circumstances, however, an entity's[1] cash flows arising from operating, investing, or financing activities may be reported on a net basis:

   a. Cash receipts and payments on behalf of customers when the cash flows reflect the activities of the customer rather than those of the entity; and
   b. Cash receipts and payments for items in which the turnover is quick, the amounts are large, and maturities are short.

(IAS 7, Para 22)

4. Cash flows arising from extraordinary items should be classified as either

   a. Operating activities;
   b. Investing activities; or
   c. Financing activities.

   Each of these items should be disclosed separately.

(IAS 7, Para 29)

5. Cash flows from interest received and dividends received and dividends paid should be classified consistently (from period to period) as either

   a. Operating activities;
   b. Investing activities; or
   c. Financing activities.

   Each of these items should be disclosed separately.

(IAS 7, Para 31)

6. In relation to cash and cash equivalents, a cash flow statement should

   a. Disclose the policy which it adopts in determining the components;
   b. Disclose the components; and
   c. Present a reconciliation of the amounts in its CFS with similar items reported in the balance sheet.

(IAS 7, Paras 45 & 46)

7. The effect of exchange rate changes on cash and cash equivalents held or due in foreign currency should be presented separately from cash flows from operating, investing, and financing activities.

(IAS 7, Para 28)

8. Noncash transactions arising from investing and financing activities should be excluded from the CFS. Such transactions do not require the use of cash and cash equivalents and thus should be disclosed elsewhere in the financial statements by way of a note that provides all the relevant information about these activities.

(IAS 7, Para 43)

9. Cash payments and receipts relating to taxes on income should be separately disclosed and classified as cash flows from operating activities unless they could specifically be identified with financing and/or investing activities.

(IAS 7, Para 35)

---

[1] *Cash flows of financial institutions may be reported on a net basis under the following cases:*

   1. *Cash flows from the acceptance and repayment of deposits with fixed maturity dates;*
   2. *Placement of deposits with and withdrawal of deposits from other financial institutions; and*
   3. *Cash advances and loans made to customers and the repayment of those advances and loans.*

(IAS 7, Para 24)

10. In relation to acquisitions or disposals of subsidiaries or other business units which should be presented separately and classified as investing activities, an entity should disclose the following:

   a. The total purchase or sale price;
   b. Portion of the consideration discharged by cash and cash equivalents;
   c. Amount of cash and cash equivalents acquired or disposed; and
   d. Amount of assets and liabilities (other than cash or cash equivalents) summarized by major category.

(IAS 7, Para 40)

11. Significant cash and cash equivalent balances held by the entity which are not available for use by the group should be disclosed by the entity along with a commentary by management.

(IAS 7, Para 48)

C. Additional Recommended Disclosures

Additional disclosures which may be relevant to financial statement users in understanding an entity's financial position and liquidity have been encouraged by IAS 7 and include the following:

1. The amount of undrawn borrowing facilities including disclosure of restrictions, if any, as to their use;
2. The aggregate amount of cash flows related to interests in joint ventures reported using the proportionate consolidation;
3. The aggregate amount of cash flows that represent increases in operating capacity separately from those cash flows that are required to maintain the operating capacity; and
4. Disclosure of segmental cash flow information in order to provide financial statement users better information about the relationship of cash flows of the business as a whole vis-à-vis cash flows from its segments.

(IAS 7, Para 50)

STATEMENT OF CHANGES IN EQUITY

A. Statement of Changes in Equity

1. As a separate component of its financial statements, an entity should present a statement showing the following four items:

   a. The net profit or loss for the period;
   b. Each item of income and expense, gain or loss which, as prescribed by other Standards, is recognized directly in equity, and the total of these items;
   c. Total income and expense for the period showing separately the total amounts attributable to equity holders of the parent and to minority interest;
   d. Transactions with equity holders, such as issuance of shares, repurchase of shares, and contracts to be settled by delivery of fixed number of shares;
   e. Transaction costs related to share issuances, deducted from equity;
   f. Distributions to owners via dividends or other means;
   g. A reconciliation between the carrying amount at year beginning and year-end, showing for each class of capital, share premium, and treasury stock each movement;
   h. Each reserve in equity, including revaluation reserves for property, plant, and equipment, for intangibles, for available-for-sale securities, hedging reserves for cash flow hedges, translation reserves, current or deferred tax adjustments for items recognized directly in equity, and equity-settled share-based payment transactions;
   i. Retained earnings; and
   j. The equity conversion feature of convertible debt accounted for as a compound instrument under IAS 32.

(IAS 1, Paras 1 & 96-97; IAS 32, Paras 22, 28, 34, 35, 59 & 94;
IAS 16, Para 77; IAS 21, Para 52; IAS 38, Para 124; IFRS 2, Para 50)

2. When a "Statement of Income and Expense Recognized in Equity" is presented, it should set forth profit or loss for the period; each item of income or expense being reported directly in equity, and the total of such items; total income or expense for the period; and for each element of stockholders' equity the effects of changes in accounting policies and corrections of errors as mandated by IAS 8.

(IAS 1, Paras 96-97; IAS 32, Paras 34, 35, 59, & 94;
IAS 16, Para 77; IAS 21, Para 52; IAS 38, Para 124; IFRS 2, Para 50)

3. When a "Statement of Income and Expense Recognized in Equity" is presented (as an alternative to the "Statement of Changes in Equity") the following three items are presented in the notes to the financial statements:

    a. Capital transactions with owners and distributions to owners;
    b. Transaction costs relating to issuance of share capital;
    c. Distributions to owners;
    d. The balance of retained earnings (referred to as "accumulated profit or loss") at the beginning of the period and at the balance sheet date, and the movements for the period; and
    e. A reconciliation between the carrying amount of each class of equity capital, share premium and each reserve at the beginning and the end of the period, separately disclosing each movement.

(IAS 1, Para 97)

NOTES TO THE FINANCIAL STATEMENTS

A. Structure of the Notes

1. The notes to the financial statements should

    a. Present information regarding the basis of preparation of the financial statements and the specific accounting policies selected and applied for significant transactions and events;
    b. Disclose information required by IAS which is not presented elsewhere in the financial statements; and
    c. Provide additional information which is not presented on the face of the financial statements but which is necessary for a fair presentation.

(IAS 1, Para 103)

2. The notes to the financial statements should be presented in a systematic manner. Each item on the face of the balance sheet, income statement and cash flow statement should be cross-referenced to any related information in the notes to the financial statements.

(IAS 1, Para 104)

3. The following order of presentation of the notes is normally adopted which assists users of financial statements in understanding them and comparing them with those of other entities:

    a. Statement of compliance with IAS;
    b. Statement of the measurement basis/bases and accounting policies applied;
    c. Supporting information for items presented on the face of each financial statement in the order in which each line item and each financial statement is presented; and
    d. Other disclosures, including

        (1) Contingencies and commitments and other financial disclosures; and
        (2) Nonfinancial disclosures.

(IAS 1, Para 105)

4. An entity shall disclose in the notes

    a. The amount of dividends proposed or declared before the financial statements were authorized for issue but not recognized as a distribution to equity holders during the period, and the related amount per share; and

     b.   The amount of any cumulative preference share not recognized.

B. Accounting Policies

    1.   The accounting policies section of the notes to the financial statements should describe the following:

        a.   The measurement basis/bases used in preparing the financial statements; and
        b.   Each specific accounting policy that is necessary for a proper understanding of the financial statements.

(IAS 1, Para 108)

    2.   Examples of accounting policies that an entity may consider presenting include, but are not restricted to, the following:

        a.   Revenue recognition;
        b.   Basis of consolidation of subsidiaries and method of accounting for investments in associates;
        c.   Business combinations;
        d.   Joint ventures;
        e.   Recognition and depreciation/amortization of tangible and intangible assets;
        f.   Capitalization of borrowing costs and other expenditures;
        g.   Construction contracts;
        h.   Investment properties;
        i.   Financial instruments and investments;
        j.   Leases;
        k.   Research and development costs;
        l.   Inventories;
        m.   Taxes, including deferred taxes;
        n.   Provisions;
        o.   Employee benefit costs;
        p.   Foreign currency translation and hedging;
        q.   Definition of business and geographical segments and the basis for allocation of costs between segments;
        r.   Definition of cash and cash equivalents;
        s.   Inflation accounting; and
        t.   Government grants.

(IAS 1, Para 99 & 110)

C. Service Concession Arrangements

    1.   All aspects of a service concession arrangement should be taken into account in determining the appropriate disclosures in the notes. Both a concession operator and a concession provider should disclose the following **in each period:**

        a.   A description of the service concession arrangement;
        b.   Significant terms of the arrangement that may affect the amount, timing, and certainty of future cash flows (e.g., period of concession, repricing dates, and the basis upon which the repricing or renegotiation is determined);
        c.   The nature and extent (e.g., the quantity, time period, or amount as appropriate) of

            (1)   Rights to use specified assets;
            (2)   Obligations to provide or rights to expect provision of services;
            (3)   Obligations to acquire or build items of property, plant, and equipment;
            (4)   Obligations to deliver or rights to receive specified assets at the end of the concession period;
            (5)   Renewal and termination options; and
            (6)   Other rights and obligations (e.g., major overhauls); and

        d.   Changes in the arrangement taking place during the period.

2. The above-mentioned disclosures should be provided individually for each service concession arrangement or in aggregate for each class of service concession arrangements. A "class" is a grouping of service concession arrangements involving services of a similar nature (e.g., toll collections, telecommunications, and water treatment services).

(SIC 29, Paras 6 & 7)

INTERIM FINANCIAL STATEMENTS

A. Minimum Components of an Interim Financial Report

1. An interim financial report should include, at a minimum, the following components:

    a. A condensed balance sheet;
    b. A condensed income statement;
    c. A condensed statement showing **either** all changes in equity **or** changes in equity other than those arising from capital transactions with owners and distributions to owners;
    d. A condensed cash flow statement; and
    e. Selected set of footnote disclosures.

(IAS 34, Para 8)

B. Form and Content of Interim Financial Statements

1. If an entity chooses the "complete set of (interim) financial statements" route, instead of opting for the shortcut method of presenting only "condensed" interim financial statements, then the form and content of those statements should conform to the requirements of IAS 1 (revised 1997) for a complete set of financial statements.

(IAS 34, Para 9)

2. However, if an entity opts for the condensed format of interim financial reporting, then IAS 34, para 10, requires that, at a minimum, those condensed financial statements should include

    a. Each of the headings, and
    b. Subtotals that were included in the entity's most recent annual financial statements, along with selected explanatory notes, prescribed by the Standard.

    (Additional line items or notes should be included if their omission would make the condensed interim financial statements misleading.)

(IAS 34, Para 10)

3. Basic and diluted earnings per share should be presented on the face of an income statement, complete or condensed, for an interim period.

(IAS 34, Para 11)

4. An interim financial report should be prepared on a consolidated basis if the entity's most recent annual financial statements were consolidated statements. As regards presentation of separate interim financial statements of the parent company in addition to consolidated interim financial statements, if they were included in the most recent annual financial statements, this Standard neither requires nor prohibits such inclusion in the interim financial report of the entity.

(IAS 34, Para 14)

C. Selected Explanatory Notes

1. The minimum disclosures required to accompany the condensed interim financial statements are the following:

    a. A statement that the same accounting policies and methods of computation are applied in the interim financial statements compared with the most recent annual financial statements or if those policies or methods have changed, a description of the nature and effect of the change;

    b.   Explanatory comments about seasonality or cyclicality of interim operations;

    c.   The nature and magnitude of significant items affecting interim results that are unusual because of nature, size, or incidence;

    d.   Dividends paid, either in the aggregate or on a per share basis, presented separately for ordinary (common) shares and other classes of shares;

    e.   Revenue and operating result for business segments or geographical segments, whichever has been the entity's primary mode of segment reporting;

    f.   Any significant events occurring subsequent to the end of the interim period;

    g.   Issuances, repurchases, and repayments of debt and equity securities;

    h.   The nature and quantum of changes in estimates of amounts reported in prior interim periods of the current financial year or changes in estimates of amounts reported in prior financial years, if those changes have a material effect in the current interim period;

    i.   The effect of changes in the composition of the entity during the interim period like business combinations, acquisitions or disposal of subsidiaries and long-term investments, restructuring, and discontinuing operations; and

    j.   The changes in contingent liabilities or contingent assets since the most recent annual report.

(IAS 34, Para 16)

2.   Disclose any other events or transactions material to understanding of current interim period.

(IAS 34, Para 16)

DISCLOSURES FOR BANKS AND SIMILAR FINANCIAL INSTITUTIONS (IAS 30)

A. Income Statement

1.   The income statement of a bank should be presented in a manner that groups income and expenses by nature and discloses the amounts of the principal types of income and expenses.

(IAS 30, Para 19)

2.   In addition to the requirements of other IAS, the disclosures in the income statement or in the footnotes should include, but are not limited to, the following items:

    a.   Interest and similar income

    b.   Interest expense and similar charges

    c.   Dividend income

    d.   Fee and commission income

    e.   Fee and commission expense

    f.   Gains less losses arising from dealing securities

    g.   Gains less losses arising from investment securities

    h.   Gains less losses arising from dealing in foreign currencies

    i.   Other operating income

    j.   Losses on loans and advances

    k.   General and administrative expenses

    l.   Other operating expenses

(IAS 30, Paras 9 &10)

B. Balance Sheet

1.   The balance sheet of a bank should group assets and liabilities by nature and list them in the order of their respective liquidity. These are to be made either on the face of the balance sheet or in footnotes.

(IAS 30, Para 18)

2.   In addition to the requirements of the other IAS, the disclosures in the balance sheet or notes to the financial statements should include, but are not limited to

a. Assets

    (1) Cash and balances with the central bank.
    (2) Treasury bills and other bills eligible for rediscounting with the central bank.
    (3) Government and other securities held for dealing purposes.
    (4) Placements with, and loans and advances to, other banks.
    (5) Other money market placements.
    (6) Loans and advances to customers.
    (7) Investment securities.

b. Liabilities

    (1) Deposits from other banks.
    (2) Other money market deposits.
    (3) Amounts owed to other depositors.
    (4) Certificates of deposits.
    (5) Promissory notes and other liabilities evidenced by paper.
    (6) Other borrowed funds.

(IAS 30, Para 19)

3. The fair values of each class of financial assets and financial liabilities, as required by IAS 32 and 39, should be disclosed. According to IAS 39, the four classifications of financial assets are: loans and receivables originated by the entity, held-to-maturity investments, financial assets held for trading, and available-for-sale financial assets. A bank should disclose the fair value of its financial assets for these four classifications, as a minimum.

(IAS 30, Paras 24 & 25)

C. Contingencies and Commitments Including Off-Balance-Sheet Items

1. The disclosures required in this regard are the following:

a. The nature and amount of commitments to extend credit that are irrevocable because they cannot be withdrawn at the discretion of the bank without incurring significant penalty or expenses.

b. The nature and amount of contingencies and commitments arising from off-balance-sheet items, including those relating to

    (1) Direct credit substitutes, which include general guarantees of indebtedness, bank acceptances, and standby letters of credit, which serve as financial backup for loans and securities;
    (2) Transaction-related contingencies, which include performance bonds, bid bonds, warranties, and standby letters of credit related to particular transactions;
    (3) Short-term self-liquidating, trade-related contingent liabilities arising from the movement of goods, such as documentary credits where underlying shipment is used as security; and
    (4) Other commitments, including other off-balance-sheet items such as revolving underwriting facilities and note issuance facilities.

(IAS 30, Para 26)

D. Maturities of Assets and Liabilities

1. An analysis of assets and liabilities into relevant maturity groupings based on the remaining period at the balance sheet date to the contractual maturity date should be disclosed.

(IAS 30, Para 30)

E. Concentrations of Assets and Liabilities

1. Any significant concentration of assets, liabilities, and off-balance-sheet items should be disclosed. Such disclosures should be made in terms of geographical areas, customer or industry groups, or other concentrations of risk.

2. The amount of significant net foreign currency exposures should be disclosed.

(IAS 30, Para 40)

F. Losses on Loans and Advances

1. The following disclosures are prescribed with respect to "losses on loans and advances:"

    a. The accounting policy describing the basis on which uncollectible loans and advances are recognized as an expense and written off;

    b. Details of the movements in the provision for losses on loans and advances during the period, disclosing separately the amount charged to income in the period for losses on uncollectible loans and advances, the amount charged in the period for loans and advances written off and the amount credited in the period for loans and advances previously written off that have been recovered;

    c. The aggregate amount of the provision for impairment losses on loans and advances at the balance sheet date; and

    (IAS 30, Para 43)

2. Any amounts set aside in respect of losses on loans and advances in addition to those losses that have been specifically identified, or potential losses which experience indicates are present in the portfolio of loans and advances, should be accounted for as appropriations of retained earnings. Any credits resulting from the reduction of such amounts should be treated as increases in retained earnings and not included in the determination of net income.

    (IAS 30, Para 44)

G. General Banking Risks

1. Any amounts set aside in respect of general banking risks, including future losses and other unforeseeable risks or contingencies in addition to those for which accrual must be made under IAS 10, should be separately disclosed as appropriations of retained earnings. Any credits resulting from the reduction of such amounts result in an increase in retained earnings and are not included in the determination of net income.

    (IAS 30, Para 50)

H. Assets Pledged as Security

1. The aggregate amount of secured liabilities and the nature and carrying amount of the assets pledged as security should be disclosed.

    (IAS 30, Para 53)

I. Related-Party Transactions

1. When a bank has entered into transactions with related parties, the nature of the relationship, the type of transaction, and the elements of the transaction should be disclosed. The elements that are to be disclosed include the bank's lending policy to related parties and, in respect of related-party transactions, the amount included in or the proportion of

    a. Each of the loans and advances, deposits and acceptances, and promissory notes—disclosures may include the aggregate amounts outstanding at the beginning and end of the year as well as changes in these accounts during the year;

    b. Each of the principal types of income, interest expense, and commissions paid;

    c. The amount of the expense recognized in the period for the losses on loans and advances and the amount of the provision at the balance sheet date; and

    d. Irrevocable commitments and contingencies and commitments from off-balance-sheet items.

    (IAS 30, Para 58)

J. Trust Activities

1. If a bank is engaged in significant trust activities, wherein banks commonly act as trustees and in other fiduciary capacities that result in the holding or placing of assets on behalf of individuals, trusts, retirement benefit plans, and other institutions, and such relationships are legally supported, disclosure of that fact and an indication of the extent of those activities should be made.

    (IAS 30, Para 55)

INSURANCE CONTRACTS

1. An insurer shall disclose information that identifies and explains the amount in its financial statements arising from insurance contracts.

(IFRS 4, Para 36)

2. To comply with IFRS 4, paragraph 36, an insurer shall disclose

   a. Its accounting policies for insurance contracts and related assets and liabilities, income, and expense;
   b. The recognized assets, liabilities, income, and expense (and, if it presents its cash flow statement using the direct method, cash flows) arising from insurance contracts. Furthermore, if the insurer is a cedant, it shall disclose

      (1) Gains and losses recognized in profit or loss on buying reinsurance;
      (2) If the cedant differs and amortizes gains and losses arising on buying reinsurance, the amortization for the period and the amounts remaining unamortized at the beginning and at the end of the period.

   c. The process used to determine the assumptions that have the greatest effect on the measurement of the recognized amounts described in b. When practicable, an insurer shall also give quantified disclosures of those assumptions.
   d. The effect of changes in assumption used to measure insurance assets and insurance liabilities, showing separately the effect of each change that has a material effect on the financial statements.
   e. Reconciliation of changes in insurance liabilities, reinsurance assets and if any, related deferred acquisition costs.

(IFRS 4, Para 37)

3. An insurer shall give the information to understand the amount, timing, and uncertainty of future cash flows from insurance contracts.

(IFRS 4, Para 38)

4. To comply with IFRS 4, paragraph 38, an insurer shall disclose

   a. Its objectives in managing risks arising from insurance contracts and its policies for mitigating those risks.
   b. Those terms and conditions of insurance contracts that have a material effect on the amount, timing, and uncertainty of the insurer's future cash flows.
   c. Information about insurance risk (both before and after risk mitigation by reinsurance), including information about

      (1) The sensitivity of profit or loss and equity to changes in variables that have material effect on them;
      (2) Concentrations of insurance risk;
      (3) Actual claims compared with previous estimates (i.e., claim development). The disclosure about claims development shall go back to the period when the earliest material claim arose for which there is still uncertainty about the amount and timing of the claims payment, but need not go back more than ten years. An insurer need not disclose this information for claims for which uncertainty about the amount and timing of claims payments is typically resolved within one year.

   d. The information about interest rate risk and credit risk that IAS 32 would require if the insurance contracts were within the scope of IAS 32.
   e. Information about exposures to interest rate risk or market risk under embedded derivatives contained in a host insurance contract. If the insurer is not required to, and does not, measure the embedded derivatives at fair value.

(IFRS 4, Para 39)

5. An entity need not apply the disclosure requirements in this IFRS to comparative information that relates to the annual period beginning before January 1, 2005, except for the disclosure required by IFRS 4, paragraph 37(a) and (b) about accounting policies, and recognized assets, liabilities, income and expense (and cash flow if direct method is used).

(IFRS 4, Para 42)

6. If it is impracticable to apply a particular requirement to comparative information that relates to annual periods beginning January 1, 2005, an entity shall disclose that fact. Applying the liability adequacy test to such comparative information might sometimes be impracticable, but it is highly unlikely to be impracticable to apply other requirements to such comparative information.

(IFRS 4, Para 43)

7. When an entity first applies this IFRS and if it is impracticable to prepare information about claim development that occurred before the beginning of the earliest period for which an entity presents full comparative information that complies with this IFRS, the entity shall disclose this fact.

(IFRS 4, Para 44)

AGRICULTURE

A. General

1. An entity should present the carrying amount of its biological assets separately on the face of its balance sheet.
2. An entity should disclose the aggregate gain or loss arising during the current period on initial recognition of biological assets and agricultural produce and from the change in fair value less estimated point-of-sale costs of biological assets.

(IAS 41, Paras 39 & 40)

3. An entity should provide a description of each group of biological assets.

(IAS 41, Para 41)

4. If not disclosed elsewhere in information published with the financial statements, an entity should describe

    a. The nature of its activities involving each group of biological assets; and
    b. Nonfinancial measures or estimates of the physical quantities of

        (1) Each group of the entity's biological assets at the end of the period; and
        (2) Output of agricultural produce during the period.

(IAS 41, Para 46)

5. An entity should disclose the methods and significant assumptions applied in determining the fair value of each group of agricultural produce at the point of harvest and each group of biological assets.

(IAS 41, Para 47)

6. An entity should disclose the fair value less estimated point-of-sale costs of agricultural produce harvested during the period, determined at the point of harvest.

(IAS 41, Para 48)

7. An entity should disclose

    a. The existence and carrying amounts of biological assets whose title is restricted, and the carrying amounts of biological assets pledged as security for liabilities;
    b. The amount of commitments for the development or acquisition of biological assets; and
    c. Financial risk management strategies related to agricultural activity.

(IAS 41, Para 49)

8. An entity should present a reconciliation of changes in the carrying amount of biological assets between the beginning and the end of the current period. Comparative information is not required. The reconciliation should include

   a. The gain or loss arising from changes in fair value less estimated point-of-sale costs;
   b. Increases due to purchases;
   c. Decreases due to sales;
   d. Decreases due to harvest;
   e. Increases resulting from business combinations;
   f. Net exchange differences arising on the translation of financial statements of a foreign entity; and
   g. Other changes.

   (IAS 41, Para 50)

9. Disclose (grouped or otherwise) the amount of change in fair value less estimated point of sale costs included in net profit or loss due to physical changes and price changes.

   (IAS 41, Para 51)

B. Additional Disclosure for Biological Assets Where Fair Value Cannot Be Measured Reliably

1. If an entity measures biological assets at their cost less any accumulated depreciation and any accumulated impairment losses at the end of the period, the entity should disclose for such biological assets

   a. A description of the biological assets;
   b. An explanation of why fair value cannot be measured reliably;
   c. If possible, the range of estimates within which fair value is highly likely to lie;
   d. The depreciation method used;
   e. The useful lives or the depreciation rates used; and
   f. The gross carrying amount and the accumulated depreciation (aggregated with accumulated impairment losses) at the beginning and end of the period.

   (IAS 41, Para 54)

2. If, during the current period, an entity measures biological assets at their cost less any accumulated depreciation and any accumulated impairment losses, an entity should disclose any gain or loss recognized on disposal of such biological assets and the reconciliation required by IAS 41, para 50, should disclose amounts related to such biological assets separately. In addition, the reconciliation should include the following amounts included in net profit or loss related to those biological assets:

   a. Impairment losses;
   b. Reversals of impairment losses; and
   c. Depreciation

   (IAS 41, Para 55)

3. If the fair value of biological assets previously measured at their cost, less any accumulated depreciation and any accumulated impairment losses, becomes reliably measurable during the current period, an entity should disclose for those biological assets

   a. A description of the biological assets;
   b. An explanation of why fair value has become reliably measurable; and
   c. The effect of the change.

   (IAS 41, Para 56)

C. Government Grants

1. An entity should disclose the following related to agricultural activity covered by this Standard:

a. The nature and extent of government grants recognized in the financial statements;
b. Unfulfilled conditions and other contingencies attaching to government grants; and
c. Significant decreases expected in the level of government grants.

(IAS 41, Para 57)

Exploration for and Evaluation of Mineral Resources

1. An entity shall disclose information that identifies and explains the amounts recognized in its financial statements arising from the exploration for and evaluation of mineral resources.

(IFRS 6, Para 23)

2. To comply with paragraph 23, IFRS 6, an entity shall disclose

   a. Its accounting policies for explorations and evaluation of expenditures including the recognition of exploration and evaluation assets.
   b. The amounts of assets, liabilities, income and expense, and operating and investing cash flows arising from the exploration for and evaluation of mineral resources.

(IFRS 6, Para 24)

3. An entity shall treat exploration and evaluation assets as a separate class of assets and make the disclosures required by either IAS 16 or IAS 38 consistent with how the assets are classified.

(IFRS 6, Para 25)

4. If an entity applies IFRS 6, *Exploration for and Evaluation of Mineral Resources,* for a period beginning before January 1, 2006, it shall disclose the fact.

(IFRS 6, Para 26)

5. Exploration and evaluation assets shall be assessed for impairment when facts and circumstances suggest that the carrying amount of an exploration and evaluation asset may exceeds its recoverable amount. When facts and circumstances suggest that the carrying amount exceeds the recoverable amount, an entity shall measure, present, and disclose any resulting impairment loss in accordance with IAS 36.

(IFRS 6, Para 18)

ILLUSTRATIVE FINANCIAL STATEMENTS PRESENTED UNDER IFRS

This appendix contains three comprehensive sets of financial statements presented in accordance with international accounting standards.

The first example, Simple Traders Inc., illustrates how a relatively simple business' financial statements might be presented. The second example, Simple Manufacturing Inc., is for a more advanced operation and involves a greater number of financial reporting issues, including those unique to financial instruments, related-party transactions, and manufacturing operations. The final example, Simple Bank Inc., illustrates the extensive disclosures prescribed under IAS for this specialized industry and also incorporates disclosures relevant to publicly held companies (disclosures like segment reporting, etc.). Taken together, these examples will convey a range of effective communications of the accounting policies and practices under existing international accounting standards.

It is not the intent to suggest that these example financial statements are all-inclusive of either industry practices or the reporting and disclosure standards under IAS. Rather, these are merely illustrative of common practices at this time, from which readers may construct disclosures apropos to their individual needs and circumstances.

I. Illustrative financial statement—Simple Traders, Inc.

Simple Traders Inc.
Balance Sheets
As of June 30, 2005 and 2004

(In euros)

	Notes	2005	2004
Assets			
Current assets:			
Cash and banks	4	2,292,282	2,517,806
Trade and other receivables	5	53,734,494	57,878,976
Amounts due from related parties	6	85,286	3,148,260
Inventories	7	5,956,454	8,318,928
		62,068,516	71,863,970
Noncurrent assets:			
Loan to related party	6	14,000,000	--
Property, plant, and equipment	8	25,237,506	20,902,178
Intangible assets	9	148,494	188,466
		39,386,000	21,090,644
Total assets		101,454,516	92,954,614
Liabilities and Owners' Equity			
Current liabilities:			
Due to bank	10	8,328,494	5,126,280
Trade and other payables	11	25,335,556	27,736,648
Amounts due to related parties	6	163,116	1,127,360
		33,827,166	33,990,288
Noncurrent liabilities:			
Long-term loans	12	14,508,888	--
End of service gratuity		4,795,754	4,583,796
		19,304,642	4,583,796
Owners' equity:			
Share capital	13	22,000,000	22,000,000
Statutory reserve		6,051,887	6,051,887
Proposed dividend		--	2,000,000
Retained earnings		20,270,821	24,328,643
Owners' equity		48,322,708	54,380,530
Total liabilities and owners' equity		101,454,516	92,954,614

The accompanying notes form an integral part of these financial statements.

Simple Traders Inc.
Statements of Income
For the Years Ended June 30, 2005 and 2004

(In euros)

	Notes	2005	2004
Revenue:		101,552,746	94,630,010
Cost of sales		(100,262,898)	(83,977,434)
Gross profit:		1,298,848	10,652,576
Other operating equipment		846,624	459,306
Distribution costs		(174,990)	(86,372)
Administrative expenses		(7,864,204)	(5,543,316)
(Loss)Profit from operating activities:	14	(5,902,722)	5,482,194
Finance costs		(155,100)	(34,382)
Net (loss)profit for the year		(6,057,822)	(5,447,812)

The accompanying notes form an integral part of these financial statements.

Simple Traders Inc.
Statements of Changes in Equity
For the Years Ended June 30, 2005 and 2004

(In euros)

	Share capital	Statutory reserve	Proposed dividend	Retained earnings	Total
As at July 1, 2003	22,000,000	5,507,106	--	29,425,612	56,932,718
Net profit for the year	--	--	--	5,447,812	5,447,812
Transfer to statutory reserve	--	544,781	--	(544,781)	--
Dividend proposed	--	--	10,000,000	(10,000,000)	--
Dividend paid*	--	--	(8,000,000)	--	(8,000,000)
As at June 30, 2004	22,000,000	6,051,887	2,000,000	24,328,643	54,380,530
Reversal of dividend proposed	--	--	(2,000,000)	2,000,000	--
Net loss for the year	--	--	--	(6,057,822)	(6,057,822)
As at June 30, 2005	22,000,000	6,051,887	--	20,270,821	48,322,708

*   *Dividend paid per share for the current year NIL (previous year USD 363.6 per share)*

The accompanying notes form an integral part of these financial statements.

Simple Traders Inc.
Statements of Cash Flows
For the Years Ended June 30, 2005 and 2004

(In euros)

	Notes	2005	2004
Cash flows from operating activities			
Net cash from operating activities	16	3,173,990	17,864,176
Cash flows from investing activities			
Purchase of property, plant, and equipment		(10,212,504)	(663,522)
Proceeds from sale of property and equipment		1,240,102	6,160
Acquisition of intangibles		(81,844)	(32,748)
Net cash used in investing activities		(9,054,246)	(690,110)
Cash flows from financing activities			
Decrease in due from related parties		3,062,974	2,591,534
Decrease in due to related parties		(964,244)	(12,709,336)
Proceeds from long-term bank loan		2,460,000	--
Repayment of long-term bank loan		(1,279,112)	--
Loan from related party		14,000,000	--
Loan to related party		(14,000,000)	--
Increase in bank overdraft		2,530,214	3,433,966
Interest paid		(155,100)	(34,382)
Dividends paid		--	(8,000,000)

	Notes	2005	2004
Net cash from (used in) financing activities		5,654,732	(14,718,218)
Net (decrease) increase in cash and cash equivalents		(225,524)	2,455,848
Cash and cash equivalents, beginning of year		2,517,806	61,958
Cash and cash equivalents, end of year	4	2,292,282	2,517,806

The accompanying notes form an integral part of these financial statements.

Simple Traders Inc.
Notes to the Financial Statements
For the Years Ended June 30, 2005 and 2004

(All amounts in euros)

Note 1: Establishment and operations. Simple Traders Inc. (the "company") is a limited liability company registered in the country XXX. The company's business principally comprises trading in mosaic tiles. The address of the registered office of the company is 2001 Expensive Street, New Wish City, Country XXX.

Note 2: Adoption of New International Accounting Standards. In the previous year, the company adopted IAS 39, *Financial Instruments: Recognition and Measurement,* which has introduced the concept of reporting financial instruments (including "off-balance-sheet" financial instruments) at their respective fair values. The adoption of this standard by the company has not resulted in any significant impact on these financial statements.

Note 3: Summary of significant accounting policies. The financial statements are prepared under the historical cost convention and in accordance with International Financial Reporting Standards. The significant accounting policies adopted are as follows:

a. **Property, plant, and equipment.** Property, plant, and equipment are stated at cost less accumulated depreciation. Depreciation is computed on the straight-line basis over the estimated useful lives as follows:

	Years
Buildings	10
Plant, machinery, and equipment	7
Furniture, fixtures, and office equipment	4
Motor vehicles	3

   Capital work-in-progress is not depreciated. Depreciation is charged on the assets from the date on which they come in to use.

b. **Intangible assets.** Intangible assets are amortized using the straight-line method over their estimated useful life of four years.

c. **Inventories.** Inventories are stated at the lower of cost and net realizable value. Cost is arrived at using the weighted-average method. Cost comprises invoice value plus applicable handling charges. Net realizable value is based on estimated selling price less estimated costs to completion and disposal.

d. **End-of-service gratuity.** Provision is made for end-of-service gratuity payable to employees at the balance sheet date in accordance with the labor laws of country XXX.

e. **Foreign currency translations.** Transactions in foreign currencies are translated into US dollars at the rate of exchange ruling on the date of the transaction. Monetary assets and liabilities expressed in foreign currencies are translated into US dollars at the rate of exchange ruling at the balance sheet date. Gains or losses resulting from foreign currency transactions are taken to the Statement of Income.

f. **Statutory reserve.** A statutory reserve is created by the limited liability company by allocating 10% of its net profit for the year as required by commercial companies law of country XXX. The company can discontinue such annual transfer when its statutory reserve totals 50% of its paid-up share capital. The reserve is not available for distribution except as provided in the XXX Law.

g. **Revenue.** Revenue represents the net amount invoiced for goods supplied.

h. **Borrowing costs.** Borrowing costs are recognized as an expense in the period in which they are incurred.

i. **Cash and cash equivalents.** Cash and cash equivalents comprise cash and bank current account.

j. **Financial instruments.** Financial assets and financial liabilities are recognized on the Company's balance sheet when the Company has become a party to the contractual provisions of the instrument.

Trade receivables

Trade receivables are stated at their nominal value as reduced by appropriate allowance for estimated doubtful amounts.

Trade payables

Trade payables are stated at their nominal value.

k. **Dividends payable.** Dividends payable are presented as a separate component of equity.

Note 4: Cash and banks.

	2005	2004
Cash on hand	60,000	60,000
Bank balances	2,232,282	2,457,806
	2,292,282	2,517,806

Note 5: Trade and other receivables.

	2005	2004
Trade receivables	51,921,552	54,326,624
Other receivables	1,269,220	1,048,716
Less: Allowance for doubtful receivables	(1,120,616)	(34,314)
	52,070,156	55,341,026
Advances	872,786	357,402
Prepayments	543,052	1,938,048
Deposits	248,500	242,500
	53,734,494	57,878,976

Note 6: Related-party transactions. The company enters into transactions with other companies that fall within the definition of a related party contained in IAS 24. Such transactions are in the normal course of business and at terms that correspond to those on normal arm's-length transactions with third parties.

Related parties comprise companies under common ownership and/or common management control. At the balances sheet date, trade and nontrade balances with related parties were as follows:

	2005	2004
Included in trade receivables	3,145,768	4,811,048
Included in trade payables	17,617,476	17,772,796
Disclosed as amounts due from related parties	85,286	3,148,260
Disclosed as amounts due to related parties	163,116	1,127,360
Disclosed as loan from related party	14,000,000	--
Disclosed as loan to related party	14,000,000	--

The nature of significant related-party transactions during the year and the amounts involved were as follows:

	2005	2004
Sales	8,857,316	10,509,302
Purchases	33,211,776	27,926,464
Interest expense	155,100	34,382

The company also provides funds to and receives funds from related parties as and when required for working capital purposes. Interest is charged or paid at commercial rates. The loan from a related party bears interest rate of US Prime plus 1%. This loan is unsecured and is without any fixed repayment schedule. The loan to a related party is interest-free and has no repayment schedule.

Note 7: Inventories.

	2005	2004
Trading material	2,246,894	3,476,594
Stores and consumables	6,114,010	7,146,082
Less: Allowance for slow moving inventories	(3,074,648)	(2,371,068)
	5,286,256	8,251,608
Goods in transit	670,198	67,320
	5,956,454	8,318,928

Note 8: Property, plant, and equipment.

	Buildings	Plant, machinery, and equipment	Furniture, fixtures, and office equipment	Motor vehicles	Capital work in progress	Total
Cost						
As at July 1, 2004	11,133,094	77,920,256	3,365,862	2,157,500	354,698	94,931,410
Additions during the year	--	--	7,266	307,000	9,898,238	10,212,504
Transfer during the year	--	9,711,560	63,834	--	(9,775,394)	--
Disposals during the year	--	(6,137,964)	(491,608)	(511,200)	(301,002)	(7,441,774)
As at June 30, 2005	11,133,094	81,493,852	2,945,354	1,953,300	176,540	97,702,140
Accumulated depreciation						
As at July 1, 2004	8,449,534	61,334,260	2,489,256	1,756,182	--	74,029,232
Depreciation for the year	255,798	4,554,888	313,346	258,500	--	5,382,532
Adjustments relating to disposals	--	(6,137,946)	(348,994)	(460,190)	--	(6,947,130)
As at June 30, 2005	8,705,332	59,751,202	2,453,608	1,554,492	--	72,464,634
Net book value						
As at June 30, 2004	2,683,560	16,585,996	876,606	401,318	354,698	20,902,178
As at June 30, 2005	2,427,762	21,742,650	491,746	398,808	176,540	25,237,506

Note 9: Intangible assets.

	Computer software	Patents and trademarks	Total
Cost			
As at July 1, 2003	1,235,736	43,650	1,279,386
Additions during the year	81,844	--	81,844
As at June 30, 2004	1,317,580	43,650	1,361,230
Accumulated amortization			
As at July 1, 2003	1,080,018	10,902	1,090,920
Amortization for the year	89,068	32,748	121,816
As at June 30, 2004	1,169,086	43,650	1,212,736
Net book value			
As at June 30, 2003	155,718	32,748	188,466
As at June 30, 2004	148,494	--	148,494

Note 10: Due to bank.

	2005	2004
Bank overdraft	7,656,494	5,126,280
Current portion of long-term bank loan (note 12)	672,000	--
	8,328,494	5,126,280

Bank overdraft is secured by personal and corporate guarantee of shareholders and bears an interest rate of a fixed percentage above US Prime.

Note 11: Trade and other payables.

	2005	2004
Trade payables	22,993,574	25,402,922
Accruals	2,138,152	1,516,562
Other payables	203,830	817,164
	25,335,556	27,736,648

Note 12: Long-term loans.

	2005	2004
Long-term bank loan	1,180,888	--
Less: Current portion (note 10)	(672,000)	--
	508,888	--
Loan from related party	14,000,000	--
	14,508,888	--

Bank term loan is secured by corporate guarantees of the shareholders and bears an interest rate of 1.5% over US prime with a minimum of 7.50% per annum.

Note 13: Share capital.

Authorized, issued, and fully paid—
22,000 shares of USD 1,000 each, owned as follows:

Imperial Investment Co. LLC	10,000,000
Excellent Investments Inc.	12,000,000
	22,000,000

The company's ultimate parent is Exuberant Inc., incorporated in Isle of Man.

Note 14: Loss/profit from operating activities. Loss/profit for the year from operating activities is stated after charging

	2005	2004
Salaries and benefits	14,843,550	12,209,898
Depreciation	5,382,532	5,629,350

Note 15: Number of employees. The number of employees of the company at the end of the year was 200 (June 30, 2004: 175).

Note 16: Net cash from operating activities.

	2005	2004
Net (loss)profit for the year	(6,057,822)	5,447,812
Adjustments for noncash items		
Depreciation of property, plant, and equipment	5,382,532	5,629,350
Gain on sale of property, plant, and equipment	(745,458)	(6,152)
Amortization of intangible assets	121,816	100,914
Allowance for slow moving inventory	703,580	537,396
Allowance for doubtful receivables	1,086,302	--
Provision for end of service gratuity	857,026	--
Interest expense	155,100	34,382
	1,503,076	11,743,702
Decrease in trade and other receivables	3,058,180	10,101,970
Decrease in inventories	1,658,894	1,962,772
Decrease in trade and other payables	(2,401,092)	(5,524,168)
Cash generated from operations:	3,819,058	18,284,276
End-of-service gratuity paid	(645,068)	(420,100)
Net cash from operating activities	3,173,990	17,864,176

Note 17: Financial instruments: credit, interest rate, and exchange rate risk exposures.

a.   **Credit risk.** Financial assets which potentially expose the company to concentrations of credit risk comprise, principally, bank current accounts, trade and other receivables, and amounts due from related parties. The company's bank accounts are placed with high credit quality financial institutions. Trade and other receivables are stated net of the allowance for doubtful recoveries. At the balance sheet date the company did not have any significant exposure to credit risk from customers situated outside the XXX. There are no significant concentrations of credit risk amongst individual customers.

b. **Interest rate risk.** Bank borrowings are at floating rates of interest generally obtained in the XXX, which are negotiated with the banks at US Prime plus a negotiated margin.

c. **Exchange rate risk.** At the balance sheet date, there are no significant exchange rate risks as substantially all financial assets and financial liabilities are denominated in US dollars.

Note 18: Financial instruments: fair values. The fair value of a financial instrument is the amount for which an asset could be exchanged, or a liability settled, between knowledgeable, willing parties in an arm's-length transaction. At the balance sheet date, the fair values of the company's financial assets and financial liabilities approximate to their carrying values.

Note 19: Commitments and contingent liabilities.

	2005	2004
Letters of credit	1,909,666	315,495
Letters of guarantee	50,000	--
	1,959,666	315,495

Note 20: Comparative figures. Certain previous year figures have been reclassified to conform with current year's presentation.

II. Illustrative financial statement—Simple Manufacturing, Inc.

Simple Manufacturing Inc.
Balance Sheets
As at June 30, 2005 and 2004

(In euros)

	Notes	2005	2004
Assets			
Current assets:			
Cash and cash equivalents	4	350,180	25,166
Trade and other receivables	5	19,904,772	16,816,106
Inventories	6	18,482,662	15,961,120
Amounts due from related parties	7	1,235,796	404,144
		39,973,410	33,206,536
Noncurrent assets:			
Property, plant, and equipment	8	117,796,980	111,810,436
Intangible assets	9	2,282,508	2,251,721
Investment property	10	3,610,000	3,510,000
Investment in associates	11	1,890,000	1,500,000
Available-for-sale financial assets		2,000,000	1,990,000
		127,579,488	121,062,208
Total assets		167,552,898	154,268,744
Liabilities and Shareholders' Funds			
Current liabilities:			
Due to banks	12	3,889,328	17,594,858
Trade and other payables	13	40,365,452	35,873,644
Amounts due to related parties	7	60,844,520	52,855,170
		105,099,300	106,323,672
Noncurrent liabilities:			
Interest-bearing liabilities—long-term portion	14	14,680,000	300,000
Other long-term liabilities	15	2,757,656	4,398,414
		17,437,656	4,698,414
Shareholders' funds:			
Share capital	16	5,000,000	5,000,000
Statutory reserve		2,500,000	2,500,000
Retained earnings		5,015,942	3,246,658

	Notes	2005	2004
Shareholders' equity		12,515,942	10,746,658
Subordinated loans from shareholder	17	32,500,000	32,500,000
		45,015,942	43,246,658
Total liabilities and shareholders' funds		167,552,898	154,268,744

The accompanying notes form an integral part of these financial statements.

Simple Manufacturing Inc.
Statements of Income
For the Years Ended June 30, 2005 and 2004

(In euros)

	Notes	2005	2004
Revenue:		67,497,474	71,196,018
Other operating income		3,193,502	2,345,794
		70,690,976	73,541,812
Operating expenses:			
Materials consumed		31,449,162	33,154,690
(Increase)decrease in inventories of finished goods		(63,314)	516,748
Salaries and benefits		8,090,312	9,569,694
Depreciation		7,920,074	7,890,238
Amortization		427,992	423,402
Other operating expenses		12,714,536	13,222,344
Total operating expenses		60,538,762	64,777,116
Profit from operating activities:		10,152,214	8,764,696
Finance costs	18	(8,882,930)	(7,539,960)
Fair value adjustment—investment property		100,000	--
Fair value adjustment—available-for-sale financial instruments		10,000	
Share of profit from associates		390,000	250,000
Net profit for the year		1,769,284	1,474,736

The accompanying notes form an integral part of these financial statements.

Simple Manufacturing Inc.
Statements of Changes in Shareholders' Equity
For the Years Ended June 30, 2005 and 2004

	Share capital	*Statutory reserve*	*Retained earnings*	*Total*
Balance at July 1, 2003	5,000,000	2,500,000	961,922	8,461,922
Increase in fair value (investment property)	--	--	510,000	510,000
Increase in fair value (available-for-sale financial instruments)	--	--	300,000	300,000
Net profit for the year	--	--	1,474,736	1,474,736
Balance at June 30, 2004	5,000,000	2,500,000	3,246,658	10,746,658
Net profit for the year	--	--	1,769,284	1,769,284
Balance at June 30, 2005	5,000,000	2,500,000	5,015,942	12,515,942

The accompanying notes form an integral part of these financial statements.

Simple Manufacturing Inc.
Statements of Cash Flows
For the Years Ended June 30, 2005 and 2004

	Notes	2005	2004
Cash flows from operating activities			
Net cash from operating activities	20	16,137,770	4,614,106
Cash flows from investing activities			
Purchase of property, plant, and equipment		(14,638,072)	(6,584,858)
Purchase of investment property		--	(3,000,000)
Proceeds from sale of property, plant, and equipment		716,812	19,160
Payments for intangible assets		(458,728)	(734,166)
Net cash used in investing activities		(14,379,988)	(10,299,864)

Cash flows from financing activities

Proceeds from long-term bank loans	14,680,000	12,000,000
Repayment of long-term bank loans	(6,900,000)	--
(Decrease) increase in due to banks—excluding term loans	3,963,410	(7,105,530)
Repayment of supplier's loans	(2,107,238)	(10,508,252)
Net cash from (used in) financing activities	(1,432,768)	5,455,158
Net increase (decrease) in cash and cash equivalents	325,014	(230,600)
Cash and cash equivalents, beginning of year	25,166	255,766
Cash and cash equivalents, end of year (4)	350,180	25,166

The accompanying notes form an integral part of these financial statements.

Simple Manufacturing Inc.
Notes to the Financial Statements
For the Years Ended June 30, 2005 and 2004

Note 1: Establishment and operations of the company. Simple Manufacturing Inc. (the "company") is a limited liability company incorporated in country XXX. The company manufactures widgets and accessories. The address of the registered office of the company is...... The financial statements for the year ended June 30, 2005, were authorized for issuance by the board of directors on...... The ultimate parent of the company is YYY which is incorporated in Channel Islands.

Note 2: Changes in accounting policies resulting from first-time adoption of International Financial Reporting Standards. Effective July 1, 2003, the company has adopted the following International Financial Reporting Standards for the first time, which has resulted in changes in accounting policies as explained below.

IAS 39, *Financial Instruments: Recognition and Measurement,* introduced a comprehensive framework for accounting for all financial instruments. The effect of adopting this standard is that the investment in listed equity securities (classified as an "available-for-sale" financial instrument) will be carried at fair value, with changes in fair value being reflected currently in earnings.

IAS 40, *Investment Property,* addresses measurement issues relating to investment property. The effect of adopting this standard is that the company will carry investment property at fair value (instead of at cost less accumulated depreciation, which was its policy previously), with unrealized gains or losses from changes in fair value of investment property being reflected currently in earnings.

The effect of the change in accounting policy resulting from adoption of IAS 39 is to increase (decrease) the net income for the year ended June 30, 2005, by €...... and equity by €......(2004: €.....). The effect of the change in accounting policy resulting from adoption of IAS 40 is to increase (decrease) the net income for the year ended June 30, 2005, by €...... and equity by €.....(2004: €.....).

Note 3: Summary of significant accounting policies. The financial statements are prepared in accordance with International Financial Reporting Standards (IFRS) and under the historical cost convention, except in case of investment property and certain financial instruments, which are carried at fair value in accordance with IFRS. The significant accounting policies adopted are as follows:

a. **Property, plant, and equipment.** Property, plant, and equipment are carried at cost less accumulated depreciation. Property, plant, and equipment are depreciated using the straight-line method over their respective estimated useful lives as follows:

	Years
Factory and office buildings	20
Plant, machinery, and equipment	5 – 20
Furniture, fixtures, and office equipment	5
Vehicles	5

Capital work-in-progress is not depreciated. Depreciation is charged on the assets from the date on which they are placed in service.

b. **Amortization of intangible assets.** Goodwill arising from purchase business acquisitions, patents and trademarks, development costs, and software development expenditures are amortized using the straight-line method over their estimated useful lives as follows:

	Years
Goodwill	10
Patents and trademarks	10
Development costs	5
Computer software	5

c. **Investment property.** Investment property represents commercial real estate held for the purpose of earning rental income, and is stated at fair value at the balance sheet date. The changes in fair value of the investment property are reflected currently in the income statement. Fair values have been determined based on valuations undertaken by an independent qualified appraiser. These valuations were conducted with reference to market prices of similar properties.

d. **Investment in associates.** Investment in associates represents investments in entities over which the company has the power to exercise significant influence, through participation in the investees' financial and operating policy decisions. Such investments are accounted for under the equity method, whereby the investments are initially recorded at cost and are subsequently adjusted based on the company's share of the subsequent profits or losses of the investees.

e. **Inventories.** Inventories are stated at the lower of cost or net realizable value. Cost is arrived at using the first-in, first-out (FIFO) method. Cost comprises invoice value plus applicable landing charges in the case or raw materials, packing materials, spares, and consumables. Finished goods comprise cost of materials plus attributable labor and overhead charges. Net realizable value is based on estimated selling price less estimated costs to completion and sale.

f. **Employees' end-of-service indemnity.** Provision is made for end-of-service indemnity payable to employees at the balance sheet date in accordance with the labor laws of country XXX.

g. **Foreign currency translations.** Transactions in foreign currencies are translated into US dollars at the rate of exchange ruling on the date of the transaction. Monetary assets and liabilities expressed in foreign currencies are translated into US dollars at the rate of exchange ruling at the balance sheet date. Gains or losses resulting from foreign currency transactions are taken to the statement of income.

h. **Statutory reserve.** A statutory reserve, as required under the Companies Corporate Law of country XXX, is created by appropriating 10% of the net profit for the year, which procedure is to be discontinued once the statutory reserve is equal to 50% of the share capital, after which no further transfers are required. This reserve is not available for distribution except as provided in the XXX Law.

i. **Revenue.** Revenue represents the net amount invoiced for goods supplied during the year.

j. **Borrowing costs.** Borrowing costs are recognized as an expense in the period in which they are incurred except those that are directly attributed to the acquisition and construction of an asset that takes a substantial period to get ready for its intended use. Such borrowing cost are capitalized as part of the related asset.

k. **Cash and cash equivalents.** Cash and cash equivalents comprise cash on hand, bank current accounts, and other bank deposits free of encumbrances and having maturity dates of three months or less from the respective dates of deposit.

l. **Financial instruments.** Financial assets and financial liabilities are recognized on the company's balance sheet when the company has become a party to the contractual provisions of the instrument.

Receivables

Receivables are stated at nominal value as reduced by appropriate allowance for estimated doubtful amounts.

Available-for-sale financial instruments

Available-for-sale financial instruments represent investments in listed equity securities and are initially recorded at cost, on trade date. Subsequently these investments are measured at fair value, which are determined based on quoted market prices. Any changes in fair value are included in the income statement in the periods these occur.

Payables

Payables are stated at nominal value.

Due to/due from related parties

Due to/due from related parties are stated at nominal value.

Borrowings

Interest-bearing bank loans and overdrafts are recorded at the proceeds received, net of direct issue costs. Finance charges are accounted for on an accrual basis.

Note 4: Cash and cash equivalents.

	2005	2004
Cash on hand	47,930	36,320
Bank balances in current accounts	102,250	(11,154)
Bank fixed deposit	200,000	--
	350,180	25,166

At June 30, 2004, a negative balance in the bank current account, amounting to €11,154, has been offset against cash on hand since it represents a temporary accommodation by the bank under a special program offered to high net worth bank customers, referred to by the bank as "bounce protection plan." Such negative balance in the current account with the bank resulted from outstanding checks cleared at balance sheet date in excess over deposited checks uncollected by the bank at that date.

Note 5: Trade and other receivables.

	2005	2004
Trade receivables	20,494,366	16,969,458
Less: Allowance for doubtful accounts	(1,440,000)	(1,000,000)
	19,054,366	15,969,458
Advances	205,180	169,190
Prepayments	502,216	608,678
Deposits	143,010	68,780
	19,904,772	16,816,106

Note 6: Inventories.

	2005	2004
Raw materials	5,421,064	2,767,142
Packing materials	11,152,118	7,490,388
Finished goods	2,738,868	2,675,554
Spares and consumables	521,560	784,010
	19,833,610	13,717,094
Allowance for slow moving inventories	(1,350,948)	(500,000)
	18,482,662	13,217,094
Goods in transit	--	2,744,026
	18,482,662	15,961,120

Note 7: Related-party transactions. The company enters into transactions with other entities that fall within the definition of a related party as set forth by IAS 24. Such transactions are in the normal course of business and are at terms which correspond to those on normal arm's-length transactions with third parties.

Related parties comprise companies under common ownership and/or common management control. At the balances sheet date, trade and nontrade balances with related parties were as follows:

	2005	2004
Included in trade receivables	6,000,656	5,555,222
Included in trade payables	27,365,088	22,381,594
Disclosed as amounts due from related parties	1,235,796	404,144
Disclosed as amounts due to related parties	60,844,520	52,855,170

The nature of related-party transactions during the year and the respective amounts were as follows:

	2005	2004
Revenue	1,060,786	762,714
Cost of sales	1,857,094	1,989,140
Distribution sales	1,729,818	1,255,246
Finance costs	7,928,170	5,628,082

The company receives/provides funds from/to related parties as and when required for working capital. Interest, whenever applicable, is paid at commercial rates. Subordinated loans from shareholder are interest-free (see note 17).

Note 8: Property, plant, and equipment.

	Factory and office buildings	Plant, machinery, and equipment	Furniture, fixtures, and office equipment	Vehicles	Capital work in progress	Total
Cost						
As at July 1, 2004	20,589,226	100,495,370	4,500,746	5,518,130	7,810,504	138,913,976
Additions	--	71,578	173,300	45,000	14,348,194	14,638,072
Transfers	--	10,711,822	--	--	(10,711,822)	--
Disposals	--	(644,000)	(27,800)	(380,734)	--	(1,052,534)
As at June 30, 2005	20,589,226	110,634,770	4,646,246	5,182,396	11,446,876	152,499,514
Accumulated depreciation						
As at July 1, 2004	5,976,464	15,560,480	2,568,548	2,998,048	--	27,103,540
Depreciation for the year	1,029,462	5,165,070	672,678	1,052,864	--	7,920,074
Adjustments relating to disposals	--	(69,766)	(10,192)	(241,122)	--	(321,080)
As at June 30, 2005	7,005,926	20,655,784	3,231,034	3,809,790	--	34,702,534
Net book value						
As at June 30, 2004	14,612,762	84,934,890	1,932,198	2,520,082	7,810,504	111,810,436
As at June 30, 2005	117,796,980	13,583,300	89,978,986	1,415,212	1,372,606	11,446,876

Plant and machinery includes interest capitalized during the year of €5,555 (previous year: €555,000). The capitalization rate used was the actual borrowing cost (refer note 21).

Note 9: Intangible assets.

	Goodwill	Patents and trademarks	Development costs	Computer software	Total
Cost					
As at July 1, 2004	566,088	599,518	2,197,366	--	3,362,972
Additions during the year	--	288,414	79,612	90,702	458,728
As at June 30, 2005	566,088	887,932	2,276,978	90,702	3,821,700
Accumulated amortization					
As at July 1, 2004	226,432	147,770	736,998	--	1,111,200
Amortization for the year	56,608	63,468	297,326	10,590	427,992
As at June 30, 2005	283,040	211,238	1,034,324	10,590	1,539,192
Net book value					
As at June 30, 2004	339,656	451,748	1,460,368	--	2,251,772
As at June 30, 2005	283,048	676,694	1,242,654	80,112	2,282,508

Note 10: Investment property.

As previously stated at July 1, 2004	3,000,000
Fair value adjustment at July 1, 2004 (on adoption of IAS 40)	510,000
Fair value at July1, 2004 (as restated)	3,510,000
Change in fair value during the current year	100,000
Fair value at June 30, 2005	3,610,000

Note 11: Investment in associates.

Balance at July 1, 2004	1,250,000
Share of profit	250,000
Balance at June 30, 2004	1,500,000
Share of profit	390,000
Balance at June 30, 2005	1,890,000

Note 12: Due to banks.

	2005	*2004*
Overdrafts	2,683,928	9,789,458
Current portion of long-term loans (note 14)	1,205,400	7,805,400
	3,889,328	17,594,858

Bank facilities are secured by floating charge on the inventories of the company, pledge of plant and machinery, subordination of loans from shareholder, corporate guarantees of companies owned by the shareholder as well as corporate guarantees of other related parties.

Note 13: Trade and other payables.

	2005	*2004*
Trade payables	32,648,812	31,298,690
Accruals	4,742,660	2,242,164
Advances received from customers	865,536	224,538
Current portion of supplier loan (note 15)	2,108,444	2,108,252
	40,365,452	35,873,644

Note 14: Interest-bearing liabilities—long-term portion.

	2005	*2004*
Long-term bank loans	15,885,400	8,105,400
Less: Current portion (note 12)	(1,205,400)	(7,805,400)
Long-term portion	14,680,000	300,000
The borrowings are repayable as follows:		
Within one year	1,205,400	7,805,400
In the second year	4,893,334	300,000
In the third to fifth years inclusive	9,786,666	--
Amount due for settlement after twelve months	14,680,000	300,000

Note 15: Other long-term liabilities.

	2005	*2004*
Supplier loan	3,162,664	5,269,902
Less: Current portion (note 13)	(2,108,444)	(2,108,252)
	1,054,220	3,161,650
Employees' end-of-service indemnity	1,703,436	1,236,764
	2,757,656	4,398,414
The borrowings are repayable as follows:		
Within one year	2,108,444	2,108,252
In the second year	1,054,220	2,108,444
In the third to fifth years (inclusive)	--	1,053,206
Amount due for settlement after twelve months	1,054,220	3,161,650

Note 16: Share capital.

	2005	*2004*
Authorized, issued and paid up:		
5,000 shares of USD 1000 each	5,000,000	5,000,000

Note 17: Subordinated loans from shareholder. These represent interest-free unsecured loans from the principal shareholder without any fixed repayment schedule.

Note 18: Finance costs.

	2005	*2004*
On long-term bank loans	383,196	1,085,402
On other bank loans and overdrafts	571,564	826,476
On amounts due to related parties	7,928,170	5,628,082
	8,882,930	7,539,960

Note 19: Number of employees. The number of employees at the end of the current year was 550 (previous year: 490).

Note 20: Cash generated from operations.

	2005	*2004*
Net profit for the year	1,769,284	1,474,736
Adjustments for		
Depreciation of property, plant, and equipment	7,920,074	7,890,238
Amortization of intangible assets	427,992	423,402
Provision for employees' end-of-service indemnity	488,318	614,932
Allowance for doubtful accounts	440,000	631,374
Allowance for slow moving inventories	850,948	200,000
Loss on sale of property, plant, and equipment	14,642	--
Share of profits from associates	(390,000)	(250,000)
Fair value adjustment to investment property	(100,000)	--
Fair value adjustment—available-for-sale financial instruments	(10,000)	
Finance costs	8,882,930	7,539,960
Operating profit before changes in operating assets and liabilities	20,294,188	18,524,642
Increase in trade and other receivables	(3,528,666)	(3,184,564)
(Increase) decrease in inventories	(3,372,490)	2,477,500
(Increase) decrease in amounts due from related parties	(831,652)	1,485,766
Increase (decrease) in trade and other payables	4,543,120	(15,759,612)
Increase in amounts due to related parties	7,989,350	9,351,718
Cash generated from operations	25,093,850	12,895,450
Employees' end-of-service indemnity paid	(21,646)	(563,220)
Interest paid	(8,934,434)	(7,718,124)
Net cash from operating activities	16,137,770	4,614,106

Note 21: Financial instruments: credit, interest rate, and exchange rate risk exposures.

    a.   **Credit risk.** Financial assets, which potentially subject the company to concentrations of credit risk, comprise, principally, trade and other receivables and amounts due from related parties. Trade and other receivables are stated net of the allowance for doubtful accounts. At the balance sheet date, the company's maximum exposure to credit risk from two customers amounted to €5,555,440 (previous year: €3,999,999).

    b.   **Interest rate risk.** Term loans, bank overdrafts, and bank borrowings are at floating rates of interest generally obtained in the country XXX, which are negotiated with the banks at LIBOR plus a negotiated margin. Loans from shareholder and loans from supplier are interest-free. Amounts due to related parties are at fixed rates of interest that are comparable to interest generally obtained from third parties.

    c.   **Exchange rate risk.** There are no significant exchange rate risks as substantially all financial assets and financial liabilities are denominated in US dollars.

Note 22: Financial instruments: fair values. The fair value of a financial instrument is the amount for which an asset could be exchanged, or a liability settled, between knowledgeable, willing parties in an arm's length transaction. At the balance sheet date, the fair values of the company's financial assets and financial liabilities approximate to their book values except in case of available-for-sale financial assets.

Note 23: Commitments and contingent liabilities.

	2005	2004
Letters of guarantee	5,155,444	2,220,000
Capital commitments	6,333,888	7,474,333

Note 24: Comparative figures. Certain prior year figures have been reclassified to conform to the current year method of presentation.

III. Illustrative financial statement—Bank

Consolidated Balance Sheet of Erste Bank at December 31, 2004

EUR thousand	*Notes*	*December 31, 2004*	*December 31, 2003*
Assets			
Cash and balances with central banks	12	2,722,931	2,548,758
Loans and advances to credit institutions	1, 13	15,513,265	13,140,025
Loans and advances to customers	1, 14	72,721,800	67,766,224
Risk provisions for loans and advances	2, 15	(2,748,775)	(2,771,653)
Trading assets	3, 16	4,628,261	5,259,294
Investments available for sale	4, 17	9,140,806	7,379,239
Financial investments	5, 18, 19, 49	28,866,928	26,454,438
Intangible assets	6, 19	1,823,409	1,868,201
Tangible assets	7, 19	1,722,576	1,814,078
Other assets	11, 20, 21	5,290,610	5,116,649
Total assets		139,681,811	128,575,253
Liabilities and shareholders' equity			
Amounts owed to credit institutions	22	28,551,355	25,703,928
Amounts owed to customers	23	68,212,546	64,838,840
Debts evidenced by certificates	9, 24	19,886,962	16,944,124
Provisions	10, 11, 25	7,328,240	6,366,096
Other liabilities	26	6,178,548	5,514,814
Subordinated capital	27	3,048,309	3,537,729
Minority interests		3,128,790	2,878,953
Shareholders' equity	28	3,347,061	2,790,769
Total liabilities and shareholders' equity		139,681,811	128,575,253

The accompanying notes form an integral part of these financial statements.

Consolidated Income Statement of Erste Bank
For the year ended December 31, 2004

EUR thousand	*Notes*	*2004*	*2003*
1. Interest and similar income		5,228,778	5,209,459
2. Interest paid and similar expenses		(2,533,270)	(2,622,618)
I. *Net interest income*	29	2,695,508	2,586,841
3. Risk provisions for loans and advances	30	(406,185)	(406,428)
4. Fee and commission income		1,358,449	1,181,614
5. Fee and commission expenses		(217,381)	(185,047)
Net commission income (Net of 4 and 5)	31	1,141,068	996,567
6. Net trading result	32	216,481	214,551
7. General administrative expenses	33	(2,592,923)	(2,460,755)
8. Income from insurance business	34	34,819	32,944
9. Other operating result	35	(27,737)	(202,132)
10. Extraordinary result		–	–
II. *Pretax profit for the year*		1,061,031	761,588
11. Taxes on income	36	(273,759)	(224,191)
III. *Profit for the year*		787,272	537,397
12. Minority interests		(242,751)	(184,094)
IV. *Net profit after minority interests*	37	544,521	353,303

Earnings per share

Earnings per share constitutes net profit after minority interests divided by the average number of ordinary shares outstanding. Diluted earnings per share represents the maximum potential dilution (increase in the average number of shares), which would occur if all issued subscription and conversion rights were exercised.

		2004	*2003*
Net profit after minority interests	in EUR thousand	544,521	353,303
Average number of shares outstanding[1]	number	238,576,585	237,845,836[2]
Earnings per share	in EUR	2.28	1.49
Diluted earnings per share	in EUR	2.26	1.47
Dividend per share	in EUR	0.50	0.38

[1] *Including those shares representing minority interests*
[2] *After stock split*

Consolidated Statement of Changes in Shareholders' Equity

EUR million	*Subscribed capital*	*Add. paid-in capital*	*Retained earnings*	*Distributable profit*	*Total 2004*	*Total 2003*
Shareholders' equity at						
December 31 previous year	436	1,445	820	90	2,791	2,481
Translation differences	--	--	115	--	115	(46)
Own shares	--	--	(27)	--	(27)	55
thereof shares acquired	--	--	(632)	--	(632)	(268)
thereof shares sold	--	--	591	--	591	307
thereof result	--	--	14	--	14	16
Dividends	--	--	1	(90)	(89)	(73)
Capital increases	47	(16)	--	--	31[*]	6
Net profit after minority interests	--	--	424	121	545	353
Other changes	--	--	(19)	--	(19)	15
thereof cash flow hedge	--	--	(19)	--	(19)	24
thereof deferred tax	--	--	5	--	5	(7)
thereof other	--	--	(5)	--	(5)	(2)
Shareholders' equity at						
December 31	483	1,429	1,314	121	3,347	2,791
Cash flow Hedge Reserves at December 31					38	57

[*] *Capital increase from reserves and from ESOP/MSOP 2004, special reserve for convertible bond and special reserve for stock options*

Changes in number of shares (see also note 28)

(in units)	*2004 post stock split*	*2003 post stock split*	*2003 before stock split*
Shares outstanding at January 1	225,138,004	221,728,868	55,432,217
Acquisition of own shares	(13,195,346)	(13,588,700)	(3,397,175)
Disposal of own shares	12,395,744	16,523,060	4,130,765
Capital increase due to ESOP and MSOP	1,667,660	474,776	118,694
Shares outstanding at December 31	226,006,062	225,138,004	56,284,501
Own shares[*]	15,436,830	14,637,228	3,659,307
Number of shares at December 31	241,442,892	239,775,232	59,943,808
Average number of shares outstanding	238,576,585	237,845,836	59,461,459

[*] *Including those shares held by members of the Haftungsverbund Agreement*

Cash Flow Statement

EUR million	2003	2002
Profit for the year	787	537
Noncash adjustments for items in net profit		
Depreciation, amortization, revaluation of tangible assets, financial investments as well as investments available for sale.	342	489
Allocation/release of provisions (including risk provisions)	463	454
Profits from the sale of financial investments and tangible assets	(105)	(91)
Other adjustments	(110)	330
Changes in assets and liabilities from operating activities after adjustment for noncash components		
Loans and advances to credit institutions	(2,407)	2,447
Loans and advances to customers	(5,017)	(2,314)
Trading portfolio	631	(1,766)
Investments available for sale	(1,696)	(635)
Other assets	(619)	(964)
Amounts owed to credit institutions	2,901	(1,012)
Amounts owed to customers	3,374	2,326
Debts evidenced by certificates	2,927	2,747
Other liabilities from operating activities	1,532	1,070
Cash flow from operating activities	3,003	3,618
Proceeds from the disposal of		
Financial investments	6,594	5,832
Fixed assets	257	818
Payments for the acquisition of		
Financial investments	(8,676)	(9,123)
Fixed assets	(443)	(1,323)
Acquisition of subsidiaries (net of cash and cash equivalents acquired)	(72)	(482)
Cash flow from investing activities	(2,339)	(4,278)
Capital increases	31	6
Dividends paid	(90)	(74)
Other financing activities	(473)	136
Cash flow from financing activities	(532)	68
Cash and cash equivalents at beginning of period	2,549	3,181
Cash flow from operating activities	3,003	3,618
Cash flow from investing activities	(2,339)	(4,278)
Cash flow from financing activities	(532)	68
Effect of translation differences	42	(40)
Cash and cash equivalents at end of period	2,723	2,549
Payments for taxes, interest and dividends	2,558	2,496
Payments for taxes on income	(138)	(90)
Interest and dividends received	5,229	5,209
Interest paid	(2,533)	(2,623)

On April 20, 2004, Erste Bank expanded its ownership interest in Slovenská sporitel'ña by 10% to a total of 80.01%. The purchase price was EUR 72 million and goodwill arose at EUR 31.1 million.

Notes to the Consolidated Financial Statements of the Erste Bank Group

General information

Erste Bank der oesterreichischen Sparkassen AG is Austria's oldest savings bank and the largest wholly privately owned Austrian credit institution listed on the Vienna stock exchange. Since October 2002 it is also quoted on the Prague stock exchange. Erste Bank's registered office is located at Graben 21, 1010 Vienna, Austria.

The Erste Bank Group offers a complete selection of banking and financial services, such as saving, asset management (including investment funds), lending, mortgage loans, investment banking, securities and derivatives trading, portfolio management, project financing, foreign trade financing, corporate finance, capital market and money market services, foreign exchange trading, leasing, factoring and insurance.

Unless otherwise indicated, all amounts are stated in millions of euros. Rounding differences may occur in the accompanying tables.

Acquisitions

On January 27, 2004, the ownership structure of Erste & Steiermärkische Banka d.d. (Croatia) changed as planned: Steiermärkische Bank und Sparkassen AG increased its interest in Erste Steiermärkische Banka d.d. by 2.4 percentage points through a voluntary tender offer to minority shareholders and by 17.5 percentage points through a share purchase from Erste Bank, to a new total of 35.0%. The purchase price of a total of EUR 46.3 million paid by Steiermärkische Bank und Sparkassen AG to Erste Bank had no direct effect on the consolidated income statement of the Erste Bank Group, as these transactions occurred between Group entities.

On April 20, 2004, Erste Bank increased its ownership interest in Slovak subsidiary Slovenská sporitel'ña by 10 percentage points to a total of 80.01%. The purchase was made under an option that had been agreed in 2001 between the Slovak Finance Ministry and Erste Bank regarding the privatization of Slovenská sporitel'ña. The purchase price of the 10% tranche was EUR 72 million and goodwill of EUR 31.1 million was recognized.

In a continuation of the strategy of streamlining the branch network in the Austrian savings bank group, the Annual General Meeting on May 4, 2004, passed a resolution to transfer the Erste Bank branches in Kitzbühel, Kufstein, Krems and Korneuburg to the local savings banks for payment in cash. The volume of business involved was negligible. The consolidated net sale proceeds in the form of the cash payments totaled EUR 5 million. As well, Erste Bank sold its ownership interest of 43.71% in Sparkasse Bregenz to Sparkasse Dornbirn. The sale closed in October 2004.

Effective September 1, 2004, Erste Bank Hungary merged with Posta bank to become Erste Bank Hungary Rt. This created the second largest retail bank in Hungary. The integration led to a reduction in the number of branches from 195 in the previous year to 169 at the end of 2004. There was no effect on the consolidated financial statements of Erste Bank.

In 2000 Erste Bank's New York branch concluded an investment consulting contract with New York-based High Peak Funding LLC. This company with a special legal form is owned by Global Securitization Services, LLC (registered office: New York), which does not form part of the Erste Bank Group. Global Securitization Services LLC specializes in the management and administration of companies whose business purpose is structured financing. The establishment of High Peak Funding allowed asset-backed commercial paper to be issued for international investors and to be invested in internationally rated American asset-backed securities. This company's investment policy is subject to stringent contractual rules under which, among other factors, risk diversification (i.e. risk spreading in terms of the international ratings of the individual investments) is defined and continuously monitored. Based on the ratings assigned by Moody's and Fitch, at least 80% of the overall portfolio must have a rating of between A1/A+ and Aaa/AAA and at least 60% of the securities portfolio must be rated Aa2/AA or better. The risk associated with this portfolio can thus be classified as low. No investments may be made in instruments with a rating below Baa3/BBB. Additionally, Erste Bank's New York office extends short-term credit facilities to this company for the eventuality that the investments cannot be completely funded with the investment vehicles issued by High Peak Funding. Erste Bank's New York branch also has a financing obligation in the event that a security is assigned a credit rating below Aa3/AA- and that High Peak Funding's portfolio contains more than ten securities with this rating. Erste Bank's New York location has no guarantee obligation or financing obligation in the event that a securities issuer does not meet its payment obligations, nor is it liable if High Peak Funding itself becomes insolvent. For the activities described here, Erste Bank's New York branch receives commissions. As of December 31, 2004, the financing portfolio of High Peak Funding amounted to about USD 2.0 billion. Given the company's particular legal and ownership structure, it was not included in the Erste Bank Group's consolidated financial statements.

Shareholdings in significant companies and their representation in the consolidated financial statements are detailed in Note 49.

Relationship to largest shareholder

At the end of 2004 DIE ERSTE österreichische Spar-Casse Privatstiftung, a foundation, held 32.48% of the shares of Erste Bank AG, making it the largest shareholder.

The purpose of the foundation, in addition to holding a substantial equity interest in Erst Bank, is to support social, scientific, cultural, and charitable institutions as well as generally promoting the guiding principles of the savings bank philosophy.

By a decision of the foundation's supervisory board on March 11, 2004, Dietrich Karner was appointed to the foundation's managing board, replacing Reinhard Ortner. At present, Andreas Treichl, Franz Ceska and Dietrich Karner are the members of this managing board. The supervisory board of the foundation had nine members at the end of 2004. Three of these members also sit on the Supervisory Board of Erste Bank AG.

Accounting policies

The consolidated financial statements of Erste Bank for the 2004 financial year and the comparable data for 2003 were prepared in compliance with the International Financial Reporting Standards (IFRS, formerly IAS) published by the International Accounting Standards Board (IASB) and with their interpretations issued by the International Financial Reporting Interpretations Committee (IFRIC, formerly SIC), thus satisfying the prerequisites set forth in Section 245a Austrian Commercial Code and Section 59a Austrian Banking Act on exempted consolidated financial statements prepared in accordance with internationally recognized accounting principles. The disclosure requirements of the European Union were also met.

Points in which the consolidated financial statements prepared in accordance with IFRS differ from Austrian reporting methods are outlined in section VI of these Notes.

Under new standards that took effect in 2004, accounting policies changed materially in the following areas in particular:

The new IFRS 3, *Business Combinations* published in 2004, in conjunction with IAS 36, *Impairment of Assets* and IAS 38, *Intangible Assets*, addresses the measurement, presentation and impairment testing of goodwill. The most important change compared to the old standards arises from the fact that the straight-line amortization of goodwill has been replaced with annual impairment tests. The option existed to already apply these new standards from January 1, 2004, and the Erste Bank Group elected to do so. Based on the required impairment tests, this resulted in the recognition in the income statement (in other operating result) of goodwill impairment losses totaling EUR 80 million. This involved a write-down of EUR 45.6 million on the goodwill of Tiroler Sparkassen AG to EUR 32.8 million and a write-down of EUR 24.8 million on the goodwill of Salzburger Sparkassen AG to EUR 22.3 million. The other EUR 9.6 million represented other subsidiaries. The total goodwill impairment loss of EUR 80 million is disclosed in the segment information for the Corporate Centre segment.

Erste Bank also opted for the early application of the new IFRS 2, *Share-Based Payments* from January 1, 2004. As a result, and based on the associated exercise dates, personnel expenses of about EUR 3.3 million were recorded for the stock ownership scheme and stock option plan for the period.

On December 17, 2003 the IASB issued the revised IAS 32, *Financial Instruments*: *Disclosure and Presentation*, and IAS 39, *Financial Instruments: Recognition and Measurement*. These revised standards must be applied to financial statements for periods beginning on or after January 1, 2005. For the 2004 financial year the recognition and measurement rules of the current, prerevision IAS 39 were therefore still applied.

The effects of applying the new revised IAS 39 in the Erste Bank Group arise mainly in the securities business and in credit valuation. Current assets include a category of securities (available-for-sale) for which the net result of remeasurement is recognized in equity until changes in value are realized. In addition, the current assets of Erste Bank also include the category "fair value through profit and loss" that is newly created by the standard and for which the valuation changes are recognized in the income statement. Credit valuation is refined by the introduction of impairment testing at the portfolio level. In accordance with the transition rules of the revised IAS 39, in the 2005 financial year the value adjustments resulting from the implementation of the new standard will be recognized retroactively in equity at January 1, 2004. The total effect of the changeover on equity after taking account of deferred taxes and minority interests is an increase of EUR 34.7 million. This breaks down into an increase of EUR 61.0 million from the securities business and a decrease of EUR 26.3 from lending operations.

Assets and liabilities stated in foreign currencies and pending foreign-currency spot transactions are converted at ECB reference rates; forward exchange contracts are converted at the forward rate at the balance sheet date.

In translating the financial statements of foreign subsidiaries reporting in foreign currencies, the ECB reference rate of exchange at the balance sheet date is applied in the case of the balance sheet and the annual average rate is used for the income statement. Translation gains and losses resulting from the inclusion of foreign subsidiaries in the consolidated financial statements are taken directly to retained earnings.

Hedging

The hedging activities of the Erste Bank Group focus on measures to protect net interest income and control market risk. Cash flow hedges are used to minimize interest rate risk. Fair value hedges are employed to reduce market risk.

Basis of consolidation

All significant subsidiaries controlled by Erste Bank AG are included in the Consolidated Financial Statements.

Erste Bank is a member of the Haftungsverbund Agreement of the savings bank group. This Haftungsverbund was established in 2001 and took effect in January 1, 2002. At the balance sheet date almost all of Austria's savings banks formed part of this system.

The provisions of the Haftungsverbund Agreement are implemented by a Steering Company (s Haftungs- und Kundenabsicherungs GmbH). Erste Bank AG directly holds at least 51% of the share capital of the Steering Company. Two of the four members of the Steerning Company's managements, including the CEO, who has the casting vote, are appointed by Erste Bank AG. The Steering Company is invested with the power to establish the common risk policies of its members and monitor adherence to these policies. As well, if a member encounters serious difficulties—this can be discerned from the specific indicator data that is continually generated—the Steering Company has the mandate to provide the support measures described later in this section and/or to intervene as required in the business management of the affected member savings bank. As Erste Bank AG owns a controlling interest in the Steering Company, which by virtue of its rules of procedure can exercise control on the business strategy of any of its members, in accordance with IFRS all members of the Haftungsverbund Agreement have been fully consolidated since January 1, 2002.

Significant equity interests of between 20 and 50% (associates) are stated at equity. For lack of applicable IFRS rules, interests in insurance companies are accounted for on the basis of financial statements prepared in accordance with national accounting standards.

Proportionate consolidation is not applied in the consolidated financial statements (IAS 31.28). Subsidiaries whose overall influence on the Group's financial position and the results of operations is small and undertakings whose assets are subject to restrictions under the Non-Profit Housing Act were not consolidated.

The other strategic equity holdings are reported at fair value. If fair value cannot be reliably determined, they are reported at cost or, in the event of material impairment, at remeasured amounts.

Business combinations are accounted for using the purchase method by comparing the acquisition cost against the parent company's share in identifiable assets and liabilities at fair values. Resulting goodwill arising after January 1, 1995, is recognized as an asset. Since January 1, 2004, as a result of the early adoption of the new IFRS 3, *Business Combinations,* in conjunction with IAS 36, *Impairment of Assets,* and IAS 38, *Intangible Assets,* the straight-line amortization of goodwill has been replaced with an annual impairment review.

Minority interests in acquired identifiable assets and liabilities are determined on the basis of proportionate equity.

Intercompany balances, intercompany income and expenses and intercompany profits and losses are eliminated if significant.

1. Loans and advances

Loans and advances to credit institutions and customers are reported at amortized cost. Credit losses which were not provided for are directly written off in this item.

Impairment of credit assets is disclosed as risk provisions for loans and advances on the face of the balance sheet.

Premiums and discounts—the differences between amounts paid out and par values—are reported on an accrual basis as interest income or interest expense under other assets or other liabilities.

Interest receivable is not recognized as revenue in the income statement if, regardless of any legal claims, it is very unlikely to be collected.

Unlisted securities (with the exception of negotiable credit substitutes) are reported within the appropriate securities item (the trading portfolio, investments available for sale or held-to-maturity portfolio). Since January 1, 2001 (when application of IAS 39 began) an exception has been made for asset swaps, which have since then been reported within loans and advances to credit institutions or loans and advances to customers.

2. Risk provisions for loans and advances

The special risks inherent in the banking business are taken into account by forming adequate specific provisions, which are made using the same measurement methods throughout the Group and which reflect any collateral where present. The transfer risk from lending to borrowers in foreign countries (country risk) is measured using an internal rating system which takes into consideration the respective economic, political, and regional situation.

The total amount of risk provisions for loans and advances, inasmuch as it relates to on-balance-sheet assets, is reported on the face of the balance sheet under assets as a line item deduction below loans and advances to credit institutions and loans and advances to customers. The risk provisions for off-balance-sheet transactions (particularly warranties and guarantees as well as other lending commitments) are included in the separate item "provisions."

3. Trading assets/ liabilities

Securities, derivatives, and other financial instruments held for trading purposes are reported at their fair values at the balance sheet date. Negative fair values are reported in the balance sheet in "other liabilities." Listed products are measured at quoted stock exchange prices. The fair values of nonlisted products are measured by the net present value method or using suitable valuation models.

All realized and unrealized gains from such items are reported in the income statement within net trading result. Also included in this item are interest and dividend income earned on the trading portfolio, and the portfolio's funding cost.

4. Investments available for sale

Securities which, under the Group's internal guidelines and IAS 39, are assigned neither to the trading portfolio nor to financial investments are reported at fair value in investments available for sale.

The gains and losses of this portfolio are included in other operating result.

5. Financial investments

This item includes, among other assets, bonds intended to be held to maturity and other fixed income and floating-rate securities, provided they have a fixed maturity. This portion of financial investments is assigned to the held-to-maturity portfolio. Also included in financial investments are investments in associates and other companies, ownership rights in nonconsolidated companies and property intended primarily for leasing to outside parties. Investments in associates are accounted for by the equity method. Equity holdings that are intended for sale in the short to medium term are stated at fair value (or in the case of listed companies, at the quoted price) at the balance sheet date.

Financial investments intended for leasing to outside parties are reported at cost (less normal periodic depreciation in the case of leased property) using the cost method permitted by IAS 40. In the case of impairment the asset is written down as required. If the reasons which led to the write-down cease to apply, the impairment loss is reversed, to no more than the original cost.

6. Intangible assets

Intangible assets consist mainly of goodwill resulting from acquisitions and of software. Until December 31, 2003, they were valued at cost less amortization.

From the first-time application date of IFRS 3 (in conjunction with IAS 36 and IAS 38) of January 1, 2004, an annual impairment test is carried out for all cash-generating units (CGUs) to review the value of existing goodwill.

The impairment test is to be performed for all CGUs to which goodwill is allocated. The calculation of the expected cash flows is based on the normalized projected earnings of the CGU (or the individual company in the case of minority-owned entities). As a rule, the basis for the normalized projected earnings is the reported pretax profit before minority interests in local currency.

To determine future cash flows, the projected normalized IFRS-based pretax profit of the subsequent three years is translated at the average exchange rates used in the forecast and discounted to present value at a pretax discount rate.

The discount rate usually used is the moving three-year average of the five-year swap rate (risk-free rate) in local currency. To this rate, as a rule, a risk premium of 80% is added for domestic subsidiaries or of 100% for foreign subsidiaries. Based on the above parameters, the entity's value is calculated in EUR every December.

The subsidiary's proportionate or full value is compared, respectively, to the sum of proportionate or full equity in the subsidiary and of goodwill. If the proportionate or full enterprise value exceeds the sum of, respectively, proportionate or full equity and goodwill, an impairment loss is recognized in the amount of this difference. The impairment loss is allocated first to writing down the CGU's goodwill, and any remaining impairment loss reduces the carrying amount of the CGU's other assets, though not to an amount below their fair value. There is no need to write goodwill down when the proportionate or full value of the CGU is higher than or equal to, respectively, the sum of proportionate or full equity and goodwill. Once recognized, impairment losses on goodwill cannot be reversed in later periods.

Software produced internally is recognized as an asset if the future economic benefits associated with the software are likely to flow to the Group and the cost can be reliably determined. Such software is amortized over the estimated useful life, which is generally deemed to be four to six years, the same range assumed for acquired software.

Impairment losses are recognized for decreases in value that are expected to be permanent.

7. Tangible assets

Tangible assets—land and buildings, office furniture and equipment—are stated at cost, less depreciation corresponding to their estimated useful life. Permanent impairment losses are recognized.

The assumed useful lives of tangible assets are presented in the table below.

	Useful life in years
Buildings	25-50
Office furniture and equipment	5-20
Computer hardware	4-5

8. Leasing

The leasing agreements in force in the Erste Bank Group almost exclusively represent finance leases, defined as leases in which all of the risks and rewards associated with the leased asset are transferred to the lessee. Pursuant to IAS 17, the lessor reports a receivable from the lessee amounting to the present value of the contractually agreed payments and taking into account any residual value.

In the case of operating leases (defined as leases where the risks and rewards of ownership remain with the lessor), the leased asset is reported by the lessor in financial investments and depreciated in accordance with the principles applicable to the type of fixed assets involved. Lease payments are recognized as income, spread over the term of the lease.

9. Debts evidenced by certificates

Debts evidenced by certificates in issue are stated at their redemption value or par value. Bonds with long maturities (e.g. zero coupon bonds) and similar debt securities in issue are reported at their present value.

10. Provisions

In compliance with IAS 19, *Employee Benefits*, long-term employee provisions (obligations for pensions as well as for termination and jubilee benefits) are determined using the projected unit credit method. Pension provisions pertain only to already retired employees, as the pension obligations for current staff were transferred to retirement funds in previous years.

Future obligations are determined based on actuarial expert opinions. The calculation takes into account not only those pensions and vested rights to future pension payments known at the balance sheet date, but also anticipates future rates of increase in salaries and pensions.

The most important assumptions used for the actuarial computation of pension obligations are an annual discount rate (long-term capital market interest rate) of 5.5% and an annual rise in salaries of 3.5% for active employees. The premises for pension provisions for retirees (the obligation for existing retirees' pensions was not transferred to a pension fund) are a discount rate of 5.5% and an anticipated statutory increase in pension benefits of 1.5% per year.

Obligations for termination and jubilee benefits are also calculated based on an annual discount of 5.5% and an average annual increase in salary of 3.8%. The assumed retirement age is 60 years for women and 65 for men.

Long-term employee provisions (obligation for pensions as well as for termination and jubilee benefits) were calculated in accordance with current mortality tables ("AVÖ 1999 P – Rechnungsgrundlagen für die Pensionsversicherung" by Pagler & Pagler).

Other provisions are made for contingent liabilities to outside parties in the amount of the expected utilization of benefits.

11. Taxes on income—deferred taxes

Deferred tax assets and liabilities are included in the items other assets and other provisions. Deferred tax assets and liabilities are recognized at the tax rates at which the taxes are expected to be paid to or credited by the tax authorities concerned.

In measuring deferred taxes, the balance sheet liability method is used for temporary differences. Under this method the carrying amounts are compared with the tax base of the respective Group company. Differences between these amounts represent temporary differences for which deferred tax assets or deferred tax liabilities are reported regardless of when such differences cease to exist. The deferred taxes for the individual Group companies are measured at the local future tax rates that are expected to be applied. The deferred tax assets and deferred tax liabilities of any one company are netted only if the taxes on income are levied by the same tax authority.

Deferred tax assets for unused tax losses and liabilities are recognized if it is likely that the entity will generate corresponding amounts of taxable profits in future periods. Deferred taxes are not discounted.

Information on the Consolidated Balance Sheet

12. Cash and balances with central banks

EUR million	At Dec. 31, 2004	At Dec. 31, 2003
Cash in hand	1,282	1,243
Balances with central banks	1,441	1,306
Total	2,723	2,549

13. Loans and advances to credit institutions

EUR million	At Dec. 31, 2004	At Dec. 31, 2003
Loans and advances to domestic credit institutions	2,495	2,193
Loans and advances to foreign credit institutions	13,018	10,947
Total	15,513	13,140

14. Loans and advances to customers

EUR million	At Dec. 31, 2004	At Dec. 31, 2003
Loans and advances to domestic customers		
Public sector	2,899	3,004
Commercial customers	26,147	25,977
Private customers	17,892	16,650
Other	106	127
Total loans and advances to domestic customers	47,044	45,758
Loans and advances to foreign customers		
Public sector	2,695	2,996
Commercial customers	15,851	13,861
Private customers	6,937	4,949
Other	195	202
Total loans and advances to foreign customers	25,678	22,008
Total	72,722	67,766

Loans and advances to customers included receivables from finance lease agreements totalling EUR 3,802 million (2003: EUR 2,997 million). The gross investment in the leases was EUR 4,871 million (2003: EUR 3,591 million); the related unearned finance income totaled EUR 1,051 million (2003: EUR 601 million).

15. Risk provisions

EUR million	Dec. 31, 2003	Translation difference	Allocations[2]	Use	Releases[2]	Reclassification	Dec. 31, 2004
Risk provisions	2,691	19	788	(322)	(456)	(42)	2,678
Suspended interest	81	1	21	(10)	(21)	(1)	71
Risk provisions for loans and advances[1]	2,772	20	809	(332)	(477)	(43)	2,749
Other risk provisions[3]	26	3	24	(1)	(4)	43	91
Provision for guarantees	57	1	45	(2)	(36)	–	65
Total	2,855	24	878	(335)	(517)	–	2,905

[1] *Risk provisions for loans and advances are reported in balance sheet asset item 4.*
[2] *Additions to and releases of risk provisions pertaining to lendings, including guarantees, are reported in the income statement in risk provisions for loans and advances. Suspended interest is recognized in net interest income and other risk provisions are included in other operating result.*
[3] *Includes provisions for legal proceedings, risks associated with investments, realization losses and liabilities for statements made in offering circulars.*

16. Trading assets

in EUR million	At Dec. 31, 2004	At Dec. 31, 2003
Bonds and other fixed-income securities		
Listed	2,671	3,586
Unlisted	181	190
Shares and other variable-yield securities		
Listed	301	89
Unlisted	261	355
Positive fair value of derivative instruments		
Currency transactions	209	152
Interest rate transactions	999	868
Other transactions	6	19
Total	4,628	5,259

17. Investments available for sale

EUR million	At Dec.31, 2004	At Dec. 31, 2003
Bonds and other fixed-income securities		
Listed	5,313	4,136
Unlisted	531	442
Shares and other variable-yield securities		
Listed	333	198
Unlisted	2,964	2,603
Total	9,141	7,379

18. Financial investments

EUR million	at Dec 31, 2004	at Dec 31, 2003
Bonds and other fixed-income securities	16,276	14,657
Listed	4,293	4,475
Unlisted		
Variable-yield securities		
Listed	9	70
Unlisted	661	670
Equity holdings		
In nonconsolidated subsidiaries	124	123
In associates accounted for at equity		
Credit institutions	85	63
Noncredit institutions	77	72
In other investments		
Credit institutions	57	85
Noncredit institutions	143	154
Investments of insurance companies	5,979	4,989
Other financial investments	1,163	1,096
Total	28,867	26,454

Other financial investments include assets under operating lease agreements (carrying amounts of EUR 217 million; December 31, 2003: EUR 187 million).

19. Movement of fixed assets and financial investments

EUR million	At cost Dec 31, 2003	Currency translation (+/–)	Additions (+)	Disposals (–)	At cost Dec. 31, 2004
Intangible assets	2,727.8	25.2	209.5	(67.0)	2,895.5
Goodwill	1,810.8	0.1	31.1	0.0	1,842.0
Other	917.0	25.1	178.4	(67.0)	1,053.5
Tangible assets	3,529.0	87.7	269.4	(416.9)	3,496.2
Land and buildings	2,051.3	48.8	121.2	(261.2)	1,960.1
Office furniture and equipment	1,477.7	38.9	148.2	(155.7)	1,509.1
Financial investments	2,036.7	4.1	487.7	(433.4)	2,095.1

EUR million	At cost Dec 31, 2003	Currency translation (+/−)	Additions (+)	Disposals (−)	At cost Dec. 31, 2004
Nonconsolidated subsidiaries	170.2	1.2	75.7	(82.2)	164.9
Associates accounted for at equity	164.4	0.9	103.9	(73.3)	195.9
Other equity holdings	295.7	1.4	29.8	(95.7)	231.2
Other financial investments (particularly property used by third parties)	1,406.4	0.6	278.3	(182.2)	1,503.1
Total	8,293.5	117.0	966.6	(917.3)	8,459.8

EUR million	Accumulated depreciation (−)	Currency translation (+/−)	Amortization and depreciation (−)[1]	Impairment (−)[2]	Carrying amounts Dec. 31, 2004	Carrying amounts Dec. 31, 2003
Intangible assets	(1,072.1)	9.1	(141.1)	(81.0)	1,823.4	1,868.1
Goodwill	(402.5)	0.1	0.0	(80.0)	1,439.5	1,482.7
Other	(669.6)	9.0	(141.1)	(1.0)	383.9	385.4
Tangible assets	(1,746.6)	45.7	(205.2)	(11.3)	1,722.6	1,814.0
Land and buildings	(649.1)	34.5	(57.2)	(10.2)	1,311.0	1,378.4
Office furniture and equipment	(1,097.5)	11.2	(148.0)	(1.1)	411.6	435.7
Financial investments	(446.1)	3.2	(42.3)	(20.1)	1,649.0	1,593.8
Nonconsolidated subsidiaries	(40.6)	0.8	(0.3)	(4.8)	124.3	122.8
Associates accounted for at equity	(33.9)	1.0	0.0	(5.3)	162.0	134.5
Other equity holdings	(31.6)	0.8	(1.4)	(7.3)	199.6	239.9
Other financial investments (particularly property used by third parties)	(340.0)	0.6	(40.6)	(2.7)	1,163.1	1,096.6
Total	(3,264.8)	58.0	(388.6)	(112.4)	5,195.0	5,275.9

[1] Including depreciation expense of companies not engaged in the banking business which is reported under other operating result.
[2] Impairment is included in other operating result.

20. Other assets

EUR million	At Dec. 31, 2004	At Dec. 31, 2003
Income from accrued interest and commissions	1,476	1,341
Prepaid expenses	99	101
Deferred taxes	292	362
Securities lending and other repurchase agreements	1,454	1,258
Positive fair values of derivatives (banking book)	565	548
Sundry assets	1,405	1,507
Total	5,291	5,117

Sundry assets consist largely of payments on account for construction in progress and capitalized funding costs.

21. Deferred tax assets and liabilities

EUR million	Deferred tax assets Dec. 31, 2004	Deferred tax assets Dec. 31, 2003	Deferred tax liabilities Dec. 31, 2004	Deferred tax liabilities Dec. 31, 2003
Temporary differences relate to the following items:				
Loans and advances to customers	(5)	(1)	24	22
Investments available for sale	(1)	(1)	(39)	(42)
Financial investments	79	78	(25)	(7)
Tangible fixed assets	27	14	(7)	(10)

	Deferred tax assets		Deferred tax liabilities	
EUR million	*Dec. 31, 2004*	*Dec. 31, 2003*	*Dec. 31, 2004*	*Dec 31, 2003*
Amounts owed to customers	1	5	(20)	(24)
Long-term employee provisions	40	66	29	27
Other provisions	18	25	(8)	(12)
Tax loss carryforward	122	123	2	5
Other	11	17	(32)	(30)
Subtotal	292	326	(76)	(71)
Reclassification		36		(36)
Total	292	362	(76)	(107)

In compliance with IAS 12.39, no deferred taxes were calculated for temporary differences relating to investments in subsidiaries in the amount of EUR 296.9 million (December 31, 2003: EUR 285.9 million).

Deferred tax assets are reported under other assets; deferred tax liabilities are shown under provisions.

22. Amounts owed to credit institutions

EUR million	*At Dec. 31, 2004*	*At Dec. 31, 2003*
Amounts owed to domestic credit institutions	6,658	5,583
Amounts owed to foreign credit institutions	21,893	20,121
Total	28,551	25,704

23. Amounts owed to customers

	Domestic Dec. 31		Foreign countries Dec. 31		Total Dec. 31	
EUR million	*2004*	*2003*	*2004*	*2003*	*2004*	*2003*
Savings deposits	29,879	29,587	8,080	7,748	37,959	37,335
Other						
Public sector	442	470	1,198	946	1,640	1,416
Commercial customers	6,500	6,151	5,890	5,070	12,390	11,221
Private customers	4,567	4,293	10,506	9,915	15,073	14,208
Sundry	204	166	947	493	1,151	659
Total other	11,713	11,080	18,541	16,424	30,254	27,504
Total	41,592	40,666	26,621	24,173	68,213	64,839

24. Debts evidenced by certificates

EUR million	*At Dec. 31, 2004*	*At Dec. 31, 2003*
Bonds	13,684	11,527
Certificates of deposit	2,866	2,187
Other certificates of deposits/name certificates	1,673	1,695
Mortgage and municipal bonds	1,278	1,222
Other	279	222
Profit-sharing rights	107	91
Total	19,887	16,944

For 2004 the size of the debt-issuance program (DIP) launched in 1998 was agreed at EUR 15 billion. The DIP is a program for issuing debt instruments in any currency, with a wide array of available structures and maturities.

In 2004 under the DIP 57 new issues with a total volume of about EUR 1.8 billion were floated. As of December 31, 2004, the DIP's utilization rate was about 75%.

The size of the Euro-commercial paper program (including certificates of deposits) remains EUR 3 billion. Under this program, Erste Bank placed 49 new issues in 2004 with total proceeds of approximately EUR 1.8 billion. As of December 31, 2004, the utilization rate was about 25%.

25. Provisions

EUR million	*At Dec. 31, 2003*	*At Dec. 31, 2002*
Long-term employee provisions	1,080	1,097
Other provisions	6,248	5,269
Total	7,328	6,366

a. Long-term employee provisions

EUR million	Pension provisions	Termination provisions	Jubilee provisions	Total long-term provisions
Net present value at Dec. 31, 2002	827	314	44	1,185
Unrecognized actuarial losses	(68)	–	–	(68)
Long-term employee provisions at Dec. 31, 2002	759	314	44	1,117
Service cost	–	13	2	15
Interest cost	43	17	2	62
Payments	(70)	(8)	(4)	(82)
Actuarial gains/losses	90	(25)	10	75
Net present value at Dec. 31, 2003	822	311	54	1,187
Unrecognized actuarial losses	(90)	–	–	(90)
Long-term employee provisions at Dec. 31, 2003	732	311	54	1,097
Service cost	1	12	5	18
Interest cost	43	17	3	63
Payments	(71)	(29)	(4)	(104)
Actuarial gains/losses	97	6	(2)	101
Net present value at Dec. 31, 2004	802	317	56	1,175
Unrecognized actuarial losses	(95)	–	–	(95)
Long-term employee provisions at Dec. 31, 2004	707	317	56	1,080

Applying the current AVÖ 1999 P mortality tables ("AVÖ 1999 P—Rechnungsgrundlagen für die Pensionsversicherung," by Pagler & Pagler), as of December 31, 2004, the present value of the pension obligations for future benefits was EUR 802 million. The increase of EUR 95 million between this amount and the pension provisions reported in the balance sheet essentially results from the use of the current mortality tables.

b. Other provisions

EUR million	at Dec. 31, 2003	Currency translation	Allocations	Use	Releases	Reclassifications	At Dec. 31, 2004
Provision for taxes[1]	222	6	112	(114)	(13)	0	213
Provision for off-balance-sheet and other risks	83	4	69	(3)	(40)	43	156
Insurance reserves	4,829	18	1,021	(54)	(74)	0	5,740
Sundry other provisions[2]	135	5	54	(37)	(17)	(1)	139
Total	5,269	33	1,256	(208)	(144)	42	6,248

[1] *Regarding deferred tax liabilities, see Note 21.*
[2] *This item consists mainly of restructuring provisions and provisions for litigations.*

26. Other liabilities

EUR million	At Dec. 31, 2004	At Dec. 31, 2003
Liabilities relating to trading		
Currency transactions	88	113
Interest rate transactions	951	769
Other transactions	7	40
Deferred income	219	242
Accrued interest and commissions	716	633
Securities lending and other repurchase agreements	1,611	1,290
Negative fair values of derivatives (banking book)	288	514
Sundry liabilities	2,299	1,914
Total	6,179	5,515

Sundry liabilities primarily represent current balances from securities transactions, derivatives and ongoing payment transactions as well as other current accounts.

27. Subordinated capital

EUR million	At Dec. 31, 2004	At Dec. 31, 2003
Subordinated liabilities	1,194	1,434
Supplementary capital	1,854	2,104
Total	3,048	3,538

28. Shareholders' equity

Subscribed share capital as at December 31, 2004, was EUR 482.9 million (previous year: EUR 435.6 million), consisting of 241,442,892 voting bearer shares (ordinary shares) with no par value.

Capital increase from reserves pursuant to the Austrian Capital Adjustment Act prompted by the stock split, employee share ownership plan (ESOP 2004) and management share option plan (MSOP 2002)

- The Annual General Meeting of Erste Bank held on May 4, 2004, passed a resolution to increase the subscribed share capital from an accounting value of EUR 435,628,641.82 to EUR 479,550,464.00 by the conversion of EUR 43,921,822.18 of additional paid-in capital and to change the number of shares outstanding from 59,943,808 bearer shares without par value to 239,775,232 such shares by means of a four-for-one stock split. These resolutions were entered in the commercial register at the Vienna Commercial Court on June 25, 2004.
- As a result of the capital increase, the amount of Erste Bank's subscribed capital represented by each share rose from the original level of EUR 7.27 to EUR 8.00. This permitted a four-for-one stock split where each resulting share represented EUR 2.00 of the subscribed capital of Erste Bank. The stock split was effected as at July 8, 2004. After the entry of the new shares from the ESOP 2004 into the commercial register on June 26, 2004, the exercise of options under the MSOP 2002 and the execution of the stock split, the number of shares outstanding is 241,442,892, representing subscribed share capital of EUR 482,885,784.

Capital increase from reserves retroactive to January 1, 2004, under the Capital Adjustment Act 1967 as amended (KapBG) and creation of special reserves for contingent capital.

- The capital increase of EUR 43,921,822.18 from reserves was performed entirely by reassigning additional paid-in capital from the July 2002 capital increase.
- In compliance with Section 5(3) KapBG, a dedicated reserve of EUR 4,396,299.50 for additional paid-in capital was created for contingent capital of EUR 43,603,700.50 that had been authorized for the purpose of issuing conversion rights associated with convertible bonds. This contingent capital represented a maximum of 6,000,000 shares before the stock split or 24,000,000 shares after the split.
- Likewise, a reserve of EUR 1,254,580.79 for additional paid-in capital was created for the contingent capital intended to cover the potential exercise of stock options under the ESOP and MSOP. This reserve corresponds to the balance of authorized contingent capital of EUR 13,697,856, or up to 6,848,928 ordinary shares.
- Like the adjustment of the accounting value per share, the two special reserves were created by reassigning additional paid-in capital from the 2002 capital increase.

Employee stock ownership plan and management stock optional plan

MSOP 2002: The MSOP comprises a maximum of 4,400,000 ordinary shares of Erste Bank after the stock split, represented by 1,100,000 options. This total includes 60,000 options for the five members of the Managing Board at the time (12,000 per person) and an additional 8,000 options for the sixth member, who joined the Managing Board on January 1, 2003. The remaining 1,032,000 options were designated for distribution to eligible management staff and other eligible employees of the Erste Bank Group.

- Terms of MSOP 2002: Each of the options, which are granted free of charge, entitles the holder to subscribe for four shares; the transfer of options inter vivos is not permitted. The options granted in 2002 are delivered in three tranches by crediting the options to recipients' accounts: For the Managing Board and other management, on April 24, 2002, April 1, 2003, and April 1, 2004; for performance leaders among employees, on June 1, 2002, June 1, 2003, and June 1, 2004. The exercise price for all three tranches was set at the average quoted price of Erste Bank shares in March 2002 (rounded down to the nearest half euro), which was EUR 66 per share. After the stock split performed in July 2004, the exercise price remains EUR 66. This means that each option confers the right to purchase four shares of Erste Bank for a total of EUR 66. That corresponds to a subscription price of EUR 16.50 per share. The option term begins at the delivery date (the date on which the options are credited to the option account) and ends on the value date of the exercise window (described below) of the fifth calendar year after the delivery date. Every year, declarations to exercise may be submitted beginning on the day after publication of the preliminary consolidated net profit for the most recent completed financial year, but no earlier than April 1 and no later than April 30 of the year. This period represents the exercise window. It is followed by the lockup period, which ends on May 10 of the year following exercise of the option. No more than 15% of the purchased shares may be sold during the lockup period.

The options credited to recipients' accounts to date are distributed as follows:

	2002	*2003*	*2004*	*Total*	*Exercised*
Andreas Treichl	4,000	4,000	4,000	12,000	8,000
Elisabeth Bleyleben-Koren	4,000	4,000	4,000	12,000	7,000
Reinhard Ortner	4,000	4,000	4,000	12,000	8,000
Franz Hochstrasser	4,000	4,000	4,000	12,000	6,000
Erwin Erasim	4,000	4,000	4,000	12,000	6,000
André Horovitz	0	4,000	4,000	8,000	4,000
Received by virtue of Managing Board membership:	20,000	24,000	24,000	68,000	39,000
Christian Coreth (not by virtue of Managing Board membership)	1,000	1,000	1,000	3,000	2,000
Total received by Managing Board members	21,000	25,000	25,000	71,000	41,000
Other management	173,000	179,500	190,500	543,000	234,953
Other staff	93,211	116,959	95,748	305,918	71,227
Total option credited	287,211	321,459	311,248	919,918	347,180

- The contingent capital increase as per clause 4.4.3 of the Articles of Association (ESOP and MSOP) was carried out inasmuch as 416,915 bearer shares with an accounting value of EUR 3,335,320 were subscribed for in 2004 by employees, managers, and members of the Managing Board of Erste Bank and its subsidiaries under the MSOP 2002 and ESOP 2004 initiated by the Managing Board and approved by the Supervisory Board. Taking into account the resolutions of the Annual General Meeting of May 4, 2004, (four-for-one stock split), the number of shares subscribed for was thus 1,667,660.
- Of this total, under the 2002 MSOP, 347,180 options were exercised in the exercise window of April 2004. At an exercise price of EUR 66, the proceeds were EUR 22,913,880, of which EUR 2,777,440 was allocated to subscribed share capital and EUR 20,136,440 was assigned to additional paid-in capital. Of the exercised options, 181,312 represented the first tranche (Managing Board members: 20,000 options, other management: 125,445, staff: 35,867). The spread between the exercise price and the market price at exercise for the first tranche was between EUR 59.20 and EUR 62.80 for Managing Board members and between EUR 58.85 and EUR 62.80 for other management and staff. From the second tranche, 165,868 options were exercised (19,000 by Managing Board members, 111,508 by other management, and 35,360 by staff). The spread between the exercise price and the market price at exercise for the second tranche was between EUR 59.90 and EUR 62.50

for Managing Board members and between EUR 58.85 and EUR 62.80 for other management and staff.

- The exercise price of the individual options—the average of all daily closing prices recorded in March 2002—rounded to the nearest half euro was EUR 66.00. The market price (the fair value) of the individual options at the balance sheet date of December 31, 2004, for options credited in 2002 was EUR 91.60, that of the options credited in 2003 was EUR 91.60 and that of the options credited in 2004 was EUR 91.44.

ESOP 2004: Under the ESOP 2004, between May 10 and 21, 2004, employees subscribed 69,735 shares at an exercise price of EUR 101.00.

- The resulting issue proceeds of EUR 7,043,235.00 plus EUR 1,410,041.70 (from the difference between the issue price of EUR 101.00 and the quoted price of EUR 121.22 on the value date of May 26, 2004, charged to personnel expenses) amounted to a total of EUR 8,453,276.70. Of this amount, EUR 557,880.00 was assigned to subscribed-share capital and the balance of EUR 7,895,396.70 was assigned to additional paid-in capital.
- The 69,735 shares subscribed for under the ESOP 2004 in May 2004 were increased to 278,940 shares by the stock split. Of these, 162,460 shares were purchased by management and staff of Erste Bank, including 100 by members of the Managing Board (Andreas Treichl).

Information about holdings of and transaction in Erste Bank shares by members of the Managing Board and Supervisory Board

Managing Board members: (number of shares, after stock split)

	At Dec. 31, 2003	Purchase 2004	Sale 2004	At Dec. 31, 2004
Andreas Treichl	80,840	32,400	9,200	104,040
Elisabeth Bleyleben-Koren	8,840	28,000	12,440	24,400
Reinhard Ortner	73,200	32,000	0	105,200
Franz Hochstrasser	12,728	24,000	8,472	28,256
Erwin Erasim	400	24,000	3,600	20,800
Christian Coreth	8,000	8,000	0	16,000

At the balance sheet date of December 31, 2004, the following members of the Supervisory Board held Erste Bank shares in the numbers shown:

	Shares held
Klaus Braunegg	3,280
Werner Hutschinski	480
Georg Winckler	960
Günter Benischek	280
Joachim Härtel	400
Anton Janku	328

As far as can be determined, persons related to members of the Managing Board or Supervisory Board held 5,055 shares of Erste Bank at December 31, 2004.

Authorized but unissued capital and contingent capital remaining at December 31, 2004

Clauses 4.4. as well as 4.4.1. and 4.4.2. of the Articles of Association authorize, for a five-year period from the date of registration of the amendment to the Articles of Association in the commercial register, the issuance of up to 80,000,000 shares with an accounting value of EUR 160,000,000. The Managing Board is authorized by the Articles to exclude the shareholders' subscription rights, with the consent of the Supervisory Board, for the issue of shares against noncash contributions or inasmuch as the capital increase serves to issue shares to staff, management and Managing Board members of Erste Bank or of its subsidiaries.

Clause 4.4.3. of the Articles of Association authorizes, for a period of five years from the date of registration of the amendment of the Company's Articles of Association in the commercial register, the issue of capital with an accounting value of EUR 18,168,208.54 in the form of 2,500,000 ordinary bearer or registered shares to be used to grant share options to employees, management, and members of the Managing Board of Erste Bank or of its subsidiaries. After the exercise of options in 2002 and 2004, and the stock split in July 2004, the unissued balance of this authorized capital at December 31, 2004, stood at 6,848,928 ordinary shares with an accounting value of EUR 13,697,856.

As approved by the extraordinary general meeting held on August 21, 1997, and as per clause 4.5. of the Article of Association, there is authorized capital for a contingent increase in capital by 24,000,000 ordinary bearer shares with an accounting value of EUR 48,000,000, to be carried out inasmuch as holders of convertible bonds exercise their conversion rights.

Another employee share ownership plan (ESOP 2005) is planned for the 2005 financial year, subject to approval by the Supervisory Board.

The qualifying capital of the Erste Bank Group as determined under the Austrian Banking Act had the composition shown below.

EUR million	At Dec. 31, 2004	At Dec. 31, 2003
Subscribed capital	482	436
Reserves	4,375	3,940
Less intangible assets	(480)	(464)
Core capital (Tier 1)	4,377	3,912
Eligible subordinated liabilities	2,528	2,696
Revaluation reserve	230	198
Qualifying supplementary capital (Tier 2)	2,758	2,894
Short-term subordinated capital (Tier 3)	316	340
Total qualifying capital	7,451	7,146
Deductions according to Section 23 (13) and Section 29 (1–2) Austrian Banking Act	(165)	(137)
Total eligible qualifying capital	7,286	7,009
Capital requirement	5,594	5,315
Surplus capital	1,692	1,694
Cover ratio (in %)	130	132
Tier 1 ratio (in %)	6.7	6.3
Solvency ratio (in %)	10.7	10.7

The risk-weighted basis pursuant to Section 22 (1) Austrian Banking Act and the resulting capital requirement showed the following changes:

EUR million	At Dec. 31, 2004	At Dec. 31, 2003
Risk-weighted basis acc. to Section 22 Austrian Banking Act	65,384	62,188
Of which 8% minimum capital requirement	5,231	4,975
Capital requirement for open foreign exchange position acc. to Section 26 Austrian Banking Act	49	14
Capital requirement for the Trading Book acc. to Section 22 b (1) Austrian Banking Act	314	326
Capital requirement	5,594	5,315

Information on the Consolidated Income Statement

29. Net interest income

EUR million	2004	2003
Interest income from		
Lending and money market transactions with credit institutions	588.1	788.0
Lending and money market transactions with customers	3,009.2	2,883.7
Fixed-income securities	1,269.2	1,154.0
Other interest and similar income	86.5	70.8
Current income from		
Shares and other variable-yield securities	173.9	163.9
Investments		
– in nonconsolidated subsidiaries	9.2	10.7
– in associates accounted for at equity	13.7	56.9
– in other investments	13.5	14.2

EUR million	2004	2003
Property used by outside parties	65.5	67.3
Total interest and similar income	5,228.8	5,209.5
Interest expenses for		
Amounts owed to credit institutions	(494.7)	(600.3)
Amounts owed to customers	(1,208.2)	(1,214.9)
Debts evidenced by certificates	(611.1)	(577.2)
Subordinated capital	(212.8)	(223.3)
Other	(6.5)	(7.0)
Total interest and similar expenses	(2,533.3)	(2,622.7)
Net interest income	2,695.5	2,586.8

Net interest income includes the net interest income of EUR 137 million (2003: EUR 139 million) from finance leases.

30. Risk provisions for loans and advances

EUR million	2004	2003
Allocation to risk provisions for loans and advances	(857.3)	(745.1)
Release of risk provisions for loans and advances	497.0	374.9
Direct write-offs of loans and advances	(61.2)	(59.8)
Amounts received against written-off loans and advances	15.3	23.6
Total	(406.2)	(406.4)

The above figures do not include the allocations to and releases of risk provisions netted in net interest income (suspended interest). See the explanation provided in Note 15.

The allocations to and releases of other risk provisions that do not pertain to lendings are included in other operating result (see Note 35). The above figures include the allocations to and release of provisions for off-balance-sheet credit risks.

31. Net commission income

EUR million	2004	2003
Lending business	178.7	160.1
Payment transfers	443.7	384.7
Securities transactions	303.1	248.8
Of which investment fund transactions	133.6	111.2
Custodial fees	44.9	43.9
Brokerage	124.6	93.6
Insurance business	61.6	59.0
Building society brokerage	35.9	38.3
Foreign exchange transactions	40.9	50.5
Other	77.2	55.2
Total	1,141.1	996.6

32. Net trading result

EUR million	2004	2003
Securities and derivatives trading	89.9	97.6
Foreign exchange transactions	126.6	117.0
Total	216.5	214.6

Listed products are valued at the prices quoted on the balance sheet date. The fair values of nonlisted products are measured by the net present value method or using suitable options pricing models. All realized and unrealized gains are reported in the income statement within net trading result. Also included in this item are interest and dividend income earned on the trading portfolio, and the portfolio's funding cost.

33. General administrative expenses

EUR million	2004	2003
Personnel expenses	(1,480.4)	(1,422.3)
Other administrative expenses	(772.2)	(691.9)
Depreciation and amortization	(340.3)	(346.6)
Total	(2,592.9)	(2,460.8)

Personnel expenses

EUR million	2004	2003
Wages and salaries	(1,080.9)	(1,031.4)
Compulsory social security contributions	(292.7)	(273.5)
Long-term employee provisions	(87.0)	(62.0)
Other personnel expenses	(19.8)	(55.4)[1]
Total	(1,480.4)	(1,422.3)

[1] *This includes EUR 32.0 million from onetime payments made to pension funds under Section 48a of the Austrian Pension Fund Act as amended.*

Average number of employees on payroll during the financial year (in full-time equivalents)

	2004	2003
Employed by Group	36,533	36,661
Domestic	14,765	15,213
thereof Haftungsverbund savings banks	6,843	6,958
Foreign countries	21,768	21,448
thereof Ceská sporitel'ňa Group	11,805	12,823
thereof Slovenská sporitel'ňa	5,233	5,300
thereof other subsidiaries	4,730	3,325

In addition to the headcount given above, during the reporting period an average of 73 people (2003: 68) were employed in nonbank Group companies (hotel leisure segment).

At the end of 2004, loans and advances to members of the Managing Board totaled EUR 138,000 (2003: EUR 150,000). Loans to members of the Supervisory Board amounted to EUR 1.973 million (2003: EUR 2.397 million). The applicable interest rates and other terms (maturity dates and collateralization) are in line with typical market practice. In 2004 members of the Managing Board made loan repayments totaling EUR 12,000 (2003: EUR 11,000) and members of the Supervisory Board repaid EUR 424,000 (2003: EUR 218,000) on loans. Loan extended in the 2004 financial year to parties related to the Supervisory Board carried market rates of interest and were in line with market practice in their other terms.

In 2004 the then members of the Managing Board received remuneration (including noncash compensation) in their capacity as Managing Board members totaling EUR 11.672 million (2003: EUR 5.911 million), which represented 0.8% of total personnel expenses of the Erste Bank Group.

In financial 2004, EUR 683,000 (2003: EUR 599,000) was paid to former members of the Managing Board or their surviving dependents.

The breakdown of the remuneration of the members of the Managing Board in 2004 was as follows:

EUR thousand

Managing Board member	Monetary compensation salary	Monetary compensation bonus	Other compensation	Total
Andreas Treichl	1,200	3,000[1]	345	4,545
Elisabeth Bleyleben-Koren	900	750	205	1,855
Reinhard Ortner	750	625	172	1,547
Franz Hochstrasser	750	625	172	1,547
Erwin Erasim	500	420	117	1,037
Christian Coreth from July 1, 2004	200	0[2]	48	248
André Horovitz until June 30, 2004	218	364	311	893
	4,518	5,784	1,370	11,672

[1] *Including a one-time bonus of 2,000*
[2] *Bonuses are paid out in the first half of the year.*

In 2004 the Managing Board of Erste Bank AG did not receive supervisory board emoluments or other compensation from subsidiaries majority-owned by Erste Bank. The item "other compensation" represents pension fund contributions and various noncash compensation. The compensation of the members of the Managing Board depends on the individual's responsibilities, the achievement of corporate targets and the Group's financial situation.

The Supervisory Board members of Erste Bank in 2004 were paid EUR 349,000 (2003: 467,000) for their board function. Members of the Supervisory Board received the following compensation for board functions in fully consolidated subsidiaries of Erste Bank: Heinz Kessler: EUR 7,632.51; Klaus Braunegg: EUR 12,538.88. Other transactions resulted in the following payments to members of the Supervisory Board or companies related to them.

For legal services to assist in debt recovery, the law firm Braunegg, Hoffman & Partner, a company related to Mr. Klaus Braunegg, received gross fees in 2004 totaling EUR 133,015.95, including value added tax and court fees in the amount of EUR 41,146.27. For various legal consulting to Erste Bank and Erste Bank's fully consolidated subsidiaries, Braunegg, Hoffmann & Partner in 2004 received total gross fees of EUR 53,588.00 including value added tax and disbursements.

Dorda Brugger Jordis Rechtsanwälte GmbH, a law firm related to Theresa Jordis, in 2004 invoiced a total of EUR 112,770.58 (excluding value added tax and disbursements) for consulting contracts with fully consolidated subsidiaries of Erste Bank.

PwC PricewaterhouseCoopers GmbH, a company related to Friedrich Rödler, in 2004 invoiced a total of EUR 91,395.00 for consulting contracts with fully consolidated subsidiaries of Erste Bank.

The following amounts of compensation were paid to the individual members of the Supervisory Board:

EUR thousand

Supervisory Board member	Supervisory Board compensation	Meeting fees	Total
Heinz Kessler	27	12	39
Klaus Braunegg	27	12	39
Theresa Jordis	21	10	31
Bettina Breiteneder	0	4	4
Dietrich Blahut until May 4, 2004	18	1	19
Elisabeth Gürtler	18	3	21
Jan Homan	0	2	2
Wolfgang Houska until May 4, 2004	18	3	21
Werner Hutschinski	18	9	27
Dietrich Kamer until March 10, 2004	18	0	18
Josef Kassler	18	4	22
Lars-Olaf Ödlund	18	2	20
Friedrich Rödler	0	7	7
Hubert Singer	18	3	21
Georg Winckler	18	10	28
Gunter Benischek	0	2	2
Erika Hegmala	0	5	5
Ilse Fetik	0	3	3
Joachim Härtel	0	8	8
Anton Janku	0	9	9
Christian Havelka	0	3	3

Other administrative expenses

EUR million	2004	2003
IT expenses	(194.5)	(162.1)
Expenses for office space	(153.4)	(140.7)
Office operating expenses	(138.6)	(135.7)
Advertising/marketing	(114.7)	(103.5)
Legal and consulting costs	(74.8)	(71.4)
Sundry administrative expenses	(96.2)	(78.5)
Total	(772.2)	(691.9)

Depreciation and amortization

EUR million	2004	2003
Software and other intangible assets	(136.9)	(132.3)
Real estate used by the Group	(53.9)	(60.0)
Office furniture and equipment and sundry tangible assets	(149.5)	(154.3)
Total	(340.3)	(346.6)

34. Net income from insurance business

EUR million	2004	2003
Premiums earned	1,013.5	937.1
Investment income from technical business	320.4	252.4
Claims incurred	(249.0)	(285.8)
Change in underwriting reserves	(856.6)	(693.6)
Expenses for policyholder bonuses	(75.0)	(67.7)
Operating expenses	(106.0)	(102.9)
Sundry underwriting profit/loss	17.6	(10.0)
Underwriting profit/loss	64.9	29.5
Financial profit/loss	290.3	255.8
Carryforward—underwriting	(320.4)	(252.4)
Total	34.8	32.9

35. Other operating result

EUR million	2004	2003
Other operating income		
Income from measurement/sale of securities held to maturity	11.7	14.2
Income from real estate/properties	36.4	45.5
Income from release of other provisions/risks	11.4	7.5
Proceeds of the sale of the Czech property insurance business	88.0	--
Sundry operating income	67.9	94.3
Total other operating income	215.4	161.5
Other operating expenses		
Expenses from measurement/sale of securities held to maturity	(12.7)	(15.3)
Losses from real estate/properties	(25.1)	(27.3)
Amortization of goodwill (Since 1/1/2004 impairment)	(80.0)	(81.2)
Expenses from allocation of other provisions/risks	(35.2)	(26.4)
Expenses from making deposit insurance contributions	(54.0)	(41.5)
Other taxes	(18.1)	(10.7)
Provisions for litigations	(44.5)	(19.7)
One-off expenses for noncapitalized software	(17.3)	(33.4)
Sundry operating expenses	(117.6)	(108.4)
Total other operating expenses	(404.5)	(363.9)
Other operating result		
Results from measurement/sale of securities held as investments available for sale	60.9	9.6
Measurement of the sale of Investkredit	67.2	--
Results from measurement/sale of shares in unconsolidated subsidiaries	33.3	(9.3)
Total other operating result	(27.7)	(202.1)

Sundry operating income/expenses consist primarily of items not attributable to the ordinary banking activities, such as operating costs, cost of goods purchased for resale, sales revenues generated by providers of banking support services and by other nonbanks, and licensing income.

36. Taxes on income

The taxes on income are made up of the current taxes on income calculated in each of the Group companies based on the results as reported for tax purposes, corrections to taxes on income for previous years, and the change in deferred taxes.

EUR million	2004	2003
Current tax expense	(232.4)	(179.0)
Deferred tax expense	(41.4)	(45.2)
Total	(273.8)	(224.2)

The following table reconciles the transformation of pretax profit and the Austrian tax rate to the income taxes reported in the income statement:

EUR million	2004	2003
Pretax profit for the year	1,061.1	761.6
Income tax expense for the financial year at the domestic statutory tax rate (34%)	(360.7)	(258.9)
Impact of different foreign tax rates	42.6	14.7
Tax reductions due to tax-exempt earnings of investments and other tax-exempt income	134.7	178.4
Tax increases due to nondeductible expenses	(74.0)	(137.4)
Tax expense/income not attributable to the reporting period	(16.4)	(21.0)
Reported taxes on income	(273.8)	(224.2)

37. Appropriation of net profit

EUR million	2004	2003
Net profit after minority interests	544.5	353.3
Allocation to reserves	(423.8)	(263.4)
Profit carried forward	0.1	0.2
Distributable profit of the parent company	120.8	90.1

The Managing Board proposes to the Annual General Meeting that shareholders be paid a dividend of EUR 0.50 per share (2003 after stock split: EUR 0.375 per share) and that the remaining retained profit under Section 65 (5) Austrian Stock Corporation Act be carried forward.

38. Segment reporting

Segmentation by business activities

In the 2004 financial year the accounting segment structure of the Erste Bank Group remained unchanged.

The first-order segmentation consists of the three market segments Austria, Central Europe, and International as well as Group Corporate Centre.

Austria segment: The Austria segment comprises all business units and subsidiaries operating in Austria. It is further segmented according to business activity into Haftungsverbund, Retail and Real Estate, Large Corporate Customers and Trading and Investment Banking.

The Retail and Real Estate segment also encompasses those savings banks in which Erste Bank holds a majority stake (Salzburger Sparkasse, Tiroler Sparkasse and Sparkasse Hainburg-Bruck-Neusiedl). The savings banks that are consolidated as a result of their membership in the Haftungsverbund Agreement or in which Erste Bank holds no interest or only a minority interest are grouped in the Haftungsverbund segment.

Central Europe segment: The Central Europe market segment, which is subdivided into the entities operating in the individual countries, encompasses the results of Ĉeská sporiteľňa a.s. (the Czech Republic segment), Slovenská sporiteľňa (Slovakia segment), Erste Bank Hungary Rt. (Hungary segment) and Erste & Steiermärkische banka d.d. (Croatia segment). The results for the 2004 financial year of Postabank (acquired at the end of 2003 and merged as of September 1, 2004 with Erste Bank Hungary) are included under Erste Bank Hungary.

International segment: This reporting segment includes both the International Business unit in Vienna and the commercial lending business of the London, New York, and Hong Kong profit centers.

Corporate Centre segment: Corporate Centre encompasses all performance components that cannot be attributed directly to other segments, as well as consolidating entries.

The allocation of results to the segments is based on the profit contribution report at the business unit level. Net interest income is determined based on opportunity cost (market spread, maturity mismatch), with the contribution from maturity transformation attributed entirely to the Trading and Investment Banking segment. Fees and commissions, net trading result and other operating result are allocated to the business units where they are generated.

General administrative expenses are reported on the basis of activity-based costing (product cost, indirect costs and general overhead) at the business unit level.

Segmentation by geographic markets

The following regional segmentation underlies this segmental analysis:

- Austria
- Central Europe (Czech Republic, Slovakia, Hungary, Croatia)
- Rest of Europe
- North America
- Central and South America
- Asia
- Rest of world

The Austria geographic segment captures the contributions generated in Austria and Corporate Centre, subdivided by core business areas. The Central Europe segment represents the contributions from Central Europe.

The International segment, subdivided by core business activities, is distributed across the geographic segments according to customer location.

Segment reporting/overview

	Total		Austria		Central Europe	
EUR million	*2004*	*2003*	*2004*	*2003*	*2004*	*2003*
Net interest income	2,695.5	2,586.8	1,607.9	1,622.8	950.9	829.4
Risk provisions for loans/advances	(406.2)	(406.4)	(341.3)	(374.6)	(49.9)	(9.7)
Net commission income	1,141.1	996.6	722.1	680.2	404.3	345.3
Net trading result	216.5	214.6	117.6	137.1	101.4	71.2
General administrative expenses	(2,592.9)	(2,460.7)	(1,613.0)	(1,655.6)	(897.0)	(766.7)
Income from insurance business	34.8	32.9	26.4	25.9	8.4	10.2
Other operating result	(27.7)	(202.1)	(32.0)	(26.4)	(44.8)	(167.1)
Pretax profit for the year	1,061.1	761.6	487.8	409.4	473.2	312.6
Less taxes	(273.8)	(224.2)	(113.4)	(128.4)	(107.8)	(78.1)
Less minority interests	(242.8)	(184.1)	(158.7)	(112.3)	(43.3)	(44.7)
Net profit after minority interests	544.5	353.3	215.7	168.7	322.1	189.7
Average risk-weighted assets	66,470.4	61,888.0	46,484.0	44,771.0	13,318.7	10,162.1
Average attributed equity	3,022.8	2,578.2	1,731.0	1,549.1	860.8	611.0
Cost-income ratio (in %)	63.4%	64.2%	65.2%	67.1%	61.2%	61.0%
ROE based on net profit after minority interests (in %)	18.0%	13.7%	12.5%	10.9%	37.4%	31.1%
Funding costs	(163.1)	(142.0)	(70.6)	(73.0)	(64.8)	(44.4)
Amortization of goodwill	(80.0)	(81.1)	0.0	(18.5)	0.0	(54.4)

	International Business		Corporate Centre	
EUR million	*2004*	*2003*	*2004*	*2003*
Net interest income	150.8	146.8	(14.1)	(12.1)
Risk provisions for loans/advances	(15.5)	(26.1)	0.6	3.9
Net commission income	22.5	21.1	(7.9)	(50.0)
Net trading result	1.7	0.1	(4.2)	6.2
General administrative expenses	(33.4)	(34.0)	(49.5)	(4.4)

EUR million	International Business		Corporate Centre	
	2004	*2003*	*2004*	*2003*
Income from insurance business	0.0	0.0	0.0	(3.2)
Other operating result	(5.7)	(13.8)	54.8	5.2
Pretax profit for the year	120.4	94.1	(20.3)	(54.5)
Less taxes	(26.7)	(24.0)	(25.8)	6.3
Less minority interests	0.0	0.0	(40.7)	(27.1)
Net profit after minority interests	93.6	70.1	(86.9)	(75.3)
Average risk-weighted assets	6,262.0	6,387.5	405.7	567.3
Average attributed equity	404.7	384.0	26.2	34.1
Cost-income ratio (in %)	19.1%	20.2%	(189.7%)	(7.4%)
ROE based on net profit after minority interests (in %)	23.1%	18.3%	(331.3%)	(220.6%)
Funding costs	0.0	0.0	(27.7)	(24.5)
Amortization of goodwill	0.0	0.0	(80.0)	(8.3)

Segment reporting/Austria

EUR million	Austria		Savings banks		Retail and real estate	
	2004	*2003*	*2004*	*2003*	*2004*	*2003*
Net interest income	1,607.9	1,622.8	849.6	841.3	516.1	521.8
Risk provisions for loans/advances	(341.3)	(374.6)	(184.5)	(198.1)	(118.9)	(132.4)
Net commission income	722.1	680.2	318.8	321.5	280.4	264.1
Net trading result	117.6	137.1	18.8	29.3	10.5	16.7
General administrative expenses	(1,613.0)	(1,655.6)	(801.7)	(820.5)	(634.8)	(653.0)
Income from insurance business	26.4	25.9	0.0	0.0	26.4	25.9
Other operating result	(32.0)	(26.4)	(11.8)	(22.3)	(5.5)	(2.5)
Pretax profit for the year	487.8	409.4	189.1	151.3	74.2	40.5
Less taxes	(113.4)	(128.4)	(46.6)	(46.7)	(15.7)	(15.5)
Less minority interests	(158.7)	(112.3)	(133.8)	(101.5)	(14.8)	(5.3)
Net profit after minority interests	215.7	168.7	8.7	3.1	43.7	19.8
Average risk-weighted assets	46,484.0	44,771.0	22,986.2	22,179.7	12,844.7	12,185.8
Average attributed equity	1,731.0	1,549.1	242.3	190.8	813.8	732.7
Cost-income ratio (in %)	65.2%	67.1%	67.5%	68.8%	76.2%	78.8%
ROE based on net profit after minority interests (in %)	12.5%	10.9%	3.6%	1.6%	5.4%	2.7%
Funding costs	(70.6)	(73.0)	(16.2)	(15.3)	(37.0)	(39.5)
Amortization of goodwill	0.0	(18.5)	0.0	(5.9)	0.0	(12.6)

EUR million	Large corporate customers		Trading and investment banking	
	2004	*2003*	*2004*	*2003*
Net interest income	139.9	147.7	102.4	112.1
Risk provisions for loans/advances	(37.9)	(44.1)	0.0	0.0
Net commission income	71.2	53.1	51.7	41.5
Net trading result	1.2	1.5	87.1	89.6
General administrative expenses	(83.0)	(81.2)	(93.5)	(100.9)
Income from insurance business	0.0	0.0	0.0	0.0
Other operating result	(7.7)	9.1	(7.0)	(10.8)
Pretax profit for the year	83.7	86.1	140.8	131.5
Less taxes	(17.9)	(25.6)	(33.3)	(40.6)
Less minority interests	(10.1)	(6.0)	0.0	0.3
Net profit after minority interests	55.8	54.6	107.5	91.2
Average risk-weighted assets	6,860.9	6,918.9	3,792.1	3,486.6
Average attributed equity	434.7	416.0	240.3	209.6
Cost-income ratio (in %)	39.1%	40.2%	38.7%	41.5%
ROE based on net profit after minority interests (in %)	12.8%	13.1%	44.8%	43.5%
Funding costs	(14.6)	(15.7)	(2.8)	(2.5)
Amortization of goodwill	0.0	0.0	0.0	0.0

Segment reporting/Central Europe

EUR million	Central Europe		Česká sporiteľňa		Slovenská sporiteľňa	
	2004	*2003*	*2004*	*2003*	*2004*	*2003*
Net interest income	950.9	829.4	506.6	460.8	185.8	234.7
Risk provisions for loans/advances	(49.9)	(9.7)	(15.8)	1.3	0.8	3.3
Net commission income	404.3	345.3	268.6	252.3	66.4	51.6
Net trading result	101.4	71.2	41.0	38.1	16.5	10.8
General administrative expenses	(897.0)	(766.7)	(498.5)	(474.1)	(158.5)	(157.3)
Income from insurance business	8.4	10.2	8.4	10.2	0.0	0.0
Other operating result	(44.8)	(167.1)	3.9	(75.7)	(25.4)	(81.9)
Pretax profit for the year	473.2	312.6	314.1	212.9	85.6	61.3
Less taxes	(107.8)	(78.1)	(92.5)	(75.2)	(7.2)	(5.6)
Less minority interests	(43.3)	(44.7)	(12.3)	(15.2)	(18.8)	(22.9)
Net profit after minority interests	322.1	189.7	209.4	122.5	59.6	32.7
Average risk-weighted assets	13,318.7	10,162.1	7,491.5	6,287.5	1,890.2	1,493.2
Average attributed equity	860.8	611.0	484.2	378.0	122.2	89.8
Cost-income ratio (in %)	61.2%	61.0%	60.5%	62.3%	59.0%	52.9%
ROE based on net profit after minority interests (in %)	37.4%	31.1%	43.2%	32.4%	48.8%	36.5%
Funding costs	(64.8)	(44.4)	(26.4)	(27.7)	(11.1)	(6.2)
Amortization of goodwill	0.0	(54.4)	0.0	(40.2)	0.0	(12.0)

EUR million	Erste Bank Hungary		Erste Bank Croatia	
	2004	*2003*	*2004*	*2003*
Net interest income	174.0	58.5	84.5	75.4
Risk provisions for loans/advances	(30.0)	(7.5)	(4.9)	(6.9)
Net commission income	52.6	28.8	16.7	12.5
Net trading result	31.3	11.6	12.6	10.7
General administrative expenses	(175.7)	(69.3)	(64.3)	(66.1)
Income from insurance business	0.0	0.0	0.0	0.0
Other operating result	(21.0)	(7.6)	(2.3)	(1.8)
Pretax profit for the year	31.3	14.7	42.2	23.7
Less taxes	0.3	(1.7)	(8.5)	4.3
Less minority interests	(0.1)	0.1	(12.1)	(6.7)
Net profit after minority interests	31.5	13.2	21.6	21.3
Average risk-weighted assets	2,031.2	920.8	1,905.9	1,460.6
Average attributed equity	131.3	55.4	123.2	87.8
Cost-income ratio (in %)	68.1%	70.0%	56.6%	67.1%
ROE based on net profit after minority interests (in %)	24.0%	23.8%	17.6%	24.2%
Funding costs	(21.5)	(3.2)	(5.8)	(7.3)
Amortization of goodwill	0.0	0.0	0.0	(2.2)

Segment reporting by region

EUR million	Austria		Central Europe	
	2004	*2003*	*2004*	*2003*
Net interest income	1,596.0	1,628.5	964.4	837.7
Risk provisions for loans/advances	(340.7)	(370.6)	(50.0)	(12.3)
Net commission income	711.5	626.8	406.9	348.5
Net trading result	111.1	141.6	101.4	71.2
General administrative expenses	(1,637.9)	(1,659.7)	(917.1)	(769.1)
Income from insurance business	26.4	22.7	8.4	10.2
Other operating result	23.5	(32.7)	(43.5)	(167.1)
Pretax profit for the year	490.1	356.6	470.5	319.1
Less taxes	(136.9)	(117.5)	(109.9)	(80.1)
Less minority interests	(199.7)	(139.4)	(43.1)	(44.7)
Net profit after minority interests	153.5	99.7	317.6	194.3
Average risk-weighted assets	48,338	46,238	13,856	11,402

EUR million	Rest of Europe		North America	
	2004	*2003*	*2004*	*2003*
Net interest income	30.2	28.1	56.7	44.4
Risk provisions for loans/advances	(4.4)	(2.5)	(3.5)	(13.4)
Net commission income	7.3	5.2	6.2	8.3
Net trading result	1.3	0.3	1.3	0.5
General administrative expenses	(14.1)	(13.3)	(15.4)	(11.6)
Income from insurance business	0.0	0.0	0.0	0.0
Other operating result	(3.8)	(2.4)	(4.6)	0.0
Pretax profit for the year	16.6	15.4	40.8	28.2
Less taxes	(1.3)	(4.7)	(18.6)	(8.7)
Less minority interests	0.0	0.0	0.0	0.0
Net profit after minority interests	15.3	10.7	22.2	19.4
Average risk-weighted assets	1,585	1,373	1,394	1,587

EUR million	Central/South America		Asia	
	2004	*2003*	*2004*	*2003*
Net interest income	1.8	2.6	42.8	14.9
Risk provisions for loans/advances	(0.1)	(0.3)	(4.9)	(2.6)
Net commission income	4.4	2.6	4.4	4.4
Net trading result	0.0	0.0	1.4	(0.6)
General administrative expenses	(1.0)	(1.0)	(7.0)	(4.9)
Income from insurance business	0.0	0.0	0.0	0.0
Other operating result	0.0	0.0	0.8	0.0
Pretax profit for the year	5.1	3.9	37.5	11.2
Less taxes	(1.2)	(1.2)	(6.0)	(3.5)
Less minority interests	0.0	0.0	0.0	0.0
Net profit after minority interests	3.9	2.7	31.5	7.7
Average risk-weighted assets	112	180	1,057	642

EUR million	Other		Total	
	2004	*2003*	*2004*	*2003*
Net interest income	3.4	30.7	2,695.5	2,586.8
Risk provisions for loans/advances	(2.6)	(4.7)	(406.2)	(406.4)
Net commission income	0.4	0.9	1,141.1	996.6
Net trading result	0.0	1.6	216.5	214.6
General administrative expenses	(0.4)	(1.1)	(2,592.9)	(2,460.7)
Income from insurance business	0.0	0.0	34.8	32.9
Other operating result	(0.1)	0.0	(27.7)	(202.1)
Pretax profit for the year	0.7	27.3	1,061.1	761.6
Less taxes	0.0	(8.5)	(273.8)	(224.2)
Less minority interests	0.0	0.0	(242.8)	(184.1)
Net profit after minority interests	0.6	18.9	544.5	353.3
Average risk-weighted assets	129	467	66,470	61,888

39. Additional information

Only non-Euro-area currencies are now reported as foreign currencies.

EUR million	At Dec. 31, 2004	At Dec. 31, 2003
Assets	60,624	53,874
Liabilities	49,297	45,986

Unconsolidated foreign investments and goodwill are not reported as assets and liabilities denominated in foreign currencies.

Foreign assets and liabilities:

EUR million	At Dec. 31, 2004	At Dec. 31, 2003
Assets	69,763	59,609
Liabilities	63,736	54,807

40. Loans and advances to and amounts owed to unconsolidated subsidiaries and investments

EUR million	At Dec. 31, 2004	At Dec. 31, 2003
Loans and advances to credit institutions		
Unconsolidated subsidiaries	--	1
Associates accounted for at equity	46	42
Other investments	398	377
Loans and advances to customers		
Unconsolidated subsidiaries	529	466
Associates accounted for at equity	323	107
Other investments	734	598
Investments available for sale		
Unconsolidated subsidiaries	2	3
Associates accounted for at equity	36	36
Other investments	62	61
Financial investments		
Unconsolidated subsidiaries	--	1
Associates accounted for at equity	4	7
Other investments	4	67
Amounts owed to credit institutions		
Unconsolidated subsidiaries	2	3
Associates accounted for at equity	22	29
Other investments	2,296	2,020
Amounts owed to customers		
Unconsolidated subsidiaries	46	56
Associates accounted for at equity	72	19
Other investments	124	164
Debts evidenced by certificates		
Unconsolidated subsidiaries	5	5
Associates accounted for at equity	26	26
Other investments	114	44
Subordinated capital		
Unconsolidated subsidiaries	--	--
Associates accounted for at equity	5	9
Other investments	7	26

41. Assets pledged as collateral

Assets in the amounts stated below were pledged as collateral for the following liabilities and contingent liabilities:

EUR million	At Dec. 31, 2004	At Dec. 31, 2003
Amounts owed to credit institutions	1,307	202
Amounts owed to customers	349	788
Debts evidenced by certificates	1,088	1,314
Other obligations	19	21

The following assets were pledged as collateral for the abovementioned liabilities:

EUR million	At Dec. 31, 2004	At Dec. 31, 2003
Loans and advances to credit institutions	1	5
Loans and advances to customers	1,275	1,920
Trading assets	78	122
Investments available for sale	217	204
Financial investments	1,555	363
Tangible assets	1	1

42. Fiduciary transactions

The fiduciary operations (not reported in the Balance Sheet) are broken down as follows:

EUR million	*At Dec. 31, 2004*	*At Dec. 31, 2003*
Loans and advances to credit institutions	53	103
Loans and advances to customers	2,263	2,449
Investments available for sale	768	597
Assets held in trust	3,084	3,149
Amounts owed to credit institutions	27	260
Amounts owed to customers	2,430	2,224
Debts evidenced by certificates	627	665
Liabilities held in trust	3,084	3,149

43. Risk management policies

Risk policy and strategy

The Erste Bank Group's approach to risk management seeks to achieve the best balance of risks and returns for earning a sustained high return on equity. The risk management strategy of the Erste Bank Group is marked by a conservative approach to risks facing a bank that is driven both by the requirements of customer-centered banking and by the legal environment. Under this risk management strategy, the Erste Bank Group uses an enterprise-wide system of risk monitoring and control designed to identify all risks throughout the Group (market, credit, business and operational risks), measure these risks in terms of Value-at-Risk (VaR) and ultimately enable the management to exert active control over the identified and measured risks in order to attain the goal of optimizing the risk-return relationship.

Risk management organization

In keeping with relevant law (especially the Austrian Banking Act), the central responsibility for risk management lies with the Group Managing Board. One way in which the Managing Board performs this task is by setting an aggregate bank limit based on value-at-risk at the quarterly meeting of the Risk Committee.

As set down in the Erste Bank Risk Rulebook, the role of the Risk Committee is to approve amendments to the rules where appropriate, allocate capital at the macro level, set an aggregate risk limit for the bank as a whole based on the bank's risk absorbing capacity, set an aggregate limit based on value-at-risk for market risk activities on the trading book, and define medium-term objectives for risk management.

In order to ensure comprehensive and integrated oversight of risks across the Erste Bank Group, independent risk control function and management are Managing Board–level functions exercised by the Chief Risk Officer. The Chief Risk Officer's sphere of responsibility includes the following service units:

- Strategic Risk Management
- Credit Risk Management Austria/CEE
- Credit Risk Management International
- Credit Restructuring

The Strategic Risk Management unit supports the Chief Risk Officer in furthering the disciplined handling of risks and in harmonizing risk management applications for all risk types in the business units. Working closely with the risk management departments of the business units, this unit also ensures the implementation of the risk management strategy.

At every level of the risk management process—particularly concerning market and credit risks—the measurement and monitoring functions are exercised independently of the front-office functions to be supervised (separation of front-office and back-office function).

In addition, the Chief Risk Officer is responsible for the development, implementation and monitoring of limit compliance, of risk reporting, of the risk management strategy, and of the associated standards and processes.

The Chief Risk Officer also has oversight of credit risk control for the Erste Bank Group. Under the Chief Risk Officer's leadership, standards are defined for credit policy and processes, credit portfolio management and risk-adjusted pricing. As well, the Chief Risk Officer is the functional head of the entire credit risk management organization.

In view of the growing demands placed on risk control, and in the interest of a clear definition of the roles and areas of authority of all units involved, the Group credit risk management and risk control activities are combined and bundled in the Strategic Risk Management service unit.

CHIEF RISK OFFICER (CRO)
Strategic Risk Management

Group risk control	*Group credit risk management and reporting*
Group market risk control	Group credit risk reporting & monitoring
Group credit risk control	Group credit risk management
Group operational risk control	

Risk control

The Group Risk Control department forms part of the Strategic Risk Management unit. Group Risk Control acts as a central and independent risk control unit as required by the Austrian Banking Act (Section 39[2]) and formulates Group guidelines for processes relating to risk management (these guidelines are codified in the Erste Bank Risk Rulebook). As an organizational entity independent of the business units, Group Risk Control thus ensures that all measured risks are within the limits set by the Managing Board.

The core competencies of Group Risk Control in the risk control process include the daily computation, analysis, and reporting of market risks for the whole Group and the timely and continuous monitoring of credit, business and operational risks on the basis of value-at-risk. Another key function is the aggregation of all risks (market, credit, business and operational) into a measure of total bank risk (economic capital) as part of the determination of the Group's risk absorbing capacity. Finally, Group Risk Control also provides regular reports to the Managing Board based on value-at-risk.

To do justice to this broad mandate, Group Risk Control is divided into three groups that respectively concentrate on market, credit, and operational risk. These subunits each calculate value-at-risk on an ongoing basis with the help of specialized models. Their other responsibilities include the refinement and updating of the models and measurement methods employed and the rollout of the risk control process in the Group.

Risk control process

The Erste Bank Group's independent risk control process has five elements.

1. **Risk identification** at the Erste Bank Group means the detection of all relevant risks related to banking operations. A systematic and structured approach to this task is emphasized. Aside from existing risks, potential risks also need to be identified. The aim of risk identification is the permanent, timely, rapid, complete and cost-effective detection of all individual risks that have a bearing on the achievement of the Erste Bank Group's business targets. However, risk identification is concerned not only with the early detection of risks themselves, but also the most complete possible recognition of all sources of risk.

2. **Risk measurement** at the Erste Bank Group means the valuation and analysis of all quantifiable risks on the basis of value-at-risk.

    The expected loss is the average amount which Erste Bank loses per year in its business activities. This represents the average annual observed historical loss over the course of an economic cycle. These foreseeable costs enter into pricing as a risk premium (standard risk costs) and must be recouped through the terms extended to customers. The expected loss thus does not pose a risk for Erste Bank, but simply a "cost of doing business."

The unexpected loss (equivalent to value-at-risk) is the maximum actual loss in excess of this expected loss for a given observation period and a predetermined probability of occurrence (expressed in terms of a confidence level). For this unexpected loss, equity capital must be set aside.

In addition, stress scenarios are defined, with the goal of quantifying the losses that may be triggered by extremely adverse, albeit highly unlikely, events. The information gained from test scenarios complements value-at-risk results, making it easier to predict the effects of potential extreme market movements.

3. **Risk aggregation** refers to the compilation of the results of value-at-risk-based risk measurement for the individual risk types (taking into account diversification effects) into an aggregate potential loss from the assumption of risk. This resulting aggregate measure is known as economic capital (representing value-at-risk at a confidence level of 99.95% over a one-year time period). In a multistage process, this aggregate total potential loss from the assumption of risk (economic capital) is compared to the resources (earnings potential, reserves and equity) available to cover potential losses. At Erste Bank this is done as part of the determination of risk–absorbing capacity.

4. **Risk limit–setting** at Erste Bank refers to the setting of a loss ceiling (aggregate bank limit) by the management through the Risk Committee based on the periodic determination of risk–absorbing capacity, which takes into account the bank's equity base and profitability situation.

5. **Risk reporting** at Erste Bank means continual reporting to management of the results of the various value-at-risk calculations in the individual risk types (daily value-at-risk report by the Market Risk Control group via Erste Bank's electronic management information system, monthly and quarterly reports, and risk–absorbing capacity calculation).

Risk types

Market risk. Fluctuation in interest rates, exchange rates, share prices and commodity prices creates market risks. Market risks derive both from short-term trading (the trading book) in instruments whose prices are quoted daily and from the traditional banking business (the banking book).

Taking into account the Bank's risk-absorbing capacity and projected earnings, the Managing Board sets the aggregate limit in the Risk Committee. The aggregate limit is then allocated by the Market Risk Committee based on a recommendation from the decentralized Financial Markets Risk Management unit. All market risk activities are assigned risk limits that, in the aggregate, are statistically consistent with the aggregate value-at-risk limit covering all market risks of Erste Bank. Limit compliance is verified at several levels: by the appropriate local risk management unit, by Risk Management Financial Markets and also by the independent Group Risk Control unit.

A key step in limit setting is the estimation of the potential losses that could be caused by market movements. This amount—value-at-risk—is calculated at Group level on a daily basis and reported to the Managing Board via the electronic management information system. Value-at-risk is determined by the historical simulation method. In its analysis Erste Bank uses a 99% confidence level and holding periods of one and ten days. The validity of the statistical methods applied is constantly checked by backtesting.

Extreme market situations can exert a strong influence on the value of trading positions and thus have extraordinary effects on trading results. The main such events are market movements that have a low probability of occurrence. Relying on purely statistical methods such as value-at-risk to measure risk does not adequately take into account the consequences of crisis situations. For this reason Erste Bank reinforces its value-at-risk-based risk measurement with stress testing by several methods (historical worst, extreme value theory, scenario analysis). The results of these assessments are made available to the Managing Board via the electronic management information system.

The market risk model approved by the Austrian Financial Market Authority is used to determine the minimum regulatory capital requirements of the Erste Bank Group under the

Austrian Banking Act. The calculation employs the most favorable multiplier possible (3), assigned by the Financial Market Authority on the basis of an appraisal by the Austrian National Bank.

Credit risk

Credit risk arises in traditional lending business (losses incurred by the default of obligors or by the need to provision assets as a result of the deteriorating credit quality of borrowers) as well as from trading in market risk instruments (counterparty risk). Country risks are recognized implicitly in the calculation of credit risk.

The task of the Group Credit Risk Control unit within the Group Risk Control department in this context is the measurement of credit risk, using a portfolio model based on credit value-at-risk, for the entire credit business of Erste Bank AG and the largest foreign and domestic subsidiaries. Neither the Group Risk Control department nor the Group Credit Risk Control unit is involved in the operational credit decisions. That responsibility falls entirely to the three decentralized credit risk management units (Group Credit Risk Reporting & Monitoring, Credit Risk Management International and Credit Risk Management Austria/CEE).

Measurement of credit value-at-risk is based on confidence levels of 95% and 99.95% (as in the total bank risk management calculation of risk-absorption capacity) and a risk horizon of one year. The central risk drivers in the portfolio model—the probabilities of default and transition probabilities for each customer segment—are determined based on the Group's own rating history and used in the calculation of credit value-at-risk.

In 2004, Group Credit Risk Control developed a new model of standard risk cost that takes account of, among other factors, the Basel II parameters. The use of the new model is scheduled for 2005 and is thus intended to ensure the operational application of the Basel II provisions to credit pricing.

Operational risk

As early as March 2000 a project was started for the first bankwide identification (Erste Bank AG) and measurement of operational risks. It was completed in April 2001 with the implementation of a model for calculating operational risk in value-at-risk terms.

Erste Bank uses the same definition of operational risk as the Basel Committee on Banking Supervision (Basel II): "the risk of loss resulting from inadequate or failed internal processes, people or systems, or from external events." In keeping with current practice at most international banks, the responsibility for operational risks rests with line management. The identification and measurement of operational risks employs quantitative and qualitative methods.

The quantitative measurement methods are based on internal loss experience data. To assist in the capture of this data, an intranet-based data collection tool was launched in mid-2004. The data collected since 1998 was migrated to the new tool. The proper transmission of loss reports is verified by the Internal Audit department. In order to factor in losses which have not occurred to date but are nevertheless possible, external data and scenarios are also used.

On the qualitative side, risk assessments have been employed since the beginning of 2003. The first pass through all business lines of Erste Bank AG was completed in 2004. Based on the qualitative information thus obtained, a potential further step would be to develop risk management instruments to support line management in making decisions aimed at reducing operational risk. In order to be able to assess potential risks at an early stage in the future, Erste Bank is in the process of defining key risk indicators.

Since the beginning of 2004 the insurance cover obtained by the Erste Bank Group is combined in a group-wide insurance program. By means of this approach, the cost for the Group's traditional property insurance needs was reduced, making it possible to buy additional insurance for previously uninsured banking-specific risks. The combination of potential economies and additional insurance cover, without an increase in overall cost, is achieved by retaining part of the losses in a captive reinsurance firm, thus permitting diversification of risk in the Group.

Business risk (fixed-costs risk)

Business risk, or fixed-costs risk, is defined by Erste Bank as the risk that an unexpected decline in revenues will lead to a loss because of the inflexibility of fixed costs. Known also as operating leverage risk, business risk thus reflects the degree of volatility of the major income and revenue items in Erste Bank's contribution margin accounting. Such unexpected fluctuations in income may be caused by changes in the competitive environment or customer behavior or by technological advances.

Controlling Erste Bank's overall risk

At Erste Bank AG, the regulatory requirements for qualitative risk management that result from pillar 2 of Basel II (Supervisory Review Process) and from the ICAAP (Internal Capital Adequacy Assessment Process) consultation paper are fulfilled by the risk absorbing capacity calculation which has been in use for years and by risk-adjusted performance measurement.

Determination of risk-absorbing capacity

It follows from the formula for risk-absorption calculus that the objective of an overall risk – control function must be to ensure the credit institution's continued solvency. The central tool for safeguarding this is the calculation of risk-absorbing capacity. In this computation, the value-at-risk resulting from the different risk types is aggregated to arrive at the total potential loss from the assumption of risk (economic capital) and this loss potential is then compared in a multiple-stage process to the resources (earnings potential, reserves and equity) available to cover these potential losses. Aside from the risk actually measured, a safety buffer and the existing risk limits are also taken into account on a value-at-risk basis. The point of this comparison is to determine the extent to which the bank is in a position to absorb potential unexpected losses (calculation of the risk-absorbing capacity). Risk-absorbing capacity thus represents a limit for aggregate risk activities at Erste Bank. Based on the bank's measured ability to bear risk, the Managing Board establishes an aggregate bank limit at the quarterly Risk Committee meeting.

The measure of risk used to calculate this aggregate bank limit is the economic capital that the bank must hold in order to cover its risk. This economic capital is defined as the minimum capital necessary on an annual basis to cover unexpected losses at a confidence level of 99.95%, derived from the default probability of Erste Bank's target rating. The objective of calculating this figure is to determine the amount of capital needed in order to ensure Erste Bank's continued viability even in extreme loss scenarios. This figure also allows for comparative measurement and aggregation of all risks. In parallel with this approach based on economic capital, the risk-absorbing capacity is also calculated at a much lower confidence level of 95% and conveyed to the management as supplementary information.

Erste Bank AG's aggregate risk by risk type (unaudited)

Allocation of economic capital (99.95% confidence level) at December 31, 2004

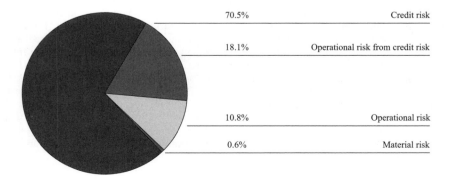

70.5%	Credit risk
18.1%	Operational risk from credit risk
10.8%	Operational risk
0.6%	Material risk

Risk-adjusted performance measurement (RAPM) and shareholder value added

Building on this calculation of risk throughout the bank based on value-at-risk for the different types of risk, Erste Bank can use the economic capital determined for each business area as the crucial component in the calculation of risk-adjusted Return On Economic Capital (ROEC). This figure compares all revenue with the risk that is taken in generating it, using economic capital as the measure of risk. As part of measuring risk-adjusted performance, a comparison is drawn between the results of marginal costing based on regulatory capital and the results based on economic capital.

Return on economic capital is determined for each business unit. This extends the existing controlling tools, such as marginal costing, by also making available to management the information it needs to view the entire bank through the lens of risk-return ratios. Going beyond the determination of regulatory capital adequacy, this parallel computation also lays the foundation for risk-efficient capital allocation based on risk-adjusted performance measurement (RAPM). Thus, economic capital and ROEC combine risk limit-setting aimed at preserving the Bank's continued existence with active risk and capital management geared to increasing Erste Bank's enterprise value for its shareholders (adding shareholder value).

Decentralized risk management

The decentralized Financial Markets Risk Management group within the Treasury business unit is responsible for the day-to-day control of the market risk associated with trading activities. It oversees market risk limits and counterparty limits. Other key duties include risk reporting, supporting the trading desk, legal support, testing of new products and—in coordination with Group Risk Control—market risk management.

The Treasury unit is also where market risks relating to the banking book are measured. The Balance Sheet Management group submits monthly reports to the Asset Liability Committee (ALCO) on the interest rate risk of Erste Bank Group and the savings bank group, to be used as a basis for adjusting balance sheet risks.

The responsibility for operational credit risk management rests with two service units: Credit Risk Management Austria/CEE and Credit Risk Management International. Foreign branches and subsidiaries have their own risk management units as required.

Basel II

In order to fulfill the requirements of the new capital adequacy regulations (Basel II/EU), a dedicated Basel II program was set up in the Erste Bank Group. Its technical direction is provided by the Strategic Risk Management unit.

Advanced approaches to measuring credit, market and operational risk

Erste Bank AG is an active participant in the consultation process shaping the new capital adequacy regulations for banks. Erste Bank's goal is to qualify for advanced approaches (according to the Basel II definition) when the new provisions enter into force.

For credit risk, Erste Bank seeks to apply the Advanced IRB Approach in the retail segment and the Foundation IRB Approach in all other Basel segments. For the measurement of market risk in the trading book, an internal model approved by the Austrian Financial Market Authority is already in place, and the model for measuring interest rate risk in the banking book already satisfies the Basel II requirements to a large extent. In the area of operational risk, Erste Bank is working to qualify for an Advanced Measurement Approach (the loss distribution approach) when the new provisions take effect. The decision as to which approach will ultimately be used to determine capital adequacy depends on the final form of the qualitative and quantitative requirements.

Qualification for the Foundation IRB Approach and Advanced Measurement Approach (loss distribution approach) is expected to have a corresponding beneficial effect on the regulatory capital requirements of the Erste Bank Group.

Credit exposure

EUR million	Total loans and advances to credit institutions and customers (including fixed-income securities)	Guarantees/ letters of credit	Total Dec. 31, 2004	Total Dec. 31, 2003
Banking and insurance	40,499	2,558	43,057	39,246
Consumers	23,349	105	23,454	20,760
Public administration, social security	19,139	938	20,077	17,774
Manufacturing	6,461	1,505	7,966	7,642
Real estate	11,499	677	12,176	10,582
Retail	7,332	623	7,955	7,233
Construction	3,152	956	4,108	4,096
Hotels and restaurants	2,686	198	2,884	2,906
Transport and communi- cation	2,400	345	2,745	2,849
Energy and water supply	1,390	180	1,570	1,871
Other	5,572	250	5,822	5,472
Total	123,479	8,335	131,814	120,431

The total comprises loans and advances to credit institutions and customers, fixed-income securities held in the trading portfolio, held as available-for-sale securities (investments available for sale) and as financial investments (held to maturity), and finally off-balance-sheet credit risks.

The changes in risk provisions are explained in Notes 15 and 30.

Interest rate risk

Interest rate risk is the risk of adverse change in the fair value of financial instruments caused by movement in market interest rates. This type of risk arises when mismatches exist between assets and liabilities (including off-balance-sheet items) in respect of their maturities or of the timing of interest rate adjustments.

In order to identify interest rate risk, all financial instruments, including transactions not recognized in the balance sheet, are grouped in order of maturity bands according to their remaining term to maturity or term to an interest rate adjustment.

The following tables list the open fixed-income positions held by the Erste Bank Group in the three currencies that carry significant interest rate risk: the euro, Czech koruna and Slovak koruna.

Only those open fixed-income positions are shown which are not allocated to the trading book. Positive values indicate fixed-income risks on the asset side (i.e. a surplus of asset items); negative values represent a surplus on the liability side.

Open fixed-income positions not assigned to the trading book (unaudited)

in million	1–3 years	3–5 years	5–7 years	7–10 years	Over 10 years
Fixed-interest gap in EUR positions at December 31, 2004	(1,569.2)	985.1	801.3	136.5	(31.3)
Fixed-interest gap in CZK positions at December 31, 2004	(18,383.2)	(16,746.9)	24,089.0	13,646.1	10,090.0
Fixed-interest gap in SKK positions at December 31, 2004	(5,505.4)	5,164.0	1,132.4	10,082.5	162.2

Hedging

The goals of market risk management for the banking books of the Erste Bank Group are to optimize the risk position while taking into account the economic environment, competitive situation, market value risk and effect on net interest income; to maintain an adequate liquidity position for the Group; and to centrally manage all market risks inherent in the banking book via the Group's Asset Liability Committee.

In keeping with the goals of risk management, hedging activities focus on the two main control variables—net interest income and market value risk. Two kinds of instruments are available with which to manage these variables: Cash flow hedges are used to mitigate interest rate risk. Fair value hedges are employed to reduce market risk.

Fair value hedges are currently used to turn fixed-income or structured transactions into variable-income transactions. The current policy on debts evidenced by certificates is to use fair value hedges to convert those issues that are not money-market-linked into issues that are. Other fair value hedges were set up for part of the syndicated loan portfolio and for fixed-interest loans.

Interest rate swaps and floors are the main instruments used for these fair value hedges. In connection with issuance, fair value is also hedged by means of cross-currency swaps, swaptions, caps, floors and other options.

Cash flow hedges are used for three objectives: to turn money market-linked transactions into fixed-interest transactions and thus reduce interest rate risk; to safeguard a minimum interest rate via floors; and to hedge anticipated foreign-currency interest income against exchange-rate risk. Some of the revolving money market liabilities are currently converted into fixed-interest transactions. Floors are used to secure a minimum interest rate on money-market-linked loans in case of declining market interest rates.

Interest rate swaps and floors were employed to hedge interest cash flows. Currency risk was hedged with spot transactions.

44. Total volume of unsettled derivatives as of December 31, 2004

in EUR million	Nominal amount by remaining maturity				Fair value	
	≤ 1 year	1-5 years	≥ 5 years	Total	Positive	Negative
Interest rate contracts						
OTC products						
Interest rate options						
Purchase	14,290	7,524	5,733	27,547	2,563	(11)
Sell	14,456	10,699	5,323	30,477	14	(2,618)
Interest rate swaps						
Purchase	94,426	35,665	21,007	151,098	5,677	298
Sell	101,194	33,445	15,418	150,058	418	(5,141)
FRA's						
Purchase	18,259	1,508	--	19,767	7	11
Sell	17,178	1,553	--	18,731	18	(7)
Listed products						
Futures						
Purchase	4,724	65	73	4,861	2	--
Sell	2,914	411	392	3,717	--	--
Interest rate options						
Purchase	1,219	--	302	1,521	1	--
Sell	1,219	--	29	1,248	--	--
Currency contracts						
OTC products						
Currency options						
Purchase	5,413	136	17	5,566	62	--
Sell	4,769	72	17	4,858	--	(44)
Currency swaps						
Purchase	26,468	1,464	1,728	29,660	849	(607)
Sell	23,844	1,619	1,701	27,205	630	(569)
Listed products						
Futures						
Purchase	185	--	--	185	1	--
Sell	138	--	--	138	--	(3)
Currency options						
Purchase	--	--	--	--	--	--
Sell	--	--	--	--	--	--
Precious metal contracts						
OTC products						
Precious metal options						
Purchase	4	--	--	4	--	--

in EUR million	Nominal amount by remaining maturity				Fair value	
	≤ 1 year	1-5 years	> 5 years	Total	Positive	Negative
Sell	3	--	--	3	--	--
Listed products						
Futures						
Purchase	6	--	--	6	--	--
Sell	--	--	--	--	--	--
Precious metal options						
Purchase	--	--	--	--	--	--
Sell	--	--	--	--	--	--
Securities-related transactions						
OTC products						
Stock options						
Purchase				92	25	(2)
Sell				214	2	(14)
Listed products						
Futures						
Purchase				99	--	--
Sell				174	--	--
Stock options						
Purchase				606	4	--
Sell	451	--	--	451	--	(6)
Total	332,214	94,298	51,773	478,285	10,271	(8,714)
Thereof OTC products						
Purchase	158,873	46,344	28,515	233,733	9,182	(312)
Sell	161,609	47,476	22,461	231,546	1,082	(8,394)
Thereof listed products						
Purchase	6,836			7,278	7	0
Sell	4,896			5,728	--	(9)

45. Fair value of financial instruments

In the table below, the fair values (unaudited) of the balance sheet items are compared to the corresponding carrying amounts.

Fair value is the amount for which a financial instrument could be exchanged or settled between knowledgeable, willing parties in an arm's-length transaction. Market prices were used in measurement where available.

For items without a contractual fixed maturity, the carrying amount was used. Where market prices were not available, internal valuation models were applied, in particular the present value method.

in EUR million	At Dec. 31, 2004		At Dec. 31, 2003*	
	Fair value	Carrying amount	Fair value	Carrying amount
Assets				
Cash and balances with central banks	2,723	2,723	2,549	2,549
Loans and advances to credit institutions	15,532	15,513	13,149	13,140
Loans and advances to customers	73,210	72,722	68,187	67,766
Risk provisions	(2,749)	(2,749)	(2,772)	(2,772)
Trading assets	4,628	4,628	5,259	5,259
Investments available for sale	9,141	9,141	7,379	7,379
Financial investments	29,580	28,867	26,830	26,454
Derivatives in banking book (other assets)	564	564	548	548
Liabilities				
Amounts owed to credit institutions	28,590	28,551	25,733	25,704
Amounts owed to customers	68,220	68,213	65,034	64,839

in EUR million	At Dec. 31, 2004		At Dec. 31, 2003*	
	Fair value	Carrying *amount*	*Fair value*	Carrying *amount*
Debts evidenced by certificates	19,887	19,887	16,944	16,944
Trading liabilities (other liabilities)	1,046	1,046	922	922
Subordinated capital	3,048	3,048	3,538	3,538
Derivatives in banking book (other liabilities)	288	288	514	514

* *The previous year's data was restated to reflect the new treatment of items without contractual maturities. Demand deposits with a market value below their carrrying amount are measured at the carrying amount.*

46. Contingent liabilities and other obligations

in EUR million	At Dec. 31, 2004	At Dec. 31, 2003
Contingent liabilities	8,692	7,068
– From guarantees and warranties	8,335	6,955
– Other	357	113
Other obligations	19,221	15,926
– Undrawn credit and loan commitments, promissory notes	16,655	15,047
– Amounts owed resulting from repurchase agreements	1,772	328
– Other	794	551

In connection with the accession to the European Union, the European Commission is screening state aid granted by the governments of the accession countries in the past with respect to their conformity with EU standards for the period after the accession date of May 1, 2004. The European Commission's examinations of the restructuring of the Czech Republic's Česká sporitelňa, a.s. and of the Slovak Republic's Slovenská sporitelňa were completed in 2004 with a positive outcome: The European Commission found that the restructuring measures have no effect on the period after the accession date.

With respect to the Republic of Hungary's Postabank the European Commission has completed its examination under the Interim Procedure in October 2004 with the following outcome: The European Commission found that all but one of eighteen measures in favor of Postabank, including an "indemnity for threatened litigation claims" granted by the Republic of Hungary to Erste Bank in the share purchase agreement on the sale of 99.9% of Postabank (in the course of the privatization of Postabank, following a public two-round tender proceeding), have no effect on the period after the accession date. With regard to one particular measure notified by the Hungarian Government and reviewed by the European Commission, an "indemnity for unknown claims" which was granted by the Republic of Hungary to Erste Bank in the same share purchase agreement, the European Commission has informed the Republic of Hungary that it has serious doubts about the compatibility of this particular indemnity with the acquis communautaire and that it has therefore decided to object to that measure and to initiate the formal investigation procedure laid down in Article 88(2) of the EC Treaty.

Certain assertions made by an Austrian competitor at the end of 2003 to the Austrian Financial Market Authority and to the Austrian Federal Competition Authority allege that Art. 30 (2a) of the Austrian Banking Act (BWG) conflicts with European law and that the formation of the Haftungsverbund between Erste Bank and the participating Austrian savings banks does not comply with European and/or national legislation. Art. 30 (2a) BWG has the effect that a co-operation such as the Haftungsverbund Agreement existing between Erste Bank and the other members qualifies as a banking group. The banking group forms the basis for Erste Bank's consolidation of qualifying capital (required under Art. 24 BWG) and of risk-weighted assets (required under Art. 22 BWG) of the members of the Haftungsverbund.

The examination by the Financial Market Authority of the validity of the competitor's allegations has already been completed with the conclusion that it shall not prohibit the consolidation on the basis of the Haftungsverbund.

The Haftungsverbund-related consolidation of the qualifying capital of member savings banks made a difference of about 55 basis points (0.55%) in the Tier 1 ratio of the Erste Bank

Group upon first consolidation in September 2002. Even without inclusion of the Haftungsverbund savings banks, the legal minimum requirements for regulatory capital are fully met.

The review initiated by the Cartel Court upon rerquest from the competitor (and the Federal Competition Authority) of the question of the applicability of European competition law to the cooperation under the Haftungsverbund between Erste Bank and the member savings banks under the Haftungsverbund has not yet been completed. The cooperation is based on exemptions granted under Austrian competition rules.

Erste Bank is confident that the review by the Cartel Court will come to the conclusion that the formation of the Haftungsverbund is in full compliance with all applicable laws and regulations.

In December 2004 Erste Bank has, jointly with the Haftungsgesellschaft and some other members of the Haftungsverbund, filed an application with the Cartel Court for a declaratory decision that the cooperation of the applicants under the Haftungsverbund qualifies as a Zusammenschluss within the meaning of the cartel merger rules. This procedure does not alter in any way the principles on which the Haftungsverbund is based.

In 2003, in connection with the financial collapse at the end of the 1980s of the WEB-IMMAG group, a conglomerate of real estate and finance companies in Salzburg, Austria, a trial court passed criminal judgements against three former managers of Salzburger Sparkasse. The three retired managers were charged with being accessories to acts of embezzlement committed by the individuals responsible at the WEB-IMMAG conglomerate, who were already convicted by the court of last instance. Since the beginning of 2004, with reference to these sentences and the alleged liability of Salzburger Sparkasse for the acts of its former managers, some three thousand former WEB-IMMAG investors, with the support of the Verein für Konsumentenschultz, an Austrian consumer protection association, have brought civil suits against Salzburger Sparkasse claiming alleged damages in an amount of EUR 61 million plus interest in an amount of EUR 66 million. The hearings at the court of first instance were scheduled to start in February 2005. Right before the beginning of the hearings the claimants have considerably reduced their claims— they are now claiming damages in the total amount of EUR 44 million plus interest/loss of profit in the amount of EUR 10 million. Salzburger Sparkasse is contesting these claims. In view of the complex legal and factual issues involved it is expected that it will take several years before a final judgment will be available.

As well, both Erste Bank and some subsidiaries are involved in legal disputes of a nature typically encountered during the conduct of ordinary business activities. It is currently unlikely that these legal proceedings will have a material negative impact on the financial position or the results of operations of Erste Bank, as either appropriate provisions have already been made, or Erste Bank has rights of recourse, or the cases in question are of insignificant magnitude in the aggregate.

47. Breakdown of remaining maturities as of December 31, 2004

in EUR million	On demand	Up to 3 months	3 months– 1 year	1-5 years	>5 years
Loans and advances to credit institutions	2,278	10,348	1,517	1,054	316
Loans and advances to customers	5,680	8,082	9,675	20,374	28,911
Securities held in the trading portfolio	497	337	362	1,603	1,829
Securities held as investments available for sale	540	595	635	2,034	5,337
Securities held to maturity	22	1,286	2,994	9,431	7,506
Total	9,017	20,648	15,183	34,496	43,899
Amounts owed to credit institutions	2,605	21,437	2,389	706	1,414
Amounts owed to customers	25,403	11,714	9,613	10,732	10,751
Debts evidenced by certificates	440	1,787	2,348	7,391	7,921
Subordinated capital	--	23	95	456	2,474
Total	28,448	34,961	14,445	19,285	22,560

Events after the balance sheet date

On January 10, 2005, Erste Bank acquired from the European Bank for Reconstruction and Development (EBRD) the 19.99% of Slovenská sporiteľňa that it did not already own. Erste Bank now holds 100% of the shares of Slovenská sporiteľňa. The preliminary purchase price for this last tranche is a total of EUR 122.3 million. This corresponds to a price/book value ratio of about 1.6 based on the expected shareholders' equity of Slovenská sporiteľňa at the end of 2004 using IFRS accounting. Upon ratification of the financial statements by the Supervisory Board and approval of the dividend, the final purchase price will be adjusted if required.

The Austrian tax reform legislated in 2004 took effect on January 1, 2005. The changes most relevant to Erste Bank are the reduction in the corporate income tax rate from 34% to 25% and the introduction of new rules for the taxation of groups.

APPENDIX C
Comparison of IFRS and US GAAP

IFRS 2006 chapter	Topic	US GAAP treatment	IFRS treatment
1	Introduction to IFRS	No comprehensive guide to statement presentation is offered; however, basic financial statements are the same under both sets of standards; GAAP departures when necessary are audit reporting issue.	Comprehensive guidance on presentation of financial statements provided; minimum line items identified for all financial statements; fair presentation goal may necessitate IFRS departures.
		FASB's *Conceptual Framework* is similar to IASB's *Framework for the Preparation and Presentation of Financial Statements.*	FASB's *Conceptual Framework* is similar to IASB's *Framework for the Preparation and Presentation of Financial Statements*; latter is less detailed.
		Comparative financials urged, but not required (required for SEC filings); greater specificity as to location of disclosures in body of statements or in notes.	Comparative financials are required, including footnote data; disclosure can often be optionally in financials or in notes.
		Formal GAAP hierarchy defined under US auditing literature (FASB is planning to establish hierarchy in new standard).	No hierarchy established beyond IAS, but suggested by language of IAS 8
2	Balance Sheet	Limited guidance on offsetting of assets and liabilities; classified balance sheet not required, but definition of current/noncurrent differs from IFRS somewhat.	Specific guidance on offsetting of assets and liabilities; classified balance sheet not mandatory, some difference from GAAP definitions of current/noncurrent.
		Some differences from IFRS re: exclusion of long-term debt being refinanced, etc.	Some differences re: exclusion of long-term debt from current liabilities, etc.
		No offsetting of assets and liabilities with different counter-parties	Some offsetting of assets and liabilities with different counter-parties permitted when legal provision exists.
3	Statements of Income, Changes in Equity, and Recognized Income and Expense	Estimated operating results of a discontinuing operation are included in the measurement for the expected gain or loss on disposal; timing of segregation of discontinuing operations from continuing operations may differ from that under IFRS; direct continuing cash flows or involvement in operations preclude discontinuing operations display	Actual operating results of a discontinuing operation are reported as incurred; timing of recognition of gain or loss in discontinuance and income or loss from activities of the discontinuing operation may differ from US GAAP.
		Restructuring costs recognized when there is little discretion to avoid costs; most costs recognized when later incurred.	Restructuring costs recognized when announced or commenced, which is earlier than under US GAAP.
			Separate statement of changes in equity required.
		Display of total comprehensive income is mandatory, but various modes of presentation are allowed.	Display of total comprehensive income is optional, but current project may result in closer approximation of US GAAP method.

IFRS 2006 chapter	Topic	US GAAP treatment	IFRS treatment
3	Statements of Income, Changes in Equity, and Recognized Income and Expense	Extraordinary item classification still permitted.	Extraordinary item classification now banned.
		Broader definition of discontinued operations than under IFRS, either a reportable business or geographical segment, or reporting unit, subsidiary, or asset group.	Narrow definition of discontinued operations as being reportable business or geographical segment or major component.
4	Statement of Cash Flows	Interest paid and dividends received must be classified as operating cash flows, and dividends paid must be classified as financing cash flows.	Choice allowed in classifying 1. Dividends and interest paid or received as operating cash flows, or 2. Interest or dividends paid as financing cash flows and interest or dividends received as investing cash flows.
		Overdrafts cannot be included in cash (show as financing source of cash).	Overdrafts can be included in cash under defined conditions.
5	Cash, Receivables, and Financial Instruments	No specific guidance offered under US GAAP or IFRS.	No specific guidance offered under either set of standards.
		Stricter definition of "sales" resulting in more recognition of secured borrowing transactions.	Slightly looser definition of "sales" of financial assets.
		Basis adjustment arising from firm commitments and forecasted transactions not in initial measurement of hedged item; hedging gains and losses on cash flow hedges recorded in other comprehensive income when they occur, reclass to income with hedged item.	Hedging gains and losses from cash flow hedges of firm commitments and of forecasted transactions can be included as part of the initial measurement of the cost basis of the related hedged item (basis adjustment).
		Hedging for part of term of hedged item not permitted.	Hedging for part of term of hedged item permitted if effectiveness can be shown.
		Hedging effectiveness can be assumed in limited circumstances (using "shortcut method").	Hedging effectiveness must be demonstrable.
			New option to designate any financial asset or liability for measurement at fair value with changes in current income.
		"Macrohedging" not permitted.	"Macrohedging" is permitted.
		Reclassifications to "trading" required under certain conditions, but reclassification from trading not permitted.	New, unified disclosure requirement applicable to all financial instruments, including those held by financial institutions, set forth in IFRS 7, effective 2007.
6	Inventory	Recognition in interim periods of inventory losses from market declines that reasonably can be expected to be restored in the fiscal year not required.	Recognition in interim periods of inventory losses from market declines that reasonably can be expected to be restored in the fiscal year is required; guidance in the areas of disclosure and accounting for inventories of service providers offered.

IFRS 2006 chapter	Topic	US GAAP treatment	IFRS treatment
6	Inventory	Allowable methods include FIFO, average cost, and LIFO.	LIFO costing now banned.
		Certain costs (idle capacity, spoilage) cannot be added to overhead charge in inventory cost, conforming to IFRS rule.	Certain costs (idle capacity, spoilage) cannot be added to overhead charge in inventory cost.
		Lower of cost or market adjustments cannot be reversed.	Lower of cost or market adjustments must be reversed under defined conditions.
7	Revenue Recognition, Including Construction Contracts	No standard on revenue recognition in general, but SEC requirements offer guidance.	More possibility for up-front revenue recognition when performance has occurred.
		Generally must amortize revenue over service period, no up-front recognition under GAAP	
		Revenue recognition deferred on delivered part of multi-element contract if refund would be triggered by failure to deliver remaining elements.	Revenue recognized on delivered part of multielement contract even if refund triggered by failure to deliver remaining elements, if delivery is probable.
		Use of completed contract method for construction projects under certain circumstances is required; revenue-cost and gross-profit approaches to percentage-of-completion both allowed.	If percentage cannot be reliably estimated, use of cost recovery method required; "revenue-cost" approach to percentage of completion mandatory for construction projects.
		Assorted guidance offered for specific situations	Specific guidance on revenue recognition principles for selected industries.
		Joint project with IASB may result in completely new conceptual foundation for revenue recognition based on "asset and liability recognition" approach.	Joint project with FASB may result in completely new conceptual foundation for revenue recognition based on "asset and liability recognition" approach.
8	Property, Plant, and Equipment	Change in depreciation method treated as cumulative effect item, but IFRS method may be adopted.	Change in method accounted for prospectively.
		Mandatory capitalization of construction period interest costs, only interest costs subject to capitalization.	Optional expensing or capitalization of construction period interest; ancillary costs also can be capitalized.
		Major overhauls generally expensed.	Major overhauls added to asset cost.
		Impairment suggested when book value exceeds gross expected future cash flows; second step to measure impairment uses discounted present value of cash flows.	Impairment suggested when book value exceeds greater of value in use (discounted cash flows) or fair value less cost to sell.
		Impairments cannot be reversed.	Impairments reversed under defined conditions.

IFRS 2006 chapter	Topic	US GAAP treatment	IFRS treatment
8	Property, Plant, and Equipment	Cost basis required.	Alternatively can use cost basis or revaluation to fair value.
			IFRS has been brought into closer conformity with US GAAP as to component depreciation, accrual of asset retirement obligations.
		Like-kind exchanges of productive assets measured at fair value, with gain or loss recognized, converging to IFRS method with FAS 153 adoption.	Like-kind exchanges measured at fair value, with gain or loss recognized.
			Investment property can be carried at depreciated cost or fair value (see Chapter 10).
		Decommissioning (asset retirement) obligations not recomputed after initial computation, generally.	Decommissioning (asset retirement) obligations recomputed at current risk-adjusted rate each balance sheet date.
		Investment property must be carried at depreciated cost.	
9	Intangible Assets	Research and development costs are all expensed, related cash flows in "operating"; goodwill not amortized, but tested for impairment; trigger for impairment recognition excess over fair value; cost basis required for intangibles.	Research costs expensed, but development capitalized and amortized with cash flows shown as "investing;" goodwill amortized; revaluation of intangibles permitted.
		Impairment implied when book value is greater than undiscounted cash flows to be derived from use of asset	Impairment implied when book value is greater than higher of value in use or fair value less costs to sell.
		Measurement of impairment done with reference to fair value (often operationalized as discounted cash flows).	Measurement of impairment done with reference to higher of value in use or fair value less costs to sell.
		Estimated residual often defined by present value of expected disposal proceeds.	Estimated residual value defined by current net selling price assuming asset is age, condition as of expected end-of-useful-life.
		Measurement of goodwill impairment uses special method, requires first comparing fair value of cash generating unit to book value including goodwill, then comparing implied goodwill to carrying value; measured at level of business segment or one level below that.	Measurement of goodwill impairments similar to other long-lived assets, requires only single-step computation; measured at lowest level goodwill can be assigned (cash-generating unit).
		No reversals of previously recognized impairments.	Impairments can be reversed, under defined conditions, except for goodwill.
		Revaluations never permitted.	Revaluation of intangibles permitted under limited circumstances.

IFRS 2006 chapter	Topic	US GAAP treatment	IFRS treatment
10	Interests in Financial Instruments, Associates, Joint Ventures, and Investment Property	Classification as trading, available-for-sale, or held-to-maturity limited to securities; equity method required for investee accounting.	Classification as trading, available-for-sale, or held-to-maturity applies to all types of financial assets, not just to securities; choice of equity, cost, fair value methods for some investees.
		If held-to-maturity securities are sold, use of this category is thereafter prohibited	"Fair value option" allows any financial asset or liability to be designated at inception to be accounted for at fair value with changes reported in current earnings.
		No parallel under US GAAP to the IFRS "fair value option."	If held-to-maturity securities are sold, use of this category is prohibited for next two years.
		Equity method of accounting similar under US GAAP and IFRS.	Investments in unlisted securities can be valued at fair value, if reliable measure available.
		If held-to-maturity securities are sold, use of this category is prohibited thereafter.	Derecognition of financial assets based on risks-and-rewards and control analyses; partial derecognition permitted; no parallel to QSPE rules under GAAP.
		Investments in unlisted securities valued at cost.	Joint ventures accounted for by equity method or proportional consolidation.
		Derecognition of financial assets based on risks-and-rewards analysis; partial derecognition prohibited; Qualifying SPEs permitted.	Need to conform investor and investee accounting policies.
		Joint ventures generally accounted for by equity method, but some industries (e.g., construction) use proportional consolidation.	Passive investments in nontraded equities can be valued at fair value or cost.
		No need to conform investor and investee accounting policies.	Investment property can be accounted for by cost (and depreciation) method, or by fair value method with changes taken to income.
		Passive investments in nontraded equities can be valued only at cost.	
		Investment property must be accounted for by cost (and depreciation) method.	
11	Business Combinations and Consolidated Financial Statements	Poolings prohibited by FAS 141; consolidation rules effectively based on majority ownership criterion, but special consolidation requirements apply to Variable Interest Entities (VIE); closing date generally used for recognizing acquisitions (purchases).	Poolings (unitings) eliminated by IFRS 3; consolidation rules based on control criterion; control date used for recognizing acquisitions (purchases).
			VIEs not yet addressed by IFRS.
		Acquisition date based on closing of transaction.	Acquisition date based on passing of control.
		Recognize postacquisition obligations only for exiting activities begun before merger, to be completed in one year.	Recognize postacquisition obligations only for provisions recognized by acquired entity.
		"Qualifying" SPEs to be consolidated if QSPE exceptions not satisfied.	Special-purpose entities to be consolidated if controlled.

IFRS 2006 chapter	Topic	US GAAP treatment	IFRS treatment
11	Business Combinations and Consolidated Financial Statements	Consolidation of majority owned subsidiaries required unless control is not exercised by parent.	Consolidation required unless control is not exercised by parent, or unless control is temporary (to lapse within twelve months).
		No promulgated rules governing "parent company only" financial statements, but use of equity method would be acceptable.	In "parent company only" financials, the investment in subsidiaries, equity investees, and joint ventures may be presented at cost or under rules for investments in securities, but equity method cannot be used.
			Consolidate controlled SPEs.
		Not necessary to conform parent and subsidiary accounting policies	Need to conform parent and subsidiary accounting policies.
		Minority interest in consolidated subsidiary can be presented in liabilities, in equity, or in special category.	Minority interest included in equity.
		Purchased in-process R&D expensed.	Purchased in-process R&D capitalized.
		Subsequent expenditures on acquired in-process R&D expensed.	Subsequent expenditures on acquired in-process R&D generally capitalized.
		Negative goodwill credited against nonfinancial assets acquired, with excess as gain.	Negative goodwill credited to gain immediately.
		Use pooling-type accounting for mergers of entities under common control.	Use pooling-type accounting for mergers of entities under common control.
12	Current Liabilities, Provisions, Contingencies, and Events After the Balance Sheet Date	Different recognition threshold for timing of recognition of liabilities associated with a restructuring than under IFRS; recognize under GAAP only if event occurs making this a present obligation.	A variety of recognition criteria for different items that may enter into the measurement of a provision are identified, missing under US GAAP; recognize when formal plan is announced.
		Short-term debt refinanced before statement issuance date can often be shown as noncurrent.	Short-term debt refinanced before balance sheet date can be shown as noncurrent.
		Provisions (estimated liabilities) measured by reference to low end of range of amounts needed to settle, sometimes but not always discounted to present value.	Provisions measured by reference to best estimate to settle, discounted to present value.
		Fair value of guarantee obligations must be recognized apart from contingent aspect.	Fair value of guarantee obligations must be recognized apart from contingent aspect.
13	Financial Instruments—Long-Term Debt	Convertible debt classified as liability.	Convertible debt assigned to both debt and equity, based on fair values of liability portion and residual amount allocated to equity.

IFRS 2006 chapter	Topic	US GAAP treatment	IFRS treatment
13	Financial Instruments—Long-Term Debt	Noncurrent presentation of defaulted debt if waiver granted before statement issuance date.	Noncurrent presentation of defaulted debt if waiver granted before balance sheet date only.
			New requirement to recognize liability for disposal of electronic equipment.
14	Leases	Similar to IFRS, but with more guidance on specialized topics; deferral of profit on sale-leasebacks.	Very similar to US GAAP; profit recognition on sale-leasebacks permitted if fair value priced.
		Separate accounting for land and building in combined lease depends on terms and materiality of land.	Separation of land and building components of lease is now mandatory.
		Third party guarantees cannot be included in minimum lease payments to determine whether capital lease criteria are met.	Third-party guarantees must be included in minimum lease payments to determine whether capital lease criteria are met.
		Present value of lease payments computed using incremental borrowing rate.	Present value of lease payments computed using implicit rate.
		Output contracts are leases.	Output contracts are not leases.
		Leasehold interest in land accounted for as prepayment.	Leasehold interest in land can be accounted for as investment property, valued at fair value with changes in current earnings; or else as prepayment.
		Gain on sale/leaseback not recognized in current earnings, but deferred and amortized.	Gain on sale/leaseback recognized in earnings.
		Lease obligations disclosures more extensive than under IFRS.	Lease obligations disclosures less than under GAAP.
15	Income Taxes	Recognize effect of rate changes when enacted.	Recognize effects of rate changes when "substantively enacted" which may precede US GAAP recognition.
		Prohibits recognition of effects of temporary differences related to 1. Foreign currency nonmonetary assets when the reporting currency is the functional currency, and 2. Intercompany transfers of inventory or other assets remaining within the company.	
		Deferred tax assets and liabilities are current or noncurrent based on related asset or liability.	Deferred tax assets and liabilities are noncurrent.
		Post–business combination recognition of deferred tax asset eliminates goodwill, then other intangible assets, with any excess taken to income.	Post–business combination recognition of deferred tax asset eliminates goodwill with any excess taken to income.
		Several specific exemptions to general requirement to provide deferred tax on all temporary differences are set forth.	No exceptions to general principle that all temporary differences in carrying amount of assets and liabilities require deferred taxes.

IFRS 2006 chapter	Topic	US GAAP treatment	IFRS treatment
15	Income Taxes	Recognize deferred tax asset in all cases, provide reserve when realization is not "more likely than not."	Recognize deferred tax asset when realization is probable, which means "more likely than not" per IFRS 3.
		Effect of change in rates or change in assessed likelihood of realization on deferred tax related to item originally recognized in stockholders' equity must be reported in current earnings.	Effect of change in rates or change in assessed likelihood of realization of deferred tax related to item originally recognized in stockholders' equity must be reported in equity.
		Subsequent year realization of tax benefit from business combination reduces goodwill, then other intangible assets, and only then excess reported in current earnings.	Subsequent year realization of tax benefit from business combination reduces goodwill, then excess reported in current earnings.
		Rate reconciliation based on domestic federal rate times pretax profit from continuing operations only.	Rate reconciliation based on applicable rates times accounting profit.
		Tax effect of intercompany transactions recognized at seller entity's tax rate.	Tax effect of intercompany transactions recognized at buyer entity's tax rate.
16	Employee Benefits	Expense recognition for certain types of equity compensation benefits; opposed to mandatory stock compensation expensing; prior service cost to be amortized over the expected service life of existing employees; contributions to multiemployer plans expensed.	Expense for equity compensation benefits not recognized, but current agenda item; prior service cost related to retirees and active vested employees to be expensed; benefit obligation for multiemployer recognized.
		Past service costs amortized over service period or life expectancy of workers.	Past service costs expensed immediately.
		Actuarial gains and losses cannot be recognized in equity.	Actuarial gains and losses can be recognized in equity under amendment to IAS 19 adopted in 2004.
		Recognition of a minimum liability on the balance sheet to at least the unfunded accumulated pension benefit obligation.	No minimum liability to be reported in the balance sheet.
		No limitation on recognition of pension assets.	Limitation on recognition of pension assets.
		Curtailment gains recognized only when employees terminate or plan suspension is adopted, computed differently than under IFRS.	Curtailment gains or losses recognized when announced; computed differently than US GAAP.
		Anticipating changes in the law that would affect variables such as state medical or social security benefits expressly prohibited.	Anticipate changes in future postemployment benefits based on its expectations in the law.
		Termination benefits expensed when employees accept and amount can be estimated, recognize contractual benefits when it is probable that employees will accept.	Termination benefits expensed when employer is committed to pay these.

IFRS 2006 chapter	Topic	US GAAP treatment	IFRS treatment
17	Stockholders' Equity	Mandatorily redeemable preferred shown as liability with dividends deducted as expense.	Mandatorily redeemable preferred shown as liability with dividends deducted as expense.
		Fair value method now required for share-based compensation plans; special simplified method for nonpublic companies.	Mandatory income statement recognition of effect of stock-based compensation measured at fair value; no special rules for nonpublic entities.
		Fair value measurement of goods and services acquired for stock from nonemployees using counterparty's commitment or actual performance date.	Fair value measurement of goods and services acquired for stock from nonemployees using modified grant date method.
		Tax benefits related to share-based payments credited to equity.	Tax benefits related to share-based payments credited to equity only if in excess of compensation expense.
		Tax benefits related to share-based payments based on GAAP expense, later adjusted when actual tax effects are realized.	Tax benefits related to share-based payments based on expected applicable tax deduction.
18	Earnings Per Share	Very similar to IFRS, but with more detailed guidance on calculations.	Similar to US GAAP.
		Report basic and diluted EPS on continuing operations, discontinued operations, extraordinary items, cumulative effect of change in accounting, and net income.	Calculation of year-to-date EPS (versus previously reported interim data) varies from US GAAP.
			Report basic and diluted EPS on continuing operations and net income.
		For interim reporting, average the interim periods' incremental shares to compute EPS.	For interim reporting, use treasury stock method on year-to-date results, unlike US GAAP approach.
19	Interim Financial Reporting	Some timing differences in recognition of interim revenues and expenses vs. IFRS.	Some timing differences in recognition of interim revenues and expenses vs. US GAAP.
		Basic principle is that interim period is integral to full year, but actual requirements depart from this in many instances.	Basic principle is that interim period is discrete period, but actual requirements depart from this in many instances.
20	Segment Reporting	"Management approach" provides flexibility in defining segments; segment results using internal managerial approach OK, even if these differ from financial statements.	Specific requirements governing the format and content of a reportable segment; segment results using same accounting policies as financial statements.
		Disclosures based on primary classification, with some additional "entity-wide" items (major customers, etc.), not necessarily lines of business or geographical areas however.	Both primary and secondary classifications have disclosure implications (line of business and geographical areas, in either order).
		No segment result definition given.	Segment results defined.

IFRS 2006 chapter	Topic	US GAAP treatment	IFRS treatment
21	Changes in Accounting Policies and Estimates, and Corrections of Errors	Correction of errors must be prior period/opening retained earnings adjustment; cumulative-effect method for changes in accounting principle, although restatement of prior periods is required for certain changes.	Choice permitted re: correction of "fundamental" errors; either prior period/opening retained earnings, or else current income effect; changes in principle can be restatement, cumulative effect, or prospectively; no guidance on changes in entities.
		Change in depreciation method is treated as change in accounting policy, handled as cumulative effect change, but US GAAP will likely converge with IFRS approach.	Retrospective restatement for correction of errors now mandatory.
			Change in depreciation method is treated as change in estimate, handled prospectively.
		Effect of voluntary changes in principles reported as cumulative effect in year of change in most cases, but US GAAP will likely adopt IFRS approach for years after 2005.	Voluntary changes in principles require restatement of prior years' financials, if practicable.
22	Foreign Currency	Exchange losses to be expensed in all instances.	Exchange losses on a liability for the recent acquisition of an asset invoiced in a foreign currency either as 1. Charge to expense, or 2. Add to the cost of the asset when the related liability cannot be settled and there is no practical means to hedge.
		Current exchange rate used to translate all balance sheet items, including goodwill and fair value adjustments.	Either current exchange rate or historical exchange rate permitted in translating goodwill and fair value adjustments to assets and liabilities arising from purchase accounting for acquisition of foreign entity if foreign currency is functional currency.
			Goodwill and fair value adjustments are deemed part of acquired assets/liabilities and translated at current rate.
23	Related-Party Disclosures	Similar to IFRS, but disclosures of relationships in absence of transactions is often missing.	Extensive disclosures required under IFRS, including those about control relationships even in the absence of actual transactions.
24	Specialized Industries	No primary guidance for government grants, agriculture.	Guidance provided for government grants, agriculture, reporting by banks, insurance contracts.
		Specialized guidance on inventories related to the motion picture, software, and agricultural industries, and others, found in "secondary" GAAP sources such as AICPA Guides, SOP, etc.	No guidance offered on range of industries covered by AICPA's Audit and Accounting Guides and Statements of Position; there is no "secondary" source for IFRS guidance.

IFRS 2006 chapter	Topic	US GAAP treatment	IFRS treatment
25	Inflation and Hyperinflation	Similar to IFRS, with some limitations.	General inflation accounting rules have been withdrawn; for hyperinflationary economy, financials must be presented based on balance sheet date measuring unit, with comparative (prior period) statements restated on same basis.
26	Government Grants	No rules promulgated under US GAAP, but IFRS-like approach would be acceptable.	Government grants received as compensation for expenses already incurred are recognized as income once conditions are met; revenue-based grants deferred and matched as expense incurred; capital grants amortized as depreciation recognized.